Iɴ ᴛʜᴇ ᴘʀᴇsᴇɴᴛ perplexing times, amid what seems to be the gravest crisis in world affairs, an extraordinarily large discussion goes on, mainly of a pessimistic nature, about our historic Western civilization.... I have scant sympathy with contemporary criers of doom. I unblushingly persist in believing that our Western civilization has long been and still is a great liberal and progressive civilization—the greatest the world has ever produced—and that, having survived other troubled ages, it is likely to survive the present one.

Carlton J. H. Hayes (1882-1964)
Raymond Fred West Memorial Lectures
at Stanford University, 1954

HISTORY OF
WESTERN CIVILIZATION

HISTORY OF

The Parthenon.
Courtesy of the Royal Greek Embassy Information Service, Washington, D.C.

WESTERN CIVILIZATION

Second Edition

CARLTON J. H. HAYES
MARSHALL WHITHED BALDWIN
CHARLES WOOLSEY COLE

The Macmillan Company, New York
Collier-Macmillan Limited, London

Second Printing, 1968

Earlier Editions

History of Europe by Carlton J. H. Hayes, Marshall W. Baldwin, and Charles W. Cole, Copyright 1949 by The Macmillan Company; also published in separate volumes as follows: *History of Europe, Volume I, To 1648*, by Carlton J. H. Hayes and Marshall W. Baldwin; *History of Europe, Volume II, Since 1648*, by Carlton J. H. Hayes and Charles W. Cole; *History of Europe Since 1500* by Carlton J. H. Hayes, Marshall W. Baldwin, and Charles W. Cole.

History of Europe, Revised Edition, by Carlton J. H. Hayes, Marshall W. Baldwin, and Charles W. Cole, © 1956 by The Macmillan Company; also published in separate revised volumes as above.

History of Western Civilization by Carlton J. H. Hayes, Marshall W. Baldwin, and Charles W. Cole, © 1962 by The Macmillan Company; also published in separate volumes as follows: *History of Western Civilization, Volume I, To 1650*; *History of Western Civilization, Volume II, Since 1650*; *History of Western Civilization Since 1500*.

Library of Congress catalog card number: 67–13596

The Macmillan Company, New York
Collier-Macmillan Canada, Ltd., Toronto, Ontario

Printed in the United States of America

Prefatory Note

This work is a new edition of the volume published originally in 1962. That in turn was based on the authors' *History of Europe*, which first appeared in 1949 and was revised in 1956. As befits its title, *History of Western Civilization*, it treats, at considerable length, of cultural as well as political and economic development. The new edition brings the story down to date, through more than two decades of the troubled times that have followed World War II.

The publishers have given the work an attractive and useful format, with double-columned pages, with a profusion of pertinent maps and illustrations, with select lists of supplementary readings for each of the twelve parts into which the text is divided, and with an exhaustive index. Of the hundred maps, about half are adapted from excellent ones provided originally for *History of Europe* by Mr. Vaughn S. Gray. The other half have been drawn anew by Dr. Francis Barkóczy, to whom the authors gratefully acknowledge their indebtedness. The authors are likewise particularly indebted to Mr. and Mrs. Frederick J. Woodbridge for artistic advice in selection of illustrations, and to Mrs. Dixon Ryan Fox for her photograph of Rome which appears on page vi.

This work is made available by the publishers in a single volume, in a two-volume edition with 1650 as the dividing date, and also in partial form in a volume covering the period since 1500.

Rome. The Forum and the Arch of Septimius Severus.

CONTENTS

France and Isolation of Britain (1940–1941). c. Break between Germany and Russia, and Participation of the United States (1941). D. Passing of Axis Powers from Offensive to Defensive (1942–1944). E. Allied Victory (1944–1945).

Sculpture of peasant from facade of Cathedral at Chartres.

Maps

HISTORY OF
WESTERN CIVILIZATION

Geographically, Europe is usually designated a continent. As such it is the smallest (except Australia) of the six continents which constitute the bulk of the Earth's surface. Actually, however, Europe is not a continent in the strict sense of the word. It is not a major area completely or almost completely separated by water, like the American continents or Africa or Australia, from other large landed areas. Rather, it is only a western extension of Asia—a minor part of the vast land mass geographers call Eurasia.

But Europe is not simply an arbitrary geographical expression. It signifies something much more important. It denotes a particular kind of historic civilization. And it is this distinctively civilizing Europe which in modern times has spread far beyond the merely geographical Europe, encompassing the American continents and Australia and exerting no little influence on the whole world. It is Europe in this cultural sense whose long historical development will concern us in the following pages.

At the outset we should note that Eurasia, at once the most extensive and the most diverse land mass on our globe, and yet lying largely in the north temperate zone, is the seat of several great and enduring civilizations. Each of these is commonly distinguished by the geographical section of Eurasia where it arose and flourished. Thus, "Far Eastern" civilization is peculiar to China and Japan; "Middle Eastern" and "Near Eastern" civilizations, to India, Persia, and Arabia; "Western" civilization, to Europe. These civilizations have existed longer and been much more fruitful than any native culture of America or Africa or Australia. Though they have touched one another in many ways throughout the countless ages of their formation and development, and though particularly in recent times their interrelationship has been greatly quickened, they are still distinctive. There is as yet no single "world civilization."

To this day, the manners and customs and thoughts of the Chinese are basically determined by their heritage of Far Eastern civilization, just as those of the Persians and Arabs are principally derived from the legacy of Near Eastern civilization, and our own from that of European, or Western civilization. It is this last of which Americans, as well as Italians, Englishmen, Scandinavians, and Germans, are heirs. It has conditioned our past. And whether we are aware of it or not, it conditions our present and future.

In what does this "Europe"—this Western civilization—consist? *First,* in the results of a fusing of ancient peoples and empires of the eastern Mediterranean into a conscious community of settled life, commercial intercourse, expansive effort, and artistic and literary achievement. *Second,* in the

INTRODUCTION

added Graeco-Roman tradition, with its abiding heritage of literature and language, of philosophy, of architecture and art, of law and political concepts—monarchy, aristocracy, democracy, dictatorship. *Third*, in the superimposed Judaeo-Christian tradition, with its fructifying spirituality and ethics, its permeating influence on personal and social behavior, its continuing distinction between the individual and the race, between liberty and authority, between mercy and justice, between what is Caesar's and what is God's. *Fourth*, proceeding from joint effects of the first three, it comprises distinctive traditions of both individualism and socialism, of limitations on the state, of social responsibility, of repeated revolt and revolution. *Finally*, and likewise proceeding from the others, it includes a pretty constant tradition of expansiveness, of missionary and crusading zeal, which has inspired a steady pushing out of European and Western frontiers—from the Mediterranean to the Arctic and across the Atlantic, in turn over lands of Latins, Celts, Germans, and Slavs, over the full width of both American continents, and beyond to at least the Philippines and Australia.

"Europe," in the sense of its distinctive historic civilization, is not a matter of geography or race or nationality. From its origins, it has embraced a variety of peoples, differing from one another in heredity and habitat, in speech and local culture. Predominantly, its inhabitants have been describable as "white" or "Caucasian," and its languages as "Indo-European" or "Aryan." But "white" or "Caucasian" are generic terms covering many racial strains and mixtures, some of which are found outside the area of European civilization, while numerous non-whites (including American Negroes) have been brought within its orbit. In like manner, the words "Indo-European" and "Aryan" merely denote a big family of distantly related languages, not only the Greek, Latin, Celtic, Germanic, and Slavic traditionally associated with Europe, but also the Sanskrit, Hindustani, and Persian of the Middle East; while within Europe have flourished quite alien languages, such as Semitic (Hebrew and Arabic), Turkish, Magyar, and Finnish.

"Europe," that is, the "West," has always had a multiplicity of nationalities, and since ancient times none of the repeated attempts to subject it to political unity has met with any real or lasting success. Yet in the domain of civilization and culture, it has long possessed a unity and distinctiveness marking it off from "Asia," whether of the "Far East," "Middle East," or "Near East." How "Europe" began, and how, during the past three thousand years, it grew and expanded, is the theme of the present book.

The story is long and complicated. It can here be told only in bald outline.

1

Prehistoric Art. The Lascaux
Cave Paintings (see p. 6).
*Courtesy French Government Tourist
Office, New York*

PART I
THE MEDITERRANEAN CRADLE

OF WESTERN CIVILIZATION

THE FIRST part of the story of European, or Western, civilization covers a very long period of time, roughly from 4000 B.C. to A.D. 300. It starts with a gradual rise and fusing of peoples and cultures in lands adjacent to the eastern end of the Mediterranean, in what is known as the ancient "Near East" of Egypt, Mesopotamia, Asia Minor, Syria, Phoenicia, Crete, and the Aegean.

Eventually, the civilization, thus developed in the Near East, is carried westward across the Mediterranean, and modified and added to, first by the Greeks and then by the Romans. Finally, when the entire Mediterranean basin (southern Europe and northern Africa, as well as southwestern Asia) is brought under Greek cultural influence and Roman imperial sway, Christianity, springing from Palestinian Judaism, provides new religious faith and ideals for the Mediterranean world. Without the original, many-sided heritage of the ancient Near East, without the added intellectual and artistic heritage of Greece, without the heritage of law and order of Roman Republic and Empire, and without the Judaeo-Christian spiritual heritage, Europe could not be the Europe of the last nineteen hundred years, nor the home of the Western civilization of today.

Civilized Europe, throughout its early formative period, does not embrace the geographical continent of Europe. It is evolved in, and confined to, the Mediterranean. To the north of a line drawn from Britain up the Rhine and down the Danube to the Black Sea, there still prevails, in the third century A.D., a primitive barbarism analogous to that of most American Indians in the time of Columbus. The expansion of Western civilization over the whole continent of Europe belongs to a later part of our story. And still later is its extension over the American continents.

Queen Hatshepsut of Egypt from the temple at Thebes, c. 1490–1480 B.C. (see p. 11).

Courtesy Metropolitan Museum of Art, New York

CHAPTER 1

Original Heritage of the Ancient Near East

A. Origins in the "Near East"

The origins of what we understand as European civilization are to be found, not in Europe itself, but in the eastern Mediterranean basin and the adjacent hinterland. Although modern geographical classification includes this area in either northeastern Africa or southwestern Asia, the achievements of its inhabitants in ancient times constitute the first important heritage of Mediterranean and hence of European civilization. Long before Europeans as such had emerged from barbarism, men had reached a relatively high degree of civilization in the lands bordering the eastern Mediterranean.

The geographical explanation of this development becomes clear as one studies a map, for that region includes two vast river basins, the Nile and the Tigris-Euphrates, and the intervening coastal lands of Syria and Palestine. Partly because these lands encircle the "desert bay" of Arabia, the whole area has been called the "fertile crescent." And from earliest times peoples of the neighboring territories—northeast Africa, inner Arabia, and the lands north and west of the Tigris-Euphrates valley— were attracted to the "fertile crescent." Moreover, it is possible that there were also contacts with ancient centers of culture in the Indus valley of northwest India. At any rate, the culture of the Nile and the Tigris-Euphrates and of intervening lands was the achievement of many different peoples.

The peoples throughout the Near East were already, in ancient times, of mixed blood. There was no purity of race among them, except only that most of them could be described in a very general way as "white," rather than "yellow" or "black." They belonged to many different tribes, or nationalities, each with a distinctive language. Some of these diverse languages, by reason of similarity in vocabulary and syntax, can be grouped together in the so-called Indo-European (or Aryan) "family" of languages, which embraces the ancient Hindu (or Sanskrit) of India and also Persian, Armenian, Greek, and Latin, as well as most modern European tongues. Another "family" of languages is the Semitic, which in the ancient Near East characterized the bulk of the peoples in the valley of the Tigris-Euphrates, in Syria, Palestine, Arabia, and in a few isolated areas elsewhere. As the Persians and Armenians were Indo-European (or Aryan), so the ancient Hebrews, Arabs, Phoenicians, Babylonians, and Assyrians were Semitic. A related "family" of languages was the Hamitic, spoken by Egyptians, Ethiopians, and certain other peoples of northern Africa. In addition, there were some languages, such as the Hittite in Asia Minor and the ancient speech on the eastern Mediterranean island of Crete, which do not appear to be related to any of the three language "families" already mentioned.

An important caution should be entered

5

here against confusing language with race. Language is a badge of common nationality, but not necessarily of blood-relationship. Whites and blacks may speak the same language, and such terms as Aryan, Semitic, and Hamitic refer to languages, not to races. This was true of the ancient Near East, as it is true of modern Europe.

The Near East, with its "fertile crescent," is one of the oldest habitations of man, if not absolutely the oldest. Here man dwelt for many thousands of years before the existence of any written records, before even the most primitive inscriptions were carved in rock or on clay tablet. In that distant "prehistoric" time, man devised tools and weapons of stone, from the character of which we divide time, for convenience sake, into a Palaeolithic (or Old Stone) Age and a Neolithic (or New Stone) Age. The exact beginnings or precise duration of these Ages can, of course, never be determined. The Palaeolithic may tentatively be said to have ended about 8000 B.C., while the Neolithic lasted in the Near East until about 4000 or 3500 B.C., and in the more backward Europe until a later date.

Inscriptions and other written records appeared earlier in the Near East than elsewhere, as did also the use of copper for tools and weapons. The resulting transition from the prehistoric New Stone Age into an historic Bronze or Copper-Bronze Age occurred in the Near East about 4000 B.C. In Europe copper was not generally used until two thousand years later, and writing was correspondingly backward. Finally, iron metallurgy, with its Iron Age, which represented a still more important advance over copper, began in Mesopotamia perhaps as early as 2500 B.C. and was certainly well developed in Asia Minor by 1300 B.C.

The northeastern part of the "fertile crescent" is the land between the rivers, or Mesopotamia, as the Greeks called it. Both the Tigris and the Euphrates flow down from the Armenian highlands in courses which, though varied, are roughly parallel. At modern Bagdad, the two rivers are only about twenty miles apart. Thence the valley broadens into the vast alluvial plain of Babylonia where the annual overflow of the rivers deposits a rich soil, and the gradual silting of the river mouths has added to the length of the plain through the ages at the rate of perhaps three miles a century. But nature, though generous to Babylonia, has occasionally brought disaster. Accordingly, from very early times men had to learn how to build dikes against floods and to construct irrigation works to make agriculture possible during the long dry seasons. Yet so great were the natural advantages of the region that it is easy to understand why it early became a center of civilization.

Equally important to the inhabitants of its basin was the Nile River. The longest of all African rivers, the Nile rises in east central Africa many miles south of Egypt. Somewhere near the modern Khartum it is joined by a great tributary, the Blue Nile. Thence it flows northward through Nubia where a number of rocky rapids, commonly called cataracts, make navigation difficult but not impossible for small boats moving with the current. Near Syene (Aswan) the rapids cease and the valley broadens into a vast depression averaging a dozen miles in width and some five hundred miles long, bounded by the edges of a desert plateau. As this great stream approaches the Mediterranean it divides into the several branches of the delta, so called because it resembles in shape the Greek letter Δ. Adequate rainfall is lacking in this region, but every year the Nile overflows its banks for a period of about two months. And as the waters recede they leave a deposit of exceedingly fertile sediment. Thus from time immemorial Egyptian peasants have seen their soil renewed. And they also discovered various methods of impounding water for local irrigation. Fertile soil and a warm dry climate have combined to make civilized life possible for the Egyptian.

Despite the unique configuration of the river valley, ancient Egypt was not completely isolated from other lands. Caravan routes led from the Nile eastward to the Red Sea, and the river itself, despite the rapids, was a line of communication from the south. Moreover, the delta region was accessible from both sides, and passage eastward to the Sinai peninsula and to Syria was by no means difficult. Notwithstanding, throughout most of its history Egypt was rather less affected by outside influences than any other ancient state.

B. Ancient Kingdoms and Empires of the Near East

It would be manifestly impossible here to rehearse in detail the history of the successive kingdoms and empires of the Near East during some four thousand years before Christ. What is important, however, in our study of European civilization, is some understanding of those achievements in government, social and economic organization, and science and art, which were passed on to the West. Accordingly, what will be attempted here is a brief outline of ancient history designed to show how the culture of the Near East was brought into contact with the more primitive Europe and contributed to its civilization.

The earliest evidences of settled political and social life appeared about the same time—during the fourth millennium before Christ—in both the Nile and the Tigris-Euphrates valleys.[1] But since Egypt attained to a political unity somewhat earlier than Mesopotamia, it will be well to commence our story with the origins of political life in the Nile valley. Sometime around 3000 B.C. a number of formerly separate communities were consolidated into the two kingdoms of Upper and Lower Egypt. The former included the valley south of the delta. The latter was the region of the delta itself. Sometime late in the third millennium before Christ the two kingdoms were united, with Memphis, a city near the borders of the upper kingdom, designated as capital. Then began what is called the dynastic period in Egyptian history, the dynasties being distinct lines of rulers, or pharaohs as they were called.

An important aspect of early Egyptian history is the expansion of its authority over neighboring lands. As early as the sixth dynasty (2420–2270 B.C.), for example, the tribes of lower and upper Nubia were subjugated, and Egyptian sovereignty was extended southward as far as the second cataract. The Sinai peninsula with its mineral deposits was also exploited, and commercial expeditions took the Egyptians by sea and land as far as Punt (modern Somaliland)

---

[1] Also, interestingly enough, at almost as early a time, in the valleys of the Indus (in India) and of the Yellow River (in China).

on the lower Red Sea coast. Then, following a protracted period of political trouble, civil war, and even foreign invasion, the pharaohs of the eighteenth dynasty (1580–1356 B.C.) embarked upon a new career of conquest. Security from attack was the initial motive. But, as has so often happened in history, adequate frontier protection seemed to demand expansion over adjacent buffer states. At any rate, during these years, especially under the great Thutmose III (about 1500 B.C.), Egypt advanced to occupy Palestine, Syria, and Phoenicia, which were garrisoned with Egyptian troops and required to pay tribute. Even Crete, Cyprus, and other eastern Mediterranean islands were forced into alliance with Egypt.

The Egyptian Empire, however brilliant, exceeded its own strength as army after army was sent out of the country. A protracted struggle with the Hittites, a people who, as will presently be explained, had moved eastward and southward from Asia Minor, was ended by a treaty (1280 B.C.) which delimited spheres of influence and which, in fact, marks the culmination of the power of both states. Thus by the thirteenth century before Christ, Egypt's days as an expanding world power were over. But contacts with the rest of the Near East had been established and subsequent events there were to affect the course of Egypt's history.

Meanwhile, in Mesopotamia, by the second half of the fourth millennium a people known as the Sumerians had developed a culture superior to any then existing. Around 3200 B.C. the evidence justifies somewhat fuller discussion. Then we hear of a number of separate city-states both in northern Mesopotamia (Akkad) and in the south (Sumer). During the period after 3200, Semitic peoples appeared in increasing numbers, especially in Akkad, and eventually the Sumerian people became submerged. Not, however, until the reign of Sargon (about 2637–2581 B.C.) did a Semitic dynasty rule over Sumer and Akkad.

Toward the end of the third millennium before Christ, a new Semitic people, the Amorites, entered Mesopotamia and settled at Babylon in western Akkad on the Euphrates. Thenceforth, Babylon, which up to that time had not figured prominently in

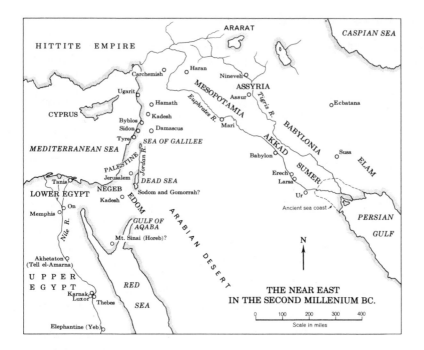

The map contains the following labels:

ARARAT
CASPIAN SEA
HITTITE EMPIRE
Carchemish
Haran
Nineveh
ASSYRIA
Ugarit
Assur
Ecbatana
MESOPOTAMIA
Euphrates R.
Tigris R.
Hamath
CYPRUS
Kadesh
Byblos
Mari
Sidon
Damascus
BABYLONIA
Tyre
SEA OF GALILEE
AKKAD
MEDITERRANEAN SEA
Jordan R.
Babylon
Susa
SUMER
ELAM
PALESTINE
Jerusalem
DEAD SEA
Erech
Tanis
Larsa
LOWER EGYPT
NEGEB
Sodom and Gomorrah?
Kadesh
Ur
EDOM
Ancient sea coast
On
ARABIAN DESERT
PERSIAN
Memphis
GULF OF AQABA
GULF
Nile R.
N
Mt. Sinai (Horeb)?
Akhetaton (Tell el-Amarna)
UPPER EGYPT
RED
THE NEAR EAST
Karnak
IN THE SECOND MILLENIUM BC.
Luxor
Thebes
SEA
0   100   200   300   400
Elephantine (Yeb)
Scale in miles

Mesopotamian history, was to take the lead. And the rulers of Babylon, after first merely maintaining their independence, began a career of expansion. Hammurabi (1947–1905 B.C.), the sixth of the Babylonian kings, challenged the rival and threatening power of the 'Elamites to the north, effectively subdued all Sumer and Akkad, and even extended his sway toward Assyria, the region north of Babylonia. Thus what was to become a remarkable centralized administration commenced to develop throughout Mesopotamia.

The military and political successes of Hammurabi did not long endure, for shortly after his death the unity of the old Babylonian kingdom was broken, partly because of internal dissension, but principally as a consequence of invasion by neighboring peoples. The most important of these invaders, the Hittites, destroyed Babylon in 1750 B.C. and, a little later, established a strong state centering in Asia Minor. The origin of the Hittites is still a matter of dispute, although it seems probable that they migrated from the region north of the Black and Caspian Seas. Presumably the ruling classes were Indo-European, though not, apparently, the main body of the population. The importance of the Hittites lies

partly in their introduction of the domesticated horse and their progress in the manufacture of iron implements. But perhaps even more significant were their contacts with neighboring peoples. For it was the Hittites who, as a consequence of their occupation of Asia Minor, formed one of the links between the ancient Near East and the primitive culture of the Aegean and eastern Mediterranean. Further, their pressure southward into Syria threatened Egypt and brought about a long rivalry which, as has been explained, curbed Egyptian expansion. Not until around 1200 B.C. did the Hittite power begin to show signs of decline.

The meeting between the cultures of the Nile and the Tigris-Euphrates, which was a consequence of Egyptian expansion northward and Hittite pressure southward, focuses attention on the intervening coastlands of Palestine and Syria. Moreover, the decline after the thirteenth century B.C. of Egyptian and Hittite prestige provided an opportunity for the independent development of the peoples inhabiting those coastlands, especially the Aramaeans, Hebrews, and Phoenicians. The Aramaeans, a Semitic people, had gradually moved into Syria from the lands bordering on Mesopotamia. As they established themselves in cities like

Damascus and obtained control over the caravan routes, they forsook their earlier nomadic ways for settled agriculture and commerce. Their language was widely adopted and remained, even after their dispersion by the Assyrians, a kind of universal tongue in the Near East. It was presumably the speech of Jesus Christ and was certainly the language of important parts of the Bible.

The Hebrews were also Semitic nomads who entered Palestine probably around the middle of the second millennium B. C., at a time when the western part of the country was under Egyptian control. Many sojourned for a considerable period in Egypt, but eventually the "Exodus" took place, and probably by the middle of the thirteenth century the Hebrews were well established in the region west of the Jordan. The Canaanites, former inhabitants of the land, were defeated, but subjection again followed at the hands of the Philistines. Then, after the first efforts toward liberation under Saul and Samuel in the late eleventh century, there came the final triumph of David of Judah (1020–975 B.C.). During the reign of his son, Solomon (975–935), the old Hebrew kingdom reached its height.

The Semitic Phoenicians are chiefly noted as sailors, traders, and colonizers. Their famous cities on the coast of northern Palestine, especially Tyre, Sidon, and Byblos, flourished first under Egyptian domination. By the end of the second millennium B.C., the Phoenicians had not only outstripped the Egyptians, but were founding colonies throughout the length and breadth of the Mediterranean and even penetrating the Atlantic.[1] Thus, like the Hittites in Asia Minor, the Phoenicians formed a link with the Mediterranean world. But as traders and colonizers their contacts to the west were at once more frequent and spread over a larger area. Greek merchants visited their harbors and, among other things, imitated their method of writing. And at Carthage (near modern Tunis), their most famous colony, the Phoenicians developed a commercial and political power which dominated the central and western Mediterranean until the expansion of Rome.

Another important intermediary between

the ancient Near East and the culture which was later to flourish in Greece was the island of Crete, for it seems likely that Cretan culture was first developed by immigrants from Egypt perhaps as early as the fourth millennium before Christ. Later came settlers from Asia Minor and, finally (about 1400 B.C.), invaders, presumably from the Greek mainland, who destroyed the distinctive institutions of the island. Of necessity Cretans were a sea-faring people. Their mariners plied the sea to Egypt and western Asia and extended Cretan influence to the Aegean islands, the Greek mainland, and Asia Minor. Two of the earliest examples of Cretan influence were Mycenae in southern Greece and Troy in northwestern Asia Minor. Indeed, the "sea kings" of Crete exercised authority over a considerable maritime empire.

Clearly, then, with the decline of the old Egyptian and Mesopotamian land states, the westward expansion of Phoenicia, and the emergence of Crete, we pass into a new age in the ancient Near East. But before undertaking an examination of the subsequent centuries, we must attempt an estimate of the contributions made toward the perfecting of government and the advancement of art and science.

C. Institutions and Cultural Contributions

Generally speaking, the ancient Near East was organized on a basis of absolute monarchy. Moreover, monarchy was closely associated with religion, and the ruler's authority was commonly regarded as of divine origin. This was especially true in Egypt where the monarch was a theocratic despot—that is to say, he was chief priest as well as supreme law-giver and judge. Indeed, he was regarded as the incarnation of a god and bore various titles emblematic of his divine character. He was the "son of Ra," the sun-god, and later, after the Theban god Amen was introduced, the "son of Amen-Ra."

Over all his people the pharaoh possessed unlimited authority. Not only did he levy taxes, promulgate laws, and administer justice, but, since he was regarded as owner of all the land, he decided for each farmer how many and what fields should be culti-

[1] See map, below, p. 18.

vated. The products of artisans and the exchanges of merchants were similarly regulated. In practice, theocratic absolutism was exercised through officials placed over the various provinces and districts. There developed an administrative bureaucracy. And, as a consequence of the identification of religion and government, a priest class acquired considerable authority even outside the purely religious sphere. The vast majority of the population, however, was composed of peasants living as serfs on the estates of the nobles or of the king. Until recent times, history offers few comparable examples of such complete regimentation of life by the state.

Centralized bureaucratic administration fostered a number of necessary public works. Reservoirs and canals, for example, made possible at least a partial control over the life-giving waters of the Nile and facilitated irrigation. Indeed, the absolute dependence of Egyptian agriculture on water control necessitated a large measure of governmental intervention. But the government also encouraged commercial expeditions abroad, which enhanced and varied Egyptian life.

Although in Babylonia, no less than in Egypt, the pressures of corporate life left little opportunity for the individual, the autocracy there seems to have been tempered somewhat by a greater regard for individual rights to both life and property. This is evident in a famous ancient Babylonian code of law which bears the name of Hammurabi, who coördinated and systematized earlier practices. In fact, this famous code, perhaps the first of its kind, presumably mirrors Mesopotamian life of an even earlier date. Class distinctions were recognized. There were wealthy landed magnates, a priest class, petty landowners, tenants bound to the soil, and various categories of persons engaged in agriculture and trade. Slavery also existed. Punishments, often severe, and in many cases based on the primitive "eye for an eye" principle, were graded accordingly. But there is evidence, too, of a more enlightened and humanitarian attitude. Woman's position was generally higher than in other lands. Slaves enjoyed certain very definite rights, even over property. Thus, although in Babylonia religion and govern-

ment were theoretically inseparable and the king's power was considered to be of divine origin, a regard for individual rights and property moderated an otherwise autocratic governmental system.

It should not be thought that the association of the ruler with divinity exhausted the religious aspirations of the ancients. Babylonians believed in some form of existence after death and lavishly adorned the subterranean tombs of their kings. In the course of time more attention was paid to temples and palaces. Egyptian preoccupation with death and the life hereafter is also evident in their funeral customs. The bodies, at least of the great, were mummified, some existing mummies being of considerable antiquity. The pyramids and the many smaller and later temples were in reality tombs designed and equipped to serve the departed in another world. Although Amenophis IV (*d.* 1358 B.C.) of Egypt changed his name to Ikhnaton ("pleasing to Aton," the god of the sun's disk) and tried to enforce this cult as the sole worship, the ancients were, in general, polytheists— that is, worshippers of many deities. The persistent loyalty of the Hebrews to the one god, Jahveh, is, therefore, highly significant and will merit further discussion in a subsequent chapter.

Both Babylonians and Egyptians made important contributions to the art of writing. The Semitic Babylonians adapted to their own language the earlier Sumerian method of writing. This was a script composed of wedge-shaped or cuneiform (from *cuneus,* wedge) characters which could be made relatively easily on rock or clay tablets. Symbols were provided for some five hundred syllables. Thus, the Babylonians had progressed beyond the more primitive stage of picture writing. The Egyptians were able to designate certain sounds of the human voice by single letters. But in their hieroglyphics, they did not abandon signs for syllables or even for words and ideas. The Egyptians also developed papyrus, a writing material made by pressing together certain reeds which were plentiful in their country. Papyrus rolls served as the books of the ancient world.

It remained for the Phoenicians to produce a set of symbols, adapted from the

Egyptian Sculpture (from about 1400 B.C.). The Temple of Karnak at Luxor.

Courtesy Egyptian State Tourist Administration, New York

writing of other peoples, which represented twenty-two consonants (vowels were not written until later). Named and arranged in order, these symbols constituted an alphabet in the modern sense of the term. And it was this alphabet which was adapted and carried to the west by the Greeks and to the east by the Aramaeans. Thus, even in ancient times, it came to be known from India to the Atlantic. Further, since a great deal of the Egyptian papyrus used by the Greeks was obtained at the Phoenician port of Byblos, completed written works came to be known as *biblia*. Hence, there has come down to us from ancient Phoenician, through Greek and Latin, not only the word paper but the word-root so familiar in such terms as bible and bibliography.

As a consequence of their belief that heavenly bodies influenced the course of human events, the ancient Babylonians made a number of astronomical discoveries. They named the days of the week after the planets, divided the year into twelve months, and the day and night into twelve hours

each. This sexagesimal computation was also used in dividing hours into sixty minutes, minutes into sixty seconds, and the circle into three hundred and sixty degrees. In Egypt, scientists also observed the heavenly bodies with simple instruments and distinguished between planets and fixed stars. And probably in the third millennium before Christ, though possibly earlier, the Egyptians reckoned time by a solar year of twelve thirty-day months with an added five extra days. The scientific lore of the ancients was passed on to their successors. And it is significant that it was the Greeks of Ionia in Asia Minor, those whose contacts with the Near East were closest, who were pioneers in the advancement of Greek science.

The most familiar and most striking evidences of ancient culture are to be found in the architectural monuments of Egypt. For the Egyptians achieved a grandeur and massiveness rarely, if ever, surpassed in human history. And stone monuments of astonishing size were possible in a civilization where the king commanded an unlimited supply of forced labor. The oldest and in many ways the most impressive structures were the pyramids which date from the IVth dynasty. In fact, the period from about 3200 to 2500 B.C. is sometimes called the Pyramid Age. Vast funeral monuments, the pyramids reflect the power of this ancient civilization and, taken all together, they form a veritable "city of the dead." In the empire period were completed the great temples at Karnak and Luxor, with their tremendous columns and their brilliantly colored sculptured reliefs. From the same period the huge seventy-foot statues of the pharaohs and the colossal figure of Rameses II (*d.* 1255 B.C.), carved out of the face of a rock, stand in mute testimony to the skill of sculptors thousands of years ago.

Egyptian artistic achievements were not confined to the gigantic, for Egyptians also excelled in portrait sculpture and in the minor arts of the jeweler and the goldsmith. Some of the smaller statues and sculptured busts are exquisite. And the jewels and furnishings of the lately discovered tomb of Tut-ankh-Amen, the successor of Ikhnaton, display a remarkable wealth of artistic talent.

No structures comparable to the Egyptian have survived from Mesopotamia, largely because scarcity of stone forced builders to use unburnt brick, a far more perishable material. Nor was the portrait sculpture of Mesopotamia as remarkable as that of Egypt. But the Babylonians developed to a high degree of perfection the carving of intricate scenes and groups.

To moderns, these ancient masterpieces are important in themselves. But we are also concerned with the cultural influence of the Ancient Near East on Greece and Europe. It is important to observe, for example, that the early Greek sculptors imitated the Egyptians. It is appropriate, therefore, to conclude this section with a word about Cretan art. For Crete was one of the links between the ancient Near East and the Mediterranean civilization which was first to develop in the Aegean area. Although scholars have in part been able to decipher a form of Cretan script, it is not yet possible to present a clear picture of Cretan political life. Other evidence, however, points to a highly developed culture. During the "golden age" (2200–1500 B.C.) Cretan builders raised large palaces, especially at Cnossus, and devised water conduits and drainage systems. Artists adorned walls with handsome frescoes, created beautiful figurines of gold, silver, and bronze, and painted pottery. Curiously enough, although the Greek writer Thucydides alluded to a great maritime empire on the island of Crete, his statement was long discounted and it was not until recent times that archaeologists have disclosed the actual existence of this great ancient culture.

D. The Empires of Assyria and Persia

The scene of our narrative thus far has shifted repeatedly from Egypt to Mesopotamia, with brief glances at the small states in Palestine and Syria and the island of Crete. And, while there has been evidence of cultural relations between these three areas, there has been no sign of any political coördination. The last thousand years before Christ witnessed the formation of new empires, each greater than its predecessor. As a consequence, the predominant characteristic of the first millennium before Christ was the welding together of formerly disparate cultures into unity. Indeed, this is the beginning of a process which reached a climax under the later leadership of Rome.

The first in this succession of empires was the achievement of a Semitic people who around 3000 B.C. had built in northeastern Mesopotamia a city called Assur, whence the name Assyrian. Subjected for many centuries to the Babylonians, the Assyrians developed a civilization influenced by Sumerian culture, but none the less distinctive. Their opportunity for expansion came toward the beginning of the first millennium with the decline of the Egyptian, Babylonian, and Hittite states. A people remarkably efficient in war and employing new weapons and tactics, the Assyrians soon overran Mesopotamia, Syria, and Palestine, and for a time occupied Egypt. Under Sargon II (722–705 B.C.) and his successor, Sennacherib, the Assyrian empire attained the summit of its power. Although often ruthless in their treatment of enemies and conquered peoples—thousands of Jews, Aramaeans, and others were deported to Mesopotamia—the Assyrians were noted for institutions of centralized government and administration which excelled those hitherto developed either in Egypt or in Babylonia. Absolute monarchical power was secured by such measures as an efficient postal service which enabled the king to keep in constant touch with outlying provinces. In spite of this, a large degree of municipal autonomy was permitted within the framework of the central administration.

Assyrian strength was at length challenged by a combination of Indo-European Medes and Persians and Semitic Chaldeans who encompassed the fall of Nineveh, the Assyrian capital, in 612 B.C. The Medes and Persians were destined ultimately to gain the mastery, but for a brief interlude Babylon again achieved an outstanding if temporary brilliance with the rule of the Semitic Chaldeans. Under Nebuchadnezzar, (604–561 B.C.), the capital city reached its maximum size and surpassed in magnificence all other cities. Under Nebuchadnezzar, too, the Jews were again defeated, Jerusalem destroyed, and many Jews endured a half century of captivity, the "Babylonian Captivity" of the Bible.

The passing of the Assyrian and Chaldean

Mesopotamian (Assyrian) sculpture of the ninth century B.C. Alabaster winged lion from the palace gate of Ashur-nasir-apal II, 885–860.

Courtesy Metropolitan Museum of Art, New York; gift of John D. Rockefeller, Jr., 1932

empires brings to a conclusion an era of ancient history marked by the supremacy of Semitic civilization, for the coming of the Medes and Persians heralded the beginning of a long predominance of Indo-European peoples over the Near East. Thus far, Indo-Europeans have not figured prominently in our narrative. In the period we have been considering, they inhabited for the most part the vast grassland, plain, and steppe country to the north, which stretches from central Asia through southern Russia into the Danube basin. When they moved south and west into the Mediterranean region, the lands of eastern and southern Europe began to come into prominence, as our next

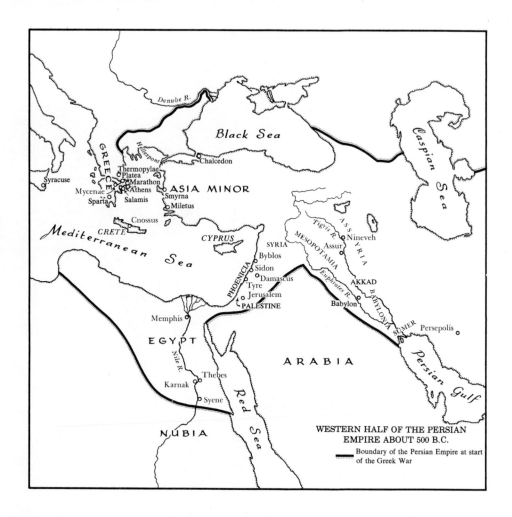

WESTERN HALF OF THE PERSIAN
EMPIRE ABOUT 500 B.C.
━━━ Boundary of the Persian Empire at start
of the Greek War

chapters will indicate. But one Indo-European people, the Iranians,[1] of whom the Medes and Persians were the most prominent, pushed southward into the fertile crescent. At the time of the destruction of the Assyrian empire, to which they contributed heavily, the Medes were dominant, the Persians in a state of vassalage. But under their chieftain Cyrus, the Persians turned the tables on their kindred and followed their triumph over the Medes by successful attacks first on the kingdom of Lydia in Asia Minor, then on Babylon which fell in 539 B.C. When Cyrus's successor, Cambyses, conquered Egypt (525 B.C.), the Persian empire embraced the entire ancient Near East from the Nile delta and the eastern Mediterranean to the borders of India.

Persian civilization owed much to its predecessors. Its architecture seems largely derived from the Egyptian, Babylonian, and Assyrian. Throughout the entire western part of the empire Aramaic was an official language. But the Persians also devised a cuneiform alphabet of thirty-nine letters.[2] It seems probable that Hebrew religious influence was not inconsiderable, although in the field of religion the Persian contribution was largely original. Through the *Magi* (or priestly "wise men") of the Medes had been preserved beliefs and rituals of

---

[1] Iran, which is derived from "Aryan," has become the name of the plateau stretching from the Zagros mountains to the Indus river, and has been adopted as a name for the modern state of Persia.

[2] Among the inscriptions on the famous triumphal monument carved out of a huge rock face at Behistun, near Ecbatana, was a passage in Persian, Babylonian, and Susian, which has provided a key to the language of old Babylonia.

great antiquity, which among other things emphasized the ceaseless struggle of good and evil, of the spiritual powers of darkness and light. It remained for Zoroaster (probably seventh century B.C.) to teach a kind of monotheism which exalted the power of Ahura-Mazda, the supreme god of good. Among Ahura-Mazda's helpers was Mithras. And Mithraism, as an offshoot of Zoroastrian beliefs, developed in a later time into a serious rival of primitive Christianity.

Ancient Persia's most significant contribution lay in the field of government. Never before in the ancient world had so large an area been administered so efficiently. The entire empire was divided into provinces (satrapies), some twenty in all, each under the supervised control of a local governor. The authority of each satrap was checked by the presence of a secretary and a military commander, both responsible directly to the emperor. Moreover, government officials, the famous "eyes and ears of the monarch," constantly traveled over the numerous and excellent roads on the emperor's business. Beneath this superstructure of centralized administration, local life and customs went on much as before. Different religions were tolerated, and Cyrus permitted the Jews to return to their Palestinian homeland and rebuild their temple at Jerusalem.

As we have mentioned, the rise of Persia ushered in an age of great empires. In their expansion the Persians turned north and west in an attempt to subjugate Greece, where a brilliant culture had already developed. Accordingly we shall direct our attention westward from Asia to Greece and the developing civilization of Europe.

Egyptian Sculpture, Queen Nefertiti c. 1375 B.C., Berlin Museum.

Courtesy Marbury Art
Reference Bureau

Greek Architecture in Magna Graecia. The Greek
Theater at Syracuse, Sicily.

Courtesy Italian State Tourist Office, New York

Fourth or fifth century B.C. Greek-Athenian
vase. Combat of Greeks and Amazons.

*Courtesy Metropolitan Museum of Art, New
York; Fletcher Fund, 1944*

CHAPTER 2

Added Intellectual and Artistic Heritage of Greece

A. The Greeks in the Aegean and the Mediterranean

In the previous chapter we were concerned with the achievements of successive cultures in the ancient Near East. With the study of Greece we encounter the very foundations of European and Western civilization. For not only is the Greek peninsula in Europe proper, but Greek habits of life and especially Greek artistic and intellectual accomplishments are recognizable as integral parts of our distinctive Western culture. Greek art has inspired countless artists from the days of Rome to the present. Indeed, there is hardly a city in the western world which does not in some of its buildings reflect Greek influence. The contribution of the Greek mind is less apparent, but no less real and important. Down through the centuries Greek literary forms, Greek scientific achievements, and, perhaps above all, Greek skill in rationalizing the problems of life have repeatedly left their mark.

The Indo-European ancestors of the Greeks moved through the Balkans into the Greek peninsula about the time that the Indo-European Medes and Persians were wandering southward east of the Caspian Sea (about 1300–1100 B.C.). Somewhat later they began to occupy the Aegean islands, Crete, and the coast of Asia Minor. Thus the ancient Greek world included the entire area washed by the Aegean Sea. The irregular and indented coasts of both Asia Minor and Greece are rich in excellent harbors. As the Greek peninsula is broken not only by bays, inlets, and gulfs, but by rugged mountains, communication even in ancient times was often less difficult by sea than by land. It would seem inevitable that the inhabitants of such a region should become a seafaring people.

As the early Greeks came into contact with the ancient Near East, they were particularly influenced by the Cretans. In fact, Crete was a kind of intermediary between the old culture of the west Asiatic mainland and the new world of the Aegean and Mediterranean. The Cretans, it will be recalled, had established settlements of considerable size at Mycenae in southern Greece and at Troy in northwestern Asia Minor. Not only did the Greeks absorb these Cretan outposts, but they invaded Crete itself. The tables were turned. The old Cretan civilization declined and became merged with the new culture of Greece. Thus, about the time of the famous siege of Troy (about 1184 B.C.), immortalized by Homer, the Greeks were beginning to develop customs of their own.

Although the ancient Greek world was one of separate city-states which did not form an administrative national unity, there did develop among them a sense of cultural nationality based upon the many elements of life which all Greeks held in common. Foremost among these was a common language, for, despite differences of dialect, men from various parts of the Greek world could understand one another. Literature

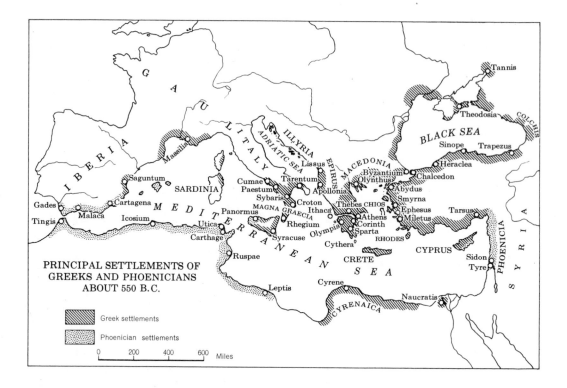

PRINCIPAL SETTLEMENTS OF
GREEKS AND PHOENICIANS
ABOUT 550 B.C.

Greek settlements

Phoenician settlements

0   200   400   600   Miles

and religion also fostered common traditions. Through the Homeric epics all Greeks became familiar with the same gods and with the heroic deeds of their own ancestors. Representatives of Greek communities occasionally met to arrange for such common religious celebrations as the famous festivals of Olympia, which date from the early eighth century. The oracle of Apollo at Delphi was also universal in its attraction. Thus it was that the Greeks became conscious of themselves as culturally distinct from others. They gradually began to think of themselves as Hellenes, one and all descended from a common legendary ancestor, Hellen. Hellas was a culture, if not a nation.

A striking manifestation of a community of culture can be seen in Greek colonization, a feature of Greek life which began in the eighth and extended into the seventh and sixth centuries before Christ. Greek colonization was motivated as much by political as by economic factors. In certain cities such as Corinth and Miletus (Miletus founded more colonies than any other Greek city) the original area was so limited that emigration was almost a necessity. Prestige was not unimportant in coloniza-

tion; nor, of course, was the desire to increase the opportunities for trade. However motivated, Greek colonial expeditions were thoroughly organized and equipped. Colonists, when they had established themselves, kept on good terms with their mother city while at the same time jealously preserving the sovereign independence of the new community.

Geographically, Greek colonization spread westward throughout the entire Mediterranean area and eastward along the shores of the Black Sea. The Thracian coast, the Straits where the Greek city of Megara founded the colonies of Chalcedon and Byzantium, and the whole length of the Black Sea coast, including the northern shore, attracted Greek settlers. Intrepid pioneers reached the shores of the Iberian peninsula. The modern French city of Marseilles was once a Greek colony. Cyrene (Cyrenaica) and Naucratis, near the later Alexandria, were established in North Africa. The most important Greek colonies were in Southern Italy and Sicily, an area later known as *Magna Graecia*. For there, from centers like Syracuse, founded by Corinth in 735 B.C., Cumae on the bay of Naples, or Croton on the boot of Italy,

Greek ways of life first influenced the Romans.

To a surprising degree the new settlements retained a distinctively Greek character. The architectural and artistic forms of the homeland were employed. Greek speech persisted, and the religious and political institutions of the mother city were set up. As a consequence, colonization proved to be the means of an extraordinary expansion of a truly Greek culture. The modern traveler may visit Greek temples in Sicily, and the modern archaeologist may uncover Greek statues in Africa.

Another evidence of community of feeling among the Greeks is the capacity of at least some of them to coöperate against common danger. This was demonstrated in the fifth century before Christ, when Greeks stood off successive attacks from mighty Persia. In the preceding chapter, we followed the expansion of the Persian empire and its conquest of Asia Minor. This involved the subjugation of Ionian Greek cities. These, however, revolted; and Athens, sensing the ultimate threat to the Greek peninsula, sent twenty ships to assist them. In retaliation, the Persian king Darius launched an attack on Greece and in 490 B.C. successfully landed an army on the shores of Attica in the bay of Marathon. The Athenians mustered a citizens' army and sought aid from Sparta and other Greek cities. Though outnumbered two to one, the Athenians were fortunate in having in Miltiades a capable commander who was familiar with Persian tactics. Instead of awaiting a Persian assault, his army advanced to the hills overlooking the plain of Marathon. The Persians, unable to lure the Greeks from their advantageous position, finally marched towards Athens, thereby exposing their flank to a Greek attack. The result was a resounding Greek victory. The surviving Persians took refuge in their ships and sailed away.

A decade later, Xerxes, Darius's successor, renewed the struggle. Having built a formidable fleet with the assistance of the Phoenician cities, he planned a combined sea and land attack on Greece, together with an advance on Sicily from Carthage. But the Athenians, as a result of the first Persian campaign and the insistent advice of Themistocles, had strengthened their navy; and Sparta helped them with an army under its king, Leonidas. n this occasion (480 B.C.), a big Persian army, supported by the fleet, crossed the straits and moved southward toward the Greek peninsula. It was the Greek plan to fight a delaying action on land until the Athenian navy could overcome the Persian fleet. The plan succeeded only in part. The Persian fleet was halted but not defeated. Meanwhile, the heroic Leonidas, with a force of some four thousand Hellenes, fell at the historic pass of Thermopylae; and the Persians marched into the peninsula, devastating it and burning Athens.

The Greeks were rallied by Themistocles; and presently the Persian fleet was drawn into an attack on the Athenian navy, which had taken up a favorable position in the bay of Salamis. After an engagement which lasted all day, the Persian fleet was disastrously defeated. Themistocles urged that the victory of Salamis be followed up by an attempt to cut off the Persian army, but the Spartans at first hesitated to risk so bold a maneuver. As a consequence, the war dragged on into the following summer, and Attica was again devastated. Then the Spartan King Pausanias, with the combined armies of Athens and Sparta, defeated the Persian host at Plataea (479 B.C.), while the Athenian navy overwhelmed the remnants of the Persian fleet north of Miletus. Already, Syracuse had repulsed the Carthaginians in Sicily. Thus the entire Greek world was saved from conquest. It was a splendid achievement, and the following age was a time of unparalleled brilliance in Greek civilization.

B. City-State Politics of the Greeks

The political development of the Greeks was characterized, not by the formation of a Greek nation, but, doubtless much influenced by geographical conditions, by the growth of separate city-states. Yet even a brief examination of early Greek political life reveals a remarkable political maturity. Many of the governmental terms still in current use, such as monarchy, democracy, tyrant, politics, to mention only a few, are of Greek origin. The conception of a city-state is in itself important, and it lasted into Roman times and far beyond. Indeed, the Greek word for city, *polis*, has been absorbed into words of governmental significance in more than one Western language. The term means a sovereign and independent state whose area is either confined to the environs of a single city or, perhaps, includes several smaller communities dominated by one large city.

Despite the political diversity which is evident in the history of the Greek city-states, there were certain developments which many experienced in common. In early times most cities were petty monarchies. But by the time of the great expansion, that is, around the eighth century before Christ, the predominance of the aristocracy was fairly general, and most kings were overthrown. The mercantile tendencies which characterized that age produced profound social and political changes. In the cities of Ionia, the Greek coastland of Asia Minor, which had been in the van of economic progress, and in the commercially progressive cities of the Greek mainland and Sicily, seizure of power by violence was not uncommon. Dictators made their appearance. Some were beneficent rulers and championed the oppressed lower classes. Indeed, the word "tyrant" did not then have its modern sinister meaning. Nevertheless, benevolent tyranny could and sometimes did degenerate. And there were tyrants who were removed by the same methods which had maintained them in power. By the sixth or fifth century before Christ the principal Greek city-states had developed that form of government which, in general, they were to maintain, and some were beginning to achieve a certain prominence which singled them out over their neighbors. Corinth, for example, owed much to its favorable location at the head of the Gulf of the same name. Sparta was to attain prestige in the south. Miletus, Ephesus, and Phocaea on the mainland of Asia Minor, and certain of the islands such as Naxos or Lesbos remind us that the ancient Greek world embraced both sides of the Aegean Sea.

Since it would be impossible here to trace the development of all the Greek city-states, it must suffice to discuss two famous and strikingly different cities, Sparta and Athens. Spartan social and political organization was not typical. But its peculiar militaristic culture undoubtedly contributed to Spartan predominance in the Peloponnesus, the peninsula of southern Greece. Unlike commercial Athens, Sparta was an agricultural state with an exaggerated emphasis on the military discipline of its citizens. Rigorous training under the aegis of the state began for boys at the age of seven and continued through early manhood. Even girls were required to undergo physical training. Such preoccupation with things physical and military left little time for the finer things of life, and Spartan contribution to the arts was negligible. But Spartan discipline, though not typical of Hellenic civilization, had its importance and in some measure justified itself in the military trials with Persia and later with Athens.

Although the democratic institutions for which Athens became famous were noticeable early in the city's history,[1] the climax of Athenian political development came in the fifth century before Christ. This was a brilliant period in Greek history which followed the long and successful defense of the homeland against Persian attacks, a defense in which Athens played a major part. In accordance with a pronounced tendency toward more popular government, the authority of the old aristocratic council of elders, which formerly met on a hill called the Areopagus, was curtailed. A popular council of five hundred citizens, divided into small groups, now conducted most of the state business. Citizen juries were enlarged to include about six thousand citizens divided ordinarily into smaller units of five hundred and one. To enable poor citizens to serve, jurors were paid, As these juries gained prestige they became, together with the popular assembly, virtual law-making bodies.

The right to hold office was extended to all men who possessed some property, and the choice of office-holders by lot was introduced. This practice, although

---

[1] It was at Athens that any citizen could write the name of a person deemed dangerous to the state on a broken piece of pottery or *ostracon* (hence our word "ostracize").

democratic, had its obvious disadvantages, and it is noteworthy that the important post of military commander (*strategos*) remained elective. The president of a body of ten generals might, as the principal elected official, wield considerable power. Pericles, for example, champion of the now popular cause of reform and progress, was elected *strategos* (461 B.C.) and, since he was re-elected repeatedly, became virtual dictator of Athens for a period of nearly thirty years.

Athenian democracy was also qualified by the restriction of its advantages to citizens. Citizens included only the children of free-born parents. Thus, the foreigners (*metics*) resident in Athens, numbering more than 25,000, and the 115,000 slaves of Attica, not to mention most workingmen, were denied the privileges of citizenship. And no women enjoyed the franchise. Athenian democracy, however full for those who shared its privileges and responsibilities, was severely limited as to the number of those participating.

Of far greater importance than any single political achievement was the impact of the Greek mind on politics. In Greece, perhaps for the first time in history, the greatest thinkers sought to rationalize the theory as well as the practice of government. Above all, they were concerned with ethics as applied to the life of the city-state. As Athens developed a popular government, an increasing number of men sought an education, at least in things political and moral. They acquired, too, a training in persuasive speech. A group of teachers called sophists (Greek *sophia*, "wisdom") helped fill this need. And although their practices degenerated later into an emphasis on mere tricks of speech and reasoning (sophistry), the sophists at their best contributed much to Greek intellectual development.

Indebted to the sophists, and yet standing apart from them, was Socrates (*d.* 399 B.C.). Professing to be an earnest seeker after truth, particularly an inquirer into such things as abstract justice and goodness, Socrates became a notorious questioner. He embarrassed and evidently irritated many of those whom he interrogated by the ease with which he cast doubt on established beliefs. With disarming frankness he pretended to know nothing and sought to lead others toward a more sound rationalization of their own ideas. Posterity has paid his method of teaching the supreme compliment of imitation.

Plato (*d.* 347 B.C.), Socrates' famous pupil, presented a reasoned picture of the ideal state governed by the "philosopher-king" in his book *The Republic*. And finally Aristotle (*d.* 322 B.C.) not only pondered over the nature of ethics but examined the constitutions of some 158 city-states in his treatise on *Politics*. The rational examination of political institutions has ever since been characteristic of Western civilization. The Greeks gave us the foundation and much of the technique for this rationalization.

C. Hellenic Culture

The rationalization of politics is, of course, only one example of Greek intellectual achievement. The interests of Greek thinkers were wide and deep. The word "philosophy" is of Greek origin and means, literally, "love of wisdom." Moreover, Greek philosophers took all knowledge as their province. Philosophy to them included what would today be designated the natural sciences, such as physics, astronomy, and mathematics, as well as the more narrowly "philosophical" subjects of logic, ethics, and metaphysics.

The earliest Greek thinkers of prominence were primarily concerned with the nature of the universe. And because of its closer contacts with the ancient Near East, Ionia (the Greek coast of Asia Minor) witnessed the beginnings of Greek natural science. Thales of Miletus, on the basis of Babylonian calculations, correctly predicted an eclipse of the sun (585 B.C.) and proclaimed, contrary to former beliefs, the dependence of the heavenly bodies on natural laws. Somewhat later came Pythagoras (*d.* about 500 B.C.), who, in addition to enunciating a famous geometrical theorem, was a philosopher and something of an educational theorist. He conducted a sort of "model school" at Croton in southern Italy. Students graduating from our modern medical schools still take a professional oath which is a paraphrase of the words of Hippocrates of the island of Cos (born about 460 B.C.). For centuries physicians followed Hippocrates's teaching.

The sophists were not interested in political matters exclusively. They also laid the foundations for the systematic study of rhetoric and logic. In emphasizing clarity of speech and in giving precise meaning to words they helped to form the tradition of rationalism which became characteristic of Greek intellectual life. Moreover, Socrates and Plato posed the great questions of all philosophy: What is being? What exists? Plato insisted on the reality of abstract ideas—justice, goodness, and the like —which existed in the mind of God and only as pale imperfect reflections in the world of sense. This philosophy of "idealism" has profoundly affected later thinkers, even into modern times.

Aristotle, Plato's illustrious pupil, was a painstaking scholar, who, in addition to his interest in the theory of politics, gathered an enormous amount of information on biology, anatomy, zoölogy, and other sciences, which he systematically classified. In the realm of metaphysics, while conceding that the human mind could "abstract" the general from the particular and, for example, classify into *genus* and *species*, he insisted on the reality of the individual. Aristotle's voluminous writings on almost every conceivable subject constitute a veritable encyclopedia of ancient knowledge. On many matters his authority was unquestioned for centuries. As late as the fourteenth century the Italian poet Dante could hail him as "the master of those who know."

Both Plato and Aristotle strengthened the Greek tradition of rationalism which lies at the foundation of Western thought. Moreover, in their striving to understand the nature of the universe and of man, and, in particular, in attacking the central philosophical problem of being, the Greek philosophers were gradually led away from the primitive polytheism which had characterized Greek popular religion. Although the gods of Olympus continued to figure prominently in literature and art, they began to lose their appeal as objects of real religious worship. More important, Plato and Aristotle presented, at least to intellectuals, the rational conception of a single supreme being, a "first cause" or "prime mover," which was to be of increasing significance.

The Greek literary tradition, which commenced with such works as the Homeric epics, *The Iliad* and *The Odyssey*,[1] includes the lyric verse of Pindar of Thebes, and Sappho, poetess of Lesbos, and, above all, the tragedies of Aeschylus (*d.* 456 B.C.), Sophocles (*d.* 406 B.C.), and Euripides (*d.* 406 B.C.). Their dramas, as also the "comedies" of Aristophanes (*d.* about 385 B.C.), found intelligent and critical audiences in Athens. So skillful was the handling of the timeless themes of life, death, fate, and religion that Greek tragedies have become "classics" for every subsequent age. Athens also produced three renowned historians—Herodotus (*d.* 425 B.C.), chronicler of the Persian wars; Thucydides (*d.* 400 B.C.), who somewhat later described the decline of Athenian hegemony in Greece; and Xenophon (*d.* 355 B.C.), who was an essayist as well as an historian.

Pericles, the great statesman who guided the destinies of Athens in the period after the Persian wars, was also an enthusiastic and discerning patron of the arts. And while it would be incorrect to associate Greek art solely with the "age of Pericles" or even exclusively with Athens, nevertheless it remains true that his régime produced an unrivalled effort of artistic creation. It was distinguished by a revival of building, especially by a rebuilding of the Acropolis, the hill in the heart of the city. Athenians spent little on their private dwellings, but they supported Pericles' appeals for expenditure on the public edifices which adorned the famous hill. Thus they made possible such a masterpiece as the Parthenon, the temple of Athena, designed in the Doric style by Ictinus. The Doric is the most severely simple of Greek architectural styles. The plain columns are surmounted with unadorned "capitals." Yet it seems

---

[1] These famous epics were composed presumably in the second half of the ninth century before Christ. They reflect, however, Greek life in the period before 1000 B.C.

ideally suited to the Parthenon. Harmoniously proportioned, faultless in every detail, it is one of the most nearly perfect temples ever erected.[1]

The Parthenon and the many other public buildings on the Acropolis and elsewhere bear witness to a combination of architectural skill and artistic taste which has seldom been equaled. In addition to the Doric style which reached its perfection in the Parthenon, there was also the Ionic, employed in the delicately ornamented Erechtheum, and the Corinthian with its more elaborate capitals. Subsequent ages, in paying Greek architecture the compliment of conscious imitation, have made Doric, Ionic, and Corinthian columns and capitals familiar throughout all Europe and America.

Greeks also excelled in sculpture. The Parthenon housed the colossal bronze statue of Athena, while above the stately rows of columns was the carved marble frieze displaying a procession of Athenians. These creations of Phidias (d. about 432 B.C.) and his pupils display a capacity to handle a variety of subjects and attitudes and an ability to produce adequate detail without destroying the harmony of the whole composition. Praxiteles and others maintained in the fourth century the high standards set in the era of Pericles.

Greek painting is perhaps less appreciated than Greek sculpture. But the achievements of Phidias were equalled by his contemporary, Polygnotus the painter. Indeed, Phidias probably learned a great deal from Polygnotus' work. Best known for his large frescoes, Polygnotus also influenced the art of vase painting. For the best Greek artists were not unwilling to identify themselves with the efforts of craftsmen. And nowhere is the close association of art and industry more evident than in ceramics.

Hellenic culture reached its full flowering in the period following the Persian wars. Although the defeat of the Persians was a splendid achievement, it brought only temporary unity to the Greek city-states.

---

[1] The frontispiece of this volume depicts the Parthenon as it is now.

For some thirty years, Athens, through the Delian League, dominated the northern half of the peninsula, together with most of the Aegean islands and Ionian towns, and even threatened the south. But what may be called an Athenian empire was opposed by some cities. Finally, Sparta, leader of the cities of the Peloponnesus, challenged Athenian domination in a series of conflicts known as the Peloponnesian War (431–404 B.C.). There followed a brief period of Spartan and then Theban hegemony.

Evidently, temporary military or naval alliances among Greek city-states did not prove adequate foundations for political unity. Thus it was that the peninsula fell an easy prey to a conqueror less distant than Persia. And this Macedonian conquest which we are about to describe brought to a close the splendid age of the Greek city-states. Thenceforth, Hellenic civilization was spread far and wide and merged with the culture of many other peoples.

D. Alexander's Empire and the Hellenistic Age

The regions to the north of Greece proper —Thrace and Macedonia—had lagged far behind their southern neighbors. In Macedonia, however, Greek influence had penetrated and, at the court of its king, Philip II, Greek culture was so highly respected that the king engaged the philosopher Aristotle as tutor for his son, Alexander. Further, well aware of the opportunities offered by the chronic political disunity of the city-states, he dreamed of welding the entire peninsula together under one government capable of challenging once and for all the dominion of Persia. Part of this dream was realized when he defeated the Greeks at the battle of Chaeronea (338 B.C.) and assumed the leadership over a league of Greek states.

Philip, however, was not destined to carry his plans to fruition, for his untimely death (336 B.C.) left that tremendous task to his twenty-year-old son, Alexander. Alexander inherited his father's admiration for Greek civilization, an admiration strengthened by the tutelage of Aristotle. Moreover, his romantically ambitious spirit was fired by the Homeric epics, and he not only

dreamed of establishing a united Greece as a Mediterranean power but deemed it his mission to spread Greek civilization abroad. A young man of action as well as a dreamer, Alexander possessed the military qualities necessary for so gigantic a task. Assisted by a body of competent and devoted colleagues trained in the service of his father, he embarked upon one of the most amazing careers of conquest the world has known.

The first step in the accomplishment of his great design was a bold invasion of Asia Minor. Then, following two brilliant victories over Persian arms, Alexander declined a peace offer which would have flattered many a greedy conqueror and which olders advisers urged him to accept, for the Persian King Darius III was willing to concede the Euphrates as a boundary between the Greek and Persian empires. Alexander hesitated, but not for long. His mission was not yet accomplished. Advancing southward he occupied Syria and all the Phoenician ports, thus neutralizing the Persian fleet which soon dispersed. Egypt, now exposed, fell easily. Persia was overrun, and the immense treasures of the Persian kings at Susa and Persepolis fell into his hands. Then, to the amazement of everybody, this youthful conqueror pressed still farther eastward. For six years (330–324 B.C.) he led his armies north and east across the Oxus river, even across the Indus into the Ganges valley. And only the complaints of his weary soldiers forced him to turn back.

What was the political result of the stupendous conquest? Alexander had far-reaching political designs which were not merely the result of personal ambition. When he had himself deified at the temple of Amen-Ra in Egypt, he was establishing a kind of religio-political order which he hoped would facilitate a world unity of Greeks and Asiatics. And although the outward manifestations of divine right offended many of his sturdy old companions-at-arms, Alexander doubtless calculated that he might thus win the loyalty of Egyptians and Asiatics, to whom such customs were familiar. His plan for Hellenizing the entire Near East involved the establishment everywhere of cities on the Greek model. Actually some seventy were founded, many of them bearing his name. The most famous, Alexandria in Egypt, remained one of the foremost Mediterranean ports for centuries. Alexander did not live long enough to enjoy the fruits of his conquests. Estranged from his former associates and worn out by exertions and dissipation, he died while still a young man in 323 B.C.

The Empire as a unit did not long survive its creator. It was soon divided into separate kingdoms, some of them ruled by Alexander's generals. But since the various states and kingdoms of the post-Alexandrian period were all monarchies after the original model, a characteristic political order did remain as the legacy of the original single state. Further, there developed in the age following Alexander a civilization which, though diversified, was common to a great part of the area of the Macedonian's conquests. We speak of this age as "Hellenistic," a word which denotes the predominantly Greek basis of its culture yet avoids the connotation of "Hellenic," or the purely Greek. For Alexander's dream of Hellenizing the Orient was realized to a surprising extent, while in its dispersal Greek culture was fused with the oriental.

The significance of Hellenistic culture, therefore, lies partly in the fusion of Greek and oriental culture, but more in the spread of Greek institutions and thought over a wide area. In fact, the heritage of Greece was eventually to be transmitted not only to the Near East but westward by Rome to Europe. It was, therefore, Hellenistic, not Hellenic, culture which directly influenced subsequent civilizations.

It was a prosperous age, a time of commercial and industrial expansion, which affected the entire Mediterranean as well as western Asiatic areas and is evident in the building of cities and in the development of banking. Unlike Athens, where most of the energy went into beautifying the Acropolis, most Hellenistic cities boasted broad and straight streets, sumptuous residences, handsome public buildings. Even the smaller towns had their libraries, assembly halls, baths, theaters, and public squares. It was, therefore, a frankly luxurious and materialistic society, and the cleavage between rich and poor was marked.

Although the subsequent loss of the greater part of Hellenistic literature makes adequate criticism difficult, it is evident that this was preëminently a literate age. Moreover, the Greek political predominance forced all important public servants to learn the tongue of their conquerors. Thus, diplomats, men of commerce, and, most

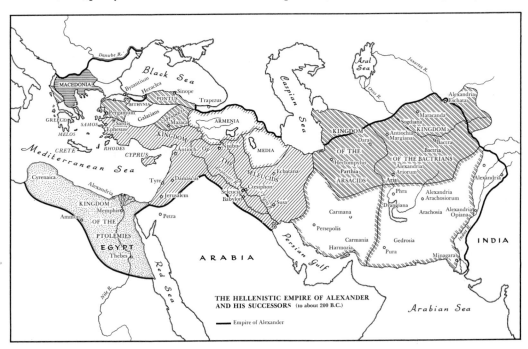

THE HELLENISTIC EMPIRE OF ALEXANDER AND HIS SUCCESSORS (to about 200 B.C.)

——— Empire of Alexander

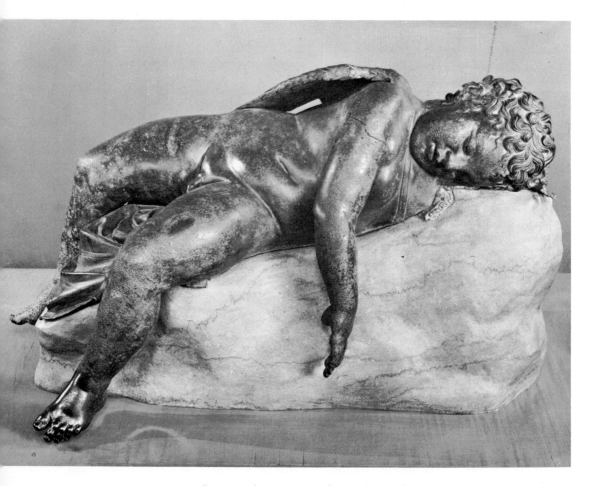

Hellenistic sculpture. Bronze figure of Eros sleeping.

important, men of learning made Greek a virtually universal language throughout the entire area. For this larger audience many books were written, and in certain cities important libraries were collected. The most famous was the library at Alexandria which helped to make that metropolis the foremost center of Hellenistic learning.

Although there are some who hold that Hellenistic art failed to maintain the exacting standards of the Hellenic period, the artists of the later age continued the work of their predecessors. Technical skill and mastery of material were perfected. Painting, especially mural painting, enjoyed a wide popularity. Greek architectural forms persisted, becoming under oriental influence more ornate. Corinthian capitals were es-

pecially popular. The large and grandiose had great appeal. The lighthouse at the entrance to the harbor of Alexandria, the Colossus of Rhodes, a huge bronze statue of the sun-god, 105 feet high, and the third temple of Diana at Ephesus were numbered among the traditional seven wonders of the world.

The crowning achievement of the period was in science where the climax of Greek thinking was reached. This was the age of Euclid, who taught at Alexandria and compiled a treatise on geometry wherein he coordinated the work of many predecessors, both known and unknown. Equally famous is the name of Archimedes of Syracuse, who again reminds us that the Greek world extended westward into the Mediterranean. Primarily a mathematician, Archimedes made important inquiries in the fields of mechanics and hydrostatics. Hipparchus of Nicaea was an astronomer of renown whose positive contributions were somewhat dimmed, at least in the eyes of modern critics, by his attack on the heliocentric theory of the universe as proposed by Aristarchus of Samos. The weight of his authority, along with that of Euclid, decided the matter for ancient times. Hipparchus also made a number of important additions to the sum total of astronomical knowledge and its mathematical implications, including a great deal of trigonometry. The *Almagest* (about A.D. 140) of Ptolemy, for centuries the foundation of western astronomical thinking, was based largely on the work of Hipparchus. And lastly we may mention Eratosthenes of Cyrene, who compiled a treatise on geography and whose computation of the earth's circumference was in error by only some two hundred miles.

Hellenistic philosophy failed to live up to the promise of its past. Aristotle, to be sure, lived and worked as the tutor of Alexander, but he was, after all, of the Hellenic tradition. The escapist arguments of Epicurus of Samos, who sought happiness in the intelligent pursuit of pleasure, failed to satisfy many. Stoicism, so named because its first proponent, Zeno, taught at the *Stoa Poecile* (Painted Porch), had a more lasting influence, though its devotees were never numerous. For the Stoic, morality was inseparable from religion, and man must surrender to the will of God who is Nature and the Law of the World. Thus the man who does not question the course of Nature, even though it bring evil or pain to himself, finds peace. Stoicism was a noble philosophy and it reflected a hunger for the spiritual which was increasingly noticeable as the old paganism lost its appeal.

The subject of the preceding pages has been the development of a culture which lies at the foundation of western civilization. Not much has been said of Greek political history, still less of economic progress. For the legacy of Greece to subsequent generations was not economic or political. Rather, it must again be emphasized, it was the rationalization of man, his place in society and, indeed, in the universe of things seen and unseen. Evidences of the pervading influence of Greek thought will multiply as our narrative progresses. And in art, the touch of Greek genius is apparent throughout the west and not a little of the east. Thus what germinated in the relatively restricted area of the Aegean and the central Mediterranean was eventually to flourish throughout the European world.

A Roman wall painting of the first century B.C.

Courtesy Metropolitan Museum of Art, New York; Rogers Fund, 1903

CHAPTER 3

Fusing Heritage of Roman Republic and Empire

A. Formation of the Roman Republic

The geographical center of Alexander's Empire had been in western Asia. Roman civilization developed first in the central Mediterranean region, then expanded westward as well as eastward to include the entire Mediterranean basin. Under Rome, Mediterranean civilization embraced for the first time all the coast lands of southern Europe, north Africa, and, finally, considerable areas to the north in Europe.

Less speculative and philosophical than the Greeks, the Romans were far more practical, and their greatest achievements were in the fields of law and government. Rome was able to remedy the political failures of the Hellenistic world and to preserve and transmit the Hellenistic cultural heritage. The remarkable combination of the Greek and the Roman achievement, which we call Graeco-Roman culture, lies at the base of our western civilization.

The Mediterranean basin which was the scene of this Graeco-Roman civilization is a natural geographic unit. From earliest times it has been an avenue of communication. As we have already seen, the ancient Phoenicians and Greeks founded colonies throughout its length and breadth. Compared with the Atlantic it is a body of water more easily navigated by small vessels. As a consequence, there has been, at least since Roman times, an intimate connection between southern Europe and northern Africa. At the Strait of Gibraltar, Europe

and Africa are in close proximity. Many historically significant crossings have been made there. Sicily is not far from the African coast. And in the eastern Mediterranean we have already noticed the contacts between Egypt, Crete, and Greece. The climate of northwestern Africa is roughly comparable to that of southern Europe. The Atlas mountains contribute largely to this condition by breaking the winds which blow over the Mediterranean and the eastern Atlantic, causing precipitation, and impeding the hot airs which blow north out of the Sahara.

Midway in the Mediterranean, and extending southward from Europe toward Africa, is the long peninsula of Italy. This is at least three times as large as Greece and it is the cradle of Roman civilization. Three distinct peoples contributed to the early development of civilization in Italy. A western wing of the Indo-European peoples entered the peninsula from the north sometime after 2000 B.C. To these the Greek colonists of southern Italy later gave the name "Italic." Around 1000 B.C. the Etruscans, a people of unknown origin but more advanced than the early Italic peoples, came, perhaps from Asia Minor, and occupied large sections of western Italy. Then came the Greeks to southern Italy and Sicily. The latter two of these peoples, with their relatively advanced cultures, were to affect the development of the more primitive Italic people. Indeed, it is remarkable that it was these and not one of their more advanced rivals who were des-

Etruscan chariot of the fourth or third century B.C.

Courtesy Metropolitan Museum of Art, New York

tined finally to dominate the peninsula. Meanwhile, the Carthaginian descendants of the Phoenician colonists, builders of a formidable sea power and commercial state in north Africa, were branching out to include parts of Sicily, Sardinia, and Corsica.

South and east of the Tiber river lies the plain of Latium. There, in various scattered communities, had settled an Italic people known as Latins. One of their settlements was a kind of trading-post, at a point where an island and shoals in the Tiber made possible a crossing and an ancient bridge. Overlooking the shallows was the Palatine hill, and on the lowlands along the bank was the market-place or Forum. Sometime before 800 B.C. the more powerful Etruscans on the north bank overran the Latin settlements and coordinated them into a nucleus which came to be known as Rome. Thus Rome commenced its political history as a monarchy under a line of Etruscan kings.

Under Etruscan domination Rome progressed in many ways, learning both from its conquerors and from the Greeks of southern Italy with whom it continued to trade. Greek coins and oriental measures of length and weight made their appearance as, also, did Greek vase-painting and architectural forms. The Latins had preserved their own language and now they began to adopt, with some modification, the Greek alphabet which thus became part of our general European heritage. Many Greek words also found their way into Latin. And the Romans discovered that some of their own traditional gods had their counterparts among the Greek deities.

Meanwhile, the Roman people had developed certain political ideas and practices which they were able to bring to maturity after the overthrow of the monarchy (about 500 B.C.). A council of older men, the Senate (from *senex*, old), had acquired considerable influence. And this was enhanced by the high esteem the ancient Romans had for the father as head of the family. A family (*familia*) could include an entire household, relatives, and servants, as well as members of the immediate family group. Moreover, the father's authority (*patria potestas*) was supreme. Then, as a natural consequence of the passing of monarchy, the Romans came to think of their government as a "public thing," a notion preserved in the expression *respublica*, or "republic." Sovereignty, or *imperium* as they called it, rested ultimately in the people, who entrusted it temporarily, or for long periods of time, to their rulers.

Immediately after the overthrow of the kings, the Romans gave form to these ideas by entrusting political power to elected magistrates. Two *consuls*, holding office for a year only, served as an executive. And in the early days of the republic only wealthy patricians served as *consuls* and sat in the Senate. Moreover, they dominated the assembly which elected the magistrates. But since the poorer citizens and peasant farmers, the *plebs*, were indispensable in time of war, the aristocratic element was forced to concede to the *plebs* the right to elect in their own assembly officials known as tribunes who could veto a magistrate's action.

As the volume of state business grew, other magistracies were added. *Quaestors* cared for financial matters. *Censors* kept lists (*census*) of citizens and assessed taxes. *Praetors* were judges who relieved the *consuls* of many judicial matters. And in the event of dire emergency it was decided that supreme power could be entrusted to one person (*dictator*).

Having acquired the protection of the tribunician authority, the people were able to achieve certain additional objectives. About 450 B.C. Roman laws were written

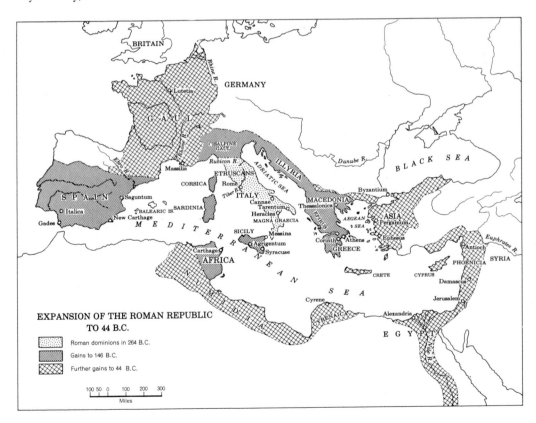

EXPANSION OF THE ROMAN REPUBLIC
TO 44 B.C.

Roman dominions in 264 B.C.

Gains to 146 B.C.

Further gains to 44 B.C.

100 50 0   100   200   300
Miles

down for the first time, being engraved on the famous twelve bronze tablets. In the making of new laws the plebs also enjoyed some influence in legally constituted assemblies. Gradually the right of any citizen to hold office as *censor, praetor,* and at length even as *consul* was conceded. In addition, the formerly exclusively patrician Senate came to include ex-magistrates. Thus was formed a kind of new nobility of office-holders along with the patrician land-owners.

Despite the increase of popular influence in the Roman government, the republic remained to the end a predominantly aristocratic state. This resulted largely from the unique position held by the Senate. Although no formal additions to its constitutional powers were made, it gained markedly in political influence. First, it was a permanent assembly, its members serving for life. And, with the addition to its membership of ex-magistrates, it included the wisest and most experienced men in Rome.

Moreover, especially in time of war, when many younger men were away from the city on military service, it was frequently difficult to assemble the other bodies, whereas the senate could always be convened with a minimum of delay. Thus it was that, although in theory the senate's functions were advisory only, magistrates often found themselves listening to proposals from the senate instead of initiating measures themselves.

B. Expansion and Corruption of the Republic

In its early days the Roman republic was no more than a small city-state. But since the neighboring Latin tribes realized that for purposes of defense Roman leadership was indispensable, they consented to incorporation into a Latin league of cities, a league which was later replaced by separate treaties negotiated with each city. In this way Etruscan supremacy in the region north of the Tiber was effectively challenged and other unfriendly Italic tribes or cities subdued. Then the Romans turned southward and conquered the various Greek colonies in southern Italy. And in so doing

they exposed themselves even more than before to the elevating influence of Greek culture.

Thus by about 275 B.C. Rome had become master of all Italy south of the Po valley.[1] Moreover, to the Latin inhabitants of the territory immediately surrounding Rome, comprising about one-sixth of the peninsula, full citizenship was granted. Elsewhere colonies of Roman citizens were planted or the conquered cities were regarded as allies and given a number of the privileges of citizenship. Voting, impractical anyway because of distance, was not included, but rights under Roman law were universally granted. This policy, so far-sighted in contrast with that of the Greeks, insured the Romans a peasant citizen-army which could expand as need arose, and facilitated Roman domination over Italy.

Roman expansion over Italy had been primarily agricultural in nature. It was accomplished by a small agrarian city-state. But this very expansion, especially as it included the Greek cities of the south, increased the commercial opportunities of Roman and Italian merchants and added to the responsibility of Rome as the protector of its allied communities. This became particularly apparent as Roman merchants looked out over the central and western Mediterranean only to find the commerce of that region monopolized by Carthage. Carthage, originally a Phoenician colony, had developed into a large and prosperous city. All of the north coast of Africa from Cyrenaica to the Atlantic, the southern coast of Spain, the Balearics, Corsica, Sardinia, and lately Sicily had fallen under Carthaginian control. In fact, it was feared that the Carthaginians might, by seizing the Sicilian city of Messina, close the passage to Roman ships. It was inevitable that further commercial expansion on the part of Rome would necessitate challenging the power of Carthage.

The long struggle between the two Mediterranean powers ended in the defeat and destruction of Carthage. In three separate periods of armed conflict, known as

---

[1] The Celtic Gauls who had invaded the Po valley were later subdued.

the Punic Wars (264–146 B.C.), the Romans, often in dire straits, proved their strength on land and sea against a truly formidable adversary. For if in the illustrious Hannibal, Carthage possessed a commander of outstanding qualities, Scipio, surnamed "Africanus," performed brilliantly for the Romans. At home the Romans displayed remarkabl fortitude in the face of successive emergencies. In the end Carthage was completely destroyed.

Dominion over the central and western Mediterranean made Rome an imperial power which, to protect itself, felt obliged to oppose any other Mediterranean state whose strength rivaled its own. Thus, expansion led to further conquest until the entire Mediterranean world was brought under Roman domination. A pretext for intervention in the eastern Mediterranean arose shortly after the fall of Carthage. Further, this region was ripe for conquest after the disintegration of Alexander's Empire. Accordingly, Macedonia, Greece, Syria, and even Egypt were conquered. Moreover, after a league of Greek cities which had taken up arms had been crushed, as though to teach the Greeks a lesson comparable to that of Carthage, Corinth was burned (146 B.C.) and thousands of Greeks sent to Rome as slaves. The city-state of Rome was henceforth mistress of the entire Mediterranean basin.

This spectacular transformation from humble Italian city-state to mistress of a far-flung empire was not accomplished without tremendous changes in the political, social, and economic life, especially of Rome and Italy, but also of the entire imperial area. So profound were the effects of conquest that they ultimately produced a revolution in the Roman way of life. First, the administration of conquered areas involved a host of new problems. In these areas Roman "provinces" were set up. Regulations were made by the senate and carried out by provincial governors whose authority was, in turn, supported by a sufficient number of troops. Although provincial governors or *proconsuls* often held office for only a year, not all were experienced and not all resisted the temptations for great private gain and personal power.

Another result of conquest was the marked increase in wealth. But since the wealth was not evenly distributed, Rome began to face the problem of a large and impoverished proletariat whose tastes, in this age of increasing luxury, seem to have run to the bloody and brutal gladiatorial contests. Moreover, many a political aspirant sought election by wholesale bribery of the Roman electorate. This added to the debasement of the proletariat. Finally, the state offered food and entertainment, the famous *panem et circenses* (bread and circuses).

Rural conditions were little better. The long campaigns of the Punic Wars had devastated many agricultural districts of Italy beyond repair. A new grain supply was now available from Africa, Egypt, and Sicily. And in Italy and Sicily great estates appeared, bought up by the senators and other wealthy Romans. These large-scale farms, worked by slave labor of which the conquests had unfortunately produced an ample supply, were far beyond the competition of the small farmer. Thus the yeoman citizen-farmer, the backbone of the republic and its army, faced ruin. Many gave up and joined the ranks of the city proletariat.[1]

Extensive and rapid conquest also created new military problems, for the new frontiers required constant vigilance. Critical military situations frequently presented themselves to plague a government already shaken at home. In short, the Roman republic, a government which had arisen to answer the needs of a city-state, was now faced with domestic and external difficulties which proved too formidable for its limited capacities. The last century of the republic, one of intermittent revolution and civil war, demonstrated that a city-state government could not manage an empire.

[1] One important consequence of the wars, representing a change from former ways, was the patronage by rich and educated Romans of Greek literature and art. Such was the vogue of Greek that well-to-do Roman children were commonly educated in schools conducted by emancipated Greek slaves. Greek, therefore, became the language of culture, and Latin literature developed in a large degree as an imitation of the Greek.

C. Transition from Republic to Empire

While it would be impossible to describe the civil war in detail here, it can easily be imagined that it proved disastrous for the institutions of republican Rome. As we have seen, actual power had fallen largely into the hands of the senate. Therefore, as the plight of the small farmer became acute, remedies sought by popular leaders were likely to be blocked. For the senate represented the aristocratic element in Roman society and above all the large landowners. When in 104 B.C., despite a hostile senate, Marius, a farmer's boy who had risen to be a successful general, was elected consul, it seemed as though the popular element had found a worthy champion. Unfortunately, although he was an excellent general and had instituted important reforms in the army, Marius was no statesman. Riots accompanied his election as consul for the sixth time (100 B.C.), and after his retirement the senate also found a military champion in Sulla, one of Marius' officers. Ignoring popular opposition, Sulla marched his troops into Rome and forced the passage of several new laws which destroyed the power of the popular assembly. Thus, for the first time, military power was openly used to secure political action. But this led to open civil war in which, as each side won temporary advantage, it avenged itself ruthlessly on its hapless adversaries. With the death of Marius (86 B.C.) and the retirement of Sulla (79 B.C.), the first period of the revolution ended.

Not only did civil war endanger republican institutions; it provided an opportunity for ambitious opponents of Roman expansion. Mithradates, king of Pontus in Asia Minor, challenged the Roman protectorate over Greece. At the same time his ally, Tigranes of Armenia, occupied Syria and Judaea while Cilician pirates terrorized the seas to the shores of Italy itself. Finally, the presence of foreign danger increased a tendency, already dangerously prevalent, for the military to assume political powers.

The careers of Gnaeus Pompey and Julius Caesar illustrate this emergence of the generals into public life. Pompey, des-patched to the east by the senate, effectively crushed both Mithradates and Tigranes, overran Judaea, and captured Jerusalem. A new eastern frontier, comprising newly created provinces and certain areas under indirect Roman influence, carried Roman dominion to the line from the upper reaches of the Euphrates to the Arabian desert. In the many negotiations and treaties involved in the creation of the new border, Pompey acted on his own initiative; and when the senate refused to sanction his decisions, he sought the help of Julius Caesar, the other consul of 59 B.C. Caesar secured the ratification of Pompey's measures and in return was given the military command in Gaul.

Transalpine Gaul, which at that time included only parts of what is today southern France, was then threatened both by the Germanic *Suevi* and the Gallic *Helvetii*. Caesar's successes and his ultimate conquest of the entire area west of the Rhine to the English channel are well known. Equally familiar is the jealousy of the senatorial leaders who refused to abandon the constitution and persuaded Pompey to oppose the successful general. But Caesar was a man of sufficient stature as a statesman to identify himself with the best interest of Rome. Thus not only did he defeat Pompey and his armies in Italy, in Spain, and in Greece, but, as dictator, inaugurated a number of much needed reforms. The assassins who struck him down in 44 B.C. undoubtedly regarded themselves as patriotically removing a tyrant. But Caesar was more than a tyrant. Though a general and an authoritarian, he possessed many statesmanlike attributes.

Caesar's death plunged Rome once again into civil war which lasted until 31 B.C. We need not follow its gloomy details. Mark Antony was the first to gain prominence by seizing Caesar's fortune and securing his own election to the consulship. More important was his acquisition through military power of the eastern half of the empire and his marriage to Cleopatra, queen of Egypt. But the mantle of Caesar's power eventually fell on his nephew Octavian. Too young, at first, to be taken seriously, he gradually strengthened his position, and as some of Antony's legions came over to

A Roman of the first century B.C.

*Courtesy Metropolitan Museum of Art,
New York*

him he prevailed upon the senate to declare war on Egypt. In a combined land and sea engagement at Actium his forces triumphed. The long civil war was over, and to Octavian was given the golden opportunity to reorganize the Roman government and save the empire.

Octavian, whom we may as well now refer to as Augustus,—the title a grateful people bestowed on him,—was eminently fitted for the stupendous task of imperial reorganization. Though not a general, he was a statesman in the best sense of the word and, despite recurring ill health, he kept persistently at the work he had assigned himself. He was capable of bold, resolute action, but never acted impetuously. During his tenure of power (31 B.C.– A.D. 14) the revolution was consummated and a governmental system devised which endured for nearly three hundred years. The beginning of the Roman Empire is customarily reckoned from his reign.

After the battle of Actium, what the entire Mediterranean world most desired was peace and order. Augustus sensed this. He also realized that although the Roman citizens of Italy were still jealous of the ancient city-state constitution, this had to be brought into harmony with the new situation. For henceforth a city-state was to govern the entire Mediterranean world. Augustus, therefore, developed a system of government which was in a sense a combination of monarchy and republic, an empire under republican forms. Sometimes described as a "dyarchy" (double rule), it has usually been designated the "principate," because Augustus himself preferred the title of *princeps*, or first citizen, which the senate conferred upon him.

Augustus preserved the forms of republican government by maintaining the senate and the magistracies in the administration of the city of Rome. But outside the city the senate's powers were limited. Further, Augustus prevailed upon a grateful senate to elect him to all the key offices. Thus, in addition to being *imperator*, or commander-in-chief, with control over the military forces, he possessed the tribunician authority, by which he could veto the acts of the senate. And as *censor* he could in a measure control its membership. He was also *pontifex maximus*, head of the pagan state religion, and the proconsular authority made him supreme in the provinces. Provincial governors were appointed by and directly responsible to him, and their activities were frequently checked. Yet even here he wisely shared power with the senate to whose charge he entrusted the inner provinces. Those on the frontiers where military power was significant he reserved to himself.

Augustus endeavored within the framework of this system to carry out various reforms. Italy was pacified and cleared of bandits. Rome was adequately policed and a rebuilding program commenced. Augustus counseled against any further conquests, a bit of advice prompted by the defeat of his legions east of the Rhine. Britain, however, was added later in the century. He realized, too, that the events of the past century had weakened the old devotion to the state and had created no new loyalty capable of enlisting the support of Romans and provincials alike. As a consequence, he sought to reinvigorate the Roman religion. Nor was it mere personal ambition which led him to accept the senate's enrolling him among the gods. It is possible that he urged Vergil to compose a poem glorifying the deeds of his family. Certainly

THE ROMAN EMPIRE ABOUT 120 A.D.

The Empire in 120 A.D.

0   100   200   300   400   500

Scale in miles

The Aeneid is an epic whose hero Aeneas, in whom are found all the old Roman virtues, is held to be the ancestor of the Julian family.

Augustus deserved well of the Roman people, and his reign inaugurated a period of internal peace unparalleled in duration and in the wide area affected. As the years passed the powers granted the Princeps, which were in a sense emergency measures, became permanent. Thus the word *imperium*, which originally signified sovereignty, came through its new association with one man to mean monarchical rule over a vast state. And *imperator* similarly acquired its later connotation of single ruler, or emperor. Moreover, the system Augustus created was even able to survive a number of bad emperors during the first century A.D. Since the republic had never formally been abolished, there could never be adequate provision for the succession. This was the most conspicuous weakness in the system. Augustus associated Tiberius with him and he was accepted after his death. But there were occasions when the rival claims of army and senate caused serious disturbances. Yet the Roman government survived, despite the faults of men like Caligula (37–41) and Nero (54–68), and passed in the second century into the age of the "good emperors."

Under a series of remarkable men Mediterranean civilization prospered as never before. Here we can only name these rulers and then conclude with a brief survey of life during this brilliant period. Trajan (98–117) is perhaps best known for incorporation of the province of Dacia, north of the Danube, and an extension of the eastern frontier to include Armenia, Mesopotamia, and Assyria, and for his correspondence with Pliny the Younger, governor of Bithynia. His remarks concerning the treatment of Christians will be discussed in a later chapter. It is significant that Trajan, who was born in Spain, was the first provincial to hold the imperial title. Hadrian (117–138) built the wall protecting the province of Britain from the north, and commenced the coördination of Roman law. Finally, we must mention the two Antonines, Antoninus Pius (138–161) and Marcus Aurelius (161–180), both men of pre-eminent ability, the latter a philosopher as well. With his death this happy age passed into more troubled times.

D. Life in the Roman Empire

The unity of the Mediterranean world within the Roman Empire was maintained by a disciplined standing military force and an admirable system of communication. Augustus had attempted to restore the citizen character of the Roman army, but with the passage of years the legions were composed more and more of provincials and mercenaries. Sometimes citizenship was the reward for service, and army pensions often included a plot of land on which veterans could settle. The Romans had organized the army into units called legions, each containing about 4,500 men, the majority of whom were heavily armed infantry. These were variously divided, the smallest unit being the century, originally one hundred men, later usually less, commanded by a centurion. Every mile of the long frontier was policed, and no point was far from a Roman encampment. Great permanent fortifications were erected, for example, to protect Britain, as already mentioned, or to connect the upper Rhine and Danube. Except for Dacia, the two rivers constituted the northern frontier in Europe proper.

The Romans were skillful road-builders. Roadbeds and stone block surfaces were designed for durability as well as speed of travel. Primarily military, they served civilian traffic and a postal system. They greatly aided overland commerce, and made possible the profitable exploitation of the mineral resources of Spain, Gaul, and Britain. Sea traffic showed less progress. Although Roman galleys regularly plied the Mediterranean, the Atlantic was little used.

Not only did the Romans divide the Mediterranean world into provinces, they established cities everywhere—unless these already existed. A Roman *civitas* often resembled the mother-city and boasted a forum, theaters, arenas, and the like. Roman expansion into the provinces was no log-cabin pioneering. Rather, it was a veritable transportation of everything familiar at

Rome. It is possible for a traveler today to gaze on the ruins of an amphitheater at Nîmes in southern France, to visit a Roman theater at Orange, to view mighty aqueducts in southern France and Spain or a forum in north Africa. In the east, most cities were already built, though even there Roman influence was by no means negligible. In the newer western provinces, a tribal center was often chosen as the original nucleus of a *civitas*, a practice reflected in names which have survived to the present. Paris (*Parisii*), Soissons (*Suessiones*), and Trier (*Augusta Treverorum*) are examples.

The *civitates* were of the essence of Roman civilization. To understand the empire it is essential to grasp their significance. Indeed, it has often been said that the principate was a federation of partially self-governing communities.

In the realm of the mind, the Roman contribution is less impressive than the Greek. Indeed, the educated Romans themselves paid tribute to Greek culture by learning Greek, and their writers, by imitating Greek forms. And yet the Latin language as perfected by the Romans became the vehicle for some of the greatest works of our western civilization. Surely literature is the richer for the works of Cicero, the poetry of Vergil and Horace, the histories of Livy and Tacitus, the dramas of Plautus and Terence, to mention only a few. And the Latin tongue lived to become the language of the Catholic church, a language sufficiently flexible to meet the demands of theological precision as well as of religious poetry.

One of the greatest of Rome's legacies was its law. This had grown from the time of the Twelve Tables to the time of Augustus and later into a formidable mass of literature. Judges' (*praetors'*) decisions became precedents. The opinions (*responsa*) of legal experts (*juris prudentes*), at first unofficial, then some officially sanctioned, added to the volume. Moreover, the jurisdiction of Roman law expanded with the extension of citizenship. Thus it came to include first all Italians. Finally, under Caracalla (212), it was extended over the entire imperial area. Just as Greek practices affected the laws of the early republic, so new procedures came in as the entire cosmopolitan citizenry enjoyed rights under Roman law. Such a vast literature finally required codification, a work begun much earlier but not completed until the reign of Justinian in the sixth century. As later chapters will indicate, Roman law has directly or indirectly affected the laws of almost every European country.

Next to law and government, architecture most clearly represents the character of Graeco-Roman civilization. It can be styled Graeco-Roman because Roman builders owed so much to the Greeks whom they sometimes rather slavishly imitated. The Greek orders, especially the Corinthian, were widely used. But, generally speaking, Roman building lacked the exquisite proportions of the Greek. Roman structures were more massive and grandiose. Moreover, many, such as triumphal arches, the Colosseum, and the baths in Rome, were frankly built for pleasure or display. There were, of course, innovations. The round arch, taken probably from the Etruscans, was employed not only by itself but as the structural base of a dome or a vault. Roman engineering also achieved some notable triumphs. The city was supplied with water from fourteen aqueducts, the water being conducted in stone conduits both over and under the ground. Huge dams and drains were constructed and sewage was surprisingly well disposed of. Roman building reflects the Roman emphasis on organization, wealth, and material success in general. It also manifests, even to the modern traveler, the expanse and cultural unity of the Mediterranean world. For from the borders of Scotland to the olive groves of north Africa and from Portugal to the Arabian desert, the all-pervading influence of Rome is still evident in its monuments.

The very existence of the Roman Empire with its uniting of the Mediterranean world left an indelible impression on men's minds. The centuries during which the Empire flourished became the "golden age" for subsequent generations to venerate. So great was the spell cast by Roman civilization that men ever afterwards continued to imitate many of its features. And Rome as the city of the popes, the heart of Christianity, was to live on in a new spiritual empire. Truly, Rome may be called "eternal."

A second century sculptured representation of the Founder of Christianity, now in the Lateran Museum in Rome.

Alinari Photo

CHAPTER 4

The Judaeo-Christian Spiritual Heritage

A. Origins of Christianity in Judaism

Now it came to pass in those days that there went forth a decree from Caesar Augustus that a census of the whole world should be taken. This first census took place while Cyrinus was governor of Syria. And all were going, each to his own town, to register.

And Joseph also went from Galilee out of the town of Nazareth into Judaea to the town of David, which is called Bethlehem—because he was of the house and family of David—to register, together with Mary, his espoused wife. . . . And . . . while they were there . . . she brought forth her firstborn son, and wrapped him in swaddling clothes, and laid him in a manger, because there was no room for them in the inn.[1]

In these words a Palestinian physician, living in the early decades of the Roman Empire, described an event which a substantial proportion of the world's population today regards as the most important in history. It is a simple, straightforward account, but it gives us a glimpse of the Roman administrative system at work in the census ordered by the Emperor, and it reveals much about Christ's birth. The Founder of a great religion was born in humble circumstances, and lived His entire life within the orbit of Roman civilization. The influence of Christianity upon Rome and of Rome upon Christianity is of vital importance to our understanding of both.

It was Judaea, an eastern province of the Empire and one inhabited by a people despised by the Romans, which provided the scene for a history unique in ancient times. Judaea (or Palestine) was the repository of a religious tradition unlike that of any other country of its day. The Roman governmental tradition and the Hebrew religious heritage were two significant formative influences in the development of Christianity.

The Jewish religion was unique, because in a world characterized by various forms of polytheism the Jewish people had persisted in their loyalty to the one God. Moreover, to them, Jahveh was a God of spirit, creator of the world, ruler of the universe, and not a deity fashioned after man's own imperfect imagination. As the ancient psalmist so eloquently put it:

But our God is in heaven: he hath done all things whatsoever he would.
The idols of the Gentiles are silver and gold, the works of the hands of men.
They have mouths and speak not; they have eyes and see not.
They have ears and hear not: they have noses and smell not.
They have hands and feel not, they have feet and walk not; neither shall they cry out through their throat.[2]

Successive Hebrew prophets had striven to convince their people of the gravity of sin. They had preached repentance and emphasized the idea of sacrifice in atonement for sin. And the offering of sacrifices to God became an essential part of Jewish ritual. Finally, the prophets had taught that man-

---

[1] Luke, II, i–vii.

[2] Psalm CXIII, iii–vii.

41

kind, in a fallen state since Adam in pride rejected God's command, required a redeemer. Thus they had long foretold the coming of a Messiah or Savior.

The teachings of the prophets, along with the inspired poetry of the psalms and many books dealing with the creation of the world and of man and with Hebrew history, amounted to a literary as well as a religious heritage of extraordinary richness. Moreover, since Christianity embodied a number of Jewish religious ideas, it was only natural that the sacred writings of the Jews should have been incorporated into Chris-

tian literature. They formed, in fact, the "Old" Testament, distinct from the specifically Christian "New" Testament books.

The religion preached by Christ was, to his followers, a fulfilment of the Hebraic heritage. They believed Him to be the promised Messiah, both God and man— God who, in the person of Christ, had assumed a human nature from His Virgin Mother, Mary. This doctrine, known as the "Incarnation," is indissolubly linked with man's "Redemption" in the minds of Christians. To them, Christ's crucifixion and death constituted the one perfect sacri-

Saints Peter and Paul depicted on a Christian glass and gold leaf bowl of the fourth or fifth century.

Courtesy Metropolitan Museum of Art, New York; Rogers Fund, 1916

ANCIENT PALESTINE

10   0   10
Miles

Sidon
MT. LEBANON
MT. HERMON
Damascus

Tyre
Litani R.
PHOENICIA
Dan

LAKE HULEH

Acre
Capernaum
BASHAN

GALILEE
Cana
SEA OF GALILEE
Yarmuk R.

Tiberias

Nazareth

Gadara

MT. CARMEL
Kishon R.

Dor
Megiddo
Ramoth-Gilead

Caesaria
GILEAD

Beth-Shan
(Scythopolis)
Gerasa

PLAIN OF SHARON

Samaria

Shechem
Jabbok R.

Appollonia

Antipatris
SAMARIA

Joppa

Lydda
Rabbath Ammon

Bethel
Jericho

Gezer
Emmaus
AMMON

Jerusalem (Dead Sea Scrolls found here)

Beth-Shemesh
MT. NEBO

Ascalon
Bethlehem

Gath

Gaza
Hebron

Raphia
DEAD SEA
Arnon R.

Gerar
J U D A E A

Sharuhen
Beer-Sheba

EGYPT
WILDERNESS OF ZIN

MOAB

Zered R.

EDOM

Petra

T R A N S J O R D A N

MEDITERRANEAN SEA

Jordan R.

fice for men's sins. Humanity was reconciled with divinity, and all men were offered the hope of life after death in a "kingdom not of this world."

Christ startled and dismayed some of His Jewish audiences by His seeming departure from Hebrew tradition. To over-strict observance of the "old" law, as evidenced by the Pharisees, He gave short shrift. Rather, as in His famous *Sermon on the Mount*, He exalted true humility, meekness, even suffering and poverty. His first faithful followers were mostly untutored men. His sympathy for the poor and unfortunate was unbounded, and He commanded His disciples to "love one another."

B. Christian Doctrine and Church Organization

Christ's teachings were both moral and theological. The former, embodying the noble concept of the brotherhood of man, are perhaps the more familiar today. However much they have been disregarded, they still form the ethical basis of European, or Western, civilization. The theological teachings, on the other hand, have been the subject of many controversies. As a consequence, it will be well here to mention briefly the principal beliefs of early Christianity. Later chapters will discuss controversial matters as they arise.

The kernel of Christian teaching is the doctrine of the Trinity, that God is triune, three distinct persons in one divine nature, the Father, Son, and Holy Ghost, to use the familiar terms. Christ frequently insisted on His "oneness" with the Father. And before He took leave of His apostles, He promised that His Father would send them the "Paraclete," the "Spirit of Truth." In the person of Christ, therefore, were united, it was taught, a divine and a human nature. This mystery is an important corollary to the doctrine of the Trinity, for from it developed the Christian teaching with regard to the relation of man and God and, indirectly, the idea that the Christian church was divine as well as human.

As a consequence of belief in the Incarnation, or Christ's taking a human nature, there could not be in Christianity any view of flesh and matter as intrinsically evil such

as was held by the ancient Zoroastrians of Persia or by the Manichaeans, of whom there were considerable numbers in the Roman Empire. On the contrary, Christ provided the means by which, after His departure from the world, future disciples might continue that union with divinity enjoyed in a different way by those who associated with Him on earth. These means were later called sacraments and, to quote a formal definition, were "outward signs instituted by Christ to give grace." By "grace" was meant a supernatural gift of God freely bestowed on man to prepare him for eternal life. Among the sacraments, baptism was the one which made a person a Christian, while the eucharist, as the sacrificial repetition of Christ's last supper, became the central act of Christian worship.[1]

It has already been pointed out that the early Christians appropriated the sacred scriptures of the Jews and added others of their own, known as the New Testament. The New Testament included the three gospels of St. Matthew, St. Mark, and St. Luke, which tell the story of the life of Christ. Though they evidently existed in oral tradition considerably earlier, they were probably not reduced to writing until thirty or forty years after the crucifixion. The fourth gospel, that of St. John, written towards the end of the first century, is quite different and relates many incidents not found in the others. In addition to the gospels there were the *Acts of the Apostles*, an historical account of the earliest days of the infant church, the *Apocalypse* or book of *Revelation*, and a number of letters, especially those of St. Paul.

The New Testament was only the beginning of Christian literature, for the various struggles against the Roman government, as well as the inner controversies within Christianity itself, occasioned many works of an apologetic nature. These were treatises justifying, explaining, and defending the faith against its adversaries. Although distinct from the Bible ("book"), as the Old and New Testaments came to be called, some of these writings which were regarded as especially inspired or particularly impor-

---

[1] Other sacraments, as subsequently defined, were confirmation, penance, extreme unction, holy orders, and matrimony.

tant received a kind of official sanction. Their authors were known as the "Fathers" of the church. Among the most famous were St. Ambrose of Milan, St. Jerome, and St. Augustine of Hippo, whose works will be described more fully in a later chapter.

The infant church founded in Jerusalem spread with remarkable rapidity throughout the Roman Empire. Indeed, the Empire by virtue of its very existence immensely aided the progress of the new religion. The *pax Romana* (Roman peace) guaranteed safe travel, and hence made possible the passage of ideas as well as the materials of commerce. As a consequence, the early Christian communities were ordinarily found in the cities. Moreover, it frequently happened that the original nucleus of a Christian community was a group of Jews, many of whom had been dispersed far and wide and had commonly settled in the cities. Any and all Christians were, in those days, "missionaries," for in the course of their travels they brought the faith to others. But there were also some who dedicated their lives to the spread of Christianity and were, therefore, in a more formal sense missionaries. Such, of course, were the immediate apostles of Christ and those closely associated with them.

Foremost among the early missionaries was St. Paul. Paul (originally Saul) of Tarsus was an educated Jew and a Roman citizen who became one of the earliest converts to Christianity. Since he was thoroughly conversant with Hellenistic thought, he was admirably fitted to synthesize the Christian tradition with the Greek and the Hebrew. Although he preached and wrote to his own people, particularly those "Hellenized" Jews who were to be found throughout the Roman world, he firmly believed that the Christian gospel was intended for all races and nations. Hence he traveled the length and breadth of the Empire as an "apostle to the Gentiles." He was especially successful in interpreting Christian theology to educated minds influenced by the Greek philosophical tradition. His epistles which are included in the New Testament are the letters he wrote to the communities where he had preached and founded churches.

Christianity early developed a visible human organization known as the church (*ecclesia*). Those whose function it was to administer the sacraments were known as the clergy, distinct from the body of the faithful or laity. The twelve apostles, the immediate associates of Christ, had been, as it were, the original clergy. And their successors came to be called bishops (*episcopi*). Moreover, since the first Christian communities were in the towns, a bishop's "see" (seat) was invariably a city. The entire area of his jurisdiction, known as a diocese, a word borrowed from Roman usage, was customarily coterminous with a Roman *civitas*. The various smaller parish churches within a *civitas* were administered by priests, who in turn were assisted by deacons.

An episcopal (or bishop's) see founded by an apostle enjoyed a preëminence, and among these Rome came to have a unique position. First, an early tradition held that at Rome, where both St. Peter and St. Paul suffered martyrdom, the former founded his bishopric. And, as was recorded in St. Matthew's gospel,[1] Christ had singled out St. Peter as the leader of his apostles. These things combined with the city's political position to give to the Roman see a supremacy over all others. This was not, of course, so evident in the days of persecution as later. Moreover, records for those early days are scanty. But even as early as 95 A.D., St. Clement, bishop of Rome, exhibited a strikingly authoritative tone in a letter addressed to the Corinthians. During the first century, therefore, the Christian church began to take shape as an hierarchical organization.

C. Christianity and the Roman Empire

The Roman government did not, at first, welcome Christianity. Customarily tolerant of all faiths, the Empire officially banned Christianity and on frequent occasions made determined efforts to suppress it. This was partly because the early Christians usually lived apart and, as a consequence, were often popularly suspected of engaging in various questionable practices in secret meetings. But the principal reason for persecution was the fact that the conscientious Christian

[1] XVI, 17–19.

Rome. The Colosseum, place of Christian martyrdoms, as seen through the Arch of Titus.

refused the one act of pagan worship still required of everyone. This was a formal outward obeisance to the shrine of the god-emperor. To the Christian such an act was idolatry and signified repudiation of the eternal God. To the Roman government, on the other hand, the refusal was tantamount to treason and punishable by death. The result was an impasse which drove Christians to worship in secret and at the risk of the martyrdom which many suffered. Yet so bravely did men and women, even the very young, face the lions in the public arena that others were inspired by their heroic example. Persecution did not succeed in its objective. It was not continuous, but burst forth sporadically, on the impulse of an irresponsible ruler like Nero, or as a consequence of the considered judgment of a statesman like Marcus Aurelius. Actually most emperors were more lenient than cer-

tain provincial governors who were sensitive to the pressure of popular anti-Christian feeling. But for many intervening years the policy of the Roman government was that outlined by Trajan in a famous letter to Pliny, the governor of Bithynia. So long as Christians did not openly flaunt their faith, they were to be left alone.

By the early fourth century it became evident that despite governmental measures, whether severe or moderate, the number of Christians had so increased that some form of recognition was inevitable. Accordingly, in A.D. 313, the Emperor Constantine issued the famous Edict of Milan, which legally tolerated Christianity and placed it on an equal footing with all other religions. The motives which prompted Constantine to this act are not clear. According to an ancient account, he called on the God of the Christians in a critical battle and be-

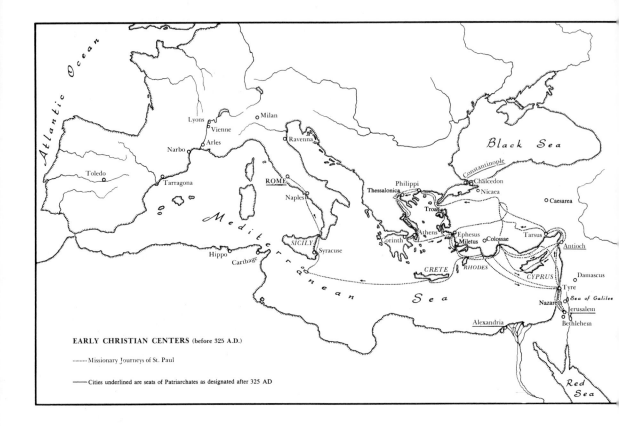

EARLY CHRISTIAN CENTERS (before 325 A.D.)

--------- Missionary Journeys of St. Paul

———— Cities underlined are seats of Patriarchates as designated after 325 AD

held in the sky the sign of the cross and the words *In hoc signo vinces* (In this sign thou shalt conquer). Constantine did not, however, become a Christian himself until shortly before his death many years later. And he never entirely abandoned, at least in the east, the concept of a god-emperor. But whatever Constantine's own ideas may have been, the future lay with Christianity. A temporary pagan reaction under Julian "the apostate" (A.D. 361–363) merely served to emphasize the power of the new faith. By the reign of the Emperor Theodosius (*d.* 395) public profession of paganism was proscribed and Christianity thus placed in a privileged position. As a consequence, the Roman Empire, before it disintegrated, was a Christian Empire. The persecutor became the ally.

The tremendous mystery of the rise of Christianity, from its humble beginnings among unlettered men in an obscure corner of the Roman Empire to its triumphant recognition as the imperial religion, lies hidden in the hearts of those who became Christians. In a secular history, such as this,

we can at best only enumerate contemporary conditions which seem pertinent. Accordingly, we have emphasized material facts, the *pax Romana*, the admirable Roman system of communication. There are also certain developments in the fields of intellectual and religious history which will bear examination. First, it is significant that at the time of the beginnings of Christianity Graeco-Roman paganism had already lost much of its former appeal. Greek intellectual achievements had weakened the belief in the Homeric deities and, with Plato and Aristotle, had pointed toward a rational monotheism. Much the same thing occurred in Rome. Augustus tried in vain to restore the veneration of the ancient Roman gods. But virtually all that remained was an emperor-worship which actually was a religion of the state. Educated, high-minded Romans like Cicero and Seneca turned to Stoicism.[1]

Philosophical rationalization of religious questions could not satisfy the common man. He craved a more tangible, a more

[1] See above, p. 27.

emotionally satisfying faith. And this explains the popularity of various so-called mystery religions which made their way, usually from the Near East, into the Graeco-Roman world. All of these cults seem to have had in common an appeal to the emotions through elaborate ritual. Some embodied the important idea of purification, even of sacrifice. The most popular oriental cult, especially in the Roman army, was that of Mithras. This was of Persian origin, Mithras being the helper of Ahura Mazda and thus elevated into a sort of sun-god.[1] Elaborate and arduous initiations served to give the devotees a sense of fellowship. The military virtues were stressed and a future life was promised. The cult of Mithras was for a time a serious competitor with Christianity.

During the time of Christianity's early growth, educated people were inclined to seek the answer to the riddle of life in some sort of philosophical speculation, while common folk looked to the sensuous rituals of the East. And although the philosophy called Neo-Platonism, as expounded by Plotinus, did in some measure bridge the gap, it is significant that Christianity appeared in a world strikingly barren of real religion. Moreover, it appealed to rich and poor, to educated and illiterate. Christ's teachings gave comfort and hope to those on whom the burdens of life pressed heavily. His promise of beatitude in Heaven was simple and clear. And yet, as explained by a St. Paul or elaborated by the early apologists, Christianity could and did satisfy the intellectual aspirations of the learned. And in contrast to the vague myths of the mystery religions, the Christ of the New Testament appeared as a distinct, historic personality, born into a recognized Jewish family, a man who had lived under Roman governors recorded by name and who had walked and talked with real people.

D. The Problem of Heresy

Even before the days of toleration, the infant Christian Church faced the problem of heresy. Heresy meant deliberate departure from the accepted doctrines of the church.

[1] See above, p. 15.

It was intellectual and spiritual dissent and concerned the beliefs of Christianity, not the morals of its adherents. It was distinct, therefore, from the ordinary human moral failings or sins, however great. When heretics were numerous, the church was forced to act as an organization. In fact, the inner organization of the church was materially strengthened as a result of combating heresy. Two types of action were called forth by the prevalence of a particular heresy: first, formal and precise definition of the dogma questioned; and, second, disciplinary measures to suppress heresy.

Most of the heresies of the early centuries of Christianity concerned the doctrine of the Trinity. This mystery, admittedly difficult to understand, puzzled many especially in the Hellenistic East where subtle philosophical speculations were extraordinarily popular. Questions were raised with regard to the person and nature of Christ and his relation to the Godhead. Most important was the heresy known as Arianism, from its founder Arius. Arius held that Christ had not co-existed eternally with the Father. This implied a denial of Christ's equality with God the Father and undermined the entire theology of the Incarnation and Redemption. Arianism acquired a considerable vogue despite the efforts of such stalwart champions of the Trinitarian doctrine as Athanasius of Alexandria. Finally, under the auspices of the Emperor Constantine, there assembled at Nicaea (A.D. 325) a council of bishops and prelates from all over the Christian world. This, the first great ecumenical council, affirmed the orthodox doctrine of the Trinity and in a formal statement of faith, the Nicene Creed, carefully defined Christ's co-eternity and consubstantiality with the Father.

Arianism persisted for some years. But ultimately, and partly with the assistance of the imperial government, orthodoxy triumphed throughout the Empire. Arian missionaries had, however, taught their faith to various German tribes beyond the frontiers, thus creating serious problems, both religious and political, during the later period of the Germanic invasions.

Arianism tested the ability of the early church to coördinate its authority against its enemies. Moreover, the practice of holding universal councils was continued. The church recognizes seven ecumenical councils within the first seven centuries of its existence, as well as many local councils. The Council of Ephesus (431) again upheld the Trinity against the teachings of Nestorius who held that the two natures in Christ, the divine and the human, amounted to two personalities and that the Virgin Mary was the mother of his human personality alone. In condemning Nestorianism the Council of Ephesus affirmed Mary's title of "Mother of God" and thus officially sanctioned the popular veneration of the Virgin Mary, as the greatest of the saints, which has become so characteristic of Catholic Christianity.

Going to another extreme the Monophysites held that Christ possessed only a single combined nature. This doctrine was condemned by the Council of Chalcedon in 451, a council which was further distinguished by the active leadership demonstrated by Pope Leo I. It was his letter to the Patriarch of Constantinople which was accepted by the assembled prelates as the authoritative expression of orthodoxy on this matter. It is worth noting that the Monophysite heresy persisted in Eastern parts of the Roman Empire, especially Syria, Palestine, and Egypt, and considerably embarrassed later emperors.

By the fifth century Christianity had not only emerged from the "catacombs" and triumphed over external enemies, it had overcome inner schism. It had also commenced a work destined to be in a sense perennial, that of perfecting its organization and adapting it to the conditions of the world about. This important task was retarded, as we shall presently see, by the chaos into which the Roman Empire was plunged in the fifth and sixth centuries.

E. Summary of Europe's Ancient Inheritance from Mediterranean Lands

In looking back upon ancient civilization, philosophers of later days sometimes conceived of the legacy of the past as symbolized by three cities—Athens, Rome, and Jerusalem. For Athens signified the supremacy of the intellect, Rome the benevolent authority of law, and Jerusalem the spiritual heritage of religion. It would be difficult to find a more appropriate summary of the material of the preceding chapters. All that was best in the science and art of the ancient Near East was fulfilled and surpassed in Greece. The Romans were a race of conquerors with a genius for law and government. But as their own poet, Horace, remarked, they were "conquered" culturally by their Greek captives. And as we have just seen, Rome, before its fall, was a Christian empire. Therefore, perhaps the greatest achievement of the Romans was the fusion of the ancient heritage into one organic whole.

With Rome, civilization moved westward to embrace the entire Mediterranean basin. Thus was formed what might appropriately be called a Mediterranean community. Moreover, for several centuries to come the center of gravity of civilization remained within the limits of that community. But Julius Caesar and his successors advanced the Roman standards well into Western Europe. And before many years had passed, new peoples in eastern as well as western Europe were to come under the influence of Graeco-Roman-Christian civilization. What we have been describing is not merely the development of a series of ancient cultures, but the very foundations of European civilization, its inheritance from the past.

Christian marble sarcophagus, fourth century, Allegory of the Last Judgment, the separation of the sheep from the goats.

Courtesy Metropolitan Museum of Art, New York

Greek Coin from Syracuse, c. 400 B.C.

Courtesy Frederick J. Woodbridge

SELECT SUPPLEMENTARY READINGS FOR PART I

Note. The books listed here and at the end of the other Parts of the volume are exclusively in English, and are only a very few of the many important historical works relating to the present text. For additional titles, students should consult the bibliographies in the more recent general books cited below, and also the *Guide to Historical Literature* (new ed., 1961). Two useful surveys of Western civilization, copiously illustrated with artistic material from successive periods, are: *Life Picture History of Western Man* (1951), and F. van der Meer, *Atlas of Western Civilization* (tr. 1954). Useful surveys of art are: H. W. and P. J. Janson, *History of Art* (1963); H. Gardner, *Art Through the Ages* (new ed., 1959); N. Pevsner. *An Outline of European Architecture* (1957); W. H. McNeill, *The Rise of the West* (1963) is a suggestive synthesis.

General for Part I. The standard work of reference for the ancient world is the *Cambridge Ancient History*, 12 vols. (1923–1939). Other comprehensive treatments are: E. Barker, G. N. Clark, and P. Vaucher, *The European Inheritance*, vol. I (1952); J. H. Breasted, *Ancient Times* (1935); W. G. De Burgh, *The Legacy of the Ancient World* (3rd ed., 1960); T. R. Glover, *The Ancient World* (1935); M. I. Rostovtsev, A *History of the Ancient World*, 2 vols. (1923–1939).

Chapter 1. J. H. Breasted, A *History of Egypt* (1942); V. G. Childe, *What Happened in History* (1946), and *The Dawn of European Civilization* (1958); C. H. Dawson, *The Age of the Gods* (1933); H. M. Orlinsky, *Ancient Israel* (2nd ed., 1960).

Chapter 2. W. R. Agard, *What Democracy Meant to the Greeks* (1942), and *The Greek Mind* (1957); G. W. Botsford and C. A. Robinson, *Hellenic History* (4th ed., 1956); C. M. Bowra, *The Greek Experience* (1957); G. L. Dickinson, *The Greek View of Life* (1958); E. Hamilton, *The Greek Way* (1930); H. D. F. Kitto, *The Greeks* (1951); S. Barr, *The Will of Zeus, a History of Greece* (1961); M. I. Rostovtsev, *The Social and Economic History of the Hellenistic World*, 3 vols. (1941); M. Hadas, *Hellenistic Culture* (1959); A. Zimmern, *The Greek Commonwealth* (1931).

For Greek (and Roman) art, see the works of Gardner and Pevsner, cited above.

Chapter 3. M. Hadas, *Imperial Rome* (1965); R. H. Barrow, *The Romans* (1949); J. Carcopino, *Daily Life in Ancient Rome* (tr. 1940); S. Dill, *Roman Society from Nero to Marcus Aurelius* (1920); D. Dudley, *The Civilization of Rome* (1960); H. Mattingly, *Roman Imperial Civilzation* (1959); F. G. Moore, *The Roman's World* (1946); M. I. Rostovtsev, *Rome* (new ed. by E. J. Bickerman of vol. II of *History of the Ancient World;* 1960); H. Scullard, *From the Gracchi to Nero* (1959); C. Starr, *The Emergence of Rome as the Ruler of the Ancient World* (1953).

Chapter 4. R. Bainton, *Early Christianity* (1960); P. Carrington, *The Early Christian Church*, 2 vols. (1957); P. Hughes, A *History of the Church*, vol. I (1934); A. H. M. Jones, *Constantine and the Conversion of Europe* (1949); K. S. Latourette, A *History of the Expansion of Christianity*, vol. I (1937).

Roman building in the provinces. The Arena at Arles.

Courtesy French Government Tourist Office, New York

PART II

CONTRACTION OF THE ROMAN
OF THE

From
Marcus Aurelius
to
Gregory the Great

St. Paul. Late sixth or early seventh century ivory
plaque from Roman-Frankish Gaul.

Courtesy Metropolitan Museum of Art, New York

EMPIRE AND EXPANSION
CHRISTIAN CHURCH

A Roman aqueduct in southern
Gaul. The Pont du Gard.

Courtesy French Government Tourist Office, New York

THE second part of the story of Western civilization extends from the close of the third century to the beginning of the seventh. It is marked by social decay and political reorganization of the Roman Empire, by the practical loss of the western provinces of the Empire (Spain, Gaul, Britain, and most of Italy) to Germanic invaders and settlers, and by the consequent shift of the center of gravity of the Empire from old Rome to newly founded Constantinople. The Empire continues, but henceforth it is described more properly as Byzantine (or Greek) than as Roman; and it confronts, on one hand, a quite different civilization to the east in Asia, and, on the other hand, a relative barbarism among Slavs and Germans to the north and west in Europe.

This part of the story is also marked by consolidation and expansion of the Catholic Christian Church. Indeed, the Church now succeeds the Empire as the chief agency in preserving and extending the Western civilization of the Mediterranean. It gradually converts and helps to civilize the Germanic and Slavic invaders and settlers in southern Europe, and begins to push its missionary and civilizing work northward beyond the former confines of the Roman Empire.

At the same time, Christianity loses the eastern and southern shores of the Mediterranean to the new and rival religion of Mohammed—the religion of Islam. Henceforth, the old traditional unity of the Mediterranean world is broken. Half of it (Syria and northern Africa) becomes identified with the Near and Middle East in an essentially Islamic civilization, while Western and Christian civilization becomes more strictly European.

CHAPTER 5

THE THIRD AND FOURTH CENTURIES:

Decay and Reorganization of the Roman Empire

A. Military and Social Factors in the Collapse of the Augustan Principate

A preceding chapter has described the Roman Empire at the height of its prosperity in the second century. Although a succession of powerful emperors had gradually implanted a habit of autocratic rule, the principate (or dyarchy) founded by Augustus had, in the main, been preserved. Unfortunately, peace and prosperity did not last into the third century; and in the hundred years from the death of Marcus Aurelius (A.D. 180) to the accession of Diocletian (A.D. 284) the Augustan system collapsed. Political disturbances were accompanied by economic and social disintegration, while military anarchy was followed by military despotism until, under Diocletian and his successors, the whole constitutional order was openly changed into an absolutism of the Oriental type.

Thus, at the threshold of European history—at the very time in the third century when Christianity was spreading throughout the Roman Empire and becoming a mark of the advanced civilization of the whole Mediterranean basin—we meet the great problem of the decay of that Empire and the decline of its civilization. It is a problem because our modern attitude of mind, conditioned as it still is by the notion that human history represents continuous progress, rebels at the thought of a great civilization in decay.

Probably no question has engaged the attention of more scholars or produced more varied explanations than the so-called "fall of Rome." According to predilections of various writers, different phases of Rome's decline have been emphasized—the political, the economic, the military, the religious, the agricultural, even the biological. Moreover, to the old question of "why" has been added in recent years the question "when." Obviously, no definitive statements as to the causes or even the chronology of Rome's decay can be given, least of all within the brief compass of this chapter. We must be content with a short description of the transformation of ancient society during the third and fourth centuries, and we must pay particular attention to the new forms which that society assumed. Further, it will become increasingly evident that the drama of the "decline of Rome" was enacted principally in the western and central portions of the Mediterranean basin. The continuing political and economic stability of the eastern provinces is a noteworthy feature of this period.

A primary cause of the troubled conditions which afflicted the Empire was the renewal of the struggles over the imperial throne. This was not new; and the absence of any system of succession has already been noticed. But in the third century the disorder spread beyond Rome to the provinces. As the army discovered its power to make and unmake "barrack emperors," civil war with its destruction of property, including the plunder of cities, ended the long Augustan peace. Since each new emperor owed his power to the army, the soldiers were privileged at the expense of others. Constitutional forms and civilian rights were increasingly disregarded.

Meanwhile the composition of the army changed. Partly because of peace and prosperity, partly because military service became almost exclusively frontier guard duty, the city bourgeoisie were no longer willing to assume the burdens of defense. More and more, therefore, in the third century the army was recruited from the peasants of the less Romanized provinces. Military leaders and even some of the emperors were drawn from non-Italian peasant stock. Ultimately, as numbers of barbarians were settled within the frontiers, the army ceased to be Roman in the old sense. A soldier's loyalty was to his commander rather than to the state, with whose cultural traditions he was apt to be unfamiliar.

The influence of the military was further enhanced by foreign war, for the internal anarchy of the third century invited attacks on the formerly quiet frontiers. In the east, for example, the new Sassanid dynasty of Persia (A.D. 226) was able to capture and temporarily hold the city of Antioch. The province of Dacia north of the Danube was abandoned. Goths and other Germans raided and even penetrated the frontiers from the Black Sea and the Aegean to Gaul. So serious was the crisis that it was deemed necessary to fortify many cities of the interior and finally Rome itself.

The social and economic deterioration which accompanied the military crisis is less easily explained. Certain developments, however, seem clear. To the ravages of civil war was added pestilence. The population markedly declined. Large tracts of land were left uncultivated. With government disorganized, bandits infested the roads, and pirates again roamed the Mediterranean. It is also probable, although exact statistics are not available, that the balance of trade between the western provinces and the eastern Mediterranean favored the latter. At any rate, it seems that a drainage of cash eastward was accompanied by a decrease in the productivity of the European mines. Besides, when the government, in the sec-

ond half of the third century, resorted to the expedient of debasing the coinage, inflation and speculation followed and trade between east and west was further curtailed. Also, although Rome had formerly exploited the growing trade of the area beyond the northern frontier through its contacts north and east of the Danube and the Rhine, these contacts now diminished.

Whatever the cause of the commercial decline, economic disintegration went hand in hand with a distintegration of local political life, especially in the western provinces. Moreover, it must be remembered that the cities of the Romanized west were newer than those of the east. In many instances their growth reflected that artificial political and military aspect which characterized a great deal of Roman expansion. It is significant, as a later chapter will indicate, that, throughout the disturbances of the third century, the older urban centers of the east successfully maintained themselves. Whether economic deterioration was accentuated by the increasing intervention of the central government, or whether the failure of local initiative left a void which had to be filled, is a debatable question. Certainly city self-government was demoralized and municipal officials and bourgeoisie were ruined by the arbitrary exactions of the military despotism. Public office-holding, which in better times was considered an honor, was now only a burden. The more fortunate left the towns to become farmers, often in a dependent status. Many remained to swell the ranks of the proletariat enjoying the "bread and circuses" which a paternalistic central government dared not curtail. The moral and material decline of the *civitates* is of the highest significance, for upon them and upon the political vitality of the bourgeoisie rested the whole fabric of the Augustan system.

As a result of these depressing economic conditions, the enervation of the municipalities, and the inroads of military despotism, Roman citizenship, once a privilege, became a burden. It was also cheapened by the edict of Caracalla (212) which granted citizenship to all freemen in the Empire. No longer were Italians the privileged ruling class. But if Gauls, Spaniards, Africans, Syrians, and Greeks were thenceforth equal before the law, that law now reflected absolutist tendencies. Further, since the depression had curtailed the taxing facilities of the government, it is permissible to interpret Caracalla's edict as an extension of obligations rather than of rights.

In marked contrast to the poverty of the city bourgeoisie and proletariat and the small farmers was the wealth of the large landowners. Those who were fortunate enough to inherit or to acquire great estates were able to weather the political and economic storms of the later empire. Their extensive villas were sufficiently large to include small local industries as well as large fields. Members for the most part of the so-called senatorial class, the landowners were also politically privileged. They were now powerful enough to defy government agents and tax-gatherers. In competition with them the small farmers were helpless. To escape the tax-collector large numbers of these gave up their independent status and became tenants on great estates. Usually these *coloni*, as they were called, retained the use of their land in return for service. A villa, therefore, was normally composed of a large tract of land cultivated for the owner and an indefinite number of smaller plots, often widely separated, of the *coloni*. These, legally free at least in theory, were economically dependent, while the great landowner was further enriched in both land and service. Large-scale cultivation on an efficient basis was now possible. Thus the best and most carefully managed of these villas became virtually independent principalities over which the central government's power was tenuous in the extreme. The western provinces of the Empire—Gaul, Spain, and parts of North Africa and Italy—ceased to be the home of thriving urban centers with a politically active bourgeoisie. Instead, a new social order based on the country was emerging.

It is evident that the federation of free self-governing municipalities under the enlightened guidance of philosopher-statesmen had been destroyed. The Augustan principate had collapsed. The only hope for the preservation of the state lay in stabilizing the military despotism. This is the meaning of the reorganization inaugurated by Diocletian (284–305) and carried forward by

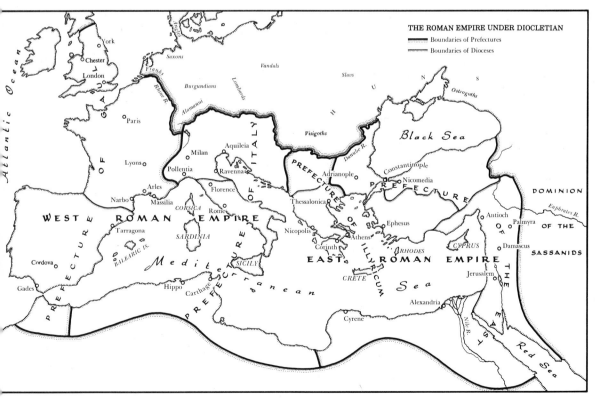

Constantine (306–337) and his immediate successors.

B. Diocletian and the Establishment of Imperial Absolutism

Diocletian was born of Dalmatian peasant stock. Service in the army brought him prominence and eventually acclamation by the troops as Emperor. Thus his career illustrates both the political power of the army and its non-Italian composition. He was distinctly a man of his age. But he had never known and therefore would never understand the cultural and political traditions of the early Empire. A soldier, he viewed the crisis as military. The Empire must be protected against its external enemies at whatever cost.

Diocletian's first move was to exalt the person and power of the emperor. The senate was deprived of all its functions in the central government and became merely a Roman municipal council. A new, elaborately graded and titled hierarchy of officials, dependent solely on the emperor, controlled every phase of life from the central government down to the smallest municipality. Thus the old dyarchy of senate and emperor with its maintenance of republican forms was replaced by a frankly absolute monarchy resting on a huge centralized bureaucracy. Mindful, perhaps, of the discredit into which the imperial dignity had fallen during the days of the "barrack emperors," and realizing that an army could confer power but not the prestige of constitutionally established authority, Diocletian set up an elaborate court with all the paraphernalia of oriental despotism. The "divine" character of the imperial office was given a new emphasis.

Diocletian also decided that the Empire was too big to be governed efficiently by one man. Accordingly he divided it into two parts, each part being further subdivided into two sections (prefectures). Two *Augusti* (himself and Maximinian,), assisted by two Caesars, governed the sections. Since the latter were to succeed the former, it is possible that he intended in this way to settle the thorny question of the imperial succession. This plan, however, did not succeed, although during the fourth and fifth centuries there were commonly two co-emperors, one for the eastern half and one for the western. The four prefectures were further divided into dioceses and provinces. The latter, designed to be roughly uniform in size, were much smaller than the former provinces and numbered over one hundred. All administrative heads were appointed and shifted about by the emperor and subjected to constant supervision by special agents. Moreover, practically all civil servants were stripped of military authority.

Although local political power was in this way curbed, various personal privileges continued to exist. Officials of the government service formed a hierarchy of nobility with high-sounding titles of rank: *illustres, spectabiles, clarissimi, perfectissimi, nobilissimi.* Members of the senatorial order, whose actual duties were, for the most part, now only theoretical, were *clarissimi.* All these noblemen—and their number increased as the emperor rewarded old servants or created new ones—were granted various immunities from taxation and other governmental obligations. Many of them rarely left their great estates in the provinces. Moreover, although offices were not hereditary, they tended to become so, since men in other walks of life were prevented from changing their occupations.

The army was similarly reorganized and its own hierarchy of officers rigidly subjected to imperial control. The policy of fortifying the interior cities was continued. Since the frontier legionaries had become resident and privileged landowners, a new and mobile force was created in which infantry and cavalry were separate units. To fill the desired quota of some half million men, "barbarian" Germans, Arabs, Moors, and others, were admitted not only as auxiliaries, but even into the "citizen" legions. Whole tribes were allowed to cross the frontier as allies (*foederati*).

Diocletian's efforts to reëstablish the Empire's economic life were no less far-reaching. They involved control of the currency and prices, a new system of taxation and rigid restrictions on all mercantile and agricultural enterprise. Only the outlines of this policy can be given here. The greatest problem was financial and was made more difficult by the inevitable expense of the bureaucracy. Diocletian did succeed in restoring the coinage,[1] but specie remained scarce and many taxes as well as wages had to be paid in kind. Soldiers, for example, were paid in land, and since they were permitted to marry, they thus became an agrarian peasant class. Food prices had soared during the chaos of the third century and Diocletian sought without appreciable success to achieve stability by price-fixing.

Trades essential to the state, which virtually meant those required by the military, were rigidly restricted. Most of these were already organized into guilds (*collegia*) which proved to be convenient units for taxation. Since many artisans hesitated to undertake contracts because of the depressed condition of business, the government now made a minimum production compulsory and required sons to succeed their fathers in their positions. Merchants and artisans, therefore, became a hereditary caste. The military needs of the state were met, but private enterprise was gravely hampered if not ruined.

Although real local self-government had disappeared from the provincial *civitates*, some of the burdens of local administration remained. Tax collecting was among the most onerous. As commercial decline increased the difficulty of obtaining taxes, the government made members of the local senates (*curiae*)—the *curiales*—personally responsible for certain amounts. Their task was difficult. Any deficit had to be made up out of their own pockets. For a time the system worked and, under the immediate successors of Diocletian, provided the state with revenue. But as their burdens became intolerable, many *curiales* sought to avoid their responsibilities. Here again the government intervened and in no less than one hundred and ninety-two edicts throughout the fourth century closed the army, the church, and the civil service to the *curiales* and forbade their travel abroad. Finally, as in the guilds, membership in the curial class was made hereditary. Nevertheless, despite all these measures, many did escape. Some managed to enter the less important guilds, others placed themselves under the protection of the powerful landowners, even giving up their own property and becoming *coloni*.

[1] Constantine introduced a gold *solidus* which remained a standard coin for centuries.

Some even escaped to the desert of Egypt to become hermits. The "flight of the curiales," indicative of the ruin of the middle class throughout the Empire, is a significant feature of late Roman society.

The long arm of the government also reached out to the countryside, although there the influence of the great landowners limited its effectiveness. Notwithstanding, the peasant was the basis of the state, and land taxes were an important source of revenue. Therefore, the *coloni*, who composed the bulk of the tenants on the villas, were forbidden to leave and became a hereditary caste of laborers. The responsibility for the collection of the tenants' taxes was placed upon the landlord. But, unlike the curial, he was wealthy and powerful and able to defy the government's collector and sometimes to retain the revenues for himself. In the course of time, other governmental duties, including even local police power, devolved upon the landlords, thus completing the formation of another hereditary caste, the great landed magnates. It should be remembered, nevertheless, that, although landowners were in some measure able to defy centralized control, the production of their villas remained an integral part of the organization of defense.

In evaluating the reforms of Diocletian and his successors it must first be emphasized that they resulted from a realistic appraisal of a desperate situation. The heritage of the third century left little opportunity for innovation. The principate with its theoretical division of power between senate and "citizen" emperor had long since ceased to function in the original manner. Diocletian did not set out to destroy Augustan institutions; he found them nearly defunct. Neither did he attempt to revive them. He proceeded along lines familiar to himself, a former peasant and soldier, to establish a regime of discipline and force. What were the results? In certain respects they were noteworthy. Order was restored. The frontiers were held for another century. Diocletian's successor, Constantine, ended one source of unrest by tolerating Christianity, and built a new and magnificent capital on the shores of the Bosphorus. Economic life was restored at least enough to support the army and the bureaucracy.

C. Continuing Social and Cultural Decline

Despite these successes, Diocletian's system in the long run only perpetuated the evils which had appeared during the third century. Moreover, the cost in human freedom and individual enterprise was so terrific that the cure proved worse than the disease. The leveling process by which peasants and proletariat were favored at the expense of the bourgeoisie really resulted in a kind of enslavement of all classes to the state. With all freedom of movement between occupations prohibited, society was divided into fixed castes. For the less fortunate—the *curiales*, the artisans, the small landowners, the *coloni*, even the soldiers—there was no escape. The result was a widespread feeling of resignation. If it is permissible to speak of a Roman spirit which had enlivened the institutions of the Augustan age, the prevailing mood of the late fourth century was a sort of discouraged apathy. Barbarian invaders found little resistance left in the fifth century.

The internal disintegration of Roman society is reflected in the realms of culture and the old pagan religion. Classical culture was the product of the city and its religion. This was true of ancient Greece as well as of Rome. The best efforts in the arts and in literature belonged to the periods when civic consciousness was alive and bourgeois prosperity unimpaired. The decline of classical culture, therefore, followed the decay of the city community and the disappearance of the city's gods. It is a phenomenon both spiritual and material. As the central government crushed the community politically, community spirit, manifested in loyalty to the city's gods, disappeared. The incentive to build and dedicate handsome buildings was no longer present either in Rome or in the provinces. The establishment of paternalistic despotism destroyed the old Roman religion, because that religion had been so closely identified with the earlier and freer state. Therefore, until Christianity provided a new source of inspiration, art remained a feeble imitation of the past. Finally, poverty destroyed the material basis upon which the patronage of art rested.

So also it was with secular Latin literature, a faint reflection of the golden age. Ausonius (*d.* about 400) was a poet of some distinction, and Symmachus (*d.* 405) wrote eloquently in defense of a dying paganism. Ammianus Marcellinus (*d.* 400) produced a useful and occasionally vivid continuation of Tacitus's *Histories*. Certain works of compilation were likewise valuable. Dona-

Roman building in the provinces. A Roman amphitheatre at Palmyra, Syria.

Courtesy Syrian Government Tourist Office, New York

tus' (fourth century) treatise on grammar was regarded as the standard work for centuries, and the *Marriage of Philology and Mercury* by Martianus Capella (late fourth century) introduced the classification of learning by the "seven liberal arts" so familiar in the middle ages. Furthermore, some responsibility for preserving the heritage of old Graeco-Roman culture was assumed by the best of the aristocracy on the great estates. From the letters of men like Sidonius Apollinaris, Gallo-Roman country gentleman of the fifth century, later a Christian bishop, and from fragments of mosaics and the extant ruins of villas, comes a picture of a life of genteel ease with a lively appreciation of Rome's cultural tradition. Thus the cultivation of grammar and rhetoric, while not productive of an original literature, kept alive some of the achievements of the past and handed them down to a later age.

D. Development of Christian Literature and Art

In this generally dismal picture of Roman society in the fourth and fifth centuries there are, however, two bright spots. First, what the decadent state now failed to offer, an opportunity for loyal and capable service and an inspiration to intellectual and artistic energy, was being supplied by the rapidly expanding Christian church. Second, the eastern half of the Empire not only remained stable, but in some respects experienced a revival.

Among the representatives of Christian learning in the later Empire were certain men who have been designated the "fathers" of the church. This term was applied to those religious writers whose works were of sufficient importance to warrant a special recognition as authoritative sources of the church's doctrine. All were educated men, steeped in the classical learning of their age and versed in its literature and philosophy. Owing to the general cultural decline of the west, the work of the "Latin" fathers, so-called to distinguish them from their colleagues, the "Greek" fathers of the east, is of particular significance in the intellectual history of that area. In a real sense the Latin fathers were the interpreters of an age that was passing to a new age that was beginning.

The life of St. Ambrose of Milan (*d.* 397) demonstrates how an educated and energetic young man could find a stimulating career in the church. The son of a Roman official, Ambrose advanced in the imperial service to the governorship of Milan. Then, on the death of the bishop of the city, he was chosen by popular acclaim as successor. Accepting this new responsibility, Ambrose became as successful in ecclesiastical administration as he had formerly been in the service of the state. Moreover, though never an accomplished scholar, his writings were of sufficient importance to warrant his inclusion among the Latin Fathers.

The writings of two other Latin Fathers further illustrate how the church enlisted the best intellectual energies of the late Roman period. St. Jerome (*d.* 420), like Ambrose formally educated according to contemporary standards, was an enthusiastic devotee of secular Latin literature, especially the writings of Cicero. But he too entered the church and during a sojourn in Syria learned Hebrew. This enabled him to accomplish his most important work, a complete Latin translation of the Bible. Known as the Vulgate, Jerome's version is still recognized by the Catholic Church as authoritative.

St. Augustine of Hippo (*d.* 430) was one of those rare figures whose destiny it was to influence subsequent generations in an outstanding manner. Born in Numidia, the son of a pagan father and a Christian mother, he too was educated in grammar, rhetoric, and law. Throughout a wayward youth, he was given to intellectual pursuits and especially the study of philosophy, and he was constantly searching for a religion which would satisfy the mind. For a time he embraced Manichaeism, a cult then moderately popular in the Empire, stemming from the Zoroastrian dualism of Persia. But eventually, and apparently owing in no small measure to the preaching of St. Ambrose, he returned to the Christian faith of his youth. Thus, as he relates in his remarkably frank memoirs, the *Confessions*, the prayers of his saintly mother, Monica, were answered. Augustine was finally made Bishop of Hippo in North Africa where he completed a distinguished career and died as the German Vandals besieged the city.

No author was more widely read during the middle ages than Augustine and there is hardly a theological or philosophical question that he did not consider. Since he had been influenced by contemporary Neo-Platonism, the philosophical trend of the early middle ages was Platonic. Perhaps he is best known for his monumental and discursive *City of God*, a work occasioned by the Gothic sack of Rome in 410. Written in part as an answer to the pagan accusation that the abandonment of Rome's gods had caused her fall, the *City of God* presents, for the first time, a Christian philosophy of history. Divine providence is seen in all earthly events, and men's minds are directed from the transitory vicissitudes of human affairs to things eternal.

Another result of the new inspiration which Christianity offered was the beginning of a Christian religious poetry. Ambrose, for example, had composed a number of Latin hymns. More important in the development of hymnody was Prudentius (*d.* 405), who is regarded as one of the founders of the great tradition of Latin religious verse. Indeed, a number of Prudentius' hymns have become familiar in English versions.

Early Christian art had developed in the catacombs where modern archaeology has discovered some remarkable frescoes and sculpture, in particular carved stone tombs or *sarcophagi*. But except for the building of small underground chapels (*cubicula*), the development of architecture had perforce to await the days of toleration. Since the catacombs contained the tombs of martyrs, a number of the earliest churches, not only in Rome but in the provinces, were built over such burial places. Frequently, private dwellings served as places of worship. Portions of these early edifices have been found beneath later structures. The first formal buildings devoted exclusively to worship were, as a rule, adaptations of the Roman basilica. In fact the depression in Roman society had put a number of these typical public buildings out of use. Many early Christian basilicas were actually secular structures made over.

The basilica was a rectangular building with a flat roof supported commonly by two and sometimes four rows of columns which separated the main body of the church from the aisles. At one end, to house the altar, an apse was added, usually semicircular in shape with a quarter-sphere dome. At the other end of the basilica was often a sort of lobby (narthex) and an outer court. For in primitive Christianity, the catechumens—those not yet baptised—were not permitted to view the sacred ceremonies in their entirety. Apse and walls above the columns were decorated with mosaic, a form of pictorial art which flourished widely both in the west and in the east. Finally, it is important to note that comparatively recent studies of mosaic, sculpture and pictorial decoration justify the contention that early Christian art even in the west was not exclusively Latin. Rather does it show definite traces of oriental influence. But most important of all is the fact that Christian church-building so vividly symbolizes late Roman society. For here in the realm of architecture is an absorption by the Christian religion of a venerable secular tradition. And as it was in art, so it was in literature and in virtually every human activity.

E. Orientalizing the Empire and Transfer of Its Capital to Constantinople

In the eastern provinces of the Empire, the economic depression had been less disastrous. Here, the older and more stable cities retained their commercial contacts with the Asiatic hinterland—with Persia and India and even the Far East. Moreover, bureaucratic despotism was not a novelty to the eastern Mediterranean. The vast state socialism which the new system implied closely resembled the political and economic organization of ancient Egypt. The idea of a god-emperor which Diocletian and Constantine, despite the latter's recognition of Christianity, deliberately inculcated was indigenous to the ancient Near Eastern empires. Indeed from the time of Augustus the Egyptians had regarded him and his successors as heirs of the pharaohs rather than chiefs of a republic. It is not

Fifth century Roman mosaic at Ravenna. The Tomb of Galla Placidia, half-sister of the Emperor Honorius, wife of the Visigothic King Athaulf, later of the Roman general, Constantius, and mother of the Emperor Valentinian III.

Courtesy Italian State Tourist Office, New York

surprising to find that the later emperors recognized the importance of the eastern part of the Empire and even preferred it to Rome as a place of residence. Further, during the third and fourth centuries the most dangerous frontiers were in the east. For this reason, Diocletian moved the imperial residence to Nicomedia in Asia Minor, and Constantine finally decided to build a new capital on the shores of the Bosphorus. We conclude this chapter with discussion of the new city and its influence in the later Empire.

The decision to move the capital, already foreshadowed by Diocletian's abandoning of Rome, probably resulted from a combination of the developments described in this chapter. Rome and the western provinces no longer seemed to be the natural center of imperial life. Moreover, as the home of once thriving republican institutions, it no longer attracted men who completed their destruction. Byzantium, an old Greek colony and the site of the new city, was ideally situated at one of the great gateways to the east where trade continued to flourish. Its location, surrounded on three sides by water, possessed marked natural advantages for defense. Great walls across the fourth side rendered it impregnable to ancient methods of attack. Finally, it was near the important Danube frontier where

constant vigilance would alone preserve the Empire intact. In 325 the construction of the new capital began, and in 330, although a great deal of building remained to be done, the city was officially dedicated.

This city which Constantine founded and named after himself was destined to become the seat of a flourishing culture which historians have called Byzantine from the name of the original Greek colony. The story of its development belongs to a later chapter. We are concerned here only with the fact that its foundation by no means signified a surrender of the western provinces or any sudden change in the traditions of the Roman state. Constantinople was the "new Rome," the new seat of the old Empire, not the capital of a new state. When, as was often the case after Diocletian's reorganization, two coemperors were named, one for the east and one for the west, this signified the desire to preserve the Empire intact. It is a mistake to speak of the "eastern empire" and the "western empire" as though they were two separate units. And although the two parts developed along diverging lines, the sense of imperial unity was too strongly implanted to disappear. It was to survive the shock of the barbarian invasions which shook the Empire to its foundations in the fifth century.

Theodoric's tomb at Ravenna. The top is a single piece of stone.

Courtesy Italian State Tourist Office, New York

CHAPTER 6

Barbarian Neighbors and German Settlers on West Roman Soil

A. German Tribesmen Beyond the Roman Frontier

Beyond the long frontier of the Roman Empire lived peoples of many different nationalities. Some of these, like the Persians, who had held the upper Euphrates against Roman advance for centuries, represented civilizations more ancient than the Roman. Most of the frontier peoples, however, were still in a relatively primitive stage of culture and were regarded by the Romans as barbarians.[1] By the third century the regions beyond the northern and northeastern boundary were being occupied by Germans. First appearing centuries earlier in northern Europe, they had gradually moved, sometimes by devious routes, in a generally southward direction. Occasionally their progress toward, and ultimately across, the border of the Empire was hastened or disrupted by periodic pressure from Asiatic nomads in back of them.[2]

Little is known of the primitive Germans. Julius Caesar mentioned them briefly. A hundred and fifty years later, the Roman historian Tacitus gave a more detailed picture, colored somewhat by his attempt to shame his "decadent" fellow Romans with a description of the "simple, virtuous, and rugged Germans." What struck the Romans particularly was the reddish or blond hair, blue eyes, great stature, and generally powerful physique—in short, what popular imagination still denotes as "Nordic."

In general, German society was tribal, that is, it emphasized the relations and loyalties of kinship rather than of citizenship. An injury to an individual, for example, was an injury to his kin and must be avenged by them unless they were compensated by a graded system of penalties known as *wergeld*. Some tribes, however, had coalesced into groups which, for lack of a better term, might be called "nations." Over such nations ruled kings, at first hardly more than war leaders, elected by the freemen and subject to their wishes. But by the time they entered the Empire there was already a tendency to choose rulers from the same family, thus paving the way for hereditary succession.

Since certain fairly distinct "nations" were later to migrate into the Empire, it will be well to mention the most important. On the lower Rhine were the Franks. Ultimately the strongest of all the German nations, they were originally divided into two groups, the Ripuarian (from *ripa*, riverbank) and the Salian (from *sal*, salt, signifying sea). The Alamans (*Alamanni*, whence the French word "allemand" for German) had occupied the lands between the upper Rhine and the Danube and had

---

[1] The Latin word, *barbarus*, was used by the Romans in the sense of "foreigner," and had no such depreciatory connotation as is conveyed by the modern English word, "barbarian."

[2] Along the African frontier, Berbers and Moors frequently caused minor problems as did the Arabs in Syria and Palestine. Behind the Germans in eastern Europe were Slavic peoples who later invaded the eastern part of the Empire.

been pushed aside by the Burgundians who came toward the Rhine from central Germany. Behind were the Vandals and Suevi in the interior, the Saxons and Angles along the North Sea in what is now Holland and Western Germany, and last of all, the Lombards who in their southward migration, did not reach the limits of northern Italy until the middle of the sixth century. On the Danube and north of the Black Sea were the Goths, divided into the West Goths (Visigoths) and East Goths (Ostrogoths). By the end of the fourth century A.D., therefore, Germanic peoples had settled along the entire northern frontier from the Black Sea to the North Sea.

It is difficult to estimate how numerous were these Germans. Larger nations, like the Goths, numbered perhaps 80 to 120 thousand. Only about one-fifth of these were freemen or warriors. At any rate, all the German peoples together constituted but a fraction of the total population of the Roman Empire.

On the eve of the fifth-century invasions, the Germanic world was still far from stable. Tribal jealousies and wars enabled the imperial authorities to play one German nation against another. It is a great mistake to think of the Empire as menaced by united German hosts. And as a result of close contact with Roman civilization over a period of centuries, most Germans had become acquainted with Roman ways and some had acquired a veneer of Roman culture. Some of the Germans had also been subjected to influences emanating from the Middle East. In the area north of the Black Sea the Goths, for example, had been preceded by the Sarmatians, an Indo-Iranian people with contacts reaching into Persia. Accomplished horsemen and archers, they used a coat of chain mail and a conical helmet and introduced into Europe stirrups and spurs. Moreover, from them the Goths learned the art of making jewelry of cloisonné enamel, an art form which they carried westward.

It must also be remembered that those Germans who had taken up a position along the boundary, had been preceded across the line by thousands of their compatriots. Individual Germans had crossed to become peasants or *coloni* or to serve in the Roman

Visigothic gold and silver work of the seventh century. Facsimile of the crown of King Swinthila.

Courtesy Hispanic Society of America

army. Occasionally a whole tribe was settled as allies (*foederati*) and given the congenial duty of guarding the border against other Germans. Indeed, the Romans felt no particular racial animosity to those Germans whom many had come to regard as neighbors.

It should be borne in mind, too, that the Roman legions of the late fourth and early fifth centuries were composed largely of German and other "barbarian" troops. The attitude of these Romanized Germans has been admirably summed up in the often quoted phrase: "The Empire was not an enemy but a career." They were not, to use a modern phrase, a "fifth column" seeking to destroy the Roman state. To a considerable degree their attitude of respect for the Empire was shared by the Germans beyond the frontier. The Roman Empire was part of the world they knew. Its institutions and fertile fields were superior to anything they had encountered. They wanted nothing more than to become a part of it, to settle peacefully within its frontiers. For their chieftains, as some of them frankly stated, there was no greater honor than high position in the imperial service. This feeling persisted even after the Empire in the west had crumbled.

B. First Germanic Migrations into the Empire

By the end of the fourth century, thousands of Germans had peacefully entered the Empire and in varying degrees had become Romanized. Beyond the frontier many more had settled and turned their eyes toward the broad cultivated acres and the more secure life to the south. There were times when the pressure on the boundaries was very great, presumably during those periods when the perennial German desire for fertile fields as well as for freedom from attack was more impelling. It is possible that the process of peaceful penetration could have gone on indefinitely and that the entire German world, which was not overwhelmingly numerous, could ultimately have been absorbed without the violent upheaval which came in the fifth and sixth centuries. That this was not the case was largely owing to the coincidence

of two factors: first, the weakness of the imperial government which the previous chapter has explained; and, second, the pressure on the Germans from Asiatic nomads, in particular the Huns.

Across the steppes and deserts of central Asia and Russia there have come into central and southeastern Europe at periodic intervals roving nomadic peoples who have terrorized wide areas. Because they inhabited the region between the Ural and Altai mountains, their similar languages have been designated Ural-Altaic. Such a people were the Huns whose round heads, flat noses, slanting eyes, swarthy complexion, and dark hair distinguished them from their Indo-European adversaries whether German or Roman. Dependent on their flocks and herds, they followed the pasturage south in winter and north in summer, often ranging a thousand miles. They became excellent horsemen, and what pastoral life failed to provide they took in raids which terrorized or enslaved more settled agricultural peoples. Their endurance and their ability to withstand hunger and thirst for incredibly long periods were phenomenal.

By the end of the fourth century A.D., after many struggles along the way, the Huns had reached eastern Europe. Shortly thereafter they attacked the Goths north of the Black Sea and the Danube and precipitated a major crisis in both German and imperial affairs. In A.D. 375 the Ostrogoths were overwhelmed and remained for several decades in subjection to the Huns, except for a few who fled westward into Dacia. But when the Huns advanced on the Visigoths, the latter sought permission from the imperial authorities to cross the Danube frontier.

This request of the Visigoths was a turning point in the relations between the Romans and the Germans. As we have seen, many groups of Germans had entered the Empire, but never before had a whole nation sought admission. Though embarrassed by the request, the Emperor, Valens (364–378), could hardly refuse, and the Visigoths were settled as *foederati* south of the Danube. Thus the first German nation to cross the frontier *en masse* came as suppliants, not as invaders. Unfortunately, the incompetent and high-handed officials in charge of the crossing and the subsequent settlement so angered the Goths that they commenced to loot the neighboring provinces. Valens led an inadequate force against them which was badly defeated, and he was killed at Adrianople (378). Though significant as the first victory of Germans over Romans within the Empire and a demonstration of the superiority of Gothic cavalry over Roman infantry legions, the battle of Adrianople can be overestimated and it must be understood in relation to contemporary events. Actually it was a mutiny of Gothic troops who were technically a part of the Roman army. Moreover, under Theodosius (379–395), one of Rome's great emperors and a worthy successor of Diocletian and Constantine, the Goths were again settled peacefully as *foederati*, bound to furnish contingents for the imperial army in return for an annual tribute. Although a considerable territory was in Gothic hands and the Romans' capacity to absorb the Germans was put to a new test, the Empire was still intact under a strong ruler.

It was Rome's misfortune that Theodosius was the last emperor to rule both the eastern and the western parts of the Empire. He was succeeded by his two incompetent sons, Arcadius and Honorius, who divided the Empire, Honorius taking the west and Arcadius the east. Since neither was qualified to assume the responsibility of government, actual power fell to subordinates. In the west, Stilicho, a Romanized German of exceptional ability who had risen in the imperial service, now virtually ruled as *magister militum* or commander-in-chief. Indeed, he was called upon to meet one of the gravest crises in Rome's history. For, under their new king, Alaric, the Visigoths, sensing the weakness of the imperial government, had become dissatisfied with their position and marched through the Greek peninsula, looting as they went. After a temporary occupation of the Illyrian provinces, they appeared in north Italy, entered the Po valley and attempted an assault on Milan. Stilicho temporarily stopped them by a resounding victory at Pollentia (402). But, at this fateful moment in Rome's history, a court clique persuaded the weak and jealous Honorius to have Stilicho, the last hope of the western provinces of the Empire, executed for treason (408).

Meanwhile, the removal of troops from Gaul and Britain, in order to strengthen Italy, left those frontiers vulnerable to attack. In 406 the Alans, Suevi, and Vandals crossed Gaul and the Pyrenees and established themselves in Spain, though still nominally as *foederati*. Alaric, seizing the moment to reverse the defeat at Pollentia, led his Visigoths into Italy again. In 410 he marched on Rome and his troops pillaged the city for three days.

Although the famous sack of Rome by Alaric was not particularly devastating, it was a terrible blow to Roman morale. As has been mentioned, St. Augustine of Hippo felt called upon to write his famous book, *The City of God*, to refute the charge that the abandonment of the old pagan gods had caused Rome's fall. Even hermits of the desert came to St. Jerome in Palestine seeking counsel. The Empire's weakness was now apparent to everybody.

Seventh century Visigothic pottery tablet.

Courtesy Hispanic Society of America

ANGLO-SAXON, PICT AND CELTIC BRITAIN

ORKNEY IS.

N O R T H

S E A

PICTS AND SCOTS

IONA DALRIADA

Firth of Forth

BERNICIA

NORTHUMBRIA

STRATHCLYDE

Firth of Clyde

Solway Firth

Durham

DEIRA Whitby

ISLE OF MAN

York

I R E L A N D

IRISH SEA

Humber R.

Lincoln

The Wash

Chester

Nottingham

WALES

MERCIA Ely

EAST ANGLIA

Oxford

London

ESSEX

Thames R. Canterbury

ISLE OF THANET

KENT Dover

WESSEX

Winchester SUSSEX

Hastings

ATLANTIC   OCEAN

CORNWALL Exeter

ENGLISH CHANNEL

0   50   100   160

Miles

FRANKS

The Visigoths did not remain in Italy. Since they were still facing a serious food shortage, Alaric led them south with the intention of crossing to Sicily. But a storm ended this plan by destroying his ships. Discouraged, he turned north again only to meet a premature death in Calabria. Somewhat later, the imperial government, still attempting to save itself by playing one German nation against another, commissioned one of Alaric's successors to drive the Vandals out of Spain. This the Goths did, virtually destroying the Alans in the process, and leaving only the Suevi in the northwest. Thus was established a Visigothic kingdom, which included southern Gaul and (somewhat later) Spain.

The importance of sea power was further demonstrated by those Vandals who survived the Visigothic attacks on Spain. Temporary control of the Spanish ports and mastery over the Roman fleet of Spain enabled them, under a new and vigorous king, Gaiseric, to cross the strait of Gibraltar to Africa. Thence Gaiseric pushed eastward and overpowered the resistance of the Roman governor. Accordingly, the imperial government, following its now customary procedure of accepting what it could not prevent, established the Vandals as *foederati* in Numidia. But the famous city of Carthage was too tempting a prize for Gaiseric to resist. Its fall in 439 completed the Vandal conquest of North Africa from the Atlantic eastward to modern Tunisia. Meanwhile the Vandal fleet took heavy toll of Mediterranean shipping. Finally, in 455 the Vandals raided Italy and delivered Rome over to a second pillage lasting two weeks.

Along the northern frontiers of Gaul and Britain, Rome had to concede territory. Britain had been denuded of troops in the crisis and left prey to raids from Picts on the north, Scots from Ireland, and Saxon pirates along the east coast. The latter, accompanied by Angles and Jutes, eventually occupied most of what is now England, driving many of the Celtic and Romanized Britons into the remote regions of Wales and Cornwall. No trace of Roman government remained in Britain, and the Anglo-Saxon victors were not regarded as *foederati*.

Meanwhile, the Franks and Burgundians had been installed as *foederati* within the Rhine frontier. The Franks settled along the lower Rhine and westward along the North Sea in what is now Belgium. The Burgundians, after unsuccessful conflicts with Aetius, the harassed Roman commander in Gaul, occupied the territory around Geneva, from which they later spread southward into the Rhone valley. The territory left vacant along the upper

Rhine and in Switzerland was taken over by the Alamans. It was precisely at this juncture that the Huns appeared in western Europe.

It will be recalled that the Huns had subjugated the Ostrogoths and driven the Visigoths to seek shelter across the Danube. Continuing their conquests, the Huns gained control over the vast area between the Don and the Danube and captured many German peoples. In 444 Attila, a frightening man, cruel and treacherous, but a capable leader of his people, became their king. Under this "scourge of God," who was to become a sort of legendary figure, the Huns invaded the Balkan peninsula and exacted from the imperial government at Constantinople a yearly tribute, thinly disguised as pay for military service. In 451, with an army composed of Huns and thousands of captured Germans, Attila moved westward and commenced the invasion of Gaul. Sensing the danger, the Visigoths and other Germans made common cause with the Romans under Aetius. The result was a defeat for Attila at Châlons, which stemmed the Asiatic invasion and proved that Roman-German co-

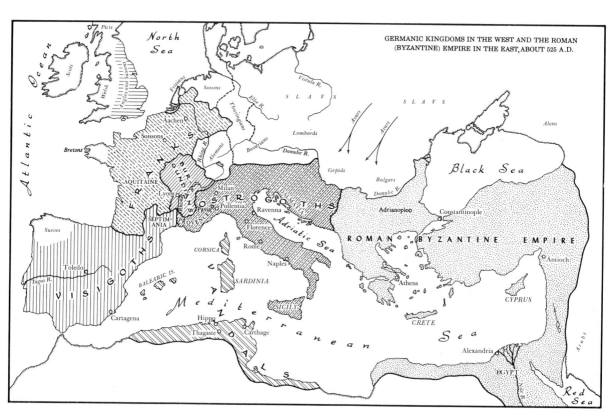

GERMANIC KINGDOMS IN THE WEST AND THE ROMAN (BYZANTINE) EMPIRE IN THE EAST, ABOUT 525 A.D.

operation was not impossible. Attila's army had not been destroyed, however, and he moved south into Italy. There, he was persuaded to turn back by Pope Leo the Great. When the Hunnic chieftain died in 453 his great empire disappeared completely and his people found their way back to Asia.

C. *Collapse of Imperial Government in the West*

The fact that it was the Pope, not the Emperor, who went out to meet Attila is eloquent testimony of the low state to which the imperial government in Italy had fallen. The details of the pitiful story of the last co-emperors in the west need not detain us here. When the Theodosian dynasty came to an end (455), there followed a series of puppet co-emperors controlled by German military leaders with no consistent opposition from the Emperor at Constantinople. The last of these puppets was Romulus "Augustulus," the son of Orestes, an ex-secretary of Attila, who had temporarily gained control of the Roman army. When Romulus was deposed (476) by Odovakar, another German chieftain, no successor was chosen and the imperial insignia were sent to Constantinople.

For a few years Odovakar ruled Italy in the name of the Emperor at Constantinople, but without his express approval. Meanwhile, the Ostrogoths, now liberated by the defeat of the Huns, had become dangerously powerful. Settled as *foederati* in the Danubian province, they had developed remarkable political cohesion under their king, Theodoric. Theodoric had spent many years at Constantinople. He was familiar with Roman administration and a great admirer of Roman ways. At one time he had been named one of the consuls of the city. But he was anxious to further the interests of his people. Accordingly, the Emperor Zeno decided to placate Theodoric by commissioning him to remove the usurper, Odovakar. In a few years (489–493), Theodoric mastered the Italian peninsula. Odovakar was invited to a banquet and murdered. Italy itself, the heart of the old Empire, was now a German kingdom, nominally dependent on the emperor at Constantinople, actually governed independently by Theodoric, the Ostrogothic King.

Fortunately for the Italians who had endured many decades of chaos, the wise rule of Theodoric (493–526) brought a generation of peace and prosperity. Genuinely devoted to Roman ideals and scrupulously correct in all his relations with Constantinople, Theodoric attempted to devise a system whereby Roman ways of life could be preserved under German military control. The Roman civil administration was continued. Consuls and magistrates were maintained and Theodoric surrounded himself with officials bearing the familiar Roman titles. Although his capital was at Ravenna where some of the later co-emperors had resided, the city of Rome was not neglected. Its aqueducts were repaired and its people fed and amused. Ravenna was adorned with buildings, some of which still stand; and Theodoric brought to his court the greatest scholars of the day, including Boethius and Cassiodorus. Both of these served as important government officials. Although an Arian, Theodoric protected the Roman church and was even asked on one occasion to settle a disputed election to the papacy.

As a permanent development, however, Theodoric's work must be reckoned a failure. Toward the end of his reign, the jealousy of the Romans and their active hostility to Gothic Arianism finally embittered the Ostrogothic King and led to such unfortunate acts as the imprisonment and execution of Boethius. Not long after Theodoric's death, the Ostrogothic kingdom fell before a new conquest.

Meanwhile, the Franks, who had not figured prominently during the first wave of invasion, were coming into prominence. In fact, they were destined to play a far more important role than any other Germanic nation. Under Clovis (481–511), a Salian Frank, one of the earliest and certainly one of the most important kings of the Merovingian dynasty, the Franks began a remarkable career of expansion.[1] In successive campaigns on the part of

---

[1] The name Merovingian presumably comes from Merovech, Clovis's grandfather.

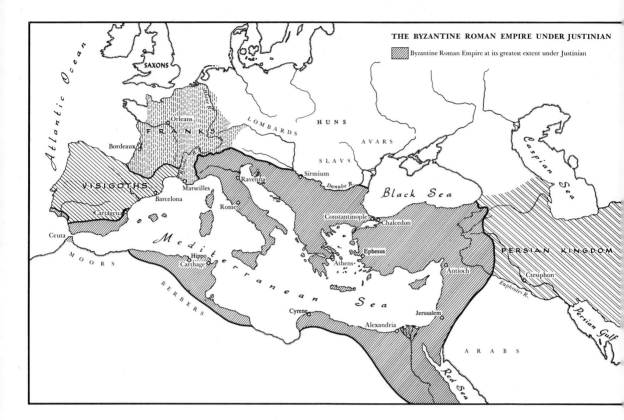

Clovis and his successors against Romans, Alamans, Visigoths, and eventually Burgundians, most of Gaul was taken. As Clovis became convinced that the Christian God had given him victory over the Alamans, he accepted Catholic Christianity. Clovis's Catholic baptism, which led to the acceptance of Catholicism rather than Arianism by the Franks, was an event of capital significance. It assured Clovis a welcome by the Gallo-Roman clergy as the champion of orthodoxy against heresy. Thus the Franks had an advantage in their relations with the native Roman population which other German kingdoms did not at first possess.

The expansion initiated by Clovis differed from other German invasions. Goths, Vandals, Burgundians, and others had left their Germanic homeland and migrated into Roman territory where their Teutonic institutions lost much of their vitality. The Franks, on the other hand, remained on both sides of the lower Rhine and expanded southward into Roman territory. No less respectful of Roman institutions, they never

lost touch with their Germanic homeland. Eventually their remarkable expansion carried them eastward as well. In the Frankish kingdom there took place a real fusion of the two cultures, the German and the Roman, not merely an absorption of German population by Rome.

D. Temporary Imperial Recovery and Renewed Invasions

Little has been said thus far of the attitude of the emperors at Constantinople toward the new situation in the western half of the Empire. Indeed, little can be said because for many years they were powerless to change the course of events. Therefore, they temporarily accepted what they could not prevent and saved a vestige of their authority by installing the Germans as *foederati*. Most of the German kings admitted the formal suzerainty of Constantinople. It is important to notice that at Constantinople there was no thought of abandoning the west or of accepting the new situation permanently.

Toward the middle of the sixth century a great Emperor, Justinian (527–565), thought the moment propitious for recovering actual control over the western provinces. Theodoric's kingdom had collapsed, the Franks were divided, and neither Visigoths nor Vandals were any longer formidable. Justinian's career will merit further attention in the next chapter. We are concerned here only with his keen interest in Latin culture and his desire to reunite the entire Empire. Although his capital was Constantinople, a city now more Greek and oriental than Roman, it was he who codified Roman law and recovered, at least partially, the west.

Justinian's first efforts were directed toward Africa where his famous general, Belisarius, destroyed the remnants of Vandal rule in six months (533). Roman provincial administration was restored, although the turbulent Moors, who took this opportunity to revolt, were never entirely pacified. Meanwhile, Belisarius had moved northward and occupied Sicily, Naples, and Rome as another force reconquered Dalmatia.

But Justinian and Belisarius under-estimated the power of Gothic resistance. Not for another twenty years (553) did Narses, who replaced Belisarius, bring the war to an end. Ostrogothic rule was completely erased, and no significant vestiges of it remained except the buildings erected by Theodoric.

The long campaign had sadly devastated Italy. Five sieges and the destruction of the aqueducts ruined Rome and reduced the population to a miserable few thousand in the lower city along the Tiber. Justinian made no attempt to restore the ancient capital, and its administration passed into the hands of papal officials. Ravenna, rebuilt and refortified, became the seat of the exarch, as the imperial representative in Italy was now called. The recovered territory was divided for purposes of administration into units called duchies.

Justinian extended his conquests to Sardinia, Corsica, the Balearics, and a portion of southern Spain. But the major part of Spain and all of Gaul escaped him. Important as his success was, he failed to restore the Empire to its former greatness. The long campaigns so weakened his military system that his successors were unable to maintain what he had regained. North Africa continued another century under Roman rule, but Italy succumbed to the attacks of the Lombards a few years after Justinian's death (565).

Unlike former Germanic invaders, the Lombards possessed no particular reverence for Roman institutions. They had moved from the German forest after the Empire had lost its western provinces. Once in Italy they occupied the valley of the Po (572) with Pavia as the seat of their monarchy. Powerless to thwart them, the exarch concentrated his energies on retaining Ravenna and parts of southern Italy and Sicily. The Lombards overran all the rest of the peninsula except Rome and its environs. But the Lombard monarchy was not strong; and from the first, various dukes, whom the kings set up in imitation of the system established by Justinian, rivaled each other in establishing principalities. No longer could imperial authority be maintained even under a fiction of "alliance"— and indeed there was none in the case of the Lombards. The future of Italy and the west lay with others.

The transformation of the western part of the Empire was now complete. In the space of some two centuries this entire area had succumbed to barbarian attacks and had been forced to permit their entry *en masse*. Everywhere, Germanic kingdoms had replaced the Roman provincial administration. The conquest was not, however, a cataclysmic, sudden development. The fact that it has been described here in a few pages should not mislead the reader. In human history two centuries are a long time. Throughout this gradual process, for it was gradual, Roman civilization— its law, its language, and its institutions— retained sufficient strength to influence the conquerors to a marked degree. Military power, it is true, rested with the Germans. But they were relatively few compared with the Roman population, and the traditions of centuries lay behind Rome even in defeat. The extent to which the Germans preserved Roman institutions and the importance of their own customs will be discussed in the following sections.

E. Institutions of the German Kingdoms

The German kingdoms on Roman soil represent a gradual mixture of Roman institutions and Germanic customs. This was not, however, a meeting between the Romans of the Augustan age and the Germans of the primitive forests. It is evident from the preceding pages that both had changed. The Germans were but a small minority of the total population and totally lacking in any sense of German "unity." Moreover, as some Roman provinces had been less deeply affected by Roman ways than others, so some German peoples preserved their own customs less well than others. The Franks, it will be remembered, did not migrate as did Goths and Vandals, and, as a consequence, kept closer touch with their Germanic background. And the Lombards, who entered Italy late in the sixth century when Roman ways had been altered by time and long years of war, were lacking any sense of respect for things Roman. We must expect to encounter considerable variation in the degree of Romanization. And the following pages must, in emphasizing the characteristics common to all the German kingdoms, note many exceptions.

It should likewise be observed that, for at least the first century of the German occupation, there was a disposition on the part of both natives and invaders to live side by side, as it were, rather than to achieve a fusion into one society. Germans were proud of being Goths, Burgundians, Franks, or Vandals. They wore German costumes and followed German customs. Romans continued to regard them as aliens temporarily quartered in their midst. Only later did a real fusion take place.

Most of the German nations had developed into monarchies, mainly elective in principle, but with tendencies toward dynastic succession. Superficially, the German kings maintained a "court" consistent with their dignity as lieutenants of the emperor. They surrounded themselves with officials bearing high-sounding Latin titles and wore purple vestments on state occasions. Theodoric most nearly approached the Roman system in this respect. But appearances may be deceiving. Although to his own people a German ruler was king, to the Roman natives he remained merely the *magister militum* (master of the troops). Moreover, the Roman conception of the state as a public thing (*res publica*) was hardly understood by the Germans. They viewed territory and governmental authority which went with it as a kind of patrimony, the estate or personal possession of the king. The king's court, therefore, was the center of attraction for the powerful magnates, Roman and German, rather than the seat of a highly developed administrative system. And, of course, military authority was everywhere German. Germans were the conquerors and, although they were willing to preserve Roman institutions, they had no intention of letting military control slip from their hands.

Local government preserved its Roman aspect longer. Since the German peoples had not, as a rule, developed any permanent administrative organization, Roman administrative machinery was retained under German supervision. Latin remained the language of government, and natives continued to occupy civil positions. In Italy, for example, Theodoric, the Ostrogoth, preserved the senate and the magistrates—indeed, all the Roman civil administration—and dated his edicts (as did the Burgundian monarchs) after the year of the consuls whom he named in collaboration with the emperor at Constantinople. Roman provincial divisions and financial organization were commonly retained. The latter proved indispensable to most German kings; and the lot of the remaining *curiales* was not bettered.

Some German kingdoms followed the Roman practice of systematizing their law. Visigothic, Frankish, Burgundian, and Lombard legal codes were drawn up in Latin. These codes, especially the *Lex Salica* of the Salian Franks, present an excellent picture of German society in its new environment. German law was still fundamentally the product of ancient custom and generally reflected an earlier pastoral existence and a strong individualism. More settled conditions never entirely removed these earlier characteristics, but they did produce an increased emphasis on public responsibility for preserving order and dispensing justice. Accordingly, while the relatives of the victim of a crime were still free to take vengeance on the criminal or his kin, or to receive the stipulated money payment (*wergeld*), it was more emphatically insisted that all disputes be settled before the regularly constituted tribunals.

Germanic courts were groups of tribesmen. When an accused appeared he might clear himself, if the court so ruled, by summoning a specified number of men who would swear either to his innocence or to the validity of his oath. This process, called compurgation, required no evidence and was more often accepted in the case of noblemen. Trials by ordeal continued for several centuries. An ordeal consisted in the successful endurance of some physical test such as carrying a hot iron for some specified distance. The ordeal by battle was especially popular. It was believed that in an ordeal God would directly reveal the guilt or innocence of the accused.

Class distinctions were recognized in Germanic law. According to the tariff of *wergeld*, it was more expensive to injure a nobleman than a person of modest means. Great importance was attached to injuries done to or committed by cattle. Burgundian law fixed the death penalty for stealing a cow. On the other hand, since Roman agricultural customs were widely imitated, Germanic codes gave ample protection to enclosed lands, vineyards, and gardens.

The distinction between German and Roman is clearly evident in the attitude of the two peoples toward law and social practices. Both the Visigoths and the Ostrogoths, for example, followed the Roman usage and forbade intermarriages between Goths and Romans. The *wergeld* was invariably higher for an injured German than for a Roman. Romans generally had to pay larger fines and even to suffer capital punishment for lesser offenses against Germans. And although the Germans governed themselves according to their own legal customs, they usually preserved Roman law for Roman provincials.

The distinction between Roman and German, evident in law, was accentuated by difference in religion. With the exception of the Franks, practically all the Germanic peoples who settled on Roman soil were Arians. On the other hand, the bulk of the Roman population was Catholic. There is no doubt that the mutual hostility felt by Catholics and Arians aggravated the natural antipathies of nationality. This situation did not remain permanent. The Franks were converted directly to Catholicism, as has been described. By the end of the sixth century the Visigoths had adopted Catholicism. Gundebaud, king of the Burgundians, was converted to Catholicism as early as 517, and he proscribed Arianism. The conquest of Justinian restored orthodox Catholicism to Italy and North Africa. Even the Lombards who ruined Justinian's work in Italy were converted soon after the middle of the seventh century.

Economic life was not profoundly modified by the Germans. Late Roman provincial society had already become predominantly agricultural owing to the prolonged depression since the third century. Germans easily fitted into this society. The German magnates who settled on Roman soil became landowners and lived on great estates or villas just as their Roman contemporaries. Since the Germans were established in an official capacity, an orderly method of dividing the land had to be devised. Usually the former public domain went to the king. In Gaul the Visigothic magnates took two thirds of the private land. In Italy Theodoric's troops took only one third. But the method was the same and the results roughly comparable. It was not a geographical division of territory, with certain areas Gothic and others Roman. Each domain, that is, the sum total of the cultivated estates belonging to an individual, including the dependent population of *coloni* and slaves, was partitioned. An Ostrogothic magnate probably received one third of a larger domain. Provincial Roman proprietors, therefore, were deprived of at least a portion of their patrimony. While German and Roman magnates lived as neighbors, the latter in somewhat reduced circumstances, the dependent slaves and *coloni*, perhaps both Roman and German, continued their former life uninterrupted except for a change of masters.

The commercial system of the later Empire was less drastically affected by the

German invasions than was once believed. Contacts between the eastern and western provinces were not cut off. Syrian and Jewish merchants peddled their wares in Gaul. The western Mediterranean ports of Marseilles and Narbonne continued to preserve their relations with the eastern Mediterranean. As the Germans sought, at least in theory, to preserve the political unity of the Mediterranean world, so they did not deliberately interfere with its economic life. True, they added nothing to it, and economic life continued to stagnate. Industry languished as before, and the transition from urban to agricultural economy continued. But the economic unity of the

Mediterranean world, which the Roman Empire had made possible, they did not destroy. This was endangered only by a new and hostile invasion, that of the Arabs, which will be discussed in a later chapter. Its effects began to be felt in the later seventh century.

F. Gradual Fusion of German and Roman Society: Romanizing the Germans

Thus far we have emphasized the factors which tended to keep Germans and Romans apart. It must not be supposed, however, that the separation was permanent. In the

Sixth century basilica. Sant'Apollinare in Classe, Ravenna.

Photograph by M. W. Baldwin

course of the late sixth and seventh centuries many of those elements which separated German from Roman disappeared, and it is possible to speak of a gradual fusion of the two peoples. First, religious disagreement was removed with the decline of Arianism and the conversion of the Germans to Catholicism. Second, the inability of the imperial government at Constantinople to maintain any semblance of authority, outside of certain parts of Italy, destroyed even the fiction of imperial power throughout the western provinces. Therefore, with confessional differences removed, Hispano- and Gallo-Romans and Italians were no longer unwilling to admit the sovereignty of a German king, now *de facto* ruler of their native province. In short, they came to accept the new situation as permanent and legal. Roman magnates served with the troops of German kings. Nobles—German, Roman, and ecclesiastical—often combined to curb the power of an over-ambitious monarch.

As administrative institutions and popular customs changed, the separation of the two legal systems became less marked. In 654, for example, a Visigothic king promulgated a code of law applicable to both Roman and German subjects. Intermarriages became frequent, and it is significant that late in the sixth century a Visigothic king officially removed the ban on them. As a consequence, racial antagonism between Goths and Romans declined and eventually disappeared. The descendants of the Hispano-Roman aristocracy gloried in Gothic ancestry. Romans in Gaul began to adopt Frankish names, and during the seventh century Gallo-Roman and Frankish magnates fused into a single aristocracy.

Not only did Latin remain the official language of government and church, but Germanic speech apparently disappeared in an area only slightly smaller than the former western half of the Empire. Throughout this territory, which is sometimes referred to as *Romania*, a speech derived from the spoken Latin of the natives survived. Many Germans words were added, more in Frankish Gaul and Lombard Italy than elsewhere. But basically this *lingua Romana*, as it was called, was a Latin speech, and out of its

various dialects came the Romance languages of later times. The boundary between *Romania* and the peoples of Germanic speech has hardly changed through the centuries, and has proved far more stable than political frontiers. The border provinces along the Rhine and Danube frontiers were Germanized. Therefore, the dividing line must be drawn west of the Rhine and south of the Danube. The inhabitants of most of what is today eastern Belgium, Alsace, eastern Switzerland, Bavaria, and Austria—speak a Germanic tongue. The only exception is modern Rumania where a Romance language has survived.

It is evident that during the course of the seventh century, if not before, a process of fusion had begun and it is no longer correct to speak of two separate societies. Broadly speaking, the Roman element predominated in this fusion. After all, the Germans were not numerous, and Rome represented an older and much more highly developed civilization. Its language triumphed over German as a written medium of official and intellectual intercourse. Spoken tongues derived from the Latin displaced the speech of the invaders. Arianism disappeared and Catholicism spread. Roman law, although in a greatly modified form and unsupported by any Roman political institutions, survived in some towns. Centuries later it could be deliberately revived with considerable success. Roman economic life, its agricultural system, and what was left of its commerce, the Germans adopted.

Thus by the year 700 a new society was being formed in the western provinces of the old Emipre. Profoundly changed as it was by the German migrations, it had not entirely lost its fundamentally Roman character. Nor had its contacts with the ancient seat of civilization in the eastern Mediterranean been completely severed. Meanwhile, beyond the frontier those Germans who did not move southward, together with other peoples, were also contributing to the formation of a new society, a European as distinct from a Mediterranean civilization. But before proceeding further, it will be well to cast a glance at the fate of the eastern half of the Empire during the same sixth and seventh centuries.

Interior of the church of Santa Sophia showing the pendentives.[1]

Courtesy Turkish Information Office, New York

[1] For an exterior view see below, pp. 346–347.

CHAPTER 7

Byzantine Continuation of the Roman Empire in the East

A. Byzantine Institutions

The barbarian invasions, which disturbed the Roman Empire in the fifth century and resulted in the formation of Germanic kingdoms in its western part, did not permanently disrupt life in the eastern part. Gothic and other tribesmen attacked and even passed through the eastern provinces, but they did not remain to form kingdoms. Nor was the prolonged economic depression which we described in an earlier chapter so disastrous in the eastern provinces. Therefore, while the whole Empire suffered, the collapse which we have been considering was primarily a western phenomenon.

As time went on, the east became separated politically from the former western provinces, and a culture developed there which was a somewhat different composite of Roman, Greek, and Oriental elements from what obtained in the west. This East European culture is generally referred to as Byzantine, a term derived from the old Greek town of Byzantium upon whose site Constantinope had been founded. Although derived mainly from earlier cultures, especially from ancient Near Eastern, the Byzantine possessed a vitality and originality of its own which was particularly manifest in the realm of art. Moreover, as the traditions of "old Rome" proved to be the civilizing influence on the western barbarians, so the institutions of "new Rome," or Constantinople, profoundly affected the development of the eastern European peoples.

Basically, the culture of the Balkan peninsula and Russia is still Byzantine. Even Sicily and parts of Italy show traces of the temporary Byzantine occupation of those areas. Some knowledge of Byzantine institutions is, therefore, essential to an understanding of European history, particularly in the east.

Byzantine government was mainly a continuation of the institutions devised by the later Roman emperors. The conception of imperial authority as absolute and divinely instituted, which Diocletian and Constantine had emphasized, was perpetuated. It will be recalled that the "god-emperor" idea was native to the east, and deeply implanted in it; and this conception was now given a Christian form in the Byzantine Empire. The patriarch of Constantinople, theoretically representing the electors and expressing, as it was held, the will of God, anointed the new ruler. The emperor thus became the anointed of God and was expected to fulfill the will of Heaven. While the method of choosing the emperor remained uncertain, senate and army usually concurring in the choice, there developed a marked tendency toward dynastic succession. Such ruling families as the Justinianean, the Heraclian, the Comnenian, the Paleologian, and others are famous in Byzantine history.

Since all pretense of free republican or popular forms had long disappeared, administrative routine was carried out by an elaborate bureaucracy. Well paid and on the whole educated and efficient, the civil service was something on which the Byzantines could justly pride themselves. The reorganization of the Empire into prefectures, dioceses, and provinces, undertaken by Diocletian, was maintained, as was his practice of separating the civil and military jurisdictions. One was a check on the other. The vicars who were in charge of the dioceses were appointed by and responsible to the emperor and exercised a restraining influence on the prefect. The separation of the two jurisdictions also made for greater efficiency, although there developed in the civil jurisdiction a strong administrative conservatism. While this traditionalism sometimes prevented reforms, it did serve to stabilize Byzantine government and to curb the vagaries of a willful emperor.

Inevitably, special circumstances dictated modifications. The exarchs of Italy and Africa, created by Justinian, were military commanders to whom the civil administration was subordinate. In the seventh century the Empire, then greatly reduced in size, was redivided into "themes" for military reasons. In a theme, the military governor had precedence. The Isaurian dynasty in the eighth century took a further step and combined the civil and military jurisdictions.

While Roman imperial ideas and practices formed a basic substratum in all matters of government, native influences, Greek and Oriental, became increasingly evident. This was particularly true after the final loss of Italy and the west. We have already noticed the appropriation of the oriental idea of the god-emperor. And while Latin remained the official language through most of the sixth century, it afterwards gave place to Greek. Roman law was codified for the last time in Latin by the Emperor Justinian (527–565), but even he was forced to publish later imperial laws in Greek and could not prevent the appearance of Greek paraphrases of the original code.

Generally speaking, the Byzantine army, though small, was excellently trained and equipped. While many earlier Roman practices were continued, others were abandoned. The old Praetorian guard, with its baneful influence on government, was abolished. New frontier forces were created

(the *limitanei*) and the soldiers were rewarded with inalienable grants of land. Cavalry troops, medical services, and engineers' corps were parts of an effective organization, and several contemporary books on tactics have survived which give evidence that the Roman scientific military tradition was faithfully and intelligently carried forward.

Naval power was developed by the Byzantines far more than it had been by republican or imperial Rome. Constantinople was defended (673–678; 717–718) against the Arabs with the aid of ships, and the highly inflammable and explosive Greek fire was used with telling effect.

The secret of Byzantine political and military strength lay largely in its continued economic prosperity. The development of the eastern Roman provinces presents a marked contrast to the fate of the west. The same regimentation of life, the same oppressive taxation, necessary to support the civil service and the military establishment, which ruined the western half of the Empire, fell on the east. Here also, broadly speaking, agricultural society became stratified, with large estates worked by *coloni* or dependent peasants, bound to the soil. Yet the eastern provinces survived and actually flourished because they possessed old cities whose commercial life was based on well established trade contacts and a thriving native industry. Constantinople, the newest great city, became the depot for merchandise from all over the known world and its fabulous wealth and exotic eastern wares astonished travelers from western and northern Europe.

While products reached Byzantium from southwestern Europe, her great commercial wealth resulted from trade with the east. And although a few Syrian and Alexandrian merchants visited the Far East and returned with wondrous tales of Ceylon and India, or even ventured down the African coast to the marts of Ethiopia, most of the eastern trade, especially that in silk, was monopolized by Persia. Since the shortest route to the Far East by Samarkand and Bokhara lay through Persian territory, the Persian monopoly could only be avoided by occasional use of the old northern route by the Black and Caspian Seas or through contact with the merchants of Ethiopia. Ethiopian ships regularly plied the Indian Ocean and Ethiopian traders penetrated the interior of Africa. To Adule on the Red Sea they brought their wares and met the ships and merchants of Byzantium.

Since silk was increasingly in demand for ecclesiastical vestments and altar draperies, and for private luxury use by the wealthy, measures were taken to bargain with Persia. Most important, however, was the smuggling of silk worm eggs from China by Byzantines. This eventually made possible a thriving native silk industry.

To all this evidence of Byzantine economic prosperity there should be added, finally, the stability of its coinage. The gold besant (Byzant) was the standard coin of the Mediterranean region for centuries.

The heart and center of the Byzantine imperial system was Constantinople. To make this city, the "new Rome," worthy of its dignity as the capital and successor of the "old Rome," Constantine and his successors spared no expense. Not only was it admirably fortified, but great churches, palaces, public buildings, with gilded domes, marble steps, and magnificent mosaic decorations, made the city a show place of the east. In the center of the city was a great marble paved square, the *Augusteum*, its very name reminiscent of Roman grandeur. On the north side of the *Augusteum* was the famous church of Santa Sophia. Opposite was the imperial palace which also overlooked the blue waters of the Bosphorus and the Sea of Marmora.

Near the *Augusteum* was the Hippodrome which, despite its dedication to circus games, public shows, triumphs, and even executions, played a not inconsiderable part in the political life of the Empire. Gathered in its sixty thousand seats the populace cheered their favorite charioteers and, on occasion, denounced the policies of the government. By the sixth century there had appeared two rival circus factions, the Blues and the Greens. Not only did each of these factions support a particular set of charioteers, but, urged on by a turbulent crowd, they intervened in politics. Ministers, judges, even emperors, for they were often present in the lofty royal box, favored or belonged to one faction or the other. Outrages and assassinations occasionally followed victory or defeat in the Hippodrome. As a result, a dangerous popular influence over policy, based on an emotional factional loyalty, threatened to undermine orderly administration. When Justinian attempted to discipline both factions, he was faced with an insurrection, the famous *Nika* ("conquer") riots, which nearly cost him his throne. Only the slaughter of some thirty thousand people and the destruction of a section of the city ended the menace. Thereafter, the political influence of the Hippodrome crowds diminished.

But the ill controlled and somewhat degraded populace of Constantinople did not represent Byzantine society in its entirety. The citizens of the Empire were profoundly interested in matters of religion, and nowhere did religion play a greater role in political and social life than in the Byzantine Empire. Not only did emperors take an active part in ecclesiastical affairs, but the average citizen was absorbed in the great theological controversies of the day and habitually discussed them with his friends in the market place. It will be recalled that it was in the east that the early heresies like Arianism and the Monophysite doctrine of the single nature of Christ developed. Religious asceticism, both in its individual or hermit form and in its communal or monastic aspect, flourished in the eastern provinces. Christian monasticism originated in the east. Monks or hermits from the desert ranked with the charioteer as popular heroes, and pilgrims journeyed far to visit them. On occasion mobs of desert monks from the Thebaid region south of Alexandria even entered that great city to applaud or denounce the policies of the bishop.

B. Policies and Achievements of the Emperor Justinian

The most famous of the Byzantine Roman Emperors of the sixth century was Justinian the Great (527–565). Although of humble, Latin-speaking, Illyrian peasant stock, he possessed, as a man, that dignity which becomes a ruler. He was intelligent, industrious, and concerned with every detail of government. He expected all his subordinates to be equally diligent, and he insisted on, and to a large degree secured, an honest, efficient administration. An enthusiastic patron of the arts, he was also a great builder and many churches in Constantinople were started during his reign, the most celebrated being the great Santa Sophia. Justinian was also a religious poet and composer of hymns. His weaknesses were a want of that capacity for decisive action which a ruler so often needs, and a tendency to overemphasize details.

Justinian's wife, Theodora, was the daughter of a bear-trainer at the Hippodrome and a former circus performer herself. Of somewhat dubious reputation, she was a strange consort for the rather strait-laced Justinian. Yet she made an excellent Empress and her resolute will often strengthened her wavering spouse. It was her refusal to flee at the time of the Nika riots that galvanized the more timid Emperor into the action which suppressed the rebellion and saved his throne. Throughout the reign her influence over her husband and over imperial policy remained considerable, and after her death Justinian was pathetically irresolute. Not without reason did the artists who created the beautiful mosaics of the church of San Vitale in Ravenna portray both Emperor and Empress.

Two great aims guided all of Justinian's policies: the restoration of the Roman Empire to its former greatness, and the championship of Catholicism. If there was a strong tendency for Byzantine culture to become increasingly Hellenized, it was Justinian's distinctly Latin and Roman policy which limited that tendency and preserved in Byzantine civilization an important substratum of Roman influence. The codification of Roman law stands as one of his greatest achievements; the recovery of the western provinces was the task to which he bent most of his energies.

By the sixth century Roman law was in a confused state. The old law (*ius vetus*), composed of statutes of the republic and empire, decrees of the senate, comments of jurists, judicial decisions and the *responsa*

of the *jurisprudentes*, had become a mass of ill ordered and often conflicting material. The so-called new law (*ius novum*), or the provisions of later emperors, being more recent, was in somewhat better shape. Hence Justinian first appointed a commission headed by a distinguished jurist, Tribonian, to purge the new law of repetitions and inconsistencies. The result, known as the Code (*Codex Justinianus*), was a greatly reduced amount of material contained in some ten volumes.

The success of this first attempt emboldened the Emperor to appoint another commission to reorganize the *ius vetus*. An enormous amount of material was reduced and compiled into the fifty books comprising the *Digest* or *Pandects*. There were added the *Institutes*, a statement of legal principles, and the Novels (*Novellae*) or new imperial laws which came into existence as the work was being carried forward. The four parts, Code, Digest, Institutes, and Novels, came to be known as the *Corpus Juris Civilis* (Body of Civil Law).

It is impossible to overestimate the significance of the Justinian code. It was compiled at a time when Greek and oriental influences threatened to overpower the Roman. These influences are noticeable in the work of Justinian's jurists. Nevertheless, the *Corpus Juris Civilis* is basically Roman. In feudal western Europe, Roman law soon ceased to be practised as a scientific system. Yet the *Corpus Juris Civilis* was never lost. And when in the eleventh and twelfth centuries a more settled society in the west again demanded a scientific law, the Justinian code proved to be the instrument of a remarkable legal renaissance. Subsequent generations in almost every corner of the earth have been greatly influenced by Roman law.

The partial recovery of the western provinces was perhaps Justinian's most spectacular achievement. It was natural that his Roman policy should lead to an attempt to restore the Empire to its former glory. A Roman Empire permanently separated from Old Rome was to him unthinkable. The suppression of Arianism was in accord with Justinian's Catholic policy. But despite their theoretical subjection to the Emperor's rule, which had never been abandoned, the western barbarian kingdoms, by the middle of the sixth century, were fast losing touch with Constantinople. Justinian's task in this respect was not an easy one. Nor did he ever bring it to completion.

We have already related the story of Justinian's western campaigns and demonstrated how, after a comparatively easy conquest of North Africa, it took his generals, Belisarius and Narses, twenty years to subdue the Ostrogoths in Italy. A few years later imperial armies entered Spain, but could only wrest the southern coast and the Balearics from the Visigoths.[1] Justinian's reconquest was, therefore, not complete. In a sense the Mediterranean was again a "Roman lake," but Britain and Frankish Gaul and most of Spain remained untaken. Nor was Roman administration everywhere reinstated. True, the African provinces were restored to something like their former prosperity. The old systematic irrigation was revived and olive culture again flourished. The

[1] See map, p. 70, above.

Arianism of the Vandals was effectively suppressed in line with Justinian's policy of championing Catholic orthodoxy. But the Berbers and Moors took advantage of the Vandal war to revolt and were never entirely pacified. It will be remembered that in Italy twenty years of warfare had left widespread devastation.

The cost of Justinian's wars was terrific and increased the tax load on his already overburdened subjects. Further, war in the west necessitated a neglect of the eastern frontiers and spread dangerously thin the empire's military forces. Therefore, in spite of the numerous frontier fortresses which Justinian built, and the organization of border patrols (*limitanei*), his conquests scarcely survived his death. In the next generation Italy was again invaded by the Lombards and the Danube frontier broken, and a serious crisis with Persia emerged. The latter had arisen before Justinian's death. The Emperor's western conquests merely added temporary glory. In the long run they weakened the Byzantine state.

The Empress Theodora and her court. Sixth century mosaic in the church of San Vitale, Ravenna.

Photograph by John M. Woodbridge

It is a mistake to regard Justinian's western policy as entirely fruitless. It must be considered as part of his plan to recover the entire Roman heritage, to preserve its religion and its law. Moreover in parts of Italy where Byzantine rule lasted for upwards of two centuries, Byzantine culture left an ineradicable impression. This was especially true in the south, in the region around Ravenna, seat of the imperial exarch, and later in Venice. Thus by a strange paradox one result of Justinian's Latin policy was the Byzantinizing of sections of Italy. Byzantine art, for example, was employed in Italy and influenced other areas of western Europe. The Greek language was maintained in monasteries in southern Italy where Greek monks chanted the Byzantine liturgy.

The second great aim of Justinian was the championship of Catholicism and the maintenance of the unity of Christianity. He was deeply interested in religious affairs, and regarded the church as legitimately subject to him as absolute ruler. He appointed bishops and even interfered in theological controversies. And since he regarded religious uniformity as essential to political unity and internal peace, all pagans and heretics felt the heavy hand of official intolerance.

Paganism still existed, although it was fast dying out. A number of pagan philosophers still frequented the schools at Athens, and Justinian considered these vestiges of a once great tradition important enough to suppress. The schools were closed and the scholars scattered. But since the Athenian "Academy" then represented only a faint reflection of earlier glory, the consequent loss to scholarship was slight.

Heretics constituted a more formidable problem, especially the Monophysites who were numerous and powerful in Syria, Palestine, and Egypt. Justinian's early policy of close relations with Rome and the papacy, particularly his enforcement of the decrees of the Council of Chalcedon which condemned the Monophysite doctrine, aroused considerable discontent in the eastern provinces. Here was a religious problem with serious political implications. To appease the west meant to alienate important areas

in the east. For a time the Emperor attempted to bring about a theological compromise, a course which resulted in satisfying neither party. One pope was summoned to Constantinople and virtually held prisoner for several years. Toward the end of his life, under the influence of Theodora, Justinian favored the Monophysites. Thus he did not establish religious uniformity and the Monophysite provinces remained a religio-political problem until their conquest by the Arabs in the seventh century.

C. Narrowing of the Byzantine Empire in the Seventh Century

Justinian's reign marked the culmination of Latin influence in Byzantine civilization. Thereafter, while certain Roman ideas continued to determine the course of Byzantine history—the emperors never ceasing to regard themselves as the legitimate successors of Augustus—Greek and Oriental influences prevailed. Greek became the official language of the administration and of the law as it had been of the church in the east.

Besides, the loss of the western provinces rendered contact of the east with Rome and Italy more difficult. It is true that southern Italy, Rome, and Ravenna were not taken by the Lombards, but continued as nominal possessions of the Emperor. Yet imperial power in Italy was tenuous in the extreme. More and more, people there turned for guidance, even in temporal matters, to the pope rather than to the exarch. The unity of eastern and western Christianity was also endangered by this loss of contact between the Latin—and, in the Byzantine view, barbarian—west and the Greek east. Finally, Justinian's successors were forced to deal with pressing eastern problems which he had neglected. Foremost among these was the defense of the frontiers.

During Justinian's reign communities of southern Slavs had been established along the northern Byzantine frontier. The Slavs were an Indo-European people who migrated in various directions from the region of the Pripet marshes. In later chapters we shall notice the western Slavs of Bohemia and Poland and the eastern Slavs of Russia. Here we are concerned with the south Slavs

Interior of the basilica of San Vitale at Ravenna built by the Emperor Justinian, sixth century.

Alinari photograph

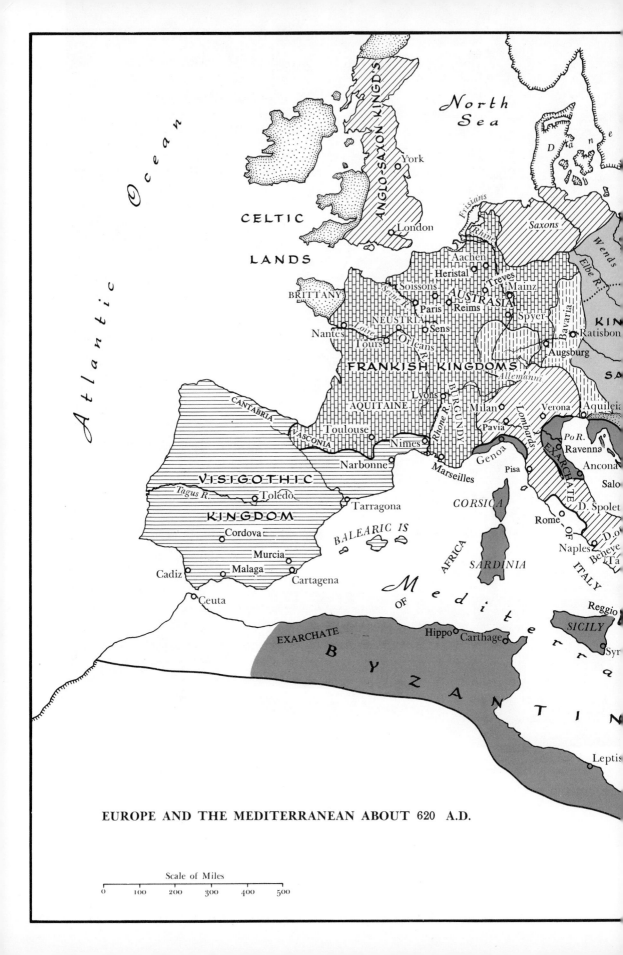

EUROPE AND THE MEDITERRANEAN ABOUT 620 A.D.

Scale of Miles

0   100   200   300   400   500

(or Yugoslavs) who by the fifth and sixth centuries had settled in some numbers north of the Black Sea. Although they had frequently suffered at the hands of Germans and also of Asiatic nomads, they were tenacious and prolific and maintained their identity. Unlike the nomads, they had reached an agricultural stage of civilization.

In the sixth century, much as the Goths had previously been driven on by the savage nomadic Huns, large numbers of south Slavs were pushed by the Avars, another Hunnic people, into the Balkan peninsula. Sometimes in conjunction with the Avars, but finally on their own initiative, they advanced into imperial territory. By the end of the century a great many had settled in Thrace and Greece. And in 620 the Emperor Heraclius officially recognized a number of them as allies against the Avars. Somewhat later, as Avar raids continued, these Yugoslavs, ancestors of the modern Serbs and Croats, moved into the Illyrian provinces.

Thus it was that the Roman Empire of the east was forced in its turn to permit barbarian immigration. And although it was many years before the Yugoslavs were able to form stable kingdoms, the ethnic character of the Balkan peninsula was permanently changed.

Meanwhile, the Avars remained a formidable military menace. In 591, in 619, and again in 626, together with Slavs, they appeared before Constantinople. But the redoubtable fortifications of the city frustrated all their attacks. Thereafter, the Avars ceased to trouble the Byzantine Empire seriously, and the Slavs settled down within its frontiers.

Defense of Constantinople was complicated by an even more serious menace to the eastern frontier. This resulted from a remarkable resurgence of Persian power. Under their King Chosroes, the Persians passed through Armenia and Syria and advanced into Palestine. Capturing Jerusalem, they carried away part of the relic of the Holy Cross, the Cross upon which Christ had been crucified. That the Emperor Heraclius (610–641) was able to cope with this situation is a tribute to his skill and courage as well as to the inherent strength of the Empire. The Avars were temporarily appeased, and between 622 and 627 a series of brilliant campaigns not only drove the Persians from Syria and Palestine, but carried the Emperor to a signal victory near the ruins of Nineveh on the Tigris. In the following year Chosroes's successor sued for peace. Meanwhile Constantinople had successfully withstood Avar assaults by sea and land. In 629 Heraclius returned in triumph to Constantinople bearing with him the relic of the True Cross. He was a savior of the Empire.

But except in name it was no longer a Roman Empire. The Balkans were henceforth predominantly Slavic, for the Yugoslavs, profiting from the exploits of the destructive Avars, were now firmly settled in the Balkan peninsula. And though they were presently converted to Christianity and nominally incorporated in the Empire, they retained their own Slavic speech and ignored both Latin and Greek. Moreover, the long Byzantine war with Persia exhausted both countries and left them a prey to the Arabs, who, even before Heraclius' death, had invaded Egypt, Syria, Palestine, and Mesopotamia.

Thus the Empire of the early eighth century consisted only of Constantinople, a portion of the Balkan peninsula, Asia Minor, and a few areas in Italy and Sicily. But even in its reduced state—and more losses were to follow—the Byzantine Empire was to remain for centuries a rampart of Graeco-Roman and Christian civilization in the eastern Mediterranean.

CHAPTER 8

Consolidation and Expansion of the Catholic Christian Church

A. Conversion of Celts, Germans, and Slavs

In an earlier chapter we described how the Christian church became in the fourth century the official religion of the Roman Empire. The hundred years of comparative peace between 325 and the German invasions of the fifth century permitted the church to spread throughout the Empire and to develop as a stable institution. As the history of many subsequent centuries testifies, much remained to be accomplished in church organization and in making its operation more effective. But the fundamental principles upon which the organization was based—hierarchy, pope, and bishops—were clear. When the Roman political structure disintegrated in the fifth century, the organized church already possessed sufficient stability to survive and to exert a growing influence over society. In a sense, it replaced the Roman Empire as the principal civilizing agent of Europe.

Not alone did the church develop as an organization; it spread geographically beyond the bounds of the Roman state. With the Saxon conquest of Britain, Christianity had been almost destroyed there and completely isolated. In the fifth century St. Patrick (d. 461), who as a youth had spent six years in captivity in Ireland, and then become a monk in Gaul, returned to evangelize the land of his former captors. Before his death he had the satisfaction of seeing the bulk of the Irish people Christian and imbued with missionary zeal. Irish mis-sionaries followed St. Columba (d. 597) across the water to the northern coast of England where they found inhabitants of a similar Celtic speech. Since the Latin name for these Irishmen was *Scoti*, the northern part of Britain came to be known as Scotland. Other Irish crossed to Celtic Brittany whence they penetrated the Frankish kingdom which was then still largely pagan. St. Columbanus (d. 615) was a famous Celtic missionary to the continent.

Late in the sixth century (597), Pope Gregory sent a monk, St. Augustine, to convert the Saxons of southern England. Thus was started a movement which later converged with the Celtic Christianity of the north. And it was not long before Anglo-Saxon missionaries were carrying the gospel to those parts of the Frankish kingdom where paganism still flourished. The Northumbrian, Willibrord, after an education in Ireland, so successfully labored among the Frisians of the Rhine estuary that he was called to Rome and made bishop of Utrecht. Another Saxon missionary, Winfrid, later known as Boniface (d. 754), was a man of exceptional ability. He established the church in the East Frankish dominions and organized its hierarchy under direct papal authority. Even today most Germans regard St. Boniface as their patron saint.

In the east, a century later, the Greek Saints Cyril and Methodius, who were brothers, labored with considerable success in Moravia. The Germans, who aspired to dominance in this Slavic region, were hostile, but Rome upheld the efforts of Cyril and Methodius and sanctioned the Slavonic liturgy they introduced and for which they had devised an alphabet (Cyrillic, Glagolithic). Although Slavonic did not remain the liturgical language of Bohemia and Moravia, it did persist, along with the Cyrillic alphabet, among many Slavic peoples.

Wherever the church spread, its religious ideas permeated all life—political, economic, and social. The church's mode of operation, however, necessarily differed according to the manifold and changing conditions of post-Roman society. In the east, for example, under the stable political institutions of the Byzantine Empire, the development of the church took on a different aspect from its progress in the west where political instability was the rule. Such things must be considered in any discussion of the church in the fifth, sixth, and seventh centuries. And yet the essential unity of Christendom, though jeopardized by the cultural estrangement of east and west, persisted despite political divisions. This is an historical fact of no little significance. It is appropriate, therefore, to treat the church in the period after the Germanic invasions in its entirety, making whatever distinctions geographical variation may require.

B. Consolidation under the Papacy from Leo I to Gregory I

One of the most significant developments during the decline of the Roman Empire was the increasing prestige of the bishops of Rome in both spiritual and temporal matters. We have seen that the supremacy of these bishops as successors of St. Peter was of primitive origin and had been asserted in the days of persecution. In the period of Roman decline, despite the transference of the seat of Empire to the east, the Roman see and papal supremacy became more effective.

This is particularly noticeable in the case of the church's action against heresy. Most of the early heresies—Arianism, Monophysitism, and the like—had developed in the east and were in the beginning, at least, problems for the eastern bishops. The first seven ecumenical councils which were called primarily to deal with such matters were all

held in the east. But Rome's decisive leadership in the resulting definition of orthodox dogma was impressive. At the Council of Nicaea (325), the Roman formula on the "consubstantiality" of the Father and the Son was adopted. Two Roman priests were present as representatives of Rome and it is probable that Bishop Hosius of Cordova, who presided at most of the sessions, was actually a papal legate. Similarly, when the bishops in the Council of Chalcedon (451) failed to reach an agreement, Pope Leo I issued his famous *Tome*, or letter, which ended the controversy and upheld the doctrine that Christ possessed two natures, human and divine, in one divine person. Thus the Monophysite belief in a single combined nature was condemned largely as a result of papal initiative.

In the sphere of jurisdiction, that is, the actual power of the pope as supreme governor in administering the church's daily affairs, various political developments of the post-Roman world gravely impeded the pope's freedom of action. In the former western provinces, unstable conditions hampered communications. In place of a single political jurisdiction there were now four or five German kingdoms. For some time, all but one of these, the Frankish, had Arian rulers. Moreover, bishops who had originally been selected by the clergy and people of a city were, by the sixth and seventh centuries, often appointees of the German kings. Under such conditions effective papal jurisdiction was extremely difficult.

Notwithstanding these and other difficulties, there were certain distinct gains, especially in the northwest. Celtic Christianity long retained many local peculiarities which resulted partly from the tribal organization of the Irish. Most of these, such as the calculation of the date for Easter, were in themselves of minor significance, but they represented to their adherents aspects of a whole ecclesiastical system. Scottish and north English Christians clung tenaciously to the practices taught them by the Celtic monks in the face of the determined opposition of the disciples of St. Augustine in the south. Accordingly, when the synod of Whitby (664) accepted the Roman method

Ruins of the St. Simon monastery in Syria.

Courtesy Syrian Government Tourist Office, New York

of determining the date of Easter, something far more important than a date was decided. For the acceptance of the Roman formula signified that the English church—and eventually the Irish—was thenceforth an integral part of Roman Christianity. And it will be recalled that it was with a strong sense of the importance of papal supremacy that the Saxons, Willibrord and Boniface, carried the faith to the continental dominions of the East Franks.

In eastern Europe, the persistence of imperial power meant the continuance of the ecclesiastical organization which had already been developed and which was based largely on the imperial administrative system. As long as the Byzantine Empire remained a unit, so too within its boundaries did the church in the east.

Byzantine Christianity was centered in Constantinople. This had not always been the case, because an old tradition which the west emphasized placed the foundation by an apostle as the criterion of the precedence of a bishopric. But in the east, after Diocletian's reorganization of the Empire, political and ecclesiastical administrative units were identical. Thus "it was a city's position in the civil hierarchy which decided its precedence in the ecclesiastical sphere." [1] Moreover, the Council of Constantinople (381) officially sanctioned this position, at least as far as the east was concerned, by giving Constantinople first place after Rome, "because Constantinople is new Rome." Thenceforth the patriarch of Constantinople, while recognizing the apostolic supremacy of the Roman see of Peter, claimed jurisdiction over all the eastern churches. Only Alexandria seriously contested Constantinople's supremacy. And this was partly because Egypt had always occupied a unique position within the Roman Empire, amounting almost to a kind of autonomy, and partly because Alexandria under Athanasius had so valiantly championed orthodoxy against the Arians. But in the fifth century Constantinople successfully asserted its primacy over the bishops of Alexandria.

Thus it can be seen that the jurisdiction of the pope over the eastern bishops was not direct, as in the west, but was exercised through the patriarch of Constantinople. Moreover, the latter's position was not an independent one, for the continuation of stable imperial government in the east meant the persistence of imperial interference in matters of religion. Even in purely ecclesiastical affairs, the relation of pope and emperor was of paramount importance. Almost from the very moment of imperial toleration of Christianity, the problem of the emperor's position with regard to the church existed.

And it was soon discovered that imperial protection was not an unmixed blessing. The Council of Nicaea met under imperial auspices and Constantine presided over its initial sessions. Later, Justinian regarded himself as head of the church, appointed the bishops in the east, and occasionally interfered in religious concerns. Fortunately, Justinian's strong Roman propensities and

---

[1] N. H. Baynes, *The Byzantine Empire*, p. 77.

his anxiety to promote orthodoxy led him to give full recognition and support to the pope's position. But even with Justinian there were difficult moments, especially during that period when the Emperor attempted to effect a compromise with the Monophysites. Pope Vigilius was virtually prisoner at Constantinople for several years.

When imperial authority was temporarily reëstablished in the west by Justinian, the interference of the Byzantine emperors became a factor even in Italy. The archbishop of Ravenna and other bishops in Byzantine territory were often encouraged by the imperial exarch to resist such expressions of papal authority as the confirmation of an episcopal election or the attendance at a papal synod. Finally, it should be remembered that Justinian's Roman policy scarcely outlived him and that many of his successors wavered in their orthodoxy. And in so far as they gave support to the Monophysites or other heretical groups they tended to turn away from Rome and to encourage the patriarch of Constantinople to do likewise.

An acute issue between Rome and the east was raised early in the eighth century. Partly as a result of the rise and spread of Mohammedanism, whose followers accused the Christians of making gods of their saints and idols of their images, there arose a sort of puritanical faction in the church in Asia Minor which attempted to do away with all statues and images and to repudiate the traditional veneration of saints. Since some of the adherents of this view carried their beliefs into action, they became known as the Iconoclasts (image-breakers). And when their cause was supported by certain emperors, notably Leo III (717–741), a real ecclesiastical crisis developed. The church in the east was nearly rent asunder in the struggle between the imperially supported Iconoclasts and the defenders of the proper use of images led by the patriarch strongly backed by the monks. Fortunately, the church in the east was not permanently divided. The defenders of the traditional veneration of saints held their ground and Iconoclasm eventually disappeared. Although Iconoclasm did not greatly affect the church in the west, the pope as head of the entire church was seriously concerned. He upheld the patriarch and defended the veneration of saints. As a result of the policy of Leo, relations between the pope and the emperor were badly strained.

It should be emphasized that as the eastern and western provinces of the old Roman Empire drew apart politically, a similar tendency toward division developed in the ecclesiastical sphere. There had long been minor doctrinal and liturgical divergencies. The Christians in the east followed in their public services the Byzantine rite in the Greek tongue, while those in the west used Latin in their liturgy. The more sophisticated, cultured, and economically prosperous east inclined to regard the west as barbarian. There was a noticeable reluctance on the part of some patriarchs to admit that the bishop of the populous and flourishing "new Rome" should be subordinate to the bishop of what had become a comparatively small Italian town. In spite of papal protests, the title "ecumenical patriarch" was adopted and occasionally used by the bishops of Constantinople. During the seventh and eighth centuries the rift widened and there were actually one or two temporary schisms or separations between the two churches.

But none was permanent and it is important to note that, despite political and cultural divergencies and occasional disputes, the religious unity of Christendom was not formally broken for centuries thereafter. Indeed between 650 and 750 there were no less than six popes of Greek or Syrian origin. Nevertheless, papal jurisdiction over Byzantine Christianity was hampered by imperial interference, by the growing cultural differences between east and west, and by the ambitions of several patriarchs.

An important aspect of church history during the period of the invasions was the growth of papal authority outside the purely ecclesiastical sphere. This was the time when the foundations of papal temporal power—a power of great importance in subsequent centuries—were laid. In the first place, the failure of imperial authority in the west left a void which had to be filled. Except for Theodoric's reign, Italy was in constant turmoil. Owing to the prestige of the papal office, the pope was often regarded as the only real symbol of authority and stability. It was Pope Leo I, not the emperor, who went out to meet Attila, the Hun. The popes, like all bishops in the late Roman period, were magistrates. And since a decree of Constantine had empowered the church to own property, the papacy had received many donations of land. Most of these were in the environs of Rome and eventually formed a sizeable strip of territory along the coast north and south of the city, known as the Patrimony of St. Peter. But some estates were as far away as Sicily. Both magisterial authority and the fact that they were large landowners forced the popes in an unstable age to assume the duties and responsibilities of civil government. This was especially true after the Lombard invasions had separated the various sections of Italy which were still claimed by the Byzantine sovereigns. From the sixth century it was the popes who governed the city of Rome and the Patrimony, fed the populace with the grain shipped from the papal estates in Sicily, and, since the imperial exarch rarely fulfilled his proper functions, negotiated with the Lombard kings.

All the tendencies in papal history which we have described were exemplified in a most brilliant manner by Pope Gregory the Great (590–604). Gregory was a Roman of noble family, educated in the Roman tradition. He knew no Greek, little church history, and generally held style and classical scholarship to be of secondary importance. But he was an intelligent student of the Bible and the Church Fathers.

After beginning a political career which carried him to the office of prefect of the city, he gave up his possessions to charity and converted his house into a monastery. Later he was called from monastic seclusion to the position of archdeacon of Rome, a post of high importance in the papal administration. Twice he visited Constantinople, once as a papal representative. Throughout his career as pope, he consistently upheld the legitimate authority of emperors. But with equal insistence he resisted those imperial policies which either aimed at subjecting the church in

Italy or bowed to Monophysite or other heretical opinion. Moreover, since imperial help against the Lombard invaders of Italy was entirely lacking, he was forced to political measures of the type we have described and which to all intents and purposes transferred political authority over Rome and parts of central Italy to the papacy.

Gregory was also zealous in his concern for the church's welfare beyond the Alps. The Frankish kingdom was Catholic, and even in Visigothic Spain Catholicism was making progress. Gregory's letters to bishops and rulers indicate his constant solicitude. Saxon England, of course, was a more decisive conquest. And after St. Augustine's mission was established, it was Gregory's intelligent direction which laid the foundations for the English church's full communion with Rome in the seventh century. As a former monk, he was naturally deeply interested in the progress of monasticism, and the weight of his authority contributed largely to its development.

Gregory was not merely a competent administrator. His deep interest in the church's liturgy induced him to instigate an arrangement of church music then in use at Rome. As a result, the official chant of the church has borne his name ever since (Gregorian chant). Among his many published sermons and writings were the *Pastoral Care*, written for the guidance of bishops and priests, and the *Moralia*, a commentary on the book of Job, and the *Dialogues*. His works earned him the designation of a "Father" of the church. All in all, St. Gregory was one of the great figures in the history of the papacy. And while papal supremacy was by no means perfectly realized in practice, the way was paved for the triumphs of his successors.

C. The Bishops

Emphasis on the prestige of the papacy should not obscure the significant activities of bishops, priests, and monks, for it was through them that the ecclesiastical organization touched the life of every community. Since the ecclesiastical organization had been based on the Roman administrative system, each *civitas* possessed an episcopal church presided over by a bishop. As a consequence, most of the later *dioceses* took their names from the Roman *civitates*. In the eastern provinces the heart of a *civitas* usually remained a metropolis, a city in the actual sense of the word. In the west, where city life declined, the *civitas* was often no longer a flourishing town, but simply a community inhabited by the bishop, his clergy and a population dependent on them. These would consist of the bishop's principal assistants, of whom the most important was the archdeacon, and the clergy of the cathedral who, especially in the west, were usually organized into a community and known as canons. Then in addition to the clerical population, there were the servants in the episcopal household, shopkeepers, and tenants or laborers on the episcopal estates. Finally, since bishops were also magistrates and since the bishop's court was frequented by suitors in a variety of cases, civil and ecclesiastical, there would probably be a considerable transient population. The entourage of a bishop might constitute a fairly sizeable community.

Parish organization tended to become identified with the *latifundia* and great estates. For throughout Christendom the powerful landed magnates maintained small churches or chapels for themselves and their dependents, the *coloni*. Often, despite the decrees (or canons) of church councils, the proprietors exercised a right of patronage over these village churches which thus became the forerunners of the rural manor parishes of the middle ages.

While the bishops of the east had to combat the various heresies which have been mentioned, western bishops, after the decline of Arianism, had to contend with survivals of paganism and with the low moral tone of a semi-barbaric society. Numerous local church councils held in Gaul in the sixth century attest to their activity in this regard. And the decrees of these councils indicate the church's interest in the sanctity of marriage and its concern for the poor and for slaves. As the Roman civil administration passed out of existence, people looked to the local bishop, the representative of a great and stable institution, as a guide and protector in temporal as well as spiritual affairs. Many bishops like St. Caesarius of Arles, St. Remigius of Reims, St. Germanus of Auxerre, St. Avitus of Vienne, and Gregory of Tours, historian of the Franks, gained considerable prestige which they used to further their spiritual missions.

Unfortunately, not all bishops were so active or themselves such shining examples of godly living. All too many sank nearer to the level of the rude society in which they lived. Although bishops were supposed to be elected by the clergy and people of a city and the choice approved by the other bishops of the province, there was actually considerable interference on the part of kings and magnates. And as Frankish and other German kings began to influence episcopal elections or even to appoint bishops, too many selections were made for political or personal reasons. The result was a deterioration of the clergy, and a number of prelates behaved like secular princes and warriors. Notwithstanding, most of the bishops of Spain, Gaul, Africa, and Italy strove valiantly and with no little success to uphold the principles of personal and social morality. Their civilizing role in a barbarian world was of paramount significance.

D. Development of Monasticism

Monasticism is a way of life. It means a complete or partial withdrawal from the world and voluntary abstinence from certain of the ordinary lawful activities of life for the sake of undisturbed prayer and worship of God. True monasticism, as distinct from the solitary life of the hermit, also signifies life in a community according to a fixed rule or daily routine. Monasticism is not exclusively a Christian institution. In various forms it has flourished in other world religions. In fact, asceticism or self-denial, combined with the urge to remove oneself from the world for the sake of religious contemplation, has appealed to people of many races and faiths.

In the days when Christianity was repressed and persecuted by the imperial Roman government, most Christians were called upon to lead a life of self-sacrifice, even of danger, as a matter of course. But after official toleration and support had removed the threat of persecution, an increasing number of heroic souls felt that ordinary life no longer provided the constant challenge to self-denial which a good Christian should face. In the eastern provinces, many such persons betook themselves to remote places to live as solitary hermits. The desert of the Thebaid south of Alexandria, where the climate made such an existence possible, was especially popular. Some, like St. Anthony (d. 355), achieved a real sanctity through fasting and prayer. But too many, mistaking the means for the end, fell into excessive self-mortification, vying with their fellows in a strange sort of ascetic competition. The hermit was a popular figure with the average Byzantine citizen who regarded him, despite his excesses, as a sort of spiritual hero. In the west the solitary hermit life was not unknown, but it had less appeal and was less prevalent.

In the main, the asceticism of the solitary hermit did not commend itself to the ecclesiastical authorities. All forms of religious expression, they felt, must be brought within the scope of the church's jurisdiction. The solitary, for his own good as well as for that of the church, must be restored to contact with the community. There arose the demand for a regulated asceticism and there were not lacking men who combined the ascetic spirit with an organizing ability. Three of these deserve mention here, St. Basil in the east, St. Columbanus and St. Benedict in the west.

St. Basil (329–379) elaborated a rule of life to be practiced, not by individual hermits each following his own inclinations, but by a community of monks wherein the individual will was subjugated to the will of the group. Basil felt that solitary asceticism was unfruitful and that prayer was more likely to be spiritually satisfying when varied with labor in the field. He insisted that prayer according to the official liturgy of the church was the foundation of spiritual life. A daily routine of public prayer and worship was added to individual meditation. This was true monasticism, a life of prayer and fasting, but a life lived with others and regulated in every detail. The Basilian rule was soon adopted by many communities throughout the eastern provinces. The Council of Chalcedon (451) ordered that monasteries be subject to the local bishop, and the Emperor Justinian authorized the rule and urged its spread. Its success is indicated by the fact that it is still followed by monasteries in the eastern church and by some in the west.

A number of separate monastic communities had arisen in the west during the later Empire. St. Martin of Tours (*d.* 397) founded a community at Marmoutier. St. John Cassian, who had visited eastern monks, formulated a rule for his community at Marseilles. In Ireland, which was evangelized during the fifth century by St. Patrick, monasticism dominated the Christianity of that land. Early Ireland was predominantly tribal and rural in its organization. Ecclesiastical and social life centered around the great abbeys, and in many cases the abbot, the head of a monastery, was a far more important personage in the community than the bishop.

Irish monks were also missionaries. Many of them went across to Scotland and northern England, whence, as has been explained, they traveled through Saxon England and ultimately to the continent. One of the greatest of these "Scoti" was St. Columbanus (*d.* 615). A native of Ireland, he traveled widely on the continent and founded a number of monasteries in Gaul and northern Italy, of which Luxeuil and Bobbio were the most famous. For all these foundations he also drew up a rule which was markedly ascetic and was later modified under the influence of the rule of St. Benedict.

Most famous of all the monastic founders and the author of the rule which eventually superseded most others in western Europe and influenced all later rules, was St. Benedict of Nursia (about 480–543). St. Benedict was originally a hermit. Subsequently, in association with other hermits who had sought his guidance, he founded a community of monks at Montecassino in southern Italy. There in 529 he published the rule of life which bears his name. It has been said that the Benedictine rule admirably combines the Greek ascetic spirit with the Roman love of law. Every detail of the daily life of the monks was provided for, thereby forestalling laxity or excess. Before taking the irrevocable threefold vow of poverty, chastity, and obedience, each candidate was required to spend a year of trial as a novice (the novitiate). The head of each

monastery was the abbot whose rule was supreme. Food and clothing were simple but adequate. Like St. Basil, St. Benedict believed that "idleness is the enemy of the soul," and work and religious study were provided for. Above all, the Benedictine rule carefully outlined the daily life of public prayer, the *opus dei*, as it was called, for this after all was the purpose of the monastic life. In addition to daily Mass, the religious observances of the monastic day consisted of eight "offices" or services. Prime, Terce, Sext, None and Vespers, named after the Roman hours, divided the day into three hour intervals. Compline came at nightfall. Matins and Lauds were the night "vigils." And while the times varied according to latitude and season, matins was invariably sometime not long after midnight. Three or four of the Psalms formed the nucleus of each office, and the entire Psalter was recited in the course of each week.

The Benedictine Rule did not, however, win immediate acceptance in western Europe. In fact, Montecasino was destroyed before the end of the century. Early in the ninth century, through another St. Benedict (of Aniane), and the later Frankish rulers, Benedictine monasticism gradually predominated. Meanwhile other systems continued to flourish. With St. Augustine, Benedictine monasticism penetrated Saxon England, and the later Saxon missionaries introduced it into the newer parts of the Frankish kingdom and ultimately into Scandinavia as well.

By the strictness of their life, the regular clergy, as the monks came to be called (from *regula*, rule), set an example to those members of the secular clergy (from *saeculum*, time) living in the world who strayed from the path of duty. Without doubt they raised the standards of all religious life. As time went on, some monasteries emphasized learning more than others. Thus in monastic libraries were preserved and copied the writings of the ancients, both religious and secular. Diaries, or rather annals, of local happenings were kept, many of which later expanded into important sectional chronicles. Knowledge gained from Roman books on agriculture, combined with experimentation and above all with an orderly and steady regimen of work, made of many a monastery, perhaps originally built in a secluded wilderness, a kind of model farm for the neighborhood. Cattle-breeding, sheep raising, viticulture, the brewing of wine and beer were all activities in which the monks excelled and others learned from them. The tradition of hospitality which developed from St. Benedict's admonition that every traveler should be "received as though he were Christ" made each monastery a kind of inn. For centuries the monasteries were virtually the only establishments for travelers. In short, in a world where agriculture, not commerce, was the prevailing basis of existence, Benedictine monasticism was of paramount importance religiously, culturally, and economically.

E. Church and Culture: Education, Literature, and Art after the Barbarian Invasions

The great Roman tradition of secular learning and education passed with the decay of Roman society. Even in the east, where an educated civil service was still required and where the systematic practice of law long persisted, learning and literature were profoundly affected by the religious spirit of the age. Alike in east and west most scholars and men of letters in the sixth and seventh centuries were churchmen. Although the Latin literary traditions were preserved in the west and the Greek classics cultivated in Byzantium, learning and education became increasingly the monopoly of the clergy.

In the east, a great flowering of Byzantine culture, especially in art and architecture, came during the sixth century and owed much to the patronage of the Christian and Catholic Emperor Justinian. His reign might be said to have marked a period of Greek literary revival in both poetry, especially religious poetry, and prose. Justinian himself composed some hymns. In prose, perhaps the greatest achievements were in the field of historical writing. Procopius, secretary and adviser to Belisarius, and therefore in a positiion to obtain valuable information, produced three significant works: the *History in Eight Books*; the *Buildings*, which lauds the Emperor by de-

scribing all his manifold building operations, and is therefore important from an artistic, military, and economic standpoint; and the *Secret History*. In the last, the author, by a strange shift of opinion, relates all the scandal of Justinian's court and villifies the Emperor, his wife Theodora, and others.

Two other historians who deserve mention were Agathias and John of Ephesus, whose *Ecclesiastical History* in Syriac contains interesting and important material on the Monophysites. And although Cosmas Indicopleustes in his *Christian Topography* set out to prove that the earth was shaped like an oblong box similar to Moses's tabernacle, and was not round as Ptolemy had claimed, he contributed, nevertheless, a vast amount of information on geography and commerce.

Generally speaking, the sixth-century Byzantines produced very little original literature. Their foremost contribution was the preservation of the knowledge of Greek and of the Greek classics. After Justinian, the knowledge of Latin disappeared rapidly in the east.

Perhaps the most striking Byzantine cultural achievement was its art. A number of manuscript miniatures and beautiful religious ivory carvings have come down to us from the sixth and seventh centuries. More widely known are the Byzantine mosaics, a form of art which had already been developed to a notable degree in the west. The most famous are those in the interior of Santa Sophia which, although whitewashed by the Turks in the fifteenth century, have recently been partially restored.[1] There are also Byzantine mosaics in the churches built by Justinian and his predecessors at Ravenna.

In the realm of architecture, the Byzantines carried on the Roman tradition and added something of their own. Justinian was a prodigious builder, and the influence of the style of Constantinople was felt throughout the Empire, west as well as east. The churches of San Vitale and Sant'Appolinare in Ravenna and the monastery of St. Catherine on Mount Sinai [2] are examples. Justinian's most famous creation was Santa

[1] See p. 76.
[2] See pp. 74, 83, 89.

Sophia in Constantinople. For this work he chose two gifted architects, natives of Asia Minor, Anthemius and Isidore. The building was completed in five years, and it accomplished what hitherto had not been deemed possible, the raising of a huge circular dome over a rectangular substructure. This was done by means of pendentives (spherical triangles of masonry) and half domes. Santa Sophia was the glory of Justinian's reign. Indeed, there are those who consider two things as justifying his title "the Great": the Law Code and Santa Sophia.

In the former western provinces, civil education and learning gradually died out. And while a number of lay folk, mostly of the upper classes, could read and write (the number is greater than was once supposed), practically all the schools of the sixth and seventh centuries were maintained by the church, either by the bishops or by monasteries. Since most of those who attended such schools did so with the intention of entering the clergy, secular or regular, the content of the education was largely religious. Pope Gregory the Great held the pursuit of profane learning to be merely time taken from more important things. Nevertheless, the ability to study the church fathers and other religious works presupposed a knowledge of Latin, and helped to preserve the classics. The study of the great Latin writers, even for the sake of mastering the language, kept alive a literary spark which others in a later and more peaceful time could fan into a flame.

Among the chief literary figures in the period of the German kingdoms, Boethius (*d.* 524) stands out. He was one of the last of the Romans to be educated in the secular tradition. He entered the service of Theodoric, the Ostrogothic king, firmly believing that in doing so he was serving the best interests of Roman society. It will also be recalled that as a result of a tragic misunderstanding he spent his last days in prison awaiting execution. But there, out of adversity, he produced one of the literary masterpieces of the west, the *Consolation of*

Twelfth century cloister at Moissac, France.

Photograph by Frederick J. Woodbridge

Early medieval manuscript illumination. An initial page from the *Book of Kells*, a manuscript of the Gospels executed in Ireland about the year 800.

Courtesy Library, Trinity College, Dublin

Philosophy. This is not a treatise on philosophy. Rather, it is the voice of a philosopher rationalizing suffering and sorrow with calm resignation. While not specifically Christian, it breathes a truly religious spirit and is by no means incompatible with Catholic Christianity which, it seems clear from his other works, Boethius professed.

More important in the long history of learning was Boethius' attempt to translate the works of Aristotle and Plato. Appreciating that the knowledge of Greek was fast disappearing, he hoped to preserve the thought of the ancient philosophers by translating them into Latin. Unfortunately, he only finished part of Aristotle's logical treatises and some of the comments of Plotinus, a neo-Platonist. Yet what he did

accomplish had a tremendous importance in the history of western philosophy.

A contemporary of Boethius, Cassiodorus also felt the passing of the old learning. It was he who, by introducing the practice of copying manuscripts in the monastery where he lived, commenced that all important activity which spread to other monasteries. He too may be called one of the "transmitters" of the ancient heritage.

In the Frankish kingdom, Bishop Gregory of Tours (*d*. 594) represents what was left of the literary tradition in Gaul. His *History of the Franks*, despite its ungrammatical and badly spelled Latin, faults which Gregory himself recognized and lamented, has great vigor and originality and is a priceless record of the times. Bad Latin however, is not necessarily characteristic of the period. Fortunatus, a sixth-century poet, composed two beautiful hymns which still form part of the church's official liturgy, the *Vexilla regis prodeunt* and the *Pange lingua*. Meanwhile in Visigothic Spain, Isidore, bishop of Seville (*d.* 636), wrote his *Etymologies*, a curious compound of fact and fancy which preserved some of the scientific and literary learning of the past.

Perhaps the most striking example of the preservation of ancient culture during the centuries after the disappearance of the Roman Empire in the west is found in Ireland. For Irish monasticism produced in the sixth and seventh centuries a remarkable flowering of classical learning. Scholars who fled Gaul to escape the turmoil of the continent found a haven in Ireland. And there both Greek and Latin literature were not only studied as steps toward the mastery of sacred learning, but enjoyed with true literary enthusiasm. And this is the more remarkable because with the Irish scholars theology formed the goal of all other learning. A tangible evidence of the Irish achievement consists in the handsomely lettered and decorated manuscripts which have come down to us from that remote period. The *Book of Kells* (after 800) is perhaps the most famous.

Irish missionaries, the *Scoti*, carried their enthusiasm and their knowledge to the continent, but especially to Scotland and England. A veritable "renaissance" of learning flowered in Saxon England in the seventh and eighth centuries. This Anglo-Irish culture was strengthened by the renewed contacts with Rome which followed St. Augustine's mission and the synod of Whitby. Especially important was the appointment of Theodore of Tarsus (*d.* 690) as archbishop of Canterbury. For Theodore was formerly a Greek monk and was consecrated by Pope Vitalian himself at a time when Greek influence in Italy and Rome was more than usually prominent.

Under Theodore's direction the school of Canterbury became renowned and the ties between England and Rome were strengthened. Meanwhile, other schools were founded. Malmsbury was made illustrious by Aldhelm who taught from 675 to 705. Benedict Biscop, a convinced adherent of Rome's authority, founded a monastery and school at Jarrow which was destined to become famous as the home of Bede.

Bede (*d.* 735), surnamed the Venerable, was the most famous of all the Saxon scholars. As priest and monk he was, of course, devoted to sacred learning and theology. But his interests were extraordinarily wide. He knew Greek, which he probably learned from some Irish-trained teacher. He was interested in and wrote treatises on scientific questions. Above all a teacher with an absorbing interest in the problem of religious education, he composed works on grammar and spelling for the monastery school pupils.

Most of Bede's works, and those most frequently referred to by his contemporaries, were his commentaries on the Bible. But the production which has earned the acclaim and gratitude of later generations was his *Ecclesiastical History of the English People*, a history of the English to the year 731. And while the first chapters were compiled from older writers, the author took great pains to secure information from every available source. Fortunately, he was constantly encouraged as well as aided by a number of contemporary clerics. One even consulted the papal archives in Bede's behalf. The *Ecclesiastical History* is an indispensable source for English history, both ecclesiastical and secular, before the early eighth century.

Thus in the distant British isles, where Roman influence had been slight or nonexistent, there began a revival of learning which was later to prove of great assistance to continental scholarship in recovering its ancient heritage and in building upon it. In fact, largely because it was uncontaminated with a similar popular speech, the Latinity of the Celts and Saxons was often more correct than that of Gaul. Unfortunately, as the Greek east lost contact with Latin, so the Latin west gradually lost the knowledge of Greek. The Irish monks were familiar with Greek, and Greek literature was studied in Saxon England as late as Bede (*d.* 735). Charlemagne is said to have understood Greek slightly. But apparently after the eighth century Greek survived in the west only in a few places in Byzantine Italy. As a consequence a cultural rift between east and west was accentuated.

CHAPTER 9

Rise and Conquests of Islam

A. Role of Arabs Different from that of Germans and Slavs

For centuries all lands surrounding the Mediterranean, and embraced in the Roman Empire, had shared in a common Graeco-Roman civilization, and latterly Christianity had become a central characteristic of this civilization. The Germans who invaded the western regions of the Empire in the fifth century were gradually assimilated and converted, and became a part of the Graeco-Roman world. Ensuing Slavic invaders of the Balkans were similarly affected. This was not true, however, of the seventh-century Arab invasions into eastern and southern regions of the Empire. For the Arabs were fanatical Moslems, devotees of a new religion—Islam, or Mohammedanism. They spurned conversion to Christianity or other assimilation into the Roman world.

The rise and spread of Islam brought an alien and disruptive force which finally broke the unity of the Mediterranean world. The previous Graeco-Roman-Christian civilization of the entire southern shore of that sea—and most of its eastern shore—was transformed by conquest into an essentially Arab-Moslem civilization. And the conquest proved decisive and complete. Henceforth the Mediterranean was no longer the center of a common civilization but a dividing line between two quite different civilizations, which for centuries were to be largely hostile. The one is "Western," or "European," civilization; the other is "Near Eastern" and

"Middle Eastern" civilization. Although each has borrowed heavily from the other, Christendom and Islam have remained two separate worlds.

In the early years of the seventh century no one could have predicted the extent of the assault that was to split the Mediterranean world. Least of all would anyone have suspected that it was to originate in Arabia. Relatively little was then known of the Arabian peninsula, and to the outside world it seemed unimportant. On its fringes were a number of petty quarrelsome states, and a few towns of some commercial significance, including Palmyra and Petra (Arabia Petraea of the Romans) in the north, and Mecca and Medina near the Red Sea coast. The first two of these towns were in contact with the Roman Empire, and the last two with the African kingdom of Ethiopia. Most of the interior of Arabia was arid, and was inhabited by nomadic Bedouin tribes, typical desert Arabs of popular imagination. These were warlike people whose unsettled life was largely given over to predatory raids on neighboring tribes or passing caravans. Yet hitherto they had always been held in check by the more settled border states which in turn were supported by Rome or Persia. Both of these powers considered the Arabs merely a perennial frontier problem.

Why the seventh century brought revolutionary change to Arabia is not entirely clear. It is possible that economic conditions in the period just before Mohammed created a special wave of unrest among the tribesmen, and certainly the economic needs of the Arabs, town dwellers as well as nomads, played a part in the Islamic movement. But material circumstances alone can hardly explain the great Arabian upheaval which had such far-reaching effects. Mohammedanism was first and foremost a religion, and it was the fanatical devotion of the Arabs to that religion which proved to be the driving force in their expansion.

Prior to the advent of Mohammed, Arabia had been subjected to a number of outside religious influences which varied with the geographical environment. Jewish and Christian influences had entered the northwest by way of Syria and Palestine, and the southwest from Ethiopia, while the northeastern Arabs had been affected by the Zoroastrian religion of the Persians. Such external influences had mingled with a native and rather degraded heathenism which manifested itself in the worship of idols or sacred objects of nature, and especially in the veneration of a black stone lodged in the Ka'aba, a temple at Mecca. But there had been no indication that these varied religious trends could be welded into a religious unity, any more than that the perennial conflicts among the tribesmen could be submerged in a national thrust outward, for Mohammed was born (570) at a time when Arabia was a land materially and spiritually divided.

B. Mohammed and His Religion of Islam

Mohammed came of a fairly well regarded, though not wealthy, Arab family of Mecca. After some years in the service of a rich widow, Kadijah, he married her and became financially independent. He was familiar with the merchant people and, generally speaking, possessed their outlook on life and their contempt for the lawless desert Arab. But he also had some of the daring of the latter and, no doubt owing to his travels in the service of Kadijah, he was familiar with the desert way of life. He also had some partial familiarity with Judaism and Christianity.

Mohammed's character is difficult to appraise. For his followers there was hardly a fault, while to his enemies he was everything

The Mosque of Ibn Tulun, Cairo, 876–79.
Courtesy Egyptian State Tourist Administration, New York

that was evil. He was highly sensitive, and in some manner came to believe himself the repository of divine revelation. His utterances, therefore, often communicated to his followers in a remarkable rhythmic prose, were regarded as the word of God given directly to Mohammed by the Angel Gabriel. These sayings, many of which were taken down or remembered later by his disciples, constitute the Koran, the "bible" of the Mohammedan religion. Mohammed finally became convinced of his mission to regenerate his people. Two ideas especially seem to have animated him: submission to the one God, Allah (hence *Islam*, submission, and *Moslem*, one who has submitted); and elevation of the moral tone. As time went on his own position as God's last and greatest prophet received more emphasis.

So long as he confined his teaching to his family and immediate friends, Mohammed was tolerated as a harmless eccentric, but when he tried to convert the Meccans he met considerable resistance. The merchants were alarmed at what seemed to them a subversive doctrine and the ordinary town folk were scandalized by his attacks against their idols. So great was the opposition that he was forced to leave Mecca. This was the friendly Yathrib, which was subsequently renamed Medina. The year of the *Hejira* (622) is year one of the Moslem calendar.

At Medina, Mohammed won a large following, and his religion and with it the life he preached were put on a more established basis. Laws and regulations began to form a sort of penal code. The first mosque, or place of worship, was erected. At Medina, too, Mohammed was forced to satisfy the economic needs of the many nomads who espoused his cause. Attack on the Meccan caravans was regarded as religiously justifiable. Thus began in a small way the holy war (*Jihad*), which later turned the warlike energies of the desert Arab from blood feud to national conquest.

Mohammed was able to avenge his early defeat at the hands of the Meccans, for the pillaging of caravans soon led to a war in which Mohammed and his followers were victorious. In 630 he returned to Mecca in triumph. Dramatically he destroyed the idols of the temple, but discreetly kept the black stone of the Ka'aba, already sacred to many Arabs, as the symbol of his one God. Mecca, the town of his birth, thus became the religious center of Islam. When Mohammed died two years after his return, his religion was well established in western Arabia and his military successes had won him prestige throughout the peninsula. Within a few years of his death, his religion overspread all Arabia and served to unify the country.

The religious precepts of Islam, or Mohammedanism, are very simple. The Moslem God is the God of Judaism and of Christianity, and strict emphasis on monotheism is paramount. Mohammed did not reject the Old Testament prophets. Christ he regarded not as divine, but as the next to the last in the line of prophets which culminated in himself, the last and the greatest, the messenger (*rasul*) of Allah. Paradise, pictured in vivid imagery, awaited the faithful believers after death, especially those who died in battle against the infidel. A frightful hell punished the damned.

Mohammed's moral teachings were equally simple. Polygamy was permitted, each man being allowed four wives, a number less than had been customary. (By a special dispensation Mohammed himself had thirteen.[1]) Slavery was also condoned. Otherwise the moral code was almost puritanically strict. A rule that compensations, when offered, must be accepted was designed to limit the blood feud. Pork and wine were prohibited. Alms were to be given to the poor. All believers were to constitute a single fellowship.

Islam has neither priesthood nor sacraments. There are, however, a number of ritualistic observances. Prayer in common at the mosque is recited after a leader, and usually consists of passages from the Koran. Prayer five times a day facing Mecca is a strict requirement and has to be preceded by elaborate ablutions and prostrations. Mohammed was very particular about cleanliness. Every Moslem is required to fast from sunrise to sunset each year during the Arab month of Ramadan, and, provided he can afford it, to make a pilgrimage to Mecca at least once during his lifetime.

Such is the faith and practice of Islam. The simplicity of it appealed to the desert folk and yet it is not exclusively the religion of the nomad, for it has flourished in great cities. Moreover, its later exponents and teachers, in seeking to reconcile it with philosophical and scientific knowledge, rationalized it into a complicated moral and theological system. In the early decades after Mohammed's death, however, it was a fighting faith; and the desire to conquer and subdue the infidel, to subject all people to Allah, was in a large measure the secret of the amazing success of Arab Moslem arms.

C. Arab Moslem Conquests

The rapidity and extent of the early conquests of the Arabs, fired by their new religion and national unity, are astonishing. A century after Mohammed's death, the territory over which the crescent banners of Islam waved stretched from the Pyrenees

---

[1] Mohammed's marriages were dictated in large part by political considerations and helped to consolidate the tribes of Arabia.

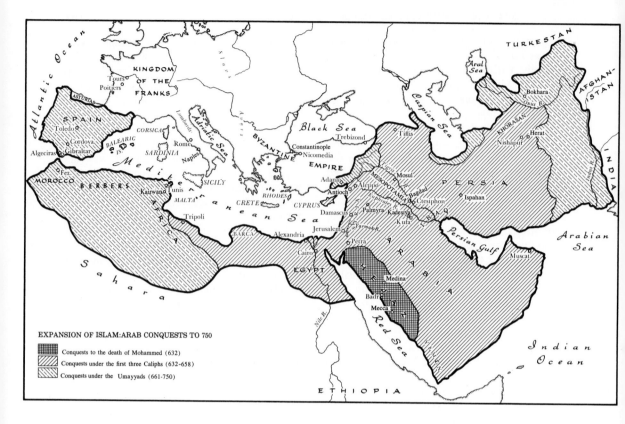

EXPANSION OF ISLAM: ARAB CONQUESTS TO 750

▓ Conquests to the death of Mohammed (632)
▨ Conquests under the first three Caliphs (632-658)
▨ Conquests under the Umayyads (661-750)

and southern France to the Indus river. But the reasons for such prodigious success are not far to seek.

First, the conquerors were militant Arabs, whose new-found Moslem faith inspired them with a kind of fanaticism. It was not simply that they expected the rewards of Paradise. They gloried in the subjection to Allah of other peoples, often of more advanced culture. It was a sign of their own superiority. Then too, the desert Arab has always been a fighter, and now his bellicose propensities were channeled, so to speak, into one great undertaking. He was serving a cause at once national and religious.

Equally important as explanations of Moslem military success were the weakness of the opponents, and the disaffection of many of the subject peoples in the conquered countries. Both the Byzantine and Persian Empires had been exhausted by long war between them. The triumphs of the Byzantine Emperor Heraclius over the Persian King Chosroes left the former's forces so weakened that he was unable to cope with the advancing Arabs. Persia was an

even easier prey. Moreover, there were thousands of Roman Byzantine subjects in Egypt, Syria, and Palestine—Jews and heretical Christians especially—who were only too glad to exchange Byzantine masters for Mohammedan. For the latter promised them religious toleration and imposed upon them a smaller tribute than the Byzantine tax. Egyptian Coptic monks, for example, sang chants of rejoicing at the downfall of the Byzantine "heretics."

The conquest was not an elaborately planned affair. After the unity of Arabia had been won, border raids, long familiar to Arab warriors, betrayed unexpected weaknesses in Byzantine and Persian defenses and tempted the Arab Moslems to more extensive efforts. The Byzantine Emperor Heraclius, after losing Damascus and other Syrian cities, made a determined effort to throw the invader back. But early successes were nullified in the decisive battle of Yarmuk (636). By 640 the fate of Palestine and Syria was sealed. These provinces of the old Roman Empire, with their Christian and Jewish population, passed under Arab rule. Meanwhile, Arab raids into Mesopotamia developed into an extensive campaign, and at the battle of Kadesiya (637) a Persian force was so badly defeated that by 650 the Persian Empire had ceased to exist as an independent state and had been incorporated in the Arab Empire. Thence the impetus of conquest carried the followers of the Prophet through western Turkestan into India and to the shores of the Indus river.

More significant to the ultimate fate of the Graeco-Roman and Christian Mediterranean was the conquest of Egypt. Alexandria fell in 642 and the Moslem conquerors moved the Egyptian capital to Cairo. With Egypt in Arab hands, any danger of a flanking movement by the Byzantines was removed. Alexandria had been a great Byzantine naval base, and in the hands of Moslems it gave them power in the Mediterranean.

The conquest of north Africa followed that of Egypt, though compared to the earlier successes it proved to be slow going. Berber resistance was formidable. But the foundation of a city at Kairwan in Tunisia and the winning of the Berber chieftains over to Islam eventually weighted the scale heavily in Moslem favor. Nevertheless the Berber and Moorish tribesmen remained a problem for the Arabs, and the necessity of offering them booty was partly responsible for the continuation of the Moslem march across north Africa and into Spain.

The Moslem attack on Spain (711) began as a glorified raid. But Visigothic resistance proved so pitifully weak that with the assistance of the Spanish Jews, anxious to avenge their own persecution, the Moslem Arabs and Berbers overran Spain, drove past the Pyrenees, and occupied Narbonne. Later they captured the Balearic Islands. In Frankish Gaul their drive spent itself. And although the great defeat at Tours (732), accomplished by Charles Martel, Frankish *major domus* (mayor of the palace), must still be considered one of the world's decisive battles, it is hardly probable that Moslem armies could have continued their uninterrupted series of successes. Meanwhile in north-western Spain the tiny kingdom of the Asturias harbored what was left of the Gothic armies, which were being reinforced

steadily. Not long afterwards Asturias provided the base for a gradual Christian reconquest of Spain.

Meanwhile, in the eastern Mediterranean, Moslem marauders, now joined by sea raiders, were menacing Constantinople itself. Therefore, Emperor Leo III's stout defense of Constantinople in 717–718 deserves recognition as a very important military engagement. Thereafter the defeated Moslem armies retired behind the Taurus mountains and for three centuries Asia Minor remained a Byzantine province. Byzantine Africa, Syria, and Palestine were lost, but eastern Europe was saved.

In only one other area was Christendom to fall back during the early middle ages. In the ninth century the Moslems of north Africa, based at Kairwan, pushed across the Mediterranean, occupied Sicily, Sardinia, and Corsica, and repeatedly harried the coasts of Italy and southern France. They sacked Rome in 846.

D. The Moslem Empire of the Seventh and Eighth Centuries: the Caliphate

The conquest we have just described was tremendous in its geographical extent. And although much of the occupied territory was of desert character and therefore sparsely populated, the countries of Egypt, Syria, Palestine, and Persia were the seats of old cultures vastly superior to that of the relatively primitive Arabs. The early Moslem rulers realized this, and it is to their credit that for the most part they did not destroy what they found.

Moreover, they were now faced with the serious problems of government which could not be solved by religious fervor alone. Although their conquering zeal was maintained for the better part of a century, the Moslems were forced to become statesmen as well as warriors. Two problems called for immediate solution: the treatment of subject peoples; and the choosing of a ruler who would succeed to the mantle of Mohammed and preserve the political as well as religious unity of Islam. On the whole the first problem offered less difficulty than the second.

In general, the Moslem Arabs did not

seek to convert their newly won subjects. "Tribute or the sword" sums up their attitude, at least to all those who possessed a "Book," that is, a collection of sacred writings which they themselves understood and respected, like the Old and New Testaments. Tribute from the unbeliever was a tax, usually not greater than that formerly paid to the Byzantine or Persian empires. To the Moslem overlord it was a symbol of subjection to Allah, and it was an important source of revenue which the infant government needed. The conversion of large numbers in the conquered areas was not a feature of early Islam. That came later when Islam was more firmly established as a government, when its brilliant material successes gave it added prestige, and when the civil rights and privileges enjoyed by all the faithful tempted many unbelievers into conversion to Islam. As a consequence, except for occasional sporadic persecution, the denial of certain legal privileges, and the requirement of special dress, Christian and Jewish communities continued to exist within the Moslem world. Churches were maintained, even monasticism continued. The principal difficulties for the Christians were, first, the maintenance of contact with their co-religionists in non-Moslem lands, and, second, the social pressure upon them to turn Moslem.

In the early days, the plunder of caravans and the division of the spoils constituted the Moslem financial system. The Arabs were then a kind of army of occupation living from the tribute of the unbeliever. But such a simple system could not meet the demands of stable government. As far as the routine of administration was concerned, the Arabs appropriated or copied Byzantine and Persian systems. And in the course of time many Greeks, Syrians, and Persians held office under Moslem supervision. Thus the daily life of large areas continued with little change except for new masters.

The method of choosing a successor to Mohammed, as political and religious head (or Caliph) of the Moslem world, proved a bone of contention. On this problem of what might be called central government of a farflung empire, the primitive politicoreligious unity of Islam was destroyed. Since Mohammed left no son, the idea of hereditary succession was not at first accepted, and "orthodox" Moslems always held that the caliphate was elective. Since they also respected traditions (*sunna*) which were not included in the Koran, they were known as Sunnites. The first caliphs or "successors" of Mohammed were respected personal associates of the Prophet—Abu Bakr, Omar, and Othman. After the brief reign of Ali (655–661), Mohammed's cousin and son-in-law, which ended in his assassination, the Umayyad family got possession of the caliphate and held it until 750. In this way, hereditary succession finally found a place in the Mohammedan system. But with its acceptance came the confused and bitter rivalries—personal, geographical, tribal, and national—which mark the history of the Islamic "dynasties." Only the bare outlines can be indicated here.

The principal opponents of the Umayyads were the *Shi'a* (Shiites), or partisans of Ali, Mohammed's son-in-law, who held that the succession must be in the family of the Prophet. Except for the reign of Ali, the Shiites were only temporarily and locally successful. They may be described as a powerful minority which existed in many parts of the Moslem world; and in encompassing the murder of Othman they commenced the bloody rivalry between Shiite and Sunnite which created a permanent schism in Islam. Meanwhile other claimants appeared and strange "heresies" developed. Almost from the beginning, Islam was divided religiously and politically.

The Umayyad family ruled from Damascus and under their auspices Syria was the center of the Moslem world, with Damascus and Jerusalem enjoying remarkable prosperity. But Syrian predominance was not acceptable to Persia, where a large number of non-Arab inhabitants had embraced the new faith and found themselves, notwithstanding, in a position of political and social inferiority. A great reaction swept the Umayyads from power, and in 750 Abu'l-Abbas became the first of the Abbasid dynasty which was to rule for several centuries from Bagdad.

One member of the Umayyad family escaped, found his way to Spain, and there proclaimed a virtually independent state

Arabic decorative art.
The ceiling of the
Manial palace, Cairo.

*Courtesy Egyptian State
Tourist Administration,
New York*

(756), which in 929 became a second caliphate. A generation later (972) a third
caliphate was set up in Cairo by the Fatimites, a Shiite dynasty of north Africa.
Meanwhile throughout the Moslem world,
and especially in north Africa, various administrative divisions became virtually
independent. It was one of these, Tunisia,
which spread Moslem power throughout
the islands of the western Mediterranean
in the ninth century.

These political and religious schisms did
not destroy certain aspects of Moslem unity.
Every Moslem learned the same Koran,
recited similar prayers, and made the pilgrimage to Mecca. Since the only authorized version of the Koran was in Arabic,
every Moslem, whatever his nationality, had
to know at least enough Arabic to recite it.
Thus the Arabic tongue became a medium
of communication over a large section of
the world. As an instrument in spreading
Islamic culture this was of incalculable
importance.

A further evidence of Moslem unity is
seen in the extent of its commercial prosperity. Men of similar faith and speech now
controlled the Mediterranean from end to
end, and likewise the western terminals of
the great trade routes to the Far East.
Appropriation of Byzantine sea bases in the
eastern Mediterranean, together with occu-

pation of the islands in the western and central Mediterranean, guaranteed a common Moslem sea control which was virtually unchallenged before the eleventh and twelfth centuries. Rarely has history witnessed a more extensive commercial monopoly.

The fall of the Umayyads in 750 and the removal of the caliphate to Bagdad marks the end of the first era of Moslem history. At Bagdad a new spirit entered. The faith spread with Islamic material success. With increasing social pressure, conversions from Christianity and other religions became more frequent, until Islam no longer signified a privileged minority of Arabs ruling subject peoples. Thus the way was paved for a continuous expansion in the following centuries, southward into Africa and eastward into Asia and eventually to Indonesia and part of the Philippines. Moreover, as the Moslem empire lost its predominantly Arab character, there commenced that remarkable assimilation of Persian, Byzantine, and Hellenistic culture for which it became so noted during the later middle ages, and which was to prove so important in the cultural progress of medieval Europe.

E. Disruptive Effects on Christendom

The immediate effects on Christian Europe of the early Moslem expansion were serious. In the first place, in so far as the Arabs removed from the control of Christian Europe all the eastern and southern coastal lands of the Mediterranean, including Spain and Sicily, which had formerly belonged to the Roman Empire, their conquest constituted a major military setback for Europe. And since Europe was not willing to admit the losses as permanent, warfare between the two continued. The Spanish reconquest commenced almost immediately with the formation of a little Asturian kingdom. Byzantine resistance strengthened in the ninth and tenth centuries. Later, Italian sailors and Norman adventurers cleared southern Italy and the mid-Mediterranean. These advances were followed in time by the organized crusades of the eleventh and twelfth centuries. Christian Europe's first response to the Arab

conquest was military, and military hostility remained a feature of Christian-Moslem relations for centuries. War was not constant and did not prevent, in later times, highly significant commercial and cultural interrelationships which affected the civilization of both. But until modern times, Europe lived under the shadow of a Moslem menace.

A second consequence of the rise of Islam was a major numerical and territorial loss to Chrisianity. It is true that, for the most part, the Moslems were fairly tolerant. Yet the Christians in Moslem lands were isolated, and many, especially in Syria, Palestine, and Egypt, were already disaffected toward the churches of Rome and Constantinople and hence more inclined to accept the Moslem faith as well as Arab rule. Then, too, the material successes of Islam and the legal and social privileges offered to the believers induced many conversions from Christianity to Islam. While Christian communities with surprising vitality survived in Spain and Sicily and, to a much lesser extent, in Syria, Palestine, and Egypt, north Africa (and later Asia Minor) became almost entirely Moslem. The Moslem control of the Mediterranean weakened the contacts between Rome and Constantinople and accentuated the already marked tendency toward political and religious separation. Religiously and culturally, the old Mediterranean world was disrupted. So also were economic ties broken or imperiled.

A third important result of Moslem expansion which can appropriately be considered here is economic. By occupying the Mediterranean coasts from southern Gaul to Asia Minor, together with Sicily and the other principal islands, the Moslems for a time virtually monopolized Mediterranean trade. Western European commerce was gravely impeded and an already weakened economic system was further damaged. Certainly an accelerated trend toward agrarianism and the accompanying deterioration in trade are features of eighth and ninth century western economy. But before many decades trade with the Moslem area began to grow. Accordingly, although the initial rise of Islam must clearly be considered a disruptive force in European history, there were also to be positive contributions.

F. Moslem Culture and Its Influence on Europe

Although Moslems might disagree over the succession to the caliphate and might form innumerable petty states, in all essential matters religious unity remained. In the intellectual sphere, unity of language was also significant, for every good Moslem, whatever his native vernacular, was expected to know the Koran, or at least something of it, in the original Arabic. It is, therefore, possible to speak of an Islamic culture, and what scholars of Bagdad did soon became the common property of their confrères at Cordova.

The classic age of Islamic culture, the age of its foundation and formation, was the first hundred and fifty years of the Abbasid caliphate (750–900). During the preceding period of the Umayyads the Moslems had been content to adapt to their own uses the institutions of the conquered peoples. And this was true not only of the political and economic institutions. Mosques were frequently converted churches, or else buildings newly erected in Graeco-Roman style with columns, capitals, and marbles taken from older Christian edifices.

The accession of the Abbasids (750) did not at once usher in a period of originality. Islamic culture was and is an essentially borrowed and adapted culture. But when the capital of the Moslem world was moved to Bagdad, it was exposed to the influence of an ancient and richly variegated civilization.

Moslem cities came to resemble those of the old Roman Empire and were in striking contrast to the small urban communities in contemporary western Europe. Bagdad, as early as the reign of the Caliph Harun al-Rashid (785–809), was a fabulously prosperous city with many public buildings, markets, residences, baths, and hospitals. So also was distant Cordova in Spain. Under the Abbasids, therefore, Moslem savants found themselves in an intellectual atmosphere which was many-sided and already thousands of years old. And, just as the Mohammedan world was composed of diverse nationalities, so Islamic culture was produced by the amalgamation of various component elements. The particular genius of the Mohammedan scholars was their ability to organize the achievements of others into a harmonious system of their own.

This composite Moslem culture was derived principally from three sources: the Greek, or rather the Hellenistic; the Hindu; and the Persian. The Hellenistic heritage was philosophical and scientific rather than literary or artistic. Classical Greek literature and art were too closely bound up with the polytheism of the old pagan Greek religion to appeal to the severely monotheistic Mohammedans. On the other hand, the writings of the great Greek philosophers, especially Aristotle, had been preserved and studied by the Monophysite Christians of Syria and the Nestorians in Persia, both of whom were in close touch with their Mohammedan conquerors. Of primary importance was the work of translation, and this, too, was often accomplished by Christian or Jewish scholars, or recent converts, who knew Greek and Syriac as well as Arabic, and who passed it on to the Islamic world. The patronage of the caliphs in the diffusion of knowledge was also extremely important. Mamun the Great (813–833) went so far as to found at Bagdad a "House of Wisdom" with a library and observatory— in short a university which proved to be the model for similar schools of higher learning elsewhere.

Greek mathematics and medicine especially interested the Moslems who devoted their attention to Euclid, Galen and Hippocrates, Ptolemy and Archimedes, in addition to Aristotle. But an especially significant mathematical contribution of the Moslems came from India. Thence, sometime before the end of the eighth century, was brought the principle of decimal numeration and of computation with the cipher (o). This the Europeans later named Algorismus after al-Khwarizmi, the Persian mathematician in whose works the system was developed. The same author also composed an important treatise on algebra.

From Persia, which was the home of a series of ancient civilizations, the Arabs gained medical lore that added considerably to the Greek systems of Galen and Hippocrates. Moreover, Persian literary forms influenced contemporary Moslem literature, especially such famous tales as those included in the *Arabian Nights*. In Persia, too, was produced such famous poetry as that of the *Rubaiyat* of Omar Khayyam (*d.* 1123).

Moslem art was also an ingenious amalgam of earlier and varied forms found or developed in different parts of the Mohammedan world. Byzantine, Persian, Egyptian, even Visigothic elements can be discerned in Moslem building and decoration. In time all these diverse features became common Moslem property and Moslem art became a distinctive creation in its own right. Multicolored decoration, geometric design later known as arabesque, "horseshoe" arch, ample cupola, and colonnaded halls can be found throughout the length and breadth of the Islamic world. Two famous structures in Europe might be mentioned here as examples: the mosque of Cordova, and the palace of the Alhambra at Granada.

Moslem civilization which developed in the ninth and tenth centuries as an appropriation or fusion of the higher and more ancient cultures of Greece, Mesopotamia, and India began in the eleventh century to display considerable originality of its own. This took the form at first of a notable clarification of the diverse material which had been assimilated. Then, especially in mathematics, medicine, and astronomy, Moslem scholars surpassed their ancient masters. Avicenna (Ibn-Sina, 980–1037) was not only the greatest of the Moslem philosophers, but an accomplished medical scholar as well. Omar Khayyam (*d.* 1123) was an astronomer as well as a poet. Al-Farabi (*d.* 950) discussed the theory of measured music. Others, whom even a brief treatment should mention, were al-Razi (865–925), composer of a famous treatise on small-pox, and al-Biruni (973–1048), a general scientist. The fact that most of these men came from the region of the Oxus, where the Mohammedanism of Persia touched the civilization of India, illustrates the cosmopolitan character of Mohammedan culture.

In medicine, Islam contributed most to pharmaceutical knowledge. Although in surgery there was some slight advance, it was hampered by a slavish devotion to the authority of Galen and by religious opposition to dissection. The persistence of ancient superstitions with regard to the transmutation of metal, made "alchemists," rather than real scientists, of most Moslem students of chemistry and medicine. But superstition did not prevent treatises on animals, trees, dyes, glass, and miscellaneous subjects.

In the field of astronomy, the names of many stars and such terms as zenith and nadir illustrate the remarkable observations and discoveries of Moslems. These were all based on Ptolemy's conception of a geocentric universe. As in chemistry, so in astronomy, the ancient lore of Mesopotamia survived in the belief that heavenly bodies exercise a determining influence over earthly events. As a consequence Moslem astronomers were also astrologers.

The wide extent of Moslem commerce naturally fostered a special interest in geography and navigation. And in these fields Mohammedans made significant practical contributions. One of the most famous medieval geographers, the Moslem Idrisi, resided at the court of King Roger II of Sicily in the twelfth century. And Moslem trade with the Middle and Far East brought to Europe useful new knowledge from China, and such things as fireworks, paper, and block printing.

Inspired partly by the breadth and diversity of the knowledge opened to them, and partly by the Greek, especially the Aristotelian, philosophical tradition, certain Moslem scholars attempted with considerable ingenuity to embrace and coördinate all human knowledge in one great synthesis. Philosophy to men like Avicenna was not merely metaphysics. Physics, astronomy, cosmology, theology, indeed all knowledge, must be reconciled to and combined with metaphysics. Such was the all embracing encyclopedic ideal of men like al-Kindi, al-Farabi, and especially Avicenna. The reception of Aristotelian philosophy by the Mohammedans raised those same problems of science and faith which were later to trouble the Christian world. Aristotle was hardly compatible with orthodox Moham-

Moslem architecture in Spain. Interior of the Mosque at Cordova. Eighth and ninth centuries.

medanism. In the main, the philosophy of the Moslem scholar remained apart from the faith of the orthodox religious teacher. Yet Moslem rationalism persisted and exercised no small influence, as we shall later see, on the European scholasticism of the twelfth and thirteenth centuries.

By the eleventh century Moslem culture was formed. Although its debt to past civilization was enormous, it possessed a brilliance and a synthetic originality which insured it an important place in the history of man's material and intellectual progress. That Mohammedan civilization of the ninth, tenth, and early eleventh centuries, in its material aspect at least, was in advance of feudal Europe's is obvious. Early in the twelfth century Christian scholars of western Europe, making contact with Moslem centers of learning, especially in Spain and Sicily, began through translations to acquaint their fellows at home with Arabic learning, and to stimulate a veritable intellectual renaissance. But before we can understand this notable development, we must consider what western Europe had accomplished by the middle of the eleventh century with its own resources.

Byzantine cloisonné enamel on gold of the twelfth century or later. St. John the Evangelist

Courtesy Metropolitan Museum of Art, New York; gift of the estate of Mrs. Otto H. Kahn, 1952

SELECT SUPPLEMENTARY READINGS FOR PART II

General. Two standard works of reference for the entire period from the fall of Rome to 1500 are the *Cambridge Medieval History*, 8 vols. (1911–1936), and the *Cambridge Economic History of Europe*, 3 vols. (1941, 1952, 1961). See also C. W. Previté-Orton, *The Shorter Cambridge Medieval History*, 2 vols. (1952); S. Baron, *A Social and Religious History of the Jews*, vols. III–V (1957–1958). An important guide for further study is L. J. Paetow, *Guide to the Study of Medieval History* (2nd ed., 1931); J. B. Morall, *Political Thought in Medieval Times* (1958); W. Ullmann, *Principles of Government and Politics in the Middle Ages* (1961). L. Bernard and T. B. Hodges, *Readings in European History* (1958) is designed to accompany this volume.

Particularly relevant to the period covered in Part II are: W. C. Bark, *Origins of the Medieval World* (1958); C. D. Burns, *The First Europe* (1947); C. Dawson, *The Making of Europe* (1932); M. Deanesly, *A History of Early Medieval Europe, 476–911* (1956); E. S. Duckett, *The Gateway to the Middle Ages* (1938). H. St. L. B. Moss, *The Birth of the Middle Ages, 395–814* (1935); A. Jones, *The Later Roman Empire, 284–682*, 3 vols. (1964); R. E. Sullivan, *Heirs of the Roman Empire* (1960). J. M. Wallace-Hadrill, *The Barbarian West, 400–1000* (1952). A discussion of some of the problems of the interpretation of this period can be found in A. F. Havighurst, *The Pirenne Thesis* (1958).

Chapter 5. R. M. Haywood, *The Myth of Rome's Fall* (1958); J. B. Bury, *History of the Later Roman Empire*, 2 vols (1923); S. Dill, *Roman Society in the Last Century of the Empire* (1910); S. Katz, *The Decline of Rome and the Rise of Medieval Europe* (1955); F. Lot, *The End of the Ancient World* (new ed., 1961). For the cultural life of the later Empire, see W. L. MacDonald, *Early Christian and Byzantine Architecture* (1962); C. R. Morey, *Christian Art* (1958) and *Medieval Art* (1932); E. K. Rand, *The Founders of the Middle Ages* (1928); H. O. Taylor, *The Classical Heritage of the Middle Ages* (1911), also newly edited by K. M. Setton, *The Emergence of Christian Culture in the West* (1961).

Chapter 6. J. B. Bury, *The Invasion of Europe by the Barbarians* (1928); S. Dill *Roman Society in Gaul in the Merovingian Age* (1926); A. Dopsch, *The Economic and Social Foundations of European Civilization* (1937); C. Gordon, *The Age of Attila* (1960).

Chapter 7. In addition to J. B. Bury, *Later Roman Empire,* already mentioned, N. H. Baynes, *The Byzantine Empire* (1926); N. H. Baynes and H. St. L. B. Moss, *Byzantium* (1948); C. Diehl, *Byzantium: Greatness and Decline* (1956); G. Ostrogorsky, *History of the Byzantine State* (1957); G. Downey, *Constantinople* (1960); J. Hussey, *The Byzantine World* (1957); S. Runciman, *Byzantine Civilization* (1933); A. A. Vasiliev, *History of the Byzantine Empire,* 2 vols. (1928).

Chapter 8. For ecclesiastical history in general: A. F. Flick, *The Rise of the Medieval Church* (1909); P. Hughes, *A History of the Church,* vol. II (1935); H. Daniel-Rops, *The Church in the Dark Ages* (1959); K. S. Latourette, *A History of the Expansion of Christianity,* vol. II (1938); H. K. Mann, *The Lives of the Popes in the Middle Ages,* 18 vols. (1906–1932).

On the rise of monasticism: Dom J. Chapman, *St. Benedict and the Sixth Century* (1929); Dom David Knowles, *The Monastic Order in England* (1940); J. McCann, *St. Benedict* (1958); L. J. Daly, S.J., *Benedictine Monasticism* (1965). For intellectual developments, in addition to the citations for chapters 5 and 7: H. M. Barrett, *Boethius* (1940); E. S. Duckett, *Anglo-Saxon Saints and Scholars* (1947); M. Laistner, *Thought and Letters in Western Europe, 500–900* (1957). On the relation of religion to medieval civilization: C. Dawson, *Religion and the Rise of Western Culture* (1958).

Chapter 9. Tor Andrae, *Muhammad, the Man and His Faith* (1956); T. W. Arnold and A. Guillaume, *The Legacy of Islam* (1931); R. V. C. Bodley, *The Messenger: the Life of Mohammed* (1946); E. Dermenghem, *Muhammad and the Islamic Tradition* (1957); H. A. R. Gibb, *Mohammedanism* (1949); G. E. von Grunebaum, *Medieval Islam* (1946); P. K. Hitti, *History of the Arabs* (1946), and *The Arabs: a Short History* (1956); A. Jeffery, *Islam: Muhammad and His Religion* (1958); B. Lewis, *The Arabs in History* (1950); A. Guillaume, *Islam* (1954).

Hispano-Moorish ivory box, tenth century.
Courtesy Hispanic Society of America, New York

Carolingian art. The figure of St. Mark from an illuminated manuscript of the Gospels produced at Reims at the time of Archbishop Hincmar, 845–882.

Courtesy Pierpont Morgan Library, New York

PART III
THE EARLY MIDDLE AGE IN THE
NORTHWARD PROCESS OF

Norman architecture in England. Peterborough Cathedral. Nave with Norman arches. Flat, pointed wooden ceiling of the twelfth century.

Courtesy British Information Services, New York

From Charlemagne to Hildebrand

WEST AND THE EUROPEANIZATION

Medieval warfare. A thirteenth century French manuscript presented by the pope to the shah of Persia in the seventeenth century and annotated at his direction.

Courtesy Pierpont Morgan Library, New York

"MIDDLE AGES" is a term invented in modern times to describe the thousand years of European history from the break-up of the Roman Empire in the fifth century to the so-called renaissance of classical Roman culture in the fifteenth century. Nobody who lived in those thousand years imagined he was living in any "middle age." And certainly those ten centuries witnessed more of continuity than of change in the development and expansion of European and Western civilization.

True, the thousand years had certain peculiar features which may justify us in applying to them a special label, and for this purpose the conventional label of "Middle Ages" will do as well as any. Moreover, in order to distinguish various stages of development during the period, we may conveniently divide it into three parts: (1) an "Early Middle Age," from the seventh to the eleventh century; (2) a "Middle Age proper," from the eleventh to the thirteenth century; and (3) a "Late Middle Age," of the fourteenth and fifteenth centuries.

The immediately ensuing chapters treat of the Early Middle Age, which is often called the "Dark Age." Though doubtless the sun shone as brightly then as in any other age, it was a time when European civilization suffered a series of grave set-backs and something of an eclipse.

While Germanic tribes are gradually emerging from their earlier barbarism, they fall far short of attaining the settled life and rich culture of the old Roman Empire. For a time in the eighth and early ninth centuries, a line of Frankish rulers—the Carolingian—makes valiant efforts, in coöperation with the papacy, to restore order in the West; and under Charlemagne, the greatest of the line, a new empire is constructed, embracing not only Gaul and northern Italy but also the Netherlands and Germany, and fostering throughout its territories a revival of learning and a spread of Christianity. But this promising advance is halted by fresh incursions of fierce Saracens from the south, of barbarous Slavs, Bulgars, and Magyars from the east, and of piratical Scandinavians from the north. Again commerce declines, disorder increases, and ordinary government collapses.

To meet the most pressing needs of the hour—especially the assurance of local security and the production of a minimum food supply—feudalism appears and becomes characteristic of medieval society. To this feudalism and its agricultural support we shall devote special attention.

In the late tenth century, and during the eleventh, matters slowly mend, thanks in no small degree to ecclesiastical activity. Originally inspired by a new monastic movement, centering at Cluny, and eventually headed by one of the greatest medieval popes (Hildebrand, or Gregory VII), the Church manfully opposes the disintegrating and demoralizing tendencies of the age. Simultaneously, ardent missionaries spread Christianity and church influence northward over Scandinavia and eastward among the Slavic peoples. The European continent as a whole is becoming Christian.

Then, too, wherever the Church is established, it contributes to the building up of European states, as yet basically feudal, but already embryonically national. In this connection we shall note the development of France under Capetians, of Germany under a newly founded western "Roman Empire," of England and southern Italy under Norman kings, and of other emerging Christian kingdoms for Scandinavians, Czechs, Poles, Magyars, and Russians. We shall likewise refer to the beginnings of Christian reconquest of Spain from its Moslem invaders.

Finally, we must stress that the Early Middle Age—the so-called "Dark Age" of intellectual and cultural eclipse—is temporary and limited. It is peculiar to western and central Europe. There is no comparable slump in the continuing Byzantine Empire of southeastern Europe, and there is an extraordinary brilliance of Moslem culture from Syria and Persia around northern Africa into Spain. From the Moslems and from Byzantium, as well as from increasing internal stability and education, Europe will presently derive impetus for a real flowering of its own Western civilization in the succeeding Middle Age of the twelfth and thirteenth centuries.

St. Michael's Church, Fulda, one of the oldest in Germany, c. 800.

Courtesy German Tourist Information Office, New York

CHAPTER 10

Rise and Disintegration of the Frankish Empire

AND NEW BARBARIAN INVASIONS OF THE NINTH CENTURY

A. The Frankish State: Transition from Merovingian to Carolingian Rule

The consolidation and expansion of the Frankish kingdom under the Merovingian chieftain, Clovis (*d.* 511),[1] was followed by a period of confusion. The kingdom was soon divided into two large units: Austrasia, comprising the Rhine country and lands west of it; and Neustria, the "newest" territory, lying along the Seine. Further subdivisions resulted from the chronic weakness of the monarchy and the Frankish practice of dividing the kingdom, as though it were a private estate, at the death of a ruler. The Merovingian family degenerated, and the seventh-century descendants of a great house have been styled the do-nothing kings (*rois fainéants*). As a consequence, political authority was exercised by the king's principal subordinate, the mayor of the palace (*major domus*). In 687, Pepin, the second of the name and mayor of the palace in Austrasia, defeated the Neustrian mayor in a battle which again brought together the two halves of the Frankish kingdom. Thereafter, the descendants of Pepin continued to occupy the position of mayor and, although they did not as yet possess the royal title, were actually a ruling dynasty.

Two of the most famous of the mayors were Charles Martel (714–741), whose defeat of the Moslems at Tours (732) we have already noted, and Pepin III "the

Short" (741–768). Pepin was a ruler whose capabilities were second only to those of his illustrious son and successor, Charlemagne. Lingering separatist tendencies were suppressed. Frisia and all Septimania on the Mediterranean were added to the kingdom, the latter removing from Moslem control the commercially important coastal region west of the Rhone and bringing Frankish power to the Pyrenees. Following in the footsteps of Charles Martel, Pepin supported the organizing activities of the church and the efforts of St. Boniface, a monk who was a product of the religious and cultural revival in Saxon England, together with other missionaries, to convert the Germans beyond the Rhine. Equally significant were his relations with the papacy.

The success of the Franks in reëstablishing political order, in defeating the Mohammedans, and in spreading the Christian faith had attracted the attention of the papacy. The Lombards, who had caused trouble for the popes ever since the time of Gregory the Great, had acquired renewed vigor in Italy. At times even Rome was threatened. Normally such a situation would have induced the pope to seek the assistance of the Byzantine Emperor. But the support given the iconoclasts by Emperor Leo III had accentuated the estrangement between Rome and Constantinople.[2] In 739 the pope had sent messengers to Charles Martel; and although Charles had been

---

[1] See above, pp. 69–70.

[2] See above, p. 90, and below, p. 150.

unable to render any assistance, a new development in papal relations with the Franks was imminent.

It was doubtless this friendly atmosphere which prompted certain Frankish prelates to consult Pope Zacharias on the state of the monarchy. The pope handed down a judgment that he who possessed actual authority deserved the title of king. Accordingly, in 751 an assembly of Frankish chieftains acclaimed the Mayor of the Palace, Pepin III, as King, whereupon he was solemnly anointed by St. Boniface and other bishops as King Pepin I. Thus, with papal sanction, the now decadent Merovingian dynasty was set aside, and succeeded by the Carolingian.

Three years later Pope Stephen II moved one step farther in the orientation of papal policy toward the Franks. The Lombard King Aistulf occupied the exarchate and the duchy of Spoleto and, in recognition of his sovereignty, demanded tribute from Rome. The Pope, to make sure of Frankish assistance, actually journeyed across the Alps to Aachen, where he personally anointed King Pepin and threatened with excommunication all who resisted his lawful authority. His reward came when in two expeditions (754, 756) Pepin decisively defeated the Lombards and restored the territory of the exarchate, not to the emperor at Constantinople but to the pope. Although the papal lands along the west coast of Italy (the Patrimony of St. Peter) were already considerable, Pepin's "donation" is sometimes regarded as the foundation of the papal states.

This whole episode of Franco-Papal cooperation is highly significant and amounted almost to an alliance, and Italy became an area of Frankish activity.[1]

B. Charlemagne and His Administration

Pepin's son and successor, known to history as Charlemagne or Charles the Great, was well endowed physically and mentally with qualities which make a successful

ruler. His secretary, Einhard, has left a vivid picture of this extraordinary man. According to Einhard, Charlemagne was over six feet tall with limbs in proportion. Like most men of his day he was fond of exercise and especially of hunting. Though not abstemious in food and drink, he abhorred drunkenness. Under the influence of the churchmen at the royal court Charlemagne, despite a flexible attitude toward his own matrimonial affairs, developed a deep piety and a sense of the religious purpose of government. Indeed, there was a marked Old Testament flavor about the King's administration. He delighted in being called "David," modeled his regime after the ancient Hebrew kings', and regarded himself as a latter-day moral and religious leader of a chosen people. He felt an obligation not only to protect the church, but to promote a healthy moral and religious life within his realm and to spread the faith to those outside.

Charlemagne was not a genius, nor given to the elaboration of far-sighted plans. But he was persistent in the face of obstacles and setbacks. Above all, he was a man of abundant energy, who allowed no detail of administration to escape him. His capitularies, as the royal decrees are designated, reveal a comprehensive grasp of the realities of the world in which he moved.

Like his predecessors, Martel and Pepin, Charlemagne was a warrior whose conquests further expanded the Frankish dominions. The Lombard power he ended once and for all by decisively defeating King Desiderius and then assuming the Lombard crown himself. He extended his dominion southward, occasionally intervened in Spoleto and Benevento and, as a matter of course, regarded himself as overlord of Rome and the papal states. The longest of his campaigns was with the pagan Saxons who inhabited the territory lying roughly between the lower Rhine and the Weser. Although all of Charlemagne's campaigns were in a sense "holy" wars, and priests always accompanied the armies, the Saxon War was especially so because it signified the conversion—albeit forcible—of an entire people. Saxon opposition to both conquest and conversion was so stubborn that it required 33 years to overcome. But eventually, young

---

[1] At about this time there appeared a charter known as the *Donation of Constantine*, later shown to be a forgery. By it the Emperor Constantine had supposedly bestowed Rome and Italy on Pope Sylvester I.

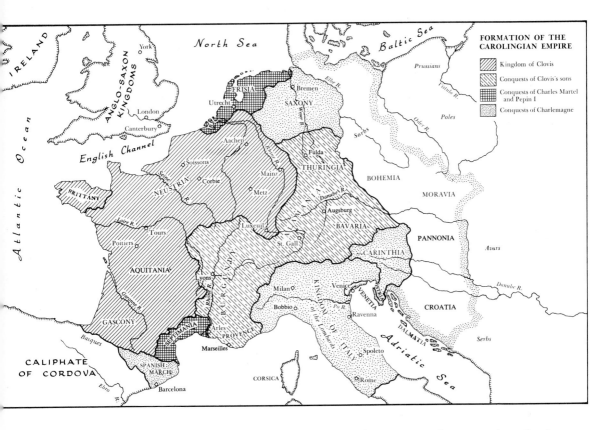

Saxon men were educated for the priest-hood, a bishopric was created at Bremen, and monasteries soon flourished in the land. Moreover, the inclusion of Saxony in the Frankish empire prevented the emergence of a non-Frankish Germany and assured to the future German nation the influence of Carolingian culture.

Charlemagne likewise subdued Slavic tribes in the region of the Elbe river and commenced the *drang nach osten*, or pressure eastward, which was to become a characteristic feature of later German policy. He was equally successful in south-central Germany. Bavaria, hitherto dubiously loyal, was forced again into obedience. The Avars, who from their settlements had menaced both Frankish and Byzantine lands, were crushingly defeated. The Carolingian frontier, therefore, reached from Saxony to the upper Adriatic and included Carinthia along with Bavaria and Thuringia. Beyond lay a series of loosely organized Slavic states—Croatia, Pannonia, Moravia, Bohemia, and the northern Slavic and Baltic peoples. These paid tribute and for the most part were to become Marches (border provinces)

in later times. In the west the effective work of his predecessors enabled Charlemagne to push southward and to form a march south of the Pyrenees in Spain.

In governing this greatly enlarged domain, Charlemagne followed the pattern set by previous rulers and added certain important innovations made necessary by contemporary conditions. The principal agents of administration were dukes and counts appointed to govern various divisions of the domain, and margraves (*Markgrafen*, counts of the march) who were given special powers over frontier provinces. Charlemagne also elaborated a system whereby the activities of each count could be supervised. Every district of the realm was periodically visited by two men, usually a bishop and a layman, who investigated each county, heard the grievances of any persons, and generally checked upon all the affairs of the district. Since these agents were sent from the King's entourage, they were called *missi dominici*. All matters religious and secular came under their supervision and their own actions were governed by detailed instructions from the King.

Charlemagne's capacity for practical organization and his desire to promote a healthy moral and religious tone can also be noticed in his efforts to regulate economic life. Certain capitularies (or decrees), following papal or conciliar precepts, dealt with money-lending and usury. Others were concerned with weights and measures and food prices. Slavery still existed, but the slave trade was restricted. Metal currency was scarce and the standard coin of the day, the *denarius*, was silver. But Charlemagne insisted on the exclusive right of the palace mint to issue coins or to authorize their issue.

Since the decline of trade and city life which had commenced in the later Roman period continued unabated, the organization of the great landed estates was of first importance, for these provided in last analysis the stable income and economic basis of political power whether of king or of magnates. To the stewards of his own private estates, which he expected to be always ready for his personal use, Charlemagne issued detailed instructions, and he expected his magnates to exercise comparable care and to keep accurate accounts. Moreover, a glance at the King's directive on his farms, the capitulary "On Villas," with its minute regulations on such matters as tenants, cattle, fowl, agricultural produce, cloth-making, forests, mines, and forges, reveals not only a concern for the details of farm administration, but also the fact that a Carolingian *villa* was something more than an agricultural institution. It was, in fact, a center of local industry.

Important as were the great domains of the Carolingian kingdom, two factors must be emphasized further. First, every large domain or *villa* included, in addition to the reserve land cultivated for the landlord, a considerable and often widely scattered collection of tenant farms. Second, it seems clear that there existed throughout the Carolingian period a large number of small privately owned farms. Thus continued the trend toward smaller individualized exploitation which was to become a feature of medieval agriculture.

The administrative procedures devised by Charlemagne seem impressive, and he was doubtless a more capable administrator than most rulers of his time. But directives are not necessarily accomplishments. The decentralizing tendencies of the day were slowed, but not halted. In the gradual transformation of Europe from the cosmopolitan, urban, and unified society of the Roman Empire to the congeries of feudal monarchies of the Middle Ages, the Carolingian kingdom represents a brief pause, a significant but temporary recovery.

That the church should play a major role in Carolingian administration was characteristic of the age. According to current practice bishops were invested with considerable governmental authority and many bishoprics and abbeys were conceded grants of immunity from the jurisdiction of the local count. Thus bishops and abbots were in a position analogous to that of secular magnates.

It was equally natural that the King should make little distinction between the secular and ecclesiastical administrations and should regard religious affairs as his responsibility. Episcopal elections often followed the King's wishes. The papal states in Italy were governed by the pope, but under the King's suzerainty. Indeed, somewhat more than half of the Carolingian capitularies dealt with ecclesiastical matters. To all intents and purposes, therefore, Charlemagne was as much the head of the western church as the emperor at Constantinople was of the eastern. And since, in contemporary theory, church and government were regarded as but supplementary branches of a single society, the position of Charlemagne took on a quasi-religious aspect. He was "God's vicar," the "leader and guide of all Christians."

C. Coronation of Charlemagne as "Roman Emperor"

The politico-religious form of society headed by Charlemagne, despite his generally beneficent attitude and his many excellent reforms, could not be entirely acceptable to the papacy. The situation was not without serious dangers for the future freedom of the church.[1] Unfortunately, the

---

[1] Even under Charlemagne there were serious problems. In 787 the second Council of Nicaea had condemned the iconoclasts in the Byzantine

pope was between two fires. The Byzantine emperor had removed certain Italian bishops from papal jurisdiction. Now the Franks, on whom the papacy had come to rely, were in a too commanding position. To break with both would have meant complete isolation. The church in the eighth century relied on the support of the secular power, and, so great was the force of the Roman imperial tradition, that it still conceived of secular power as normally and properly the Roman Empire. Prayers for the Roman emperor had long been included in the Roman liturgy. These things must be considered if we are to understand what was perhaps the most spectacular event of Charlemagne's life, his coronation as Roman Emperor by the pope.

In the year 800 Charlemagne celebrated Christmas at Rome. At the solemn Mass, Pope Leo III stepped down from the altar, placed a crown on the Frankish King's head, and proclaimed him Emperor. The interpretation of this event has occasioned innumerable controversies among historians from that day to this. Particularly in the thirteenth century the adherents of pope and emperor discovered all sorts of implications of papal or imperial supremacy, of which Charlemagne and Leo probably never dreamed. The coronation acquired a religious and symbolic value in the later history of what came to be known as the Holy Roman Empire.

As far as Charlemagne's reign is concerned, the coronation altered nothing. He continued to govern the church and to claim suzerainty over Rome as before. As a matter of fact, the interminable arguments over the bearing of the coronation of the year 800 on the relations between emperor and pope have tended to obscure what was really of central importance about it. Actually it consummated a revolution whereby the political suzerainty of the Byzantine "Roman" Empire of the east

over the pope or over western Europe was irrevocably repudiated. To Byzantium the coronation was sheer usurpation, and it was only after Charlemagne intervened in Venice that a Byzantine government, hard pressed by eastern invaders, reluctantly admitted the existence of a rival "empire" in the west. Thus Charlemagne's coronation marked the last step in the political separation of Rome and Constantinople.

D. Emergence of Feudal Kingdoms

It cannot be overemphasized that calling Charlemagne's state a "Roman Empire" obscured its real character. The imperial title and other Roman designations gave only an appearance of the sovereignty that had been exercised by the ancient Roman government. In reality, Charlemagne's Empire was a semi-feudal kingdom held together by the genius and energy of one man. The forces of decentralization which he had temporarily stayed proved too powerful for his successors. In addition, the natural tendency of the Frankish kingdom to break up into smaller units was hastened by a wave of invasions far more devastating than those of the fifth century.

An immediate cause of disintegration was the Frankish practice of dividing the royal domains among the sons of the ruler, a practice which had never been abandoned, even by Charlemagne. Since magnates ordinarily followed suit, each major division of the realm was further subdivided.

Royal power was also weakened by the lapse of those checks which Charlemagne had instituted, such as the *missi* and the practice of regular supervision. As a consequence, within each section of the original Empire, the counts, bishops, and other local magnates were practically unhampered in their natural propensity to pursue independent policies. Other developments helped to crystallize this tendency toward local autonomy into a sort of system. Counts came to be succeeded in office by their sons. Thus the great administrative offices became hereditary, and, as the restraints were lessened, innumerable petty dynasties emerged. As the power of the magnates became greater, each Carolingian king or

---

church and upheld traditional veneration of saints and proper use of images. In 794 Charlemagne summoned a council of bishops at Frankfurt, which questioned the decision of Nicaea. Frankish churchmen added to the Nicene Creed: "The Holy Ghost proceeds from the Father [and the Son]." The pope was embarrassed, and the alteration in the creed was seriously opposed in the east.

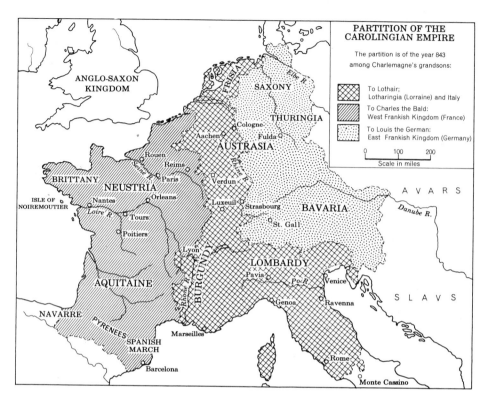

PARTITION OF THE
CAROLINGIAN EMPIRE

The partition is of the year 843
among Charlemagne's grandsons:

To Lothair;
Lotharingia (Lorraine) and Italy

To Charles the Bald:
West Frankish Kingdom (France)

To Louis the German:
East Frankish Kingdom (Germany)

"emperor," in order to win support, was constrained to purchase it, in the only way possible, by grants of land. But this process diminished the royal estates and revenues which had already been curtailed by the divisions. The diminution of the Carolingian estates in relation to the lands of the magnates is a major factor in the decline of the Empire.

Although Charlemagne, following the Frankish custom, had provided for the division of his Empire, only one son, Louis, survived. Known as Louis the Pious (814–840), he failed to maintain his father's system. Norse raids, frontier wars, and local rebellions punctuated his troubled reign. Strongly influenced by clerical opinion regarding the indivisibility of the Empire, Louis arranged a division which conceded the imperial title and a position of superiority to his eldest son; but after his death his already rebellious sons transferred their quarrels to each other. Louis, known as the German, because he had been given Bavaria and other regions east of the Rhine, joined with Charles the Bald against Lothair. To Lothair, the oldest of the three, had been entrusted Italy and the im-

perial crown and, by implication, a superior authority. In 842 Louis and Charles solemnized their pact by oaths which each had written in the language prevalent in the territories of the other. Historically these "Strasbourg Oaths" are important as early written examples of the *lingua romana* and the *lingua teudesca*—Romance and Germanic languages. In the following year (843), after Charles and Louis had defeated Lothair, an important political settlement was reached in the treaty of Verdun, which became the foundation of all later divisions. Three kingdoms were formed. Charles the Bald governed the land west of an irregular line running from the Scheldt to the Rhone and the Mediterranean. Louis the German reigned over the territory east of the Rhine, exclusive of Frisia. Lothair was left the imperial title and a middle kingdom stretching from the North Sea to the southern boundary of the papal states.

The eastern and western kingdoms of Louis and Charles were relatively homogeneous and proved comparatively stable. As the kingdoms of the East and West Franks, respectively, they became the nuclei of the later feudal kingdoms of Germany and France. Although the middle kingdom included the main lines of communication between Italy and northern Europe, its boundaries were vulnerable and it lasted only a short time in its original form. Lothair died in 855 and, according to Frankish tradition, his middle kingdom was divided among his three sons whose individual fortunes we cannot follow here. One of them, however—Lothair II—had a northern section which thereafter was called *Lotharii regnum* and hence Lotharingia or Lorraine. On Lothair II's death, the weakness of his kingdom proved an irresistible source of temptation to Charles the Bald and Louis the German, who appropriated and partitioned it by the Treaty of Mersen (870). Henceforth a territory of varying boundaries, known as Lorraine, was to be disputed between the eastern and western kingdoms, that is, between Germany and France. The treaty of Mersen also provided a boundary which made these two countries contiguous. So they have remained until now.

Meanwhile, the southern portion of the original middle kingdom was divided into a kingdom of Italy, whose history was indescribably turbulent, and the kingdoms of Upper and Lower Burgundy (Provence) in the Rhône valley.[1] The imperial title passed from one branch of the Carolingian family to another, but the office had little meaning. Charles the Bald held it for two years, 875–877. In 884 the magnates chose Charles the Fat, son of Louis the German, and then in 887 deposed him. He died in 888.

To all intents and purposes the year 888 marks the end of the Carolingian Empire. The political future lay with the more stable of the states then existing, particularly with the eastern and western kingdoms—Germany and France. For many years the strongest of the local counts and dukes within these kingdoms provided such protection and stability as remained. It was Count Odo of Paris who saved his city

from one of the worst Norse raids (885–886). For this exploit Charles the Fat made him duke of the Franks, and the grateful magnates later elected him King of the West Franks (888). Thereafter for a century his successors alternated with the later Carolingians as kings of the West Franks, or of "France." Finally, in 987, following the death of the last Carolingian, a descendant of Odo—Hugh Capet—was elected and started the new French dynasty which bears his name.

In the East Frankish kingdom of Germany, the Carolingian line died out earlier, and in 918 the election of Henry the Fowler commenced the Saxon dynasty there. The confused history of Italy and the Burgundian kingdoms during the ninth and tenth centuries need not trouble us. Their ultimate inclusion in the kingdom of Germany will be noted in a later chapter.

E. Education and Culture under Charlemagne and His Successors

Among the concerns of Charlemagne was an anxiety to improve the schooling and general cultural conditions in his dominions, especially among the clergy. There was great need of improvement, for the cultural and educational level of West Christian Europe in the eighth century was far below that of the Byzantine Empire or of the Moslem world. In Gaul, the real center of the Carolingian Empire, the old Roman schools had completely disappeared, and surviving institutions for training the clergy were few and of inferior grade. To help him in his educational task, Charlemagne assembled at his court at Aachen such scholars as he could obtain from other Christian regions of the West, notably Italy, Spain, and England, where something of the old Graeco-Roman tradition of scholarship had survived.

The most distinguished of these scholars, and the Emperor's trusted confidant on many matters, was Alcuin of York (730–804). Alcuin was a product of that flowering of culture in Saxon England which had profited from both Irish and Roman traditions. As a boy he had known the reputation of Bede, and had received his education

---

[1] A small kingdom of Navarre in southwestern France, reaching across the Pyrenees into northern Spain, was a sixth section of the original Carolingian Empire.

and then had taught at a cathedral school at York founded by one of Bede's pupils. In 781, on his return from a journey to Rome, Alcuin met Charlemagne, who prevailed upon him to take up his residence at the Frankish court. There, and later as Abbot of Tours, he carried on his invaluable work as supervisor and as teacher. Thus the Carolingian intellectual revival was, to a large extent, an outgrowth of previous Anglo-Saxon scholarship.

Charlemagne appreciated that a solid intellectual foundation was necessary if his church reforms were to succeed. He strove to provide enlarged facilities for education. Under the immediate auspices of leading prelates of the Empire—bishops and abbots—many of whom were trained by Alcuin or associated with him, two types of schools were fostered. These were the cathedral schools and the monastic schools. Both were concerned with the religious education of the clergy, but their aims were not identical. The cathedral schools were more practically motivated because they were principally engaged in the training of young men for the clergy. In them, too, under Alcuin's direction, there was a certain amount of specialization. Some, for example, specialized in music, and uniformity of ritual and chant throughout the realm was expected.

Monastic schools were likewise concerned with the religious training of young men, but by reason of their more detached position they were often centers of higher learning. In writing rooms attached to them were copied and preserved the texts of both secular and ecclesiastical authors which any advanced scholar would find indispensable. The importance of the work of the Carolingian monastic copyists is illustrated by the fact that the great majority of the classical texts which have come down to our day date from the Carolingian era. And to the same copyists we owe a beautifully executed form of lettering known as the Carolingian minuscule (lower case letter).[1]

As a kind of crown to his educational

reforms, Charlemagne instituted, or rather reorganized, a royal palace school at Aachen for the training of his own children and those of his relatives and chief magnates. Under his predecessors such a school had existed simply to give the royal children the rudiments of military education. Charlemagne injected into it the intellectual element. Although he himself never learned to write, he could read and understand Latin and knew some Greek, and he was an enthusiastic patron of learning. Accordingly the palace school was a favorite creation of the Emperor, who frequently attended its conferences and enjoyed familiar discourse with the scholars he had assembled. Indeed, aside from the education of a few young persons closely associated with the royal family, the principal function of the palace school was to provide a place for the congregating of learned men.

The Carolingian revival was not productive of many original literary works. Rather it produced a significant, if limited, educational curriculum and preserved the contributions of the past. The principal emphasis in the schools was on grammar and rhetoric. But grammar and rhetoric implied the mastery not only of the classical Latin grammarians, but also of the most prominent of the Latin authors of antiquity. There emerged, especially later in the ninth century, a love of literature and a real humanist spirit, out of which grew a desire not only to learn but to create. And while the first step in composition proved to be conscious imitation of the style and form of ancient writers, this training enabled some to produce works of considerable importance and not a little originality. This was especially true of history and poetry.

A few writers merit attention. We have already mentioned Einhard, author of the *Life of Charlemagne*. Paul the Deacon, after sojourning at Aachen, returned to his native Italy and there wrote a *History of the Lombards*. Abbot Lupus of Ferrières possessed an unusually fine library and became a polished letter writer. Mention should also be made of John Scotus Erigena, a philosopher markedly influenced by Neoplatonic ideas, but withal an original thinker. His *On the Division of Nature* appeared around 865.

---

[1] Later renaissance humanists admired the Carolingian minuscule and imitated it. Thus it came to be adopted by fifteenth-century printers in Italy and has survived to our own day as "Roman" type.

Carolingian art. A ninth century silver-gilt and jewelled binding for the Gospels.

Courtesy Pierpont Morgan Library, New York

There were several poets of some distinction. Not only did they add to the treasury of medieval religious poetry and hymnology, but they sang of nature and human emotions. Paul the Deacon left two gems, one a description of Lake Como, another a plea to the Emperor to liberate his brother. Alcuin also wrote poetry, although it was in the manner of a classical teacher and more imitative than inspired. Theodulf of Orléans, on the other hand, showed real poetic feeling and skill.

Carolingian art also showed a modest but significant revival and exhibited the same diverse influences that are observable in learning. The Emperor's chapel at Aachen was octagonal and evidently inspired by Justinian's church of San Vitale at Ravenna. Indeed, Pope Hadrian permitted Charlemagne to use marbles taken from Ravenna. Such "round" churches were popular as stone gradually replaced wood

in building. Some architects also modified the rectangular form of the Roman basilica by enlarging the apse and sometimes adding chapels. Theodulf of Orleans, who came from formerly Visigothic Spain, built a church at St. Germigny-des-Près which is strikingly reminiscent of the Romano-Visigothic style of his native country. Carolingian illuminated manuscripts show not only strong Byzantine characteristics but also barbarian, and especially Celtic, influences in design. Some bibles or gospel-books were handsomely bound with ivory-carved, or gold-and-jewel, covers.

Although the Carolingian intellectual revival had its limitations, arising from the ideals of the age and the purposes of the Emperor, it was a big step forward. Because it was one of those occasions in western European history when there was a deliberate reaching back for inspiration to the Graeco-Roman past, it has been called the "Carolingian renaissance." Moreover, it was not as ephemeral as the Carolingian Empire. It is true that Charlemagne's educational system suffered considerable damage from renewed barbarian invasions of the ninth and tenth centuries. But not all was lost. The greater cathedral and monastic foundations at Fulda, Tours, Corbie, St. Gall, Reichenau, Lorsch, Orléans, Reims, Pavia, *etc.*, remained centers from which came later cultural revivals. And it is a tribute to Charlemagne's energy and foresight that such was the case.

As the Carolingian Empire disintegrated, there survived no single center of cultural activity comparable to the palace school of Charlemagne. It was left to local cathedral and monastic schools and to an occasional enterprising local ruler to carry on the tradition. Alfred the Great in England (871–901) proved to be a devoted patron of learning, although his efforts bore fruit in the vernacular Saxon language rather than in Latin. He fostered the development of the *Anglo-Saxon Chronicle* and had certain of the works of Gregory the Great translated. With respect to the vernacular, Saxon England was ahead of the continent. The great heroic epic, *Beowulf*, dates from about the eighth century.

F. Ninth-Century Attacks from South and East: Saracens, Slavs, Bulgars, and Magyars

The principal invaders of the ninth century were Norsemen, Slavs, Bulgars, Magyars, and Saracens. All except the Norsemen attacked from the south or the east, and none of them felt the respect for the institutions of Roman Christendom which had animated the German invaders of the fifth century. Nor was the supremacy of European culture as apparent in the two centuries following Charlemagne's death as it had been in the fifth century. For ninth- and tenth-century Christendom, beleaguered from north and east, was encircled on its southern side by Islamic civilization which, in its material aspects at least, was far superior.

Yet the situation was not hopeless. In the west, as we have seen, strong centers of local resistance often succeeded where central government failed. And in the Byzantine Empire, as a later chapter will explain, there was a significant recovery. More important, Europe, thanks especially to the vitality of the church and the surprisingly durable quality of Roman-German institutions, retained remarkable powers of assimilation. In the end most of the barbarians were civilized.

Western Europe's capacity to assimilate its enemies did not, however, extend to Moslems. For in the Moslems, Europe faced not barbarians but the possessors of a rival civilization which had encircled the southern fringes of Christendom. Their ninth-century depredations were an aftermath of the great conquests of preceding centuries. From Tunisia, Moslems—or "Saracens," as these were now called—expanded across the sea to envelop Sicily and menace southern Italy. In 846 Rome was sacked and the tombs of the apostles profaned, with the result that Pope Leo IV encircled the Vatican palace and St. Peter's with a wall.[1] Montecassino was also ravaged and various Italian and Provençal ports were taken and held for some time. Saracen raids on land reached as far as the Alpine passes. Since Corsica, Sardinia, and the Balearics also fell under Moslem control, European commerce was virtually swept from the western and central Mediterranean for many years.

Slavic raids along the northeastern frontier of the East Frankish kingdom were often a source of considerable danger. But even during the period of decline the Germans occasionally renewed their eastward pressure with some success against primitive Slavic states in Poland, Bohemia, and Moravia. Both Slavs and Germans were greatly affected by the advance of two other peoples, the Bulgars and the Magyars. The former, originally Asiatic kindred of the Huns, had expanded into the Balkan peninsula. At one time they almost captured Constantinople. But the Bulgars were anxious to emulate the civilized ways of their neighbors. The kahn or king assumed the Roman title of tsar (Caesar). Their native speech was gradually transformed into

---

[1] The area thus enclosed, the "Leonine city," roughly corresponds to the present-day Vatican City.

a predominantly Slavic tongue. Finally, in 871, the Bulgar King Boris I accepted Christianity under Byzantine jurisdiction.

The Magyars, also of Asiatic origin, invaded the Carpathian basin once occupied by the Avars, and conquered Moravia. They destroyed a promising Slavic state centering in Moravia, and separated the Balkan Slavs, the South- or Yugo-Slavs, from their cousins, the western Slavs, in Bohemia, Moravia, and Poland. This proved to be a major disaster for the Slavic peoples, for the division accentuated other cultural differences and undoubtedly contributed to the lack of unity later evident in Slavic history. Meanwhile, the Magyars, who came to be known as Hungarians because of a supposed resemblance to the ancient Huns, terrorized the borders of the East Frankish kingdom and Italy. In their most devastating raids they penetrated as far as Lorraine and Burgundy. Not until their defeat by the German King Otto I in 955 did they settle down to form a stable kingdom. In 1000, under their King Stephen, they accepted Christianity and the spiritual authority of Rome, and opened the way for the entrance of Western civilization into Hungary.

G. Norse Incursions and Settlements

The far northern Scandinavian lands were practically unknown to Carolingian Europe. Their inhabitants, loosely called Danes or Vikings, had only occasionally appeared as raiders. Like the Franks, they were a Teutonic people, but of a distinct speech and culture. The heavily forested Danish peninsula and the rocky soil of Norway and Sweden offered limited facilities for agriculture and turned their naturally rugged and warlike inhabitants to the sea. The deep coves and fiords of Norway formed ideal harbors. In their long double-ended boats manned by warriors who set up their shields along the gunwales as they took the oars or managed the small sails, or in the broader and deeper craft not uncommon in the Northern seas, Norsemen fearlessly ventured across unknown waters. Their skill in navigation, their uncanny knowledge of winds and currents surpassed anything Europe was to see until the compass was developed.

The extent of Norse expansion is amazing. Late in the eighth century Viking attacks were felt on the east coast of England, a land then divided into separate Saxon kingdoms. The raids continued through the ninth century, increasing in size as news got back home of easy successes. Finally, the English King Alfred the Great (871–901), after years of stubborn defense, reached a compromise with Guntrum, the Dane, whereby the entire northeastern half of England was given over to the latter, while the rest of England was spared. The territory given the Danes was known as the *Danelaw*, and although the Danes became Christian and professed an allegiance to Alfred, the *Danelaw* was actually independent. In the course of the next century, however, despite a constant influx of Danes, the *Danelaw* was reconquered, and gradually the Danes adopted Saxon ways.

Ireland, though suffering some Danish raids, became one of the principal areas of

The carved prow of a Viking ship. The Ose-berg Ship.

Courtesy Norwegian Information Service,
New York

Norwegian activity. Norwegians also explored the islands north of Scotland and established colonies in the Faroë, Shetland, and Orkney islands, in the Hebrides, and as far south as the Isle of Man. Thence, guided by the Irish, they pushed on to Iceland where, in the later ninth century, colonization began and a thoroughly Norse state was formed. Even Iceland did not prove to be the limit of Norse expansion westward. Greenland was discovered and a small colony established, which by the twelfth century was considered important enough for the institution of a Catholic diocese. Thence Leif Ericson, accompanied or perhaps preceded by Bjarni Herjolfson, went on to the northern coasts of the North American mainland, where, perhaps journeying southward by land, they reached a place which they called Vinland.[1] While the exact location of Vinland remains a matter of dispute, and so far as we know no perma-

[1] Recent investigations by Norwegian archeologists have uncovered convincing evidence of Norse settlements in Newfoundland. A recently published map dating from the fifteenth century indicates Vinland as an island with rather vague western outlines. R. A. Skelton, T. E. Marston, G. D. Painter, *The Vinland Map and the Tartar Relation* (New Haven, 1965).

nent settlement resulted, the Norse voyages to America may confidently be regarded as fact.

Of more immediate influence on Europe was the Viking penetration of the continent. Swedish traders and adventurers had crossed the Baltic at an early date, perhaps in the sixth century, and had begun to ascend the northern Russian rivers into the interior. Thence some descended the Volga to the Caspian and thus made contact with Persia and the Moslem world. Others followed the Dnieper to the Black Sea and established contact with Constantinople and the Byzantine Empire. These early Norse rovers were called *Rus* or *Varangians*. The trade route across Russia to Constantinople was known as the "Varangian route." Russia in those day were merely a collection of small Slavic principalities, some of which employed bands of Vikings or gradually fell under their domination. The leader of one such band was Rurik who in 862 became the prince of Novgorod, a thriving northern metropolis, and whose kinsmen, led by Oleg, later appropriated Kiev on the Dnieper. The principality of Kiev was destined to be the chief Russian state during the early middle age. Although intercourse be-

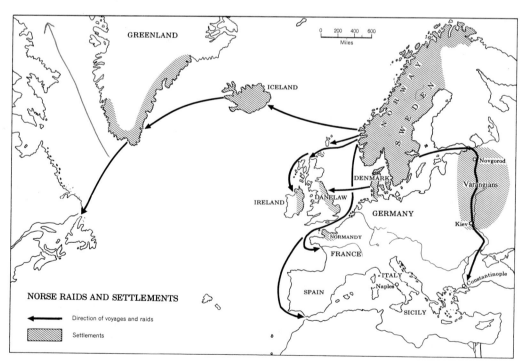

NORSE RAIDS AND SETTLEMENTS

→ Direction of voyages and raids

Settlements

tween the Varangian principalities and the Scandinavian homeland was maintained, the Norse, as was their habit, adapted themselves to their new surroundings and were gradually lost in the development of these early Slavic principalities of Russia.

The western European mainland was also the scene of extensive Norse raids. The French coast, Spain, Mediterranean ports, and Italy were visited by their long boats. The many rivers of the Low Countries and France provided excellent avenues of inland penetration, and toward the end of the ninth century Norse raids in France were noticeably intensified.

One of the greatest attacks on an inland city was the siege of Paris in 885–886 where the heroic defense of Count Odo held several thousand Vikings with a large number of vessels at bay for ten months and saved the city. Even then the French King, Charles the Fat, was forced to pay a tribute. It was evident that the Norse were too firmly entrenched on the lower Seine to be dislodged, and so King Charles the Simple came to terms with the Norse chieftain, Rollo. In the treaty of St. Claire-sur-Epte (911) a statesmanlike compromise was arranged. The Norsemen were permitted to retain that part of the northern Frankish coast which lay between Brittany and the Low Countries, with a hinterland including Rouen, which became their capital. In return, Rollo embraced Christianity and became a vassal to King Charles for what came to be known as the duchy of Normandy.

Although Rollo probably understood but imperfectly the implications of vassalage, the creation of the duchy of Normandy brought the sturdy Vikings of northern France into the orbit of European civilization. Within a surprisingly short time these former marauders were building monasteries instead of pillaging them. And instead of destroying churches they were developing a noteworthy style of ecclesiastical architecture. Yet despite a thorough assimilation of the Latin civilization of western Europe, the Normans, as the inhabitants of Normandy were later called, did not lose the vigor and adventurous spirit of their ancestors. In the eleventh century, Normans carried their fused Norman-French culture to England and to southern Italy and Sicily.

It is difficult to overemphasize the results of the Norse expansion. Its geographical extent was tremendous. Everywhere the Norsemen went they stimulated trade. Skilled sailors, they advanced all the arts of the sea and gave to sea-borne commerce a new impetus. Equally significant was the effect of European civilization on the Norsemen. Everywhere they adopted Christianity, and the church experienced a notable growth. Moreover, while the adventurous Vikings roamed abroad, those who remained at home were forming the three kingdoms of Sweden, Norway, and Denmark. Soon missionaries from the continent and from England were carrying the gospel to heathen Norse in their homeland. By the year 1000, or shortly thereafter, an entirely new and hitherto unknown area had become a part of European Christendom.

That the two centuries following Charlemagne's death were a dark period in European history is undeniable. Political decay was followed by disorder, pillage, and widespread devastation. The losses, both material and spiritual, were terrific. However, it is not inappropriate to conclude this chapter on a happier note. Slavs, Bulgars, Magyars, and Norsemen, were, in the last analysis, absorbed and brought within the orbit of European civilization. Meanwhile, the inhabitants of western Europe were devising a new way of life made necessary by the breakdown of the Roman and Carolingian systems. The result was a slow but steady recovery which will occupy our attention in the following chapters.

Spanish thirteenth century sculpture. Marble relief of a mounted knight in helmet and mail shirt.

Courtesy of the Metropolitan Museum of Art, New York; Dodge Fund, 1913

CHAPTER 11

The Beginnings of Recovery: Feudalism and Feudal Society

A. Origins of Feudalism

The organization of society characteristic of the Early Middle Age is known as feudalism. Although feudalism arose out of the disturbed conditions preceding and following the reign of Charlemagne and may be associated, therefore, with the disintegration of the Roman and Carolingian states, it contained elements of stability and strength. Most important, it made possible a recovery of western European society on a local basis which in turn was to contribute to integration on the wider plane of feudal kingdoms. The latter process, which is first notable during the tenth century, is part of the larger phenomenon of western European recovery—economic, religious, and cultural, as well as political.

Feudalism developed as a kind of amalgam of earlier Roman, German, and perhaps even Celtic practices, modified to suit current needs. Practices varied from place to place and from time to time. There is no typical or "ideal" feudalism. Yet while allowing for very many local exceptions, some sort of general description is possible.

Two kinds of relationships run through the whole development: the personal bond between man and man; and the holding or tenure of land. The former is illustrated by the institution known as "vassalage," an honorable relationship between men based on military service. Though the origin of vassalage is a controversial matter, it appears that in Carolingian times a vassal was a professional fighting man serving someone of higher rank. Meanwhile various magnates—bishops and counts—many of whom held large tracts of land, became associated with the king as his *fideles* or *homines*, that is, as his "faithful men." Further, after the early Carolingians discovered that the great need in combating the Moslems was a well equipped cavalry, the vassal was given a special grant of land in return for service. Such a grant was called a "benefice" and enabled the vassal to meet the added expense of mounted service. Eventually, all landlords, including magnates, were expected to contribute to the military establishment. As customary procedures gradually became fixed as law, they were further emphasized by ceremonial. In becoming the "man" (*homo*) of his lord, the vassal performed some act of "homage." Since his loyalty was all important, he also took an oath of fealty.

Hence landlords, both lay and ecclesiastical, in order to provide military service in proportion to the size of their domains, gave out sections of these as benefices. Carolingian policies also added other elements to the benefice. The holder of a benefice usually retained complete jurisdiction over the dependent peasants. This was an obvious necessity since the land was to provide the economic support for military service. Moreover, a general political jurisdiction over a benefice by its holder was acquired either by a grant of "immunity," which conferred official release from the jurisdiction of the central government, or,

The fortunes and misfortunes of war at the Battle of Hastings.

From the Bayeux Tapestry

as was often the case, simply by appropriation.

The benefice system, which had developed out of late Roman procedures, had not originally or always been associated with military service. Hence a new term, "fief," came into use to designate this novel military benefice developed by the Carolingians. From its Latinized form, *feodum*, is derived the word feudal. A fief was land held in return for military service, but, because governmental jurisdiction was included, it was also an office. In the areas of the former west Frankish kingdom where the Carolingian county system was well developed, inheritance of fiefs came to be, as a rule, by primogeniture (that is, by descent to the eldest male heir). In the east division of the Frankish kingdom, divided inheritance tended to prevail for a longer time.

Then, too, by a process known as "subinfeudation," a vassal holding a fief could subdivide it into smaller fiefs. As a consequence there were sub-vassals (rear vassals) as well as vassals, and fiefs within fiefs. Such fiefs originated out of feudalism itself. They were not former administrative divisions of the Carolingian Empire.

B. Feudal Procedures

The essence of the feudal relation, whether it was between a king and one of the magnates who held directly from him,

sometimes called a tenant-in-chief, or between a lesser lord and his vassal, was its contractual nature. Lord and vassal each had reciprocal duties and privileges. Since all lords were also vassals and all but the humblest vassals were also lords, there existed a definite social equality among all the nobility from the king to the poorest knight. Each had similar responsibilities and rights. When we describe the ordinary duties of a vassal toward his lord, we must remember that he expected the same from his own vassals. Vassalage was an entirely honorable estate and implied none of that humiliating subjection which the modern connotation of the word has acquired.

The mutual obligations of vassal and lord were not the same everywhere in Europe and they changed from century to century; but they were sufficiently similar in nature to warrant a general summary. They followed logically from the character of the fief as both a piece of land and an office. First, every vassal was expected to perform the act of homage, that is, to kneel and place his hands between the palms of his lord and take the oath of fealty. Broadly speaking, a vassal's duties can be summarized as governmental or judicial, financial, and military. He had to attend the lord's court at certain intervals or whenever summoned. There he advised his lord on policy or sat in judgment with other vassals, his own peers (*pares*), to decide a case involving one of them. Whatever decision was reached he was required to help carry out. The feudal court attended by those who held directly of the king was usually called the *curia regis* and was the nucleus of such central government as existed. In fact, all the services owed directly to the king were significant in the development of feudal monarchy.

Financial assistance amounted to financial contributions, varying with the size of the fief, on certain specified occasions, such as the marriage of the lord's daughter, the knighting of the lord's eldest son, or the provision of ransom in case the lord was captured. These were the three famous feudal "aids," and like all feudal payments were regulated by custom. One other normal payment, the "relief," recalled the days before the fief was hereditary. It was usually a fairly heavy tax and was expected of every vassal who inherited a fief from his father. A lord might also occasionally profit handsomely from the *droit de gîte*, or compulsory lodging, if he traveled through his vassal's land.

Military service was one of the principal reasons for the feudal system. Each vassal was expected to serve his lord personally (if he had more than one, presumably his liege lord) as a mounted knight. If his fief were large he would have to provide a number of mounted men. These he would secure from his own sub-vassals through sub-infeudation. But military service, however exacting, was limited. A common custom, at least in northern France, stipulated that it should not exceed forty days, although garrison duty at the lord's castle might also be required.

It is obvious that every lord would seek to protect himself from rebellious or otherwise undesirable vassals. If a vassal seriously defaulted in his obligations, the lord had the right, after due trial by peers, to declare the fief forfeit—that is, to expel the recalcitrant vassal and take over the property. Such a procedure required that the lord have adequate force at his disposal and this usually meant the full support of his other vassals. If a vassal died, leaving an unmarried daughter as heiress, it was the lord's privilege to choose a husband for the young lady. Meanwhile, the right of wardship permitted him to administer the fief and collect its revenues. He exercised similar rights over the fief of a young boy whose father died before the son reached his majority.

The obligations of a vassal were counterbalanced by certain definite rights. We have already alluded to the much prized privilege of trial by one's peers. The lord also engaged to protect his vassal in his fief and to support him in righting wrongs done him. Contemporary writers, emphasizing the loyalty due a lord, insisted that the lord ought to act in like manner toward the vassal in all things. It was entirely possible for the lord to violate the feudal contract. And although in theory a vassal might repudiate the agreement because of his lord's default, his chances of redress were, in the nature of things, not great.

Nevertheless, since a lord depended on faithful vassals, he dared not press them too far. Feudalism implied limited, not absolute, sovereignty on the part of the king as well as of other lords. This is its greatest contribution to the theory and practice of free government in western Europe.

Feudalism had many complications. There was nothing to prevent a noble, naturally anxious to enlarge his holdings, from becoming the vassal of more than one lord. The counts of Champagne, for example, had nine lords. As a consequence, any baron attending the court of his lord might find there, doing homage to the same man, one of his own vassals. It was possible to be both the lord (or vassal) and the equal (peer) of the same person.

Such situations necessarily complicated the matter of allegiance. Hence arose the practice of *liege* homage, whereby a vassal designated one of his lords as his liege lord to whom he admitted superior allegiance and whom he served personally. In the case of a dispute between two of their lords, most barons followed the course which conscience or apparent self-interest (whichever was stronger) dictated. Feudalism was not without its confusion, its conflicting loyalties and jurisdictions. Feudal warfare, one of its greatest evils, was chronic. But to a marked degree feudal wars, at least in the minds of those involved, were to redress wrongs or to protect rights. Turbulent as were the nobles of the ninth and tenth centuries, they were not entirely lacking in a sense of moral responsibility.

C. Chivalry and Feudal Warfare

The emphasis on fidelity to contract, to plighted word and agreement, is particularly evident in the development of chivalry. Chivalry is not easily defined, for it was never a clearly developed institution. Our principal sources are the great medieval epic poems written in the vernacular.[1] It was natural that the noble audiences for whose entertainment these romances were composed would appreciate most easily

---

[1] See below, pp. 251–252.

those things which were familiar to them. Derived from the French word for horse (*cheval*), chivalry represents at once a code of conduct and a sort of loose indeterminate fellowship of the warrior class, where king and humble knight were equal. Probably of German origin, and at first purely military and secular, it emphasized courage, loyalty to one's superior, and devotion to military duty. Later, especially in the twelfth and thirteenth centuries, when society was somewhat more sophisticated and more Christianized, the ideas of protection for the weak and defenseless and of courtesy toward women entered. The church also influenced the development of chivalry by inculcating the ideal of the Christian knight sworn to defend the faith against its enemies, in particular Mohammedans. But despite the addition of all these new elements, chivalry retained the predominantly military and secular character of its early days.

Since fighting was the principal occupation of the nobility, a few words about medieval warfare are in order. Private warfare was the great scourge of early medieval society. Yet, in comparison to modern war, it was not especially sanguinary or devastating. For the most part it involved only the noble class and was a privilege which they jealously guarded. Only the necessities of new strategy, required in combating the Moslems, led to the introduction of infantry, bowmen in particular, from the nonfeudal classes. And as late as the fourteenth century, the mercenary infantry troops were despised by the proud French knights. The masses of the population—the peasants—experienced war only when it passed over their crops or when perhaps their lord and his knights were victims of a siege.

Clothed in a long cloak of chain mail, the hauberk, and a conical steel helmet, and carrying shield, sword, and spear, the mounted knight could be knocked down, bruised, and wounded, but less often killed. His ransom was usually more desirable than his life.

The earliest type of castle, and one long considered adequate, was the *motte-and-bailey*. This was a wooden block-house or square tower known as the keep (*donjon*), usually situated on a mound and surrounded by stockades and possibly by a moat and drawbridge. The first stone keeps were also square. Round towers were then developed and, during the period of the crusades more elaborate integrated construction appeared with inner and outer circles of walls forming a concentric design. Towers placed at intervals commanded every section of the walls. The advantage in a siege usually lay with the besieged unless inadequate provisioning made starvation possible. But since only kings or a few virtually independent magnates were likely to afford such edifices, complicated stone castles were never numerous.

The more thoughtful elements in society realized the evils inherent in excessive private war, and various steps were taken, particularly by the church, to curb it. In the late tenth and early eleventh centuries the bishops of France instituted the Peace of God and the Truce of God. The former was designed to protect ecclesiastical persons and property, the poor, and even merchants. Some lords responded by forming societies and taking vows to respect its provisions, but the results were on the whole disappointing. The Truce of God, which prohibited war on weekends and during certain seasons, was somewhat better observed.

The crusades of the twelfth and thirteenth centuries and the earlier wars of reconquest in Spain also diverted much warlike energy. But the most effective deterrent was the growth in authority, either of the central government, as in France, England, and Sicily, or of certain powerful magnates. The duke of Normandy was able to police his duchy and to prevent castle building without his special permission. Other instances could be cited. But such developments marked the decline of feudalism and the recovery, at least locally, of governmental authority. In the high feudal age the problem of private warfare was never really solved.

If fighting was a knight's chief occupation, mock fighting and hunting were his favorite amusements. Tournaments held on festive occasions were little dress-rehearsal wars consisting of a series of jousts, wherein individual knights were paired and rode at each other with lances set, and of an ensuing mêlée or "free for all' which usually resolved itself into individual combats. The fact that tournaments were forbidden, albeit ineffectively, by the church (1179) indicates that they were no mere child's play. Another favorite sport was hunting the deer or wild boar, which provided men of active life with both exercise and food. Falconry, also, became a highly developed art and was enjoyed by women as well as by men.

The position of women under feudalism was considerably improved by the later, more sophisticated chivalry; and their importance as gracious mistresses of considerable households was enhanced by the larger manor houses and castles of the subsequent middle ages. The poetry of romantic love, which had a certain vogue in the twelfth and thirteenth centuries, may also have changed some men's attitudes toward women.[1]

Under feudalism women were regarded primarily as necessary housekeepers and mothers of children, and marriages among the nobility were for the most part arranged for dowries and fiefs, not for love. Nevertheless women could, and often did, administer fiefs by reason of the absence or death of their husbands. And feudal custom jealously guarded woman's rights of inheritance and control over property.

As we have already intimated, feudalism developed spontaneously to meet critical conditions. It must be judged in this light and not by unfair comparison with previous or following ages. It was not perfect, but it enabled western Europe to resist and assimilate barbarians; it provided a rough and ready law and order. Many of its customs have become embodied in the laws of modern states. Trial by peers is still a prized privilege. The concepts of limited sovereignty and individual rights were fundamental to feudal government.

D. Feudalism and the Church

The position of individual churchmen under feudalism, like that of all other members of society, was determined by the con-

ditions of land tenure. Bishops and abbots, as custodians of property, were lords or vassals (or both) under the feudal regime, and at the same time proprietors of peasants on ecclesiastical estates. Many served as government officials. Members of the clergy acquired a dual function. They were members of the ecclesiastical order with appropriate duties and, at the same time, they were forced to assume many of the responsibilities normally expected of laymen.

The evils inherent in such a situation were many. Preoccupation with worldly problems necessarily detracted from spiritual concerns. Many a bishop and abbot in the feudal age seemed more statesman than churchman. Moreover, in a very natural way a number of practices developed which were damaging to the church's welfare. Successful kings and great nobles endeavored in every way to control their vassals. As a consequence, the normal process of electing bishops was seriously disturbed. The canons of a cathedral church might formally elect, but the king or neighboring duke or count frequently nominated, the candidate. Younger sons who would not inherit a fief could often be nominated to an ecclesiastical benefice. Such baronial prelates, hurried through Holy Orders without adequate preparation, were seldom fit for their sacred office. A goodly number declined to let their churchly duties interfere with their customary mode of life. Although churchmen were forbidden to bear arms and were not as a rule expected personally to perform military service, too many in the early, rough feudal age were indistinguishable from any other knights. Eventually, there developed the practice known as lay investiture. A king or great lord "invested" the nominee to a bishopric or abbacy, not only with the customary symbols of authority over his fief, but also with the ring and crozier, symbols of his spiritual authority. This implied lay control over matters of ecclesiastical jurisdiction.

All these practices, unfortunate though they were, were a normal consequence of feudalism. More serious was the resultant breakdown of ecclesiastical discipline. Simony, the traffic in church offices, became fairly widespread; and the earlier injunction that clerics must not marry was rather

---

[1] See below, pp. 253–254.

widely disregarded. Even monasteries were not exempt from the general moral decline.

Not only did feudalism create problems for churchmen as individuals; it seriously endangered the church as an institution. As lay control over ecclesiastical offices increased, the church was in grave danger of becoming decentralized and brought everywhere under the domination of local political authority. For the universal decentralization of western European society accentuated a tendency on the part of certain prelates to assume a quasi-independent ecclesiastical jurisdiction.

It is also true that the machinery of centralization, the means whereby the pope could maintain close contact with bishops and abbots throughout the Christian world, was not yet adequately developed. To build an effective monarchical constitution on the basis of the primacy of the Roman See was one of the great tasks facing the church as it emerged from the Roman Empire. But the fulfilment of this objective was impeded, first, by the disorder of the invasions, and, second, by the development of feudalism.

This dangerous condition was aggravated by an especially acute feudal anarchy which persisted in central Italy. After the collapse of the Carolingian Empire the papal territories fell under the control of nobles of the Roman district. These men were a particularly unruly lot who regarded the bishop of Rome primarily as their temporal ruler—which he was—and paid scant attention to his prerogatives as head of the entire church. Like feudal lords elsewhere in Europe, they attempted, unfortunately with considerable success, to thwart the control of their suzerain. Members of their own families were elected at their behest until the choice of the highest official in Christendom was determined by the factional struggles of a petty local nobility. Needless to say, many of the candidates were unworthy characters and grossly negligent in their duties. There were periods in the late ninth and early tenth centuries when the papacy seemed to have reached the depths of degradation. In such a state, it could offer little leadership to a church caught in the meshes of feudalism.

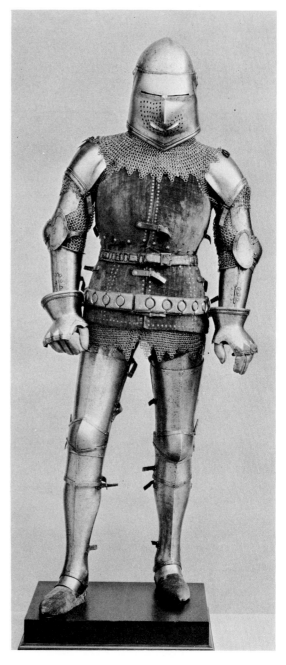

Medieval armor. Italian about 1400.

Courtesy Metropolitan Museum of Art, New York; The Bashford Dean Memorial Collection, gift of Helen Fahnestock Hubbard, 1929, in memory of her father, Harris C. Fahnestock

It would be incorrect to overemphasize the worst aspects of a very bad period in the church's history. There were a number of local efforts to bring about reform. Individual bishops and isolated abbeys struggled to maintain the proper standards, sometimes with notable success. And it must be remembered that, then as now, notorious evil-doers always attract more attention than the rank and file of conscientious people. A number of princes, although jealously guarding their self-assumed prerogatives of appointing bishops and abbots, were, as Charlemagne had been, sufficiently religious, as well as statesmanlike, to be genuinely interested in improving the condition of the church.

Indeed, there was often a real *rapport* between the ecclesiastical authorities and the secular rulers. We have mentioned that many nobles coöperated in maintaining the Peace and Truce of God. Endowment of religious foundations was general. Moreover, the practice of investing clerics aroused no serious objections on the part of the church until toward the mid-eleventh century. And it should be remembered, too, that in contemporary thinking the king was regarded, as Charlemagne had been, as a quasi-religious figure. He was *rex et sacerdos*, king and priest, entitled on solemn occasions to appear in the sanctuary of the church. Accordingly, the church upheld royal authority and expected the king to assist in enforcing ecclesiastical discipline. The ideal of the tenth and eleventh centuries was a coöperation of the two powers, the religious and the secular, to promote a Christian society.

The Romanesque Cathedral of Bamberg. The See of Bamberg was founded in 1007 by the German Emperor Henry II as a missionary diocese and outpost of defense against the Slavs. It became famous for its school and as a resort of the emperors.

Courtesy German Tourist Information Office, New York

CHAPTER 12

Emerging Feudal States
of the Tenth and Eleventh Centuries

During the tenth century, after the worst storms of invasion had passed and many of the new peoples had been absorbed, political consolidation was once again possible. The Europe which emerged resembled neither the Roman nor the Carolingian Empire. Rather it was a collection of separate feudal kingdoms. Yet even in the face of political separatism, most of Europe managed to maintain and develop a common culture based upon common religious and political traditions. And it is this unity of culture which justifies, by the eleventh century, the interchangeable use of the words Europe and Christendom.

Political practices in those centuries were generally based on feudalism. This, as we have already seen, had originated in the former Carolingian domains. Elsewhere it developed sometimes in imitation, and sometimes through new settlers to whom feudal institutions were familiar. Invariably it was modified by local conditions. In general, we may say that a feudal kingdom was a collection of fiefs in which the size and management of the fief belonging to the reigning family, the "royal domain," were of first importance as the ruler's primary resource. Beyond this domain the authority of a feudal king was circumscribed by the customary law which evolved from the practical operation of the feudal contract. The idea that a ruler is bound by law and not superior to it is an outgrowth of feudalism. A feudal monarch was "suzerain," not sovereign.

Tenth- and eleventh-century Europe included: (1) those states which had formerly been divisions of the Carolingian Empire; (2) territories consolidated following feudal expansion; (3) kingdoms formed by erstwhile invaders who had settled down and adopted the institutions of the civilization they had previously attacked.

There was also, on an older and different basis, the Byzantine Empire which, though reduced in size, recovered notably in the ninth and tenth centuries and maintained important contacts with central and western Europe. All these will be considered in turn.

A. Capetian France

The former Carolingian kingdom of the West Franks was in the tenth and eleventh centuries considerably smaller than the later French state. Although it extended northward to include Flanders and southward to embrace Barcelona below the Pyrenees, the entire Rhone valley and all of upper Lorraine belonged to neighboring kingdoms. At the accession of Hugh Capet (987),[1] the kingdom was a collection of fiefs loosely bound together. Most of these were larger than the royal domain, the *Ile-de-France*, and many had developed distinctive customs. In Brittany, parts of Flanders, and the southern provinces, different speech prevailed. It would, therefore, be more appropriate to speak of Normans, Angevins,

---

[1] See above, p. 123.

IRELAND

ENGLAND

English Channel

FLANDERS

VERMANDOIS

Rouen

Reims

NORMANDY

Paris

ILE DE
(FRANCE)

TROYES
(CHAMPAGNE)

Chartres

BRITTANY

MAINE

B
L
O
I
S

Orléans

A
N
J
O
U

NEVERS

BURGUNDY

Nantes

Poitiers

BOURBON

G U I E N N E
(AQUITAINE)

AUVERGNE

Lyons

Angoulême

Bordeaux

ROUERGUE

GOTHIA

GASCONY

T
O
U
L
O
U
S
E

Toulouse

Mediterranean
Sea

BARCELONA

HOLY ROMAN EMPIRE

FEUDAL FRANCE

//// Royal Domain

The boundaries of the principal·fiefs are approximate

Burgundians, or Flemish, than of Frenchmen. Certainly the history of early medieval France is the history of its fiefs.

Of the first four Capetians who ruled from 987 to 1108 there is little to be said. Hugh set an important precedent for the future by having his eldest son crowned during his own lifetime, thus insuring an orderly succession. The undisputed succession of the early Capetians did much to secure the throne in the family, and hereditary succession by primogeniture became a feature of the French monarchy. Although the early Capetian kings exercised little if any influence outside the *Ile de France*, it must be remembered that there was no unity among the great fiefs which surrounded the royal domain. The perpetual quarrels which marked the relations of the great vassals with each other did much to save the monarchy. A significant event in early Capetian history was the conquest of England (1066) by the Duke of Normandy, for thenceforth France and England were in an unusually close relationship.

B. Germany and the Formation of the Holy Roman Empire [1]

The history of the former East Frankish kingdom (Germany) during the tenth and eleventh centuries differs markedly from the development of feudal France which we have just noted. First, the Carolingian dynasty came to an end in Germany in 911, seventy-five years before the accession of Hugh Capet in France, and Germany's consolidation under a new line of Saxon kings commenced earlier. Second, feudalism developed rather later and differently in the eastern Frankish realm. Inheritance of fiefs, for example, was slow to be established. Carolingian traditions of sovereignty lingered longer in Germany than in France. Thirdly, the early German monarchy differed from the French in the location of the

[1] Although the designation "holy" was not applied until later, it has become customary to antedate it to the time of Otto I in 962.

crown lands, for the East Frankish monarchs had not lost control of all the Carolingian domains and they retained property scattered throughout the realm. For a time, these were a valuable asset in the early growth of the German monarchy.

The failure of any single dynasty to establish itself for more than a century meant that the elective principle in German kingship was never entirely lost. On a number of occasions the power of the magnates as electors was of special significance. As a result of the crown's passing from one dynasty to another, it was difficult to establish a compact royal domain. And while this was not important during the period under consideration in this chapter, it was a factor in Germany's later development. Finally, the German kings steadily pushed forward their eastern frontiers against the Slavs.

Like its neighbors to the west, the East Frankish kingdom during the period of Car-

An eleventh century amphibious military operation. The invasion of England by William the Conqueror, 1066. Transporting horses.

From the Bayeux Tapestry

North Sea

POMERANIA

Gnesen

POLAND

Breslau

MARCH OF THE BILLUNGS

NORTH MARCH

Hamburg

Bremen

Weser R.

Elbe R.

Oder R.

FRIESLAND

Utrecht

SAXONY

Brandenburg

Magdeburg

SAXON EAST MARCH

THURINGIA

THURINGIAN MARCH

LOWER

Cologne

Rhine R.

Aachen

LORRAINE

FRANCONIA

Frankfurt

Prague

BOHEMIA

MORAVIA

Trier

Mainz

UPPER

LORRAINE

NORDGAU

Danube R.

BAVARIAN

Meuse R.

ALSACE

Strassburg

SWABIA

Augsburg

Lechfeld

BAVARIA

EAST MARCH

Salzburg

FRANCE

Saône R.

Besancon

CARINTHIA

Drava R.

STYRIA

KINGDOM

CARNIOLA

HUNGARY

Rhone R.

Lyons

OF

Milan

LOMBARDY

MARCH OF VERONA

Venice

MARCH OF ISTRIA

Rhone R.

Po R.

CROATIA

BURGUNDY

(K. OF ARLES)

Genoa

Bologna

Ravenna

Arles

Florence

Arezzo

TUSCANY

PAPAL

Adriatic Sea

CORSICA

Tiber R.

STATES

SPOLETO

Rome

Benevento

**FEUDAL "ROMAN" EMPIRE
OF OTTO THE GREAT**

NAPLES

Salerno

olingian decline had become divided into a number of semi-independent principalities. At the time of the accession of Henry I "the Fowler" (918–936), the first of the Saxon dynasty, there were four major duchies—Saxony, Franconia, Swabia, and Bavaria. Later other areas, counties, duchies, and marches were added.[1] But Henry the Fowler, so named because the messenger sent to announce his election found him engaged in that traditional feudal amusement, was primarily interested in his own domain of Saxony. For the most part he left the other dukes alone, requiring only a recognition of his royal authority. To secure the frontiers of Saxony and Thuringia against Slavic and Magyar inroads, Henry established numerous fortified communities (*Bürgwärde*). His successors continued this practice and encouraged Germans to settle in the vicinity, thus laying the foundations not only of military security but of German colonization eastward. It was Henry's military reorganization which made possible on the Unstrutt River in 933 the first real victory over the invading Magyars.

Otto the Great (936–973) was even more successful both in protecting and in expanding the kingdom's frontiers. More forts were built by his subordinates in eastern Saxony and in the Slavic marches between the Elbe and the Oder. The northern frontier was pushed forward at the expense of the Danes and a new march of Schleswig created. The Slavic Czechs in Bohemia and Moravia proved sufficiently formidable to warrant a campaign led by the King, with the result that in 950 the Czechs recognized his suzerainty and promised him an annual tribute. Wherefore, the duchy of Bohemia, including the march of Moravia, became a feudal principality within the German kingdom. One of Otto's most signal triumphs was the decisive defeat of the Magyars near Augsburg in the battle of Lechfeld (955).

Otto the Great, not content with a the-oretical suzerainty over the East Frankish kingdom, made an important contribution to governmental policy in Germany through his alliance with the church. Bishops and archbishops were given lands and immunities. Some even acquired the jurisdiction of counts. Obviously this policy could succeed only so long as the crown actually controlled the episcopate. Under Otto and his immediate successors this was the case. Bishops were formally elected, but royal nominees were commonly chosen. As a result, tenth-century German bishops were usually loyal feudal servants of the king. They attended court, administered royal lands, gave the king lodging on his travels, and acted as diplomats and regents. They supplied the bulk of the king's troops, and some defied the canon law of the church and appeared in person with their levies.

The successes of Otto in consolidating the German realm must be viewed in the light of his imperial designs. He regarded himself as successor to the Carolingians and, after the manner of his illustrious predecessors, he interested himself in the affairs of Italy. In north and central Italy, originally part of the middle kingdom created by the sons of Louis the Pious,[1] no stable regime had emerged and feudalism degenerated into anarchy. South of Rome the political power was divided among the semi-independent duchies of Spoleto and Benevento and the Byzantine Empire. The peninsula was ripe for foreign intervention.

The occasion for Otto's first transalpine venture was a combination of personal rivalries. Adelaide, widow of one of two candidates for the Italian throne, was imprisoned by the rival. Her brother Conrad, king of Arles (the combined kingdom of Provence and Burgundy), had already fallen under the protection of Otto. On his first expedition across the Alps (951), Otto secured from the Italian king the recognition of his own overlordship and the hand of Adelaide as well.

Some years later Pope John XII was the victim of the now chronic anarchy in Rome. Otto responded to his appeal, and on this occasion, supported by a formidable army, he assumed the Italian crown and in 962

---

[1] Aside from the eastward expansion and the incorporation of northern Italy which will be described below, the principal additions were Lorraine, taken from the West Frankish kingdom in the reign of Henry I, and (1033) the former kingdom of Burgundy (Arles) which was willed to Conrad II by a king who died childless.

[1] See above, p. 122.

received an imperial coronation at the hands of the Pope. Thus Otto, as Charlemagne before him, assumed the title of emperor, a title which gave greater sanction to his extensive annexations. The danger that a hostile prince might reign in Italy was obviated and a tradition set for his successors. Somewhat later Otto suppressed an insurrection of the Romans, had John deposed by a subservient synod, and secured the election of his own secretary as pope. This success in controlling the papacy and central Italy was not duplicated in the south. But Otto, like Charlemagne, entered into negotiations with Constantinople, and it was agreed that his eldest son, the future Otto II, should marry a Byzantine princess, Theophano.

In the main, Otto's successors were guided by the policies which he had inaugurated. The church remained an important element in government, and imperial domination over the popes was strengthened. Otto III (983–1002), an exceptionally imperially-minded ruler, actually appointed a pope. This was the famous scholar and teacher, Gerbert of Aurillac, who took the title of Sylvester II.

Conrad II (1024–1039), first of the Salian (Franconian) line of German kings and Roman emperors, introduced an important innovation in domestic policy by supporting lesser nobles against the great dukes and by recognizing their fiefs as hereditary. Careful not to deplete the crown lands and rights any more than was absolutely necessary, he made most of his grants to *ministeriales*. These were servants of the monarchy—officials and men-at-arms drawn from the non-noble classes—who, it was hoped, might prove especially loyal and devoted to the King's interests. Finally, Henry III (1039–1056) successfully controlled the magnates in Germany, exercised wide authority in ecclesiastical matters, and in 1046 had three rival claimants to the papal throne deposed and his own candidate, a German bishop, nominated. A second imperial nominee was the reforming Pope Leo IX.

Both the political and the ecclesiastical authority exercised by the German Roman Emperors down to the time of Henry III was destined to pass. Henry III was succeeded by a son, Henry IV (1056–1106),

then only six years old, and the period of his minority afforded an opportunity for rapacious nobles to seize whatever royal property and rights they could. Even more significant was the revived prestige and authority of the papacy, for by the middle of the eleventh century, as subsequent pages will explain, the papacy had become strong enough openly to condemn imperial control over the German and Italian episcopate. Obviously such a challenge to royal domination over the church was an attack upon the very foundations of imperial policy. The resultant struggle between empire and papacy halted, at least temporarily, the consolidation of the medieval German kingdom. The details of this controversy will be explained presently.

Meanwhile Otto the Great attempted to imitate Charlemagne's cultural work, as he did his political. He showed zeal in monastic reorganization and in reconstituting libraries. His son and especially his brother, Archbishop Bruno, were both men of letters. And one of his subjects was the remarkable Saxon nun, Hroswita, who wrote Latin poetry and a series of prose dialogues in the style of Terence. Gerbert (*d.* 1003), archishop of Reims and director of its cathedral school, was a friend and confidant of Otto and later became Pope Sylvester II. Gerbert was an accomplished classicist who apparently acquired, from a visit to Barcelona, some acquaintance with Arabic scientific lore. He did special work in mathematics and knew the Hindu numerals one to nine. But the fact that he wrote a treatise on the old Roman system of calculating with an abacus, two hundred years after the Arabs had begun to employ the decimal system and the zero for calculation, indicates the backwardness of scientific knowledge in the western Europe of his time.

By the eleventh century, political and social conditions were again sufficiently settled in western Europe to render possible a greater and broader intellectual revival. Modern scholars have long been accustomed to the term "twelfth century renaissance." The foundations for that achievement were laid in the eleventh century and were particularly marked in the liberal arts, and in law, medicine, and architecture.

At Salerno, in southern Italy, was a center of medical studies which had already won considerable renown as the foremost institution of its kind in Europe. In northern Italy, there developed at Bologna, toward the end of the eleventh century, a center of legal studies, inspired by renewed interest in Justinian's *Digest*, while at the same time Guido of Arezzo produced some remarkable writings on musical theory. In Italy, too, there was considerable secular education.

In France, the liberal arts newly flourished, along with philosophy, theology, and poetry. Here, the intellectual primacy, once held by monastic establishments, was now passing to the cathedral schools. Of the latter, those of Orleans, Chartres, Reims, and Liege were especially prominent, while that of Paris was soon to become the seat of a great university. Fulbert, bishop of Chartres (1007–1029), was an accomplished and versatile scholar, poet, and man of letters, as well as a noted teacher. In Normandy were educated two scholarly archbishops of Canterbury—Lanfranc (*d.* 1089) and St. Anselm (*d.* 1109)—the latter becoming one of the great medieval philosophers.

C. Kingdoms in Northern and Southern Europe

The expansive capacities inherent in feudalism contributed to the formation of new frontier states. Feudal expansion exhibited certain general characteristics. Among the noble classes, love of adventure and the perennial desire for new fiefs sent many young men to distant lands. This often resulted in the adoption by adventurous knights of news ways and a new nationality. Spain and Sicily provided careers for many a French and Norman knight. The gradual expansion of the eastern German frontier, on the other hand, was the joint achievement of knight, peasant, and missionary. Here was a real colonization, the movement of a whole people into a new area. Medieval expansion was often associated with war against the infidel, especially against the Moslem. Pilgrimage to distant shrines was also an inspiration. One of the best illustrations of feudal

expansion is the formation of medieval Spain. There, not only did the church encourage the war against the Moslem conquerors of the peninsula, but the land re-won offered great opportunities for new fiefs. Moreover, at Compostela was the immensely popular shrine of St. James (*Santiago de Compostela*). From every part of France came a horde of knights eager for combat. Medieval Spain was almost as much the achievement of French knights as of the Spanish themselves.

Unfortunately, the Christian armies lacked cohesion; and despite the prodigies of individual valor on the part of men like Rodrigo Diaz whose exploits won him everlasting, if legendary, fame as *El Cid Campeador*,[1] progress was slow. Toledo, the heart of "new" Castile, was taken in 1085. But not until the third and fourth decades of the twelfth century were the boundaries of Castile and Portugal pushed farther south.

The Spanish territory thus re-won was not united. In some respects it resembled feudal France, except that there were four or five separate kingdoms instead of the great fiefs. By 1100 Aragon, Navarre, Leon, and Castile were distinct, and the county of Portugal was soon to become independent. Moreover, French feudal influences which were so important a factor in the reconquest of Spain remained significant in its later political and cultural development.

Southern Italy, also an ideal spot for the activities of restless knights-errant, became the special preserve of Normans. Nominally, southern Italy comprised a few small principalities formerly under Lombard suzerainty: Apulia and Calabria, loosely held by the Byzantine emperors; and the city-republics of Gaeta, Naples, and Amalfi. The entire area was subject to the forays of Saracens who controlled Sicily, Sardinia, and Corsica. Moreover, the presence at Monte Gargano of a shrine to St. Michael, whom the Normans as Christians had adopted as a patron saint, was an added attraction. For pilgrimage demands travel, and travel leads to adventure.

By 1030 one Norman knight had already won a fief near Naples. The news spread, and more Normans arrived, of whom the

[1] On the medieval Spanish epic *El Cid*, see below, p. 252.

The fourteenth century gateway of Battle Abbey. The abbey was established originally by William the Conqueror on the site of the battle of Hastings, 1066.

Courtesy British Information Services, New York

most prominent were the many sons of Tancred of Hauteville. Soon Robert Guiscard (*d.* 1085) and his brother Roger (*d.* 1101), the most famous of twelve brothers, were well on the way toward the conquest of the entire southern part of the peninsula and were even planning an invasion of Saracen Sicily.

Robert's successes eventually brought him into conflict with the papacy. Pope Leo IX led a military expedition against the Normans, who badly defeated him and took him prisoner. A later pope, Nicholas II, in 1059 officially recognized the Norman conquests by formally investing Robert with southern Italy as a papal fief. In addition, the projected conquest of Sicily received the papal blessing as a sort of holy war. It was completed by Roger in 1091. Thus both parties gained—the papacy, an ally; and the Normans, official sanction for their depredations. In the course of time the two states of southern Italy, Naples and Sicily, were united as a kingdom destined to be one of the more important in medieval Europe.

Another famous accomplishment of the Normans was the conquest of England by Duke William (1066). Pre-Norman or Saxon England had never achieved a real stability and had only rarely been blest with a ruler of the stature of Alfred the Great (871–901) who dealt with the Danish invaders. As late as the eleventh century, English weakness was a source of tempta-

tion for strong neighbors in Scandinavia and Normandy. For a generation England was part of a Danish empire which also included Sweden and Norway and which was capably governed by King Knut (1016–1035). Knut was a civilized, Christian ruler, not a semi-barbarian Viking. When Harold, the "last of the Saxons," came to the throne in 1066, he was faced with two invading armies, one from Norway led by Harold Hardrada and one from the continent under Duke William of Normandy. Although Harold worsted Hardrada, he went down at Hastings before William.

The Norman conquest is an event of capital importance in English history, for William's occupation of England profoundly affected every aspect of English life. Especially did it bring England more closely within the orbit of western Christendom. These things will become clearer in subsequent chapters.

The temporary incorporation of England into a Danish empire is evidence of important political progress in Scandinavia. During the great period of Norse expansion a considerable degree of stabilization had been achieved under the growing influence of European civilization. As we have seen, Christianity had been introduced and the church organized. During the tenth century and after, three Christian kingdoms begin to. appear as distinct. Harold Bluetooth (*d.* 985) boasted of the reduction of all

Denmark. And by the early eleventh cen-tury, Denmark under King Knut was strong enough temporarily to subdue Norway and even England.

Harold Fairhair's trumph over rival nobles (about 872) began the development of a Norwegian monarchy which gained strength under the saintly King Olaf (1016–1029). Moreover, Norway managed to maintain a kind of overseas empire. Olaf received the submission of the colonies in the Faroes, Shetlands, and other islands off the Scottish coast. Contacts with Greenland were kept up, and the Icelanders, though enjoying political independence, were origi-nally of Norwegian stock and were given equal rights with natives when in Norway. Sweden also seems to have emerged as a separate kingdom by the year 1000. Thus the homeland of the Viking marauders became an integral part of Europe.

D. Eastern Frontier Kingdoms

In the period after Charlemagne's death, Slavs and Magyars had pressed against the frontiers of the East Frankish kingdom. By the middle of the tenth century the tables were turned and the historic German *drang nach osten,* or eastward pressure, was acquir-ing a real impetus. As a consequence, the states which were forming in east-central Europe often developed cohesion as they resisted the German advance.

Slavic resistance was not uniformly suc-cessful. The early development of the Czechs had been associated with the ancient princi-pality of Moravia. It was there that the missionaries, Cyril and Methodius, had in-troduced the Slavonic liturgy.[1] But after the Magyar invasions and the fall of old Moravia, Bohemia replaced Moravia as the Czech political center of gravity. German and western ecclesiastical influences in-creased and Latin replaced Slavonic in the church's liturgy. Eventually, as we have already remarked, it was the des-tiny of this young West Slavic principality to become an hereditary fief of the Holy Roman Empire.[2] Yet Czech culture proved

[1] On Cyril and Methodius, see pp. 87–88, 151.

[2] The suzerainty of Otto the Great was recog-nized in 950. See above, p. 143.

stubbornly resistant to German pressure. The political authority of the duke within his own domain was, for that age, extensive and the imperial administrative system was never introduced into Bohemia.

The West Slavs who inhabited the basin of the Warthe and Vistula rivers were more successful in maintaining their independ-ence. Under the Piast dynasty (960–1370) a loose confederation of tribes was organized into a duchy of Poland, which eventually became the most powerful state in east-central Europe. The shrewd Miesko I mar-ried a Czech princess and accepted western Christianity (966) at the hands of Czech rather than German clergy. A native Polish bishopric was established at Poznan and, somewhat later, Poland was taken under the special protection of the Holy See. Bole-slav the Brave (992–1025), in wars against Germans, Czechs, and Russians, extended the frontiers of Poland to include eastern Galicia, Silesia, and some territory beyond the Carpathians. His religious policy also tended to confirm the independence of the young state. Gniezno, shrine of the dis-tinguished Adalbert of Prague who won a martyr's crown as a missionary to the Prus-sians (997), was made an archepiscopal see. Shortly before his death, Boleslav was crowned king, thus signalizing the establish-ment of a new and promising Slavic king-dom.

Meanwhile, the Magyars were also laying the foundations of an independent state. Under their early rulers, of whom St. Stephen (997–1038) was the most famous, the Hungarians had adopted Catholic Chris-tianity and a settled mode of life. The ecclesiastical organization was kept care-fully free of German domination. And the crown with which Stephen assumed the title of king was blessed by the pope, Syl-vester II.

Farther east, the Russian Slavs were mak-ing remarkable progress, particularly in the principality of Kiev, which was established by the Norsemen. A development of the first importance was the marriage of Prince Vladimir to a Byzantine princess and his conversion to Christianity (988). There-after, with the growing influence of the church, Byzantine cultural influences per-meated Russia. Under Yaroslav (1016–

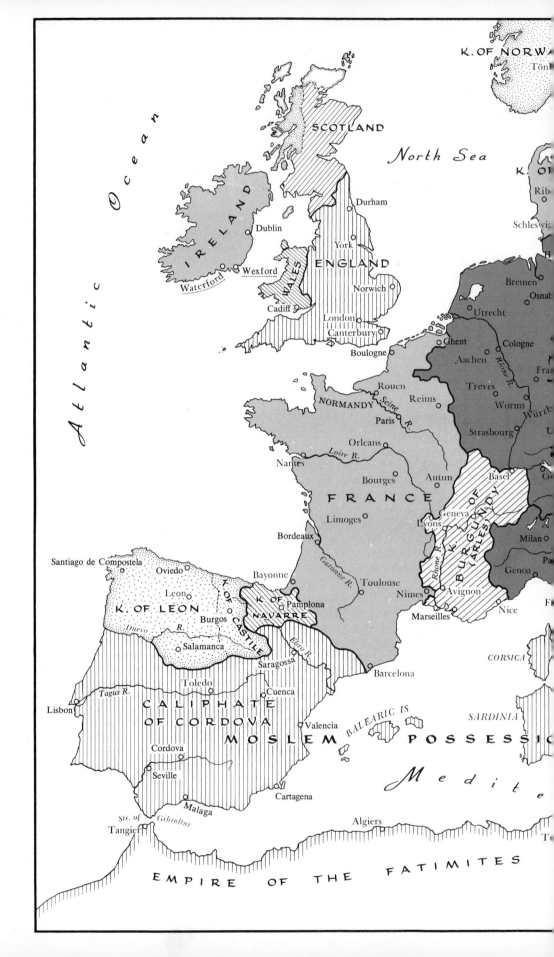

K. OF NORW...
Tön...

K. OF ...
Rib...
Schleswi...

SCOTLAND

North Sea

Durham

York

ENGLAND

Norwich

Bremen
Osnab...

Utrecht

Ghent
Cologne

Aachen

Treves

Worms

Würzb...

Fra...

O
c
e
a
n

A
t
l
a
n
t
i
c

IRELAND

Dublin

Wexford
Waterford

WALES

Cadiff

London
Canterbury

Boulogne

Rouen
Reims

Seine R.

NORMANDY

Paris

Strasbourg

Rhine R.

Orleans

Loire R.

Nantes

Bourges

Autun

Basel

FRANCE

Limoges

Lyons

Geneva

K. OF BURGUNDY (ARLES)

Milan

Pa...

Genoa

Bordeaux

Garonne R.

Toulouse

Nimes

Avignon

Nice

Marseilles

Rhône R.

CORSICA

Santiago de Compostela

Oviedo

Bayonne

Leon

K. OF LEON

K. OF CASTILE

K. OF NAVARRE

Pamplona

Burgos

Duero R.

Salamanca

Ebro R.

Saragossa

Barcelona

Toledo

Cuenca

SARDINIA

Tagus R.

Lisbon

CALIPHATE OF CORDOVA

MOSLEM

BALEARIC IS

POSSESSIO...

Cordova

Valencia

Seville

Cartagena

Medite...

Malaga

Str. of Gibraltar

Algiers

Tangier

T...

EMPIRE OF THE FATIMITES

EUROPE ABOUT 1000 A.D.

Scale in miles

0   100   200   300

1054) the state of Kiev attained the zenith of its power. A thriving commercial metropolis, second only to Constantinople in eastern Europe, it was noted especially for its churches. St. Sophia and the many other edifices, richly adorned with frescoes and mosaics, rank among the finest examples of medieval Byzantine art. Unfortunately, the brilliant promise of eleventh-century Kiev was not to be fulfilled, for in the period following Yaroslav's death the state was divided among the various branches of the old Kievan dynasty. Medieval Russia suffered from chronic political division.

The Byzantine orientation, so noticeable in old Russian culture, was also characteristic of the Serbs and other southern Slavs who were separated from their northern brethren by the intrusion of the Magyars.

There were exceptions, however. The inhabitants of Croatia-Dalmatia, close to the old dividing line between the east and west parts of the Roman Empire, remained within the orbit of Western Christendom. First conquered by the Franks, Croatia became a kingdom when in 924 Tomislav accepted a crown from the pope. In 1102 Croatia joined with Hungary, thus firmly establishing its western cultural orientation.

E. Political and Cultural Revival in the Byzantine Empire

The Byzantine Empire never entirely recovered from the disasters of the seventh century. Some territories—Egypt and North Africa—were permanently lost. Others—Syria, Macedonia, and Thrace—were regained only temporarily. The political recovery of the ninth and tenth centuries did not restore the Empire's former boundaries. It was, however, of great importance, and since it was accompanied by a revival of the Greek classical tradition and a marked advance in art and architecture, it had vital significance for the cultural history of Europe at large.

Military stabilization began to be reestablished under the soldier emperors of the eighth century. It was the Emperor Leo III (717–741) who completed the reorganization of the Empire into the *themes*, in which the civil and military jurisdictions were combined. The army was recruited from the peasants of the eastern provinces.

It was also Leo III who launched the campaign of Iconoclasm against church images.[1] We have hitherto treated of Iconoclasm as a factor in the political separation of east and west, but it should be emphasized here that it caused a severe upheaval in Byzantine society. Temporarily, Emperor, army, and eastern provinces were pitted against the patriarch of Constantinople and the monks. Iconoclasm was really a form of puritanism not uncommon in oriental culture, which disparaged the material element in life and denied its capacity, as in the case of images, to represent the divine and supernatural. As a consequence, and this is more pertinent to the present discussion, when the Byzantine church outlawed Iconoclasm at the second council of Nicaea (787), a notable artistic revival was made possible.

Emperors of the Macedonian dynasty (867–1054) carried the military recovery further. The advance of the Bulgars was first halted, and finally the Bulgar "empire" was conquered and annexed (1018). Thus a portion of the Danube frontier was for a time restored. During the tenth century the Russians of Kiev under their Norse rulers were becoming formidable north of the Black Sea. It was significant that in 988 Emperor Basil II made a treaty with Prince Vladimir of Kiev whereby the latter agreed to become Christian and to furnish the Emperor with 6,000 troops—the famous "Varangian guard." Also during the tenth and eleventh centuries, Byzantine armies re-won ground from the Moslems in Syria, along the upper Tigris-Euphrates valley, in Crete and Cyprus, and in southern Italy. Antioch was a particularly important reconquest (909).

As is so often the case, political success was accompanied by cultural revival. After the defeat of iconoclasm, literature and art were predominantly religious, but they were less exclusively monastic than they had previously been. There was also a rebirth of secular learning marked by a renewed interest in the ancient Greek masters. The university of Constantinople was reëstablished in 863. Men like Michael Psellus, who revived

---

[1] See above, pp. 90–91, 117.

Platonic philosophy, and Constantine Porphyrogenitus, author of the *Book of Ceremonies*, a manual of court ceremonial, forecast, in their literary tastes and their conscious imitation of classical style, the humanists of the later Italian renaissance. This relatively early revival at Constantinople was not one of great creative genius, but it represented an achievement far in advance of anything then extant in western Europe.

Art, released from the restriction of iconoclasm, exhibited a trend toward naturalism. Painting, ivory carving, illuminated manuscripts, even ecclesiastical mosaics, all showed Hellenic tendencies. Tenth- and eleventh-century Byzantine architecture was less clearly classical, except in the practice of decorating exteriors, porticos, and facades.

Unfortunately, the Byzantine revival was short lived, for the later eleventh century brought, especially at the hands of the Seljuk Turks, new defeats from which the Empire never fully recovered. Yet the "Byzantine Renaissance" of the ninth and tenth and early eleventh centuries profoundly affected the cultural development of many other peoples who came within the sphere of its influence. A few illustrations will make this clear.

Even before the reduction of the Bulgarian "empire" and its incorporation into the Byzantine system, the Bulgarians, though constantly menacing Byzantine frontiers, had developed an admiration for the higher culture of the Byzantines. This was especially true after the Bulgarian Tsar Boris, by becoming Christian in 866, had opened the way for Byzantine influence. Moreover, most of the southern as well as western Slavic peoples (and the Bulgarians were already noticeably Slavic in their speech and customs) were indebted to the civilizing and Christianizing work of Saints Cyril and Methodius. These two famous missionaries had labored in the second half of the ninth century (862–885), especially in Bohemia and Moravia.[1] But the fact that most of the Slavic Christians adopted the "Cyrillic" alphabet, an adaptation of Greek letters to the Slavonic tongue, is proof of the much wider influence of Cyril and Methodius. The late ninth and early tenth centuries witnessed in Bulgaria the formation, through translations from the Greek, of a Christian Slavonic literature which was passed on to other Balkan Slavs and to the Russians.

Byzantine influence greatly increased in Russia during the eleventh century, following the conversion of Vladimir. Greek bishops and missionaries taught the Russians the Slavonic script and brought with them the architectural and artistic traditions of Constantinople. And although the churches and monasteries of Kiev with their Byzantine mosaics are particularly famous, the more northern centers of Novgorod and Moscow, later to become the heart of Russian life, felt the influence of this higher culture.

Direct Byzantine influence in western Europe was significant, though less pronounced than in the east. This was the result partly of the Frankish conquest of the exarchate of Ravenna and the Norman conquest of southern Italy, and partly of a growing cultural and religious rift between eastern and western Christendom.[2] Nevertheless, the Byzantine renaissance was influential throughout Dalmatia and northeastern Italy, and in southern Italy through the Greek-speaking monasteries of Calabria. Byzantine art, as exemplified by St. Mark's at Venice, became in time an inspiration for artists and architects throughout the west.

Such was the Europe of the eleventh century. Though divided politically, it was beginning to manifest signs of governmental consolidation. And this was accompanied by recovery in both economic and religious spheres. To these we shall now turn.

[1] See above, pp. 87–88.

[2] This will be explained later. See below, p. 167.

A tenth century bell tower. A thirteenth century copy of a tenth century Spanish manuscript which substituted, at the right, figures of laymen with drawing instruments for the original monks.

CHAPTER 13

Economic Conditions Under Feudal Society

A. Commerce and Industry in the Early Feudal Period

In the preceding pages we have noted the predominantly rural character of western European life in the Carolingian age. Such trade as survived was mostly, though by no means exclusively, local; and the many markets for agricultural goods or the products of domain industry were patronized by farm folk. But some necessities and a few luxuries came to the manors from the outside. Salt, iron, grindstones, salt fish, to mention only a few items, were seldom procurable locally. Hence, these and the few oriental luxury products—like spices, pepper, silks, incense, enamels, and ivories which the age sought and could afford—had to be provided by professional traveling merchants.

For some time transportation difficulties were well nigh insuperable. Roads were incredibly bad because no public authority existed with sufficient sense of responsibility to repair them. It was often necessary for monasteries, local benevolent associations, or groups of merchants to repair such roads and bridges as remained. Brigandage was common. And almost equally vexatious were the innumerable local tolls levied by rapacious lords at every crossroad or bridge. Not without reason did the church include merchants in the protection it sought to extend by the Peace of God.[1]

Such a picture of Europe's commercial

---

[1] See above, pp. 134, 137.

life is not complete, for the recovery in political life which has been described was paralleled by a corresponding economic growth. Slower in some areas than in others, but everywhere marked by a steady rise in population, this economic expansion which commenced in the tenth century gradually created a new Europe, a Europe different both geographically and economically from the ancient Roman world. Although remaining predominantly agrarian, the New Europe was characterized by a notable increase in the volume of commerce and industry and in the number and size of towns. It is the beginning of this process in the tenth and eleventh centuries which will be described in the present chapter.

The Byzantine Empire never suffered the economic fate of the west either in the fifth or the ninth century. Despite the loss of Syria and Egypt, its naval and military power had preserved Constantinople and (until the eleventh century) Asia Minor. Further, although the Moslems took Sicily, the towns of southern Italy—such as Naples, Amalfi, and Bari—continued for a while under Byzantine sovereignty. And when the southern Italian towns were eventually taken by the Normans in the eleventh century, Byzantine commercial contacts with the west were maintained in Venice. For that city, founded on the islands and lagoons at the head of the Adriatic by refugees from the Germanic invaders, was destined by nature to live from commerce. It would be hard to find a more striking contrast than that between commercial Venice and agrarian Europe of that day. Venice was never incorporated into the Carolingian state or into the Holy Roman Empire. Instead, it continued to develop under Byzantine auspices. And when Byzantine sovereignty gradually disappeared, Venice was left an independent republic.

The Venetians did not confine their commercial operations to Constantinople. Undeterred by religious scruples, they made contacts with the Moslems of Africa and Syria, drove a lucrative traffic in slaves, and even sold to Moslems the timber and iron which were undoubtedly used against their fellow Christians. By 1100 Venice, already a great sea power, had mastered the Adriatic and established trading posts all along the coasts of Dalmatia and Greece. In fact, in 1082 the Byzantine Emperor Alexius granted the Venetians privileges and exemptions for trade in his territory which made them a group more favored than his own subjects nearer home.

Ultimately, Venetian enterprise was imitated by cities on the west coast of Italy. Perhaps less exclusively inspired by the love of gain, the Pisans and Genoese required the additional inspiration of religious faith. Their expansion was also an attack on the infidels of Sardinia and north Africa. The Pisan conquest of Mahdia in Tunis (1087) was a crusade in which the Bishop of Modena took part. The cathedral of Pisa was built to commemorate this success. Meanwhile, with Genoese help, the Pisans also established themselves early in the eleventh century in Corsica and Sardinia. Other Mediterranean seaboard towns, including Marseille, were likewise active in this early period.

The commercial and maritime civilization which was emerging during the eleventh century in the Mediterranean had its counterpart in the north. The Norse, it will be recalled, had made contact with the Black Sea and Byzantium and with the Caspian where they met Jewish and Moslem merchants from Bagdad. Honey, furs, and slaves from the north were exchanged for spices, wines, silks, and other luxuries from the orient. Quantities of Arabic and Byzantine coins have been found in Russia. The island of Gothland in the Baltic off the

coast of Sweden became a great depot for Scandinavian-Oriental trade, and even greater quantities of Greek and oriental coins have been unearthed there. Moreover, as the three Scandinavian kingdoms developed politically, and as England, particularly in the tenth century, increased its stability, the entire northern area, extending from the British Isles to Russia, moved commercially forward.

It should also be noted that northwestern Europe, especially Flanders, was an early center not only for trade but of a native textile industry. Flemish woolen cloth was everywhere in demand, even in the east. As an article of export, it helped in some measure to restore the balance of east-west trade which was generally unfavorable to the west. As early as the tenth century it proved necessary for the Flemings to import wool from England, their own supply being insufficient. There resulted an economic bond between the Low Countries and England which was subsequently to have important political repercussions.

Also, the quantity of mineral output commenced to increase. Certain areas of north, central, and eastern Europe beyond the old Roman frontiers began to produce not only gold and silver, but iron. The discovery of the Rammelsberg silver mine (960) near Goslar in Saxony might be cited as an example.

Along with the increasing volume of trade and industry, and in part the cause of it, was the increase in the number and size of town communities, that is, those containing a population living by trade and industry, even in inland areas. In Germany which, as we have seen, early enjoyed a measure of political stability, this phenomenon is noticeable even in the tenth century. Owing doubtless to a slower political development this primitive urbanism, outside of such Roman municipalities as had survived, was not common in France or elsewhere before the eleventh century.

B. Agricultural Revival

Urban growth, even of a limited extent, demanded expanded agricultural production. So also, of course, did an expanding population whether in country or town. As

The close association of town and country. Sheep under the walls of Avila, Spain. Sheep-raising has been an important part of Spanish economy since early times.

Courtesy Spanish National Tourist Department, New York

a consequence there followed systematic efforts to effect a more rational use of the land. These took two forms.

First, certain technical improvements were devised. In part these antedated the population rise, and resulted from an initial decline in agricultural man-power caused by the destructive invasions. Slavery, which had persisted into Carolingian times, largely disappeared and with it the human motor-force it supplied. It is noteworthy, for example, that the water-mill for grinding grain, known but not exploited by the Romans, now came into greater use.

Horse-shoes, horse-collar, and tandem harness increased the availability of animals for farm work. As agrarian exploitation moved northward into damper climates and heavier soils, it became necessary to invent a heavier wheeled plow with mould board. It was also discovered that in large areas of northern Europe certain grains could be planted in the fall and harvested early in summer. Romans had commonly employed a two-field rotation, one field being left fallow each year to recover its fertility. In the damper northern areas a three-field rotation (including a fall planting) was possible and therefore correspondingly greater annual yield. Experiments were tried with three, four, and five fields, and, in places where soil was plentiful but poor, a continuous shift of the arable land was made as soon as the soil became unusable.

The second important change in western Europe's agrarian economy was the increase in the total area under cultivation. Begun toward the end of the tenth century and gathering momentum in the eleventh, this phenomenon revolutionized what might be described as the agricultural map of Europe. Though not discernible on ordinary political maps, except those of sufficient scale to show the multiplication of villages, the changes were as important to the history of Europe as the shift of national boundaries.

How were these changes accomplished? A considerable extension of eventually usable land was obtained by diking along the lowlands of the northwest coasts of the Low Countries. Monasteries often pioneered in this enterprise. Comparable techniques were employed in draining swamp areas along the eastern frontiers of Germany. Indeed, skilled Flemings were sometimes employed to further the work. By far the greatest amount of new land was brought under cultivation by systematic deforestation. Abbeys, enterprising landlords, individual peasants, all joined in this pioneer work. Into a new area first came the loggers, charcoal-burners, and the like, who moved on when their work was done. Then came the peasant settlers, often known as *hospites*, and usually given privileged or free status. Although much deforestation took place along actual frontiers which were continually expanding, a great deal was done within the already existing kingdoms. Accordingly, much of what was once forest became a land of alternate woodland and clearing. There persisted, for some two or three centuries, what might be described as frontier conditions which constantly reacted on the older or less recently settled areas.

Finally, it should be noted that in addition to the divergencies between the older southern regions and the more recently exploited north and west, innumerable variations of local custom and differences of soil and climate dictated widely varying farming methods. What is suitable to fertile plains will not suffice in mountain regions. Viticulture, sheep and cattle raising, require techniques different from those for the cultivation of cereal crops. It is in the light of all these possible and actual differences that we must now consider the predominant agricultural institution of western Europe in the feudal age, the seigneurial regime.

C. The Seigneurial Regime

The seigneurial regime [1] may be loosely defined as the exploitation of land by a landlord (*seigneur*) or by a single institution such as an abbey, with the aid of a dependent peasantry over whom he (or it) exercised certain governmental and legal functions. For like the feudal relation between lord and vassal, the relation between seigneur and peasant was political and legal as well as economic. It was, in short, a unit of government as well as an economic institution. The seigneurial regime emerged in the post-Carolingian age, when, as a consequence of invasion and general turbulence, the large Carolingian domains were mostly destroyed. Parts of these older domains were delegated to or appropriated by individual landlords and the few remaining free villages or small free farms were absorbed. The

Page from a twelfth century English bestiary (book of animals, etc.) Showing a "saw fish" and a contemporary single-masted ship.

Courtesy Pierpont Morgan Library, New York

system, therefore, marks a further stage in the development of individualized, smaller-scale farming which, it will be recalled, had existed even in the Carolingian period.

Students of medieval economy have found so many different types of peasant community that they have been unwilling to admit that there is such a thing as a "typical" settlement. Speaking from a territorial standpoint, and allowing for many variations, it is possible, however, to distinguish two main types of settlement, the village and the hamlet. The former was a nucleus of houses with fields, often divided up into long narrow individual holdings, occupying a common area outside. It prevailed throughout most of northern and western Europe, the area of predominantly three-field cultivation. The hamlet, on the other hand, was commonly composed of houses with small plots nearby, and other, usually rectangular, fields outside; it was common in the south and in certain extremities of the northwest, for example in Wales, Scotland, and Brittany.

---

[1] The words manor or manorial regime are usually employed in describing English agrarian organization. A manor, however, signified a complex of relationships between peasants and landlord, and not necessarily a single farm community.

The property under the jurisdiction of seigneur or monastery might all be contiguous and form a single agrarian complex. But it was equally common for parts of villages or hamlets to be held by different lords. The seigneur, or the lord of the manor, to use the expression common in England, was the holder of a collection of rights and obligations owed him by the peasants possibly of one, but often of more than one, community, each separate from the others. Manifestly, it was also possible for a peasant to be obligated to more than one landlord.

Most of the peasants on whose labor the seigneurial exploitation depended were neither slaves nor entirely free. As slavery declined, so also the turbulence of the ninth century tended to reduce the status of the remaining free men. The latter did not disappear, but the typical peasant of the eleventh century was dependent legally and economically on his landlord, owed him services and taxes, and was usually called a serf.[1]

There were, in fact, many gradations of serfdom. Not all peasants, even on the same manor, paid precisely the same taxes or were required to do the same amount of work. Local arrangements of long standing dictated the individual relations of lord and serf. Gradations of manorial peasantry resulted from property. Although the average serf's holding in a manor's separate strips amounted to about thirty acres, many held more, some less. Thrift, inheritance, and marriage (as in fiefs) might expand a peasant's tenure over the years. A few peasants —the cotters—held no land and simply possessed a rude dwelling (cottage, cot) and perhaps a small kitchen garden. Their livelihood was almost entirely the result of labor for the lord. We must not neglect to mention the lord's household servants—the skilled craftsmen, millers, bakers, smiths,

carpenters, leather-workers, and the like— whose relations to the lord must have differed from those of the peasant who labored in the fields. There were also certain manorial offices held by men of servile status, such as the reeve, who supervised the manorial economy and prepared its annual accounts.

In general, the status of the peasants with regard to their lord, their rights as well as their obligations, and their relations with one another were regulated by long standing custom which had come, with the passing of years, to have the force of law. It is impossible to overestimate the importance of long established custom in medieval agrarian economy.

D. Peasant Obligations and Rights

Broadly speaking, every serf was dependent on his lord, and theoretically required to do whatever work and to pay whatever taxes the lord demanded. Actually, old customs set limits both to work and to taxes. Some lords were cruel, but most of them were sensible, hard-headed farm managers, who recognized that a starving serf was a poor farmhand. Although serfs could be sold off the manor, they could not of their own will leave it, and custom guaranteed that a serf's tenures were his to cultivate and hand down to his son, much as a vassal handed down his fief.[2]

A serf was valuable primarily because of the work he could do, secondarily for the taxes he could pay. Although there were many ways of regulating the serf's labor, a fairly widespread practice stipulated that a certain number of days, commonly three each week (week work), be given over to the lord's demesne, together with extra days (boon work) at especially busy times. Food and drink were often supplied by the lord on such occasions. In the village where open field cultivation prevailed, work was of necessity communal. Each peasant might hold his own land and enjoy its fruits, but, especially after the invention of the heavy plow, he had to pool such draft animals as he possessed with those of his fellow-peasants. Similarly, sowing and harvesting were found

---

[1] In England the term *villein* was more common, whereas in France the term *vilain* or *franc vilain* ordinarily meant freeman. The student should guard against associating modern connotations of "freedom" or "unfreedom" with medieval serfdom. The status of freeman and serf on a medieval estate did not differ greatly in actual practice and one was not necessarily superior to the other. Freedom of movement, legally conceded the freeman, could often not be denied a serf who chose to escape.

[2] Inheritance customs varied in different parts of Europe.

to be more effectively accomplished if all worked together. The up-keep of roads and bridges was also generally required of serfs. From military service, except in cases of siege or dire emergency, the serf was usually free. The feudal knights placed no high value on the military capacity of the peasant.

The payments expected of an average serf were many, but here again ancient custom and the stern school of experience limited the lord's caprice. The subject is too complicated to treat adequately here. We must content ourselves with a few illustrations. Since money was scarce, payments were usually made in produce, but as the volume of money in circulation increased in the later middle ages, it appears that manorial taxes were sometimes paid in coin.

Some dues grew out of the very conditions which governed manorial economy. If a serf's daughter married outside the manor, involving, at least potentially, a loss to the lord, a payment (*formariage*) was demanded. Marriages outside the manor had formerly been prohibited, but the church's insistence that families not be broken up helped to produce this compromise. A serf's son, on succeeding his father, paid an inheritance tax (*heriot*); and as a serf was not regarded as having the right to inherit movable property, his death might mean the loss to the lord of some of his chattels, possibly his best beast. *Chevage* (head tax) was occasionally levied, and *banalités* were payments resulting from the lord's monopoly over certain necessary services such as wine-press, oven, and mill. Fines imposed in the manorial court were also a source of revenue. And, finally, the peasant owed a tithe (tenth) to the local parish church.

Practically every manor had its church. The parish limits usually, though not always, corresponded with it. In some cases, a monastery had control of the local church and appointed a vicar (substitute). The parish priest had his little land, the *glebe*, along with the rest, and often, if he were a good sort and, as was frequently the case, peasant-born, he lent a hand in the village work. Many a faithful village priest, in addition to regular duties, gave advice, settled disputes, solaced the sorrowing, and

A shepherd depicted in a mid-thirteenth century French manuscript.

Courtesy Pierpont Morgan Library, New York

even gave the rudiments of an education to especially promising peasant lads. It is necessary to add, however, that few parish priests in the early middle age were themselves educated beyond the rudiments of their religion. Facilities for clerical education were woefully inadequate. The efforts of the church to improve this situation will be noted in subsequent chapters.

The peasant's life was undeniably hard. He worked from sunrise to sunset and returned to his little one-or-two-room thatched cottage. It may have lacked a wooden floor and been simply furnished with stools, table, and wooden couch with a straw mattress big enough for the whole family. Cattle were housed in adjacent out-buildings or at the end of one of the rooms. Primitive sanitation (in such matters, the nobles were not vastly superior) fostered disease, and pestilence spread rapidly. Fire was an ever present hazard and, once started in one cottage, could easily wipe out a whole village. Though probably adequate in quantity, the peasant's food was coarse in quality.

It would be a mistake to dwell over long on the hardships of the medieval peasant's life or to picture the medieval agricultural community as absolutely static. Not only did the increase of towns and new farming communities offer opportunities to venture-some peasants; their development reacted on the management of the older settlements. Even before 1100 a tendency is noticeable to commute services into fixed payments, and obligations into rents. This tendency was notably to increase in the later middle ages.

The Monastery Church at Cluny as it appeared before it was dismantled following the French Revolution.

CHAPTER 14

Religion and Society in the Feudal Age

An earlier chapter has indicated the grave problems which feudal decentralization presented for the church: lay control, often exercised for personal or family aggrandizement, over bishoprics and abbeys; the prevalence of simony; the widespread disregard of clerical celibacy which had come to be the rule in the west. It has also been remarked that the picture was not entirely bleak. It is now time to analyze the measures taken to remedy this situation, the church's part in the general renewal of society which characterized the tenth and eleventh centuries. Three aspects of this story will engage our attention: a monastic reform; the reorganization of the secular clergy and the elaboration of a machinery of centralization under the pope; the religious life of the laity and its relation to the renewed church.

A. Cluny and Monastic Reform

Owing perhaps to the shrewdness of a monastic notary, the charter of foundation granted in 910 to the abbey of Cluny in Burgundy guaranteed absolute independence in elections and in all internal affairs. The first Cluny monks devoted themselves to the strict observance of the Benedictine rule but with certain important modifications. Farm work was no longer a major part of the monk's day; it was carried on by peasants, some of them often living under a semi-monastic regime. Instead, the monastic community spent a longer time in the solemn chanting of the liturgy which now became the principal emphasis of the daily life. The Cluny idea spread to other daughter houses established by or adopted by monks from the original abbey. Unlike the typical Benedictine communities, these daughter houses maintained their connection with the mother house at Cluny, each being governed by a prior under the jurisdiction of the abbot of Cluny. Even when, in the course of a century or more, some three hundred Cluniac monasteries had been established in France, Burgundy, western Germany, Spain, and England, there still remained only one abbot. Inevitably the abbot of Cluny was an ecclesiastic of major importance and not a few were men of real distinction.

The growth of the Cluny movement was also significant in Europe's cultural development. The emphasis on liturgy stimulated in the succeeding years a notable development of ecclesiastical music, the chant. Since a larger proportion of Cluny monks were priests, an abbey church needed added chapels or side-altars. In the case of the abbey church at Cluny size was also a factor. And there was dedicated in 1130 the largest church in the west, one of the longest, indeed, ever constructed in the Christian world.[1]

---

[1] 187 meters. St. Peter's, including the vestibule, is about thirty feet longer. Owing to neglect the great church at Cluny collapsed early in the nineteenth century. From the ruins measurements have been taken and scale reconstructions made.

B. The Gregorian Reform

While it is undoubtedly true that the Cluny achievement affected other areas of the church's organization and that in the reform of the secular clergy and the papacy a markedly monastic spirit prevailed, the two developments were not the same. The more general ecclesiastical renewal has been called the Gregorian reform after Pope Gregory VII (1073–1085), its most zealous promoter. In many respects it was a radical, almost revolutionary, movement which stemmed from earlier efforts, some in north Italy, some in Lorraine, and which aimed at a total reorganization of Christian society.

With the appointment by Henry III of Pope Leo IX (1049–1054), a native of Lorraine and formerly bishop of Toul, this movement reached Rome, and it was in the company of Leo that the future Gregory, then known as Hildebrand, first joined the papal administration. Hildebrand was of humble Tuscan peasant stock. Although not particularly prepossessing in manner, appappearance, or voice, he was a man of indomitable will and genuine spirituality. Less intransigent, more diplomatic and flexible, and more patient, but no less dedicated, was Urban II, a Frenchman perhaps best known for his launching of the First Crusade. As reform proceeded, France was to become one of its major areas of support.

Under the auspices of such men, there were taken what have sometimes been considered the first steps in building the modern constitution of the church. Certainly for the first time since the invasions it was possible to begin to create an ecclesiastical constitution with the pope actually, not merely theoretically, at the head, and a governmental procedure supported by canon law. Certain of these initial measures may be mentioned here. It was stipulated by a decree of 1059, for example, that only the principal or "cardinal" clergy of the Roman district should elect the Pope. These cardinal clergy were specifically designated. The seven (later six) cardinal bishops of the suburban sees of Rome actually elected the pope. A somewhat larger number of cardinal priests and deacons, attached to the principal Roman churches, confirmed the election. The role of the "people," who according to ancient traditions were expected to participate, was reduced to mere "acclamation." Thus the interference of the Roman nobility was avoided. With regard to the emperor's rights in the matter, only those enjoyed by the existing ruler were admitted; nothing was conceded to his successors.

While Pope Leo personally traveled a great deal, his successors, notably, Gregory, relied increasingly on legates. Papal legates, usually cardinals clothed with full papal power, were sent everywhere to correct abuses, hold synods, enforce the canons against clerical marriage and simony, even to depose recalcitrant prelates.

Though imbued with the monastic spirit, the Gregorian reformers were not unmindful of the interests of the secular clergy. They supported a tendency on the part of many secular priests to associate themselves with others in communities which adopted a quasi-monastic rule, usually one associated with the name of St. Augustine. Clergy living in such a way were called canons, and their community, sometimes connected with a cathedral church, sometimes with a large town parish or "collegiate" church, was called a chapter.[1] This development helped to restore a spiritual prestige to the town clergy whose reputations had been somewhat tarnished partly as a consequence of their own shortcomings, partly by comparison with the monks.

C. The Church and the Laity

The measures just described were but the beginning of a task which was to occupy the church for centuries. Moreover, its purpose was the sanctification not merely of clerics and monks, but of the vast population of laymen. To understand the magnitude of this problem it will be well to consider briefly the state of lay religion in the feudal age. Owing to the scarcity of evidence any generalizations regarding the religious life of the agrarian or town popu-

---

[1] One organization of canons founded in 1120 at Premontré by St. Norbert became a new religious order, the Premonstratensians, devoted to the service of parishes.

Italian Romanesque architecture. Orvieto.

lation which comprised the majority of Christians must be tentative. But there were occasional demonstrations of considerable religious feeling, though often irrational and disorganized. Hermits, particularly in France, were not uncommonly the objects of popular veneration, and a number of popular preachers—not all of them orthodox—made their appearance. The cult of saints and martyrs, particularly those of local fame, and of their relics was a notable feature of popular religious life. Apparently the attempts to thwart feudal war and banditry and to punish the offenders against the peace sometimes enlisted the support of the peasantry. Many, indeed, were killed in the attempt. There was a disposition to criticize a clergy whose lives were deemed unworthy of their sacred calling. In short, there was among the lower orders of medieval society a religious as well as an eco-

nomic and social restlessness which in some instances was capable of leading to movements or "crusades" of some magnitude. And in some manner many of the humble folk managed to make pilgrimages to distant shrines.

Somewhat more clear are the religious aspirations of the nobility. Here the church had been at some pains to curb and, at least in part, to Christianize the innate warlike vigor of the typical feudal knight. This is the meaning of such institutions as the Peace and Truce of God and the religious element in chivalry. Knighthood, the status of the noble as a warrior, was originally a purely secular thing. The young squire, his training completed, received a simple accolade, or blow on the back of the neck, sometimes with the flat of a sword, from another knight. Thus he was admitted into the fellowship of the warrior class. But as ecclesiastical influence increased, the candidate spent the previous night in vigil before an altar on which his arms reposed. In the morning his arms were blest in an elaborate ritual, and he took a long and detailed oath symbolizing the ideals he hoped to live up to as a true Christian knight.

During the eleventh century bellicose tendencies were often channeled toward what was coming to be considered a "Holy War," the war against Islam. As early as 1063, for example, papal approbation was given to the expedition of French knights into Spain. Thus the already popular pilgrimage to Santiago de Compostela came to be associated with the great military offensive against the Moslems, the *Reconquista,* a movement by no means exclusively or even predominantly religious, but none the less manifesting a somewhat unsophisticated and enormously heroic sort of religious sentiment quite characteristic of the age.

All these emotions and aspirations, the typical melange of religious, political, and social ambitions, are dramatically and unforgettably expressed in the popular poetry of the time, the *chansons de geste,* composed in the language of northern France, the *langue d'oil.*[1] Originating in the eleventh century or before, many of these epics center around the figure of Charlemagne whose campaigns in Spain now appear in the guise of a great struggle with the Moslem world and who in the popular mind becomes a saint. Prodigious blows are given and taken in battles against countless thousands of Saracens. But battle is always preceded by religious ceremony, the blessing by the priest or by the emperor. Thus religious piety and bloody carnage are mingled together without discrimination. There is much emphasis on vassalage and feudal loyalty, but none on women or romantic love. All in all these epics let their readers and listeners see the Carolingian heroes perform as they would like to perform themselves.

The most famous of the *chansons de geste* is the *Song of Roland,* the story of a gallant but eventually unsuccessful rearguard action fought by Charlemagne's nephew, Roland, when he was ambushed in the Pyrenees by overwhelming thousands of Saracens. Although the story may have originated from an actual incident in Charlemagne's career, what little historical truth remains is highly colored to fit the tastes of later listeners. It must be read to be appreciated. One becomes acquainted in it with great characters of fiction: the knightly Roland; the traitor Ganelon; the fighting archbishop Turpin, who at one moment invokes the Deity, the next, "in the thick of the press, deals well more than a thousand buffets." [2]

Another aspect of the religious life of the upper feudal classes has already been mentioned, the widespread control of religious foundations by rulers and feudal magnates. This had involved, it will be recalled, the intrusion into ecclesiastical office of many men unfit for such duties, an alarming increase of simony, and the usage of lay investiture whereby a bishop was invested with the symbols of his jurisdiction by a layman. The continuance of lay participation in ecclesiastical affairs did not, however, always or necessarily lead to corrupt practices. Many nobles and not a few rulers regarded their religious responsibilities as a solemn obligation. So, for example, did the Emperor Henry III consider his interventions in papal affairs. As we have explained, contemporary opinion held the ruler to be a partly religious figure. And until the advent of the Gregorian reform there had been no consistent objection to lay investiture.[3]

Accordingly, when the Gregorian reformers came to regard the evils of lay intervention in church matters as outweighing the good, and concluded that lay investiture must be abolished, they were proposing a revolutionary reversal of current procedures and they were challenging the traditionally accepted religious character of kingship. These things became evident during the pontificate of Gregory VII in what has been called the "Investiture Controversy," for Gregory felt that lay investiture was the

---

[1] See below, p. 252.

[2] *The Song of Roland,* tr. by Isabel Butler, in the "Riverside Literature Series," No. 157, p. 77.

[3] The Emperor Henry II (1002–1024), who appointed and invested a considerable proportion of German bishops, is an officially canonized saint.

cause of much of the simony and corruption. The principal offender was the Emperor Henry IV who appears to have been more interested in the political aspects of lay control than in the improvement of the church. Thus the issue was squarely joined. Two men, equally resolved to uphold opposing positions on the matter of lay investiture, stood face to face.

D. The Investiture Controversy

In a famous synod held at Rome during the Lenten season of 1075, the Pope added to the now usual decrees against simony and clerical marriage the first outright prohibition of lay investiture. Henry disregarded the papal order. Moreover, when he received from the Pope a letter threatening excommunication and deposition,[1] he summoned a synod of German bishops (1076) who showed their loyalty to Henry by voting the deposition of the Pope.

Faced with such defiance, Gregory's only course was to carry out his threat of excommunication and deposition and to absolve all of Henry's subjects from their oath of fealty. All bishops who failed to make their peace with the Holy See were similarly placed under the ban of the church. Some submitted. A few, like Bishop Herman of Metz, braved the Emperor's wrath and supported the Pope throughout the entire bitter controversy. This first excommunication of an emperor not only frightened some of the bishops, but was eagerly seized upon by a large number of Henry's lay vassals as a religious sanction for rebellion against him. After consultation with Gregory's legates, the rebels demanded of Henry that he obtain absolution or forfeit their loyalty. The Pope was invited to cross the Alps and preside over a synod at Augsburg where Henry's position was to be discussed. Overjoyed at this apparent expression of loyalty, Gregory set out, stopping on the way at Canossa, the castle of a devoted friend, the Countess Matilda.

Henry's shrewdness did not fail in the

---

[1] Since no good Christian was supposed to associate with an excommunicated person, the deposition of such a ruler was a logical consequence.

crisis. Realizing that he must become reconciled to the church before he could hope to subdue his insurgent vassals, he decided to force the Pope's hand before the proposed council could meet. With a handful of followers he eluded his enemies, crossed the Alps in mid-winter, and appeared as a penitent before the Pope at Canossa. There, according to contemporary accounts, he appeared barefoot and without royal insignia on three successive days. At length, on the solicitation of those around him and doubtless much moved by this show of penitence, Gregory gave Henry absolution and reinstated him in his office.

This famous scene has been repeatedly cited as a symbol of the subjection of temporal to spiritual power. Henry's spectacular penitence does not tell the whole story. As events were to show, no permanent advantage was obtained by the Pope. Henry had now righted himself and was again the lawful sovereign, and his rebellious vassals were deprived of all justification for resistance. It soon became abundantly clear that Henry was returning to his old ways. Accordingly, nearly four years after Canossa, the Pope again excommunicated and deposed the Emperor.

Gregory's second sentence found Henry in a stronger position and in no mood for another public penance. The fortunes of the struggle began to go against the Pope. The archbishop of Ravenna was elected anti-pope as "Clement III" by the imperial faction. In 1081 the Emperor invaded Italy, and the year 1084 saw him in possession of Rome with the Pope besieged in the castle of St. Angelo. At this critical juncture Gregory called upon his vassal Normans of southern Italy for assistance. Robert Guiscard responded, but the Norman army was as much interested in sacking Rome as in rescuing the Pope. Since he was not safe elsewhere, Gregory went with them when they retired to the south. The imperialists were again masters of the Eternal City, and Gregory died at Salerno in 1085, a virtual prisoner of his rescuers.

Henry IV's victory over Gregory VII was a triumph over one pope, but not over the papacy. Gregory's successors carried on the struggle. And the added strength which the papacy gained as a result of the reforms

The Bury St. Edmunds Cross. Carved walrus-
ivory. English twelfth century.

*Courtesy the Metropolitan Museum of Art,
New York, The Cloisters Collection*

gradually began to tell. The last years of
Henry's reign were troubled by renewed
rebellions in which even his own son participated. And although Henry V continued his
father's policies and invaded Italy, he was
eventually defeated by his enemies and in
1122 was ready to negotiate.

The Concordat of Worms (1122) between Emperor and Pope permitted the
former to invest a new incumbent of a
bishopric with the symbols of temporal rule
only. Ring and crozier, symbolizing ecclesiastical jurisdiction, he was no longer to
bestow. Episcopal elections were to be conducted, in the manner then customary, by
the cathedral chapter. The emperor, however, was allowed to be present and to
decide in the event of a disagreement.[1] The

concordat was a compromise in that neither
party gained the full measure of its demands. Lay investiture was a thing of the
past, but interference in episcopal elections
was not permanently avoided. Nevertheless,
the time when emperors could dominate
popes was passing.

The spectacular nature of the controversy between Popes and Holy Roman Emperors tends to obscure the more normal
relations between the popes and certain of
the other European kings. William I of
England, for example, appointed bishops
and ruled the English church, but he promoted reforms. Therefore, except for a brief
period of strain, Anglo-Papal relations were
friendly. In France Philip I did not resist
the threat of excommunication and papal
legates achieved considerable success, although here it was the magnates as much
as the king who were guilty of lay investiture.[2]

The Gregorian reform opened a new era
in the history of the church and of Europe.
A new morale was evident which had considerable popular support and which continued to animate the church in the following decades. Yet the age of reform was not
without its losses. Not all ecclesiastics sympathized with what seemed the overly
rigid and sometimes markedly monastic
character of the movement. The challenge
to the ruler's religious position endangered
the *rapport* between king and church, and
subsequent decades were to witness considerable tension in certain areas. Excommunication and deposition, even for purely
religious reasons, had political consequences
and amounted to a claim, albeit vague, of
the spiritual power to authority over the

---

[1] There were minor variations for Italy and
Burgundy. A settlement reached in England
(1107) seems to have provided a model for
the arrangements in the Concordat of Worms.

[2] At this time certain rulers entered into a
formal feudal relationship with the Holy See.
Papal suzerainty might bring prestige and protection to a king whose position was legally insecure. For the pope a contractual relation
seemed to offer, in addition to a regular revenue,
the assurance that ecclesiastical policy would
have the support of the local government. The
actual extent of Gregory's feudal policy was not
great. Hungary, Croatia-Dalmatia, the principality of Kiev, the Norman kingdom of southern
Italy and Sicily, and a few small principalities
accepted papal suzerainty, although in certain
instances only temporarily. Others were added
by later popes.

temporal. In the current confusion caused by the intimate association of religion and politics, Gregory laid the foundation for papal claims to political supremacy. He did not himself bring this idea to realization, and he probably had not such an intention. But his acts, whatever their motive, set important precedents for his successors. Another unfortunate development of the period which was in part related to the reform in the west was the tragic rift with the church in the east. By the middle of the eleventh century deep-seated cultural, linguistic, and political, as well as certain minor religious, divergencies had produced an estrangement and occasionally an outright, if temporary, break between the two ecclesiastical worlds. Certain recent events, for example the Norman occupation of Byzantine Italy, including dioceses formerly under Constantinople's jurisdiction, accentuated the tension. Most important, the Gregorian conception of an effective jurisdictional supremacy of Rome worried a Byzantium long accustomed to a nominal primacy.

In 1054 a papal legate was sent to Constantinople. He was Cardinal Humbert, an exceptionally able person, but one of the more intransigent Gregorian reformers and notably lacking in diplomatic finesse. The patriarch of the time, Michael Cerularius, was a man not without personal ambition. The details of their contretemps need not concern us here. Suffice it to say that each excommunicated the other. Certainly neither man regarded his action as involving anyone beyond those present. Nor for many decades did either side look upon 1054 as constituting a formal schism. A number of popes, and of eastern prelates, continued their efforts at reconciliation. Nevertheless, the Byzantine church which now included the bulk of the south Slavic population of the Balkans and also the Russians, gradually drifted into schism, and this schism has never been healed. To this day most of the east European churches continue to reject the jurisdiction of the pope.

E. The First Crusade

Toward the end of the eleventh century in the midst of the investiture controversy, there occurred an event which in many respects epitomizes all that western feudal society had come to be. This was the First Crusade to the Holy Land. It would therefore seem appropriate to conclude this chapter of our story with a consideration of that unique achievement.

The origins and causes of the First Crusade have long been the subject of controversy, and have been ascribed to a great variety of human motives, spiritual and material. Certainly the desire to acquire new fiefs, the mainspring of feudal expansion, was one. Another was the urge to extend contacts with lucrative oriental trade. But it must be remembered that the great majority of the participants did not remain in the east. They were moved, it would seem, by a spirit of high religious adventure, an attitude thoroughly characteristic of the age and perhaps of no other period in the history of the West. For the First Crusade was the culmination of the "holy war" against the "infidel." Such war, encouraged by the church, had been going on locally in Spain and elsewhere for some time. Its extension to the east followed certain important developments in the Moslem world, in particular the expansion of the Seljuk Turks in the eleventh century. These people, migrating from Turkestan, overran Moslem Persia and pushed south into Syria and Palestine. After becoming Moslems themselves, they decisively defeated a Byzantine army at Manzikert in Asia Minor (1071). Thereafter bands of Turks commenced an occupation of large sections of Asia Minor, thus bringing a resurgent Islam to the very gates of Europe.

Largely because the Seljuks were only a ruling minority in the conquered territories, there was considerable disorder for a time in Syria which interrupted or endangered Christian pilgrim travel to Jerusalem. Contemporary accounts bear witness of serious mistreatment of pilgrims, with a resulting curtailment of pilgrimages. This was not a permanent situation, but reports reached the west and stimulated a desire to take defensive measures against the Seljuk Turks and to ensure the safety of the Holy Sepulchre, the place of the entombment of Christ, at Jerusalem.

By the eleventh century, indeed long before, pilgrimage had become a venerable

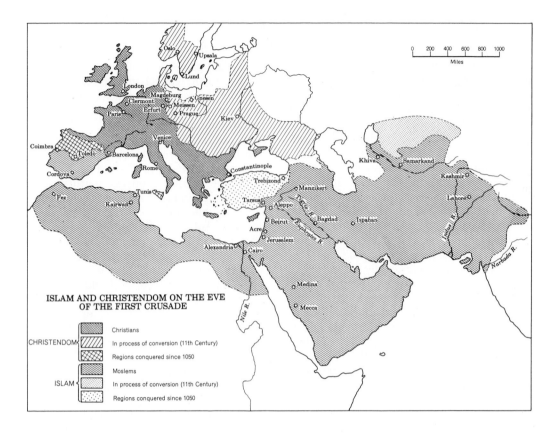

ISLAM AND CHRISTENDOM ON THE EVE
OF THE FIRST CRUSADE

CHRISTENDOM
- Christians
- In process of conversion (11th Century)
- Regions conquered since 1050

ISLAM
- Moslems
- In process of conversion (11th Century)
- Regions conquered since 1050

Christian practice. In fact, from the very early days of Christianity, men and women of all walks of life had formed the habit of visiting the places hallowed by the events of Christ's life or by the shrine of a great saint. Sometimes such journeys were prescribed as penances. More often a pilgrimage was a purely voluntary pious act. Rome and Santiago de Compostela were famous pilgrimage centers. But the most famous was Jerusalem, despite its remoteness from western Christendom, for here were the Holy Sepulchre and a portion of the relic of the True Cross of the Crucifixion. Nearby were Nazareth and Bethlehem and many other spots intimately associated with Christ's life. In a sense, the crusades were armed pilgrimages.

The First Crusade was launched as the immediate result of a famous sermon delivered by Pope Urban II at a church council in Clermont, France, in 1095. Urban, a man of broad statesmanship with a remarkable ability to grasp the significance of the current crisis, perceived the danger to all of Europe in the Moslem resurgence. He saw

that it existed in Spain as well as in the Orient. Above all, he understood how the safety of eastern Europe depended upon the survival of the Christian Byzantine Empire. Only a few months before his appearance at Clermont, he had received envoys from the Byzantine Emperor Alexius Comnenus I, requesting western assistance against the Seljuk Turks. Evidently, the Pope was thinking in terms of a defensive war. Urban was a Frenchman and a former monk and abbot of the French monastery of Cluny; and it was to Frenchmen, who had already contributed heavily to Christian fighting against the Moslems in Spain, that he made his epochal appeal at Clermont in 1095.

Precisely what Urban said on that famous occasion we do not know. The accounts we have of his sermon were written years after the event. But in calling for an organized effort against the Moslems in the east, he evidently knew how to arouse his audience. He spoke in their native vernacular. His appeal was religious, but not entirely so. He urged his listeners to abandon their fratricidal feudal warfare and to expend their fighting energies in a more worthy cause. He dwelt on the unhappy plight of the eastern Christians, but he also pictured the Levant as a "land of milk and honey." Finally, to all participants who died repentant was offered a plenary indulgence.[1]

The response was immediate; and, according to the chroniclers, a great cry of "God wills it (*Deus lo vult*)" greeted the Pope's words. There is reason to believe that the numbers volunteering for service, and taking the cross, far exceeded Urban's expectations and plans.[2] Large-scale organization had to be provided immediately, and, in order that the expeditionary forces should be properly directed, the Pope appointed Bishop Adhemar of Puy as papal legate in charge. Provision was also made to protect, under threat of ecclesiastical censure, the property and families of those who enlisted. Women had to be specifically prohibited from going without their husbands' consent, and monks and priests without the authorization of their superiors. August, 1096, was set as the departure date for the crusading army.

The first contingent to set out was a miscellaneous, ill-organized band under a fanatical itinerant preacher named Peter "the Hermit." A second was a similar though somewhat better equipped band, led by another fanatic, Walter "the Penniless." Neither of these was of any real military significance, and both were decimated by the Turks in Asia Minor. But the fact that such bands went at all is eloquent testimony of popular enthusiasm for the crusade.

The real military expedition set out in the summer and fall of 1096. As might have been expected, practically all its members were French. Germany, which might otherwise have participated, was then torn by the investiture controversy, and its Holy Roman Emperor, Henry IV, had recently been excommunicated. As a consequence, the term "Frank" became almost synonymous with "Crusader." The expedition as a whole consisted of several separate divisions, each under a distinguished feudal leader.

Though they all agreed to meet at Constantinople, there was no effective unified command.

At Constantinople, trouble arose out of conflicting aims of the Crusaders and of the Byzantine Emperor Alexius. The latter had requested assistance in recovering lost territory for his Empire. The Crusaders, on the other hand, were intent on keeping for themselves whatever land they conquered, at least in Syria and Palestine. And the Western divisions of eager and often truculent knights were a source of potential danger to Alexius until he could shepherd them safely over into Asia Minor. Between the Byzantines and the Westerners, differences of language and customs, as well as of war aims, were aggravated by the recent rift between the eastern and western churches.[3] Though some temporary agreements were reached between them, real coöperation, so essential to any permanent success, was never achieved.

In crossing Asia Minor the Crusaders demonstrated an ability to defeat armies of the Seljuk Turks, and, despite hunger and thirst, to triumph over such natural obstacles as the hot Anatolian plateau and the rugged Taurus mountains. At Antioch in north Syria they began the siege of a major city.[4] Lacking siege engines and needful supplies, they were forced to await the arrival of an Italian fleet before pressing the siege in earnest. This intervention of Italian shipping was a development of special significance. For the Crusaders, in their advance southward, were no longer dependent on land communication with the Byzantines, but rather on sea communication with Italy. In this way, commercial contact between the Levant and western Europe was at last revived. The Italians soon learned to exact a high price for their invaluable assistance, and before long traders from Genoa, Pisa, and other Italian city-states were firmly established in Syrian and Palestinian ports.

Meanwhile, the divisions which were to

---

[1] A *plenary* indulgence signified the remission of all the temporal punishment due to sin. See below, pp. 351–352.

[2] Because those volunteering wore the cross, at first rudely made of cloth, on their armor they were called *crucesignati* or "crusaders."

[3] See above, p. 167. It is probable that Pope Urban hoped that Western aid might create an atmosphere favorable to ending the schism. If so, his hopes were disappointed.

[4] Nicaea had been taken shortly after the Crusaders left Constantinople.

A French twelfth century polychrome oak statue of the Virgin and Child.

Courtesy Metropolitan Museum of Art, New York; Gift of J. Pierpont Morgan, 1916

plague the crusading movement to its very end had already begun to appear. One group had left the main army before the siege of Antioch and had begun operations along the upper Euphrates which eventuated in the capture of the city of Edessa (1098). And it was only a general clamor among the rank-and-file shortly after the fall of Antioch which compelled the leaders to reunite their forces and resume the march to Jerusalem.

Jerusalem, the goal of the expedition, was captured after a six-week siege on July 15, 1099, three years after the crusade had set out and four years after Pope Urban's sermon.[1] The Pope died on July 29, before the news of victory could reach him. When eventually the news did reach western Europe, it was received with the utmost enthusiasm and exultation. The victory crowned a long sustained effort, which cannot be explained by mere ambition for material gain. It betokened a zeal, an idealism, a stubborn persistence against formidable obstacles, and a spirit of high adventure, which have rarely been equalled.

The First Crusade may be taken as marking the climax of the early medieval world. It was unique, both in its character and in being the only one of the crusades which really succeeded. Those Crusaders—and they were the minority—who remained in the east to found principalities, together with the Italian merchants who controlled the trade in the ports, came to be, if they were not already, men of a different stamp. Like their contemporaries in Europe they now set out to build institutions of law and of government, to live and deal with the Moslems as well as to fight them. But such developments were characteristic of a more mature stage in the growth of Western civilization, the stage which may be called the "Middle Age proper" and to which we shall next turn.

---

[1] Jerusalem was taken from the Shiite Egyptian Moslems who had captured the city from the Sunnite Turks in the preceding year.

SELECT SUPPLEMENTARY READINGS FOR PART III

General. Same as for "General" under Part II, p. 110; in addition: R. W. Southern, *The Making of the Middle Ages* (1953); C. Brooke, *Europe in the Central Middle Ages, 962–1154* (1964).

Chapter 10. For the rise and decline of the Carolingian Empire, and the culture of the period: J. A. Wallace-Hadrill, *The Long-haired Kings* (1962); E. S. Duckett, *Alcuin, Friend of Charlemagne* (1951) and *Alfred the Great* (1956); S. C. Easton and H. Wieruszowski, *The Carolingian Empire* (1961); H. Fichtenau, *The Carolingian Empire* (tr. 1957); M. Laistner (cited above, Chapter 8); G. Schnürer, *Church and Culture in the Middle Ages,* vol. I (1956); R. E. Sullivan, *The Coronation of Charlemagne* (1959); R. Winston, *Charlemagne* (1954). On the Norsemen and other invaders: H. Arbman, *The Vikings* (1961); J. Brondsted, *The Vikings* (1940); F. Dvornik, *The Slavs: Their Early History and Civilization* (1956); T. D. Kendrick, *History of the Vikings* (1930); A. R. Lewis, *The Northern Seas* (1958); C. A. Macartney, *The Magyars in the Ninth Century* (1930); F. Mowat, *Westviking* (1965); C. Turville-Petrie, *The Heroic Age of Scandinavia* (1951).

Chapter 11. M. Bloch, *Feudal Society* (new ed., 1961); F. L. Ganshof, *Feudalism* (1952); S. Painter, *Medieval Society* (1951) and *French Chivalry* (1940); E. Prestage, *Chivalry* (1928); C. Stephenson, *Feudalism* (1942).

Chapter 12. G. Barraclough, *The Origins of Modern Germany* (1947); F. Dvornik (cited above, Chapter 10); R. Fawtier, *The Capetian Kings of France* (1960); R. Menendez-Pidal, *The Cid and His Spain* (1934); C. Petit-Dutaillis, *Feudal Monarchy in France and England* (1936); F. M. Stenton, *Anglo-Saxon England* (2nd ed., 1947); J. W. Thompson, *Feudal Germany* (1928); D. Whitelock, *The Beginnings of English Society* (1952); P. Blair, *Introduction to Anglo-Saxon England* (1959).

Chapter 13. H. S. Bennett, *Life on the English Manor* (1937); M. Bloch, *Feudal Society* (1961); G. G. Coulton, *The Medieval Village* (1925), reprinted as *Medieval Village, Manor, and Monastery* (1960); H. L. Adelson, *Medieval Commerce* (1962); R. Latouche, *The Birth of Western Economy* (tr. 1960); A. R. Lewis, *The Northern Seas* (1958); N. Neilson, *Medieval Agrarian Economy* (1936); H. Pirenne, *Economic and Social History of Medieval Europe* (1937); S. Painter, *Medieval Society* (1951); E. Power, *Medieval People* (1924).

Chapter 14. In addition to the general works on church history cited above, p. 49: R. H. Bainton, *The Medieval Church* (1962); G. Tellenbach, *Church, State, and Christian Society at the Time of the Investiture Contest* (1940); W. Ullmann, *The Growth of Papal Government in the Middle Ages* (1955) and *Medieval Papalism* (1949). For the Eastern church and the crusades: S. Runciman, *A History of the Crusades,* 3 vols. (1951–1954), and *The Eastern Schism* (1955); K. M. Setton and M. W. Baldwin, eds., *A History of the Crusades,* vol. I (1955); H. Daniel-Rops, *Cathedral and Crusade* (1957); M. A. Deanesley, *History of the Medieval Church, 590–1500* (1954).

Twelfth century military architecture. The Barbican Gate at Carisbrooke Castle, Isle of Wight.

Courtesy British Information Services, New York

*From Urban II
to Dante*

Gothic architecture in Spain. The elaborate interior of the Cathedral at Burgos.

Courtesy Spanish National Tourist Department, New York

PART IV

THE MIDDLE AGE OF THE

CENTURIES AND THE

TWELFTH AND THIRTEENTH
FLOWERING OF EUROPE

173

Late twelfth or early thirteenth century Champlevé enamel work from the famous center of the industry at Limoges, France.

Courtesy Metropolitan Museum of Art, New York

DURING THE MIDDLE AGE of the twelfth and thirteenth centuries, European civilization, with its Graeco-Roman and Judaeo-Christian traditions, is no longer confined to Mediterranean lands, as it had been in antiquity; nor is it diluted with barbarism, as it was in the Early Middle Age—the "Dark Age"—from the sixth to the eleventh century. It is now the civilization of the entire continent of Europe, and it is remarkably lusty and progressive.

True, two major subdivisions of European civilization, long in the making, now become definitive through a rupture of church unity. The "East," including the Byzantine Empire, the Balkans, and Russia, follows a separate Orthodox Church, with strongly Greek and oriental influence, while the "West," embracing western and central Europe, continues to adhere to the Catholic Church under the Roman papacy and with Latin liturgy and usages. Henceforth there is an aloofness, and a more or less open hostility, between "West" and "East."

It is the "West" which flowers in the Middle Age proper, and with which we are here chiefly concerned. The flowering takes many forms. It is evidenced in a great crusading movement against Moslems in the Near East and the Iberian peninsula, in colonial experiments outside Europe in Syria and Palestine, and in pioneer contacts with faraway China. It is shown, too, in the expansion of maritime and inland trade, the increase of commodities, industry, and money, the growth of cities, and the extension of agriculture. It is further exemplified in the consolidation of feudal monarchy, in the development of representative institutions, in the seeming brilliance of the Holy Roman Empire, and in the very real "Drang nach Osten"—the West's "Drive to the East."

Central to this Middle Age in the West is the Catholic Church, which develops a strong papal monarchy, sponsors such new religious orders as the Franciscan and Dominican, successfully combats heresy, and exerts an all-pervasive popular influence. In close connection with the Church, universities arise, scholastic philosophy flourishes, and notable progress is made in science, medicine, and law.

It is an age, moreover, of highly important popular literature and art. Epics and romances and Dante's *Divine Comedy* appear in the ordinary spoken (vernacular) languages, and both romanesque and gothic architecture reach a climax.

CHAPTER 15

New Frontiers

A. The New Frontiers of Western Europe

Earlier chapters have emphasized the expansive character of feudal society. Expansion continued to be characteristic of European civilization during the twelfth and thirteenth centuries—the Middle Age proper—and it was accentuated by such factors as a general rise in population, increasing commerce, and a heightened emphasis on waging a "holy war" against the infidel. Not only was the area of Christendom enlarged by the establishment of new frontier settlements, but venturesome souls journeyed to remote lands prompted by the desire to open new avenues of trade or to carry forward the banners of holy religion. By 1300, Europeans of varied nationality had extended their political boundaries, added to their knowledge of other civilizations, and generally broadened and deepened their own.

From far northern Europe had gone out in all directions the Scandinavian Vikings, or Norsemen. From their settlements in French Normandy, their descendants in the eleventh century went to southern Europe and to England. The *wanderlust* was certainly in their blood, for from all three places young knights pushed on to further adventures. The Norman kingdom of Sicily developed commercial contacts along the north coast of Africa. And Norman-Sicilian barons were active in the crusades in Palestine. Meanwhile, Anglo-Norman warriors and traders helped to extend the territory

of the English monarchy, particularly at the expense of the Scottish kingdom, which had included a large section of English-speaking Northumbria. Into this "lowland" area and even into the Celtic "highlands" of Scotland came many knights from the south, especially during the reign of the Scottish King David I (1124–1153), who was receptive to southern and feudal ideas.

A somewhat similar situation developed in Wales. The Anglo-Norman border knights, or "Lords Marchers" as they were called, drove the Celtic Welsh farther into their rugged hills and established new fiefs and towns. Finally King Edward I conquered Wales (1276–1284) and incorporated it into the English monarchy. Since then the heir to the English throne has usually borne the title of "Prince of Wales."

Nor was Ireland immune to Anglo-Norman expansion. Although many Scandinavians had settled there, adopting Christianity and mingling with the native Irish, the Viking raids had left the island a turmoil of warring clans. In 1171 an Anglo-Norman contingent invaded Ireland, ostensibly to aid an exiled chieftain, but actually to establish English barons in new fiefs. Two years later King Henry II placed a royal official in Ireland, organized the east coast under his jurisdiction, and even received the homage of a number of Irish chieftains of the interior. During the thirteenth century the area under English domination increased.

In southern Europe, the Iberian peninsula continued to attract restless French as well as native knights in search of material or spiritual rewards. The formation of Portugal affords an excellent example of what happened. First, a group of northern Crusaders en route to Jerusalem assisted in the conquest of Lisbon (1147) from the Moslems. Then Portugal, already a fief of the Holy See (1143), was recognized as a separate kingdom (1179) through the authorization of Pope Alexander III.

In the expanding Christian kingdoms of Spain, papal influence was especially noticeable under Innocent III (1198–1216). The king of Aragon, for example, submitted his state to the protection of the Holy See in 1204. And during a crisis of temporary Moslem recovery, it was Innocent's organizing activities which procured added assistance from the north and united the several Christian Spanish states into some sort of common front. As a consequence, the Moslems were defeated in a great battle at Las Navas de Tolosa in 1212. Never again was Christian Spain seriously menaced by Moslem advance.

During the thirteenth century the consolidation and expansion of Christian Spain was furthered, first, by the union of the kingdoms of Leon and Castile (1230), and, second, by the growing preëminence of the kingdom of Aragon in the western Mediterranean. Though Aragon lost Languedoc (except Montpellier) to the French monarchy, it conquered Valencia from the Moslems (1245) and won temporary footholds on the north African coast. It regained the Balearic Islands in 1235. Then in 1282, the King of Aragon, Peter III (1276–1285), taking advantage of a popular revolt in Sicily—the so-called "Sicilian Vespers"—intervened in the island and took possession of it.[1] Thus Aragon secured a predominance throughout the Western Mediterranean, and shared the bulk of the Iberian peninsula with three other Christian states—Castile, Navarre, and Portugal. Only Granada, in the extreme south, remained in Moslem hands.

Meanwhile, there had been a notable German expansion eastward in north-central Europe. This had begun, on a wide front from the Danube to the Baltic, under

the early Saxon emperors. The internal strengthening of the Slavic states of Poland and Bohemia and the Magyar state of Hungary had at first prevented major extension of the German frontier at their expense, but not the immigration within them of many German settlers. The twelfth and thirteenth centuries did witness, however, an impressive advance of the German frontier along the Baltic. There, in a concerted and often highly systematic movement, thousands of German peasants, merchants, and townsmen followed the leadership of such feudal magnates as Adolf of Holstein, Albert "the Bear" of Brandenburg, and Henry "the Lion" of Saxony.

New towns, bishoprics, and monasteries were founded and German settlers and missionaries introduced. Gradually, the original Slavic inhabitants were submerged by the influx of German peasants in Mecklenburg, Brandenburg, and Pomerania. In this Germanizing process, the church and especially such monastic orders as the Cistercians and the Premonstratensians zealously coöperated. The church's official support of the movement went beyond the organization of missions and the establishment of local hierarchies. In 1147, at the time of the Second Crusade to the Holy Land, the church promised the same spiritual rewards for fighting Slavic "infidels" as for warring against Moslems.

German expansion eastward and northward along the Baltic was speeded in the thirteenth century by religio-military orders, particularly the Knights of the Sword and the Teutonic Knights. The former of these, founded early in the century by Albert, missionary bishop in Livonia, completed the conversion and conquest of that province and extended its sway into Estonia and Kurland. In these regions a kind of ecclesiastical state was founded under a Grand Master of the German Knights of the Sword, and with immigrant German nobles as feudal landlords. Here was a transplanted feudalism, topped by a German aristocracy and supported from below by a conquered and Christianized native peasantry.

The Teutonic Knights, originally established for service in the Holy Land, transferred their activities first to eastern

---

[1] Later, during the fourteenth and fifteenth centuries, Aragon appropriated Sardinia from the Pisans and Genoese.

Hungary and then (1228), on the invitation of a Polish prince, to Baltic-speaking Prussia, east of the Vistula river. The Grand Master of the Order, Hermann of Salza, then sought and obtained from the Holy Roman Emperor Frederick II confirmation of the "rights" of the Teutonic Knights to all future conquests in Prussia. Many younger sons of German nobles joined the Knights in warfare against the native Prussians. But these Prussians were stubborn fighters, and it took fifty years for the German forces to subdue them. Eventually Teutonic Knights not only reduced the Baltic Prussians along the coast and in a considerable hinterland, but blocked the Polish kingdom from access to the Baltic. This meant a revival of Polish-German rivalry and enmity, with important consequences for the future. Meanwhile, in 1237, the Teutonic Knights absorbed the Knights of the Sword and succeeded them as rulers of Livonia and Kurland. With the conquest of Prussia, and the final acquisition of Estonia from Denmark in 1346, the Teutonic Order and its Germanizing influence were of paramount importance along the whole Baltic coast from the Vistula to the Gulf of Finland.

The expansion which has just been described was one of the major achievements of the German people in the middle ages. A large area which had formerly been Slavic or Baltic was Germanized: Holstein, Mecklenburg, and Brandenburg in what is now the heart of north Germany; Lusatia and Silesia, on the upper Oder; Pomerania and Prussia, on the Baltic. Besides, German rulers and landlords now dominated the northeastern Baltic lands of Livonia, Kurland, and Estonia.

But in considering this achievement, its long-term effect on Germany's neighbors must not be forgotten. The kingdom of Poland was forced to seek expansion southward. Lithuania, threatened with conquest, made common cause with Poland. And the Russians resented and resisted the attempts of the Teutonic Knights to compel their conversion to the Roman church. All these peoples were to provide formidable opposition to the Germans in later years. German eastward expansion reached its climax in the thirteenth and early fourteenth centuries.

B. Western Christian States in the Levant

An earlier chapter has described the First Crusade to the Holy Land, a movement which led to a somewhat different form of feudal expansion. The states which the Crusaders founded in Syria were not the result of frontier expansion. Rather, they were settlements of Europeans, predominantly Frenchmen, living in a distant land and in a foreign environment. Four states were established: the county of Edessa; the principality of Antioch; the county of Tripoli; and, farthest south, the kingdom of Jerusalem. The last contained, in addition to the sacred towns of Jerusalem, Bethlehem, and Nazareth, the important ports of Tyre, Beirut, Acre, Sidon, Jaffa, and Ascalon. Its first ruler was Godfrey of Bouillon who was content with the title of Advocate, or Defender, of the Holy Sepulchre, but on his death in 1100 his brother, Baldwin, was given the title of king. Thus was established a feudal monarchy, rather than an ecclesiastical or even a Crusaders' principality. A temporary and largely theoretical suzerainty of the kingdom of Jerusalem over the other states was soon replaced by the actual independence of each.

Each of the states was divided, in typical western feudal fashion, into fiefs and baronies, the vassals forming a feudal *curia*. Thus a superstructure of western feudal administration governed the relations among crusading nobles and knights in the Near East; and these relations were minutely described, so far as the kingdom of Jerusalem was concerned, in the thirteenth-century *Assizes of Jerusalem*, an important compilation of feudal law. Beneath such a superstructure of European feudalism, which represented the usages of the ruling minority, lived the numerous and cosmopolitan native population, Christian and Moslem. Doubtless these people lived in much the same manner as before. The Moslem rulers left the country, and their agricultural estates were parceled out among new Christian masters. But townsmen continued

CRUSADER STATES IN THE NEAR EAST

Areas within heavy outline were held until 1265-1291. Others were reconquered by Saladin 1187-1191.

Map labels: BYZANTINE EMPIRE; SELJUK TURKS; KINGDOM OF ARMENIA; COUNTY OF EDESSA 1098-1144; Edessa; Tarsus; Antioch; PRINC. OF ANTIOCH; Aleppo; SELJUK TURKS; Tigris R.; Euphrates R.; ASSASSINS; Hamah; Nicosia; CYPRUS; Famagusta; Tripolis; C. OF TRIPOLI; Beirut; Damascus; Mediterranean Sea; Acre; Caesarea; Jaffa; Jerusalem; KINGDOM OF JERUSALEM; Jordan R.; Dead Sea; Gaza; Kerak; Arabian Desert; Alexandria; Damietta; Nile R.; FATIMITE CALIPHATE OF CAIRO; Cairo; Red Sea; Elim

---

to carry on their business and farmers to till the soil or tend their cattle. Mohammedans were not persecuted, and the various native Christian sects flourished. Some of these, like the Maronites, were reunited with Rome and the papacy. Gradually relations between Crusaders and natives became quite normal and friendly. Crusaders adopted native customs, food, and dress; and they habitually employed native physicians. In short the Franks, as all the Crusaders were called, became acclimated to the orient, and learned by experience the best methods of governing a native population on foreign soil.

A Latin ecclesiastical hierarchy was speedily established in communion with the pope and under the immediate jurisdiction of the patriarchs of Jerusalem and Antioch, two venerable sees of apostolic foundation. Western monasticism also made its appearance, and most of the European religious orders maintained houses in the Levant. The close association of church and government, so characteristic of the west,

was equally noticeable in the Latin orient. Ecclesiastics were active in political matters. An occasional prelate, like the famous Archbishop William of Tyre, chancellor of the kingdom of Jerusalem and historian, exhibited superb qualities of statesmanship.

Economic life centered in the coastal towns where the Italian merchants obtained lucrative monopolies. Usually they were given outright control over a section of a port. Since their transport services were indispensable to the furnishing of supplies and reinforcements, privileges were heaped upon them by both ecclesiastical and lay authorities. And in the Western recovery of commercial contact with the eastern Mediterranean, Genoese and Pisans took the lead, breaking thereby the virtual monopoly of eastern trade formerly enjoyed by Venice.

A permanent military establishment was organized to meet the ever present needs of defense against renewed Moslem attacks. Such attacks were frequent if intermittent, and sometimes involved large-scale campaigning. Each barony was expected to provide a stipulated number of men-at-arms, both mounted knights and foot-soldiers, for the common army. The crusaders learned by bitter experience that heavy cavalry unsupported by a disciplined infantry, especially bowmen, were helpless against the Saracen light-armed horsemen and mounted archers. Strong fortresses were erected at vulnerable points along the frontier, and important advances were made in the art of castle building.

Many of the castles were garrisoned by Knights of the Temple or of the Hospital. These were orders of military monks whose lives were dedicated to perpetual "holy war." The Templars were first organized to protect pilgrims on the way to the Holy Sepulchre. Their headquarters were on the site of Solomon's temple, hence their name. The Knights of St. John, or Hospitallers, originally founded to care for sick pilgrims, later assumed military functions. Both Orders required, though not irrevocably, the customary monastic vows in addition to military service. After many privileges and exemptions had been granted them by successive popes, they formed a virtually independent, as well as a permanent, military force.

A great weakness of the Crusaders' states was the lack of numbers, for many of the original Crusaders returned home, and reinforcements from the west were irregular and rarely sufficient. Newcomers were inexperienced in Levantine life and tactics and hence were often as much a nuisance as a help to the "native" Latin Christians. Another difficulty resulted from the rather typical feudal decentralization. Only crises brought effective common action within or among the four states, and even then Antioch, Tripoli, and Jerusalem acted as separate units. There were several attempts to revive the alliance with the Byzantine Empire, for, despite obvious sources of discord, there was great need for coöperation. Unfortunately all attempts proved unsuccessful. Consequently, whenever the surrounding Moslem states achieved a semblance of unity among themselves, they could be a grave menace to the divided and isolated Latin Christian states in Syria and Palestine.

Crusaders' fortifications in Syria.

Courtesy Government of Syria Tourist Office, New York

Such occasions were rare, however, and the Crusaders, though divided themselves, learned to profit by Moslem disunion and to achieve a sort of Near Eastern balance of power. Antioch and Tripoli, and to a lesser extent Jerusalem, were admirably protected by nature. The northern portion of the kingdom of Jerusalem, virtually all of Tripoli, and most of Antioch were guarded by mountainous frontiers. Hence it is not surprising that Edessa, the least protected, was the first to be reconquered by the Moslems, in 1144, and that Tripoli and Antioch survived the Moslem reconquest of Jerusalem in 1187 by at least a century.

Altogether the crusading Christians successfully established and for over a century maintained centers of Western European culture on an alien soil, and though they were influenced by ideas and customs in the new environment, they did not become entirely "orientalized." Some learned Arabic, but all habitually conversed and occasionally wrote in a European, principally French or Italian, vernacular. Chronicles were composed and documents issued in Latin. Churches were erected in contemporary

Moslem fortifications east of the Crusaders' states. The Citadel at Aleppo.

Courtesy Government of Syria Tourist Office, New York

styles of West European architecture. In short, although owing no allegiance to any specific European kingdom, the Latin states in the Levant were western European colonies outside of Europe.

C. Later Crusades

The rise of Saladin, Sultan of Egypt (1171–1193), brought a temporary, though tremendously effective, unity to the Moslems throughout Syria and Egypt; and his success in suppressing the rival Fatimite caliphate of Egypt and in unifying his co-religionists happened to coincide with disastrous political and personal dissensions in the Latin Christian kingdom of Jerusalem. These, rather than any clear-cut military superiority, enabled Saladin to defeat a Christian army at Hattin near the Lake of Tiberias in 1187 and to open the way to the re-conquest, in the same year, of the city of Jerusalem. By 1191 only a few ports in the former state of Jerusalem, together with the little states of Tripoli and Antioch, remained in Christian hands.

The Third Crusade,[1] organized as a result of the fall of Jerusalem, is perhaps the best known after the First, because it was led at the outset by two kings and an emperor, Philip Augustus of France and Richard I of England and the Holy Roman Emperor Frederick Barbarossa. The last was drowned while crossing a stream in Asia Minor on his way to the Holy Land, and Philip soon pleaded an excuse of illness to return to more inviting French concerns. Though Richard conquered the island of Cyprus, successfully besieged the important port of Acre, and buttressed the Latin Christian states of Tripoli and Antioch, he was unable to recover Jerusalem. This remained under control of Saladin and the Moslems. Both Richard and Saladin, despite many passages at arms, were honorable, one might almost say friendly, enemies. Both displayed the best characteristics of medieval chivalry.

------

[1] After the First Crusade, many other expeditions set out from the West. The most important have been given numerical titles (Second, Third, Fourth, etc.), but these major organized ventures represent only a part of a continuous effort in which many individuals and smaller groups participated.

During the thirteenth century there was a growing apathy in the West toward crusading. The ardor of 1095 was lacking. Only occasionally did a prince, such as St. Louis IX of France (1226–1270), devotedly take the cross. And since his genuine zeal was shared by few of his associates, his two expeditions, one to Egypt (the Seventh Crusade), and the other to Tunis (the Eighth Crusade), in which he met his death, were fruitless. In the meantime, a great deal of crusading energy was diverted by the popes to their European enemies— heretics of southern France and Hohenstaufen rulers of the Holy Roman Empire. Worldly interests, political, diplomatic, and economic, engaged the attention of Europeans in the thirteenth century so that oversea crusading against Moslems seemed to many a distant and unprofitable undertaking.

Perhaps the most conspicuous example of the predominance of diplomatic and economic motives over religious was the so-called Fourth Crusade. Inaugurated at the beginning of the thirteenth century by one of the greatest of medieval popes, Innocent III, and planned originally for the Holy Land, it was diverted first to Zara in Christian Hungary and then, despite papal censures, to Constantinople which was captured in 1204. This diversion resulted partly from diplomatic intrigues involving a pretender to the Byzantine throne, and partly from financial demands of the Venetians. These shrewd traders had been engaged to transport the crusading army, but finding part of the expected payment lacking, they insisted on compensation through an attack on the wealthy capital of the Christian Byzantine Empire. With Constantinople in western hands, the Venetians not only made its commerce a virtual monopoly of their own, but were enabled to gain more of the other oriental trade which the earlier crusades had fostered for the Genoese and Pisans. Pope Innocent III, at first profoundly disturbed, finally accepted the inevitable and seized the opportunity to organize in the conquered Byzantine provinces a Latin hierarchy in communion with Rome.

The Latin Empire of Constantinople and Greece, which the Fourth Crusade erected in 1204, lasted only until 1261, when the Byzantines, who had held out in Asia Minor, reconquered Constantinople and most of Greece. The net result of this warfare between Greek and Latin, between Christian East and Christian West, was a profound and enduring hostility. Coöperation against the common Moslem enemy was henceforth impossible, and the chances of ecclesiastical reunion of the Catholic and Eastern Churches were more remote than ever. And, despite its restoration, the Byzantine Empire was irreparably weakened by the temporary Latin conquest.

Increasingly neglected by the West, the little Christian states in Syria which had survived the fall of Jerusalem in 1187 gradually became the prey of internal quarrels and external Moslem pressure. In the latter part of the thirteenth century, they were gradually reduced by a remarkable Moslem commander, Baybars, at the head of an Egyptian force known as the Mamelukes. Acre, the last Christian stronghold in the Levant, fell in 1291.[1]

D. Results of the Crusades

It has sometimes been claimed that the Crusades were responsible for all the great developments—commercial, political, and intellectual—which occurred in Western Europe during the twelfth and thirteenth centuries. This is a gross exaggeration. While they doubtless contributed to many of those developments, in the main they merely strengthened some previously existing trends. In commerce, the Crusades simply accelerated a revival already well under way. Italian fleets completed a reconquest of the Mediterranean and reestablished with the Levant a regular sea traffic, which survived the loss of the Christian colonies that the Crusades had planted there. The result was a greater familiarity with, and a greater demand for, eastern products—spices, sugar, textiles, etc. Returning crusaders helped to transform what had once been luxuries into articles of ordinary trade. Moreover, skillful Europeans,

[1] A western Christian kingdom continued on the island of Cyprus. It passed under Venetian control in 1489.

A thirteenth century book about animals. The earliest surviving example of Persian art after the Mongol invasions and the fall of Bagdad, 1258.

Courtesy Pierpont Morgan Library, New York

notably Italians, managed to appropriate or imitate certain eastern techniques, for example, in glass-making and in the preparation of dyes. A silk industry appeared in Palermo and later in Lucca. An enterprising Italian named Zaccaria "cornered" the alum production of northwestern Asia Minor. In return for assisting the Byzantine emperor to recover Constantinople in 1261, the Genoese obtained trade privileges in the Crimea which subsequently led to further commercial penetration into the Mongol empire. But such achievements, however important, were only incidentally related to the Crusades.

Similarly, the effect of the Crusades on the political and ecclesiastical institutions of twelfth- and thirteenth-century Europe was not great and for the most part it was indirect. While the success of the First Crusade undoubtedly increased the prestige of the reformed papacy at the time of the investiture struggle, subsequent failures and such episodes as the Fourth Crusade served only to discredit the endeavor and the ecclesiastical authorities who sponsored it.

Another indirect result of the Crusades was the promotion of Christian missions to the Moslems. Franciscan and Dominican friars, whose convents were established in the Crusaders' states, made some attempts to convert Moslems.[1] But in general these remained stubbornly resistant to Christian teaching, and continued (and still continue) to compete with Christians for the conversion of pagans. Nevertheless, the efforts of the friars marked the beginning of organized and active missions to non-European peoples, which were to persist long after the collapse of Crusader states in the Near East.

To the notable renaissance of learning in western Europe in the twelfth and thirteenth centuries, the Crusades made a small, though significant, contribution in the field of historical writing. The Crusades were the most spectacular achievement of the era, and they inspired several participants to write vivid accounts for the edification of interested people at home. One of the best of these was the *History of Deeds Done Beyond The Sea*, which was written by William, archbishop of Tyre and chancellor of the kingdom of Jerusalem, and which traced the crusading history down to 1183. Histories in the vernacular, in poetry as well as prose—for the Crusade was the great *geste* of the age—were added to those in Latin. *L'Estoire de guerre sainte*, written by an Anglo-Norman minstrel, recounts the expedition of King Richard of England. Villehardouin's chronicle of the Fourth Crusade is an early prose work in old French. On the other hand, western Christian contacts with Arabic learning in the Levant were insignificant. Spain and Sicily, not Jerusalem or Antioch, were the centers of that important intellectual exchange.

In the field of military science the crusades contributed to an advance in castle building and to an increased use of infantry in coöperation with cavalry. The ultimate failure of the Crusades should not obscure the fact that, despite the disastrous rift between Constantinople and the West and the weakening of the Byzantine Empire, the Mohammedans were kept back from the gates of eastern Europe for two centuries.

Finally, the Crusades made real, for a brief time, the Christian ideal of unified endeavor, the dedication of all to a holy cause. So powerful was this ideal and so striking the initial success of the holy war, that the word "crusade" became customary in describing subsequent undertakings in other fields. "Crusades" were preached against Slavs of northeastern Europe, against heretics of southern France, against Hohenstaufen enemies of the papacy. Such diversions undoubtedly helped to lessen support for real crusading in the Holy Land, but they bear testimony to the power of an idea. Even in our own day, one of the surest ways to enlist support for a popular cause is to call it a "crusade."

The idea of crusading against Moslems persisted into the fourteenth and fifteenth and even sixteenth centuries, in the form of a number of projects for the recovery of the Holy Land, including even an economic blockade of the Mohammedans; and occasionally an expedition was launched. But little or nothing was actually accomplished. The later middle age was a period of national monarchies, incipient power politics, and diversified commerce. Although in many respects unique, the crusades were primarily a product of the feudal age, of its religious and material interests. They illustrate the exuberant energy of a feudal day. It is significant that they did not survive the passing of feudalism.

E. The Mongols, and European Medieval Contacts with China

Just before the middle of the thirteenth century, when Christian Europeans were still fighting Moslems, there suddenly irrupted in the Near East a mighty Asiatic power which most gravely threatened both Christendom and Islam. It was the Mongol power. The Mongols, or Tatars as they were more often called by Europeans,[2] were Asiatic nomads who in the first part of the thirteenth century swept over and subju-

---

[1] Some efforts were also made to teach Arabic and other oriental languages in Europe but with scant success. Ramón Lull, a missionary who was a celebrated proponent of such teaching, met his death in North Africa.

[2] Or, more popularly, *Tartars*. The name is derived from that of the Ta-ta Mongols.

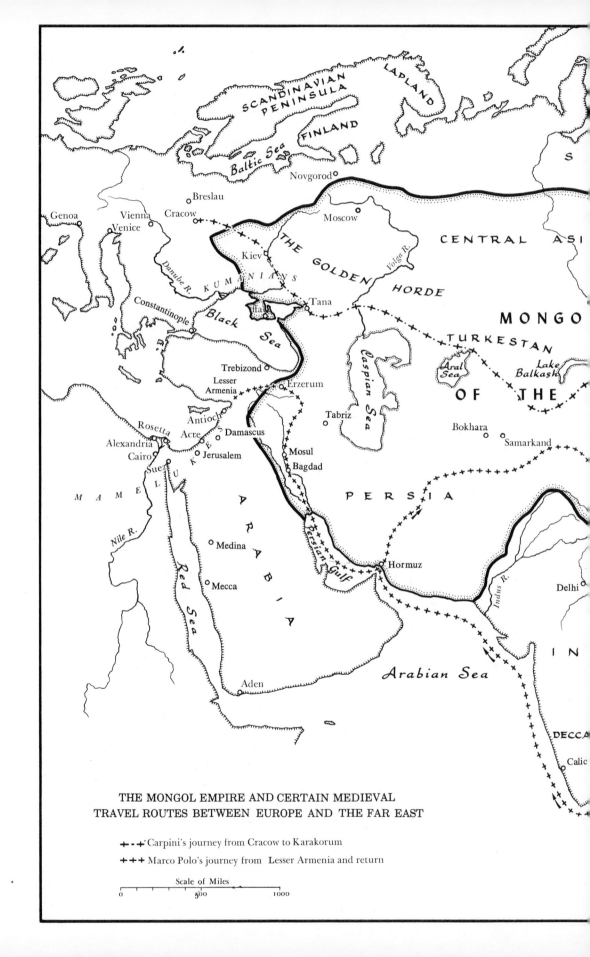

THE MONGOL EMPIRE AND CERTAIN MEDIEVAL
TRAVEL ROUTES BETWEEN EUROPE AND THE FAR EAST

+ – + Carpini's journey from Cracow to Karakorum

+++ Marco Polo's journey from Lesser Armenia and return

Scale of Miles

0   500   1000

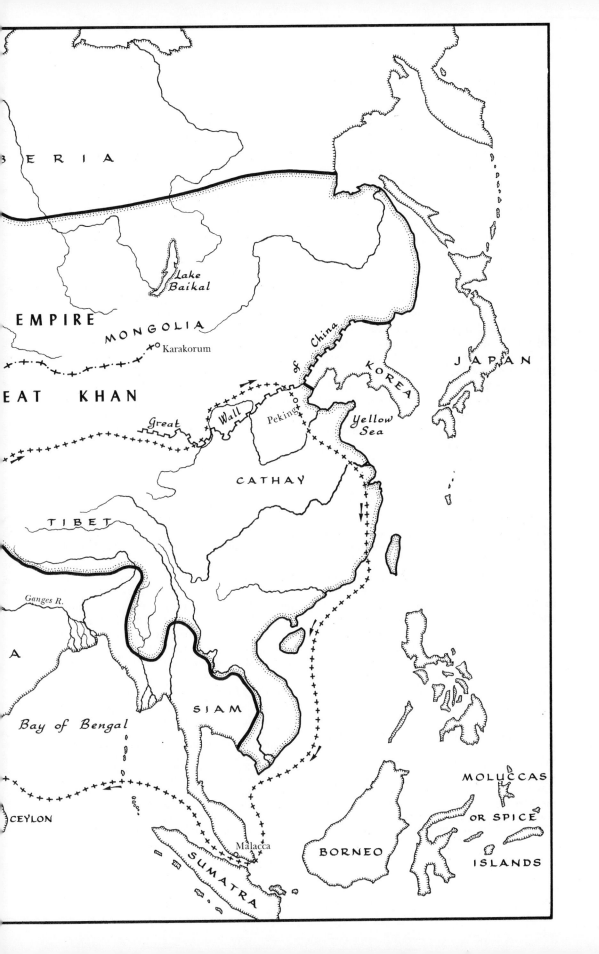

gated an area exceeding all other known empires before or since. Under the redoubtable leadership of Jenghiz Khan (*d.* 1227) and his immediate successors, they conquered the whole Chinese Empire, reduced west-central Asia (including Afghanistan and Persia), and invaded eastern Europe, overrunning southern Russia, Poland, and Hungary. In 1258 they overthrew the Abbasid caliphate of Bagdad and attacked the Moslems in Syria. Wherever they penetrated, whether into Moslem or Christian lands, they displayed a terrifying disregard of life and property.

The Mongol Empire proved too extensive. It soon broke into several "Khanates," which encountered stiffening resistance both in the Near East and in Europe. In 1260, a Moslem force, under the command of Baybars, decisively turned back the Mongols from Syria. And in Christian Europe, while Poland and Silesia suffered further spasmodic raids, only Russia remained under Mongol occupation for any length of time.

Thereafter, the Tatars devoted most of their energies to eastern and central Asia, where they consolidated their territories and gradually abandoned some of the ruthlessness of their conquering days. Before long they became surprisingly tolerant. Under Kublai Khan (*d.* 1294), they made the Chinese Empire their own and frankly adopted Chinese ways. Partly because they felt the Moslems to be their most dangerous enemies and partly because their own religious ideas were ill-developed, the Tatars in China welcomed Christian missionaries and traders. As a consequence, there began a noteworthy period of intercourse between Europe and China, which lasted until the fall of the Mongol dynasty in 1368 and the advance of Mohammedanism into central Asia.

Meanwhile popes and kings in Europe nurtured the hope that the Mongols might prove to be Christendom's allies against Islam. Although this hope proved vain, Western missionaries were able to penetrate the Middle and Far East.[1] A Franciscan friar, John of Plano Carpini, was sent to the court of the Khan, then at Karakorum in Mongolia. So far as is known, he was the first westerner who penetrated inner Asia and returned to describe his travels. His detailed account of the two-year journey is invaluable. In 1253 another Franciscan, William of Rubruquis, also journeyed to the east hoping to found a mission. His account is equally important. Finally, John of Monte Corvino (*d.* about 1330), also a Franciscan, was able to found an archdiocese at Peking, of which he was the first incumbent. The Franciscan Chinese mission lasted only into the second half of the fourteenth century when contacts with the West were lost.[2]

Missionaries were followed by the venturesome Venetian traders, Nicolo and Maffeo Polo, who made two extended visits to China (1255–1266 and 1271–1295). On the second journey, after entering the Chinese emperor's service, they returned part of the way by sea along the coast of southern Asia. Nicolo's son, Marco, who accompanied them, wrote an account of his experiences which was translated into several languages. Among other things he mentioned many ports along the southeastern coast of China and indicated that the China Sea was not separate from adjacent bodies of water. He referred to the island of Zipangu (Japan). And he reported a great many useful things, much of it hearsay, but much too from his own observation, about the East Indies, Ceylon, the coast of India, the Red Sea region, and even the islands off the east African coast. Unfortunately, further pioneering toward the Far East was halted after the middle of the fourteenth century. For then the penetration of Islam into the Middle East and the passing of the Mongol rule in China interrupted communication between Europe and China.

---

[1] Nestorian Christian missionaries had entered the Middle and Far East as early as the fifth century. In the twelfth century a letter, presumably a hoax and purporting to come from an oriental Christian priest-king, reached the west. For centuries various travelers hoped to find the kingdom of "Prester John."

[2] The ravages of the Black Death in the mid-century, the advances of Islam in Middle Asia, and the supplanting of the Mongol dynasty by the Ming (1368) combined to make the maintenance of the mission impossible.

It is evident from the preceding pages that medieval expansion profoundly altered the map of Europe. The West's economic and institutional progress, which must now be described, affected an area far greater than that occupied by the emerging feudal kingdoms of the year 1100.

The belfry and cloth hall at Bruges. Civic architecture of the thirteenth and fourteenth centuries.

Courtesy Belgian National Tourist Office, New York

CHAPTER 16

Economic Development in the Twelfth and Thirteenth Centuries

A. Expansion of Maritime and Inland Trade

An earlier chapter has described the beginning of Europe's economic recovery in the tenth and eleventh centuries. This expansion continued in the following two centuries along with a steady rise in the population. Three areas were principally concerned in this development: the northern seaboard from the Atlantic to the eastern Baltic, the Mediterranean littoral, and the inland continental region between. One of the achievements of the age was a closer linking of these three areas.

Although trade along the North and Baltic Seas had been stimulated originally by the Scandinavians, these were being rivaled in the twelfth and thirteenth centuries by Germans and Flemings. German expansion eastward, it will be recalled, included not only agricultural settlements, but urban foundations along or near the Baltic coast or on the northern German rivers. Lübeck and Danzig, for example, became important trade centers. But many towns, large and small, made their appearance, and commercial contacts reached as far east as Novgorod in Russia and as far north as Bergen in Norway.

In northwestern Europe, the most important commercial region continued to be the Low Countries. The cloths of Ghent, Bruges, Ypres, Lille, and Arras, woven from English wool, were exported everywhere, even to the Levant. Since the Flemish themselves were more interested in industry than in commerce, foreigners flocked to their country to procure their goods. Flanders attracted English, Scandinavian, and German merchants from the North Sea and Baltic regions, and French, Spanish, and Italian merchants from the Mediterranean. Bruges was the Flemish commercial metropolis, enjoying a reputation in the north comparable to that of Venice in the Mediterranean.

The bulk of the trade of northern and western Europe, except for the important cloth exports of the Low Countries, was in raw materials such as copper, iron, tin, timber, hides, wool, or certain food stuffs, including fish, salt, beer, and grain. The wines from France and from the Rhine and Moselle valleys were in widespread demand. Bordeaux was a major center of wine export. But, as the standard of living rose, there was also exchange of luxury products.

Even before the First Crusade, Genoese, Pisans, Normans, and others had challenged the Moslem and Venetian monopoly of Mediterranean commerce. The Crusades clinched European dominance in the Mediterranean, and since the Crusaders were dependent for the transport of troops and supplies on the maritime towns of Europe, these, and especially the Italian, were enabled to drive hard bargains. Most of the Near Eastern ports, or at least important sections in them, were controlled by merchants of Genoa, Pisa, Amalfi, Venice, Provence, or Aragon. Thus traders from southern Europe were established at the terminals of the chief commercial routes to the east.

Meanwhile, other maritime regions felt the impetus of commercial expansion. Sicilians obtained a temporary foothold in African Tripoli and Tunis (1134–1135). Genoese were active in Ceuta, pushed southward along the Atlantic coast of Morocco, and, following the Fourth Crusade, further accentuated a growing rivalry with Venice by establishing bases in the Crimea. Meanwhile, considerable numbers of Italians, especially Venetians, were taking up permanent residence in the Byzantine Empire and appropriating much of its commerce. Aragon also became a flourishing maritime state with its control over the Balearics and its annexation of Sicily.

Much, though by no means all, of Mediterranean trade was in the luxury products of the east. Oriental spices, which were in general demand throughout Europe for seasoning and preserving foodstuffs, and which had provided a powerful impetus for the expansion of medieval commerce, continued well into modern times to occupy the foremost place. But many other eastern wares were also in demand: certain foodstuffs, such as oranges, apricots, and figs; dyestuffs, textiles like damask (Damascus), muslin (Mosul), gauzes (Gaza), cotton, and raw silk. In exchange, Europe exported some of its primary raw materials, notably timber and iron, and certain manufactured goods, especially Flemish woolens.

The expansion of sea-borne trade was accompanied by, indeed it required, a corresponding progress in shipbuilding and navigation. This was particularly noticeable in the Mediterranean. The galley remained the common type of vessel, but it was enlarged and some Genoese and Venetian craft were upwards of a hundred feet long and with two or three decks. The sailing ships of the North and Baltic Seas were smaller, higher in the water, and of broader beam. Boat construction was generally improved. Better sails, masts, and spars came into use. Perfecting of the stern rudder in the thirteenth century eliminated the earlier and clumsier lateral steering methods. Development of the fore-and-aft rig, known in the Mediterranean as early as the ninth century, came into more general use, though often in combination with square-rigged sails. As sailing became less dependent on wind variation, the number of oarsmen in galleys could be reduced and cargo space correspondingly enlarged. There was also great improvement in ballasting, cargo stowing, and the provision of life-boats. The Venetian government devised a remarkably efficient system of ship inspection which curbed the parsimonious propensities of profit-seeking merchants. Important improvements were also made in harbor facilities, beacons, and lighthouses. Venice and Bruges were noted for their effective management of docks, lighters, and cranes.

Discovery of the properties of the magnetized needle, and its use in the compass, practically revolutionized navigation. Whether Europeans gained this now indispensable knowledge from the Moslems, or *vice versa,* is still a disputed point. At any rate, Europe had knowledge of the magnetized needle in the twelfth century, and put it to practical use in the thirteenth. By the fourteenth century the needle, suspended over a card indicating directions, was coming to be standard equipment for sailing vessels. The astrolabe, an instrument developed by the Arabs for determining latitude, seems to have been more slowly introduced. But taken altogether, these innovations made possible longer voyages out of sight of land. Some of the human obstacles were more formidable than those of nature. And since piracy remained a largely unsolved problem throughout the middle ages, most merchant vessels sailed armed and in fleets.

The inland trade of western Europe progressed less rapidly, because the obstacles to land transportation were removed far more slowly. These obstacles, it will be recalled, were both physical and political: bad roads, bridges, and wagons, and the persistence of man-made impediments in the way of brigandage and innumerable tolls. Some new roads were built and old ones improved. Bridges seemed to have fared somewhat better, and a number of canals were cut. European rivers were as indispensable to medieval trade as they are to-day; and more of them were navigable to the small sea-going ships of the middle ages than to the ocean liners of to-day.

The man-made obstacles to inland trade were both legal and illegal. Tolls, levied by local feudal lords, were numerous. Central government was slow to remedy the abuses of such tolls, and for many years it was powerless to prevent brigandage. Even in France and England, where central government was being strengthened, police jurisdiction long remained local and inefficient or obstructive. Broadly speaking, the "robber-barons," though not extinct, were mainly confined by the thirteenth century to out-of-the-way places. Wherever governmental authority was lacking, merchants took matters into their own hands, formed mutual protective associations, and traveled in large bands whenever possible. German towns, for example, often associated themselves in leagues.

A flourishing commerce requires adequate facilities for the marketing or exchange of goods. In the early middle age, when the volume of trade was small, the individual traveling merchant disposed of his wares as best he could. Markets were usually local and feudal, and concerned chiefly with the exchange of agricultural commodities. But as the quantity and variety of commodities expanded and the number of merchants rose, the older markets proved to be woefully inadequate. Solution of the marketing problem was now found partly in the development of urban communities—a feature of medieval commercial revival which will presently engage our attention—and partly in the institution of fairs.[1]

Fairs sprang up during the middle ages in all parts of Europe, but principally they were established in places through which passed an habitually used trade route, or in some locality sufficiently central to enable merchants from various countries to attend. A fair was not simply a large market; it was a very special kind of institution. Markets were of local and restricted economic importance. Fairs were universal in scope, and customarily privileged by law; they were held under the jurisdiction of a king or high feudatory who offered protection, regulation, and other inducements in order to attract the largest possible number of merchants and prospective buyers. Usually a special court was maintained for the settlement of all law-suits arising out of trade at the fair. In England, this was called the "pie powder" court (*pie poudreus*, dusty feet). Moreover, the convenience of traders was served by

---

[1] The name "fair" comes from the Latin, *feria*, "feast day." The day on which the fair opened was usually a saint's day or other holy day.

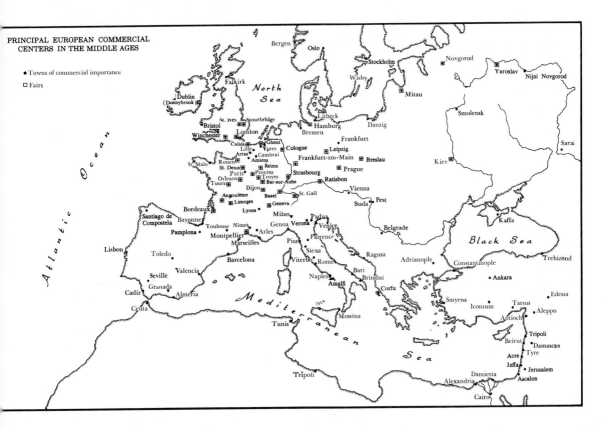

PRINCIPAL EUROPEAN COMMERCIAL
CENTERS IN THE MIDDLE AGES

• Towns of commercial importance
□ Fairs

bureaus of exchange for the various moneys in circulation. *Lettres de foire* ("fair letters") were also used. These were promises to pay at some future date, and were sometimes redeemable at a merchant's home establishment. They were early letters of credit.

In addition to the attractions of business, the medieval fair, like its modern counterpart, the county fair, had its social aspects, its amusements and side shows. Strolling jongleurs and acrobats would frequent fairs as they would any large gathering of people. And we may. be sure the various prizes and contests which attract people in modern times were equally alluring in the middle ages. The fairs were thoroughly popular institutions.

Although fairs were held all over Europe with similar procedures, those of Champagne were the most famous. These had a peculiarly favorable location at a crossroads of inland commerce. The counts of Champagne were not slow to capitalize on such a location and to afford special encouragement. Moreover, the Champagne fairs performed an especially important function in providing the first large-scale, regular contact between the northern seaboard area and the Mediterranean. Flemish cities built warehouses in the Champagne fair towns and regularly dealt with representatives of Italian business concerns who traveled north. Small wonder that during the thirteenth century there was hardly a time of year when one fair or another was not in progress in the county.

B. Medieval Industry, Money, and Credit

Medieval industrial advance, exclusive of those crafts devoted to local or town consumption, was considerable. There was marked advance in the manufacture of woolen cloth in Flanders. For dyeing it, Florentines and Venetians imported dyes from the Near East, and learned to make new colors. Before long, Florentines were "finishing" Flemish textiles for reëxport, and creating a cloth manufacturing industry of their own. We have mentioned the silk industry at Palermo and Lucca and the glass manufacture which flourished at Venice.

Limoges in France was renowned for its enamel ware.

Progress in mining and metallurgy was furthered by certain technical advances in pumping out and draining the pits, in the smelting of the ore, and in the use of waterpower for crushing ore and operating lifts. Iron was in far greater demand for building than had been the case in ancient times. The Tyrol, Bohemia, Carinthia, and Sweden were all important iron producing 'regions. Some iron ore as well as tin was also obtained in Spain and in England. Copper was procurable in Sweden. Of the precious metals, gold was mined in Bohemia, Hungary, Carinthia, and Spain; silver in Bohemia and Hungary. Coal pits were opened near Liege in the Netherlands.

The expansion of commerce created a need for a more mobile and more stable currency, and before the end of the thirteenth century the monetary situation had greatly improved, although it still left much to be desired. Among the new coins struck were the Venetian silver groat (1192) and the Florentine florin (1252), the latter marking the return of a relatively stable gold coinage to Europe. Unfortunately there remained too many types of coins issued by different feudal principalities. No comprehensive monetary system was attained in the middle ages.

Ordinary demands of economic life require credit, and the borrowing and lending of money. Credit was provided for in the middle ages by the "fair letters" we have previously mentioned. Money lending, on the other hand, was impeded by the stand which the church took against usury, or the charging of interest on loans. In the early middle age, loans had been made, but they were mainly for consumption, and not for productive purposes, and only non-Christians—chiefly Jews—were supposed to charge interest for them. But in the twelfth and thirteenth centuries there is ample evidence that, while the services of Jewish money-lenders were still in demand, traffic in money was becoming widespread among Christians, notably Italians. Successful merchants obtained capital for their expanding enterprises by permitting one or more partners to contribute money in return for a share in the profits. Thus a business partnership was established. Many such associations (and they were increasingly numerous wherever business flourished) also lent money to kings or even to the church. In general, money-lenders were also merchants. Banking as a separate occupation came later.

It seems evident that the church's prohibition of usury was not strictly heeded. What actually happened was, first, the elaboration of various methods of disguising the taking of interest, and, second, a gradual recognition on the part of ecclesiastical authorities of a distinction between legitimate "interest" and prohibited "usury." Nevertheless, the church's formal prohibition remained, and the problem of dealing with it or getting around it continued to plague both clergy and laity.[1]

In another though less obvious way, the teachings of the church ran counter to the spirit of the whole commercial revival. To trade for the sake of gain, for the accumulation of profit rather than simply to provide for the necessities of life, even to charge more than a "just price,"[2] was regarded as falling into the sin of avarice. In the medieval church's outlook on life, there was little room for the kind of capitalistic enterprise which we have described. Yet a genuine and vigorous capitalism did develop and the successful entrepreneurs often attempted to salve their consciences by endowing charitable institutions, churches, and monasteries, and by leaving funds for Masses to be said for the repose of their souls after death. Evidently the conflict between the spirit of gain and the Christian way of life was very real in the middle ages. Medieval capitalism did not entirely deaden the consciences of men who were never allowed to forget the church's teachings.

C. Development of Urban Communities

In our discussion of the commercial revival in the middle age of the twelfth and thirteenth centuries, we have repeatedly referred to towns as economic centers. We have taken them for granted. We must now examine more carefully their development and their relation to the revival of trade. Among the various and conflicting theories as to the origin of medieval towns which still engage the attention of scholars, one thing seems certain. Whatever its former site or the manner in which it came into existence, a medieval town was the creation of enterprising merchants working together. Merchants naturally sought out communities which offered them protection and a market. Those most favorably situated from an economic point of view, on navigable rivers, portages, river junctions, crossroads, or harbors, inevitably attracted the largest number of traders.

In turn, a congregation of traders soon attracted artisans who saw a greater opportunity to dispose of their wares and to procure the raw materials for their craft. Thus a type of settlement appeared whose inhabitants lived a very different kind of life from the ordinary feudal community. Often it was called a "new" *burg* or *faubourg* (*foris burgus*, outside the *burg*), or suburb (*suburbium*).[3] And in countless instances the *faubourg* became larger than, or even engulfed, the original settlement. Since the *faubourg* was usually enclosed by a wall and, as a consequence, became in its own right a *burg*, or fortified community, such terms as "burgher," "bourgeois," or "burgess," came to be applied to its inhabitants. Thus the extension in meaning of a now well-known word illustrates the importance of these new communities.

The communities of merchants and artisans formed an essentially new element in feudal society. The inhabitants of a *faubourg* were not typical feudal personages. Being neither nobles nor peasants, they did not fit into the feudal organization as individuals. Feudal law did not provide for the freedom of movement or for the right to possess movable property which were vital to a mercantile society. Consequently, the members of these new communities strove for some sort of autonomy. Many cities won their freedom dearly against determined

---

[1] It is worth noting that questions regarding usury were reserved to the ecclesiastical courts.

[2] Theologians held that the "just price" should include the cost of material and labor plus a profit sufficient to enable the craftsman to live according to his station in life.

[3] A *burg* was originally a fortified settlement of peasants, knights, and clergy commonly located in a frontier region.

The Cathedral and Leaning Tower at Pisa.

opposition and at the price sometimes of years of actual fighting. For many nobles, both ecclesiastical and lay, saw in the rise of towns a threat to their traditional feudal jurisdiction. The association thus forced on the burghers gave rise to a new term, "commune," often used in medieval town history.

Other more fortunate urban communities found their neighboring feudal lord amenable to reason or to regular money tribute. Many lay magnates saw possible advantages to themselves in the development of adjacent commercial towns; and during and after the twelfth century, a number of princes were prompted for reasons of profit to establish towns, often with privileges guaranteed by a written charter. Kings frequently protected cities within the domains of their great vassals. Everywhere, the characteristic feature was the banding together of merchants into corporations in order to deal as legal entities with the nobility and the central government.

However achieved and whatever the degree of freedom attained, self-government of the towns guaranteed personal liberty. And eventually it signified not only a freedom granted to certain individuals, but to the town itself. Town liberty became territorial.[1] Thus the town inhabitants—the

bourgeosie—became in reality a privileged class. Moreover, the rights of the merchants and artisans of a *faubourg* were in time extended to include even the inhabitants of the original settlement, the whole forming a single urban community. Not all medieval towns achieved precisely the same degree of independence. The largest measure of autonomy was acquired in those regions, like north Italy or Germany, where monarchical centralization failed. For the flood tide of commercial prosperity coincided with the decline in power of the Holy Roman Empire. As subsequent pages will show, the resistance of the Lombard towns of north Italy contributed largely to the failure of imperial power. By 1250 they were independent in all but name.[2] And during the same period the so-called "imperial cities" of Germany were actually communities which, having thrown off immediate feudal control, were only nominally responsible to the Holy Roman Emperor. In countries like

---

[1] According to a widespread custom, residence in a town for a year and a day guaranteed freedom.

[2] In the Italian communes there were two factors not usually present elsewhere. First, most of them expanded to include the surrounding countryside, and became city-states. Second, as a result of expansion, the local nobility were drawn into the communal movement. Unlike the French, English, or German landlords who preferred their country castles, the Italian nobility took part in urban life. Only in some towns of southern France and of Spain were there similar developments.

France and England, where royal authority was enhanced, political independence such as the Italian cities enjoyed was rare. Here, even in those instances where autonomy had once been achieved, central government usually gained the upper hand sooner or later.

D. Town Institutions

In matters of internal administration, the burghers were breaking new ground, for there were few earlier institutions to guide them. Town councils, designated by the burghers, took charge of routine matters and displayed remarkable ingenuity in tackling such practical matters as food supply, schools, police, local taxation, and, of course, the regulation of commerce and industry.

The types of government devised by medieval townsmen varied with the degree of autonomy they possessed. And quite commonly single towns passed through extraordinary vicissitudes and many changes in their own institutions. But even in cities with limited rights of self-government, there developed a cohesive civic patriotism. The town became a miniature state, pledged to protect its citizens politically and economically. The outside world (including other towns) was "foreign" soil.

The characteristic institution for the regulation of economic life within the town was the guild. The earliest form of guild, and one that could be found practically everywhere, was the merchant guild, an association of merchants formed to protect and forward their mutual interests. Somewhat later the craft guild appeared. By this, each industry, or craft, devoted to the production of a particular kind of manufacture for local consumption, was organized into a separate guild whose function was to promote and protect the interests of the workers in that craft.

Most craft guilds were organized on a threefold hierarchical basis, embracing masters, journeymen, and apprentices. An apprentice was a young boy bound by his parents, according to a fixed contract and for a stipulated number of years, to some master craftsman. During his apprenticeship, he would live in the master's house,

work for him, and be completely under his control. In return the master was required to provide for the moral and physical needs of the apprentice and to educate him, especially in the techniques of the craft.

A journeyman was a young man who worked for some master as a hired day laborer (*journée*, day). So long as the guild system operated for the benefit of all in the craft, there was rarely any unemployment; and the journeyman worked in the master's shop on terms of familiarity if not equality with him.

In order to be accepted by the craft guild as a master and admitted into the full privileges of the association, a former apprentice or journeyman had to demonstrate upon examination his skill as a craftsman. Usually he had to create a "masterpiece," a completed product according to the standards of the guild and often while other masters watched. Then, after paying certain fees and perhaps banqueting his future associates, he became a full-fledged master.

Since the purpose of the guild was to protect its own members, it insisted first of all on a monopoly of its product in the town. Guild wardens periodically inspected their own and other crafts and reported infringements on the monopoly. Thus the guild system exhibited that extreme of protectionism which was characteristic of medieval town life. Since it was felt that the maintenance of a standard quality of output was essential to the good reputation of a craft guild, all guild production was regulated and inspected, and commonly the craftsmen were required to work near a window in full view of passersby. A standard fixed price prevented undue competition and assured the guild's monopoly.

Like the merchant guild, the craft guild was also a social and benevolent organization having its banquets and celebrations and caring for its own members or their families in time of trouble. Through the guilds the citizens expressed their civic pride, even much of their religious devotion. Guilds usually had a patron saint whose feast day they honored. And many beautifully stained glass windows in churches and cathedrals were donated by guilds.

At their best, that is in the late twelfth and thirteenth centuries, the guilds provided an organization of local industry without undue profit and with a high standard of work. Masters, apprentices, and journeymen worked together at the same table and in the same shop. And since every apprentice or journeyman presumably had the opportunity one day of becoming a master, the class distinction between employer and employee, so prominent in modern machine industry, hardly existed. Besides, the masters in any craft had perforce to be real craftsmen themselves. There was always, too, a direct exchange from producer to consumer. Competition was at a minimum, and no master was allowed to acquire property or a volume of trade so great as to be injurious to his fellows.

Such conditions could endure only in relatively small communities where the market was known and limited. With commercial expansion and resulting change in circumstances, there was evidence, even before the end of the thirteenth century, that the guild system, as originally conceived and operated, was breaking down. Competition for markets prompted masters to limit the number of apprentices. Requirements for guild membership were deliberately raised, and many apprentices and journeymen were prevented from becoming masters. In some cases, only members of guild families or the sons of wealthy friends were admitted. What was originally a protective monopoly was narrowed, and the relation between master and journeyman tended to become that of employer and employee, while unemployment increased. In short, the guilds evinced embryonic capitalistic tendencies. Further, the guild system inevitably discouraged industrial inventiveness.

It should also be borne in mind that the guilds controlled industrial life only within the town. Over expanding enterprises affecting wider areas, they had no control. In these, the craftsmen usually worked for some wealthy merchant as hired laborers, and, unlike the local guildsmen, they did not themselves sell the product of their own work but rather had to be content with letting their employer dispose of it abroad, perhaps in the Levant or in some other distant market. Although the workers in export industries organized themselves into guilds,

their relation to the merchants for whom they labored was that of employee to employer.

It is obvious from what we have said that the condition of craftsmen in the main middle age was not universally satisfactory. Whether because of growing exclusiveness of the masters of local guilds or because of

A medieval fortified town. Carcassonne.

Courtesy French Government Tourist Office, New York

competition in the export trades, journeymen were frequently exploited. Before the end of the thirteenth century, there were in relatively wealthy and populous Flanders a number of journeymen's strikes, which were drastically curbed by the town authorities representing the merchant class. Unemployment, poor wages, and wretched living conditions are not a monopoly of modern times.

A few words should be added about the appearance of medieval towns. Usually walled, they were apt to be very congested. Houses of five or even six stories were not uncommon, and since the upper stories jutted beyond the first, the streets were dark. Some attempts were made at "zoning."

Reims had a quaint regulation prohibiting houses higher than the level of the eaves of the cathedral. Venice permitted no houses higher than seventy feet. Florence, Paris, and Toledo limited buildings to one hundred, sixty, and seventy-five feet respectively. There was a good deal of overcrowding, and to discomfort was added the hazard of fire, since all houses except those of the very rich were built of wood. An ordinance of King Richard I of England required the separating of houses by at least a two-foot wall. Overcrowding was not evident everywhere within a medieval town, any more than it is in a modern city. There was always a public square or market place, usually in front of the cathedral or other principal church. And we read of gardens and orchards, even of small farms, within town limits. Within a medieval town, there were often distinctive "quarters" for particular or associated trades.

Town authorities, interested in the physical upkeep of the town, were concerned first with its defense. "Watch and ward" on the walls was always necessary, and the maintenance of fortifications was provided by taxation. Despite the popular notion that all medieval towns were extraordinarily dirty, many enterprising urban administrations, at least in the twelfth and thirteenth centuries, made important improvements in sanitation and cleanliness. It is true that in the previous period the narrow streets were unpaved and unlighted, and that refuse was thrown in a common gutter in the middle. But already in the twelfth century London and other cities had latrines and sub-surface sewers. Many communities provided a water supply from without, relieving the inhabitants of the necessity of relying entirely on wells. Cologne and Lübeck paved their market places and adjacent streets, and King Philip Augustus of France paved the street in front of his palace in Paris. By the thirteenth century, many municipal hospitals were established. The population of towns at the time cannot be determined accurately. A community of twenty thousand was considered a rather large town. Probably a majority were under ten thousand. Although a figure of one hundred thousand or over has been attributed to Venice and Paris, only a few others, such as Florence,

Milan, and Genoa, exceeded fifty thousand.

Outside the town proper there was usually a belt district, called in France the *banlieu*, which fell under the jurisdiction of the municipal authorities. It was often dotted with villages and farms and was indispensable to the provisioning of the town. Many of the artisans also lived in the *banlieu*.

E. Agricultural Development

The twelfth and thirteenth centuries constituted a period of significant agrarian as well as commercial development. This was in part a continuation of the expansion which had begun in the early middle age, but the growth of trade and urban life also radically affected the economy of the rural manor. Since much of the surplus population was drawn to the towns and since towns depended on food brought from the outside, a heightened agricultural production was necessitated. And the provisioning of towns opened up the possibility of farming for profit, rather than merely for local manorial consumption. Thus the clearing of new agricultural land from the forest, which had commenced in the early middle age, reached its climax in the twelfth and thirteenth centuries. Afterwards, for several centuries, there was not much further addition to cultivated land in central or western Europe. A great deal of the new farming was done in districts opened up along the frontiers, but much also was done within the older regions, where there was forest land to be cleared. Technological improvements furthered agricultural progress. The wheelbarrow, which came into use in the thirteenth century, was helpful; and the appearance of windmills in the same period was of marked utility, especially in areas where natural waterflow was sluggish.

An important role in the agricultural advance was played by the Cistercian monasteries. The Cistercian order was established early in the twelfth century with the idea of observing monastic rules more strictly. Whereas the older Benedictine and Cluniac foundations usually held estates or manors which had long been under cultivation, the Cistercians set themselves to clear new land.

This was accomplished not entirely by the monks themselves, who, according to the Cistercian rule, led extremely strict lives, but often by lay brothers, called *conversi*, who took the monastic vows but did not live the full monastic life. The Cistercians also employed numbers of agricultural laborers knowns as *hospites*. These were free laborers, whatever their original status, who, as a result of overcrowding on the older manors, sought new openings as pioneer farmers.

Not all *hospites* went to Cistercian farms. Many found their way to the fringes of forest borderland not part of any estate under cultivation, where they usually obtained from the nominal proprietor ready permission to settle. Eventually, enterprising landlords sought to attract *hospites* to villages deliberately established in hitherto undeveloped areas. Such settlements were known as *villeneuves* (new towns); and, although agricultural in nature, they often imitated the merchant communities and secured a charter and a measure of self-government. Not quite as independent as the real urban communities, for most lords retained certain rights over the land in the *villeneuves*, they were nevertheless very different from the older manors.

Pioneer free farming was the rule in new frontier regions. But it was also true of the "frontier" of the Low Countries, in the land won from the sea by diking. This work, as we have indicated, began in the early middle age. It continued with the encouragement of the counts of Flanders and often under the direction of monasteries. The Cistercians were particularly active. The abbey of the Dunes, for example, had nearly twice as much diked land as undiked.

The effects of the rise of towns on agriculture were striking. Manors which in the early feudal age produced only for home consumption were now able to produce a surplus for sale outside. Grain became an article of mercantile circulation, brought by the peasant to the town or sold to the merchant who traded in foodstuffs. As a consequence, money circulated more freely in the countryside. Peasants were able to buy freedom or to become tenant farmers paying a fixed rent. Some became laborers for hire. The size of holdings could be increased more readily by hard-working peasants who invested their savings in more land. Even the bourgeoisie speculated in land. The immobility of the manorial relationship was broken.

Since the dues and rents exacted by the landlords were usually fixed by immemorial custom and did not fluctuate, and since the general increase in money caused a rise in prices, many landlords—nobles, abbeys, and bishops—faced serious financial loss if not ruin. These, in order to keep their serfs from running away to the towns and if possible to increase their revenues, were forced to enfranchise serfs and to accept money rent. Since the process of emancipation was primarily the result of economic change, it was more rapid and widespread in the regions where commercial development was most advanced. Accordingly, in western and central Europe, by 1300, a substantial proportion of the peasants were in reality tenant farmers, not serfs in the older sense. In eastern Europe, on the other hand, serfdom was more general and lasted longer.

Another significant effect of the commercial revival was the tendency toward agricultural specialization. Certain regions concentrated on one product. Some landlords devoted all their acres to a crop which could be exported. The Cistercian abbeys of England, for example, were famous for their wool. In certain favorable areas, vineyards spread at the expense of grain growing. All these tendencies quickened in the later middle age.

It should be evident from the preceding pages that the economic life of the twelfth and thirteenth centuries was far from static. Western Europe was now dotted with thriving urban communities whose way of life altered medieval society. Simultaneously there were significant changes in the countryside, many of them induced by the commercial revival. But we must beware of exaggerating the importance of the medieval towns. Europe was still largely agrarian. Only in relatively recent times has European and Western civilization taken on the predominantly urban aspect which it now has.

Château-Gaillard, built by Richard I of England to control the route along the Seine.

Courtesy French Government Tourist Office, New York

CHAPTER 17

Consolidation of Feudal Monarchy in Western and Southern Europe

Political developments of the twelfth and thirteenth centuries followed a similar pattern in France, England, Spain, and Sicily. By 1300 feudal monarchy in these countries was evolving into more centralized royal states.

England and France were bound together by the fact that after 1066 the English rulers, royalty and aristocracy alike, were Norman Frenchmen who spoke French and held large domains in France. Copying and borrowing one from the other was inevitable. And since many French knights sought careers in Spain, French feudal influences persisted there. The Norman occupation of Sicily and southern Italy provided a Norman-French background for political institutions in those regions. In all the countries mentioned, though only temporarily in Sicily, governmental progress was marked.

A. English Monarchy in the Twelfth and Thirteenth Centuries

Among the most important consequences of the Norman conquest of England in 1066 was the introduction of Norman-French feudalism. Although William the Conqueror preserved whatever Saxon practices he found useful, he skillfully utilized such Norman institutions as emphasized the power of the overlord rather than the rights of the vassal. The typical Saxon local divisions—the shires and the hundreds—were maintained, although the shires were now often called counties. The sheriff (shire reeve) became a royal official, commanding the chief castle in the shire. He was appointed by and responsible to the king. Most important of all, the estates of the Anglo-Norman nobles were scattered. Except in the case of the Welsh and Scottish border marches, there were no compact fiefs in England with extensive governmental rights such as prevailed on the continent. A comprehensive and detailed survey of all landed properties as they existed before the conquest was ordered by William in 1086. The results were recorded in a document known as *Domesday Book*, one of the most important sources of information concerning English landholding in the eleventh century.

The foundations laid by William I proved their worth during the twelfth century. Under Henry I (1100–1135) feudal courts declined and many more cases were brought before the king's court (*curia regis*) than had been customary previously. While the *curia* itself accompanied the king wherever he went, agents of it were appointed as itinerant justices (*justices in eyre*) to hear cases on specifically designated circuits in regions not personally visited by the king.

Henry I left no sons, and a generation of feudal anarchy disturbed England until the accession of Henry II (1154–1189), the son of Henry I's daughter, Matilda, and of Count Geoffrey Plantagenet of Anjou. Henry II, the first of the Plantagenet, or Angevin, kings of England, was not merely ruler of England and Normandy, which he inherited from his mother. Maine had been added, and from his father he inherited Anjou and Touraine. In 1152 he married Eleanor, heiress of Aquitaine. As a consequence, although he remained a vassal to the king of France for his French holdings, he personally ruled a domain stretching through England and France, from the Scottish marches to the Pyrenees.

In spite of the manifold responsibilities which obliged him to spend more time on the continent than in England, Henry II was one of England's greatest kings. Perhaps the most famous of his reforms was the employment of juries as a regular part of judicial procedure. The origins of the jury can be traced to much older continental practice, perhaps to practice in the Roman Empire. Its immediate predecessor was the sworn inquest, adopted by the Normans from the Franks. In order to cope with violent crime, a legacy from the turbulent days before his accession, the King ordered (Assize of Clarendon, 1166) that twelve men from each hundred and four from each village should be present when an itinerant justice held a county court. These men who were to tell under oath the names of those suspected of crime formed a jury of presentment or indictment. Usually, the actual trial of a person thus indicted was the early medieval method of ordeal.

In certain kinds of civil cases, particularly those having to do with the land, Henry II directed that the actual trial should be by a smaller (*petit*) jury of twelve men. These twelve were presumed to possess some special knowledge of the case. They were witnesses and jurors combined. Not for many years did a distinction between juror and witness begin to be recognized, and consequently Henry II's use of the jury was only the germ of our modern system of trial by jury. Jury trials in criminal cases, although occasional, were not common much before the end of the thirteenth century.

Two consequences of Henry II's legal reforms should be emphasized. First, they contributed in a large measure to the development of what came to be known as the "common" law, that is, the law common to the entire realm. Second, through the use of the jury the king invaded and curtailed the local jurisdiction of the barons. Accordingly, the twelfth-century jury should be regarded as an extension of royal power, rather than as a curb on arbitrary government.[1]

In one important instance, the extension of royal justice ran into conflict with ecclesiastical jurisdiction. Since the Norman conquest had brought the English church into closer touch with Rome, the procedure in English ecclesiastical courts kept pace with the development of canon (church) law. There were, in twelfth-century England, two parallel and well organized legal systems, one of the king and the other of the church. And in view of the intimate relations of church and state, the possibilities of disputes over jurisdiction were very real. The case of clerics convicted of crime in ecclesiastical courts gave rise to a famous controversy between Henry II and a celebrated archbishop of Canterbury, Thomas Becket. Becket had originally been chancellor of the kingdom and a devoted servant of the king. Henry arranged that he be given the see of Canterbury in the hope that, as archbishop, he might coöperate in the king's plan to subordinate the church to the state. But Becket was a person who threw himself wholeheartedly into whatever task he assumed; and to the king's dismay, Becket resigned his chancellorship and became a stubborn champion of ecclesiastical rights.

The king had insisted that "criminous clerks," after conviction in ecclesiastical courts, should be handed over to the king's courts for punishment. These and other matters, for example the curtailment of the right of appeal from English ecclesiastical courts to Rome, were incorporated into a document called the Constitutions of Clarendon (1164). Becket at first gave his consent, with some reservations. But later he changed his mind and resisted to the last. He was forced to spend many years in exile in France. In the course of the protracted struggle, Henry let drop a chance remark

---

[1] The privilege of bringing suit before the king's justices was obtained by the purchase of a writ, and such purchase money enriched the royal treasury.

which he doubtless did not really mean, but which a few of his followers interpreted literally. For these sought out Becket in the cathedral of Canterbury and there murdered him.

The assassination shocked all Christian Europe, including England, and Henry, genuinely remorseful, submitted to papal legates, took an oath that he had no part in the murder, and conceded on the matters of criminal clerics and freedom of appeals to Rome. Various other matters were settled by subsequent negotiations between papal legates and the king's lawyers. Becket, the martyr, was canonized, and his shrine speedily became the object of popular pilgrimage.

The ensuing century—the thirteenth—was particularly significant in the development of English government, for two reasons. It opened with a struggle between King John (the son of Henry II) and his barons, leading to Magna Carta; and it closed with the summoning by King Edward I of the so-called Model Parliament (1295). Unfortunately both events have received exaggerated emphasis as a result of later interpretations placed upon them. In a certain sense, the really determining development of the century was the growth of the monarchy as an institution governing the realm.

An important feature of John's reign was the loss of all the French possessions except Aquitaine. The details of this change in the relations of the kings of France and England will be described in the following section. What is important to point out here concerning the loss of French possessions by the English king is, first, that it was a serious blow to the king's prestige, and, second, that it necessitated a relinquishing by his English barons of their feudal holdings abroad. These barons tended to become more exclusively English in their outlook, more jealous of their own rights as against those of the king, and more outraged by John's arbitrary actions and occasional injustice. That the reckoning was delayed until 1215 is a tribute to the basic strength of the Norman-Angevin monarchy.

In addition to the protracted struggle over the French lands, John from 1205 to 1213 was engaged in a bitter controversy with Pope Innocent III. A disputed election to the see of Canterbury had been appealed to Innocent, who took the opportunity of persuading the electors present at Rome to accept his own candidate, Stephen Langton. Stephen was an excellent choice, but the king saw in the Pope's action a denial of his own claim to nominate to English sees. He refused to accept Stephen and confiscated the episcopal estates. For seven years

The murder of Thomas Becket from a thirteenth century English manuscript.

Courtesy Pierpont Morgan Library, New York

John defied papal interdict [1] and excommunication, and attacked those who obeyed the Pope, even seizing as hostages the sons or daughters of recalcitrant barons. Eventually all classes of the population were affected by the king's misrule and his conflict with the church. Finally, Innocent III, hearing of a baronial conspiracy against the king, proclaimed his deposition, absolved his subjects from their allegiance, and summoned the assistance of the king of France. But John was clever enough to appease one opponent in order to face others. Not only did he submit to the Pope (1213) and agree to accept Stephen Langton, but he made over his kingdom to the papacy as a fief and promised an annual payment to Rome of a thousand marks. Thereby he solicited papal support against the now rebellious barons in England. But when he returned from a finally unsuccessful attempt to recover his French possessions, he had to face a formidable combination of discontented and defiant nobles. He submitted to their demands at Runnymede and signed the Great Charter in 1215.

Viewed in relation to the situation in thirteenth-century England, Magna Carta was not a revolutionary document. Rather, it was feudal and conservative, a reëmphasis on that fundamental characteristic of all feudalism, the mutual contract between lord and vassal. John had violated such a contract, and no king was to do so again. Yet the conditions of the granting of the charter, as well as the actual wording of certain of its provisions, were susceptible, especially in later times, of a more revolutionary interpretation.

The very act of calling a ruler to account, even though the motive was feudal, together with the somewhat clumsy provision that his acts were to be supervised by a committee of barons, was of the very essence of *limited* sovereignty. Although the clause, "no freeman shall be arrested and imprisoned, or dispossessed, or outlawed, or banished, or in any way molested, nor will we set forth against him, nor send against him, unless by the lawful judgment

of his peers and by the law of the land," did not guarantee trial by jury, it did assure, in cases of arrest, an orderly procedure governed by accepted custom. Further, while in 1215 the word "freeman" had a limited meaning, by the seventeenth century it signified almost everyone.

Magna Carta was confirmed six times during the thirteenth century, and many times more during the later Middle Age. For later generations it became an arsenal of rights. It hardly had such significance in the year 1215.

The reign of Henry III (1216–1272) was important principally because a series of royal difficulties with the nobility confirmed the limitations on monarchical power laid down in Magna Carta. In 1258 the king was forced to submit to various baronial restrictions on his authority set forth in an additional document, the Provisions of Oxford. In 1264 he was defeated and captured by a number of magnates led by Simon de Montfort. Only the death of Simon and the more successful maneuvers of Henry's son, Edward I, saved the royal prestige.

Under Edward I (1272–1307), one of England's ablest kings, the worst controversies of the earlier period were avoided and a more normal progress rendered possible. In many respects his policy was more English and less continental than that of his predecessors. Wales was conquered (1276–1284). Scotland was subjugated, although its people soon rebelled under the leadership of Robert Bruce, who defeated Edward II at the battle of Bannockburn (1314) and reëstablished Scottish independence.

Under Edward I there also appeared more clearly than before a distinction within the *curia regis* between an inner group of councillors who met regularly with the king and the more cumbersome and less frequently summoned great council of all the major barons and prelates. Certain meetings of the latter were called parliaments. And in order to obtain a closer contact with elements of the population hitherto not represented, Edward began to summon representatives, chosen locally, from the shires and the boroughs, the

---

[1] Interdict is the prohibition of normal religious functions within a specified area.

knights and the burgesses. Because all the elements which were to become associated with English practice in this regard were present at a meeting in 1295, this came to be called the "model parliament." [1] It met in four separate groups, not in two as in later times. And though not regarded as particularly important at the time, this meeting marked the beginning of what was to become a celebrated institution.

Edward I had no such serious trouble with the church as Henry II or John had had. He was personally devout and on good terms with the popes, with whom he often coöperated in taxing the English clergy. On one matter he clashed with Pope Boniface VIII. When the latter declared in the letter, or "bull," *Clericis laicos* (1302), that the clergy should not be taxed by lay rulers without papal consent, Edward replied by refusing the clergy access to the royal courts. Edward's stand against Boniface proved successful, though not as spectacularly so as that of his French contemporary, Philip IV.

The foundations of the English constitution were laid in the medieval feudal period. The significance of the developments we have described did not escape contemporary Englishmen. Ranulf de Glanvill, Henry II's justiciar, wrote a *Treatise on the Laws and Customs of the Kingdom of England*. Henry de Bracton produced a similar work in the thirteenth century. These and other writings, together with the recorded decisions of the king's justices, formed an important body of literature on the government and law of England. It is well for modern English-speaking students to appreciate the extent of our debt to the medieval past.

B. French Monarchy in the Twelfth and Thirteenth Centuries

In the twelfth century the strictly royal domain of France—the Île-de-France—was still surrounded by large fiefs with old traditions of independence. In the thirteenth century, however, large areas were added to the royal holdings, and as in England a century earlier, institutions of centralization were elaborated within the framework of feudalism. It is evident that the key to the understanding of medieval French history is the geographical growth of the royal domain.

Toward the end of his reign, King Louis VI (1108–1137) arranged a marriage between his son and Eleanor, the heiress of the duchy of Aquitaine. As sometimes happened in such marriages, the royal couple proved to be ill matched, and the husband, Louis VII (1137–1180), was able in 1152 to procure from a council of French clergy an annulment of the marriage. Thus the French king lost control of Aquitaine, a large fief including the greater part of southwestern France. Eleanor's marriage two months later to Henry Plantagenet, the future Henry II of England, has already been mentioned. It transferred control of Aquitaine to the English crown, which already controlled Normandy, Maine, Anjou, and Touraine, and presently gained Brittany. Thus roughly two thirds of France owed immediate fealty to the English King Henry II. True, Henry was in turn the vassal of the French King Louis VII for these territories, but Henry was a vastly more powerful sovereign than Louis. In the circumstances it is a tribute to the latter's ability that he held his own against the former.

Philip II (1180–1223), generally known by the surname "Augustus," was a wily sovereign and very successful. He occupied Artois and Vermandois, and, after Henry's death, acquired part of Berry and Auvergne. For personal and political reasons, his English contemporary, King John, had married the fiancée of one of his own vassals in Poitou, Hugh of Lusignan. Hugh complained to Philip as John's overlord, although such appeals from a sub-vassal to the king were then rare. Philip bided his time until he felt strong enough to challenge his royal vassal. Then, in 1202, he summoned John to answer Hugh's charges at his court. And when John refused to appear after the customary three summons, Philip declared John's French fiefs forfeit. Though perfectly legal in feudal law, this

---

[1] In 1295 two knights from each shire and two burgesses from each town were summoned in addition to the principal ecclesiastics and barons.

was a bold maneuver. It succeeded. In the ensuing war Philip was able to drive John from northern France, including all of Normandy, Brittany, Anjou, Maine, and Touraine, and subsequently he conquered Poitou. When John attempted to repair his fortunes and made alliances with the Holy Roman Emperor Otto IV, with the count of Flanders, and with a number of other magnates, Philip, with the support of Otto's imperial rival, Frederick II, decisively defeated John's allies at Bouvines (1214). The French royal domain was trebled in size, and the prestige and power of the Capetian monarchy immensely increased.

It was also during the early thirteenth century that Pope Innocent III proclaimed a Crusade against the Albigensian heretics of southern France.[1] This was espoused by

[1] On Innocent III's policies, see pp. 176, 181, 227, 235.

Philip II's successors and utilized to extend their control southward. In 1229, after a devastating struggle, it was arranged that Count Raymond VII of Toulouse, the son of Raymond VI whose refusal to proceed against the heretics had occasioned the conflict, should be allowed to retain only the small part of his lands which had not yet been conquered, but even this reverted to the French crown on the death of Raymond's successor without heirs.[2] Since many northern barons were also rewarded with fiefs in the south, a veritable northern "invasion" added to the devasta-

[2] The French King Louis VIII (1223–1226) had given certain of his younger sons royal fiefs called *apanages*. Two especially deserve mention here: Charles was given Anjou and Maine, to which he later added Provence, east of the Rhone. Alphonse was given Poitou and Auvergne, to which he added Toulouse through his marriage to the daughter of Count Raymond VII.

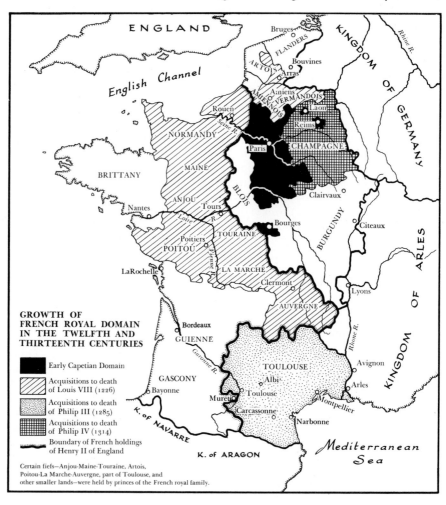

GROWTH OF FRENCH ROYAL DOMAIN IN THE TWELFTH AND THIRTEENTH CENTURIES

■ Early Capetian Domain

▨ Acquisitions to death of Louis VIII (1226)

░ Acquisitions to death of Philip III (1285)

▦ Acquisitions to death of Philip IV (1314)

Boundary of French holdings of Henry II of England

Certain fiefs—Anjou-Maine-Touraine, Artois, Poitou-La Marche-Auvergne, part of Toulouse, and other smaller lands—were held by princes of the French royal family.

tion wrought by the war and further strengthened the political hegemony of the north over the south. Finally, in the latter part of the century, King Philip IV married the heiress of Champagne and Navarre. Thus, in the space of a hundred years the French royal domain expanded from the Île-de-France to include the greater part of the whole kingdom of France.[1]

French institutional development of the period hardly kept pace with the English. In the first place, it was not until the reign of Philip II (Augustus) that the amount of territory under direct royal control was really significant. Secondly, in many of the lands incorporated during the thirteenth century, as well as in the great fiefs which remained outside of the royal domain, local customs and usages persisted. Nevertheless, as the king's lands increased to the point where he controlled an aggregate of former fiefs far larger than the domain of any existing magnate, the occasions when his authority was exercised outside his domain became rapidly more numerous. Appeals to the king's court, which were exceptional in the days of Louis VI and Louis VII, henceforth became the rule. And, although the kings still traveled frequently, Paris in the thirteenth century was developing into a permanent royal residence and the capital of the French feudal monarchy.

Some of the men who accomplished these things are deserving of special mention. Suger, abbot of St. Denis, a learned man and an ascetic, was also a capable administrator. He was a tower of strength as chief minister for Louis VI and Louis VII. Philip Augustus is naturally best known for his territorial acquisitions, but he also instituted, for his newly expanded domain, a system of local administration modeled on that of the Anglo-Norman-Angevin rulers. Bailiffs (in the north) or seneschals (in the south), drawn usually from the petty nobles or royal knights of the *curia*, supervised alloted districts. As delegates of the

king's court, they made royal authority felt in outlying areas. Louis IX strengthened the system by ordering periodic inquests and issuing special ordinances for the conduct of bailiffs and seneschals.

Louis IX (1226–1270), more often known as Saint Louis, was brought up devotedly, but strictly, by his capable mother, Blanche of Castile. It was she who instilled in him an intense loyalty to the Christian religion and a conscientious devotion to the ideal of a true Christian monarch. As regent for eight years during her son's minority, she ably administered the kingdom, and remained a wise adviser to him after he came of age. Louis possessed that rare combination of a deeply religious temperament with a capacity for bold action. No ruler has ever surpassed his zeal for justice. So universal was the confidence in the wisdom of his decisions that he was invited to arbitrate disputes in other lands. And although on occasion his generous impulses got the better of his judgment, his whole reign was one long effort to protect rights and to see that obligations were fulfilled. Thus the "crowned saint" was an exceptionally capable ruler with a remarkable judgment in matters of government.

The character of Philip IV (1285–1314), known to history as Philip the Fair, is less easy to appraise. Certain of his policies and acts, though possibly dictated by influential advisers, have given him a sinister reputation as a ruthless and unscrupulous monarch. Some of these will be described in subsequent pages,[2] but it is appropriate to suggest here that the portrait of Philip as an evil king has perhaps been overdrawn. He regarded himself as following in the steps of his sainted grandfather.

As in England, the chief business of the *curia regis* (or royal court) in France was judicial. As the number and variety of cases increased, the court required the services of professional lawyers who sat in on sessions known as *parlements*. These men were trained, presumably in feudal law, and, as the thirteenth century wore on, many also in Roman law. Thus there came into being a permanent corps of judges resident at Paris which later was

---

[1] In an agreement with the king of Aragon (1259), the French King Louis IX gave up claims to Catalonia and Roussillon which dated from the formation of the Spanish march in the time of Charlemagne, in return for a relinquishment, on the part of Aragon, of all claims north of the Pyrenees except Montpellier.

[2] See below, pp. 205, 207–209, 227.

to become a separate body known as the *Parlement*, the highest court in feudal France. Since the *curia regis* was occasionally in session for financial matters exclusively, there eventually appeared a specialized personnel, the germ of what in the fourteenth century was called the *chambre des comptes*.

There also appeared in France a general assembly, or Estates General. Philip IV first summoned such an assembly in 1302 during a sharp crisis in his relations with the pope. It comprised representatives of three Estates—clergy, nobility, and third estate—and was the beginning of an institution which at first resembled the English parliament, but whose later history was quite different. The Estates General strengthened rather than limited the French monarchy. It should be remembered that there were also provincial or regional estates.

The summoning of the Estates General indicates the rising importance of the bourgeoisie and the towns. In fact, monarchy and towns were natural allies against the feudal nobility. Louis VII, occasionally,

The young King Louis IX (1226–1270), from a French manuscript of the thirteenth century.

Courtesy Pierpont Morgan Library, New York

and Philip Augustus, more consistently, granted and confirmed town charters and encouraged the formation of communes. The latter found town militias of considerable assistance. During the reign of Louis IX, however, many towns were under the control of oligarchies of rich guildsmen whose policies often weighed heavily on the poor and whose mismanagement of finances endangered the royal revenues. Accordingly, although Louis IX confirmed some old charters and reëstablished municipal privileges where royal officers had abused them, he founded only one new commune.[1] And wherever possible, he attempted to bring towns, especially their financial administration, under royal supervision.

The signal advance of the French monarchy had been paralleled by an equally impressive establishment of effective papal supremacy. The papacy of the twelfth and thirteenth centuries, as a later chapter will explain more fully, was in a position to challenge royal encroachments on ecclesiastical liberties. The case of John of England was an illustration. Moreover, Innocent III, one of the great popes of the middle ages, felt it his duty to discipline a monarch for grave immorality. When Philip Augustus repudiated his wife and she appealed to Rome, Innocent ordered the King to reinstate her. Philip refused, but after defying excommunication and interdict for several years, he eventually relented. On the other hand, he would not let the Pope arbitrate his quarrel with the English king, and he maintained his own control over the French clergy by appointing the bishops in his dominions. Even Louis IX, saint that he was, resisted any ecclesiastical interference with what he considered his legitimate authority. For all his intense loyalty to his religion he felt that in political matters pope and bishops might be mistaken.[2]

If Louis IX's relations with the church had been characterized by a pious loyalty

---

[1] This was Aigues-Mortes, a naval and commercial establishment, founded in connection with crusading.

[2] Note also Louis's attitude toward the controversy between Innocent IV and Frederick II. See below, pp. 220, 237.

mingled with reserve, a famous controversy between his grandson, Philip the Fair, and Pope Boniface VIII was marked by spectacular violence. Boniface was an accomplished canonist, devoted to the extreme temporal claims of the papacy as enunciated by some of his predecessors. Unfortunately, he was deeply involved in the factional and family quarrels of thirteenth-century Italy. Moreover, he was a man singularly lacking in diplomatic finesse. In his bull, *Clericis laicos*, Boniface had forbidden kings to tax the clergy without papal permission. Philip replied by stopping the export of money and precious metals from France to Rome. Later, when the Pope attempted to defend a bishop against the arbitrary decisions of a secular court and issued two other bulls, Philip, by summoning the first Estates General, sought to enlist the support of the country against the Pope. Whereupon Boniface issued still another bull, *Unam sanctam*, which reëmphasized papal supremacy in the strongest language.

Assured of the backing of the Estates General, and following the advice of his minister, Nogaret, Philip intensified the campaign against the Pope. A mission was dispatched to bring the pontiff to trial before a general council. Nogaret, joined by Italian factions, sought out Boniface at Anagni where the Pope met his enemies with great dignity. Nevertheless, he was insulted and seized. And although Nogaret was subsequently forced to release him, the aged pontiff died soon afterwards (1303).

The affair of Philip and Boniface has often been regarded as the first striking victory of the "national state" over the medieval papal theocracy, a sort of "Canossa" in reverse. Such, in a sense, it was. Thirteenth-century France was already becoming a national state. Yet it should be borne in mind that although Philip the Fair was a powerful monarch, he was still only a suzerain over considerable areas. France lacked a common law and even a common language. In 1300 Frenchmen were still Normans, Bretons, Burgundians, Gascons, or Poitevins. French royal power, like that in England, was limited. But it was limited less by constitutional curbs than by considerations of distance and communication,

and, above all, by the varied cultural backgrounds of the different parts of the country.

Finally, it should be emphasized that thirteenth-century France, a thriving country with an expanding population, had obtained an eminent position in the cultural life of Europe. It was at once the home of the great university of Paris, of Gothic architecture, and of a vernacular literature of widespread popularity. Such matters will receive more extended consideration in later chapters.

C. Developing Christian Kingdoms of the Iberian Peninsula

The rugged mountainous nature of much of the Iberian peninsula and the prolonged wars for its reconquest by Christians from Moslems combined to delay its political unity. Moreover, the constant influx of French knights to participate in the local crusades served to perpetuate in the peninsula the feudalism which was passing in France. As late as 1300, the peninsula was still divided into four Christian kingdoms— Portugal, Navarre, Castile, and Aragon— and a Moslem state of Granada. Political separatism was also accentuated by cultural and linguistic differences. In those years which saw the rise of vernacular languages and literature, the Hispanic peninsula had four different ones—Portuguese, Castilian, Catalan, and Basque, not to mention Arabic.

Communities of *Mozarabs*, Christians who had in large measure adopted Moslem culture, were incorporated in one or another of the expanding Christian kingdoms, or utilized as new settlers on conquered territory. *Mudejares*, free Moslem Arabs, were also numerous in conquered areas and some degree of autonomy was customarily guaranteed them in the treaties of surrender. Jews likewise constituted an important element in the peninsular population. The same Moslem resurgence which threatened Christian Spain toward the end of the twelfth century and in the early years of the thirteenth, led to persecution of Jews in Moslem Spain, and at the time large numbers of them found a cordial reception in Christian areas. Upwards of ten thousand, for example, were welcomed to Toledo, where they were subsequently permitted to hold public office. Only in the later Middle Ages and early modern times did popular and official resentment toward Jews become a factor in Spanish life.

All such elements increased the diversity of Spain's population, while notably enriching its culture. Yet despite political and cultural divergences, there were certain common features of Christian civilization in the Iberian peninsula which it will be well to consider.

The chief difference between the fundamental agricultural life of Spain and that, let us say, of France, was the prevalence of grazing in the former. For while the upland plains and mountainous regions of the peninsula could support many sheep and cattle, they were not suitable for any large-scale cultivation. Thus, while medieval Spain fostered a privileged, land-owning nobility in common with most of western Europe, the type of agrarian community characteristic of western feudalism had scarcely taken root in Spain. But there were a considerable number of towns enjoying

special privileges under royal charters (*fueros*). Cities were often founded in reconquered territory, and liberties promised as an inducement to settlers. Leagues or brotherhoods (*hermandades*) of towns, formed usually as a means of protection against the nobles as well as against Moslems, played an important part in Spanish political life and were often highly useful to the kings.

As far as institutions of central government were concerned, considerable progress was made in the larger states. In Castile, Alphonso X "the Wise" (1252–1284) was not only a patron of general learning, but the author of *Las Siete Partidas*, a code of laws based on Roman principles of centralized monarchy. In both Castile and Aragon, *cortes* or parliaments antedated the English Parliament and the French Estates General. The *cortes* of Castile was an assembly summoned by the king and comprising nobles and clergy together with representatives from the towns chosen by lot. Like their counterparts elsewhere, the Castilian *cortes* met only at the king's pleasure, but their powers somewhat ex-

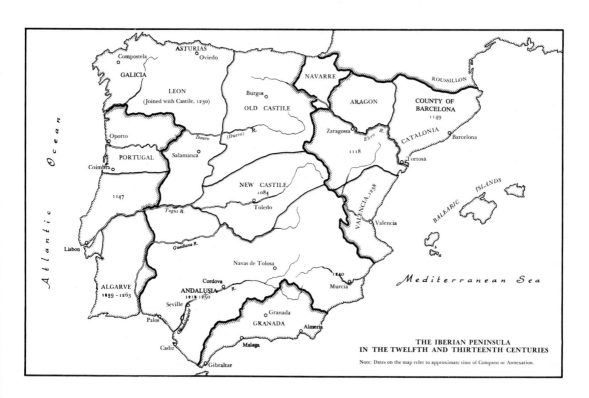

THE IBERIAN PENINSULA
IN THE TWELFTH AND THIRTEENTH CENTURIES

Note: Dates on the map refer to approximate time of Conquest or Annexation.

ceeded those of the French Estates. The *cortes* of Aragon possessed much wider powers, as did also the local *cortes* in each of the provinces composing the realm—Aragon proper, Catalonia, and Valencia. They were all divided into four estates: one of the clergy, another of the chief nobles, a third of the knights, and the fourth of the commoners. England was by no means the only land in which there developed during the middle ages a monarchy constitutionally limited by a parliament.

D. Norman Kingdom of Sicily and Naples

One of the most successfully centralized kingdoms in Europe was the Norman kingdom of Sicily. It will be recalled that Normans from Normandy in the eleventh century had occupied Apulia and Calabria in southern Italy and then conquered Sicily from the Moslems. Under Count Roger, southern Italy and Sicily were united and all attempts at interference by popes, Holy Roman emperors, or Byzantine emperors were frustrated by a skillful combination of force and diplomacy. In 1130 Roger II assumed the title of king, a title the Pope was eventually obliged to recognize. Not content with his existing domains, Roger contemplated a Mediterranean empire and actually secured, at least temporarily, certain holdings in north Africa. His immediate successors continued his policies.

In 1186, with the marriage of the Norman heiress, Constance, to the future Emperor Henry VI, the kingdom was linked with German fortunes and came under the rule of the imperial Hohenstaufen dynasty.[1] Under the brilliant Frederick II (*d.* 1250), the kingdom reached the peak of its development.

In many respects the government of Sicily

[1] See below, p. 217.

was unique. Although composed of disparate elements long accustomed to different rulers, it attained a high degree of centralization. The inhabitants were variously Greek, Saracen, Italian, Jewish, Lombard, and Norman French. Roger had shrewdly drawn on all these elements to weld his state into a notably compact unit. Three languages—Latin, Greek, and Arabic—were officially recognized, while royal agents had also to be familiar with Italian and French. Religious toleration for non-Christians was obviously essential, though the Catholic rulers suppressed heresy and strictly controlled the clergy. A heterogeneous army and bureaucracy owed complete loyalty to the king and enabled him successfully to curb the feudal aristocracy. In 1231 Frederick II reconstituted all these institutions and further centralized the state in the *Constitutions of Melfi*, which clearly showed the influence of Roman law. In economic policy Frederick was particularly progressive and leaned heavily on Moslem precedents. Internal tolls were abolished, tariffs being levied only at the frontiers. Fairs were encouraged. The kingdom prospered.

The fall of the Hohenstaufen dynasty, which will be explained in the following chapter, marked also the decline of Naples-Sicily as a strong state. The brother of Louis IX of France, Charles of Anjou, to whom the papacy entrusted the kingdom, lost Sicily to Aragon, and thus retained only Naples and southern Italy. This should not obscure the fact that during the twelfth and thirteenth centuries the Norman kingdom of Sicily-Naples was an important European state, far more important, indeed, than contemporary England. In Mediterranean diplomacy and commerce, it played a highly significant role. Moreover, as the meeting ground of Latin, Greek, and Arabic cultures it contributed in large measure to the medieval revival of learning.

Gothic architecture in Spain. The Cathedral at Toledo.

Courtesy Spanish National Tourist Department, New York

CHAPTER 18

Medieval Empires and Border States of Central and Eastern Europe

A. Emperor Frederick Barbarossa; His Effort to Build a Consolidated Feudal Monarchy in Germany

In the German lands of north-central Europe, various factors combined to prevent the formation of a strong feudal monarchy such as arose in the western countries of France and England. Among these factors were: (1) certain peculiarities of German feudalism, (2) frequent changes of dynasty, (3) prevalence of civil strife, and (4) a pursuit of Italian as well as German policies on the part of German kings. These kings, it must constantly be borne in mind, persisted in regarding themselves as the successors of Charlemagne and Otto the Great: Roman emperors as well as German kings.

The years of the investiture controversy with its attendant civil wars had halted the promising progress of early medieval Germany.[1] Although the kings of that time had fairly successfully curbed the greater dukes, many lesser vassals had seized the opportunity, sometimes with royal encouragement, to establish their own power even to the extent of building castles and surrounding themselves with bands of knights. Nevertheless, in the German kingdom—and in this it was unlike the former western Frankish domains—many royal rights (*regalia*), taxes, mining rights, etc., were still claimed or contested by the king within the various duchies. In other words, feudalism was neither universally nor systematically

[1] See above, pp. 164–166.

rooted. Further, despite the setback which the German crown had received as an outcome of the investiture controversy, most German rulers continued to try to use the church in support of the monarchy.

The death of the Emperor Henry V in 1125 without direct heirs confirmed the German practice of election by the chief feudal lords. Two families, in particular, were rivals for the kingship and imperial title—the Hohenstaufen and the Guelf. The former stemmed from the duchy of Swabia, and found supporters in both Germany and Italy, who were usually styled "Ghibellines," presumably from the name of the family's castle of Waiblingen. The Guelf family were dominant in Saxony and Bavaria. After much struggling and disorder, the Hohenstaufen gained the upper hand, and in 1152 the head of the family became Holy Roman Emperor as Frederick I.

Frederick I "Barbarossa" (1152–1190) has become the legendary German hero-king. Handsome, well built, with golden red hair, he could attract by his affable disposition and command with authority. A young man of energy and ability, he was the perfect embodiment of the knightly chivalrous ruler.

Generally speaking, Frederick I strove to do for Germany what his contemporaries in England and France were doing, namely to strengthen the state and to establish monarchical institutions grounded on a constructive feudalism. His relations with Henry "the Lion" of Saxony and Bavaria, the head of the rival house of Guelf, illustrates the king's policy with regard to the great duchies and incidentally the lesser nobility. For several years Frederick left Henry unmolested and in practical independence. But though he was deeply engaged with Italian affairs, he apparently did not lose sight of the ideal of making Germany a federation of great duchies bound to him by ties of vassalage. Manifestly such an ideal could not be realized if any duchy was too strong. As time went on, Frederick became alarmed at the success with which Henry was utilizing his independence to build up a formidable domain. Henry was consolidating the duchy of Saxony, patronizing towns, and generally promoting prosperity; he was also extending his sway into Brandenburg and Pomerania. Frederick finally challenged Henry; and his method was typically feudal and not unlike the procedure of Philip Augustus with King John of England.

In 1180 Henry, whose successes had not been won without alienating many of his smaller neighbors, was summoned to the royal court to answer charges. His refusal brought from Frederick a declaration of the forfeiture of his estates. In the ensuing struggle, Henry's forces were crushed, his duchies of Saxony and Bavaria were divided into smaller fiefs dependent on the crown, and only two castles were left to him. Of the previous large duchy of Saxony, only the small eastern part continued to bear the name. The western part was cut off and formed into a new duchy of Westphalia; this was temporarily assigned to the archbishop of Cologne. By thus overcoming and penalizing Henry the Lion, the Emperor redressed in his own favor the balance of power between the duchies and the crown and gave dramatic emphasis to the obligations of vassalage. By dividing Henry's lands and securing the dependence of smaller territories, he put himself in a position to ensure that balance. Like Philip Augustus of France, he was utilizing feudal law and practice to strengthen the monarchy.

There were two other significant aspects of Frederick Barbarossa's German policy: his attempt to build up a royal domain governed by some sort of administrative system; and his continued use of the church.

In western and south-central Germany, especially in Franconia, Swabia, and neighboring Alsace, he labored to consolidate his own territories and to exercise an effective control of monastic and other properties. His marriage to Beatrice, heiress to the kingdom of Burgundy, was a significant move. He also won support of numerous cities, particularly in the Rhineland, by granting them liberal privileges. It was not a compact domain in the geographical sense, but Frederick strove to make it so. Moreover, within this expanded royal territory, Frederick hoped to ensure control through the appointment of officials dependent on the crown. As a consequence, *ministeriales* were stationed at appropriate places. The German monarchy was less successful in exercising control over the new frontier districts in the northeast, for there the princes were usually able to establish a relatively unrestricted authority of their own.

With regard to the church, Frederick continued to dominate the German bishops, at least in political matters. He made the most of the right to invest a new incumbent with the temporalities of his see, a right, it will be remembered, conceded by the pope in the Concordat of Worms.[1] Thereby, ecclesiastical princes were associated with the crown. All in all, Frederick Barbarossa made a promising start toward building a consolidated feudal monarchy in Germany.

B. The Hohenstaufen Emperors and Italy

What distinguishes German medieval history from that of other countries is the Italian or "imperial" policy of its monarchs, for, as the years passed, they came to regard themselves as the successors of Charlemagne, the heirs of a Roman Empire. The wisdom of pursuing such a course in the twelfth and thirteenth centuries when Italy, though divided, presented such formidable obstacles as a strong southern kingdom, a revived papacy, and prosperous and powerful northern cities, has been questioned. To some historians it has seemed the principal reason for the failure of a truly constructive

---

[1] See above, p. 166.

GERMAN (HOLY ROMAN) EMPIRE
UNDER THE HOHENSTAUFEN

▬▬ Boundary of the Empire
▨ Territory added during Hohenstaufen period
▨ Patrimony of St. Peter
▨ Other lands claimed by Papacy
■ Venetian possessions

K = Kingdom   D = Duchy   C = County
M = Mark   L = Landgraviate

By 1300 the great duchies were broken into smaller feudal divisions.
By 1300 French influence was strong in the Kingdom of Arles
and imperial power in Italy was slight.

DENMARK

PRUSSIA

Danzig
Pomerelia
POMERANIA
C. Holstein
Slavonia
Hamburg
FRISIA
Elbe R.
M.
BRANDENBURG
POLAND
C. Oldenburg
Brunswick Lüneburg
D. SAXONY
Magdeburg
M. Lausitz
Vistula R.
Guelders
Munster
Brunswick
Oder R.
Weser R.
SILESIA
D. BRABANT
C. Loos
Cologne
Mühlhausen
Antwerp
Rhine R.
C. Berg
L. THURINGIA
Aachen
Hesse
M. Meissen
C. Hainaut
Fulda
Luxemburg
Prague
Mainz
K. BOHEMIA
Trier
Worms
D. FRANCONIA
M. Moravia
Ratisbon

FRANCE
D. LORRAINE
ALSACE
Ulm
Augsburg
Danube R.
D. Vienna
Breisgau
D. SWABIA
D. BAVARIA
Austria
S. Constance
Salzburg
C. Burgundy
D. Styria
A L E S
D. Carinthia
Geneva
C. Savoy
Trent
Friuli
M. Carniola
Chartreuse
Cortenuovo
M. Verona
Legnano
Milan
Venice
Rhone R.
LOMBARDY
Cremona
Alessandria
Roncaglia
Po R.
Zara
C. Provence
(to Anjou, 1266)
Genoa
Romagna
Florence
Pisa
M. Ancona
Ancona
TUSCANY
D. Spoleto
Ragusa
CORSICA
Patrimony
Rome of St. Peter
To Pisa until 1285
then to Genoa
S. Germano
Apulia
Hohenstaufen, 1194
Anjou, 1266
Melfi
K.
Naples
SARDINIA
TWO
To Pisa and Genoa
to Aragon 1296-1326
SICILIES
Calabria
Palermo
SICILY
Hohenstaufen, 1194
Anjou, 1266
Aragon, 1282

HUNGARY

German policy.[1] But Frederick, it must be remembered, viewed the world from a twelfth-century, not a nineteenth- or twentieth-century standpoint. To his kingdoms of Germany and Burgundy he must add the kingdom of Italy, traditionally associated with the German monarchy. No doubt the wealth of Italy he needed. Moreover, his rival, Henry the Lion of Bavaria and Saxony, was close to the Alps and had relatives in Tuscany. To have permitted consolidation by the Guelphs would have seriously endangered his work in Germany. It is possible, therefore, to argue that solid realistic reasons prompted Frederick's moves to the South.

All three areas of Italy—the northern cities, the papal lands, and the Norman kingdom of the south—were concerned in one way or another with Frederick's policies. Under Pope Hadrian IV, the only English pope, relations, despite certain tensions,[2] were reasonably friendly. Opinion among the cardinals favored the traditional coöperation of Pope and Emperor. As a consequence, Frederick assisted the Pope in subduing a revolt of the Roman citizenry and captured and executed Arnold of Brescia, an agitator-reformer. In 1155 Frederick was crowned by the Pope.

However, a growing number of cardinals led by Roland Bandinelli, who was soon to become Pope as Alexander III, was becoming uneasy about Frederick's control of ecclesiastical affairs in Germany as well as the possibility of a real instead of a nominal

---

[1] For a summary of the long controversy over German medieval imperial policy, and a presentation of the traditional adverse criticism, see J. W. Thompson, *Feudal Germany* (Chicago, 1928), Chapter VIII. Since Thompson, himself, figures in the controversy, the student is advised to consult the appropriate pages in G. Barraclough, *The Origins of Modern Germany* (Oxford, 1957), and his "Frederick Barbarossa and the Twelfth Century," *History in a changing world* (1956).

[2] On their first meeting, Frederick refused for two days to perform the usual courtesy of holding the Pope's stirrup. In 1157 a legate, in referring to favors done the Emperor by the Pope, used the word "beneficia." This was translated "fiefs" by the imperial chancellor and was immediately protested. Hadrian later acknowledged that the word meant "benefits," not "fiefs."

control over northern and perhaps central Italy. Thus in 1156 a Treaty of Benevento was negotiated with the Norman kingdom of the south that was distinctly favorable as regards the ecclesiastical privileges of the monarchy and that Barbarossa regarded as incompatible with a previous Treaty of Constance of 1153 with the Empire.

Meanwhile, Frederick had begun the consolidation of his authority in northern Italy. In a famous imperial Diet held at Roncaglia (1158), after overcoming resistance in Lombardy, the Emperor proclaimed, according to the principles of Roman law then being revived in Italy, his sovereign rights over the cities. Although he had no intention of doing so in all cases, he reserved the right in each to appoint an official, a *podestà*, and to collect certain taxes. But if Frederick's regalian claims were more precisely stated than had been the case previously, so also were the cities better able to resist, for, as we have seen, this was the period of the flowering of town administration throughout Europe and preëminently in Italy.

Such was the situation when Pope Hadrian died and Cardinal Roland was elected to succeed him as Alexander III (1159–1181). A minority of cardinals disputed the election and chose a rival Pope whom the Emperor supported. Most, but not all, of the German bishops—some, no doubt, under pressure—also accepted the anti-Pope and his two successors. And though the Emperor's superior force drove Alexander to refuge in France, the Pope had no intention of surrendering and managed to maintain the papal administration for some years in exile.

Although Frederick was at first successful in Italy and crushed a rebellious Milan his triumph proved only temporary. The Pope soon won the support of other monarchs and of the majority of the clergy everywhere. Moreover, most of the defeated cities formed a Lombard League (1168) to defend their privileges. A few cities and factions remained loyal to the Emperor and were called "Ghibelline." On the other hand, the name of "Guelf" was applied to the Lombard League and others who opposed the Emperor and supported the Pope. The Norman king, and occasionally even the Byzantine emperor, who was anxious to recover influence in the west, gave assistance. Finally at Legnano in 1176 Frederick suffered a crushing defeat. But in the peace of Venice (1177) he managed, by astute diplomacy, to separate Pope Alexander, whom at long last he recognized, and the Lombard cities with whom final settlement was deferred. In 1183, by the peace of Constance, the emperor conceded the rights of self-government for which the Lombard cities had fought. But in return they acknowledged his suzerainty, including the right to hear appeals from their courts and to receive occasional contributions.

Although partially thwarted in northern Italy, Frederick was more successful in Tuscany and other parts of central Italy. Besides, in the years after the treaty of Constance, he managed to neutralize the formerly hostile south by arranging a marriage between his son, the future Emperor Henry VI, and Constance, daughter of the King of Sicily.

In 1189 this Frederick I, Barbarossa, good Christian knight that he was, embarked for the Holy Land on a Crusade. Did he perhaps hope to lay new foundations of power in the east? It is difficult to say, for the great emperor did not live to complete his project. He died while fording a stream in Asia Minor. Thus ended the distinguished, if not entirely successful, career of one of Germany's most engaging rulers.

It so happened that Constance, the wife of Frederick's son and successor, became sole heiress to the southern kingdom. Hence with the reign of Henry VI (1190–1197) Hohenstaufen policies were more deeply involved than ever in Italian and Mediterranean affairs. But although Henry made the most of his inheritance, subduing his newly acquired kingdom of Sicily, and mastering central and northern Italy, premature death cut short his successes.

Henry VI's death gave the papacy a much needed respite, of which the young and vigorous Pope Innocent III (1198–1216) knew how to take advantage. Henry's heir was his son Frederick, then only three years old. With great energy and skill, but not without considerable difficulty, Innocent recovered the bulk of the papal lands and managed to entrust the remainder to princes loyal to himself. In Germany, the imperial and royal titles were withheld from the boy Frederick, while in Sicily his mother, anxious to obtain papal support for her son,

Gothic architecture in Germany. The Cathedral, formerly abbey, at Altenberg, north Rhineland.

Courtesy German Tourist Information Office, New York

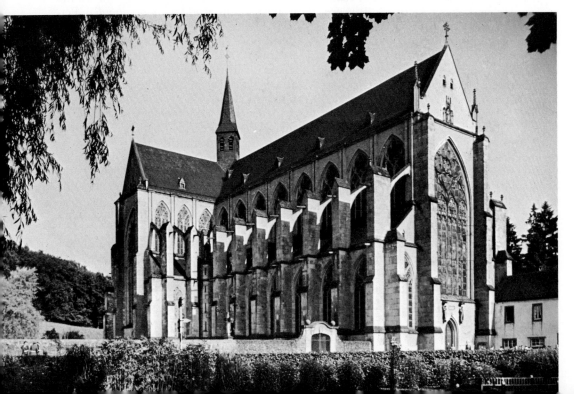

recognized anew the old feudal suzerainty of the Holy See over the kingdom. Consequently, when she died in 1198, the young Frederick II, as King of Sicily, automatically became a ward of the papacy. Thus Innocent was enabled to sever the union between Sicily and Germany.

In Germany itself, the refusal of the princes to accept the young Frederick II precipitated a renewed outbreak of the Guelf-Hohenstaufen feud. Philip of Swabia, Barbarossa's youngest son and candidate of the Hohenstaufen faction, was opposed by Otto of Brunswick, a son of Henry the Lion. Before long, the civil war involved most of Europe, as the English Angevin kings joined the Guelfs and the French Capetian kings threw in their lot with the Hohenstaufen.

Pope Innocent III was at first neutral. He had no desire to question the German custom of electing a king, although he reserved to himself the rights of approving the choice and of reviewing a disputed election —rights implied in his privilege of crowning Holy Roman Emperors. Gradually, because Otto seemed the more conciliatory and Philip refused to agree to any arbitration, the Pope swung his powerful support to the former (1201). But not until Philip was killed (1208) was Otto's position secure.

Unfortunately for all concerned, the Guelf Otto, once he was crowned Emperor, proved to be as tenacious of imperial claims as any Hohenstaufen. As a consequence, Innocent's maneuvers were in vain, and in 1210 he was forced to break with his erstwhile candidate. And when, in 1211, a Diet of rebellious princes finally elected the young Frederick, the Pope gave his backing to his Sicilian ward. Frederick II repeated the protestations of loyalty to the papacy made by Otto and, on Innocent's insistence, made two additional promises. He agreed to undertake a Crusade; and he promised never to unite the Sicilian and German kingdoms under one crown. Then when Frederick, with the aid of Philip Augustus of France, defeated Otto and John of England at Bouvines (1214), Innocent's position seemed secure. Europe was pacified and could, so he hoped, unitedly carry forward the crusade which was so dear to his heart. In 1216 the great Pope died, little realizing

how untrustworthy his former ward was to prove.

C. *Frederick II, German Emperor and King of Sicily*

Frederick II (1211–1250) was one of the most brilliant rulers of his time. Unlike his chivalrous grandfather, who exemplified the Teutonic hero-king, Frederick was the subtle, shrewd, and unscrupulous diplomat. He was far more attached to Sicily with its cosmopolitan culture than to his northern German realm. Although Frederick, like others of his day, had a firm belief in astrology, he was well educated and a good deal of a scholar, with a real intellectual curiosity, especially in matters of science. He arranged for a number of experiments, and transported on his journeys a whole menagerie of birds and animals. He even wrote an important treatise on falconry, displaying considerable scientific knowledge (*De arte venandi cum avibus*). Under his patronage, Moslem, Christian, and Jewish scholars took up residence in Sicily.

Frederick II was known as a skeptic, and contemporary gossip attributed to him the authorship of an anonymous pamphlet entitled, *The Three Imposters: Moses, Christ, and Mohammed*. It was also alleged that he kept a sort of harem in Mohammedan style. Small wonder that his astonished contemporaries spoke of him as the wonder of the world (*stúpor mundi*). Perhaps Frederick's propensity to defy current theological and moral standards has been somewhat exaggerated owing to his long struggle with the papacy. It is noteworthy, at any rate, that in Sicily he treated heresy as a civil crime.

Frederick II was thoroughly devoted to the Hohenstaufen conception of empire which he regarded as divinely ordained to bring about a reign of justice. Only, in his case, the center of the empire would not be Germany, but rather Sicily. In this southern kingdom, with its admirable governmental traditions, Frederick was more at home.

Fortunately for the young Emperor, Innocent III was succeeded by Honorius III (1216–1227), an elderly man not disposed to insist too strictly that Frederick fulfill

Castel del Monte, built by the Emperor Frederick II in southern Italy.

Courtesy Italian State Tourist Office

his promises. The latter readily found reasons for postponing the Crusade, and easily persuaded Honorius to agree to the election of Frederick's infant son as "King of the Romans," or heir-presumptive to the headship of the Holy Roman Empire. Meanwhile Frederick conceded important privileges to German princes, ecclesiastical and lay, as he energetically extended his sway throughout Italy. For a time, it seemed as though the ambition of Frederick Barbarossa was to be realized by Frederick II, and all Italy and Germany joined under the strong rule of a Holy Roman Emperor.

But Honorius's successor, Pope Gregory IX (1227–1241), despite his eighty-odd years, was as stout a champion of papal prerogatives as Innocent III had been. He insisted that Frederick set out for the Holy Land in fulfillment of his promise, and the Emperor, who had recently married the heiress to the Latin Kingdom of Jerusalem, actually made a pretense of going. He conveniently fell ill, however; and his failure to depart brought an excommunication from Gregory. Though still under the ban of the church, Frederick left in the following year for the Holy Land. There he managed, by skillfully playing on the jealousies of the Moslem chieftains, to win a temporary control of Jerusalem. Meanwhile, the doughty Gregory refused to lift the ban and attempted to rouse Frederick's subjects against him. Eventually, in 1230, the Emperor submitted, pledging himself to respect church privileges in Sicily and to protect the papal territories, and was then absolved by the Pope.

Peace with the papacy afforded Frederick II the opportunity to resume pursuit of his imperial plans. After suppressing an insurrection in Germany, he turned his attention to Italy. Claiming that he was not bound by the promises which his grandfather had made at Constance in 1183, he demanded the submission of the Lombard cities. But for these cities, Constance had been a kind of charter of independence, and they now formed a second Lombard League. Their resistance was shattered, however, by a victory of Frederick's forces at Cortenuova (1237). The Emperor followed up his triumph by conquering all north Italy and imposing upon it a Sicilian type of administration under trusted officials of his own. Each city was placed under an imperial *podestà*, the forerunner of the Italian "despot" of the next century. Moreover, since the Pope had sided with the Lombard League, Frederick invaded the papal states. At this point Gregory IX died (1241).

When it was learned that Gregory's successor had been a personal friend of Frederick, the latter, despite his pleasure at the choice, is said to have remarked "no pope can be a Ghibelline." And, indeed, Innocent IV (1243–1254) continued with vigor the struggle against the Emperor. Compelled to flee from Rome, the Pope took refuge at Lyons in France, and there summoned a general church council, in which he solemnly excommunicated and deposed Frederick and proclaimed a Crusade against him. Never before had the ideal of papal predominance over the kings of Christendom been so clearly expressed. But Innocent could not organize forces sufficient to overcome the Emperor and once again it was death which thwarted the imperial plans. Frederick was within sight of the mastery of all Italy when he died in 1250.

The death of Frederick II virtually brought to an end the Hohenstaufen dream of empire. Frederick's son, Conrad IV (1250–1254), survived him only four years; and the grandson, Conradin, who was next in succession, was only a boy. In vain, an illegitimate son of Frederick, Manfred, attempted to stem the tide that was setting in against the Hohenstaufen. The papacy preached a new Crusade against the last representatives of the imperial family, and invited Charles of Anjou, a brother of St. Louis IX of France, to take possession of the kingdom of Sicily. Manfred died in battle and Conradin was finally captured and executed.

All this did not bring peace to Italy. Towns freed from imperial rule presently resumed quarreling and fighting with one another; while the new French Angevin kings of Sicily and Naples soon proved themselves almost as ambitious and dangerous to the papacy as the former Hohenstaufen had been. In 1282, a rebellion broke out in Sicily against the French Angevin ruler, and although he retained control of Naples and adjacent territory in the southern part of the Italian peninsula, he lost Sicily to the King of Aragon, who utilized the rebellion to occupy the island. In this way, the once great Norman kingdom of Sicily and Naples was broken into two parts and sadly weakened.

In a sense, the outcome was a triumph for the papacy, which had prevented the formation of a consolidated Italian monarchy that might have been dangerous to its own independence. But the triumph was achieved at heavy cost. As will later be explained, the political hegemony of the papacy proved as short-lived as that of the Hohenstaufen Emperors.

A just estimate of Frederick II's career must include passing reference to his achievements in Sicily and also in Germany. Sicilian by birth, more Sicilian than German in temperament, he devoted some of his best energies toward furthering the progress of the former Norman kingdom. The results we have described elsewhere. But he did not neglect entirely his northern German realm. Indeed it is possible that the rights conceded to the princes he regarded as a temporary expedient and that he intended ultimately to impose a "Sicilian" regime in Germany. Frederick did foster eastward expansion by encouraging and confirming the Teutonic Knights in their Prussian conquests.[1] He also defended the eastern frontiers against the Mongols. But this very frontier policy worked in the long run against the Hohenstaufen design for a monarchically unified Germany. For it shifted the balance of power within the country farther away from the west, where Frederick Barbarossa had commenced to consolidate a royal domain, to the pioneering and more independent east.

Germany emerged in the later Middle Ages as an agglomeration of principalities, large and small, ecclesiastical and lay. With the fall of the Hohenstaufen went the last attempt to create a crown domain strong enough to dominate the entire realm in manner comparable with that of the Capetian kings in France. Some historians see in this the key to the medieval and much of the modern history of Germany. As we have indicated, another explanation is that the imperial policy of the Hohenstaufen entailed their neglect of Germany and its consolidation; that they sacrificed national to imperial interests. If this be true, there is a temptation to condemn the German rulers of the twelfth and thirteenth centuries for pursuing a policy which lacked realism. This is unfair. Nationalism is a

---

[1] See above, pp. 176–177.

modern, not a thirteenth-century, conception. If the Hohenstaufen were imperialists in the Roman sense, they were seeking to realize the highest political ideal their contemporaries knew, that of a single empire for all Christendom. Today, we are accustomed to look ahead for progress. In the thirteenth century, men still looked back to what seemed to them the golden age of the past, the days of Charlemagne.

D. Northern and East-Central Europe

As we turn from Germany proper to northern and eastern Europe we pass into areas of varying political development. In the latter region, the Tatar invasion [1] had considerably more than temporary significance. Then, too, in many instances throughout both regions, the institutional influences of the older kingdoms, particularly of Germany, were marked. But perhaps the most striking feature about all the smaller or border states of northern and eastern Europe is their membership in the community of Christendom. We shall begin our survey with a brief glance at the Scandinavian lands in northwest Europe.

During the twelfth and thirteenth centuries the three Scandinavian kingdoms of Denmark, Norway, and Sweden developed, in varying degree, the institutions of feudal monarchy. The struggles between crown and nobility, so characteristic of western Europe, were evident in each; and in Denmark the nobles forced from King Eric V a charter (1282) not unlike the English Magna Carta.[2] In Norway and Sweden regular parliaments of the nobility were assembled. But, in general, royal power remained a reality in Scandinavia, while the peasants retained a large measure of personal freedom. The thirteenth century also witnessed here, as in Europe generally, the growth of towns and commerce, the latter stimulated by German capital and German merchants. The fishing industry flourished, and mining came to play an increasingly important role, especially in Sweden. Ecclesiastical organization was also perfected with the establishment of new dioceses, and the

[1] See above, p. 186.
[2] See above, p. 204.

growth of monasticism. The institution of archdioceses in each of the kingdoms freed the Scandinavian churches from their earlier dependence on the archbishop of Bremen.

Meanwhile, the northern descendants of the Vikings were not entirely inactive beyond their own frontiers. Norway retained its contacts with Iceland and Greenland, and its hold over the islands off the north coast of Scotland. King Eric IX (1150–1160) of Sweden led a Crusade into Finland, and the Danes were active all along the Baltic coast until their efforts were frustrated by the Germans.

To the east of Germany proper were two Slavic states of growing importance in the middle ages—Bohemia and Poland. Bohemia, peopled largely by Slavic Czechs, was closely connected with Germany and included within the Holy Roman Empire. Both in its internal affairs and in its relations with the imperial government, however, Bohemia retained a very large measure of autonomy. It is true that Frederick Barbarossa's centralizing policies threatened Bohemian independence. But the danger passed with the failure of his efforts and with the simultaneous cessation of internal conflict within Bohemia. In the closing years of the twelfth century and the early years of the thirteenth, the Bohemians were able to utilize for their profit the contemporary political difficulties of their imperial suzerains. Ottokar I (1197–1230), for example, won confirmation for his title of king from both factions in the German civil war, and likewise from the pope (1207). Still more important, Ottokar obtained from the Emperor Frederick II the Golden Bull of 1212, which specifically limited Bohemia's obligations to the Empire and recognized the right of the Bohemian nobility to elect their own king. This latter concession, together with Ottokar's own provisions for the royal succession, resulted in a customary "election" of the king's eldest son and the practical establishment of a hereditary succession to the crown of Bohemia.

Subsequent decades witnessed not only further diminishing of imperial interference in Bohemia, but increasing participation on the part of the Bohemian kings in

German affairs. Their position as imperial electors came to be officially recognized. And partly as a consequence of the chaotic conditions in the Empire attendant upon the fall of the Hohenstaufen, Ottokar II (1253–1278) was able temporarily to extend Bohemian territorial boundaries. Furthermore, despite the fact that many of the clergy in Bohemia were German rather than Czech, the period witnessed a notable development of Czech culture. Several Bohemian chronicles and tales were written, including Cosmas's *Chronicle of the Bohemians*. Finally, the opening of Bohemian silver mines proved important in the economic development of the kingdom.

Though Poland, the other Slavic state in central Europe, was not included within the Holy Roman Empire, its relations with the Germans assumed special significance during the twelfth and thirteenth centuries. The Polish King Boleslav III (1102–1138) successfully withstood the Emperor Henry V, and, by capturing Pomerania, gained access to the Baltic. Less auspicious was his division of the state into five principalities for his sons. Cracow, the old capital, went to the eldest member of the ruling house, with the title of Grand Duke. Resulting quarrels over the succession materially weakened Poland. Furthermore, the country was restricted by the conquest of the adjacent region of Prussia by the Teutonic Knights who, ironically enough, had first been summoned by one of the Polish dukes. Eventually, German settlers outnumbered the native inhabitants. Poland likewise suffered from Mongol raids and the devastation they wrought. It is true that the settlement of Teutonic Knights and other Germans in northern Poland was of immediate advantage for common defense against the Mongols and for the economic development of the region, but it sowed seeds of future rivalry and conflict between Poles and Germans.

In east-central Europe, like a wedge between the West Slav Poles and Czechs and the South Slavs (Yugoslavs) of the Balkans, lay the Magyar kingdom of Hungary. In the twelfth century its rulers reduced to vassalage the Slavic state of Croatia on the Adriatic, but their efforts to extend the Hungarian realm farther into the Balkans were successfully resisted by the Byzantine Emperor at Constantinople. For a short time, the Byzantine Emperors managed to exercise a suzerainty over Hungary.

In the early thirteenth century Hungary was raided and devastated by Mongols, and to protect the country against renewed raids, the nobility were authorized to build castles which increased their power at the expense of that of the kings. Already King Andrew II (*d.* 1235) had disposed of large tracts of the royal domain in order to finance a crusade. And in the Golden Bull of 1222, another document in some measure comparable to the English Magna Carta, he agreed to periodic meetings of a parliament, or diet, and to other curtailments of royal power by the nobility. Thus, medieval Hungary took on a feudal and agrarian character, with a strongly entrenched aristocracy.

E. Russia, the Byzantine Empire, and the Balkans

In eastern Europe, Russian history of the twelfth and thirteenth centuries was marked by two significant developments: (1) the rise of several new principalities following the decline of Kiev; and (2) the Tatar, or Mongol, occupation. Some inhabitants of the Slavic principality of Kiev migrated northward to the region of the upper Dnieper and Dvina rivers, where they contributed to the formation of a distinctive Byelorussian ("White Russian") nation. Others moved in a more north-easterly direction toward the upper Volga and Oka rivers, where they intermarried with other Slavic and Finnish peoples to form the "Great Russian" stock. Still others went west and south into Volhynia and Galicia, which became the historic homeland of the Ukrainians or "Little Russians." In all these regions new settlements were founded or older communities strengthened.

Russia, alone of all the countries of Europe, was forced to endure a prolonged occupation by the Tatars. Practically all the Russian principalities, except Novgorod in the north, came under the Mongol yoke and suffered varying degrees of devastation. In the course of time, however, Tatar dominance came to involve little more than

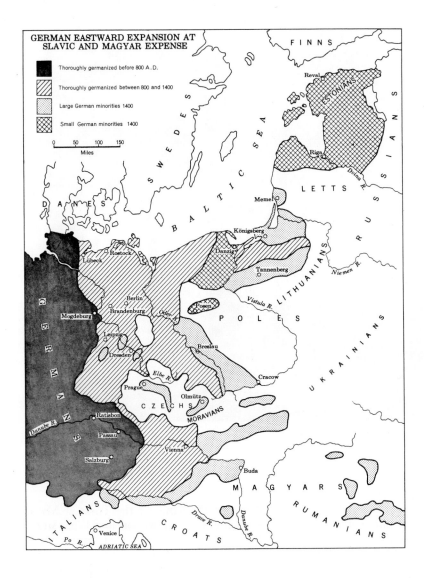

GERMAN EASTWARD EXPANSION AT
SLAVIC AND MAGYAR EXPENSE

Thoroughly germanized before 800 A.D.

Thoroughly germanized between 800 and 1400

Large German minorities 1400

Small German minorities 1400

0   50   100   150
Miles

tribute paid by native Russian princes and magnates for lands they actually ruled. And since the Mongols failed to construct any strong central states, their power was wielded by several different, and usually rival, "Khanates."

The Tatar invasions had driven many Russians north and northeast along the rivers and deep into the forests which afforded them escape from assault. One result was the rise of a new principality centering in the town of Moscow—a principality which was destined to be the starting-point for the rise of a great and unified Russian state.

Thus, despite the protracted occupation of a large part of Russia by the Mongols,

some independent Russian life and culture precariously survived throughout the middle ages and even gave promise of later resurrection and expansion. This culture had been derived mainly from Constantinople, and it continued to be fundamentally Eastern and Byzantine.

The period immediately following the Mongol conquest was not without occasional moments of native Russian brilliance. For example, one of the grand-dukes of the principalities of Novgorod and Vladimir, Alexander Nevski (1236–1263), defeated the Swedes and the Teutonic Knights, and secured peace with the Mongols and an easing of the tribute they exacted.

In southeastern Europe, the history of

Russian medieval architecture. Cathedral of St. Sophia at Novgorod. Dating from the eleventh century, restored.

Sovfoto, New York

the Byzantine Empire and the Balkan lands during the twelfth and thirteenth centuries is a troubled and confusing story. The Emperor Alexius Comnenus, whose request for assistance from the West against the Seljuk Turks helped to precipitate the First Crusade, was succeeded by John (*d.* 1143) and Manuel (*d.* 1180), both of whom were able statesmen. Manuel continued his efforts to retain influence in the west, as we have seen, by assisting Pope Alexander, and by attempting, although unsuccessfully, to maintain a foothold in southern Italy. The Peace of Venice (1177), which terminated Alexander's long controversy with Barbarossa and brought peace to Italy, marked the end of these efforts. Venetians and Sicilians forced the Byzantine Emperor to confirm their trading privileges; and Venetians, it will be recalled, along with other Italians, were migrating in considerable numbers into the Byzantine dominions.

Meanwhile the Emperor suffered a major defeat at the hands of the Turks at Myriokephalon in Asia Minor in 1176. And a Bulgarian insurrection forced the Byzantine government to cede a large area in the Balkan peninsula to a practically independent Bulgaria. Thus was inaugurated what is called the Second Bulgarian Empire, which reached its apogee under Tsar John Asen II (1218–1241).

The climax of these misfortunes for the Byzantine Empire was the Fourth Crusade (1204) and the establishment of a Western "Latin" Empire at Constantinople. Greece was divided into feudal principalities after the French fashion, and Venice clinched her control of the Adriatic by annexing a number of islands and portions of the Greek mainland. Further, a Roman Catholic hierarchy was established in the Eastern Empire, and papal political influence was temorarily extended to the Balkans. A Serbian and a Bulgarian monarch were crowned by papal legates. The Byzantine government doggedly held out at Nicaea in Asia Minor and established a state at Trebizond which enjoyed brilliant if precarious existence.

Even after the Byzantines, under Michael Paleologus (1261–1282), recaptured Constantinople with the aid of the Genoese, rivals of the Venetians, western influences continued. A Latin duchy of Athens and principality of Achaia and a Venetian principality of the Archipelago remained for some years, while Venetian commercial pre-dominance in the eastern Mediterranean was more firmly entrenched than ever. Other western influences were to be felt in the ensuing years.

Thus the Byzantine recovery was both incomplete and temporary. The Fourth Crusade had irreparably weakened the once great empire. It had also rendered extremely difficult, if not quite impossible, any rapprochement between the eastern and western branches of the Christian Church.

Byzantine architecture in Italy. Interior of the Church of San Marco, Venice. Dating from the eleventh century.

Courtesy Brogi Art Reference Bureau

Gothic architecture in France. The interior of Amiens.

Courtesy French Government Tourist Office, New York

CHAPTER 19

The Church in the Twelfth and Thirteenth Centuries

A. The Papal Curia

It was remarked in an earlier chapter that the Gregorian reformers of the eleventh century took certain significant steps in developing the church's monarchical constitution. The further internal institutional growth of the twelfth and thirteenth centuries should be viewed in connection with the contemporary renaissance of legal studies, canon and civil, and with the progress of secular government. It is significant that after 1150 most of the popes, notably Alexander III (1159–1181), Innocent III (1198–1216), Gregory IX (1227–1241), and Innocent IV (1243–1254), were canon lawyers. As men trained in the law, they left their imprint upon the papal curia and monarchy.

Ecclesiastical government was developed to promote the spiritual welfare of the faithful.[1] Accordingly, it is important not to concentrate too much attention on certain spectacular activities of the papacy, such as crusades and the conflicts with emperors and kings. Even a cursory examination of papal letters will reveal that the vast majority of them deal not with such exceptional matters, but with the many day-to-day concerns of priests, monks, and laymen.

[1] That is, of almost everyone throughout the greater part of Europe. Outside of the church were, of course, groups of Jews in various countries and a Moslem minority in Spain. And most Christians in the Byzantine Empire and Russia adhered to the Eastern Orthodox Church which by the thirteenth century was no longer in communion with the church of the west.

In an age keenly aware of things legal and constitutional, the supremacy of the pope in matters of ecclesiastical jurisdiction was at once more precisely defined and more widely effective. The pope was, as Innocent III said in describing his own position, the "vicar of Christ." As successor of St. Peter, his office was recognized as of divine institution and sanction. His court, the papal *curia*, was a supreme court of appeal from all other ecclesiastical courts, and also a court of first instance.

The principal members of the papal *curia* were the cardinals, who represented the chief clergy of Rome and its vicinity and who elected the pope.[2] As a result of the expansion of papal jurisdiction, what had once been a purely local body became the

[2] In 1179, the right of cardinal priests and deacons as well as of cardinal bishops to participate in papal elections was recognized, and a two-thirds majority was required for such elections. There was an implied jurisdictional equality between cardinal bishops, priests, and deacons. It gradually came to pass that all cardinals outranked other clergy. In modern times, bishops have commonly been appointed cardinal priests and deacons. In 1274, in order to avoid delay (sometimes the result of political pressure), it was ruled that within ten days after the death of a pope, the cardinals were to be placed behind locked doors until they reached a decision. This was the conclave (*clavis*, key), and with minor modifications, the procedure has been continued to the present day. The modern practice whereby a cardinal resides permanently away from Rome was not the rule in the Middle Ages.

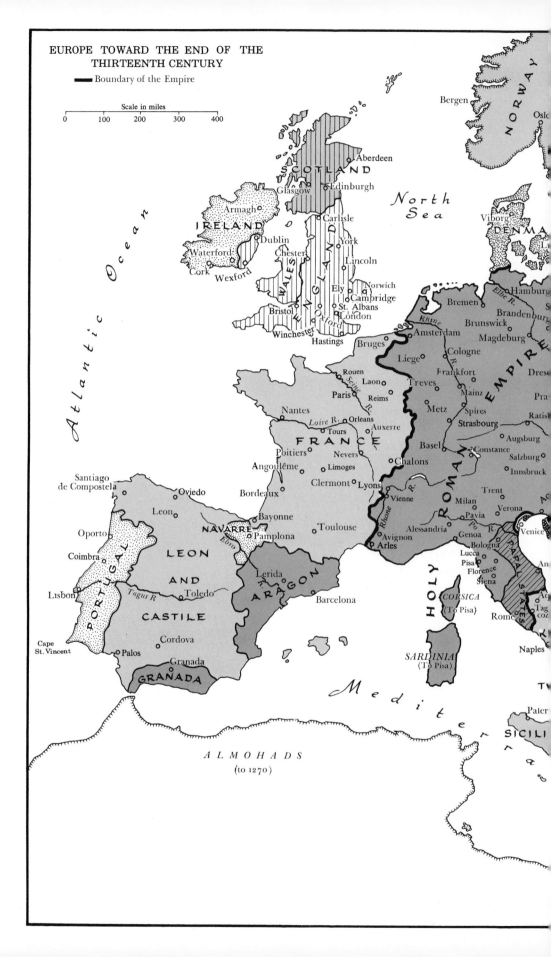

EUROPE TOWARD THE END OF THE
THIRTEENTH CENTURY

▬ Boundary of the Empire

Scale in miles

0   100   200   300   400

Atlantic Ocean

North Sea

NORWAY

Bergen

Oslo

SCOTLAND

Aberdeen

Glasgow   Edinburgh

IRELAND

Armagh

Carlisle

Viborg

DENMA

Dublin   York

Waterford   Chester   Lincoln

Cork   Wexford   WALES   ENGLAND

Ely   Norwich

Cambridge

Bristol   St. Albans

Oxford   London

Winchester   Hastings

Hamburg

Elbe R.

Bremen   Brandenburg

Brunswick

Bruges   Amsterdam   Magdeburg

Liege   Cologne

Rouen   Treves   Frankfurt   Dresden

Seine R.   Laon   Pra

Paris   Reims   Mainz

Metz   Spires   Ratis

Nantes   Strasbourg

Loire R.   Orleans   Augsburg

Tours   Auxerre   Basel   Constance

FRANCE   Salzburg

Poitiers   Nevers   Chalons   Innsbruck

Angoulême   Limoges

Clermont   Lyons   Trent

Vienne   Milan   Verona

Santiago   Bordeaux   Pavia

de Compostela   Oviedo   Alessandria   Genoa   Venice

Leon   Bayonne   Po R.

NAVARRE   Avignon   Lucca   Bologna

Oporto   Pamplona   Arles   Pisa   PAPAL STATES   An

Coimbra   Ebro   Florence

PORTUGAL   LEON   Lerida   Siena

Lisbon   Tagus R.   Toledo   ARAGON   HOLY   CORSICA   Rome   coz

AND   Barcelona   (To Pisa)

CASTILE

Cape   Cordova   Naples

St. Vincent   Palos

Granada   SARDINIA

GRANADA   (To Pisa)

Mediter

ranea

ALMOHADS   SICILI

(to 1270)   Paler

ROMAN EMPIRE

SWEDEN
FINLAND
Upsala
Wisby
Baltic Sea
mar
Danzig
Posen
POLAND
Olmütz
Vienna
Pressburg
Gran
Kalocsa
HUNGARY
Semlin
Spalato
Ragusa
Durazzo
(to Sicily)
Corfu
(to Sicily)
M
NE

KURLAND
LIVONIA
TEUTONIC KNIGHTS
Memel
Riga
Samogitia
Kovno
LITHUANIA
Warsaw
Vladimir
Lvov
Cracow
Halicx

to Denmark
Ladoga
Novgorod
Pskov
TERRITORY OF NOVGOROD
Moscow
Polotski
Tchernigov
Kiev
RUSSIAN STATES
(Tributary to Mongols)
Dnieper R.
Prust R.

Yaroslav
Vladimir
MONGOL KHANATE OF THE GOLDEN HORDE
Volga R.
Don R.

CUMANS
WALLACHIA
Danube R.
SERBIA
Nissa
BULGARIA
Philippopolis
Adrianople
BYZANTINE EMPIRE
EPIRUS
THESSALY
Thessalonica
Larissa
Corfu
ATHENS
Thebes
Athens
ACHAIA
RHODES
CRETE
CYPRUS

Black Sea
Sinope
EMPIRE OF TREBIZOND
Trebizond
Constantinople
Nicomedia
Nicaea
Mongol Dominions
(Seljuk Turks)
Iconium
ARMENIA
Seleucia
Euphrates R.
Antioch
Tripoli
TURKS
Damascus
Acre
Jerusalem
Sea
MAMELUKES
Cairo

governing body of the entire church. Although there could then be fifty-two cardinals (six bishops, eighteen priests, and twenty-eight deacons)—later seventy cardinals and nowadays still more—the number was rarely complete. In 1179 the cardinals were officially constituted as a corporation or *collegium*, whence arose the familiar term "college of cardinals." The cardinals administered the important affairs of the universal church, but they did not legally limit papal authority. Popes could and did consult them and take their advice, but were not bound to do so. And only the pope could create cardinals.

A full meeting of the cardinals with the pope was known as a consistory. And it was through consistories that most of the important affairs of the church were administered even into the thirteenth century. Since added pressure of business required division and specialization, there was a tendency to reserve consistories for particular occasions and to leave routine matters to departments of the *curia*. There were two distinct curial departments by the twelfth and thirteenth centuries, the chancery and the camera. The chancery, one of the oldest of papal bureaus, was responsible for the sending and receiving of letters and bulls.[1] The camera was the papal treasury, headed by a *camerarius* or chamberlain, always a cardinal bishop.[2] Papal curial procedure, especially in regard to finances, has been a subject of criticism from the middle ages to the present. Some of this criticism is certainly justifiable. Delays were frequent, and at times there was considerable financial corruption in the transaction of curial business. Yet the fact remains that, with all its shortcomings, the papal *curia* was better organized and conducted than any secular

government of the period and that from it were derived many features of later political organization.

The papal *curia* was organized to care for all the ordinary routine of centralized administration. There were occasions, however, when a pope wished to discuss with prelates from all Christendom important matters of doctrine or policy affecting the entire church. This was done by requiring all the bishops and abbots to attend a general church council. The most famous of these gatherings in the middle ages, the Fourth Lateran Council at Rome (1215), was attended by over four hundred bishops, some eight hundred abbots and priors, and a number of lay delegates. It was this council, together with its predecessor the Third Lateran (1179), which issued a number of canons designed to raise the standards of clerical conduct. And while success in this respect was by no means complete, the general level of clerical efficiency and morality in the mid-thirteenth century was undoubtedly higher than it had been a hundred years earlier.

The Fourth Lateran Council also concerned itself with important matters of faith. The intellectual revival of the twelfth and thirteenth centuries with its marked emphasis on language and logic, particularly where theological or philosophical terminology was involved, raised a demand for more precise definition of certain dogmas. For example, although it had always been believed that in the sacrament of the Eucharist the bread and wine were miraculously transformed into the Body and Blood of Christ, the Fourth Lateran Council solemnly defined the doctrine of "transubstantiation." This meant that while the inner reality, or "substance," [3] of the bread and wine was changed as the priest pronounced the words of consecration, the appearance, or "accidents," remained the same.

These are only examples of the many matters which engaged the attention of the Fourth Lateran Council. And since Innocent III had committees carefully prepare its agenda beforehand, all the work was

---

[1] A bull (from the Latin, *bulla*, seal) was a more formal communication than the ordinary letter.

[2] Since the receipts from papal lands in Italy were no longer adequate for its expanding organization, and since such payments as the *census* from papal fiefs and Peter's pence (originally a sort of hearth tax in England and certain northern states) were irregularly paid, the popes were forced to levy income taxes and benefice taxes on the bishops and to charge fees for letters, bulls, and litigation at the *curia*.

[3] There is no adequate English equivalent of the medieval Latin term, *substantia*. The usual material connotation of the modern English word "substance" is very misleading.

Gothic architecture
in France.
The Cathedral
at Chartres.

Courtesy French Government Tourist Office, New York

completed in a surprisingly short time. The Council was at once a testimony of a smoothly functioning organization, and a tribute to the administrative genius of a remarkable pope.

B. The Secular Clergy

The success of any government, however centralized, depends on its subordinate officials. In the case of the church, the most important of these were the bishops. In order more adequately to regulate them, the papacy repeatedly sought to bring their elections under some sort of control. By 1300 it ordinarily confirmed the appointment of all archbishops and many bishops and abbots,

and increasingly made "provision" (appointment) even to minor benefices. Papal supervision over prelates once elected, was also made more effective. The system of legates was expanded. Every archbishop was required to receive a *pallium*, the symbol of his office, from the pope, and all bishops were expected to make periodic visits to Rome. More numerous appeals to the papal *curia* were facilitated by the appointment of special judge-delegates to act locally. This diminished the jurisdiction of local episcopal courts, as did also the deliberate "reservation" of certain types of cases, notably those concerning heresy, for papal jurisdiction only.

In spite of the surrender of a good deal

of his formerly independent authority to Rome, the average bishop was burdened with cares both ecclesiastical and secular. First, he presided over a cathedral church, of which the priests, or canons as they were called, were organized into a corporation known as the cathedral chapter. Since it was the bishop's duty to supervise the parish priests of his diocese, he had to travel on regular tours of inspection, and, as a rule, he required his parochial clergy to attend an annual synod. The regular clergy were also a concern, for not all monasteries were exempt from episcopal jurisdiction. To relieve themselves of some of the burden, most bishops either delegated a great deal of their routine to a diocesan official, the archdeacon, or appointed other agents.

The bishop also had obligations to his superiors, the archbishop and the pope. There were frequent provincial synods which the archbishop expected him to attend, and even occasional controversies over judgments rendered in his episcopal court. With more effective papal supremacy there were increasingly numerous dealings with Rome. Bishops were often required to act as judge-delegates in papal cases. Most important of all were the journeys to Rome, either to make the periodic visit, to attend a Lateran council, or simply to participate in a litigation in which he was personally concerned. Moreover, in the Middle Ages, a trip to Rome was long, arduous, and sometimes dangerous. Finally, as previous chapters have indicated, the average bishop's life could not be wholly devoted to the service of the church. He was responsible for the supervision of the episcopal estates with all that entailed in a feudal world, and frequently he was involved in the political life of his country.

What sort of men were the bishops of the twelfth and thirteenth centuries? It is impossible, of course, to generalize. Probably a large majority, though certainly not all, were of noble birth. As a whole they were fond of power and display. A few were wealthy enough to bequeath considerable property to their cathedrals, to monasteries, or to the poor. According to contemporary critics (who were many and outspoken), they were too fond of worldly things.

But we must beware of accepting the tes-timony of detractors who often exaggerate. Actions speak louder than words. If the worst bishops were little better than robber barons, and the despair of popes and reformers, the best were excellent administrators of their dioceses, faithfully fulfilling the duties of an exacting, even perilous, position. Eudes Rigaud, bishop of Rouen in the thirteenth century, has left in his record of diocesan visitations a priceless source of information, and the evidence of his own conscientious devotion to duty. Maurice of Sully, bishop of Paris in the twelfth century, was the son of a peasant, who, somewhat in the manner of the modern student who works his way through college, begged his food and waited on rich scholars at Paris. Having become Master of Theology, he rose in the church and won renown as a preacher and as a remarkably efficient administrator of his diocese. Like Maurice, a number of bishops were scholars and theologians with a university education. Many were builders, for we must not forget that the great cathedrals, perhaps the most striking contribution of medieval art, were partly the result of episcopal energy and initiative. The bishop's task was essentially an administrative one which left little time for the systematic pursuit of personal sanctity.

It will be remembered that some parish priests of the towns were organized into corporations ("colleges") much as were the cathedral canons, and that their churches were known as collegiate churches. The rural parish priest faced different problems. He was often appointed and to some extent controlled by the local *seigneur*. His duties were manifold and included not only the maintenance of his church and its functions, but often a responsibility for parish discipline. He was always very close to the people of his parish and potentially an important influence for good.

Unhappily, repeated fulminations of popes and councils, together with the reports of episcopal visitations, indicate a continuing need for reform among the parish clergy. Moreover, although better facilities for education became available with the rise of schools and universities, they remained generally inadequate throughout the middle ages.

Doubtless many a parish priest faithfully

fulfilled his duties, and thus attracted no particular attention. But his opportunities to raise the standard of his own life and thus more deeply influence his people were meager.

C. The Regular Clergy

Among the new religious orders founded in the twelfth century, the Cistercians were the most important.[1] The Cistercian order, so named from the original settlement at Cîteaux in Burgundy, was actually established in 1098. But its importance in the ecclesiastical life of Europe dates from the career of its most famous son, St. Bernard of Clairvaux (1090–1153). It was the purpose of the Cistercians to restore the Benedictine observance in all its strictness, for by the twelfth century many Benedictine and Cluniac houses had strayed from the path of primtive discipline. Thus the Cistercian monks were to the twelfth century what the Cluny foundation had been to the era of Hildebrand.

Greatest of all the Cistercians was St. Bernard. In fact so widespread was the influence of this outstanding abbot of Clairvaux, that the designation, "the age of St. Bernard," seems quite appropriate to the mid-twelfth century. For St. Bernard was not only a remarkable ascetic, gifted with an extraordinary capacity to detach himself from worldly affairs in the contemplation of things divine. He was a man of action as well. It was St. Bernard who preached the Second Crusade, aided the pope against his enemies, helped the king of France settle various ecclesiastical problems, and withstood the prominent scholar, Abelard. Many of his sermons and hymns have been published and several of the latter have remained popular to this day.[2] Rarely has a man so towered above his contemporaries.

Until the thirteenth century monasticism had commonly been associated with the countryside. But it was particularly in relation to the growing towns that a new type of regular clergy now appeared under the name of "friars." These, like the monks of earlier times, took vows and lived under a rule. But whereas the monk's life of prayer and contemplation normally centered in a cloister, the friar's life was one of religious activity. He was expected to go out into the world and to serve the laity in particular work associated with his order. There were several different orders of friars, of which two were especially important—the Franciscan and the Dominican.[3] Each of these reflected the character of its founder.

---

[1] The Cistercians adopted a policy midway between Cluniac centralization and Benedictine separatism. Each monastery was governed autonomously by an abbot, but a system of annual meetings of all Cistercian abbots and periodic visitations by the abbot of Cîteaux ensured uniform practices. In the thirteenth century, the Cistercians obtained exemption from local episcopal control.

[2] *Jesu, dulcis memoria* (Jesus, the very thought of Thee) is the best known of St. Bernard's hymns. He also composed for Eugenius III, the first Cistercian monk to be chosen pope, the *de Consideratione*, a notable treatise on the papal office and its responsibilities.

[3] In addition, there were the Carmelite, the Augustinian, and the Servite.

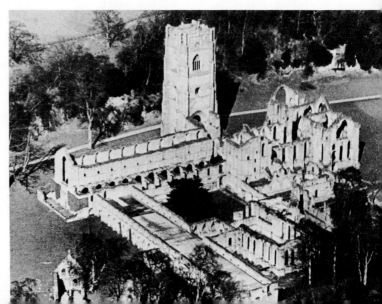

A monastic complex of buildings. The ruins of the Cistercian abbey of Fountains, Yorkshire, twelfth and thirteenth centuries.

Courtesy British Information Services, New York

St. Francis of Assisi (about 1181–1226) was the son of a wealthy Italian merchant. As a young man, he passed through a deep crisis in his own spiritual life which ended in a resolution to embrace a life of poverty. To live as the apostles, to be poor with Christ and to minister to Christ's poor, enduring the same hardships as they; that was the course ahead of him. This radical decision was accompanied by no morbid melancholy. Rather it seems to have enhanced his naturally buoyant temperament. In a spirit of romantic chivalry which never left him, he devoted himself to his "Lady Poverty."

Although this resolve meant a separation from his family and former associates, Francis with a few faithful followers persisted in the new way of life. He received sympathy and counsel from the bishop of Assisi, and in 1210 he sought papal confirmation for his undertaking. Although Innocent III was opposed to the formation of new orders, he was impressed with the sincerity and persistence of Francis and shrewd enough to see the possible value of his work. As a consequence, he gave a verbal consent to the Franciscan rule of life. This rule, revised later to meet the demands of larger numbers, was confirmed by Pope Honorius III in 1223. It was a simple statement of the Franciscan ideal of apostolic poverty, with needful practical directions for an expanding organization.

It is difficult to overestimate the significance of the Franciscans (or Friars Minor, as they were officially termed) in the Europe of the early thirteenth century. They were simple, sincere men, who, in a world prospering materially, but whence much religious fervor of an earlier day had departed, devotedly ministered to townsfolk who were often inadequately served by the local secular clergy.

The Franciscan order expanded rapidly, becoming numerically the largest in the church. Moreover, before the end of the thirteenth century the activities of the order had expanded far beyond the simple ideal of the founder. Franciscans went as missionaries to distant lands. They maintained schools at the universities and produced famous scholars like Roger Bacon and St. Bonaventure. But never, even when in later times many Franciscans succumbed to the temptations of wealth, did they entirely forget poverty and the poor.

Dominic Guzman (1170–1221)—St. Dominic—differed in temperament and emphasis from Francis of Assisi, and the Dominican order which he founded differed from the Franciscan. Dominic was a Spaniard and primarily a scholar, theologian, and preacher. He was a cathedral canon when, as an associate of a Catalan bishop on a preaching mission, he first came into contact with the Albigensian heretics of southern France.[1] Later, with a small band of followers, officially recognized by the bishop, he began to preach in Toulouse, a hotbed of the heresy. Like St. Francis, Dominic sought papal recognition for a new organization. But since the Fourth Lateran Council (1215) had formally prohibited new orders, the Pope urged him to adopt one of the already existing rules. Dominic then adapted to his own purposes the so-called rule of St. Augustine, which was familiar to him as a cathedral canon. Dominic's rule was formally confirmed by Honorius III in 1216.[2]

Like the Franciscans, the Dominicans lived on the alms of the faithful, and they too were welcomed in the towns where they helped to fill a real need, particularly in preaching. In fact, the official title of their organization is the Order of Friars Preachers. But they were also missionaries, scholars, and teachers. One has only to recall the name of St. Thomas Aquinas, perhaps the greatest of medieval theologians and philosophers, to realize their influence. In 1277 there were three hundred and ninety-four Dominican convents situated in all parts of western and central Europe and in Greece and the Holy Land.

D. Preservation of the Faith Against Heresy

From its beginning, hardly a century passed in which the church did not have to oppose some heresy. But since the disappearance of Arianism and other heresies of

---

[1] See above, p. 206, and below, p. 235.

[2] The Dominican rule was a constitutional masterpiece, providing for provinces and chapters of the Order, and for representative democracy in its central government.

the fourth and fifth centuries concerning the Trinity and the nature of Christ, heretical movements had been only temporary or of local importance, until the twelfth century. Then, two different heresies arose and attracted a sufficiently numerous following to create a formidable problem for the ecclesiastical authorities. Moreover, heresy was also a concern of governments which, so close was the relation between religion and secular affairs, usually regarded heresy as treason. Not uncommonly, too, heretics were the victims of mob violence.

What at first seemed an innocuous movement was that of the Waldensians, so-called from the name of its founder, Waldo, a rich merchant of Lyons. Waldo was a man of no particular learning, but he possessed generosity and a love of the poor. His followers who preached to the poor were at first not unlike the Franciscans and were known as the Poor Men of Lyons. Pope Alexander III gave official approval to their work on condition that they obtain the sanction of the local clergy. But the Poor Men soon defied clerical discipline, and in censuring publicly and severely the ordinary clergy of the day they adopted a markedly anti-clerical attitude. At length, in 1184, the Waldensian movement was condemned by an ecclesiastical council at Verona, and it passed from simple anti-clericalism to acceptance of the heretical doctrine that personal holiness availed more than the sacrament of Holy Orders. Although Waldensianism spread from southern France into Spain and even into central Europe, it was gradually overcome and eventually survived only in a few places in northern Italy.

The other, and far more formidable, heresy of the time was known as Catharism, from a Greek word, *cathari* (the pure), or as Albigensianism, from the town of Albi in southern France, one of its strongholds. Though it gained an especially large following among the Provencal population, particularly around Toulouse and in Languedoc, its origin seems to have been in the Near East. At any rate, it resembled an ancient Persian religion of "Manichaeism," and in the early middle age it had spread in Bulgaria and thence to Italy and southern France.

The central doctrine of Catharism was a belief in an eternal struggle between a god whose dominion was the realm of the spirit and an evil deity, or the devil, who ruled the material universe. All matter and flesh were considered evil, and their propagation serviceable only to the devil. The Christian belief in the resurrection of the body was also rejected. An important element in Catharism, and one which accounts in some measure for its popular appeal, was the distinction it made between pure or "perfect" believers and ordinary believers. The former, usually numbering only a few members of a community, lived lives of extreme asceticism, and, in some cases, they hastened their release from the flesh by suicide. The ordinary believer was merely required to venerate the "perfect."

Catharism flourished in the lax and sophisticated atmosphere of southern France where clerical wealth and corruption were especially prominent and, as Pope Innocent III himself bluntly remarked, were powerful inducements to loss of faith. The combined efforts of bishops, papal legates, and preaching missions like that of St. Dominic had only limited success in reconverting the heretics. When the local secular ruler, Count Raymond VI of Toulouse, flatly refused to coöperate with the church in suppressing Catharism, he was excommunicated by Pope Innocent III's legate, Peter de Castelnau, and his lands were placed under an interdict. A few months later Peter was murdered by one of the Count's men.

The death of Castelnau was the signal for the abandonment, at least temporarily, of peaceful persuasion and the adoption of more drastic methods in dealing with the Catharist heresy. The Pope now proclaimed a holy war against the Count of Toulouse, and offered the same indulgence to the participants as was promised to those who went to the Holy Land. The ensuing Albigensian Crusade soon developed into a protracted, sanguinary war, in which the conflicting political ambitions of the leading participants overshadowed its original purpose. Northern French barons seized the opportunity to pillage and acquire new lands in the south, and French kings, to extend their power. Count Raymond VI was finally defeated at the battle of Muret (1213), but not until 1229, when his son, Raymond VII, once again submitted and renewed his father's promises to prosecute heretics, was the Albigensian war finally liquidated.

The eradication of Catharism was only obtained by the establishment of a special ecclesiastical tribunal, called the Inquisition. This medieval Papal Inquisition, was a court for judicial inquiry, with a regular procedure based primarily on canon law and secondarily on Roman civil law.[1] From the latter was derived the practice of torturing accused persons in order to obtain confessions from them—a practice which Pope Innocent IV authorized (1252) in "stubborn cases."

The Inquisition recognized various gradations of heretical crime, including mere suspicion of being a heretic, and a harboring of heretics. Lesser offenses, duly confessed, were lightly punished. But even suspects were sometimes required to undertake expensive and difficult pilgrimages, or to wear distinctive markings on their clothes. Fines and confiscation of property were fairly frequent. Only in more severe cases was imprisonment the penalty; and for only two kinds of cases was the death penalty recommended: (1) a final refusal to recant, and (2) a relapse after recantation. In these cases, the recommendation usually meant burning the condemned at the stake, and it was invariably carried out not by the ecclesiastical but by the civil authorities. It is worth noting, too, that such recommendations of the medieval Inquisition were relatively few.[2] After all, though it may seem very strange to us, the medieval Inquisitors were striving to convert the heretic. They did not desire his death, but rather the saving of his immortal soul.

E. Church and Laity

There were two levels on which the church organization dealt with the layman. It had official dealings with rulers, and, more important, it was concerned with the spiritual life of all the faithful. In its dealings with the rulers of Europe, the church of the thirteenth century developed a comprehensive temporal policy. Its purpose was the attainment of peace and justice in Christendom through the universal recognition of papal political predominance. This did not mean direct papal government of Europe. Rather, it implied a kind of administrative unity or federation of European states under papal supervision. Indeed, it was a kind of ecclesiastical counterpart of the Holy Roman Empire, an attempt to revive, under papal rather than imperial suzerainty, the ancient dream of world unity—of a Pax Romana. Thus, although the thirteenth-century popes were still concerned with the protection of the papal states and with the prevention of secular dictation to the clergy, they aspired to something broader and higher. It was their hope that Christendom could achieve an inner harmony necessary to the furtherance of Christian life and to adequate defense against the ever menacing Moslems.

The juridical claims of the papacy to preeminence over the several European realms varied considerably. In the first place, those over the Holy Roman Empire were grounded on a traditional relationship dating from the time of Charlemagne's coronation by the Pope in the year 800. It was strife between Emperors and Popes which occasioned some of the most striking medieval pronouncements regarding papal preeminence.

Second, the papacy utilized contemporary feudal practices to assert and establish its preeminence. Thus, among its fiefs, besides a numbers of towns and petty principalities, were the kingdoms of Portugal, Aragon, Poland, Sicily, Hungary, and, temporarily, England.[3]

Still other opportunities for papal intervention in secular states were afforded by local infringement of clerical privileges, by violation of marriage vows on the part of a ruler, by disputes between kings, etc. The cases of John of England and Philip Augus-

---

[1] Gregory IX (1227–1241) seems to have definitely established the Papal Inquisition and to have first appointed members of the Dominican Order as its judges, or "Inquisitors."

[2] Over a period of seventeen years, Bernard Gui, generally regarded as a particularly efficient Inquisitor, recommended the death penalty in forty-five cases, while imposing prison sentences in 307 cases, out of a total of 613 adjudged "guilty." Incidentally, the medieval Papal In-

quisition should not be confused with the more notorious Spanish Inquisition of the fifteenth and sixteenth centuries.

[3] The first systematic list of pontifical fiefs was included in the *Liber Censum* (1192). Insistence on payment of the *census*, or feudal tax, was often an added occasion for papal intervention.

tus of France were thirteenth-century examples.

Although the actions of Gregory VII implied a substitution of papal for royal predominance, the popes of the twelfth century were, despite occasional tension, hesitant about pressing this. Alexander III's patience, for example, in the controversy between Henry II and Thomas Becket, was resented by some of the Archbishop's supporters, and during the long struggle with Barbarossa there was no mention of an anti-Emperor.

It remained for Innocent III, mentioned often in these pages, to be the most brilliant exponent of a papal theocracy. A careful lawyer and a skilled diplomat, he examined the legality of each case before he acted. Later popes asserted more emphatically the papal temporal claims, but no pope before or since has so nearly succeeded in making effective the idea of a Christian commonwealth of nations under the supremacy of the Apostolic See. England, France, the Empire, and many smaller states felt the power of his exalted office. And in most instances, it will be recalled, Innocent III won his point. It is true that several of his successors also won certain triumphs, but their claims to political supremacy went unheeded even by such pious monarchs as Henry III of England and St. Louis IX of France.[1] Philip IV's rejection of Boniface VIII's bull, *Unam Sanctam*, was even more spectacular. In the later ages, the development of monarchies demanding unrestricted control over their territories prevented the realization of the papal dream of a federated Christendom.

The success which the medieval church attained in promoting a genuine spirituality among the laity and in raising the standard of individual and social morality is difficult to estimate. Religion was a real part of every man's life, and modern preconceptions make it easy to forget that religion played a great part in the daily lives of the laity throughout the middle ages and that the average layman was constantly brought into contact

[1] During the struggle between Innocent IV and Frederick II, St. Louis promised to protect the Pope if he were attacked at Lyons where he was then staying, but he attempted to mediate in the dispute. Both Louis of France and Henry of England continued to address Frederick as Emperor after the Pope had pronounced his deposition.

with the all-embracing ecclesiastical organization. Indeed, the laity constituted the vast majority of the "body" of the church. Spiritual matters were intermingled with temporal concerns in a manner baffling to the modern student. Various activities which today are frequently secular, such as education or the care of the poor and sick, were, in the middle ages, ecclesiastical responsibilities. Frequently hospitals for the sick and kindred institutions for lepers, for women and children, or for the aged, were organized under ecclesiastical direction by religious confraternities of laymen. Ecclesiastical courts claimed jurisdiction over all cases involving clergymen and over many matters affecting everybody, such as domestic relations, wills, oaths, and usury. As a consequence, any layman would have recourse to the courts of the church.

Saint Francis preaching to the birds, from a Franco-Flemish manuscript of the thirteenth century.

Courtesy Pierpont Morgan Library, New York

There is also ample evidence of popular devotion. We have seen that while some nobles and kings attacked church property or sought to control the church for their own purposes, others went on crusades and pilgrimages and generously contributed to churches and monasteries. A townsman might laugh at satirical and often ribald stories about clerical shortcomings. But his guild was dedicated to a patron saint and he shared in giving a stained glass window to the cathedral. He was often also a member of a religious confraternity devoted to a charitable or purely devotional purpose.

Medieval popular devotion is evident, too, in the increased veneration of the saints, and especially the Virgin Mary. From early times, and particularly after the Council of Ephesus (431) had solemnly proclaimed her the "Mother of God," Mary had been the chief recourse for pious seekers of spiritual, and even temporal, favors. But it was especially in the main middle age that popular devotion to Mary flourished. Saints, of course, had always been honored

in the church and their shrines had been objects of pilgrimage. The saints, in short, were very real to the average medieval man. He constantly sought their intercession. He prayed to them and he swore by them.

Although it seems clear that ecclesiastical and secular authorities working together—and they were part of a single society—did noticeably improve the quality of medieval religion, there remained much that was imperfect. Lay participation in the sacraments, for example, was not always frequent. It is notable that at the Fourth Lateran Council (1215) it was felt necessary to prescribe that every Christian must receive the sacraments of penance and the eucharist at least once a year under pain of excommunication. The medieval church's achievement was principally in perfecting an organization capable of bringing religion into men's daily lives. It was exercising its influence more widely and deeply in the twelfth and thirteenth centuries, but there was much still to be done.

CHAPTER 20

The Medieval Revival of Learning

The intellectual revival of the eleventh century in western and central Europe, rendered possible by increasing political and social stability, was quickened into what modern historians often call the "renaissance of the twelfth century." This was marked by a notable increase in the number of students and teachers and a corresponding demand for better organization of instruction. Two aspects of this revival will concern us here: the content of medieval learning, and the development of schools and universities.

A. Medieval Intellectual Interests: Liberal Arts and Philosophy

The purpose of medieval education was practical, the improvement of the student's position in church, state, or commerce. To some a grounding in the traditional liberal arts sufficed. These numbered seven, it will be remembered, and were divided into the *trivium* and the *quadrivum*, or the "three ways" and the "four ways." [1] The *trivium*, consisting of grammar, rhetoric, and logic, was the basis for all further advanced study. And it is important to notice the use of the terms "art" and "way." Together they designate facility or competence, and also method. They were the instruments of literary expression and thought, what today are sometimes called "skills." Before a scholar could hope to enter the fraternity of higher learning, he must first master the tools. He must be thoroughly competent in the Latin language (grammar), be able to express his

[1] See above, p. 59.

ideas clearly (rhetoric), and, perhaps most important, know how to think and reason correctly (logic). Hence the *trivium*, the basis of all education, came to be the core of instruction.

A growing number of students sought further instruction in the three advanced subjects of the day—theology, law, and medicine—which most often led to employment or promotion, and which formed the principal curricula of the medieval universities. It should also be remarked that many scholars, however concerned they might be with professional advancement, acquired at various stages along the way a love of learning for its own sake. Both motives, the practical and the purely intellectual, must be considered in estimating the medieval achievement.

The mastery of grammar and rhetoric involved the study not only of grammatical and rhetorical treatises, but acquaintance with the works of the great classical men of letters. And rhetoric required at least imitation, if not original skill. Hence there appeared during the eleventh and twelfth centuries a genuine literary humanism, a both wider and deeper knowledge of the ancient authors. The quality of Latin composition improved notably. To mention only one example, John of Salisbury, a student and later bishop at Chartres, counsellor of popes and kings, friend of Thomas Becket, was an excellent Latinist. His letters, especially, are masterpieces of style. This was the age, too, of the great Latin hymns, and of poems on nature and love, youthful student songs, satires, all in excellent Latin. And the twelfth century likewise produced some notable historians whose works reveal considerable acquaintance with the ancients.

Medieval Latin differed from the Latin of Cicero in style and vocabulary. For it continued to be a living language, capable of absorbing ecclesiastical, feudal, and Germanic words and philosophical ideas. Despite a persistent popular notion to the contrary, medieval Latin was not barbarous or ungrammatical.

In the west, medieval literary classicism was exclusively Latin. Greek works were known only in translation, and knowledge of the Greek language was generally confined to parts of southern Italy and Sicily or to those ecclesiastics and diplomats who had dealings with Byzantium. A notable advance in this matter resulted, however, from the establishment of the Latin empire at Constantinople after the Fourth Crusade.

As grammar and rhetoric blossomed into literary appreciation and skill, so logic inspired inquiries into philosophy. And so fascinated were scholars by the problems of logic and philosophy that toward the end of the twelfth century philosophical studies predominated over the humanistic. Thus the thirteenth century, the great "age of the universities," was a period of philosophical and theological, rather than of literary, interest. Men were absorbed by the attempt to understand the nature of the world and of man and to explain the existence of God and the meaning of creation. Above all, they sought answers to the questions which philosophers have always asked and doubtless always will. What is? What exists? What is being? And since these questions were threshed out in the schools, the solutions and reasonings of the medieval "schoolmen" have been called "scholastic philosophy" or "scholasticism."

To the average medieval thinker, philosophy was not an end in itself. It should lead him to truth, and in particular to theological truth, which he deemed the highest of all. The schoolmen did not believe that the truths of revealed religion could be strictly proven, but they did insist that they could be rationally explained, that they could be made to satisfy the human intellect. There emerged a scholastic theology, related to and dependent on, yet intellectually distinct

from, scholastic philosophy. A few examples may help to explain the distinction. It was held that the human intellect was capable of understanding the things of nature and of man—his virtues, his vices, his physical and moral attributes. It could also reason from man and nature to God; it could, in fact, demonstrate the existence of a supreme being and in a limited manner understand the divine nature. But there, having reached the limits of what some have called "natural theology," the independent function of philosophy—of the mind unaided by revelation—ended. Beyond that, philosophy was merely the handmaid of theology, the "queen of sciences." As such, it provided the rational basis for an intelligent discussion of what God revealed to man, such as the Incarnation, the Trinity, the sacraments, the theological virtues, divine grace, etc.

Although the basis of logical studies throughout the early Middle Age had largely been those parts of Aristotle's *Organon* which Boethius had translated from Greek into Latin in the sixth century, most of Aristotle's other treatises were then unknown. As a consequence, and also owing to the veneration with which the semi-Platonist works of St. Augustine were held, it was the general philosophy of Plato, rather than of Aristotle, which gave chief direction to European thought well into the twelfth century. On the fundamental question of being, for example, it was held, with Plato, that abstract ideas or "universals," such as justice, goodness, man, etc., were the true realities. Thinkers who entertained such views were called "realists." [1] St. Anselm, scholar and archbishop of Canterbury, was a prominent "realist" in this tradition. His *Cur Deus Homo* was a widely read treatise and contained a famous proof of the existence of God, reflecting the "realist" school of thought.

Medieval Platonic "realism" did not remain uncontested. A veritable revolution in thought resulted from western Christendom's deriving from the Moslems fuller knowledge of the whole philosophical heri-

---

[1] It should be noted that the modern connotation of the term "realism" is radically different. "Idealism" would more nearly approach the medieval meaning.

Gothic architecture in England. Salisbury Cathedral.

Courtesy British Information Services, New York

tage of ancient Greece. Bit by bit the long forgotten or neglected works of Aristotle reappeared in Latin translations from the Arabic. By the middle of the thirteenth century, practically the complete writings of Aristotle were available. Under this new, or rather ancient, but radically different intellectual influence, the validity of "realism" was challenged. It was urged that universals did not possess true reality, but were only arbitrary collective names. Hence, arose, in the mid-twelfth century, a "nominalist" school of thought.

But we must not overemphasize the controversy over universals. Significant though it was to the understanding of being, it was but one example of the current enthusiasm for the new Aristotelian logic. Meanwhile, men like Peter Abelard (*d.* 1142) were pioneering in methods of reasoning and argumentation. In a treatise called *Sic et Non,*

Abelard stated a series of propositions and cited from various authorities opinions for and against each. Since the reader was expected to resolve the contradiction himself, the method aroused considerable criticism. It had, however, many advantages, and later writers adopted it, while usually suggesting solutions to the questions posed. Peter Lombard, who became bishop of Paris in 1159, applied the technique in his *Book of Sentences,* one of the first systematic treatises on theology.

Although Abelard was a remarkable teacher he was as self-assured as he was brilliant. He dared openly to challenge at Paris the most noted realist of the day, William of Champeaux, and soon the latter's students were deserting him and flocking to Abelard's lectures. Abelard's popularity undoubtedly contributed to the reputation of the University of Paris in its early days.

On the matter of universals, too, Abelard made a distinct contribution. To him individual things possessed reality, but universals or abstract ideas, he admitted, had validity as concepts of the mind. This "conceptualism" of Abelard's proved to be a basis for rationalizing the problem of being —a basis which gradually gained wide acceptance. Fortified and modified by further knowledge of Aristotle, it led to the "moderate realism" of St. Thomas Aquinas in the thirteenth century.

Unfortunately Abelard's real gifts were all too often nullified by his egotism.[1] On one occasion his enthusiastic rationalizing brought him into conflict with ecclesiastical authority. Partly at the instigation of St. Bernard, who probably did not fully understand Abelard's purposes, certain of his propositions were publicly condemned. But Abelard was not a heretic and never questioned either the fundamental truths of the faith or the authority of the church. He was simply attempting to make the truths of religion understandable to the human mind through the instrument of logic. Opposition resulted partly from his own somewhat intemperate manner and partly from a mistrust of the new logic which disappeared as soon as it was better understood.

Scholastic philosophy became associated with another intellectual tendency characteristic of the thirteenth century. It was firmly believed that all knowledge, whether it be natural science, metaphysics, or theology, was interrelated and could be fused into an organic whole. As a consequence, there were many efforts to synthesize the sciences and a number of treatises appeared bearing the title "Summa" ("the whole"), or some similar designation. In this endeavor to coordinate all knowledge as well as to rationalize theology, the foremost figure was St. Thomas Aquinas, the greatest philosopher of the middle ages, and one of the greatest of all time.

St. Thomas (*d.* 1274) was a Dominican friar and as such belonged to an order with a tradition of learning, which had already made significant contributions to the coordinating of Aristotelian rationalism with Catholic thought. He was a disciple of Albertus Magnus, also a Dominican, who taught at Paris and stoutly defended the study of the great Greek philosopher at a time when many were questioning its propriety.[2] Firmly convinced that the truths of faith and of natural reason could not conflict, since both were from God, Aquinas set about preparing his synthesis. In the manner of Aberlard's *Sic et Non*, he posed questions and quoted contrary opinions from Greek, Christian, and Arabic sources, and then offered resolutions of the contradictions for each question. Meticulous care was exercised in citing authorities and in distinguishing the conclusions reached by the author. St. Thomas's *Summa theologica*, his greatest work, is, as its title indicates, a complete compendium of theological knowledge. But it is a theological work in the broadest sense and contains a tremendous amount of material on philosophical, psychological, moral, and scientific subjects as well, and all presented in a logical and orderly manner. Not without reason is the *Summa theologica* universally regarded as one of the world's masterpieces.

We must not assume that the thirteenth-century penchant for synthesis resulted in perfectly harmonious systems being universally accepted. For the disputes between rival philosophies and rival schools of thought, always provided they did not question the fundamental truths of revealed religion, were many and acrimonious. We have already mentioned the controversy over universals. Both the Platonic tradition of

---

[1] Abelard is perhaps best known to moderns for his famous love affair with Héloise, his pupil, an affair which not only interrupted his academic career, but brought poignant tragedy into two lives.

Abelard, after a condemnation of certain of his writings, was given asylum at Cluny. Héloise became an abbess. The two corresponded until Abelard's death in 1142.

[2] The original study of Aristotle at Paris occasioned some misgivings. Certain teachings of Aristotle seemed incompatible with Christian thought and much of the work appeared in translation from the Arabic with commentaries by Moslem philosophers. Although Aristotle's scientific writings were temporarily banned in Paris early in the thirteenth century, by 1254 his chief works were required for the degree of master of arts.

realism and an extreme nominalism persisted. The highly gifted Franciscan, St. Bonaventure, following generally the former trend, stoutly championed the importance of the will against the emphasis laid on the intellect by Aquinas.

More damaging to the reputation of Aquinas was the work of certain thinkers at Paris who followed a more uncompromising Aristotelianism and were influenced by the writings of the great Moslem commentator, Averroes. A general condemnation in 1277 by the bishop of Paris included several propositions of Thomas. Although these were later removed, the cause of Thomism was seriously damaged. The teachings of Aquinas were generally not followed in the succeeding two centuries.[1]

B. Law, Medicine, and Science

Although the scholastic method of reasoning—the citing of authorities and the balancing of contradictory opinions—is primarily associated with the study of philosophy and theology, it was also generally employed in law and medicine. The renaissance of legal studies is preëminently associated with the city of Bologna and was stimulated by the revival of Justinian's *Digest* of Roman law late in the eleventh century. About 1140 there also appeared the *Decretum*, a codification of canon law by a monk, Gratian.[2] Teachers of both Roman and canon law then appeared, and Irnerius, one of the most famous, established himself at Bologna in the early decades of the twelfth century and attracted many students. In the course of this century, Bologna became the center for

an impressive number of other distinguished jurists. But although its law faculty was the most celebrated, Bologna early had a good liberal arts faculty and subsequently established a school of medicine which was the equal of any in Europe.

Medicine had long been studied at Salerno in southern Italy and at Montpellier in southern France. With the revival of learning in the twelfth and thirteenth centuries, other institutions surged ahead, notably Bologna, Padua, and Naples, which eventually absorbed the medical school at Salerno. The fundamentals of medical knowledge continued to be derived from the writings of Galen and Hippocrates, the famous physicians of the Hellenistic age. Indeed, the respect with which the authority of those ancients was held tended to retard progress. But the Arabs had made later and important contributions to the chemistry of medicine, and Moslem textbooks were now widely studied. Little progress was made in surgery in either Christendom or Islam, but toward the end of the thirteenth century, despite adverse popular opinion, occasional dissections of human corpses were performed and the way paved for later advances.

Recent studies have revealed that more progress was made during the middle ages in mathematics and the natural sciences than was once supposed. Mathematics flourished particularly at Oxford where one of the leading lights was Robert Grosseteste (*d.* 1253), one-time chancellor of the university. A pupil, Roger Bacon, a Franciscan friar, won considerable publicity through his eloquent criticisms of contemporary learning. Because of his somewhat stormy temperament, his remarks, many of them justified, often aroused antagonism rather than support. Thus his pleas that mathematics, languages, even oriental languages, and, above all, experimentation be given greater emphasis were not always heeded. In the manner of his day, Bacon conceived of all knowledge, including theology, as one organic whole, but one in which natural science should have a place.

The popularity of scientific and mathematical studies at places like Oxford indicate that European scholars were receiving from the Moslems not only Greek philosophy, but Greek and oriental science. As a result

---

[1] Extreme Aristotelianism and what came to be called Latin Averroism later obtained an important following at the university of Padua in Italy. The principal theological problems involved were Aristotle's teaching on the eternity of matter, and Averroes' questioning of the immortality of the individual soul and his doctrine of the "double truth," that is, one for philosophy or science, another for religion.

[2] The full title of the *Decretum—Concordantia discordantium canonum* (Concord or Harmony of Discordant Canons)—indicates that the canonists faced the same kind of problems in reconciling conflicting authorities as did the civilians.

Gothic Exterior. Notre Dame, Paris

Courtesy French Embassy Press and Information Division, New York

of the work of certain pioneer translators, Graeco-Arabic mathematics, astronomy, geography, chemistry—in short, natural science generally—became available to Christian Europeans. In both Western and Moslem traditions the persistence of ancient superstitions retarded progress, though they did not prevent it. For astronomy was confused with astrology, and chemistry was burdened with the alchemist's dream of transmutation. Generally speaking, natural science did not enjoy the popularity of the arts, theology, or law in the thirteenth century. What advances there were in it, and these were not inconsiderable, were - made chiefly outside of the universities.

C. Schools, and the University of Paris

The first universities were not, of course, "founded." They sprang up naturally and more or less spontaneously in the twelfth century, when increasing material prosperity, especially in the towns, combined with new intellectual interests to multiply the number of students and to tax the facilities of existing monastic and cathedral schools. Monastic schools, which had been the best, if not the most numerous, educational institutions in Europe since the early middle age and which were usually located in rural places, were now being eclipsed in quality and popularity by cathedral schools in urban centers. This was the time, it should be remembered, when cities were growing in size and wealth, developing merchant and craft guilds with much civic pride and vying with one another in building great cathedrals and expanding cathedral schools. Chartres, for example, boasted a school of considerable renown. But at Paris, which was becoming the capital of the French monarchy, the cathedral school became so expanded and famous and so attractive to students from all parts of Christendom that it evolved into what was called a *studium generale* ("general study-place"), or "university."

At Paris, the cathedral school of Notre Dame was located on a little island in the Seine, the *cité*. During the course of the eleventh and twelfth centuries the school drew so many students and teachers that they overflowed the island to the high ground across the river where there were certain other schools associated with the abbey of Ste. Geneviève. In this way, the site of the university of Paris came to be the historic "left bank" of the Seine, "the latin quarter" of later days, so named because of the scholarly language spoken there.

Medieval scholars were not primarily concerned with location or buildings. Actual instruction and its organization first engaged their attention. It was early determined that no one should give instruction without a "teaching license," to be issued by the bishop's chancellor. Still more significant, the scholars early sought an autonomous organization of their own through which they might control their own affairs, determine their own curriculum, and license their own teaching staff. For this they quite naturally borrowed the type of organization then coming into general use in towns—namely, the guild. From the Latin word sometimes used to designate a guild—the word "universitas," meaning corporation—was derived the popular name for the new *studium generale,* or "university."

Thus the unique feature of the university, as distinct from other contemporary schools, was its organization as a corporation after the manner of a guild. Since their "trade" was the liberal arts, it was the "master of arts" who controlled university affairs. Upon the completion of a designated curriculum, an "apprentice" in arts received a certain official recognition as "bachelor" (*baccalaureus*).[1] Later he might be admitted to the guild as a "master" after formal "inception," an elaborate ceremony of investiture with appropriate oaths of obedience. Moreover, since the baccalaureate was a "step" toward becoming a master, it was a *gradus* or "degree." The whole familiar paraphernalia of guild customs now appeared in this academic organization.

The arts guild at Paris became so large that it was found necessary to subdivide it into what were called "nations." The term "nation" in medieval Paris did not signify what it does today. A "nation" was then any convenient grouping of scholars from

---

[1] The term *baccalaureus* seems to have been borrowed from the contemporary terminology of chivalry, in which it signified the knight bachelor or knight without others serving under him.

particular regions. There were originally four: French, Picards, Normans, and English. And the absence of nationalism in the terms as then used is indicated by the fact that the English "nation" at Paris included Germans, and that all southern Europeans were grouped with the French. Each "nation" was headed by a *proctor*, and, toward the middle of the thirteenth century, a *rector* was chosen to supervise the entire institution.

Since liberal arts remained the fundamental basis of medieval education and were doubtless sufficient for the needs of most people, the great majority of students at Paris pursued their studies under a "faculty of arts." But there soon developed at Paris and elsewhere a demand for instruction in other more advanced and specialized subjects. This was provided by higher "faculties," as they were called, dealing with such fields of learning as theology, civil and canon law, and medicine. Rarely did any one university provide for all "faculties." Paris, for example, specialized in those of theology and canon law. The higher faculties, as well as the faculty of arts, were organized on the guild model with similar terminology, although the term "dean," designating the head of a higher faculty, was borrowed from ecclesiastical usage. There were masters of theology and of law, as well as masters of arts. Meanwhile, the titles "doctor" and "professor" were introduced—titles signifying teacher and used interchangeably with "master." As these academic titles were often sought by men who had no intention of teaching, they came to be, like our modern degrees, certificates indicating the successful completion of specified courses of study.

The University of Paris became a federation of guilds. And perhaps owing to the basic importance of the liberal arts and the greater number of arts students, the original arts guild retained its primacy. After a certain amount of protest on the part of the deans of higher faculties, the rector of the arts faculty was recognized as superior to the others. Moreover, although the term *studium generale* remained in contemporary usage, the word *universitas* gradually replaced it.

In the course of its incorporation as a self-sufficient teaching organization, the university—or federated guilds of masters and scholars—found it necessary to regularize its relations with the civil and ecclesiastical authorities. Toward the end of the twelfth century, comparatively early in the history of the institution, the problem of police jurisdiction over students became serious. Since not all scholars were hardworking, and not all students serious, there were recurrent troubles between "town" and "gown," that is, between officials and citizens of Paris on the one hand, and members of the university on the other. Shortly after one bad riot and a consequent suspension of university activities, King Philip Augustus decreed (1200) that the masters and scholars of Paris should be officially immune from the interference of ordinary civil authority. Masters and scholars were thus confirmed in the privilege of responsibility only to themselves and to the ecclesiastical authorities.

The university rather resented the continued supervision of the bishop and his chancellor, who, in turn, were not altogether pleased at the spectacle of their intellectual child, now grown to man's estate, and demanding an end of paternal control. A series of difficulties between bishop and masters ensued, necessitating papal intervention. The result was that, in the early decades of the thirteenth century, Popes Innocent III and Gregory IX recognized the university as a corporate entity and confirmed its right to determine its own course of study. The *studium generale* at Paris was henceforth a fully independent institution responsible only to itself and to the pope.

In the thirteenth century the new orders of friars sought to establish themselves within the university. At first they were not welcome. The university had been developed by the secular clergy and they were jealous of any encroachment on the part of the "regulars." But the friars eventually won the right to lecture as masters in theology, though not to participate in the faculty of arts.

Teaching and learning are processes which change very little. In the early days of the university of Paris, any available buildings were used for lectures and the students sat on whatever chairs or benches they could find or on the floor. The principal difference between medieval instruction and our own was the scarcity of books, which, of course, were written laboriously by hand and were expensive. More was accomplished orally than is the case today. A medieval lecturer often read aloud the text of some important work and added his own comments as he went along. His auditors might scribble some notes, but we may be sure that memory was normally more depended upon than notebooks. Examinations were oral and the candidate for a degree was commonly required to sustain a "thesis." That is, he was presented with a proposition which he had to defend in the face of vigorous questioning.

Medieval scholars lodged where they could or formed little societies to provide in common the necessities of life. For the poorer among them the pursuit of learning inevitably entailed real hardship. By the thirteenth century, however, conditions improved. The friars provided houses for their own members, and about 1258 Robert de Sorbon endowed for students in theology a hostel or "college," as it was called, which proved to be the first of many similar foundations. Thus the term "college" originally signified merely a place of residence. Pres-

ently it included a library and even some instruction. In the later middle ages, many universities came to be dominated by endowed and well-organized colleges which were attached to them and which often boasted teaching staffs of distinguished masters. In the university of Paris, the *Sorbonne* has continued to occupy an important place.

D. Bologna and Other Medieval Universities

While the *studium generale* at Paris was growing into the foremost university of western and northern Europe, a similar institution of higher learning was developing in southern Europe, at Bologna. Here, as we have remarked, the study of law—both civil and canon—prevailed.

The university of Bologna differed in organization from that of Paris. While in both institutions the masters formed guilds to regulate their own affairs and to deal collectively with the students, at Bologna it was associations of students, rather than of teachers, which exercised real control. For these associations were able to pre-

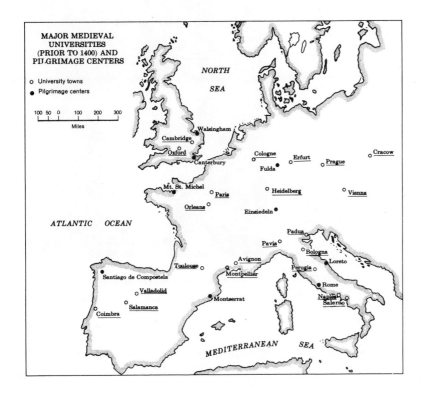

MAJOR MEDIEVAL
UNIVERSITIES
(PRIOR TO 1400) AND
PILGRIMAGE CENTERS

o University towns
• Pilgrimage centers

100 50 0   100   200   300
Miles

scribe and enforce minute regulations governing the conduct of their professors, including hours of lectures, presentation of subject-matter, absences, fees, etc. Even the powerful civic authorities of Bologna were brought to terms by threats of boycott or migration on the part of the students. The chief explanation of this striking role of the student body at Bologna lies in the fact that they were usually older and more mature than the student body of Paris. Legal study, which was the main pursuit at Bologna, attracted men of business and nobles with estates to manage, as well as younger men anxious to obtain administrative positions.

The examples of Paris and Bologna were soon followed elsewhere. In general, the universities which emerged in northern and western Europe adopted the type of organization at Paris, while those in southern Europe took Bologna as their model. Sometimes new universities started as offshoots from an older one. Padua, for example, was an offshoot of Bologna. Toward the end of the twelfth century a number of masters who had been at Paris took up residence at Oxford, and in the next century a similar migration resulted in the formation of a second English university at Cambridge. It was especially at Oxford that the colleges which, as at Paris, were originally boarding establishments with some equipment for teaching, came to enjoy a dominant position in the university organization.

Salamanca, chartered and privileged by kings of Castile and by the pope toward the middle of the thirteenth century, was the first important Spanish university; and Coimbra, the first in Portugal. The university of Toulouse received a papal charter in 1233, as a sequel to the Albigensian crusade; and in the mid-thirteenth century a university of the papal *curia* was established. Naples, founded by the Emperor Frederick II in 1224, and Montpellier in southern France, dating from about the same time, together with Bologna, soon surpassed older Salerno [1] as famed centers for medical study.

Medieval towers at Bologna.
Courtesy Italian State Tourist Office, New York

---

[1] Salerno had been famous as a health resort with competent physicians as early as the tenth century, though references to a formal "school" of medicine are later. Its geographical location gave it access to Latin, Greek, Arabic, and Jewish medical lore.

Montpellier was also noted for its instruction in law.

Not until the fourteenth century did universities appear in countries on the Continent north of France and Italy. Then were founded Prague in Bohemia, Cracow in Poland, Vienna in Austria, and Heidelberg in Rhenish Germany. Thenceforth there was a steady spread and multiplication of universities throughout Europe.

E. Medieval Students

Various contemporary sources give the impression that medieval students were an unruly, turbulent lot. Apparently, many were very young, some only fourteen or fifteen. They were likely to be far from home and parental discipline, and in an institution which exempted them from ordinary police jurisdiction. It is not surprising that they got themselves into trouble. But we must beware of exaggerating. The unusual always attracts more attention than the ordinary. The average conscientious student was taken for granted and passed unnoticed.

Some student correspondence has survived. Though commonly composed in the stilted style of professional letter writers, the subject matter—requests for money on the part of students and concern on the part of parents over frivolous behavior and neglect of studies—is perennial.

A unique source of information about medieval students is their verse. Especially in the early days when the universities were in process of formation, there was a great deal of informal changing by students from one place to another. Scholars dissatisfied with a teacher, or merely restless or bored, simply moved elsewhere. Probably they begged en route. In this atmosphere was produced what has been called Goliardic poetry, for the students were the wandering Goliardi, so named perhaps because they pretended to be followers of Goliath the Philistine. The principal themes of these are the time-honored "wine, women, and song." But there is also in many of them a nostalgic melancholy which reflects the uncertainties of life and the rapid passing of youth. Composed in Latin, they demonstrate that the admirable linguistic skill acquired by medieval students could as easily be put by them to the service of a lively full-blooded humanism as to a technical treatise or a hymn.[1]

The remarkable and varied achievements of medieval students, as well as medieval masters, indicate that a very important intellectual class was coming to the fore in Europe of the twelfth and thirteenth centuries—a class which commanded increasing respect. Evidently, the academic or university estate—the calling of the scholar—was coming to be so highly regarded that all the chief authorities in Christendom were only too eager to give it their protection and patronage. Medieval society at large must have believed that the students were pursuing something eminently worth while, and must have acquired a respect for education which our own generation can appreciate.

Thirteenth-century achievements in law, medicine, and theology, and in philosophy in the most inclusive sense of the word, indicate that, at least in university circles, interest in the technical was now surpassing the earlier enthusiasm for the literary and humanistic. But though formal learning in the thirteenth century lacked the humanistic spirit of the twelfth, there emerged a notable literature in the vernacular tongues. This, too, ranks among the major accomplishments of the period, and will be treated in the following chapter.

---

[1] An important collection of medieval student literature was preserved in the monastery of Benediktbeuren in Germany and hence called *Carmina Burana.*

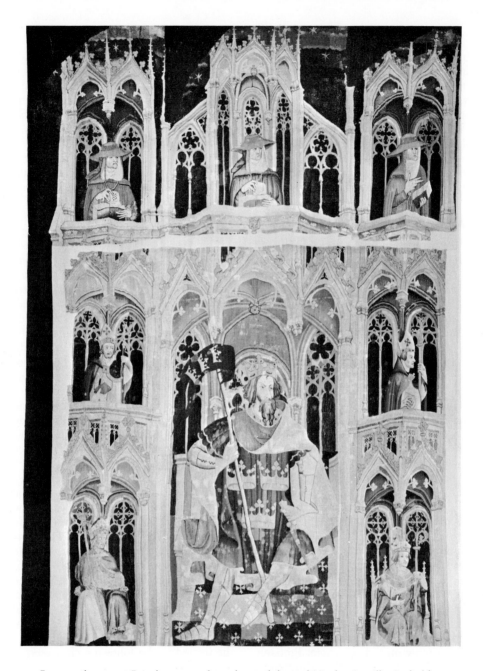

Fourteenth century French tapestry from the workshop of Nicolas Bataille. Probably King Arthur with cardinals.

CHAPTER 21

Popular Literature and Art of the Middle Age

A. Epics and Romances

Throughout the Middle Ages, all over Western Christendom, educated people knew Latin, and scholarly writing was done in it. Professors and students used the same Latin language in university work, whether at Paris, Bologna, Oxford, Salamanca, Prague, or Heidelberg. But alongside the scholarly Latin, and quite distinct from it, were many different spoken languages or dialects, the so-called "vernaculars" of the common people. Some of these had developed, in late Roman and early medieval times, out of a "vulgar" spoken Latin—the *lingua romana*—differing from "classical" written Latin, and had become the parent tongues of the later "romance languages" —French, Italian, Provençal (and Catalan), Castilian, Portuguese, and Rumanian.

Other vernaculars had been developed from early Teutonic speech: Low German, in northwestern Germany and the Netherlands; High German, in southern and eastern Germany; Anglo-Saxon, in England; and distinctive Scandinavian dialects in Denmark, Norway, and Sweden. Besides, different Slavic vernaculars were spoken by Czechs (in Bohemia), Poles, Yugoslavs, and Russians, while Celtic vernaculars survived in Ireland, Scotland, and Wales, and in Brittany (in western France). "Middle English," becoming the common vernacular of England in the thirteenth century, was a combination of Anglo-Saxon with Norman French.

In the early middle age, there was relatively little writing in any of the vernacular languages, beyond some translations of the Bible and of church service books for the religious instruction of newly converted peoples. But gradually the amount of vernacular literature increased and became popular. Having little or no connection, as Latin had, with technical intellectual concerns, it was written primarily to amuse; and, far more than Latin, it reflected the fashions and tastes of secular lay society.

This was especially evidenced by the growing number of medieval "epics," which were long poems recounting deeds of adventure and usually sung by minstrels to the accompaniment of a lute or some similar instrument. Such epics appeared fairly early in Germanic vernaculars. The Anglo-Saxon *Beowulf* dated from the eighth century or even earlier. The *Hildebrandslied*, of which a fragment from the end of the eighth century has survived, was in the old Saxon dialect. The half legendary, half historical Norse sagas, many of which were actually composed in Iceland in the time of the Vikings, are essentially epics in content and form.

Broadly speaking, France produced the most popular and influential vernacular literature of the middle age. France was then, both politically and culturally, the leading kingdom in Europe, and the two vernacular languages which had developed within it were adapted to the production of popular literature. One of these was the *langue d'oil,* or "French," spoken throughout northern France and, after the Norman conquest of England in 1066, by the English court and upper classes. The other was the *langue d'oc,* or "Provençal," spoken in southern France and, with only slight differences of dialect, in northeastern Spain, where it was known as "Catalan.' Each of these vernaculars became the vehicle for a distinctive written literature, which was widely read and imitated abroad.

Some of the literature of the *langue d'oil,* the *chansons de geste,* we have already described as a reflection of early feudal society.[1] The appeal of the *chansons de geste,* especially of the Carolingian cycle, was not merely French; it was broadly European. There were Scandinavian, German, and Italian translations of them.

Meanwhile other heroic epics were appearing in the vernacular languages of Northern Europe and of Spain. Of particular importance was a Germanic cycle which in various forms embodied the tragic stories of *Siegfried* and *Brünhilde.* One version, the *Volsunga-Saga,* was a twelfth-century prose composition, while the more familiar *Niebelungenlied,* originally produced in the late twelfth century, was subsequently remodeled. Then, too, from twelfth-century Spain came the *Poema del Cid,* which celebrated the deeds, largely legendary, of Rodrigo Diaz, a Castilian warrior of the eleventh century. Like the *chansons de geste* of France, the *Cid* reflects the atmosphere of the epic struggle for the liberation of Christian lands from the Moslems.

Side by side with the *chansons de geste,* though not, it would appear, greatly influencing or being influenced by them, there appeared another kind of popular vernacular literature. This was the so-called "courtly romance." One of the most famous examples dealt with the British King Arthur and his court. Original material for this had come from Celtic legends, but it had been added to by Norman Englishmen, in particular by Geoffrey of Monmouth (*d.* 1154), whose *History of the Britons,* while purporting to be a presentation of historical fact, seems to have been largely manufactured out of whole cloth. At any rate, poets and minstrels were thereby pro-

[1] See above, pp. 123–125.

vided with numerous suitable themes for the courtly romances which speedily became favorites with aristocratic audiences. Perhaps the most famous poet who so used the Arthurian material was Chrétien de Troyes who wrote in French. But it was also drawn upon by a number of German writers of the thirteenth century, including Wolfram von Eschenbach in his *Parzifal,* and Gottfried von Strassburg in *Tristan,* one of the best renderings of the famous Celtic love story of *Tristan and Iseult.* The courtly romances, unlike the *chansons de geste,* were composed by individual poets, many of whose names are known. Moreover, they evidently catered to a more exclusively aristocratic taste than was the case with the *chansons de geste.* On the whole, the romances reflected that more sophisticated chivalry which idealized woman and romantic love and which emphasized the distinction between the knights and persons of lower estate.[2]

B. Other Vernacular Literature, the Troubadours, and Dante

Epics and courtly romances were only a part of the vernacular literature which appeared and flourished in the twelfth and thirteenth centuries. Examples of several other types and forms may be cited. The *Romance of the Rose* by Guillaume de Lorris was an allegory in French, in which the characters typified vices and virtues. The *Romance of Reynard,* also in French, consisted of a series of parodies on chivalry. *Aucassin and Nicolette* was a delightful novelette, half prose, half poetry. Such German works as *Der Arme Heinrich* of Hartmann von Aue and *Meier Helmbrecht* by Werner der Gartenaere dealt with peasants and their life. Also, there were numerous and very popular *fabliaux,* which were coarsely humorous stories in verse, poking fun at contemporary characters and sparing none, not even the clergy. Equally popular in appeal were the simple scenes,

[2] In addition to the Carolingian cycle of *chansons de geste,* and the Arthurian court romances, mention should be made of contemporary "Roman" epics, in which ancient worthies, such as Alexander, Caesar, Joshua, or David, were celebrated as feudal heroes.

with appropriate dialogue, which were enacted in churches on major feast days, and the more elaborate "mystery plays" which developed from them and constituted a medieval form of drama.

A special literary form, rather different from anything so far mentioned, arose in the sophisticated society of southern France and northeastern Spain. For the land of the *langue d'oc* (that is, of Provençal and Catalan) was peculiarly productive of lyric poetry dedicated primarily, though not exclusively, to various themes of romantic love. The southern composers were called *troubadours*. Most of them were well born, and the names of some four hundred have come down to us from the middle ages. Duke William IX of Aquitaine (1071–1127) was an early and especially famous *troubadour*.

Though the distinctive culture of southern France suffered a good deal from the Albigensian crusade in the early part of the thirteenth century, the influence of its lyric poetry was extensive after, as well as before, that political-religious struggle. *Troubadours* roamed and sang from Provence to Catalonia throughout Spain, France, and Italy, and in all these regions they were welcomed and acclaimed. Moreover, the marriages of Eleanor of Aquitaine, granddaughter of Duke William IX, first to the French King Louis VII and then to the English King Henry II, had literary as well as political importance, since it served to establish southern lyric poetry at the royal courts of both France and England. Before long, this type of literature ceased to be a monopoly of southern *troubadours*. It was successfully practiced in northern France by *trouvères*, and in Germany by a swarm of *minnesingers*. Among the latter, Walther von der Vogelweide was an outstanding lyric poet.

In Italy, the Emperor Frederick II patronized poets using the Sicilian dialect. Meanwhile, a group, greatly influenced by these as well as by the Provençal and Catalan *troubadours*, commenced writing in the thirteenth century in the northern Italian vernacular. The most famous was Dante Alighieri (1265–1321), who utilized for his poetry the idiom of his native Tuscany. He is regarded not only as the greatest of all Italian poets but also as one of the most distinguished literary artists of all time.

Dante came of good Florentine stock and was active in the government of his native city until the vicissitudes of politics drove him into exile. Always a patriot, he retained a deep love for Florence, though he bewailed the petty strife which disturbed it and which divided Italy as a whole; and he dreamed of the restoration of the traditional Holy Roman Empire. Though a layman, he was exceptionally well educated. In fact, the breadth and depth of his learning reveal the advances made in medieval education. Dante had a remarkably wide acquaintance with classical literature and an excellent command of Latin. This language he used for his serious prose works, such as *De Monarchia*, a defense of the idea of empire, and *De vulgari eloquentia*, a reasoned justification of the use of the vernacular. Dante was likewise profoundly versed in theology, and had evidently immersed himself in the writings of the scholastics.

Giotto (d. 1337). Portrait of Dante. National Museum, Florence.

Alinari photograph

Dante's most important work, the *Divine Comedy*,[1] which he wrote in vernacular Italian, is a long allegorical and narrative poem. The symbolic setting of the *Comedy* is the author's imaginary pilgrimage through Hell, Purgatory, and Paradise. After seeing the hopeless torments of the damned and the hideousness of evil, he passes through Purgatory, the abode of those departed spirits whose sufferings are lightened by the hope of Heaven, into the dwelling place of the saints and the presence of God. Thus the poet's own journey is made to represent the general theme of the salvation of the soul. But as he holds converse with many figures famous in Italian and European affairs, Dante boldly criticizes those whom he holds responsible for the evils of church and state. A poem of great vividness and emotional beauty, it is also a work of deep philosophical, theological, and moral significance. Indeed, it has been described as the theology of St. Thomas Aquinas in poetic form. To convey in brief compass the merit of this most famous of poems is manifestly impossible. It must be read and re-read to be understood.

C. Medieval Music

To the modern listener, medieval music may seem remote and difficult to understand. This is because our ears have become accustomed to modern harmonies and rhythms which have created for us an entirely different musical atmosphere. The actual changes in the art of music subsequent to the middle ages are more radical than those in the other arts.

The most significant musical advance made during the main middle age was an increasingly successful experimentation with combinations of more than one voice, that is, with polyphony. It will be recalled that the so-called Gregorian chant had enriched the church's liturgy with a variety of melodies designed to be sung in unison. The liturgical tradition of the chant persisted—its subordination to the text, its fitness for performance in church, even the very melodies of earlier days. But now, for the first time, the chant is enriched or

[1] Dante's title was simply *Commedia*. The word "Divine" was added later.

Gothic sculpture. The Cathedral at Bourges.

Courtesy French Government Tourist Office, New York

Stained glass. French thirteenth century.

Courtesy Metropolitan Museum of Art,
New York

supplemented by association of two or more melodies simultaneously.

As early as the eleventh century, a practice known as *organum*, the use of voices singing in parallel fourths, fifths, or octaves, appeared. A bit later, contrary motion in a second part was introduced. Thereby different intervals became marked, and a more varied second melody was possible. This was at first called "descant," and later, in the thirteenth century, "counterpoint." Several varying parts began to be incorporated, as contrasting melodies with the central one, not necessarily altogether, but more usually following one another. This provided opportunity and incentive for invention, not so much in the original melody as in the contrasting parts. The central melody, as a rule, continued to be a traditional chant, based on one or another of the earlier medieval modes. It was mainly ecclesiastical, although a few secular melodies were introduced. And this central melody, with which other parts were sung contrapuntally, was called the *cantus firmus*.

Counterpoint, rather than harmony, represents the principal musical achievement of the time. Inevitably, however, the varied intervals which contrapuntal singing produced led toward harmony. And the theory of measured music, necessary in order that notes in different parts should sound together, was familiar to the Arabs and presumably known to Europeans by the thirteenth century. In writing music, a certain Guido of Arezzo (*d.* 1050) seems to have popularized the use of a four (later five) line staff, while square notes, with various symbols to indicate time value, were introduced.

Stringed instruments were, of course, familiar to medieval musicians and especially to the *troubadours*. A bow seems to have appeared in the tenth century and to have provided means for developing many of our modern instruments. Some sort of organ with sliders instead of keys was in use as early as the ninth and tenth centuries. Keys seem to have come into use by the thirteenth century.

D. Romanesque Art and Architecture

Because so much is visible to us in the buildings still standing and in our museums, medieval art is better known than any other feature of medieval civilization. Here we possess tangible evidence of a combination of artistic taste and technical skill rarely equaled in world history. Medieval art was predominantly religious, for in those days the church was the main inspiration and support for the genius of artists and its patronage often best rewarded their efforts. Besides, the flowering of medieval art was a product of that same religious revival which was in back of Cluny and the Cistercians, the medieval papacy, and the friars. Finally, medieval architecture, especially the great cathedral-building of the thirteenth century, represented a popular awakening and movement.

The art of western Europe during the eleventh and twelfth centuries is generally called "romanesque." [1] As the name indicates, romanesque art owed a great deal to the art of classical Rome. But somewhat as the romance languages evolved from ancient popular speech, so romanesque art often developed from provincial rather than strictly Roman models. Moreover, Byzantine influence was highly important. Romanesque building was predominantly monastic, for it flourished especially in the age of Cluny and Cîteaux, and most of it, even in the case of cathedral churches, was supervised by monks. Romanesque churches were also associated with pilgrimages by reason of the fact that so many monasteries in that style were established along the roads to popular shrines.

Among the characteristic features of romanesque church building was a ground plan designed in the form of a cross—the cruciform plan, as it has been called. The basic rectangle, or nave (*navis*, ship), of the ancient basilica was enlarged, and a transept, or crossing, added. Beyond the transept a choir and apse increased the total length. The side aisles of the church were also bigger, sometimes double, and were continued into an ambulatory completely encircling the apse. Finally, a series of chapels or side altars was placed in the semi-circle of the apse.

This more elaborate ground plan was accompanied by corresponding changes in the superstructure. Moreover, frequent losses by fire had created a demand for all-stone structures. Therefore, wooden roofs were replaced by stone vaulting. And the added weight of a stone roof required a substructure of considerable strength. Because the graceful slender columns of the basilica could not bear the weight of a stone roof, they were replaced by rows of massive piers joined by higher and wider semi-circular arches and flanked by correspondingly higher and wider aisles. Above the arcade of the main piers, the wall often extended upward in a second set of smaller round arches (the *triforium*), and these were finally topped by the windows of a clerestory.

The simplest form of stone roof was the so-called barrel vault. This might be described as a plain semi-circular arch extended tunnel-like. Its weight fell equally on all points of the supporting wall, which necessarily had to be massive. Indeed, the outer walls were supported by piers or buttresses built against the side of the building. In some of the later romanesque churches, groined- or cross-vaulting was formed by adding arches which passed diagonally across the piers of the nave and served to distribute some of the weight of the roof.

There were a number of variations in romanesque building which are noticeable in different regions. A distinctive Norman style found its way into England. Southern French types were evident in Spain, thus affording further evidence of the cultural inter-relationship of the two regions. And a north Italian or Lombard school of architecture was also popular in Germany, especially in the Rhineland. Taken all in all, romanesque architecture was by no means mere imitation of the Roman or Byzantine. It was distinctive and original.

Sculpture kept pace with building. Columns were surmounted with carved designs, sometimes reminiscent of the classical orders, but more often departing radically from them. Romanesque sculpture is perhaps seen at its best in the ornamental reliefs and figures adorning the portals of churches. Interior decorative features were surprisingly varied. Mosaics continued to be popular, and polychrome frescoes made their appearance. The romanesque period likewise witnessed advances in the technique of stained glass.

Among the minor arts were metal work and enamels. At Limoges in France, new methods of applying and firing the enamel made possible a greater flexibility, and established a lasting fame for Limoges enamel. Meanwhile, comparable skill and artistry were being displayed by miniaturists who illustrated or "illuminated" manuscripts, and by ivory carvers who produced exquisitely formed articles such as combs, chessmen, or small boxes.

---

[1] Romanesque art developed in the early Middle Age and reached what might be called the peak of its development in the twelfth century. In many parts of Europe, however, romanesque churches were built long after 1200.

E. Gothic Architecture

Gothic architecture,[1] which many people still revere as the supreme achievement of medieval civilization, reached the summit of its development in a comparatively short space of time, roughly between 1150 and 1350. While the style spread to England, western Germany, northern Italy, and Spain, the most famous gothic cathedrals were erected in north-central France.

The Gothic was intimately bound up with contemporary social and economic developments. If romanesque was a monastic architecture, gothic reflected the new town life. Bishops, of course, took the initiative in cathedral building, but they were earnestly supported by citizens and by the guilds. Guilds usually contributed chapels and stained glass windows. While an initial impetus or "drive" may have enlisted general popular participation, the medieval cathedral was a skilled professional enterprise. Many architects were friars, but an increasing number were laymen and graduates of universities. Masons' guilds contracted with the bishop for their labor. Naturally there was keen competition, as the bishop and townsmen of one city sought to erect a "bigger and better" structure than that being completed by a neighboring community. Gothic building represents, therefore, a unique and fortuitous combination of civic pride, religious zeal, technical skill, and aesthetic understanding.

A number of structural problems were solved by the gothic builders. In particular, they discovered how to achieve greater height and breadth without so enlarging the walls as to shut out light. It was not entirely an accident that grey northern France, rather than the sunnier south, was the locale for the original experimentation. Three distinctive structural features were

devised: the groined vault; the pointed arch; and the flying buttress. One of these alone did not necessarily make a building gothic, for, as we have already noticed, a groined vault and even a slightly pointed arch had been employed in earlier romanesque churches. It was rather the combination of all three features just mentioned which constituted the gothic.

The use of a pointed arch enabled the builder to increase the ratio of height to width, for the extra space could be bridged by a number of pointed arches of different heights. This in turn made possible more varied cross-vaulting and the bridging of rectangular as well as square areas. In the simple semi-circular cross-vaulting of the romanesque, only two arches intersected. Gothic vaulting might be quadripartite or sexpartite or even more complicated, while the ridges between the stone panelling were emphasized by ribs which went up fanlike from pier to roof.

There was the problem of the outward, as well as the downward "thrusts," from the weight of a heavy stone roof. This had been met in romanesque churches by increasing the thickness of the supporting walls. In gothic buildings it was solved by a series of "flying buttresses," of stone arcs, which swept out from high points in the main walls, over the roof of the side aisles, to pier buttresses built out alongside the foundations. A gothic church was indeed a miracle of structural engineering, and the skill of its builders is perhaps best proven by the fact that their seemingly delicate creations still stand, resistant to the storms of nature and the bombardments of war.

Since arched vaults and flying buttresses relieved the walls of much of their weight-carrying functions while heightening the whole structure, it was possible to install many glass windows. And this provided far more opportunity than in romanesque churches for the introduction of stained glass. The term "stained glass" is somewhat misleading. Actually the glass was colored in its molten state and part of the design etched and fused. Then innumerable pieces were inserted and held together with strips of lead and masonry. Some of the large "rose windows" commonly placed over the

---

[1] The term "gothic" is really a misnomer. It has nothing to do with primitive German tribes of Goths. It was invented by an Italian writer of the sixteenth century, Giorgio Vasari, as a contemptuous description of what he deemed a style of architecture very inferior to the classical. Vasari's view, unfortunately, was widely accepted from his time until the romantic revival of "Gothic" in the nineteenth century.

broad front entrance of cathedrals required consummate skill in balancing glass, lead, and supporting masonry. The total effect was singularly imposing and beautiful.

Just as the raising of a cathedral required the coöperation of a whole community, clergy and laity alike, so gothic sculpture and decoration emphasized the union of man and nature in God. Front and side portals were flanked with figures of Christ, the Virgin, and the saints, together with characters from both Old and New Testaments, rulers, scholars pagan as well as Christian, and peasants and artisans at work. And a scene of the Last Judgment invariably completed the cycle of religious life. Innumerable carvings of flowers and leaves, not the formalized acanthus of the classical orders, but real oak leaves and floral garlands, testified to an awareness and love of nature and to a desire that it, too, should glorify God. At the same time, gaiety and humor were evident in accompanying gargoyles and grotesques, some of which adorned inaccessible niches that only the birds could see. And not only did the guilds contribute windows, but in the stained glass which they put into them, they portrayed themselves at work.

Altogether, the Gothic cathedral mirrored the rich life of the age in all its fullness, in its vitality, and, above all, in its movement. Romanesque retained something of classical tranquillity and sense of proportion. With Gothic architecture—and it is equally true of manuscript illumination, of painting, and of vernacular literature—we are in an age of romanticism.

French twelfth century architectural sculpture. A capital from the abbey of St. Michael and St. Germain, Cuxa. Birds and grotesque men.

New York; The Cloisters Collection, Purchase, 1925 Courtesy Metropolitan Museum of Art

SELECT SUPPLEMENTARY READINGS FOR PART IV

General. Same as for "General" under Parts II and III (pp. 110, 171, above); in addition, F. Heer, *The Medieval World* (1962).

Chapter 15. For the expansion of European frontiers, see under the appropriate countries mentioned under Chapter 12 (p. 171) and Chapter 17 (below). For the crusaders' states, in addition to the works mentioned in Chapter 14 (p. 171): J. L. La Monte, *Feudal Monarchy in the Latin Kingdom of Jerusalem* (1932); D. C. Munro, *The Kingdom of the Crusaders* (1935); G. Slaughter, *Saladin* (1955). For the Mongols and European travelers to Asia: C. R. Beazley, *The Dawn of Modern Geography*, 3 vols. (1897–1906); Kim Setton, R. L. Wolff, H. W. Hazard, eds., *A History of the Crusades*, vol. II (1962); L. Olschki, *Marco Polo's Precursors* (1943) and *Marco Polo's Asia* (1960); M. P. Prawdin, *The Mongol Empire, Its Rise and Legacy* (1940); P. M. Sykes, *The Quest for Cathay* (1936); J. K. Wright, *Geographical Lore of the Time of the Crusades* (1925).

Chapter 16. H. Adelson, *Medieval Commerce* (1962); P. Boissonade, *Life and Work in the Middle Ages* (1927); M. V. Clark, *The Medieval City State* (1936); R. S. Lopez and I. W. Raymond, *Medieval Trade in the Mediterranean World* (1955); J. H. Mundy and P. Reisenberg, *The Medieval Town* (1958); S. Painter, *Medieval Society* (1951); H. Pirenne, *Economic and Social History of Medieval Europe* (1937) and *Medieval Cities* (1949); C. Stephenson, *Borough and Town* (1933).

Chapter 17. In addition to the books cited for Chapter 12 (p. 171): W. C. Atkinson, *A History of Spain and Portugal* (1960); F. Barlow, *The Feudal Kingdom of England* (1954); A. Castro, *The Structure of Spanish History* (1954); H. J. Chaytor, *The History of Aragon and Catalonia* (1933); J. T. Appleby, *John, King of England* (1959); S. B. Chrimes, *An Introduction to the Administrative History of England* (1959); D. C. Douglas, *William the Conqueror* (1964); C. L. Haskins, *The Growth of English Representative Government* (1948); A. Kelly, *Eleanor of Aquitaine and the Four Kings* (1950); H. V. Livermore, *History of Portugal* (1948); R. L. Poole, *Domesday Book and Magna Carta* (1955); S. Painter, *The Reign of King John* (1940); M. Powicke, *The Thirteenth Century* (England) (new ed., 1962); F. M. Stenton, *The First Century of English Feudalism* (1932); D. M. Stenton, *English Society in the Early Middle Ages* (1951); W. Warren, *King John* (1961).

Chapter 18. In addition to the works cited for Chapter 12 (p. 171): G. Barraclough, "Frederick Barbarossa and the Twelfth Century" in *History in a Changing World* (1955), pp. 73–96; H. B. Cotterill, *Medieval Italy* (1915); O. Halecki,

Borderlands of Western Civilization (1952); E. Kantorowicz, *Frederick II* (1931); G. Slaughter, *The Amazing Frederick* (1937); G. Vernadsky and M. Karpovich, *A History of Russia*, vols. II and III (1948, 1953).

Chapter 19. The general works on the church cited for Chapter 8 (p. 110) contain material pertinent to this chapter. For more special topics: M. W. Baldwin, *The Mediaeval Church* (1953); R. P. Bennett, *The Early Dominicans* (1937); S. R. Packard, *Europe and the Church Under Innocent III* (1927); A. C. Shannon, *The Popes and Heresy in the Thirteenth Century* (1949); W. Ullmann, *The Growth of Papal Government in the Middle Ages* (1955) and *Medieval Papalism* (1949); E. Vacandard, *The Inquisition* (1924). See also the following biographies: T. S. R. Boase, *St. Francis of Assisi* (1936) and *Boniface VIII* (1933); Fr. Cuthbert, *St. Francis of Assisi* (1913); J. Jorgenson, *St. Francis of Assisi* (1912); B. S. James, *St. Bernard of Clairvaux* (1957); B. Jarrett, O.P., *Life of St. Dominic* (1924); C. E. Smith, *Innocent III, Church Defender* (1951); W. Williams, *St. Bernard* (1944).

Chapter 20. F. B. Artz, *The Mind of the Middle Ages* (1952); F. Coppleston, *Medieval Philosophy* (1961); A. C. Crombie, *Augustine to Galileo* (1952), reprinted as *Medieval and Early Modern Science*, 2 vols. (1959); C. G. Crump and E. F. Jacob, *The Legacy of the Middle Ages* (1926); E. Gilson, *Heloise and Abelard* (1960), *History of Christian Philosophy in the Middle Ages* (1955), and *Reason and Revelation in the Middle Ages* (1938); C. H. Haskins, *The Renaissance of the Twelfth Century* (1927) and *The Rise of the Universities* (1932); P. Kibre, *The Nations in the Medieval Universities* (1948), and *Scholarly Privileges in the Middle Ages* (1962); G. Leff, *Medieval Thought* (1958); H. Rashdall, *The Universities of Europe in the Middle Ages*, 3 vols. revised by F. M. Powicke and A. B. Emden (1936); L. Thorndike, *University Records and Life in the Middle Ages* (1944) and *The History of Magic and Experimental Science*, vols I–IV (1923–1934); D. Knowles, *The Evolution of Medieval Thought* (1962); H. O. Taylor, *The Medieval Mind*, 2 vols. (1930); L. J. Daly, S. J., *The Medieval Universities* (1961).

Chapter 21. There are many available editions and translations of medieval literary works. A convenient selection is given in C. W. Jones, *Medieval Literature in Translation* (1950) and in *Medieval Epics*, Modern Library (1963). See also W. P. Ker, *The Dark Ages* (1904) and *Epic and Romance* (1897). On art, see Gardner, *Art through the Ages*, and Morey, *Medieval Art and Christian Art*, cited above for Chapter 5; J. Gimpel, *The Cathedral Builders* (1960); E. Mâle, *The Gothic Image* (1958); N. Pevsner, *An Outline of European Architecture* (5th ed., 1957); R. Branner, *Gothic Architecture* (1961); W. R. Lethaby, *Medieval Art* (rev. D. Talbot Rice, 1949); H. Saalman, *Medieval Architecture* (1962). For music, P. H. Lang, *Music in Western Civilization* (1941); G. Reese, *Music in the Middle Ages* (1940).

PART V
LATE MIDDLE AGE:

Gloucester Cathedral. An example of English perpendicular style (see p. 322).
Courtesy British Information Service, New York

THE FOURTEENTH
AND FIFTEENTH CENTURIES

The Alba Madonna. Raphael (d. 1520),
(see p. 320).

National Gallery of Art, Washington, D.C.;
Mellon Collection

From Edward III of England
to Leonardo da Vinci

THE fourteenth and fifteenth centuries may be designated as the "Late Middle Age." This phrase implies a difference, perhaps a decline, from the particular features of civilization which characterized the preceding two centuries and which may be regarded as strictly "medieval." But the same period includes what has also commonly been called the "renaissance," a term which connotes the revival of a culture long dead or dormant. The period, moreover, was climaxed by certain novel and highly significant developments: the emergence of national monarchy, the invention of printing, the opening of new routes to India, and the discovery of a new world across the Atlantic—developments which have been described as heralding the coming of the "modern age."

It should be remarked that the distinctive cultural movement associated with the term "renaissance" was largely confined, during the fourteenth and fifteenth centuries, to Italy and affected northern Europe only gradually and later. Hence it is possible to speak of a cultural revival in Italy and a lag elsewhere. But this geographical distinction is hardly satisfactory as an explanation of a remarkably complex period. The arc and music of the north, for example, rivaled that of Italy; and in economics, recent studies have indicated that throughout Europe, including Italy, the Late Middle Age, at least until near its close, was one of protracted and occasionally acute depression accompanied by a decline in population.

For years scholars have debated about the "renaissance." Doubtless they will continue to do so. Two observations may be made here. First, while there is general agreement that the concept of a sharp break between middle ages and renaissance must be abandoned, it remains true that if much in the fourteenth century is reminiscent of an earlier day, the civilization of the fifteenth century does differ in certain important respects from that of the preceding middle ages. Second, and most important, the student should realize that in studying this transitional period he is confronting one of the most difficult problems of interpretation in the entire course of European and Western history.

CHAPTER 22

Social and Economic Developments of Late Middle Age

A. "Closing the Medieval Frontier," and Economic Depression

Earlier chapters have described the long process of growth which characterized western European civilization: the winning of new land from forest, swamp, and shore; the expansion of commerce and the growth of town life. Before the middle of the fourteenth century this forward movement had apparently reached its peak and a recession had begun. Europe's population, except in east-central areas, leveled off and became relatively stationary. This involved a cessation of the continent's internal colonization, whether through the founding of new towns or the occupation of new agricultural lands. In short, an important "pioneering" aspect of European life was coming to an end. This process has been described as "the closing of the medieval frontier." [1]

In part the recession seems to have been the normal termination of a movement of centuries' duration which had finally run its course. But it was also in large part the result of disturbed political and social conditions in the fourteenth century and the first part of the fifteenth. France suffered grievously from the Hundred Years' War, and England in the fifteenth century was plagued with lawlessness and wars of royal succession. Spain was divided, and

[1] The phrase is that of A. R. Lewis, "The Closing of the Medieval Frontier," *Speculum,* XXXIII (1958), 475–483.

the Byzantine Empire which had never recovered from the Fourth Crusade was now beleaguered by Turks, Slavs, and Mongols, not to mention French, Italian, and Catalan merchants and adventurers.

Partly, too, the change resulted from natural calamities of famine and pestilence. In the second decade of the fourteenth century a major famine afflicted large areas of Europe. And most terrible of all pestilences was the epidemic of bubonic plague, or "Black Death," which in 1348–1350 ravaged all Europe and carried off an estimated fourth or third of its population. The congested districts of the towns were hardest hit, but the countryside was not spared. All classes of society were affected. There was an especially heavy mortality among the secular clergy, who, with physicians, ministered to the sick and dying; and even isolated monasteries fell prey to this greatest plague in all European history. Economic life, in the circumstances, could not fail to be adversely affected not only by the Black Death itself and by repeated occurrences of pestilence, but by the shortage of labor which followed in its wake.

Gradually, during the second half of the fifteenth century, an economic recovery occurred. This, with the new geographic discoveries, heralded a new era. Hence, as we consider various aspects of European life during the late Middle Age, we must do so with understanding of their setting in a long depression followed by gradual economic restoration and advance.

B. The Land and the Landed Classes

Europe remained throughout the fourteenth and fifteenth centuries predominantly agrarian. But the effects of an expanded commercial and urban life, and of a money economy with consequent rise in commodity prices—effects which were noticeable well before 1300—were now accentuated. It was more common for landlords to pay agricultural laborers with money, and for peasants to lease their holdings for fixed sums of money in lieu of personal services. In short, most peasants in England, the Netherlands, France, and the Rhineland became rent-tenants or farm laborers for hire. And in general the customary law of the land guaranteed to peasants the permanent possession of the holdings for which they paid rent. Thus the French tenant became a *censier* (from *cens*, "rent"), and the English tenant a "copyholder." [1] Since most such leases were on a long-term basis, the landlord was at a disadvantage in an age of rising prices.

Thus what was left of serfdom in western Europe diminished further. Although opportunities to migrate to new farms were lessened, the possibilities for a more flexible rent-relationship with a *seigneur* were enhanced, as were also the opportunities to sell surplus produce to landlords or to town.

The agrarian changes of the period in western Europe were by no means an unmixed blessing for the peasants. The greater flexibility which characterized the western areas was apparently not matched in various parts of Germany and eastern Europe where serfdom persisted. In some places the old coöperative manors were transformed into capitalistic estates practically owned by an individual landlord, and on these the peasants found themselves deprived of the security which manorial organization had afforded them, and transformed into mere hired agricultural laborers, underpaid and possessing nothing they could call their own. Besides, the virtual cessation in the settling-up of new lands removed an important outlet for depressed peasants anxious

to improve their lot. There was less opportunity for peasants to leave the manor or estate, and the landlord, knowing this, felt less disposed to ameliorate their living and working conditions. Even for those peasants who enjoyed a relatively low rent, the rise in prices of articles which many now felt they needed could be a real burden.

The change was unsettling, and especially in the fourteenth century it gave rise to widespread peasant disorders and insurrections throughout western Europe. Some of these, like the "Jacquerie" in France, which followed the Black Death and the devastations of the Hundred Years' War, were undoubtedly inspired by dire material distress and active hostility to landlords. But others, such as the Peasants' Revolt in England (1381) and similar uprisings in Flanders in the third decade of the century, seem to have been the work of peasants who were relatively well off and conscious of their strength; and in the case of the revolt in England, there was a well formulated peasant pronouncement of "revolutionary" doctrines concerning the equality of all men. While the peasants' rebellions of the fourteenth century were suppressed by force, the very fact of their occurrence indicated on the part of masses of peasants a class consciousness and ambition unknown in an earlier day.

The landowning classes, nobility and upper clergy, were in general adversely affected by political and economic change. Politically, the rise of monarchical power and the extension of its judicial authority, and in fifteenth-century Germany the integration of some of the larger principalities, deprived the nobility of their functions as governors of fiefs. Long-term rents, as we have seen, proved disadvantageous as prices rose. At the same time, the average noble's normal expenses increased for his now more complex and costly arms and armor, and for luxuries which commerce made more available, which current social convention dictated, and which he, and more particularly his wife and daughters, now desired.

One way to recoup a lost or falling fortune was to enter government service and to become associated with a royal court. Other possibilities were to arrange a mar-

---

[1] The term "copyholder" signified that the tenant held a "copy" of the manorial court roll which stated the conditions of his tenure.

Early fifteenth century French illuminated manuscript. *The Très Belles Heures* of the Duke of Berry done by the Limbourg brothers, Jean, Pol, and Herman.

Courtesy Metropolitan Museum of Art, New York; The Cloisters Collection, Purchase, 1954

riage with the daughter of a wealthy bourgeois or to encourage younger sons to enter the church. Many nobles sought employment in military service. Royal military forces in this age were largely composed of contingents serving for pay from funds which kings were able to obtain from taxes. While such forces now included archers, pikemen, and other infantry troops drawn from the lower orders, nobles of all ranks continued to serve, not as a feudal obligation, but for pay definitely contracted for. The armies of the Hundred Years' War were in many respects still "feudal," that is, composed of mounted knights in armor. But these were professional soldiers, recruited by and serving under captains. Unhappily, many such companies under English, Irish, French, or Flemish captains remained in arms between formal campaigns, and sold their services to warring factions of France, England, or Italy, or went on distant and often ill-planned expeditions to Spain, Sicily, North Africa, or the Near East, or simply engaged in methodical pillage. In short, the nobles of the late middle age, no longer administrators of fiefs or feudal warriors in the old sense, were extraordinarily restless and generally ill-adjusted to the conditions of life which confronted them.

Perhaps because they felt a challenge to their hitherto dominant position in society, the nobles of the late middle age clung tenaciously to the outward symbols of prestige, to those things which represented the ideals of their class. Hence emphasis was put on an exaggerated and essentially unreal brand of chivalry. When war or distant expeditions failed to provide opportunities for deeds of daring, tournaments abounded. These were at once more formal than in the earlier middle ages and more costly. Full plate armor, though doubtless beyond the means of many petty nobles, came into fashion early in the fifteenth century. Barriers were set up between the contestants, heralds announced the opening of a joust, and ladies in gala attire graced the gallery. And although only the chosen few could join, such elaborate institutions as the *Order of the Golden Fleece*, created by the duke of Burgundy, set a tone for aristocratic society.

It is probable that such institutions also reflected a desire to escape from the crudity, brutality, and suffering which characterized the actual existence of many townsmen and peasants. It savors of paradox, not easily explained, that an age of economic depression should be also an age of fantastic luxury. Certain it is that the royal court of France and the court maintained by the dukes of Burgundy, who were also rulers of the Netherlands, were unparalleled in lavish display and in costly and minutely ordered ceremony of court life. This was not entirely wasteful, for most of the rulers were intelligent and discriminating, as well as generous, patrons of art.[1] But if the modern student can thank these men for making possible some of the most beautiful of tapestries, illuminated manuscripts, and paintings, he should remember the cost. Not without reason was the prodigal and art-loving French duke of Berry hated by his subjects as grasping, dishonest, and totally unconcerned with their welfare.

C. Industry and Banking

It was suggested at the opening of this chapter that the persistence of economic depression did not mean that the capitalistic enterprise which had begun to characterize the economic life of the twelfth and thirteenth centuries now ceased or that large fortunes were not made. Indeed, the contrary is true. Although more evident in the later fifteenth century, progress is notable in the fourteenth. Certain general trends may be mentioned first.

In the preceding age, private capitalistic enterprise had been checked by such essentially coöperative institutions as the craft and merchant guilds, or it had been discouraged by the church's teaching regarding the just price and the taking of usurious interest. Even before 1300 these restraints were weakening. Churchmen were beginning to compromise on the matter of usury and to distinguish between it and "interest," a

---

[1] Under the auspices of the dukes of Burgundy, Flemish painting reached its apogée, and Flemish influences penetrated Burgundy and other parts of France. The artist Jean Fouquet became court painter to King Louis XI. These are but a few examples of such patronage.

legitimate return on loans. Loaning money at interest was no longer a despised profession of Jews and other non-Christians, but an accepted as well as lucrative occupation of Christian bankers, with whom even popes now had high financial dealings. In this respect, as in so many others, the influence of the church lessened during the late middle age.

Equally significant was the decay of the guilds, with resulting sharpened cleavage between wealthy merchants and poor artisans. Already, prior to 1300, we have had occasion to remark a tendency within the craft guilds toward a rift between master and workman.[1] Apprentices and journeymen were finding it more difficult to become masters. At the same time certain larger industries which depended on distant markets were beginning to break loose from any guild organization or control.

True, guilds persisted through the fourteenth and fifteenth centuries. But after 1300 they underwent a profound alteration. In some parts of Europe, especially in national states, they were seized upon and utilized by monarchs as convenient instruments of governmental control over industry. In regions where the demand for goods outran the supply from local guilds, enterprising merchants established new centers of production, with workmen outside of the guild system and free from its restrictions.

[1] See above, p. 196.

Burgundian cannon of the late fourteenth or early fifteenth century (mounting modern).

Courtesy Metropolitan Museum of Art; The Bashford Dean Memorial Collection, Purchase funds from various donors, 1929

Thus, in Flanders, smaller towns without guild organizations, and sometimes with the encouragement of the ruling dukes of Burgundy, flourished at the expense of older guild cities such as Bruges, Ghent, and Ypres. Large-scale operators would employ workmen widely scattered in various localities, providing them with raw wool and disposing of the finished cloth. Such workmen were often part-time farmers, part-time weavers.

The cloth guilds of Florence, founded much earlier—the *Arte della Lana* and the *Arte di Calimala* [2]—were essentially capitalistic. They monopolized the clothing business of the city, buying out small weavers, and controlling raw materials, dyeworks, transportation facilities, and warehouses. But if Florentine cloth was a rival of Flemish, it, too, was facing serious competition in the latter part of the fifteenth century.

In London, a number of guilds, particularly those engaged in large-scale buying and selling, obtained royal charters of incorporation permitting them to monopolize the trade in designated types of goods. They enriched themselves as monopolists and capitalists, and in the latter role they gained a commanding position in city affairs and in royal councils. And what occurred in London and Florence, became a common occurrence in most other European cities during the late middle age. Even in towns where the market remained fairly static, guilds tended ever more to become closed corporations dominated by wealthy masters and offering little opportunity to aspiring journeymen.

With the decay and alteration of the guilds, the lot of the small artisan in the fourteenth and fifteenth centuries was not a happy one. True, he did not have to experience all the evils of the later factory system. But he was an employee dependent upon various vicissitudes of employment, and with very little likelihood of becoming a master himself. It must not be supposed, however, that artisans submitted quietly to capitalistic exploitation. Journeymen's guilds began to appear, even before 1300, and, though not nearly as powerful as modern trade unions, they participated in strikes and

[2] The *Arte della Lana* manufactured cloth, the *Arte di Calimala* "finished" imported cloth.

urban disorders which increased in frequency during the late middle age and testified to growing unrest of an artisan class.[1]

Broadly speaking, as the feudal order passed, there vanished with it those checks and balances which had made it endurable. Developing capitalism not only rendered possible a great access of wealth; it caused widespread poverty. Political and military complications added to the strains and stresses of economic change. Moreover, the lower classes of society, both urban and rural, had no organs for orderly expression of their political and economic views. Town governments were closed to them. Parliaments and Estates of the national monarchies were representative only of the relatively well-to-do.

Insurrection, therefore, was a crude means of self-expression. But it would be a mistake to interpret the frequency of urban and rural disorder merely as evidence of injustice. Injustice there was in plenty. But violent outbursts reflected the desires of people already conscious of some change for the better and demanding more.

Although there was a tendency, especially in the fifteenth century, for banking to become an independent business of particular families or firms of capitalists, many bankers were, as in earlier days, prosperous merchants who developed money-lending as a side line. Some catered to royal needs or proved themselves useful intermediaries between the papal treasury and its collectors throughout Europe. Several of the chief banking families were Italian. The foremost in the fourteenth century were the Bardi and Peruzzi families, the latter having branch banks in sixteen cities and five different countries, including England. Like some later bankers, the Bardi and Peruzzi families eventually met reverses and failed. The English tariff duties which they administered fell into arrears. The king of Naples repudiated a debt of two hundred thousand florins he owed them, and interest payments from the king of England were suspended. And finally they lost heavily at home in a war between Florence and Pisa.

No banking house could stand such a combination of strains, and both families went bankrupt.

What proved to be a bigger and more illustrious banking family, the Medici, profitted by the mistakes of the Bardi and Peruzzi and established financially autonomous branch banks in various key localities. In the middle and second half of the fifteenth century, Cosimo de' Medici and his successor, Lorenzo "the Magnificent," headed this opulent family whose financial ramifications extended throughout the greater part of Europe. Not only did they become "bosses" in their own city of Florence, but they saw their sons elevated to the papacy; and, somewhat later, their daughters married French kings. Meanwhile, there was arising, in the German city of Augsburg, another famous banking family—the Fuggers—who in the early sixteenth century were to outstrip all others.

An example of a great financier and business man who served his country's interest as well as his own was the Frenchman, Jacques Coeur of Bourges (*d.* 1456). Born of a merchant family, he followed a commercial career, dealt in a variety of goods, and owned warehouses in several French cities. He operated mines and owned a fleet of ships which plied the Mediterranean. He even obtained special papal permission to trade with the Moslem Turks. With his enormous fortune and manifold financial connections, he was welcomed as steward of the French king's household and later was appointed master of the royal mints at Bourges and Paris. Members of his family married into high society or were given handsome ecclesiastical benefices; and in return he advanced money to the king, to the pope, and to many of the French nobility. But his conspicuous patriotic service was the raising of sufficient sums to enable French arms to reconquer Normandy from the English. And, as a reward, this merchant's son accompanied his king on the latter's triumphal entry into Rouen in 1449. But if Jacques Coeur's career illustrated the heights to which the wealthy bourgeoisie could rise, it also, by a queer turn of fortune's wheel, demonstrated that those who thus rose might fall. Convicted on a preposterous charge of having poisoned the

---

[1] Political motives combined with social and economic to produce certain insurrections, such as the Matins of Bruges (1302) and the Sicilian Vespers (1282).

king's mistress, he was banished and his property confiscated. He finally met his death fighting the Turks as a captain of a papal army.

Although the Medici were deep in the politics of their native city and Jacques Coeur served his king, the capitalists of the time rarely sought to influence policy other than to seek privileges, monopolies, mining rights, etc., for themselves. They generally did not aspire to become statesmen, but were content as men of wealth to promote their own and their relatives' private fortunes, or to see their sons and daughters rise in noble or ecclesiastical society.

D. National Economy and Commercial Expansion

To a limited degree, the successful national monarchies of the fourteenth and fifteenth centuries began to foster a national as distinct from an urban economy. As early as 1381 the English government attempted to restrict English trade to English ships. About the same time the English Parliament tried to regulate agricultural wages, which led, in this case, to a peasants' revolt. In the same century, an English company, known as the Merchants of the Staple, was given a virtual monopoly of the export of wool, hides, and tin, and for a time was subjected to close governmental supervision. Partly as a consequence of the dislocation caused by the Hundred Years' War, an English wool industry appeared which began to rival the Flemish. After the middle of the fifteenth century English economic policy was further promoted by a series of measures prohibiting the importation of continental cloth and restricting the activities of foreign merchants within the country. King Henry VII (1485–1509) sponsored the organization of a company of "Merchant Adventurers" to operate, under close governmental supervision, in foreign trade. It should be remembered, however, that until the accession of Henry VII the English government was far from stable, and that until 1453 it was occupied in the French war. Although this had some economic implications regarding trade between England and southwestern France, it seems that many Englishmen who were regularly

committing acts of piracy against Flemish, Dutch, and Germans would have preferred a hostile policy aimed at the Netherlands rather than an alliance with them.

France, by reason of the protracted Hundred Years' War fought on its own soil, did not adopt a corresponding national trade policy before the reign of Louis XI (1461–1483). Louis surrounded himself with bankers and men of business, attempted with some success to promote a silk industry, and in other ways sought to protect French merchants. Similar developments occurred in Spain and Portugal.

National economic policy was limited and did not preclude the continued economic development fostered by the relatively autonomous cities or city-states of the Netherlands, Germany, or Italy. It only foreshadowed the more consistent national mercantilism of the following century.

Despite economic depression, Europe's commerce continued to be geographically extensive. Italians, for example, remained active in the Near and Middle East. It was a Genoese base at Caffa in the Crimea whence, it is believed, the Black Death was carried to western Europe. Italian commercial depots (*fondachi*) were to be found in the Mongol hinterland. The discovery, early in the present century, of the Datini archives (1360–1410) has revealed a vast commercial enterprise organized with great sophistication, including double-entry accounting. The Venetians, perennial rivals of the Genoese, maintained a number of areas of exploitation in Greek islands and mainland, which they detached from the Byzantine Empire, at least until conquests of the Ottoman Turks in the fifteenth century menaced the entire area. Nor were Italians the only ones to exploit Byzantine weakness. A Catalan company appeared in the fourteenth century and was followed by Navarrese.

The connection between the commerce of the Mediterranean region and that of northern Europe had been made overland in the twelfth and thirteenth centuries, particularly through the instrumentality of the Champagne fairs. Early in the fourteenth century Venice, employing larger and more seaworthy ships, was able to establish and maintain a regular sea contact with Flanders. A Venetian "Flanders galley" was 120 to 150 feet long, and was manned by a crew of from one hundred to two hundred. The oarsmen were signed on—the use of galley "slaves" was a later development—and the entire ship was under the command of a captain who was usually a representative of the Venetian aristocracy. Though his authority on shipboard was absolute, he was governed by specific instructions from the owners.

During the fourteenth and early fifteenth centuries Bruges remained, as it had been, the principal commercial depot of the north. It was at once the "staple," that is the terminal, for English wool export and a factory of the Hanseatic League. This league, or *Hanse* as it was called from a German word for mercantile association, eventually included some two hundred towns, villages, and districts in an area stretching from England and Flanders on the west, through Scandinavia in the far north, to Russian Novgorod in the east. Moreover, the league came to include not only cities of the Baltic and North Sea coasts, but inland river towns like Magdeburg and Breslau. Though predominantly German, the Hanseatic League was an international affair. In addition to Bruges, it possessed foreign trading centers, or factories, at London, at Bergen in Nor-

way, and at Novgorod in Russia. Documents recording agreements made with the city of Bruges in the mid-fourteenth century appear to be the first official use of the phrase German *Hanse*.

An objective of the League was the securing of trading privileges in foreign ports for merchants of the member cities and eventually the acquisition of a monopoly of northern Europe's export trade. It also devoted itself to the imports of northern Europe and to the protection of the inland trade routes of northern and central Europe. Of necessity, the protection of members required strict rules of trading at home and abroad, and this in turn led to a form of organization. Never rigid, this amounted to little more than occasional meetings and assemblies. There were no league officials and no common treasury or army. Lübeck, Hamburg, and certain other towns came to be recognized as leaders of groups within the whole League. Nevertheless, the League could and did bring recalcitrant members into line by withholding privileges, or forcing the hand of a foreign power by boycott. Moreover, on occasions the League actually went to war to defend its rights, levying contributions of men, money, and ships. The most notable occasion was the struggle with and defeat of Denmark in the four-

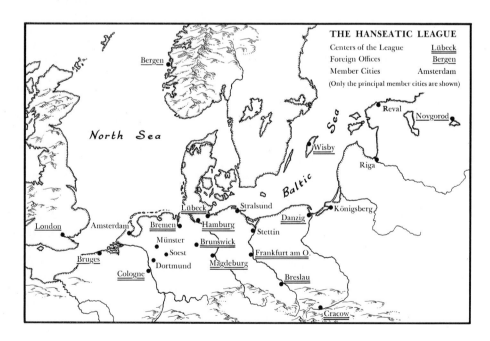

The thirteenth century Wall of Wisby, Isle of Gotland. Wisby was one of the outposts of the Hanseatic League.

Courtesy Swedish National Travel Office, New York

teenth century and the subsequent restoration there of the League's privileges (treaty of Stralsund, 1370).

By the fifteenth century the Hanseatic League was troubled by domestic dissensions. It also suffered from the defeat of the Teutonic Knights, an important ally, by the united kingdom of Poland-Lithuania.[1] Besides, it began to encounter more determined opposition from England, and likewise from the Netherlands under the dukes of Burgundy. Even nature contributed to the woes of the League, as the herring, among the most important items of its trade, became less plentiful in the Baltic and more so in the North Sea.[2]

Important changes also developed within the Netherlands in the second half of the fifteenth century. Bruges now suffered loss of its commercial primacy, partly as a result of serious silting of its harbor with consequent inability to accommodate larger and more numerous ships, partly owing to the persistence of old and now outdated restrictions, and partly because of the promising development, with the encouragement of the dukes of Burgundy, of such other ports as Amsterdam and Antwerp. As the middle ages came to a close, Antwerp with its magnificent harbor, some distance from the

[1] See below, p. 296.
[2] The movement of the herring, presumably following a change in the ocean *flora*, may have resulted from what is now held to have been a

progressive deterioration of the climate of the northern areas during the late middle age. A southward movement of the polar ice cap, which lowered northern mean temperatures, may also have accounted for the decline and disappearance of the Norse colony in Greenland.

sea on the river Scheldt, became the leading commercial depot of the north. By 1500 it had surpassed Bruges and other cities and was the seat of a flourishing *bourse* or stock exchange.[1]

E. Improving Technology: Mining and Navigation

Mining of both precious and baser metals had declined during the depression of the fourteenth and early fifteenth centuries. Then, too, many mines, formerly successfully exploited, were abandoned because a point had been reached where water seepage was too great for contemporary drainage techniques to handle. In the later fifteenth century when general economic conditions improved, there were important improvements in mining techniques. Some of these dated from an earlier time, but could now be more fully developed and exploited. They included such things as longer mine passages for gravity drainage, horse-driven pumps, larger and more effective blast furnaces, and bellows driven by water-power which could produce cast iron "pigs" in greater quantity. In the middle of the century an improved method for separating silver from copper ore was devised by Johannes Funcken.

Although fifteenth-century mining was still hardly more than extensive quarrying, the new techniques indicate a combination of technology and industry which had important implications for the future. Moreover, since these techniques were expensive, exploitation tended inevitably to become more capitalistic. Miners' associations which in an earlier day had managed their own affairs under contract with a landlord, were now often forced to borrow money to continue operation. As a consequence, many fell under control of their creditors.

Control over mining, particularly where the precious metals were concerned, was also a political concern. In the Holy Roman Empire, a constitutional document of 1356,

the Golden Bull, conceded to the several princes what had previously been jealously guarded regalian mining rights. The princes, in turn, generally conceded the actual management of mining to merchants whose wealth made possible a successful large-scale exploitation. Mining, for example, played an important role in the rise of the fortunes of the Fugger banking family. Independent capital was also important in England and Scotland, but in France the regalian claims of the crown were generally maintained. It should be added here, that, although the cleavage between capital and labor became more marked during the fifteenth century, the miner was still regarded as a substantial member of society.

The commercial and technical achievements of the late middle age made possible, toward the end of the period, a venturing beyond Europe's historic coastal seas. The arts of shipbuilding and navigation were well developed. In the fourteenth century a large number of carefully drawn portable maps (*portolani*) were available, indicating shore lines, harbor channels, and the like; and at least for the well-traveled routes, they were quite accurate. Simultaneously, improvements were made in the compass, and the astrolabe was already known if not universally used. In the fifteenth century, the sailing vessel known as the caravel was developed, usually having three masts.

There had been some venturing into the Atlantic before the fifteenth century. Even in ancient times, both Greek and Phoenician sailors had sailed out beyond the straits of Gibraltar and discovered what they called the "Fortunate Isles" or what we know as the Canaries. Though these Atlantic islands had afterwards been neglected and forgotten, they seem to have been rediscovered in the year 1270 by a Genoese navigator, Malocello by name. Thenceforth, other Genoese penetrated the Atlantic fairly frequently, and certainly visited Madeira and the Azores as well as the Canaries. Moreover, they learned something of the northwest coast of Africa and may well have considered the possibility of reaching India by encircling that continent. Apparently, however, the first European to explore the Atlantic coast of Africa was not a Genoese but a Frenchman, Anselm Desalquier of Toulouse, who

---

[1] Maritime law codes associated with Lübeck, with Barcelona, and with Oléron, a town on the western coast of France, and generally similar in nature, facilitated the settlement of disputes between merchants, ship-owners, sailors, and governmental authorities in widely separated parts of the continent.

visited Guinea, lived in the Niger region for several years, and returned in 1417 with the story of his exploits. We have already mentioned the regular trips of the Venetian galleys to Flanders.

There was also some penetration into the interior of Africa. Venetians went up the Gambia River in 1455, and a Florentine expedition reached Timbuktu in 1469. In the long run, however, Italians did not profit from these ventures. Rather, it remained for national states along the Atlantic seaboard—Portugal, Spain, England, and France—to be the pioneers in this endeavor. Hence before considering the great voyages of discovery, it will be well to trace the development of the states of Europe in the late middle age.

Fifteenth century air-conditioning by Leonardo da Vinci (d. 1519). A full story-high wheel, partly driven by water-power, forced cool air into the apartment of Beatrice d'Este, the wife of Leonardo's patron, Ludovico Sforza (see p. 320).

Courtesy the IBM Collections

The Pietà of Avignon by an unknown French painter of the mid-fifteenth century.

Courtesy Louvre Museum, Paris

CHAPTER 23

The Hundred Years' War and its Aftermath

Previous chapters have traced the development of the French and English monarchies up to the early decades of the fourteenth century. It will be recalled that, despite considerable progress toward governmental integration, neither country—and this is particularly true of France—had achieved real national unity. This was further retarded in succeeding decades not only by the economic depression described in the previous chapter, but also by protracted war between the two countries and bitter internal strife. Not until late in the fifteenth century was either monarchy able to promote national consolidation in any systematic fashion.

A. The Hundred Years' War, 1337–1453: First Stage

The Hundred Years' War was so named, not because actual fighting was continuous for a whole century, but because certain issues which precipitated the struggle were settled only after that long period of time. Foremost among these was the continued possession by the kings of England of lands in southwestern France. These were Guienne and Gascony, the residue of the great fief of Aquitaine which had first been acquired by Henry II.[1] The French government, which aspired to take over these provinces, continually harassed the English administration with various claims to jurisdiction, especially the hearing of appeals.

A further source of conflict was the French insistence, according to treaties made between Louis IX and Henry III (1259), that the English king must do liege homage for these lands.

A more serious bone of contention was Flanders, a fief of the French crown, but closely associated economically with England. The Flemish burghers had been irked by efforts of Philip IV to curtail their traditional liberties and to strengthen French authority over them. Following a victory at Cassel (1328) by Philip VI and further curtailment of privileges, many Flemish emigrated to England.[2] Somewhat later, the Count of Flanders, doubtless acting on the suggestion of King Philip, arrested English merchants. Whereupon Edward III of England, perhaps hoping to stimulate a revolt in Flanders, retaliated by placing an embargo on the export of English wool to Flanders and by arresting Flemish merchants in England.

Minor irritations also contributed to the outbreak of war. English and French sailors frequently came to blows over fishing rights in the English channel, and bloody reprisals occurred. Then, too, just as the English supported the Flemish, so the French maintained an alliance with the Scots, who successfully resisted efforts of English kings to incorporate them into the English monarchy.

---

[1] See above, p. 205.

[2] The town where most of them settled, Worsted, is appropriately memorialized as the name of a type of cloth.

FRANCE
IN THE EARLY STAGES
OF THE HUNDRED YEARS'
WAR 1328-1360

All these sources of disagreement were critically complicated by a disputed succession to the French throne. With the death in 1328 of the last of the sons of King Philip IV,[1] the direct male line of the Capetian sovereigns of France came to an end. Actually, the nearest surviving male relative was King Edward III of England, who, through his mother Isabelle, was Philip IV's grandson. But the French, maintaining that the royal succession could not pass through a woman,[2] chose Philip of Valois, son of Philip IV's brother. He became King of France as Philip VI (1328–1350).

In the critical years 1337 and 1338 Edward made formal claim to the French crown,[3] and the Flemish under the expert leadership of Jaques van Artevelde, a weaver of Ghent, launched a revolt against the French. After a brief period of neutrality,

the Flemish formally allied themselves with the English, and an Anglo-Flemish fleet won a victory off the Flemish coast at Sluys (1340). Meanwhile, highly destructive raiding expeditions were conducted in northeastern France and in Flanders.

The death of the Flemish leader, Artevelde, in 1345, temporarily deprived the English King of military support on the continent. Notwithstanding, he fitted out in England an expeditionary force of some 10,000 men, which he landed in Normandy, moved eastward, put across the lower Seine at low tide, and advanced to a hill at Crécy near the Flemish border. Philip VI, with a larger army, followed the English, but failed to trap them at the Seine; in 1346 he joined battle with them at Crécy, the first important land engagement of the war.

The battle of Crécy was important, not only as a signal triumph for the English, but as an example of the newer methods of warfare which they had learned in recent fighting with the Welsh and Scots. For the traditional feudal cavalry, upon which the French chiefly relied, was mowed down by a veritable hail of arrows from English

[1] See above, p. 207.
[2] The authority for this was the so-called "Salic law," presumably derived from the law of the Salian Franks.
[3] Edward quartered the French lilies on his coat of arms and adopted the French motto, "Dieu et mon droit."

infantrymen, armed with the highly effective long bow. This weapon, a simple though powerful arched bow held upright, was capable of a greater rapidity of discharge than the more cumbersome cross-bow of the French.[1] Crécy was a step in the decline of feudal methods of warfare.

We must not exaggerate the speed or intensity of warfare resulting from the new military tactics employed at Crécy. Compared with modern warfare, the fighting in the Hundred Years' War moved at snail's pace. Except for the capture of the important channel port of Calais by the English, and a certain amount of desultory skirmishing, there were no immediate results of the battle of Crécy. It was ten years before another significant engagement was fought. Then the "Black Prince," Edward III's eldest son, who had moved north from Guienne with a small force, inflicted another defeat on the French at Poitiers (1356). The French King John II "the Good," who meanwhile had succeeded Philip VI, was taken prisoner.

Fortunately for France, John's eldest son, Charles "the Dauphin," [2] took over the reins of government with such admirable courage and efficiency that in 1360 Edward III agreed to peace with him and signed the treaty of Calais (or Brétigny). Thereby the English King formally renounced his claims to the French crown, and in return was ceded in full sovereignty the territories of Aquitaine (including Poitou), Calais, and Ponthieu. John II was to be ransomed, but as the full amount could not be collected, this old French King, honorable knight that he was, and perhaps hopeful of negotiating further, returned voluntarily to England and died there in 1364.

The reigns of Philip VI and John II were marred not only by military defeat, but by spells of political and social disorder. In addition to strife between factions of nobles, there were insurrections known as Jaqueries

—so designated from the common name for peasant (Jaques)—and pillagings by the so-called "free companies." These were bands of soldiers who between formal campaigns were organized, often with considerable skill, by various English, French, Flemish, and Irish captains, and who conducted a terrorizing but methodical pillage. Added to all these woes were the ravages of the Black Death (1348–1350) which, as has been explained, carried off perhaps a quarter of the population.

Meanwhile, the Estates General (or embryo parliament) at Paris took advantage of King John's captivity in England and the accompanying disorders within France to assert extensive authority over revenues and expenditures and even over the royal ministers. For a short period in the middle of the fourteenth century it seemed as though the French Estates General might securely establish itself as a paramount factor in French political life. One of its leaders, Étienne Marcel, member of the third estate and champion of a sort of bourgeois revolutionary movement in Paris, discredited the Estates General by his activities. He and his followers murdered a number of the king's unpopular ministers, and he intrigued with Charles of Navarre, properly nicknamed "the Bad," who was a would-be claimant for the French throne. Eventually, Marcel was repudiated by his native Paris and killed. Another obstacle to the Estates General at Paris was the jealousy of local provincial estates throughout the country. Paris was not France; and the efforts of Marcel and the Estates General had little support outside of the capital.

The Dauphin eventually succeeded to the French throne as Charles V, and throughout his reign (1364–1380) French fortunes fared well. Charles "the Wise," as he was popularly called, combined political insight with a cautious though statesmanlike conservatism. These qualities enabled him to stabilize the disturbed political condition of the country and to restore to the crown much of the prestige it had previously lost. Finances were reorganized, and a number of military reforms accomplished. Particularly important was the liquidation of the "free companies." With the help of Bertrand du Guesclin, a Breton noble who was

---

[1] The "long bow" was apparently first developed by the Welsh, many of whom were now serving in the English forces.

[2] The title of Dauphin, subsequently held by the French king's eldest son, was derived from the province of Dauphiné, east of the Rhône, which had been secured by Philip VI when its Count died childless.

his Constable and who was a competent commander and tough fighter, Charles managed to disperse some of the companies and to incorporate the others into the French army. As a result of the king's efforts a more effective French fighting force was available for continuing the war with the English.

Despite the peace treaty of 1360, the war did continue. The French king would not recognize as permanent a settlement which deprived him of a large and rich part of of France. Avoiding such full-scale battles as Crécy and Poitiers, Du Guesclin allowed the English forces to penetrate and scatter far in hostile country before he attacked them. Thereby he could overcome them piecemeal. He was aided, too, by a weakening of the English command. The "Black Prince," the ablest of the English generals, became involved in the politics of Castile and presently fell ill and died; and his aging father, King Edward III, encountered rising disaffection within England. By 1380, the French under Charles V and Du Guesclin had been so successful that the English retained in France only the coastal towns of Bordeaux, Bayonne, and Calais.

B. The Hundred Years' War: Second and Final Stages

In that year (1380), both Charles V and Du Guesclin died, and with them ended a period of great promise for a unified France. The succeeding period was marked by renewed disasters, the result not so much of any immediate resurgence of English power as of an outbreak of civil war in France. Since the new king, Charles VI (1380–1422), on his accession was too young to rule alone, the administration was shared by various uncles, including the dukes of Burgundy, Anjou, Berry, and Bourbon. Inevitably there was jealousy, and each sought to promote his own interests at the expense of the country at large. Wherefore, if, as the previous chapter suggested, the world was the richer for the art patronage of the dukes of Berry and Anjou, the French people were the poorer. And the misfortune was tragically prolonged when in 1392 the king was afflicted with recurring insanity.

The most prominent of the royal uncles was Duke Philip "the Bold" of Burgundy (1363–1404). He had been entrusted with the duchy of Burgundy by his brother, Charles V, and encouraged to marry the heiress of Flanders, Margaret, in order to break the traditional alliance between England and Flanders and to bring the latter into alliance with France. Shortly afterwards, Philip was further invested with that part of eastern Burgundy, known as Franche-Comté, which was a fief of the Holy Roman Empire rather than of the French monarchy. Gradually, by various means, he acquired most of the territory between Burgundy and Flanders. Thus it transpired that the wealthy Flemish domain in the Netherlands was combined with a territorial state of considerable size and importance on the northeastern borders of France.

For a time Duke Philip exercised a commanding influence over his royal nephew. But gradually a rival influence was exerted by the king's younger brother, Duke Louis of Orléans,[1] until finally the competition for influence at the royal court developed into active hostility between a Burgundian and an Orleanist faction. After the death of Philip "the Bold" of Burgundy in 1404 and the succession of his son, John "the Fearless," the latter instigated the assassination of the Duke of Orléans. This was the signal for the outbreak of civil war between "Armagnacs" (as the former Orleanists were now called [2]) and "Burgundians." And to make matters worse, Paris fell prey to serious industrial riots led by Simon Caboche, a butcher.

Meanwhile the unrest and internal troubles which had disturbed England during the later years of Edward III and throughout the reign of Richard II (1377–1399), the gifted but erratic son of the "Black Prince," were allayed by an enterprising prince of the Lancastrian branch of the royal family who obtained the throne with the title of Henry IV (1399–1413). This monarch's vigorous son, Henry V (1413–

---

[1] Orléans married Valentina Visconti, daughter of the ruler of Milan. This combined with the Angevin claims to Naples to involve France increasingly in Italian affairs.

[2] Their leader, succeeding the Duke of Orléans, was the Count of Armagnac.

1422), perceived in the French civil strife an excellent opportunity to fulfill his ambition to renew claim to the French crown. Hence during several decades of the fifteenth century English energies were diverted from more constructive pursuits at home to the maintenance of costly military operations in France.[1]

In a well-planned invasion, Henry V led his army across the Channel, took Le Havre, and won a signal victory at Agincourt (1415), a victory comparable with the earlier ones at Crécy and Poitiers. And while Armagnacs and Burgundians contested the mastery of Paris and control of the French government, Henry V proceeded to capture Rouen (1419) and to master all Normandy. In vain, a reconciliation was sought between the two French factions in order to present a united front against the English. It failed by reason of a second murder. John of Burgundy, then in control of Paris, met the Armagnac leaders and the heir to the French throne—the Dauphin—at Montereau. As

[1] On the economic implications of Henry V's policies, see above p. 271.

they conferred on a bridge, angry words led to a scuffle in which the Duke of Burgundy was killed. In revenge, the Burgundians allied themselves again with the English.

Faced with the combined English and Burgundian military strength, the French were forced to make peace. The resulting Treaty of Troyes (1420) was most humiliating. By its terms the unfortunate French King Charles VI was to be succeeded at his death, not by his son, the Dauphin, but by Henry V of England, who was married to Charles's daughter. Two years later both Charles VI and Henry V died, and the rights of the latter to the throne of France passed to his infant son, Henry VI, now formally King of both England and France.

The Duke of Bedford, regent for France during Henry VI's minority, consolidated English control of northern France, gave Normandy an excellent administration, and prepared, with Burgundian support, to overcome French resistance in other parts of the country. Nevertheless, the English position was insecure in many ways. Bedford's regime, however efficient, was not popular with the majority of native French-

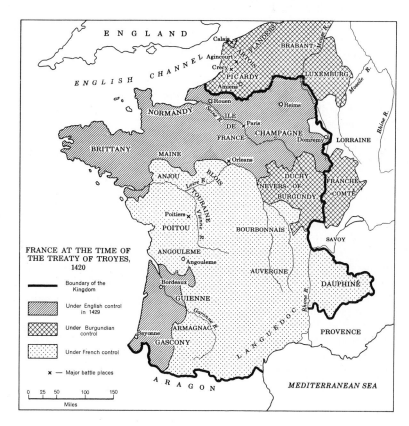

FRANCE AT THE TIME OF
THE TREATY OF TROYES,
1420

▬▬▬ Boundary of the Kingdom

▨ Under English control in 1429

▩ Under Burgundian control

⠿ Under French control

✕ — Major battle places

0 25 50   100   150
Miles

men, who recognized the English as being of different speech and nationality and derisively called them "goddams." Then, too, the Dauphin, the son of Charles VI, refused to recognize the Treaty of Troyes which had disinherited him. He assumed the title of Charles VII, established a temporary capital at Bourges, and maintained some forces in the field. The Armagnacs adhered to his cause, as did most other Frenchmen who disliked the Burgundians. Even the Burgundians were not thoroughly loyal to their English alliance. They regarded it merely as a temporary means of overcoming their Armagnac rivals in France.

The Dauphin, Charles VII, was not exactly a prepossessing figure. He was slight and bandy-legged, and he was nicknamed by his adversaries the "king of Bourges." But he also acquired the appellation of "the Well Served." The first who served him well was a remarkable peasant girl named Joan of Arc.

The story of Joan of Arc has had such universal human appeal as to have become almost a legend. Indeed, much has been claimed for her which never happened. She did not single-handedly drive the English from France. Her military exploits were extraordinary, but not in themselves decisive. But she did help to crystallize an incipient French patriotism. This was her real achievement.

Joan was a humble peasant girl of Domrémy,[1] near the Lorraine frontier, a region which had witnessed a great deal of fighting between Burgundians and Armagnacs. She disliked the Burgundians and was well aware of the distraught condition of France. Though uneducated, she possessed an unusual native intelligence and quick wit. She was deeply religious, much given to meditation, and especially devoted to Saints Michael, Catherine, and Margaret. To their "voices" she listened. They told her to go to the King and bring him to Reims to be crowned. She approached a local lieutenant of the Dauphin, and he was sufficiently convinced by her to give her some sort of escort. That she finally reached Charles VII at Chinon, after traveling some three hun-

[1] Her father's name was Jaques Darc. The name was later changed to d'Arc.

dred miles through hostile territory, is a tribute to her inner conviction and her persistence. The King's advisers were naturally very skeptical of this peasant girl dressed in man's clothing, but she convinced the King himself of her sincerity by picking him out of a crowd of courtiers. As a consequence, Charles provided her with armor, a horse, and command over a small contingent.

Joan was not commander-in-chief of the French army, but her presence in it aroused a strange new enthusiasm among a hitherto apathetic and discouraged soldiery. She set a new tone, and, by urging action and more action, raised the morale of the French troops who were convinced that they now had the aid of a saint. Her first military exploit was the driving of English besiegers from the city of Orléans (1428), and so miraculous did it seem that not only were her French soldiers confirmed in their belief that she was "la Pucelle" (the Maid) sent from heaven, but the English became convinced that she was a witch, actuated by the devil.

After the relief of Orléans, the irresolute Charles VII would have preferred to revert to his accustomed lethargy, but Joan, faithful to continuing "voices" of her saints, prevailed upon him to make the journey to Reims, where he was solemnly crowned and anointed in her presence. From a purely military viewpoint, an attack on Paris might have been better, but the coronation at Reims, in the traditional place and manner, was a symbol to the whole country that the "king of Bourges" was now truly King of France. For a moment, Charles could be persuaded to no further activity, and Joan had at first deemed her mission fulfilled when the King was properly crowned. Yet it seems she was persuaded to continue, and presently she was captured by the Burgundians who turned her over to the English. After an imprisonment of nine months, she was tried at Rouen in Normandy, by a local court of the Inquisition, for witchcraft and heresy (1431).

The trial was one of the most famous in history. The judges, presided over by Bishop Cauchon of Beauvais, were French sympathizers with the English and doubtless

LE TRESVICTORIEVX ROY DE FRANCE

CHARLES SEPTIESME DE CE NOM

Charles VII of France about 1444.
Jean Fouquet.

Courtesy Louvre Museum, Paris

believed, like them, that Joan was bewitched by the devil. They asked her if she was willing to permit the church to decide whether her voices were really of heavenly inspiration or merely the promptings of the devil. Refusal would render her guilty of heresy. For ten weeks the simple peasant girl insisted before the hostile tribunal on her supernatural inspiration and skillfully parried the subtly worded leading questions. Only when worn out in body and mind, and threatened with torture and death, did she admit that the "voices" had been an hallucination. But returning to her cell, she rallied and retracted this admission. Whereupon the inquisitors found her guilty of being not only a heretic and witch, but a relapsed heretic, and as such subject to the extreme penalty. She was turned over to the civil authority, which was English, and by it was burned at the stake in Rouen.

Twenty-five years later, the papacy ordered a posthumous re-trial of Joan's case. This time the earlier verdict was quashed and she was pronounced innocent. Much later, in our own century, the church sol-

emnly canonized the "maid of Orléans" as a saint, not, of course, because of her military exploits, but rather in recognition of the undoubted reality of her personal sanctity and of her intimate converse with things divine. It was the inspiration of her valor and enthusiasm, rather than any military achievement, which counted in the national cause of France.

Following Joan's death, King Charles VII displayed more energy and statesmanship. He opened negotiations with the Burgundians, and at the Congress of Arras (1435), by ceding certain territories to them, he got them to break their alliance with the English. Thereafter, although hostilities with the latter dragged on for another twenty years, the French had the upper hand. Charles obtained appropriations from the Estates General and additional loans, as we have seen, from the banker Jacques Coeur.[1] With such financial backing, he reorganized and enlarged his army. Gunpowder, already in use in the fourteenth century, made possible a primitive sort of artillery. The

[1] See above, p. 270.

English were driven out of Normandy, and in 1453 they lost Bordeaux, their last stronghold in southern France. Only Calais, on the Channel coast, remained to them for another century as a remnant of the former vast possessions and claims of English kings in France.

C. Expansion and Strengthening of the French Monarchy

After the final defeat and expulsion of the English, the French monarchy had still to cope with a number of princes and nobles who in the preceding years had managed to build up a considerable local authority. Most menacing was Burgundy, which had steadily grown in size and strength under the leadership of a line of able and ambitious dukes. Already, Duke John "the Fearless" (1404–1419) possessed not only Burgundy proper, with Franche Comté, part of Lorraine, and Flanders, but also nearly all of the Low Countries, or "Netherlands" (Holland and Belgium). His successor, Duke Philip "the Good" (1419–1467), added Namur and Luxembourg and exercised chief control over the neighboring bishoprics of Utrecht, Liége, and Cambrai. It was possible, therefore, for Philip and his successor, Duke Charles "the Bold" (1467–1477), to build up a strong domain, and even, perhaps, an independent "middle kingdom" between France and the Holy Roman Empire. To this end Charles rounded out the Burgundian-Netherlands possessions by acquiring further territories in Lorraine and upper Alsace. And, as though to prove to the rest of Christendom that Burgundy was actually a great power, the dukes magnified their court and spent money lavishly. Philip founded the celebrated order of chivalry, the Order of the Golden Fleece. The dukes liberally patronized the arts and letters and especially fostered a golden age of Flemish painting. They aspired to be at least the equals of the kings of France, and they succeeded in being a most serious threat to them.

Yet eventually the ambitions of the dukes of Burgundy, and particularly of Charles the Bold, were thwarted by the subtler maneuverings of a French king who had little use

Portrait of Maria Baroncelli. Hans Memling (d. 1494).

Courtesy Metropolitan Museum of Art; Bequest of Benjamin Altman, 1913

for the external trappings of royalty. This was the son of Charles VII, the remarkable Louis XI (1461–1483). Louis was small, unprepossessing in appearance, and frequently afflicted by illness. But he possessed an abundant nervous energy, traveled incessantly, and was passionately fond of the chase. He surrounded himself with able associates, few of whom were of the noble estate, and one or two of whom were of very dubious origin. Often preferring devious to direct methods, Louis earned the reputation of being an intriguing, sinister monarch. This reputation was enhanced in his later years, when, made miserable by his illnesses, he more and more withdrew from society. A hostile Burgundian writer spoke of him as "the Spider King," a sobriquet which has come down through the years and which obscures the more positive side of Louis' character. Although, as we have remarked, he was not fond of court ceremonial, he was by no means uninterested in things cultural. He fostered the establishment of printing in France and invited the celebrated artist,

Jean Fouquet, to be court painter. We have mentioned his concern for the economic development of the country. All in all, Louis was a capable ruler, an accomplished diplomat, and more than a match for the impetuous Charles the Bold of Burgundy.

Charles managed to form against Louis a league of discontented French nobles anxious to frustrate progress in the royal centralization which was proceeding apace since the close of the Hundred Years' War. This "League of the Common Weal" represented a feudal reaction and proved, with Burgundy, to be a powerful combination. Against it, however, Louis XI succeeded, by diplomacy and bribery, in arraying Alsatian subjects of the Duke of Burgundy and also the Swiss, who were fearful of further Burgundian expansion; and when Charles the Bold attempted an invasion of Switzerland, he was defeated and killed (1477). With his death, the League of the Common Weal collapsed.

Louis utilized the occasion not only to overawe rebellious nobles in his own territories, but also to break up and annex a large part of the Burgundian possessions. Duke Charles' only heir was his daughter, Mary, who was unable to prevent Louis from appropriating, in 1482, the original duchy and county of Burgundy, together with Picardy and Artois (in southern Flanders). The remainder of her inheritance—the Low Countries, or Netherlands (including the former French fief of Flanders)—she managed to retain only by marrying Maximilian of Habsburg, Archduke of Austria and heir to the Holy Roman Empire, whose power and threats gave pause to Louis. Although Louis' successor on the French throne, Charles VIII, was obliged subsequently to re-cede Artois and the county of Burgundy (Franche Comté) to Mary and Maximilian, Burgundy proper (the duchy) and also Picardy remained permanently with France.

Meanwhile, Louis XI, on the extinction of the direct line of noble rulers of the old feudal fiefs of Anjou and Maine (to which Provence had recently been added) extended direct monarchical control over them. Then, when Charles VIII, the son

FRANCE
AT THE CLOSE OF THE
HUNDRED YEARS' WAR
(1453) AND ITS
EXTENSION (1453-1500)

Boundary of the Kingdom in 1453

Extension of France by 1500

English possession after 1453 limited to Calais

0   25   50   100   150
Miles

of Louis XI, married Anne, Duchess of Brittany, this large fief in western France and the only remaining feudal estate of first-rate importance in the country, passed to the crown and was incorporated in the royal domain.

Although the early decades of the fifteenth century had brought to France military disaster and civil war, governmental progress was again possible during the later years of Charles VII's reign. In order to effect the military reorganization which brought the Hundred Years' War to a conclusion favorable to France, the Estates General empowered the King to levy a direct land tax, the *taille*. This tax, voted as a permanent right to a monarch then successful in war, went a long way toward making the crown financially independent. As a consequence, the French Estates General had no effective means of controlling royal policy, and it became a rather useless body. Louis XI seldom convoked it. And since Louis not only repressed the nobles but also consistently sponsored the interests of the bourgeoisie, the latter came to regard the old urban liberties, and the Estates General on which these depended, as less desirable than the security which a strong monarchy could now ensure.

Important military reforms were also begun by Charles VII. Since no formal treaty concluded hostilities in 1453, royal ordinances regarding the organization of companies, including companies of artillery, provided for a standing army. The church in France had also been largely brought under royal control, as a contemporary crisis in the papacy permitted an arrangement, called the Pragmatic Sanction of Bourges (1438), whereby the French king would appoint the bishops.[1]

By 1500, the French crown had subdued most of the older feudal lords, had become mainly dominant over the towns, and had furthered the development of governmental institutions. France was not yet an absolute monarchy, however, and the government was still far from centralized. There remained many local differences of custom, of law, and even of language. Moreover,

French kings beginning with Charles VIII, the successor of Louis XI, were tempted by the divisions in the Italian peninsula to expend valuable energy and resources in asserting dynastic claims there. But royal authority, though far from uncontested, was now paramount, and the direction of future political progress clearly indicated.

D. English Political Developments in the Fourteenth and Fifteenth Centuries

Like other European countries, England passed through a period, from 1300 to 1500, characterized by the decline of medieval institutions. Unlike France, where the long Hundred Years' War was actually fought, England escaped its devastation and the depredations of unemployed soldiery. But the Black Death visited England as well as France and occasioned equally profound social disturbance. Nor was the protracted warfare in France without important effect on the development of English government. In the fourteenth century England witnessed a growing constitutional limitation of monarchy by Parliament. The exigencies of foreign war and its consequent drain on the finances had early forced Edward III (1327–1377) to summon frequently the English Parliament; and during his reign it began to assume a bicameral (or two-chamber) form unlike the contemporary Estates on the Continent, which met in three or even four bodies.

In the English Parliament, the upper house, or House of Lords (Peers) to use its later designation, included such tenants-in-chief as had customarily constituted the king's Great Council, together with the bishops and abbots many of whom were bound by ties of kinship to the nobility.[2] At the same time, the lesser gentry, consisting of baronets and knights of the shires

---

[1] On the contemporary papal crisis of the Great Schism, see below, pp. 325–327.

[2] The representatives of the lower clergy dropped out and never became a part of Parliament.

It is important to distinguish between the king's Council in parliament and the king's Council out of parliament. The latter was the group of officials and regular consultants of the king who assisted him in the daily routine of government.

(or counties) associated themselves with the town representatives and sought a "common" place of meeting. This House of Commons, as it came to be called, was not at the outset the powerful legislative body it is today. For in the fourteenth and fifteenth centuries the nobles in the House of Lords usually took the initiative in political matters. But the Commons, and the burgesses in particular, having more money than anyone else, were not slow to make their influence felt. In the long run, they would prevail.

The functions and powers of the English Parliament, though still relatively undeveloped, were extended and clarified in the fourteenth century. As the king's council, Parliament was primarily a judicial body, a high court where complaints could be heard and decisions rendered on formal petition. But from the king's point of view, Parliament was also a means of obtaining revenue. As a consequence, it was discovered, especially by the Commons, that when the king was in financial straits subsidies could be withheld unless grievances were redressed. And the king's demands for money increased during the Hundred Years' War. Unlike the French Estates General which gladly voted subsidies to a king who would rid the country of an invader, the English Parliament only grudgingly supported a foreign war. Thus there grew in England a tendency toward financial dependence of the king on Parliament. Edward III, for example, was forced in 1340 to agree that no tax should be levied without the consent of Parliament, and in 1343 he promised to make no change in customs duties without parliamentary approval.

Progress toward a general legislative function of Parliament was also evident, though less marked. Some, but by no means all, statutes were promulgated by the king in answer to parliamentary petitions, but even in these cases, they were apt to be issued after an adjournment of Parliament and to undergo royal alteration. Similarly, parliamentary attempts to control the king's ministers and the appointment of royal officials met with only limited success. In the latter part of the fourteenth century Parliament did succeed in establishing a procedure for "impeachment" of officials, whereby they could be indicted by the Commons and tried by the Lords. Broadly speaking, the English Parliament was acquiring a considerable authority and prestige. The lower house was exercising wide powers in financial matters, while the upper house was continuing and developing the restraints over monarchy which had been set forth in Magna Carta.

During the reign of Richard II (1377–1399), the King's high-handed methods and defiance of Parliament aroused a formidable baronial opposition in Parliament, which ultimately brought about his deposition. The role of Parliament in bringing about the succession of Henry IV (1399–1413) of the house of Lancaster added considerably to its prestige.

Following a general tendency of the time throughout Europe, the English government attempted to limit papal jurisdiction within the country. In 1351, a Statute of Provisors prohibited papal appointments to English benefices, and in 1353 the Statute of Praemunire limited appeals to the papal *curia*. These measures indicated an incipient national consciousness, doubtless accentuated by the fact that, during most of the fourteenth century, the popes were resident at Avignon in France and on particularly friendly terms with French kings, with whom the English were at war. Simultaneously, heresy appeared in England, and, as a later chapter will explain more fully, the teachings of John Wyclif attracted a considerable following known as "Lollards." [1] The Lollards were suppressed by government action. In general, English religious opinion continued to be staunchly Catholic. Such measures as were taken against the pope's jurisdiction did not indicate any widespread departure from the faith.

Although England was not devastated by war, the ravages of the plague had important social and economic consequences. For a time after the Black Death, which affected England as disastrously as it affected the continent, the relative scarcity of labor caused a rise in wages. Then in 1351 a Statute of Laborers fixed the wage rate as it had been before the plague. In the resulting atmosphere of discontent, radical political

---

[1] See below, p. 328.

and social ideas found a hearing. In 1381, after the government decreed a poll tax, there was a formidable peasant revolt, which was put down by the cool hard effort of the young King Richard II. As the preceding chapter has indicated, such revolts were characteristic of the transition from an old order to a new. The English peasant was attempting to get a hearing. And it may further be remarked that he had a spokesman in William Langland whose *Vision of Piers Plowman* reflects much of the social unrest of the age.

Henry V (1413–1422) who led England again to continental invasion was followed by Henry VI (1422–1461). Since the claim of the Lancastrians to the throne was not unassailable and in fact was challenged by their cousins, the Yorkists, and since Henry VI was a weak ruler, factional strife developed over the control of, and ultimately the succession to, the throne. Thus it was that after the conclusion of the Hundred Years' War in 1453, with English defeat, the country was torn by a series of civil wars known as the Wars of the Roses. These were wars over the royal succession between rival houses of Lancaster and York, the former with a red rose as its emblem, and the latter with a white rose. The struggle involved much disorder and violence, and in the course of it a large part of the old nobility was killed, while Parliament, split into factions, was temporarily weakened. For a time the Yorkists had the upper hand under Edward IV (1461–1483). But the strife was not ended until Henry Tudor, indirectly connected with the Lancastrian house, gained a decisive victory over the Yorkist King Richard III in 1485 and assumed the crown as Henry VII and married a surviving Yorkist princess.

During the Wars of the Roses, there had been shocking disregard or manipulation of the usual judicial processes. Nevertheless, although common law procedures were endangered by violence and intimidation, they did not collapse. Then, too, in the realm of local administration, officials known as justices of the peace, and appointed by the crown from among the lesser landowners, acquired in the fourteenth and fifteenth centuries considerable administrative, police, and judicial authority.

When Henry VII (1485–1509), the first Tudor, came to the throne, the country was generally sick of war, disorder, and anarchy, and ready to welcome a strong monarchical rule which would put an end to the internal troubles that had so long disturbed the kingdom. And Henry did, in fact, repress disorder with a heavy hand. He established the Court of Star Chamber and other royal or "prerogative" courts which were not bound by the ordinary rules of common law procedure. They could, for example, make the accused testify against himself by means of torture. These courts were used to try political cases and to convict great nobles or important people who might have overawed a regular court.

Realizing that financial difficulties could weaken his position, Henry VII practised careful economy. By a foreign policy of peace, he reduced expenditures. At the same time, he increased his revenues by prudent management of the crown lands, by regular collection of feudal dues and taxes (such as import and export duties), and by imposing fines and "benevolences" (forced gifts) on the wealthy. Thus the king was less dependent on Parliament. And since he promoted foreign trade he won the support of many merchants. With Henry VII began the Tudor policy of controlling, manipulating, bribing, but not abolishing, Parliament.

In international politics, Henry VII sought to increase his prestige by arranging marriages for his children. His son Arthur was married to Catherine, daughter of Ferdinand and Isabella of Spain and aunt of the future Holy Roman Emperor Charles V. When Arthur died a few months after the wedding, Catherine was married to his brother Henry, the King's second son. The King's daughter Margaret was married to King James IV of Scotland, thereby paving the way for the union of the crowns of England and Scotland just a hundred years later (1603). When Henry VII died in 1509, he left to his son Henry VIII a kingdom strengthened internally by peace and good management, used to strong rule, and bolstered by marriage alliances abroad.

CHAPTER 24

Central and Eastern Europe in the Late Middle Age

A. Disintegration in the Holy Roman Empire

In the fourteenth and fifteenth centuries, while France and England were overcoming separatist tendencies of feudalism and were emerging as strong national monarchies, the course of events in Germany was in the opposite direction. Here, instead of more centralization, there was less. Instead of a unifying monarchy, there were multiplying local sovereignties.

One explanation of this peculiar development is that the Holy Roman Emperors had never regarded themselves simply as kings of Germany. As previous chapters have indicated, their domains included Slavic Bohemia, part of the Netherlands, much of French-speaking Burgundy and Provence, northern and central Italy. And until at least the middle of the thirteenth century the imperial title still seemed a valuable prize.

With the death of the Hohenstaufen Emperor Frederick II in 1250 and the extinction of his line shortly afterwards, any prospect of bringing both Germany and Italy into a single solid Empire was dispelled. Subsequent emperors made a few desultory attempts to assert claims south of the Alps, but in the main they abandoned the pretense of controlling Italy and retained only a nominal suzerainty over a few city-states in the north of the peninsula.

Although the relinquishment of Italy enabled the emperors of the fourteenth and fifteenth centuries to concentrate their attention upon the affairs of Germany, they were not able to develop a strong German monarchy. The time had passed when such an eventuality was practicable. For the preceding emperors had so privileged their German vassals and so depleted the royal domain that a policy of centralization was out of the question. What their contemporaries were accomplishing in France and England could not now be commenced in Germany.

There were now in Germany hundreds of fiefs, large and small, ruled by princes, who, under various titles such as dukes, counts, margraves, knights, etc., aspired to ever greater independence of central authority and to ever widening territories for themselves. Most of the larger and more prosperous towns had gained charters as free imperial cities. The policy which earlier emperors had pursued of favoring ecclesiastical vassals as a counterpoise to undependable lay vassals, had served to build up several large, and practically independent, ecclesiastical states, such as the "prince-bishoprics" of Cologne, Mainz, Trier, Liége, Magdeburg, Passau, and Salzburg. The history of Germany was already becoming the history of its many different states—ecclesiastical, lay, and "free cities"—rather than the history of Germany as a whole or of the Holy Roman Empire.

But ancient tradition, and particularly the ancient tradition of some sort of an Empire for Christian Europe, died hard. Despite ample evidence of its actual disintegration the Holy Roman Empire continued with a formal semblance of authority. After an interregnum (1256–1273)

A fifteenth century German woodcut of the "Dance of Death." Heidelberg, 1488.

Courtesy Pierpont Morgan Library, New York

which followed the fall of the Hohenstaufen, a new emperor was elected by the German princes. He was Rudolf of Habsburg (1273–1291), a Swabian prince whose ancestral lands centered in Alsace and Switzerland. Rudolf concerned himself less with trying to rule Germany or the Empire than with utilizing what prestige and influence he had as Emperor to establish an important state for his family within Germany. It so happened that during the preceding interregnum, a particularly ambitious prince of the Empire, Ottokar II of Bohemia, had extended his sway far into the Danube valley.[1] Now, on Ottokar's refusal to recognize Rudolf or to attend his court, the Emperor resorted to force and, after winning a decisive victory at Marchfeld (1278), appropriated for himself the territories of Austria, Styria,

Carinthia, and Carniola. These provided the historic center of subsequent Habsburg power and the nucleus for many other possessions acquired by the Habsburg family.[2] However, the very fact that Rudolf was so successful in improving his family fortunes militated against his securing an hereditary Habsburg succession to the Empire. The other princes insisted upon the right of electing the Emperor, and they were averse to electing one who, through too large possessions of his own, might dominate them.

Hence, while Habsburg descendants of Rudolf strove for the imperial title, they were repeatedly thwarted in the fourteenth and fifteenth centuries by rival princely families, especially by the Wittelsbach family of Bavaria and the family of the Dukes of Luxembourg. From the latter was elected in 1308 the Emperor Henry VII, who was haunted by the imperial dream of the Hohenstaufen and attempted to realize it by once more invading Italy. In this he failed dismally. Far more significant was his effort, in imitation of Rudolf of Habsburg, to construct a big family inheritance within Germany. By arranging a marriage of his son with the heiress of Bohemia, he temporarily joined this important state with his original duchy of Luxembourg.

But the other German princes had the same reaction toward Luxembourg power as they had previously had toward Habsburg power. They would have no emperor too strong for them. Consequently, on Henry's death, they chose Louis of Bavaria, a member of the Wittelsbach family, who assumed the imperial crown without papal sanction. His reign (1314–1347) was marked by a controversy with Pope John XXII over the relation of the imperial power to the papacy and the control of Rome and central Italy. Various proponents of anti-papal political theories found refuge at Louis' court. Although the Emperor's attempts to exercise a real power in Italy failed, he did succeed in aggrandizing the Bavarian possessions of the Wittelsbach family and establishing it as one of the major dynasties in Germany.

On Louis' death, the electors transferred

[1] See above, p. 222.

[2] Franche Comté and the Netherlands were added by the marriage of Maximilian of Habsburg (1493–1519) to Mary of Burgundy. See above, p. 285.

the imperial title back to the Luxembourg-Bohemian family in the person of Charles IV (1347–1378). Charles did make an effort, albeit ineffectual, to maintain some authority in Italy. More important was his contribution to the constitution of the Empire in Germany by recognizing its essentially federative character and by regularizing the procedure of electing its emperors. The latter he provided for in a document called the "Golden Bull" (1356). Henceforth there were to be seven electors: three ecclesiastical (the prince-bishops of Cologne, Mainz, and Trier), and four lay (the count palatine of the Rhine, the duke of Saxony, the margrave of Brandenburg, and the king of Bohemia). Within a month of an emperor's death, the seven would meet at Frankfurt-am-Main, and within another month they must choose his successor. If they took more than a month, they would be put on a diet of bread and water. Although papal confirmation was not specifically repudiated, the Golden Bull made no reference to any need of an election's being confirmed by the pope.

The Golden Bull further provided that none of the states of the seven electors should be divided and that, with the exception of Bohemia which was privileged to elect its king, the lay states were to pass from father to son by the rule of primogeniture. Conspiracy against the life of an elector was designated as high treason, and no appeal was allowed from electoral courts. Mining and coinage rights, formerly regarded as imperial *regalia*, were relinquished. Many of these measures, though stipulated for the electoral states, were imitated elsewhere. They operated to preserve the major states of the Empire and to contribute to the acceptance of a divided or federalized Germany.

The seven electors also constituted a kind of upper house to an imperial parliament, or Diet, as it was called. This assembly had developed, in the century before Charles IV, from a council, or court, of the suzerain's feudal vassals in much the same way as simultaneously the English Parliament and the French Estates General had developed. The German Diet consisted at first of the chief nobles and clergy who met as two separate estates. Gradually, the "free" imperial cities were invited to submit recommendations, although it was not until the century after Charles IV that burghers constituted a regular "third estate" of the Diet. Altogether, the Diet was unwieldly in size, and its members were so jealous of their respective rights and privileges that it could seldom take any effective action. Its powers remained extremely vague, and as time went on it was called together only in the face of some extraordinary emergency.

Charles IV was succeeded by his son Sigismund (1410–1437), the last of the Luxembourg-Bohemian line.[1] Sigismund was greatly concerned over the contemporary schism in the papacy, as well as over the spread of heresy in Bohemia which resulted from the teachings of John Hus. As will presently be explained, the Council of Constance, which Sigismund was instrumental in assembling, ended the schism and disposed of John Hus.[2] But the heresy persisted and provoked a series of conflicts—

---

[1] Charles' first son, Wenceslas (1378–1400), was deposed because of drunkenness and general incapacity.
[2] See below, p. 330.

Page from the Constance Missal. Gutenberg. Possibly the first printed book.

Courtesy Pierpont Morgan Library, New York

the Hussite wars which disturbed the following decades. Sigismund had married the heiress of Hungary, and as so frequently happened in the later history of the Empire, he found his energies absorbed outside of Germany.

After Sigismund's death in 1437, the imperial electors, again fearing a too powerful ruler, turned to a member of the Habsburg family, Albert II (1438–1439). His short reign proved to be the beginning of a long tenure of the imperial throne by members of this family. His successor, Frederick III (1440–1493), the last Emperor to be crowned at Rome, was chiefly noted for his skill in avoiding serious problems throughout a long and rather dull reign. But his son, Maximilian (1493–1519), attempted to improve matters by strengthening the imperial judiciary and by creating, at the Diet of Cologne in 1512, ten imperial "circles" for better enforcement of law and order.

Such measures were taken too late in the history of the Empire to prove efficacious or to halt its development into a collection of states rather than a unity. Moreover, its weakness had tempted more fortunate neighbors. In the course of the fourteenth and fifteenth centuries, France had appropriated Lyons (1307), Dauphiné (1349), and Provence (1481), and had exercised considerable influence in such areas as Lorraine and imperial Burgundy (Franche Comté).

B. Major Separate States within the Empire

Really to understand Germany and the Holy Roman Empire in the late middle age, attention must be directed to the separate states. Particularly in the second half of the fifteenth century, certain of the German principalities managed to overcome local particularism, to control or coördinate local estates or diets, and to effect a reasonably successful administrative consolidation. In certain cases, such as the Habsburg lands,

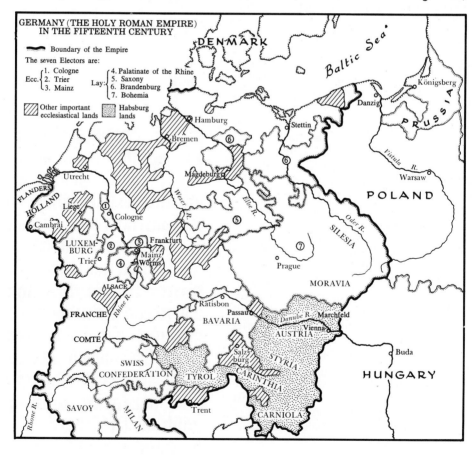

GERMANY (THE HOLY ROMAN EMPIRE) IN THE FIFTEENTH CENTURY

geographical expansion thwarted centralization. For to the already widely scattered territories in the south and southeast of Germany, Maximilian, it will be remembered, added imperial Burgundy and the Netherlands. But other states fared better with consolidation. In 1423 when the previous ruling line of the electorate of Saxony died out, the Emperor Sigismund conferred it upon the Wettin family which already possessed the principalities of Meissen and Thuringia.[1] Both the family and the consolidated Saxony were to play important roles far into modern times.

It was similar with the electorate of Brandenburg in northern Germany. As an original frontier state (*mark*) against the Slavs, it early had considerable military significance. It acquired a new line of rulers (*margraves*) when the Emperor Sigismund in 1415 conferred it upon Frederick of Hohenzollern. Thereby, a previously inconspicuous Swabian family, whose name was derived from a castle on the heights of Zollern, came into possession of territory that would eventually raise the Hohenzollerns to a leading position in Germany, in Europe, and in the world.

German Switzerland differed greatly from Brandenburg or Saxony. It was not a compact state or a rich country. Originally a part of Swabia and the old kingdom of Burgundy, it had developed into a number of mountain and forest communities, or cantons, owing principal feudal allegiance to the Habsburg family of Austria. Three of the forest cantons—Uri, Schwyz, and Unterwalden—had importance because they controlled the main passes through the Alps from Germany to Italy; and transalpine traffic promoted the growth of several Swiss towns. Both townsmen and mountaineers resented outside interference with their local liberties; and in behalf of these they were disposed to seek guarantees or to fight.

The canton of Uri obtained its freedom in 1231 through negotiation with the Habsburg overlord. But when, a few years later, Rudolf of Habsburg became Holy Roman

The Emperor Maximilian (d. 1519). Etching and engraving by Lucas van Leyden.

Courtesy Museum of Fine Arts, Boston

Emperor and attempted to enforce his authority over the cantons, the hardy Swiss resisted him.

By a "Perpetual Pact" of 1291 the three forest cantons agreed to united action, and thus laid the foundations for the Swiss Confederation. They administered a stinging defeat to Austria and the Habsburgs in 1315, and in the same year they solemnly renewed their Pact. Fighting continued intermittently for a long time. Occasionally the Swiss suffered reverses in their struggle for independence, but they stubbornly kept on opposing each fresh attack upon them. Gradually the three forest cantons were joined by others, including the towns of Lucerne, Zürich, Berne, Fribourg, and Basel, until by the early sixteenth century there were thirteen cantons in the Swiss Confederation. With increasing strength, they won several victories in the fourteenth and fifteenth centuries over the Habsburgs, sometimes with the assistance of rival Emperors. At length, Maximilian, after still another unsuccessful attempt to subdue the

---

[1] This Electorate of Saxony consisted of a mark (or outpost) of the much older Saxony, which had been divided by Frederick Barbarossa in the twelfth century after his defeat of Henry "the Lion." See above, p. 214.

Swiss, confirmed their liberties by the Treaty of Basel in 1499.[1]

Their long war of independence, lasting more than two centuries, gave the Swiss the reputation of being the best fighters in Europe. Consequently they were widely employed as mercenaries by foreign rulers. There was long a Swiss Guard in the French army, and there is still a Swiss Guard for the pope.

Bohemia occupied a unique position in the Empire. Its population was predominantly Slavic, and its history continued to be associated, as it had been in the past, not only with Germany but with the kingdoms beyond the eastern frontiers of the Empire. Bohemia quite naturally attained an especial prominence under the Emperor Charles IV of the Luxembourg-Bohemia dynasty. He understood the people of his own kingdom, the native Czechs, and spoke their language. In 1344 he obtained the separation of the bishopric of Prague from the German ecclesiastical province of Magdeburg and its erection into an independent archdiocese. In 1348 he founded the university of Prague. Charles was also a patron of the arts and letters and a friend of the humanist Petrarch who at one time visited Prague.

Although many Germans had penetrated into various regions of Bohemia and neighboring Moravia and were playing a prominent part in the life of the country, a Czech national feeling was growing in the late middle age and was manifested in the multiplicity of Czech literary works and by the warm reception accorded to such popular preaching in the vernacular as that of John Hus.[2] Under Wenceslas, the successor of Charles, the former German domination of the university was ended.

When Sigismund, the last of the dynasty, began to occupy himself with the affairs of Hungary, the fate of the Bohemian kingdom became increasingly linked with developments in eastern Europe. It retained, however, its identity as an important Slavic kingdom within the central European complex of individual states which the Holy Roman Empire was fast becoming.

C. Scandinavia, the Baltic Lands, and East Central Europe

The development of the Scandinavian kingdoms was affected by the expansion into that region, and the appropriation of much of its commerce, by the Hanseatic League. As a consequence, the kings of Denmark, Norway, and Sweden were not able, as were the kings of France and England, to utilize an active native middle class against the dominance of landed magnates. Until late in the middle ages the nobility of all three kingdoms played a leading role in military, political, and social life.

Toward the end of the fourteenth century, an extraordinary woman gave promise of improving the political situation. This was Queen Margaret, daughter of a Danish king and wife of a Norwegian king. Following the deaths of father and husband, she joined Norway (and Iceland and Greenland) with Denmark. Then, after protracted negotiations, and no little fighting, she managed to overcome opposition of both nobility and Hanseatic League in Sweden and to secure this country's adherence to the so-called Union of Kalmar (1397), whereby all three Scandinavian kingdoms agreed to form a single monarchy and to accept a common sovereign named by Margaret. Unfortunately, the sovereign so named lacked Margaret's diplomatic and military ability, as did also his successors during the fifteenth century. One of them, Christian I, ceded the Orkney and Shetland Islands to Scotland in 1468 as dowry for his daughter on her marriage into the Scottish royal family. Within the Scandinavian kingdom there was much political disorder and backwardness.

Culturally there was progress. A university was founded at Copenhagen, in Denmark, in 1476, and another at Upsala, in Sweden, in 1477. Both speedily became important centers of intellectual life, and Upsala gave special impetus to nationalist sentiment in Sweden.

The Swedes never took kindly to the Union of Kalmar. They repeatedly challenged it and demonstrated a constant

---

[1] This was internationally guaranteed by the chief European powers in the Peace of Westphalia of 1648. See below, p. 402.

[2] The Hussite movement drew upon the Czech element and Czech national feeling. See below, p. 330.

The Prodigal Son. Albrecht Dürer (d. 1528).

disposition to break away from it and to set up a separate national monarchy of their own. Moreover, many of them migrated northward and eastward into Finland, and brought this area into subjection to Sweden. Viborg, which would have great modern importance in the northern Baltic, was already, in the fifteenth century, a strongly fortified Swedish outpost.

It had seemed in the thirteenth and early fourteenth centuries as if the greater part of east central Europe, from the northern Baltic to the southern Danube basin, might be dominated by the German expansion eastward which was being promoted militarily and politically by the crusading Order of Teutonic Knights, and commercially by the Hanseatic League. The Teutonic Knights in

1346 added Estonia, just south of the Gulf of Finland, to their earlier conquests of Prussia and other lands along the southern and eastern coasts of the Baltic. Towns on these coasts, such as Riga and Danzig, were being monopolized by Hanseatic merchants, while German colonists, overrunning Prussia, were seeping into Poland and Lithuania. Still farther south, Germans were settling in Slavic Bohemia.[1]

Against the influx and threatened dominance of Germans, not only the Czechs of Bohemia, but also the Slavic Poles and the Baltic Lithuanians developed, in the fourteenth century, a protective national spirit which eventually set limits to German expansion and helped to establish large and powerful Slavic kingdoms in east-central Europe. In 1386 was arranged a union between the kingdom of Poland and the principality of Lithuania which had recently been greatly expanded at the expense of Russians, Tatars, and South Slavs. Jadwiga, heiress of Poland, married Prince Jagiello -of Lithuania, who, as part of the agreement, accepted Catholic Christianity with all his people and became joint King of the two countries. Thereby the Teutonic Knights were deprived of the religious basis for their "crusade" against the pagan Lithuanians, and were confronted with combined forces superior to their own. In 1410 a Polish-Lithuanian army invaded Prussia and decisively defeated the Teutonic Knights near Tannenberg. This historic battle not only regained for the victors the province of Samogitia (on the Baltic, between Prussia and Estonia) but it marked the decline of the Teutonic Knights as a military power. Their internal discipline decayed, and a second attack upon them ended in 1466 in the ceding by them to Poland of West Prussia [2] (Pomerelia), including Danzig and its hinterland in the Vistula basin. East Prussia, henceforth separate from Germany, was retained by the Knights, but as a fief of the Polish king. Early in the sixteenth century the territories of the Teutonic Order were secularized, East Prussia being henceforth designated a duchy.

German eastward expansion, a movement of several centuries' duration and one of the major achievements of the German people during the middle ages, was thus finally halted. It had permanently altered the linguistic and national complexion of the coastal area stretching from the Elbe to the Gulf of Finland. The region of Prussia had been thoroughly Germanized, and the Baltic regions to the northeast had acquired, above the native peasantry, a German landholding class. Moreover, Bohemia and Poland, although retaining their essentially Slavic character, had received a considerable number of German settlers. Though Germany failed to become a national state in the middle ages, the eastern areas which it then colonized were to be objectives for the German national state of our modern twentieth century.

As a result of its victories over the Teutonic Knights, the Polish-Lithuanian state achieved great prominence in the affairs of eastern Europe. Already in the fourteenth century, especially during the reign of Casimir III the Great (1333–1370), Poland was making notable advances both politically and culturally. Though forced to admit the absorption of Silesia by Bohemia and of Polish Pomerania (Pomerelia) by the Teutonic Knights, he added to the kingdom's southeastern territories by occupying the Lithuanian (and formerly Russian) province of Galicia, thus increasing the Ukrainian element in an already heterogeneous population. There were many immigrants, not only Germans, but also Jews and Armenians, who swelled the population of Poland, especially of its towns. Something of the development common to the states of western Europe took place in Poland, as the number of cities and the volume of trade increased. Besides, in establishing in 1364 at the capital city of Cracow a school which in 1400 was raised to the rank of a first-rate university, King Casimir enabled Poland to assume a position of leadership in the intellectual and cultural life of east-central Europe.

South of the Polish-Lithuanian state was the Magyar kingdom of Hungary, which for a century after the extinction of its native dynasty (the Arpad) in 1308, was contended for by rival foreign princes of Angevin, Luxembourg, and Habsburg families,

---

[1] See map above, p. 223.

[2] This territory of "West Prussia" was roughly the same as the Polish "corridor" of 1919–1939.

RUSSIA AND ITS NEIGHBORS
ABOUT 1500

Boundary of the Holy Roman Empire

0   100   200   300
Miles

and also by Polish kings. Sigismund of Luxembourg-Bohemia and the Holy Roman Emperor, for example, was also King of Hungary, and Ladislas I, who died fighting the
Turks at Varna (1444), was King of Poland as well as of Hungary. But in no case
did rule by a foreign king mean the political
incorporation of Hungary into any other
state.

The Magyars were intensely jealous of
their national independence, and their patriotism was heightened by chronic warfare
with the Ottoman Turks who were overrunning southeastern Europe. In this struggle, a leading figure on the Hungarian side
was a frontier nobleman, John Hunyadi by
name, whose son became one of the country's most famous kings—Matthias Corvinus
"the Just" (1458–1490). Matthias built up
an efficient administration and patronized
scholarship. He collected a celebrated library, the *Bibliotheca Corvina,* containing
a large number of valuable books and manuscripts. His successor, Ladislas II, also King
of Bohemia, arranged marriages for members of his family with the Habsburgs, thus
paving the way for the ultimate succession
of both kingdoms in 1526 to the Habsburg
family.

D. Byzantine Empire, the Balkans, and Russia

As explained in an earlier chapter, the
Byzantine Empire suffered territorial losses
in the twelfth and thirteenth centuries to
Moslem Turks in Asia Minor, to Christian
states of Serbia and Bulgaria in the Balkans,
and to the Venetians in Greece.[1] For a
time, as the result of the Fourth Crusade,
Latin Emperors supplanted Byzantine (or
Greek) at Constantinople. Though the latter were restored in 1261, the Empire was
never able to recover its former power or
prestige.

The rising Yugoslav kingdom of Serbia in
the Balkans experienced a notable expansion under King Stephen Dushan (1331–
1355). He dominated the whole area from
the Danube to the Isthmus of Corinth, subjugated Bulgaria, and even aspired to the
imperial throne at Constantinople.

But eventually all three states—Serbia,
Bulgaria, and the now diminished Byzantine Empire—proved powerless to withstand the steady advance of the Ottoman
Turks in the fourteenth and fifteenth centuries, some details of which we shall nar-
rate in the next chapter. Suffice it here to
state that the Turkish conquest of southeastern Europe not only gravely menaced all

[1] See above, p. 224.

Christendom but finally extinguished the Byzantine Empire in 1453 and subjected Greece and the Balkans to several centuries of alien and stagnating rule.

One consequence of the Moslem Ottoman conquest of Constantinople and the Greek Orthodox East was an added significance of Russia as the only remaining independent country whose cultural heritage, however modified by later events, stemmed originally from the Byzantine Empire. For, it was during the fourteenth and fifteenth centuries, while the Byzantines were losing their independence to the Turks, that Russia was winning its independence from the Tatars. This new Russia was not centered as in earlier days around Kiev, which had fallen under Lithuanian jurisdiction, but in the north-central principality of Moscow, which gradually emancipated itself from the Tatar yoke.

The most noted fifteenth-century Duke of Moscow was Ivan III "the Great" (1462–1505), who annexed Novgorod and other rival principalities, conquered certain border territories in White Russia (Byelorussia) and Little Russia (Ukraine) at the expense of Lithuania, and then, after repulsing a final push of Tatars toward Moscow, made his whole dominion entirely independent. After his marriage to Sophia Paleologus, niece of the last Byzantine Emperor, Ivan III emulated contemporary monarchs in pursuit of glory and prestige. He rebuilt the ducal palace at Moscow (the Kremlin), adopted an elaborate court ceremonial, and styled himself "Autocrat of All the Russias."

The church also played an important part in the development of Russia in the later middle age. There had been a notable growth of monastic life. A metropolitan see had been established, first at Vladimir, then in Moscow. And there was growing sentiment that Russia should be, as the Byzantine Empire had latterly been, the exponent and defender of the Orthodox Eastern Church against the Pope and the Catholic Church of the West. Shortly before the fall of Constantinople in 1453, the Byzantine Emperor and a number of prelates of the Eastern Church had agreed at the Council of Florence (1439) to unite with the Western Church.[1] Ivan III's predecessor imprisoned the Russian Archbishop, Isidore of Kiev, who had supported the union, and appointed another. The union lasted, therefore, only temporarily in some southwestern areas, and Russian religious sentiment came to be more and more associated with an incipient national feeling. It was suggested, for example, that as Constantinople had been called the "second Rome," so Moscow was to be the "third Rome." Later, in 1589, the Russian Church was placed under a Patriarch of Moscow whose subordinate relation to the Tsar was analogous to that of the Patriarch of Constantinople to the Byzantine Emperor.

Thus by 1500, though still blocked in the south by Tatars and Turks, and in the west by Poland, Lithuania, the Teutonic Knights, and Sweden, what came to be known as the Grand Duchy of Moscow was emerging as an important state in eastern Europe.

---

[1] See below, p. 331.

CHAPTER 25

Mediterranean Europe, Conquest of the Atlantic

AND ADVENT OF OTTOMAN POWER

Our distinctively Western civilization had originally developed around the Mediterranean. This area remained, throughout the period of the Roman Empire, and on down through the middle ages, the central avenue of cultural as well as commercial progress for the rest of Europe. And although during the late middle age the center of gravity, so to speak, had begun to move northward, events in the lands bordering the Mediterranean continued to be of great significance to the whole of Europe. In the west, much of the ancient Mediterranean unity was still apparent in the close interrelationship of Italy, southern France, and the Iberian peninsula. Such was not the case, however, in the east, where the Moslem Ottoman Turks overran what was left of the old Byzantine Empire and extended their conquests through the Balkans to the Adriatic and across north Africa to Morocco. At the close of the middle ages, a resurgent Islam again menaced European civilization as it had done at the time of the First Crusade in the early middle age.

With the foregoing reflections in mind, we shall now proceed to consider specific happenings in each of the Mediterranean countries during the fourteenth and fifteenth centuries.

A. Portugal and Overseas Expansion

Political life in the Iberian peninsula followed a pattern not unlike that of France and England. True, there was no Hundred Years' War. But there were numerous disputes about royal succession and rebellions on the part of feudal lords or would-be independent towns and provinces; and, until late in the fifteenth century, the peninsula remained divided into the four states of Portugal, Castile, Aragon, and Moslem Granada.

The great achievement of Portugal during the fifteenth century was the exploration of the African coast and the discovery of an all-water route to India. The first step was King John's capture of Ceuta, across the strait of Gibraltar, in 1415. The Portuguese, like the Spaniards, had fought so long to overcome Moslems that crusading was a vital part of their life and thought. Thus they bestirred themselves, at the very time when England and France were locked in mortal combat at Agincourt, to carry the Christian cross into Africa. The conquest of Ceuta was at once a crusading achievement and an incentive to further national expansion.

King John of Portugal had a brilliant son, who, through the greater part of the fifteenth century, was the central figure in Atlantic exploration. This was Prince Henry, commonly styled "the Navigator" (1394–1460). Although he did little navigating himself, he inspired and patronized a vast deal. He was essentially a scientist, intensely desirous of enlarging man's knowledge. Being also a patriot, he aspired to win land and gold and glory for Portugal. And being likewise a devout Christian, he was anxious to gain converts from Islam and to link up European Christendom with the fabled Christian kingdom of "Prester John," formerly thought to have been in Asia, but in the fourteenth century more usually associated with the African Christian Kingdom of Ethiopia. On Cape St. Vincent, whence he could look out upon the broad expanse of the Atlantic, Prince Henry established his headquarters. There he collected and studied all available maps and charts, prepared and equipped expeditions, collated and interpreted reports of returning captains, and constantly encouraged his men and urged them to ever greater endeavor. Incidentally, he employed a number of Genoese as well as Portuguese.

The success of the Portuguese expeditions under Prince Henry's direction was remarkable. Madeira and the Azores were occupied and their colonization begun (1418, 1427). At first, the sailors showed great reluctance to venture southward along the African coast beyond Cape Bojador, but Henry was insistent and the Cape was rounded in 1434. Thereafter progress was more rapid, and Henry's fame mounted. The year 1445 witnessed the passing of Cape Verde, and shortly afterwards Portuguese trading fleets were plying the southern Atlantic. Commercial companies were chartered, and some of them inaugurated a traffic in Negro slaves from the Guinea coast. In 1445 Portugal obtained from the pope an award of all non-Christian territory which its explorers might discover south and east as far as the Indies.

The death of Prince Henry in 1460 did not halt Portuguese advance down the Atlantic coast of Africa. In 1486, Bartolomeo Diaz reached the southernmost tip of the continent, the Cape of Good Hope. Eleven years later, another Portuguese captain, Vasco da Gama, made the first voyage around the Cape into the Indian Ocean, whence he sailed on to Calicut on the western coast of India. This exploit, despite the loss of two of da Gama's three original ships, brought an enormous profit and proved to be the start in the formation of a great Portuguese commercial empire in the sixteenth century.

B. Spain and Overseas Expansion

In both Castile and Aragon, but more particularly in Aragon, the cortes, or parliament, continued during the fourteenth century to play an important part in government. The Castilian cortes obtained the right to propose laws in the form of petitions to the king, who usually accepted them. It also insisted upon its assent to any extraordinary taxation which the king might wish to levy, and upon freedom of speech of its members and their immunity from arrest by the king. The Aragonese cortes possessed even greater powers. It held the king to strict accountability for practically all his actions; and within the kingdom of Aragon, local affairs were regulated by subsidiary provincial cortes for Catalonia and Valencia, as well as for Aragon proper. The English parliament was no unique example of medieval representative government. But just as in France and England, so in Castile and to a large extent in Aragon, monarchy was strengthened in the late fifteenth century through its alliance with the rising middle class; and parliamentary institutions, which had developed out of feudal society, suffered eclipse.

While royal power was being strengthened in Castile and Aragon, an important step was taken toward joining the two kingdoms under a common crown. This was the marriage in 1469 of Queen Isabella of Castile with King Ferdinand of Aragon. They were both highly competent, and quite determined to round out and centralize the common kingdom, henceforth known as Spain. In pursuit of this policy, they resumed warfare with the Moslems in the southern part of the peninsula, and after a long siege they finally, in 1492, captured Granada and incorporated that last Moorish stronghold in their dominions. At Granada still fittingly repose the mortal remains of Ferdinand and Isabella, the "Catholic sovereigns," who brought to successful conclusion the centuries-long crusading of Christians against Moslems in Spain.

In internal policy, Ferdinand and Isabella were confronted with such deep-rooted local patriotism in Aragon and Castile that they retained separate administrations and parliaments for each. Gradually they introduced common practices in both, built up an efficient super-administration, and reduced the meetings and powers of the several cortes. In place of an unreliable feudal force, they established a semi-popular constabulary, called the Holy Brotherhood and subject entirely to the crown. Many feudal castles were destroyed, and privileges of the feudal nobility and knights were notably curtailed. Likewise the charters, or *fueros*, of the towns were revised so that local officials were no longer chosen by the citizens or guilds but appointed by the sovereigns.

The "Catholic sovereigns" were as intent upon cultural and religious as upon political uniformity. Although the long wars of reconquest had bred surprisingly little religious intolerance, measures were now adopted, despite the reluctance of Isabella to accede to her husband's designs, which resulted in the expulsion from Spain of both Moslems and Jews.[1] By means of the ecclesiastical court of the Inquisition, which in Spain passed from papal to royal control, thousands of converted Jews (the *Maraños*) and of converted Moslems (the *Moriscos*) were convicted of heresy and put to death. Though doubtless many of these had professed conversion to Christianity while secretly adhering to their former faith, the wholesale executions were severely criticized abroad. The Pope protested bitterly in 1483, accusing the Spanish sovereigns and their Inquisitors of motives other than religious. But the sovereigns did not desist from their efforts to secure uniformity. They decreed in 1492 that all Jews must accept Christianity or leave Spain. And shortly after the conquest of Granada, despite previous promises of toleration, a similar decree was issued against all Moslems throughout Castile. Thus religious uniformity was forcibly achieved, at the expense of peoples who had contributed largely to Spain's economic and cultural life.

In treating of Spain, we should note that the union of Castile and Aragon combined a vigorous inland state which had dominated the central portion of the peninsula,

---

[1] It should be observed that much of the anti-Jewish feeling was popular in origin and occasionally the result of inflammatory preaching.

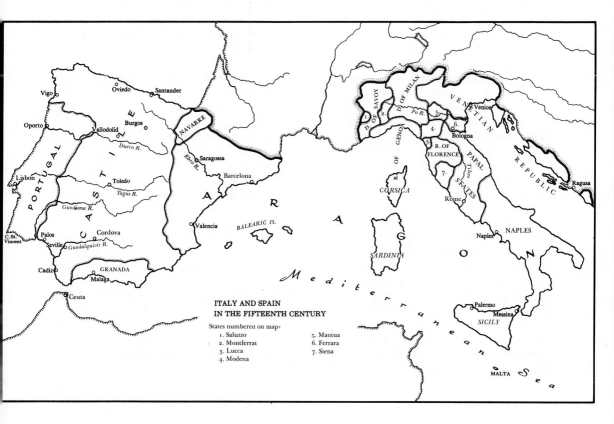

**ITALY AND SPAIN
IN THE FIFTEENTH CENTURY**

States numbered on map:
1. Saluzzo
2. Montferrat
3. Lucca
4. Modena
5. Mantua
6. Ferrara
7. Siena

and which looked westward, with a wealthy maritime state with extensive Mediterranean interests. Aragon had acquired Sicily in 1282. Naples and southern Italy—the other half of the former Norman-Hohenstaufen kingdom of the "Two Sicilies"—remained under Angevin control until 1442 when, as will presently be explained, it too passed into the possession of Alphonso of Aragon. On his death in 1458, the kingdom of Naples was again separated from Aragon, though ruled by kings of the same family until its final incorporation into the united Spanish kingdom of Castile and Aragon in 1504. Meanwhile, before the end of the fourteenth century, Sardinia was also acquired. These acquisitions, together with Malta and a number of ports along the north African coast, constituted a Mediterranean empire of considerable size and strength.

In addition to these possessions, the Spanish, at the very end of the fifteenth century, laid the foundations of what was to become a celebrated and extensive empire overseas. Indeed, in 1492, the very year of the conquest of Granada, Queen Isabella authorized Christopher Columbus to make an attempt to reach eastern Asia and the Indies by sailing due west across the Atlantic.

Columbus' decision to sail west resulted, much as did the Portuguese ventures southward, from a combination of practical experience and theoretical knowledge. The idea of a spherical earth was by no means new; it had been believed by educated men since the days of the ancient Greeks. And although the commonly accepted Ptolemaic geography postulated an earth smaller in size than that of modern calculation, some professors with whom Columbus discussed the matter had made fairly accurate estimates of the Earth's circumference. But Columbus stubbornly clung to his own estimates which were smaller even than those of Ptolemy. As it turned out it was fortunate that he did. With the equipment and supplies at his disposal, he could not possibly have covered the actual distance to the East Indies.

It must not be supposed, however, that Columbus' preparation was inadequate for Atlantic voyaging. A native of Genoa, a city with long-standing maritime traditions, he was a sea captain of much experience which included sailing in the Atlantic. He had studied pertinent geographical writings and he knew Marco Polo's descriptions of the island of Japan and the ports of the China coast. Even so, he had no little difficulty and delay in obtaining needful support for his undertaking. He did receive encouragement from the Franciscan friars at La Rábida, and eventually, in 1492, he secured the invaluable patronage of Queen Isabella. Moreover, he enlisted the practical aid of two Spanish captains, the Pinzon brothers, who supplied him with ships and crews. Incidentally, we may remark that the three ships thus provided (the *Santa Maria*, the *Pinta*, and the *Nina*), though diminutive in comparison with present-day ocean liners, were entirely seaworthy and admirably adapted to the purpose of Atlantic exploration.

After hearing Mass with his men in the little monastery of La Rábida near Huelva on the morning of August 3, 1492, Columbus set sail, and on October 12 made land just about where he had calculated the East Indies should be. It proved to be an island (San Salvador or Watling Island) in the Bahamas off the coast of North America. In the following days, still thinking that he was near the Asiatic coast, he discovered other islands, including Cuba and Hispaniola (Santo Domingo). On the latter island he left a few men to found the first Spanish colony overseas and to locate the gold which he heard about from native "Indians." He then returned to Spain, bringing along some of the natives, and at Barcelona he was received by the Spanish monarchs and their court as a conquering hero. He was fêted and entrusted with a continuing mission of exploring and colonizing lands across the Atlantic.

Columbus made three subsequent voyages to the "Indies," cruising through the Caribbean and finally touching the mainland of South America. The settlers he originally left he could not find again, and in other respects he suffered frustration and disillusionment. True, he eventually founded a permanent settlement at Santo Domingo (1496)—the oldest European town in the New World—but he showed little ability in colonial administration. And, as he failed to disclose any considerable amount of gold or any connection of lands he visited with Asia or the East Indies, his reputation waned in Spain and among his fellow mariners. He died in 1506, ill, worn-out, discouraged, and still imagining that he had reached Asia. He had discovered America without knowing it.

Presently, the truth dawned in Europe that the lands across the Atlantic were not Asia or the East Indies, but a "new world." In 1503 an Italian explorer named Amerigo Vespucci, a native of Florence, claimed to have discovered the "new world." Four years later a German professor suggested that the newly discovered lands should be called "America." The suggestion stuck, and people ever since have described the lands on the western side of the Atlantic as "America" or the "West Indies." just as they have continued to refer to the original inhabitants there as "Indians."

Meanwhile, in 1493, after Columbus's first voyage across the Atlantic, Pope Alexander VI was called upon to arbitrate rival claims of Spain and Portugal to newly discovered lands and seas. He did so by drawing a "line of demarcation" from the north to the south pole, a hundred leagues west of the Azores, and awarding a monopoly east of the line to Portugal and a similar one west of the line to Spain. Portugal protested the award, and the next year, by mutual agreement between the two countries, the line of demarcation was shifted 270 leagues farther west.

Thus it was that at the opening of the new century the states of the Iberian peninsula were not only furthering monarchical consolidation, but were leading the way to new commercial exploitation and the establishment of a new world. At the other end of the Mediterranean, however, an old empire which had stood for centuries as a bulwark against invasion from the east was facing a new and ultimately overpowering attack.

C. End of the Byzantine Empire and Rise of the Ottoman

While England and France were engaged in the Hundred Years' War, and while the Holy Roman Empire was disintegrating into separate German states, the historic Byzantine Empire was nearing its end. Weakened by the effects of the Fourth Crusade and the subsequent appropriation of much of its territory and commerce by French, Venetians, and others, it was no longer capable of playing its traditional role as defender of eastern Europe against invasion. As a consequence, when a new and formidable Moslem power, the Ottoman Turks, appeared in the late middle age, it menaced Christendom as gravely as had the Arab conquests in the early middle age.

The Ottomans originated as a small group of Turkish tribesmen who had settled in northwestern Asia Minor following the Mongol conquests in the thirteenth century. They became converts to the religion of Islam, and from the name of their chieftain, Osman, were known as "Osmanli," or, in English, Ottomans. And under Osman and members of his family who succeeded him, they displayed a fighting valor and a fanaticism which rapidly expanded their small territory and population. By 1349 they had breached the Byzantine defenses in northern Asia Minor and captured Brusa, Nicomedia, and Nicaea.

The Ottomans were soon enabled to take advantage of a dispute between rival claimants to the throne of the Byzantine Empire in order to gain for themselves a foothold on the European continent. One of the claimants invited assistance from the Sultan, and in 1356 an Ottoman army crossed the Dardanelles to Gallipoli. Within a few years it subjugated most of Thrace, and the Sultan Murad I (1359–1389) moved his capital from Asia Minor to Adrianople. The conquest of Bulgaria followed, and in 1389 the Serbs were overwhelmed in the battle of Kossovo and their country incorporated in the Ottoman Empire.

With a resurgent and expanding Moslem Empire on the shores of the Danube, western Europe began to take serious notice. The Hungarians were most directly menaced, and their King Sigismund, who was also Holy Roman Emperor, at once joined the pope in urging and sponsoring a new crusade. A temporary lull in the Hundred Years' War made possible the raising of an expeditionary force in the West; and Christian chivalry, mainly French, once more

RISE OF THE OTTOMAN EMPIRE AND EXTINCTION OF THE BYZANTINE, 1355-1481

Ottoman Empire in 1355	Byzantine Empire in 1355	Expansion of Ottoman Empire to 1481

Note: Crete, to Venice, 1204-1669; Cyprus, Crusader Kingdom to 1489, then to Venice until 1571; Rhodes to Knights Hospitallers, 1309-1523

rode against the "infidel." But the Ottoman armies, under the Sultan Bajazet, were more than a match for the new crusaders. At Nicopolis on the Danube, the latter were badly beaten in 1396.

What saved Europe temporarily was a sudden new irruption of Mongols into Asia Minor under an extraordinary military genius, the Emperor Tamerlane. Tamerlane had already overrun and subjugated northern India, Afghanistan, Persia, and Syria, and he was now invading Asia Minor. Against him the Ottoman Sultan Bajazet, abandoning a contemplated siege of Constantinople, hurried with a Turkish army, only to meet defeat and be captured at Ankara in 1402.

This proved but a temporary set-back to the Ottoman Turks. Tamerlane failed to take advantage of his victory; and his empire was too loose and too far-flung, too much the product of marauding successes, to have any permanence. It began to disintegrate almost as soon as it was formed. Only in northern India did it survive as a compact state. From Asia Minor, the Mongols soon disappeared, leaving the Turks in control and stronger than ever. The fate of

Constantinople was delayed but not prevented.

Byzantine Emperors repeatedly pleaded for aid from the west, and these efforts were associated with moves to reunite the eastern and western churches.[1] Successive popes endeavored to enlist crusaders, but they were unable to overcome the divisive forces within Christendom which prevented effective united action. We have already mentioned the attempted crusade of 1396 and its defeat at Nicopolis on the Danube. A half century later, Ladislas, joint King of Poland and Hungary, defeated the Ottoman Turks under the Sultan Murad II at Nish in Serbia, but as he advanced toward the Black Sea he met decisive defeat at Varna in 1444. The Sultan was now master of the entire Balkan area, and ready not only to extend his Moslem Turkish Empire northward into Hungary but also to extinguish, southward, what was left of the Byzantine Empire.

Shortly after the death of Murad II, his successor, the Sultan Mohammed II, laid siege to the venerable Christian Byzantine capital. Only a handful of Venetians were available for help to the hard-pressed Greek

[1] See below, p. 330.

defenders. They fought gallantly, but against overwhelming odds. Constantinople, cut off by land and sea, its walls battered for seven weeks by bronze cannon of the Turks, its last Christian emperor slain, finally capitulated in 1453. Thus fell the "second Rome," the capital of an empire which had continued in unbroken succession the Roman Empire of antiquity.

The Ottoman Empire henceforth centered in Constantinople, or Istanbul as the Turks called it. In a way, it was itself a continuation of the Byzantine, and hence of the old Roman, Empire. But it was Moslem, not Christian; and it represented not a bulwark, but a threat to European Christendom.

Discussion of the government of the Ottoman Empire, of its growing maritime as well as military power, and of its further expansion to include Egypt and nominally, at least, the entire north African coast, must await a subsequent chapter. We would here merely note that Christianity was not extinguished in Greece and the Balkans. Following the usual Moslem practice, Christians in the Ottoman Empire were permitted freedom of belief and worship, subject to the payment of a special tribute. The Orthodox Patriarch of Constantinople was accorded jurisdiction over, as well as responsibility for, all Byzantine Christians. Byzantine administrative procedures were adopted, and many Christian Greeks were retained in civil administrative posts. Under the Ottomans, trade continued and revived throughout the entire eastern Mediterranean region. But it must not be supposed that the lot of the Empire's Christian subjects was entirely happy. They were the *rayahs*, the "cattle" of the Sultan. The great cathedral of Santa Sophia at Constantinople and other famous churches were transformed into mosques. Moslem custom and law favored those who adopted the faith of Islam. Moreover, part of the Sultan's army was obtained by imposing a tax on every Christian family of one boy in five. These were then separated from their families, brought up as Moslems, and indoctrinated with a fanatical loyalty to the Sultan. Reminiscent of the ancient Roman Pretorian guard, they were known as the *Yeni Cheri* (new troops), or Janissaries.

Although persecution of a physical nature was not officially condoned by the Sultans, it was occasionally practiced by subordinates. Nevertheless, the Greek and Balkan Christians not only stubbornly persisted in the practice of their religion; they kept alive the memory of the Byzantine Empire and of the once independent states of Serbia and Bulgaria. Thereby were sowed the seeds of the later intense nationalism in the Balkans.

The impact of the Ottoman power was felt not alone in Christian Europe. Its extension through Syria and Palestine and across north Africa entailed the downfall of other and older Moslem states and the subordination of the Arabs. In the early sixteenth century the Ottoman Empire was the dominant political force in the whole Moslem world. Moreover, the Sultans were champions of the Sunnite, or orthodox, Moslem faith, and, as such, the Sultan Selim I (1512–1520) assumed the title of Caliph, or supreme religious head of Islam. His successors followed his example until the end of the Empire in our own century, so that they were at once Sultans of a political and military state and Caliphs of the religion of Islam.

D. Disunited Italy and Its City States

Italian history in the fourteenth and fifteenth centuries was much affected by the developments in the eastern and western Mediterranean areas which have just been described, but it presents certain features peculiar to itself. It is really the story of separate Italian states, of their internal development, and of their relations with one another and with the outside world. The failure of the Holy Roman Empire of the Hohenstaufen had left the peninsula destitute of any semblance of political unity. Even Germany, divided as it was, still had at least a nominal emperor and a confederation of native princes. In Italy, no prince emerged as a symbol of national loyalty or political federation; no national dynasty claimed the allegiance of all Italians or secured their coöperation.

The defeat of the Hohenstaufen liberated Italy from German domination, but other foreign influences and pressures continued. As has been indicated, French Angevin and Spanish Aragonese dynasties contested control of the south. French interest in Piedmont, Genoa, and Milan added to the problems of those areas. All these external pressures complicated the already chronic rivalries among the separated states of the peninsula.

A further divisive element in Italian history was the absence of the papacy. From 1309 to 1377 the popes resided at Avignon on the frontier of the French kingdom. And for some thirty years after their return to Rome in 1378, a papal schism divided the western Christian world. A subsequent chapter will discuss the religious consequences of these events.[1] Here we are concerned with the political effect on Italy. Not only was a potentially unifying factor temporarily removed, but the absence or weakness of authority in the papal state of central Italy provoked encroachment by neighboring states and usurpation of power by various petty rulers.

While it might appear that all these factors combined to produce a state of hopeless confusion, there is a kind of pattern, not only in internal administration, but also in inter-state relations, which Italian history generally followed in the late middle age. In the fourteenth century, certain of the northern city-states succeeded in expanding at the expense of their smaller neighbors and becoming principalities of some size and strength. Milan and Florence are examples. To some extent, this process continued in the fifteenth century.[2] Venice, hitherto primarily interested in expansion along the Adriatic, pushed westward and southward to become an important land power, and the Papal State acquired a greater stability. But what particularly characterized the developments of the fifteenth century was the creation of an equilibrium, albeit precarious, among the major principalities—Naples, the Papal State, Florence, Milan, and Venice. The equilibrium was precarious, it must be emphasized, because almost without exception these states retained expansive ambitions. Alliances and

leagues. therefore. proved temporary.[3] And most dangerous for the future of the peninsula was the tendency, in time of supposed or actual crisis, to seek foreign aid. But it must also be remembered that the danger of foreign intervention which seems so clear to the modern student was evidently not apparent to, certainly not understood by, the Italians of the fifteenth century.

The petty imperialisms of the Italian cities and kingdoms required the maintenance of standing armies more effective than the former communal militias. The common practice was to hire mercenaries who served under, and were organized by, competent captains. From the contract (*condotta*, literally, "leadership"), which was drawn up outlining the terms of service, the armies or "companies" were called *condottieri*. Some of the captains acquired considerable fame. Some changed sides and served more than one city. A few came from outside the peninsula. Manifestly such a system demanded strong government, one able to dominate the troops it employed. In many instances, the *condottieri* system contributed to the decline or abandonment of communal republican institutions.

In internal administration, there is evident a general tendency toward some form of absolutism. Centralization, it is true, was hampered in Naples by survivals of feudalism, the lingering animosity toward a foreign dynasty, and the rivalries of the houses of Anjou and Aragon. And papal government, exceptionally difficult to manage during the Avignon period and the schism, was further endangered by the appearance of local petty despots. Nevertheless, in both these states, an effective monarchy was the goal which their respective rulers sought.

While some of the northern cities boasted old established dynasties, many, as a previous chapter has explained, had adopted some form of republican constitution. But under the pressure of late medieval political and economic conditions, and owing, as we have seen, to the necessity of maintaining companies of *condottieri*, republican

---

[1] See below, p. 327.

[2] For major states in fifteenth-century Italy, see map above, p. 301.

[3] It is important to note that modern interstate diplomacy and formal diplomatic usages developed first among the Italian states of the late middle age.

government tended to break down. Power was conceded to or seized by a single person, the lord of the city (*signore*) as the Italians called him. Some—the "despots," as they have often been styled—were descendants of old families. Some were locally prominent citizens who, in one way or another, managed to acquire political power, a few were upstarts, captains of *condottieri*. Often such a ruler was able to secure the support of the less fortunate classes, the *popolo minuto*, against the republican oligarchy, *popolo grasso*. Not uncommonly, too, the *signore* sought from pope or emperor some sort of official sanction as papal or imperial vicar.

A notable example of the development of one-man rule was Milan. Toward the end of the thirteenth century, out of the confusion which had resulted from persistent conflicts of nobles, burghers, and craft guilds, had emerged a rivalry between two great families, the della Torre and the Visconti, in which the latter finally won out. Otto Visconti became archbishop of Milan (1262) and actual ruler of the city. His nephew, Matteo, was appointed imperial vicar, and thus began a succession which was to last until the middle of the fifteenth century.

The Visconti ruled Milan successfully and expanded its domain to the point where it menaced the security of its neighbors. This expansion began, while the popes were at Avignon, with Archbishop Giovanni (1349–1354) and reached a climax under Gian Galeazzo Visconti (1378–1402), who at the time of his death seemed on the point of taking over a large part of northern Italy. This was one of the major crises in fifteenth-century diplomatic history. From the Emperor Wenzel, Gian Galeazzo purchased the title of Duke, and he entered into relations with France by marrying a French princess and by securing for his daughter, Valentina, a marriage with Louis of Orléans, brother of Charles VI. Thus began a diplomatic connection which was ultimately to prove more dangerous than helpful.

Filippo Maria, Gian Galeazzo's successor, was unable to maintain the enlarged Milanese state in the face of Florentine opposition and of Venetian expansion westward. On his death in 1447 there was a brief revival of the republic which, in turn, was followed by the rule of Francesco Sforza (1450–1479), an able captain of *condottieri*. Successful achievement, not dynastic legitimacy, enabled the Sforza family to rule in Milan. Ludovico Sforza (*il Moro*) was something of an economist and promoted agricultural betterment in the surrounding countryside. He was also a patron of arts and letters and brought the celebrated Leonardo da Vinci to Milan.

Ludovico, however, in order to thwart the hostile plans of Naples and Venice, felt it necessary to seek French aid. No doubt he believed that, as had happened often in the past, the threat would suffice. But this time the French were in earnest. The resulting French invasion (1494) will presently be discussed more fully. It was to open a new and unhappy chapter not only in Milanese, but in Italian, history. Ludovico himself miserably ended his days in prison (1508).

The city of Florence rose to eminence in Italy as an industrial and banking center. Commercial success led to imperialism and Florence soon mastered the neighboring towns of Tuscany. Pisa, which controlled the mouth of the Arno on whose banks Florence is situated, resisted for a considerable time, but finally submitted in 1406. Meanwhile, Florence had had its share of class warfare and domestic disturbance. In 1378, a kind of proletarian rebellion, the insurrection of the Ciompi,[1] threatened temporarily the political domination of the aristocratic guilds. Eventually, the Medici, then the leading banking family of the city, gained control of the republican organization. Cosimo, who returned to Florence in 1434 after a brief exile, ruled as a kind of political "boss." His son, Piero, and grandson, Lorenzo "the Magnificent" (1469–1492), built up a strong following and, despite occasional opposition, maintained control over the government. Thus, although Florence remained formally a republic, the Medici were no less *signori*, or "despots," than the Visconti or Sforza.

No less than the Visconti, the Medici sought to promote family interests. Lorenzo,

---

[1] The leader of the revolt was a certain Michele Lando. The *ciompi* were wool carders.

Lorenzo de' Medici. Verrocchio (d. 1488).

*Nation Gallery of Art, Washington, D.C.;
Samuel H. Kress Collection*

for example, was able to obtain for his son, Giovanni, whom he had destined for the church, important ecclesiastical benefices at an early age. These culminated in his nomination as cardinal at the age of fourteen. We shall hear more of him in the early years of the sixteenth century as Pope Leo X.

The Medici, it should be added, were among the most generous and discriminating of patrons. With the exception of Rome, no city contributed more to the development of art and learning than did Florence. This will be discussed later at some length. But it should be noted here that Lorenzo, as a boy, was brought up to regard some of the greatest artists and men of learning as his companions. Rarely has it been given a head of state to live in such distinguished company.

Toward the end of Lorenzo's career, a Dominican friar, Savonarola, preached a series of sermons which not only won him renown as a popular orator, but carried him to heights of dubious fame in Florentine politics. His eloquent denunciations of current morals and politics gained him a large following among the discontented workmen; and for a few months after Lorenzo's death, Savonarola virtually ruled a city which, in the enthusiasm of the moment, dedicated itself to God. But Savonarola was far from being a prudent or moderate statesman. Moreover, he saw in the invasion of the French King, Charles VIII, God's instrument to purge Italy of its sins.

Savonarola had many enemies, and Medici influence was powerful at Rome. As a result of his defiance of Pope Alexander VI who ordered him to stop preaching, he incurred ecclesiastical censure. In the end, he was tried and burned at the stake in Florence amid the jeers of people who had formerly acclaimed him.

When the Medici returned, they lacked prestige of earlier times. Florence, as all of Italy, now had to adjust itself to foreign invasion.

In many respects Venice stood apart from the main currents of Italian life. Never included in the Holy Roman Empire, it had long maintained close relations with Constantinople. Besides, it was primarily a commercial, not an industrial, metropolis. Its governmental development was conditioned by none of the Guelf-Ghibelline feuds of the Lombard cities and by far less internecine class warfare. Most important, Venice was governed, not by a despot, but by a commercial oligarchy. True, there was a *doge* (duke) who nominally headed the state, but his office was elective and his power originally limited by a popular assembly. Gradually, however, the popular element in the Venetian constitution disappeared. A great council of magnates replaced the popular assembly in 1171, and this in turn was subordinated to a Council of Forty and then to a Council of Ten. Finally, membership in the Great Council was restricted (1297) to those whose paternal ancestors had formerly sat in that body.

Venetian imperialism was of relatively early origin and continued well into modern times. Venice's chief rival, Genoa, was finally worsted and its sea power badly impaired in a war of 1378–1381. During the fifteenth century the Venetian republic possessed the major portion of the Istrian and Dalmatian coasts, various parts of southern Greece, Corfu, Euboea, Crete, Cyprus, and a number of islands in the Aegean. Before the end of the century, however, the Venetians were forced to surrender some of these possessions to the Ottoman Turks. Meanwhile, as we have remarked, Venice, by pushing westward, had become one of the major land powers of northern Italy and a rival of Milan, Florence, and the Papal State.

E. The Papal State and the Kingdom of Naples-Sicily

Milan, Florence, and Venice have been singled out for special mention because in different ways they represented the brilliant, prosperous, secular culture of the city-states of late medieval Italy. Two other states remain to be considered: the Papal State in the middle of the peninsula, and the kingdom of Naples-Sicily in the south.

This latter kingdom, founded by the Normans, had passed to the Hohenstaufen and had then been conceded to Charles of Anjou, brother of Louis IX of France. Following the rebellion of the Sicilian Vespers (1282), Sicily fell under the control of the Spanish house of Aragon, but Naples remained under Angevin kings until 1443 when Alphonso of Aragon temporarily

The Venetian Doge, Andrea Vendramin. Gentile Bellini (d. 1507).

reunited the two parts of the dual kingdom. Again separated on his death (1458), though Naples was still ruled by a member of the family, the two parts were finally brought together in 1504 by Ferdinand, husband of Isabella of Castile. Thus the kingdom of the "Two Sicilies," as it came to be called, formed part of a formidable sixteenth-century Spanish empire.

Although the previous brilliance and power of the southern kingdom did not last into the late middle age, and although it was constantly disturbed by discontented nobles and by the claims of Angevin-French pretenders, it continued to play a major role in Italian politics. Under Alphonso "the Magnanimous," the Neapolitan court enjoyed a certain eminence as a resort of scholars and artists.

The Papal State stood apart from the other Italian principalities as the temporal domain of the Holy See. Yet as a territorial state in the very center of the peninsula, it could not escape the vicissitudes of Italian power politics. During the fourteenth century when the popes were resident in Avignon, the papal lands were menaced by encroachments on its frontiers as well as by considerable internal usurpation of power. For a few years a remarkable individual, Cola di Rienzi (d. 1354), gained control over the government of Rome. Playing upon the veneration for past institutions which Romans never lost, Rienzi styled himself "tribune." Temporarily losing his influence, he was driven from the city only to return two years later with the support of the pope. Once again he failed to maintain his power and was killed.

The actual defense and rehabilitation of the Papal State was chiefly the work of Cardinal Albornoz (d. 1367) whose combination of military and administrative skill brought a real improvement. But much remained to be done. Ladislas of Naples was in occupation of a large part of the Papal State at the time of his death (1414).

The popes of the second half of the fifteenth century felt compelled to enter the arena of local power politics by raising armies, waging war, and arranging alliances. Moreover, they concluded that, since prestige was then measured by the external display of a court, Rome should be second to none. And Sixtus IV (1471–1484), noting that secular rulers usually had sons and daughters who could profit their countries by holding important offices, contracting useful marriages, and furthering diplomatic policies, decided to make like use of his own numerous nephews and nieces. Systematic "nepotism" had certain advantages, but it was highly dangerous, since the character of nephews greatly varied. A climax may be said to have been reached when Pope Alexander VI (1492–1503), of the Catalan family of Borgia, provided handsomely not only for nephews but for children.

But if the student of religious history is repelled by the career of the notorious Alexander VI, the student of politics can see in the same pope an extremely capable politician and prince. For when Charles VIII of France entered Italy, to the great dismay of all except those who saw him as an ally, Alexander, with consummate skill, made necessary concessions, won over the impressionable King by his affability, ushered him out of Rome into the kingdom of Naples, and then proceeded to build up an alliance behind his back. Once in Naples, disease as well as military inefficiency brought the venture of Charles VIII to an end.

A few years later, Alexander reversed his policy toward the French and secured an alliance with King Louis XII who was making claims to Milan. It happened that Caesar Borgia, Alexander's son, was married to a French princess; and the Pope hoped, with French aid, to break the northern Italian power and thereby to strengthen and enlarge the Papal State. That it did not turn out so was owing in large measure to a new diplomatic orientation which brought Ferdinand of Aragon into possession of Naples in 1504, one year after Alexander's death. This was a critical event in the history of Italy. For to the French in the north were now added the Spanish in the south. Moreover, as we have remarked, Ferdinand represented not merely the dynasty of Aragon, but a united Spain, already a great power.

Shortly after these events a brilliant Italian writer, Niccolò Machiavelli, published a book called *The Prince* (1513),

in which, citing examples from Italian history of his time, he outlined the policy which a ruler ought to follow in order to succeed—political expediency and "reasons of state," subordinating all considerations of justice and morality to the needs of the commonwealth. Machiavelli's book, in addition to being the classic expression of what has come to be called "Machiavellianism," has come down through the centuries as an image of fifteenth-century Italy, a land of great brilliance and sophistication, but bereft of unity and lacking in moral integrity, a land of the artist, the artist in statecraft as well as the artist with brush or pen. This, however, is a highly romanticized picture of fifteenth-century Italy. Machiavelli, it must be remembered, was writing in that bleak atmosphere after the French and Spanish invasions had begun. *The Prince* is the treatise of a seasoned but disillusioned politician who has lived to see his hopes shattered and who is groping for an explanation and for a formula for future action. To attribute to Italians an exceptionally large share of unscrupulous political behavior is to misread the history of the age. There were political murders in Italy, it is true.[1] But there was coarse brutality and shocking violence in the north, and calculated intolerance in Spain.

Italy was destined to suffer invasion in the sixteenth century as a consequence of its lack of unity. But Italians had not tried to achieve unity. Rather they sought to create, and in considerable measure succeeded in creating on a small scale, a sense of statehood. To do this they drew on the many sources of their varied political heritage. These were tempered by a searching study of what Rome had once meant and might mean to "Romans" of a later generation. This is one of the significant aspects of what is called the Italian Renaissance and to which we shall now turn.

---

[1] Two murders often singled out as "typical" were the Pazzi conspiracy against the Medici (1478) as a result of which Lorenzo was wounded and Giuliano killed, and the assassination of Galeazzo Maria Sforza (1476). Both were carried out in church. To these might be added Caesar Borgia's "liquidation" of a number of conspirators at Sinigaglia, an affair which Machiavelli described as splendidly executed.

A panel from the door of the Baptistery at Florence. Ghiberti (d. 1455).

Alinari photograph

Courtyard of the fifteenth century Bevilacqua palace, Bologna.
Alinari photograph

CHAPTER 26

Learning and Art in the Late Middle Age

THE RENAISSANCE

A. Italian Humanism and the Italian Renaissance

Preceding chapters have indicated that the political and economic life of the late middle age presented less uniformity than had earlier centuries. Nascent national states were fostering national cultures, and the intellectual and artistic developments of the fourteenth and fifteenth centuries were correspondingly diversified. Yet there was a pervasive cultural trend which, first noticeable in Italy, ultimately affected almost all Europe. This was a vigorous effort to restore certain important elements in Europe's classical heritage. Although by no means entirely novel—Europeans had repeatedly looked back to Greece and Rome for inspiration—the late medieval emphasis on the ancient inheritance was so extensive as to justify the term "renaissance" (rebirth). In course of time the word, renaissance, has come to signify a period of history, a civilization in all its aspects, political as well as cultural, including, in short, the material of the preceding chapters dealing with European life in the late middle age. Here, however, we are concerned with the renaissance as an intellectual and artistic movement. Basic to it was the literary vogue known as humanism.

Humanism has been variously defined. But in the fourteenth and fifteenth centuries it denoted an enthusiastic devotion to the literature of classical or Graeco-Roman antiquity, the *litterae humaniores* or "humane letters." Latin literature had formed the basis of most medieval education, and during the twelfth century there had developed, as we have seen, a classical culture which might be considered a forerunner of fourteenth-century humanism. That a century elapsed before the literary promise of the twelfth century was fulfilled was largely owing to the more technical spirit of thirteenth-century scholasticism and science which took possession of the universities. The pursuit of metaphysics and the purposeful study of law, medicine, and theology did not, of course, cease in the late middle age. But alongside of these, there grew up, mainly outside of the universities, a veritable cult of antiquity and a searching for those things which, it was felt, would give fullest meaning to the spiritual and intellectual development of the individual man. Thus, although humanism signified to its devotees a fuller appreciation of the good things of this world, it by no means excluded the supernatural or was hostile to traditional Christianity.[1] Indeed, many of its most ardent promoters were ecclesiastics.

It was in Italy, seat of a thriving bourgeois culture and a land where the consciousness of the Roman past had never been lost, that renaissance humanism arose.

---

[1] The student should realize that at the heart of the present-day debate over the interpretation of "renaissance" lies the question whether it was secular, and "this worldly," as opposed to the "other-worldly" middle ages. See above, p. 264.

313

Many Italian communities contributed to it, though none more brilliantly than Florence and Rome. And the first of the pioneering humanists, often styled "the father of humanism," was Francesco Petrarca, or Petrarch (1304–1374), who was born of a Florentine family that, like Dante, had gone into political exile. With an absorbing fondness for Latin literature, Petrarch set about collecting the works of ancient Latin authors, and in his many travels he discovered in monastic libraries a number of forgotten manuscripts which he rescued and publicized. Like most succeeding humanists, he was devoted to the works, especially the letters, of Cicero; and in an endeavor to emulate the Ciceronian style, he wrote numerous Latin letters and incidentally composed a lengthy epic poem, *Africa*. Although he failed to master Greek, he appreciated its significance to a well-rounded humanism and encouraged others to study it.

Although Petrarch as a scholar enjoyed the solitude of his country estate near Avignon and retired in later life to a retreat near Padua, he did not hold himself aloof from the life of his time. His travels took him to the Avignon of the popes, and to the Prague of the Emperor Charles IV, as well as to many cities of Italy. Among the many honors which he received was the crown of poet laureate bestowed on him at Rome. He lamented the divisions of Italy and pleaded for the return of the popes from Avignon to Rome. Petrarch was by no means an irreligious man, and one of his most interesting works, the *Secret*, consists of an imaginary dialogue between himself and St. Augustine and reveals the struggle in his soul between the claims of the world and those of eternity. In addition to all these activities Petrarch wrote poetry in his native Italian vernacular. This, as will be explained later, won him undying fame as one of the greatest poets in the history of the western world.

Petrarch as a highly regarded scholar was the center and inspiration of a group of devoted admirers. Among these was Giovanni Boccaccio (1313–1375). Since Boccaccio is best known as the author of the *Decameron*, a collection of stories in Italian,

it is easy to forget that he was a classical Latin scholar who managed to obtain some proficiency in Greek. He also lectured in Florence on Dante, a subject of abiding interest to Florentines.

Toward the end of the fourteenth century, a fuller knowledge of Greek considerably broadened the field of classical study and opened the way for that complete humanism to which Petrarch aspired. Manuel Chrysoloras (d. 1415), a Byzantine Greek who had been sent to Italy on diplomatic missions, became a much sought-after teacher of his native language and held a professorship at the University of Florence. Among the learned Greeks who attended the Council of Florence (1438–1439) and who remained in Italy were Plethon and Bessarion. Plethon suggested to Cosimo de' Medici the idea of establishing an "academy" to further the study of Plato's works. A coterie of scholars rather than an institution, the resulting academy gained distinction under the direction of Marsiglio Ficino and the patronage of Lorenzo.[1] Bessarion, formerly bishop of Nicaea, later became a cardinal of the Roman church, and a highly respected churchman and scholar. One of the finer products of the revival of Greek studies was Angelo Poliziano (d. 1494), who, like so many humanists and artists, was a friend of Lorenzo de' Medici and whose public lectures in Florence won much acclaim. Finally, it should be noted that the Greek works which were added in the period to the West's classical heritage were principally though not exclusively literary— writings of dramatists, poets, and historians which had not been acquired from the Moslems during the earlier middle ages.

In addition to Greek, certain scholars, in an effort to absorb the entire ancient heritage, mastered Hebrew. The most noted was Pico della Mirandola (d. 1494), a brilliant scholar in many fields, whose breadth of learning, acquired in a brief career, was phenomenal. He attempted to

---

[1] The marked interest in Plato was in part a reaction against the Aristotelianism of the thirteenth century, but in part resulted from the humanist desire for a complete classical heritage. "Neo-Platonism" deeply influenced renaissance thought, but did not supersede the study of Aristotle.

coordinate all knowledge in a single system; in addition, he was an extremely devout man, much influenced by the Dominican friar Savonarola.

Although humanists were men of letters primarily, they were not unmindful of other aspects of human life and they recognized the obligations of the scholar to society. Indeed, the ideal of the humanist, as is evident in the educational treatises or experiments of such persons as Guarino da Verona and Vittorino da Feltre who conducted model schools for the rulers of Ferrara and Mantua respectively, or of Leon Battista Alberti, writer as well as architect, was the well-rounded individual whose training should include not merely classical literature, but art, music, athletics, dancing, military skill, "proper bearing," and the study and practice of religion. Thus, although much of the inspiration for this ideal came from pagan Greece and Rome, fifteenth-century humanists, with few exceptions, remained practicing Christians and continued to emphasize the freedom of the individual will and the salvation of the individual soul.

It is not surprising, therefore, that a considerable number of Italian humanists were ecclesiastics or that Rome rivaled Florence as a center of renaissance patronage. Nicholas V (1447–1455) has been called a humanist pope: he invited to Rome Lorenzo Valla who, in a previous service with Alfonso the Magnanimous of Naples, another renaissance patron, had demonstated the falsity of the celebrated "Donation of Constantine." [1] Pope Pius II (1458–1464), the former Aeneas Silvius Piccolomini, was a humanist of wide learning who among other things was concerned with the preservation of Roman remains, thus lending official support to another facet of the Italian renaissance, archaeology.[2] All these activities reached their apogée during the pontificate of Leo X (1513–1521), the son of Lorenzo de' Medici, who brought to Rome as a young cardinal that love and knowledge of classical culture which was his birthright.

The development of humanism from an intellectual fashion to a general and pervasive vogue, and the principal basis of education, was not—indeed, could not have been—the work simply of humanists who represented a relatively small number of highly educated scholars. It resulted partly from the libraries established or expanded during the fourteenth and fifteenth centuries, partly owing to a limited though important penetration of humanism into the universities, and partly as a consequence of the invention of printing.

Many humanists, commencing with Petrarch, were avid collectors and their efforts uncovered a number of classical manuscripts which might otherwise have been lost. Cosimo de' Medici, with the assistance first of Niccolò Niccoli, the humanist, and later of a remarkable book dealer, Vespasiano da Bisticci, assembled many volumes and housed them in the convent of San Marco which he endowed. The collection grew and subsequently was named the Laurentian after his grandson. Cardinal Bessarion gave his fine collection to Venice, and Nicholas V reëstablished and housed what was to become a celebrated collection, the Vatican library. These are but a few examples.

To account fully for the expansion of humanist interests in Italy and their extension to northern Europe, mention must be made of their impact on the existing institutions of formal education—the universities. What seems to have happened is that most universities continued to provide instruction in the arts and in the still indispensable subjects of theology, law, and medicine. But many, usually simply by expanding the offering in the arts, added the humanistic program of Latin and Greek letters. This was true of such new universities as Florence (founded in the fourteenth century and moved to Pisa in the fifteenth), and Pavia, and of such older universities as Padua, Bologna, Rome, and others outside of Italy. In a few instances, such as the *Collège de France*, founded by Guillaume Budé early in the sixteenth century, humanistic studies constituted an exclusive interest. In one way or another,

---

[1] See above, page 118, footnote 1.

[2] A Roman Academy, not unlike its Florentine counterpart, expressly dedicated itself, among other matters, to archaeology.

humanism was gaining acceptance as an educational principle.

B. Invention of Printing, and Humanism in Northern and Western Europe

Printing was invented in Germany. The materials necessary, paper, types of ink, etc., had long been known in western Europe, and the printing of full pages or illustrations from blocks of wood was common early in the fifteenth century. All that was additionally necessary was the invention of movable type. And the first to capitalize on this invention, perhaps to have made it, was Johann Gutenberg of Mainz in the decade of the 1440's. The few extant Gutenberg bibles are priceless treasures.

Soon Gutenberg's countrymen were setting up presses in other lands. Two of them, Swenheim and Pannartz, speedily introduced the invention in Italy, and others brought it into Spain. The first press in England was installed by Caxton in 1476. In a surprisingly short time, printing establishments were to be found all over Christendom, including Mexico and Peru. The Aldine press at Venice, named after Aldus Manutius, its founder, was particularly famous.

The effects of printing on the general development of Western civilization were tremendous. The availability of extant works was increased immeasurably, since presses could turn out copies by the thousand while a scribe labored over a few pages. Accuracy, or at least uniformity, was now reasonably assured. And most of the early printers were editors as well. That is to say, they found it necessary to ascertain from perhaps several manuscripts of a given work what was the correct text. Printing, of course, gave an impetus to humanism, although individual humanists were no longer so much in demand. But the fifteenth-century presses also turned out copies of the Bible, the Fathers, and theological, scientific, and legal treatises. In short, the output reflected the varied interests of the age.

In a sense, too, the printing press forms a link between the humanism of Italy and the humanism of the northern countries. For although the new learning was not unknown north of the Alps in the days before Gutenberg, the first half of the sixteenth century was the golden age of northern humanism. Its more rapid spread and shorter life resulted in no small degree from the fact that so much was already accomplished and readily available. Indeed, although it may have been desirable, it was no longer necessary to travel to Italy.

Among the German humanists was Nicholas of Cusa (*d.* 1464), a prominent ecclesiastic and eventually a cardinal, a man of wide intellectual interests which included science as well as classical literature, and withal something of a mystic. Rudolf Agricola (*d.* 1485) spent ten years studying in Italy; and through his subsequent teaching, he made Heidelberg a humanist center.[1] Conrad Celtes (*d.* 1508) also studied in Italy, was crowned poet-laureate at Nuremberg in 1487, and taught at Ingolstadt in Bavaria and at the University of Vienna. Johann Reuchlin (*d.* 1522) visited Italy in 1482 and 1490 and acquired from Pico della Mirandola an enthusiasm for Hebrew studies which led him to devote his attention to critical examination of the text of the Old Testament.

Many German humanists were associated with the schools of the Brethren of the Common Life, a religious and educational society which will be discussed in the following chapter. When Alexander Hegius (*d.* 1498) became head of their principal school at Deventer in the Netherlands, a humanist program, including the teaching of Greek, was introduced into the schools of the society. There was, therefore, in these schools an intimate association of humanism and religion which tended to characterize the northern movement and to distinguish it from the Italian.

Preoccupation with ecclesiastical reform was especially characteristic of the greatest of all the non-Italian humanists, Desiderius Erasmus (1466–1536). A native of Rotterdam, Erasmus received his early education

---

[1] Erfurt was another German university where humanistic studies flourished. Martin Luther studied there as a young man.

at Deventer and later pursued theological studies at Paris. Thoroughly absorbed in the new learning, he was an excellent Latinist and obtained a good knowledge of Greek. As his scholarly reputation grew he met many people and became a kind of peripatetic scholar and writer and a welcome guest at princely and university establishments everywhere. He corresponded with scholars throughout western Europe and his letters are a mine of information about contemporary conditions. Among his most happy years were those spent in England, where he formed fast friendships with John Colet and Thomas More. To the latter he dedicated his famous *Praise of Folly* (*Encomium Moriae*). This work and the *Familiar Colloquies* show Erasmus as a master of wit and gentle satire directed especially against decadent scholasticism, corrupt and ignorant clergymen, and the foibles of his day generally.

Erasmus' renown does not rest alone on satire. His *Adagia*, a compendium of selections from classical authors with critical commentary intended for young students, went through many editions including one at the Aldine press in Venice. He dedicated to his patron, Charles I of Spain, ruler of the Netherlands and later Holy Roman Emperor, his *Education of a Christian Prince* (1516), an earnest plea for peace and for an application to government of the principles of Christianity. His most ambitious undertaking was a critical edition of the Greek New Testament. Erasmus' later years were saddened by the shattering of his high hopes for a peaceful regeneration of society.

In England, John Colet (1466–1519) and Thomas More (1478–1535), both friends of Erasmus, stand out. Colet, dean of St. Paul's Cathedral in London, won fame for his critical lectures on the Pauline epistles, an excellent example of the religious earnestness in northern humanism. He also founded at his own expense a grammar school at St. Paul's which was devoted to the new learning. With Thomas More, classical humanism was an avocation. He was a busy man of affairs, a competent lawyer, and ultimately Lord Chancellor of England. Moreover, as his *Utopia*, a kind of Platonic vision of the ideal state, indi-

cates, he grasped the pressing problem of social reform.

French humanism, of which there were indications as early as the reign of Charles V (1364–1380), hardly flourished before the end of the fifteenth century when Greek teachers were brought to Paris and Greek works collected.[1] Francis I (1515–1547) was a patron of learning and established the *Collège de France* with special professorships in Latin and Greek literature. Guillaume Budé was his principal agent in this matter, and in founding the Bibliothèque Nationale.

In Spain the new learning took a distinctly religious turn under the direction of Cardinal Ximines de Cisneros (d. 1517). Ximines' objective, a thoroughgoing reform of the Spanish church, required an educated clergy. For this purpose he founded the university of Alcalà which among other accomplishments produced the famous *Complutensian Polyglot*, an edition of the Bible with the original languages and the Latin in parallel columns. Although an awareness of social problems is evident in the literary work of Juan Luis Vives (d. 1540), Spanish humanism, generally speaking, took second place to religious reform.[2]

C. Science and Philosophy

Humanism, being a primarily literary movement, contributed to science only incidentally by uncovering and, after the mid-fifteenth century, reprinting certain important classical works. To cite but two examples, Ptolemy's *Geography* reappeared in 1410 and Hippocrates began to supersede Galen in medical teaching. Meanwhile, in both practical and theoretical fields notable progress was made, particularly in the fourteenth century. At the

---

[1] It has been suggested that the expedition of Charles VIII into Italy (1494) was a means of bringing Italian renaissance ideas into France. This is scarcely true of intellectual matters, but it seems likely that Italian villas with their formal gardens influenced the artistic taste of French nobles.

[2] Erasmus' works, at first well received in Spain, were later banned.

universities of Paris and Oxford, as well as continuing at Padua, there was vigorous re-examination of Aristotle's scientific theories and of Ptolemy's cosmography, and a more penetrating use of mathematics. Nicholas Oresme, Jean Buridan, and Albert of Saxony, among others, developed theories of motion which proved to be important steps toward what Galileo was to demonstrate years later.

Perhaps the most significant applications of applied science were in navigation. We have mentioned the undertakings of Prince Henry the Navigator. Nowhere, in fact, was there a closer association of theoretical and practical science than at the Portuguese court. Portuguese navigators were able to determine latitude by observing with astrolabe or quadrant the vertical angle of the Pole Star, or as they voyaged south-ward, by observing the sun at noon. For the latter procedure Abraham Zacuto produced in 1478 a table of solar declinations. So also about the same time did Johannes Müller (Regiomontanus), who was later invited to Rome by Pope Sixtus IV to discuss calendar reform.

Medical professors of the fourteenth century regularly dissected human bodies as part of their instruction, and in their surgery they no longer uncritically followed the ancients. The *Anatomy* of Mundinus (1316), in use for the next two centuries, was printed at Padua in 1478; as also was a treatise on surgery by Guy de Chauliac (1363), which, though highly important, was hardly fair to its predecessors. Some progress was also made in the prevention of infection and in the diagnosis of certain diseases previously unknown. During the Black Death (1348–1350) many doctors acquired considerable information, and some displayed notable heroism in ministering to the afflicted.

The fifteenth century seems to have been less productive of scientific accomplishment than the fourteenth, but it is important to observe that the works of the late medieval scientists were printed and that they were known and used by the scientists of the sixteenth and seventeenth centuries.

It was noted in a previous chapter that in 1277 an episcopal commission at Paris condemned a number of propositions held by those scholars known as extreme Aristotelians.[1] And it was further noted that one of the consequences was the transference of this school of thought to the Italian university of Padua. Since the adherents continued to profess the Averroistic doctrine of the double truth—one for science, another for religion—they came to be known as Latin Averroists. Meanwhile, an English philosopher, William of Ockham (*d.* 1349), a Franciscan friar and a nominalist, concluded that rational speculation, however useful for the understanding of man and nature, was of dubious and only "probable" validity as a support for religious truth. Thus in different ways, each of these modes of thought diverged from the basic concept of the unity of all knowledge which Thomas Aquinas had proposed for philosophy and theology, and to which such thinkers as Robert Grosseteste and Roger Bacon had wanted to add natural science, and with which the humanists, in their way, were in accord. The implications for theological teaching will be discussed in the following chapter. Here, it may be observed that since these two streams of thought were to persist into the early sixteenth century, precisely through the period of the origins of modern science, there was gradually produced a dichotomy between religious and scientific thought which had not been prominent earlier, but which was to raise many acute problems regarding the relation between religion and science in later times.

E. Progress of Vernacular Literature

If the classicism of the humanists represented a special interest of scholars, the vernacular literature of the late middle age embraced a broader range, both secular and religious. Petrarch and Boccaccio, both humanists, won enduring fame for their works in Italian. Petrarch perfected the poetic form of the sonnet. Boccaccio, in his *Decameron*, a collection of lively and often bawdy tales preceded by a vivid description of the plague in Florence, proved

[1] See above, p. 243.

An unique equestrian portrait of Geoffrey Chaucer from a manuscript of about 1410.

Courtesy Henry E. Huntington Library and Art Gallery, San Marino, California

himself a master of Italian prose. In the fifteenth century the versatile Leon Battista Alberti defended the use of the vernacular on the interesting "classical" grounds that the Romans had used their own native language. Lorenzo de' Medici, the patron, and Poliziano, the humanist, both composed in Italian. Somewhat later, two Italian epics, Boiardo's *Orlando Innamorato* (1486) and Ariosto's *Orlando Furioso* (1515) testified to the enduring popularity of the Roland theme.[1] Although formal treatises were still composed in Latin, historical writing was increasingly done in the vernacular as is evidenced by the *Florentine Chronicle* of Giovanni Villani (*d.* 1348), and by the more skillful histories of Niccolò Machiavelli (*d.* 1527) and Francesco Guicciardini (*d.* 1540).

French literature of the fourteenth and fifteenth centuries was enriched by the satirical works of Jean de Meung (*d.* 1305); by the poetry of Christine de Pisan (*d.* 1430), a celebrated lady of letters, and of Charles, son of the murdered Louis of Orléans (*d.* 1465); and by the lively, vivid, and often pathetic verse of François Villon (*d.* 1463). To these may be added the historical works of Jean Froissart (*d.* 1405) and Philippe de Commines (*d.* 1509).

In England, the days when Norman nobles spoke French and peasants spoke

[1] See above, p. 164.

Saxon had passed, and a common national language, compounded of Germanic and Romance elements, had emerged as "middle English" and was being utilized in the fourteenth century for literary purposes. An early example was the *Vision of Piers Plowman*, written by William Langland in the first half of the fourteenth century. But the outstanding figure in this formative period of English literature was a poet, Geoffrey Chaucer (*d.* 1400), with his famous *Canterbury Tales*. In the following century there appeared a notable prose work, Sir Thomas Malory's *Morte d'Arthur*.

There was a considerable amount of German literature in the fourteenth and fifteenth centuries, and it reflected varied interests of contemporary middle-class people in the German cities. It embraced popular satirical works, like Sebastian Brant's *Ship of Fools* (1498), a good deal of poetry, including ballads and the somewhat artificial pieces which meistersingers used in their singing contests, and also many popular books of devotion. Several German versions of parts of the bible appeared before the end of the fourteenth century, and the first printed edition emanated before 1456, presumably from the press of Gutenberg.

Altogether, it was evident that, though Latin continued to be the language of scholarship, most popular and a good deal of serious writing was now being done in the several vernacular languages. The illustrations mentioned in this section are only a few among many that could be cited. Even governments, like the English, French, and Castilian, were now admitting the respective national tongues to official usage. This encroachment of the vernaculars on a former monopoly of Latin was one of the most significant cultural developments of the late middle age. And it is one of the ironies of history that it occurred amid the humanistic renaissance of classical Latin. In the realm of literature, as in so many others, the growing consciousness of nationality was marked.

F. Painting

The late middle age of the fourteenth and fifteenth centuries witnessed achievements in the fine arts, especially in painting, sculpture, and architecture, which have made that period, artistically, one of the greatest and most amazing in all human history. It will be possible here to mention only a few of the artistic accomplishments and to relate these to the history of the age.

The art of the period, while still largely religious in subject-matter, was no longer so exclusively fostered by the church. It was more often patronized by lay princes or wealthy townsmen, or commissioned by town governments. Moreover, the vicissitudes of contemporary diplomacy often affected the transference of artistic trends. It is important to remember that Italians often resided in the north, that the Holy Roman Empire had a French-Luxembourg dynasty, that the French Angevins were in and out of Naples, that the popes resided during most of the fourteenth century in Avignon, and especially that the dukes of Burgundy controlled the Netherlands.

Fourteenth-century painting, in Italy as well as in northern Europe, is today generally classified as still within the "international Gothic" age. By this is meant that everywhere in Europe painters continued what the medieval miniaturists and designers of stained glass had begun, a departure from the conventionality of Byzantine art. In short, they pushed further in the direction of a freer naturalism. It was the Florentine Giotto (*d.* 1336) who most notably illustrates this trend and who set a fashion for a number of followers during the fourteenth century.[1] Meanwhile, there flourished at Siena, in the first half of the century, Duccio, Simone Martini, and the Lorenzetti brothers. Martini was invited by the pope to come to Avignon. In France, to the already remarkable technique demonstrated in illuminated manuscripts was added Flemish influence. An earlier chapter has indicated the generous patronage of the royal and ducal courts of the late fourteenth and early fifteenth centuries, and the notable development of miniatures and tapestry. French artists were also doing panel-painting and achieving re-

markable success with portraits. Meanwhile, Italian and French influences appeared in the Empire and in Prague.

By the fifteenth century art was being notably influenced by contemporary humanism. Along with religious subjects, it became fashionable to depict characters from Greek and Roman literature. Even the essentially Christian representations were not all designed for churches; many were now produced for private residences, and local persons were used as models. Painters grappled harder with the problems of perspective and space, strove for an ever greater naturalism and a more faithful representation of the human form. By the end of the century some, as, for example, Leonardo da Vinci (*d.* 1519), were making careful studies of anatomy. Leonardo was an exceptional genius, versatile in many fields, who served the Sforza in Milan and subsequently the king of France. Moreover, before him had been a series of artists who helped to make possible what he was able to do. Many of these enjoyed the patronage of the Medici and virtually all owed much to Massaccio (1401–1428) who in a short life started the new post-Giotto trend which many followed. A long list of names could be made, and among the outstanding would be Fra Angelico (*d.* 1455)[2] who did the frescoes in Cosino's convent of San Marco, Benozzo Gozzoli who executed those in the Medici palace, Fra Filippo Lippi, Ghirlandaio, and finally the universally popular Sandro Botticelli (*d.* 1510).

Distinguished as was the Florentine school of painting, it was but one, albeit in many ways the chief, of several Italian schools. There was also a Venetian school represented by Gentile da Fabriano, the Bellini brothers, Mantegna, and, in the sixteenth century, Titian (*d.* 1576). From Umbria came Raphael (*d.* 1520), a pupil of Perugino (*d.* 1524). Raphael was one of the celebrated artists who, toward the end of the fifteenth century and early in the next, were brought to Rome. For after the death of Lorenzo the Magnificent (*d.* 1492), the cultural and artistic primacy in Italy passed from Florence to Rome. This

---

[1] See example of Giotto's work, above, p. 253.

[2] See example of Fra Angelico's work below, p. 324.

is the "high renaissance," the "golden age," and will be considered later in connection with the papacy in the sixteenth century. Here it may be mentioned that Raphael was not only the creator of several famous Madonnas and of the frescoes of the *stanze* in the Vatican palace, but was commissioned to supervise the preservation and restoration of ancient Roman monuments and works of art.

The fifteenth century also brought a flowering of art in northern and western Europe, equally impressive qualitatively, though smaller quantitatively. This included French and Flemish painters, some of whom were also miniaturists who carried that technique into their panel-painting. Jan van Eyck (*d.* 1441), Roger van der Weyden (*d.* 1464), and Hans Memling (*d.* 1494) who came to Bruges from Cologne, are especially to be noted among the Flemish artists. French fifteenth-century art included the remarkable Avignon *Pietà* by an unknown artist, and the portraits by Jean Fouquet (*d.* 1481), court painter of Louis XI. In Germany, the paintings of Albrecht Dürer (*d.* 1528) show Italian influence, and he was equally skilled as an engraver and wood carver. Hans Holbein the Younger (*d.* 1543), whose work shows somewhat greater Italian influence, won renown as a portrait painter. He spent a number of years in England, and to him we owe the likenesses of a number of early sixteenth-century notables of that country.

G. Sculpture, Architecture, Music

As has been explained, medieval Gothic sculpture had made remarkable progress both in free-standing polychrome wood and stone figures and in those designed to adorn the portals of cathedrals. This forward movement continued; and there was added a greater mastery of technique and, especially in Italy, an increased classical influence. Niccolò Pisano (*d.* 1278) who, despite his name, came from Apulia, was probably influenced by work in that area as well as by Roman *sarcophagi* (carved stone coffins) in the Pisan area where he worked. His most famous creations were

The David of the Casa Martelli. Donatello (d. 1466).

National Gallery of Art, Washington, D.C.; Widener Collection

a pulpit at Pisa and another at Siena, and his work was continued by his son, Giovanni (*d.* 1328), and by his pupils. As in other fields, so in sculpture, Florence excelled in the fifteenth century. And the visitor there today will still marvel at the gilded-bronze doors of the baptistery by Ghiberti (*d.* 1455), the statues of Donatello (*d.* 1466), and Verrocchio (*d.* 1488), whose work inspired the young Leonardo; and the glazed terra cottas of Luca (*d.* 1482) and Andrea (*d.* 1525) della Robbia. The versatile Michelangelo (*d.* 1564) began his work in Florence before he joined the company of artists at Rome.

Outside Italy, special attention should be called to the Dutch sculptor, Claus Sluter (*d.* 1405), who was brought to Burgundy by its dukes and whose most notable works are in Dijon. In both France and Germany, medieval skills in both stone and wood-carving continued to flourish, although design and taste was gradually influenced by what was being done in Italy.

In northern and western Europe Gothic building continued into the fifteenth century. In France, it developed into the more intricately articulated and decorated style known as "flamboyant." In England, structural changes in vaulting made possible the elimination of flying buttresses, and the emphasis on vertical and horizontal lines led to a further modification called "perpendicular." In both countries, Gothic features were incorporated into private residences.

Fifteenth-century Italian architecture did not at first or everywhere show classical influence. The *duomo*, or cathedral, of Florence retained much of the Gothic spirit: Giotto designed its campanile, or bell tower, and Brunelleschi (*d.* 1466) its octagonal dome. But classical influences grew

Renaissance architecture. The Rucellai Palace, Florence. Alberti (*d.* 1472).

Alinari photograph

apace during the century. There was a striving for symmetry, a noticeable revival of classical capitals and entablatures, and an effort to conceal structural features. Renaissance palaces, for example the Medici residence in Florence designed by Michelozzo (*d.* 1472), and the Rucellai palace designed by Alberti (*d.* 1472), show skillful use of capitals, entablatures, pilasters, and cornices. Each enclosed an interior court with classical arcade. Certain churches in Florence designed by Brunelleschi, and the church of San Andrea in Mantua, designed by Alberti, are good examples of the application of the classical style to ecclesiastical building. Most striking is the acceptance of the new style in Rome. But since the fulfillment there came in the following century we shall reserve a discussion of Renaissance Roman building to a later chapter. By the end of the fifteenth century the vogue of classicism in architecture had begun to affect every country in Europe.

The development of music during the renaissance was also significant. The art of contrapuntal composition progressed, especially in England, the Netherlands, and northern France. With the work of Dunstable (*d.* 1453), Okeghem (*d.* 1495), and Josquin des Prés (*d.* 1523), skill in counterpoint reached a high degree of technical perfection and tonal beauty. This was an important achievement in the evolution of modern musical forms and techniques.

It should be evident from the preceding pages that the late medieval, or "renaissance," cultural progress was both impressive and varied. Moreover, despite much political disorder, violence, pestilence, and in certain respects a spirit of pessimism, the prevailing humanist mood was one of optimism. Erasmus, in writing early in the sixteenth century to Pope Leo X, expressed his joy that Christendom was led by a man so much in sympathy with the new learning and under whose enlightened guidance church and society might be regenerated. This hope Erasmus lived to see dashed in the confusion of religious strife. And while the sixteenth-century upheaval was associated with many factors other than religious, it was, at least at the outset, essentially a religious matter. It is, therefore, appropriate to conclude our study of the middle ages with an examination of the state of the church in order that we may better understand the events of early modern times.

Miracles of St. Zenobius. Botticelli (d. 1510).

CHAPTER 27

The Church
in the Late Middle Age

A. The "Babylonian Captivity" of the Papacy

The story of the church in the fourteenth and fifteenth centuries presents a melancholy contrast to the record of its brilliance in the thirteenth century. Indeed, this period in its long history has often been entitled "the decline of the church." It is true that both in its functioning as an institution and in its influence over European society, the church of the Late Middle Age showed deterioration. The difficulties which now engulfed it were not all the result of internal weakness or personal derelictions, though these were present. The basic trouble lay in the complex circumstances of the age which we have been describing in preceding pages. It was an age of growing secularism which obscured spiritual ideals and weakened ecclesiastical influences over society.

The particular problems which beset the church included (1) a governmental crisis threatening the position of the pope in the ecclesiastical system, (2) the growth and persistence of heresy, and (3) serious malfunctioning of the administrative system calling for drastic reform. All of these were associated with, and in part caused by, what has been called the "Babylonian Captivity," the residence of the popes for some seventy years (1309–1377) at Avignon in southern France. The removal of the papacy from Rome was an indirect consequence of the fateful conflict between Pope Boniface

VIII and Philip IV of France.[1] In 1305 a Frenchman was elected Pope as Clement V (d. 1314). Although he had little strength of character and in certain matters sought to appease the French King, he did stand out against Philip's constant pressure that he publicly condemn the actions of Boniface VIII. The Pope's most notorious concession was his acquiescence in French demands for the suppression of the Crusading Order of Knights Templar.[2] Apparently in the hope of stopping hostilities between France and England and promoting a crusade, Clement remained in France and eventually established the papal *curia* at Avignon.[3]

Although Clement V doubtless intended to stay only temporarily at Avignon, his appointment of a large number of French cardinals led to the election of a series

---

[1] See above, p. 209.

[2] The Templars had undoubtedly outlived their usefulness as a crusading order and had acquired considerable wealth and landed property in Europe, largely as a result of their banking operations. Clement permitted an investigation of various charges brought against them by French royal commissioners coöperating with the Inquisition. Torture produced confessions and many suffered the death penalty for heresy. The Pope decreed that their property should be turned over to the Knights Hospitallers, but the King had already appropriated most of it for himself.

[3] Actually, Avignon was an enclave of papal territory, outside, but surrounded by, French territory. It was purchased from the heiress of Provence in 1348.

The Palace of
the Popes at Avignon

*Courtesy Marbury Art
Reference Bureau*

of French popes. These showed less and less inclination to leave Avignon, particularly as conditions in the papal lands in Italy became increasingly turbulent. Eventually a large and sumptuous palace was erected at Avignon to house the *curia*. Criticism from outside of France was inevitable, and the Avignon popes were accused by rulers and people of other countries of subordinating their policies to the kings of France. The English, then engaged in the Hundred Years' War, were especially prone to make the accusation. Both Dante and Petrarch lifted their voices to lament the "captivity." But it should be borne in mind that the French monarchy was in a lamentably weak condition during most of the period, and that, with the exception of Clement V, the Avignon popes were not coerced by it or unduly subservient to it.

Actually, after the entire machinery of administration had been moved from Rome to Avignon, the government of the church went on much as before, and several significant policies were energetically pursued. It was Clement V who answered John of Monte Corvino's plea for assistance by establishing missionary dioceses in China. John XXII (1314–1334), an able administrator, was also a proponent of missions to the Far East.

Particularly important at Avignon was the continued centralization of ecclesiastical administration in the papal *curia*. This was especially significant in the financial realm. Papal taxation increased and was more efficiently collected. Income taxes on benefices were regularized, notably the "annates," payments of the first year's income from a benefice. Papal appointments, or "provisions," to benefices throughout Europe were increased. But while these served to counteract the prevalent tendency on the part of secular rulers to dominate the clergy in their respective realms, papal provisions too often involved questionable financial payments and the appointment of aliens who performed a minimum of service and were resented as "foreign" clerics.[1]

While papal finances at Avignon were a major source of criticism, much of it justified, it seems evident that needful expenses of expanding administration were increasing. In addition, considerable expenditure was necessary to reconquer papal lands in Italy from the various local *signori* and *condottieri* who had appropriated them. There was also, it will be recalled, a greater demand for the higher priced consumer goods, and a relative diminution in revenues derived from land. At the same time, venality and luxury, however exaggerated

[1] Two statutes enacted by the English government illustrate contemporary opposition to Avignon policies. The statute of *Provisors* (1351) forbade papal appointment to English benefices; the statute of *Praemunire* (1353) forbade appeals to Rome. Neither statute was consistently enforced in subsequent years.

by contemporary critics, were indubitably present at Avignon. If the popes themselves were able and honest men, and not notably extravagant, the cardinals, mostly French, lived in sumptuous residences and resisted attempts to curtail expenses; and there were too many "hangers on" who were maintained in comfort and comparative idleness.

In spite of the long residence at Avignon, it had never been deemed a permanent change and return to Rome was delayed only because of conditions in central Italy. Cardinal Albornoz was despatched to restore order in the Papal State, and before his death (1367) he had accomplished a great deal. At length, after considerable hesitation, and encouraged by the letters of two saintly women, St. Brigid of Sweden and St. Catherine of Siena, Gregory XI left Avignon in 1377 to take up residence in the Eternal City.

B. The Great Schism

The return of the papacy to Rome proved but the prelude to a new and even graver crisis. On Gregory's death in 1378, as the cardinals assembled to choose his successor, the Roman populace, milling around outside the conclave, demanded a Roman or an Italian pope. As a compromise, the cardinals elected Urban VI, a Neapolitan—not a Roman, but at least an Italian and not a Frenchman. Urban proceeded in summary fashion to cleanse the *curia* of many abuses for which it had been justly criticized. But his high-handed and tactless methods so antagonized the cardinals that several members of the Sacred College fled Rome into the kingdom of Naples, where they met and declared that the votes they had cast for Urban had been extorted by the threats of the Roman mob, and that Urban's election was consequently void. They then elected Cardinal Robert of Geneva, a Frenchman, who subsequently set himself up in Avignon as "Clement VII." Needless to say, Urban stoutly maintained the validity of his own election and anathematized Clement and the French cardinals.

Western Europe was thus treated to the scandalous spectacle of a pope at Rome and a rival claimant at Avignon. But this was not all. For there were now two *curias,* two sets of legates, conflicting bulls of excommunication, and what was most irksome, two organizations for the collection of revenue. And since successors were elected at both Rome and Avignon on the death of the original incumbents, the "Great Schism" bade fair to continue indefinitely. Pious folk were confused and knew not which way to turn for although this was not the first time that western Christendom had been faced with a schism between a pope and an "anti-pope," previous schisms had usually been rather obviously the result of external pressure on the part, say, of an emperor. In the new case, however, the two claimants had nearly equal support and there was genuine doubt in many minds as to which was the true pope.

Broadly speaking, Europe divided its allegiance in a way characteristic of the time, namely along lines of nationality. France, the Spanish kingdoms, Naples (after changing sides), Sicily, and Scotland followed the popes at Avignon, while England and the Scandinavian kingdoms supported the Roman popes. But the division was by no means clear. Germany and northern Italy were divided in their allegiance, and at one time France questioned the status of the Avignon incumbent.

C. Deterioration in Ecclesiastical Morale and Growth of Heresy

The long papal residence at Avignon and the years of the great schism aggravated various conditions in the church which badly needed remedying. The general standard of clerical conduct and competence had deteriorated. In large part, this was the result of the ravages of the Black Death and the consequent necessity of filling vacancies with imperfectly trained nominees. Thereby the policy, inaugurated by the thirteenth-century popes, of promoting university-trained clerics was badly hampered. Sometimes even worse was the number of dispensations given—often after a payment —to hold an ecclesiastical post without proper ordination, or to remain absent for considerable periods of time. Thus in many areas the faithful lacked proper parochial, and sometimes even episcopal, care. To these ills was added a recurrence of simony. And monasticism, badly hit by the Black Death, suffered greatly both materially and morally.

At the same time that the church was faced with the administrative crisis of the schism and a decline in its morale, it was also confronting serious heresy. Heresy had always been a problem for the church, as preceding chapters have shown. In the fourteenth and fifteenth centuries, it flourished as never before, and in certain instances the discipline of the church proved inadequate for its suppression. The explanation of the marked prevalence of heresy lies partly in the weakness of the church of the time. Corruption in it invited criticism and simultaneously so slackened its internal discipline as to unfit it for coping with its critics and opponents. But ecclesiastical failings were not alone sufficient to account for the volume of dissent. The age was a restless one, in which serfs and artisans engaged in spasmodic rebellions, and scholars broke from old traditions. Something of the spirit of change seems to have permeated the religious sphere as well.

In the fourteenth century, a group known as "Spiritual Franciscans" aroused considerable agitation in ecclesiastical circles. Certain members of the Order of Friars Minor, or Franciscans, sought first to restore the practice of strict poverty as it had originally been taught by St. Francis of Assisi. But in their zeal to reject all the compromises by which the Order held or administered property, the Spirituals went on to insist as a matter of doctrine that Christ and the Apostles had possessed no property whatever. Although condemned by Pope John XXII (1323), the Spirituals persisted for some time, and some found refuge at the court of the Emperor Louis of Bavaria (1314–1347), who for a time was at odds with the papacy.

Also at the imperial court was Marsiglio of Padua (d. 1343), a prominent advocate of the conciliar theory of church government. His *Defensor Pacis* is one of the most remarkable political treatises of the age. For Marsiglio conceived of the state as an institution devoted to purely earthly ends and not dependent on any church. He advocated a monarchy limited by a species of popular sovereignty which was to operate, not through a democratic legislature in the modern sense, but through an assembly of the wiser and richer citizens. Further, Marsiglio held that the church was subordinate to the state, and that ecclesiastical authority rested not with the pope and the clergy, but with the community of the faithful (*universitas fidelium*).

If Marsiglio was concerned mainly with questioning the organization of the church, John Wyclif (1320–1384) went further to question fundamental religious doctrine. Wyclif, an English scholar and master at Oxford, was an enthusiastic student of the Bible. At first scandalized, no doubt like many other Englishmen, by the residence of the popes at Avignon, he limited his criticisms to the temporal possessions of the church which, he insisted, the civil government might and should control. Up to this point he had the support of several highly placed persons, including King Edward III's younger son, John of Gaunt. But this support he lost when he denied papal supremacy and rejected the miracle of transubstantiation in the Mass. Wyclif's doctrines were condemned by an ecclesiastical convocation at Canterbury, and he was banished from Oxford. He died in retirement in 1384.

Wyclif's followers, the "poor priests" or "Lollards" as they were called, persisted for some time despite sporadic official action against them. In the main, however, the English rejected Wyclif's doctrines, and throughout the early decades of the fifteenth century civil and ecclesiastical authorities combined to suppress Lollardry.

As a consequence of contacts between England and Bohemia—the marriage of the English King Richard II with a Bohemian princess, and the exchanging of visits by students and diplomats—Wyclif's teachings had considerable influence far from the country of their origin. At the same time, a movement directed toward ecclesiastical reform and including popular preaching in the Czech vernacular was developing at Prague.

The most conspicuous native of Bohemia whose beliefs were derived in part from Wyclif was John Hus. He, too, was a uni-

The Crucifixion.
Fra Angelico
(d. 1455).

Courtesy Metropolitan Museum of Art, New York

versity man, dean of the Faculty of Arts at Prague, canon of the cathedral, and popular preacher. Although Hus rejected some of the English master's teachings, notably that on transubstantiation, he seems to have been markedly influenced by Wyclif's questioning of ecclesiastical authority and by his views on the importance of scripture. Hus won considerable support, as did also his associate, Jerome of Prague, one of those who had introduced Wyclif's writings into Bohemia.

D. Age of the Councils

It is evident that at the beginning of the fifteenth century the western church was faced with major heresy as well as divided by schism. These, together with the matter of reform, were featured on the agenda of an important church council which met in 1414 at Constance. For some time before this gathering, attempts had been made to persuade one or the other of the papal claimants to withdraw. Since all these attempts had proved unavailing, many groups of Christians, both ecclesiastical and lay, bestirred themselves to devise new means for reuniting Christendom. And it was natural that the means they eventually elaborated should reflect contemporary

political ideas and practices. Thus it was proposed that when the head of the church and its central governing body were in default, the entire church could and must assert itself through the instrumentality of a general council. To some, notably the experts in canon law, conciliar action in opposition to a pope was envisaged only as a temporary emergency measure. Others, however, claimed for the proposed council a permanent association with the pope as the supreme governing body of the church. To such theorists it seemed particularly fitting that the government of the church should be parliamentary, and papal authority limited, at a time when parliaments and estates were seeking to restrict monarchical power.[1]

It was, therefore, in an atmosphere of considerable controversy that several prelates, under the auspices of cardinals from both Rome and Avignon, assembled at Pisa in 1409. Too hastily convened and too ill prepared for constructive work, the Council of Pisa lacked general support. Neither

---

[1] The idea of conciliar supremacy had been advocated in the fourteenth century by Marsiglio of Padua. Early in the fifteenth century somewhat more moderate proposals emanated from the university of Paris. Jean Gerson was a leading proponent of moderate conciliarism.

papal claimant would recognize its validity. Consequently its hasty action in electing a new pope, under the name of John XXIII, did not heal the schism. Rather it broadened and deepened it, for there were now three, instead of two, claimants—Roman, Avignon, and Pisan.

This trebly scandalous situation did not long endure. Five years later a more widely attended and better prepared council was assembled at Constance under the patronage of the Emperor Sigismund. Present were not only churchmen, but numerous representatives of cities and kingdoms. In a sense it was a cross-section of the society of the time, and it proceeded to devote itself to three principal problems: the schism, heresy, and reform.

John XXIII, the Pisan claimant, apparently hoping to wreck the council, left Constance after a brief appearance and was then deposed. Somewhat later (July 1415), Gregory XII, the Roman pope, agreed to resign on condition that the Council accord him the right of officially convoking it. By gaining acceptance of this condition, Gregory not only preserved the papal conception of ecclesiastical government wherein a council must be summoned or approved by the pope, but he secured recognition of himself and his Roman predecessors since Urban VI as the legitimate popes. It likewise followed that a decree concerning conciliar supremacy over the pope which had been issued at a date prior to Gregory's convocation had no validity. At length, in 1417, a group of cardinals of the Pisan and Roman obediences met at Constance, and, with certain deputies of the Council, elected a pope for the whole church, Martin V. The Avignon claimant, now a very stubborn old Spaniard, defied the Council and refused to resign. But he soon lost all his following and lapsed into the position of an insignificant anti-pope.

Even before the delicate matter of the schism had been settled, the prelates at Constance had taken up the matter of heresy. In 1414, under a safe conduct of the Emperor, John Hus appeared, seemingly anxious to defend his views. His safe conduct was not honored and he was imprisoned. After some months he was presented with a list of propositions which he was asked to abjure. He replied that he would recant only those which he had actually professed and only if he were convinced that they were contrary to scripture. In short, he chose to stand for private judgment based on scripture as opposed to the authority of the church. The consequence was that he was condemned by his judges, turned over to the civil authorities, and burned at the stake at Constance in 1415. A year later, Jerome of Prague met a similar fate.

The execution of Hus and Jerome did not put an end to the Hussite heresy in Bohemia. It persisted in parts of the country, associated to some degree with a nascent Czech national feeling, and it occasioned a series of "crusades" on the part of the Emperor. All of these failed. Ultimately a moderate wing accepted a temporary compromise with the ecclesiastical authorities in 1432.[1] The extremists, known as "Taborites" from their mountain retreat which they called "Mt.. Tabor," and under the remarkable military leadership of two generals, Procop and Ziska, held out against all attacks. Thus, for the first time in its history, the church had failed to stamp out a major heresy.

Perhaps because it was so occupied with the schism and with heresy, the Council of Constance, despite much talk of "reform of the church in head and members," failed to inaugurate a reform movement of significant proportions. After many discussions, a program was drawn up and formally promulgated, but its implementation was left to future councils which, it was decreed, should be held at regular and frequent intervals. But the popes, fearful of a resurgence of the conciliar theory of ecclesiastical government, were markedly unsympathetic.

Pope Martin V grudgingly acted upon the recommendation of the Council and summoned a council at Pavia (1423), which

[1] These "Compacts," as they were called, permitted the reception by the laity, in the sacrament of the eucharist, of both the consecrated bread and wine, instead of the bread alone as was customary. Hence the moderates were known as "Utraquists" (Latin, "both") or "Calixtines" (Latin, "chalice"). The Compacts were never permanently ratified by the pope.

accomplished nothing. Then, under Pope Eugenius IV another council met at Basel (1431), which had a long and turbulent history. Disagreements between some of its members and the Pope prompted the latter to transfer the council to Bologna and thence (1438) to Ferrara. A minority, refusing to follow Eugenius, remained at Basel, reasserted their superiority over the Pope, and even went so far as to elect an anti-pope. But the Basel assemblage lacked popular support, and the papacy was adept in securing the backing of secular governments. In 1449 the council at Basel came to an inglorious end.

Meanwhile in 1439, the council at Ferrara-Florence (it was moved once again to the latter city) carried on negotiations with representatives of the Eastern, or Orthodox, Church of the Byzantines and Russians, which had been separated from Rome since the eleventh century. Contemporary military pressure of the Moslem Ottoman Turks against the Christian East stimulated serious efforts for reunion of the Churches, and eventually an agreement was reached at Florence, by which the Orthodox Church of the East, like the Catholic Church of the West, would recognize the Pope as spiritual head of all Christendom. When, however, the agreement was made known in the East, it was repudiated by the ecclesiastical authorities at Constantinople and at Moscow.[1] Thus, although the last Byzantine emperors remained personally loyal to the arrangements made at Florence, the two churches remained separate.

Only one thing, therefore—the ending of the Great Schism—was accomplished by the church councils of the fifteenth century. Heresy persisted, and so did the crying need for reform. The papacy, it is true, had survived a major crisis. Its very position in the church had been under attack, and naturally it felt obliged to devote much energy to defending and maintaining its position. This required, as the popes viewed the world in the unstable period of the councils and the Italian wars, a firm hold on the Papal State and the support of the powerful secular rulers of the day.

To the former task the popes, as we have seen, dedicated considerable energy and no little expenditure. Scarcely less demanding of time and money was their patronage of art and letters. Such things, entirely justifiable in themselves, were often pursued at the expense of urgent needs of the church as a whole; and worldly considerations of government, even of art and literature, too frequently took precedence over spiritual concerns.

In dealing with secular rulers, the popes, largely as a consequence of the schism and the conciliar movement, found themselves at a disadvantage. It is noteworthy that the concordats, or arrangements made with contemporary monarchs, usually conceded to them the right of patronage. A notable example is the Concordat of 1516 made by Pope Leo X with King Francis I of France.[2] Similar arrangements had been made with certain German emperors and princes. And to the Spanish monarchy the papacy granted exceptional controls over the court of the Inquisition. Thus, to assure the assistance —or avert the hostility—of monarchs, fifteenth- and sixteenth-century popes conceded what their predecessors since the eleventh century had struggled to preserve. But the early modern monarch, unlike his eleventh-century predecessor, was not a quasi-religious figure in a religio-political society, "priest and king." Rather he was ruler of a secular state which, as it perfected its political machinery, was ready to use this to control the ecclesiastical establishment.

The new system of royal control over

---

[1] Two Eastern prelates who accepted the union, Bessarion of Nicaea and Isidore of Kiev, returned to end their days in the west after brief visits to their respective homelands. The former, it will be remembered, was highly venerated as a Greek scholar.

[2] The Concordat of 1516, it should be added, did follow a great French victory (Marignano, 1515) in Italy. Moreover, the Pope gained two important concessions. He retained the right of investiture, and he obtained the promise that the Pragmatic Sanction of Bourges (1438), which had included a statement of the superiority of Council over Pope and had proclaimed the virtual autonomy of the French church, would be renounced. The Pragmatic Sanction, it may further be added, is an early example of what came to be known as "Gallicanism," the concept of a partially independent French church.

church affairs did not, in general, promote ecclesiastical reform, but rather the opposite. There was an increase in the number of dispensations, often granted to the relatives of important personages, to hold more than one benefice or to hold ecclesiastical office before reaching the minimum canonical age. The number of major sees whose incumbents during the last half of the fifteenth century were absentees was scandalously high.[1] Similar conditions afflicted many parishes. That this had a disastrous effect on the religious life of the time is obvious. Indeed, such conditions were far more significant than the misconduct, however spectacular, of individual members of the clergy.

In one instance, however, royal control over the ecclesiastical establishment did eventually facilitate an important movement of reform. This was Spain where, it will be recalled, Cardinal Ximenes, an archbishop of Toledo, primate of the Spanish church, and grand inquisitor, obtained extensive powers which he used to promote clerical education and generally to restore proper conditions. Ximenes met much opposition, but he persisted. Moreover, the reform which he inaugurated was not at first, like that of the Gregorians in the eleventh century, an ecumenical effort. Rather it was the Spanish national church which he was restoring. But it so happened that from this Spanish reform came much of the spirit and no small part of the energy for the larger reform of the following century.

E. Popular Religious Life in the Late Middle Age

Clerical shortcomings, especially when they were widespread, or, as in the case of the Great Schism, distinctly spectacular, were bound to affect the religious attitudes of the lay masses. Religion continued to be a powerful, possibly a dominant, influence in the life of the average European. At the same time, many persons, especially among the wealthy bourgeoisie, were affected by the prevailing spirit of worldliness. Perhaps for this very reason, there was evident a greater emphasis on religious externals. Popular veneration of relics bordered on the superstitious. Pilgrimages retained and increased their popularity.

In matters of popular devotion, the border line between superstition and orthodox practice is often hard to draw. The majority of Christians in the fifteenth century were illiterate and often came into contact with poorly trained priests. And perhaps because of a general loosening of ecclesiastical discipline, various weird beliefs became alarmingly popular. One was the peculiarly sinister belief in witchcraft.[2] Almost anyone who acted oddly, and especially lonely old women who perhaps had fallen into the habit of talking to themselves, became the object of popular suspicion and resentment as bewitched allies of the devil and sources of all manner of temporal and spiritual evil. So widespread was the delusion that many authorities shared and acted upon it; and in the course of the fifteenth century there developed a kind of epidemic of searching out "witches" and putting them to death.

The witchcraft delusion was but one example of a markedly pessimistic outlook on life which prevailed in the late middle age, especially in northern Europe. Perhaps men were abnormally absorbed in the contemplation of death because, in an age of much violence and recurring pestilence, death was ever present, and life for many was hard. At any rate, popular preachers could hold audiences by discourses, not so much on the hell fires of the hereafter, as on the spiritual struggles of the dying. Treatises on *The Art of Dying* had considerable vogue, as did contemporary woodcuts which abounded in skeletons and portrayed the "dance of death." [3]

---

[1] A famous example, often cited, is the case of Valencia, all of whose bishops for a period of a hundred years were Borgias, none of them resident.

[2] Witchcraft was a distortion of the church's teaching about the real existence of evil spirits—the devil and the fallen angels—into the popular notion that man could call such evil spirits to aid him against his enemies, and that some persons, "witches," were in communion with, and actually worshipped, the devil.

[3] For an example of the vogue in art, see above, p. 290.

If the historian must describe evil or unfortunate trends in the religious life of the late Middle Age, he cannot fail to remind his readers that the irregular is always more noticeable than the average. No doubt many, perhaps the great majority, of the clergy faithfully discharged their duties without attracting attention. There were fewer canonized saints than in earlier periods, particularly among the higher clergy, but there were some. It is also noteworthy that a considerable number of persons strove for a greater inner "experience of things divine." Such striving is known as mysticism. It was not novel to the fourteenth and fifteenth centuries. Far from it. But it stood out then against a background of worldliness and it represented, too, a spiritual reaction against scholastic rationalism and against mere externalism in religion. Mystical preachers seem to have appealed particularly to townsmen, who were now less under ecclesiastical influences than formerly.

Prominent among the noted mystics of the day was a German Dominican friar, usually known as Master Eckhart (d. 1327). A man of intellectual training who fully accepted the doctrines of the church, Eckhart preached to the common folk of the towns. Eschewing the customary scholastic methods, he sought rather to move the hearts of his hearers. Although he left no writings, his influence was great, especially in the Rhineland, and can perhaps best be judged by the lives and writings of some of his disciples. Of these, the best known were John Ruysbroeck, a Dutchman, and John Tauler and Henry Suso, both Germans.[1]

A similar spirit of longing for intimate personal communion with Christ can be seen in the life and work of Gerard Groote (1340–1384) of Deventer in Holland. Groote founded the organization known as the Brethren of the Common Life to which we have already referred.[2] In 1395 the Brethren adopted the Augustinian rule, and each separate house or monastery devoted itself to the copying of manuscripts and to teaching. Indeed, the pedagogical activities of the Brethren stimulated an educational reform throughout northwestern Europe. A number of famous scholars, including the great humanist Erasmus, were alumni of their schools. But above all, the Brethren inculcated a deep love of God and of one's fellow man. This movement came to be known as the "Devotio moderna," and from it, possibly from the pen of Thomas à Kempis (d. 1471), came one of the most popular devotional books of Christian literature, the *Imitation of Christ*.

Generally speaking, the *Devotio moderna* was unsympathetic to intellectualism or rational speculation in matters of religion. Instead, it was in line with an important trend of the late middle age in theological teaching—putting emphasis on the will rather than on the intellect. An earlier chapter called attention to the direction given philosophical studies by William of Ockham (d. 1349) and his followers. Ockhamism, with its questioning of the validity of rational speculation in matters of faith and its denial of any correspondence to reality of universals, or general ideas, was prevalent in the schools of the late middle age. Partly for this reason and partly because thirteenth-century scholasticism had given way in many places to pedantic and seemingly fruitless discussion of details, there was a marked lack of vigor and originality in contemporary theological teaching.

The church in the fifteenth century had successfully frustrated all attempts to alter its ancient constitution. This was an achievement of the first importance. In its espousal of the new learning and in the promotion of art, it had given brilliant leadership. But a comparable leadership in promoting much needed spiritual renewal was lacking. It seems evident that, as an organization, the church was not meeting or reducing the tensions of the early modern age.

---

[1] An exaggeration of Eckhart's teachings led to a type of mysticism which was condemned by the pope. Martin Luther, at a later date, seems to have been influenced by doctrines of this nature.

[2] See above, p. 317.

SELECT SUPPLEMENTARY READINGS FOR PART V

General. The interpretation of the period known as the late middle age or the renaissance has been and continues to be a subject of lively discussion, much of which revolves around the classic work of J. Burckhardt, *The Civilization of the Renaissance in Italy,* first published in German in 1860 and republished and translated many times since. See the recent edition, with introduction by B. Nelson and C. Trinkhaus, 2 vols. (1958). For further study of the concept of "renaissance," see K. H. Dannenfeldt, *The Renaissance, Medieval or Modern?* (1959); W. Ferguson, *The Renaissance in Historical Thought* (1948) and *Renaissance Studies* (1963); T. Helton, ed., *A Symposium on the Renaissance* (1961). Other general works are: *Cambridge Medieval History,* vols. VII and VIII; *New Cambridge Modern History,* vol. I (1957); E. P. Cheyney, *The Dawn of a New Era* (new ed. 1960); D. Hay, *The Italian Renaissance in Its Historical Background* (1962); J. H. Plumb, ed., *The Italian Renaissance* (1964); E. Lucki, *History of the Renaissance,* 5 vols. (1963–1965); M. P. Gilmore, *The World of Humanism* (1952); J. Huizinga, *The Waning of the Middle Ages* (1927); G. C. Sellery, *The Renaissance, Its Nature and Origins* (1950).

Chapter 22. *Cambridge Economic History of Europe,* 3 vols. (1941, 1952, 1961); R. de Roover, *The Medici Bank* (1948), also *Money, Banking and Credit in Medieval Bruges* (1948) and *Rise and Decline of the Medici Bank* (1963).

Chapter 23. A. Buchan, *Joan of Arc and the Recovery of France* (1958); H. Cam, *England before Elizabeth* (1950); O. Cartellieri, *The Court of Burgundy* (1929); P. Champion, *Louis XI* (tr. 1929); E. F. Jacob, *The Fifteenth Century* (England) (1961); M. M. McKisack, *The Fourteenth Century* (England) (1959); A. R. Myers, *England in the Later Middle Ages* (1952); E. Perroy, *The Hundred Years' War* (1951); G. M. Trevelyan, *England in the Age of Wycliffe* (1909); R. Pernoud, *Joan of Arc* (1961).

Chapter 24. G. Barraclough, *The Origins of Modern Germany* (1947); J. D. Clarkson, *A History of Russia* (1961); O. Halecki, *Borderlands of Western Civilization* (1952); A. W. A. Leeper, *A History of Medieval Austria* (1941); G. Vernadsky and M. Karpovich, *A History of Russia,* vol. III (1953).

Chapter 25. T. J. Oleson, *Early Voyages and Northern Approaches, 1000–1632* (1964). On Spain and Portugal, in addition to books cited above for chapter 17: J. H. Mariéjol, *The Spain of Ferdinand and Isabella* (tr. 1961). For the discoveries: B. W. Diffie, *Prelude to Empire: Portugal Overseas Before Henry the Navigator* (1960); J. E. Gillespie, *A History of Geographical Discovery* (1933); S. E. Morison, *Admiral of the Ocean Sea* (Columbus), 2 vols. (1942, and also a one-volume edition); S. E. Morison and M. Obregón, *The Caribbean as Columbus Saw It* (1964); A. P. Newton, *The Great Age of Discovery* (1932); E. Prestage, *The Portuguese Pioneers* (1933); E. Sanceau, *Henry the Navigator* (1947); C. McK. Parr, *Ferdinand Magellan, Circumnavigator* (1964); C. E. Nowell, ed., *Magellan's Voyage Around the World: Three Contemporary Accounts* (1962); P. Sykes, *A History of Exploration* (new ed., 1960). For Italy: W. M. Bowsky, *Henry VII in Italy* (1960); H. B. Cotterill, *Italy from Dante to Tasso* (1919); F. Chabod, *Machiavelli and the Renaissance* (1959); G. Mattingly,

Renaissance Diplomacy (1955); F. Schevill, *The Medici* (new ed., 1949), *History of Florence* (new ed., 1961), and *Siena* (new ed. with introduction by W. M. Bowsky, 1964).

Chapter 26. In addition to the books cited under "General," above: R. Bolgar, *The Classical Heritage and Its Beneficiaries* (1954); R. W. Chambers, *Thomas More* (1935); J. Fletcher, *The Literature of the Italian Renaissance* (1934); J. Huizinga, *Erasmus* (tr. 1924); P. O. Kristeller, *The Classics and Renaissance Thought* (1955, new ed., 1961). On science, H. Butterfield, *The Origins of Modern Science* (1949); A. C. Crombie, *Medieval and Early Modern Science* (1959). For art, in addition to Gardner. Janson, and Pevsner cited above, p. 49; B. Lowry, *Renaissance Architecture* (1962); O. Benesch, *The Art of the Renaissance in Northern Europe* (1945). On music: P. H. Lang, *Music in Western Civilization* (1941). On printing: P. Butler, *The Origin of Printing in Europe* (1940); D. C. McMurtrie, *The Book, the Story of Printing and Bookmaking* (3rd ed., 1943).

Chapter 27. L. E. Binns, *Decline and Fall of the Medieval Papacy* (1934); A. C. Flick, *The Decline of the Medieval Church* (1930); P. Hughes, *A History of the Church*, vol. III (1947); A. Hyma, *The Christian Renaissance, a History of the "Devotia Moderna"* (1924); J. Gill, *The Council of Florence* (1959); G. Mollat, *The Popes at Avignon, 1305–1378* (new tr. 1963).

From Charles V
and Luther
to Gustavus
Adolphus
and Philip IV

PART VI

EARLY MODERN

RELIGIOUS UPHEAVAL

The interior of the Jesuit church of the Gesù in Rome (Vignola, d. 1573), redecorated
seventeenth century.

TIMES AND

IN THE WEST

Sixteenth century limestone medallions of the Emperor Charles V and his consort, Isabel of Portugal.

Courtesy Hispanic Society of America

Wᴇ DESCRIBE as "Early Modern Times" the sixteenth century and the first half of the seventeenth. In most respects they are but a continuation of the "Late Middle Age" of the fourteenth and fifteenth centuries. There is continuity in the strengthening of national monarchy, in the growth of commercial capitalism, in the development of printing, classical renaissance, and vernacular literature, in the menacing advance of the Moslem Turks in the "East," and in the expansion of the "West" across the Atlantic and into America.

The outstanding novelty of Early Modern Times is a religious upheaval throughout western and central Europe. It finds expression in a forceful revolt against the Catholic Church in the northern half of Germany and the Netherlands, in Scandinavia, Switzerland, England, and Scotland, and the establishment of a variety of separate Protestant churches and sects. It also finds expression in a reformation within the Catholic Church and a renewed zeal which enables it to maintain its hold on a majority of European countries and at the same time to secure compensation for its losses in Europe by missionary gains in America and the Far East.

The religious upheaval produces extraordinary bitterness and intolerance on the part of both Protestants and Catholics, and a series of religio-political wars. These wars begin with the unavailing efforts of the Emperor Charles V, in the first half of the sixteenth century, to keep the Holy Roman Empire strong and united and to use it, in conjunction with his Spanish inheritance, to dominate the Continent. They continue with the farflung but largely unsuccessful attempts of his son, Philip II, in the second half of the sixteenth century, to secure the supremacy of Spain and the defeat of Protestantism. They conclude with the Thirty Years' War, in the first half of the seventeenth century, when religious factors yield to dynastic and commercial, when political hegemony passes from Spain to France, and when the practical collapse of the Holy Roman Empire finally dispels any hope of providing a central power for a united Western Christendom.

CHAPTER 28

Emperor Charles V in Europe, Overseas and Against the Turks

A. Charles the First of Spain and Fifth of the Holy Roman Empire

When Charles was born in Ghent in 1500, it was clear that he would one day come into an extensive inheritance, but few could have realized that he would be lord of wider dominions than had been ruled by any previous European monarch. When he was six years old, the death of his father, Philip of Habsburg, gave him possession of the Netherlands and Imperial Burgundy (Franche Comté). When he was sixteen, the death of his grandfather Ferdinand made him King Charles I of Spain, with its dependencies in Italy and overseas in America. At nineteen, the death of his grandfather Maximilian brought him all the hereditary territories of the Habsburgs and the expectation of being chosen Holy Roman Emperor.

Though the title of emperor had come down in the Habsburg family continuously since 1438, the office was still elective, and in 1519 there were in addition to Charles two young and ambitious rulers who put forward their candidacies: Henry VIII of England, and Francis I of France. The latter was the more formidable rival in the election. By diplomacy and bribes Francis sought to win the backing of the church and the votes of the electors. Charles already ruled so many lands that it could easily be argued that he would have little time to devote to Germany or to his duties as Emperor.

But in the election Charles had certain advantages. The tradition of electing the Habsburgs was strong, and as a Habsburg Charles seemed more like a German than did Francis. In addition, Charles had special friends among the bankers of the time, and with their aid he was better able to play the game of bribery than his rival. He borrowed some money for the purpose from the Medici at Florence, and still more from the Fuggers, the German banking family of Augsburg which had long been loaning money to the Habsburgs. The Fuggers now surpassed the Medici and had more funds at their disposal than any other bankers in Europe. They had branch offices in Antwerp and a dozen other cities from which they financed merchants, towns, provinces, and kings. When the head of the house of Fugger, Jacob the Rich, opened his purse to Charles, it meant that the bribes of Francis could be easily matched and exceeded. In 1519 Charles gained the election, and in 1520 he was crowned as the Emperor Charles V at Aix-la-Chapelle (Aachen).

It was a sign of the times that capitalists could help make emperors. In the fifteenth century the center of capitalistic credit and banking had been in northern Italy, and particularly with the Medici family at Florence. But in the early sixteenth century it passed to Augsburg in southern Germany, where the family firms of the Welsers, the Hochstetters, the Meutings, and others

339

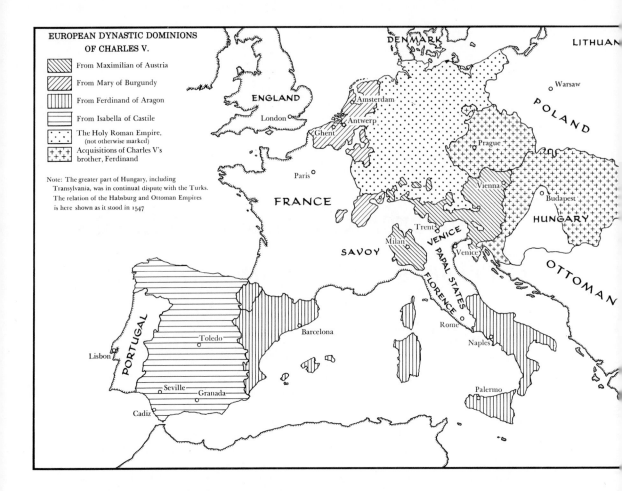

vied with the Fuggers. Many of the banker-merchants financed commercial and industrial ventures, but the Fuggers had two main interests—mining, and loans to the Habsburgs. They reaped rich profits from the copper, silver, and lead mines of the Tyrol and of Hungary. They loaned more and more money to the Habsburgs, until in 1560 Charles' son, Philip II of Spain, owed them some 4,000,000 gold gulden, a gigantic sum for those days.

Most of the great German and Italian bankers had offices in one of Charles' cities, Antwerp in the Netherlands. For by the sixteenth century Antwerp had displaced the older city of Bruges as the commercial center of northern and western Europe. There the products of the north, especially English cloth, were exchanged for those of the Mediterranean and for the new goods that began to come in from America and the Far East. Antwerp had a great Bourse, or Exchange (opened in 1460), for trade in

goods, and another (opened in 1531) for financial transactions such as loans to merchants and kings. Its river harbor was thronged with shipping, its streets crowded with drays and carts. To Charles V, it was a great source of strength that he was ruler of the rich Netherlands and of the busy city of Antwerp.

Because he had been born in the Netherlands, had lived there during his boyhood, and spoke the local language (Flemish or Dutch), Charles V always thought of himself more as a Netherlander than as an Austrian or a Spaniard. He knew how to deal familiarly and in friendly fashion with the rich burghers of the towns. They, in turn, regarded him with pride and affection and even paid the taxes he levied without too much murmuring or discontent. In Spain, on the contrary, Charles was regarded, when he went there first in 1517, as a foreigner and he did not increase his popularity by making use there of advisers

Francis I of France about 1525.
Jean Clouet.

Cuortesy Louvre Museum, Paris

and officials from the Netherlands. There was some hostility to him and even open revolt in various Spanish cities (1519–1520). But though Charles looked upon Spain merely as a source of wealth and military strength, he was able to crush all opposition and rule the country with a firm hand.

Charles was indeed an able ruler, who could adapt himself to the needs of the moment. If he was amiable in Ghent, he could be haughty in Madrid and stern in Vienna. Though he was afraid of mice and spiders, he was an able and courageous general on the field of battle. He could persuade as well as command, and he could employ guileful diplomacy as well as military force. All his life he showed a deep devotion to the Catholic faith. Thin of face and with the protruding lower jaw of the Habsburgs, Charles was anything but handsome. Yet his dignity and bearing were those of the great monarch that he truly was.

B. Wars of Charles V in Europe

During most of his reign, Charles V was at war with France. The French monarchy, which had done much to reëstablish itself following the Hundred Years' War, had, before the end of the fifteenth century, intervened actively in the affairs of Italy. The French King Charles VIII's expedition of 1494 has been discussed in a previous chapter. His successor, Louis XII (1498–1515) of the house of Orleans, continued the policy, adding the Orleanist claims to Milan to the older French-Angevin pretensions to Naples.[1] His efforts were unavailing, and they resulted, among other things, in the Spanish occupation of Naples (1504).

Louis' successor, Francis I (1515–1547), was therefore continuing an old Franco-Spanish rivalry both in pushing war into Italy and in attempting to win the Pyrenees

[1] Louis XII was the grandson of Valentina Visconti. See above, p. 280 *n.*

kingdom of Navarre which Ferdinand of Aragon had absorbed in 1512. But to Francis the entire complex of Habsburg territories offered a new problem. For it seemed as if these territories, more especially Spain, Franche Comté, and the Netherlands, were encircling France. On the other hand, Charles was determined to oppose all French pretensions beyond their frontiers and if possible to regain the French duchy of Burgundy which had been taken from his grandmother by Louis XI of France.

The war between Francis and Charles was, therefore, of wider scope than previous Franco-Spanish conflicts. Though it was fought at first mainly in Italy, it soon extended to other theatres. With various truces and treaties as interruptions, it was to be continued for more than a century. This series of conflicts was dynastic rather than national in character, in that disputes over inheritance and succession often outweighed more fundamental national interests.

By a brilliant victory at Marignano (1515), shortly after his accession, Francis regained Milan, which had been recently lost by Louis XII. But the forces of Charles V, aided by the pope, drove the French out again and went on to invade France. In turn, Francis pushed the Emperor's troops back. Finally, at Pavia in 1525, the army of Charles V completely crushed the French army and captured the French King. "Nothing is left to me," wrote Francis I to his mother, "save honor and life."

Francis won his release by agreeing to humiliating peace terms. But no sooner was he back in France, than he busied himself in winning the support of the pope and of other Italian rulers who were dismayed by the growing power of Charles. Hostilities were soon resumed, and the pope paid dearly for his change of sides, for in 1527 the unpaid and unruly soldiery of Charles V sacked and pillaged the city of Rome. Despite some aid from England, Francis made little headway, and the peace of Cambrai (1529) left all Italy under the rule or the influence of Charles V.

To make trouble for Charles, Francis sought help wherever he could find it. He made alliances with Scotland, Sweden, and Denmark, with rebellious princes in Germany, and even with the infidel Turks. Fighting occurred again from 1536 to 1538, and from 1542 to 1544. Neither the death of Francis I (1547) nor the abdication of Charles V (1556) ended the struggle, for war raged again from 1552 until the peace of Cateau-Cambrésis in 1559. By this treaty, France renounced once again its claims in Italy, leaving the entire peninsula under the control of Charles' Habsburg successors in Austria and Spain. But France gained something, for she was permitted to occupy the bishoprics of Metz, Toul, and Verdun, which were located in a position of high strategic importance on the northeast frontier of France, and gave to the French a foothold in Alsace and thus in the Holy Roman Empire.

From a larger point of view, the French gained by these many wars for they had checked somewhat the rising power of the

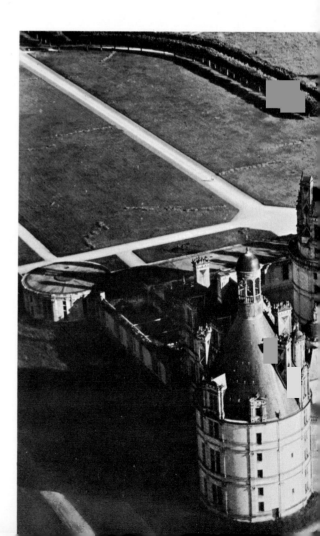

Habsburgs. In so doing they had adopted a policy of alliance with the Protestant princes of Germany which was to continue and to be intensified in the following century. Thus France had indirectly aided not only the Turks, but also the growth of Protestantism in Germany, by keeping Charles busy with foreign wars, when he might well have been putting down the ecclesiastical revolt in the Empire.

The difficulties in Germany were not merely the religious ones which will be examined in the next chapter. The German princes, great and small, were eagerly trying to increase their political power. They had made Charles, at his election as Emperor, grant them added rights over government and policy, and they could arouse a good deal of German national sentiment against him by painting him as a foreigner dominated by Spanish or other alien interests. Then, too, the rich burghers of the German

towns opposed any taxes which would have increased the Emperor's power.

The lesser German nobility—the knights—under such fiery leaders as Ulrich von Hutten and Franz von Sickingen, were the most patriotic class, proud of being German and distrustful of foreign influence. At the beginning of his reign it looked as if Charles V could depend on the knights to help him against the princes and burghers. But at this very time, many of the knights welcomed the new Protestant movement as a way to end "foreign" control of the church in Germany. Thus when Charles took steps against the Protestants (1521) he alienated the knights. The next year under von Sickingen, the knights took arms and attacked the Catholic bishopric of Trier. Since the burghers and princes hated the unruly knights, they joined together and crushed them.

Nor were these the only troubles Charles

French sixteenth century castle architecture. Chambord, the favorite residence of King Francis I.

Courtesy French Government Tourist Office, New York

had to face in Germany, for the Lutheran princes banded together in a League at Schmalkald in 1531 and waged civil war off and on from 1546 to 1555, when the Peace of Augsburg temporarily settled the religious conflict.[1] Thus Charles V had on his hands not only almost continuous war with France, a foreign foe, but also almost equally continuous difficulties within Germany. To add to his problems, there was the ever-present threat to the east, the menace of the Moslem Turks.

C. Wars of Charles V against the Turks

Charles was concerned with the Turkish menace not only as Emperor and traditionally responsible for the Empire's eastern frontiers, but more particularly as Archduke of Austria and guardian of Vienna and the Danube valley. Moreover, his reign almost coincided with that of the greatest and ablest of the Turkish Sultans, Suleiman the "Magnificent" (1520–1566).

When Suleiman came to the throne at Constantinople, the Turks had already overrun most of the Balkan peninsula and the new Sultan soon renewed the victorious drive northward. In 1521 he captured Belgrade, and all of Serbia was soon under his sway. One of his greatest victories came five years later (1526) when he overwhelmed the Hungarian army on the field of Mohács. There perished a great portion of the Hungarian knights and nobles, and the king of Hungary (Louis II) fell on the field of battle. In 1529, Suleiman led his armies onward and laid siege to Vienna itself. All Christian Europe seemed threatened as the eastern marches crumbled. So strong was the defense of Vienna, however, that Suleiman raised the siege after three weeks, though his forces ravaged the surrounding countryside.

In the meanwhile, Ferdinand of Habsburg, brother of Charles V, laid claim to the throne of Hungary, secured his election to it, and tried to carry on the war against the Turks, more, perhaps, to acquire and defend new lands for himself than to free Hungary from the infidel. In 1547, Charles and Ferdinand were compelled to recognize

---

[1] See below, p. 354.

the Turkish conquests in Hungary. By an agreement of that year, Suleiman left Ferdinand in possession of thirty-five counties of Hungary for which he agreed to pay the Turks a heavy annual tribute. The largest part of the country, including Budapest, became a Turkish province, while a third section centering in Transylvania was left under Turkish influence, though it was to be ruled by a Hungarian prince. Twice (1552 and 1566) did the Habsburgs try to conquer Transylvania, and twice Suleiman defeated them and consolidated the Turkish power. In many Hungarian towns, churches were turned into mosques.

The Hungarian King who fell at Mohács, Louis II, was also the elective King of Bohemia, still part of the Holy Roman Empire. After his death the Bohemians, in desperate fear of the advancing Turks, and wanting a ruler who could defend them, chose Ferdinand of Habsburg. Consequently, though it was not until the end of the following century that all of Hungary was recovered from the Turks, it and Bohemia were added to the Habsburg domains, to remain as such for nearly four hundred years.

Although at least nominal suzerainty over parts of central and western North Africa was claimed by the Turks, this was opposed by Charles who, as King of Spain and the Two Sicilies, was responsible for the Mediterranean interests of these countries. Since the fourteenth century the Spanish had held a small, fortified, rock island in front of the harbor of Algiers. In 1519 they sought to capture the city itself, whither had fled many of the Moors who had been expelled from Granada in 1492. The Spanish attack was repelled by a Turkish sea rover and admiral known as Khair-ed-Din, or Barbarossa (Redbeard), who had made himself master of the city and placed himself under the rule of the Turkish Sultan Suleiman the "Magnificent." Ten years later Barbarossa drove the Spanish even from their islet fortress.

To the east of Algiers, the same Barbarossa was also successful. Acting for Suleiman, he secured possession of Tunis. Then to check the expanding Turkish power in the Mediterranean, Charles V intervened. In 1535, with the Emperor in personal command of the army and a Genoese admiral, Andrea Doria, in charge of the fleet, a Spanish expedition conquered Tunis and installed a native ruler as a Spanish vassal. Though the Spaniards long held strong fortresses on the Tunisian coast, they were never able to establish a firm rule over the country and in 1574 they were driven out and Tunisia became a Turkish province.

The Turkish rule at Algiers seemed to Charles V a special threat to the safety of Spanish commerce and even to Spain itself. Accordingly, in 1541, he led a large force against the city. But his luck was bad, for a storm destroyed many of his ships and his army of 30,000 men was defeated by the Algerians under a native prince, or pasha. In the ensuing years, the Moslem Barbarossa took a fleet to the south coast of France to support Francis I against Charles V, and on his way back to Constantinople the Turkish admiral ravaged and plundered the coast of Italy.

These forays and repulses in North Africa were really part of a great renewed struggle between Christian and Moslem for naval control of the Mediterranean. On the one side was Charles V, usually in alliance with Venice whose possessions among the islands and ports of the Near East were menaced. On the other side was Suleiman the Magnificent, aided by roving sea fighters like Barbarossa. On the whole, the Turks won in the first phases of the struggle, for they increased their control of North Africa, gained strong points on the Dalmatian coast across the Adriatic from Venice, conquered island after island, and repeatedly attacked the coasts of Sicily, South Italy, and even the Balearic Islands.

The crisis of the struggle was not reached till after both Suleiman and Charles V were dead. In 1570, a Turkish fleet captured Cyprus from the Venetians. Only Malta and Crete were left as Christian outposts in the eastern Mediterranean. Inspired by Pope Pius V, Genoa, Venice, and Spain joined with him to send a great fleet of 208 ships against the Moslems. It was led by Don John of Austria, a son of Charles V. On October 7, 1571, he inflicted a crushing defeat on a Turkish fleet of 273 vessels in

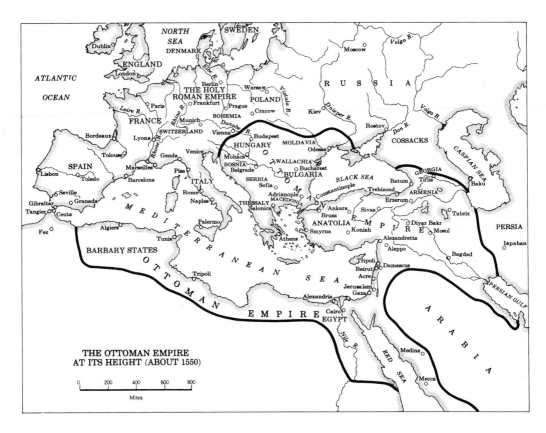

THE OTTOMAN EMPIRE
AT ITS HEIGHT (ABOUT 1550)

0   200   400   600   800

Miles

the mouth of the Gulf of Lepanto. The cannon and tactics of the Christians proved superior. Most of the Turkish warships were sunk or driven ashore. Twenty thousand Turks, it is said, lost their lives.

The battle of Lepanto was the last great sea fight fought by large fleets of galleys. It was also in many ways the last of the Crusades. But it was more than that, for it marked a check to their sea power from which the Turks never recovered. Slowly their naval strength in the Mediterranean dwindled. In the seventeenth century, Moslem activity at sea was to be mainly in the form of piratical forays from cities like Algiers and Tunis on the north shore of Africa.

D. Charles and the Spanish and Portuguese Dominions Overseas

When Charles came to the throne of Spain in 1516, the foundations of the great Spanish overseas dominion had been laid. The work of Columbus and other explorers had made known the West Indies and much of the coasts of northern South America and of Central America. In 1513 Balboa had crossed the isthmus of Panama and seen the Pacific, while in the same year Ponce de Leon had discovered Florida. It was now, of course, universally realized that these lands were not Asia or the East Indies, but a "new world;" and it had been named "America." [1] The Portuguese meanwhile had been not only exploring and conquering important eastern areas from the Persian Gulf to the Spice Islands, but had also, through the work of Cabral, discovered and laid claim to the coast of Brazil. In order to arbitrate the rival claims of Spain and Portugal, Pope Alexander VI had drawn a "line of demarkation" (1493), as we have already said, from the north to the south pole, a hundred leagues west of the Azores, and then, by subsequent mutual agreement, the line had been moved some 270 leagues farther west. All lands to the east of the line (including Brazil, Africa, India and the East Indies) were to be a Portuguese monopoly for trade and colonization. All lands to the west of it (including the West Indies, North America, Central America, and

South America, minus Brazil) were to be a Spanish monopoly.

In the years after 1516 the Spaniards pushed ahead rapidly with their tremendous work of exploring and conquering new lands. In 1519, an expedition under Alvarez de Piñeda sailed along the coast from Florida to Mexico. In the same year Ferdinand Magellan, a Portuguese in the service of Spain, set out with five ships and 243 men to open up a way to the East Indies by going south of South America. The expedition found a strait between the continent and Tierra del Fuego, crossed the Pacific, and discovered the Philippines where Magellan was killed in a fight with the natives. In 1522, one of his ships, the *Victoria*, got back to Spain with eighteen men. The world had been circumnavigated and no one could longer doubt that it was round or that the East could be reached by sailing west.

It was likewise in 1519 that the young

_____
[1] See above, p. 303.

The Sultan Ahmet (Blue) Mosque in Istanbul (Constantinople), a sixteenth century building in which the Turks developed further the structural principles of Santa Sophia (in left background).

Courtesy Turkish Information Office, New York

Spaniard Hernando Cortez landed on the coast of Mexico with six or seven hundred men, eighteen horses, and a few cannon. Within a few years, he had accomplished the seemingly impossible, and conquered the rich and populous empire of the native Aztec Indians. A few years later, Francisco Pizarro conquered the extensive South American empire of the Incas.

The great work of the conquest forced Spain to develop a colonial system for the management of her new dominions. This task had been begun under Ferdinand and Isabella, but it really took definite form under Charles. Political control of the colonies was in the hands of a Council of the Indies. This Council sat as a court in important cases, made laws like a legislature, appointed viceroys, governors, and other officials, administered church affairs, and determined policies. Through it, the King was able to maintain firm control over all phases of colonial life.

In their treatment of the natives, the Spaniards were torn by two conflicting motives. On the one hand, bishops, priests, monks and friars, who had gone out from the homeland to win souls, wished to convert the natives and to treat them in a kindly manner as potential fellow Christians. On the other hand, many conquistadores and landowners, in their lust for wealth, were tempted to exploit the natives. In general, it may be said that the laws issued by the central government at Madrid were designed to protect the natives. But, such was the great distance between Spain and America, and so many were the involvements of the Spanish monarchy in Europe, that the laws were not effectively implemented. Thus it befell, for example, that after the native kingdoms had been despoiled of their gold and silver and the Spaniards had taken over the mines, the Indians were forced to provide the mine labor.

SPANISH AND PORTUGUESE
AMERICA IN THE SIXTEENTH
CENTURY

Spanish possessions

Portuguese possessions

In 1545, Potosí in Peru, a veritable mountain of silver, was opened up, and other mines scarcely less rich were soon developed. For a century the New World was to pour a vast stream of silver into the Old. So great was this influx of precious metal that with it Spain could pay soldiers, build fleets, and bribe diplomats throughout the sixteenth century. It was this wealth, mined out of the earth by Indian laborers, that helped to make Spain the predominant country in Europe.

Not all Indians were treated badly. In the missions established by Franciscans, Dominicans, Jesuits, and other religious orders, many were protected with paternal kindness and taught the arts and crafts of civilized life. There were always some Spaniards who preached and worked against their greedy fellow countrymen and in behalf of the native Indians. For example, Bartolomé de Las Casas (1474–1566), Bishop of Chiapas in Mexico, is known as the Apostle of the Indies, because he devoted his every effort to champion the Indians and to secure laws which would improve their lot.

While the Spanish were creating a colonial empire in the new world, the Portuguese were building an empire of a different type in the east. Their far-flung possessions constituted a commercial rather than a colonial empire. The interest of the Portuguese centered in the spice trade over which they rapidly acquired a virtual monopoly. Two great leaders, Almeida, an admiral, and Albuquerque, a viceroy, followed up between 1505 and 1515 da Gama's voyage by ousting Arab traders and securing ports from the Persian Gulf to the Spice Islands. With their naval supremacy they held, fortified, and garrisoned the cities they captured and used them as centers of trade. Relatively little attempt was made to colonize or to extend Portuguese control beyond the coastal cities, for with a population of less than two million Portugal had little manpower to spare, and the Far Eastern countries were already densely inhabited.

Portuguese trade to the East was a royal monopoly, at least as regarded the all important spices. It was carried on by royal officials, with royal money, on royal ships. The profits were the king's and they were very great, for the Portuguese were able to buy pepper and other spices cheap in the East and sell them dear in Europe. Even so they undersold the Venetians, whose trade by the expensive overland routes rapidly dwindled after 1500. It was to Lisbon that ships came from all countries to secure the eastern spices. Until almost 1600, this little country of Portugal held all the storied eastern trade in its hands. When finally the Dutch and English broke into their preserve, then and only then did the Portuguese give much serious attention to their one great American colony of Brazil.

Thus it was that, for a hundred years after the original voyages of Columbus and da Gama, the countries which profited from the new discoveries were Spain and Portugal. Moreover, when the Spaniards—and later the Portuguese—settled in the New World, they were performing one of the major feats of modern history. They were transferring to that new and distant world their language, their religion, and Europe's Western civilization. By 1600 there were 150,000 Spaniards in America. Their political system was organized, and they were divided ecclesiastically into four archbishoprics and twenty-four bishoprics, including some 360 monasteries and convents. In some degree, European customs were merely superimposed on persisting native cultures. And it was some time before the schools and seminaries could rival their European counterparts. But if the universities of Mexico City and Lima had only small enrollment and limited facilities at the time of their establishment in 1551, they were the first institutions of higher learning in the New World. In many ways all the Americas south of the Rio Grande, with the exception of Brazil, were being made indelibly Spanish.

Such were the manifold concerns of the Emperor Charles V. They were, in fact, too much for one man. On his abdication in 1556, it had been decided that his eldest son, Philip, should inherit all his possessions with the exception of the Austrian lands and the presumption of election to the imperial title. These were to go to Charles' brother, Ferdinand. The formal act of abdication took place in the Netherlands where Charles had always been beloved. Worn out and broken in health by his many labors, he resigned his crowns, shed some tears, and went into retirement in a little house attached to a monastery in Spain.

Martin Luther and his friends. Lucas Cranach (d. 1553). Although John Frederick, Elector of Saxony and nephew of Frederick the Wise who had first protected Luther, dominates the picture, Luther can be seen at the extreme left, Melancthon at the extreme right, and Zwingli between Melancthon and the Elector.

Courtesy Toledo Museum of Art;
gift of Edward Drummond Libbey, 1926

Title page of Luther's German translation of the Bible. Printed by Hans Lufft, Wittenberg, 1534.

Courtesy New York Public Library

CHAPTER 29

Protestant Revolt Against the Catholic Church

LUTHERANISM AND CALVINISM

A. Catholic Beliefs

Early in the sixteenth century the Catholic church which, except for occasional heresies, had universal acceptance throughout western and central Europe, was subjected to a major revolt which resulted in the formation of several new and separate, or as they came to be called, "Protestant," churches. The original Protestant movements from which others later diverged were three in number: (1) Lutheranism and (2) Calvinism, each so designated from the name of its founder, and (3) Anglicanism, named from the country of its origin. The weakness and corruption of the early sixteenth-century church, which a previous chapter has described,[1] contributed much to the spread of Protestantism. So also did certain political and economic factors. But Protestantism, at least in its origin, was essentially religious and involved serious questionings of basic doctrines of the Catholic faith. It may be well, therefore, to review briefly the principal articles of the Catholic faith in order better to understand where Protestants diverged.

Of central importance, it will be recalled, was belief in the Trinity, in the divinity of Jesus Christ, and in a divinely established church which, under the pope, was the ordained instrument to enable sinful human beings to attain salvation in the next world. The church was the custodian and dispenser of the sacraments. These, seven in number, were baptism, confirmation, confession

---

[1] See above, pp. 325–333.

and penance, the holy eucharist or Mass, extreme unction for the sick and dying, matrimony, and holy orders. Baptism was held to be essential for salvation since it cleansed the individual of all sin. Around the Eucharist or Lord's Supper, during which, at the words of the priest, the bread and wine were considered to be miraculously transformed into the very Body and Blood of Christ (transubstantiation), there had developed the elaborate and beautiful ritual of the Mass. The Mass, it should be added, was believed to be a sacrifice, a continuation of the sacrifice of Christ in his crucifixion.

In addition to these fundamental tenets, there had developed in the course of the centuries certain beliefs and practices which, although peripheral to the central articles of faith, had obtained widespread popularity. Indeed, it was the contention of some that certain of these, such as the invocation of saints and the issuance of indulgences, were often pursued at the expense of more important matters.

Since the distribution of indulgences was to precipitate the revolt of 1517, they require special explanation here. An indulgence, according to Catholic teaching, was the remission, in whole or in part, of the temporal punishment to be meted out to a person after his death for sins for which he had been sincerely sorry and had done penance. By means of an indulgence, the punishment of a soul in purgatory, the abode of those not yet ready for heaven, might be shortened (partial indulgence) or done away with altogether (plenary indulgence) by virtue of the authority conferred by Christ upon St. Peter to hold and use the "keys of the kingdom of heaven" and to "bind and loose" upon earth. In earlier times, indulgences were obtainable only after the performance of rather arduous tasks such as pilgrimages or crusades. Latterly, it had become customary only to require the penitent to say certain prayers or to perform some simple religious act. Among these might be a contribution of money for some religious purpose. The doctrine of indulgences was an extremely important matter in the early months of the Lutheran movement. After that, not being a tenet of major importance, it dropped into the background.

B. Luther and Lutheranism

Martin Luther (1483–1546) was born into a family of modest means. His father was a miner, able to give his son an education, and hopeful that he would follow the law. But Martin, a sensitive youth, entered the religious life as an Augustinian friar. He had studied at the university of Erfurt and he later taught at Wittenberg in Saxony. Intelligent and eloquent, though making no pretense at erudition, he was much influenced by the ideas of the *Devotio moderna* and by the contemporary philosophical and theological current of Ockhamism with its questioning of the role of the intellect in religious speculation.

Luther did not find in the religious life that inner peace which he sought. And as he studied the writings of St. Augustine and St. Paul, he gradually reached the conviction that, as a consequence of original sin, man's will was so corrupt as to be unable to do any works which could be "good" in the sight of God. Man could be saved, or in this life "justified," Luther came to think, not by anything he did but only by faith in God's infinite mercy. In other words, he was developing a doctrine of salvation, or justification, by faith alone, in opposition to the traditional Catholic doctrine of salvation through faith, sacraments, and good works.

Although Luther's ideas had grave theo-

Desiderius Erasmus. Hans Holbein the Younger (d. 1543).

Courtesy Louvre Museum, Paris

logical implication, it is possible that he might not have pursued them to further conclusions had it not been for the appearance in Wittenberg of an exceptionally glaring combination of ecclesiastical abuses. Pope Leo X, absorbingly interested in raising money to rebuild the great basilica of St. Peter's at Rome, had issued indulgences for which financial payments would be made and devoted to the cause. These indulgences were not popular and were not, in fact, preached in many places in Europe. But the young Albert of Hohenzollern was willing to permit their preaching in his German lands in return for one half of the proceeds. With this money he hoped to repay a debt to the banking house of Fugger which he had incurred in order to pay the pope for a dispensation to hold three episcopal sees at one time.

Now in 1517, the agent sent to Germany to dispose of the indulgences, a man named Tetzel, was employing methods that would today be termed those of high-pressure salesmanship. The commercial aspects of the transactions were heightened by the fact that agents of the banking house of the Fuggers accompanied Tetzel and took charge of the money that came in so as to ensure the repayment of certain loans they had made. To a considerable number of both clergy and laity, it appeared as if Tetzel was scandalously selling for cash something wholly spiritual.

It was this scandal which prompted Martin Luther to post on the church door at Wittenberg ninety-five *theses* or assertions which were designed to promote debate on the subject. But it must be emphasized that in his theses, Luther, who already had questioned the efficacy of "good works," was not only objecting to Tetzel and his methods, but was also questioning a commonly accepted doctrine and even the necessity of the church as an intermediary between man and God. "The Christian who has true repentance," wrote Luther, "has already received pardon from God altogether apart from an indulgence, and does not need one."

Probably Luther had, as yet, no intention of separating himself from the church. But as his theses were translated from Latin into German and circulated widely, he found himself in the midst of a growing protest to which he soon gave effective leadership. In 1519, in debates with prominent theologians, he began openly to question the status of both pope and church council and to proclaim that ultimate religious authority resided in Scripture. Even more significant were two pamphlets issued in 1520, the one calling on the German princes to take the initiative in purging the church of error, and the other, stating more explicitly his religious beliefs. Only two of the traditional seven sacraments, baptism and the eucharist, should be retained. In the latter, which was no longer considered a sacrifice, the doctrine of "consubstantiation" was substituted for transubstantiation. This meant that the bread and wine were not transformed into the Body and Blood of Christ, but that Christ was really present *with* and *in* the elements as fire is in a hot iron, to use Luther's own figure of speech.

In 1521, Pope Leo X excommunicated Luther, and the Diet of the Holy Roman Empire, meeting at Worms, placed him under the ban. Luther, however, was protected from both Pope and Emperor by the Elector of Saxony, Frederick the Wise; and he at once devoted himself to making a new German translation of the Bible which is still prized as a monument of German literature. Thus the break between Luther and the Catholic church was complete, and, despite many attempts of reasonable and moderate men to heal the breach, it widened and deepened.

Within the next few years, the Lutheran teachings spread like wildfire throughout northern and central Germany. They appealed to devout persons who were shocked by abuses in the church, to the worldly who saw a chance to appropriate church lands and riches for themselves, to patriots who wanted to nationalize the church, and to princes and nobles who were eager to increase their political power, as well as to those university professors and students who were impressed by Luther's theological arguments. To the movement, Luther gave effective leadership. Tirelessly he preached fiery sermons and wrote inflammatory pamphlets. German princes and peasants, burghers and clergymen rose against the church, seized its property, and abolished traditional forms of worship.

The peasants, in fact, went much too far to please princes and landlords. More victimized than any other class by the existing social and economic system, and now aroused by Luther's teachings and spurred on by fanatical leaders, the peasants thought the time had come to get rid of their economic burdens as well as their allegiance to the church. To us in the twentieth century, their demands seem quite modest. They wanted such things as the abolition of serfdom, the payment of wages for work done, the right freely to hunt and fish. They rose in open revolt in 1524 not only against the church but against their landlords and princes, many of whom had already repudiated Catholicism and become Lutheran.

Luther, appealed to by both sides, had a difficult decision to make. Shocked by the excesses of the rough peasantry, he chose the side of the nobles, and ended by urging them to put down the rising by any means available. The revolt was crushed in blood, and some fifty thousand peasants were slain. As a result not only did the lot of the peasants become worse in most of Germany, but Luther's influence among them declined, especially in south Germany.

Luther also failed to win wide support from among the humanists. Erasmus, for example, first saw in Luther simply one who might force the issue of much needed reform. Erasmus, however, was opposed not only to violence, but to any alteration in the fundamentals of the Catholic faith. It is significant, too, that Erasmus chose to break with Luther by publishing a pamphlet defending the freedom of the human will.

There was one humanist, however, who followed Luther. Melancthon became his right-hand man and a sort of unofficial theologian for him. When in 1530 the Emperor, who veered between attempts to suppress Lutheranism and efforts to achieve reconciliation, asked for a statement which could be used as a basis for a discussion held at Augsburg, Melancthon produced one which was moderate and careful. The "Augsburg Confession," as it was called, proved to be unacceptable to Catholic theologians, but it remained an integral part of the official teachings of the Lutheran church.

Thus it was that the princes of the Holy Roman Empire came to be divided into a Lutheran and a Catholic party. And in 1529 when Charles V, at that time confident of his authority, ordered the laws against heretics enforced, the Lutheran princes protested and were thereafter called "Protestants," a term which was to become general for all dissenters from the Catholic faith. In 1531, they banded together in the League of Schmalkald. And so it was that Charles, distracted by many problems outside Germany, was unable to put down Protestantism. At last in 1555 a sort of stalemate was reached and the two parties agreed to the so-called Peace of Augsburg, which provided: (1) each prince was to be free to dictate the religion of his subjects; (2) the Protestants were to retain all the church property they had seized up to 1552; (3) no form of Protestantism other than Lutheranism was to be tolerated; (4) Lutherans in states ruled by churchmen were not to be forced to become Catholics; (5) any churchman who became a Protestant was to give up his position and the lands that went with it. This last provision, called the "ecclesiastical reservation," was not strictly a part of the peace, but was added later by the Emperor, and not fully accepted by the Protestants. It was to be a source of future trouble.

Thus between 1520 and 1555 Lutheranism won an established position and found general acceptance throughout the northern half of Germany. But its triumphs were not limited to Germany. To the north, Sweden broke away from Denmark in 1523 in a general uprising, and a new king, Frederick I (1523–1533), came to the throne of Denmark and Norway, while the Swedes chose Gustavus Vasa (1523–1560) as their ruler. Both the new rulers saw the possibility of increasing their political control and their power by adopting Lutheranism. Both met with considerable opposition, but by propaganda and legislation, and especially by force, they gradually converted their countries to the new faith. Catholicism died slowly in the Scandinavian lands, but before the end of the century they were firmly Lutheran.

Although the Lutheran churches established in north and central Germany and in Scandinavia were not organically united, and each was organized under the prince of the region, they retained a common faith and developed a modified liturgy in the vernacular. Moreover, much of the form of the old church organization was retained with bishops acting as administrative officials.[1] Considerable advances were made, too, in providing schools for the young. Judged in comparison with other sects, Lutheranism might be termed a moderate type of Protestantism.

C. Emergence of Radical Sects

Luther's conservatism is evident in his failure to come to any sort of agreement with certain of the more radical religious movements which emerged early in the sixteenth century. One contemporary leader, Thomas Münzer, who was denounced by Luther, and who took part in the Peasants' Revolt, went so far as to urge the overthrow of existing governments and the establish-

---

[1] At Upsala in Sweden, the title of archbishop was retained.

ment of a sort of communism. Even more shocking to conservative folk was John of Leiden (*d.* 1536), a Dutch tailor who taught that the Bible sanctioned polygamy and that he was the successor of King David. With a group of fanatical followers he seized the city of Münster and held it for a year until it was recaptured by the forces of its Catholic bishop.

A number of radical groups were what is known as "evangelical" in tendency, that is, they emphasized the emotional rather than the rational aspects of Christianity, and insisted on the literal inspiration of the Bible.[1] Most prominent among these were the Anabaptists, who believed that only adults should be baptized, since infants could not have had the necessary religious experiences. Although Thomas Münzer was an Anabaptist leader, most members of the sect were pious people who sought to lead pure and simple lives. Menno Simons (*d.* 1559), another reformer, preached a return to Biblical simplicity. He condemned as un-Christian the taking of oaths and the waging of war as well as the baptism of infants and is remembered as the founder of the Mennonite sect.

Another of Luther's contemporaries was Huldreich Zwingli (1484–1531), a well-born and well-educated Catholic priest who came to the Swiss canton of Schwyz. Though he first preached mainly against the practice of hiring out Swiss soldiers to foreign rulers, a business in which the church played a part, he soon came to attack ecclesiastical abuses and finally to denounce the supremacy of the pope and to insist that the Bible, not the church, was the true guide to faith and morals, and, as a consequence, that the ceremonies and traditions of the church were not truly Christian. Hence, he argued, the Eucharist was not a sacrament, but simply a memorial service.

Although Zwingli's teachings won considerable support in all but the original Forest Cantons, the vast majority of Swiss Protestants came to follow the doctrines of John Calvin, whose important movement we shall now consider.

---

[1] The word "evangelical" is derived from the Latin word for "gospel," *evangelium.*

D. Calvin and Calvinism

The second major branch of Protestantism—Calvinism—resembled the radical sects in departing farther from Catholic teaching. But unlike most of them, it built up a systematic body of theology and developed a strong church organization. Moreover, of all the Protestant religions it was the most international, the most widespread geographically.

The founder of Calvinism, John Calvin (1509–1564) was born of a middle-class family in Noyon in the French province of Picardy. He was educated first for the priesthood and then for a career as a lawyer. He was also, it seems, given somewhat to humanist studies then flourishing in Paris. France, like most other countries of Europe, was experiencing effects of the religious upheaval of the times, and Lutheran preachers had made themselves heard. But the French King Francis I, whose concordat with the pope (1516) conceded him wide power over the church in France, especially in the matter of the selection of bishops, adopted a stern policy toward religious dissent. He, and his successors, might find the Lutheran princes of Germany, or even the Turks, useful allies against the Catholic Habsburgs, but they were not minded, at least during the sixteenth century, to tolerate heresy within their own dominions.

At the age of twenty, Calvin became involved in the religious turmoil. He experienced a sudden "conversion" which he believed was a divine call to forsake Catholicism and to teach a purer Christianity. Despite his youth, followers soon gathered about him to learn from his lips how Christians might recapture the supposed simplicity of the early days of the church. In view of the attitude of the French government, Calvin prudently left his native country and settled at Basel in Switzerland. Here he came in contact with the teachings and the followers of Zwingli; and here he wrote his chief work, *The Institutes of the Christian Religion.* Published in 1536, the book was dedicated to Francis I, in the vain hope that it would win him over to the cause of the reformers.

Portrait of John Calvin by Lucas Cranach.

The Bettmann Archive

The *Institutes* proved of great historical importance. It is still regarded as a monument of French literature because of its cool, clear, dignified language. Orderly and concise, with an almost legal logic, it did for Protestant theology what the great medieval writers had done for that of the Catholic Church. In it are to be found the seeds, at least, of all the beliefs and practices of Calvinism.

The *Institutes* taught, and Calvin and his followers developed, certain special doctrines that have set the Calvinists apart from other sects. Like Zwingli, the Calvinists abandoned all the sacraments save baptism and the Lord's Supper, and the latter they regarded as merely a symbolic memorial. They stripped the church services of all rites and ceremonies for which they could not find express authority in the Bible. They did away with vestments, holy water fonts, stained glass windows, sacred images, incense, and organ music. The altar they set down in the body of the church and called it a communion table. They gave up the use of the crucifix and other symbols such as the ring in the marriage ceremony. In their public worship, they laid stress on the reading of scripture, the preaching of sermons, and the singing of psalms without instrumental accompani-

ment. Save for the Lord's prayer, which they found in the Bible, they used prayers devised extemporaneously for the occasion.

In church organization likewise, the Calvinists made many changes. They did away with bishops, archbishops, and regular clergy. They kept but one order of clergymen—the presbyters (priests or ministers) —who, aided by "elders" from the various congregations, governed the church through periodic local assemblies called synods.

Sixteenth-century Calvinism placed considerable emphasis on a special interpretation of the ancient doctrine of divine predestination. For it was held that the foreordination of all things by an omnipotent and eternal God precluded the freedom of the individual will. Thus, albeit with different reasoning, the Calvinists joined the Lutherans in questioning the Catholic teaching on free will. It must not be supposed, however, that the Calvinists' belief that those predestined to salvation, the "elect" or "saints," would go to heaven, the others to hell, resulted in a fatalism regarding human conduct. Few Protestants have been more systematic in promoting the good or "godly" life, few more energetic in advancing and expanding their religion. Calvinists frowned on light amusements such as dancing, games, and theatres; they insisted on a rigid observance of the Sabbath and on regular churchgoing; and they stressed the virtues of thrift, sobriety, and industry. Their way of life is known to us as "puritanical," a word coming down from the later English Calvinists.

In 1536 Calvin went to Geneva and helped to unite the followers of Zwingli and other reformers there and to throw off the rule of the Duke of Savoy who was upholding Catholicism. Soon, Calvin was made chief pastor and preacher of the city, and this position he held, save for a brief exile, till his death in 1564. Indeed, Geneva under Calvin became a theocracy, in which the civil administration was dominated by the religious governing body called the consistory. Thus offenses against religion were punished just as vigorously as crimes. When another reformer, the Spaniard Servetus, came to Geneva, Calvin had him tried for questioning the divinity of Christ, and burned at the stake. And the stern simplicity of life, the "puritanical godliness," in which Calvin believed, was rigidly enforced at Geneva.

While he was reforming Geneva, Calvin was also winning for himself the name of the "Protestant Pope." With unflagging energy he gave advice and guidance to a rapidly increasing number of followers all over Europe. Hundreds of earnest students and preachers came to Geneva to absorb Calvin's teaching. With others he carried on so extensive a correspondence his letters would fill thirty huge volumes.

E. The Expansion of Calvinism

Not only did most of Switzerland become Calvinist, but Geneva became a remarkably busy center for the propagation of Calvinism to various parts of Europe. And in those countries where it took root, often as a small but energetic minority, it was called the "Reformed Church." Thus German Calvinism came to be known as the German Reformed Church. In the northern Netherlands, where Calvinism achieved a notable success and won over a majority of the population, it was called the Dutch Reformed Church. Although Calvinist successes in Poland proved to be temporary, an important minority of the Hungarians, then under Turkish rule, adopted the Reformed faith.

In two instances, France and Scotland, the penetration of Calvinism was associated with important political developments. It was, in fact, in France, the native land of Calvin, that there occurred one of the most prolonged and dramatic struggles of the sixteenth century. We have noted that the French monarchy under Francis I (1515–1547) and Henry II (1547–1559) used its authority to repress all signs of Protestantism. In this it was not altogether successful, for Calvinism spread, especially among the middle class and in the south and west of France. By 1560 the French Calvinists, usually called Huguenots, had organized a nationwide church in Presbyterian fashion, had drawn up a confession of faith, and with their local meetings and larger synods had developed what almost amounted to a state within a state.

After the death of Henry II, his three sons, Francis II (1559–1560), Charles IX (1560–1574), and Henry III (1574–1589), ruled in succession. But most of the time, their mother, Catherine de' Medici, daughter of the Florentine banking family, was the real guide of royal policy. The whole period of these last three of the Valois kings was torn by a series of religious wars and by almost constant civil strife. Peaces and truces were made only to be broken in a few months. On the one side were the Huguenots, who had as leaders certain great nobles like Admiral Gaspard de Coligny (1519–1572), and Antoine de Bourbon (1518–1562), who was King of the principality of Navarre as well as a magnate of France. In the latter part of the wars, the leader of the Protestants was Antoine's son Henry, who took on an added importance as it became clear that Catherine de Medici's sons would leave no male heirs. Henry was only a distant cousin of the Kings, but he was next to them in line of succession to the throne.

On the opposing side, the leaders of the extreme Catholic party were a family by the name of Guise which had come to prominence in the first half of the century. Francis, duke of Guise (1519–1563), with his brother Charles who was called the Cardinal of Lorraine, played a leading role in the early stages of the religious strife. The Duke was an able general and had won renown by capturing Calais from the English in 1558. After his assassination by Protestants, his son Henry (1550–1588) became the prime leader of the Catholics. Popular with the people of Paris, Henry of Guise was able to form a powerful League to support the Catholic cause. There were moments when it looked as if he might be able to make himself king of France.

Between the extreme Protestant and Catholic parties stood Catherine de' Medici and her sons who ruled in succession. By and large, they sympathized with the Catholic cause, but they were more interested in maintaining and increasing the royal power. The devious policy of Catherine was usually aimed at playing off Protestant against Catholic so as to strengthen the crown. In this endeavor she often had the support of a group known as the "Politiques," who, though for the most part moderate Catholics, set peace and order and strong government ahead of religious considerations. France was to know no end to turmoil until those who thought like the Politiques grew strong enough to impose their views on embittered religious factions and a war-weary population.

Outside the country, the Spaniards were ever eager to fish in the troubled French waters. They supported the Catholic party with men and money. They several times invaded France with large armies. As long as France was rent by civil war, it was no threat to Spain. On the other hand, the Protestant party in France was aided from abroad, directly or indirectly, by the English who were at war with Spain, by the Dutch who were in revolt against their Spanish rulers, or by Protestant princes of Germany.

Many outrages were committed by both sides during the French wars of religion. There were assassinations and massacres of Catholics by Protestants, and of Protestants by Catholics. A particularly horrible example was the so-called massacre of St. Bartholomew's Day (1572). The Catholic party, under Henry of Guise, feared that the Protestant Coligny was winning too much influence over the mind of the weak King Charles IX. After an unsuccessful attempt to assassinate Coligny, Guise persuaded Catherine de' Medici and the King to consent to a general massacre of Protestants who had gathered in Paris to celebrate the marriage of Henry of Bourbon, King of Navarre, with the French King's sister, Margaret. When all was ready, the signal was given by the ringing of a church bell, and Guise's soldiers fell on the hapless Protestants. Coligny was murdered, and several thousand were slaughtered in Paris, and in the provinces, to which the butchery spread. Henry of Navarre escaped by rapidly feigning a conversion to Catholicism, which lasted only as long as he was in the King's power.

The later years of the French religious wars were filled with dramatic events. The last of the Valois kings, Henry III, who leaned to the Protestant side because he feared the growing power of Henry of Guise and his Catholic League, was driven from the capital city of Paris in 1588 by Guise's adherents in a rising known as the Day of Barricades. Soon afterwards, the Duke of Guise was lured to Blois by the King and assassinated by royal henchmen. The next year Henry III was assassinated by a fanatical monk. Then befell what the Catholics had dreaded. Henry of Navarre, the leader of the Protestants, became the rightful King of France as Henry IV.

For four years Henry IV waged war against his foes. But the Catholics would not willingly permit a Protestant to sit on the throne of St. Louis. At last, in 1593, the King removed most of the grounds for opposition by somewhat cynically abjuring Protestantism and becoming a Catholic. At this point, most followers of both parties were willing to come to terms, for the Catholics at least had a Catholic king and the Protestants a king whom they felt they could trust. But it was not until 1598 that the last of the rebellious nobles gave up and peace descended once more upon France. The French religious wars were over.

Henry IV marked the pacification of his kingdom by the Edict of Nantes (1598) which, for the time at least, settled the religious disputes in France. It granted to the Protestants liberty of conscience and of private worship throughout the country. Public worship was to be permitted them in two hundred towns listed by name and in the country houses or castles of something like three thousand nobles. Protestants, moreover, were accorded full civil and political rights, and, as a guarantee, they were privileged to hold and garrison some two hundred fortified towns. Thus the Huguenots, though never more than a minority of Frenchmen, won by their cohesion and by their persistence not only toleration but numerous political privileges.

In the British Isles, Calvinists were known as Presbyterians. Although never numerous in England, they did influence the development of Anglicanism. In Scotland, however, Calvinism took root and flourished. As elsewhere in Europe, there had been protests in Scotland against moral and financial abuses in the Catholic Church. But the primary causes of the religious over-turn seem to have been political. The kingdom had long been torn by the strife of great noble families, many of whom could rally small armies of clansmen from the Highlands.

In 1542, the premature death of King James V left the Scottish throne to his infant daughter Mary Stuart and opened the way for the nobles to seek more power at the expense of the Crown. In general, the Catholic clergy sided with the Crown and with the rule of the Queen's mother, a Frenchwoman, Mary of Guise. Many ambitious nobles, therefore, took up the Protestant cause as a means of reducing the royal power. Cardinal Beaton, archbishop of St. Andrews and primate of the Church in Scotland, strove to suppress Protestantism by the trial and execution of a number of its leaders. In retaliation, a group of Protestant nobles conspired together and in 1546 murdered the Cardinal and hung his body on the battlements of the castle of St. Andrews. Such was the tense situation in Scotland when John Knox appeared.

A Catholic priest born of peasant parents, John Knox (1515–1572) began openly in 1546 to attack the Catholic Church and to espouse the new religious ideas which were coming into Scotland from England and the continent. In fiery sermons, he preached the overriding authority of the Bible, and a stern puritanical morality. Mary of Guise and the Catholic court were still strong enough, however, to drive him into exile. After being imprisoned in France, Knox went to England, where he became a chaplain at the court of Edward VI and helped to swing the English church toward Protestantism. On the accession of the Catholic Mary Tudor to the English throne, Knox prudently departed for Geneva where he made the acquaintance of Calvin and discovered that in essential matters they were in agreement. From exile, Knox continued to exhort the Scottish Protestants with strongly worded letters and pamphlets.

In 1559, though still under sentence of death, Knox returned to Scotland and was soon the real leader of the Protestants. Meanwhile, Queen Mary Stuart had left Scotland, and by marriage to the short-lived Francis II had become Queen of France. Her absence weakened the Catholic cause, and local Calvinist, or Presbyterian, churches were being organized throughout Scotland. In 1560, a General Assembly of the Presbyterians met and adopted a rigidly Calvinist *Book of Discipline*, largely the work of Knox.

After the death of her husband, Mary Queen of Scots returned in 1561 to her native land. But she was too late to stem the tide of religious revolt and political opposition to the crown. The nobles prevented any increase in royal power, and Knox in public sermons fairly flayed the character and religion of the young Queen. Mary's marriage to her cousin Henry Stuart, Lord Darnley, who, like her, had a claim to the English throne, did little to strengthen her position. By him she gave birth to a son, James. Matters soon hastened to a climax. Darnley died under most mysterious circumstances. Mary married a nobleman named Bothwell who was suspected of Darnley's murder. The country was in a turmoil, and Mary was imprisoned by the nobles who opposed her. In 1568, she escaped and fled to England, to cast herself on the mercy of her cousin Elizabeth. But as a Catholic and the heir to the English throne, Mary was a dangerous person. Elizabeth kept her in confinement and eventually sent her to the scaffold.

Back in Scotland, the Presbyterians were triumphant. The Catholic adherents of Mary were put down by force of arms. Though her infant son was made King as James VI, the real power lay with groups of Protestant nobles who struggled among themselves but educated James in the new faith and imposed on the kingdom a rigid Calvinism in doctrine and church organization. By the end of the century Catholicism still lingered only in remote parts of the Highlands and among a few scattered families elsewhere.

Before the end of the sixteenth century, therefore, Calvinism had won adherents in many countries of Europe, and in some had exercised a major political as well as religious influence. Moreover, even where the official Calvinist reformed church was not established, Calvinist influences were often of great importance. Before many years, these influences, as well as official Calvinism, were to appear also in the expanding English possessions in the New World.

Th' admired Empresse through the worlde applauded, Unto the eares of every forraigne Nation.
For supreme Virtues rares t Imitation : Cannopey' d under powreful Angells winges
Whose Scepters rule fames lowde-voyc d trumpet lawdeth, To her Immortall praise sweete Science singes
Are to be sould in Popes head Alley by Io Sudbury and Geor Humble.

Queen Elizabeth I. Engraving by William Rogers (after Isaac Oliver).

Courtesy Museum of Fine Arts, Boston

CHAPTER 30

Revolt Against
the Catholic Church: Anglicanism

A. Henry VIII and the Separation of the Church of England from the Papacy

In 1500 the Catholic Church seemed as firmly rooted in England as on the continent of Europe. A century later, the church in England had split off from Rome and become a separate national church, called Anglican, or the Church of England, with the king at its head. This change arose in large part from events which took place in the reign of Henry VIII (1509–1547). Henry VIII was the second king of the Tudor dynasty which, beginning with Henry VII, had pacified England following the Wars of the Roses and had obtained a firm control over the government and over Parliament.

The English, like Europeans elsewhere, had been influenced by criticisms of church abuses by the great humanists and scholars such as Colet, More, and Erasmus. It is possible that some traces of the teachings of John Wyclif lingered among the common people. And England was, of course, affected by the events on the continent. Lutheran teachings had come into England by 1521 and had aroused discussion in Oxford, Cambridge, and London. But despite the existence of strong national feeling and a desire among many for a thoroughgoing reform of the church, there was, at the accession of Henry VIII, no sign that religious revolt was imminent.

Moreover, Henry VIII for many years seemed to be a most devoted son of the Catholic Church. With his own royal hand he penned a bitter attack on the Lutheran teachings, and dedicated the work to the pope. The pope responded by conferring on the King the title "Defender of the Faith," which, ironically, the kings of England have borne ever since. In international politics, Henry VIII was on several occasions allied with Pope Leo X. In England, Henry's chief minister at first was the ambitious Thomas Wolsey, a cardinal of the Roman Church.

Indeed, it is difficult to see how England would have soon broken off from the Catholic Church, had it not been for the peculiar marital troubles of its ruler. Henry VIII had been married for many years to Catherine of Aragon,[1] and she had borne him six children of whom all save one daughter, Mary, had died. It seemed unlikely to Henry that she would give him the male heir he ardently desired. In addition, the King became smitten by the charms of Anne Boleyn, a maid-in-waiting at the court. Whatever his reasons, Henry VIII sought to have his marriage with Catherine annulled on the grounds that church law forbade a man to marry his brother's widow. To be sure, Pope Julius II had granted a dispensation authorizing the marriage. But Henry expressed doubt whether any pope could lawfully grant such a dispensation, and in any event, he argued, one pope might undo what another had

---

[1] She had previously been the widow of his older brother, Arthur. See above, p. 288.

Henry VIII. Hans Holbein the Younger (d. 1543).

done. Further, since the Wars of the Roses were of recent memory, the absence of a legitimate male heir seemed more than usually important.

The Pope, Clement VII, would have liked to oblige Henry VIII, though he was naturally reluctant to reverse a decision of one of his predecessors, and he knew that the Emperor Charles V, who was then dominant in Italy, would be incensed if his Aunt Catherine's marriage with Henry VIII was annulled. So the Pope procrastinated, and for several years delayed making any decision, hoping, no doubt, that in the meantime the matter might resolve itself. But the Pope did accede to Henry's wishes in the appointment, as the archbishop of Canterbury, of Thomas Cranmer, a cleric of marked Protestant leanings.

As the King grew more impatient, he began a campaign against what he now regarded as papal tyranny. In 1531, he was able to force an assembly of clergy to recognize him as the "supreme head" of the English church so far "as that is permitted by the law of Christ." But this proved to be but a preliminary step. For Henry then turned to Parliament, there-

after known as the "Reformation Parliament," and secured authorization to shut off payments to Rome and to appoint bishops without papal permission. Thereupon, convinced that no annulment was to be had from Rome, he secured from Cranmer declarations that his marriage with Catherine was null and void and his marriage to Anne Boleyn was legal and canonical. Meanwhile Cardinal Wolsey, who had failed to obtain the papal annulment, was forced out of office and died in disgrace. He was replaced as Lord Chancellor by Thomas More. But Henry's real right-hand man in these and subsequent negotiations was Thomas Cromwell, a layman and former secretary to Wolsey.

In 1534 the split with Rome was widened into formal separation when Parliament passed the Act of Supremacy which declared the King to be the "only supreme head on earth of the Church of England," and established penalties of treason for anyone who should deny the King's supremacy. An Act of Succession, validating Henry's heirs by both the new and the former marriage, followed and to this all were required to take an oath. Thomas More, the saintly John Fisher who was bishop of Rochester, and several lesser persons refused to do this, and were accordingly beheaded for clinging to their belief in the supremacy of the pope.[1] A popular pro-papal uprising in the north, called the "Pilgrimage of Grace," had to be put down by force of arms.

Lutherans and other Protestants were encouraged by these events to think that Henry VIII was moving in their direction. But in reality he adhered firmly to the old Catholic beliefs. He was a schismatic in that he had split off from Rome, but he insisted that he was no heretic. In 1539, Henry got Parliament to pass a law called the "six articles" which reaffirmed the chief points of the Catholic faith, including the miracle of transubstantiation, and provided severe penalties for any dissent from these doctrines. Thus, any Catholic who upheld

[1] More was imprisoned for refusing to take an oath to the Act of Succession. Throughout months of confinement in the Tower of London, he persistently refused to accept royal supremacy over the English church.

Thomas More. Hans Holbein the Younger
(d. 1543).

Copyright, the Frick Collection, New York

the supremacy of the pope was beheaded, while any Protestant who denied transubstantiation was burned at the stake. The King's will was enforced in blood. Many died for political-religious offenses.

Meanwhile, Henry VIII had taken another significant step in an attack upon monasteries, though their alleged scandalous conduct was probably grossly exaggerated by the interested investigators whom Henry appointed and sent about the country. In general, the monks and nuns were supporters of the pope and opponents of the idea of royal supremacy, and hence were deemed disloyal. Still more important, the monasteries were possessed of broad lands and considerable wealth, and Henry was in need of funds. Accordingly, under the direction of Thomas Cromwell, the monasteries were suppressed by a series of acts and their property confiscated to the crown. Some of their wealth thus acquired, Henry used for ordinary expenses. A small portion went into new educational and charitable foundations, which were by no means an adequate replacement of those that were destroyed. A very large portion, Henry gave to his favorites and supporters, thus creating

a new class of rich nobles and gentry, bound to the crown by gratitude and committed to the new religious situation by fear lest any change back toward the papacy might cost them the wealth they had newly obtained.

By his marriage to Anne Boleyn, Henry VIII had one daughter, Elizabeth. But Anne was found guilty of adultery and hence of treason, and was executed, thus leading to the King's third marriage, that with Jane Seymour, the mother of his only son, Edward, who succeeded him in 1547.[1]

B. Edward VI and Mary, and Religious Fluctuations in England

Under Henry VIII, the Church of England had split off from Rome, but remained Catholic in doctrine. Under his son Edward VI (1547–1553), the English church moved rapidly in the direction of Protestantism. Edward was but a child of nine when he came to the throne, and real power lay with various nobles who were eager to push the country toward Protestantism. Under their influence, Calvinists and Lutherans were allowed to preach freely. New articles of religion, drawn up to establish the position of the Anglican Church, were unmistakably Protestant in tone. Catholic service books were translated from Latin into English and edited, under the auspices of Archbishop Cranmer, as the *Book of Common Prayer* (1552), which made it clear that the eucharist was not to be regarded as a miracle. This denial of transubstantiation led to other changes. The "Mass" was henceforth to be called "Holy Communion," or the "Lord's Supper." The "altar" was called a "table." In the old churches, many changes were made. Altars and images were taken down, the former service books and stained glass windows destroyed.

On Edward's death in 1553, Mary, daughter of Catherine of Aragon, became Queen of England. Against continual

---

[1] Jane died in childbirth. Henry's subsequent wives were Catherine Howard, who was beheaded for adultery; Anne of Cleves, whom he promptly repudiated; and Catherine Parr, who managed to survive him.

pressure, she had clung stubbornly to the Catholic faith; and curiously, her rights to the succession had been protected by Parliament. Accordingly, despite a plot to bring a Protestant, Lady Jane Grey, to the throne, Mary was accepted. Now, too, according to the legislation of Henry VIII, she was head of the English church, and she immediately exercised her authority to restore it to Catholic usages and to communion with the papacy. She reinstated the bishops who had been put out of office in previous years. She obtained from Parliament the repeal of the church legislation of the two preceding reigns. England made its peace with the pope. A papal legate, Cardinal Reginald Pole, sailed up the Thames with a cross gleaming from the prow of his barge, and in full Parliament administered the absolution which freed the kingdom from the guilt incurred by its schism under Henry VIII and its heresy under Edward VI.

Nor did Mary stop here. The bishops who had supported the changes or who had married were dismissed from their offices. Similarly, something like a fifth of the clergy were deprived of their benefices, though some secured new ones if they put away their wives. Laws against heresy were revived, and some three hundred persons were put to death for violating them. Among these were four bishops and Archbishop Cranmer. Twice Cranmer recanted his Protestant beliefs and denounced the work he had done. But in the end he recanted his recantations and held in the flames the hand with which he had signed them. Thus Mary gave to Protestantism a number of martyrs, as her predecessors had martyred a number of Catholics, and her successor would put more to death. One result of Mary's persecutions was unexpected. Many English churchmen escaped punishment by taking refuge in Germany or Geneva. When in later years they came back to England, they returned more firmly Protestant than ever. With all her ardor for making England Catholic again, there was one step Mary did not dare to take. To reëstablish the monasteries and give them back their lands would have deprived many nobles and gentlemen of wealth they had gained and would have alienated them from

Jane Seymour, third wife of Henry VIII and mother of Edward VI. Hans Holbein the Younger (d. 1543).

Courtesy Foundation Johan van Maurits Mauritshuis, The Hague

the crown. Mary, therefore, left the church lands in private hands.

To strengthen the Catholic pasition in England and to win foreign influence, Mary determined to marry her cousin, Philip II of Spain, although she was eleven years his senior. She took this step on the advice of the Emperor Charles V, who was not entirely disinterested in the matter, for he hoped by a union of England with the Netherlands and Spain to ring France about with hostile powers. The marriage was unpopular in England and its results were unhappy. Even those Englishmen who accepted the return to Catholicism tended to resent the influence of Philip and his Spanish courtiers. Spain was already embroiled in a war with France, and in the strife England lost to the French the port of Calais, the last remnant of the once extensive English holdings on the continent. Had an heir been born to Philip and Mary, the whole course of English and European political and religious history might have been different. But the couple were childless. When Mary died in 1558, her successor was her half-sister, Elizabeth, who by her birth was naturally inclined to uphold the Protestant position. Elizabeth was to undo all of Mary's work.

C. Elizabeth and the Final Establishment of Anglicanism

After all the shifts and changes of the preceding decades, the English church, under Elizabeth, definitely took on the form that in the future was to characterize it. And while it may seem surprising that many individual clergymen were able to accept all the revolutions of English religious policy which occurred in the mid-sixteenth century, it must be remembered that in England, as on the continent, there were many people who firmly believed in the right of the ruler to dictate the religious beliefs of his subjects. In addition, there were those who felt that to uphold royal authority in England was the only way to avoid disorder, civil war, and foreign aggression. Such sentiments were enormously intensified during the reign of Queen Elizabeth.

Elizabeth, herself, had a lingering affection for some of the older ways in religion. She liked the use of the crucifix in church services. She disliked married clergy. But her very birth made her uphold the swing back toward Protestantism, just as England's position in international affairs gradually forced her to align the country against Spain, the champion of Catholicism in Europe. And so it was that, in 1559, Parliament repealed the religious laws of Mary and passed once more the Act of Supremacy and the Act of Uniformity which enforced the use of Cranmer's *Book of Common Prayer*. Three years later Parliament enacted the *Thirty-Nine Articles*, a slightly modified version of the statement of doctrine that had been adopted under Edward. Since all but two of Mary's bishops refused to accept the new trend, Elizabeth put in a new set of bishops, including, as before, archbishops of Canterbury and York. Thus the official church of England, while embracing a modified Protestant theology, retained all the outward form of Catholic organization, save only the pope.

Elizabeth, no less than Mary, wanted all her subjects to conform to the new religious settlement. Liberty of public worship was denied to all dissenters from Anglicanism. A special court, the Court of High Commission, was set up to suppress heresy and enforce uniformity. Although royal commissioners tended at first to disregard private worship in the old faith, the persistence of plots to overthrow Elizabeth brought a change in governmental policy. For nearly twenty years (1568–1587), these plots revolved around the person of Mary, Queen of Scotland, who, it will be remembered, had been driven from her northern kingdom by a rebellious Calvinist nobility, and had sought refuge in England only to be imprisoned by Elizabeth. But Mary was not only a devoted Catholic; she was, should Elizabeth die childless, heiress to the throne of England.

Most of these plots originated outside of England and usually involved Spain. Moreover, as such activities continued, many Catholic clergy, including several Jesuits who had managed to enter England, and who were concerned simply to minister to English Catholics or to convert others, were held to be traitors. Thus, particularly from about 1583 onwards, the propagation of Catholicism in England was punishable by death as high treason, for it was held to involve political disloyalty to the Queen and support for a foreign ruler, the pope.[1] Some 250 Englishmen paid for their religious convictions with their lives. Eventually, as foreign affairs grew more tense, Elizabeth reluctantly consented to the execution of Mary (1587).

In the following year, Philip II of Spain, increasingly irritated by English attacks on Spanish shipping, made his last great effort to subdue England. The story of the Great Armada will occupy our attention in a subsequent chapter. Here two things must be noted. First, the failure of the Armada relieved England of the Spanish danger. Second, English Catholics rallied to the support of their country. The vast majority of them had nothing to do with the plots against the Queen, and wanted nothing more than to be left alone. Gradually it

---

[1] The papacy appears to have been ill-informed about religious conditions in England and overly optimistic about the strength of the Catholic cause. Pius V excommunicated Elizabeth in 1570 and declared her to be a usurper.

again became possible for them, now a small minority, by paying fines for themselves and their dependents, to worship in private.

It remains to mention another group of religious dissenters, those more extreme Protestants to whom the Anglican settlement seemed too reminiscent of the old Catholicism. Suppressed, as were Catholics, the non-Anglican Protestants were not, however, involved in accusations of treason. They did persist and gradually increased in numbers. Some were representatives of the Continental sects, Calvinists or Anabaptists. Many, much influenced by Calvinism, and known as Puritans because they wished to "purify" the Anglican church of all vestiges of Catholic practices, remained for a time nominal members of the official church. Others moved toward a democracy or congregationalism in church government. They tended to believe that each congregation should choose its own pastor, set up its own rules, and establish its own forms of worship. Such ideas were developed by Robert Browne (1550–1633). His followers, known as Brownists, Congregationalists, or Independents, were later to play an important role in both English and American history.

We have mentioned the course of religious events in Scotland. Very different was the story of the sixteenth century in Ireland. Henry VIII extended the royal authority over that eastern area of Ireland which the English managed to control. Monastery lands were seized and absorbed as greedily by Irish nobles and chiefs as were those in England by the English gentry. But, although there were abuses in the Catholic church in Ireland, there was no great popular feeling against it. As a consequence, the efforts of Edward VI and Elizabeth to introduce Anglicanism had only partial success in the Dublin area and in a few of the larger towns. During Elizabeth's reign, rebellions which were partly feudal revolts against the English conquerors, and partly religious protests against the imposition of Anglicanism, were all put down in blood. But Anglicanism made little headway and Catholicism became throughly intertwined with Irish patriotism.

D. The Elizabethan Age

Before concluding this chapter on the establishment of Anglicanism, it is important to observe that the sixteenth-century religious settlement in England occurred in an age of exceptionally brilliant national development. Various aspects of English life prospered. Parliament, though generally in support of royal policy, retained and strengthened its hold on the English government. Each change in English religious life had been promoted or ratified by an act of Parliament. Besides, England's power was being felt abroad as never before. For many years Elizabeth's complicated diplomacy, in which she played off the Netherlands, France, and Spain against each other, kept England out of open war. And at the same time English seamen, frequently with the encouragement and backing of the Queen, raided Spanish commerce and made piratical attacks on Spanish colonies. Raleigh and Hawkins, Cavendish and Gilbert, Grenville and a dozen others, won fame, fortune, and popular acclaim by "singeing the beard" of the Spanish King. When Drake returned in 1580 from a voyage around the world, his ships laden with twenty-six tons of silver not to mention coin, jewels, and gold, Elizabeth (who shared in the loot) knighted him on the quarter deck of the "Golden Hind."

The great national effort which involved the destruction of the Spanish Armada [1] and the defeat of Spain made Elizabeth, who had presided over the victory, a focus of patriotic fervor. In addition, during her long reign of nearly fifty years, England enjoyed a remarkable period of growth and prosperity, so that in later times Englishmen looked back with nostalgia to the gracious days of "good Queen Bess." The cloth industry flourished and found new markets on the continent. Companies were formed to trade with Russia, Africa, and the Near East. New industries were founded and won subsidies and support from the crown. If business was regulated by the long arm of the monarchy which reached into every sphere of life, still it also won popular support for the crown and favorable legislation. Fisheries grew and Parliament

---

[1] On the Armada, see below, pp. 388–389.

passed laws that people must, for national reasons, eat fish on Fridays and in Lent as they once had from religious motives.

Attempts were also made to found colonies. As early as 1497, a Genoese named John Cabot, in the service of Henry VII, had made a voyage from Bristol to Cape Breton Island in the Gulf of St. Lawrence. During Elizabeth's reign efforts were directed to the lands farther south, especially in "Virginia" (named after the Queen). But, though they showed the expansive energy of England, they met with no immediate success.

In agriculture, too, there was change and some prosperity. But here for the poorer classes there was suffering as well. Many of the manors changed over from grain-growing to sheep-raising, and considerable tracts of manorial land were "enclosed." Since it took fewer hands to tend a "sheep walk," many of the former cultivators were driven from their homes and into beggary. But if the peasant who lost his land, and, hounded from village to village, ended up in one of the new, prison-like national workhouses, had little cause to be enthusiastic about the trend of the times, still it was easy to forget him. The merchants with their new trade, the gentlemen with their new lands which had once belonged to the monasteries, the sailors spending their Spanish silver, all felt a sense of growth, expansion, and a most promising future.

Appropriately, there also occurred, in the time of Elizabeth, a most spectacular output of vernacular literature. The reasons for it cannot be disentangled, for they are compounded of the advent of an unusually large number of individual geniuses, the impact of the Italian renaissance, the development of a literary tradition, the freshness of a new age that was opening, the expanded horizons resulting from the geographical discoveries, business prosperity, the breaking away from the old lines of thought in religion and in philosophy, swelling pride in the nation and the monarch, and a dozen other factors. In any case, during the closing years of the sixteenth century and the opening decades of the seventeenth, there appeared in England a galaxy of writers whose work stands out

for its beauty, its freshness, its power, and its charm. Though works of many types in poetry and prose were produced, the outstanding achievements were in the field of the drama, where plays had ceased to have a religious purpose and were being produced in London for the pleasure of persons of high and low degree.

Christopher Marlowe wrote half a dozen dramas in the tragic or historical vein which, despite an almost turgid eloquence, reached at times the very peak of poetic inspiration. Ben Jonson, in his plays, mixed scholarship and wit with insight into human nature and very real poetic power. Beaumont and Fletcher, who collaborated in dozens of dramas, turned out many routine products, but their best works had a gaiety and sparkle far above the ordinary.

Over all his competitors towered William Shakespeare. He would be remembered for the magic of his sonnets, had he never written for the stage. But it is his plays that won for him a unique position in the history of literature. It is remarkable that in every type of drama he produced incomparable masterpieces: in tragedy, such works as *Othello, Macbeth*, and *Hamlet*; in historical plays, such dramas as *Henry IV* and *Richard II*; in comedy, such varying types as *The Merry Wives of Windsor, Twelfth Night*, and *The Tempest*.

Despite the fact that his plays were for the ages, Shakespeare was a man of his own time, full of patriotism for England and respect for its Queen, having a sympathetic regard for England's Catholic past yet being curious about new ideas and new lands, heir to the thought of the renaissance yet able to address the generations to come.

Thus it was, that Anglicanism, the third great branch of Protestantism, took shape during an era of English resurgence. Of all the Protestant faiths it was the most national. Indeed, it was the only one which, until the independence of the United States, was exclusively associated with the development of a single country.[1]

---

[1] Following the establishment of independence, the Anglican Church in the United States, while maintaining the identical faith and many personal and other ties with the Church of England, became officially the Protestant Episcopal Church without attachment to the Crown.

The Council of Trent in Session. French sixteenth century engraving.

Courtesy Metropolitan Museum of Art, New York; Dick Fund, 1947

CHAPTER 31

Catholic Reformation, and the Cultural Life of the Sixteenth Century

A. Reforming Popes and the Council of Trent

The religious upheaval of the sixteenth century which gave rise to Lutheranism, Calvinism, Anglicanism, and the radical sects, had its counterpart in a great reform movement which swept through the Catholic Church to leave it both purified and strengthened. If Protestantism won most of northern and much of central Europe, still a rejuvenated Catholicism retained the loyalty of the rest of the continent, west of the area in which the Eastern Orthodox Church had long held sway.

It has already been noted that the prevailing weaknesses in the Catholic church in the fifteenth and early sixteenth centuries had prompted widespread demands for reform. And it will also be recalled that a vigorous reform had been promoted in the Spanish church by Cardinal Ximines.[1] This was destined to provide much of the impetus for a broader movement. Certainly, with the widening breach between Protestantism and the church, what had formerly been desirable now appeared imperative. But partly as a consequence of contemporary political conditions, and partly owing to the lack of vigorous leadership, it was only toward the middle of the sixteenth century that effective reform was promoted from Rome.

The change was first evident in the pontificate of Paul III (1534–1549). Pope Paul inaugurated a policy of appointing to high church offices men renowned for their virtue and learning rather than for their family position, their wealth, or their political influence. During the second half of the sixteenth century, this policy was well maintained by a series of upright and foresighted popes, such as Paul IV, Pius IV, St. Pius V, Gregory XIII, and Sixtus V. By the year 1600 a remarkable reformation had gradually been wrought in the personnel of the church, from the papacy, the cardinals, the *curia*, and the bishops, down to the parish priests and the monks. The worldly bishop and the ignorant priest became increasingly rare. To meet the challenge of Protestantism, the Catholic Church strove to recruit its officers from among its ablest sons.

The reforming zeal of the popes was supplemented and reënforced by the work of a general church council—the Council of Trent (1545–1563). It was no easy task in those troublesome times to hold a general council. But despite the many difficulties which long postponed its convocation and repeatedly interrupted its labors, the council which met at Trent on the boundary between the Italian- and German-speaking peoples consummated a great reform and contributed materially to the preservation of the Catholic faith. A few Protestant delegates attended certain of the sessions, but were able to obtain no acceptance of their views. The number and renown of the Catholic churchmen who did take part were such that the

[1] See above, p. 332.

Council of Trent easily ranked with the eighteen general councils which preceded it. Its final decrees were signed among others by six cardinals, three patriarchs, and 192 bishops and archbishops.

The work of the Council of Trent was twofold—dogmatic and reformatory. It was argued that the errors of the new religions might be refuted and the beliefs of the faithful better protected by a clear statement of Catholic doctrine, particularly on those matters which had been in dispute. Thus the main points of Catholic theology as it had long been accepted by all central and western Europe were confirmed. It was declared that historic tradition as well as the Bible was to be taken as the basis of the Christian religion and that the interpretation of the Holy Scriptures belonged exclusively to the church. The Protestant teachings about grace and justification by faith alone, and about the effects of original sin on the human will were condemned. The seven sacraments were pronounced indispensable. The miraculous and sacrificial character of the Lord's Supper (Mass) was reaffirmed. Belief in the invocation of saints, in the veneration of images and relics, in purgatory, and in indulgences was explicitly upheld, but precautions were taken to clear away some of the pernicious practices that had at times been connected with these doctrines. The spiritual authority of the Roman See over all Christians was confirmed, and the pope was recognized as the supreme interpreter in matters of faith and the incontestable chief of the bishops.

A volume of regulations on discipline constituted the second great achievement of the Council of Trent. The sale of church offices was forbidden. Bishops and other prelates were ordered to live in their respective dioceses, to abandon worldly pursuits, and to devote themselves entirely to spiritual labors. Seminaries were to be established for the proper education and training of priests. While Latin was retained as the official and liturgical language, frequent sermons were to be preached in the vernacular tongues. Indulgences were not to be issued for money, and no charge was to be made for conferring the sacraments.

The work of the Council did not produce changes overnight. More than fifty years after its close there was still controversy in France as to whether its decisions should be officially published there. But the seed sown by the Council had abundant fruit in the ensuing decades. The central government of the Catholic Church was completely reorganized. A uniform catechism was prepared at Rome and, by means of it, laymen were systematically instructed in the tenets and obligations of their religion. Revisions were made in the service books of the Church, and a new standard edition of the Latin Bible—the Vulgate—was issued.

Steps were taken, too, to check the spread of the Protestant teachings. The Council of Trent had begun work on a list of dangerous and heretical books, and this list, called the Index, was completed and published under Pope Pius IV (1559–1565). All Catholics were forbidden, without special permission, to read books listed in the Index. Under Pope Sixtus V (1585–1590) a "Congregation of the Index" was established to keep the prohibited list up-to-date.

To punish lapses in faith and conduct had been the function of the medieval ecclesiastical court of the Inquisition. In most Catholic lands, and especially in Italy and Spain, the personnel of the Inquisition was strengthened in the last half of the sixteenth century, and its work was pushed forward with redoubled zeal. Because it dealt with heresy and those who fell into heretical beliefs, it became for Protestants a symbol of Catholic persecution. As in other courts of the time, the proceedings of the Inquisition were secret and torture was used to extract confessions. Heretics judged guilty were sentenced to fasting and prayer and sometimes to fines and imprisonment. The church itself formally refused to put anyone, even a heretic, to death, but obstinate cases were sometimes "handed over to the secular arm," that is, to the lay government, for execution.

B. St. Ignatius Loyola and the Jesuits

To buttress and strengthen the Catholic Church in its trials during the sixteenth

Pope Paul III. Titian (d. 1576).

century, there arose several new religious orders. The largest and most famous of these new orders, and the one which did most to maintain Catholicism in southern Europe and to arrest the spread of Protestantism in the north, was the Society of Jesus, whose members are commonly known as Jesuits. The Society was founded by a Spaniard, St. Ignatius Loyola (1491–1556) in 1534 and its constitution was formally approved by Pope Paul III six years later.

In his younger days Loyola had been a soldier and, as a patriotic Spaniard, had fought bravely against the French in the armies of the Emperor Charles V. But while he lay wounded in a hospital, his leg shattered by a cannon ball, he chanced to read a life of Christ and biographies of several saints, which, he tells us, worked a great change within him. From a soldier of an earthly king, he would now become a knight of Christ and of the Church. Thus in the very year (1521) in which the German monk, Martin Luther, became the avowed and leading adversary of the Catholic Church, this Spanish warrior was starting on that remarkable career which was to make him a chief champion of Catholicism.

After a few years' trial of his new life, a pilgrimage to Jerusalem, and several rather footless efforts to serve the Church, Ignatius determined at the age of thirty-three to learn Latin and perfect his rather scanty education. It was while he was studying the classics, philosophy, and theology at the University of Paris that he made the acquaintance of a group of scholarly and pious men who became the first members of the Society of Jesus. Among this first group was Francis Xavier, the celebrated missionary, who, like Loyola, was eventually canonized as a saint. In 1537 Loyola was ordained a priest, and, despite the fact that for a time his intense zeal aroused the suspicion of the Spanish Inquisition, he amply proved his orthodoxy. His *Spiritual Exercises*, which he completed in 1548, became even more famous and influential in Catholic circles than Calvin's *Institutes* among Protestants.

Though the Society of Jesus was at first intended primarily for missionary work among the Moslems, it was speedily turned to other ends. In its organization, it showed the military instincts of its founder. To the usual three vows of poverty, chastity, and obedience, was added a fourth vow of special allegiance to the pope. Remembering his own educational difficulties, Loyola arranged that new members were to be carefully trained during a long novitiate. The whole order was placed under the personal direction of a general, resident in Rome. Loyola was the first general and served until his death. He understood that the church was now confronted by conditions of war rather than of peace. Accordingly, he directed that his brothers

should not content themselves with prayers and works of peace, with charity and local benevolence, but should adapt themselves to the new circumstances of the time and should strive in a wide variety of ways to restore and strengthen the Catholic Church.

Thus it happened that the Jesuits, from the very start, rushed to the front in the religious upheaval and conflict of the sixteenth century. They distinguished themselves as teachers and as preachers, as advisers of kings and as diplomats, as missionaries and even as explorers. Realizing the importance of education, the Jesuits made it one of their primary duties to enlighten and train the young. As schoolmasters, they soon had no equals in Europe. No less a scholar and scientist than Francis Bacon said of Jesuit teaching, "Nothing better has been put into practice." In Catholic countries the Jesuits became the principal teachers in the universities, and their schools and colleges provided the best primary and secondary education.

By the unimpeachable purity of their lives, no less than by their learning and culture, the Jesuits won back popular respect for the Catholic clergy. In theological and philosophical controversies, they were opponents to be reckoned with. As preachers, too, they earned a high esteem by the clearness and simplicity of their sermons and instructions. Taking inspiration from their founder, many Jesuits displayed a soldierly courage and worked for Catholicism under conditions of the utmost peril. For example, the saintly Edmund Campion and the supple Robert Parsons entered England in disguise in 1580 to work and preach among the English Catholics. Though Parsons eluded the agents of Queen Elizabeth, Campion was caught and, after a partisan trial and repeated torture on the rack, was executed.

So successful were the Jesuits in their varied endeavors that they created for themselves many enemies. The Protestants came to regard them with dismay and loathing. Because of their political activities they were suspected of constant plotting. Their skill in logic led their opponents to charge that the Jesuits could make the worse appear the better reason. And in the religious recriminations of the time, their Protestant opponents accused them—quite erroneously—of believing that "the end justifies the means" and that any methods, however dubious or circuitous, were proper if they advanced the Catholic cause.

Even among Catholics there was a certain amount of opposition to the Jesuits. Older religious orders eyed their success with some envy and jealousy. But when the Society of Jesus celebrated its hundredth anniversary, it could look back on a proud record of achievements. Its eight hundred houses with fifteen thousand members represented a remarkable growth from the little band that had originally joined with St. Ignatius in Paris.

C. Catholic Revival, Political and Religious

In most of southern Europe, Protestantism in its various forms never represented more than a threat to the Catholic Church. Protestant preachers and teachers arose in Italy but they made slight headway, for Italy was bound more closely to the papal fortunes than any other country. Italians profited from the funds drawn in by the church from the rest of Europe. Italians held a large proportion of high church offices. Italian princes and nobles were often recipients of papal favors. Aided by the doctrinal clarity and the reform in discipline that followed the Council of Trent, the Catholic Church, through the Inquisition, through the Jesuits and the other new orders, and through a firm control of the schools and universities, was able to suppress all Protestant tendencies in Italy in the sixteenth century.

In Spain and Portugal, likewise, the kings supported the Catholic Church with consistency. Before the Protestant revolt broke out, Ferdinand and Isabella had persuaded the pope to transfer control of the Inquisition in Spain to the crown. Throughout the sixteenth century the Spanish Inquisition was employed for political as well as religious purposes and was supported by secular as well as ecclesiastical authority. As the champions of Catholicism in all Europe, Charles V and Philip II took good care that religious uniformity was maintained at home in Spain. In Germany, the influence of the Habsburgs and of the Catholic princes in the southern part of the country aided the forces of the Catholic revival, although in Bohemia, where the tradition of John Hus was still evident, the Habsburgs, up to the end of the sixteenth century, were not able to eliminate strong Protestant movements.

During the first half of the sixteenth century, conditions in the Catholic Church had been as bad in Poland as anywhere in Europe. It is not surprising, therefore, that Calvinists, Lutherans, and radical sects made considerable progress in Poland and that a fairly large number of Polish nobles went over to Protestantism. But here the forces of the Catholic revival soon gathered strength. King Sigismund II (1548–1572), despite his Calvinist wife, upheld the decisions of the Council of Trent and brought the Jesuits into Poland to stem the Protestant tide. As a consequence, the Catholic Church, reformed and strengthened, regained in Poland and Lithuania the ground it had briefly lost.

It was the Jesuits again, backed by the Habsburgs, who played a major role in Hungary in restricting Calvinists, Lutherans, and various heretical sects. On the other side of Europe in the Netherlands, the fate of the Catholic Church was closely tied with political developments. In the seven northern provinces, which eventually gained their independence from the Habsburgs, Calvinism became dominant, while in the ten southern provinces, where the Habsburgs continued to rule, almost all the people remained loyal to Catholicism.

In France, as has been related, Calvinism succeeded in establishing itself while still remaining the religion of a small but active minority. Toward the middle of the century the Catholic forces sought to do by propaganda and persuasion what political support was evidently failing to do. Aided by the reforms of the Council of Trent, by the activity of Jesuit preachers and teachers, and by a remarkable revival of national Catholic sentiment, the Catholic Church in France lost no more ground to the Protestants. In fact, during the first half of the seventeenth century a number of French Protestants returned to Catholicism

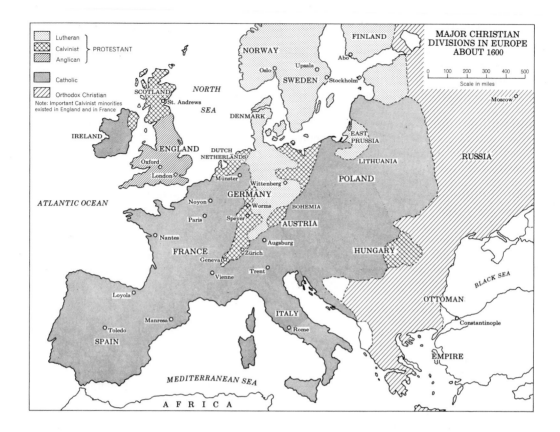

FINLAND

NORWAY
Oslo   Upsala
Abo
SWEDEN   Stockholm
Moscow

NORTH
SCOTLAND   St. Andrews
SEA
DENMARK

RUSSIA

IRELAND
EAST
PRUSSIA
ENGLAND   DUTCH
NETHERLANDS
LITHUANIA
Oxford
London   Münster
Wittenberg
POLAND

ATLANTIC OCEAN
GERMANY
Noyon   Worms
BOHEMIA
Paris   Speyer
AUSTRIA
Nantes   Augsburg

FRANCE   Zürich
Geneva   HUNGARY
Vienne   Trent
BLACK SEA

Loyola
OTTOMAN

Manresa   ITALY
Constantinople
Toledo   Rome
SPAIN
EMPIRE

MEDITERRANEAN SEA

A F R I C A

whether moved by religious conviction or by the hope of reward from the successors of Henry IV who seemed to be more sincerely devout than that monarch.

More important in the long run than ephemeral political support was a genuine religious revival. For before the end of the sixteenth century there was under way in Europe an extraordinary renewal of the Catholic faith. During the middle ages and especially in the late middle age, most Catholics had taken their religion as a habit and a mere matter of course. But the events of the sixteenth century brought about a change. Catholics had to defend their beliefs and examine their individual relations to their religious faith. Many became eager to prove by their lives and their acts that the fruits of Catholicism were both godly and goodly. They founded new orders to canalize their good works into fruitful lines. They organized new schools to educate the youth as able defenders of the faith. They wrote and read new books which proclaimed the mystical

and divine mission of the Church. They were inspired by the martyrdom of priests and laymen who died in Protestant countries for their belief in Catholic Christianity.

Though the Jesuits were perhaps the most notable and most successful of the new Catholic orders that sprang up after the Protestant revolt, they were by no means unique. Some of the new orders were devoted to special kinds of service. Thus the Theatines, founded in 1524 by St. Cajetan and Giovanni Caraffa (later Pope Paul IV) had as their object the promotion of personal piety and the combating of heresy by preaching. The Capuchins, who arose at about the same time, were an off-shoot of the older order of the Franciscans. Their chief mission was preaching to the poor and ministering to their spiritual needs. By 1619 when they were finally recognized as an independent order, they had fifteen hundred houses scattered throughout Catholic Europe.

A new kind of Catholic religious order,

called a "congregation," developed during the latter part of the sixteenth century. It consisted of secular priests, living and working together for a period under temporary vows. One such "congregation" was that of the Oratorians founded at Rome by St. Philip Neri. It grew up around evening meetings organized by St. Philip, at which there were readings, prayer, discussion, and musical selections with sacred settings which are still called "oratorios." The members undertook to preach in the evenings of weekdays at the various churches in Rome. The organization was formally recognized by the pope in 1575. Oratories, after the model of the original one, spread rapidly through Italy and France. With a loose, democratic organization, that made them in some respects almost like clubs for priests, they brought together many able men and some of the Oratories became famous for their scholars.

A somewhat similar order was that of the Oblates, founded by St. Charles Borromeo in 1578. Its members were pledged to aid the Church whenever and wherever they could, and in each diocese in which they were established, their services were at the immediate disposal of the local bishop.

While the new orders of varied types played a major role in the Catholic revival, the older organizations which had come down from the middle ages enjoyed a rebirth of activity and devotion. The Dominicans, for example, had long been famous as teachers in the universities and as the most active members of the Inquisition. In both roles, the troubled times of the sixteenth century called forth from them redoubled zeal. In most Catholic countries, the Chief Inquisitor was usually a learned Dominican. Among the Franciscans, too, there was a notable revival. Not only did this order give birth to the Capuchins, but it vied with them in promoting the Christian way of life exemplified by St. Francis of Assisi.

Amidst the revival of faith, the Catholic Church produced in the sixteenth century a number of famous saints. One of the most notable was St. Teresa (1515–1582), a Spanish Carmelite nun, whose spiritual experiences and beatific visions formed the substance of an extraordinary autobiography. St. Teresa wrote beautiful poetry as well as prose, and yet had time to found fourteen monasteries and sixteen convents. A somewhat different type was St. Francis de Sales (1567–1622). A wealthy noble of Savoy by birth, he founded the order of the Visitation for those strong in spirit but weak in body who could not endure the austerities of some of the other orders. But his greatest influence was through the gentleness, devoutness, and firmness of his personality. While still alive he was regarded by many as a saint and on a visit to Paris toward the end of his life he became the center of a veritable religious revival.

The renewal of mysticism, of devotion to the Church, and of faith in its divine mission led in the late sixteenth and early seventeenth centuries, not only to the formation of new religious orders, but also to the building of many churches, schools, and seminaries and to a remarkable growth of charitable organizations. The same impulses, combined with the fact of European expansion overseas, led to a tremendous outburst of Catholic missionary activity in far places.

D. Catholic Overseas Missions

During the sixteenth century the work of expansion overseas, of exploration and empire building, were almost exclusively in the hands of Spain and Portugal, lands which remained consistently loyal to Catholicism. From the start, one of the objectives of the Spanish and to a lesser degree of the Portuguese, in opening up new lands, was to win converts for the Catholic Church. Each expedition usually took with it priests and monks who ministered to the needs of emigrant Europeans and strove to bring Christianity to the natives.

Sometimes the conversion of native Americans or Asiatics was superficial and imposed by force. Sometimes it was strangely combined with economic oppression and exploitation. But if there was outcry against the ruthless methods of the conquerors, it came from priests like Bartolomé de las Casas who sought to protect the natives. And in America, at least in accessible areas,

Rome. St. Peter's. Facade and Piazza completed in the seventeenth century.

Christianity largely replaced the cruel native religions.

One of the most remarkable missionary careers was that of St. Francis Xavier (1506–1552), friend and co-worker of St. Ignatius Loyola, and known for his labors in the Far East as the "Apostle of the Indies." Born of a noble family in Spanish Navarre, he received a thorough classical education at Paris. Then, won over to St. Ignatius' plans, he devoted himself to religious work. In 1541 he joined a mission which was being sent to the East Indies by the Portuguese king, and reached Goa the next year. There he began his missionary work. In the ensuing years he preached and taught and converted up and down the coast of India, then pushed on to Ceylon, Malacca, and the Spice Islands. Meeting a Japanese exile in Malacca, he was inspired to carry Christianity to Japan, and reached that little-known island empire

in 1549. After a return trip to India, he died on his way to China where he had planned to continue his work.

Incredible stories are told of the hundreds of thousands of Asiatics who embraced Christianity as a result of Xavier's preaching. But it is clear that in the face of gigantic difficulties he began and organized missionary work in a dozen different areas. In Japan, indeed, so rapidly did Christianity grow in the last half of the sixteenth century that the native rulers felt called upon to suppress it by force as a threat to native institutions. The missionary activity in China of which Xavier had dreamed was actually accomplished by another Jesuit, Matteo Ricci (1552–1610), who spent twenty-seven years there. By his knowledge of science and mathematics, Ricci won the respect of the Chinese, and for a period he held an important place at the court of the emperor. It was Ricci and his fellow Jesuits who introduced western learning into China and gave Europe the first accurate knowledge of that country. Simultaneously, under Spanish auspices, the Philippine Islands were largely christianized.

On the other side of the world, Catholic missionaries—Franciscan, Jesuit, and Dominican—were laboring among the heathen in a somewhat different fashion. As Spanish rule expanded in America, the outposts of empire frequently consisted of missions organized by priests or monks to work among the natives. The mission normally consisted of a church surrounded by a small village. Here the Indians were gathered together, taught to till the soil, instructed in useful arts, protected from their Spanish rulers, and converted to Christianity. Over the mission ruled the priests or monks with a strict but kindly paternalism. As outposts, the missions had a political and military as well as a religious importance. They were indeed the knots with which the Spanish tied up the raveled edges of their empire.

In America, the Catholic missionaries accomplished a great deal that was a by-product of their religious work. Much of the exploration of Brazil and of the interior of South and Central America was accomplished by intrepid churchmen who boldly crossed mountains, sailed on rivers, and pierced jungles where no white man had ever preceded them. Into missions were introduced European plants and animals, and from them fruits and vegetables were sent back to Europe. The missionaries often compiled grammars and dictionaries of the native languages, translated the Bible into local tongues, and wrote works on the cultures and customs of the peoples among whom they labored. Thus they played an important role in Europeanizing the new lands and in introducing into Europe knowledge of overseas areas and peoples.

All the missionary activity overseas demanded organization and guidance from Rome. The demand was met in a preliminary way by Pope Gregory XIII, who originated, about 1582, a plan for the control of missionary activity. But this plan was not fully developed till 1622 when Pope Gregory XV organized the Congregation of the Propaganda and gave it charge of mission-ary work in non-Catholic countries. Five years later the College of the Propaganda was established to train missionaries.

After the close of the sixteenth century, other countries played a part in missionary endeavor. French priests explored the pathless wilderness of North America and gave their lives in efforts to convert the warlike Iroquois. England and, to a lesser degree, Holland made a beginning of Protestant missions overseas. Spain and Portugal continued their earlier endeavors. But the way had been opened, and the pattern for much of the later activity set, by the heroic efforts of the sixteenth-century pioneering missionaries who carried overseas the religious zeal and enthusiasm engendered by developments in Europe.

E. General Effects of the Religious Upheaval

It is difficult to determine clearly what were the effects of the religious events of the sixteenth century on other aspects of life, for in many cases they were entangled with older trends or with other new developments. But certain changes seem to have been closely associated with the religious revolution. One was, for example, an outburst of intolerance and fanaticism. In 1500 almost all the inhabitants of western and central Europe were Catholic Christians living in religious peace with one another. Seventy years later, in addition to Catholics, there were Lutherans, Calvinists, Anglicans, Anabaptists, Mennonites, and a dozen other sects, all quarreling with each other, persecuting and being persecuted.

Both Catholics and Protestants took arms to defend their creeds and there were battles and massacres and assassinations of the most ferocious sort. Prisoners of war and even women and children were often slaughtered without mercy. In countries remaining Catholic, the Inquisition, spies, police, and the army were employed to wipe out religious dissent. Protestants were often tortured and then burned at the stake. On the other hand, in lands which became Protestant, Catholics were banished or put to death and their property seized, while priests were hunted down like public enemies.

In the long run, but only in the long run, the Protestant revolt led to greater toleration, for in some lands two or more sects came to be so firmly established that people at length grew weary of strife between them, and governments less insistent on securing religious uniformity. Thus in Catholic France the Huguenots secured toleration by the Edict of Nantes in 1598. Poland showed signs of a tolerant policy in the sixteenth century, and Holland became quite tolerant in the seventeenth. In some American colonies of England, such as Rhode Island, Pennsylvania, and Maryland, toleration was the public policy at some time in the course of the seventeenth century. Modern religious tolerance is, however, more a result of the growth after 1700 of religious apathy and of rationalism, than a direct outcome of the religious upheaval of the sixteenth century.

One result of the fierce religious struggles that began with Luther was a growing strictness of morals and behavior. Each side accused the other of looseness and immorality. Protestants told with horror of the evil lives of Catholic priests and bishops. Catholics were equally horrified that the Protestants permitted divorce. To meet these charges both Catholic and Protestant strove to preach and to practice higher moral standards. Not only the Calvinists were puritantical. Everywhere efforts were made to put down swearing and blasphemy, to suppress lewd books, and to make sure that all ministers and priests led holy lives.

Similarly, both Catholics and Protestants were eventually driven to establish schools and improve their educational facilities. If they were to meet their opponents in debate, they must have the necessary intellectual tools at their disposal. Special efforts were made to see to it that priests, pastors, and ministers received proper instruction, and many new schools were founded especially to train them.

In a less direct way, the religious revolt may have led to an increase in individualism. The Catholic Church had always stressed unity in doctrine, and salvation through the church organization. Most of the reformers, on the other hand, tended to emphasize the relation of each individual to God. Each man was to read the Bible and interpret it for himself. The reformers were usually quite intolerant of anyone whose interpretation failed to coincide with their own. Yet in the long run, their teachings probably served to heighten the traditional Christian belief in the importance of the individual, and this not only in religious, but in economic and political life as well.

It can, for example, be argued that the religious revolt had some influence in aiding the rise of modern democracy. The emphasis on the worth of the individual is part of the democratic faith. Many of the radical sects organized their congregations in a democratic fashion. The Calvinists in France, England, Hungary, and elsewhere, because they were in a minority, stood against royal absolutism. But most of the new sects, even the Calvinists, were organized in an aristocratic fashion, and the principal Protestant leaders had little confidence in the ability of the masses to guide their own affairs.

In fact, the first effect of the religious upheaval was undoubtedly to strengthen the power of princes and kings, to increase the trend toward monarchical absolutism. In the Lutheran states of Germany and Scandinavia, in England, and even in Switzerland and Holland, the rulers added to their power by securing control of religious affairs at the same time that they increased their wealth by the seizure of church lands. In Catholic countries, too, the monarchs took advantage of the pope's difficulties to wring from him concessions that gave them greater power in church matters. In the three centuries immediately following Luther, rulers had much more absolute power than formerly.

Closely connected with this trend toward absolutism was a tendency toward "secularization," that is, the transfer to lay governments of the control of numerous activities which had formerly been handled by the church. In the middle ages, education, charity, and many legal matters had been in the hands of the church. When the power of the church was broken and its lands and endowments seized in Protestant countries, it became necessary for the government to step in to establish schools, to care for the poor and the sick, and to make laws on marriage

Statue of Moses. Michelangelo (d. 1564).

and the family. In the matter of charity, at least, the state was often a poor substitute for the church. The new work-houses were rarely an improvement on the old alms-houses.

In another sphere, the effects of the religious changes are less clear. Scholars are still arguing as to whether Protestantism hastened the rise of capitalism or not. It is clear that the church in the middle ages had disapproved not only the taking of interest on loans but also any undue eagerness to acquire wealth. It is equally clear that the Protestants and especially the Calvinists were more lenient about interest and stressed those virtues of thrift, sobriety, and hard work which are suitable to the growth of business and capitalism. But the first great capitalists arose in Catholic areas like north Italy, south Germany, and the southern Netherlands. Only later did the Protestant capitalists come to the fore. Perhaps the safest conclusion is that both the religious revolt and the rise of capitalism were caused by dozens of intertwined factors in the sixteenth century. It is, nonetheless, evident that by 1600 Calvinism was creating an environment very suitable for growing capitalism in Holland and in other areas.

F. Cultural Trends in the Sixteenth Century

The religious upheaval of the sixteenth century tended to bring to a close the great intellectual quickening of the renaissance. Italian humanism reached its climax with the pontificate of Leo X (1513–1521). Of the outstanding northern humanists, Johann Reuchlin (*d.* 1522), Philip Melancthon (*d.* 1560), John Colet (*d.* 1519). Thomas More (*d.* 1535), and the greatest of them, Desiderius Erasmus (*d.* 1536), all save Melancthon were mature men before Luther began his attacks on the church. Those who lived long enough were all diverted from their classical studies and literary work by religious controversy. It is true that the learning which they had brought to northern Europe, the knowledge of Greek and Hebrew and the critical scholarship, did not die out. But after 1520 or 1530 the new learning was put more and more to the service of theological and religious disputes. The arguments were

not now concerned with the great Latin and Greek writers, but with the interpretation of the New Testament or the origins of papal supremacy.

In art, the impetus of the earlier "golden age" continued. Michelangelo (*d.* 1564) did much of his best work in painting, in sculpture and in architecture, after Luther posted his theses on the church door at Wittenberg. Titian (*d.* 1576), Veronese (*d.* 1588), Tintoretto (*d.* 1594), and the later Venetian painters were active through most of the sixteenth century. Spain boasted of El Greco (*d.* 1614); and Holbein (*d.* 1543), the German painter, who has preserved for us the likenesses of Henry VIII and many of his contemporaries, was followed by Lucas Cranach (*d.* 1553), to whom we owe portraits of Luther. And in the Netherlands, a great artistic genius, Peter Bruegel (*d.* 1569), was able not only to portray inimitably the people of his land in their rustic occupations and in moods of gaity, but also with bitter satire to expose their sufferings under the Spanish occupation.

In Palladio (*d.* 1580) Italian renaissance architecture reached a culmination which was to lead to the baroque early in the following century. Meanwhile, in England Elizabethan gentlemen were constructing gracious "Tudor" manor houses. And in France renaissance motifs influenced, but did not entirely replace, gothic features in the wonderful sixteenth-century *châteaux* of the Loire valley.

Appropriately too, in an age of monarchical consolidation, literature in the vernacular continued to flourish. We have mentioned the popularity of the German Bible of Luther and the great surge of Elizabethan literature. And we shall note later the literary achievements of Spain. In France, Calvin followed the original Latin edition of his *Institutes of the Christian Religion* with another version in French. In the first half of the sixteenth century, Rabelais (*d.* 1553), a humanist and admirer of Erasmus, produced his celebrated satires, *Pantagruel* and *Gargantua*, in a coarse but vigorous French. Somewhat later, Ronsard (*d.* 1585) and du Bellay (*d.* 1560), the founders of a group of French writers known as the *Plé-iade*, were imparting to French literature a character at once more formal and more classical. And French literature was further enriched by the essays of Montaigne (*d.* 1592).

The sixteenth century also brought important achievements in music. Among the noted composers of the period, the name of Giovanni Pierluigi (*d.* 1594), more commonly known as Palestrina from the town of his birth, stands out. Palestrina composed a considerable quantity of ecclesiastical music, which is unsurpassed in its combination of technical skill, tonal appeal, and liturgical appropriateness. Setting himself against the over-elaborate style of some of his contemporaries, he produced masses and motets in which the music enhances and supports the words of the liturgy without dominating them. Although he exploited to the full the possibilities of polyphony, Palestrina made his music a natural accompaniment of religious worship and prayer.

In the sixteenth century there were other cultural developments which proved to be steps toward the creation of the modern spirit. These were notable advances in the field of science; and it is the influence of science, more perhaps than anything else, which distinguishes the modern mind and temper from that of earlier centuries. The scientific achievements of the sixteenth century owed much to the labors of the preceding generations, whose accomplishments at such places as Oxford, Paris, and Padua have been described. And while those men had contributed much to mathematics, chemistry, physics, and astronomy, they had, in general, not challenged the Ptolemaic concept of a geocentric universe.

In the year 1543, the year of his death, a Polish Catholic priest named Copernicus (1473–1543) put forward another theory in his work entitled *On the Revolutions of the Celestial Bodies.* He had found hints for his idea in the works of certain Greek and Roman authors. From these, by observations, calculations, and reflections, he developed the heliocentric theory, which held that the planets, including the earth, revolved around the sun.

The new theory was in every way superior to the old Ptolemaic system. It was far simpler and mathematically sounder. But it upset many old notions. Aristotle had taught that the sun moves around the earth.

The common man thought he saw it so move. And churchmen had accepted this view, for it seemed to fit in with the notions which made the earth the great central stage on which the drama of man's salvation was being played. The Copernican theory which demoted the earth and its inhabitants to a secondary role, therefore, made its way but slowly. It was not accepted by most educated men before the middle of the seventeenth century.

In the meantime, however, further work was buttressing and demonstrating the validity of the new theory. Tycho Brahe (1546–1601), a Danish astronomer, made new and better observations of the movements of the heavenly bodies. Using Brahe's observations, a German named Kepler (1571–1630) worked out three mathematical statements or "laws" which described the way in which planets moved around the sun. The simplest of them declares that the path of a planet moving around the sun is an ellipse, with the sun at one of the two foci of the ellipse.

Most important of all, perhaps, was the work of the Italian Galileo (1564–1642). A great scientist in the fields of mechanics, mathematics, and optics as well as in astronomy, Galileo by his lectures at the University of Padua demonstrated and popularized the Copernican system. With a small telescope which he built (though the telescope does not seem to have been his invention), he showed that the sun was turning on its axis and that Jupiter was attended by moons revolving about it. These facts made it easier to believe that the earth turned daily on its axis and revolved around the sun. Unfortunately for Galileo, his enthusiastic desire to convert the church at once to the new astronomy got him into trouble. The church court of the Inquisition in 1616 condemned the Copernican system and in 1632 Galileo was found guilty of upholding it and punished for so doing.

It is noteworthy that it was a pope, Gregory XIII (1572–1585), who took advantage of the increasing astronomical knowledge to reform the calendar. The Julian calendar, in use since Roman times, had gotten ten days ahead of astronomical time. The new Gregorian calendar moved the date back by ten days and arranged to keep the calendar and the solar year in line by omitting the extra leap year day in all years ending in 00 (like 1700) unless the number of the year could be divided evenly by 400 (like 1600). The Gregorian calendar was quickly adopted by Catholic countries, more slowly by others. England accepted it only in 1751, and Russia not until 1922.

As in astronomy, great advances were made in mathematics. In Italy, Tartaglia (1506–1559) and Cardan (1501–1576) vied with each other in solving cubic equations. In Holland, Stevinus (1548–1620) wrote on decimal fractions, while in Scotland John Napier (1550–1617) invented logarithms and was the first to use the decimal point. In physics, great strides were made. The compound microscope was in use by about 1590 and the telescope a decade later. William Gilbert (1540–1603) experimented with magnetism. Galileo invented an air thermometer and an astronomical clock, while his work on falling bodies disposed of the old notion that heavy objects fall faster than light ones. Medicine and physiology were advanced by Paracelsus (1493–1541), half quack though he was, and by Vesalius (1514–1564) with his great treatise on anatomy. Not long after the end of the sixteenth century, William Harvey (1578–1657) discovered the circulation of blood from the heart through the arteries and back to the heart through the veins.

Similar progress was registered in half a dozen other fields. The expansion overseas, for example, greatly stimulated work in astronomy, geography, botany, and zoölogy. Men's minds were being expanded in many directions, most of which had but little connection with religious strife and controversy. Occasionally the two areas of thought collided. Giordano Bruno (1548–1600), an intemperate and stormy Italian, fell under the spell of the new science. He espoused the Copernican astronomy, jeered at the biblical miracles, and put the Hebrew scriptures on the level with pagan myths. He tried to work out a religious conception by which the whole of nature was conceived of as embodying and expressing the divine. He aroused the ire of Protestants and Catholics alike and was eventually burned at the stake in Rome. More important was the work of Francis Bacon (1561–1626), an English lawyer, courtier, official, and writer. In a series of writings, he developed a new philosophy adapted to the new science. He pleaded for induction, observation, and experiment, and insisted on the usefulness of scientific knowledge.

While some men pushed forward the frontiers of science and of thought, and others took part in fierce religious controversies, it must not be thought that most Europeans were engaged in intellectual pursuits. The vast majority of them still could not read or write. They toiled in the fields or worked at their crafts almost oblivious of many of the new developments. For them the world was still full of magic and superstitions. Even the upper classes still believed in witches, in astrology (the theory that stars influence men's lives), and in fabulous tales about distant lands. The great contributions in every field of thought were, in the sixteenth century as always, the work of a small elite of able thinkers. Yet in the long run these thinkers had more to do with the shaping of the world of today than even the kings and generals whose pomp and power dazzled the eyes of all.

It should also be remarked and emphasized that, overwhelming as was the impact on Western civilization of the religious upheaval, this did not entirely monopolize the energies of the early modern age.

CHAPTER 32

Successes and Failures of Philip II of Spain

A. Philip II, the Man and the Monarch

As Charles V had dominated the first half of the sixteenth century in Europe, so his son Philip II (1556–1598) dominated the second half. He came to the throne of Spain at a time when that country seemed at a peak of power and influence. At his death, a beginning of Spain's decline might have been detected. But during his reign he strove mightily to fulfill the manifold obligations which birth had placed upon him.

When Philip II in 1556, at the age of twenty-eight, became King of Spain, he did not fall heir to all the lands which his father had held. His uncle Ferdinand of Habsburg, who by election and marriage had become King of Bohemia and a part of Hungary, obtained the archduchy of Austria and was chosen to succeed Charles V as Holy Roman Emperor. Philip, however, received the impressive remainder of the family inheritance which included Spain, the Netherlands, Franche Comté, Milan, Naples, Sicily, and the Spanish holdings in North Africa, America, and the West Indies, together with the Philippines which had been claimed after Magellan's discovery of them in 1521 and further explored in 1542. Moreover, if Philip relinquished the German and Austrian holdings of his father, he nonetheless felt called upon to aid his relatives in those areas, and the family ties between the Habsburgs of Spain and Austria were drawn ever closer by new alliances.

Ferdinand's son and successor married Philip's sister, and Philip's son and successor married Ferdinand's granddaughter.

Philip II has been represented as a deceitful and bigoted despot by English and Dutch writers, and by Spanish authors as the stalwart champion of Christian civilization. The judgment passed on Philip depends largely on the view taken of his policies, for the policies themselves are reasonably clear.

To begin with, Philip had a profound sense of dedication to the obligations of his office and a constant loyalty to the responsibilities placed upon him by his birth and heritage. Whatever he undertook he pursued to the end with extraordinary persistence, and no area of his scattered dominions—nor those of his Habsburg relatives in Germany—escaped his attention. Yet despite his widespread involvements, and in marked contrast to Charles V, Philip prized Spain as his native country and his most important possession. He spoke Spanish as fluently as his father had spoken Dutch. He surrounded himself with Spanish advisers, lived most of his life in Spain, and sought by every means to make Spain strong and powerful.

Finally, Philip was sincerely and piously attached to Catholicism. He abhorred Protestantism as a blasphemous rending of the seamless garment of the church and a grave menace to law and order. Confronted with a choice between the best interests of Spain and those of the church, he worked for the latter as he conceived them. His drastic use of the Inquisition, for example, undoubtedly promoted a kind of unity in Spain, but it was in the long run a unity dearly bought at the expense of the economic and political strength of the nation. No seeming failure of his policies could weaken Philip's belief in their fundamental excellence. What he did he did for the greater glory of God. Success or failure depended on the inscrutable will of the Almighty.

To carry out his policies, Philip was in some ways well-equipped. He had a boundless capacity for hard work. All day and much of the night he toiled over the reports and documents that came to him from his far-flung dominions. So conscientious was he that frequently the administration bogged down because the monarch was swamped in his paper work. He was more of a man of the desk and the pen than of the sword and the war horse. But if he preferred diplomacy to battle, he was ever ready to send his troops to fight for a cause that he conceived to be righteous. His conviction of his own righteousness made him intolerant of both political and religious dissent and led him to use wile, deceit, and even assassination to gain his ends.

Whatever his personal equipment, Philip faced tasks that in their multiplicity and difficulty were too much for any man, and he had to play a world role from a Spanish base that in itself presented many problems. Spain was a country of only nine or ten million people and it was composed of historically separate kingdoms, each with traditions and privileges. Philip II sought to further the work of national unification begun by his great-grandparents, Ferdinand and Isabella, and carried on by his father, because national unification implied uniformity and greater power for the crown. Absolutism and uniformity became the watchwords of his internal administration. Politically, Philip made little pretense of consulting the local legislatures or cortes about new laws, and although he convoked them to vote new taxes, he made it the rule that old taxes were to be considered as granted forever. Rejecting the older capitals of the Spanish peninsula, Philip embellished a formerly bleak area a few miles from Ma-

drid near the geographical center of the country and there erected the magnificent but austere Escorial—combined palace and monastery. He made the nobles ornaments of the court rather than active statesmen, and put into the important offices lawyers and other subservient members of the middle class. Philip "the Prudent," as he came to be called, was the hard-working center of a complicated administration, which gradually became entangled in formal rules and much red tape.

Economically, the burdens Philip II placed on Spain were too heavy. More and more it had to finance his costly endeavors all over the world. If silver flowed in from America, it flowed out again with amazing rapidity to buy goods and support armies, for Philip did little to encourage industry or commerce within Spain. The ten per cent sales tax, called the *alcabala,* collected on each transaction, slowed down trade and hampered production. The great sheep-herding combine, the *Mesta,* won the support of the crown at the expense of other kinds of agriculture.

The expulsion of the Jews (1492) and the Moors (1502), led to the persecution of those (*Maranos* and *Moriscos*) who, as converts to Christianity, were allowed to remain. Thus Spain lost or lessened the contribution of some economically productive elements in the population. As the burdens of Philip's policy grew, Spain's ability to bear them decreased, and by the end of the century the country was staggering under the load.

One major addition to Spain's problems came in 1580, when Philip, eager to complete the political unity of the Iberian peninsula, laid claim to the throne of Portugal, whose king had just died. Philip bought off the duke of Braganza whose right to the Portuguese crown was better than his own, and sent in Spanish troops to take over the country. Despite Philip's efforts to placate the Portuguese by recognition of their constitutional rights and his endeavor to win over the nobility and country gentry by favors, Spanish rule was unpopular in Portugal. It was to be just sixty years until the Portuguese found an opportunity to reëstablish a native ruler. But in the meantime,

King Philip II of Spain. Sixteenth century marble bust.

Courtesy Metropolitan Museum of Art; bequest of Annie C. Kane, 1926

Spain had to defend Portugal and Portuguese trade and colonies, without receiving from that country much financial or military support.

A sign of the opposition to Philip's policies in Spain was the revolts he faced there. When he tried to stamp out heresy among the *Moriscos*, the descendants of the Moors in southern Spain, they rose in a bloody revolt in 1568, and were suppressed only after two years of bitter fighting. A revolt in Aragon in 1591 had to be put down by a Castilian army, and as a result the traditional rights and privileges of that kingdom were further reduced.

B. Spain's Many Problems Abroad

Of all the difficulties which Philip faced abroad, the most serious and most permanent was the revolt of the Netherlands which began about 1566, and was still in progress at his death in 1598. The prosperous Netherlanders objected to the burdensome taxes and the attempts to regulate their economy in the interests of Spain. Cities, provinces, and nobles alike resented the curtailment of long cherished rights and privileges. In addition, since Philip never understood Dutch ways, and appointed

El Escorial, the monastery-palace-mausoleum of Philip II of Spain.

Courtesy Spanish National Tourist Department, New York

Spaniards as governors and high officials in church and state, Spanish rule came to seem more and more like government by and for foreigners. Philip, who never visited the Netherlands after 1559, offered an unpleasant contrast to his father who had been at home in the Netherlands.

Finally, despite the rapid spread of Calvinism throughout the northern provinces of the Netherlands, Philip was resolved to force Catholicism upon all his subjects. He rearranged the bishoprics and increased their number. He issued decrees against religious dissent. He strengthened the Inquisition

and employed it ruthlessly. Thus, for a combination of reasons, the Netherlanders found Spanish rule unbearable.

At first the opposition in the Netherlands was sporadic and ill-organized. But in 1566 a group of nobles and townsmen requested the Regent, Margaret of Parma, to urge Philip to abolish the Inquisition and to redress other grievances. The Regent, disquieted by the petitioners, was reassured by a courtier who exclaimed, "What, Madam, is your Highness afraid of these beggars?" The epithet was seized upon by the opponents of Philip. They called themselves

with a large army and with instructions to reduce the people to submission.

In the next six years, Alba did his best to carry out his master's wishes. To try treason cases, he created an arbitrary court which won the name of the "Council of Blood." In the period of his rule, some eight thousand persons were executed, including two great nobles, Counts Egmont and Horn, who were patriots rather than religious fanatics. Taxes were increased, property confiscated, and thousands of Calvinists were forced into exile. So ruthless was Alba's rule that the Catholic townsmen of the southern Netherlands united with the Protestants of the north to oppose the Spanish tyranny. For a leader, the country found a nobleman, German by birth, French by title, who had large estates in the Netherlands and had held high offices there. He was William of Nassau, Prince of Orange (1533–1584), usually called William the Silent, though he was actually talkative to a normal degree.

At first the nondescript forces of William of Orange were easily routed by Alba. But soon a new factor developed. In 1569, William began to charter privateers to harass and prey upon Spanish shipping. These "Sea Beggars," as they were called, were mainly a wild and unruly lot, united by hatred of Spaniards and Catholics and by hope of loot. They were competent seamen and soon laid the foundations of Dutch naval power. They raided commerce, sailed up the numerous waterways, and before long had seized coastal towns and islands which served as secure bases for further operations.

When it was clear that Alba with his harsh tactics was making little headway, Philip replaced him, in 1573, with the more politic Requesens. But the new governor died three years later having accomplished little, and shortly after his death (1576) the unpaid Spanish soldiery mutinied and sacked the great commercial town of Antwerp with fire and sword, an event known as the "Spanish fury." Shocked by this happening, deputies from all seventeen provinces met and concluded an agreement known as the "Pacification of Ghent," by which they agreed to resist the Spaniards till Philip should abolish the Inquisition and reëstablish the old liberties. But before

"Beggars" and used the old emblems of begging, the wallet and the bowl, as symbols.

Philip at first showed signs of wishing to pacify the Netherlands by concessions. But in the same year, 1566, the more radical Protestants, enraged at the religious decrees, took to arms and attacked Catholic churches, wrecking altars, breaking windows, and smashing images. The magnificent cathedral of Antwerp was irreparably ruined. To Philip there could be but one answer to such violence and sacrilege. In 1567 he sent his most famous general, the duke of Alba,

Portrait of William the Silent. Willem Key
(d. 1568).

*Courtesy Foundation Johan Maurits van Nassau,
Mauritshuis, The Hague*

long, this union was broken up. Philip's
governor from 1578 to 1592 in the Netherlands was Alexander Farnese, Duke of
Parma. Adroitly mingling war with diplomacy, Parma sowed seeds of discord between
the ten southern provinces, which were
largely Catholic and industrial and in part
French-speaking, and the seven northern
provinces, which were largely Calvinist and
commercial and wholly Dutch-speaking. In
1579 the southern provinces joined in the
League of Arras to seek a reconciliation with
Philip, while the northern provinces agreed,
by the Union of Utrecht, to persevere in the
fight for independence. Thereby the Netherlands were permanently split, and Spain
kept possession of the southern portion
(modern Belgium) throughout the next
century.

Meanwhile, in the northern (Dutch)
Netherlands, the struggle dragged on. In
1581, Philip proclaimed William of Orange
a traitor and offered a reward for his person,
dead or alive. William replied by a famous

Apology in which he justified his acts. He
was able to persuade the representatives of
the northern provinces to proclaim their independence from Spain in an "Act of Abjuration." William was assassinated in 1584
by a Spanish agent, and Farnese captured
Antwerp from the Protestants in the next
year. But thereafter the Spanish made little
headway against the stubborn Dutch.

Although the Dutch received some aid in
men, munitions, and money from the German Protestants, from England, and from
France, and, of course, profited from the
defeat of the Armada in 1588, their ability
to resist the might of Spain lay largely in
their own resources. The rise of Dutch sea
power enabled them to harass Spanish shipping and to cut sea communications between Spain and the Netherlands. At the
same time their commerce built up their
wealth and made possible the employment
of mercenary soldiers. Moreover, the Spanish were operating at a distance from their
base in difficult country peculiarly vulnerable
to such Dutch tactics as opening the dykes.

Finally, in 1609, Philip's son and successor Philip III (1598–1621), made a twelve-
year truce with the Dutch. During this
interim, Dutch wealth and power grew
apace and Holland was able to play a major
role in the ensuing Thirty Years' War. At its
conclusion in 1648, Spain reluctantly recognized that Holland was a free and independent nation.

The defeat of the Armada has been mentioned in connection with events in English history. As a major undertaking of
Philip II it deserves further treatment here.
In 1588, Philip had assembled to send forth
against England what was called the "Invin-
cible Armada," the most formidable fleet
which Christendom had ever seen—130
ships, 8,000 seamen, 19,000 soldiers, and the
flower of Spanish chivalry. It was placed
under the command of the Duke of Medina-
Sidonia, a man without important previous
experience in maritime affairs. Out of a
deeply felt sense of duty the Duke accepted
and, remedying his lack of knowledge by
careful study of all the problems he had to
face, proved to be an extraordinarily able
commander. But a combination of the failure of the Spanish authorities in the Netherlands to appear with invasion barges at the

appointed rendezvous, the weather, and the clever tactics of the lighter and more maneuverable English craft, forced a break in what had for several days been a magnificently disciplined crescent formation. For Medina-Sidonia to bring his remaining, and now badly damaged, ships back to Spain by encircling the tip of Scotland was another rare feat of seamanship. As a military venture, the Armada was another failure of Philip II. As a saga of the seas, it is one of the most extraordinary in maritime annals.

It should be added that the defeat of the Armada brought feelings of relief not only to England. The Catholic French, no less than the Protestant Dutch, could breathe more easily. Indeed, Philip's French policy was also a failure. During the religious wars in France, Philip continually gave aid to the Catholic party and for a while his troops even held Paris. It took Henry IV nine years after he came to the French throne, in 1589, to expel the Spaniards from France. But at last Philip in the year of his death was forced to recognize the trend of events. France and Spain in 1598 signed the Peace of Vervins, which merely confirmed that of Cateau-Cambrésis.[1] Philip had poured out blood and money in France, and had little to show for his efforts.

Throughout his reign, Philip had constantly before him the menace of the Moslems. He had to continue the warfare against them in the western Mediterranean and north Africa, and Spain contributed the commander and the largest contingent to the fleet that won the great naval battle of Lepanto in 1571.[2] Far away, too, on the Hungarian plains, contingents of Spanish soldiery fought to help the Austrian Habsburgs stem the Turkish tide.

Finally, Philip was the almost undisputed master of Italy. The political complications which followed the long wars of his father continued to keep Italy divided. To many Italians this was a dark period of foreign occupation, a bleak contrast to the vitality of the middle ages and the brilliance of the renaissance.

Thus in every direction, Philip was faced with pressing difficulties, for Spain seemed

so great and powerful that all eyed her with envy, and her very preëminence multiplied her enemies. Only in his overseas dominions did Philip see Spanish power wax and develop, for it was there that Spain not only maintained its position, but made notable advances.

C. Spain Overseas

In the work of developing the American conquests of Spain, the great features of the period of Philip II were the consolidation of Spanish rule, the development of mining, and the building up of the colonial system. Under the King the Council of the Indies continued, as far as the difficulty of communications permitted, to supervise the activities of the viceroys and governors in the New World. The King kept the church, too, subordinate to the crown and made it an instrument of political management as well as of religious instruction.

Interested though he might be in the growth of the church overseas, Philip was forced by his financial needs to pay even more attention to the mines of the new lands. The opening of the Potosí in Peru in 1545 and of Zacatecas in Mexico a year later had shown that the wealth to be secured by looting the old Indian civilizations was trifling compared to that which could be won by mining. Other mines were discovered and developed. The amalgam process, which employed mercury to separate the silver from the ore, came into use about 1576. It increased the yield of rich mines and made profitable the working of those of lower grade. By a happy chance Spain was the greatest producer of mercury in the world, so that the colonial demand quickly brought prosperity to the Spanish mercury mines.

In the early years of the Spanish conquest gold had outweighed silver in importance. But when Philip II came to the throne silver production was rising rapidly and in the decade 1561–1570 the imports of silver into Spain came greatly to surpass those of gold in value. Silver imports into Spain rose rapidly until they reached a peak in the last decade of the century, when they amounted to more than 1,230,000 pounds of fine silver. That figure is not very large in terms of

---

[1] See above, p. 342.
[2] See above, pp. 345–346.

modern production. But in the sixteenth century it was epoch making. These silver imports upset the economy of Spain and indeed of all Europe. They gave Spain a source of wealth and power that all the world envied. After 1600, the imports of silver into Spain slowly declined as some mines were exhausted, and more bullion was retained in America. In the decade of 1651–1660 they totaled only about 200,000 pounds.

As the wealth of the Americas became apparent, a colonial system for their economic exploitation was developed. As it grew, it came to be shaped by the importance of the silver imports. Under Philip II the chief purpose of the whole system was to secure more silver and to get it safely to Spain.

Charles V at first had let the German bankers, who were his subjects, play a part in developing America. But gradually restrictions of foreigners were increased, so that after 1556 trade and emigration were permitted only to Spaniards and, in theory at least, only to Castilians. Moreover, all merchandise was carried by royal ships, though on behalf of private merchants. All commerce with the colonies had to go in and out of the single port of Seville in Spain (from 1503 to 1717) and certain specified American ports (Havana, Puerto Bello, Nombre de Dios, Vera Cruz). For protection the ships were often sent in large fleets, and, after about 1560, two great fleets usually went each way every year. The *Flota* sailed in April for Havana and Vera Cruz, and the *Galleons* in August for Nombre de Dios. Both set out with sealed instructions and the routes were varied each time to thwart foreign pirates. From time to time stray ships were picked off, but so successful was the system that no fleet was captured till the Dutch took one in 1628, when Spanish power was already on the wane.

To control American trade and especially to keep track of the bullion, of which one-fifth went to the crown as a tax, the *Casa de Contratacion* (House of Trade) had been set up in 1503. It grew steadily in importance, and after 1543 it was aided by a sort of merchants' court called the *Consulado*, which settled disputes and tried commercial cases. The treasurer of the *Casa* had charge of receiving and registering all the bullion that came in, especially that part belonging to the crown. Stringent regulations were made and enforced by heavy penalties to prevent the smuggling of silver.

On paper Spain had a water-tight monopoly of all trade with her American colonies, and by keeping out foreigners she hoped to secure for herself all the silver produced. But from the early days, the Portuguese, the Dutch, the English, and the French cast envious eyes on the wealth of America. By the middle of the sixteenth century they were securing some share of the new riches, legally by selling goods needed for America, illegally by bribing Spanish merchants to ship goods for them and by sending vessels to the west to trade or plunder as opportunity offered. By the end of the century the Spaniards were having considerable difficulties and colonists could be tempted to trade illegally for the cheap goods brought in by foreigners, since under the restrictive Spanish system European wares sold at very high prices in America. Essentially, however, the Spanish colonial system was unshaken in 1600, and if foreigners were to nibble at its edges and even to win some of its outlying territories in the seventeenth century, it was to stand unshattered until after 1800.

One important addition to the Spanish overseas dominion under Philip II was the Philippine Islands, for it was during his reign that they were effectively occupied. In 1564, an expedition with five hundred men and four Augustinian friars was sent thither from Mexico, and the first permanent Spanish town was founded in the next year.

D. Successors of Philip II: Philip III and Philip IV, 1598–1665

Despite the many failures of Philip II, he has remained a symbol of the greatness of Spain, a greatness which endured for some decades after his death. He was followed by his son, Philip III (1598–1621), and his grandson, Philip IV (1621–1665). During the first part of this period most people thought of Spain as still the leading power

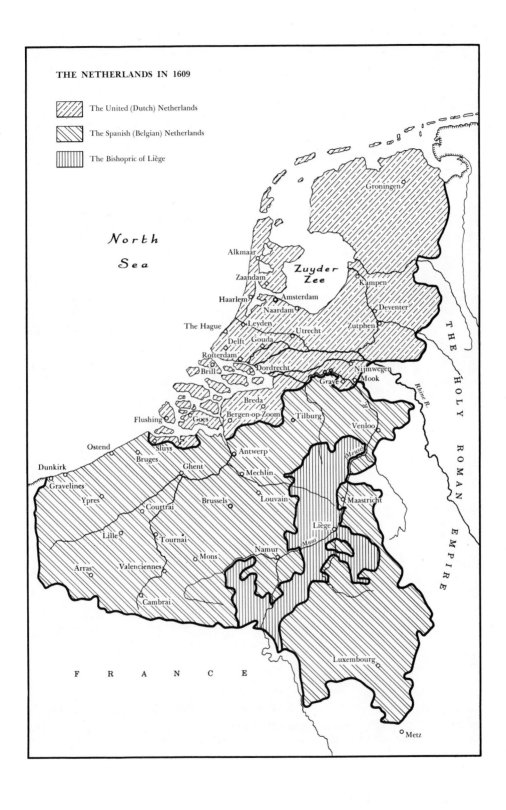

THE NETHERLANDS IN 1609

The United (Dutch) Netherlands

The Spanish (Belgian) Netherlands

The Bishopric of Liège

North Sea

Groningen

Alkmaar

Zuyder Zee

Zaandam

Kampen

Haarlem   Amsterdam

Naardam   Deventer

The Hague   Leyden   Zutphen

Delft   Gouda   Utrecht

Rotterdam   Nijmwegen

Brill   Dordrecht   Mook

Grave

Breda

Flushing   Goes   Bergen-op-Zoom   Tilburg

Venloo

Ostend   Sluys

Bruges   Antwerp

Dunkirk   Ghent   Mechlin

Gravelines   *Meuse*

Ypres   Brussels   Louvain   Maastricht

Courtrai

Lille   Liège

Tournai   Namur   *Maas*

Mons

Arras   Valenciennes

Cambrai

Rhine R.

THE HOLY ROMAN EMPIRE

F   R   A   N   C   E

Luxembourg

Metz

Cardinal Don Fernando Nino de Guevara. El Greco (d. 1614).

of Europe. By its end, Spain, impoverished and weakened through long wars, had clearly yielded the foremost place to France.

The opening decades of the seventeenth century seemed auspicious for Spain. Henry IV of France, who had disliked and distrusted the Habsburgs but after 1598 had kept peace with them, was assassinated in 1610 as he was about to attack the Spanish Netherlands. He was succeeded by his wife, Marie de Medici, as Regent, a weak ruler who sought to curry Spanish favor and who married her young son, Louis XIII, to a Spanish princess in order to promote the friendship of the two countries. Similarly in England, Queen Elizabeth, who had rallied the forces of the country against Spain, was succeeded in 1603 by James I, who admired Spain, sought a Spanish alliance, and tried unsuccessfully to marry Charles, his son and heir, to a Spanish princess. Besides, the struggle between Spain and Holland reached something of a stalemate in 1609 with the twelve-year truce negotiated between the two countries. Philip III hoped to muster Spanish forces and resources to crush the stubborn Dutch at the end of the truce in 1621. The flow of silver from America to Spain began to show signs of slackening after 1600, but since it did not drop precipitately till after 1630, Spain could continue to count on a constant influx of bullion.

Within Spain there were some signs of trouble and decay. Philip III was upright and pious, but weak, incompetent, and pleasure-loving. Unlike his father, he took little part in the affairs of government; and power was exercised by courtiers and favorites, especially the duke of Lerma and his son, the duke of Uceda. Philip II had kept the nobles at a distance or used them in his military forces. Under Philip III, they swarmed about the court seeking favors and pensions. Luxury grew apace. The expenses of the royal household increased fourfold, and money was spent lavishly and frivolously. The stiff Spanish etiquette grew yet more rigid, till court life was crowded with forms and ceremonies. Public administration became increasingly inefficient and corrupt, and foreigners began to say that any Spanish official could be bought for a price.

Meanwhile public finances and currency were falling into disorder, so that the Spanish monarchy throughout the seventeenth century was either bankrupt or tottering on the brink of bankruptcy most of the time. Religious and political intolerance led to the expulsion in 1610 of the *Moriscos* who, it was feared, might aid the Moors of North Africa in an invasion. The *Moriscos* were able artisans and farmers, and their expulsion was something of a blow to Spanish prosperity.

A sign of Spanish weakness was the inability to defend the Portuguese overseas empire which had been annexed to Spain in 1580. The English formed a competitive East India Company in 1600 and two years later the Dutch consolidated one out of several smaller companies. By the end of Philip III's reign in 1621, the Dutch were firmly established in the Spice Islands and in India and, together with the English, they had taken over a large part of the eastern trade. In 1622 the English captured Ormuz, the key to the Persian Gulf and its commerce. Eleven years later the Portuguese were driven out of Bengal.

But if Spain gave signs of decay, it also was able to make an impressive show of cultural achievement. For this was the era of the immortal *Don Quixote* of Cervantes (*d.* 1616) and the dramas of Lope de Vega (*d.* 1635) and Calderón (*d.* 1681). In painting, El Greco (*d.* 1614) was finishing at Toledo the long career which had produced so many strangely moving masterpieces, while Ribera (*d.* 1652), Velasquez (*d.* 1660), Zurbarán (*d.* 1664), and Murillo (*d.* 1682) brought Spanish artistic achievement of the era to a brilliant climax.

When Philip III died in 1621, the Thirty Years' War had been under way for some three years. For Spain this struggle was to endure not for thirty but for 41 years. In its course the hollowness of Spain's seeming strength was to be made apparent, and the proud monarchy of Charles V and Philip II was to be humbled by the Bourbons of France.

King Philip IV of Spain. Velasquez (d. 1660).

CHAPTER 33

The Age of the Thirty Years' War, 1618–1648

A. Issues at Stake in the War

In 1618 there broke out in Bohemia (modern Czechoslovakia) a struggle which was to rack Europe for a generation and more. The Bohemian revolt which began the conflict was not in any real sense its cause, but rather the spark that ignited a conflagration which had been long in the making. Though the Habsburgs of Austria had been kings of Bohemia for almost a hundred years, the monarchy there had been traditionally elective. The Habsburgs had come to look upon it as one of their hereditary dominions, but the Bohemians felt differently.

Now in 1618, the Holy Roman Emperor was Matthias, and since he was childless his heir was Ferdinand of Styria, a man of blameless life and resolute character, devoted to the cause of absolutism and intensely loyal to the Catholic Church. In Austria and Hungary, few opposed the prospective accession of Ferdinand. But in Bohemia, where three types of Protestants (Lutherans, Calvinists, and so-called Utraquists who were followers of the old Hussite doctrines) were numerous, the advent of so staunch a Catholic as ruler was regarded with dismay. Having conspired together to preserve their political and religious independence, a group of Bohemian noblemen invaded the room in the palace at Prague where some of the Emperor's envoys were stopping and threw them out the window into the moat sixty feet below. Though the envoys were but slightly injured, it was clear that the Bohemians were bent on flouting imperial authority.

The next spring, the throne of Bohemia became vacant through the death of Matthias, and the Bohemian estates formally deposed the Habsburgs and elected Frederick, Count Palatine of the Rhine, to be their King. They chose Frederick partly because he was the leading Calvinist prince of Germany and partly because they thought he would receive support from his father-in-law, James I of England. In this hope they were disappointed, for they never received from England much more than benevolent good wishes. Frederick accepted the throne and was crowned in Prague with due formality in 1619.

Despite minor sympathetic risings in Hungary and Austria, it took the Habsburgs little over a year to crush what they regarded as a revolt in Bohemia against their just rule. Ferdinand had succeeded Matthias and had been elected Holy Roman Emperor. He arranged with his cousin, Philip III of Spain, to have the Palatinate, Frederick's home territory, invaded by a Spanish army. Then securing the aid of Maximilian of Bavaria and a famous Bavarian general, Tilly by name, he invaded Bohemia and, at White Hill outside Prague, Ferdinand's forces in November 1620 inflicted an overwhelming defeat on the Bohemian army. Frederick fled and thus earned the title of the "Winter King," for he had ruled so short a period in his new kingdom. Ferdinand was reinstated as ruler of Bohemia. Many Czech nobles lost their lives and their estates. The

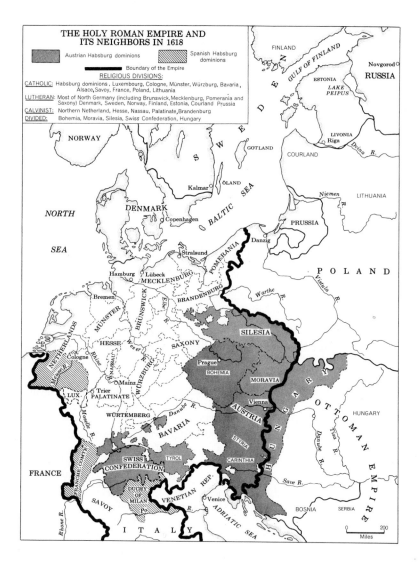

THE HOLY ROMAN EMPIRE AND
ITS NEIGHBORS IN 1618

Austrian Habsburg dominions   Spanish Habsburg
                                   dominions

Boundary of the Empire
RELIGIOUS DIVISIONS:
CATHOLIC: Habsburg dominions , Luxembourg, Cologne, Münster, Würzburg, Bavaria,
Alsace, Savoy, France, Poland, Lithuania
LUTHERAN: Most of North Germany (including Brunswick, Mecklenburg, Pomerania and
Saxony) Denmark, Sweden, Norway, Finland, Estonia, Courland Prussia
CALVINIST: Northern Netherland, Hesse, Nassau, Palatinate, Brandenburg
DIVIDED: Bohemia, Moravia, Silesia, Swiss Confederation, Hungary

practice of all forms of Protestantism was forbidden. Frederick's Palatinate was turned over to Bavaria, and Bavaria's ruler Maximilian was recognized as an elector of the Holy Roman Empire.

Most of the Lutheran princes in Germany, led by the tactful John George of Saxony, had remained aloof from the struggle, hoping to win favors and concessions from the Emperor. The war might have ended with the crushing of Bohemian independence, had there not been a whole series of issues in Germany and Europe which demanded settlement and which were sufficient to keep half the continent embroiled for three decades. Of these issues the religious was the most prominent in the early stages of the war, and the dynastic in the later

stages. But it will be simplest to discuss them all at this point.

The provisions of the religious peace of Augsburg of 1555 [1] were no longer adequate to meet new situations which had since arisen. First, it had been made before Calvinism became strong in Germany. While it gave satisfactory status to Lutherans and Catholics, it did not recognize Calvinism, and in the ensuing years the Calvinists became strong not only in Bohemia but in central and southern Germany as well. Second, the Emperor had added to the peace of Augsburg a provision called the "ecclesiastical reservation" which forbade the further alienation of Catholic lands. The Protestants refused to recognize this provision,

[1] See above, p. 354.

and Protestant rulers continued to seize church lands when opportunity offered, and there were also a number of cases where Catholic ecclesiastics, bishops or abbots, became Protestant and turned their church holdings into personal estates. The Catholic revival had now gained great strength, spearheaded in many areas by the activities of the Jesuits. Yet Protestantism was still active and seeking to gain new converts. The forces of a rejuvenated Catholicism met the advancing Protestants head on.

The Holy Roman Empire, where the Bohemian revolt had occurred, had failed completely, as previous chapters have indicated, to achieve the kind of consolidation characteristic of France and Spain. Indeed, long before the Peace of Augsburg (1555), the history of the Empire had become the history of its separate states. Certainly in the seventeenth century these states, Protestant and Catholic alike, were determined to thwart any attempt on the part of ambitious emperors to revive a long dormant imperial authority.

Furthermore, the German states which opposed the Habsburg Emperors, particularly in the final stages of the Thirty Years' War, were to be aided by the Bourbon rulers of France who in the seventeenth century, no less than their Valois predecessors of the sixteenth, felt that their country was encircled in a threatening fashion by Habsburg power and that France could gain in strength and prestige only by defeating the Habsburgs. Between Habsburg and Bourbon, therefore, the dynastic stakes were clear; they were nothing less than predominance in Europe.

In addition to the religious and dynastic issues, both of which were continuations of sixteenth-century problems, there had arisen other matters which concerned the Baltic and its trade. Denmark, through its traditional authority in the straits which gave access to the Baltic, was able to collect dues on ships passing by and was also in a good strategic position to extend its commerce and its territory. But so also was Sweden, which, having won its independence from Denmark nearly a hundred years earlier, was growing in military power and in commercial and territorial ambitions. Nor were these the only powers interested in the Baltic.

The old Hanseatic cities of Lübeck and Bremen were eager to maintain their commerce and prosperity. Brandenburg, the northern electorate of the Holy Roman Empire, was ambitious to become a Baltic power as a consequence of the war. Even Spain, France, and England were desirous of increasing their commerce with the Baltic countries. And the Netherlands, having already won a major share in the North Sea trade, was anxious to improve its position in the Baltic.

In all these matters, one factor is increasingly evident. The divided condition of Germany, accentuated by religious conflict, dynastic struggles, and economic rivalry, was inviting foreign intervention. By the early seventeenth century, the German problem was an international concern.

B. Phases and Course of the War

The Bohemian phase of the Thirty Years' War had been brief (1618-1620), and in it the religious issues had been outstanding, though Czech patriotism was likewise involved. It had ended in the triumph of the Habsburgs and of Catholicism and a ruthless crushing of Bohemian Protestantism. In 1621, Philip IV succeeded Philip III as King of Spain. Since that year marked the end of the Spanish-Dutch truce and since things seemed to be going well for the Habsburgs in Europe, the new King renewed the war with Holland in the hope of reconquering it. Both France and England espoused the cause of Holland. But the French campaign against the Spanish was badly managed, an English attack on Cadiz was repulsed, and a Dutch expedition against Brazil was driven off. In 1625, Spain's success reached a climax, for after a long and painful siege a Spanish army captured the important Dutch town of Breda.

In the meantime, the Protestant princes of Germany had grown increasingly alarmed as they witnessed the triumphs of the Habsburgs of both Austria and Spain and the expansion of Catholic Bavaria. It seemed as if the balance of power in Europe was being upset in favor of the Catholics. At this juncture, Christian IV (1588-1648) of Denmark opened the second, or Danish,

The Club-foot.
Painting by José
Ribera (d. 1652).

*Courtesy Louvre
Museum, Paris*

phase of the war in Germany. An ambitious and impulsive ruler, Christian, as duke of Holstein, was a member of the Holy Roman Empire and like most of the other princes was eager to check any increase in Habsburg power. As King of Denmark and Norway, he was desirous of extending his influence over the northern coasts of Germany and his control over the trade of the Baltic. As a Lutheran, he wished to support his fellow Protestants in their privileges and in their possession of lands seized from the Catholic Church. For these reasons, Christian IV, supported by grants of money from England and aided by many of the German Protestant princes, invaded Germany in 1625.

Against the Danish invasion, Tilly, general of the imperial forces, might have had difficulty in making headway. But fate seemed to have raised up in the nick of time another defender of the Habsburg cause in the person of a remarkable adventurer, Wallenstein. This man had made himself enormously rich out of the confiscated estates of Czech Protestants. He had secured permission from the Emperor Ferdinand II to raise an independent army of his own to restore order in the Empire and expel the Danes. By liberal promises of pay and plunder he had recruited a force of some 50,000 men, soldiers of fortune like himself. Italian, Swiss, Spaniard, German, Pole, Irishman, and Scot, Protestant and Catholic, were welcomed into his army by Wallenstein. Bound together by loyalty to its leader and hope of gain, it was made into an effective military machine by Wallenstein's genius. Supplied from his Czech lands, it became a sort of moving military state. It plundered and ravaged as it went, dragging in its train a motley throng of camp followers, men, women, and children. Where Wallenstein's army had been, it was said that a crow could scarce find sustenance.

The fighting in the Danish phase of the war was in northern Germany. At Lutter (1626), Tilly's forces, combined with those of Wallenstein, crushed the army of Christian IV. The Lutheran states were left at the mercy of the Catholics, and Brandenburg, hastily joining the Habsburg cause, aided Ferdinand's generals in expelling the Danes from German soil. Only lack of naval control in the Baltic and North Seas prevented the victors from seizing Denmark and winning complete mastery of the German Baltic coast. Thus, for example, the city of Stralsund, aided by Danish and Swedish ships which brought in supplies and evacuated non-combatants, successfully withstood an eleven-week siege in 1628 by Wallenstein, who dreamed of carving out a Baltic state for himself and who swore to take the city, "though it were chained to heaven." The desperate straits of Christian IV and the growth of suspicious activity on the part of Sweden resulted in the peace of Lübeck (1629), by which the Danish King was left in possession of Jutland, Schleswig, and Holstein, but deprived of the German

bishoprics which various members of his family had taken from the Catholic Church.

As a result of these successes, the Emperor Ferdinand II in the same year (1629) felt strong enough to sign an edict of "Restitution," which restored to the Catholic Church all the lands taken from it in violation of the principle of "ecclesiastical reservation" of the peace of Augsburg of 1555. The edict was executed by imperial commissioners, all Catholics, who worked so effectively that within three years Catholicism in Germany recovered three bishoprics, thirty Hanse towns, and nearly a hundred monasteries, to say nothing of numerous parish churches. Up till then, the weight of the Habsburg power had fallen mainly on Calvinists, but at this point the Lutheran princes became thoroughly alarmed. The enforcement of the edict of Restitution seemed likely to deprive them of many fair lands and to strengthen greatly the position of the Emperor and of the Catholic league which supported him. This dismay of the Lutherans seemed to promise a favorable opportunity for intervention by the foremost Lutheran power—Sweden. In addition, the Emperor weakened his position in 1630, by dismissing, at the behest of the Catholic league, the rapacious but able Wallenstein.

The King of Sweden was Gustavus Adolphus (1611–1632), the grandson of Gustavus Vasa who had established both the independence and the Lutheranism of his country. Gustavus Adolphus was one of the most attractive figures of his age—in the prime of life, tall, fair, blue-eyed, well-educated, and versed in seven languages, fond of music and poetry, skilled and daring in war, impetuous and versatile. A rare combination of idealist, general, and practical man of affairs, Gustavus Adolphus dreamed of making of Protestant Sweden the leading power of northern Europe, and of the Baltic sea a Swedish lake. Setting to work vigorously to achieve his ends, he had occupied Finland and Estonia and had forced Russia in 1617 to recognize these territories as Swedish possessions. Then by a stubborn conflict with Poland (1621–1629) he had secured for Sweden the province of Livonia and the mouth of the Vistula river. In these wars in the eastern Baltic, he had matured his military genius and become a master in handling both artillery and cavalry.

No sooner was his war with Poland ended than Gustavus Adolphus turned his attention to northern Germany. He feared lest the Emperor, gaining control of the coastal cities there, might build up a Baltic sea power threatening Sweden. He viewed with alarm the decline of the Protestant cause, and the edict of Restitution promised him aggrieved allies among the Lutheran princes. It was likewise at this very time that Cardinal Richelieu, chief minister of King Louis XIII of France, was seeking some effective means of prolonging the war in Germany so that France might profit from the defeat and humiliation of the Habsburgs. In Richelieu's mind, cardinal of the Roman church though he was, national and dynastic reasons had more weight than religious ones. He agreed to support Gustavus with money and arms, and asked only that the Protestant leader accord liberty of Catholic worship in conquered districts.

Gustavus Adolphus, landing in Pomerania in 1630, inaugurated the third, or Swedish, phase of the war in Germany. He proceeded to occupy the chief northern fortresses and to seek alliances with the influential but reluctant Protestant electors of Brandenburg and Saxony. While Gustavus tarried at Potsdam in these negotiations, Tilly and the imperialists succeeded after a long siege in capturing the Lutheran stronghold of Magdeburg (May 1631). The fall of the city was attended by a mad massacre of the garrison and of armed and unarmed citizens in the streets, houses, and churches. At least 20,000 perished; wholesale plundering and a general conflagration completed the havoc. Gustavus Adolphus, now joined by the electors of Brandenburg and Saxony and by many other Protestant princes of northern Germany, advanced into Saxony, where, in September 1631, he avenged the destruction of Magdeburg by decisively defeating the smaller army of Tilly on the Breitenfeld, near Leipzig. Tilly was himself thrice wounded and escaped from the field with some difficulty.

Gustavus then turned southwestward, making for the Rhine valley, with the idea of forming a union with the Calvinist princes. Only the prompt protest of his powerful ally, Cardinal Richelieu, prevented the ·Catholic archbishoprics of Cologne, Trier, and Mainz from passing immediately under Swedish control. Next, Gustavus Adolphus moved east and invaded Bavaria. Tilly, who had reassembled his forces, failed to check the invasion and lost his life in a fierce battle on the Lech (April 1632). The victorious Swedish King, now acclaimed by German Protestants as their liberator, at once made ready to carry the war into the hereditary dominions of the Austrian Habsburgs. As a last resort, Ferdinand II recalled Wallenstein and gave him full control of his free-lance army. About the same time, the Emperor concluded an especially close alliance with Philip IV of Spain.

The memorable contest between the two generals—Gustavus Adolphus and Wallenstein—was brought to a tragic close in November of the same year, 1632, on the fateful field of Lützen. Wallenstein was defeated, but Gustavus was killed. Although the Swedes continued the struggle, their army was not large, and they possessed no general of the calibre of their fallen King. On the other hand, Wallenstein's loyalty to the Emperor was suspect. He had earlier offered to coöperate with Gustavus, and rumors reached Ferdinand II that he was engaged in self-seeking negotiations with the Protestants. In February 1634, Wallenstein was assassinated in his camp by a group of imperialists whose very names (Piccolomini, Gordon, Devereux, Leslie, Butler) indicate the motley nature of the armies of soldier-adventurers warring in Germany at the time.

The removal of both Wallenstein and Gustavus Adolphus, the economic exhaustion of the whole Empire, and the eagerness of the Protestant princes, and the Emperor as well, to rid Germany of foreign soldiers and foreign intervention—all these developments seemed to point to the possibility of concluding the third, or Swedish, period of the war, not as advantageously for the imperial cause as would have been possible earlier, but at any rate by some sort of compromise. In fact, in May 1635, a treaty was signed at Prague between the Emperor and a number of the German princes, whereby the former would gain control of the military forces of the Empire, the leagues of the princes would be dissolved, captured territory would be restored, and church lands would remain in the hands of those who actually held them in 1627, two years before the edict of Restitution was issued. On this basis a fairly satisfactory peace seemed possible. But from such a peace, the Emperor would doubtless have emerged in a considerably strengthened position, and this was contrary to the desires of Richelieu and what he conceived to be the interests of France.

C. French Intervention and the Peace of Westphalia

After the death of Gustavus Adolphus it became increasingly evident to Richelieu that France might have to abandon its policy of merely aiding the enemies of the Habsburgs with money. It was the peace of Prague which made it clear that if Richelieu wished to keep the war going to weaken and defeat the Habsburgs he would have to use more direct methods. Richelieu accordingly declared open war on Spain in 1635, and began the final, or French, phase of the war, which was to last thirteen years, almost as long as the other three periods put together. In the earlier phases, religious considerations had been prominent, though German and Baltic questions were also important. In the last period, with Catholic France warring on Catholic Spain and the Emperor, the issues were clearly dynastic, and religious matters played only a secondary role. Furthermore, while Richelieu was eager to humble the Austrian Habsburgs and to add to the French holdings in Alsace, his major designs were against Austria's close ally, Philip IV of Spain. The wily French Cardinal could count upon the Swedes and a number of the German princes to keep up the fight against the Emperor, while French armies attacked the encircling dominions of the Habsburg King of Spain.

From 1635 onward Philip IV had to wage a very different war from that he had previously carried on. Before 1635 he had aided his Austrian kinsmen and sought vainly to crush Holland. After 1635, he was confronted by such violent attacks from the French in the Belgian Netherlands, in

Franche Comté, in northern Italy and in Spain itself, that he had frequently to abandon the offensive against Holland and also against the German Protestants. From the start Richelieu's keen strategic eye had discerned the importance of the Valtelline, an Alpine valley which offered the only practicable route by which the Spaniards could bring supplies and men from Italy to the Rhineland and Germany. In that valley, therefore, repeated campaigns were fought and much of the time the French were able to prevent its use by the Spanish.

At first, the Spanish armies, composed mainly of veterans of a dozen campaigns and led by able and tested generals, seemed superior to the French forces, which totaled some 200,000 men but lacked adequate training and competent commanders. In 1636 a large Spanish army invaded northern France and almost captured Paris. The next year, another Spanish force invaded southern France. Gradually, however, the balance shifted. Spanish armies made less and less headway against the French. As the latter gained in experience and acquired more capable generals, they began to press the Spaniards back in the Netherlands, in the Rhineland, in northern Italy, and in southern France.

By 1640, Philip IV was threatened with the disintegration of his dynastic empire. In that year, while the Dutch, with French aid, were successfully maintaining their independence and making inroads into Brazil, an assembly of nobles at Lisbon proclaimed the deposition of Philip IV as King of Portugal. In his place, they put John IV, the head of the native noble family of Braganza and a relative of the king whom Philip II had succeeded in 1580 when he made himself ruler of Portugal. Shortly after 1640, other revolts against Philip IV broke out in Naples and Catalonia (Aragon). Valiantly but hopelessly the Spanish struggled on. The Neapolitans were repressed and so were the Catalans eventually, despite military, naval, and financial aid they received from France. Milan was successfully defended and the Belgian Netherlands were grimly held. But these defensive endeavors quite exhausted the resources of Philip IV. He was unable to recover Portugal or to make headway against the Dutch or the French. In 1643, the long-standing prestige of Spanish arms was shattered when in a fair fight at Rocroi the brilliant young French general, later known as the Grand Condé, crushingly defeated a large body of the far-famed Spanish infantry.

Meanwhile, the fortunes of war had been fluctuating in Germany. For a time the Habsburg Emperor, with the aid of Maximilian of Bavaria and other Catholic princes, more than held his own against the Swedes and the Protestant German princes. But the waning strength of Spain enabled the French to send larger and larger forces into Germany against the Emperor, with increasingly decisive results. Though negotiations for a general peace were undertaken in 1641 by Ferdinand III (who had become Emperor on the death of his father in 1637), they bore no fruit until after the death of Cardinal Richelieu in 1642 and the occupation of Bavaria by the French in 1646. So complicated were the questions involved that after the diplomats had been conferring for many months as to the peace terms, it was decided to hold a general debate to determine what had been the issues over which the war had ·been fought. At last in 1648, by a series of treaties concluded at Münster and Osnabrück in Westphalia, the Thirty Years' War was ended and peace restored within the Holy Roman Empire. But in signing the peace treaties the Emperor, under pressure from the French, abandoned his Spanish kinsman and ally, Philip IV, and the war between Spain and France dragged on for eleven more years—years that were long and costly for the Spaniards.

The peace of Westphalia left the Austrian Hapsburgs in undisputed possession of their dominions in Austria, Hungary, and Bohemia. But its political provisions deprived them of any effective control over the Holy Roman Empire and at the same time wrought numerous changes within the Empire. (1) Practically, each prince was invested with sovereign authority in his own territory; each prince was in effect free to make war, peace, or alliances, without let or hindrance by the Emperor. (2) France obtained Alsace, except the free city of Strasbourg, and was confirmed in the possession of the bishoprics of Metz, Toul, and Verdun. (3) Sweden received the part of Pomerania controlling the mouth of the Oder, and the bishopric of Bremen surrounding the city of that name and dominating the mouths of the Elbe and Weser. (4) France and Sweden, thus securing lands in the Empire and acting as guarantors of the peace, got the right to interfere in German affairs, and Sweden got a voice in the imperial diet. (5) Brandenburg annexed eastern Pomerania and several bishoprics, while Saxony and a number of other smaller states gained or lost certain territories. (6) The Palatinate was divided between Maximilian of Bavaria and the son of Frederick, the "Winter King," and both Bavaria and the Palatinate were henceforth to be electorates. (7) Switzerland and Holland were formally recognized as states free and independent— Holland of the Spanish Habsburgs, and Switzerland of the Austrian Habsburgs.

In addition to the political provisions, the peace of Westphalia included certain stipulations about religion. (1) Calvinists were to share all the privileges of their Lutheran fellow-Protestants. (2) Any piece of church property was guaranteed to such Catholic or Protestant as held it on January 1, 1624 (1618 for Württemberg, Baden, and the Palatinate). (3) An equal number of Catholics and Protestants were to sit in certain imperial courts. (4) The ruler could determine the official religion of each German state, but (except for the hereditary lands of the Habsburgs) he must permit liberty of private worship, freedom of conscience, and the right to emigrate.

D. Results of the Thirty Years' War, and the Continuing Franco-Spanish War to 1659

The Thirty Years' War, concluded in 1648, gave a more or less definite solution to the vexing issues which had given rise to it. In the religious sphere the Calvinists won recognition and equality, and the further alienation of Catholic lands was halted. More important, the conflict between an advancing Protestantism and a rejuvenated Catholicism was ended. After 1648 there was little further change in the

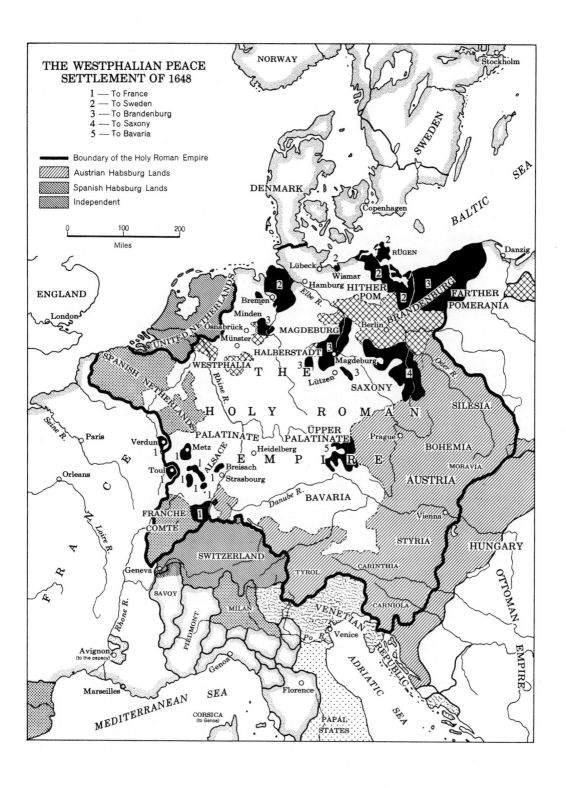

THE WESTPHALIAN PEACE
SETTLEMENT OF 1648

1 — To France
2 — To Sweden
3 — To Brandenburg
4 — To Saxony
5 — To Bavaria

Boundary of the Holy Roman Empire
Austrian Habsburg Lands
Spanish Habsburg Lands
Independent

0   100   200
Miles

NORWAY
Stockholm

SWEDEN

BALTIC
SEA

DENMARK
Copenhagen

ENGLAND
London

Lübeck   Wismar   RÜGEN
2   2   Danzig
Hamburg   2   HITHER   3   FARTHER
Bremen   POM.   2   POMERANIA
Minden   3   Berlin   BRANDENBURG
Osnabrück   MAGDEBURG
Münster   HALBERSTADT   3
WESTPHALIA   THE   Magdeburg   Oder R.
3   3   E   SILESIA
SPANISH NETHERLANDS   SAXONY   4
UNITED NETHERLANDS   Lützen   SAXONY
HOLY   ROMAN
Seine R.   PALATINATE   UPPER   Prague   BOHEMIA
Paris   PALATINATE   5   MORAVIA
Verdun   Heidelberg   EMPIRE   AUSTRIA
1   Metz   5
Toul   1   ALSACE   Breisach
1   1   Strasbourg
Orleans   1   1
1   Danube R.   BAVARIA
Loire R.   FRANCHE   Vienna
1   COMTÉ   STYRIA
HUNGARY
Rhine R.
SWITZERLAND   CARINTHIA
FRANCE   Geneva   TYROL
SAVOY   CARNIOLA
Rhone R.   PIEDMONT   MILAN   VENETIAN
Avignon   Po R.   Venice   REPUBLIC   OTTOMAN
(to the papacy)   Genoa   ADRIATIC   EMPIRE
Marseilles   Florence   SEA
MEDITERRANEAN   SEA   CORSICA   PAPAL
(to Genoa)   STATES

religious affiliation of the peoples of the various sections of Germany. In part, the cessation of religious strife in Germany after the peace of Westphalia was due to the exhaustion of the country. In part, it arose from a definite decrease in religious zeal.

Ten years before the end of the war, it had become fairly clear that the religious questions were side issues as compared with political and dynastic matters. Even the pope had been on several occasions accused of favoring the "Protestant" side in the war. Furthermore, as the seventeenth century progressed, it became clear that all over Europe religious bitterness was waning and that, through force of circumstances, tolerance was gradually increasing. In the last half of the century some of the wars had religious aspects, but more and more clearly the main issues were national and dynastic, territorial and economic.

On the whole it can be argued that in Germany the Thirty Years' War represented a victory, partial and qualified, but still a victory, for the forces of Catholicism. Not only had the further advance of Protestantism been checked, but also considerable areas had been won back for the Catholic Church. The triumphs of the Habsburgs in the early years of the war had enabled them to crush Protestantism in Bohemia. At the same time, with the aid of the Jesuits and other religious orders, they had almost wiped out Protestantism in Austria and greatly reduced it in Hungary. The Calvinists in the Palatinate and the upper Rhineland were sharply decreased in number by the course of the war and by Austrian and Bavarian influence. By 1648 the Catholic revival had won back almost all the areas that were to be recovered from Protestantism. Henceforth, its forces were to be expended in strengthening the religious life of Catholic countries in Europe and in winning converts overseas.

The Thirty Years' War helped to prepare the way for the emergence of the modern state-system of Europe, with its formulated principles of international law and diplomacy. Modern diplomatic usages had originated among the Italian states in the fifteenth century [1] and had been adopted

by the monarchs of Spain, Portugal, France, England, and other countries for the conduct of inter-state business. Yet the modern state-system could not fully emerge as long as one European power—the Holy Roman Empire—claimed even a nominal jurisdiction over states which aspired to, and were capable of, independent existence. The Treaty of Westphalia, by conceding full sovereignty to the member states of the Empire, even in matters of foreign policy, climaxed a development which had been going on since the Golden Bull of 1356 [1] and had made of the Empire merely a nominal federation of self-governing principalities.

Accordingly from the negotiations and treaties of Westphalia emerged the novel principle that all independent sovereign states, regardless of size, were essentially equal. Henceforth, the public law of Europe was to be made by diplomats and by congresses of ambassadors representing theoretically equal sovereign states. The Peace of Westphalia pointed the new path—a path that was made clearer by the fact that with the definite success of the Protestant revolt the pope could no longer speak with spiritual authority to all the rulers. To the Protestant states he was now only a petty Italian prince with somewhat sinister religious connections. Even the Catholic kings, if they still listened to the pope with respect on spiritual matters, were often inclined to ignore his behests when they interfered with political or national ambitions.

Another aspect of international relations was emphasized in the first half of the seventeenth century. It was the Thirty Years' War with its revolting cruelty which turned the attention of a considerable number of scholars to the need of formulating rules for the protection of non-combatants in time of war, the treatment of the sick, wounded, and prisoners, the prohibition of wanton pillage and other horrors which shocked the awakening humanitarianism of the time. The foremost of such scholars was Hugo Grotius (1583–1645), whose famous treatise *On the Laws of War and Peace* (1625) was published in the midst of the struggle.

---

[1] See above, p. 306 n.

[1] See above. pp. 274, 291.

In the Baltic, the results of the Thirty Years' War were somewhat inconclusive. From a political and military point of view, Sweden emerged as the strongest power. Encircled by Swedish-held lands, the Baltic was almost the Swedish lake of which Gustavus Adolphus had dreamed. But the population and resources of Sweden were not sufficient to enable it to maintain such an extensive dominion for long. Sweden was to play the role of a great power for only about seventy years after the Peace of Westphalia. Then the rise of Russia and of Prussia would thrust Sweden back into a secondary position. Commercially, the Thirty Years' War did not effect much real change. The Dutch had had the lion's share of the Baltic trade in 1617. They still had it in 1649.

In the dynastic sphere, the results of the Thirty Years' War were more definite. It marked the decline of the Habsburgs of Austria and Spain and the rise of the Bourbons of France. By French intervention, the Habsburg Emperor had been humbled, deprived of any real control of Germany as a whole, and thrust back upon his own hereditary dominions as his sole remaining source of strength. The Spanish Habsburgs had likewise been checked and weakened by 1648, but for them the war was not ended in 1648. Cardinal Mazarin, who in 1642 had succeeded Richelieu as chief minister of France, forced upon the Austrian Habsburgs the peace of Westphalia in 1648, and, despite internal troubles in France, maintained with mounting success the struggle with the Spanish Habsburgs until 1659.

The war was continued under disastrous conditions for Spain. To be sure, Philip IV had terminated the long struggle with Holland by the Peace of Westphalia. But though he had emptied the Spanish treasury and bled white the Spanish manpower to serve the Habsburg cause, though Spanish armies had borne the brunt of the fighting all over Europe and Spanish colonies and commerce had suffered repeatedly from attacks by the French, English, and Dutch, still in 1648 the Emperor Ferdinand III felt obliged to reject his cousin Philip's pleas for aid from Austria and to leave Spain to continue alone the war with the French Bourbons. Valiantly the Spanish soldiers fought on; doggedly the Spanish King declined to make concessions. But in time, French pressure became unbearable. French generals, like the brilliant Turenne, won victories in the Belgian (Spanish) Netherlands and in northern Spain. France gained an ally in Portugal and toward the end secured another ally in England. At long last, in 1659, Philip IV bowed to the inevitable and signed with France the treaty of the Pyrenees.

At the beginning of the century Spain had appeared to be the wealthiest and strongest state in Europe. The treaty of the Pyrenees formally registered the end of Spanish predominance and the beginning of that of France. Spain quickly sank to the status of a second-rate power. The provisions of the treaty were not of themselves of prime importance. But they were as favorable to France as they were unfavorable to Spain. (1) Spain ceded to France the province of Roussillon at the eastern end of the Pyrenees. (2) Spain ceded to France a southern strip of the Belgian Netherlands, including the province of Artois and several fortified towns. (3) Philip IV agreed to the marriage of his daughter Maria Theresa to the young King Louis XIV of France. In return for a large dowry, Louis XIV agreed to renounce for himself and his heirs any right to inherit the Spanish dominions. But since Spain was now poor, the dowry was never paid, and Louis XIV was left with a claim to the Spanish inheritance.

One result of the Thirty Years' War which arose from its length and extent, rather than from any issue involved, was the widespread havoc and destruction in Germany. There were few areas in the country which had not at one time or another been ravaged or plundered, and there is no doubt that the prosperity and civilization of Germany received a terrific set-back from which it took decades to recover. But the disastrous effects of the war upon Germany must not be exaggerated.[1] No section of Germany was fought

[1] Certain modern German historians, searching for an explanation of the backwardness of their country before 1870, exaggerated the disasters of the Thirty Years' War and assumed general conditions from purely local happenings.

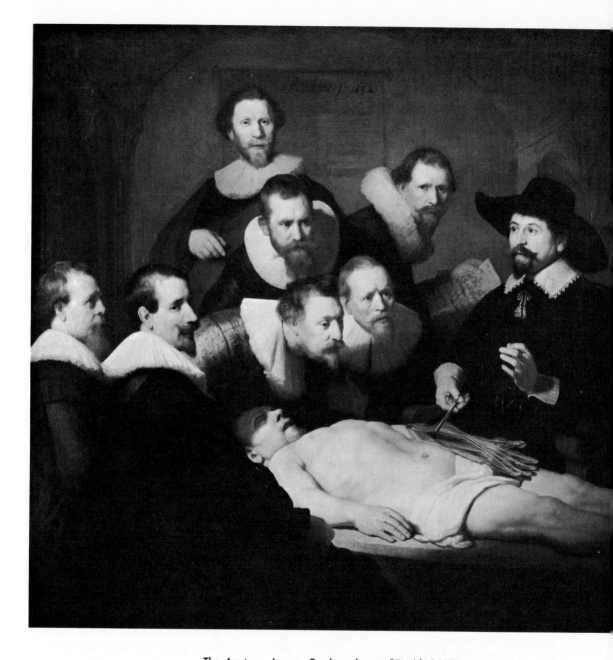

The Anatomy Lesson. Rembrandt van Rijn (d. 1669).

Courtesy Foundation Johan Maurits van Nassau, Mauritshuis, The Hague

over continuously for thirty years or even for a major portion of that time. It is also a misunderstanding of history to impute to seventeenth-century Germany a political failure. The Germans no more failed in the seventeenth century than had the Italians in the fifteenth. Indeed, the Germans of those days would have undoubtedly regarded the arrangements of Westphalia as a landmark in an important progress toward the emancipation of their respective states. Moreover, some of these states, in the course of time, participated not only in the political but also in the cultural development of Europe. The latter subject it will be well to consider briefly before passing on to a later age. But meanwhile let us say something of an

increasingly felt throughout western Europe. One of the most remarkable developments was the rise in prices which resulted largely from the imports of precious metals and which served to intensify the growth of capitalism. The quantity of gold and silver in Europe in 1500 is not known. But when all allowances are made for bullion buried, lost, used in the arts, or sent to the East, and for bullion produced in Europe, secured from Africa, or smuggled into Spain unregistered from America, it seems clear that the amount of precious metals in Europe was about tripled between 1500 and the middle of the seventeenth century.

In that same period, prices of goods and wages roughly tripled in Europe. The price rise started in Spain and moved out from that center, affecting first the nearer and then the further lands, as these secured some portion of the Spanish treasure. Wages usually tended to rise more slowly than prices, a fact which had important results, for manufacturers tended to get more for their products while paying relatively less wages. Thus, for more than a century the cards were stacked in favor of the industrialist; and the man who could make the most goods (the capitalist producer with many people working for him in a shop or under the putting-out system) made the most money. In addition, rising prices favored the merchant, for the goods he had in storage or on ships tended to rise in price while he held them. In short, the remarkable price rise favored the big business man—the new capitalist—and helped to make capitalism a success and to fix it on Europe. In a similar way, the increased supply of the precious metals speeded the transition to a money economy, made it easier to accumulate large stocks of money, and encouraged the use of credit devices, bills of exchange, and the like, based on money in both trading and banking.

We have already noted that even before 1500, landowners (including ecclesiastical establishments) whose incomes were derived from money rents, fees, and dues long fixed by custom or by contract, were at a disadvantage in an economy of rising prices. This situation was accentuated in the six-

important economic occurrence—the so-called "price revolution."

E. Economics and the Price Revolution of Early Modern Times

During the sixteenth century, when the Spanish empire was at its height, the influence of European overseas expansion was

teenth century, as fixed incomes could obviously purchase fewer of the luxury goods which were in demand. Although English landlords, many of whom had appropriated former monastic lands, or who were busy enclosing vast tracts for sheep raising, succeeded better than their French confrères in adjusting to the expanding money economy, no area in western Europe was unaffected. By the end of the sixteenth century, many big estates in France had been mortgaged and many nobles had lost their land. The buyers were officials or merchants who in one way or another had profited from the price rise. In most countries of Europe, while some nobles lost their old status, new persons appeared in the ranks of the upper classes.

The price rise, with its attendant contribution to capitalistic economy, was but one of the highly important results of overseas expansion. The new overseas trade brought to Europe a steadily increasing flow of foreign commodities and took from it a rapidly growing stream of goods needed in the Far East or in the American colonies, such as textiles, tools, munitions, hardware, glass, and trinkets. Thus, commerce grew and stimulated industry. The new fisheries off Newfoundland gave employment to thousands of Europeans, and dried or salted fish became an increasingly valuable item of consumption. It was the Atlantic that was now the highway of trade and the road to riches. The ports of the Mediterranean and the Baltic, while still busy with ships, were overshadowed by the new commercial centers on the Atlantic coast. Throughout most of the sixteenth century, the chief northern port city was Antwerp with its exceptionally fine harbor and its renowned *bourse* or "stock exchange." But Antwerp suffered during the Spanish-Dutch wars and by the early seventeenth century was being rivaled by Amsterdam. For it was the northern Netherlands which, as it won its independence from Spain, attained to the commercial supremacy of northwestern Europe.

Since Spain seemed for long to be profiting most directly and to the greatest extent from the new lands overseas, other countries strove to get some share of Spanish silver, or tried to find new lands

rich in mines for themselves. Moreover, the example of Spain fastened on Europe a pattern of economic thought and policy known as mercantilism. Almost every country adopted laws designed to bring in bullion and to retain the precious metals. Sometimes this was done directly by paying extra for bullion, forbidding its export, and limiting its use in plate, jewelry, or clothes. Increasingly, it was done indirectly by encouraging, usually by customs duties and tariff laws, a favorable balance of trade, that is, an excess of exports over imports.

The products from overseas, whether long known and now secured in increasing quantities, or brought to Europe for the first time, made possible new luxuries. Dyes like indigo, cochineal, and brazilwood, replaced older products. Silk, furs, ostrich plumes, and ivory; perfumes like musk, civet, sandalwood, and ambergris; rich rugs, carpets, and shawls, all aided the display or comfort of the upper classes. Old spices from the east such as pepper, nutmegs, cinnamon, and cloves were more plentiful; while new flavors were introduced from America, like allspice, chocolate, and vanilla. Guinea fowl were brought in by the Portuguese from Africa, and turkeys from America by the Spanish. Though they were not in common use till much later, the tomato and the potato and Indian corn (or maize) were likewise introduced into Europe from America.

It was truly an age of expanding horizons. Any year might bring word of a new land, rich and populous, or wild and strange. Any year might see some new exotic product brought in for the use of Europeans. Any hazardous voyage might win for its backers a fortune. The world was larger and stranger than anyone had thought.

F. Culture in the Early Seventeenth Century: Emergence of the Baroque

It was inevitable in the circumstances of the sixteenth and early seventeenth centuries that intellectual horizons should be broadened. The great French essayist, Montaigne (*d.* 1592), writing about Brazilian cannibals, gained a new perspective on

France. Astronomy was stimulated by the new half of the heavens seen below the equator. Geography grew by leaps and bounds as men like Gerard Mercator (1512–1594) put on to maps the new discoveries that were reported. Botany was enriched by the description of exotic plants which found their way into books like the *Herball* (1597) of John Gerard. New animals and birds were brought home as curiosities. New medicines, like quinine from South America, aided the doctors. New products like tobacco brought with them a train of social changes and opportunities for importers, manufacturers, and tradesmen.

Perhaps because the late sixteenth and early seventeenth centuries constituted an age of expanding horizons and growing fortunes, there was in art a tendency toward the grandiose and the ornate. The art of the seventeenth century is generally classified as "baroque," a term of uncertain origin, but probably first used with deprecatory connotation. But if baroque art was lavish, it was also complex, dynamic, and emotional. In southern Europe, it was closely associated with the Catholic reformation, with the Jesuits, and above all with Rome, which was fast acquiring the baroque aspect which it still possesses.

It was in the early decades of the seventeenth century that the great St. Peter's basilica was finally completed. Maderna extended the nave and added the façade. Bernini (*d.* 1680), a sculptor as well as an architect, did most of the interior decorations, including the baldachino (canopy) over the high altar, and he designed the magnificent *piazza* with its colonnades.

Early Italian baroque painters, Caravaggio (*d.* 1610) and Carracci (*d.* 1609), were followed by others who produced in churches and private palaces enormous and magnificent ceiling paintings.

It was in this same age that the Spanish painting, which was described in the preceding chapter, reached its apogée. Meanwhile, Rubens (*d.* 1640), a Flemish artist who had lived in Italy, epitomized the baroque painting of the north. Another Fleming, Van Dyck (*d.* 1641), is especially noted for his portraits.

As the northern Netherlands was winning its independence from Spain and developing a commercial empire, it was also becoming one of the cultural centers of Europe. The university of Leiden won an enviable reputation and attracted many students from abroad. And while some Dutch artists, notably Hals (*d.* 1666), painting for a bourgeois public, portrayed people and scenes from everyday life, and others, such as Vermeer (*d.* 1675), produced small pictures to hang in private homes, the great Rembrandt (*d.* 1669) was creating something much more profound.

All the aspects of the life of the early seventeenth century, political, economic, and cultural, were to find foremost expression ultimately in France and there to be modified by characteristics peculiarly French. For with the ending of Spanish military and political predominance, Spanish (and Italian) cultural preëminence notably declined. The future lay with France, and to this nation, on the eve of a period of exceptional brilliance, in which French culture matched French political achievement, we shall next turn.

SELECT SUPPLEMENTARY READINGS FOR PART VI

General. The New Cambridge Modern History, vol. II (1958); S. B. Clough and
C. W. Cole, *Economic History of Europe* (1952); A. J. Grant, *History of Europe,
1494-1610,* 2 vols. (1948); V. H. H. Green, *Renaissance and Reformation* (1952);
H. J. Grimm, *The Reformation Era, 1500-1650* (1958); E. H. Harbison, *The Age
of the Reformation* (1955); C. J. H. Hayes, *Political and Cultural History of
Modern Europe,* vol. I (1936); P. Smith, *The Age of the Reformation* (1920).

Chapter 28. K. Brandi, *Charles V* (tr. 1939); R. T. Davies, *The Golden Century
of Spain* (1937); J. Lynch, *Spain Under the Habsburgs,* vol. I, *Empire and
Absolutism, 1516-1598* (1964); J. H. Elliott, *Imperial Spain, 1496-1716* (1964);
R. Ehrenberg, *Capital and Finance in the Age of the Renaissance* (1928); C. H.
Haring, *The Spanish Empire in America, 1492-1815* (1946); H. Holborn, *History
of Modern Germany,* vol. I (1959); R. B. Merriman, *Suleiman the Magnificent*
(1944) and *The Rise of the Spanish Empire in the Old World and the New,*
vol. III (1925); F. L. de Gomara, *Cortes: the Life of the Conqueror by His
Secretary* (1964); C. Gibson, *The Aztecs Under Spanish Rule—1519-1810*
(1964); J. H. Parry, *Europe and a Wider World, 1415-1715* (1949, new ed.,
The Establishment of the European Hegemony, 1961); J. Streider, *Jacob Fugger
the Rich* (1931).

Chapter 29. Books dealing with the Reformation in general, in addition to those
cited above under "General": R. H. Bainton, *The Reformation of the Sixteenth
Century* (1952); L. Cristiani, "The Reformation on the Continent," *The Reformation* (1936), vol. IV of *European Civilization,* ed. E. Eyre; P. Hughes, *A Popular History of the Reformation* (1960); A. Hyma, *Renaissance to Reformation*
(1951); G. L. Mosse, *The Reformation* (1953); F. Mourret, *A History of the
Catholic Church,* vol. V (tr. 1930); L. Pastor, *History of the Popes,* vols. VI ff.
For Lutheranism: R. H. Bainton, *Here I Stand: a Life of Martin Luther* (1950);
H. Holborn, *History of Modern Germany,* vol. I; C. Manschreck, *Melancthon:
the Quiet Reformer* (1958); E. G. Schweibert, *Luther and His Times* (1950);
J. Clayton, *Luther and His Work* (1937). On Calvinism: A. Dakin, *Calvinism*
(1946); A. J. Grant, *The Huguenots* (1934); G. Harkness, *John Calvin: the Man
and His Ethics* (1931); R. N. C. Hunt, *Calvin* (1933); A. Hyma, *Life of John
Calvin* (1943). On France and the religious wars: F. C. Palm, *Calvinism and the
Religious Wars* (1932); J. E. Neale, *The Age of Catherine de Medici* (1943).
On the much debated question of the reformation and capitalism, including
bibliography: R. H. Green, *Protestantism and Capitalism: the Weber Thesis and
Its Critics* (1959).

Chapter 30. General histories of England: S. T. Bindoff, *Tudor England* (1950); J. B. Black, *The Reign of Elizabeth, 1558–1603* (1959); J. D. Mackie, *The Earlier Tudors, 1485–1558* (1952); J. McCollum, *The Age of Elizabeth* (1961); C. Read, *The Tudors* (1936); A. L. Rowse, *The Elizabethan Age*, 2 vols. (1951, 1955); G. W. O. Woodward, *A Short History of Sixteenth-Century England* (1963); L. Stone, *The Crisis of the Aristocracy, 1558–1641* (1965). For selected biographies and for the English reformation: R. W. Chambers, *Thomas More* (1938); C. W. Ferguson, *Naked to Mine Enemies: the Life of Cardinal Wolsey* (1958); F. Hackett, *Henry VIII* (1929); P. Hughes, *The Reformation in England*, 3 vols. (1951–1954); F. E. Hutchinson, *Cranmer* (1951); A. F. Pollard, *Thomas Cranmer* (1904), *Henry VIII* (1913), and *Wolsey* (1929); F. M. Powicke, *The Reformation in England* (1941); J. E. Neale, *Queen Elizabeth I* (1934); N. B. Morrison, *Mary, Queen of Scots* (1961).

Chapter 31. In addition to the general histories of the church, cited above for Chapter 29: J. Brodrick, S. J., *The Origin of the Jesuits* (1940) and *The Progress of the Jesuits, 1556–1579* (1947); P. Dudon, *St. Ignatius Loyola* (1950); M. P. Harney, S. J., *The Jesuits in History* (1941); G. H. Dunne, S. J., *A Generation of Giants: the Story of the Jesuits in China in the Last Decades of the Ming Dynasty* (1962); G. Sansom, *A History of Japan, 1334–1615* (1961); H. Jedin, *A History of the Council of Trent* (1957); B. J. Kidd, *The Counter-Reformation* (1933); H. Daniel-Rops, *The Catholic Reformation* (1962). For the culture of the sixteenth century: H. Butterfield, *The Origins of Modern Science* (1949); A. C. Crombie, *Science in the Later Middle Ages and Early Modern Times* (1959); M. Boas, *The Scientific Renaissance, 1450–1630* (1962); H. Gardner, *Art Through the Ages* (1959); K. Holl, *The Cultural Significance of the Reformation* (1948, 1959); P. Lang, *Music in Western Civilization* (1941); R. Murray, *Political Consequences of the Reformation* (1926); N. Pevsner, *An Outline of European Architecture* (1957).

Chapter 32. A. Castro, *The Structure of Spanish History* (1954); C. E. Chapman, *Colonial Hispanic America* (1933); B. Chudoba, *Spain and the Empire, 1519–1634* (1952); R. T. Davies, *The Golden Century of Spain* (1937); P. Geyl, *Revolt of the Netherlands, 1555–1609* (1937); C. H. Haring, *The Spanish Empire in America* (1947); J. H. Mariejol, *Philip II, the First Modern King* (tr. 1934); C. Petrie, *Philip II of Spain* (1963); G. Mattingly, *The Armada* (1959); G. J. Marcus, *A Naval History of England*, vol. I, *The Formative Centuries* (1961); R. B. Merriman, *The Rise of the Spanish Empire*, vol. IV, *Philip the Prudent* (1934); W. T. Walsh, *Philip II* (1937); C. V. Wedgwood, *William the Silent* (1944).

Chapter 33. P. Geyl, *The Netherlands Divided, 1609–1648* (1936); C. R. Boxer, *The Dutch Seaborne Empire, 1600–1800* (1965); H. Holborn, *History of Modern Germany*, vol. I (1959); M. Roberts, *Gustavus Adolphus: a History of Sweden, 1611–1632*, vol. I (1953); C. V. Wedgwood, *The Thirty Years' War* (1939). For Richelieu and French intervention in the Thirty Years' War, see p. 496 under Chapter 34. For economic and cultural developments, in addition to the books cited above for Chapter 32: E. F. Hecksher, *Mercantilism*, 2 vols. (1935); L. B. Packard, *The Commercial Revolution* (1927); J. H. Parry, *Europe and a Wider World*; P. Smith, *History of Modern Culture*, vol. I (1930); D. M. Frame, *Montaigne* (1965). On art: the works of Gardner and Pevsner, cited above for Chapter 31.

The Palace of Versailles as seen from the park.
Courtesy Bettmann Archive

Cardinal Richelieu. After a contemporary engraving.

Courtesy Bettmann Archive

PART VII

POWER POLITICS, AND THE

Molière (Jean-Baptiste Poquelin, 1622–1673).

Courtesy Bettmann Archive

From Richelieu to Voltaire

COLONIAL RIVALRY

"ENLIGHTENMENT"

DEFINITELY "modern times" are inaugurated by the age covering the second half of the seventeenth century and most of the eighteenth. In this age, Western Civilization is firmly established on the American continents, not only by Spaniards and Portuguese, but by Dutch, French, and English, while on the European continent there is an unsteady "balancing" among a set of great powers, each of which pursues its own interests under absolutist divine-right monarchs. During the greater part of the age, France under the Bourbons is chief of the great powers. It humbles the Habsburgs of Austria and makes Spain a satellite. Presently, however, two new great powers emerge: Prussia and Russia, the former at the expense of Austria, and the latter at the expense of Sweden, Poland, and the Turks.

England, unlike the Continent, experiences in the seventeenth century a protracted struggle between king and parliament, involving civil war and temporary Puritan dictatorship, and issuing eventually in rejection of absolutism and establishment of constitutional parliamentary government. Detailed treatment of this revolutionary development we nevertheless defer, in order to associate it with the great American and French liberating revolutions of an ensuing age which it presaged. Here it suffices to point out that, under its peculiar regime, England absorbs Scotland and, as the "United Kingdom" of Great Britain, wages a long and eventually triumphant duel with France for commercial, naval, and colonial supremacy. A vast British Empire is in the making. Incidentally, Britain now opposes French hegemony within Europe, as previously it had opposed that of Spain. The defeat of France by Prussia and the latter's growing prestige in the second half of the eighteenth century are attributable to British support as well as to the generalship of Frederick the Great.

The age is not exclusively one of power politics, English political revolution, or colonial conflict. Above and beyond all these, it is an age of remarkable scientific and intellectual achievement and of attendant concern with "natural law" and "natural rights." In a word, it is an "enlightened" age, when, perhaps a bit naively, there is widespread faith in "reason" and "progress," and when "reform" is in the air. Even the despotic dynastic sovereigns of the age tend to be "enlightened." Yet long after such sovereigns disappear, and indeed until our own day, ideals of "enlightenment" will have recurrent vogue and abiding effects.

The decrease in religious fanaticism and even in religious zeal, which had been noticeable in the last stages of the Thirty Years' War, and in the peace of Westphalia, became even more marked in the ensuing years, though France in the late seventeenth century was something of an exception. At first the trend was toward "tolerance," then toward "rational" or "pietist" religion, and finally, in the eighteenth century, even toward ir-religion and godlessness. French Huguenots were still to suffer for their Protestantism and Irishmen for their Catholicism, but the age of pre-dominantly religious war and combat was drawing to a close.

CHAPTER 34

The Age of Louis XIV

A. Background: Henry IV, Richelieu, and Mazarin

From about 1659 to about 1763 France was the foremost nation of Europe, and its preëminence was not clearly lost until 1815. French strength arose in part from a favorable geographic position, a relatively large population, and fertile lands. But in addition to these factors, a centralized government, an excellent army, and a considerable degree of national unity helped to make France strong. The foundations of this governmental structure were laid, or rather re-laid, by two men—Henry IV and Richelieu. The edifice was completed by Louis XIV.

For a century after the conclusion of the Hundred Years' War in 1453, a succession of French kings had been consolidating the state. But then had ensued a half-century of demoralizing civil-religious wars and foreign interventions. When these were finally ended by Henry IV in 1598, through the edict of Nantes and the treaty of Vervins with Spain, France was in a sorry state. The national treasury was empty, commerce disrupted, and agriculture impaired. With the aid of his chief minister, the Huguenot Duke of Sully, and the natural recuperative powers of France, Henry IV, by avoiding further wars, restored the prosperity of the nation.

Henry IV brought to his task certain advantages. He was personally attractive, affable and gracious to high and low. If he was self-centered and showed but little loyalty to his friends and supporters, still he was intelligent, brave, quick to decide, and firm in enforcement. Most important of all, Henry understood France and the French. In the wars, he had traveled the length and breadth of the country. Often without funds, he had known poverty and learned to understand peasants and townsmen as well as nobles. It was not without reason that his subjects called him Henry "the Great," or "Good" King Henry. Of all the long line of French monarchs Henry IV is one of two that are remembered with warmth and affection in France, the other being Louis IX (Saint Louis).

In rebuilding the prosperity of France, Sully was Henry's chief agent. Sully reformed the tax system so thoroughly and so improved collections that after 1600 there was usually a surplus of a million *livres* each year. He repaired and improved the roads and planted shade trees along them. He built bridges, encouraged fairs, and improved water ways. He zealously sought to aid French agriculture, which seemed to him the source of the country's wealth. At the same time, Henry IV had another Huguenot aide, Barthélemy de Laffemas, who as Controller-General of Commerce was equally vigorous in seeking to develop industry and trade. Under his guidance, Henry established factories for tapestries, silks, and linens, and supported them with loans, privileges, and tax exemptions. Under Henry, too, interest in colonies grew, and Quebec was founded in 1608.

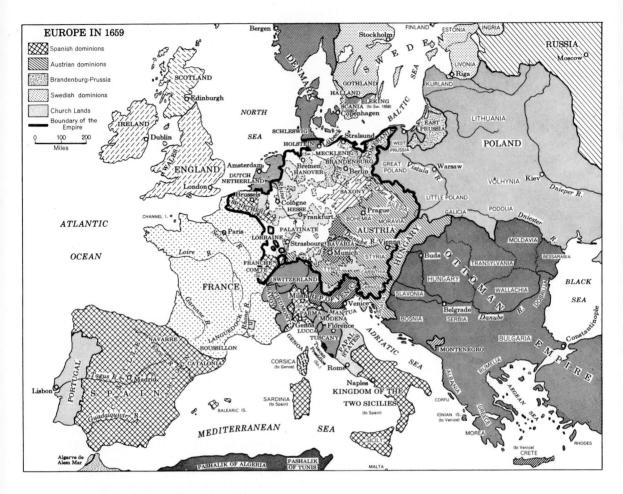

EUROPE IN 1659

Spanish dominions
Austrian dominions
Brandenburg-Prussia
Swedish dominions
Church Lands
Boundary of the Empire

0   100   200
Miles

In the long run, Henry IV's work in the political sphere was even more significant than his success in the rehabilitation of French economic life. During the religious wars, all the political elements of France had gotten out of hand. The nobles had levied taxes, raised armies, and waged wars. The Estates General (the old medieval legislature) had made laws and negotiated with foreign countries. France had come close to the old confused anarchy of early feudal times.

Again aided by Sully, Henry IV reduced France to order in a very few years and made the authority of the king and the central government paramount throughout the land. The nobles he brought to heel by pensions and favors, by a ruthless suppression of plots and fighting, and by giving much of the real power in the government to middle-class officials. As for the Estates General, he ignored it, and when he needed help and advice he summoned an Assembly of Notables whose members were hand-picked by him and were mainly bourgeois officials. The towns were made to feel the increasing weight of royal power. Henry changed their charters and reduced their financial independence.

In thus vindicating and strengthening royal authority in France, Henry IV was helped both by his personal popularity with the French people and by the fact that they were so sick of internal disorder, strife, and religious disputation that they welcomed a strong hand at the helm. Yet it seemed for a while as if all that Henry had done might go for nought, since in 1610 he was assassinated in Paris by a religious maniac. To the throne succeeded Henry's son, Louis XIII, a child of eight; while to actual power, as regent, succeeded Henry's widow, Marie de' Medici, an ambitious and scheming woman, but quite incompetent.

Surrounding   herself   with   favorites,

Marie dismissed the able Sully and other capable ministers. She tried to restrain the nobles by honors and bribes instead of firmness. In foreign policy, she sought to appease Spain at any cost. The savings of Henry IV were soon exhausted, and as a financial crisis loomed, Marie summoned the Estates General (1614). But the three estates (clergy, nobles, and commoners) spent their time in bickering with each other. They neither aided the government by voting taxes, nor took steps to increase their own power and lead France toward a constitutional monarchy. After a few weeks Marie locked the Estates General out of their meeting places and contemptuously sent them home. They were not to meet again for a hundred and seventy-five years.

After this fiasco with the legislature, matters went from bad to worse. There were revolts of nobles and of Huguenots. And Marie's pro-Spanish policy was generally unpopular with a people who looked upon Spain as their national enemy. Nonetheless the Regent arranged for the marriage of the young King to Anne of Austria, who was the daughter of Philip III and sister of Philip IV of Spain. As Louis XIII grew older he chafed under his mother's rule and at length pushed her aside. The King, however, was more interested in hunting and music than in affairs of state, and it is doubtful whether matters would have improved, if a great statesman had not risen to be chief minister in 1624. It is the principal claim to fame of Louis XIII that for eighteen years (1624–1642), in the face of all opposition, he kept Cardinal Richelieu in power.

Born of a noble family, Armand de Richelieu (1585–1642), despite early preference for an army career, had been trained for the church, and had become at twenty-one a bishop of the small diocese of Luçon. Some years later, as a delegate to the Estates General, he had attracted the notice of Marie de' Medici, who gave him a post in the government and later secured his nomination as a cardinal of the Roman Church. But Marie's favor seemed a handicap rather than a help when she was deposed by her son in 1617. Nevertheless, Richelieu handled the negotiations between

the King and Marie so adroitly that he won the respect, though not the affection, of Louis XIII. He was given a place in the ministry in 1624, and soon made himself the King's chief minister. Thereafter, though his enemies conspired against him repeatedly and sought to get rid of him, Richelieu retained the confidence of the King and remained in office till his death.

In giving Richelieu power, Louis XIII displayed excellent judgment, for the Cardinal was a great statesman, possibly the greatest that France has ever produced. A master of diplomacy, a far-sighted administrator, a skilled courtier, Richelieu had a penetrating insight into military and economic as well as political affairs. If the needs of war prevented him from reorganizing French finances as he would have liked, still he did a good deal to carry on the work of Henry IV in encouraging industry and commerce. Under him, for example, a West Indian company was formed and colonies developed in those islands, a Canadian company was organized and strengthened, and an East India company founded.

Toward the end of his life Richelieu explained his policy in a simple fashion. His aim, he said, had always been to make France strong by destroying the power of the Huguenots, abasing the pretentions of the nobles, and humbling the proud house of Habsburg. By the first two objectives, he sought to increase the power of the crown and the central government in France. By the third, he desired to win for France a preëminent position in Europe.

In destroying the power of the Huguenots, Richelieu, Cardinal though he was, was not moved by religious motives. In his devotion to France and the French crown, he seemed ever ready to sacrifice religious to political considerations. But the Edict of Nantes (1598) had given the Protestants not only religious toleration but a privileged political position. With their fortified cities, their assemblies, and their special rights, they formed a state within the state. As such they were a threat to the national unity which Richelieu desired, and their privileges were an impediment to that uniformity of administration which the Cardinal sought.

Richelieu's opportunity came when the Huguenots, egged on by England, started a revolt which centered in the seaport of La Rochelle. Richelieu went thither with the royal armies and was the real commander of the long siege (1627–1628). Eventually he forced the town's surrender by building a breakwater across the mouth of the harbor. Then, after putting down the remnants of the Protestant revolt in the south of France, he concluded with the Huguenots the peace of Alais (1629). It left them religious liberty and freedom of conscience and equal political rights— everything, said Richelieu, which a good Huguenot would think it worth dying for. But it took from them their fortified cities and their special political privileges, everything through which they could make trouble. Thereafter the Huguenots made no further difficulties in France and Richelieu's compromise lasted for more than half a century.

The repression of the great nobles was an even more serious task and one which Richelieu undertook in the face of redoubtable opposition. It had long been customary to name noblemen as governors of the various provinces and as high administrative officers of the crown. Many nobles had at their command armed troops and fortified castles. Thereby they could thwart the will of the king, and even defy him in open revolt. Moreover, the nobles at court, jealous of Richelieu's advancement and spurred on by the intrigues of Marie de' Medici and the King's weak and foolish brother, the Duke of Orleans, hampered the Cardinal at every turn and plotted against him whenever opportunity offered.

Into the ranks of the noble courtiers, Richelieu struck terror. By means of a matchless system of spies and by consummate guile, he ferreted out conspiracies and put the leaders to death. As early as 1626 he had the King decree the demolition of all fortified castles not needed for the defense of the realm, and to this day the ruins of many an ancient château bear eloquent witness to the Cardinal's activity.

The noble governorships were not abolished by the Cardinal, but their importance was reduced in two ways. First, Richelieu appointed nobles as governors in parts of the country where they had few friends or supporters. Second, he made greatly increased use of a special kind of officials called "intendants." These were usually lawyers of bourgeois origin utterly dependent on the King. Richelieu sent them out in the country with authority to try cases, to arrange for military supplies, and to put down rebellion. Gradually real power shifted into the hands of these intendants, and when, in the next reign, they were assigned for long periods to a definite locality, the noble governors became merely ornamental.

What Richelieu was really doing by developing the office of intendant was inaugurating a bureaucratic administration. The intendants were servants of the crown and had no power save as such. They became the eyes and ears of the king. Through them, the central government could enforce its will; from them, it could secure reports on conditions; by them, it could carry on the task of administering an extensive country. Dimly the country realized what Richelieu was doing, and the nobles hated him both for his aims and his accomplishments. The rest of the country, and especially the middle classes, tended to welcome a centralized all-powerful monarchy as the surest guarantee of internal peace and order.

How Richelieu set about accomplishing his third purpose—the humbling of the Habsburgs—we have already noted. By subsidizing the Swedes and then throwing the weight of France into the Thirty Years' War, he prevented the triumph of the Catholic and Habsburg causes. But he did not live to see the complete success of his policies, for he died in 1642 shortly before the death of Louis XIII, the master whom he had served so well.

It was under Louis XIII, and with some encouragement from Richelieu, that there developed a definite intellectual and cultural movement that was to quicken and flower in the next reign. The Cardinal himself created the French Academy (*Académie Française*), a group of learned and distinguished men who began purifying literary style and standardizing the French language. One of the most famous of literary hostesses, Madame de Rambouillet

(1588–1665), gathered at her town house (or *Hôtel*) a group of writers that at one time or another included the first important French dramatist, Pierre Corneille (1606–1684), the poet and critic François de Malherbe (1555–1628), the letter-writer and poet Vincent de Voiture (1597–1648), and Madame de Sévigné (1626–1696) who penned incomparable letters to her daughter and others. This self-conscious literary group, though it was somewhat affected, won for writers and their works both recognition and appreciation.

There was at the same time, in other circles, a re-awakening of Catholic religious ardor in France. Much of it went into charity, better organized than ever before by St. Vincent de Paul (1576–1660), who founded the Lazarist (Vincentian) order and the Sisters of Charity, established foundling hospitals, and even enlisted the services of society ladies of Paris. St. Francis de Sales (1567–1622), though he was bishop of Geneva, preached often and with great effect in the chief cities of France, and his books like *Treatise on the Love of God* were notable for the purity and the clarity of their French. Of quite another sort was Blaise Pascal (1623–1662). A genius in mathematics, he turned to religion in his later years and became a prominent figure in the Jansenist movement which centered in the convent of Port Royal des Champs and which was a sort of Puritan wing of French Catholicism. His writings, of which the ironic *Provincial Letters* are the best known, constitute in their style one of the high water marks of French prose.

Louis XIII was succeeded by his son Louis XIV, who at his accession in 1643 was only five years old. In spite of arrangements to the contrary made by the dead King, power passed to his widow, Anne of Austria, as Regent. Since she was a Habsburg, she might well have undone the work of Richelieu by a pro-Spanish policy (as Marie de' Medici had started to undo the work of Henry IV), save for one man. That man was Jules Mazarin (Giulio Mazarini), an Italian who had become a naturalized Frenchman and an aide of Richelieu. An astute diplomat with a real love of intrigue, Mazarin had made himself so useful to Richelieu that he had been rewarded with a cardinal's hat and posts of high responsibility. By his charm and tact, Mazarin won the respect, the trust, and even the love of Anne, the Regent, and until his death in 1661, he was her chief minister.

How Mazarin brought to fulfillment the policies of Richelieu in the Peace of Westphalia and the treaty of the Pyrenees has been described elsewhere.[1] But his brilliant successes in foreign affairs were not duplicated within France. Disliked as a foreigner, envied because he was so powerful, criticized because he made himself enormously rich, the Cardinal was soon the

[1] See above, p. 405.

Peasant Family. Mathieu Le Nain (d. 1677).
Courtesy Detroit Institute of Arts

most hated man in France. The opposition to Mazarin developed into a confused sort of rebellion, called the Fronde, which lasted from 1648 to 1653.

The Fronde had a comic-opera aspect. Noble ladies dashed around France on horseback, even leading troops on occasion. Satirical songs, called *Mazarinades*, were sung in the streets. But it had a serious side as well. Both the great French generals, Condé and Turenne, sided with the *Frondeurs*, though the latter gave them only temporary support. On several occasions the rebels were in control of Paris and the Regent had to flee with the King, while Mazarin had to retire from the scene. But the rebels had no clear-cut objectives, and when they won victories they usually did not know what to do.

Eventually the rebellion petered out, but it had some permanent importance. It was the last occasion on which the nobles in old, feudal fashion took arms against the crown. It made the French people more willing to accept strong royal rule as a guarantee against civil disorder. Finally, it made such an impression on Louis XIV that when he came to power he sternly saw to it that there were no more Frondes.

B. Louis XIV, Exemplar of Absolute Monarchy

On the death of Cardinal Mazarin in 1661, everyone wondered who would be the Richelieu or the Mazarin of the ensuing period. They were not left long in doubt, for Louis XIV, who was now of age, announced that he would be his own chief minister. The remainder of his extremely long reign (1643–1715) is known as the period of his personal rule—the Age of Louis XIV. Louis XIV had a good mind, though he was by no means brilliant, and his education had been somewhat neglected. He was short, well built, and handsome in a rather heavy-featured way. His courtesy was impeccable; his bearing most dignified; his nature imperious. He was a man of strong passions but considerable self control. Avid for glory, he wished especially to distinguish his reign by great military victories. Very seriously did Louis XIV

take his task of being king. Day after day, he went over documents, listened to reports, and sat through long council meetings. His confidence in his own judgment was unshakable. While he would give ear to various opinions at great length, once he had made up his mind he would brook no discussion or dissent.

As King of the strongest monarchy in Europe, Louis XIV had a very special position and one which he filled with great dignity. In theory his power was absolute and he was accountable for his acts only to God. His will was law. In practice, however, his authority was conditioned by difficulty of communication and enforcement, and by a vast mass of surviving traditional rights and privileges, personal, municipal, provincial, and ecclesiastical, which even the King did not consider it proper to put aside lightly. Yet the King was thought of as sacred, a monarch by divine right. It was truly sacrilege to oppose him. He was regarded, too, as the father of his people. Paris and Lyons and Bordeaux were "his good cities." Frenchmen were not citizens, but "subjects of the King." Courtiers fawned on him. Officials abased themselves before him. He was surrounded by a rigid and ceremonious etiquette from the time he got up until he went to bed.

Such was the man who, heir to the labors of Henry IV and Richelieu, built up for France a highly centralized government, which was in its day the most efficient in Europe. Louis XIV was served by a group of able ministers. Colbert handled financial and economic matters and the navy; Le Tellier and his son Louvois directed the army; Lionne, Pomponne, and Colbert de Croissy successively administered foreign affairs. With the aid of these and other ministers, Louis XIV reorganized the royal councils such as the Council of Finance, and established new ones like the Council of Commerce. These councils, which had legislative and judicial as well as executive powers, he manned with able lawyers and bourgeois officials, though for tradition's sake a duke or two was usually included on each.

The office of intendant, as developed by

Louis XIV. Hyacinthe Rigaud (d. 1743).

Courtesy Bettmann Archive

Richelieu, became the cornerstone of the administration outside of Paris. The intendants were carefully selected, and assigned for long periods to a "generality" (France was divided into some thirty generalities for financial and other purposes). An intendant who did well in an unimportant area was often promoted to a more important one and might hope to reach the highest posts in the government. While the chief duty of the intendants was to administer the collection of taxes, they became the King's general handy men. They intervened in lawsuits, raised troops, reported on crops, issued local regulations, and saw to the enforcement of the royal laws. Gradually their duties became so heavy that they had to be given assistants, called sub-delegates.

As the power and efficiency of the royal government grew, its older organs tended to become less important. The King interfered in town elections, and the local intendant saw to it that properly submissive mayors were chosen. More and more, the estates (legislatures) of the provinces which still retained them, met mainly to vote sums of money to the King. The chief business of the church assembly, which met every five years, came to be the voting of a "gratuitous gift" to the crown. The noble provincial governors, though they retained some theoretical military powers, were active mainly in public ceremonies and had no thought but to please the King. The great courts, or *parlements*, of which there were about a dozen, were kept in line by the intendants and ministers who let them know clearly what the King desired.

For the upper classes, the center of life in France came to be the royal court, first at Paris and then at Versailles. Thither flocked great churchmen, wealthy bishops and abbots, who owed their places to the King's choice and hoped for further favors from him. Thither came all nobles who could afford it, for the principal way to riches and power was through pensions and offices which the King bestowed. Henry IV and Richelieu had broken the political power of the nobility. Louis XIV completed the task by making the nobles into courtiers. To be sure, poorer nobles still lived on their estates, and all nobles were exempt from many taxes like the *taille*, or land tax, and enjoyed social precedence over commoners. But where once they had been the real rulers of the outlying districts, nobles now had but two careers open to them, that of courtier near the King's person, or that of officer in the King's army. In either case, their success depended on royal favor.

The lot of the peasant was not greatly changed. He still tilled the soil and hoped to produce enough at the harvest to carry him over the winter. But of the taxes and dues he paid, an increasing proportion went to the King, and if a peasant found himself in a law court it was more often a royal one than that of the local landlord.

Persons of the middle class could hope to attain power and even the status of a noble by becoming royal officials or members of a *parlement*. As business men they felt the weight of royal authority in two ways. First, the crown was increasingly active in regulating industry and commerce. Second, it vigorously sought to encourage production and trade in order to promote the prosperity of France.

Until his death in 1683, Colbert was the minister who had active charge of all economic matters. He was a convinced mercantilist and sought by use of the royal authority to regulate and encourage industry and commerce, so that French production would be greatly increased, so that the French would have a large merchant marine and rich colonies, and so that the masses of Frenchmen would be usefully employed. To these ends, Colbert reformed the French tariffs. By tariff act of 1664 he simplified the import and export duties. With the tariff of 1667 he declared economic war on Holland, England, and Italy by raising drastically the import duties on the goods these countries sent to France.

At the same time, Colbert reduced export duties on French goods, negotiated commercial treaties, subsidized increases in the merchant marine, and protected it from foreigners and pirates by building up a large and powerful navy. Moreover, he launched France on a period of real colonial development. Gathering up the remnants of the ventures of previous decades, he refounded in 1664 an East India Company and a West India Company and supported them lavishly with royal funds. The former, in the face of great difficulties and losses, slowly won for France a foothold in the trade to India, despite the opposition of the Dutch and English. The West India Company sent colonists to Canada as well as to the West Indies (Martinique, Guadeloupe, Santo Domingo), strengthened these colonies, increased their trade with France, and gained for the French a share of the slave trade with West Africa. Colbert also founded a Levant Company and a Company of the North which, while failures from a financial point of view, laid the foundations of future French trade in the Near East and the Baltic.

Internally, Colbert sought to increase agricultural production, and he developed French horsebreeding so that France would not have to import horses. But his main interest was in industry. By organizing companies, by granting loans, privileges, and tax exemptions, and by importing skilled foreign workers, Colbert stimulated domestic manufacture of many commodities, and made France largely independent of other countries.

At the same time that he encouraged industry, Colbert endeavored to regulate it, for he believed that quality must be maintained in order to give the domestic consumer good value and to win and retain foreign markets. Elaborate regulations were issued for the textile industry, specifying the length and width of the fabrics and sometimes the number of threads in the warp. Detailed instructions on the best dyeing methods were prepared. Royal inspectors were appointed, and arrangements were made to mark with a seal each properly woven piece of cloth.

Nor did Colbert's efforts stop here. He sought to increase the population by subsidizing large families. The poor and idle were put to productive labor. The administration of forests was reorganized. Roads were reconstructed, and canals built, the most famous of the latter being the Languedoc Canal, 175 miles long, from the Atlantic to the Mediterranean.

Moreover, Colbert drastically reorganized French finances. He chastised corrupt financiers, forced the tax farmers to bid competitively for the right to collect the royal taxes, lowered taxes like the *taille* from which the nobles were exempt, and raised those like *aides* (on beverages) which almost everyone had to pay. It was Colbert's work in rebuilding France economically which made possible many of the great cultural achievements of the reign of Louis XIV and also the long wars which that monarch waged.

C. French Cultural Leadership

With an increasing royal income, Louis XIV found himself in a position to support and encourage all sorts of cultural activities. He did so partly that he might dazzle the rest of Europe with the magnificence of his reign, partly that he might have about him a setting suitable for so great a King, and partly that he might be known to history as a patron of the arts and of learning. Nor were his efforts unavailing. His reign is known in French history as "The Great Century." The artistic style of the epoch the French call "The Great Style." Louis was known to contemporaries, French and foreign alike, as "Louis the Great" and the "Sun King."

It can be argued that French art, literature, and learning were already making rapid progress before Louis XIV came to power, and that all the King did was to subsidize and take the credit for it. Indeed, it is hard to see how a king could create men of talent and genius. Nonetheless, it is clear that he did recognize their worth and gave them an opportunity to come to the fore. In addition, he brought to France many distinguished foreigners whose presence added lustre to his court.

With the King's sanction, Colbert undertook to organize and support the arts and sciences in much the same way that he brought order and prosperity to the economic life of the country. The French Academy, composed of leading writers and literary figures, had been founded, as we have said, by Richelieu and was still a semi-private organization. Colbert took it in hand, gave it the King for a patron, lodged it in the Louvre, and told it to hurry on with the great French dictionary it was preparing. Similarly he revivified the Academy of Painting and Sculpture, enforcing its monopoly of the right to teach art.

Important, too, was the Academy of Sciences founded by Colbert in 1666 and numbering at first fifteen members. It met frequently and performed experiments of which some were perhaps more novel than significant, as for example the first dissection of an elephant's trunk. The results of its work were published in an important scientific periodical, the *Journal des Savants*. With Colbert's aid, a Royal Observatory was built and equipped at Paris. At Paris, likewise, a notable botanical garden, called the *Jardin du Roi*, was developed, and a large royal library established.

But Colbert did more than organize and regulate. With royal funds he subsidized and pensioned men distinguished in any cultural field. Thus, Jean Racine received a pension for his incomparable classical tragedies, which, despite their cold dignity, are considered by the French as the greatest dramas ever written. Pierre Corneille, known as the "father of French tragedy," had long since written his greatest works like the *Cid*, but he too received a pension. Molière was subsidized and called on to write and act in plays for court festivals. With an unsurpassed sense of the comic and a remarkable ability for biting if good-humored satire, Molière wrote comedies such as *Le Misanthrope*, *Tartuffe*, *Les Précieuses Ridicules*, and *Le Bourgeois Gentilhomme*, which have delighted later generations.

This was indeed the great age, the golden age, of French literature. For in addition to the writers already mentioned, a number of others achieved special distinction. Madame de Sévigné continued her letters, which have charmed millions of readers with their pictures of court and country life. La Fontaine, in rhymed fables about animals, satirized human foibles. Boileau won fame by his precise but witty poems. La Rochefoucauld polished his incisive epigrams and maxims. Bishop Bossuet brought the eloquence of church preaching to a rotound climax. Such was the prestige of French letters under Louis XIV, that French became the language of the polite and the learned all over Europe, at the same time that French power was making it the language of diplomacy.

As outward evidence of his glory, Louis XIV reared magnificent edifices in a new style which, though based on the principles and elements of the classical Italian renaissance (dome, pillar, pilaster, round arch), was made into something distinctively French by the genius of architects like Le Vau, Perrault, and the Mansarts. The Observatory and the Hôtel des Invalides were constructed at Paris, together with triumphal arches and new city gates. Domestic architecture for both town and country houses gained a new dignity.

But the great palace of Versailles, which cost something like 40,000,000 *livres*, outshone all else. Immense in size, set in the middle of formal gardens with walks and fountains designed by the landscape architect Le Nôtre, Versailles, with all its dignity, was more than a building. It was the symbol of the reign. With its mirrored halls, its great mural paintings, its impressive façade, its gilt and its marble, it became the seat of the court of Louis XIV. It was the setting in which the "Sun King" shone in all his splendor. That the court was now removed some eleven miles from Paris was perhaps indicative of the growing gap between the King and his people. But the people were not to make themselves felt for a century yet. And in the meantime, most European princes sought to pattern themselves after Louis XIV and to build palaces in imitation of Versailles.

To decorate Versailles and his other châteaux, Louis XIV had a whole corps of artists and other craftsmen, headed by the painter Le Brun, who turned out vast canvases depicting with classic formality the triumphs of the King in peace and war, and also thousands of designs and sketches for tapestries, rugs, and articles of furniture. The *Gobelins*, founded by Henry IV, became a state establishment where tapestries were woven, while the similar *Savonnerie* made rugs. For the furniture and interior decoration, there were numerous skilled cabinetmakers, goldsmiths, glassworkers, embroiderers, and sculptors, who made Versailles a veritable museum of all that was finest and most costly in contemporary production.

French painting of the era will be discussed in a later chapter, but it may be noted here that in all the art of the period, from the tragedies to the doorknobs, and from Versailles to the chairs inside it, there was a common spirit. It has been called the spirit of classicism because it drew its inspiration from ancient Greece and Rome via the Italian Renaissance, and because it sought magnificence, dignity, symmetry, and balance rather than charm, delicacy, or daintiness. To the modern eye, the "grand style" is a little heavy, a little stiff, a little too formal. But it was a synthesis that arose from the spirit of the time and from the organizing efforts of men like Colbert and Le Brun. It went with the manners and the clothes. It seemed definitely to fit the age, the country, and Louis XIV.

All Europe was impressed and dazzled by the achievements of the French. The upper classes all over the Continent, from England to Russia, imitated French poetry and drama, French clothes and furniture, French architecture and tapestries. France set the style, and since then it has been from France that people have sought women's dresses and perfumes, laces and fine cooking, and all those articles that make for luxury and the most civilized living.

D. Wars of Louis XIV against Spain, Holland, and the Holy Roman Empire

Had Louis XIV devoted the strength of his government and the wealth of his country to promoting the prosperity of the people and encouraging the arts of peace, the future history of Europe would doubtless have been different. Instead, he was determined to win military glory and to add to the prestige and possessions of the house of Bourbon. He wanted France, he said, to expand her territories till they reached the "natural boundaries" which God had presumably established for the country in the form of the Rhine, the Pyrenees, the Alps, and the sea. He therefore plunged France into a series of long wars which dissipated French financial resources, wasted French man-power, and impaired French prosperity. Moreover, by his aggressive tactics Louis XIV made himself hated and feared by most other nations, so that they banded together to fight off the French as they had formerly joined to strike down Spain. Such a heritage did Louis XIV leave behind him, that for a century after his death France was generally regarded as an aggressor nation, a threat to her neighbors and to the peace of Europe.

To wage his wars, Louis XIV built up a big military machine. On the sea, Colbert created, out of the decayed fleet that Mazarin had left behind, a large navy, which was powerful enough to defeat the combined English and Dutch fleets in the Battle of Beachy Head (1690). Two years later it suffered a defeat at La Hogue, and thereafter, by what was probably a crucial mistake in policy, the French devoted their main efforts to land warfare and sent to sea chiefly privateers and commerce raiders which harried enemy shipping but left in English hands the real control of the seaways and all the dominance that such control brought with it.

On land, the story was different. There, the war minister, Louvois, who encouraged his master's ardor for military glory, made the French army supreme. He regularized the enlisting and levying of men and increased the size of the forces. It was Louvois who introduced into Europe the true "standing army," a force kept continuously in being and ready for service. No longer did the French army consist of feudal levies or semi-private regiments "owned" by their colonels and called up or brought up to full strength only when war threatened. Now the royal authority was complete and apparent at all levels. Discipline was tightened. The different branches (infantry, cavalry, artillery, engineers) were more clearly distinguished and more carefully organized. Where formerly troops had struggled along the roads in nondescript costumes, Louvois made them wear uniforms and march in step. He also created an elaborate and effective system of supply. Food for the troops and fodder for the horses were collected and deposited at convenient depots. The output of cannon, muskets, swords, pikes, gunpowder, and other munitions was vastly increased in quantity and improved in quality. Under

Louvois the formation and equipping of armies became business-like and scientific.

Louvois had helpful aides. Marshal Vauban, the greatest military engineer of the time, and perhaps of all time, fortified the frontier cities, ringed France about with well-nigh impregnable fortresses, and planned elaborate siege operations against enemy fortifications. Able officers enforced the new order on the army. There was, for example, Colonel Martinet, whose very name has become a synonym for a rigid disciplinarian. In addition, there were skilled generals to command the armies in actual battle. Condé and Turenne had already distinguished themselves in the later phases of the Thirty Years' War. The Duke of Luxembourg, whose father had been executed by Richelieu, was the most brilliant general of the later period of the reign of Louis XIV.

With the strongest and best trained army in Europe, Louis XIV was not long in finding occasion to use it. In 1667–1668 he waged against Spain the "War of Devolution." The excuse for it was a quite unjustified claim he advanced, on his wife's behalf, to the Spanish Netherlands. By diplomacy, he persuaded or threatened other countries into neutrality, then threw the weight of his armies against the fortress cities of the Belgian Netherlands. His triumph was checked, however, when Holland, England, and Sweden formed a triple alliance to put a stop to the war and to preserve the "balance of power" in Europe. This caused Louis XIV to accept a compromise in the treaty of Aix-la-Chapelle, by which Spain, while retaining the greater part of the Belgian Netherlands, surrendered to France an important section, including the fortified cities of Charleroi, Tournai, and Lille. The taste for conquest of the "Sun King" was whetted, but his appetite was hardly appeased.

Louis blamed the Dutch for the check he had met. Moreover, the Dutch were the chief rivals of the growing French commerce and industry. Even Colbert, who hated wars because they were so expensive, believed it would be a good idea to destroy Dutch trade by military means. With these thoughts in mind, Louis proceeded to break

up the triple alliance by negotiating the secret treaty of Dover with King Charles, II of England,[1] and buying off Sweden with favors and pensions. Holland alone did not seem formidable, for it was a small country and was torn by civil strife. On the one side, the head of the Orange family, with the title of *Stadholder*, supported by the country districts, the nobles, and the Calvinist clergy, aspired to centralize the state and transform it into an hereditary monarchy. On the other side, the aristocrats, big business men, religious liberals, and townsfolk found an able leader in John De Witt, the "Grand Pensionary," who wished to preserve the republic and the rights of the several provinces. For over twenty years, the latter party had been in power, but as the young Prince of Orange, William III, grew to maturity, signs were not lacking of a reaction in favor of his party.

Under these circumstances, Louis XIV declared war against Holland in 1672, anticipating an easy victory. French troops occupied Lorraine, marched down the Rhine, invaded Holland, and threatened the great commercial city of Amsterdam. John De Witt, whom the Dutch unjustly blamed for their reverses, was murdered; and at the order of William III, who assumed supreme command, they cut the dikes and flooded a large part of northern Holland to check the French advance.

By refusing to accept the generous peace terms which the Dutch now offered, Louis XIV again aroused general apprehension throughout Europe. The Emperor Leopold, the Great Elector of Brandenburg, and other German rulers joined with Spain to help Holland. The French in a series of victories defeated their German opponents and invaded Spanish territory in the Netherlands and Franche Comté. But King Charles II of England was obliged by his Parliament to join the anti-French alliance, and Louis XIV decided at length that it was time to make peace. By the treaties of Nimwegen (1678, 1679), it was Spain which had to pay the penalties of Louis' second war. The Dutch lost nothing. But Spain ceded to France the long-coveted province of Franche Comté with its capital city of

[1] See below, p. 509.

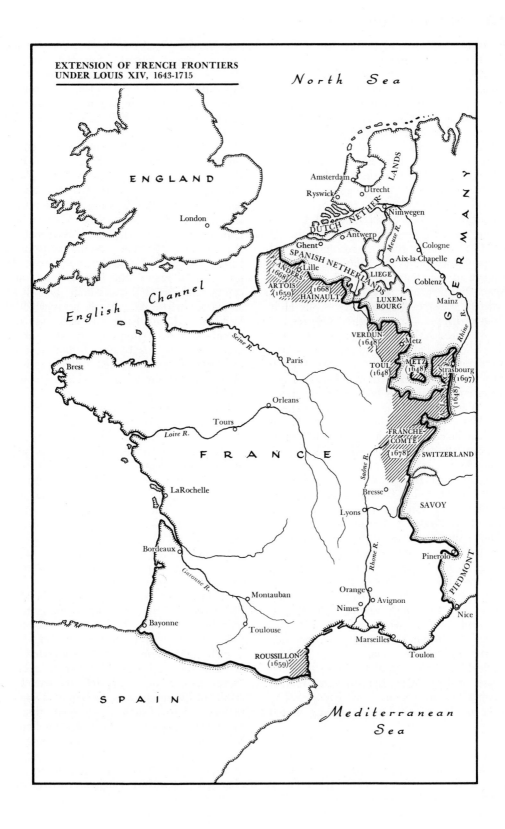

EXTENSION OF FRENCH FRONTIERS
UNDER LOUIS XIV, 1643-1715

North Sea

ENGLAND

Amsterdam

Ryswick

Utrecht

Nimwegen

London

DUTCH NETHER-

LANDS

Antwerp

Channel

Ghent

SPANISH NETHERLANDS

Cologne

FLANDERS
(1668)

Lille

Aix-la-Chapelle

English

ARTOIS
(1659)

HAINAULT
(1668)

LIEGE

Coblenz

LUXEM-
BOURG

Mainz

Meuse R.

VERDUN
(1648)

Metz

Seine R.

Paris

TOUL
(1648)

METZ
(1648)

Strasbourg
(1697)

Brest

(1648)

Orleans

Rhine R.

Tours

FRANCHE-
COMTÉ
(1678)

SWITZERLAND

Loire R.

F R A N C E

Saône R.

Bresse

LaRochelle

Lyons

SAVOY

Bordeaux

Garonne R.

Pinerolo

Montauban

Orange

PIEDMONT

Bayonne

Nimes

Avignon

Nice

Toulouse

Marseilles

Toulon

ROUSSILLON
(1659)

S P A I N

*Mediterranean
Sea*

Besançon, and several strong fortresses in the Belgian Netherlands.

Thus at great financial and economic cost, Louis had extended the French frontiers nearer the "natural boundaries." But he was not yet satisfied. No sooner was the war over than he established special courts, called "chambers of reunion," and had them adjudge to him numerous areas as "dependencies" of territories he had gained by the treaties of Westphalia and Nimwegen. In this way, he took over such important cities as Strasbourg and Luxembourg, as well as many lesser towns. At length alarmed by these encroachments, the Emperor Leopold in 1686 formed the League of Augsburg, composed of Austria, Spain, Sweden, and several lesser states, in order to preserve the territories of the Holy Roman Empire from further seizures. In 1688, Louis XIV sent a large army into the Rhenish Palatinate to enforce a preposterous claim to that valuable district. The war which resulted was Louis's third major struggle and has been variously styled the War of the League of Augsburg, or the War of the Palatinate. In America it was paralleled by a conflict between French and English colonists, known as King William's War.

In his first two wars, Louis had been able to count on the neutrality of the English King Charles II, whom he subsidized. But now a decisive change came about, since the English, for domestic reasons, drove out Charles's successor, James II, and brought in, as their new king, William III of Orange, the implacable enemy of Louis XIV. William, whose main desire was to defeat France, adroitly ingratiated himself with the English and threw all Britain's strength on the side of the anti-French alliance.

Neglecting the colonial and commercial phases of the struggle, Louis devoted French energies to the conflict in Europe. The War of the League of Augsburg lasted from 1689 to 1697. Though Condé and Turenne were now dead, the Duke of Luxembourg brilliantly led the splendidly organized French armies and won resounding victories at Fleurus (1690), Steinkirk (1692), and Neerwinden (1693). The allied armies were held at bay and France

was spared invasion, while the French ravaged the Palatinate. On the sea, the struggle went against France, and a French expedition to Ireland ended disastrously. After years of strife, ruinous to all the combatants, Louis XIV finally sued for peace.

By the treaty of Ryswick which ended the War of the League of Augsburg, Louis XIV: (1) surrendered nearly all the places adjudged to him by the "chambers of reunion," except Strasbourg, and returned Lorraine to its duke; (2) allowed the Dutch to garrison the chief fortresses of the Spanish (Belgian) Netherlands as a barrier against French aggression; (3) promised to reduce the French tariffs and commercial restrictions which had been aimed against the Dutch; (4) acknowledged William III as King of England and promised not to support any attempt to oust him from his throne. France lost no territory and even secured full recognition of its ownership of the whole province of Alsace.

But the wars of Louis were costing France dearly. Taxes and debts were increasing. Financial officials were compelled to use peculiar money-raising devices such as forcing payments from the guilds or selling new and useless offices. Industries, started so optimistically by Colbert, were languishing. The costs of winning glory for the "Sun King" seemed increasingly high.

In addition, Louis had in 1685 taken an ill-advised step. Urged by a number of his advisers, including Louvois, his war minister, he revoked the Edict of Nantes, by which the Huguenots had been granted religious toleration. Louis had been told that most French Protestants would, with a little persuasion, become converted to Catholicism, and he was eager to secure thoroughgoing unity of the country. The results of his action were disastrous. Despite ruthless pressure, such as the quartering of rough soldiery on peaceful Protestant households, most of the Huguenots clung to their religious beliefs. A hundred thousand or more left the country they loved and migrated to Holland, England, Switzerland, Germany, and even to America and South Africa. Since many of them were able merchants, manufacturers, and craftsmen, France suffered a serious economic blow. What France lost, her neighbors gained. The Huguenots took with them secrets and skills of French industry and built up commercial competition with France.

E. War of the Spanish Succession and Close of the Reign of Louis XIV

One of the reasons which led Louis XIV to negotiate the treaty of Ryswick in 1697, was the development of a situation in Spain which bade fair to give the French monarch golden opportunities for new territorial gains. Spain was still accounted a great power and held not only a vast overseas dominion but the southern (Belgian) Netherlands and much of Italy. The King of Spain at the time was a prematurely senile Habsburg, Charles II, who had reigned ingloriously since 1665 and had no direct heirs. Louis XIV might hope, therefore, to claim the Spanish inheritance for his children, on the ground that their Spanish mother's dowry had never been paid. On the other hand, the Emperor Leopold I (1658–1705) was a Habsburg and the nearest male relative of Charles II, and he was naturally eager to take over, for his line, the Spanish inheritance.

As the question of the Spanish succession loomed larger, attempts were made to solve it peacefully. Louis XIV, Leopold I, and William III of England negotiated a number of "partition treaties," which would have divided the Spanish inheritance and preserved a balance of power in Europe by preventing either France or the Empire from gaining too much. Charles II was not consulted about the matter, though as absolute ruler of Spain he was supposed to have the right to dispose of his own territories.

One of the greatest triumphs of the diplomatic art of Louis XIV was the way in which he ingratiated himself with the Spanish King whom he had so long and so often fought. French agents likewise won the favor of the Spanish people. Charles II, the last of the Spanish Habsburgs, a month before his pitiful death (1700), dictated a will that awarded his whole inheritance to Philip of Anjou, grandson of Louis XIV, with the resolute provision that in no circumstances should the Spanish possessions be divided.

When the news reached Versailles, the Sun King hesitated. The advantage of accepting the will of Charles II would be mainly dynastic; it would put the Bourbon family in a position more exalted than that of the Habsburgs under the Emperor Charles V. But the cost would be heavy, and France, already worn by a lengthening series of wars, would have to shoulder it. For other European powers would certainly strive to maintain some sort of balance between themselves and France. William III would surely not allow the French to take over the Spanish (Belgian) Netherlands without a struggle; and neither Holland nor England would willingly permit the Spanish colonies, so long closed to their ships, to be opened to French commerce. And, of course, the Habsburgs of Austria and the Holy Roman Empire were practically certain, for family reasons, as well as in German interests, to join Holland and England against any combination of France and Spain. On the other hand, if Louis XIV adhered to the previous partition treaties, he could gain considerably for France, ensure peace to Europe, and appear as an honorable and temperate ruler.

Hesitation was but an interlude. Ambition triumphed over fear, and the glory of the Bourbon family over the welfare of France. In the great hall of mirrors at Versailles, the Grand Monarch heralded his grandson as Philip V, the first Bourbon King of Spain. And when Philip left for Madrid, his aged grandfather proudly kissed him, and the Spanish ambassador exultantly declared, "The Pyrenees no longer exist."

Louis knew that war was inevitable, and he hastily prepared for it by seizing the "barrier fortresses" held by the Dutch, by recognizing the son of James II as the rightful King of England in place of William III, by negotiating alliances with Savoy and Bavaria, and by summoning up the armies of France and Spain. Meanwhile, William III and the Emperor Leopold formed against France a "Grand Alliance" of England, Holland, and Austria, to which the German states of Brandenburg-Prussia,

Hanover, and the Palatinate adhered. Later, by means of a favorable commercial agreement called the Methuen treaty (1703), England persuaded Portugal to join the Grand Alliance; and the Duke of Savoy was prevailed upon, by the promise of being recognized as king instead of duke, to change sides and enter the Alliance. It was the aim of the Allies to place the Emperor Leopold's second son, the Habsburg Archduke Charles, on the Spanish throne, to open up the Spanish colonies to foreign trade, and to set limits to the power of Louis XIV.

The War of the Spanish Succession, the fourth major war of Louis XIV, lasted from 1702 to 1713. Although William III died at its very outset, it was vigorously pushed by the English government of his sister-in-law, Queen Anne (1702–1714). On the high seas and in the colonies of America a bitter struggle known as "Queen Anne's War" ensued. And in Europe, the military campaigns were on a hitherto unprecedented scale. Fighting was carried on in the Netherlands, in southern Germany, in Italy, and in Spain. Many of the battles were in the open field, but the war was also punctuated by protracted sieges of fortress cities.

The tide of war turned steadily for several years against the Bourbons. The great French generals were all dead, and the Allies possessed the ablest military leaders of the time in the self-possessed English Duke of Marlborough and the daring Prince Eugene of Savoy. The battle of Blenheim (1704) drove the French out of Germany, and the capture of Gibraltar in the same year gave England a foothold in Spain and a naval base for the Mediterranean. Prince Eugene crowded the French out of Italy (1706); and by the victories of Ramillies (1706), Oudenarde (1708), and Malplaquet (1709), Marlborough cleared the Netherlands. On land and sea one Franco-Spanish reverse followed another. The Allies were preparing to invade France and dictate peace at Paris.

Then it was that Louis XIV displayed an energy and devotion worthy of a better cause. He appealed to the patriotism of the French people. He set an example of untiring application to toil. He melted down rich ornaments at Versailles to make coins. Nor was he disappointed in his expectations. New recruits hurried to the front. Rich and poor poured in their contributions. A supreme effort was made to stay the advancing enemy.

The fact that Louis XIV came out of the war as well as he did was owing to this remarkable uprising of the French (and of the Spaniards), and also to dissension among the Allies. The Tory party came to power in England, dismissed Marlborough, and showed some eagerness to make peace on moderate terms. Then, too, the unexpected accession of the Archduke Charles to the imperial and Austrian thrones (1711) made his claim to the Spanish crown as menacing to the European balance of power as that of Philip, for his possession of it would have made him another Charles V.

These circumstances rendered possible the conclusion of the peace of Utrecht (1713) with the following major provisions: (1) Philip V, the Bourbon grandson of Louis XIV, was acknowledged King of Spain and of Spain's overseas dominion on the condition that the crowns of France and Spain should never be united. (2) The Austrian Habsburgs were indemnified by securing Naples, Milan, Sardinia (which they exchanged for Sicily seven years later), and the Spanish Belgian Netherlands (which were known from 1713 until 1797 as the Austrian Netherlands). (3) England received the lion's share of the commercial and colonial spoils. From France she obtained Newfoundland, Nova Scotia, and Hudson Bay, and from Spain, Minorca and Gibraltar. She also secured a favorable tariff on the goods she sent into Spain through the port of Cadiz and a monopoly of slave trade to Spanish America (the Asiento), together with the privilege of sending one ship of merchandise each year to the Spanish colonies. France promised not to recognize or assist the Stuart pretenders (descendants of James II) to the English throne. (4) The Dutch recovered their barrier fortresses, whose garrisons were to be paid for in part by Austria; and the Scheldt River was to be open only to Dutch ships. (5) The Elector of Brandenburg was acknowledged as King of Prussia, an important step forward in the fortunes of the house of Hohenzollern. (6) The duchy of Savoy was likewise recognized as a kingdom, and was awarded Sicily which it had to exchange for Sardinia in 1720.

Thus France gained no territory and actually lost important colonies. In return for all her losses, for the crushing debts, the decline of trade, the mounting taxes, France had only the satisfaction of seeing a Bourbon on the throne of Spain. France might now hope for Spanish collaboration in diplomacy and war, and the Bourbons seemed clearly the foremost royal house in Europe. Louis XIV had gained dynastic ends at the cost of heavy national sacrifices.

In the wake of the War of the Spanish Succession, came to the masses of the French nation pestilence and famine, excessive taxes and debasement of the coinage, and the threat of national bankruptcy —a dangerous array of disorders. Louis XIV survived the treaty of Utrecht but two years. His long reign had seen France built up into a strong, centralized power, with its arts flourishing as never before and its people making strides forward in industry and commerce. But it had seen all the gains compromised by costly wars inspired by dynastic ambition and by desire for conquest.

La Danse dans un Pavillon de Jardin (The Minuet in a Pavilion). By Jean Antoine Watteau (d. 1721).

Courtesy The Cleveland Museum of Art. Gift of Commodore Louis D. Beaumont

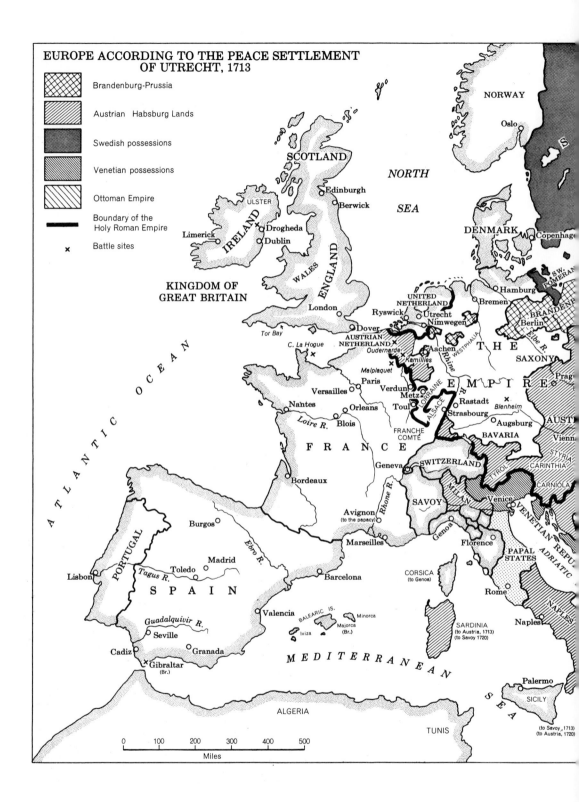

EUROPE ACCORDING TO THE PEACE SETTLEMENT
OF UTRECHT, 1713

Brandenburg-Prussia

Austrian Habsburg Lands

Swedish possessions

Venetian possessions

Ottoman Empire

Boundary of the
Holy Roman Empire

×   Battle sites

NORWAY

Oslo

SCOTLAND

NORTH

SEA

Edinburgh
Berwick

ULSTER

DENMARK   Copenhagen

Limerick   Drogheda
IRELAND   Dublin

Hamburg

S.W.
POMERANIA

Bremen

BRANDENBURG

KINGDOM OF
GREAT BRITAIN

WALES

ENGLAND

London

Ryswick   Utrecht
Nimwegen

Berlin
Elbe R.

THE

UNITED
NETHERLAND

Dover

AUSTRIAN
NETHERLAND

Utrecht

SAXONY

Tor Bay

C. La Hogue

Oudenarde

Aachen

WESTPHALIA

Kamillies

Rhine

Prag

Malplaquet

Paris

Verdun
Metz

Rastadt

Blenheim

EMPIRE

Versailles

Nantes

Orleans

Toul

Strasbourg

Augsburg

AUST

Blois

LORRAINE

ALSACE

FRANCHE
COMTÉ

BAVARIA

Vienna

Loire R.

ATLANTIC   OCEAN

F R A N C E

Geneva

SWITZERLAND

TYROL

CARINTHIA

Bordeaux

Rhone R.

SAVOY

MILAN

Venice

CARNIOLA

Avignon
(to the papacy)

Genoa

VENETIAN REPU

ADRIATIC

Burgos

Marseilles

Florence

PAPAL
STATES

PORTUGAL

Ebro R.

Madrid

Toledo

Lisbon   Tagus R.

CORSICA
(to Genoa)

Rome

NAPLES

S P A I N

Barcelona

Guadalquivir R.

Valencia

Seville

BALEARIC IS.

Minorca

Naples

Majorca
(Br.)

SARDINIA
(to Austria, 1713)
(to Savoy 1720)

Iviza

Cadiz   Granada

Gibraltar
(Br.)

M E D I T E R R A N E A N

Palermo

SICILY

ALGERIA

SEA

TUNIS

(to Savoy, 1713)
(to Austria, 1720)

0   100   200   300   400   500

Miles

FINLAND

Lake Onega

Lake Ladoga

S W E D E N

GULF OF FINLAND

INGRIA

Stockholm

ESTONIA

Novgorod

LIVONIA

Pskov

Kazan

Volga R.

Moscow

BALTIC SEA

COURLAND

Dvina R.

nigsberg

Vilna

LITHUANIA

R U S S I A

PRUSSIA

Smolensk

Oka R.

Warsaw

Voronezh

P O L A N D

Don R.

Kiev

Volga R.

Vistula R.

Dnieper R.

Astrakhan

Dniester R.

CASPIAN
SEA

TRANSYLVANIA

MOLDAVIA

Budapest

H U N G A R Y

CRIMEA

arlovitz

Belgrade

WALLACHIA

Danube R.

Varna

B L A C K   S E A

Trebizond

O

Ragusa

Samsun

MONTENEGRO

Constantinople

Vardar R.

T

Salonica

Ankara

T

O

M

A

N

E M P I R E

Smyrna

AEGEAN SEA

IONIAN IS.
(to Venice)

Mosul

Athens

Adana

Euphrates R.

Tigris R.

Aleppo

RHODES

CRETE

CYPRUS

Catherine the Great. By G. B. Lampl (*d.* 1838).

Courtesy Bettmann Archive

CHAPTER 35

Rise of Russia and Prussia

A. The Great Northern War: Decline of Sweden and Poland

During the latter part of the seventeenth century and the early part of the eighteenth, drastic changes occurred in the relative strength of countries of eastern and north-central Europe. Two states—Russia and Prussia—consolidated and extended their territories and became notably more important. Two states—Sweden and Poland—declined rather rapidly in strength and significance. One state—Austria—lost weight in Germany but gained by expansion to the east and southeast, while still another state—the previously expanding Ottoman Empire—began to recede.

At the close of the Thirty Years' War in 1648, Sweden dominated the Baltic, and was recognized as the leading Protestant power on the European continent. Much Russian and Polish trade passed through the Swedish port of Riga, and much German commerce went in and out on Swedish ships via the ports of Stettin and Stralsund. Gustavus Adolphus' successor was his brilliant but erratic daughter, Maria Christina, on whose conversion to Catholicism and retirement to Rome the Swedish crown passed to the warlike Charles X (1654–1660). He engaged in simultaneous wars with Russia, Poland, Brandenburg, and Denmark, and by a series of peace treaties with them in 1660–1661 Sweden was confirmed in its extensive Baltic possessions.

The basis of Swedish power was three-fold: commerce, army, and alliance with France. But these were not sufficient to enable Sweden to maintain its predominance in the north. Its own population was small, its resources scanty, and its administration inefficient. Its peasantry was poor and backward, its nobility self-seeking, its politics disorderly. Moreover, though its territories were extensive, they were scattered around the edge of the Baltic Sea, and control of them depended on communication by ships and thus on naval supremacy. Nor could it command any deep loyalty on the part of its subjects across the Baltic—Germans, Russians, Finns, Estonians, Latvians, Danes, or Poles. And despite subsidies and diplomatic support from France, the military strength of Sweden proved insufficent to cope with the waxing power of Russia and Prussia.

Had Sweden kept the peace, clung tenaciously to its possessions, and concentrated its attention upon internal development, its power might have endured longer. But King Charles XI (1660–1697), at the behest of Louis XIV, took Sweden into the Franco-Dutch War, with resulting defeat of Swedish forces on land and sea by those of Prussia and Denmark. Only French support secured the restoration of Sweden's territories at the peace table. In his remaining years Charles XI increased the power of the crown, bettered its finances, and strengthened the army and navy. But all his achievements were to go for nought in the catastrophe which marked the astounding reign of his successor.

Charles XII (1697–1718) came to the throne at the age of fifteen a precocious and sensitive boy filled with martial ardor and fanatical courage. When Saxony, Denmark, and Russia formed an alliance in 1699 to seize some of the Swedish territories, they expected an easy victory, for Sweden's ally France was occupied with the question of the Spanish succession. Instead, they precipitated the Great Northern War which lasted until 1721. In it, Charles XII, by the fury with which he defended his dominion, earned the title of the "madman of the North" and went down to final defeat only amid spectacular exploits and after an incredible struggle against overwhelming odds.

Seizing the initiative, Charles XII invaded Denmark and forced its terrified king to make peace (1700) and pay a huge indemnity. Then Charles hastened into Estonia and annihilated a Russian army at Narva (1700). Turning into Poland, he captured Warsaw and Cracow, forced the Polish parliament to oust King Augustus II, who was also Elector of Saxony, and place a friendly noble, Stanislaus Lesczynski, on the Polish throne (1704). Charles, youth though he was, had defeated all his enemies. Callous to the horrors of war, and arrogant with pride, he sent out orders "to slay, burn, and destroy" in the territories he had conquered. But his enemies were now aroused and stubborn. The Russian Tsar Peter reorganized his armies and occupied Karelia and Ingria. Augustus II rallied his forces and regained his Polish throne. Though Charles could still have made a satisfactory peace, he persisted, with increasing stubbornness, in the war that was bleeding Sweden.

Invading Russia, Charles XII met the armies of Peter and suffered an overwhelming defeat at Poltava (1709). Fleeing with the pitiful remnant of his forces, Charles escaped southward into the Ottoman Empire, where he stirred up the Sultan to attack Russia. While he lingered in Turkey, Charles' enemies overran all the Swedish territory except Sweden itself, Finland, and the Baltic port of Stralsund. At this port, Charles suddenly appeared (1714) with a single attendant. Though Prussia and Great Britain had now joined the coalition against him, still Charles would not sue for peace. It was while directing an invasion of Nor-

way in 1718 that Charles XII, at the age of thirty-six, met his death.

The peace which Charles would not seek was made shortly after his death, and none too soon for exhausted and enfeebled Sweden. By the treaties of Stockholm (1719–1720), Sweden gave up all her German territories except a small district in western Pomerania which included Stralsund. Denmark received Holstein; Hanover, the mouths of the Elbe and Weser rivers; Prussia, the mouth of the Oder, with Stettin. Augustus of Saxony recovered the Polish crown, while Great Britain, Denmark, and Prussia became the chief commercial heirs of declining Sweden. By the treaty of Nystad (1721), Russia secured from Sweden the territories of Karelia, Ingria, Estonia, Livonia, and a narrow strip of southern Finland which included the fortress of Viborg. By this treaty Peter the Great gained his long-sought "window to the west," and Russia's power was increased as much as Sweden's was reduced.

In the remainder of the eighteenth century, Sweden rapidly fell to the position of a second-rate power. When an ambitious and assertive party of nobles, called the "Hats," gained control and unwisely took Sweden into another war with Russia (1741) and then into the Seven Years' War (1756), the disastrous results quickly showed that even the continued support of France could not bolster Sweden or maintain it as an important factor in European politics. The economic difficulties that arose from the Swedish defeats and loss of territory led the country into some interesting experiments. A bank of Stockholm had been founded in 1656 and had issued paper notes which were much easier to handle than the clumsy Swedish copper coins, some of which weighed as much as forty-three pounds. Brought under parliamentary control and renamed the Bank of Sweden, this institution became important in the eighteenth century. By 1762, its notes in circulation had risen in amount to 45,000,000 Swedish dollars, and over-issue had led to some depreciation in their value.

The decline of Poland was more prolonged and less dramatic than that of Sweden, but it was no less painful and even more calamitous. By the end of the seventeenth century, Swedish commercial domination of the Baltic had impaired Polish prosperity. Poland's cities were not growing, nor was she developing a strong middle class of merchants and traders. Her peasantry was depressed, and the only strong class was the nobility, which owned most of the land, maintained their own political and social privileges, quarreled fiercely among themselves, and intrigued with foreign powers.

A strong national government might have remedied Poland's internal conditions and protected her against neighboring countries that were ever ready to take advantage of Poland's lack of natural frontiers to seize some of her territory. But at the very time when strong, absolute monarchies were being established in all other countries on the Continent, the Polish government was becoming almost anarchical. Since the sixteenth century the Polish monarchy had been elective, and the noble electors disfigured every reign by their squabbles about the succession. They used their power to

wrest concession after concession from their monarchs until the kings became hardly more than figureheads.

Weakened by wars with Sweden and Russia, Poland was also enfeebled by the lawlessness of the nobles. To make matters worse, the nobles insisted more and more on their political rights, such as the so-called *liberum veto*, by which any of them in the diet, or parliament, could rise in his place and, by saying "I disapprove," prevent the passage of a measure or even secure the dissolution of the session. John III Sobieski, who was king from 1674 to 1696, had led a revolt against his predecessor and had intrigued with France. Though he won immortal fame by a brilliant victory over the Turks (1673) and by defeating them again before beleaguered Vienna (1683), internal conditions in Poland, under his rule, went from bad to worse. At Sobieski's death (1697), there were eighteen candidates for the Polish throne. The election was won by Frederick Augustus, Elector of Saxony, who, to improve his chances, had hastily

SWEDEN BEFORE AND AFTER THE
GREAT NORTHERN WAR, 1699-1721

Lazienski Palace, Warsaw (XVIII Century).

become a Catholic and who arrived late on the scene with ample bribe-money when the finances of his rivals were already exhausted.

For the next sixty-six years, save when Stanislaus Lesczynski, the puppet of the Swedish King Charles XII, was precariously balanced on the throne, the electors of Saxony were kings of Poland. Such resources as Poland could muster after the long and painful war with Sweden, the Saxon rulers cheerfully used for their German projects. The nobles, as unruly as ever, increasingly sought wealth and advantages by negotiating with foreign powers, even when a betrayal of Polish interests was involved. Thus was the way prepared for the tragic partitions of Poland in the latter half of the eighteenth century, when three times (1772, 1793, 1795) her powerful and ruthless neighbors divided up her territories, and at last erased the Polish state from the political map of Europe.

Poland's fate was the result not only of foreign rule, a weak kingship, and a turbulent nobility that sought ever to increase its power, but also of other factors. Though it seemed like a geographic unit, its boundaries were mainly in open plains hard to defend. Nor was it a national unit like France or England, for it contained a large minority of Lithuanians who spoke a different language and smaller numbers of Latvians who spoke another, not to mention Ruthenians (Ukrainians) and Russian Cossacks over against the Russian border. Nor was Poland unified in religion. While the Poles and most of the Lithuanians were Roman Catholics, many of its people in the east adhered to the Orthodox Church; there were large numbers of Jews in the cities; and in the west were sizeable groups of Protestant Germans. Appeals from the Protestants to German rulers, and from the Orthodox to the Russian tsars, formed a convenient basis for foreign interference in Polish affairs.

B. Russia from Peter the Great to Catherine the Great

To the Parisian or Londoner of 1600, Russia seemed a distant half-wild land that lay so far out on the fringes of Europe as to be scarcely a factor in its life or part of its civilization. Yet developments were taking place that were to bring Russia into main currents of Western European life. The time would come when Russia would be the most populous and powerful of European states.

In the century and a half that followed the capture (1453) of Constantinople by the Turks, Russia stood out as the heir of Byzantine culture. From the old Eastern Roman Empire she had derived her religion (Orthodox Christianity), her alphabet, her art and architecture. Moreover her vigorous, ruthless rulers, Ivan III the "Great" (1462–1505) and Ivan IV the "Terrible" (1533–1584), thought of themselves as successors of the Eastern Emperors. They adopted the title of Tsar (or Czar, a form of the word Caesar), the ancient imperial symbol of the double-headed eagle, and much of the old Byzantine court etiquette. Moreover, as they enlarged the grand-duchy of Moscow into the state of Russia and shook off the Tatar yoke, they assumed something of the role of the old Eastern Empire as a barrier between the rest of Europe and the great spaces and wild tribes of Asia.

There was in Russian life a definite eastern tinge derived partly from Constantinople and partly from contact and intermixture with the Tatars and other Asiatic peoples. The Russian men wore long beards; the upper-class women were kept in seclusion; the manner of dress was more oriental than western. During the sixteenth and seventeenth centuries, Russians were spreading rapidly eastward, so that Russia thenceforward was an Asiatic as well as a European power. Russia's contacts with the nations to the west were long limited by several factors. Not only did her emigrants tend to go eastward, but the very nature of the country made agriculture more important than industry or trade, so that her commercial relations with outside lands were comparatively slight. Her Orthodox Christianity kept her aloof from both Catholics and Protestants to the west. Furthermore, as long as her immediate neighbors—Sweden, Poland, and the Ottoman Empire—were strong, Russia was shut off from the west by hostile territories. After Gustavus Adolphus secured Karelia in 1617, Russia was cut off from all contact with the Baltic and could trade directly with western Europe only by the long and difficult Arctic Ocean route.

At the close of the sixteenth century, the direct line of Ivan the Great died out and there ensued what were known as the "Troublous Times" (1605–1613). Harassed by the struggles of contestants for the throne, invaded by Swedes, Poles, and Turks, Russia seemed to be sinking into anarchy. To remedy the situation a meeting of nobles at Moscow in 1613 chose one of their own number, Michael Romanov, to be the new Tsar. Aided by his father, who was Orthodox Patriarch of Moscow, Michael slowly reduced the country to order. His successor, Alexius (1645–1676), was able, by joining with groups of frontiersmen, to wrest part of the Ukraine from Polish rule.

At the death of Alexius, there were new troubles as to the succession, but by 1694 Peter, a grandson of Michael, had become the sole ruler. Brought up amid scenes of blood and violence, gigantic in stature, subject to terrible fits of rage, ruthless and unprincipled, Peter was a remarkable leader, administrator, and statesman. His achievements won him the title of "the Great." Interested in ships from childhood, Peter, thwarted in an attempt to take Azov on the Black Sea from the Turks (1695), built a fleet which enabled him to capture that city the next year. Already eager to gain for Russia "windows" on the Black and Baltic Seas, Peter in 1697 sent a special embassy to seek the aid of the Western powers against the Turks. Those powers were too busy with the question of the Spanish succession to heed Russian pleas. But Peter, who accompanied the embassy in the guise of a sea captain, avidly absorbed useful knowledge about armies, navies, forts, shipbuilding, industry, and trade in Prussia, Holland, England, and the other countries he visited. Everywhere he went he enlisted sailors, craftsmen, engineers, and technicians, and sent them back to Russia to work on his projects.

While traveling from Vienna to Venice, Peter heard news of a mutiny among the royal bodyguard, or *streltsi*, at Moscow. Though the rising had been quickly put down, Peter hurried home to wreak a bloody vengeance and show the elements who opposed him that his authority was not to be questioned. Some seven thousand of the mutineers were executed, a number of them by Peter in person, for it amused him to demonstrate that he could behead a man with a single stroke. But Peter came back for more than vengeance.

Peter the Great. After a picture by Sir Godfrey Kneller (d. 1723).

Impressed by the superior culture and technology of western Europe, the Tsar was determined to "westernize" Russia. In part, he sought to alter external ways. Beards and mustaches were taxed heavily and Peter with his own hand cut off the hirsute adornments of some of the chief nobles. French and German clothes were made compulsory. Women were brought into the social gatherings of the court. The use of tobacco was encouraged. January 1 was substituted for September 1 as New Year's day.

Peter sought likewise to effect deeper reforms. He tried to build up trade and industry. State factories were started and manned by serfs. Shipping was subsidized, and the middle class of traders and business men, which was very small in Russia, was favored and helped. Much of the westernization was superficial. When Peter tried to establish the German guild system in Russia he met with little success. But his efforts mark a turning point in Russian history, for henceforward Russia came more and more into the main currents of Western civilization.

Determined to make Russia an absolute monarchy like that of Louis XIV, Peter acted with such skill and energy that Russian rule became more autocratic than any in the west. He created a strong army, trained and disciplined by expert foreign officers. Any remaining traces of local self-government were wiped out or enfeebled, and the old local divisions were replaced by "governments" (*gubernii*), each headed by an army officer who extorted taxes to pay for Peter's reforms. The old Duma of the nobles was changed into an advisory Senate, and each town was endowed, in western style, with a town hall and aldermen to go in it, but even here all real power rested with agents of the Tsar. The church, too, was brought under complete royal control, for though Peter, professing devotion to the Orthodox faith, harried all heretics, he also abolished the patriarchate of Moscow and transferred its authority to a "Holy Synod" whose members were chosen by the Tsar and were subservient to him. Thenceforth the Tsars exalted the Russian Orthodox Church as the source of order, while the Church rapidly became the right-hand support of Tsardom.

Effective, too, were Peter's alterations of the social structure of the country. He swamped the old nobility (the boyars) by creating tens of thousands of new nobles. To these he gave lands and privileges, and, in return, demanded that they serve him in the army and the government administration. The lands of the new nobles were worked by serfs. Until about 1600, the Russian peasants had been relatively free and had worked their lands in communal groups. During the course of the seventeenth century they had lost much of their freedom and had been bound more and more closely to the soil, at a time when most of the serfs of western Europe were gaining freedom. This trend came to completion through the work of Peter the Great. The peasants were registered by a rural census and forbidden to leave the land. They were put entirely under the control of the landowners, who regarded them more and more as a sort of livestock that went with the estates. If the nobles were to serve the Tsar, the serfs were to be forced to serve the nobles.

Peter's forceful achievements within his country were matched by success in war and foreign policy. To be sure, he made little progress against the Turks. In fact, in 1711, he had to restore Azov to them to avoid a military disaster. But against Sweden, despite his initial defeat at Narva, he was successful at Poltava and thereafter. The treaty of Nystad (1721) marked Russia's triumph. To symbolize the country's new orientation westward, Peter built on the waste marshes near the mouth of the Neva river a great new modern city and called it St. Petersburg (now Leningrad). Thither he transferred from Moscow his government. The capital of Russia was no longer to be in the old "holy city" steeped in the Russian past, with churches that bespoke Byzantium and with its memories of the Tatars. Henceforth for almost two centuries, Russia was to be ruled from a city built by Peter's orders, on land won by Peter's armies; a city linked to the rest of Europe by its position and its "western" architecture.

One of Russia's three strong neighbors— Sweden—was disposed of by Peter the Great in the early part of the eighteenth century. It remained for the Tsarina Catherine II the "Great," in the latter part of the century, to take care of the other two— Poland and the Ottoman Empire. In the interval (1725–1762) between Peter I and Catherine II, there were several disputes over the succession in Russia, and the country was ruled mainly by women more or less directly connected with the Romanov family. These female rulers were for the most part notable for their loose morals and ugly manners. Of them, Anne (1730–1740) was reared in Germany and surrounded herself with German favorites and advisers, while Elizabeth (1741–1762), a daughter of Peter the Great, hated Germans, employed native Russian advisers, and warred on Prussia.

But Catherine II, who ruled Russia from 1762 to 1796, was of a different stamp. She came of a minor German princely family and had been brought as a girl to Russia to marry a weak and half-mad heir to the throne. At once she set herself to win the favor of the Russians. She learned their language, she adopted their religion; she slighted Germans and surrounded herself with Russians. In 1762, her husband came to the throne as Peter III, and his brief rule was not without significance, for in his crazy admiration of the Prussian King Frederick II, he took Russia out of the war then raging against Prussia and aided Frederick. But within a few months Peter was removed from power by a revolt of the guards regiment abetted by Catherine. Shortly afterwards Peter died in captivity,

officially of "apoplexy," but actually by assassination.

Despite the fact that Catherine was a German with no Romanov or even Russian blood, she was proclaimed Tsarina by those who had got rid of her husband, and during the thirty-four years of her reign, her authority was never successfully challenged. Completely immoral, utterly without scruples, surrounded by favorites who were frequently her lovers, Catherine II was a strong ruler at home and notably successful in foreign affairs. Though she had no real love of learning, she was eager to be thought "progressive" and "enlightened." She founded some secondary schools and an Academy at St. Petersburg. She corresponded with learned men and philosophers in France. She discussed forward-looking reforms of all sorts and popularized French language, manners, architecture, and cookery in the court circles, with such success that French became the first and Russian the second language of the next generation of Russian nobles.

Actually, for all this show, Catherine accomplished few real reforms in Russia and these were more designed to strengthen her authority than to benefit the people. Administratively she reorganized the "governments" and "districts." The courts of justice were improved and set in order. But at the same time Catherine further subjugated the Church by taking over its lands and the million serfs that lived on them. To reward the nobles who were the class from which she derived her support, she gave to distinguished generals and administrators large estates and great numbers of serfs, and she distributed in a similar fashion much of the foreign land she acquired by conquest or diplomacy.

It was really in foreign affairs that Catherine won the right to be called "Great," for here she proved herself a worthy successor of Peter I and displayed an equal ruthlessness and an even greater cynicism. In 1764, aided by Frederick the Great of Prussia, Catherine secured the election of one of her favorites, Stanislaus Poniatowski, as King of Poland, ending the rule there of the Saxon Electors. Determined to keep Poland weak and ill-governed, Catherine not only intrigued constantly among the quarreling groups of nobles but in 1768

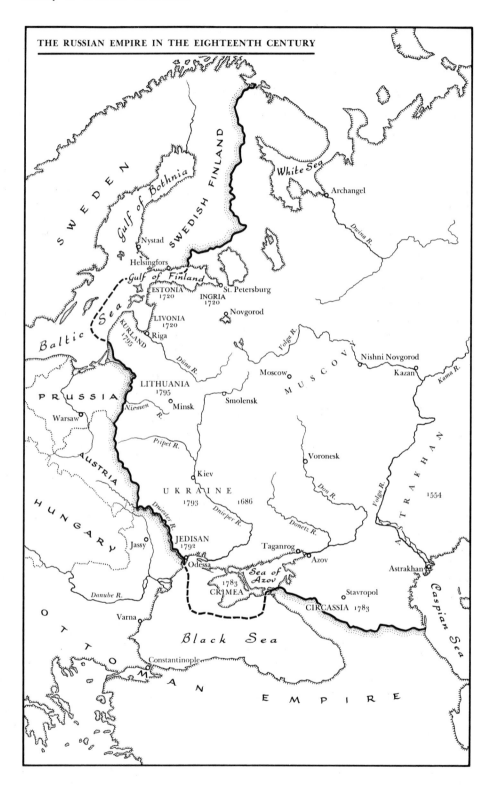

THE RUSSIAN EMPIRE IN THE EIGHTEENTH CENTURY

SWEDEN

Gulf of Bothnia

White Sea

Archangel

Duina R.

SWEDISH FINLAND

Nystad

Helsingfors

Gulf of Finland

ESTONIA
1720

INGRIA
1720

St. Petersburg

Novgorod

Baltic Sea

LIVONIA
1720

KURLAND
1795

Riga

Duna R.

Volga R.

MUSCOV

Moscow

Nishni Novgorod

Kazan

Kama R.

PRUSSIA

LITHUANIA
1795

Warsaw

Niemen R.

Minsk

Smolensk

Pripet R.

AUSTRIA

Kiev

Voronesk

Don R.

Volga R.

A S T R A K H A N

1554

HUNGARY

UKRAINE
1793

Dniester R.

Dnieper R.

1686

Donetz R.

Jassy

JEDISAN
1792

Odessa

Taganrog

Azov

Astrakhan

Danube R.

Sea of
Azov

1783

CRIMEA

Stavropol

CIRCASSIA 1783

Caspian Sea

Varna

Black Sea

O T T O

Constantinople

M A N

E M P I R E

negotiated a treaty by which the Poles promised not to reform or change their anarchical form of government without her consent.

Then by a series of negotiations with Poland's other neighbors, Austria and Prussia, Catherine prepared the way for the first partition of Poland. In 1772 all was ready. By prearrangement, and despite the frantic protests of the Poles, Prussia took from Poland West Prussia except the town of Danzig. Austria took Galicia except Cracow. Catherine seized all of Poland east of the Duna and Dnieper rivers. Thus Poland was deprived of about a fourth of its territory, a third of its population, and almost half of its wealth.

Sobered by this catastrophe, many of the Polish nobles sought to reform the government and to strengthen what remained of their nation. But Catherine always worked to prevent the fruition of their projects and stirred up dissident groups to maintain the old anarchy. In 1791 the Poles were able, by means of a new constitution, to put through a series of important improvements in their government. The *liberum veto* was abolished, and the monarchy made hereditary. But again Catherine intervened, pointing out that such changes violated the treaty of 1768. Joining with Prussia, she partitioned Poland again in 1793, defeating the Poles who were led by the heroic Kosciusko and who sought to defend their country and their new constitution. Prussia took Posen and western Poland almost up to Warsaw, while Russia occupied another large slice of eastern and southeastern Poland.

In vain did Kosciusko assume a military dictatorship and lead a desperate national revolt. He was defeated, wounded, and captured. In 1795 Prussia and Russia, again joined by Austria, completed the task of wiping Poland off the map. Though the boundaries they drew did not long endure, Poland was not to reappear as an independent national state for one hundred and twenty-three years, and, from 1815 onwards, the majority of Poles and the greater part of their country lay under Russian rule.

If acquisition of territory is the gauge of success, Catherine the Great was almost equally successful in her dealings with the Ottoman Empire. From 1768 to 1774, she waged war on the Turks and with such good fortune that the resulting treaty of Kuchuk Kainarji (1774) was a decisive turning point in the decline of Turkey and the rise of Russia in southeastern Europe.

When Catherine died in 1796 she left a record of very considerable accomplishments. If it can be said that Peter the Great made Russia a European power, it can be maintained with equal justice that Catherine the Great made Russia a great power. The eighteenth century witnessed a marvelous growth of the Russian Empire in Europe, as the seventeenth had seen it spread out over northern Asia. Russia had acquired wide lands and a capital on the Baltic. It had secured valuable ports on the Black Sea. It had pushed its boundaries westward to the middle of the continent. It now counted among its subjects, not only Russians, but Ukrainians, Byelorussians, Lithuanians, Estonians, Letts, and Poles, as well as a whole medley of Asiatic tribes and peoples.

C. Austria and the Holy Roman Empire in the Eighteenth Century

In the late middle age and early modern times, the Habsburgs of Austria, as Holy Roman Emperors, had had considerable influence and some control throughout Germany. But after 1648, a change gradually occurred. The peace of Westphalia so increased the independence of the several German states, both large and small, that Austria had to win their alliance or support almost as if she were dealing with foreign powers. Yet Austria did not sink to the position of a second-rate power, for, while it lost influence in Germany and the west, it made compensating gains in Italy, and also in the east at the expense of the Ottoman Empire and Poland. But these gains bore with them seeds of future trouble, since more and more they made of Habsburg Austria a conglomerate state of alien peoples with only a relatively small German nucleus in the old hereditary lands around Vienna.

In Germany, to be sure, the Habsburg Emperor, even after 1648, had a certain prestige. In a vague way, people still looked to him as the most important leader in German affairs. But the German states were taking advantage of their increased inde-

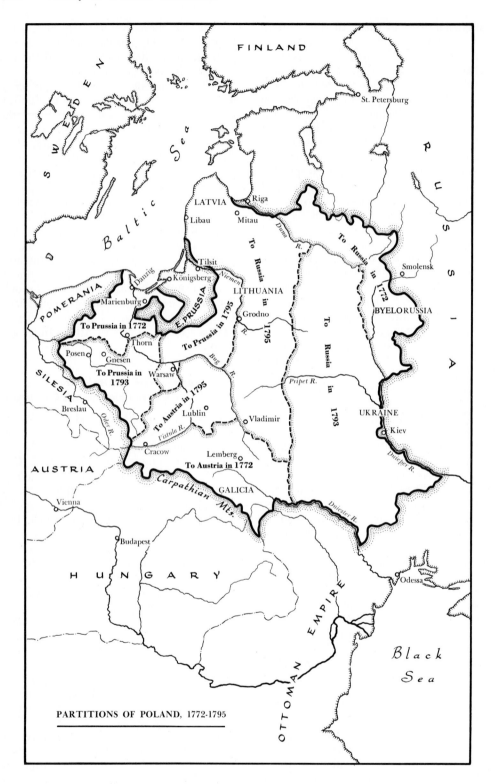

FINLAND

St. Petersburg

S W E D E N

R U S S I A

Baltic Sea

LATVIA   Riga

Libau   Mitau

Smolensk

To Russia in 1772

Tilsit

Danzig   Königsberg   *Niemen*

POMERANIA   E. PRUSSIA

Marienburg   LITHUANIA

BYELORUSSIA

To Prussia in 1772   Grodno

To Prussia in 1795

Thorn

Posen   *Bug*   To Russia in 1793

SILESIA   Gnesen   Warsaw

To Prussia in 1793   *R.*

Breslau   *Pripet R.*

To Austria in 1795   Lublin   Vladimir   UKRAINE

Vistula R.   Kiev

Cracow   Lemberg   *Dniepel R.*

AUSTRIA   To Austria in 1772

Carpathian Mts.   GALICIA   *Dniester R.*

Vienna

Budapest   Odessa

H U N G A R Y

O T T O M A N E M P I R E   Black
Sea

PARTITIONS OF POLAND, 1772-1795

pendence to pursue their own interests. In the north, Brandenburg emerged as a powerful state. In the south, Bavaria, to strengthen itself against Austria, maintained an almost constant alliance with France. The Elector of Saxony in 1697 obtained the crown of Poland, and in 1715 the Elector of Hanover became King of Great Britain. None of these states could be counted on to follow Austrian leadership, and the others did so only when it seemed to their advantage.

In the long reign of Leopold I (1658–1705), Austria secured compensation in Hungary for her weakening hold on Germany. Strengthening his administration and suppressing dissent, Leopold heightened Habsburg authority in Hungary at the expense of old local liberties. Prompted by the pope and in alliance with Poland, Leopold engaged in a long war (1683–1699) with the Moslem Turks. At the start, the Turkish armies, with something of their former vigor, surged up to the very gates of Vienna and threatened to capture the city. But the Polish King John III (Sobieski) came south with his army and drove off the Turks. Though Leopold hesitated to continue the war, Pope Innocent XI formed a Holy League which included Venice, Poland, and Russia to drive the Moslems out of Europe. Even Louis XIV for a time lent aid to the Christian cause. Success followed success. Budapest was recovered (1686); Belgrade was taken (1688); Bosnia was liberated

(1689). But then the outbreak of the War of the League of Augsburg [1] afforded a respite to the Turks; they rallied and recaptured Belgrade. In 1697, however, Prince Eugene of Savoy defeated the Turks at Zenta and a peace conference met in the next year.

The resulting peace of Karlowitz (1699) assured to the Austrian Habsburgs the whole of Hungary, instead of only the northern portion which they had formerly held. Meanwhile, Leopold had summoned a Hungarian diet and forced it to acknowledge him as hereditary rather than elective King of Hungary. Hungarian patriots rose against the Habsburgs, and though they won few battles in their long struggle (1704–1711), they at least secured a promise that some of the traditional Hungarian privileges would be respected.

Austria had been distracted from her eastern problems by wars in the west: the War of the League of Augsburg and the War of the Spanish Succession. Though in the latter she failed to recreate the empire of Charles V, she at least made significant territorial gains. As a result of the peace of Utrecht (1713), Austria obtained the Belgian Netherlands, and in Italy both the duchy of Milan and the kingdom of the Two Sicilies. The Austrian Netherlands proved difficult to defend and not particularly profitable, and the kingdom of the Two Sicilies was lost to the Bourbons of

[1] See above, p. 428.

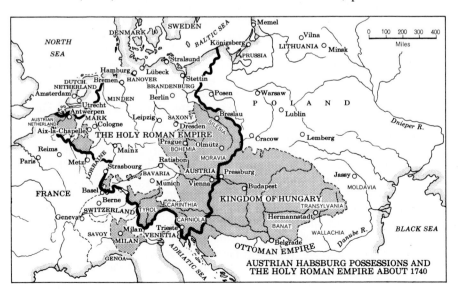

AUSTRIAN HABSBURG POSSESSIONS AND THE HOLY ROMAN EMPIRE ABOUT 1740

Spain in 1738. But Milan was held by Austria, with one brief interruption, till the middle of the nineteenth century.

The Emperor who had won these lands at the peace of Utrecht was Charles VI (1711–1740). It became clear to him early in his reign that he was going to leave no male heirs. He therefore used most of his energies and diplomacy to insure the succession of his daughter, Maria Theresa. By a document called the Pragmatic Sanction, Charles declared the Habsburg dominions indivisible and capable of being inherited by a female; and by making concessions to major foreign powers, he obtained paper promises from them that they would respect the Sanction. But, as the cynical Prussian King of the time remarked, 200,000 soldiers would have been a more useful legacy.

Austria of the eighteenth century was a collection of territories brought together by conquest, marriage, and diplomacy. It was not an Empire, for the Austrian ruler was called Emperor only if he was elected head of the Holy Roman (German) Empire. It was not a national state like England or France, for it did not comprise a single predominant nationality, nor did it have a unified administration. The common monarch of the varied lands that composed the Habsburg dominions ruled as archduke in Austria, king in Bohemia, king in Hungary, duke in Milan, and prince in the Belgian Netherlands; and the administration of each of these major areas was independent of the others and affected by local traditions and privileges. Under this complicated rule were Germans, Czechs, Slovaks, Hungarians (Magyars), Rumanians, Croatians, Slovenes, Italians, Flemings, and French-speaking Walloons.

But for all the confused and varied nature of the Habsburg domains, the Austrian rulers of the eighteenth century still had great prestige in Europe. The sheer extent of their territories and the number of their subjects made them important. They were related to most of the other ruling families of Europe. They could muster large armies. They still were thought of as the chief defenders of Christendom against the Moslem Turks. All save Maria Theresa bore the proud if empty title of Holy Roman Emperor.

D. Brandenburg-Prussia from the Great Elector to Frederick the Great

Much of the power and prestige lost by the Habsburgs in Germany was gradually gained by another house, that of Hohenzollern. In the seventeenth century, the Hohenzollerns were merely one of a number of major princely families. In the eighteenth century, they possessed the most effective military power in central Europe. In the nineteenth century, they brought all Germany except Austria under their rule. Though some of the Hohenzollerns were skilled in diplomacy and not a few encouraged the arts of peace, basically their rise rested on their armies. It was a military phenomenon.

In the tenth century, the Hohenzollerns had ruled as counts over a castle on the hill of Zollern, just north of modern Switzerland. In the twelfth century, by a lucky marriage, one of them had become Burgrave of the rich city of Nuremberg. But their real start dated from 1415 when the Holy Roman Emperor made a Hohenzollern the Elector of Brandenburg, a mark, or frontier province, in the northeast of Germany. The Protestant Revolt strengthened the Hohenzollerns, for they became Lutherans and seized broad church lands. In 1614, they acquired by inheritance the duchy of Cleves on the lower Rhine, and four years later they similarly acquired the duchy of East Prussia, then a fief of the Polish crown. In the Thirty Years' War the Hohenzollerns played a sufficiently adroit game to emerge with the wealthy bishoprics of Halberstadt and Minden and the right to succeed to that of Magdeburg, much ravaged by war, but still important.

The Elector of Brandenburg and Duke of East Prussia at the end of the Thirty Years' War (1648) was Frederick William (1640–1688), usually styled the "Great Elector." At his succession, he found himself, through the gains of his ancestors, one of the leading princes of northern Germany and likewise a leader among the German Protestant rulers. His first task was rebuilding his country, devastated by war, and reorganizing and enlarging its army. This he did so successfully that he was able to act as a strong third party in a war between Sweden and Poland (1655–1660). He made himself invaluable first to one side and then to the other, and by the end of the war he had secured recognition as the outright ruler of East Prussia, for he induced the Polish king to renounce all sovereignty over that province.

But if the Great Elector raised the prestige of his state abroad, his work of internal construction was even more important. He increased his absolute powers by crushing opposition in the estates (or legislatures) of East Prussia and Cleves. He reformed the administration of Brandenburg, improved the methods of tax collection, increased the revenues, and drew into his own hands ever more despotic power. With equal skill, he centralized the separate administrations of Prussia, Cleves, and Brandenburg, merged the local armies into one military force, and made all officials subservient to him and his ministers at Berlin. Thus Frederick William welded the scattered holdings of the Hohenzollerns into a unified monarchical state.

Utterly unscrupulous though he was, the Great Elector paid much attention to the economic welfare of his people. He strove to promote agriculture, commerce, and industry, and to make his relatively poor domains as prosperous as their resources permitted. Marshes were drained to win new agricultural lands. Commercial companies were founded. Skilled Flemish workers and traders were invited to settle in Brandenburg. When Louis XIV revoked the edict of Nantes and drove thousands of French Huguenots into exile, the Great Elector seized the opportunity. He invited the refugees to come to his dominions and granted them lands and other help. To Brandenburg they brought a vital accession of industrial and commercial knowledge in weaving, glass making, and a dozen other trades. Many of the Huguenots settled around Berlin, and that capital, which had been scarcely more than a village of 8,000 inhabitants at Frederick William's accession, was a thriving little city of 20,000 people at his death.

In the rise of the Hohenzollerns, the Great Elector played a stellar role, not so much for any accessions of territory, as for his work of organization. He made a state out of what had been a collection of family holdings, a national army out of what had been feudal levies, a centralized administration out of those who had been local officials, and a progressive country out of what had been one of the more backward areas of Europe.

Much of what the Great Elector had accomplished was solidified by his son, Frederick, whose chief ambition was to win for himself the title of King, which seemed to him much more resplendent than the titles he already bore, such as Elector (of Brandenburg) or Duke (of Prussia and of Cleves). In the War of the League of Augsburg, though Frederick helped the Emperor Leopold, the latter brushed aside his pleas to be recognized as king. But on the eve of the War of the Spanish Succession, the Emperor, anxious to secure all possible support against Louis XIV, decided that a title was a cheap price for an ally and agreed in 1700 that Frederick might become a king. The title Frederick took was King of Prussia, since his duchy of Prussia, unlike Brandenburg, was completely outside the Holy Roman Empire and there could be no question of his full sovereignty in it.[1] Early in 1701, Frederick hurried to Königsberg and there assumed the royal crown. Fulfilling his promises, Frederick aided the Emperor against France in the ensuing war, and by the treaty of Utrecht in 1713 the other European powers acknowledged the new royal title of the Hohenzollerns.

Frederick I died before the peace was signed, and, if he left kingly prestige to his son Frederick William I (1713–1740), he also bequeathed an empty treasury and a country burdened by taxes and exhausted by war. The new King, thrifty and puritanical, was quite unlike his father. As soon as he came to the throne, he busied himself with dismissing useless officials and selling off the costly French-style furniture his father had collected.

The early years of the reign of Frederick William I were marked by considerable gains of territory. By the peace of Utrecht, he acquired a large part of Gelderland. In alliance with Russia, he warred on Charles XII of Sweden and acquired a portion of Pomerania, including the valuable port of

---

[1] Technically, his title was King *in* Prussia, because his duchy consisted only of *East Prussia*. *West Prussia* (including Danzig) belonged to Poland.

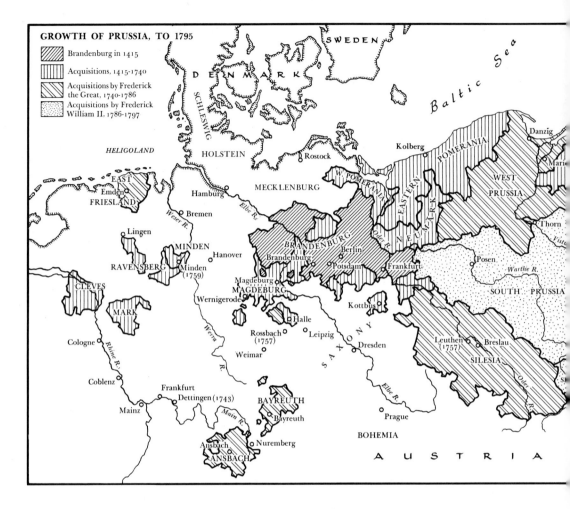

GROWTH OF PRUSSIA, TO 1795

Brandenburg in 1415

Acquisitions, 1415-1740

Acquisitions by Frederick
the Great, 1740-1786

Acquisitions by Frederick
William II, 1786-1797

Stettin, which provided a useful commercial outlet for Berlin. But the major contributions of Frederick William to the rise of Prussia were, like those of his grandfather, in the internal sphere.

By a thrift that bordered on miserliness, Frederick William I increased his standing army from 38,000 to more than 80,000 men. At his death the Prussian army was comparable in size with the military forces of the much larger and wealthier states of France and Austria. In discipline, training, and efficiency, it was probably the best in Europe. Its officers, though drawn from noble landowning families (*Junkers*), were promoted on the basis of merit and not of wealth and influence as in other lands. The equipment of the soldiers was up to date and their training was thorough.

In internal administration, the King pushed ahead the work of centralization. He organized a "general directory" to ensure

the businesslike handling of war, finance, and the royal lands. The royal estates were transformed from family holdings into crown domains and administered by public officials. The serfs on these domains were freed and encouraged to increase their productivity. For all his dislike of the French, Frederick William copied them in two respects—the creation of a bureaucracy, and the issuance of mercantilist legislation.

Though it was modeled on the French, the Prussian civil service soon surpassed it in efficiency and honesty. Junkers and bourgeois devoted their lives to the public service. The salaries and rewards were not great and the punishments for failure or laxity were severe. But a tradition was soon created of devotion to the king and to the public good. If bureaucracy brought with it formalism and red tape, it also gave Prussia a solid and honest administration.

In the field of economic legislation, Fred-

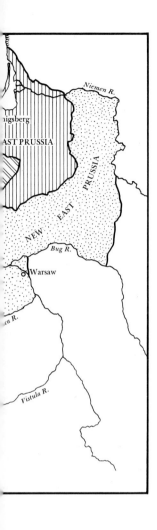

for the court, the civil service, and economic projects.

With all his abilities, Frederick William I had many personal peculiarities which highly amused Europe. Like an angry schoolmaster, he flogged his subjects with his own royal cane. Wealthy merchants were ordered to put up fine houses to improve the appearance of Berlin. Education was more or less ignored, and the King had little sympathy for philosophy, art, or literature. One craze he did have, a passion for tall soldiers. He created the Potsdam Guard of Giants and for once spent money freely. Tall foreigners he lured into his service by promises of high pay, and sometimes, it is said, hulking peasants were kidnapped that their great stature might please the King in the military reviews which were his chief delight.

During many years this crabbed and eccentric King feared that all his savings and all his labors might go for nought, since he was mightily disappointed in his son and heir. The Crown Prince Frederick showed an interest in literature, art, and music, which struck his father as nothing short of effeminate. The King abused Frederick and disciplined him. When the Prince at length ran away, the King had him arrested and then put him through an almost slave-like training in the civil and military administration, from the lowest grades upward. It was this despised and misunderstood prince who, as Frederick II, came to the throne of Prussia in 1740, just as Maria Theresa ascended the throne of Austria. Within a few months Frederick plunged Prussia and Europe into a long conflict. His achievements in war and diplomacy were so far to outshine those of his father that history has awarded him the title of Frederick the Great as a tribute to his success, though certainly not to his methods. It was Frederick II who was to complete the work of his Hohenzollern ancestors and to make Prussia a great European power.

E. Decline of the Ottoman Empire

In the sixteenth century the strength of the Ottoman Empire had been awesome indeed, though Suleiman the Magnificent

erick William followed the lines laid down by the French statesman Colbert. In the best mercantilist manner he forbade or restricted the importation of foreign manufactures and the exportation of raw materials. Industrial processes and the quality of goods were carefully regulated, and the regulations were enforced by the growing bureaucracy. In East Prussia and elsewhere, the King made every effort to improve agricultural production. He also fostered new industries, and granted rewards and protection to capable manufacturers. Yet such work of economic development was severely limited by Frederick William's thrift. He increased the state income to seven million thalers, paid off the debts left by his father, and heaped up a surplus in the treasury. But of the annual income in a normal year, five million went for military expenses, one million for a reserve fund, and only a million was left

had been checked at the gates of Vienna (1529), and the Habsburg Emperor Rudolph II (1576–1612), in the "Long War" (1593–1606), had held the Turks at bay and had even made some gains against them. In the seventeenth century, Ottoman power still seemed a major threat to Christian Europe. But in actuality it was already on the wane. The three Sultans from Mohammed III (1595–1603) to Ibrahim (1640–1648) were weak and ineffective. Under them, the government became more corrupt, palace intrigues flourished, and military strength was reduced as the Turks failed to keep up with the improvements in weapons and tactics that were being developed in the west. Indeed they missed what was a golden opportunity to make territorial gains against Austria, for troubles at home prevented them from taking advantage of the Thirty Years' War which racked Europe. Similarly at sea, the once dreaded Turkish navy fell behind as the ships, cannon, and sailing techniques of the west were steadily improved and tested by long voyages and forays on the great oceans.

When, under Mohammed IV (1648–1687), the Ottoman Empire once again took the offensive, it met a vigorous defense.[1] In the ensuing peace treaty of Karlowitz (1699), the Turks gave up all their earlier conquests north of the Danube and lost much of their power to threaten Vienna and harass the Habsburg empire.

During the eighteenth century, though the decay was not obvious to the outer world, the Ottoman Empire was subject to a kind of dry rot that slowly but surely sapped its strength and vigor. The sultans were not effective leaders and they preferred the ease of palace life to the rigors of military campaigns. Actual administrative authority became lodged more and more in a "divan" or group of ministers, and these officials were more often successful court intriguers than capable public servants. Offices and privileges came to be sold corruptly, and the officeholders recouped the cost by themselves seeking bribes. The army, which had been the primary source of Ottoman strength, declined steadily in effec-

[1] See above, pp. 346–348, 445.

tiveness as its weapons and tactics became more and more antiquated in comparison with those developed in the wars of western Europe. Even the "janissaries"—a professional military guard made up in large part of Christian boys, recruited forcibly, converted to the Moslem faith, and subjected to thorough training—were increasingly affected by corruption. But because they were better organized than other troops they tended to become the masters of the sultan and his government.

Then too, it must be remembered that the Turks in Europe had never been more than a small minority of landholding nobles and officials, who exploited the conquered Christian peasantry of half a dozen nationalities (Rumanian, Magyar, Serb, Croatian, Bulgarian, Greek). The continuation of Moslem rule depended on military force and effective government. Had the subject peoples been better organized and better educated they might have made more trouble for their Turkish masters, but they were held together mainly by their religion and by the church organizations which the Moslems tolerated and used.

One ruler who understood the growing internal weakness of the Ottoman Empire was Catherine the Great of Russia. When some Poles who had risen against Russian intervention fled into Turkish territory, Catherine's troops pursued them and brought on a Russo-Turkish war which lasted from 1768 to 1774. The decline of the Turkish army was now revealed, and the Russian forces won a series of victories. They captured Azov, took Bucharest, and conquered a large part of Rumania. At length, the Turks made peace lest worse should befall, for Catherine was even stirring up trouble among the Greeks under Ottoman rule. By the treaty of Kuchuk Kainarji in 1774, not only did Russia gain Azov which Peter the Great had briefly held, but also the Turks were compelled to renounce all rule over the petty Tatar states on the north shore of the Black Sea and to promise to give better government to the Christians under Ottoman rule in Rumania and Greece. Russia likewise obtained the right to send ships freely through the Bosporus and the Dardanelles and to act as

Russian Capture of Azov from the Turks, 1696. From an engraving
by Adriaen Schoonebeck (d. 1714).

protector of some churches in Constantinople. Catherine had not only opened a
"window" to the south as Peter the Great
had sought to do, but she had provided
Russia with excuses to intervene almost at
will in Ottoman affairs. Within a few years
Catherine had absorbed the Tatar territory
north of the Black Sea, and another treaty
in 1792 made the Dniester River the
boundary between the Russian and Ottoman
empires.

Thus by the end of the eighteenth century Ottoman power in Europe was clearly
lessening. The sultan still ruled millions of
Christian subjects and held sway over broad
lands in Europe, Asia, and Africa. But his
armies and navies were no longer able to
cope with modern forces of the west. His
administration was increasingly ineffective.
And his subject peoples were beginning to
stir as if awakening from a long sleep.

A Dutch Banker. By Rembrandt van Rijn (*d.* 1669).

CHAPTER 36

Colonial and Power Rivalries in the Seventeenth and Early Eighteenth Centuries

A. The Portuguese and Spanish Oversea Dominions

During the first decades of the seventeenth century, when Portugal was still under Spanish kings and embroiled in their wars, the earlier Portuguese monopoly of the lucrative spice trade with the East Indies was broken. The Dutch won bases in Java, while the English entered actively into the trade of mainland India. But it was during the years from 1640 to 1668, when Portugal was occupied in regaining its independence from Spain, that it lost most of its farflung Eastern dominion to the Dutch. By 1700 the Portuguese held, outside of Brazil, only some stretches of seacoast in Africa, and a few posts in the Far East—Macao, Goa, Diu, and Timor.

As their trade with the Far East declined, the Portuguese paid more attention to their extensive but hitherto neglected South American colony of Brazil. Perhaps they might compensate for the losses in Asia by gains in America. In a thirteen-year war (1641–1654), waged largely by Portuguese Brazilian colonists, Dutch intruders were ousted from the coasts of Brazil, and in 1661 Holland formally renounced its attempt to win a hold in that country. From 1645 on, the heir to the Portuguese throne bore the title "Prince of Brazil," and by 1700 Portugal's trade with Brazil was equal to its commerce with all of Europe.

Then fate took a hand to enhance still more the value of Brazil. Toward the end of the seventeenth century gold was discov-ered in the Minas Geraes district. A "gold rush" developed, and production increased rapidly. By 1780 Brazil had produced more than three-quarters of a billion dollars' worth of gold. Early in the eighteenth century diamond fields were likewise discovered, and soon Brazil was the chief diamond-producing area of the world. The government profited from the gold and diamonds by levying a head tax on the slaves brought in to work the mines. Brazil proved no mean substitute for the fabled Far East.

The Spanish overseas dominion suffered no such losses as the Portuguese in the seventeenth century. Despite the weakening of their power in Europe, the Spaniards clung to what they had won in America and the Philippines, and not only successfully defended their transatlantic colonies, but actually expanded them. Only in areas which they had not effectively occupied, did they give ground. In the West Indies, the English, the Dutch, and the French seized upon a number of islands never firmly held by the Spaniards, and in 1655 the English under Cromwell captured Jamaica. On the northeast shoulder of South America (Guiana), the Dutch and the French gained footholds; while in Central America, English logwood cutters and contraband traders were able to establish themselves in what was later to become British Honduras. At the very end of the seventeenth century, the French founded a colony near the mouth of the Mississippi and linked it up by that great waterway with their holdings in Canada.

But to compensate for these losses, the Spaniards gradually extended their sway over northern Mexico and what is now southwestern United States. In Chile, the Spanish colonists continued to war against the Araucanian Indians and to expand their settlements southward. In the fertile Plata region, despite some conflicts with the Portuguese, Spain strengthened its hold, founded new towns, and opened up new territories.

Though Spain in America was capable of making advances, it was forced into a defensive position. In the protracted wars of the seventeenth century, Dutch, English, and French vessels constantly harried Spanish shipping, and in the intervals of peace pirates of all nations continued the attack, not only in the Caribbean, but against the Peruvian coast as well. The last decades of the seventeenth century were the heyday of these "freebooters" or "buccaneers." Frequently they were protected by the governors of the Dutch, French, or English islands in the West Indies. From hidden bays they would swoop out to seize Spanish galleons and on occasion to attack, capture, and sack Spanish coastal cities in Central America.

Piratical attacks made it harder to get bullion from America to Spain. But in any case the exports of American silver were falling off rapidly. In the decade from 1651 to 1660 they amounted to less than a sixth of what they had been in the ten years from 1591 to 1600. Spain strove valiantly to guard what its American colonies produced and jealously to exclude all foreigners from its colonial trade. But even here there was a breach in the system. The importation of Negro slaves from Africa into the Spanish colonies in America had long been a monopoly of the Portuguese through an agreement known as the Asiento. By the treaty of Utrecht (1713), this Asiento was transferred to England and for some forty years afterwards it was exploited by the British.

B. Rise of Dutch Dominions

In the seventeenth century, the preëminent masters of the seaways were Dutch. In good part, they had won their independence from Spain by developing and exploiting their sea power. In the same fashion, though their country was small, their resources scanty, and their population limited, the Dutch made themselves the chief commercial nation on earth. They dominated the trade of the Baltic, taking thither cloth, French wines, and manufactured goods, and bringing back lumber, grain, furs, and naval stores. They gained a major position in the commerce with the Near East, whither they carried textiles, hardware, and silver, and whence they brought drugs, carpets, and rich fabrics. The Dutch won an important position in the trade with America; illegally they did business with Spanish, Portuguese, English, and French colonists ill-supplied by neglectful homelands; legally they developed commerce with their own American colonies, New Amsterdam and Curaçao. It was the Dutch who captured from the Portuguese the richest share of the Far Eastern trade. It was the Dutch who became the chief fishermen of Europe. By 1620, they already had some 2,000 fishing boats. They caught whales off Spitzbergen and supplied oil for the lamps and the soap of Europe. They caught herring in the North Sea and sold the dried and salted fish to the Catholic countries of Europe.

By 1660, the Dutch had won a predominant place as the carriers of Europe. Though their own products were not many or important (fine cloth, cheese, etc.), they had made their country the entrepôt of the world. Thither came goods from every clime. There Russian furs could be exchanged for East Indian cinnamon, French wine for Swedish tar, Turkish rugs for Brazilian sugar, or Caribbean tobacco for African ostrich plumes. In 1669, the French statesman, Colbert, estimated that the Dutch had some fifteen or sixteen thousand ships, as against three or four thousand for the English and five or six hundred for the French.

To a very large degree the Dutch won out in the seventeenth century because of the magnificent business organizations developed in their great city of Amsterdam, which had now far outstripped Antwerp. Dutch governments, whether of Amsterdam or of the United Provinces as a whole, were business-minded. Composed largely of

New Amsterdam (later New York) as it appeared about the time of its capture by the British (1664).

merchants, they made laws designed to aid business. For example, they, almost alone in Europe, permitted fairly free import and export of silver, and kept all tariff duties low to help the carrying trade. In making a treaty, Dutch diplomats always kept an eye on economic advantages and let lesser matters go. The Dutch fleet was ever ready to protect Dutch shipping and to fight for the right of Dutch vessels to sail anywhere. It was the Dutch who first insisted on the "freedom of the seas" as a matter of right under the slowly developing international law of the seventeenth century.

Closely associated with the government, and often run by the same men, were a number of institutions that helped Dutch trade. Insurance companies, underwriters, and brokers supplied coverage for ventures, safe or risky, at the lowest rates in Europe. The Amsterdam money market was so highly organized and so well supplied with capital that a Dutch merchant could often borrow funds at three or four per cent when his English or French competitor had to pay six or eight or ten. The Bank of Amsterdam, founded in 1609, provided a safe place to keep deposits; and bills of exchange on it were accepted all over Europe and regarded as safer and more convenient than cash.

The Stock Exchange, or Bourse, was no less important than the Bank. Though it had first been intended as an exchange center for goods, like cloth or metals or wine, it was soon a center for deals in shares of stock, for trade in coin and bullion, and for loans. In the second half of the seventeenth century the Amsterdam Bourse was the principal money market of Europe, whither needy princes, ambitious merchants, and enterprising manufacturers came to negotiate loans. Around the Bourse grew up a whole mechanism of trade and speculation that was in some respects very modern. Goods could be bought and sold subject to future delivery. Stock could be bought on a margin or sold short. "Bulls" sought to push up prices and "bears" to depress them. Fortunes could be made or lost by speculation. From 1633 to 1637 the gambling spirit ran wild in an odd fashion. Everybody tried to get rich by buying and selling tulip bulbs, whose prices went up and up and finally collapsed.

More striking even than the Bourse as an evidence of Dutch commercial genius was the East India Company. It was founded in 1602 by the union of several smaller companies which had sprung up after Philip II stopped the Dutch from getting spice at Lisbon. With a charter that gave it the right to make peace and war and to administer colonies as well as to carry on trade, with directors from the leading Dutch cities (eight of the seventeen came from Amsterdam), and with the firm support of the government, the East India Company became the instrument through which the Dutch drove out the Portuguese from the Far Eastern trade and developed it for themselves. So rich and powerful did the company become that at times it dominated the government. It paid dividends which in some years rose to seventy-five per cent and which averaged eighteen per cent a year for almost two centuries. Its stock was for long the chief object of speculation and investment on the Amsterdam Bourse.

The West India Company, founded in 1621 to develop American trade and colonies, was less commercially successful. But it proved a remarkable instrument of warfare against the Spaniards. Between 1623 and 1636 it sent out more than eight hundred ships with crews totaling 67,000 men. By it some 600 Spanish ships were captured, including nearly a hundred "famous galleons." It was said that its activities cost Spain seventy-five million guilders. After the peace with Spain in 1648, the West India Company declined in importance.

In colonial policy the Dutch in some ways resembled the Portuguese more than the Spanish or the English. By the Dutch, colonies were regarded as bases for commerce rather than as areas for settlement and development. In America, the colonial holdings of the Dutch were not insignificant. In 1640 they possessed the Caribbean island of Curaçao, the Hudson River from its mouth to above Fort Orange (Albany), a large part of Guiana, and some of the best ports on the Brazilian coast. Subse-quently, they were ousted from Brazil in the 1650's, from New York by the English in 1664, and from part of their Guiana colony by the British in 1803.

But it was in the Far East that the Dutch built up a really important dominion. By the 1680's they had replaced the Portuguese in the spice islands (except Timor) and had driven off their English competitors. The Dutch controlled the large East Indian islands of Java and Sumatra, and the smaller ones as well, by means of fortified trading ports, of which the greatest came to be Batavia (present-day Jakarta). By the early eighteenth century they were slowly beginning to expand their territorial holdings inland. It was their policy to keep up spice prices in Europe by ruthlessly restricting production, even if this meant pulling up the plants, cutting down the trees, and killing natives who objected. Though the Dutch were unable to capture Chinese Macao from the Portuguese, they did win a considerable share of the trade with China, and for a while in the seventeenth century they had forts and trading posts on Formosa. After the Japanese had driven out the Portuguese and their missionaries, they permitted the Dutch, who confined themselves strictly to trade, to maintain a small commercial depot in Japan. From 1638 to 1854 the Dutch were established on the small island of Deshima near Nagasaki and were the only Europeans permitted to trade with the Japanese.

So great was the Dutch commercial and colonial success in the seventeenth century that it created a host of enemies. Their chief rivals were the economically progressive national states of England and France. Three times in that century the English warred with the Dutch, largely for commercial reasons. Three times before 1700 the French fought the Dutch, who had previously been their allies in the long struggle with Spain. Against the Dutch the French raised their tariffs. An acute observer in 1713, at the Peace of Utrecht, would have realized that the days of Dutch commercial supremacy were drawing to a close. The future lay with the larger and stronger states of France and England. Yet throughout the eighteenth century Amsterdam remained an important trading city and the foremost financial center of Europe, and Dutch burghers still waxed prosperous on profits from commerce and from interest on the loans they made to all Europe.

C. Foundations of a British Empire

Though in population, as in area, England of the seventeenth century was definitely inferior to France or Spain, it had by 1713 secured an overseas dominion of considerable extent. The first British colony at Jamestown in Virginia (1607) was followed rapidly by a number of other foundations on the Atlantic seaboard of North America: Plymouth (1620), Boston (1630), Maryland (1634), Providence (1636), Hartford (1636), New Haven (1638), Carolina (1665). The northern and southern settlements were linked in a continuous strip of British holdings by the capture of New York (1664) with the adjacent area of New Jersey, and by the settlement of Pennsylvania, under William Penn, in the years following 1681.

Meanwhile the English had made numerous settlements in the West Indies, including part of St. Christopher (St. Kitts), Bermuda, Barbados, the Bahamas, Antigua, Nevis, Montserrat, some of the Virgin Islands, and Jamaica. On the Mosquito Coast of Honduras, the British obtained an increasingly firm hold. On the west coast of Africa, in competition with the Dutch and the French, they developed trading and slaving posts. In the East Indies, though forced out of the Spice Islands and even out of their post at Bantam (1683) by the Dutch, they developed important trading centers further to the west. At Surat in India, in the years after 1609, they built up a commercial depot. By the capture of Ormuz (1622) they gained control of the Persian Gulf. In 1639 they founded Madras and fortified it. A decade later they opened up trade with Bengal at the port of Hugli. From Portugal, England secured Bombay in 1661, and before long it became the center of their Indian trade. By 1690, despite the opposition of the native ruler, the British had established themselves at Calcutta.

Thus by the end of the century, with posts on both coasts, they were in an excellent position to expand their Indian trade.

If their aims and their holdings in the Far East were not unlike those of the earlier Portuguese and the Dutch, and if their West Indian plantations on the whole resembled those of the Spanish and the French, their North American colonies were somewhat different from overseas colonies of other European nations anywhere. In the first place, they were true colonies of settlement. To them, the English came in relatively large numbers—and not merely as individuals seeking to win fortunes, but as families, with women and children, in search of new homes overseas. In the second place, though some persons in the American colonies were active in commerce, fisheries, and the fur trade, the bulk of the population found its livelihood in agriculture and slowly moved in from the coast in search of tillable land. If some of the tobacco plantations of Virginia or the Carolinas, worked by indentured white servants or Negro slaves, were not unlike those of the West Indies, more typical in English North America was the family holding, or farm worked by the owner.

William Penn. After a painting by Sir Godfrey Kneller (d. 1723).

Courtesy Bettmann Archive

In the third place, the English rather freely permitted the emigration to their colonies of religious dissenters and people who did not like the religious restrictions at home. The French and Spanish strove to make their colonies conform in religion with the mother country. But the English colonies, in contrast, soon represented an almost bewildering mixture of creeds. English Catholics came to Maryland; English Congregationalists settled New England; English Quakers peopled Pennsylvania; while Anglicans went in numbers to Virginia and to mingle with Dutch Reformed colonists in New York and New Jersey. Presently other religious sects were added to the American scene. French Huguenots fled from France to South Carolina, various German religious radicals found refuge in Pennsylvania, and Presbyterians from North Ireland flocked to the middle colonies.

Partly as a result of this comparative religious tolerance, the English North American colonies became the most populous, for their size, of any European overseas holdings, and a high birthrate added to the effects of immigration. By 1698 the Atlantic seaboard colonies had a population estimated at three hundred thousand, and in the eighteenth century it tended to double every twenty-five years, so that by 1775 it was something like 2,500,000. Already in 1698 England's trade with these settlements amounted to about £1,600,000 a year, some fifteen per cent of its total commerce. Seventy-seven years later it had multiplied five times and represented almost a third of British imports and exports.

From the start England sought, with varying success, to regulate its colonial trade. But in the main it followed a policy that has been termed one of "salutary neglect," and, despite sporadic interference, it allowed the colonies a good deal of local self-government. The colonists had town governments of their own and provincial legislatures which advised the proprietors or royal governors, floated local loans, and often voted local taxes. As in other countries, the ignorance of colonial conditions in the motherland was immense. There were English statesmen who thought that Massachusetts was an island and Virginia was one of the West Indies.

But the English Parliament did take a lively interest in trade laws, and the country gentlemen who were so powerful in it joined with their merchant allies to try to better England's commerce by seeing that all the trade of the colonies flowed to the mother-country. The Navigation Act of 1651 provided, with a few exceptions, that overseas goods must be brought to England in English ships or in those of the country of origin. The Navigation Act of 1660 added the provision that certain "enumerated articles" (sugar, tobacco, indigo, ginger, dye-woods) should be exported from a colony only to England or to another English colony. The list of such goods was from time to time extended. The Staple Act of 1663 forbade the importation into the colonies of any goods not put on board ship in England. To keep trade between the English colonies from growing at the expense of that with England, another act of 1673 laid duties on the enumerated articles shipped from colony to colony. In 1696 an act for "preventing frauds" sought to plug existing loopholes in the trade laws.

Designed to profit England by making it the only source for goods sent to the colonies and the only destination for colonial exports, the English "colonial system" would, if rigidly enforced, have cramped colonial commercial development. But from the early days the American colonists found numerous ways to engage in profitable contraband and smuggling trade with French or Spanish colonies and with other areas. Often they paid their debts to England with foreign coin secured illegally in the Caribbean.

We have seen that the Dutch gradually succeeded in excluding the English from any major share in the trade with the East Indian spice islands. But it was as if some special providence were looking out for interests of the English and their East India Company. Slowly in the late seventeenth century, and more rapidly thereafter, the spice trade declined in importance, while the European market for other Eastern goods expanded, especially for cotton fabrics like calico. The British, pushed out of the East Indies and back to mainland India, found themselves trading at the main source of such fabrics. The English East India Company had its ups and downs, but by 1680 its imports of textiles outweighed its trade in spices and thereafter grew rapidly and proved most profitable. From Surat alone, in 1682, the English ordered 1,407,-800 pieces of textiles.

D. Struggle for a French Oversea Empire

The first successful French settlement overseas was at Quebec in 1608, only a year after the English foundation of Jamestown. But French colonial development was slower than English. In 1660 they had a few West Indian Islands—Martinique, Guadeloupe, Grenada, the Grenadines, St. Croix, St. Bartholomew, and parts of St. Martin and St. Christopher. On the last, oddly enough, the French held the two ends and the English the middle. They had also a foothold in Guiana (Cayenne), a string of small settlements along the St. Lawrence River and in Nova Scotia (Acadia), and some posts on the west coast of Africa and on Madagascar and Reunion. In Canada, there were fewer than 3,000 French settlers, and in the West Indies something like 27,000, about half of whom were slaves. The French population in the other holdings was infinitesimal.

But in 1661, Colbert came to office, determined to endow France with a colonial empire and to build for her a great Far Eastern commerce. So far as he could win the support of Louis XIV, he threw the weight of the government's influence and resources behind the effort to expand French overseas ventures. Far more than with England, French colonial development was dependent on governmental initiative, support, and supervision. Under his West India Company (1664) Colbert placed the West Indies, Cayenne, Canada, and the west African ports. By regulations and the use of naval power, he excluded the Dutch from trade with the French West Indies. By paying a bounty on every slave, he expanded the French slave trade between Senegal and Guinea in West Africa and the islands in the Caribbean. In every way, he sought to increase the population of the colonies. He sent soldiers to Canada,

François Xavier de Laval-Montmorency (1623?–1708), first bishop of Quebec.

Courtesy Bettmann Archive

then mustered them out and gave them land if they would stay. He sent over boatloads of girls to marry the male colonists. He encouraged the marriage of Frenchmen to Indians. He even tried to restrict the fur trade, on which the prosperity of Canada depended, so that the men would settle down in villages and raise families. But all his means proved far less successful than the device half negligently adopted by the British of letting religious dissenters emigrate to the colonies. At Colbert's death (1683), the population of Canada was only about 10,000, and of the West Indies only about 50,000.

More successful were Colbert's endeavors in other directions. Under an able governor, Frontenac, hostile Canadian Indians were subdued. Daring woodsmen and heroic missionaries (like Marquette) opened up the country around the Great Lakes and the upper Mississippi. The French competed vigorously with the English for the fur trade of Hudson Bay and toward the end of the century seemed to be gaining the upper hand. When Iberville planted a French colony in Louisiana (1699), it looked as if all North America, except a narrow strip south of the St. Lawrence and east of the Alleghenies, might become French.

French colonial trade likewise prospered. When Colbert came to power, commerce with the French West Indies was largely in foreign hands. At his death, some two hundred French ships were plying back and forth between France and the Caribbean. Sugar was rapidly coming to be the chief object of this trade, and its production rose until in the eighteenth century Martinique and Guadeloupe, together with Santo Domingo (or Haiti, where the French had settled the west half of the island neglected by the Spanish), became the sugar bowls of Europe.

In his efforts to promote French trade with the Far East, Colbert encountered various obstacles. Though the King poured millions of *livres* into the French East India Company and forced numerous officials to buy its stock, it proved impossible to get much financial support from the investing public. The English joined with the Dutch to attack French ships and to paralyze French trade in the ports of India. By 1675 the French had organized six trading posts there, but in the last years of the Dutch war they lost all save Surat and Pondichéry. When Colbert died, his East India Company, harassed by these misfortunes, was in serious financial straits. But in the next year (1684) it was reorganized, and slowly it began to gain strength and even occasionally to make some money. Despite heavy losses during the War of the League of Augsburg, the French under a vigorous soldier merchant, François Martin, greatly strengthened their position in India. By 1700 they had added to Surat and Pondichéry two posts on the Coromandel Coast and four in Bengal.

Both the French and the English had built up their overseas dominion at the expense of the Portuguese and the Spanish, and during the last half of the seventeenth century they both met and overcame considerable Dutch opposition. But by 1689, with William of Orange, implacable enemy of France, on the English throne and a major war just starting, it became clear that henceforth the most bitter rivalry was to be between the French and the English. During the ensuing hundred and twenty-six years, these two nations were repeatedly at war with each other. In the long run,

England, through her greater devotion to commerce and sea power, was to triumph. But the early rounds of the struggle were indecisive, and the keenest contemporary observer would have had some difficulty in predicting the outcome.

In the West Indies, the conflict began as early as 1625 with disputes about the joint occupation of St. Christopher. It consisted of naval engagements, commerce raiding, and attacks on the various islands, some of which passed back and forth between the contending powers. In North America, the Anglo-French conflict dated from 1613, when the English seized the French settlements in Acadia (Nova Scotia). They were returned to France by treaty in 1632, captured again by the English under Cromwell in 1654, restored to France by treaty in 1667, won again by England in 1710, and finally confirmed in the possession of the British by the treaty of Utrecht in 1713. By the same treaty France likewise abandoned all claims to the Hudson Bay area.

The French settlements along the St. Lawrence had similarly been seized by the English in 1629, but were held by them for only three years. Thereafter, Canada, as it grew in strength, seemed like an ever present threat to the English colonies to the southward. In the War of the League of Augsburg (1689–1697), called King William's War in the colonies, and the War of the Spanish Succession (1701–1713), termed there Queen Anne's War, bloody affrays occurred between French and English colonists in the frontier areas. Using Indian allies, the French raided to the south again and again. The massacres at Dover (1689), Schenectady (1690), Deerfield (1704), and Haverhill (1708), were only the most notable and successful of dozens of similar attacks.

But at the peace of Utrecht (1713) it was still hard to see how the American struggle would end. The English colonists were more numerous but were very loosely organized and ill-supported from England. The French had control of the St. Lawrence and Mississippi waterways, were firmly managed by the home government, and had the support of many Indian tribes. In India, too, the outcome was obscure, for the French strength there was growing. The native Mongol, or "Mogul," Empire of India was decaying and collapsing, and its heir would probably be the European nation best able to manipulate and intimidate the local rulers who were gaining more and more independent power. These issues of overseas supremacy were to be decided by wars of the later eighteenth century.

E. Russian Colonization Eastward, and Novel Commodities of Europe's Oversea Commerce

While the western European nations were engaged in embittered conflicts for possession of overseas areas and trade, the growing Russian nation was expanding eastward in quite a different fashion. To the east of Russia, with its chief cities of Novgorod and Moscow, lay the enormous unexplored Asiatic land mass. Into this area, the Russians spread by land in a movement not unlike that by which the English-speaking Americans were later to push westward toward the Pacific. The conquest of the Tatar states of Kazan and Astrakhan in the mid-sixteenth century had brought the Russians to the Urals and the Caspian Sea. As Russian rule moved eastward, the spearhead of its advance was a special type of frontiersmen, half-wild adventurers and doughty fighters drawn from a variety of sources and called Cossacks. Named after the area in which they lived, they were known as the Don, Astrakhan, Terek, Orenburg, Kuban, or Ural Cossacks. To them was granted a good deal of autonomy under their own chiefs, and in return for their privileges, they safeguarded the frontiers and extended the area of Russian dominion.

Another type of frontiersman was (as in later America) the fur trader. In the last half of the sixteenth century a wealthy merchant named Stroganov organized the fur trade in the Kama River region, built forts, and used Cossacks to defend the area. His nephews, aided by a band of brigands, defeated the Tatars and captured their chief city of Sibir, which was to give its name to the whole vast territory of Siberia. Pushing ever eastward in search of furs, the Russians founded fortified towns or posts like Tobolsk, Yeniseisk, and Yakutsk. By the mid-seventeenth century, the Russians had reached Lake Baikal, defeated the native Buriats, and founded Irkutsk. At about the same time, other fur traders, moving northward, reached the Kolyma River and the Arctic Ocean. In 1647 a little band of fifty-four Cossacks got all the way to the Pacific and, after defeating the wild fighters of the Tungus tribe, established a fort at Okhotsk. The next year, another group of Cossacks sailed from Kolyma Bay on the Arctic Ocean through the straits later to be explored by Bering and set up a fort at Anadyrsk on the Pacific. Within a century, the Russian frontiersmen had spread so far and so fast that this farthest post was 7,000 miles from Moscow.

Afterwards, the Russians pushed their explorations into the Kamchatka peninsula, the Amur region, the Manchurian borderlands, and across the straits to Alaska. This work was carried on by rough frontiersmen, fighters, and fur-traders, who overawed the natives they met or defeated them by their firearms and their courage. As bases they used fortified posts called Ostrogs, similar to the blockhouse forts of the American frontier. In the wake of the explorers who opened up the country, came settlers and traders. If there were only 70,000 Russians in all Siberia in 1662, the number increased rapidly and reached a quarter of a million by 1710. As early as 1637 a government for Siberia had been set up with its center at Tobolsk and secondary centers at Yakutsk and Irkutsk. Fur was still the basic wealth of the new land, and tribute in fur was exacted from the native tribes. To Siberia, the home government sent criminals, who were often given the opportunity to redeem themselves by opening up new areas.

When they reached the Amur river in 1644, the Russians came in contact with the Chinese, who claimed overlordship of the area. Driven out by the natives, the Russians came back, rebuilt their forts on the Amur, and began penetrating into Manchuria. In 1689, with the aid of Jesuit missionaries who accompanied the Chinese delegates as interpreters, the Russians and the Chinese signed a treaty, the first ever made by China with a European power. The Russians accepted a boundary north of the Amur, but the Chinese agreed to receive Russian traders freely. For more than two centuries peace endured between the two countries. In 1727 a new treaty permitted two hundred Russian merchants to come to Peking each year. There were not many bulky commodities sufficiently valuable to pay for transportation across thousands of miles of land to Moscow. But in exchange for their furs the Russians took costly silks and considerable quantities of tea. As a result of this early trade with China, the Russian upper classes gradually became confirmed tea drinkers.

At about the same time, the English were becoming tea drinkers too, for in the late seventeenth century their East India Company began importing this commodity, and it quickly won favor, first with the higher and then with the lower levels of society. Nor was tea the only new beverage introduced into Europe by expansion overseas. Both chocolate and coffee came into use in the latter half of the seventeenth century. Coffee houses and chocolate houses sprang up. If some claimed the new beverages to be dangerous drugs, others held them to be health-giving elixirs. In any case, people liked them. The use of these drinks increased the demand for sugar, and decade by decade the output grew, first in Madeira, then in Brazil, and later in the West Indies, while one refinery after another was built in Europe to improve the palatability of the dark sticky substance that came in the casks from America. The by-products of the growing sugar trade were also important. Rum so competed with French brandy that it was banned from France. But the English and their colonists made it in large quantities, and the English thus won an advantage in the fur trade with the Indians since rum was cheaper than the brandy of the French.

Hundreds of other new products came increasingly into the European market. Porcelain ware from China, lacquered furniture, perfumes, wall paper, drugs, silks, screens, ebony, brocades, calicos, chintz, muslins, dimities, fans, umbrellas, and even goldfish were brought in from the East. From the West, in addition to the ever growing streams of tobacco and sugar, came cabinet woods like mahogany and rosewood, codfish, naval stores, dye-woods, furs (especially beaver fur for hat making), drugs like quinine, and new vegetables and flowers. If the exotic perfumes like civet and musk were sometimes used as a substitute for bathing, the new Indian cotton fabrics led eventually to an increasing use of underwear and thus to an improvement in personal cleanliness. The wealth of new products permitted first a tremendous expansion in the luxury of the upper classes, but by the eighteenth century articles like sugar, tobacco, tea, and cotton goods were getting cheap enough to be within the reach of large numbers of people.

The trade in these new articles represented a tremendous increase in ocean-borne commerce, which had its effects on many another phase of European life. Shipbuilding boomed and the arts of navigation and map-making were steadily improved. Old European industries grew to meet the demands of overseas markets for textiles, hardware, nails, glass, arms, gunpowder, and the like. New European industries sprang up to process the imported goods, so that by the eighteenth century sugar refiners, rum-makers, hat-makers, snuff-makers, calico-printers, and many others were dependent for their raw materials on products from overseas. Each new product tended to create subsidiary industries. Thus the manufacture of snuff-boxes had become a significant if minor trade in both England and France by the eighteenth century, while at the same time efforts to imitate Indian cottons and Chinese porcelain were gradually meeting with increased success. The governments likewise profited, for they taxed the new articles such as tea and coffee, and in France and elsewhere the sale of tobacco was made a state monopoly. If Columbus and Vasco da Gama could have returned to Europe in 1715, they would have found much that was new and different, and for those differences, they and their fellow explorers had been in no small degree responsible.

F. Protracted Rivalry of Britain and France

In the major wars that raged in Europe during the late seventeenth and the eighteenth centuries there was one constant element—a duel between France and Great Britain. From the point of view of the

French, the major stakes were the maintenance of the power and leadership which Louis XIV had won for France, and the defense and extension of the country's frontiers. Secondarily, France was interested in the development of her colonial dominion and of her foreign commerce. Great Britain was much more interested than France in colonies, commerce, and naval supremacy. But it was also concerned with preserving a balance of power in Europe. To the British, France seemed too strong, and particularly too threatening to the Low Countries directly across the Channel from England. From 1689 to 1815 France and Britain were at war half the time.

At the peace of Utrecht (1713) these major opponents seemed ill matched. England, with Scotland, had a population of something like six million, while inhabitants of France numbered about twenty-four million. The foreign trade of the French was more valuable than that of the British, and their internal trade much larger. French industry was so superior to English in most lines that during the negotiations preceding the treaty of Utrecht, English business-men fearfully repulsed the suggestion that the two countries should lower the high import tariffs they levied against each other. The French army was the largest, the best equipped, and the best organized in Europe. French financial resources, if less well managed than those of England, were considerably greater. French prestige was high, French diplomacy remarkably skilled, and France had just succeeded, despite the well-nigh united opposition of Europe, in putting a Bourbon on the throne of Spain. Only in the colonies where the British population was larger and growing faster than the French, and in the naval sphere where the British, in the War of the Spanish Succession, had finally achieved supremacy, did Great Britain seem a worthy opponent of France. Yet in the long duel from 1689 to 1815 Britain gained the upper hand. In part, this was because it was better governed than France.

In part, too, the success of Britain was due to its fortunate island position. It was never, after 1066, subject to a real invasion nor could it be, so long as its navy was strong. France, on the other hand, had long land frontiers to defend and its own territory could actually be and was invaded. It seems likely that because of the recent wars French population and wealth had actually declined from 1689 to 1715, while England was growing in both respects. Then too, though both nations were adept in persuading allies to fight their battles, the British more often succeeded in using money instead of men and their financial resources were well mobilized by the Bank of England, the National Debt, and an increasingly effective system of insurance for. ships and property and of mercantile credit.

In many ways, Britain was a more modern and less feudal country than France. Neither was fully unified in language, for Gaelic was spoken in Scotland and Ireland, and Welsh in Wales just as Breton was predominant in Brittany and Basque in the southwest of France. But after 1707, when Scotland was joined with England, Britain had no interior customs duties, while France still had a tariff line dividing the north from the south and a number of minor tax systems. The old French craft and merchant guilds were still powerful, while their British counterparts were of rapidly decreasing importance. Feudal dues continued to be a weighty burden on the French peasants and had to be paid in labor, in kind, and in money. Some still existed in England, but they were no longer of real significance. Though there were notable differences between the law and the courts in England and in Scotland, France was in a much more complicated situation with some judicial power remaining in the hands of the noble landowners and dozens of different local laws, courts, and customs.

In the eighteenth century France continued the system of government developed under Louis XIV. It was an absolutist government, centralized in royal councils and in ministers chosen by the king on his own initiative. In the provinces, the intendents carried on the administration and saw to it that the wishes of the king and his councils were executed. The provincial estates, the cities, the church, and the nobles made even less trouble than they had in the days of the "Sun King." The only challenge to royal absolutism came occasionally from the higher law courts (the *parlements*), and they were privileged hereditary bodies more apt to represent the desires of the wealthy than the interests of the nation.

Likewise in the economic sphere, the traditions of Louis XIV were followed. The mercantilist regulation of industry and commerce worked out by Colbert was elaborated until it became hard and rigid. The royal finances were handled by a "controller general," who had come to be the chief minister of state. For each war, France plunged further into debt, and every effort to overcome the deficit was checkmated by the privileged classes and corporations, which paid less than their share of the tax burdens. The French monarchy was running more and more on credit, and this was lessened by every war.

Louis XIV was succeeded by his great-grandson, Louis XV (1715–1774), a boy of five years. During his childhood and young manhood the destinies of the country were guided, first for eight years by the King's cousin, the Duke of Orléans, as Regent (1715–1723), and then for many years by an elderly churchman, Cardinal Fleury, as chief minister (1726–1743). The Duke of Orléans was intellectually gifted but notoriously dissolute. His foreign policy was weak, his attempts at internal reform half hearted. His rule is most vividly remembered for the financial experiments into which he was lured by a Scottish adventurer named John Law. These led to a wild orgy of stock market speculation known as the Mississippi Bubble, which ended in a ruinous "panic" in 1721.

Cardinal Fleury was of quite different calibre. Modest, frugal, cautious, his best gift to France was seventeen years of comparative peace interrupted by only a minor war. France showed remarkable strength and recuperative powers. Commerce grew rapidly, industry flourished, and the colonies (especially the sugar islands of the West Indies) throve. But internally, Fleury was content to leave well-enough alone. He achieved no major reforms, and if he brought royal expenditures almost into line with income he made no basic improvement in the financial system. When he attempted to aid commerce by building roads with forced labor (called *corvées*), he aroused angry discontent among the peasants. Moreover, when he died at the advanced age of

ninety (1743), France had already for three years been engaged in another major war which was to undo much of the good which the years of peace had wrought.

The period of Fleury seemed one of sound rule and good government compared to the next thirty-one years when Louis XV spasmodically exercised personal power. In his youth, he had displayed some amiable qualities and for a time he was called "Louis the Well-Beloved." But as he grew to manhood, he showed himself fickle, lazy, and sensuous. Easily wearied of statecraft, he was much influenced by his mistresses, of whom Mesdames de Châteauroux, de Pompadour, and du Barry were only the most famous. Madame de Pompadour was for almost twenty years a veritable prime minister in petticoats and used her power to reward and enrich her friends and wreak her vengeance on her enemies. Under Louis XV, the maladies afflicting France grew apace. The financial disorder increased; popular discontent and criticism rose; the central government at Versailles became ever more isolated from the people.

Yet the ills of France were veiled by the wealth of the country, the success of the armies, the brilliance of the court, the distinction of the artists, writers, and thinkers. Louis XV knew that troubles were brewing, but he was confident that the old system would last for a while. With cynicism he remarked, "Après moi le déluge," "After me, the deluge." The deluge was to come in the reign of his successor, Louis XVI, a well meaning but weak monarch, whose troubles we shall have occasion to examine in another connection.

Great Britain of the eighteenth century was governed by the system of limited monarchy developed after the Revolution of 1689.[1] Real power rested in Parliament, where the House of Lords was made up predominantly of landed nobles, and the House of Commons, elected on an undemocratic basis, represented mainly the country gentlemen and the rich mercantile classes of the cities. Many seats in the lower house were controlled and sometimes sold by landed nobles or gentry. There were two parties. The Whigs controlled Parliament for more than half a century after 1713. The

[1] See below, p. 512.

Tories were influential in the countryside, and the Tory squire, who was usually the local justice of the peace, exercised in his bailiwick considerable judicial and administrative authority.

The differences between the parties were not very great. The Tories were more devoutly Anglican, supported the interests of that church, and held the Stuarts in sentimental remembrance. But when the Young Pretender (grandson of James II) landed in Scotland in 1745 and sought to rouse the country, the Tories did not respond, and the Hanoverians reigned on. The Whigs, though many of them were great landowners, had considerable association with business interests and tended to show some favor to the non-Anglican Protestant sects. But they were mainly interested in maintaining their own political power.

The administration of Great Britain and its empire was in the hands of the cabinet selected from among the members of parliament by the king (actually by the prime minister) and responsible to the majority party in parliament. For twenty-one years (1721–1742), which roughly corresponded with the ministry of Fleury in France, the British prime minister was the Whig politician Sir Robert Walpole. Like Fleury, he pursued a peaceful policy in foreign affairs. His chief object was to promote prosperity and keep the taxes low. But at the end of his ministry, he was, like Fleury, propelled into a major war.

Walpole was succeeded by a series of Whigs from great landed or titled families. They were skilled in party manipulations and more or less able in diplomacy and administration. But the mid-eighteenth century produced one Whig leader of real eminence, William Pitt, later Earl of Chatham. A member of a family which had gained wealth in the East Indies and political influence by its wealth, Pitt showed himself a brilliant politician, a great orator, and an able statesman of sturdy patriotism and imperial vision.

Kings George I (1714–1727) and George II (1727–1760), more German than English, were content to leave the governing of the country to the prime ministers and cabinets, though occasionally they exercised some influence on foreign and even on domestic

affairs. George III (1760–1820) was different in character and in objectives. Unlike his predecessors, he had been born and reared in England and was a solid family man of unimpeachable morals. Like an English country gentleman, he was interested in farming and he enjoyed considerable popularity with the British people. George III was determined to rule as well as to reign. He saw no reason why he, like some of the prime ministers, should not dominate Parliament through a judicious use of influence and favors. Gradually by such methods, George III was able to get rid of the Whig ministers, to constitute Tory cabinets, and to participate in government himself. From 1770 to 1782, the prime minister was Lord North, a Tory, loyal to the King and willing to see the royal power increase. Had George III been able to continue such a regime indefinitely, there might have been a rebirth of royal, at the expense of parliamentary, government.

G. Wars of the Polish Election and the Austrian Succession

The one war in which peace-loving Cardinal Fleury found himself entangled in the middle of his ministry arose from French interest in Poland, alliance with Sweden, and support of the Spanish Bourbons. In 1725, Louis XV had married the daughter of Stanislaus Leszczynski, the nobleman whom Charles XII of Sweden had briefly installed upon the throne of Poland [1] and who had been trying vainly since 1709 to regain his kingship. When Augustus II, the Elector of Saxony and King of Poland, died in 1733, Stanislaus hurried to Poland and secured election to the vacant throne. But Russia at once interfered and persuaded the Poles to depose Stanislaus and elect the son of Augustus II. Thereupon Louis XV sent an army to help his father-in-law, and the War of the Polish Election (1733–1738) began.

The war was quickly complicated by the ambitions of the masterful Elizabeth Farnese, wife of Philip V, first Bourbon King of Spain. Elizabeth had long been eager to regain some of the old Spanish holdings in Italy from the Austrian Habsburgs for the

---
[1] See above, p. 438.

BOURBON, HABSBURG, AND BRITISH
DOMINIONS IN EUROPE ABOUT 1740

| | Bourbon (French, Spanish) | | Habsburg | | British |

0   100   200
Miles

benefit of her sons. As the Polish war broke out and Austria was preparing to help Russia against France, Philip V, appealing to Bourbon family solidarity, persuaded Fleury to bring France into an alliance with Spain against Austria. Thus the War of the Polish Election found Russia and Austria opposed by France and Spain.

The war was not so bloody or so costly as the wars of Louis XIV; and the ensuing treaty of Vienna considerably added to the prestige of the Bourbons. Though Russia and Austria kept Augustus III on the Polish throne, Austria had to grant the duchy of Lorraine to Stanislaus Leszczynski with the understanding that after his death (which occurred in 1766) it should go to France. Austria likewise had to agree to the transfer of Sicily, Naples, and Parma from Habsburg to Spanish Bourbon control. Philip V and Elizabeth had the satisfaction of putting one son on the throne of Parma and another (Charles) on the throne of the kingdom of the Two Sicilies (Naples and Sicily).

Hardly was the War of the Polish Election over, when the more significant War of the Austrian Succession occurred (1740–1748). This was occasioned by the death of the Emperor Charles VI and the repudiation of the promises which certain other European rulers had given him that they would respect the succession of his daughter, Maria Theresa, to all the Austrian Habsburg territories. The leader in this repudiation was the ambitious and cynical Freredick II "the Great," who came to the throne of Prussia in 1740 and lost no time in trumping up a claim to the valuable Austrian province of Silesia. He enlisted against Maria Theresa the support of Louis XV of France, who planned to appropriate part or all of the Austrian (Belgian) Netherlands, and of the Elector of Bavaria, who aspired to become Holy Roman Emperor as Charles VII.

Complicating the situation was a trade war which had broken out in 1739 between Great Britain and Spain, and which was commonly called the War of Jenkins' Ear, because an otherwise obscure Captain Jenkins had aroused English feeling against Spain by relating with dramatic detail how Spaniards in America had attacked his ship, plundered it, and in the fray cut off his ear. This war was soon merged with the War of the Austrian Succession. The Spanish King Philip V, who sympathized with his fellow Bourbon, Louis XV of France, and who hoped to gain still more lands in Italy, joined the coalition against Maria Theresa. On the other hand, Great Britain, fearful of French expansion into the Austrian Netherlands and of possible Prussian designs on the German state of Hanover (which belonged to the British King), gave aid, financial and military, to Austria, and prevailed upon Holland to do likewise. Whereupon, the Franco-Prussian coalition obtained the adherence of Saxony and Savoy (Sardinia). Thus the line-up in the struggle during most of its duration (1740–1748) was Prussia, France, Spain, Bavaria, Saxony, and Savoy against Austria, Great Britain, and the Dutch Netherlands (Holland).

The War of the Austrian Succession, like others of the eighteenth century, was not so terrible or so bloody as the number of contestants might seem to indicate. The fighting was mostly in summer, and there was often, in both campaigns and battles, more maneuvering for position than actual fighting. Saxony was bribed by Austria into making peace. Spain would fight only in Italy. Savoy, as usual, changed sides. The Dutch limited themselves to activities at sea and the defense of their own lands.

Despite heroic efforts, Maria Theresa was unable to expel Frederick II from Silesia. Her generals suffered repeated reverses at his hands, and three times she was forced to recognize his possession of Silesia so as to employ her forces against Bavaria and France. By the third treaty, made at Dresden in 1745, Austria definitely ceded Silesia to Prussia. Having gained his ends, Frederick II deserted his allies and withdrew from the war. Elsewhere, Austrian arms, supported

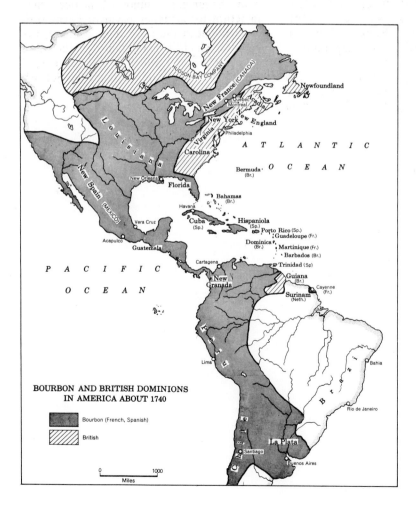

BOURBON AND BRITISH DOMINIONS
IN AMERICA ABOUT 1740

Bourbon (French, Spanish)

British

0   1000
        Miles

by British gold, were more successful. At the very time when Charles of Bavaria was, according to plan, being crowned Holy Roman Emperor at Frankfurt, and was thus breaking the long line of Habsburgs who had held that office. Austrian troops were marching into his capital of Munich. Soon Austria held all Bavaria, and the French were forced back across the Rhine, while at the same time the Austrians, with Sardinian aid, made some headway against the French and Spanish in Italy. But in the last years of the war, the French held off an Austrian invasion of Alsace-Lorraine and under a brilliant general, Marshal Saxe, conquered most of the Austrian Netherlands and threatened Holland.

The treaties which ended the War of the Austrian Succession were signed at Aix-la-Chapelle in 1748. They confirmed Prussia's conquest of Silesia. The Wittelsbach family of Bavaria recovered all its territories. Maria Theresa's husband, Francis of Lorraine, was recognized as Holy Roman Emperor. France for all her efforts and expenditures gained nothing.

The War of the Austrian Succession proved the initial encounter in a long struggle between Prussia and Austria for German leadership. It also proved an indecisive round in the long duel between France and Great Britain for colonial and commercial mastery. While fighting was going on in Europe, France and Britain had been harrying each other's commerce, the French mainly by privateering, the British by organized fleets. At the same time, the French and English colonists in North America engaged in a struggle which was called King George's War. In 1745, the English under Colonel William Pepperell of New Hampshire captured the French fortress of Louisburg on Cape Breton Island. In India, under an able politician and soldier, Dupleix, the French captured the English post at Madras and strengthened their position in the peninsula.

The treaty of Aix-la-Chapelle returned everything in the colonial sphere, including Louisburg and Madras, to the pre-war situation. Spain got a minor satisfaction, since in return for a money payment Great Britain renounced the slave trade contract, the Asiento, which it had obtained at the peace of Utrecht [1] and which it had since used illegally to force goods through the Spanish trade barriers in America.

[1] See above, p. 430.

CHAPTER 37

The Seven Years' War, and Age of the Baroque

A. The Seven Years' War in Europe, 1756–1763

Following the War of the Austrian Succession, there was a great deal of diplomatic maneuvering which so altered the alignment of European powers that it has been termed the "Diplomatic Revolution." Austria, the chief loser in that war, devoted every effort to securing allies for an attempt to recover Silesia. Saxony was readily attached to the Austrian cause, and without much difficulty Maria Theresa won as an ally the Tsarina Elizabeth of Russia, who had been much offended by the biting wit of the Prussian King Frederick II. Austria already had friendly agreements with Great Britain and Holland.

There remained the difficult task of winning the support of France. The French monarchy had been fighting the Habsburgs more or less continuously for two centuries and a half and had come to regard them as natural enemies. To Paris, Maria Theresa despatched the ablest diplomat of the age, Count Kaunitz, who sought to persuade Louis XV to abandon Prussia and join Austria, by pointing to the Prussian holdings on the lower Rhine as a possible reward in the event of a successful war. Louis XV hesitated. But Kaunitz secured the support of the King's influential mistress, Madame de Pompadour, who, like Elizabeth of Russia, had taken offense at the witty verses and sarcastic remarks of the Prussian King. Partly through Madame de Pompadour's persuasion, Louis XV finally decided to change France's traditional foreign policy and to join the Habsburg cause. A deeper reason for this action lay in the feeling that Prussia was becoming so strong as to be something of a threat to French influence in Germany.

Meanwhile, Great Britain had entered into a special agreement with Frederick II, with the object of guaranteeing the territory of Hanover and the general peace of Germany. Then, when war broke out in 1754 between French and English colonists in America, it was natural enough for Great Britain to join in a definite alliance with Prussia. Thus it befell that whereas in the War of the Austrian Succession Prussia and France had been pitted against Austria and Great Britain, in the succeeding Seven Years' War, Austria and France were in arms against Prussia and Great Britain. It will be noted that despite this change in partners the two main rivalries or duels for power were maintained. Prussia fought Austria in both wars for predominance in Germany. Britain fought France in both for commercial and colonial advantage.

The Seven Years' War lasted in Europe from 1756 to 1763. As regards the number of countries engaged, the brilliance of the generalship displayed, and the dramatic ups and downs of its course, it deserves to rank with the War of the Spanish Succession as one of the two greatest wars that Europe had so far witnessed. The coalition that was formed to check Frederick II and to make him disgorge conquered Silesia was one of the most powerful in the whole eighteenth

469

century, for, in addition to Austria, Russia, France, and Saxony, Sweden followed her old ally France into the conflict.

Learning of the coalition that was being formed against him, Frederick II did not wait to be attacked. Without any formal declaration of war he invaded Saxony (1756), exacted large money payments, drafted Saxon recruits into his armies, and moved on across the mountains into the Habsburg territory of Bohemia. Superior Austrian armies forced him to raise the siege of Prague and to fall back into his own lands. Thereupon, from all sides, the allied armies of his enemies converged on him. Russians moved into East Prussia, Swedes from Pomerania into northern Brandenburg, and Austrians into Silesia, while the French advanced in heavy force from the west.

Frederick now displayed those qualities of military genius which justify his title of "the Great." Inferior in numbers to any one of his opponents and aided only by the fact that he was fighting on "inside lines," he moved rapidly into central Germany and at Rossbach (1757) inflicted an overwhelming defeat on the French. "I cannot tell you," wrote the French commander to Louis XV, "how many of our officers have been killed, captured, or lost." No sooner had he checked the menace from the west, than Frederick was back in Silesia. He flung his army upon the Austrians at Leuthen, captured a third of their forces, and put the rest to flight.

Frederick's victories decimated his army. He still had money, thanks to subsidies which poured in from England, but he found it more and more difficult to procure men. He gathered recruits from hostile countries, he granted pardons to deserters, he enrolled prisoners of war in the Prussian ranks. No longer was he sufficiently sure of his soldiers to take the offensive and for five years he was reduced to defensive campaigns, especially in Silesia. Meanwhile the Russians rolled on. They occupied East Prussia, penetrated into Brandenburg, and in 1759 captured Berlin itself.

After the defeat at Rossbach, the French turned their efforts against Hanover. But here they encountered unexpected resistance at the hands of an army commanded by Frederick's nephew, the Duke of Brunswick. By Brunswick the French were checked, defeated, and gradually pushed back out of Germany. These reverses, coupled with disasters to the French arms in America and India, led Louis XV to call upon his Bourbon cousins for assistance. As a result, a defensive alliance called the "Family Compact" was formed among the states of France, Spain, and the Two Sicilies (1761). But the entrance of Spain into the war (1762) was too late materially to affect its outcome.

What really saved Frederick the Great was a series of unexpected events in Russia. The Tsarina Elizabeth, who hated the Prussian King, died in 1762 and was succeeded on the Russian throne by Peter III, a dangerous madman and an ardent admirer of Frederick II. With autocratic abruptness, Peter transferred his armies from the side of Austria to the side of Prussia, and gave back to Frederick all the territories conquered by the Russian armies. Peter's reign was brief, and he was quickly succeeded by his wife Catherine II. But his acts were decisive, for without Russian support, Austria was unable to wrest Silesia from Frederick.

The treaty of Hubertusburg (1763) put an end to the Seven Years' War in Europe. Maria Theresa finally, though reluctantly, surrendered all claims to Silesia. Prussia gained a rich province, clearly humiliated Austria, and became a first-rank military power. The Hohenzollerns were henceforth the acknowledged peers of the Habsburgs.

B. The Seven Years' War as a World Conflict

The inconclusive War of the Austrian Succession had left undecided a number of important issues between France and Great Britain. Could the latter attain preëminence in commerce and in naval strength at the expense of France? Could France make good its hold on the Mississippi valley from the Great Lakes to New Orleans and thus restrict the British North American colonies to a narrow coastal strip east of the Alleghenies? Would France or would Britain fall heir to the crumbling Mogul Empire in India? All these questions were definitely settled by the Anglo-French phase of

The Marquise de Pompadour (1721–1764) after an engraving by François Boucher (d. 1770).

the Seven Years' War, which saw fierce battles and long campaigns fought out thousands of miles from Europe.

In America, the conflict, called the French and Indian War, actually broke out before hostilities started in Europe. The French had been pushing into the Ohio Valley. To forestall them the British built a fort at the junction of the Monongahela and Allegheny rivers. The French captured it, enlarged it, and renamed it Fort Duquesne. Shortly afterwards a young Virginian named George Washington arrived with help for the British, but was defeated and driven off on July 4, 1754. During that same year the British American colonies sought in vain, in the face of the French menace, to form an effective union at the Albany Congress. In 1755, British regular army units under General Braddock were sent to America. In an advance on Fort Duquesne, Braddock and his men were badly defeated. British attacks on Fort Niagara and on Crown Point on Lake Champlain were likewise repulsed by the French. The British then constructed Fort Edward and Fort William Henry on Lake George, while the French replied by erecting Fort Ticonderoga.

If 1755 had been unfortunate for the British, 1756 was still worse. A British squadron was defeated in the Mediterranean and the French captured the island of Minorca, which the British had held since the peace of Utrecht. In America a British attack on the French fortress of Louisburg failed, while the French under a new and brilliant leader, the Marquis de Montcalm, captured Fort William Henry and also the British fort at Oswego on Lake Ontario. By the end of 1756, it seemed as if the French were destined to dominate North America.

At this dark juncture for the British, and especially for their American colonists, an invigorating statesman entered the ministry at London in the person of William Pitt (subsequently Earl of Chatham). He stimulated new enthusiasm at home and in the colonies, recruited soldiers, organized fleets, and raised funds. American colonial volunteers now joined with British regular soldiers to provide a force of 50,000 men for simultaneous attacks on the four chief French posts of Louisburg, Ticonderoga,

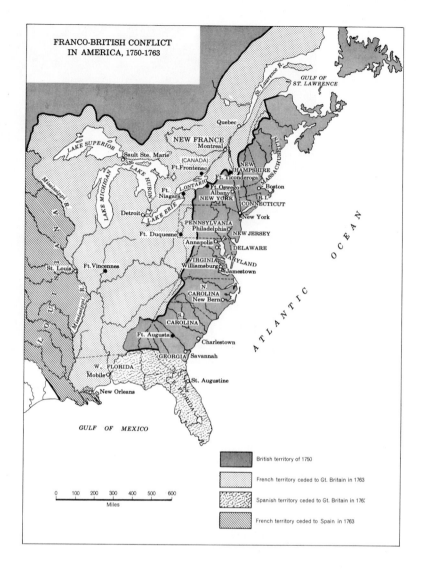

FRANCO-BRITISH CONFLICT
IN AMERICA, 1750-1763

British territory of 1750

French territory ceded to Gt. Britain in 1763

Spanish territory ceded to Gt. Britain in 176?

French territory ceded to Spain in 1763

Niagara, and Duquesne. The success of the attack on Louisburg (1758) was ensured by the support of a strong British naval squadron. Fort Duquesne was taken (1758) and rechristened Fort Pitt (now Pittsburgh). Though Ticonderoga repulsed one expedition (1758), it fell in July 1759, one day after the capture of Fort Niagara by the British.

Determined to exploit their victories, the British then launched an attack up the Hudson River valley against Montreal, and another under General Wolfe was borne on a strong fleet up the St. Lawrence against Quebec, which was defended by the redoubtable Montcalm. To capture Quebec would be well nigh decisive but very difficult. After weeks of ill success, Wolfe hit

upon a daring plan. Thirty-six hundred of his men were ferried in the dead of night to a point above the city where his soldiers scrambled up a precipitous path to a high plateau, the Plains of Abraham, commanding the city. Wolfe's presence on the heights was revealed at daybreak on September 13, 1759, and Montcalm hastened to repel the attack. For a time the issue was in doubt, but a well-directed volley and an impetuous charge threw the French lines into disorder. In the moment of victory, General Wolfe, already twice wounded, received a musket ball in the breast. His death was made happy by the news of success. But no such comfort came to the mortally wounded Montcalm.

Quebec surrendered a few days later. It

was the beginning of the end of the French empire in America. In vain the French prepared a powerful fleet against the British; it was destroyed at Quiberon Bay, in October 1759, by the English Admiral Hawke. Thus deprived of assistance from the mother country, the French city of Montreal was compelled to surrender to the British in 1760, and soon all of New France (Canada) was lost. As a last despairing gesture, France drew Spain into the war in 1762, but the two powers together were utterly unable to turn the tide in America. And already the French power was crumbling in India.

After the end of the War of Austrian Succession in 1748, the French leader in India, Dupleix, had gained control of the southern part of the peninsula by using native puppet rulers. He placed princes of his choice on the thrones of Hyderabad and of Arcot, which was capital of the Carnatic, a realm that contained both the English post of Madras and the French city of Pondichéry. To thwart the French, the English backed rival candidates. They, too, had a leader of exceptional genius in Robert Clive (1725–1774), who, beginning as a clerk in the service of the East India Company, was to end his days as a wealthy lord. Both sides used sepoys, or native troops. But Clive employed them more skillfully. In 1751, by a spectacular stroke, Clive seized the citadel of Arcot with a force of only five hundred men and held it against

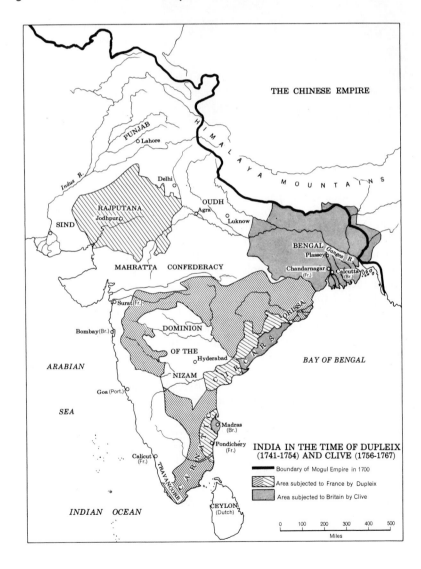

INDIA IN THE TIME OF DUPLEIX
(1741-1754) AND CLIVE (1756-1767)

— Boundary of Mogul Empire in 1700

Area subjected to France by Dupleix

Area subjected to Britain by Clive

0   100   200   300   400   500
Miles

Robert, Baron Clive. After a portrait by Nathaniel Dance (d. 1811).

repeated attacks by masses of sepoys. The English were thus enabled to place their man, Mohammed Ali, on the throne of the Carnatic, and he rewarded them richly with money and concessions. The French, instead of rushing support to Dupleix so as to recoup their losses, recalled him in disgrace.

Clive next turned his attention to Bengal, where both the French and the English had several trading centers, the British headquarters being at Calcutta and that of the French at Chandernagor. In 1756, a new, young, and violent ruler named Suraj-ud-Dowlah had come to the throne of Bengal. He quickly turned against the English, seized Calcutta, and placed 146 English prisoners in the famous "Black Hole of Calcutta," which was a tiny and stifling jail. The heat and the crowding were so severe that in one night all but twenty-three of the prisoners died. Upon receipt of the news of this atrocity, Clive organized an expedition and recovered Calcutta. Since Great Britain and France were now openly at war, Clive

seized the opportunity to capture Chandernagor. When Suraj-ud-Dowlah took the French side, Clive responded by setting up a pretender to the throne of Bengal; and the contest was decided at the battle of Plassey in 1757, where Clive won a victory as brilliant as it was unexpected. There was more fighting, and finally, in 1761, Pondichéry, the center of French power in India, was captured by the British.

Though the capture of Quebec and of Pondichéry left the outcome of the colonial struggle in America and India in no doubt, the war dragged on till 1763, when France, Spain and Great Britain signed the Peace of Paris. Of all her American empire, France retained only her main West Indian islands and the tiny fishing islands of St. Pierre and Miquelon near Newfoundland. From France, Britain secured all of Canada, all the area east of the Mississippi, and the island of Grenada in the West Indies. From Spain, Britain got Florida. To Spain, Britain restored the Philippines and Cuba which had been captured by naval expeditions, and to recompense Spain for the loss of Florida, France ceded to her Louisiana, that is, the western half of the Mississippi valley. To the French were returned their posts in India, including Pondichéry and Chandernagor, but they agreed not to use them as military bases and not to build forts or maintain troops in Bengal.

Thus in the eighteenth century, as a result of the Seven Years' War, France suffered a more humiliating defeat at the hands of the British than the Netherlands had suffered in the seventeenth century, or Spain in the sixteenth. One by one Britain had downed those powers that stood in the way of her maritime and colonial expansion. For the next century and a half, she was truly to rule the waves, to be mistress of an extensive overseas empire, and to grow wealthy from a flourishing and expanding commerce.

Despite the length and the costs and the important political results of the wars that involved so many nations for fifteen of the twenty-three years between 1740 and 1763, it would be easy to exaggerate the effect of these conflicts on the life of Europe. They were by no means "total" wars. They did not pit entire nations against one another, nor require everybody to break off all dealings with the "enemy" and to engage in some kind of "war work." Actual conflict was confined mainly to professional soldiers and sailors, and it interfered relatively little with the normal activities of the civilian population. Business men of warring nations often continued to trade with each other more or less openly. And even while hostilities were occurring, for example, between France and England, English gentlemen would sometimes sojourn in Paris, and French gentlemen might be entertained in London.

Life within a warring country was in most cases disturbed by no mass drafts of men, even though taxes might increase and rumors of victory or defeat might fly about. When a country was invaded the peasants in the path of any army suffered as they had suffered for a thousand years. But except in the case of invasion, life tended to go on in more or less normal fashion. During the wars there were long periods with little or no fighting. No continuous "front" was maintained. Rather, the relatively small and highly trained armies moved into each other's territories, advanced, retreated, maneuvered for position, laid siege to cities, and occasionally met in pitched battle.

Even the battles were somewhat stylized. With parade-ground discipline, columns were deployed into lines and efforts were made to outflank the opponent. In the colonial wars, the fate of continents was decided by the efforts of a few thousand men on each side. Nor were the numbers of men engaged in the crucial battles in Europe large by our standards. At Hohenfriedburg (1745) the Prussians had 65,000 men against 70,000 for Austria. The French won their great victory of Fontenoy (1745) with some 52,000 men against 46,000 for the allied army of British, Austrians, Dutch, and Hanoverians. Frederick the Great with 33,000 soldiers beat 82,000 Saxons and Austrians at Leuthen (1757) and with about 22,000 defeated the French and allied army of 42,000 men at Rossbach (1757).

The days of mass armies, of the "people in arms," still lay some decades ahead, and "total war" a century and a half beyond. It was not until the nature of government itself began to change that the character of war was drastically altered.

C. European Powers and Society in the Eighteenth Century

Despite recurrent wars, Europe seemed in the eighteenth century to have achieved a high degree of political, social, and economic stability. Politically, the national state was clearly the most significant form of organization. The foremost countries of the immediately preceding centuries—Portugal, Spain, Holland, Sweden, France, and England—had all been national states. On the other hand, the Holy Roman Empire was now little more than a name, and the Ottoman Empire was declining, while city states like Venice or Lübeck were playing very minor roles. To be sure, the Austrian Habsburgs had brought together an impressive aggregation of territories, which contained so many diverse peoples that they could scarcely be welded into a national state. But Prussia was very largely German and its expanding dominions were giving it an increasingly important position in north-central Europe. Russia, too, in the eighteenth century, was coming to resemble politically the national states of the west.

Most European countries were ruled by hereditary and absolute monarchs. France was perhaps the archetype of monarchial rule and the other countries resembled it rather closely. The Habsburgs were absolute rulers in their varied realms. The Romanovs in Russia, the Hohenzollerns in Prussia, the Wittelsbachs in Bavaria, the Bourbons in Spain and Italy were all autocratic rulers with but few theoretical limitations on their authority. Even in Holland with its republican tradition, the stadholders of the House of Orange succeeded in making their rule hereditary in the mid-eighteenth century. Poland, where the crown was both elective and weak, was shortly to disappear as a political entity. The only major exception to the general reign of absolutism was Great Britain.

Socially, the class structure of Europe, with some variation, seemed to display a considerable similarity and a marked stability. Everywhere the basis of society was the peasantry that worked the land and formed a large majority of the population. In the west, they were mostly freemen, and though many were tenants, a goodly number owned their land. Farther east, more of the peasants were serfs, and in Prussia, the Austrian lands, Poland, and Russia, serfdom was the normal condition of the agricultural workers. In the growing cities, there were still a considerable number of artisans and craftsmen who belonged to guilds and worked in shops much as they had in the middle ages. But there was also a steadily increasing number of workers who labored for wages in shops and shipyards and iron furnaces and factories. They became an urban proletariat.

From central Europe westward, there was an important middle class. It was composed of professional men like doctors and lawyers, of merchants and bankers who used their capital to make more money, of industrialists who employed from ten to hundreds of workers in shops and factories or who "put out" work to be done in the laborers' homes. The middle class was well-to-do and in general well educated. But while it had economic power, it enjoyed little social prestige. Social preëminence was reserved for the upper classes—great churchmen like bishops and archbishops, proprietors of large landed estates, titled nobles who formed the courts of the absolute monarchs. The nobles were relatively few in number, but they enjoyed a large share of the good things that life had to offer. They were no longer a warrior class, though many served as officers in the armies. It was not entirely clear what contribution they were making to the well-being of the various countries in return for the benefits they enjoyed.

Economically, Europe had behind it some three centuries of change which had considerably altered the old medieval conditions. In 1765 Europe was exploiting, largely by means of a commerce regulated by mercantilist principles, vast overseas areas in the Americas, in the Far East, and to a lesser degree in Africa. Everywhere in Europe, money had become important; even serfs and peasants, especially in the west, tended to pay dues in money rather than in labor and goods. Capitalism was well developed in commerce and finance. But it was largely confined to the urban areas and was perhaps most flourishing in seaport cities like London and Bristol, or Marseilles and Bordeaux, or Amsterdam and Cadiz. Industry was still mostly small-scale, though there were some large factories and mines. It was closely regulated by the state and the guilds. The hand of government lay heavily on the quality of goods produced and the techniques used in producing them. The guilds were disappearing in England. Elsewhere they had grown so rigid than an outsider had little chance of getting in. People were protesting against them and finding ways of avoiding their restrictions.

In shops, whether under guild control or outside it, there was a good deal of machinery in use. Much of it was simple, made of wood and operated by hand. But some of the machinery, such as that used in spinning silk or making stockings, was fairly complicated. There was an increasing tendency to use metals and there was a growing employment of wind and water power. Transportation had been enormously improved since the middle ages. Great sailing vessels now plied all the seas. Canals had been built in many lands, and, in some countries such as France, systems of well-made highroads had replaced the oldtime cart tracks.

In England, the eighteenth century witnessed certain peculiar agricultural developments which have sometimes been termed an "agricultural revolution." At the beginning of the century, most English agricultural land, like that on the Continent consisted of open fields worked by peasant villages. Then occurred an "enclosure movement"—a fencing in of open fields and their transfer from village community to landlord —which in the space of a hundred years destroyed the English peasantry and made England a country of large estates worked by tenant farmers and hired agricultural laborers.[1] The enclosures were authorized by acts of Parliament. There were two hundred such acts between 1700 and 1760, and nearly four thousand between 1760 and 1844 when the process was complete. More than six million acres were enclosed. Theoretically the enclosure acts protected the interests of the peasant. He was supposed to receive a consolidated block equivalent to his old holdings of strips in the open field. But the acts were instituted by landowners

---

[1] There had been an "enclosure movement" in England in the sixteenth century, but on no such scale as this one of the eighteenth century.

and maneuvered through a parliament composed of country gentlemen. Small holders were squeezed out, and many peasant holders were unable to meet the expenses of surveying and enclosing the land and had to sell all or part of the shares they received. All lost their invaluable rights of keeping cattle, sheep, and horses in the old common pastures of the village.

The people who profited from the enclosures were the big landowners who quickly became bigger landowners. The motive behind the enclosure movement was to create large unified estates on which new and improved agricultural methods could be used. The resulting crops could be sold for cash to feed growing cities like London. Among the new techniques that could be employed, were a number that had been gradually introduced from Holland in the seventeenth century. Crops were rotated so that the land was not worn out and did not need to lie fallow. Fields were drained and limed and marled. Artificial grasses like clover improved the soil, and, as hay, made it possible to keep livestock over the winter. Turnips were useful as a rotation crop and as food for animals. So enthusiastic about this vegetable did one nobleman become that he was known as "Turnip" Townshend. At the same time, experimenters like Robert Bakewell improved stock-breeding, while other innovators like Jethro Tull devised and popularized horsedrawn agricultural implements.

With the newly enclosed fields and new techniques, many English gentlemen made handsome profits from their lands. On the other hand, the dispossessed peasants were faced with the alternative of becoming agricultural wage laborers or leaving the land to go to the cities or to America. This development of the eighteenth century was peculiar to England. Though some attempts at "scientific" farming were made in France and others, under Charles III, in Spain, most peasants on the Continent continued to work on small holdings of land in the more traditional manner.

D. Baroque Art

In the arts, the eighteenth century, like the seventeenth, was persistently classical. The ideas of Greece and Rome, filtered through the sculptors, architects, and painters of the Renaissance, continued to constitute in men's minds standards of beauty and excellence. A Georgian country house in England or a Louis XV château in France looked rather different. But both used classical columns, pilasters, cornices, and decorations.

For all the persistence of conscious classicism there was development and change in the arts. In architecture the "classical" of the sixteenth century evolved into the baroque of the seventeenth and eighteenth by an emphasis on tendencies that had been evident even in Michelangelo and Palladio. Bernini (1598–1680) designed the impressive piazza with its curving double colonnades in front of St. Peter's basilica in Rome. His canopy over the high altar of that church, with its twisted and floriated columns, its crown of consoles, and its elaborate bronze work illustrates what came to be called "baroque." In baroque buildings a great use of colored marbles, gilt, rich ornamentation, broken lines, and fantastic effects was far different from the simpler tendency of the earlier period. In a number of churches founded by the Jesuits, especially in Italy, in the seventeenth century and the first half of the eighteenth, the baroque was carried to an extreme that came to be known as the "Jesuit style." Nor was the new trend confined to churches. Palaces, colleges, tombs, gardens, squares all showed its influence.

In Spain the architect Churriguera (1650–1725) evolved his own version of the baroque (called "Churrigueresque"), using light and airy decoration that was somewhat like the late Gothic in effect, but in its dramatic contrasts of line and surface, as in the façade of the Cathedral of Murcia, it becomes almost too exuberant in its richness. This Spanish style was to influence hundreds of churches and missions in the American colonies of Spain.

In France baroque architecture was more restrained. Its monuments, like the palace of the Luxembourg, the Invalides, and the great palace of Versailles with its enormous formal gardens filled with statues and fountains, have great dignity and make their impact rather by the grandeur of design than by the elaborateness of their decoration. During the eighteenth century the baroque in France became more delicate, freer, more intimate. Much use was made of stucco, of pastel shades of rose and blue, of light and fanciful ornamentation of shells, flowers, or cupids. This style, which came to be called "rococo," was widely and successfully imitated and developed in Germany and Austria in the palaces of dozens of princes and princelings.

The western architecture that Peter the Great brought to Russia was predominantly the baroque and his new city of St. Petersburg had more than its share of domes, columns, and ornate decorations. The leading architect in England was Sir Christopher Wren (1668–1710) and his masterpiece was the new St. Paul's Cathedral built to replace the Gothic edifice destroyed in the great London fire. But he designed many other churches in a style that was free in its use of classical elements but less ornate than much of the baroque of the continent. Toward the middle of the eighteenth century some architects moved toward a stricter classicism inspired by actual Greek or Roman buildings. The Pantheon in Paris, designed by Soufflot (1709–1780) and beginning in 1757, was definitely Roman, while the church of the Madeleine in the same city, begun by Constant d'Ivry in 1764, started out to be a domed building and ended up looking like a Greek temple.

During the seventeenth century, painting had been under the classical influence as transmitted by the Italian artists of the Renaissance. The paintings of Rubens (1577–1640), a native of the Spanish Netherlands who did much of his work in France, by their large size, rich color, and frequent use of mythology and of classical costumes and settings were quite like baroque architecture in effect. The leading Spanish artist Velasquez (1599–1660) in his court paintings was more restrained in manner. His unforgettable portraits of royal personages and their children are infused with a soft light. In France the painters Nicolas Poussin (1594–1665) and Claude Lorrain (1600–1682) were more strictly classical. In most of their works, the settings, the costumes, and even the subjects are derived from Graeco-Roman history or mythology and

are filled with temples, nymphs, and shepherds.

The classical tradition in art was continued in the eighteenth century by the great English portrait painters like Thomas Gainsborough (1727–1788) and Joshua Reynolds (1723–1792) and in France by a series of artists whose pictures represented in graceful and charming elegance scenes from the life of the court, usually in a pastoral or garden setting. Among these, Watteau (1683–1721) was notable for his skillful use of color, while Boucher (1703–1770) and Fragonard (1732–1806) were more delicate in their treatment and even more likely to depict cupids and goddesses. But as the eighteenth century wore on there was a movement toward greater realism, less dignity, and a choice of subjects from middle-class or even lower-class life. William Hogarth (1697–1764) painted London life in a satirical and almost exaggerated effort to show it as it actually was. Greuze (1725–1805) did softly sentimental pictures of French rustic scenes, Francisco Goya (1746–1828) almost caricatured the decadent court of Spain by painting its royal and noble personages exactly as they were.

In literature, too, there was tension between classicism and change in the eighteenth century. At first it was almost purely classical. Authors still composed epics in imitation of Homer, eclogues in the fashion of Vergil, and pastorals like those of Theocritus. For the sake of dignity, words like "dog" or "handkerchief" were barred from poetry. For the sake of form, dramas observed the "classical unities" of time, place, and action and were thus confined to a single main plot, in one spot, on one day. The English poets were also more or less limited to the rhymed couplet as were the French to the Alexandrine line. John Dryden (1631–1700) in his tragedies and poetry, Alexander Pope (1688–1744) even in his mock epic *The Rape of the Lock*, William Congreve (1670–1729) in his comedies, Joseph Addison (1672–1719) and Richard Steele (1622–1729) in their essays may all be thought of as classical in England, just as the plays and epics of Voltaire (1694–1778) or the comedies of Le Sage (1668–1747) represented classicism in France.

The Forge. By Francisco Goya (d. 1828).

New forms, however, were developing and new tendencies were appearing. The satires, savage in Jonathan Swift (1667–1745) or Voltaire's *Candide*, lighthearted in the *Marriage of Figaro* (1784) by Beaumarchais, were penetrating criticisms of contemporary society. The early English novels like the *Moll Flanders* of Daniel Defoe (1661?–1731), the *Tom Jones* of Henry Fielding (1707–1754), the *Roderick Random* of George Smollett (1721–1771) are new in both their form as long prose works of narrative fiction and in their realistic depiction of contemporary life. Other novels emphasized sentiment that often became sentimentality, as in Samuel Richardson (1689–1761) whose priggish story of the trials of the virtuous *Pamela* won a wide audience, or in *Paul et Virginie*, a tale of love among pastoral surroundings by Bernardin de Saint-Pierre (1737–1814). The novel of sentiment which would wring sighs and tears from its readers was becoming popular.

In English poetry, too, there was a foreshadowing of the romanticism which was to characterize the greater part of the nineteenth century. Romantic love of natural beauty was expressed by James Thomson in his *Seasons* (1726). Romantic liking for lowly scenes and simple emotions was voiced in the poems of Thomas Gray and especially in his *Elegy* (1750). Romantic fondness for legends and more primitive times was exemplified by Gray's *Bard*, by the *Reliques of Ancient English Poetry*, a collection of ballads and folk verse collected by the Anglican Bishop Thomas Percy and published in 1765, and by the poems of "Ossian" which the school teacher James Macpherson wrote and published in the 1760's pretending that they were translations from the Gaelic of a third-century Scottish poet. Most clearly of all the trend away from classicism and toward romanticism was marked at the very end of the century when William Wordsworth (1770–1850) and Samuel Taylor Coleridge (1772–1834) put out their *Lyrical Ballads* (1798) which dealt with nature and simple country folk, avoided the standard poetic words and verse forms of classical poetry, and appealed directly to the readers' emotions.

The same tendencies were also evident in Germany. Klopstock (1724–1803) wrote odes like those of "Ossian." Lessing (1729–1781) inaugurated a national and romantic German drama. Herder (1744–1803), an untiring advocate of folk lore, folk literature, and folk customs, published German folk poetry of earlier ages and was a decisive influence on younger literary men, notably Goethe (1749–1832) and Schiller (1759–1805). Schiller's first important play, *The Robbers* (1781), was essentially romantic as were Goethe's drama *Götz von Berlichingen* (1771) and his novel, *The Sorrows of Werther* (1774).

Like the literature of the eighteenth century, its music was predominantly classical but with new trends appearing toward the end of the period. The "classical" Italian opera developed in the seventeenth century was brought to the court of Louis XIV by Lully (1632–1687). Purcell (1658?–1695) composed operas like *Timon of Athens* and *Dido and Aeneas* for the court of Charles II and James II. An even greater master was George Frederick Handel (1685–1759) who followed George I from Hanover to England. He composed concertos, sonatas, and some forty operas, but is best remembered for the religious music of his later years, of which the *Messiah* is perhaps the greatest. His music was brilliantly appropriate to the baroque age.

One of the greatest composers of organ music, Johann Sebastian Bach (1685–1750) lived and worked at Weimar and Leipzig. Pious, humble, a good family man, and the father of twenty children, he knew little of the world. But his chorales, fugues, sonatas, concertos, and his four masses done for the elector of Saxony show his complete mastery of form and reach heights of mystical and majestic sublimity. His contemporary in France, Jean Philippe Rameau (1683–1764), continued the classical tradition of Lully but diverted it to a more pastoral mood that paralleled the rococo in art. One of his competitors was Christian Gluck, who, after leaving his native Germany for Austria, Italy, and England, settled in Paris and produced operas as classical in theme and setting as the architecture of Soufflot but with a notable lyric quality.

A greater master was Wolfgang Amadeus Mozart (1756–1791) of Salzburg and Vienna. Such a youthful prodigy that he

Sir Isaac Newton. From the painting by John Vanderbank, an English-Flemish painter who flourished at the beginning of the eighteenth century.

Courtesy National Portrait Gallery, London

began composing at the age of four, he had before his untimely death at the age of thirty-five created more than six hundred compositions including symphonies, sonatas, quartets, and world famous operas—the *Marriage of Figaro, Don Giovanni,* and the *Magic Flute.* His work has grace, charm and imagination fused by his genius into incomparable form. It was in Austria, too, that Franz Josef Haydn (1732–1809) brought the symphony to perfection. Within the rather rigid classical form of four movements, he still found scope for his talents in the more than one hundred symphonies that he composed. An even more important figure was in the making as the eighteenth century drew to a close. Ludwig van Beethoven (1770–1827), who had studied with both Mozart and Haydn, in his earlier work adhered rather closely to the predominant classicism. But in his later compositions he was to reach new heights of inspiration and new depths of emotion which led toward the romanticism of the nineteenth century.

E. Scientific Advance

Building on the earlier work of men like Copernicus, Kepler, and Galileo, scientists made rapid advances in their understanding of nature in the latter half of the seventeenth century and throughout the eighteenth. The greatest of them all, undoubtedly, was Sir Isaac Newton (1642–1727). Born of a humble family, he showed such skill in mathematics at the University of Cambridge that he was made a professor there when he was only twenty-seven years old. Almost every field of physical science felt the impact of Newton's inquiring mind, his remarkable powers of synthesis, and his mathematical insight. He developed improved tables of future astronomical movements. He created the science of hydrodynamics (the study of movements in liquids). In optics, he showed that the rainbow is caused by the breaking up of white light and proposed a corpuscular theory of light to which present-day physicists have turned back. In mathematics, he invented the crucial tool of calculus which he called the method of "fluxions." In kinetics, he pushed ahead Galileo's work and established three basic and simple "laws of motion."

But Newton's greatest and most influential contribution was the "law of gravitation." While still a young man he conceived the notion that the force which keeps the moon revolving around the earth, and the planets around the sun, is the same as that which makes an object fall when dropped. Though he long delayed publishing this idea while he checked over astronomical and other calculations, he gave it to the world in 1687 in his book, the *Principia* (Mathematical Principles of Natural Philosophy). It at once attracted wide attention in scientific circles, for the "law of gravitation" was significant in several respects. (1) It was universal. It applied to the stars in their courses and to a sparrow falling from a bush. (2) It was simple and could be stated simply: "Every particle of matter in the universe attracts every other particle with a force varying inversely with the square of the distance between them and directly with the product of their masses." (3) It brought together and unified a vast amount of work already done in astronomy and physics. (4) It seemed to indicate that man had finally penetrated God's design for the universe and had formulated one of the basic principles on which it was built.

Though there was some opposition to Newton's "law," it was soon confirmed by observation and experiment, and exerted enormous influence on every branch of thought. In sciences other than physics men sought to find similarly simple and basic mathematical laws. Soon in history, psychology, economics, political science, and religion, people were searching for Newtonian "laws." Indeed the whole intellectual spirit of the eighteenth century was to a very great degree molded by Newton's achievement.

It is notable that at first Newton's ideas on gravitation had seemed very difficult. There were essays and books to make them understandable and easy for earnest readers. But a half century after the publication of his *Principia*, they had become sufficiently commonplace to be discussed by schoolboys and society ladies.

Science depends for its progress to a considerable degree on accurate measurements, and in this period a number of new instruments were developed that made such measurements possible or permitted new kinds of experiments. The telescope and the microscope were repeatedly improved. The principle of the barometer was discovered by Torricelli in 1643. The air pump was invented by Otto von Guericke in 1650. The mercury thermometer was perfected by Fahrenheit (1686–1736). Two professors at the University of Leyden created the Leyden jar, an early form of the condenser which permitted the accumulation and sudden discharge of electricity. It was through working with such jars that Benjamin Franklin was led to experiments (published in 1751) which showed that lightning was an electrical phenomenon.

Using the Newtonian theories and the improved instruments, astronomers were able to make notable discoveries. Edmund Halley (1656–1742) catalogued the chief stars of the southern hemisphere and calculated the orbit of the great comet of 1682. When "Halley's Comet" returned (1759) as he had predicted and only a little late, the new astronomy scored another triumph. Like most of the scientists of the day, Halley had wide-ranging interests. His investigations (1693) improved the statistics of life-expectancy so that life insurance became much more practicable. Another versatile astronomer was William Herschel (1738–1822), a German by birth and a musician by profession, who was made royal astronomer by King George III of England in 1782. With improved telescopes he detected spots on the sun, mountains on the moon, and polar "snow" on Mars, and in 1781 discovered the planet Uranus, a major scientific event, since all the planets previously known were visible to the naked eye.

If Newton was the founder of modern physics, Robert Boyle (1627–1691) was the father of modern chemistry. He enunciated (1660) what came to be known as Boyle's law—that, temperature being constant, the volume of a confined gas varies inversely with the pressure. His book, *The Sceptical Chymist* (1661), helped to separate chemistry from alchemy with its magical and medieval traditions. In addition, he was one of the founders of the Royal Society, organized in 1662, which became a major factor in the exchange of scientific information and the forwarding of scientific discovery.

In the eighteenth century there was much progress in the understanding of gases. Joseph Black about 1755 prepared what he called "fixed air" (carbon dioxide). And a decade later Henry Cavendish, the son of an English nobleman, discovered "inflammable air" (hydrogen). Before long, Joseph Priestley isolated still another gas (1774) and showed that it was necessary for combustion and for the breathing of animals. Later the French chemist Lavoisier (1743–1794) gave it the name of oxygen. Cavendish went on to show that air was predominantly a mixture of oxygen and nitrogen and that water was a compound of oxygen and hydrogen. Lavoisier was able to dispose of the long-standing phlogiston theory that there was an impalpable substance which escaped from burning materials, and he laid the foundations for quantitative analysis and for the tremendous advances of chemistry in the next century.

Other sciences were moving forward too. A Scot, James Hutton, in an important paper in 1785 established the idea that the earth's crust as we have it today is the product of processes like erosion, glaciation, and vulcanism that can still be seen at work.

Malpighi (1628–1694) confirmed Harvey's theory of the circulation of the blood and was one of the first to describe the sexuality of plants. Anthony van Leeuwenhoek (1632–1723), using improved microscopes, saw protozoa, bacteria, and spermatozoa.

Information about plants, animals, and birds rapidly accumulated as specimens were brought back from overseas and placed in collections like that of Sir Hans Sloane, which at his death in 1753 became a nucleus of the British Museum. Carl von Linné (1707–1778), a Swedish botanist who is usually referred to as Linnaeus (the Latin form of his name), was able to develop a vastly improved system of classification for plants and animals which, with modifications, is still in use. His contemporary, the French zoölogist Buffon (1707–1788), brought together most of the existing information about animals in his encyclopedic *Natural History of Animals*. Buffon could not close his eyes to the resemblances among animals and remarked that were it not for the statements in the Bible one might be tempted to seek a common origin for the horse and the ass, the monkey and man. Thus he foreshadowed the evolutionary theories of the next century. just as his fellow scientists were gathering data and evolving theories on which the rapid advance of science in the future was to be based.

Voltaire. Bust by Jean François Houdon (d. 1828).

Courtesy Bettmann Archive

Beer Street. William Hogarth (d. 1764).

CHAPTER 38

Religion and the Enlightenment

A. Vogue of Rationalism and Deism

Much influenced by Newtonianism, there gradually developed a new philosophy which was essentially materialistic, that is, which tried to explain everything in the universe in terms of matter and motion, and of forces which could be detected by the human senses. Even before Newton, the French philosopher and mathematician René Descartes had worked out a philosophic system which put God and the human soul to one side as not being susceptible of human observation and which otherwise was quite materialistic. The English thinker Thomas Hobbes went further and insisted that everything, including the human soul, must be understood in terms of matter and motion. Baruch Spinoza, a gentle Jewish philosopher of Amsterdam, who made his living by grinding lenses, set forth a philosophy called pantheism. To him, what man called spirit was merely an aspect of matter; and, on the other hand, God was the natural universe. There was also a concern about materialism in the philosophy of William Leibnitz (1646–1716) who is distinguished in the history of mathematics for having discovered the calculus at about the same time as Newton. Leibnitz strove to compose the differences between Catholics and Protestants and to reconcile Christianity with the new developments in science. He put great stress on pure reason, and thought that by it man could transcend the material universe. He revived an ancient atomic theory and held that everything was made up of what he called "monads," but to him these were spiritual rather than material entities. Thus he sought to deal with matter by spiritualizing it, in contrast to Hobbes who had dealt with the spirit by insisting that it was material.

The trend toward rationalism and materialism culminated in the eighteenth century in the work of David Hume, a Scottish student of history and economics as well as of psychology and philosophy. To Hume all thought seemed based on the impressions which came through the human senses. Thought was therefore "merely a practical instrument for the convenient interpretation of our human experience." By thought, man could arrive at no truth about God, or the soul, or the after-life, or anything that lay outside of human experience, and since the truth could not be known about such matters they might best be ignored. Hume was completely skeptical about all the religious beliefs that had been accepted for generations.

Nor was Hume the only religious skeptic. True, some scientists, including Newton, accepted the Christian revelation as useful and necessary to supplement what man could find out about the universe for himself. But other scientists and most philosophers of the time were skeptical of "revelation." Hobbes and Spinoza questioned the divine inspiration and historical accuracy of the Bible.

Gradually there developed a body of religious thought which is called "Deism." Deists denied the divinity of Christ and all peculiarly Christian tenets of faith. They tried to elaborate a "natural religion" based on reason and on those beliefs that seemed common to all the different religions of mankind. By the eighteenth century, many thinkers were in general agreement as to the essential points of a "natural" and "rational" Deist religion. They could be summed up under three heads. (1) There is a God. (2) He demands righteous living of men. (3) He rewards and punishes men in a life after death. Many of the Deists agreed, likewise, that virtue could be summed up as adherence to the Christian Golden Rule.

Most of the "advanced" thinkers of the eighteenth century were Deists. Many churchmen in England and France, while performing their duties as ministers or priests and giving lip service to their respective Protestant or Catholic creeds, were really Deists at heart. But Deism was confined mainly to intellectuals. The masses and many of the upper and governing classes, and some intellectuals also, clung to Christian beliefs and fought Deism not only with word and pen but by censorship and the penalties of the law. In this controversy, the foremost of the *Philosophes*, as the advanced or "enlightened" thinkers were called in France, was a Frenchman, François Arouet (1694–1778), better known by his pen name of Voltaire. Sprung from a middle class family, Voltaire devoted his life to writing. He wrote poems and plays, histories and essays, pamphlets and books; and his personal correspondence was prodigious. Voltaire's religious views were disapproved by the royal government of France, and he spent much of his life in Lorraine, in Prussia, or finally on the Swiss border.

Wherever he was, Voltaire kept his pen busy. His writings were witty, graceful, and persuasive. Contemporaries thought them readable. In every field—social, political, or economic—Voltaire pleaded for rationalism, for the rule of "nature." As a Deist, he regarded much of Christianity as misleading mythology. As a reformer, he considered the Catholic Church, especially in France, an irrational institution handed down from the "dark ages" and designed to exploit men

by preying upon their superstitions. Seizing upon cases of religious persecution in his native country, Voltaire publicized them widely, denounced the church and its hierarchy bitterly, and pleaded for a "rational" approach to religious matters.

But Voltaire's militant Deism was not the end product of the rise of religious doubt in the eighteenth century. Soon the more skeptical were questioning the "natural and rational" religion of the Deists, including Voltaire himself. If there were no "rational" grounds for believing in the divinity of Christ, in the Christian miracles, and in the Biblical revelations, could not the same thing also be said of God and of the afterlife? A German *philosophe* named Holbach, who lived in Paris where he maintained a salon much frequented by fellow intellectuals, published two works, *Christianity Unveiled* (1767) and *The System of Nature* (1770), in which he attacked all religion and denied the existence of God. In the ensuing years Holbach's views won a number of converts, and by the end of the century there was a current of Atheism, as well as of Deism, among the intellectuals. Thus had rationalism progressed from a questioning of religious beliefs, to Deism, and finally to atheism. Yet, on the whole, Deism remained the typical religion of the *philosophes* of the eighteenth-century Age of Enlightenment. It was preached in their books and spread in their gatherings. It was furthered by secret societies like the Freemasons, which sprang up in eighteenth-century England and soon had lodges all over Europe. It profoundly shocked and disturbed the large majority of persons, who were still sincerely Christian.

The organized churches fought back at rationalism with more or less vigor. On the continent, the Jesuits were especially active in replying to the *philosophes* and striving to uphold the Catholic Christian faith. Because they had been so successful and so influential, they were singled out for the most virulent attacks by the rationalists, and these found allies among absolutist sovereigns of the age who felt themselves more "enlightened" than the Jesuits and who at the same time perceived in the Jesuits a potential menace to their own absolutism. It was "enlightened" despots who drove the

Jesuits out of Portugal in 1759 and out of France and Spain eight years later, and who in 1773 prevailed upon Pope Clement XIV to decree the formal suppression of the Society.

B. Pietism

In rural areas and small towns, and among the masses generally, Deism and other forms of rationalism made little headway. But especially in Protestant countries, there were other religious movements that did win many followers among the lower and middle classes. These movements were varied but they had certain tendencies in common. They reacted against the long theological debates of Protestant sects with one another. They minimized dogmas and emphasized the effort to lead Christlike lives. They turned away from argument and cultivated faith and religious emotions. They ignored rationalism and, frankly mystical, stressed a direct relationship of man to God.

In Germany the movement came to be called "Pietism" and can be traced to a book published by Philip Spener in 1675. Spener pleaded with his fellow Lutherans for less formal religion and more personal piety and holiness. Many welcomed the freshness and human warmth of the Pietist approach to religion, and, while Pietism never developed a separate church, it was a strong influence among eighteenth-century Protestants in Germany. Leibnitz himself was influenced by the Pietists, particularly in his interest in reducing acrimonious debate among Christians. Of a rather different sort was Emanuel Swedenborg (1688–1772), an able scientist and engineer who in 1745 had what he regarded as divine revelations and thereafter turned to writing mystical works on "divine love and wisdom" and on the "new Jerusalem." Another mystic of great power was William Blake (1757–1827) whose poems, and particularly his copper plate illustrations for them, are filled with a surging sense of divinity and eternity.

Contemporary with Spener was an Englishman, George Fox, who founded a sect, the "Friends," or "Quakers" as they were popularly known. Self-taught and by no means an intellectual, Fox was very earnest. He called churches "steeple houses," thought external observances like hat-tipping silly, and denounced war, violence, and bloodshed. He preached in England, Scotland, and America his doctrine that Christianity is no matter of clergy or churches, but a strictly personal experience. Man should be guided by the "inner light" given him by God. The Friends were soon famous for their plain-living and plain-speaking, for their refusal to take oaths, and for their staunch pacifism. While most of the Friends were humble folk, they could count among their numbers such an aristocrat as William Penn, founder of Pennsylvania.

At first the Anglican Church was little influenced by the tendencies exemplified by the Pietists or the Quakers. Yet it seemed to many in need of some sort of rejuvenation. Its services were often perfunctory and many of its clergymen worldly and even rationalist. It brought little religious emotion into the lives of the masses. The opportunity that these conditions offered was seized by John Wesley (1703–1791). At Oxford, he became the leader of a group of students who called themselves the Holy Club, but

John Wesley. After a painting by George Romney (d. 1802).

Courtesy Bettmann Archive

were nicknamed "Methodists" by reason of their methodical abstinence from frivolity and their methodical cultivation of personal piety and charity. Wesley became for a while a missionary in America and in 1738 underwent a profound religious experience, or "conversion." Then for fifty years he traveled an average of 5,000 miles a year. He preached some 40,000 sermons and with his brother Charles wrote hundreds of hymns. To Wesley anyone was a Christian who "accepted" Christ and lived methodically according to "Christian principles."

Wesley and his early associates were all Anglicans. But their emphasis on emotion, their neglect of ritual, their puritanical way of life, and their appeal to the lower classes made a breach between them and the established Church of England. Gradually the followers of Wesley came to form an independent body known as Wesleyans or Methodists, and governed by conferences of their own preachers and bishops. Before the end of the eighteenth century there were many Methodist churches in England. In North America too, Methodism rapidly became important; in fact it was as a young Anglican missionary to the Indians in Georgia that Wesley had first come into contact with Pietism through some German Protestant missionaries. George Whitefield, who was closely associated with the Wesley brothers, made several trips to America and in 1771 Francis Asbury crossed the Atlantic and gave great impetus to Methodism in the colonies. With their itinerant preachers, evangelical hymns, and their revival meetings, the Methodists made such rapid progress, especially in the frontier areas, that they became the largest of the Protestant sects in the next century.

Even within the Catholic Church there were seventeenth-century movements that somewhat resembled Pietism and persisted into the eighteenth century. One was Jansenism already mentioned in connection with Pascal. Jansen (1585–1638) was a Catholic bishop in the Spanish Netherlands who taught that above and beyond the ministrations of the church every Christian in order to be saved must experience a "conversion" and must lead a life of holiness. Louis XIV took steps against Jansenism and Pope Clement XI declared it heretical in

1713.[1] But it continued on to merge after 1870 with the sect of "Old Catholics" in the Netherlands.

The other movement, Quietism, was inaugurated by a Spanish priest named Miguel de Molinos (1640–1697); he taught that while the Catholic Church could start a man on the road to salvation, true holiness depended upon a direct indwelling of God in the individual conscience and a passive acceptance by each believer of whatever befell him. For a while Quietism won distinguished supporters in France including the famous Bishop Fénelon. But eventually it was opposed by the Jesuits and by Louis XIV and the views of Molinos were also held to be heretical.

Though the religious development of Russia was very different from that of western Europe, there were movements within its Orthodox Church that were not wholly dissimilar from Pietism. In 1654 the patriarch of Moscow had sought to revise and modernize the liturgy of the Russian Church. A number of priests and their followers clung tenaciously to the older forms, seceded from the church, and came to be known as "Old Believers." Among them arose several dissenting sects which, beside opposing the established church, tended to regard individual conscience as the final authority in religion and the sole guide to spiritual life. One of these sects, whose followers were known as Dukhobors, was composed mainly of peasants. Their beliefs were rather like those of the English Quakers, for they stressed the "inner light" and refused to do military service. The Dukhobors and similar sects were persecuted by both the government of the tsars and the Orthodox Church.[2]

The effects of Pietism were not wholly restricted to the field of religion. Pietist influence came into philosophy through the person of Immanuel Kant (1724–1804), a quiet and retiring professor of Königsberg in East Prussia. Reared in Pietist surroundings, Kant wrote on many topics but left his impress mainly by answering the ration-

[1] After 1713 the Pope specifically condemned Jansenist teachings concerning free will, grace, and predestination.

[2] A considerable number of Dukhobors later found refuge in Canada.

alism and skepticism of men like Holbach and Hume. He insisted that God, the freedom of the human will, and the immortality of the soul are subjects which cannot be understood by ordinary human reason. But man has, innately, other inner faculties by which he instinctively can know about, understand, and respond to such subjects. This philosophic point of view, known as "idealism," avoided most of the problems raised by eighteenth-century rationalism, by insisting that the basic matters of religion were not subject to reason alone. It was the basis of much of the religious and philosophic thought of the succeeding century.

C. The "Enlightenment," and Political and Economic Speculation

"Enlightened" thought of the eighteenth century expressed itself not only directly in religious skepticism and Deism, and indirectly in Pietism, but in a variety of other ways. Of course "enlightened" philosophers were not all of one mind; they differed in interests and emphases. Among most of them, however, certain general trends of thought can be discerned. (1) With the substitution of the natural for the supernatural, of science for theology, of this-worldly secularism for ecclesiastical other-worldliness, there was a stressing of *natural law*. The whole universe could now be regarded as a great Newtonian machine, perhaps originally created by God, but left by Him to function according to the rules He had established. (2) *Nature*, as man saw it, was the outer aspect of this world machine. What was natural was good. Everything worked out for the best if left alone. Man must not interfere. He must not try to go against nature. His laws should be merely explanations and declarations of what was natural. (3) Man could find out about natural law, and the workings of nature could be discovered and understood by *human reason*, as Newton had found out about gravitation. Man should trust his reason. What was *rational* was good. What was irrational or merely traditional was bad. (4) If man by reason learned about nature and natural law and sought to conform to them, if he did away with irrational laws and insti-

tutions, if he educated youth along natural and rational lines, then *human progress* would be rapid indeed. In fact man and society could by proper education approach perfection. (5) Individual human beings, endowed with reason to understand the universe, were important. They were born equal and made unequal only by education and experience. They were possessed of natural rights which should be respected. Man should treat man in a *humanitarian* fashion.

Such views slowly penetrated the field of political science and produced by the eighteenth century certain distinctive views on questions of government. Back in 1651, in the midst of civil war and troublous times in England, Thomas Hobbes had published a book called *Leviathan*. In it, he pointed to good order as the purpose of government, and strong government as the means to order. It was his notion that man in "the state of nature," before governments were established, was little better than a beast. His life was violent, nasty, brutish, and short. To escape such ills men set up a ruler and gave over to him all their rights. Thereafter they had to obey him, and even if he was unjust, they had no recourse against him.

Similar in some ways, but very different in conclusion, were the political ideas of John Locke, who lived at the time of the "Glorious Revolution," [1] approved of it, and tried in his writings to justify it. Locke believed, like Hobbes, that men in a state of nature chose a sovereign to improve their lot. But they did so mainly that he might defend the natural rights of the individual. Part of their rights men gave up to their new ruler by a "social contract." They retained under this contract, however, the rights to life, liberty, and property. If the sovereign unjustly or tyranically interfered with his subjects' remaining rights, or if he failed to protect them, then the people were entitled to drive him out and to select a new ruler who would maintain and defend their rights.

Locke's ideas were extremely popular in the eighteenth century. They led Voltaire and many of the other *philosophes* to believe that the ideal kind of government was

---

[1] In 1689. See below, pp. 511–512.

John Locke. After Sir Godfrey Kneller (d. 1723).

Courtesy Bettmann Archive

rule by a just, wise king, who was rational in his behavior, who understood nature and natural law, and who protected the natural rights of his subjects. He might be an absolute ruler, a despot, but if he were "enlightened" and ruled in an "enlightened" fashion, all was well. In fact, so great were the difficulties and dangers of rule by groups or by all the people that many held "enlightened despotism" to be the best possible form of government.

Most political thinkers spun their ideas by rational arguments from suppositions about the nature of man. But one French writer, Montesquieu, in a famous work entitled *The Spirit of the Laws* (1748), adopted another method. He studied and compared existing governments and political institutions. In England, he thought he discerned the ideal system. Because he did not fully realize how powerful the Parliament had become, he thought that in the British government the powers were divided evenly among the executive (the king), the legislature (parliament), and the judiciary (the judges). Each branch checked and balanced

the others, and, by this division of power, justice was secured and the natural rights of men preserved. Montesquieu's interpretation of British government had great influence on the formulation of the American constitution and also upon the development of the idea of *limited* monarchy as the proper form of government.

Some eighteenth-century thinkers moved beyond the notion of enlightened despotism or limited monarchy and developed democratic theories which held that the people should rule themselves. Of such thinkers, the most famous was a French Swiss named Jean-Jacques Rousseau (1712–1778). Rousseau was a pioneer in the movement which in the next century was called romanticism. Though he put his own children in an orphan asylum, his book on education, *Émile* (1762), persuaded many people that children were naturally good, and that man was evil because he was perverted by faulty teaching and by bad laws and institutions. He believed likewise that men in a "state of nature" were good, and he popularized the idea of the "noble savage." Like Locke he maintained that men set up governments by means of a "social contract," and his major political work is called the *Social Contract* (1761). But Rousseau went further than Locke, for he maintained that men are born free and they can best maintain their freedom and their rights if they are ruled by a government of their own choosing which by its acts expresses the popular will. Rousseau believed that such democracy could only work well in small states like his native Geneva. Others, however, using his vigorous phrases and his highly charged catchwords, extended the idea of democracy and of republicanism to larger countries. Within fifteen years of Rousseau's death, France itself would be experimenting with a democratic republic.

The ideas of the enlightenment gradually influenced economic thought. During previous centuries, economics had been thoroughly ensnarled with the politics of state action. It was indeed quite properly called "political economy." Almost everybody had accepted the basic mercantilist notion that individuals seeking their selfish ends must be checked and controlled by the government for the sake of the wealth, strength, and unity of the whole nation. In practice, such beliefs had led to policies of high tariffs, subsidies, industrial regulations, navigation acts, and colonial exclusiveness. In England, it is true, the destruction of a strong and effective royal government had brought about a gradual relaxation of internal controls on industry. But the parliament of landlords and merchants had maintained thoroughly mercantilist policies on imports, shipping, and colonies. In other countries, there had long been much government control of internal economic life as well as of foreign trade. Many states modeled their policies on those applied in France by Colbert.

Toward the end of the seventeenth century, complaints began to be raised in England and France about specific mercantilist regulations. Some businessmen protested against high tariffs; others denounced monopolistic companies; still others argued against the prohibition of the export of coin. There was a growing belief that nations had set too much store by gold and silver and that ships and shops and raw materials were just as important forms of wealth.

The philosopher David Hume in a series of essays insisted that the government would do well to leave foreign commerce alone, that there was no need to worry about a balance of trade, and that prosperous neighbors helped a country instead of hurting it. In France there developed a whole school of thinkers called the "Physiocrats," whose slogan was *laissez-faire* (leave alone). Led by a court physician named Quesnay, the physiocrats were mainly interested in agriculture. They held that agriculture alone really produced a national profit, a "net product." Industry and commerce were sterile, since they merely transformed goods or moved them from place to place. There was no reason, therefore, to regulate manufacturing or trade; and agriculture would be most helped by leaving commerce in farm products and especially in grain completely free. Wealth circulated best if it circulated naturally. It should be left alone. A French minister named Turgot tried to introduce physiocratic reforms in France in 1774–1776. But the opposition was too strong and he was forced out of office.

The culmination of *laissez-faire* thinking, and of eighteenth century economic thought, was reached in *An Inquiry into the Nature and Causes of the Wealth of Nations* (1776) by a Scottish professor named Adam Smith. This work was a literary masterpiece of brilliant and persuasive eloquence; it was also a notable synthesis which drew together the best of the thought of Hume and the Physiocrats and a host of earlier writers. Smith destroyed the foundations of mercantilist thought by showing that goods, not money, are true wealth, and by demonstrating that restrictions and regulations on industry and trade tended to lessen the production of goods. Wine, he pointed out, could be produced in Scotland in hothouses, if the import duty on wine were high enough. But it would cost thirty times as much as French wine. It would be better for the Scots to use their land, labor, and capital where they could employ them most effectively, and then exchange their products with France for wine.

Not only did Smith attack the reasoning which had buttressed the mercantilist regulations, but he also advanced positive arguments for *laissez-faire*. He reasoned that if men are left alone to seek their own ends they will be guided as if by "an invisible hand" to work and to use their land, labor, and capital in the way most beneficial to the whole country. Economic forces should be left alone under the sway of natural economic laws, without human interference. It is noteworthy that Smith's work which showed the folly of colonial regulations and restrictions appeared in the very year in which the American Declaration of Independence broke up the English colonial system. The lesson was not lost on some people. But though most thinkers became disciples of Adam Smith and adherents of *laissez-faire*, it was a generation or more before the British government began to adopt a *laissez-faire* policy. Other nations were still slower.

The enlightened *philosophes* of the eighteenth century were not on the whole greatly interested in history. To them the record of the past was mainly one of ignorance and superstition. They preferred, therefore, to look forward to an era of progress guided by reason, rather than looking backward. Nonetheless, there was in the period considerable development of historical method and knowledge, and some of the major figures wrote histories that reached a wide audience. Thus Voltaire's *Age of Louis XIV* and his *Life of Charles XII* (of Sweden), and Hume's *History of England* were received with enthusiasm.

Already in the seventeenth century a French Benedictine monk named Mabillon (1632–1707) had formulated the rules and scientific principles for the study and interpretation of historical documents. The monks of the Congregation of St. Maur, to which he belonged, carried his work forward, and in 1733 began to publish a monumental collection of the sources of French history. At about the same time, a learned Italian priest, Muratori, was engaged in a similar enterprise for his country. Moreover, the growth of well-ordered libraries meant that historical materials were collected and cared for more effectively than in the past. The library of the Vatican, the Laurentian library at Florence, the Royal Library at Paris, and the royal Prussian library were all greatly expanded in the eighteenth century, while the library of the British Museum grew rapidly from the nucleus of a private gift.

One of the fertile historical minds of the period was that of Vico (1668–1744), a Neapolitan professor who not only worked out theories as to the successive periods of history but also subjected the sources of Greek and Roman history to searching criticism. Vico thought of art, literature, and political institutions as all being the products of a changing historical environment. To a degree, his attitude was exemplified by Winckelmann, who has been called the founder of scientific archaeology and who published the first treatise on the treasures of the buried cities of Pompeii and Herculaneum.

The continuing interest in ancient history is illustrated by the greatest and most typical historical work of the eighteenth century, the *Decline and Fall of the Roman Empire* by Edward Gibbon (1737–1794), a well-to-do English gentleman. Gibbon was an agnostic, though he had been both a Catholic and a Protestant. With rationalism and wit he contrasted pagan "civilization" with Christian "barbarism" and attributed the decay of the Roman Empire, with all that it had meant for the well-being of mankind, to the triumph of Christianity.

More prophetic of the future was the work of Herder (1744–1803), a German Lutheran pastor. He wrote no important histories himself nor did he collect documents, but he did plead for a scientific study of history. In his *Ideas on the Philosophy of History* he urged that history should show how human actions are modified by time and place; it should explain how the human race has developed; it should be national; and it should above all be humanitarian and promote a real understanding of human nature.

D. Humanitarianism

The Enlightenment involved, with many of its devotees, a humanitarianism. For example, an Italian nobleman and professor, Beccaria, in a treatise *On Crimes and Punishments* (1761), pleaded for more humane treatment of criminals. He condemned torture and capital punishment and held that justice should seek to prevent rather than to punish crime. The Quakers denounced the slave trade, and the Pennsylvania Quakers in 1761 forbade their members to engage in it. Before long Englishmen like Thomas Clarkson and William Wilberforce were engaged in an active campaign against slavery and the slave trade, and in 1787 anti-slavery committees were organized both in England and in France.

Humanitarianism, aided by scepticism and rationalism, also affected other areas of public policy. The belief in witches which had been normal in the seventeenth century came to seem a superstition, and gradually witches ceased to be tried and executed. The last witch trial in Scotland was in 1722, the last in Germany in 1793. The same forces, combined with the insistence of dissenting sects like the Quakers, led toward a gradual rise of religious toleration. The laws against Protestants were eased in France and those against Catholics in England. Even for the Jews, who had long been clannish and subjected in most countries to repressive laws designed to keep them segregated, a new day began to dawn. Their own "enlightened" philosopher, Moses Mendelssohn (1729–1786), urged them to be more understanding of other religions, to be less clannish, and to seek to be good citizens in the countries where they resided. Despite the fact that Frederick the Great disliked and harried Jews, he began the process of giving them more rights. Joseph II of Austria in 1781–1782 repealed most of the anti-Jewish laws and even permitted them to attend universities. In England and the Netherlands, where the Jews had been tolerated for some time, they were treated progressively in the eighteenth century much like other citizens.[1]

E. The Enlightened Despots

Just after the middle of the eighteenth century, between 1751 and 1765, there appeared in France an encyclopedia composed of seventeen large volumes of text and four of illustrations. So famous that it is known as "The Encyclopedia," it forms a monument of eighteenth-century learning, rationalism, and "enlightenment." It was edited by Denis Diderot, who wrote many of the articles and who was imprisoned and constantly harried by the authorities because of the skeptical tone of the work. While some of the articles were written by hacks, others were contributed by major *philosophes.* Voltaire wrote on history, Rousseau on music, Quesnay on economics, d'Alembert on mathematics. To a degree, the Encyclopedia hid its skepticism on religious matters behind a superficial acknowledgment of orthodox views. But tucked way in unexpected minor articles were scathing, if indirect, attacks on the church, the priesthood, and traditional faith. In other fields, all the diversity, all the faith in nature and reason, all the insistence on natural rights, all the belief in man, education, and progress, which were exemplified by eighteenth-century thinkers, were spread upon the pages. So important and effective was the work that "encyclopedist" became a synonym for *philosophe* or "liberal thinker." When a churchman or a conservative wished to attack the rationalist trend of eighteenth-cen-

tury thought, he denounced the Encyclopedia.

But there were some in high places who gave heed to the encyclopedists. There were rulers who hypocritically or sincerely sought to play the role of "enlightened despots" about whom the thinkers were writing. In Austria, though Maria Theresa had striven earnestly to strengthen her realm and increase its prosperity, she was by no means "enlightened," for she was fearful of the new ideas, averse to radical changes, and quite devoted to the Catholic religion. But her son, Joseph II, who was associated with her after 1765 and was sole ruler from 1780 to 1790, was of a more "enlightened" type. He had read the *philosophes* and could quote them. While it can be argued whether he drew more of his inspiration from them or from the older Austrian mercantilist writers, there can be little doubt about his devotion to reason and reform.

With little regard to opposition or to tradition, Joseph II plunged ahead on a path of reform and tried by the despotic enforcement of his ideas to bring the Austrian domains "up-to-date." Though the masses of his subjects were Catholics, Joseph was eager not only to purge Catholicism of "superstition" but also to subject the church completely to the state. He forbade the publication of papal bulls in his territories without his permission. He nominated bishops who shared his views. He confiscated church lands. He abolished many monasteries, ordered the clergy to be trained in state schools, and gave to heretics and Jews equal rights with Catholics.

Joseph, in traditional more than philosophic manner, attempted to extend his lands by going to war with the Turks (1786). But he was also bent on centralizing his despotic government. He divided his dominions into thirteen provinces, each under a military commander. Local assemblies and legislatures were abolished and age-old customs and privileges ignored. Everything was henceforth to be managed from Vienna. The army was reorganized after the Prussian model and reluctant peasants were forced to serve in it. German was made the official language in all the diverse Habsburg lands, where so many tongues were spoken. In his effort to reconstruct society, Joseph went

---

[1] Not until the nineteenth century, however, were either Jews or Catholics admitted to the British Parliament.

still further. He ordered that all serfs were to become free men, able to marry without consent of their lord, permitted to sell their holdings, and privileged to pay a fixed rent in money rather than in labor. Nobles were to bear their share of the taxes.

Many of Joseph's social and economic reforms met with bitter opposition. The peasants disliked military service and did not understand about "freedom." The nobles resented loss of feudal rights. The provinces hated to see their assemblies and privileges destroyed. The Austrian Netherlands rose in revolt rather than surrender their local laws; the Tyrol did likewise; and angry protests came from Hungary. When Joseph II was dying (1790), he confessed that "after all my trouble I have made few happy and many ungrateful." He directed that most of his reforms be cancelled and proposed as his epitaph the gloomy sentence, "Here lies a man who, with the best intentions, never succeeded in anything."

There were other "enlightened" rulers in the eighteenth century. The English Georges and Louis XV of France were least affected by rationalist or liberal thought. Catherine the Great of Russia made at least a pretense of interest in the *philosophes*. She corresponded with Diderot, bought his library when he was in financial difficulties, and was as eager to be thought modern as she was to increase her own autocratic power. Charles IV of Naples (1738–1759) and III of Spain (1759–1788) was more genuine in his "enlightenment." He centralized and reformed the administration, reduced the public debt, built roads and canals, encouraged "scientific farming," fostered commerce and industry, reorganized the army, rejuvenated the navy, improved the government of the Spanish colonies, and sent thither emigrants from Spain. In addition, he suppressed the Jesuits and checked the activities of the Inquisition. During the reign of Charles III the revenues of Spain tripled, the population grew, and Spain's prestige increased abroad. In Portugal, Charles's neighbor, King Joseph I (1750–1777), shone in the reflected glory of a minister, Pombal, who was both an "enlightened" philosopher and an astute statesman. Under Pombal, royal authority was

strengthened, at the expense of the nobles and clergy, and was exercised to promote education and the material well-being of the middle classes.

Sweden had an "enlightened" despot in Gustavus III. (1771–1792); Sardinia, in Charles Emmanuel III (1730–1773); and Tuscany, in Leopold I (1765–1790), a brother of Joseph II of Austria and his successor as Holy Roman Emperor. But of them all the most famous was Frederick the Great of Prussia, whose exploits in war and diplomacy we have already noticed. Frederick was much more than a military genius and a ruthless diplomat. He was thoroughly imbued with the rationalist philosophy of the French thinkers whose language he spoke by choice, whose works he read, and whose company he sought. Voltaire himself came as a guest to the Prussian court, and there were long conversations and witty interchanges until the "prince of philosophers" went too far in correcting the amateur poems of the Prussian King.

Frederick took his duties as an "enlightened" despot most seriously. In a work written in French on the theory of government, Frederick declared, "The monarch is not the absolute master but only the first servant of the state." Like a faithful servant, Frederick labored many hours a day on documents and despatches, with only occasional interruptions for military parades, conversations over a coffee table, or, as relaxation, some literary work and a little flute playing. Even in the midst of his long and desperate wars, Frederick never lost his zeal for internal administration and reform.

Frederick accomplished much for the economic development of Prussia. He encouraged landowners to try out the new agricultural methods that were being introduced in England, to drain marshes, to plow waste lands, to plant fruit trees, to breed better farm animals, and to grow root crops adapted to the sandy soils of north Germany. Frederick brought in immigrants, built roads and canals, and tried to improve industry and trade. Though he kept the peasants in a state of serfdom, he was eager to reduce their financial burdens. Taxes were not light, but Frederick spent the public funds with care. He was not the man to

Frederick the Great. After a drawing by
H. Hamberg.

pices, moreover, the laws of the land were published in clear and compact form for the information of the public and the guidance of the courts. Torture in criminal investigations was abolished and other humane reforms decreed.

In religious matters, Frederick was devoid of Protestant zeal, and in fact of any zeal at all. It was part of his "enlightenment" to be skeptical about Christian faith and morals, to doubt the Bible, and to sneer at clergymen. "All religions must be tolerated," he affirmed, "and every person allowed to go to heaven in his own fashion." To the scandal of many of his Lutheran subjects, he welcomed Catholics in Prussia and told them they might build their churches as high as they pleased. To the amazement of all Christians, he declared, "If Turks should come to populate the land, I myself shall build them mosques." Only against Jews did he discriminate, and in their case not because of their religion but because of qualities which he fancied were inherent in their race. He obliged Jews to adopt surnames and to obtain special licenses to live in Prussia. He arbitrarily expelled them from this or that locality, favored them when they seemed serviceable, and at other times harassed them with restrictions.

There was another matter in which Frederick was not "enlightened." Cosmopolitan and humanitarian he might be in some respects, but he was no pacifist. Like his father he lavished time, money, and attention on the army and rebuilt it with care when it was shattered by war. Tireless drill, strict discipline, up-to-date arms, and, most of all, Frederick's enthusiasm and ability rendered the Prussian army the envy and the model of Europe in the second half of the eighteenth century. For all his "enlightenment," Frederick is best remembered for his extraordinary feats on the bloody fields of war. And in some ways he thus symbolizes the eighteenth century, which, under a veneer of rationalism among the intellectuals and polish among the courtiers, was a period in which society rested upon the exploited peasants and in which the lot of the lower classes was little bettered by all the "progress."

lavish fortunes on courtiers or mistresses like Louis XV of France. His officials dared not be extravagant for fear of corporal punishment, or, what was worse, being held up to ridicule by Frederick's sarcastic tongue.

Into the intellectual life of his time, Frederick entered heart and soul. He invigorated the Berlin Academy of Sciences and showed his faith in education by establishing numerous elementary schools. Though he disliked German literature and thought the works of Lessing and Goethe vulgar, he was fond of French writers and eagerly read the latest works from Paris.

To Frederick, the law seemed often formal and unreasonable. On one occasion, when he thought an injustice had been done to a poor man, he dismissed the judges, condemned them to a year's imprisonment, and compelled them to make good out of their own pockets the loss sustained by their victim. Under Frederick's "enlightened" aus-

SELECT SUPPLEMENTARY READINGS FOR PART VII

General. David Ogg, *Europe in the Seventeenth Century* (1925); *New Cambridge Modern History*, vol. VII (1957); C. J. H. Hayes, *Political and Cultural History of Modern Europe*, vol. I (1936); S. B. Clough and C. W. Cole, *Economic History of Europe* (1952); C. J. Friedrich, *The Age of the Baroque* (1952); F. L. Nussbaum, *The Triumph of Science and Reason, 1660–1685* (1953); J. B. Wolf, *The Emergence of the Great Powers, 1685–1715* (1951); Paul Hazard, *The European Mind: the Critical Years, 1680–1715* (1935); Preserved Smith, *A History of Modern Culture*, 2 vols. (1930–1934).

Chapter 34. A. J. Grant, *French Monarchy, 1483–1789*, 2 vols. (4th ed., 1920); *The New Cambridge Modern History*, vol. V, *The Ascendency of France, 1648–1688*, ed. F. L. Carsten (1961); Quentin Hurst, *Henry of Navarre* (1938); J. B. Perkins, *Richelieu and the Growth of the French Power* (1900), *France Under Mazarin*, 2 vols. (1886), *France Under Louis XIV*, 2 vols. (1897), and *France Under the Regency* (1892); Anthony Blunt, *Art and Architecture in France, 1500–1700* (1953); L. B. Packard, *Age of Louis XIV* (1929); James Farmer, *Versailles and the Court Under Louis XIV* (1905); N. Henderson, *Prince Eugene of Savoy* (1964); A. J. Grant, *The Huguenots* (1934); C. W. Cole, *Colbert and a Century of French Mercantilism*, 2 vols. (1939), and *French Mercantilism, 1683–1700* (1943); H. W. Van Loon, *Fall of the Dutch Republic* (2nd ed., 1924); G. M. Trevelyan, *England Under Queen Anne*, 3 vols. (1930–1934) (for the War of the Spanish Succession).

Chapter 35. Frank Nowak, *Medieval Slavdom and the Rise of Russia* (1930); Stephen Graham, *Ivan the Terrible* (1933); Eugene Schuyler, *Peter the Great*, 2 vols. (1884); B. H. Sumner, *Peter the Great and the Emergence of Russia* (1951) and *Peter the Great and the Ottoman Empire* (1949); I. Andersson, *A History of Sweden* (1956); F. G. Bengtsson, *Charles XII* (1960); E. F. Heckscher, *An Economic History of Sweden* (1954); John A. Gade, *Charles XII of Sweden* (1916); R. N. Bain, *Slavonic Europe, a Political History of Poland and Russia from 1447 to 1796* (1908); H. H. Kaplan, *The First Partition of Poland* (1962); R. H. Lord, *Second Partition of Poland* (1915); K. Waliszewski, *Catherine II of Russia* (1894); W. F. Reddaway *et al.*, eds., *The Cambridge History of Poland*, 2 vols. (1941–1950); D. Halecki, *A History of Poland* (1956); G. P. Gooch, *Maria Theresa and Other Studies* (1951); J. Stoye, *The Siege of Vienna* (1964); Mehmed Pasha, *Ottoman Statecraft* (1935); H. Gibb and H. Bowen, *Islamic Society and the West*, vol. I, *Islamic Society in the Eighteenth Century*, 2 pts. (1950–1957); Lord Eversley, *Turkish Empire* (3rd ed., 1924);

Ferdinand Schevill, *History of the Balkan Peninsula* (rev. ed., 1933); H. Holborn, *A History of Modern Germany: 1648–1840* (1964); S. B. Fay, *The Rise of Brandenburg-Prussia to 1786* (1937); C. E. Maurice, *Life of Frederick William, the Great Elector* (1926); R. R. Ergang, *The Potsdam Führer, King Frederick William I* (1941); G. P. Gooch, *Frederick the Great* (1947); W. H. Bruford, *Germany in Eighteenth Century* (1935).

Chapter 36. W. C. Abbott, *Expansion of Europe* (rev. ed., 1924); L. B. Packard, *The Commercial Revolution, 1400–1776* (1927); P. A. Means, *The Spanish Main* (1935); P. Geyl, *The Netherlands in the Seventeenth Century*, Part Two, 1648–1715 (1964); H. W. Van Loon, *Golden Book of the Dutch Navigators* (1916); V. Barbour, *Capitalism in Amsterdam in the Seventeenth Century* (1950); J. J. van Klaveren, *The Dutch Colonial System* (1953); M. A. P. Meilink-Roelofsz, *Asian Trade and European Influence in the Indonesian Archipelago Between 1500 and About 1630* (1962); C. H. Haring, *The Spanish Empire in America* (1947); C. R. Boxer, *The Golden Age of Brazil, 1695–1750* (1962); J. B. Brebner, *The Explorers of North America* (1933); J. A. Williamson, *Short History of British Expansion*, 2 vols. (1930); A. Sharp, *The Discovery of Australia* (1963); G. M. Wrong, *Rise and Fall of New France*, 2 vols. (1928); H. I. Priestley, *France Overseas Through the Old Regime* (1939).

Chapter 37. J. O. Lindsay, *The Old Regime, 1713–1763* (1957); Penfield Roberts, *The Quest for Security, 1715–1740* (1947); W. L. Dorn, *Competition for Empire, 1740–1763* (1940); W. F. Reddaway, *Frederick the Great and the Rise of Prussia* (1904); Norwood Young, *Life of Frederick the Great* (1919); J. F. Bright, *Maria Theresa* (1897); A. H. Buffington, *The Second Hundred Years' War, 1689–1815* (1929); Howard Robinson, *Development of the British Empire* (rev. ed., 1936); J. D. Perkins, *France Under Louis XV*, 2 vols. (1897); Basil Williams, *Life of William Pitt, Earl of Chatham*, 2 vols. (1913); J. S. Corbett, *England in the Seven Years' War*, 2 vols. (1907); H. H. Peckham, *The Colonial Wars, 1689–1762* (1964); H. Dodwell, *Dupleix and Clive, the Beginning of Empire* (1930); W. H. Moreland and A. C. Chatterjee, *A Short History of India* (1936); G. M. Wrong, *Rise and Fall of New France*, 2 vols. (1928); W. T. Waugh, *James Wolfe, Man and Soldier* (1928); Sir George Forrest, *Life of Lord Clive*, 2 vols. (1918).

Chapter 38. L. Gershoy, *From Despotism to Revolution* (1944); Geoffrey Brunn, *The Enlightened Despots, 1763–1789* (1941); Dorothy Stimson, *The Gradual Acceptance of the Copernican Theory* (1917); L. T. More, *Isaac Newton* (1937); J. W. N. Sullivan, *Isaac Newton* (1937); Charles Singer, *Discovery of the Circulation of the Blood* (1923); F. Masson, *Robert Boyle* (1914); A. Wolfe, *History of Science, Philosophy and Technology in the Eighteenth Century* (1939); H. Higgs, *Physiocrats* (1897); Carl Becker, *The Heavenly City of the Eighteenth Century Philosophers* (1932); Kingsley Martin, *French Liberal Thought in the Eighteenth Century* (1929); H. Daniel-Rops, *The Church in the Eighteenth Century* (1964); R. R. Palmer, *Catholics and Unbelievers in Eighteenth-Century France* (1939); E. de and J. de Goncourt, *French XVIII Century Painters* (1948); Emil Kaufmann, *Architecture in the Age of Reason* (1955); B. Willey, *The Eighteenth Century Background* (1940).

For Voltaire, see the studies by R. Aldington (1925), G. Brandes (1934), H. N. Brailsford (1935), and N. L. Torrey (1938). For Rousseau, see the studies by A. Cobban (1934), H. Fairchild (*The Noble Savage*, 1928), F. C. Green (1955), M. Josephson (1931), R. B. Mowat (1938), and E. H. Wright (1929). For Montesquieu, see R. Shackleton, *Montesquieu: a Critical Biography* (1961).

James I of England (VI of Scotland) by Pieter de Jode (d. 1634).

From Cromwell
to Napoleon

PART VIII
REVOLUTIONARY

Spanish Uprising of May Second and French Mass Shooting at Madrid. Francisco Goya (d. 1828).

Courtesy Bettmann Archive

TRANSITION

WHILE EUROPE was engaged in colonial rivalries and dynastic wars, while scientific knowledge was being greatly refined and extended, while religious attitudes were changing and thought was becoming "enlightened," there was in process, within the area of Western civilization, a special historical development which was to be of outstanding importance in laying solid foundations for the free world of the nineteenth and twentieth centuries. This development was predominantly political, though it was thoroughly ensnarled with social, religious, economic, and intellectual factors. It is a series of revolutions, beginning with those in England of the seventeenth century and including the American and French Revolutions of the late eighteenth century.

The English revolutions had definite religious origins, though the political and economic aspirations of the middle class and the country gentry gave them much of their driving force. Thereafter the revolutions sometimes had religious implications, but other factors were more significant. The American Revolution must be thought of as part of European history, for its causes were part of British imperial development and it had major repercussions not only in Britain but on the Continent. The French Revolution was the most shattering that was to occur before the twentieth century. Its effects were profound and far-reaching. Europe and the world were never, after it, to be the same again. It was to be the focus not only of political ideas of enduring influence like liberty, equality, and democracy, but also it was to create a division between "Right" (conservative) and "Left" (liberal or radical) that was permanent, and to give rise to an intense nationalism in France that was eventually to be communicated by a kind of contagion to every country on every continent.

Attempts have been made to draw parallels among the various revolutions and there are certain similarities among their courses and their events. But each arose from peculiar circumstances and each developed in a manner different from the others. It is, nevertheless, a fact that there grew up a kind of revolutionary tradition. The leaders of each successive revolt were aware of the ideas and the techniques of the previous ones and sometimes quite consciously sought to follow the examples or avoid the mistakes of their predecessors.

CHAPTER 39

The English Revolutions

A. Opposition to the Stuart Kings James I and Charles I

In almost every country of Continental Europe, the seventeenth century was marked by a tendency toward absolute monarchy.[1] At the beginning of the century, while the Tudor Queen Elizabeth was still alive, it might reasonably have been predicted that the political development of England would follow that on the Continent. Yet a peculiar combination of social, economic, and religious conditions, of political traditions, and of the personalities of Elizabeth's successors made the century's development in England unique.

When James VI of Scotland succeeded his cousin Elizabeth in 1603 and became James I of England, the first of its Stuart kings, he was already a thorough believer in strong monarchy and determined to continue the firm rule of his Tudor predecessors. Unlike these, however, he was not content to be absolute in practice. He must expound in writing the theory of divine-right monarchy, that the king derived his authority from God and was responsible only to God. The king's will was law, and the people should obey him without question, as children obey their father.

James in England faced certain disadvantages. He was regarded as a foreigner, a point emphasized by his Scottish accent. He understood the Scottish people, but the

English and their ways were something of a mystery to him. He made the mistake of giving special honors and rewards to Scottish favorites who came with him to England. Brought up in bleak, stony Scotland, James thought of England as a land blessed with milk and honey, and endowed with unlimited wealth and resources. Though he was not really extravagant, he liked display and appeared wasteful to many of his subjects, especially the Puritans.

In England James I also found certain traditional restrictions on royal power. There was a two-house parliament of lords and commons, which dated back to the thirteenth century and which in the course of time had acquired very considerable powers over taxation and legislation. The Tudors had handled it by cajolery, bribery, pressure, and popular appeal, and had called it together infrequently. Besides, there was a series of medieval charters, of which Magna Carta of 1215 was the most important. Though this dealt with medieval feudal problems, some of its wording seemed to guarantee the liberties of Englishmen against royal tyranny. There was also the common law, a collection of customs and precedents built up over centuries by English judges and governing the law courts of the land. Much of the common law was designed to protect the individual and his rights, and there were lawyers who were ready to insist that even the king was bound by it.

---

[1] The one exception was Poland. See above, p. 437.

501

BRITISH KINGDOMS IN THE SEVENTEENTH CENTURY

In addition, James I faced, though neither he nor his contemporaries understood it clearly, an almost insoluble financial problem. The flow of silver from America was forcing up prices all over Europe with startling rapidity.[1] James came to the throne in the middle of this price rise. On the one hand, his revenues were more or less fixed by custom. The King was supposed to live "of his own," that is, on the regular income of the royal estates and dues together with the customs duties. Land and other taxes were voted only reluctantly and as emergency measures. Yet every year the price of the goods and services needed by the King and his government was going up. Either James had to turn to Parliament for added grants

[1] See above, pp. 406–407.

of money, which that body would give only in return for increased control over policy, or he had to try to squeeze out added funds without recourse to Parliament, a procedure which seemed tyrannical to many people.

Finally, and perhaps most crucially of all, James was confronted by a very difficult religious problem. He approved most heartily of the Anglican Church, with its bishops, its ritual, and its tradition of royal supremacy. But within that church, there was growing up a strong body of opinion, Calvinist in tone, which wished to simplify or eliminate the ceremonies, to reduce the powers of the bishops, and to give more weight to meetings of ministers. Those who held these views were called Puritans because they wished to "purify" the Anglican Church, and they were especially numerous in certain cities, especially London, in the increasingly powerful business classes, and in Parliament. Even more radical were the thoroughgoing Calvinists, who wanted to do away with bishops altogether and to make either Presbyterianism or Congregationalism the state religion in England, and if these radicals were few in 1603, their numbers grew rapidly in the ensuing years. Both the Puritans and the more extreme "Independents" were characterized by a fanatical fear and hatred of Catholicism, by a great faith in the Bible with a strong tendency to emphasize the spirit and teachings of the Old Testament just as much as, if not more than, the precepts of the New, and by a simplicity of manner, speech, dress, and Sabbath observance that seemed like stark austerity to their more easygoing fellow-citizens.

With all these problems, it was clear that James's task as ruler was not going to be an easy one. From the start financial difficulties crowded in upon him. When Parliament refused him added revenues, the King resorted to the imposition of additional customs duties, the grant of monopolies (which interfered with free business), the sale of titles, and the solicitation of "benevolences" (forced loans). Parliament promptly protested against such practices. But Parliament's objections only increased the wrath of the King. The noisiest parliamentarians were imprisoned or sent home with royal scoldings. In 1621, the Commoners entered in their journal a "great protestation" against the King's interference. This so angered James that with his own royal hand he tore the protestation out of the journal and presently dissolved the unruly Parliament. But the quarrel continued and James's last Parliament had the audacity to impeach his lord treasurer.

The dispute with Parliament was embittered by religious conflict. The Puritans, with increasing vigor, were raising objections to Anglican ceremonies, reminiscent of "popery," such as the use of the ring in marriages. They were denouncing Maypole dances, Christmas games, and all festivities not in keeping with an austerely Calvinist view of life. In 1604, a large number of Puritan ministers presented to the King a petition on the reform of the Anglican Church

and their proposals were discussed at a conference at the royal palace of Hampton Court. Taking offence at what he believed were disparagements of the Anglican bishops, James I declared that as for those Puritans who would do away with bishops he would make them conform or "harry them out of the land." James did accede to one of the Puritan requests and appointed a board of scholars to make a new English translation of the Bible. It appeared in 1611 and is called the King James version. It is a masterpiece of English prose, despite its many authors. Fresh and colorful with the vigor of the vernacular, it greatly influenced the style and manner of many later works of English literature.

The religious bitterness was intensified by a rising tide of anti-Catholic feeling. James was suspected of harboring friendly feelings toward the Catholics and wishing to grant them toleration. But when a plot by some fanatical Catholics to blow up the King and the House of Lords was discovered (1605), public opinion forced the application of fierce penalties upon Catholic priests and their adherents. James increased his unpopularity by his foreign policy, for he showed himself determined to make friends with Catholic Spain, the hated enemy of England. To this policy he sacrificed Sir Walter Raleigh, who was executed in 1618 for attacks on Spain which would have been rewarded by Elizabeth. James's failure to take any real part in the Thirty Years' War was motivated partly by his desire to save money and partly by his eagerness to appease Spain. But the fact that he did not help his Calvinist son-in-law, Frederick of the Palatinate, added to the Puritan feeling against him.

Despite the difficulties and troubles of the reign, considerable commercial and colonial progress was made by the English under James I. The East India Company founded by Elizabeth, after some initial setbacks, and in the face of Dutch jealousy and opposition, sponsored a number of successful ventures in Asia. In America, colonies were founded at Jamestown in Virginia (1607) and at Plymouth in New England (1620). The latter was the work of Congregationalists or Separatists, who were opposed to the religious situation in England

and to the laws which punished dissent from Anglicanism. The Bermuda islands were settled in 1612, and were soon, like Virginia, growing tobacco. But the greater the growth of English commerce and colonies, the more the difficulties of the crown increased, for it was the trading classes and the London merchants who were most strongly Puritan, and whose representatives in Parliament were most eager to limit the royal power.

At the death of James in 1625, he was succeeded by his son, Charles, who had been reared in England and should have understood the English better than his father. He was handsome, dignified, and well-mannered. But he proved himself stubborn and unyielding. No less than James, he was eager to maintain all the royal prerogatives. In religion, he was a good Anglican, but he leaned toward that wing called "high church" which believed in forms and ceremonies and which, to rigid Puritans, seemed almost Catholic. From the start, Charles I was in trouble. He married a French Catholic princess who brought hated French priests in her train. He clashed with, and dissolved, his first Parliament, which had attacked his showy but worthless favorite, the Duke of Buckingham. When he made popular moves like sending a fleet against the Spanish port of Cadiz or seeking to aid the French Protestants at La Rochelle, the expeditions failed miserably. A second Parliament which tried to impeach Buckingham was dissolved, and a third was summoned only when the financial situation seemed desperate.

The third Parliament in 1628 granted subsidies to the King, but only in return for his signature to its *Petition of Right*, by which Charles promised not to levy taxes without its authorization, not to establish martial law in peace time, not to quarter soldiers on private houses, and not to order arbitrary arrests or imprisonments. But even these concessions were not enough. Only the assassination of Buckingham prevented Parliament from impeaching that unpopular minister. And soon the House of Commons was attempting to check the unauthorized collection of customs duties by the King (the customs were a major and growing item in the revenues), and to prevent the introduction of "popish" ceremonies into the Anglican Church.

Charles was now so thoroughly disgusted with Parliament that he determined to rule without it. For eleven years (1629–1640), in spite of financial and religious difficulties, he carried on a "personal," as distinct from a parliamentary, government. Had this attempt been in the long run successful, England might well have been transformed into an absolute monarchy like France, and the growth of political liberty and democracy might have been long postponed.

Without the consent of Parliament, Charles was bound not to collect direct taxes. He was therefore driven to the most peculiar expedients. He revived old feudal laws and collected fines for their infraction. He sold monopolies on wine, salt, soap, and coal for large sums, thereby enraging the trading classes, who lost business, and the people, who paid higher prices. Even more obnoxious was a device called "ship money." The king had long had the right to exact money or ships from seaboard towns for the support of the navy. But Charles now sought to regularize these contributions and to collect them from inland towns as well. To test the legality of this procedure, a certain John Hampden, egged on by his Puritan friends, refused to pay the twenty shillings required of him. The majority of the judges, subservient to the King, held that ship money was legal. But Hampden was hailed as a hero by the opponents of the crown.

Opposition to financial exactions continued to go hand in hand with bitter religious disputes. Charles had entrusted the conduct of religious affairs to William Laud, a high-church Anglican whom he named archbishop of Canterbury. Restrictions on Puritans were increased, and certain practices and vestments of the Catholic Church were reinstated in the Anglican Church. Puritan clergy were forced to read from the pulpits a royal declaration encouraging sinful Sunday sports like archery and dancing on the green.

Meanwhile Charles was creating the mechanism of arbitrary rule. Aided by Laud and the able Thomas Wentworth, Earl of Strafford, he developed a strong Privy Council which issued orders to the local justices of the peace. The prerogative courts (like the Star Chamber)[1] were strengthened, and they firmly enforced the King's will. The common-law courts were manned with judges who would support the King. Much that Charles did was worthy. Strafford gave Ireland the best English rule it had ever had. The royal government showed a real concern for the poorer classes and sought to improve their condition. Regulations against economic abuses were elaborated. But all such economic legislation only irked the Puritan business classes, and all Charles' good intentions were vitiated by his arbitrary methods.

In his Scottish policy Charles overreached himself. With the zealous aid of Archbishop Laud, he sought to reform the Scottish Presbyterian Church in an Anglican direction. The angry Scottish Presbyterians signed a covenant, swearing to defend their religion (1638); and, deposing the bishops set over them by the King, they rose in revolt. Failing to crush the rebellion and in desperate need of money for his army, Charles summoned at last another English parliament (1640). After three weeks of bootless wrangling, this so-called Short Parliament was dissolved. Still unable to check the advance of the rebellious Scots into northern England, Charles convoked (1640) a new Parliament, which, because it lasted for twenty years, has been called the Long Parliament. In both England and Scotland, absolute monarchy now faced a crisis —and indeed a rebellion.

B. The Great Rebellion and Cromwell's Puritan Dictatorship

Under the leadership of Puritans like John Pym, John Hampden, and Oliver Cromwell, the Long Parliament, confident of its own strength and the King's weakness, began to assert its authority. With blow after blow it hewed away at the royal authority. The prerogative courts were abolished. The King's financial expedients, like ship money, were forbidden. The King's power to dissolve parliament was annulled, and a "triennial act" required the legislature to meet every three years whether summoned by the King or not. Parliament went

---

[1] See above, p. 288.

further and after long proceedings forced the execution of the King's most loyal servants, Strafford and Laud.

Despite these many victories for Parliament, the King's position was temporarily improved. His armed forces turned back the Scottish invaders, and the outbreak of a rebellion in Ireland seemed to require, for its suppression, a larger royal army which might eventually be utilized to overcome the Parliament. Besides, Parliament itself was becoming divided between extremists and moderates. Charles chose this juncture to make an attempt to strengthen his position. In person he appeared in Parliament (1642) and sought to arrest five members who were his leading opponents. This act produced a definite break between the King and the legislature. Parliament proceeded to pass ordinances without the royal seal and to issue a call to arms. The levy of troops contrary to the King's will was sheer rebellion. Charles in turn raised the royal standard at Nottingham and called his loyal subjects to suppress the rebellion. The issue was squarely joined between absolute monarchy and the revolutionary forces of parliament and Puritanism.

The division of the country between King and Parliament cut across every class and section of the country. Even families were split. But in a general way the King had the support of the titled nobles, the country gentlemen or squires, the "high church" Anglicans, and the remaining Catholics. The royal cause was likewise strong in the north and west of England. In support of Parliament, on the other hand, rallied a minority of the nobility and gentry, and a large majority of the middle-class townsfolk, especially in London, together with the Puritans, Presbyterians, Congregationalists, and religious radicals. Parliament found its strongest support in the south and east of England. The lower classes were less concerned about the issues but tended to go with the leaders of their respective districts. Thus the artisans of London fought for Parliament, and the peasants of the north of England for the King. In common speech, the close cropped heads of the "God-fearing" supporters of Parliament won them the nickname of "Roundheads," while the royalist upper classes, not thinking it a sinful

Trial of Archbishop Laud, in the House of Lords. Wenceslaus Hollar (d. 1677)

vanity to wear their hair in long curls, were called "Cavaliers."

In the Long Parliament, the predominance in religious matters lay with the Presbyterians, who were more radical than those Puritans who merely wished to reform the Anglican Church, and less extreme than the Independents (mainly Congregationalists). The parliamentary majority, therefore, made a "solemn league and covenant" with the Scottish Presbyterians, to establish Presbyterianism throughout the British Isles. Though the royal army won some engagements in 1642 and 1643, it was crushed by the parliamentary forces at Marston Moor (1644). At once the Presbyterian majority in parliament abolished the office of bishop, decreed the removal of altars, and tolerated the smashing of crucifixes, images, and stained glass windows. At this point, the Presbyterians seemed ready to make peace with the King and to restore him to power, if he would accept the new religious settlement.

But the parliamentary army was growing restive. Oliver Cromwell, a stern Independent, had organized a cavalry regiment of "honest sober Christians," who charged into battle singing psalms and acquired by their steel-like invincibility the name of "Ironsides." So successful were Cromwell's troops that a large part of the parliamentary forces were reorganized on his plan into the "New Model" army. This army was strongly Independent in sympathy, hostile to Presbyterian and Anglican alike, and in favor of no compromise with the King.

The New Model army defeated Charles again at Naseby (1645) and compelled his surrender the next year. Then, after some hesitation, its leaders turned against the irresolute Presbyterian majority in parliament. A certain Colonel Pride, backed by his soldiers, "purged" the House of Commons of 143 Presbyterian members (1648), leaving only some sixty Independents to deliberate on the nation's affairs. This "Rump," or sitting part of Parliament, acting on its own authority, appointed a "high court of justice" by whose sentence Charles I was beheaded on January 30, 1649. The Rump then decreed England to be a Commonwealth with neither king nor House of Lords. In the next year, the parliamentary

Oliver Cromwell. After a mezzotint by Peter Lily (d. 1680).

Courtesy Bettmann Archive

army was placed under the supreme command of Oliver Cromwell.

During the ensuing eight years Oliver Cromwell was practical dictator in England. A country gentleman by birth, he had pleaded the Puritan cause in Parliament in 1628, and emerged as a leader of the Independents in the Long Parliament and as the ablest soldier in the civil war. In private life, Cromwell liked music, art, and a cup of wine. But everywhere he carried with him an austere Calvinist conviction that he was doing God's work, and his fiercely eloquent speeches were interlarded with Biblical phrases. His force of character was great, his temper occasionally violent, his statesmanship of a high order. Though he was the leader of the Independents (or Congregationalists) who formed only a minority of the country, the fact that he had the backing of a victorious army made him the real power in the land.

Leaving the Rump to legislate, Cromwell in 1650 put down with fire and rivers of blood the rebellion of the Irish. Then he turned against the Scots, who, dismayed at the ousting of the Presbyterians from Parliament, had rallied to the cause of Prince Charles, son of the executed King. At Worcester (1651) the Scots were defeated, and all the British Isles were at the mercy of

Cromwell and his army. The Rump meanwhile had passed the first great English Navigation Act, which aimed to restrict commerce with England to English ships and was designed to prevent Dutch vessels from trading with England. This law led to a brief Anglo-Dutch naval war, in which the English fared well, but of which Cromwell did not thoroughly approve. In fact, he was becoming disgusted with the Rump and in 1653 he turned it out saying, "Your hour is come, the Lord hath done with you."

For the next five years, Cromwell attempted to provide some legal foundation for his Puritan dictatorship, though without success. First, he assembled a legislature named by himself on the recommendation of Independent ministers. It was given the name of Barebones' Parliament after one of its members with the peculiarly Puritan name of Praisegod Barebones. But it ventured to quarrel with Cromwell, and he dismissed it. Then Cromwell had an Instrument of Government (the first important written constitution in Europe) drawn up. It conferred upon him the title of "Lord Protector" of England for life, and provided for a one-house parliament for England, Scotland, and Ireland, elected by persons not identified with the royalist party. Despite this exclusion of royalists from the polls, the Independents could not win a majority in the new parliament. Before long it was at odds with the Protector, and in 1655 Cromwell abruptly sent it home. Thereafter he made no pretense of consulting popular wishes. The British Isles were divided into areas and each was placed under the rule of a general. Cromwell's power was more absolute than that of Charles I had ever been. With a firm hand he put down Presbyterian, Catholic, and Anglican alike, and repressed the activities of extreme radicals, whether political (the "Levelers"), or economic (the "Diggers"), or religious (the "Fifth Monarchy men").

Despite the dictatorial and tyrannical form of his rule, Cromwell's authority was unshakable and he enjoyed some popularity. He was the beloved leader of an army respected for its rigid discipline and feared for its mercilessness. Under his strict enforcement of order, industry flourished and commerce throve. His conduct of foreign affairs was so skillful that it satisfied English patriotism by increasing England's prestige, and brought profit to many English purses. With the Dutch and the French, Cromwell made advantageous commercial treaties. For the first time in centuries Jews were allowed to come into England, and they brought with them capital and commercial knowledge. By an alliance with France against Spain, the English army won Dunkirk, while the English navy seized Jamaica, sank a Spanish fleet, and brought home shiploads of Spanish silver.

But with all its success Cromwell's rule struck no deep roots in England. His death in 1658 left the army without a master and the country without a government. Oliver's son Richard abdicated after a brief attempt to succeed his father. The army restored the Rump, forced it to recall the ousted Presbyterian members, and then finally obliged the reconstituted Long Parliament to summon a new and freely elected "Convention Parliament." Meanwhile, one of the generals, Monck by name, negotiated for a restoration of the Stuart family to the kingship. In 1660, King Charles II returned from exile and disembarked at Dover. His entry into London was a veritable triumph, "the wayes strew'd with flowers, the bells ringing, the streets hung with tapistry, fountaines running with wine."

England might relax from the long tension of civil war and dictatorship at this royal Restoration, but it could never be the same again. Twenty years of Calvinist rule, with sports and plays and frivolous music banned, had put an end to "Merrie England." The literature had taken on a dreary cast and the greatest poet of the time, John Milton, had latterly been busy with government work and controversial pamphlets. It was only after Cromwell's death that he turned to the composition of his great religious epic, *Paradise Lost.* The grievances and ideals that had inspired the Great Rebellion were being forgotten, and a new generation welcomed with relief the replacement of a stern dictatorship by a restored monarchy which, it was hoped, would operate within the known limits of law and custom.

C. Temporary Stuart Restoration

The narrow basis of Cromwell's popular support explains to some degree the ease with which Charles II won back the crown. The Scots and Irish had hated Cromwell as a bloody conqueror. The Anglicans and the Presbyterians in England had disapproved of his rule. The experiment with Congregationalist republicanism had convinced the majority of people that the old monarchy was a better system. All they now asked were assurances against royal despotism and, where the coin was promises, Charles II was a ready buyer. He swore to observe Magna Carta and the "Petition of Right," to respect Parliament, and to refrain from interfering with religious policy and from levying illegal taxes.

At the return of Charles II, the Anglican bishops and Cavalier nobles resumed their offices. Things seemed to slip back into the old grooves. But the strong monarchy of the Tudors or of the first two Stuarts—James I and Charles I—was not restored. The prerogative courts were not reëstablished, nor was the Privy Council given back its wide powers. Most of the King's old feudal privileges and revenues were abandoned, and there was less talk of the "divine right" of kings. Parliament emerged stronger than before, with a much firmer control of religious and financial matters. Though many a Cavalier noble or squire could not win back the estates he had sold or mortgaged under Cromwell's heavy taxation, it was the landed classes who were dominant during the restoration period (1660–1689). Charles II retained his throne and no small measure of power by coöperating with them, humoring the Parliaments in which they sat, and retreating skillfully whenever the opposition to his policies became too strong.

At the beginning of the reign, the position of the country landholder was strengthened in a way that seemed unimportant but had significant long-run implications. Parliament abolished the surviving feudal fees, dues, and services, so that it was no longer necessary to make payments to the king or another for inheriting an estate, for the wardship of a minor, the marriage of an heiress, and so on. Thus England abandoned the feudal theory that land was held in return for military service to the crown or the overlord, and confirmed the newer principle that land is private property.

In religious policy the Cavalier nobles and squires, staunchly Anglican, had their way. Two thousand Calvinist clergymen were deprived of their offices by an Act of Uniformity (1662), which required clergymen to accept the Anglican prayer-book, while a "Five Mile Act" (1665) kept them at least that distance from their old churches. A Corporation Act (1661) excluded from town offices "dissenters" from Anglicanism, and a Conventicle Act (1664) sought to prevent their religious meetings. Yet in the midst of this triumph of Anglicanism the King had his reservations.

At heart Charles II, and also his brother James, were Catholics, for their mother was a Catholic and they had grown up in exile in the strongly Catholic atmosphere of the French court. Charles, in the secret treaty of Dover (1670), promised Louis XIV, in return for a large pension, to reintroduce Catholicism into England, but, sensing the fierce hatred of "popery" even among the Anglicans, he kept his views to himself, and his formal conversion to the faith of Rome was postponed until the time of his death. James, Duke of York, and heir to the throne, was less tactful or more forthright. His conversion was announced in 1672. At the same time, Charles II, by a royal "declaration of indulgence," suspended the laws against both dissenters and Catholics. This stirred a big wave of anti-Catholic sentiment. Charles II was compelled to withdraw his declaration, and James to give up the public offices he held.

Anti-Catholic feeling reached another high point in 1678 when wild tales of a "popish plot" gained currency. There was no such "plot," but crowds rioted and several noted Catholics were executed as a sacrifice to popular feeling. In the next year, a bill was introduced into Parliament which would have excluded James and any other Catholic from the throne. The Exclusion Bill failed to pass. But from the discussions which it occasioned there gradually emerged in Parliament and in the country two parties. The one which came to be called "Whig" favored the bill and attracted the support of dissenters, of the business classes, and of those landowners who were liberal in their Anglicanism and who wished to strengthen Parliament against the King. The other party, called "Tory," was more rigidly Anglican. Since it upheld the idea of a strong hereditary monarchy and wished both to maintain the *status quo* and at all costs to avoid a renewal of civil war, it opposed the Bill. In the last years of Charles' reign the Whigs were somewhat discredited, and some of them were involved in an abortive rising which sought at Charles' death to put his illegitimate but Protestant son, the Duke of Monmouth, on the throne instead of James.

In economic matters, the Restoration witnessed a relaxation of the internal economic controls used by the Tudors and the first two Stuarts. The guilds had decayed and were unable to reëstablish their monopolies. The old regulations on industry and the grain trade were enforced with less effectiveness. The relief of the poor fell more and more into the hands of the local parish authorities. But with this decrease in the government's control of economic affairs in England, went a strengthening of the regulations on colonial and foreign trade. A Navigation Act of 1660 reënforced the one passed in 1651, and the system was further developed by acts of 1663 and 1673. These laws, taken together, were the bases of English colonial policy and an expression of English mercantilism. Their object was to build up English shipping and to make sure that the trade of the English colonies profited England alone.

This economic legislation was aimed as a direct blow at Dutch dominance in commerce and it led to two more Anglo-Dutch wars. In the first of these (1664–1667) the British seized the Dutch colony of New Amsterdam and rechristened it New York in honor of James, Duke of York. But the Dutch fleet swept the Channel clear of English shipping and the Dutch Admiral De Ruyter even sailed up the Thames and terrorized London. The second of the Anglo-Dutch wars (1672–1674) was merged in the attack of the French on Holland. During its course, the English public and parliamentary pressure forced Charles II to withdraw from

the attack on Holland and then to join the anti-French alliance. The English were coming to see that their chief rival, the real threat to their commercial and colonial progress, was not Holland but France. They were coming to realize, too, that the union of Catholicism and absolutism which Louis XIV represented in Europe was what they feared both abroad and at home. Henceforth, for nearly a century and a half, England's wars were with France.

The mid-1660's were memorable years in the history of London, which had been rapidly growing into an important center of trade and industry, and now ranked in Europe with Amsterdam or Paris or Lisbon. In 1665, London was swept by the plague. Though two thirds of the population (estimated at 460,000) fled to avoid the contagion, more than 75,000 died amid scenes of terror. The next spring the Dutch Admiral De Ruyter sailed up the Thames, burning English shipping and bringing dismay to the almost defenseless metropolis. The following autumn a great fire swept over London and reduced most of the older sections of the city to ashes. From these tribulations London rose larger and more important than ever. Its commerce kept the Thames busy with ships plying to every part of Europe, to the Near East, to the American colonies, and to India. Its merchant class was growing rapidly in wealth. The goldsmiths had become private bankers and were accepting deposits and lending out large sums.

Though parliament had voted Charles II a royal revenue that totaled about £1,200,000, the sum was insufficient for the expenses of his government. Despite his pension from Louis XIV, Charles was forced to borrow continually. In 1672, he announced that instead of paying back a million and a quarter pounds he had borrowed from a group of goldsmiths, he would consider the sum as a permanent loan. This hardly added to the popularity of the crown.

A puritanically minded business man had other reasons for disapproving of Charles, for the royal court represented a complete reaction from the austerity of Cromwell's time. Surrounded by a bevy of mistresses, Charles set an example of blatant immorality which was imitated by many of the upper

James II. After a portrait by Sir Godfrey Kneller (d. 1723).

Courtesy Bettmann Archive

classes. Manners, copied from the French, were polished, but language was coarse. Gambling was all the rage. The theatres had been opened again, and the witty dramatists of the time imitated French models with bawdy gusto. The courtiers and their imitators, with gaudy clothes and indolent manners, flocked to see such plays as William Wycherley's *The Gentleman Dancing Master*, or Sir George Etherege's *The Man of Mode or Sir Fopling Flutter*. It was all a far cry from the psalms and sermons of Cromwell's day.

It was his good-natured tact which carried Charles II sucessfully through a difficult reign of twenty-five years. Without principles, he sought only to maintain his position and to increase his authority. He was always ready to compromise or to retreat. So skillfully did he use the feeling against the Whigs, which arose from their excesses, that during the last four years of his reign he was able to rule without Parliament. When he died in 1685, the position of the crown seemed firm and even strong. But the ensuing years were to witness dramatic changes.

Uprisings in Scotland and in England (led by the Duke of Monmouth) greeted the accession of James II, but were easily put down. The country wanted no more civil war. Indeed, James might have ruled successfully had he been a Protestant, or had he been willing to play a secondary role and give real power to Parliament. It was

the combination of his Catholicism with his attempts to rule more and more despotically that roused the fear and opposition of the English leaders and of the masses of the people.

In the three years following 1685, James gave ample evidence that he was eager to increase his own power and to favor Catholicism. Even the Tories, who believed in strong royal rule, were shocked by his attempt to create a standing professional army and to officer it with Catholics. In addition, he relaxed the laws against Catholics and dissenters by a new "declaration of indulgence" (1687) and sought to place Catholics in high posts in the universities of Oxford and Cambridge, and in the town and royal governments. When he ordered a second "declaration of indulgence" read from the church pulpits (1688), seven Anglican bishops objected, and, since no jury would convict them, they were acquitted of the charges brought against them.

D. The "Glorious" Revolution of 1688–1689

Though James had alienated both Whigs and Tories, he might have kept his throne but for a change in the prospective royal succession. He was now fifty-five years old and his heirs were his two daughters by a first marriage: Mary, wife of her cousin William III, Stadholder of Holland; and Anne, married to a Danish prince. Both of these daughters and both their husbands were Protestants. So long as his heirs were Protestants, the country might have been willing to put up with James II. But in the late spring of 1688, a son was born to James by his second and Catholic wife, Mary of Modena. The boy would not only take precedence over his sisters in the succession, but obviously he would be reared in the Catholic faith. Almost at once, the English leaders, Whig and Tory alike, began conspiring to oust James and to bring in William and Mary as rulers. William listened with interest to the proposals, since he was eager to swing England into line against France for the war that was then in the making.[1]

In November 1688, William landed in

[1] See above, p. 428.

England with a small Dutch army. Welcomed enthusiastically by the Protestant masses, the Dutch Stadholder entered London without opposition. James, deserted by his army, fled to France. The revolution was quite bloodless in England. In Ireland, however, there was a popular Catholic rising in favor of James, which William was able to crush in the decisive battle of the Boyne (1690). An irregular parliament presented William and Mary with the crown as joint sovereigns, declaring that James had tried to overthrow the constitution of the kingdom, and, by his flight, had left the throne vacant.

The inner meaning of this revolution was that henceforth Parliament, not the king, was to be supreme in the British Isles. If Parliament could put aside the rightful king and his son (James, called the "Old Pretender"), and give the crown to others, then its authority was final. To be sure, the king still seemed to have considerable power, but the "Glorious" Revolution was a decisive turning point in the growth of parliamentary supremacy. It must be remembered that the Parliament of the time was by no means democratic. The system of election was such that in the country it was the big landowners who had the real influence, and in the towns and cities it was the wealthy members of the middle class. For nearly a century and a half after the Revolution, England was to be ruled by an aristocratic Parliament which represented not the people as a whole, but rather the landlords and wealthy merchants.

In establishing its own power, however, the aristocratic Parliament enacted legislation which, by limiting royal authority, did protect all citizens from royal tyranny. The Declaration of Rights (1689), which became law as the Bill of Rights, provided that the sovereign must be an Anglican, that the King could not suspend laws by declaration or otherwise, and that he could not maintain any army or levy taxes without the consent of Parliament. It provided that the King should not interfere with free speech, free elections, or free discussion in Parliament, and that the people should be allowed to make petitions to the King. It likewise demanded impartial juries and frequent parliaments. In addition, Parliament adopted a new device for strengthening its

position. From 1689 on, it granted taxes and made appropriations for the army for one year only, and it similarly passed the Mutiny Act (requiring soldiers to obey orders under penalty of court maritial) only for a year at a time. A compromise on religion was also part of the "settlement" of 1689. While the "Toleration Act" (1689) imposed exceptionally severe restrictions and penalties on Catholics and debarred non-Anglicans from public affairs, it accorded to the dissenting Protestant sects full freedom of conscience and of public worship.

Here were the first fruits of the Revolution of 1689. Absolute monarchy was finally overthrown in Britain. Parliament was entrenched in power. The Protestant character of the state was confirmed. The influence and predominance of the British aristocracy were strengthened.

William III accepted the changes in the system of government because his main interest was in bringing England into the War of the League of Augsburg (1689–1697) against France, and this he was able to do successfully, with the support of Parliament and the English people. But there were other results of the new position of Parliament. Now that taxes and expenditures were increasingly under its control, people were more ready to lend money to the government and in 1693 it became possible to organize a regular national debt. At the start people who subscribed to loans received ten per cent interest, but the rate fell rapidly to four and even three per cent. In the eighteenth century the English Government could raise large sums of money at a very low cost. In 1694, moreover, the Bank of England was founded, and though it was a private institution, it proved itself invaluable to the government in holding deposits, sending funds abroad, advancing short term credits, and managing the national debt. During the same period, England reformed and regularized its coinage, and the techniques of buying and selling stock in the various companies and of writing insurance were rapidly improved. By 1700 England not only had a more businesslike government, and one friendly to the commercial interests, but it also had a financial system that was able to meet the growing demands of the ensuing decades.

E. Triumph of Parliamentary Government

Since William III was more interested in foreign war and diplomacy than in domestic affairs, he tended to leave the management of English matters to his ministers. He found that the wheels of government turned more smoothly if, when the Whigs held a majority of seats in the House of Commons, all the ministers were Whigs. On the other hand, if the Tories gained the upper hand, it seemed better to have the king's ministers, or the "cabinet" as they began to be called, Tories instead of Whigs. Thus the tenure of a cabinet came slowly to be dependent on its ability to command a majority in parliament. In fact, as the ministers were members of one of the houses of the legislature, they came gradually to be a sort of committee whose duty it was to see that the will of Parliament was carried out. Since the cabinet enforced the laws and carried on the administration, it was clear that Parliament was getting control of the executive as well as the legislative functions of the British Government.

In 1701, Parliament again asserted its authority by determining who should succeed William III. By an Act of Settlement, it excluded the Catholic heirs of James II, together with all other Catholics, and directed that the crown should pass to Anne and her heirs. If she had no children, it was to go at her death to Sophia of Hanover and her heirs. This Sophia was a granddaughter of James I and the daughter of the Calvinist Count Palatine of the Rhine whose election as King of Bohemia had inflamed the Thirty Years' War.[1] The Act likewise provided that England should not be required to wage war on behalf of the foreign possessions of its ruler without the consent of Parliament, and it placed a number of other restrictions on the crown. Of these the most important was that royal judges should hold office "during good behavior" and not "at the king's pleasure." Unsuitable judges were to be removed only at the request of Lords and Commons. Parliament was gaining control of the judiciary as well as the executive.

Anne, who succeeded William III in 1702, was more English than he and more active

---

[1] See above, p. 395.

in English affairs. She was the last English sovereign who vetoed acts of Parliament, and toward the close of her reign she chose a Tory cabinet in the face of a Whig majority in the House of Commons. It was this cabinet that negotiated the Peace of Utrecht on terms reasonably favorable to Louis XIV. Though Anne might act as if she were sovereign by right instead of the will of Parliament, she was uneasily conscious that her half-brother, the son of James II, had a better claim to the throne than she and that this "Old Pretender," as he came to be called, had many supporters in England, and especially in Scotland, who would have liked to see him on the throne of England as James III.

It was partly to ensure the succession of the Protestant descendants of Sophia of Hanover that the parliaments of England and of Scotland in 1707 passed the Act of Union which finally fused the two kingdoms into one—Great Britain. The English Parliament at Westminster was transformed into a British Parliament by the inclusion of Scottish lords and commoners. Though the Union had been opposed in Scotland and was put through there only by bribery and pressure, it gave new prosperity to the northern kingdom by bringing it into the English commercial and colonial system and removing trade barriers between the two parts of the island. It gave to able Scots a chance to win wider political power in the new united government.

At Anne's death (1714) there were, indeed, plots to put the Old Pretender on the throne. The next year "James III" actually landed in Scotland, rallied some support, and advanced toward England. But his army of clansmen was defeated at Preston, and he soon had to return to the continent. Meanwhile, the son of Sophia of Hanover had come to London and as George I had firmly seated his ponderous form on the British throne.

George I (1714–1727) was dazzled by the fortune that thus dropped a rich kingdom in his lap. But he was slow of wit; he spoke no English; and he was far more interested in German affairs than in British. After some half-hearted attempts to carry on cabinet meetings in broken Latin, George simply stopped attending them and left his

English ministers to handle the complicated parliamentary politics which he did not understand.

George II (1727–1760) spoke broken English, but his heart, too, was in German Hanover where he was an absolutist prince. In so far as the first two Georges understood British politics at all, they favored the Whigs, who had consistently supported the Hanoverian succession, whereas many Tories had been "Jacobites," or partisans of the Stuart pretender. In general, these Kings left the Whig cabinet to rule the country, and the Whigs, profiting from the discredit of the Tories and consolidating their position by bribery and parliamentary manipulation, were able to maintain themselves in power during the whole of the two reigns. The Kings accepted every act of Parliament and never ventured to exercise the royal right of veto, which fell into disuse. The first two Georges reigned, but they did not rule. And the British were content to have it so, for to them the Kings were foreigners who were endured because they were symbols representing the Protestant royal succession.

It was during this period of Whig ascendancy that cabinet government emerged and that the office of prime minister came into existence. For twenty-one years (1721–1742) Sir Robert Walpole managed to retain the royal favor and the control of a majority in the House of Commons. Though he disclaimed any such title, he was generally recognized as "prime" minister, prime in importance, prime in executive authority, with the selection of the rest of the cabinet virtually in his hands. Thenceforth it became a tradition that the crown should appoint from the majority party in Parliament the prime minister, or head of the cabinet, and that all other cabinet ministers should be appointed by the crown upon the nomination of the prime minister.

The king was still the head of the state and in law still the ruler of his kingdom. In his name were all laws passed and treaties made. Under him both church and state were administered. But in practice, by the traditions and precedents that made up the unwritten British constitution, most of the king's functions were delegated to his "government"—to a prime minister and cabinet who were not his agents but representatives of Parliament. It was the cabinet that carried on the real business of government. Thus, by the mid-eighteenth century the king could not levy taxes, make laws, maintain an army, control the judiciary, or even appoint ministers, save with parliamentary sanction. The British system of government had evolved through two revolutions and much religious and political turmoil, from a more or less "absolute" monarchy under the Tudors, to the "limited" monarchy of the Hanoverians. The limitations on British monarchy in the eighteenth century consisted in the well-nigh complete power of Parliament, and this Parliament was dominated by a wealthy oligarchy of landowners aided by powerful commercial interests. But even under the Whig oligarchy of the eighteenth century, Britain was an object of admiration to thoughtful men on the continent of Europe, for in limiting royal powers Parliament had built up a respect for courts and for law which went far toward protecting individual rights, and Parliament itself was a forum where citizens could plead the public interests.

CHAPTER 40

The American Revolution

A. Conflict Between Britain and Its Colonies

The American Revolution was not merely a matter of British concern. It had important effects on France and indeed on the whole later history of Europe and the world. In part, it arose because the English had transported overseas, to their thirteen colonies along the North American seaboard, their own system of law and courts which protected and maintained the rights of individuals, and because they had permitted a considerable degree of self-government by provincial legislature, while at the same time they subjected the colonials to irksome mercantilist regulations. The American colonials were conscious of their rights as Britishers and had sufficient political experience to know how to organize for their defense.

Until the end of the Seven Years' War, two factors kept American discontent in check. In the first place, the British policy tended to be one of "salutary neglect." Trade laws, though strict, were enforced sporadically. Evasion was easy, and sober New England merchants smuggled their goods blithely through the loopholes they so readily found. In the second place, the existence of French Canada to the north and French Louisiana to the west kept the English colonists vividly aware of the value of the British army and navy as agencies of defense.

Both these factors were changed at the close of the Seven Years' War. Canada became British, and at the same time the British government decided to tighten up the enforcement of its trade regulations and to make the colonies pay a share of the costs of imperial defense. This program was sponsored by King George III and the ministers through whom he was trying to gain more influence in the government of Great Britain. Indeed, during the whole of the struggle between Britain and the colonies, there was a parallel political conflict within Britain. The center of the strife was King George III himself, for he was trying to build a party of his own among the ruling Whigs, so that he might regain some of the power that his predecessors had lost. By patronage, influence, corruption, and favors, the king sought to rule and to see to it that the government was in the hands of followers like Lord Bute or Lord North. In opposition to the King, the "old Whigs," like the Marquess of Rockingham, Edmund Burke, and later Charles James Fox, sought to thwart the King's efforts and to maintain the parliamentary supremacy that had been gradually built up since 1689. With this group were usually aligned the elder William Pitt (Earl of Chatham) and his large following.

In pursuance of the new policies with regard to the colonies, the British prime minister, George Grenville, in 1764 put through Parliament the Sugar Act. It actually reduced the duties on sugar and molasses brought from the British West Indies to New England, much of which was made into rum for exchange for furs and slaves.

But while the duties were cut, a determined effort to collect them and to check smuggling was made. "Writs of assistance" were issued to the customs collectors to enable them to search private houses. In the next year (1765) the Stamp Act was passed. This sought to raise £100,000 from the colonies by a stamp tax on legal documents, pamphlets, and newspapers. The opposition to these acts in the colonies was immediate and became effective when the colonists began to refuse to purchase British goods. Trade with Britain fell off precipitously. Respectable citizens formed groups called "Sons of Liberty." More important, even, nine colonies, led by Virginia and Massachusetts, sent delegates to a congress which met in New York and adopted resolutions opposing the Stamp Act as contrary to the traditional rights of the colonists.

In fact, in the debates over the Stamp Act the constitutional issue between Britain and the colonies was sharply drawn. The British government held that the colonists were "virtually represented" in Parliament just as were the new cities of Liverpool or Sheffield which elected no members to it. But the Americans, who had developed a system by which the member of a legislature actually represented the district in which he lived, insisted that they were not represented in Parliament and could not, therefore, properly be taxed by it. So violent was the colonial opposition to the Stamp Act that Grenville was forced out of office and Rockingham, the new prime minister, sympathetic to the Americans, secured the repeal of the hated law.

But in 1767 occurred a new attempt to make the colonies provide revenues. Charles Townshend, chancellor of the exchequer, put through a series of acts which levied duties on the importation into the colonies of certain goods, such as glass, lead, paper, and tea, and provided for rigorous collection. Again the colonies protested, and by agreements stopped their importation of British goods. The colonists had previously argued that external duties on trade could be imposed by Parliament and that only internal taxes were improper. Now they opposed the new levies, and their antagonism was only heightened when the legislature in Massachusetts was dissolved for expressing its disapproval of the Townshend Acts. The sale of British goods in the colonies fell off rapidly. People wore homespun cloth and drank sassafras tea.

Resistance led to violence in Boston. Customs officials were beaten up and troops were brought in from Halifax to keep order. Finally in March 1770 blood was shed. The "Boston Massacre" started mildly enough when some snowballs were thrown at the red-coated soldiers. But before it was over shots were fired and four Bostonians were killed. It was by chance that it was on the same day that the new ministry of Lord North got Parliament to repeal all the Townshend duties save only the tax on tea.

Feeling had run too high, however, to be easily soothed. The more radical of the American leaders like Samuel Adams of Massachusetts and Patrick Henry of Virginia kept up their agitation. "Committees of Correspondence" were organized and chapters of Freemasons communicated anti-British sentiments to each other. The duty on tea had been retained to maintain in principle the British right to levy taxes on the colonies, and it was to this principle that the colonists now objected. On December 16, 1773, men dressed up like Indians seized three ships in Boston Harbor and dumped 342 chests of tea into the water.

The "Tea Party" brought a quick reaction intended to cow the rebellious colonists. The British Parliament, led by Lord North, passed the famous five "intolerable acts" (1774). Massachusetts was practically deprived of self-government. Boston Harbor was closed. Troops were quartered on the colonists. In the same year, though for different reasons, Parliament passed a law that seemed to many of the colonials equally threatening. The Quebec Act was intended to settle some of the questions regarding western lands, Canada, and the Indians. But by granting complete religious freedom to the Catholics in Canada it stirred the ire of the New England Calvinists, and by assigning to Quebec all the land north of the Ohio River, it seemed to ignore the claims of four colonies to westward expansion and to eliminate possibilities of settlement, speculation, and trade with the Indians.

Thus it was that when the first Continen-

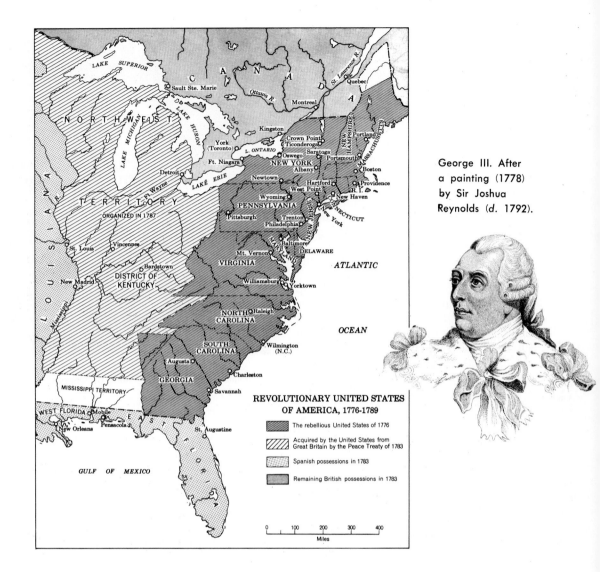

REVOLUTIONARY UNITED STATES
OF AMERICA, 1776-1789

The rebellious United States of 1776

Acquired by the United States from
Great Britain by the Peace Treaty of 1783

Spanish possessions in 1783

Remaining British possessions in 1783

George III. After
a painting (1778)
by Sir Joshua
Reynolds (d. 1792).

tal Congress met at Philadelphia in September 1774, though it had been summoned to secure the redress of grievances and concert measures of opposition that would force the British to recognize the rights of the colonists, there was much that the more radical members could point to as reason for going further. The Congress passed a Declaration of Rights and Grievances, and Lord North, under some pressure from friends of America like the Earl of Chatham and Edmund Burke, put through a Conciliatory Resolve. But this last step came too late, for in April 1775 hostilities broke out at Lexington and Concord. The American Revolution was beginning.

B. The War of American Independence

Matters would hardly have issued in armed conflict if the political and economic events just outlined had not been reënforced by other factors. Americans had long felt that they were being exploited by England and its manufacturers and merchants. Even rich Virginia planters were deeply in debt to British mercantile houses and the debts were passed on from father to son. The industries of the colonists had been throttled, their commerce restricted, and their finances restrained. The privilege of being part of the British commercial empire and collecting bounties on the production of goods like indigo and naval stores no longer seemed an adequate compensation. In addition, the British were woefully ignorant about the colonies and treated the colonials as social inferiors. They ignored even the religious needs of the colonists. There was, for instance, no Anglican bishop in America, so that an Anglican from Virginia or New York, in order to be confirmed, had to journey to England. Moreover, it must be remembered that by 1775 many of the inhabitants of the colonies were not English. There were many Scotch, Scotch-Irish, Germans, or French who had no particular ties of affection to the mother country.

Leading colonists were also much affected by the currents of eighteenth century thought. They had read Locke on natural rights and on the social contract between sovereign and subject. Some of them had read Montesquieu on the limitation of royal power and Rousseau on rule by the people. If many of the wealthier colonials put loyalty to the king above all else, the majority believed that they were being unjustly oppressed and that tyranny must be resisted as it had been in the days of Charles I or of James II. Indeed the Revolution was in some senses a civil war in both America and in Britain. In every colony there was an important minority, often including many of the leading citizens who fought for, worked for, or at least hoped for the success of the British army. More than seventy thousand "loyalists" left the colonies during the course of the war or at its close. Many more than that at length made their peace with their fellow-citizens. In Britain, in the Parliament and outside it, there were, during the whole period, many who wished for the success of the colonists, sometimes because they thought the American cause was just, often because they wanted the King to be defeated in his attempt to increase the authority of the crown. Many British officers gave up their commissions rather than fight against the Americans with whom they had marched against the French. Jeffrey Amherst, the captor of Louisburg and Montreal, refused to take command of the British troops in New England.

Practically, after Lexington and Concord, and intellectually, after the ringing sen-

Thomas Paine. After a painting by George Romney (d. 1802).

Courtesy Bettmann Archive

tences of Thomas Paine's pamphlet *Common Sense* (January 1776), there was no possibility of turning back for the Americans. But the definitive breaking point was the Declaration of Independence written by Thomas Jefferson and adopted by the Second Continental Congress on July 4, 1776. Its eloquent phrases are a summary of the best political thought of the preceding centuries and a bright beacon in the intellectual history of the Western world:

We hold these truths to be self-evident, that all men are created equal, that they are endowed by their Creator with certain unalienable Rights, that among these are Life, Liberty and the pursuit of Happiness. That to secure these rights, Governments are instituted among Men, deriving their just powers from the consent of the governed. That whenever any Form of Government becomes destructive of these ends, it is the Right of the People to alter or to abolish it, and to institute new Government, laying its foundation on such principles and organizing its powers in such form, as to them shall seem most likely to effect their Safety and Happiness.

From the start the thirteen former colonies had a major problem in securing a minimum of coöperation among themselves. The Articles of Confederation adopted by the Congress in 1777 were not ratified by the requisite number of states until 1781. Even then, lack of a federal executive or judiciary and the absence of power in Congress to deal with taxation and trade made this first attempt at federal union too weak to be effective. But gradually the neccessities of war taught the new sovereign states some lessons about working together.

Despite this increasing though very imperfect unity among the states, despite the steadfast and adroit leadership of George Washington, and despite the great difficulties that the Atlantic Ocean and the large size of the area to be reconquered imposed upon the British, it is hard to see how the Americans could have won a definite victory in the war without foreign aid. For example, from the autumn of 1776 to the very end of the war the British held the central and strategic port of New York. Or again, the Congress financed the war with larger and larger issues of paper money which rapidly depreciated in value and might have become worthless without the help of funds from abroad.

But France, still smarting from defeat in the Seven Years' War, had from the start viewed the American cause with sympathy and perceived in it an opportunity for revenge against England by helping to disrupt her empire. Influenced by the adroit propaganda of Benjamin Franklin, American emissary to Versailles, and impressed by the crushing defeat of Burgoyne at Saratoga (October 17, 1777), France in 1778 formed an alliance with the United States and declared war on Britain. The French aided the Americans with money and supplies, and also with troops and naval support. It was the momentary superiority of the French navy that enabled the Franco-American forces to compel the surrender of Lord Cornwallis at Yorktown in Virginia in 1781, an event which virtually decided the struggle in America, since all the reserve strength of Great Britain was required in the West Indies, Europe, and Asia.

In addition, French diplomacy secured the adherence of Spain to the anti-British alliance (1779). Holland, indignant at the English pressure against Dutch commerce, likewise declared war on Britain (1780). Indeed, the arrogant maritime policy of the British and their practice of stopping, searching, and seizing neutral vessels led Catherine the Great of Russia to protest vigorously. In 1780, Russia with Sweden and Denmark formed an "armed neutrality of the North" to uphold neutral rights against the British. Prussia, Portugal, the Two Sicilies, and the Holy Roman Empire subsequently confronted Great Britain with an almost unanimously hostile Europe by adhering to this "armed neutrality."

In the Mediterranean, the French and Spanish took Minorca from the British, but failed in an attempt to capture Gibraltar. In India, the French and their allies were defeated by the British. The French Admiral Suffren, however, gained such victories at sea as to threaten English maritime control in the east. It looked for a while as if the French navy, rebuilt and reconstituted since 1763, might successfully challenge British sea-power. But such hopes were dashed in April 1782, when the English Admiral Rodney overwhelmed the French fleet under De Grasse at the battle near the islands called "the Saints" in the West Indies.

Despite this naval victory, Britain, unsuccessful in America, inglorious in India, expelled from Minorca, faced with revolt in Ireland, and weary of war, was very ready for peace. But still secure behind the Channel, victorious at sea, unshaken in India, Britain was by no means humbled. Defeat, but not humiliation, was the keynote of the treaties which Great Britain concluded in 1783 with the United States at Paris and with France and Spain at Versailles.

By the treaty of Paris, the former thirteen colonies were recognized as the sovereign and independent United States of America. By the treaty of Versailles, France acquired Tobago in the West Indies and Senegal in Africa, which she had lost in 1763. Spain recovered the island of Minorca and the American territory of Florida. The Netherlands, concluding a separate peace in 1784, fared less well. It was forced to yield commercial stations in India and a share in the trade of the East Indian islands to the British.

The significance of the War of American

Independence went far beyond anything to be found in the terms of the peace treaties. It was in fact manifold:

(1) Britain lost the most populous of her colonies, and a new independent nation of European origin, destined for greatness, appeared across the Atlantic.

(2) Since the American Revolution was in good part a rising against mercantilist restrictions, it reënforced the *laissez-faire* theories of Adam Smith and cast grave doubts on the ultimate wisdom of such policies. Perhaps when other colonies became strong and wealthy they would likewise drop off the mother tree like ripe pears, and become independent. The doubts about the value of commercial restraints were accentuated by a fact which soon became evident. Before long, Britain was doing a more thriving trade with the independent United States than she had ever done with the colonies.

(3) France secured a partial revenge for her defeat in the Seven Years' War. But she did so at considerable cost. Her finances, already shaky, were cast into utter confusion by the expenses incurred. What had been a difficult financial problem now became insoluble.

(4) In Britain the ill-success of George III and his favorite ministers in the war discredited them in a very large degree and spelled the failure of the King's attempts to increase the royal power. In a very real way, the success of American (and French) arms helped to preserve limited monarchy and political liberty in Britain.

(5) The American Revolution produced a series of political innovations which were to be of the utmost importance in the coming years.

(6) The ideas and experiences of the American Revolution were ultimately to affect many lands. Almost immediately they were to have a most significant influence on France.

These last two points are of such importance that they will be treated more at length in the next two sections.

C. American Political Innovations

From the American Revolution and its attendant international war emerged the United States as an independent country basing its right to existence on popular sovereignty and successful revolution. Its very origin made this new nation a horrible example for absolute monarchs and a source of inspiration for oppressed peoples. Besides, in the course of its revolution and afterwards, the United States came to exemplify a series of very important political ideas. They can be summarized in four words: republicanism, democracy, federalism, and constitutionalism.

There had, to be sure, been republics in ancient Greece and Rome, among the Italian city states (like Venice), and in Switzerland. But the United States was far larger than the previous examples, so large that it had to invent a complicated system of representative government. It was, moreover, quite self-conscious about its republicanism. Thomas Paine's anti-monarchical slogans and their own objections to George III had convinced most Americans that the day of kings was over. There were those who had their doubts. Some would have made George Washington king. A few even thought it might legitimize the new government to have a descendant of the Stuart kings to lead it. But when the new constitution came to be written it was starkly republican and required each state to have a "republican form of government."

At first the state legislatures which supplanted the colonial assemblies were not very democratic. The franchise was limited to males and usually to landowners and the more well-to-do classes. Often, too, there were religious qualifications tending to exclude Catholics or even some kinds of Protestants. But there was no hereditary aristocracy and in a growing and developing country new people acquired wealth. If, at first, office holding was restricted to men of substance, and indirect elections were used to limit the power of the masses, still it was not long before men of the people began to rise to power. Gradually, and indeed rather rapidly, religious disabilities and property qualifications for voting or office were done away with in one state after another.

As with republics, there had also been federations before. In fact, the British empire in 1774 was a sort of a federation, since there were legislatures with some power in many of the colonies. But the United States was the first extensive, carefully and consciously thought out example of federalism. It was a working contradiction, a sovereign nation composed of "sovereign states." It pointed out a way of reconciling local and national interests and of keeping some powers close to home. It showed that diverse peoples with divergent interests could still come together under a single government for common purposes. The American example of federalism has had weighty influence on the formation of many nations, from Latin American republics (like Brazil or Colombia) to other former British colonies (Canada, Australia, India) and even to the Union of the Soviet Socialist Republics.

When a convention met in the State House at Philadelphia in May of 1787, under the presidency of George Washington, to do something about the inter-state disputes that had arisen under the old Articles of Confederation, and possibly to devise a stronger form of central government, its members were well aware of the idea of a constitution. The "Instrument of Government" in the England of Cromwell, the unwritten traditions of British government, the colonial charters, the new state constitutions, the Articles of Confederation themselves were all in one way or another examples. Yet the Federal Constitution was the first to be devised and adopted by elected representatives for a whole nation. It, so to speak, focussed and brought together all thinking on a written constitution, the experiments of the various states in forming their own governments, the experience with the (to the colonists) unfortunate flexibility of the unwritten British constitution, the writings of a hundred authors from Hobbes to Jefferson.

The Constitution, which went into effect in 1789, enshrined many important political ideas—republicanism, limited government, the separation of powers, checks and balances, representative legislatures—but it was in itself an idea of the utmost importance. Since that time, almost every new nation, whether formed by revolution or otherwise, has sought to devise a constitution and then to secure its ratification by some form of popular approval. Very shortly after 1789 another American innovation

was included in the Constitution, for the first ten amendments were declared in force in December 1791. Taken together they constitute a "Bill of Rights," designed to protect the individual citizen from the government. They guarantee the rule of law, the separation of church and state, and the freedom of speech, press, petition, and assembly.

The example of America was heightened in importance by the fact that the new ideas worked, and the government was from the start conducted with effectiveness and success. Indeed the first presidents (Washington, John Adams, Jefferson, and Madison) and their cabinet officers were men of such unusual ability and distinction that they were able rather rapidly to fill in, by setting precedents, any gaps in the constitutional framework. And from the start it was apparent that the bold American experiment had extraordinary vitality.

D. Impact of the American Revolution on France

Even before the peace treaty with the United States, George III had been forced to dismiss Lord North and his cabinet and to bring in more liberal ministers. Several reforms were soon effected. The Irish parliament was granted an almost independent position (1782) and Catholic Irishmen were given the right to vote (1793). In 1800, the Irish parliament was fused with that at Westminster,[1] and thereafter, for more than a century, the British Isles were known as the United Kingdom of Great Britain and Ireland. But even more important were the steps begun much later (1839–1849) by which former colonies were gradually transformed into self-governing dominions.

More immediate and more dramatic were the effects of the American Revolution on France. The ringing phrases of the Declaration of Independence on liberty, equality, and the rights of man woke echoes in France. The anti-monarchical writings of the Americans and their British sympathizers could be applied to Louis XVI as well as to George III. For the French such propa-

---

[1] From this, however, Catholics were excluded until 1829.

ganda was greatly reënforced by the fact that many of their navy and army officers, such as the Marquis de Lafayette, had been to America, mingled with Americans, and seen republican institutions at work. Benjamin Franklin with his great reputation as a scientist, his deliberate homespun simplicity, and his shrewd tongue had been an eloquent exponent of the new principles. French Freemasons were in contact with their American brothers.

When the American states and eventually the United States drew up constitutions, they were eagerly read and discussed in intellectual circles in France. Here was republicanism in practice. Here were the rights of men guaranteed. Here was human equality being written into law. It is not too much to say that the American Revolution was a decisive blow at both divine-right monarchy and aristocratic privilege in France. The lessons it taught were sharpened by the fact that, in good part as a result of its participation in the American war, the French monarchy was slipping into a kind of financial chaos that hampered its efforts at efficiency and reform, showed up its every weakness, and gave its opponents manifold opportunities. To understand why France was so vulnerable to new ideas and to demands for change the state of that nation in 1789 must be examined.

One factor in the situation was the fact that the seeds brought to France from America fell on ground already well plowed. The thinkers of the "enlightenment" were not merely propounding abstract notions. Much of what they said was a direct or indirect attack on the social and political order in which they lived. The existing authorities, natural upholders of traditional law, government, and religion, realized the subversive nature of the attacks; and many of the French *philosophes* spent some time in exile or in prison, while their writings were censored or banned. Yet the same authorities were fascinated by the new ideas. If condemned by church or state government, if in trouble with police or the courts, a *philosophe* could usually find a highly placed protector at home or abroad who would grant him help and refuge till the storm blew over. A book supressed in France

Benjamin Franklin. Painting by Charles Willson Peale (*d.* 1827).

Courtesy Bettmann Archive

could be published in Amsterdam. Sometimes it was printed in Paris with "Amsterdam" on the title page to deceive the censors.

It is true that the *philosophes* were constructing a positive system of thought which was to be the main basis of nineteenth-century liberalism. They stood in general for toleration (or indifference) in religion, for individual rights and limited government in politics, for greater equality between classes in society, for *laissez-faire* in economics, and for rationalism and materialism in philosophy. But inevitably, as they advocated these ideas, they found themselves attacking almost every aspect of of the existing society which was founded and organized on quite different principles. Because they wrote well and vigorously, because, despite their many quarrels and squabbles, they formed a sort of united intellectual front, because their ideas seemed modern, novel, and exciting, the *philosophes* exercised a tremendous influence in most intellectual or would-be intellectual circles. Even wealthy nobles and highly placed churchmen, who profited most from the existing order, took up the "enlightened" theories and discussed them with interest and even enthusiasm.

Rousseau well illustrates these generalizations. He was a very difficult person to get along with. He never kept a friend for long. He usually attacked his benefactors and quarreled with his supporters. But he never lacked patrons. Counts, dukes, high-born ladies took him in and gave him shelter. Louis XV would have given him a pension had he come to court when invited to do so. Society ladies wept over his *Nouvelle Héloïse,* and the salons eagerly argued about his *Social Contract.* Yet the ideas that Rousseau propounded were definitely revolutionary. He attacked the very basis and the whole fabric of the existing order.

For example, in his *Social Contract* he maintained that governments had been formed by men for their own benefit, and should have been instruments of social well-being. Instead, they had grown rigid and tyrannical. With their repressive laws and oppressive taxes, with their police and armies and officials, they destroyed liberty and enslaved men. Everywhere man was perverted from his natural goodness by bad government. The solution was to establish new and better governments representative of, and responsible to, the "popular will."

Criticism of the existing order was just as clear, if less radical, in the works of thinkers other than Rousseau. Thus it was that the late eighteenth century presented a curious picture. Intellectual leaders did not believe in the society in which they lived. In France, where the *philosophes* were most numerous, most active, and most able, the very defenders of the existing order were half convinced that what they defended was outworn and unjust. And in fact there were many things in France that were difficult to defend on any rational basis. France, it is true, was better organized and better managed than most of the other continental countries. But it was more conscious of its shortcomings.

France, in the second half of the eighteenth century, was the most advanced of all the continental countries. Its peasants were more prosperous, its financiers more wealthy, its upper classes more cultured than those in other European lands. But France under the "old regime" was a peculiar composite. Though in many basic ways it still resembled a country of the later middle age or of the sixteenth century, it had been changed by the ideas and institutions of absolutist, centralized government developed in the seventeenth century.

E. France of the "Old Regime"

The French monarchy was still based on the idea of absolutism and divine right, despite the notions of popular control that were gaining currency and despite the limitations on monarchy established in England. The king of France still treated his realm as a collection of personal and family possessions. In spite, too, of the growth of religious skepticism and the beginnings of religious toleration, the Catholic Church still held in France a privileged and exclusive position. Education and charity were almost entirely in its hands. Noble and peasant alike attended its services. If on the one hand the king selected the bishops, on the other he usually heeded their advice and supported their views. If the church lent some financial support to the government through "gratuitous gifts," it also possessed broad landholdings and collected compulsory taxes or tithes.

In a period when more and more people were talking about the equality and the "natural rights" of all men, the class structure in France showed glaring inequality and a wide variation in rights. The privileged orders, or the first two "estates of the realm," were the clergy and the nobles. The first estate, or clergy, was itself characterized by inequality. The high churchmen—archbishops, bishops, and abbots—often enjoyed great wealth drawn from church landholdings and from tithes. The Cardinal de Rohan, with an income of 2,500,000 livres a year, could astound the court with his magnificence and his gambling. Churchmen like him lived with the pomp and ceremony of princes, and were prone to neglect their ecclesiastical duties and to play the role of courtiers at Versailles. Often a noble family took care of a younger son by securing him a high position in the church, while an unmarried daughter was likely to be made an abbess. Some of the aristocratic churchmen were pious and hard-working. But others were dissipated, arrogant, and worldly.

In sharp contrast, were the lower ranks of the clergy. Many a shabby but devout country curate, with an uncertain income of less than $150 a year, was doing his best to make both ends meet, with a little to spare for charity. If among the lower clergy there was some lack of education, some sloth, and some merely routine formalism, there was also a vast deal of humble service and quiet toil in behalf of the common people. In the rural villages the priest was often the guide, philosopher, and friend of his flock. He defended them against the officials, taught their children to read, gave them the news of the day, and comforted them in their troubles.

Marquis de Lafayette. From a French print of 1781.

There was a similar contrast in the second order or "estate"—the nobility. There were thousands of lesser nobles who lived on their estates, patched up their crumbling châteaux, and showed pride in their coats of arms, their horses, and their dogs. If they could ever afford to come to Paris or Versailles, they were treated like country bumpkins. Their clothes were old fashioned, and it was held that they smelled faintly of the barnyard. Some of the country nobles were fairly well-to-do. Many of them were on friendly terms with their peasants and tenants. But their influence was largely local. They had no real function in the state as a whole.

Much more conspicuous were the great nobles, the courtiers. Some of them still were of use as officers in the army. But to a large degree they had become merely decorative. They formed a background for the king. The real work of government was done by lawyers and other middle-class folk. The nobles at court sought eagerly for royal attention, since that might mean pensions, gifts, and salaried (if honorary) posts. At Versailles, many of them rarely did anything more worth while than to invent a delicate compliment, or to patronize an art, or to pose as "enlightened." Their morals were not of the best—it was almost fashionable to be vicious. But their manners were perfect. Meanwhile, the landed estates of these absentee lords were in charge of salaried agents whose duty was to squeeze money out of the peasants.

Whether rich or poor, at court or in the country, the noble enjoyed special privileges. He was thought of as finer and better than common men. He was addressed in terms of respect—"my lord"—"your grace"—or the like. For him the best places were reserved in the church or in the theatre. Ordinary people drew aside to let him pass and bowed or doffed their hats. His noble birth, if it prevented him from marrying "below his class," admitted him to polite society and allowed him to seek preference in the army, in the church, or at court.

More substantial were the actual possessions of the noble. Each noble usually bequeathed to his eldest son a mansion or château, together with more or less territory from which rents and dues could be collected. High churchmen, on taking office, came into similar properties belonging to the church. Though nobility and clergy together held a large portion of the fairest lands of France, substantial pensions from the crown, and many well salaried offices, they paid far less than their share of the taxes. They were exempt from the burdensome *taille*, or land tax. While they were supposed to pay certain direct taxes like the *vingtième* and the *capitation*, their influence was such that they could usually scale down their contributions to a minimum. Even taxes like the *aides* on wine they could escape by maintaining their own vineyards. Thus the chief burden of taxation fell, not on those who were richest and best able to pay, but chiefly on the lower classes and especially on the peasantry.

The third estate which did pay taxes, consisted of all those who were not clergymen or nobles. Here, too, there were wide differences, for the wealthy merchant was in a position quite distinct from that of the humble peasant. The most powerful element of the third estate was the bourgeoisie—the merchants, bankers, businessmen, manufacturers, and professional men who lived in towns or cities. Industry, commerce, and finance had all been growing rapidly in France, as in the rest of Europe, since the late middle age, and with them the bourgeois had grown in wealth and power. By the late eighteenth century, the richest group in France were financiers. They made most of their money by collecting the taxes farmed out on contract by the government and by loaning money to it. If the government got hard up, that merely meant fatter profits for the tax-farmers, because they could then secure better terms on their contracts and higher interest on the loans.

There were many wealthy merchants. France, even after the Seven Years' War, enjoyed a most lucrative trade in sugar from the West Indies, in eastern textiles and other goods from India, and in products from the Near East. Trade was also extensive with the Baltic, with Germany and the Low Countries, and with southern Europe. There were several kinds of industrialists, some of whom were very well-to-do. There were manufacturers of the old medieval type, who belonged to guilds and made goods in their shops with the aid of journeymen and apprentices under the protection of the monopoly established by their guilds and confirmed by the government. There were "putting-out" capitalists, or merchant-employers, who bought the raw materials, sent them out to be worked up by laborers in their homes, and then sold the finished products. There was also a growing number of manufacturers who possessed large shops much like factories, where they employed dozens or even hundreds of people.

Associated in one way or another with these important groups of bourgeois, were others of varying significance. There were great numbers of shopkeepers, large and small, wholesalers, brokers, commission merchants, and bankers. To handle legal matters there were numerous lawyers, some of whom grew wealthy, while others eked out a precarious livelihood. Most of the government and municipal officials were drawn from the bourgeoisie. Indeed, many a lawyer found his career in government service rather than in private practice. If the officials were dependent on, and for the most part loyal to, the government, they were none the less bound by close family ties to the business classes.

Since the sixteenth century, the bourgeoisie had grown in numbers and wealth and also in education. Most of the French *philosophes* were of bourgeois origin, and from that class came most of the persons who read the latest books on science or philosophy or government, who responded sympathetically to the current pleas for rationalism or to the criticisms of the existing order, and who eagerly discussed questions of political theory or economic policy. There was growing among these bourgeois a sense that they did not have social esteem, political influence, or economic privileges corresponding to their numbers, their wealth, or their education. They felt themselves to be the backbone of the country and the basis of its prosperity. It irked them to see a foppish noble or an idle churchman take precedence over them in society or at court, and even escape payment of most of the taxes. To the bourgeois it seemed that the privileged classes who contributed little to national well-being were getting far more than a fair share of the good things of life. The situation seemed clearly out of line with the teachings of Rousseau, or Adam Smith, or Voltaire.

Yet if there was cause for discontent, the peasantry had more reason to be restive than the bourgeoisie. France was still a predominantly agricultural country, and it was on the backs of the peasantry that the other classes were borne. It was the peasantry who raised the food and produced the raw materials. It was the peasantry who paid the bulk of the taxes, tithes, and dues. But they enjoyed no political power whatever. If they failed to pay the taxes which they had no voice in levying, they lost their land or their equipment.

Though there were relatively few serfs left save in the most backward areas of France, conditions for the peasantry had not changed much from those of the middle ages. Peasant villages still were organized for the most part on the old "open field" system. The peasant cultivated scattered strips and followed the traditional agricultural procedures of the village. Some peasants now owned their land. Many were tenants paying money rents or a share of the crop.

But whatever his status, the peasant was subject to a number of vexatious burdens. If he owed no labor, he paid a "quit rent." If he sold his farm, part of the price usually went to the lord. If he took his goods to market, he often had to pay market fees or dues. Under a system of *banalités*, his grain must be ground, his grapes or olives pressed, and his bread baked at the lord's mill, press, or oven, and a fee paid for the privilege. Only the lord could hunt, and he could and sometimes did run his horses and dogs over the peasant's crops. To the church the peasant paid a tithe (often a twelfth or a fifteenth) of his crop.

The royal taxes were still more burdensome. The *taille* was sometimes a land tax, sometimes one on the peasant's whole re-sources. It varied from year to year, and the village had to choose collectors who went to jail if the expected sums were not forthcoming. To the *taille* were added the *capitation* and the *vingtième*, which had originally been intended as a kind of income tax but which in practice were collected more or less like the *taille*. Often the peasant would let his house go to pieces so that he would be thought poor and might thus be taxed less. In many parts of France, there was a heavy salt tax, or *gabelle*, and in some sections the peasant was required to buy a given amount of salt each year. Beer, wine, and other beverages bore heavy taxes called *aides*. Roadmaking was a duty of the peasant, and by the *corvée* he was forced to discharge it for the crown without pay.

All these burdens left the average peasant little for himself. There were districts where the peasants were prosperous and lived in comfortable cottages. But more often they were wretched, miserable, and sometimes even hungry. They ate black bread and thought a bit of meat a luxury. They lived in thatched huts and wore rough woolens frequently patched. Their tools were few and crude. They were ignorant, superstitious, and mainly illiterate.

Yet when all has been said, the French peasants were probably better off than those anywhere else on the continent of Europe except perhaps in the Low Countries. In France serfdom was disappearing, while it was still common in Germany, the Habsburg lands, and Russia. For all his wretchedness, the average French peasant was better fed, clothed, and housed than his fellows to the east.

As with the peasantry, so with the other classes. France, for all its outworn and traditional organization, was the most advanced country on the continent. The bourgeoisie were more numerous. better educated, and more ambitious than elsewhere. The intellectuals were abler, more critical, and more vociferous than those in other lands. The nobles and high clergy were not only more polished than in other countries, they were also a little less certain about the justice of a system which gave

Jean-Jacques Rousseau (d. 1778).
Courtesy Bettmann Archive

them so many privileges. If called on to defend their "rights," some of them would do so half-heartedly or not at all. Such was the France which heard the news from America of republicanism, liberty, equality, and constitutions which ensured the freedom of all men. Such was the France which was facing the worst financial crisis of the old regime.

Marie-Antoinette and her children. Painting by Mme. Vigée-Le Brun (d. 1842).

CHAPTER 41

The French Revolution

A. The Financial Crisis of the French Monarchy, 1783–1789

There had been those in France who had opposed war on Great Britain in 1778, for fear of the financial costs. Four years earlier Louis XV had been succeeded by his grandson, Louis XVI. The new monarch was virtuous but dull-witted, well-meaning but lacking in decision. He was too awkward and shy to preside with dignity over the court or the royal councils. He liked to shoot deer or to play at lock-making. He had many amiable virtues, but not those which could make him a forceful or an enlightened ruler.

When Louis XVI came to the throne, hopes had at first run high, for Turgot, friend of Voltaire and other encyclopedists, was named minister of finance, and reform was in the air. But Turgot's attempts to remove the old restraints on commerce and industry, to aid agriculture, to revise the financial system, to reduce the burdens on the peasants and to tax the nobles and clergy, ran into the stubborn opposition of the privileged, and seemed to threaten the traditional rights of guilds, towns, provinces, nobles, and churchmen.

Having accomplished but little, Turgot was dismissed in 1776, and amidst general relief his reforms were abandoned. Turgot, the theorist, was succeeded by a hard-headed Swiss banker, Jacques Necker. During his five years in office (1776–1781) Necker sought to apply business methods to government finances. He borrowed 400,000,000 *livres* from his banker friends and tried to reduce expenses and improve tax collections. In 1781 he pretended to inform the public about the condition of the royal treasury by issuing a report, or "Account Rendered." The report, though favorably received, was something less than a full and honest one, for Necker was eager to secure further loans; and expenditures on the American war were rapidly mounting.

At court, Necker had a powerful enemy in the Queen, Marie Antoinette, daughter of Maria Theresa of Austria. Gay and frivolous, she was disliked by many people as a foreigner and as a symbol of the alliance with Austria which had proved so disastrous in the Seven Years' War. The young Queen had little serious interest in politics and less understanding of them, but when her friends came to her with complaints about Necker's miserly economy she begged the King to dismiss him. Well-intentioned Louis XVI could not bear to deprive his irresponsible wife and her charming friends, the courtiers, of their pleasures. He appointed as the new finance minister the suave and obsequious Calonne, who found more money for the court, but only by floating new loans at high rates of interest.

By the end of the American war (1783), the financial problem was desperate. It was indeed insoluble without the reforms which would have upset the old order in France. The country could easily have borne heavier taxes, but only if the upper classes were made to bear their fair share of the burden. To a bishop or a noble it seemed ridiculous to expect a high-born person to pay taxes like a merchant or a peasant. The privileged classes were so intrenched in the courts, the church, and the government, and so well defended by law, tradition, and precedent, that they were able to block any attempt to alter the existing system.

In 1786 the interest payments on the public debt totaled more than 160,000,000 *livres* and, since the regular income fell far short of meeting the regular expenses, the government was running deeper into debt every month. In addition, it was becoming increasingly difficult to float new loans even at very high interest rates. Something had to be done. In desperation the King convened (1787) an Assembly of Notables— 145 of the chief nobles, bishops, and officials—in the vain hope that they would consent to the taxation of the privileged classes. They contented themselves, however, with recommending some minor reforms, urging that Calonne be dismissed, and declaring that the question of taxation should be referred to the Estates General. But in all their suggestions there was no real help for the treasury.

The new minister of finance, Archbishop Loménie de Brienne, politely thanked the notables and sent them home. He made so many fine promises that he was able to float a new loan. But the *parlement*, or high court, of Paris soon saw that there was nothing substantial behind his promises and refused to register new loans or taxes. Encouraged by popular approval of its stand, the *parlement* went on to draw up a declaration of rights and to assert that new taxes should only be granted by the nation's representatives—the Estates General. This sounded almost subversive, and the *parlements* were closed. At once, there was popular protest. Soldiers refused to arrest the judges. Excited crowds gathered in Paris and in provincial cities and clamored for the summoning of the Estates General. Menaced with revolt, Louis XVI finally gave way to the popular demand. In 1788, he summoned the Estates General to meet at Versailles, in May, 1789.

The Estates General was no novel institution. To be sure, it had not met for 175 years. But prior to 1614, kings had not infrequently summoned representatives of the clergy, the nobles, and the rest of the people (the "third estate") to advise them. Since each estate had met separately and had voted as a unit, the clergy and the nobles (the privileged classes) could outvote the third estate two to one. Moreover, the powers of the Estates General had been advisory, and if worse came to worse its advice could perhaps be ignored and it could be dismissed. No, the summoning of the Estates General might after all be useful and it did not seem too dangerous to the monarchy. The fact that this reasoning was to prove false arose from conditions that neither Louis XVI nor his ministers could be expected fully to grasp.

The general economic situation in France was in some ways as ominous as the strictly financial. The economic difficulties were very real, despite the fact that France was basically sound and was progressing in industry, commerce, and agriculture. A recent problem had been created by the Eden treaty negotiated between France and Great Britain in 1786. In line with the ideas of freer trade upheld by Adam Smith and other economists of the time, this treaty had reduced the import duties levied against each other's goods by the two countries. The British had agreed to receive French wines at the rates charged on the favored Portuguese wines, but had quickly nullified any advantage the French might thus have gained by lowering still further the rates on the Portuguese product. Though Britain had refused to lower the duties on French silks, France had cut the rates on English cotton goods, and just at this time the British were producing more and better cotton stuffs at costs decreased by the application of new inventions in spinning. As a result of the treaty, commerce between France and Britain had notably increased and the age-old profession of smuggling across the Channel had been hard hit. But France had been quickly flooded with English cottons and other goods. For this reason and probably for others as well, French business had entered upon a period of depression. By 1788, unemployment had become serious and business men were protesting.

To add to these problems there was a basic long-run trend which has only recently been explored and understood. From about 1735 prices of goods had been rising, while wages had risen much less rapidly. This development benefited the big landowners (who did not pay their share of the taxes), since they got more for their products and paid relatively less in wages. For this reason, land rents had been rising significantly. But it was very hard on the working classes since they got relatively less money for their labor and had to pay higher prices for their food and clothes. It has been estimated that a worker in France could, in the period 1785–1789, buy about 25 per cent less goods with his wages than a similar worker in the period 1726–1741. Nor were the peasants wholly unaffected since large numbers of them pieced out their livelihood by working part time for wages.

Before the nineteenth century, business depressions were normally associated with bad harvests and high grain prices. Such was the case in 1788–1789. The harvest of 1788 was a poor one. Soon the price of grain was going up. During the early months of 1789 it rose rapidly to a peak in the month of July, at which time the price of grain was

Mirabeau. Bust in the Louvre Museum by Jean Antoine Houdon (d. 1828).

higher than it had been since 1709, a year of great famine and suffering. When it is remembered that the French lower classes spent something like two-thirds of their total income for food and that their ability to buy food had already been seriously impaired by the current trend of prices and wages, some notion may be derived of how serious was the situation.

In considering the events of 1789, it is well to bear in mind that many members of the lower classes were hungry, fearful, and discontented. The mobs that appeared suddenly like actors on the stage came together in part at least because the people were so wretched and miserable that they felt something must be done, and the government in its financial weakness was unable to start public works or give relief or distribute cheap grain as had been done in crises in the past.

B. The National Assembly, 1789

France in the winter of 1788–1789 was undergoing a serious crisis, but that this would develop rapidly into a revolution which would overthrow divine-right monarchy and the old regime, and affect all subsequent history, was anticipated by no one. France had met and surmounted crises before. Its monarchy and social system had been so long established and had achieved such impressive success in the past that they seemed indestructible.

Elections to the Estates General were held amidst much discussion and a frantic search for precedents of two centuries earlier. In accordance with old custom and at the King's request, the groups of electors drafted reports on local conditions and made recommendations as to reforms they felt desirable. These reports and recommendations were called cahiers, and they were numerous. Almost every group of voters of each of the three estates prepared one. Though the cahiers almost uniformly expressed loyalty to the monarchy, most of them breathed a spirit of reform. In line with the "enlightened" thought of the day, they urged the removal of social inequalities and of economic, financial, and political abuses. Even the privileged orders—clergy and nobility—quite generally recognized some need for reform.

The Third Estate was naturally most insistent. Two thirds of its elected representatives were lawyers and judges, most of whom admired limited monarchy of the British sort and were well acquainted with the writings of the *philosophes*. The Third Estate had grown to be much more important than it had been in 1614, and Louis XVI had recognized this change by providing that the number of representatives of that estate should equal the number of representatives of the other two combined. The commoners naturally enough concluded that they would be the most influential group when the Estates General met.

Among the men elected by the Third Estate were two spokesmen, Mirabeau and Sieyès, both of whom belonged to the privileged classes but gladly accepted election by the unprivileged. Mirabeau was the son of a marquis who had written books on the economic principles of the physiocrats. The son had proved so wild and unruly that the father had repeatedly had him put in prison to keep him out of mischief. In 1789 he found opportunity to employ his almost superhuman energy in working for the constitutional government in which he believed. Not so forceful was the priest Sieyès, who was much less a devout Catholic than a devotee of the critical philosophy of the day. In a pamphlet issued on the eve of the meeting of the Estates General, Sieyès asked, "What is the Third Estate?" "It is everything," he replied. "What has it been hitherto in the political order? Nothing! What does it desire? To be something!"

When the Estates General finally met at Versailles in May 1789, neither the King nor his ministers had worked out a program for it. The King welcomed its members, and apparently expected them to devote themselves to financial problems. He did direct them to vote by order, that is, as three separate bodies, so that the nobles and clergy together would be able to outvote the Third Estate. If the nobles and most of the higher clergy approved this adherence to tradition, the Third Estate did not. They wished all the delegates to meet together and to vote "by head" or as individuals, so that their extra numbers would give them real power,

and so that the assemblage would represent the French nation as a whole and not the separate classes of the country.

In support of its views, the Third Estate was firm, while the King shilly-shallied, to offend no one. At length, on June 17, 1789, the Third Estate proclaimed itself a "National Assembly" and invited the other orders to sit with it and to work together for the reformation of France. Three days later, finding that the King had locked them out of their assembly hall, the Third Estate took a truly revolutionary step. Led by Sieyès and Mirabeau, they proceeded to a large nearby building used normally as a riding-hall or tennis court; they listened to a number of fiery speeches; and amid intense excitement and with upraised hands, they took an oath, as members of the "National Assembly," that they would not separate till they had drawn up a written constitution for France.

This "Tennis Court Oath" was the actual beginning of the French Revolution, for in it the representatives of the Third Estate were going against the orders of the King and far beyond the purposes for which they had been summoned. Unexpectedly, the indecisive King took no forceful action against the revolutionary commoners. Soon these were joined by a number of the lower clergy and a few liberal nobles. "We are here by the will of the people," they declared in the words of Mirabeau, "and we shall not leave our places except at the point of a bayonet." The King gave way. Just a week after the scene at the tennis court he reversed his position and directed the three estates to sit together and vote "by head" as members of a National Constituent Assembly.

The stage was now set for the new National Assembly to proceed with the work of drawing up a constitution for France. But it was not to proceed calmly, for France, in the throes of depression and near famine, was deeply stirred by the events at Versailles, and in the ensuing months a number of events occurred which gravely affected the attitude and work of the Assembly.

Early in July rumor spread that the King was concentrating troops on Versailles. Although this move may have been intended

The Tennis Court Oath. Painting by Jacques Louis David (d. 1825).

to protect rather than to overawe the Assembly, there resulted three day of wild disorder in Paris. Shops were looted and royal officers expelled, while angry crowds rioted. On the third day—July 14, 1789—a mob attacked the royal prison-fortress of the Bastille. It contained few prisoners and they were unimportant, yet it was somehow a grim symbol of Bourbon despotism. The mob took the Bastille and slaughtered the scanty garrison who sought to defend it.

The fall of the Bastille was both the first serious act of violence in the Revolution and a sign that the Parisian populace were behind the Assembly. Matters now proceeded apace, for during the disorder prominent citizens of Paris set up a new city government, or "commune," and organized a militia called the National Guard. In an attempt to allay the excitement, Louis XVI recognized the new government of Paris and confirmed the appointment of Lafayette, of American fame, as commander of the National Guard. The King did more. He visited Paris in person, praised what he could not prevent, and wore a new tricolor cockade combining the red and blue of Paris with the white of the Bourbons. The French still celebrate July 14 as the anniversary of the birth of their popular freedom.

During the summer of 1789, revolutionary violence spread to the provinces. In many regions, peasants rose, and, attacking the châteaux of nobles, burned the rolls which recorded the dues and fees they owed. Some monasteries were pillaged, some landowners were murdered. Amid the confusion, intendants and other officials left their posts and courts ceased to function. The old regime was in fact crumbling. Much affected by reports of these events, the Assembly was debating on August 4 what should be done about them, when one of the nobles—a relative of Lafayette—declared that the peasants were attacking injustices and that the remedy was not to repress the peasants but to remove the injustices. It was immediately moved and carried that the Assembly should proclaim equality of taxation for all classes, and the suppression of feudal dues. Then followed a scene of wild excitement; nobles vied with clergymen in renouncing the vested rights of the old regime. Game laws were repealed, manorial courts suppressed, serfdom abolished, tithes canceled, and all special privileges of classes, cities, and provinces swept away. Within a week the various measures had been put together into an impressive decree "abolishing feudalism." To be sure, the peasants were already abolishing it, and presently the Assembly in calmer mood was voting money compensation for surrendered privileges. Still the "August Days" wrote into law the dissolution of the traditional class society and the substitution of an individualist society.

While peasants burned châteaux and the Assembly voted decrees, many nobles were leaving France in fear or in protest, and the Queen and the King's two brothers (the Count of Provence and the Count of Artois) were urging Louis XVI to use the army against the revolution. It is doubtful whether the well-intentioned King would have done so, but news of an officers' banquet at Versailles reached Paris and once again a mob took action. On October 5, 1789, numbers of the poorest women of the city and some men dressed as women, all armed with clubs and screaming "Bread, bread!", straggled along the highway from Paris to Versailles. Lafayette with his National Guard followed them.

At the royal palace, Lafayette undertook to guard the royal family, but the night was a wild one and rioters actually broke into the palace and killed some of the Queen's bodyguard. In the morning, the King took a fateful step. He agreed to move with his family to Paris. In a lumbering coach, attended by Lafayette and surrounded by the mob, Louis XVI, Marie Antoinette, and their children took their way to Paris on October 6, while the mob shouted, "We have the baker and the baker's wife and the little cook-boy—now we shall have bread!" The National Assembly soon followed the King to Paris, and thenceforth both Louis XVI and the Assembly were no longer at Versailles full of memories of Louis XIV, but in Paris ever subject to the influence and threats of the populace.

C. New Order in State, Church, and Society, 1789–1791

The National Assembly, both at Versailles and at Paris, was accomplishing an

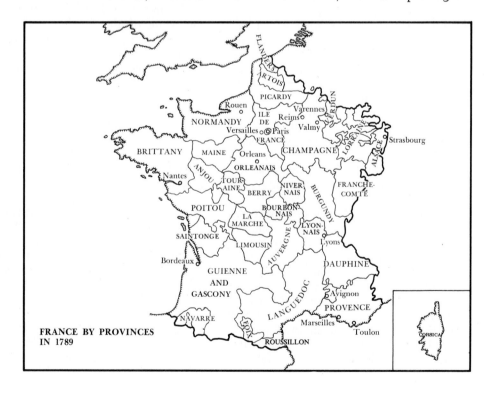

FRANCE BY PROVINCES IN 1789

important work—tearing down the old regime and building a new order. Much of what it did would become a lasting part of French political life. Its slogans and its principles would provide the basis for French liberalism.

The first major accomplishment of the National Assembly had been the destruction of the old order in the "August Days." Its second was the assertion on October 2, 1789, of the principles on which the new order was to be built—the "Declaration of the Rights of Man." This declaration reflected the influence of *philosophes* like Rousseau and borrowed ideas and phrases from the English Bill of Rights and the American Declaration of Independence. It affirmed the principles of religious toleration, freedom of speech, and freedom of the press. It proclaimed that "private property is an inviolable and sacred right," and upheld the basic tenets of democracy by declaring that "Law is the expression of the general will. Every citizen has the right to participate personally or through his representative in its formation. It must be the same for all." It announced that "Men are born and remain free and equal in rights," and it defined these rights as "liberty, property, security, and resistance to oppression." "No person," it said, "shall be accused, arrested, or imprisoned, except in the cases and according to the forms prescribed by law."

A third and more practical achievement of the National Assembly was its reorganization of the country's administration. It swept away the old overlapping subdivisions, and abolished special privileges of guilds, towns, and provinces, the traditional local variations of justice and taxation, and even the provincial names of Burgundy, Normandy, Brittany, etc., that had endured for centuries. To replace what it was demolishing, the National Assembly set up a new and uniform system. The whole country was divided into eighty-three "*départements*," named after rivers or mountains, and each *département* was subdivided into cantons, and the cantons into communes or municipal units. Local officials were not to be appointed by the king, but elected by the people, and a new system of courts with elected judges was established. To this day

France has retained the system of local divisions devised by the National Assembly.

In its reforms the National Assembly emphasized the national unity of France. Indeed the fostering of nationalism was one of the most impressive features of the French Revolution. The Estates General had renamed itself the *National* Assembly. The new citizen militia was called the *National* Guard. The Declaration of the Rights of Man insisted that "all sovereignty resides essentially in the Nation." While the Assembly discussed plans for national military service and national education, patriotic rites to celebrate the new spirit of national unity were devised. On July 14, 1790, there was a spectacular patriotic festival at Paris, and in the provinces "altars to the fatherland" were erected and before them patriotic ceremonies were conducted. But the National Assembly went even further and preached the rights of people outside of France to national self-determination. It encouraged the people of Avignon, a city on the Rhône long owned by the papacy, to vote by plebiscite in 1791 to join France, despite protests of the Pope. Already nationalism was complicating international relations.

The Assembly could not ignore the financial difficulties which had been the occasion for its meeting. These had grown more acute, since, amid revolutiionary conditions, people simply ceased to pay taxes. Moved by a sense of national need and by anticlerical ideas which the *philosophes* had preached, the National Assembly tried to

FRANCE BY DÉPARTEMENTS
IN 1791

solve the financial problem at the expense of the Catholic Church in France. It decreed in November 1789 the confiscation of the landed estates held by the church, and against this property as security it issued paper money (called *assignats*). Since the paper money could be used to buy the confiscated land, it served as a mechanism by which the middle class and the peasants acquired the properties the state had seized. As often happens, however, too much paper money was issued; the *assignats* fell in value and a serious inflation of prices occurred.

As a partial indemnity for the confiscation of church property, the state undertook to pay the salaries of the clergy, who were thus made dependent on the state. But the National Assembly soon went further and undertook to reorganize the whole ecclesiastical system in France. In February 1790, the monasteries and other religious communities were suppressed. In July, a "Civil Constitution of the Clergy" was enacted. By this new law, the bishops and priests were reduced in number; they were to be elected by the people, paid by the state, and only nominally associated with the "foreign" pope.

Naturally enough, the Pope, Pius VI, protested vigorously against the new legislation in France. He condemned the "Civil Constitution of the Clergy" and forbade French clerics to take the required oath of loyalty to it. The issue was squarely joined. Those who took the oath—"the juring clergy"— were excommunicated by the Pope. Those who refused to take it—"the non-juring clergy"—lost their posts and salaries and were threatened with imprisonment. Many of the lower clergy who had sympathized with the course of the Revolution were now forced by their consciences to oppose the Assembly and its acts. Some priests and churchmen stayed in France and incited the devout to work against the revolutionary trend. Others left the country and swelled the numbers of the *émigrés*. A minority acquiesced in the revolution. In general, from this period dates a deep split in France between anti-clerical and devout.

Meanwhile the National Constituent Assembly was drafting the written constitution which would establish in France a limited monarchy. It was completed in 1791 and reluctantly signed by the King. Like the slightly earlier American Constitution, it provided for a "separation of powers" among executive, legislative, and judicial branches of government. But chief power was actually centered in a one-house "Legislative Assembly." The middle-class men who framed the constitution showed their distrust of the masses by arranging a complicated system of indirect election for members of the legislature, and by limiting the right to vote to "active citizens" who paid taxes, and the right to hold office, to property owners. The king's powers were reduced to a shadow and he was given only "a suspensive veto" over legislation. He could delay but not prevent the passage of laws of which he disapproved. By a decision which has been much criticized, but which was intended to show their lack of self-interest, the members of the National Constituent Assembly made themselves ineligible to sit in the new Legislative Assembly which met on October 1, 1791, amid public rejoicing, to inaugurate the era of constitutional limited monarchy in France.

Before that meeting took place, certain developments occurred which boded ill for the success of the new government. Opposition to the religious and political changes was rising within France. The number of *émigrés* was increasing and they were urging foreign rulers to intervene in France. Mirabeau, who, with his personal prestige, was a major support of limited monarchy, died prematurely in April, 1791. Worst of all, the King showed that he was out of sympathy with what was happening. In June 1791, accompanied by Marie Antoinette and the royal children, he fled from Paris in an effort to escape from the country. Detected and stopped by chance at Varennes near the border, the royal fugitives were ignominiously brought back to Paris. Louis subsequently swore to uphold the constitution. But how much faith could be placed in a monarch who had sought to leave the country and join the enemies of the new regime, and whose brothers had already fled? The King's personal popularity waned rapidly, while distrust and hatred of his wife, "The Austrian woman," grew apace.

D. Limited Monarchy and Start of Revolutionary War, 1791–1792

When the Legislative Assembly met on October 1, 1791, it faced enormous difficulties. Its members were new and untried, and the whole country was divided into contending factions. While many Frenchmen were willing to accept the new constitutional monarchy and hoped for its success, there were large groups of conservatives who thought things had gone too far, and of radicals who thought they had not gone far enough.

Many of the reactionary nobles had become *émigrés* by fleeing the country. Numbers of them gathered just over the northern and eastern frontiers, especially at Coblentz, and agitated against the new regime. Within France it was believed (correctly) that the King's closest advisers were in sympathy and in touch with the *émigrés*. Conservative clubs, moreover, had been formed in Paris and other cities by members of the upper classes. In certain sections of western France, especially in Brittany, Poitou (La Vendée), and Anjou, the peasants, devoted to Catholicism and influenced by the nonjuring clergy, had become outspokenly hostile to the revolutionary changes that were going forward.

More dangerous to the orderly working of the new government were the radicals. Elated by progress already made and eager to put into practice the theories of the extreme *philosophes*, many middle-class people wished to eliminate the king altogether, to set up a republic, to establish manhood suffrage, to root out all surviving traces of privilege, and to reduce still further the role of the clergy and the church. Such radicals could usually count on the support of urban working people to whom the Revolution thus far had not given bread or jobs or (since they did not pay direct taxes) the right to vote.

The power and influence of the radicals was greatly enhanced by the fact that they were beginning to be well organized. Back in the early days of the National Assembly, eating clubs had been formed by like-minded delegates, and informal groups had gathered at cafés for political discussion. From such a beginning a number of political clubs had grown up, of which two were especially important. Known popularly by the names of confiscated monasteries in which they met, one was called the Cordelier, the other the Jacobin, Club. The former had been organized as a "society of the friends of the rights of man and of the citizen," and from the start it was radical. The Jacobin Club had originated as a "society of friends of the constitution," with such moderates as Mirabeau, Sieyès, and Lafayette. Subsequently under the leadership of Robespierre, it had become quite as radical as the Cordelier. It exercised nation-wide influence through its policy of organizing branch clubs of middle-class radicals all over France and showering them with propaganda—pamphlets, newspapers, letters.

Among the radical leaders, three may be mentioned—Marat, Danton, and Robespierre. Marat had been a skillful and learned physician. He had traveled in England and noted the aristocratic nature of its government. The meeting of the Estates General turned his attention to politics, and in vigorous pamphlets he had opposed the idea that the new French government should be modeled on Britain's. As demagogic editor of a newspaper, *Ami du peuple* (Friend of the People), he contended that reform must benefit all the people and could be secured by direct popular action. By 1791 he had a hold on the people of Paris, many of whom regarded him as their champion and prophet.

Less extreme and more statesmanlike was Danton. A lawyer by profession, he was a shrewd debater, and possessed a mighty voice and powerful physique. Remaining calm while he worked his hearers into a frenzy of enthusiasm, Danton was an immensely effective orator. He had become influential among the people of Paris and a leading member of the commune, or city government. With Marat he had founded the Cordelier Club, and there in 1791 and 1792 he spoke and worked against the King and for a republic.

A lawyer, too, was Maximilien Robespierre. A devout follower of Rousseau, he had taken his place among the extreme radicals of the National Assembly in the early days when they were few in number. When he failed to gain much influence in that body he turned to the people of Paris for support, and in 1791 became leader of the Jacobin Club. In a chilly way, Robespierre was a fanatic. He was ready to go to any lengths for his ideas and plans.

When the Legislative Assembly met, it became apparent that about half of its 750 members voted more or less independently on various issues before it, while the other half was divided into two camps—the Feuillants (so called because they met in a former convent of that name), and the Girondists (several of whose leaders came from the department of the Gironde). The Feuillants were relatively conservative in that they wished to uphold the new constitution and were even willing to strengthen the royal power. The Girondists were radical in that they favored a republic. They were intensely patriotic, and fond of "classical" references to the ancient republics of Greece and Rome. Among the Girondists were Brissot, an organizer; Vergniaud, an orator; Condorcet, a philosopher; Dumouriez, a general. At the home of the wealthy Madame Roland, they had a salon where they met for political discussion.

In internal affairs, the Legislative Assembly accomplished little, since from the start foreign problems loomed large. The foreign powers had at first welcomed the disturbances in France, since they seemed likely to weaken French influence in Europe. But the upper classes throughout Europe, including Great Britain, were soon horrified by the trends in France toward social equality and mob violence. This reaction was enshrined in Edmund Burke's eloquent *Reflections on the Revolution in France* (1790), which was widely welcomed as a telling defense of the old order of things. In August 1791, Frederick William II of Prussia joined with the Emperor Leopold II in the Declaration of Pillnitz, which announced that the restoration of order and monarchy in France was an object of "common interest to all the sovereigns of Europe." Such verbal interference in their affairs enraged patriotic Frenchmen and weakened the position of Louis XVI.

War might not have resulted if the chief political factions in France had not desired it. The moderate Feuillants, under such leaders as Lafayette, thought it would consolidate the French people in loyalty to the new constitutional regime. The radical Girondists believed it would discredit the monarchy and result in the establishment of a French republic and the general triumph of revolutionary ideas all over Europe. Only such extreme radicals as Marat and Robespierre, outside the Assembly, opposed war for fear it might lead to reaction or a military dictatorship.

Obtaining control of the government, the Girondists demanded that the Emperor Leopold II withdraw his troops from the French frontier and expel the *émigrés* from his territories. When he did not comply, the Girondist ministers prevailed upon Louis XVI to declare war, April 20, 1792. Leopold had just died, but his successor, Francis II, joined with King Frederick William II, of Prussia to gather an army of 80,000 men at Coblentz for the invasion of France. Among the French, patriotic enthusiasm rose to fever heat. Troops coming up from Marseilles sang a stirring new hymn, known as the *Marseillaise* (though it was written at Strasbourg). But, for all their enthusiasm, the French were ill-equipped and ill-organized for war, and the conflict opened with a series of French reverses.

As the military danger grew, many Frenchmen became convinced that they were being betrayed by the royal family. On June 20, 1792, a Paris mob jostled into the palace of the Tuileries and threatened the King, though it did him no violence. A month later, the French were further aroused by a manifesto from the Duke of Brunswick, commander-in-chief of the Austro-Prussian armies, which announced the intention of the Allies to restore absolute monarchy in France, and to punish the revolutionaries, while threatening dire penalties if meanwhile any harm was done to the royal family. The reply of Paris to the Duke of Brunswick was a bloody insurrection on August 9–10, 1792. A mob, led by extreme radicals of the middle class, rose against the constitutional monarchy. They replaced the city government with a new revolutionary commune in which Danton was the leading figure. They invaded the royal palace, massacred the Swiss Guards, and forced the royal family to take refuge with the Legislative Assembly. On August 10, the terror-stricken deputies voted to suspend the King from office and to authorize the immediate election by universal manhood suffrage of a National Convention to draw up a new constitution for France.

For the next six weeks, France was in a state of practical anarchy. The royal family was imprisoned. Lafayette, in protest, resigned his command of the French army and surrendered himself to the enemy. And the allied forces kept advancing.

Danton, now virtually dictator, decided that "the way to stop the enemy" was "to terrify the royalists," while Marat posted fierce placards calling for the blood of "aristocrats." When news reached Paris on September 2 that the fortress of Verdun was invested, a wholesale massacre of royalists began. Men, women, and children, priests, bishops, magistrates, and nobles to the number of two thousand, were hauled out of prisons and murdered.

Meanwhile Dumouriez had replaced Lafayette, and at Valmy on September 20 he checked the allied advance. On the same day, the newly elected National Convention met at Paris.

E. The National Convention and Revolutionary Republic, 1792–1795

The news of Valmy reached Paris on September 22, and simultaneously the National Convention decreed "that royalty is abolished in France." It proceeded to adopt a new calendar with September 22, 1792, as the first day of Year I of the Republic. During the next three years the Convention performed the twofold work of consolidating the Revolution within France and of waging successful foreign war. But it accomplished these tasks by terror, bloodshed, and dictatorship.

In composition the Convention was quite different from the Legislative Assembly. On the right sat nearly two hundred Girondists who were now the conservatives, since, though they desired a democratic republic, they represented the well-to-do middle class and believed in moderation. On the high seats at the left sat a group of about a hundred extreme radicals called the "Mountain" (from their position in the hall) or "Jacobins" (because of the affiliation of many of their leaders with that club). In the center sat a large group—the real majority—called the Plain. It had no settled convictions and no outstanding leaders. At first it tended to vote with the Girondists, but later the course of events and the clamor of Paris mobs inclined it toward the Mountain.

Louis XVI was brought to trial before the Convention on a charge of treason, found guilty by a vote of 387 to 334, and condemned to death. On January 21, 1793, he was beheaded in the Place de la Révolution (now Place de la Concorde). The dignity with which he met his death was the most kingly behavior of his reign.

Meanwhile the tide of Austrian and Prussian invasion was being rolled back from France. After Valmy, Dumouriez drove the foreign armies across the Rhine, invaded the Austrian Netherlands, and seized Brussels. Whereupon the Convention proposed to propagate "liberty" throughout Europe. By a decree of December 1792, it announced its opposition to all princes and privileged classes and its eagerness to help every people found "free and democratic governments."

Thus republican France definitely challenged monarchical Europe. Though the challenge was welcomed by some middle-class intellectuals in foreign lands, the masses of people outside France still gave unquestioning loyalty to their respective rulers. Even in France, a royalist reaction led to civil war in the Vendée, and the able Dumouriez, disgusted by increasing radicalism at Paris, deserted to the Austrians.

The foreign powers accepted the challenge of the French revolutionaries. The outraged monarchs of Austria, Prussia, Great Britain, Holland, Spain, and Sardinia formed a coalition against France. The allied armies reoccupied Belgium and the Rhineland and again invaded France. Against the threat, the National Convention acted with energy and dispatch. All young men were made subject to military conscription, and a new "national" army was organized under the competent direction of Lazare Carnot. Munitions and supplies for it were multiplied. Trusty young officers were trained and commissioned. By the end of 1793, Carnot had some 500,000 men under arms and most of them were fanatically devoted to France and the Revolution.

Not only did the new revolutionary principle of "the nation in arms" provide a large army, but Carnot, unhampered by tradition, was able to make important military innovations. He created the "division" as a military unit, improved the service of supply, and sent members of the government as "deputies on mission" to watch the generals and send home for execution any who faltered or showed themselves incompetent. Moreover, in the revolutionary army, men, regardless of their birth, could reach high rank. Gradually a new group of impetuous republican generals came to the fore and skillfully employed new tactics which took advantage of the numbers and ardor of their troops. Soon the French army was a powerful military force with a dash and vigor which made its opponents, with their tactics of the time of Frederick the Great, seem old-fashioned.

In this way, France met a coalition which would have staggered Louis XIV and won victories which would have dazzled him. The country was cleared of foreign foes. The war was pressed in the Netherlands, along the Rhine, into Savoy, and across the Pyrenees. So successful were the French that Carnot, at first called the "organizer of defense," earned the title of "organizer of victory."

Before the National Convention adjourned in 1795 the anti-French coalition was disrupted. Charles IV of Spain was compelled to make peace and to contract a close alliance with the Republic that had put his Bourbon cousin to death. Frederick William II of Prussia by treaty (1795) gave France a free hand on the left bank of the Rhine and turned his attention to a third partition of Poland.[1] William V, Stadholder of Holland, was deposed, and his country transformed into a "Batavian Republic" in alliance with France. French troops held the

[1] See above, p. 443, and map on p. 444.

Austrian (Belgian) Netherlands. Though Austria, Great Britain, and Sardinia still remained in arms, they seemed powerless to check the triumphant advance of the French.

But the victories of the Republic were won at a terrible cost. Pride in military triumph gradually overshadowed republican enthusiasm and democratic faith. Economic life in field and shop was increasingly directed to the maintenance of the army. The very victories of the French heightened alarm in other countries, and the plundering of conquered lands made many of the "liberated" dubious about the advantages of the new freedom. At home, the new military power had been mercilessly used to stamp out domestic protests and insurrections, whether of Catholic and royalist peasants of La Vendée, or of other provincials who opposed the radicalism of Paris.

Success abroad and at home arose not only from the new militarism but also from the strong central government established by the National Convention and by the policy of terrorism which that government pursued. In the spring of 1793, under the threat of foreign invasion, the National Convention entrusted supreme executive authority to a Committee of Public Safety composed of nine (later of twelve) members. Though the Girondists sought to control it, and though Danton was at first its leading figure, power in it gradually came into the hands of a group of Jacobins headed by Robespierre, St. Just, and Carnot. Through the local Jacobin societies and through a ruthless exercise of power, the Committee enforced its will on all France.

The policy of the Committee in suppressing dissent in the provinces and rival factions in Paris was terrorism, and the period of its chief work is called the Reign of Terror. So sensational were the methods used and so numerous were the victims who went to the guillotine (an efficient beheading device) that many writers treat the Terror as the central episode of the Revolution. In reality it was but an awful incident in a great political and social movement, an incident induced by the need for united action in crushing enemies at home and abroad, and perhaps, too, by bitter personal rivalry accentuated by fear.

The chief agencies used by the Committee of Public Safety in its terrorism were the Revolutionary Tribunal and the Law of Suspects. By the former, arrested persons were arbitrarily tried and condemned to death, while by the latter anyone could be arbitrarily arrested who was an "aristocrat" or was "suspected" of disloyalty to the Republic. It is estimated that at Paris some 5,000 persons were thus executed by the guillotine. The Terror spread also to the provinces. Local tribunals arrested suspects, and local guillotines beheaded them. At Lyons, hundreds were put to death. At Nantes, a brutal Jacobin, Carrier by name, loaded victims suspected of connection with the insurrection in the Vendée onto old hulks which were towed out into the Loire and sunk.

But royalists and "aristocrats" were not the only ones to be executed. At Paris, there was a constant flux, as factions strove for power. Those who lost in the struggle went to the guillotine. The Girondists were discredited by their moderation and by the treason of Dumouriez. At the end of May 1793, the Convention, incited by Marat and a Parisian mob, expelled its leading Girondist members, many of whom were afterwards guillotined. In revenge, a Girondist young woman stabbed Marat to death, and then she too was executed.

In March 1794, followers of Danton combined with followers of Robespierre against a group of extremists, led by a certain Hébert, who were intent upon destroying all Christian churches and establishing Atheism. These were outmaneuvered, condemned, and executed. Whereupon Robespierre turned against Danton, who was counseling moderation, and in April succeeded in sending him, with his closest followers, to the guillotine.

For a hundred days, Robespierre was virtual dictator of France, trying to establish a Rousseau-like "republic of virtue" and a Deistic religion. But in the Convention, members who feared that they would be victims of the next purge conspired against him. On July 27, 1794 (ninth Thermidor, Year II, in the new revolutionary calendar), Robespierre was seized and hurried to the guillotine. The death of Robespierre ended the Reign of Terror. The "Thermidorian Reaction," as this event is called, marked

also a turning away of the bourgeoisie from revolutionary radicalism. The Committee of Public Safety had exercised an economic as well as a political dictatorship. It had fixed prices, requisitioned goods, and threatened to confiscate property. Businessmen, lawyers, and "solid" citizens generally were anxious for a regime that would respect property and permit normal business and profits. And throughout the country there was widespread desire to end the "Terror" and to return to more normal conditions.

Despite foreign war and civil strife, the National Convention accomplished some long-range reforms. It devised a plan for national education, began the task of compiling a national code of laws, abolished slavery in the colonies, protected women's property rights, forbade primogeniture (inheritance of property by the eldest son alone), and established the simple and convenient metric system of weights and measures which eventually won acceptance in all save English-speaking and backward countries. With less enduring results, the Convention devised a calendar in which the months had new names (Brumaire, Thermidor, etc.) and the weeks had ten days. It authorized a "religion of reason" in the stormy days of '93, but two years later, while maintaining the ban on non-juring clergy, it promised religious toleration and restored many church buildings to Christian worship.

In republican enthusiasm, the Convention decreed that all persons be addressed as "citizen." Knee breeches (*culottes*) of the old regime went out of fashion, and were replaced by the long trousers of workingmen (*sans-culottes*). But after Thermidor, republican radicalism waned, and France edged away from revolutionary excesses. The last rioting of a Paris mob was suppressed in October 1795 by a "whiff of grape-shot" discharged at the command of a young and then obscure artillery captain named Napoleon Bonaparte.

In 1793 the Convention had drafted a radically democratic constitution based on universal manhood suffrage. But it had never gone into effect, and after Robespierre's death a new and more conservative document was worked out under the guidance of Sieyès. This, which went into effect in 1795,

THE FIRST FRENCH REPUBLIC AND
ITS SATELLITES, 1795-1799

French Republic 1799

Dependent Republics 1799

German Church States to be absorbed by
other German States under French auspices

200 Miles

is called the Constitution of the Year III, and the republican government which it established is known as the Directory. It provided for a two-chamber legislature elected by indirect and somewhat restricted suffrage and for an executive of five Directors chosen by the legislature. It was hoped that the new government would give stability to the French Republic. But in fact it lasted little more than four years.

F. The Republic under the Directory, and Advent of Napoleon Bonaparte

That the Republican Directory did not long survive was owing to a combination of factors. It was harried by pressures from radicals on one side and conservatives on the other. To have consolidated the country after six years of revolutionary upheaval would have required hard and honest labor on the part of men of distinct genius. Yet almost without exception the Directors were men of mediocre talents, and some of them were flagrantly dishonest.

In marked contrast with the mediocrity

of the Directors was the genius of the soldier whom they promoted to command a major French army and entrusted with the task of pressing the foreign war against Austria and Sardinia. This was Napoleon Bonaparte. In 1796, with lightning rapidity, infectious enthusiasm, and brilliant tactics, he crossed the Alps, humbled the Sardinians, and within a few months disposed of five Austrian armies. Soon all northern Italy was in his hands. Sardinia surrendered, and ceded Nice and Savoy to France. When Bonaparte's army approached Vienna, even Austria stooped to make peace with this amazing republican general. By the treaty of Campo Formio (1797), France obtained the Austrian (Belgian) Netherlands, and Austria, while permitted to annex the Venetian Republic, had to promise not to interfere elsewhere in Italy. Only Great Britain was left at war with France.

So great was Bonaparte's prestige as a result of his Italian campaign that the Directors were relieved when they found a way of getting rid of him temporarily. At his own suggestion, a French expedition was sent in 1798 to Egypt, with himself in command, in order to sever communications between England and India. There Bonaparte won some battles, sent home glowing reports, and encouraged scientists he had brought with him to study Egyptian monuments. But as the British Admiral Lord Nelson won a great naval victory off the mouth of the Nile, the French army in Egypt was cut off and isolated. Bonaparte himself, eluding the British warships, returned to France, where he was received as a kind of savior. For while he had been away, matters had been going very badly for France. There had been increased domestic unrest; and the foreign policy which, since the peace of Campo Formio, the Directory had pursued of installing puppet republican governments in Holland, Switzerland, and Italy, had led to the formation of a Second Coalition (Russia and Austria with Great Britain) against France.

Thanks to money subsidies supplied by the British prime minister, the younger William Pitt (1759–1806),[1] the new Allies were enabled to put large armies in the field and in 1799 they won repeated victories. The French were driven from Italy, and most of the puppet republics collapsed. Thus when Bonaparte returned from Egypt in October 1799, he found France defeated, and the public eager for a change that would remedy the situation.

Within a month the young general was able to overthrow the Directory. Adroitly intriguing with Sieyès, one of the Directors, he surrounded the Legislature with a cordon of troops, and on November 9, 1799 (eighteenth Brumaire), secured by a show of force the overthrow of the government. This *coup d'état* (blow at the state) was promptly followed by a new constitution which made Bonaparte First Consul of the French Republic. Those who had plotted with him had hoped to use him as a tool. But it quickly became clear that Bonaparte was master.

Thus, only ten and a half years after the Estates General had met in Versailles, parliamentary government fell by the sword. As Marat and Robespierre had feared, foreign war brought a military dictator to power.

[1] Son of the William Pitt who became Earl of Chatham. See above, pp. 465, 471.

The way to real liberty and democracy, never fully cleared by the French Revolutionaries, was now blocked by a reactionary dictatorship.

Yet in a sense the advent of Bonaparte did not end the French Revolution. The revolutionaries had advanced certain principles which they summed up in the words "Liberty, Equality, Fraternity." These words had been carried into foreign lands by the French armies. They brought fear to monarchs and nobles; they connoted evil to a host of devout Christians; and to many an ignorant peasant they might seem strange and dangerous. But to many of the middle class, heirs of the eighteenth-century "enlightenment," to many a dreamer or altruistic intellectual, to many a workingman in the cities, the words appeared full of hope and of the promise of better days to come when justice should reign and all men be brothers. Bonaparte did not erase "Liberty, Equality, Fraternity" from the monuments. Far from denouncing them, he applauded them. He called himself "the son of the Revolution" and declared he would complete its work. True, he twisted the principles to his own use. If he maintained equality, he sacrificed liberty.

William Pitt, the Younger. After a portrait by John Hoppner (d. 1810).

Yet to our own day, the principles of the French Revolution have had great and enduring significance. "Liberty" has implied certain political ideals. Government should be exercised, not autocratically by divine right, but constitutionally by the sovereign will of the governed. The individual should not be subject to the arbitrary rule of a king, but should be guaranteed possession of personal liberties which no state might abridge. Such were liberties of conscience, worship, speech, and publication. The liberty of owning private property was proclaimed by the French Revolution to be an inherent right of man.

"Equality" has signified the social principles of the Revolution. It meant the abolition of privilege, the end of serfdom, the destruction of the feudal system. It assumed that all men were equal before the law. It carried the hope that every man might have an equal chance with every other man in the pursuit of life and happiness.

"Fraternity" was the symbol of the idealistic brotherhood of those who sought to make the world better, happier, and more just. At the same time, it was the watchword of the new French nationalism. For the sake of humanity the French nation should be exalted. Schools, armies, even religion should be nationalized. No longer should mercenaries fight at the behest of despots for dynastic aims. Henceforth a nation in arms should be prepared to do battle under the banner of "fraternity" in defense of whatever it believed to be the nation's interests.

Political liberty, social equality, national patriotism—these three have remained the ideals of all who have looked for inspiration to the French Revolution.

CHAPTER 42

Career of Napoleon, 1799–1815

A. The French Republic under Bonaparte's Consulate, 1799–1804

From 1799 to 1814 the history of France and of all Europe was so closely tied to the career of Napoleon Bonaparte that these years have been called "the era of Napoleon." During this period France experienced a molding of previous revolutionary achievements into permanent institutions and yet at the same time was subjected to a military dictatorship. French militarism triumphed briefly, and French armies helped to spread revolutionary ideas all over Europe, arousing nationalism in other countries. During the first five years of the period France remained nominally a republic, with Bonaparte as First Consul. From 1804 to 1814, he ruled as Emperor Napoleon I over a French Empire.

In 1799 General Bonaparte was thirty years of age. Short, stocky, quiet, with cold grey eyes, he had already an imperious and commanding manner. Born in Corsica, he had received a military education in France and had become a junior artillery officer in the royal army. Restless and ambitious, he threw in his lot with the Jacobins after the Revolution broke out and achieved some distinction in the recapture of Toulon (1793) and the defense of the Convention (1795). But it was his First Italian Campaign of 1796 that made him famous. Bonaparte was selfish and ruthless, but he had qualities which convinced his associates that he was "a man of destiny." He was a mili-tary genius, knowing how to use the new tactics evolved for the mass armies that had been created by the Revolution. He had an amazing memory and a sense of the dramatic. He was an exceptionally able organizer and administrator. He understood politics and diplomacy, and, being unrestrained by religion, morality, or sentiment, he was prepared to use any means to gain his ends.

When Bonaparte seized power in 1799 he appreciated that the French people were weary of weak government and disorder. He set himself a constructive program which he carried into effect within a few years. First, he devised a new government for France (Constitution of the Year VIII), under which a semblance of democracy was retained by a three-house legislature, but in which real authority was centered in Bonaparte as First Consul and in his appointed Council of State. Submitted to the people in a plebiscite, the new constitution won an overwhelming majority. The vote was really one of confidence in Bonaparte and of disapproval of the Directory.

Within France, the First Consul's firm hand soon reduced the country to order. He repressed royalists on one hand, and Jacobins on the other. The press was subjected to rigid censorship; and under Fouché, an ex-Jacobin, a pervasive secret police and spy system was developed to keep watch over the citizenry.

Bonaparte effected a permanent reorganization of local government in France. In 1800 he abolished the elective officials in the *arrondissements* and *départements* and vested their functions in prefects and sub-prefects appointed by, and responsible to, the First Consul. Elective councils were retained but with very limited powers. While village mayors were to be appointed by the prefects, mayors and police officials of cities would be named directly by the chief of state. Thus Bonaparte completed the work of centralization begun by Richelieu. The system was hardly democratic but it was efficient.

Bonaparte also effected an ecclesiastical settlement in France. In 1799 the country was still divided into two camps—that of devout Catholics who were hostile to the revolutionary restriction and persecution of the church, and that of liberals and radicals who wished to maintain a separate French church or to do away with Christianity altogether. In 1801 Bonaparte negotiated a concordat (or treaty) with Pope Pius VII. By it, the Pope accepted the confiscation of church property and the suppression of monasteries in France. In return, the Republic undertook to pay the salaries of the clergy. The First Consul would nominate the bishops, the Pope would invest them with their office. Priests would be appointed by the bishops. Thus was the Catholic

Church officially restored in France, but it was tied to the state even more closely than in the days of Louis XIV. So advantageous did this concordat appear that it continued in force for over a century and under a dozen different governments. Bonaparte made similar arrangements with the Protestant churches and Jewish synagogues in France.

The First Consul put French finances in order. By rigid economy, exacting collection of taxes, and contributions levied on conquered lands, Bonaparte balanced the French budget. He completed the work of the Directory in establishing sound currency, and he set up the Bank of France (1800) as a central credit and note-issuing institution.

Surrounding himself with expert legal advisers, Bonaparte pushed through the wholesale reformation of French law which had been begun in the revolutionary period. The resulting civil code (1804)—the Code Napoléon—was followed by a code of civil and criminal procedure, a penal code, and a commercial code. Into the new legal structure were written many of the major achievements of the Revolution—equality before the law, religious toleration, abolition of

Napoleon's Crowning of Josephine (1804). Painting by Jacques Louis David (d. 1825).

Courtesy Bettmann Archive

serfdom, of feudalism, and of privilege, and equality of inheritance. If harsh punishments and the legal subjection of women were maintained, still the codes were so clear and otherwise so enlightened that they were later adopted or imitated in many other lands. Bonaparte was rightly hailed as a second Justinian.

Public works of various sorts also distinguished Bonaparte's rule. Highways were built, bridges constructed, canals and harbors improved. Paris and other cities were beautified by public buildings and monuments in the classical style, and many of them commemorated the triumphs of Napoleon Bonaparte.

In one matter, however, Bonaparte failed signally. He hoped to reëstablish the old French colonial empire. To Haiti he dispatched his brother-in-law, General Leclerc, with an expeditionary force to subdue the slaves who had revolted and killed or expelled their French masters. Spain was forced by Bonaparte to give back to France the territory of Louisiana (west of the Mississippi) which France had ceded in 1763. But Leclerc's efforts failed miserably, and anticipation of war with Great Britain determined Bonaparte to sell Louisiana to the United States in 1803.

One task which he had set himself in 1799—defeat of the Second Coalition of Britain, Austria, and Russia—Bonaparte was eminently fitted to perform. He inspirited the French army, perfected the system of supply, and appointed able officers to commands. By flattery and diplomacy, he induced the half-insane Tsar Paul (1796–1801) of Russia to withdraw from war against France and even to revive (with Prussia, Sweden, and Denmark) an armed neutrality of the North against Great Britain. Then in 1800, with lightning swiftness, Bonaparte led his armies through the Alps, and at Marengo in Italy overwhelmed the Austrian forces. Another French army crushed the Austrians at Hohenlinden in Germany. In 1801 Austria signed the treaty of Lunéville which reaffirmed the peace of Campo Formio.[1] and reëstablished French dominance in Italy. Though the British were still masters of the sea, though Nelson broke up the armed neutrality of the North

---

[1] See above, p. 542.

in 1801 by bombarding Copenhagen (without a declaration of war), and though the remnants of the French Egyptian expedition were compelled to surrender, still France seemed clearly unconquerable on the continent. Under these circumstances Great Britain and France signed, at Amiens in 1802, a treaty which was designed to inaugurate a peace, but which proved to be only a truce.

In a few short years, Bonaparte as First Consul had brought France order, prosperity, victory, and peace. If his rule was a thinly disguised dictatorship, yet he had maintained many of the social and legal gains of the Revolution. The future of France promised to be golden. Secure and firmly governed, there seemed nothing to prevent her from consolidating her position and her internal well-being. But instead, the story of the ensuing years is one of military glory culminating in disaster.

B. Creation of the Napoleonic Empire and Its Triumphant Expansion

After the peace of Amiens was signed, Bonaparte felt strong enough in France to take another step toward absolute power. A new constitution (Constitution of the Year X) was devised in 1802, submitted to the people, and approved by an overwhelming majority. It was very similar to the previous one, with the exception that Bonaparte was now made First Consul for life, and that his powers, as against those of the hand-picked legislative bodies, were strengthened. There remained only one more step for the ambitious general to take. Two years later, by still another constitution and still another plebiscite, Bonaparte assumed the title of Napoleon I, Emperor of the French. On December 2, 1804, amid imposing ceremonies in the cathedral of Notre Dame at Paris and in the presence of Pope Pius VII, Bonaparte placed a crown upon his own head. The peculiar nature of the new government was symbolized by the inscription on French coins of the time, "French Republic, Napoleon Emperor." Nor was the heritage of the recent revolutionary past eliminated by the Empire. The social gains were still intact. The tricolor was still the country's flag. The words, "Liberty, Equality, Fraternity," still appeared on public buildings.

There were changes, however. As a form of address, "monsieur" replaced "citizen." The republican calendar fell into disuse. Old titles of nobility were restored, and new ones created. The revolutionary generals who accepted the new regime became "Marshals of the Empire." Distinguished service to the Emperor was rewarded by membership in a newly created Legion of Honor. Some of the noble *émigrés* came back to add social graces to the imperial court, where they rubbed elbows with men of lowly origin who had won fame on far-flung battlefields.

If the Consulate had brought peace and reform, the Empire involved almost continuous war. Even before the Empire was established, war had broken out again (May, 1803) with Napoleon's inveterate enemy, Great Britain. Though the Revolution was in a real sense over in France, many Englishmen felt they were fighting its personification by opposing Napoleon. Moreover, in the expansion of French control there was an economic or strategic threat to Britain, especially in the Low Countries and in the Mediterranean. During the next decade, whatever else happened on the continent, Britain warred against France by every means at its disposal.

In part, the Franco-British conflict was naval. Here the British won an early and decisive victory. On October 21, 1805, their fleet under Lord Nelson crushed combined French and Spanish fleets off Cape Trafalgar (near the Strait of Gibraltar). Nelson lost his life in the battle, but Britain won unquestionable supremacy on the seas. So effective was Napoleon's censorship, however, that no French newspaper mentioned the naval disaster till after the fall of the Empire.

Before Trafalgar, Napoleon had planned to invade England and had even gathered troops along the Channel coast (1803–1804) for the purpose. He was diverted, however, by events in Austria; and after Trafalgar, British sea power rendered any such plan too hazardous. Napoleon was reduced to attacking Great Britain by indirect

means. In true mercantilist fashion, he sought to bring Britain to its knees by closing its markets and thus reducing its exports. By a series of decrees, he prohibited the importation of British goods, not only into France, but into all the other parts of Europe which he controlled. This method of trying to ruin Britain was known as the "Continental System," and much of Napoleon's effort was spent in attempting to enforce it, and to persuade other Continental countries such as Russia to adhere to it.

Britain replied to the Continental System by a series of royal "Orders in Council" designed to keep neutral ships from going to French-held ports and to oblige them to come to England. Thus a neutral ship could go almost nowhere in Europe without breaking either the French or the British regulations. In enforcing their orders, the British had the advantage of sea power, and so ruthlessly did they use it in violation of neutral rights that the youthful United States at length (1812) felt impelled to declare war on Great Britain.

In the long run, Napoleon's Continental System failed of its purpose. Many British goods were in great popular demand on the Continent, and even Napoleon found himself obliged to license the importation of certain ones. There was much smuggling, and countries which were subject to Napoleon, or allied with him, sought to alleviate their shortages by buying British products and overseas goods supplied by the British, whether legally or illegally. Moreover, British sea power secured the markets of the whole world, except Europe, for British merchants, who rapidly expanded their trade in distant areas such as Spanish America.

Though the commercial war went against Napoleon and slowly sapped French strength, land victories for a while seemed to offer ample compensation. In vain Great Britain organized and subsidized a Third Coalition, with Austria, Russia, and Sweden against France. Abandoning his projected invasion of England, Napoleon rapidly marched his armies into Germany and defeated the Austrians at Ulm (October 20, 1805). Moving on, he occupied Vienna, then turned northward, and crushed an Austro-Russian army at Austerlitz in Mora-

Battle of Trafalgar. By Clarkson Stanfield (*d. 1867*).

Courtesy Bettmann Archive

via on December 2, his "lucky day." Austria was thus forced out of the coalition, and by the treaty of Pressburg the Austrian Emperor Francis I ceded Venetia to Napoleon and the Tyrol to Bavaria.

Prussia had not originally joined the Third Coalition, but now its King Frederick William III, relying (unwisely) on a military reputation inherited from Frederick the Great, and fearing a complete French triumph, entered the war and sent an army under the aged Duke of Brunswick against Napoleon. The French and Prussian armies met at Jena (October 14, 1806), and the

Prussians were defeated in disastrous and most humiliating fashion. At a stroke, the Prussian military prestige evaporated. Napoleon entered Berlin and occupied most of Prussia. Prussian Poland was torn away and erected into a Grand Duchy of Warsaw under Napoleon's ally, the Elector of Saxony, and Prussia was compelled to reduce her army to 42,000 men.

Russia remained to be dealt with. In a bloody winter battle at Eylau in East Prussia, Napoleon won a partial victory; and then at Friedland, he was completely successful. At Tilsit, on a raft in the middle of the Niemen River, Napoleon and the young Tsar Alexander I (1801–1825) met to discuss peace terms. Alexander was dazzled by Napoleon's personality and by his generosity, for the victor exacted hardly an inch of Russian soil and asked only that Russia join in excluding British trade from Europe. On the other hand, Alexander was given to understand that he might deal as he would with Finland and the Ottoman Empire. "What is Europe?" exclaimed the emotional Tsar, "where is it, if it is not you and I?"

Thus was the Third Coalition liquidated, with Sweden paying a heavy price for having adhered to it. In 1808 Russia seized Finland, which had long been Swedish. In 1809, Sweden recognized the Russian conquest, and agreed to exclude British goods. The Swedish King Gustavus IV was compelled to abdicate in favor of his aged and childless uncle, Charles XIII, who soon named as his heir one of Napoleon's generals, Marshal Bernadotte.

By 1808, Napoleon's French Empire was at its height. Northern Italy had been made into a kingdom with Napoleon as King and his stepson Eugene Beauharnais as Viceroy. The kingdom of Naples was ruled by his brother Joseph, as was Holland by his brother Louis. The Pope, the King of Spain, and the King of Denmark were his allies. The Russian Tsar called him friend and brother. Sweden was being brought into line. The Grand Duchy of Warsaw was a recruiting ground for his army. All Germany was under his influence. Prussia and Austria had become second-rate powers.

Germany was being entirely made over by the impact of Napoleonic France. The left bank of the Rhine had been incorporated into France, and in subsequent rearrangements scores of petty independent states east of the Rhine had been wiped out. Altogether, the number of German states was reduced from more than three hundred to less than one hundred. Bavaria, Württemberg, and Baden in the south had been enlarged to reward them for aiding Napoleon, and the rulers of Bavaria and Württemberg, and also of Saxony, had been further compensated with the title of king.

Besides, in 1806 the South German states and a number of others virtually seceded from the Holy Roman Empire and formed a Confederation of the Rhine under Napoleon's protection. Napoleon announced that he no longer recognized the Holy Roman Empire, and on August 6 the Habsburg Emperor Francis II resigned the imperial crown which had been worn by his ancestors for centuries. The work of a long line of French kings and statesmen was completed by Napoleon, and the Holy Roman Empire had come to an inglorious end. Its last Emperor contented himself with assuming the new title of Francis I, Hereditary Emperor of Austria.

By 1808, all Germany was at the mercy of Napoleon. Prussia was shorn of half her lands, the Confederation of the Rhine enlarged, and a kingdom of Westphalia carved out of northern and western Germany for Napoleon's brother Jerome. Most significant of all, wherever French rule extended, there followed the abolition of feudalism and serfdom, the recognition of the equality of all citizens before the law, and the enlightened principles of the Code Napoléon.

The humiliations of Austria were not at an end. Far from accepting French dominance, Francis I, with the aid of two patriotic assistants—the Archduke Charles and Count Stadion—busied himself with reforming the army, mustering the national resources, and stimulating national spirit. In 1809, when Napoleon was involved in difficulties in Spain, an opportunity seemed to have come for Austria to strike. Francis I declared war, and the Archduke Charles led an army into Bavaria. But with his usual rapidity Napoleon rushed from Spain, forced the Austrians back upon Vienna, and seized their capital once more. In May, the Austrian commanders inflicted a reverse upon Napoleon at Aspern but failed to follow it up, and then at Wagram in July Napoleon won a victory which induced the Austrians once again to make peace. This time, they had to yield Austrian Poland to Russia and to the Grand Duchy of Warsaw, and the Illyrian provinces on the Adriatic to France. As an additional pledge, Napoleon shortly afterwards married Maria Louisa, daughter of Francis I. The French Emperor had long desired an heir to his throne, and he made the new marriage possible by securing an annulment of his previous marriage with Josephine Beauharnais. Fate still seemed to smile on the Corsican, for in 1811 Maria Louisa bore him a son who was given the title of King of Rome.

Yet all was not well with the Napoleonic fortunes. The troubles in Spain alluded to above were beginning to be a bleeding wound in the side of the French Empire. In 1807 Napoleon had poured troops into Spain and Portugal. He had seized Lisbon and announced that Portugal, long Britain's ally and commercial vassal, was now part of the Continental System. In the next year Napoleon had lured to France the aging Spanish King Charles IV, together with the heir to the throne, Prince Ferdinand, and the flashy chief minister of Spain, Godoy. Then he had forced both King and Prince to resign all claims to the Spanish throne. Napoleon's brother Joseph was thereupon promoted from the kingship of Naples to that of Spain, while a brother-in-law, Joachim Murat, was given the vacant Neapolitan throne.

In July 1808, Joseph was crowned at Madrid. But in August he was driven out by an angry uprising of Spaniards. At last the triumphant advance of the French, inspired by their new nationalism, had run into the aroused patriotism of another people, and they were to find this much more difficult to deal with than divine-right monarchs and professional armies. Spanish priests and nobles made common cause with bourgeois and peasants. When they could not put an army in the field they employed guerilla tactics, which cut French communications and bewildered the best French generals. Moreover, the British sent an army under Sir Arthur Wellesley (later Duke of Wellington) to Portugal in August 1808, and quickly, with the aid of Spaniards and Portuguese, he expelled the French from that country. Thus began the Peninsular War, which lasted until 1813 and brought eventual disaster to the French. Napoleon might put Joseph back on the throne at Madrid. He might seize cities and win battles. But he could not subdue the Spanish people nor could he oust the stubborn British.

C. Decline and Fall of the Empire

From 1808 to 1814 Napoleon's power was on the wane, though for some time the decline was concealed by victories like that at Wagram. Certain limitations of Napoleon's genius and of his dictatorship were becoming apparent. He was growing older and less energetic, while his ambition and lust for conquest kept on increasing. He was becoming more averse to taking advice. Moreover, the armies, on which his power really rested, were changing in character. They had once been composed almost wholly of patriotic Frenchmen fighting with enthusiasm for the fatherland and the Revolution. Now, more and more, they included Poles, Germans, Italians, Dutch, and Danes recruited more or less forcibly and held together mainly by discipline and faith in the Emperor. Nor were the French officers the dashing young patriots of the earlier days. They were more cautious, more self-seeking. Some of the best had died in battle.

In the conquered and allied lands, there had been many who originally viewed the coming of the French apathetically, or else hailed with enthusiasm the introduction of the revolutionary principles and reforms. But liberty and equality somehow proved to be mirages. For the subject countries, French rule was harsh. There were taxes and requisitions, there were confiscation (or even looting) and conscription, and there was always another war to drain off resources in men, goods, and money. Gradually other European peoples came to look upon the French as conquerors who were more oppressive than the old divine-right rulers. Conquered countries became nationalistic.

Everywhere, too, the Continental System came to be hated. It led to shortages, high prices, and stagnant trade. Smuggling grew apace and the loopholes that were opened up were too numerous for the French to plug. Despite constant pressure from Napoleon, the continental states simply could not be kept in line. They bought British goods when and how and where they could. When Pope Pius VII objected to both the Continental System and Napoleon's treatment of church matters, the Emperor made

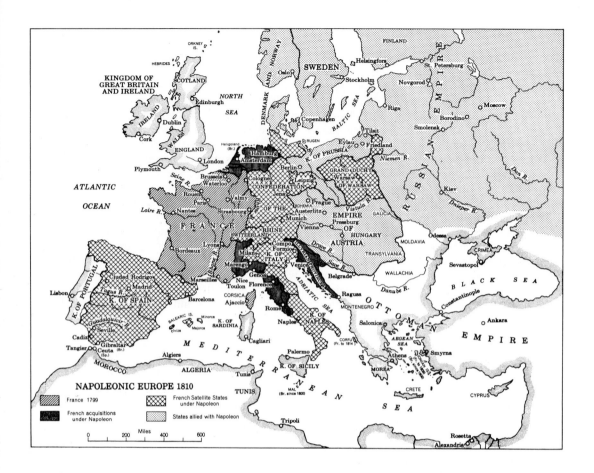

NAPOLEONIC EUROPE 1810

France 1799
French acquisitions under Napoleon
French Satellite States under Napoleon
States allied with Napoleon

him prisoner and seized the Papal State (1809). The next year he deposed his brother, Louis, for admitting English goods into Dutch territory, and incorporated Holland into France. And all the while French generals and their armies were trying vainly to subdue Spain and Portugal and expel British forces from the peninsula.

After Wagram (1809), it seemed for a time as if Napoleon need expect no more trouble in central Europe. But the very magnitude of the French victories was raising a new kind of opposition. In Prussia, King Frederick William III turned to new advisers who, between 1807 and 1813, wrought a veritable regeneration in that kingdom. The chief of these were Baron vom Stein and Chancellor Hardenberg, who felt that only by renovating the state and removing abuses could Prussia be made strong again. Under their leadership, serfdom was abolished (1807) and the peasants were made absolute owners of part of their holdings; the administration of the government

was simplified and improved; and modernized agencies of local government were set up. At the same time two military reformers, Scharnhorst and Gneisenau, were remaking the Prussian army, despite limitations put on it by Napoleon.

To check these developments in Prussia, Napoleon forced the dismissal of Stein, who proceeded to turn to Austria and Russia, preaching hatred of the French as he went. Stirred by reforms, humiliated by defeats and aroused by French arrogance, the Prussian people, and other Germans as well, felt the stirrings of a new national patriotism. Through the work of societies like the *Tugendbund* (League of Virtue) and the writings of authors like Fichte and Arndt, a new loyalty to the fatherland was rapidly created. No longer did the French have a monopoly of national patriotism. As for liberty, to a Prussian in 1810 it seemed that it could be secured only by ousting the French conquerors.

In Austria the ill-timed campaign of 1809

was but a stage, not an end, of national effort. The army was rebuilt; diplomatic channels to Napoleon's other victims were kept open; Austria was biding her time. Meanwhile the Spanish war continued. In 1812, Wellington, with British and Spanish troops, won a resounding victory at Salamanca, captured Madrid, and drove out the French. In the same year, groups of liberal Spaniards, who had learned revolutionary doctrines from both French and British, gathered at Cadiz and drafted a new constitution for Spain. This document long served as a model for liberal constitutions throughout southern Europe. Under it, sovereignty was vested in the "nation," legislative power in a single-house legislature (or *cortes*), and executive power in the king and his ministers. But the king was to have only a suspensive veto over acts of the *cortes*. The constitution proclaimed individual liberty and legal equality. While it recognized Catholicism as "the religion of the Spanish nation," it abolished the Inquisition and limited church property.

Though the four fateful defects in the Napoleonic Empire—Napoleon's own character, the changing nature of his army, the impracticability of the Continental System, and the rise of nationalism among the peoples of Europe—were now painfully evident, it was a break between Napoleon and the Tsar Alexander that ushered in the final disasters. Alexander had been irritated by the enlargement of the Grand Duchy of Warsaw after Austria's defeat in 1809. He had been impeded, rather than aided, in his designs on the Ottoman Empire. He had been annoyed when Napoleon dethroned one of the Tsar's relatives in German Oldenburg and annexed that duchy. But most of all, he was alienated by Napoleon's efforts to enforce the Continental System on Russia. Russia needed to import manufactured goods from England and to export grain thither. Gradually Alexander permitted the resumption of trade with Britain. Napoleon had either to fight for his system—his sole weapon against Great Britain—or see the system collapse in northern Europe. Napoleon chose to fight.

Early in 1812, Napoleon was busy preparing for war against his recent ally. He forced Prussia and Austria to promise aid,

and he gathered an army of 430,000 men. Less than half were French veterans; the rest were Germans, Poles, Italians, Dutch, Swiss, Danes, Yugoslavs. Nor was Alexander inactive. He made peace with the Ottoman Empire, reached understandings with Great Britain and Sweden, negotiated secretly with Austria and Prussia, and mobilized an army. Napoleon declared war on June 22, 1812, crossed the Niemen river two days later, and proceeded into Russia. Refusing to engage in open battle, the Russians retreated slowly, merely harassing the French advance. Unable to defeat or capture his foe, Napoleon penetrated ever deeper into Russia. Only once, at Borodino on September 7, did one of the Russian generals, Kutusov, fight a real battle. Both sides lost heavily, but the French were able to move on and to take Moscow a week later.

On the very night of Napoleon's triumphal entry, Moscow was set on fire. Supplies were burned up; the inhabitants fled. Already, the Russians in their long retreat had adopted a "scorched earth" policy of destroying provisions that might aid the French. Now, lack of food made it impossible for Napoleon to winter his army in Moscow. To advance was futile. He could only retreat. On October 22, he evacuated Moscow and began to retrace his steps toward Germany. The Russian forces followed, still risking no major engagements but ever attacking the French rear and cutting off stragglers.

Napoleon's retreat from Moscow is one of the most famous and horrible episodes in history. Downpours of rain changed to sleet and snow. Swollen streams checked the march. Food was short. The French forces abandoned their baggage. They ran out of ammunition. They froze to death in snow drifts. They fell from exhaustion. The retreat became a rout, the rout a disaster. It was only a pitiable and starving remnant of the *Grande Armée* which on December 13 recrossed the Niemen into Germany. Fully half a million lives had been sacrificed upon the fields of Russia to Napoleon's ambition. Yet he sought to reassure the afflicted French people by announcing, "the Emperor has never been in better health."

For a moment Alexander hesitated, for

Russia was now free. But urged on by Baron vom Stein and his own desire to play the role of deliverer of Europe, he decided to attempt the final overthrow of his rival. On January 13, 1813, Alexander led his troops across the Niemen and proclaimed the liberty of the European peoples. It was the beginning of the War of Liberation.

Russia was promptly joined by Prussia, together with all northern and central Germany. On the other side, Napoleon speedily gathered a new army of 200,000 men from France, southern Germany, and Italy. On May 2, he defeated the Prussians and Russians at Lützen, but lack of cavalry prevented him from following up his victory.

At this point, Metternich, chief minister of Austria, arranged an armistice and proposed a general peace which would have left France many of its conquests. But Napoleon only wanted time to gather more forces for a decisive victory. By the utmost effort, he got together an army of 120,000 men; and then he rejected the peace proposals. Whereupon Austria joined the coalition of Russia, Prussia, Sweden, and Great Britain.

Though at Dresden, in August, Napoleon won another victory against the Austrians, his forces were gradually hemmed in by the converging Allies. At Leipzig, in October he fought a three-day "Battle of the Nations." Outnumbered, deserted in the midst of battle by his Saxon troops, he went down to defeat. A fortnight later, Napoleon led a remnant of his army back across the Rhine. Germany was freed.

After the "Battle of the Nations" the French allies and puppets were either overwhelmed or deserted to the other side. Only the King of Saxony, on whom Napoleon had conferred the additional title of Grand Duke of Warsaw, remained loyal. Yet in the face of these events Napoleon rejected still another peace offer from Austria that would have left him a France bounded by the Alps, the Rhine, and the Pyrenees. Needlessly he prolonged the war on French soil, with the remains of his defeated army and with hastily gathered recruits.

Early in 1814 three large foreign armies moved in on France from the north and east, while Wellington, having cleared Spain of French troops, led still another army into southern France. At the end of March, de-spite a brilliant and desperate defense on the part of the Emperor, Paris surrendered to the Allies. Thirteen days later, by a personal treaty of Fontainebleau, Napoleon abdicated his throne, renounced all rights to France for himself and his family, and in return was granted sovereignty of the little island of Elba (off the northwest coast of Italy), an annual pension of two and a half million francs, and the Italian duchy of Parma for his wife, Maria Louisa. After an affecting farewell to his Old Guard, Napoleon departed for Elba, where he dwelt for ten months.

In 1793 European monarchs had banded together to restore divine-right monarchy and the old social order in France and to stamp out revolutionary ideas. But in 1814, while they restored a Bourbon to the throne, and gave him a France with the boundaries of 1792, they did so with the understanding that he would recognize and confirm the chief social and political reforms of the Revolution. The Restoration was engineered, in the name of "legitimacy," by the unscrupulous Talleyrand, ex-bishop, ex-revolutionist, ex-Napoleonic minister, who now courted the Tsar Alexander.

The "legitimate" heir of Louis XVI was his brother, the Count of Provence, a stout and cynical old gentleman, who had been living quietly in England these many years and who now made a solemn entry into Paris. The new king kept what forms of the old regime he could. He assumed the title of Louis XVIII, "King of France by the Grace of God." He reckoned his reign from the death (1795) of his nephew, the dauphin ("Louis XVII"). He replaced the tricolor with the lilied white flag of his family. At the same time, however, he granted a constitutional "charter," making France a limited monarchy. He confirmed the liberty and equality won by the Revolution. He left the church lands in private hands. Simultaneously there were restorations elsewhere in Europe. Ferdinand VII came back to Spain; Pope Pius VII returned to Rome; Victor Emmanuel I mounted the throne of Sardinia.

But the last had not been heard of Napoleon. He found Elba irksome and longed to get back to the Continent. By February 1815, circumstances seemed favorable. His enemies were divided, Austria and Great Britain being at odds with Prussia and Russia over the fate of Saxony and Poland. In France the return of the *émigrés* with their old airs and the tactless treatment of Napoleonic veterans were arousing ill-feeling, while the concessions of Louis XVIII did not render the majority of Frenchmen enthusiastic about the return of a Bourbon monarchy.

With a small bodyguard Napoleon escaped from Elba, eluded British warships, and landed at Cannes on March 1, 1815. Troops sent out to arrest him could not resist the familiar uniform; and without firing a shot Napoleon entered Paris on March 20. Louis XVIII was already jogging over the Belgian frontier. By an astute manifesto, Napoleon clinched his hold on France. He promised to renounce war and conquest, to maintain liberty and equality, and to establish a constitutional government. The French either rallied to Napoleon or remained quiet.

But if Napoleon was right about France, he was wrong about the rest of Europe. The four great powers forgot their differences, renewed their alliance, and rushed troops toward France. To oppose them Napoleon raised a new army and marched into Belgium. There on June 18, at Waterloo, he fought the final great battle of his remarkable career. The defeat administered by Wellington with a British-Dutch-German army was, at the close of the day, turned into a rout by the arrival of Blücher and his Prussians. Even had Napoleon won at Waterloo, he could not have hoped to make head against the combined and determined armies of Britain, Russia, Prussia, and Austria. The return from Elba was a really hopeless venture from the start. On June 22, Napoleon abdicated again, and before long the Allies reoccupied Paris, bringing Louis XVIII back "in their baggage train."

Napoleon surrendered himself to the British, and this time no chances were taken. The former Emperor was sent to the lonely and rocky island of St. Helena in the south Atlantic. There he lived for five and a half years until his death in 1821. There he dictated his memoirs, subtly compounded of truth and falsehood, in which he sought to depict himself as the true son of the revolution, the friend of oppressed nationalities, the lover of peace, who had been driven to war and disaster by wiles of the British and of despotic European monarchs. These writings in exile were to become the basis of a "Napoleonic legend" which would contribute in time to seat another Bonaparte on the throne of a second French Empire.

D. Abiding Influence of the French Revolution and Napoleon

The events of the French Revolution and the era of Napoleon brought into Europe a new kind of government based on ideas of the eighteenth-century "enlightenment" and in harmony with a social structure in which the middle class was especially strong. The new regime consisted of a highly centralized government based on the doctrine of popular sovereignty, supported by a national army and national schools, inspired by national patriotism, and capped by a parliament representing citizens rather than classes. The new society was individualistic, and insistent on the political rights and liberties of its members. Special privileges of all sorts were banished. All religions were tolerated. This was the new system so firmly rooted in France by 1815 that no restored Bourbon could overturn it. It was in France, and in Europe, to stay.

The new regime, belief in which constituted "liberalism," was in Europe to stay because it was strong in France and had also become the goal of many revolutionary liberals outside of France. The extension of direct French rule into the Netherlands, Germany, and Italy had accustomed persons there to a centralized state, to an individualistic society, to equality before the law, and to the modern Code Napoléon. Even in areas not directly ruled from Paris, like Spain or Naples or southern and central Germany, rulers dependent on France had abolished feudalism and serfdom and instituted a more liberal form of government. The ideas of democratic rule, social equality, and religious toleration, though but briefly experienced, were not forgotten. Moreover, in countries like Prussia and Austria, humbled by Napoleon, some farsighted statesmen appreciated the value of the new institutions and perceived that the old divine-right monarchies must be reformed if they were to be strong and popular.

Of all the lessons France taught Europe between 1789 and 1815 the most impressive was nationalism, and so well and so fast did Europe learn it, that nationalism has been a major and rapidly growing force in European life down to the present day. The soldiers of Napoleon who bore the tricolor flag of France from Naples to Moscow, and from Lisbon to Berlin, were effective messengers of the new nationalist gospel—the *nation* bound together by ties of language and culture and history, the nation one and indivisible, the nation as the regenerator of human society, the nation above any class or religion, the nation as the supreme object of human devotion and sacrifice, the nation with a "mission."

Wherever they went the French aroused nationalism in two ways—positive and negative. Positively they showed the peoples of Europe what nationalism was and what a nation in arms could do. Negatively by their conquests they made themselves hated as oppressors and roused a fierce national patriotism in *opposition* to French nationalism.

In Germany and Italy, where the French, at the start, were greeted by many as deliverers who were bringing liberty from old tyrannies, their rule at length fanned a fierce patriotism that led to reforms, to nationalistic books, poems, and hymns, and to patriotic societies. In Poland, where national patriotism had developed in response to the partition of the country by Russia, Austria, and Prussia, Napoleon intensified it by his partial recreation of a Polish national state in the Grand Duchy of Warsaw. Even in the conglomerate Ottoman Empire, the Napoleonic era had its repercussions. Napoleon's invasion of Egypt brought western ideas to Ottoman territory. Among the Yugoslavs (Serbs, Croats, Slovenes) revolutionary and nationalist ideas were introduced by Napoleon's occupation of the Dalmatian coast.

Russia, too, experienced a new surge of patriotism and a new sense of national unity. The victorious war against Napoleon was a "fatherland war," and in the hatred roused by invaders the Russians found a deeper love for their own country. The Napoleonic wars also stimulated opposition and patriotism among the Austrian peoples. But the disparate nature of these prevented the rise of a single national patriotism for the whole Austrian Empire. If there was an increase of devotion to the Habsburg Emperor, there was at the same time an increased nationalist sentiment among the several peoples—German, Hungarian, Italian, Yugoslav, and Czech—which boded ill for the Empire's future unity. Great Britain, alone among the major powers, witnessed no fighting on its own soil in the long wars. But Britain was the very heart and center of the resistance to Napoleon. Her money, her ships, and in the end her soldiers were chief instruments in breaking the power of the Corsican. Britain's role in the long struggle and her final success led to a tremendous increase in British national patriotism.

Thus, in all Europe, while monarchs were restored and many of the trappings of the old regime were brought back by 1815, and while conservatism seemed triumphant everywhere, still there were forces at work that could not permanently be held down or ignored. These forces were the new ones brought to life in revolutionary France—liberalism and nationalism—and the greater of these proved in the long run to be nationalism.

CHAPTER 43

Conservative Restoration and Liberal Rebellions, 1815–1840

A. The Congress of Vienna and Peace Settlement of 1815

At Vienna in the autumn of 1814 assembled leading statesmen of Europe to conclude the long series of revolutionary and Napoleonic wars with what they hoped would be a permanent peace settlement. Among them were the Tsar Alexander of Russia, Talleyrand as agent for Louis XVIII of France, the Duke of Wellington and Lord Castlereagh representing Great Britain, and Stein and Hardenberg, the former of these serving as adviser to the Tsar rather than to the Prussian King. Foremost in the assemblage was Prince Clemens Metternich, chief minister of Austria.

Metternich came of a distinguished Rhenish family, and his wife was a daughter of Count Kaunitz, the Austrian diplomat of the eighteenth century.[1] He had entered the Austrian diplomatic service and had rapidly advanced in it until in 1809 he became chief minister, a position he was to hold for thirty-nine years. He helped Austria recover from its defeat at Wagram. He arranged the marriage of Maria Louisa with Napoleon and at the same time schemed against the French Emperor. So well did he plan that Austrian intervention was the decisive factor in the campaign of 1813 and Austria thus became the foremost power among the victorious allies—a fact which was recognized by the choice of Vienna as the place for the peace conference.

The so-called Congress of Vienna was

hardly a congress in the usual sense. Delegates of all the participating countries met together only to sign a general treaty, the terms of which had been largely determined beforehand by the "Big Four"—Austria, Prussia, Russia, and Great Britain. True, Talleyrand so skillfully took advantage of disputes among the four, and so persuasively composed their differences, that gradually he was admitted to their inner councils. Thereby defeated France had a voice in some of the most important decisions.

The chief cleavage among the "Big Four," which gave Talleyrand his opportunity, was over the fate of Poland and Saxony. Before 1813, the Tsar Alexander had promised Austria and Prussia to give them back the Polish territories they had held in 1795. But subsequently he aspired to reconstitute the old Polish kingdom with himself as King, and he accordingly proposed that Prussia, instead of receiving its former large part of Poland, should annex Saxony (whose king had stood by Napoleon to the end). Prussia accepted the proposal, but Great Britain and Austria opposed it, and the deadlock was so serious that for a while war seemed imminent among the victors. Finally, through efforts of Castlereagh and Talleyrand, a compromise was effected. Prussia got part but not all of Saxony, and the Tsar got the greater part of Poland (henceforth called Congress Poland). Of Polish territories, Austria retained Galicia, and Prussia kept Posen and the "corridor" separating East Prussia from the rest of the Prussian kingdom.

[1] See above, p. 469.

Congress of Vienna with Metternich presiding. After a painting by Jean-Baptiste Isabey (d. 1855).

One principle underlying the whole settlement of Vienna was the restoration, so far as practicable, of the boundaries and reigning families of Europe as they had been before 1789. It was much the same as the "legitimacy" which Talleyrand was urging in order to preserve France and to enable her, though defeated, to play a major role in the councils of Europe. In line with this principle, the Bourbons were reinstated in Spain and in the Two Sicilies, the house of Orange in Holland, the house of Savoy in Sardinia, the pope in the Papal State, and a number of German princes in their former possessions. In the name of legitimacy, likewise, Austria recovered the Tyrol and most of the other lands she had lost, and the Swiss confederation was restored under a guarantee of neutrality.

A second principle, and one at variance with the first, involved "compensations," in order to reward those who had played major roles in defeating Napoleon or to build strong states around the borders of France as a check against future French aggression. Great Britain was rewarded with the French islands of St. Lucia, Tobago, and Mauritius, with the important Dutch Colonies of Ceylon and South Africa, and, in addition, with Malta, Heligoland, the Ionian islands, and part of Dutch Guiana. To "compensate" the Dutch for their colonial losses, as well as to create a stronger country on the border of France, the southern (Austrian) Netherlands were transferred to Holland. To "compensate" Austria for this change, she was given a commanding position in Italy. To Austria went the historic Venetian Republic and the duchy of Milan, while members of the Austrian Habsburg family were seated on the ducal thrones of Tuscany, Parma, and Modena.

Russia was "compensated" with Finland and additional Polish territory, while Sweden was "compensated" for the loss of Finland, and Denmark punished for its loyalty to Napoleon, by taking Norway from the latter and giving it to the former. Prussia made notable gains to reward her contribution to the victory and to strengthen her against France. She received Swedish Pomerania, all of Westphalia, most of the Rhineland, and two fifths of Saxony, though the rest of Saxony was restored to its legitimate ruler despite his long fidelity to Napoleon. The additions to Prussia gave her mineral resources which were to be of the utmost importance in the next century, and in the long run tended to transform her from an agricultural into the leading industrial state of Germany. The kingdom of Sardinia made advances too, for not only were its former lands restored but to them was added the port of Genoa with its surrounding territory. It was hoped that an enlarged Sardinia, together with a strengthened Prussia and Holland, would keep France in check.

In reconstituting Germany, few people wanted to push legitimacy so far as to restore the hundreds of petty states of 1789, and there was no serious effort to reëstablish the Holy Roman Empire. Stein would have liked to unite Germany into a single national state under the Prussian king. But Austria and the south German rulers opposed any such plan. Since states-rights' ideas were still strong in Germany, the result was the creation of a loose German Confederation of the thirty-eight remaining states, with a Diet consisting of delegates of the various rulers. Austria presided over the Diet and dominated the Confederation.

There was little concession in the peace settlement of 1815 to the forces of liberalism or nationalism, and no sympathy indicated for new ideas about individual rights, political liberties, and constitutional government. Some humanitarianism was exhibited by adoption of a declaration sponsored by Britain, to the effect that the slave trade should be abolished, though the several countries were left free to fix their own dates for its abolition. And some significant contributions were made at Vienna to existing international law, not only concerning precedence among ambassadors and ministers, but also provision for free navigation of certain international rivers, notably the Danube and the Scheldt.

Metternich was especially anxious to prevent the recurrence of revolutionary violence and international war. For this purpose he (and other leading members of the Vienna Congress) relied, not on any world league or super-state, but on joint action of a continuing Quadruple Alliance of Austria, Prussia, Russia, and Great Britain. Later in 1815, after the adjournment of the Congress of Vienna, the Tsar Alexander proposed the formation among European sovereigns of a "Holy Alliance," in which they would promise in both domestic and foreign affairs to take as "their sole guide" the precepts of Christianity, "the precepts of justice, Christian charity, and peace." Out of deference to the Tsar, this curious "alliance" with him was signed by Frederick William III of Prussia and the Emperor Francis I of Austria, although the latter confessed he did not know what it meant. Eventually all the rulers of Europe subscribed to it, except the Pope, the Sultan of Turkey, and the Prince-Regent of Great Britain.

In the minds of later liberals, the Holy Alliance became the symbol of a conspiracy of reactionary monarchs to stamp out nationalism, liberalism, and social justice. But this was unfair. The Holy Alliance never really functioned. It was the *Quadruple Alliance* of the "Big Four" which, under Metternich's guidance, provided a temporary bulwark against forces of disorder and change.

B. Metternich and the Concert of Europe

The period from 1815 to 1848 has usually been called the "Era of Metternich," for during those years the Austrian statesman was the central figure in Europe. His policies were frankly conservative. He wanted to conserve peace between states and to conserve the old regime within each country. Believing that nationalism and liberalism and other revolutionary principles were responsible for the devastating wars which had afflicted Europe from 1792 to 1815, he did his utmost to discourage and repress any reassertion of those principles in the Habsburg territories and wherever else he could bring his influence to bear. For some fifteen years, Metternich's efforts were largely successful, though afterwards he found himself obliged to accept compromises with liberalism in several parts of Europe outside of Austria, and finally in 1848 even Austria rebelled against him and his conservative system.

During the early part of this period

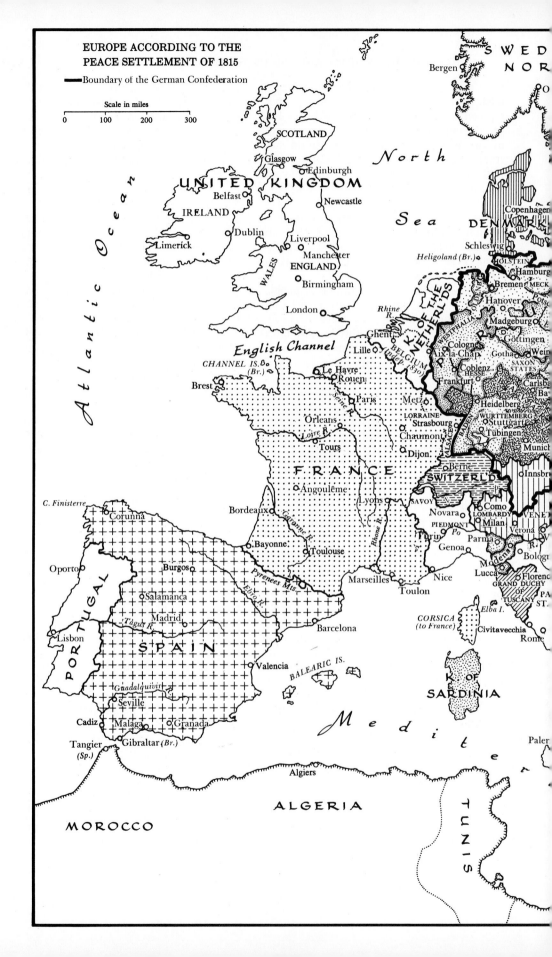

EUROPE ACCORDING TO THE
PEACE SETTLEMENT OF 1815

—— Boundary of the German Confederation

Scale in miles

0   100   200   300

SCOTLAND

Bergen

SWED
NOR

Glasgow
Edinburgh

North

UNITED KINGDOM

Belfast
Newcastle

IRELAND

Sea

DENMARK

Copenhagen

Dublin
Liverpool
Manchester
ENGLAND

Schleswig

Heligoland (Br.)

HOLSTEIN

Hamburg
MECK

Atlantic Ocean

Birmingham

Bremen

Hanover

Po

London

Rhine
R.

Madgeburg

Göttingen

English Channel

Ghent

THE
NETHERLDS

WESTPHALIA

Colognes

Wein

CHANNEL IS.
(Br.)

Lille

BELGIUM
(to Fr. 1830)

Aix-la-Chap.

Gotha

SAXON
STATES

Le Havre

Coblenz

HESSE

Carlsba

Brest

Rouen

Frankfurt

Ba

Seine R.

Paris

Metz

Heidelberg

WÜRTTEMBERG

Orleans

LORRAINE

Strasbourg

Stuttgart

Loire R.

Chaumont

Tübingen

Tours

Dijon

Munich

FRANCE

Angoulême

Berne

SWITZERL'D

Innsbr

Lyons

SAVOY

Como

Novara

LOMBARDY

VENE

C. Finisterre

Corunna

Bordeaux

Garonne R.

PIEDMONT

Milan

Verona

Rhone R.

Turin

Po

Oporto

Bayonne

Toulouse

Genoa

Parma

V
R.

PORTUGAL

Burgos

Pyrenees Mts.

Marseilles

Nice

Lucca

Modena

Bologr

Salamanca

Ebro R.

Toulon

GRAND DUCHY
OF
TUSCANY

Florence

PA
ST.

Lisbon

Tagus R.

Madrid

CORSICA
(to France)

Elba I.

Civitavecchia

Rome

SPAIN

Barcelona

Guadalquivir

Valencia

BALEARIC IS.

K. OF
SARDINIA

Seville

Cadiz
Malaga
Granada

Mediter

Tangier
(Sp.)

Gibraltar (Br.)

Paler

Algiers

MOROCCO

ALGERIA

TUNIS

FINLAND
Helsingfors
Cronstadt
St. Petersburg
Reval
G. of Finland
Stockholm
Volga R.
Nishni Novgorod
Novgorod
Baltic Sea
Riga
Moscow
Smolensk
Danzig
Niemen
Königsberg
LITHUANIA
R U S S I A
K. OF
Vistula R.
Posen
Warsaw
POLAND
Kiev
Breslau
Rep. of Cracow
(to Austria 1846)
UKRAINE
Troppau
Lemberg
Ekaterinoslav
Don R.
Dniester R.
BESSARABIA
Kherson
Dnieper R.
Sea of Azov
AUSTRIAN EMPIRE
Pressburg
Jassy
MOLDAVIA
Odessa
Crimea
Kerch
Budapest
HUNGARY
(1856)
Sevastopol
Drava R.
Temesvar
WALLACHIA
DOBRUJA
Black Sea
Bucharest
Sava R.
Belgrade
Danube R.
BOSNIA
SERBIA
Plevna
Varna
MONTE-
NEGRO
Sofia
BULGARIA
Scutari
Adrianople
Constantinople
Unkiar Skelessi
Kiuprili
Scutari
Durazzo
Salonica
Gallipoli
A N A T O L I A
E M P I R E
Brindisi
Janina
CORFU
Larissa
Mitylene
Konieh
Alexandretta
KINGDOM
OF THE
SICILIES
(Fr. 1807)
Cephalonia
(Br. 1815)
Missolonghi
Chios
Smyrna
Taurus
Reggio
Patras
Athens
Samos
Catania
Zante
GREECE
(Indep. Kindom 1830)
Navarino
Aegean Sea
RHODES
CYPRUS
Beirut
MALTA (Brit.)
Acre
CRETE (Candia)
Jerusalem
Jaffa
Sea
Aboukir B.
Damietta
Alexandria

Metternich counted on support of the so-called "Concert of Europe." This was really the Quadruple Alliance of Austria, Prussia, Russia, and Great Britain, which in 1818, by the inclusion of France, was expanded into a Quintuple Alliance. The "Concert," under Metternich's guidance, dealt with threats to peace by a series of conferences— at Aix-la-Chapelle in 1818, at Troppau in 1820, at Laibach in 1821, at Verona in 1822. These conferences became the means of concerting measures not only for the prevention of international conflict, but also for the suppression of liberal and nationalist movements within the various countries. At Troppau in 1820, Russia and Prussia formally agreed with Austria to act jointly against revolutionary distrubances anywhere in Europe. From this decision Great Britain dissented, and henceforth the "Concert" was practically a Continental affair.

With only minor exceptions the period from 1815 to 1830 was one of triumphant conservatism. In Austria, Metternich set an example of repression of nationalists and liberals. He maintained a strong army, established a rigorous censorship of publications and theatrical performances, created an efficient police system, and put conservative ecclesiastics in charge of education. The reforms that Joseph II had attempted in Austria before the French Revolution were ignored and more or less forgotten.

So far as he could, Metternich saw to it that the same sort of policies were applied throughout Germany and Italy. Austrian influence was able to block most of the attempts to give the other German states the constitutions which their princes had quite generally promised during the patriotic War of Liberation. The Duke of Saxe-Weimar was an exception, for he conceded a constitutional government. But he brought down on himself a joint protest of the reactionary powers when in 1817 some students at the Wartburg, celebrating the tercentenary of Luther's theses against indulgences, burned various symbols of the old regime. Two years later a conservative spy named Kotzebue, in the pay of Russia, was assassinated by a liberal student. This event gave Metternich an opportunity for action. He summoned a meeting of German states-

men at Carlsbad and secured the promulgation of the resulting "Carlsbad decrees" by the Diet of the German Confederation. The decrees provided for close supervision of university professors and students, for muzzling the press, and for the establishment of a committee to investigate revolutionary plots. They likewise forbade the granting of any constitution "inconsistent with the monarchical principle."

No less complete was Metternich's influence in Italy. Austria ruled in the north, Habsburg princes and the pope in the center, and the Bourbon Ferdinand I in the south. All joined in reëstablishing the old regime. Police, troops, and spies held down all liberal agitation, and the fact that in much of Italy the repressive hand was a foreign one made it especially irksome to Italian liberals and nationalists. Only in the kingdom of Sardinia was there a ruler with exclusively Italian interests. Even here, Victor Emmanuel I, at the behest of Metternich, disavowed any idea of introducing liberal reforms. Officially all Italy was conservative and reactionary.

In France, Louis XVIII, who was restored a second time to the throne of his fathers in 1815, sought to follow a policy of compromise. He retained many Napoleonic institutions like the Legion of Honor, the Bank of France, the concordat with the pope, and the system of state education; and he recognized the Napoleonic nobility. The charter he granted, while by no means democratic, since the suffrage was limited to the very wealthy, did guarantee personal liberties as well as giving France a constitutional government and providing a legislature where public matters could be discussed. The first legislature so elected proved more royalist and reactionary than the King, who dissolved it in 1816. The second was more moderate and during the next years finances were improved, the electoral law simplified, and the censorship of the press relaxed. But in 1820, the King's nephew, the Duke of Berry, was assassinated by a fanatical liberal. Once more reaction set in. Strict censorship was reëstablished. Control of the Catholic clergy over education was strengthened. The electoral law was again modified in a conservative direction. The police and spy systems were made more effective, and the army was used to overawe any opposition.

These conservative tendencies in France were accentuated in 1824 when Louis XVIII died and was succeeded by his brother, Charles X, who had long been the leader of the ultra-royalists. He was crowned with old-fashioned pomp. He surrounded himself with conservative and reactionary advisers. He promised an indemnity of a billion francs to émigré nobles who had lost their lands during the Revolution.

In Great Britain, it was the conservative Tory faction which had won the long war against Napoleon, and, under the leadership of Castlereagh and Wellington, it maintained its control in the post-war period. Aging George III had become hopelessly insane in 1811. His son acted as prince-regent till 1820 and then on the death of his father ascended the throne as George IV. In both capacities he showed himself a thoroughgoing conservative in public affairs and an immoral fop in private life. Under such guidance Britain did not at first vary much from Metternich's idea of sound government. The repressive measures of the war period were renewed and strengthened. The press was censored and suspensions of the right of *habeas corpus* made arbitrary arrests possible.

Mass meetings of protest were held, and one of them at Manchester was broken up by troops who killed six persons. Parliament then (1819) passed still more repressive laws—the so-called Six Acts, which restricted seditious writings and public meetings, provided for the searching of private houses for arms and the speedy trial and punishment of offenders, and levied a heavy stamp tax on newspapers to keep them from the hands of the masses. When violent radicals responded in 1820 by plotting to assassinate the Tory cabinet, this "Cato Street Conspiracy" was ferreted out and five of its participants were hanged. Even in Britain liberalism seemed to be ebbing.

C. Spanish American, and Greek Revolutions

Under the muffling blanket of Metternich's conservative system, liberalism and nationalism were concealed but not eliminated. They became underground forces ready to flare into activity when opportunity offered. In Germany, university students formed secret societies (*Tugendbund, Burschenschaft,* etc.) in behalf of national unity and liberal reform. Occasionally, they organized demonstrations noisy enough to cause uneasiness in Vienna and Berlin.

In southern Italy, the secret society of the *Carbonari,* with its oaths and passwords, was more active. It inspired in 1820 a rebellion in Naples against the tyrannical Ferdinand I (1815–1825). The King, terrified when he found that his army would not support him, accepted a liberal constitution

Royal Restoration of Law and Order in Naples. Honoré Daumier (d. 1879).

modeled after the one drawn up in Spain in 1812. But the next year, at the international conference at Laibach, he "invited" an Austrian army to Naples "to restore order." To Metternich's satisfaction, Ferdinand, supported by Austrian bayonets, annulled the constitution and began a savage campaign of reprisals, which helped to give the Two Sicilies the reputation among liberals of being the worst governed state in Christendom.

Crushed in southern Italy, liberals had a brief day in the north. In 1821, soldiers in Piedmont mutinied and seized Turin, the capital. King Victor Emmanuel I abdicated in favor of his brother, Charles Felix, while the liberal Prince Charles Albert, next in line for the throne, was made Regent. Charles Albert at once proclaimed a liberal constitution. Here again, Metternich intervened with Austrian troops. The Regent was expelled, and absolutism was restored under Charles Felix.

Even in Russia, least liberal of the great powers, there was some trouble. When Alexander I died suddenly in December 1825, revolutionary societies, led by young officers and a group of intellectuals imbued with ideas which they had learned from the French and from Freemasonry, attempted to alter the succession to the throne. Alexander had designated his second brother Nicholas as his successor, passing over his liberal but erratic first brother Constantine. The revolutionaries, with "Constantine and Constitution" as their slogan, organized a mutiny of troops at St. Petersburg. But Constantine would not aid the movement, and Nicholas quickly suppressed it. The leaders of this December revolt, who were later known as Decembrists, were severely punished. But they had shown that even Russia was not wholly unaffected by liberal undercurrents.

In Spain there was active liberal opposition to King Ferdinand VII, who, on his restoration in 1814, had abolished the constitution of 1812 and brought back the old absolutism, exempted the clergy and nobles from taxation, and reëstablished the Inquisition. The opposition centered in secret societies like the Carbonari and Freemasons, and permeated the army which the King assembled at Cadiz in 1819 for shipment to America to suppress revolts that had broken out in the colonies during the Napoleonic period. A mutiny occurred in the army, and presently rioting broke out in various parts of Spain. In March 1820, Ferdinand, quaking with fear, gave his royal oath to restore and support the constitution of 1812. In a subsequent declaration, he said, "Let us advance frankly, myself leading the way, along the constitutional path." The insurgents took him at his word and laid down their arms.

The hypocritical Ferdinand had no intention of keeping his word. While pretending to be a constitutional monarch, he was scheming to restore absolutism. The Spanish liberals themselves, mainly middle class in origin, fell to quarreling; nobles and clergy objected to reforms that were attempted; the peasants were for the most part apathetic. Meanwhile the Concert of Europe under Metternich was much disturbed by the events in Spain. The Tsar Alexander wanted to lead a Russian army thither to crush the revolution. But the French were not eager to have foreign troops march across their soil. Finally, at the Congress of Verona in 1822, it was agreed that France should send an army to Ferdinand's aid.

Early in 1823, after the Spanish liberals had rejected a joint demand from France, Russia, Austria, and Prussia to abolish the constitution of 1812, the Duke of Angoulême, nephew of Louis XVIII, led a French army across the Pyrenees. The invaders this time met no such national opposition as Napoleon had encountered, for the Spanish people were sorely divided and the conservative majority generally welcomed the French. In May, the French captured Madrid and the Spanish liberal ministers fled to Cadiz, taking Ferdinand along as a hostage. On October 1, they released the King on the understanding that he would grant a general pardon and set up a moderate government. Cadiz thereupon surrendered. But once safe in the French lines, the King annulled his promises and pronounced the death sentence on all constitutionalists. In vain Angoulême advised moderation. Hundreds were executed and other hundreds were jailed or exiled.

Events in Spain, and the threats of the

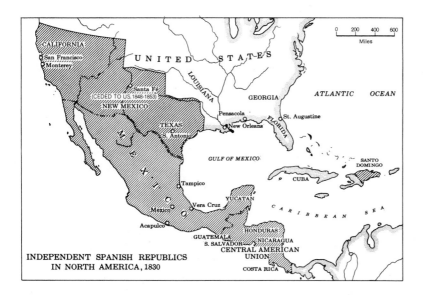

INDEPENDENT SPANISH REPUBLICS
IN NORTH AMERICA, 1830

SPANISH AND PORTUGUESE
SOUTH AMERICA, 1830

Independent Spanish republics

Independent Portuguese Empire of Brazil

great powers, likewise helped to put an end to a simultaneous liberal revolt in Portugal and to install a reactionary government in Lisbon. But in this confused period Brazil declared its independence (1822) and became a separate Empire under a member of the Portuguese royal house.

The backing of King Ferdinand VII of Spain by most of the Concert of Europe might have enabled him to carry out his project of subduing the rebellious Spanish colonies in America except for two facts. First, the British since 1789 had developed a thriving trade with Spanish America, and they had no wish to see reëstablished a colonial system which would once more shut out their goods. Second, the United States was thoroughly sympathetic with the movement in the Spanish colonies to free themselves from Spain. Encouraged by the British, the American President James Monroe announced in 1823 a policy since known as the "Monroe Doctrine." Thereby, the United States made clear its intention of refraining from any intervention in European affairs, but at the same time insisted that any intervention by European powers in the Americas would be regarded as an unfriendly act. With the British and American navies prepared to back up the Monroe Doctrine, no foreign aid was forthcoming for Ferdinand overseas, and within a brief period all Spanish American colonies, except Cuba and Puerto Rico, were independent republics.

Meanwhile, in eastern Europe, in the confines of the Ottoman Empire, there were developing other cracks in the conservative attempt to maintain the *status quo*. In 1817, a Serbian peasant named Miloš Obrenović, who had first followed the earlier Serb leader Karageorge and had later had him murdered and who had since led a popular uprising against the Turks, won from the Sultan grudging recognition as "supreme prince" of Serbia. In 1821, a Greek prince named Ypsilanti rebelled in Moldavia in expectation of Russian help, which Metternich persuaded the Tsar to withhold. The revolt was crushed and Ypsilanti ended in an Austrian prison.

But soon afterwards occurred a general Greek revolt, to which the Turks replied with severe reprisals, including a massacre of Christians. To Metternich, the Greeks were rebels against a "legitimate" sovereign, and he would do nothing for them. But Russia, bound by ties of religion to the Greeks, was sympathetic, and western Europe was deeply stirred. Liberals saw in the Greek revolt a popular uprising for liberty. Romantics saw in it an attempt to revive the ancient glory that was Greece. Even conservative Christians could approve it as a crusade against the infidel. Money, volunteers, and arms flowed to the Greeks. The English poet Lord Byron died in Greece where he had gone to fight for Greek independence.

For a while the Greeks held their own. Then the Sultan called in the aid of fierce troops from Egypt under Ibrahim Pasha, who swept up and down the Greek peninsula with fire and sword and sold thousands of Christians into slavery. Indignation in Europe rose. When the Sultan in 1827 rejected the request of Great Britain, France, and Russia for an armistice, the fleets of these countries destroyed the Turco-Egyptian naval squadron at Navarino. The next year the Tsar Nicholas I declared war on the Ottoman Empire, and, with some help from the Serbs, the Russians fought their way almost to Constantinople and compelled the Sultan to sign the treaty of Adrianople. The treaty was a milestone in the dismemberment of the Ottoman Empire, for by it the Sultan virtually recognized the independence of Greece, and granted autonomy, not only to Serbia under Miloš Obrenović, but also to the Rumanian principalities of Moldavia and Wallachia. Despite Metternich, the status quo was being seriously altered. Nationalism was making significant gains.

On the other side of Europe also, conservatism was waning, for in Great Britain, though the Tory party still held power, new leaders were coming to the fore who favored reform. George Canning as foreign minister had encouraged the United States to oppose the Concert of Europe in the Monroe Doctrine. William Huskisson, much interested in new industries, secured reductions in the tariff and removal of the most constrictive features of the old Navigation Acts. It was a Tory parliament, too, that freed Protestant Dissenters (those not belonging to the Anglican Church) from political disabilities (1828), and admitted Catholics to parliament and public affairs (1829). But such steps seemed paltry to the growing body of liberal sentiment in England. The rising industrial towns were demanding representation in parliament. Radicals were urging that the suffrage be extended even to workingmen. Conservatism in England was weakening.

D. Liberal Revolts and Reforms of the 1830's

If Metternich's system was jarred in the 1820's, it was cracked (though not destroyed) in 1830. In France, middle-class liberals and urban workingmen had been growing restive under the increasingly reactionary regime of King Charles X. In 1829, in defiance of the legislature, he appointed as prime minister a former *émigré*, Prince Polignac. After repeated votes adverse to the premier, the King dissolved the lower house and called for new elections. But the chamber which was returned was even more hostile to Polignac

than the one which it replaced. Then the King decided on what amounted to a destruction of the constitutional charter. On July 26, 1830, he published four arbitrary ordinances which tightened restrictions on newspapers, dissolved the newly elected chamber, changed the electoral law so as to eliminate most of the middle-class voters, and called for new elections. With incredible lack of foresight the King did not concentrate any extra troops in the capital.

Paris responded immediately with armed insurrection, and after three days of sporadic street-fighting, Charles X abdicated in favor of his young grandson, the Count of Chambord, and left hastily for England. Thus with but little bloodshed the "July Days" of 1830 ended divine-right monarchy in France. The victors, however, were by no means in agreement on what the ensuing government should be. Some were republicans, others liberal monarchists, and there were even a few Bonapartists. The liberal monarchists, headed by a journalist, Adolphe Thiers, and a wealthy banker, Jacques Laffitte, proposed, as a new king, Louis Philippe, Duke of Orléans, heir of the

GREECE AND THE BALKANS
IN 1832

Independent Greece

Autonomous Serbia and Montenegro

Boundary of the Ottoman Empire

Miles
0   100   200   300   400

younger line of the Bourbons, and son of a Philippe "Egalité" who had voted for the death of Louis XVI in 1793. The republicans (radical intellectuals and Parisian workers mainly) were won over to this proposal by the aging Lafayette. Louis Philippe had fought in the revolutionary army in 1792, and after that, whether in exile or in France, had lived a life of bourgeois respectability.

The accession of Louis Philippe to the throne was peculiar. It was not based on inheritance, nor on plebiscite, nor on constitutional processes. It was the result of the decision of the leaders of a brief but successful Paris revolution, later endorsed by the national legislature. From the start Louis Philippe tried to win middle-class support and to conciliate republican sentiment. He restored the tricolor flag, called himself "King of the French" (not "King of France"), and accepted his role as a constitutional monarch under the somewhat liberalized Charter. The establishment of the "July Monarchy" was so clearly a triumph of the middle class that it is often called the "Bourgeois Monarchy."

It was a saying of the time that when France caught cold all Europe sneezed. Such was the case in 1830. The suddenness and the success of the July Revolution at Paris alarmed conservatives and heartened liberals everywhere. In the Belgian Netherlands, forces of liberalism and nationalism were let loose by the events at Paris. The Belgians had been for fifteen years unhappy and restive under the Dutch rule imposed on them by the peace of Vienna, for not only were the two parts of the Netherlands divided by more than two centuries of history, tradition, and conflict, but the Belgians were industrial and Catholic, while the Dutch were agricultural or commercial and largely Calvinist. The Dutch King William I had, moreover, irritated his Belgian subjects by favoring Dutch law, language, religion, and officials. In 1830, the news of the revolution at Paris started riots in Brussels. The riots developed into a revolt; and when William refused to concede to them a separate legislature, the Belgians declared their independence (October 1830).

The international situation favored the Belgians. Metternich and the Tsar Nicholas had other matters on their minds, and the British and the new French government approved of a separate Belgian state. In 1831 an international conference at London reached an agreement by which Belgium would become an independent state with a German prince, Leopold of Saxe-Coburg, as its constitutional King. But the Dutch King William I was stubborn. It took pressure from the British navy and the French army and the lapse of eight years before he finally recognized the separation of Belgium from Holland and signed a treaty of peace and friendship. At this time (1839) all the great powers—Britain, France, Russia, Prussia, and Austria—guaranteed the independence and neutrality of Belgium, a guarantee that was to be respected for seventy-five years. In Belgium, liberalism and nationalism had scored a notable victory, marked by the definitive secession of Britain and France from Metternich's Concert of Europe.

What occupied Metternich and Tsar Nicholas in 1830, so that they could spare little thought for Belgium, was revolutionary disturbance in central, southern, and eastern Europe. In Germany, riots and demonstrations by liberals scared some of the rulers into granting constitutions. In the Papal State, liberals raised a new tricolor flag (red, white, and green) of Italian nationalism and democracy and repudiated the temporal rule of the new Pope Gregory XVI, while outbreaks in Parma and Modena forced their Habsburg rulers to flee to Vienna. But Metternich rushed into Italy Austrian troops, which soon restored "order" and the "legitimate" sovereigns.

It was Poland which gave trouble to Tsar Nicholas. He might favor nationalism in Greece, but Poland was another matter. Late in 1830, Poles, eager to reëstablish an independent nation and hopeful of aid from revolutionary France, rose in Warsaw against Russian rule. It took the armies of the Tsar nearly all of 1831 to crush the gallant Poles, who obtained words of sympathy but no practical assistance from France and Great Britain.

With the liquidation of the Polish and

Liberty Leading the People (1830). Ferdinand Delacroix (d. 1863).

Italian revolts, Metternich's conservative system seemed firmly entrenched once more in most of Europe. True, France and Belgium had now been added to Greece, Serbia, and Spanish America as areas where Metternich's beloved *status quo* had been drastically altered. It must be noted, however, that the alteration was not so violent as it seemed. Before many years Louis Philippe, despite his liberal gestures, showed himself so conservative at heart that he became quite friendly with Metternich.

Great Britain experienced no revolution in 1830. Yet the forces of liberalism were at work there, too, and they were strengthened by the growing importance of industry and the growing strength of the middle class. Britain already had national unity, a limited monarchy, and a good deal of individual liberty. It did not, however, have anything approaching democracy. The hereditary House of Lords wielded much influence, and the House of Commons was unrepresentative of the masses of people. Thriving industrial cities like Manchester, Birmingham, Sheffield, and Leeds had no representatives in Parliament, while, under the centuries-old system of apportionment, certain towns that had disappeared were still represented by two men in the House of Commons. In addition to these "rotten boroughs," there were also "pocket boroughs" where wealthy landlords controlled elections because the voters were few. Thus it was that great landlords, titled or otherwise, dominated the House of Commons as they did the House of Lords. And it was for this reason that the growing middle class of the cities, who wanted a government responsive to the needs of business, added their clamor to the outcries of liberals and radicals.

In 1830, demand for liberal reform of the House of Commons led to the resignation of the Tory ministry. The new Whig government under Earl Grey put a parliamentary reform bill through the lower House in 1831, but it was defeated by the House of Lords. New elections gave Grey a Whig majority in the Commons. But the Lords turned down a second reform bill. Then in 1832 noisy demonstrations in the cities, coupled with the inability of the Tory Duke of Wellington to form a government and with the King's reluctant pledge to create enough Whig peers to pass the bill in the House of Lords, had their effect. Enough Tory peers stayed away from the crucial vote to enable a third reform bill to pass and become law.

The reform of 1832 was a very moderate affair. It took 143 seats away from small towns and "rotten boroughs" and gave them to the new towns and cities and the most populous counties. It provided new and uniform qualifications for voters which in effect increased their number somewhat and gave the ballot to prosperous members of the urban middle class. Thus political power was henceforth shared between the landed and the business classes, and the latter were growing while the former declined in strength. Those who now had control regarded this solution as a happy and permanent one, a concession to democracy which did not endanger order or stability and would not lead to "mob rule." This arrangement, later to be called the "Victorian Compromise," carried Britain still further away from conservatism.

The reform of 1832 hastened certain changes that were already under way in Great Britain. It strengthened the Whigs who won the first elections under the new system, and who, in gratitude for the support of the industrial middle class, sponsored certain liberal reforms and indeed began to call themselves Liberals. Thus the Whig party was transformed into the Liberal party which was now composed of a right wing of tolerant aristocrats (the old Whigs), a center of ambitious business men (the real Liberals), and a small left wing of intellectuals and reformers (the Radicals). At the same time, the Tory party underwent changes. Its mildly "liberal" element was reënforced by the defeat in 1832 of the die-hards like Wellington. It accepted a

new leader in Sir Robert Peel, himself a factory owner. It began to call itself the Conservative party, and, if its right wing was still devoted to the landed interests, the Anglican Church, and intense nationalism, its left wing was not unsympathetic to business and not unwilling to coöperate on occasion with the Liberals.

The work of the reformed parliament moved England still further in a liberal direction. In 1833 Negro slavery was abolished throughout the British Empire, though the slave owners received financial compensation. In the same year, there was introduced a system of subsidizing private (church) schools from public funds so as to make education available to more people, and three years later the University of London was created by Parliament to compete with conservative Oxford and Cambridge. Other acts pushed forward the reform of the penal law, created a governmental bureau of public health, and prescribed more merciful treatment for debtors.

The reform of the "corn laws," advocated by liberal economists, was not so easy. England, which had exported grain till the mid-eighteenth century, had become, as the population grew, dependent in years of bad harvest on imports of grain ("corn") from abroad. To keep up the price of grain for the benefit of the landlords, a system of protective import duties had been developed. The lower the price of grain in England, the higher went the import duties on a "sliding scale." To the landlords who made the enclosures and adopted improved agricultural methods, these corn laws seemed like the keystone of national prosperity and the assurance of reasonable profits from their lands. Without them, they argued, England would become dependent on foreigners for food. But to the middle class and the new industrialists, the corn laws seemed like a way of raising the price of food (and thus of wages) so as to subsidize the conservative landlords.

Backed by such interested manufacturers as Richard Cobden and John Bright, there was formed in 1838 an Anti-Corn-Law League which launched a strenuous campaign of propaganda by speeches and pamphlets. The urban middle class was easily convinced. The workers thought the reform would give them cheaper food. Nature assisted the free-traders. In 1845, the English wheat crop was ruined by rain, and the blight of the potato crop in Ireland ushered in a period of starvation and emigration for that island. In Parliament the Conservatives had a majority. But in this crisis their own leader, Sir Robert Peel, deserted them. Aided by the Liberals he put through the repeal of the corn laws in 1846 and established free trade in grain.

It was the central group of the Liberal party, satisfied with the reform of 1832, which had the most influence in succeeding decades. But there were a few Radicals in Parliament and a good many outside it, who were urging further changes in a democratic direction. By 1838 groups of workers and some middle-class reformers agreed on a "People's Charter" of six points which would have made Great Britain a real democracy. The six points were: (1) universal manhood suffrage; (2) annual election of parliament; (3) equal electoral districts; (4) vote by secret ballot; (5) removal of property qualifications for members of parliament; (6) salaries for members of parliament so that poor men could afford to sit in it. For a time the "Chartists," by widespread agitation and propaganda, seemed to be gaining ground. But in Parliament the Liberals joined the Conservatives in rejecting their proposals; the government showed itself ready to put down any violence by force; and the Chartist leaders fell to quarreling among themselves. After 1842 the Chartist movement declined in numbers if not in noise. Enough of it remained, however, to cause a near-crisis in 1848.

France, despite the liberal July Revolution of 1830, did not move in a democratic direction under Louis Philippe. The right to vote was restricted by property qualifications to a quarter million owners of landed or industrial properties, and legislation was chiefly for the benefit of business men. The construction of railways was subsidized. A protective tariff was maintained. Workers' organizations remained illegal.

In one respect, Louis Philippe rather hesitantly pushed a policy inaugurated by Charles X. In 1830, to avenge an insult to a French consul by the ruler of Algiers,

and in the hope of winning some glory for his regime, Charles X had sent a military expedition to that country. After much wavering, Louis Philippe and his government decided to occupy, not only the city of Algiers, but the interior as well. Soon they found themselves with a full-fledged war on their hands, for a native leader, Abd-el-Kader, rallied the tribesmen against the French. Not until 1847, after long fighting, was Algeria subdued. But by then it was a French possession, with some 40,000 Frenchmen settled in it.

Within France, while the bourgeois monarchy of Louis Philippe pleased some of the wealthy middle class, it commanded little popular support. Gradually, at least six large groups crystalized in opposition to it: (1) *Legitimists*—nobles, clergy, and some peasants—who looked upon the Count of Chambord, grandson of Charles X, as the rightful King; (2) *Catholics*, both legitimist and liberal, who objected to existing restrictions on church schools and other anti-clerical legislation; (3) *Patriots*, who thought Louis Philippe's foreign policy of peace-at-any-price inglorious, and, inspired by the "Napoleonic Legend," looked back with longing to the glories of the Empire; (4) *Reformers*—middle class liberals—who wanted an evolution of the monarchy in a democratic direction; (5) *Republicans*, radical workers, artisans, and intellectuals who looked back with sympathy to 1793 and desired a popular democracy; and (6) *Socialists*, who were disturbed by social problems and the growth of an impoverished urban working class. Some of these last sought to establish Utopian coöperative communities. Others, like Louis Blanc, wanted to end unemployment by setting up coöperative factories called "national workshops." Still others followed Proudhon, who wished to abolish private property and authoritarian government and to create a new order based on anarchistic, voluntary coöperation. With such widespread dissent, the bourgeois monarchy was shaky.

Throughout continental Europe, except in France and Belgium, the conservative regime sponsored by Metternich and maintained in the face of the troubles of the 1820's and of 1830, still seemed solid in the early 1840's.

SELECT SUPPLEMENTARY READINGS FOR PART VIII

General. C. J. H. Hayes, *Political and Cultural History of Modern Europe,* 2 vols. (1932–1939); S. B. Clough and C. W. Cole, *Economic History of Europe* (1952); *Cambridge Modern History,* vols. VI–X (1904–1910); R. R. Palmer, *The Age of the Democratic Revolution: a Political History of Europe and America, 1760–1800,* 2 vols. (1959, 1964); M. S. Anderson, *Europe in the Eighteenth Century* (1961).

Chapter 39. W. Croft, *Scotland from Earliest Times to 1603* (1961); M. Ashley, *Great Britain to 1688, a Modern History* (1961); Godfrey Davies, *Early Stuarts, 1603–1660* (1937); G. P. V. Akrigg, *Jacobean Pageant: or the Court of King James I* (1962); G. E. Aylmer, *A Short History of Seventeenth Century England* (1963); C. Hill, *A History of England,* vol. V, *The Century of Revolution, 1603–1714* (1961); I. D. Jones, *The English Revolution* (1931); William Haller, *The Rise of Puritanism* (1938); C. V. Wedgwood, *The King's Peace, 1637–1641* (1955) and *Thomas Wentworth, First Earl of Strafford, 1593–1641: a Revaluation* (1962); John Buchan, *Cromwell* (1934); M. P. Ashley, *Financial and Commercial Policy Under the Cromwellian Protectorate* (1934); G. P. Gooch, *English Democratic Ideas in the Seventeenth Century* (2nd ed., 1927); G. N. Clark, *The Later Stuarts, 1660–1714* (1934); Arthur Bryant, *King Charles II* (1931); D. Ogg, *England in the Reign of Charles II,* 2 vols. (1934), and *England in the Reigns of James II and William III* (1955); Sir George Clark, *Three Aspects of Stuart England* (1960); G. M. Trevelyan, *English Revolution, 1688–1689* (1939) and *England Under Queen Anne,* 3 vols. (1930–1934); Winston Churchill, *Marlborough, His Life and Times,* 6 vols. (1933–1938); A. F. Pollard, *Evolution of Parliament* (1920); R. W. Harris, *A Short History of Eighteenth Century England* (1963); G. E. Mingay, *English Landed Society in the Eighteenth Century* (1963); J. H. Plumb, *Sir Robert Walpole,* 2 vols. (1956, 1961); Andrew Lang, *History of Scotland,* vol. III (1905); G. S. Pryde, *Scotland from 1603 to the Present Day* (1962); Richard Bagwell, *Ireland Under the Stuarts and During the Interregnum,* 2 vols. (1909).

Chapter 40. Additional to books listed for chapter 38: Leo Gershoy, *From Despotism to Revolution, 1763–1789* (1946); Henri Sée, *Economic and Social Conditions in France During the Eighteenth Century* (tr., 1926); J. B. Perkins, *France in the American Revolution* (1911); L. H. Gipson, *The British Empire Before the American Revolution,* 12 vols. (1936–   ); J. Steven Watson, *The Reign of George III, 1760–1815* (1960); L. Namier and J. Brooke, *Charles Townshend* (1964); C. L. Rossiter, *Seedtime of the Republic* (1953); S. F. Bemis, *The Diplomacy of the American Revolution* (1935); R. Coupland, *American Revolution and the British Empire* (1930); J. F. Jameson, *The American Revolution Considered as a Social Movement* (1926); W. H. Nelson, *The American Tory* (1961); N. Callahan, *The Royal Raiders: the Tories of the American Revolution* (1963); A. Whitridge, *Rochambeau* (1965); C. L. Becker, *Declaration of Independence, a Study in the History of Political Ideas* (1922); R. L. Schuyler, *Constitution of the United States, an Historical Survey of Its Formation* (1923). See also the new *American Nation* series edited by R. B. Morris and H. S. Commager, especially the volumes by L. H. Gipson, L. B. Wright, and J. R. Alden.

Chapter 41. Crane Brinton, *A Decade of Revolution, 1789–1799* (1934); G. Lefebvre, *The Coming of the French Revolution* (1947); P. H. Beik, *The French Revolution Seen from the Right* (1956); Leo Gershoy, *French Revolution* (1935); Albert Mathiez, *French Revolution* (tr. 1928) and *After Robespierre, the Thermidorean Reaction* (tr. 1931); Louis Madelin, *French Revolution* (tr. 1916); F. V. A. Aulard, *French Revolution, a Political History*, 4 vols. (tr. 1910); M. J. Sydenham, *The Girondins* (1960); Crane Brinton, *The Jacobins* (1930) and *The Lives of Talleyrand* (1936); G. G. Van Deusen, *Sieyès* (1933); Louis Barthou, *Mirabeau* (tr. 1913); J. S. Schapiro, *Condorcet* (1934); Louis Gottschalk, *Marat* (1927); Louis Madelin, *Danton* (tr. 1914); J. M. Eagen, *Maximilien Robespierre* (1938); Geoffrey Brunn, *Saint-Just* (1932); R. R. Palmer, *Twelve Who Ruled* (1941); W. T. Laprade, *England and the French Revolution* (1909); G. P. Gooch, *Germany and the French Revolution* (1920); C. J. H. Hayes, *Nationalism* (1960) and *Historical Evolution of Modern Nationalism* (1931); S. B. Clough, *France, a History of National Economics, 1789–1939* (1939).

Chapter 42. Geoffrey Brunn, *Europe and the French Imperium, 1799–1814* (1838); F. M. Kircheisen, *Napoleon* (tr. 1931); J. C. Herold, *Bonaparte in Egypt* (1962); J. H. Rose, *Life of Napoleon* (11th ed., 1934); August Fournier, *Napoleon*, 2 vols. (tr. 1911); J. M. Thompson, *Napoleon Bonaparte, His Rise and Fall* (1952); E. K. Knapton, *Empress Josephine* (1963); F. M. H. Markham, *Napoleon and the Awakening of Europe* (1954); V. J. Esposito and J. R. Elting, *A Military History and Atlas of the Napoleonic Wars* (1964); Sir Charles Oman, *Studies in Napoleonic Wars* (1929) and *History of the Peninsula War*, 7 vols. (1902–1930); R. G. Burton, *Napoleon's Campaigns in Italy* (1912); K. von Clausewitz, *Campaign of 1812 in Russia* (tr. 1843); R. B. Mowat, *Diplomacy of Napoleon* (1924); E. F. Heckscher, *The Continental System* (1922); H. A. L. Fisher, *Studies in Napoleonic Statesmanship: Germany* (1903); G. S. Ford, *Stein and the Era of Reform in Prussia* (1922); R. M. Johnston, *The Napoleonic Empire in Southern Italy and the Rise of the Secret Societies*, 2 vols. (1904); A. T. Mahan, *Influence of Sea Power upon the French Revolution and Empire, 1793–1812* (10th ed., 1898) and *Life of Nelson* (1899); J. H. Rose, *William Pitt the Younger*, 2 vols. (1911); Philip Guedalla, *The Duke of Wellington* (1931); Lord Rosebery, *Napoleon, the Last Phase* (1901); J. Marshall-Cornwall, *Marshal Massena* (1965).

Chapter 43. Sir Charles Webster, *Congress of Vienna, 1814–1815* (1920) and *Foreign Policy of Castlereagh* (1925); Harold Nicolson, *The Congress of Vienna, a Study in Allied Unity, 1812–1822* (1946); Algernon Cecil, *Metternich* (1933); Arthur May, *The Age of Metternich, 1814–1848* (1933); F. B. Artz, *Reaction and Revolution, 1814–1832* (1934); W. A. Phillips, *The Confederation of Europe* (1914); F. B. Artz, *France Under the Bourbon Restoration, 1814–1830* (1931); J. M. S. Allison, *Thiers and the French Monarchy* (1926); T. E. B. Howarth, *Citizen-King: the Life of Louis Philippe, King of the French* (1961); Élie Halévy, *History of the English People, 1815–1841*, 3 vols. (1924–1928); H. B. Clarke, *Modern Spain, 1815–1898* (1906); W. R. Thayer, *Dawn of Italian Independence*, 2 vols. (1892); C. M. Woodhouse, *The War of Greek Independence* (1952); William Miller, *A History of the Greek People, 1821–1921* (1922); H. W. V. Temperley, *History of Serbia* (1917); W. W. Kaufmann, *British Policy and the Independence of Latin America, 1804–1828* (1951); G. Masur, *Simon Bolívar* (1948).

From Mazzini
to Napoleon III

PART IX
ROMANTIC AND

Westminster Houses of Parliament, rebuilt in Gothic style. By Sir Charles Barry (d. 1860).

LIBERAL EUROPE, 1848–1871

THE PERIOD from 1848 to 1871 opens with revolutions which upset the conservative system of Metternich but do not lead at once to a triumph of either liberalism or nationalism. The ensuing years are, however, ones in which nationalism makes great progress. It gradually becomes an inspiring goal for conservatives as well as liberals. Through a series of brief wars considerable progress is made in redrawing the map of central Europe along national lines. A united Italy, a united Rumania, and a very strong and united Germany emerge.

At the same time, liberalism does progress too. Not in a leap, but by a series of changes, all western and central Europe moves toward liberal democracy. France, for example, at the end of the period substitutes for the quasi-liberal dictatorship of Napoleon III a democratic republic. Only in eastern Europe, in the Russian, Austrian, and Ottoman Empires, do barriers remain against nationalism and popular government, and even here there are signs of weakness in the barriers.

The age is one of romanticism in the arts not unrelated to the nationalism in political life. Artists, writers, and composers throw off the bonds of classic restraint and exuberantly seek for color, emotion, and vitality.

There is an increasingly rapid progress in science, and the results of scientific research begin to be applied to technology. Great Britain is transformed from a predominantly agricultural and commercial society to one which is preponderantly industrial. And industry begins to grow apace in Belgium, France, Germany, and across the Atlantic in the United States.

All this change is not accomplished without protest. On the one hand, some conservatives bemoan and resist the new developments. And on the other, radical protests begin to be heard from industrial workers and those who seek to speak for them.

By the end of the period, an age of optimism is dawning. It seems to many as if science and industry are actually bringing the kind of progress that which was foreseen in the Enlightenment of the eighteenth century and that the cure for surviving ills is more democracy, more liberalism, more nationalism, more science, more industry.

CHAPTER 44

Romanticism
and Scientific Progress

A. Romantic Movement in Literature and Art

For more than four centuries, from the fourteenth through the eighteenth, Europe had chiefly sought its models of taste and excellence in art, literature, architecture, philosophy, and politics by looking backward to ancient Greece and Rome. At the height of the "Enlightenment" in the eighteenth century, most dramatic writing followed classical rules; poetry dealt with classical themes and assumed classical forms; architecture was inspired by classical remains; education was in the classics. Portraits of statesmen frequently depicted them as clad in Roman togas. Revolutionaries like the French Girondists thought of themselves as playing roles of a Brutus or of the Gracchi.

In the latter half of the eighteenth century there were signs of reaction against classicism. The reaction gained ground in the early years of the nineteenth century. Between 1815 and 1848 it became the dominant note in the artistic and intellectual life of Europe. It is called romanticism.

Romanticism defies definition. Basically it was a revolt against the conventions and restraints of classicism. But the revolt took many different forms, and among its exemplars were revolutionaries and reactionaries, poets and business men, agnostics and devout Christians. The most important characteristics of romanticism were: (1) its emphasis on sentiment and nature as against reason and artificiality; (2) its glorification of the individual as against society as a whole; (3) its insistence on diversity and change as against uniformity.

With some romantics, the central theme was the veneration of nature, not as an abstract force imbued with laws and mathematics, but as something sweet and lovely, compounded of hills and fields, lakes and waterfalls, stormy seas and trackless forests. With others, romanticism meant an intense interest in history, not of Greece and Rome, but of the middle ages and the European peoples, not for the sake of the "lessons of the past" but for the sake of color, adventure, and pageantry. Still other romantics turned their attention to distant lands and peoples, to imaginary Utopias in the future, or to the exotic and the unusual. They looked before and after, and pined for what was not. Many of them were revolutionaries. Many found solace in mysticism and religious experience.

The sources of the romantic movement were manifold. In part, it arose from a disillusionment with the eighteenth century, with the "enlightenment" and its faith in reason and natural law, which had apparently led only to bloody wars and revolutions. In part, it sprang from a reaction against the growing drabness of urban life. In part, too, it was a recognition of great achievements of immediately preceding centuries, achievements which made those of classical antiquity appear pallid.

It was in English poetry that romanticism took earliest and strongest hold. In 1798,

Wordsworth and Coleridge published their joint volume of *Lyrical Ballads*, which found its inspiration in a mystical approach to life and the beauty of the commonplace in nature. Coleridge later added other strangely magical poems like *Kubla Khan* and *Christabel* to *The Ancient Mariner*, while Wordsworth described his emotional response to nature and to life in *The Prelude* and *The Excursion*. Soon Sir Walter Scott was composing historical ballads like the *Lady of the Lake* on Scottish love and valor. But the startling success of a new poet, Lord Byron, turned Scott to the long series of the romantic Waverley novels. Byron's stirring poems proclaimed his rebellion against society and the world, although they had, perhaps, less real poetic feeling than the word pictures of Keats, or the lyrics of the revolutionary Shelley.

Literature on the continent underwent a similar change as the nineteenth century advanced. Goethe, who had heralded romanticism in the eighteenth century, and then won fame as a classicist, completed his romantic masterpiece, *Faust*, just before his death in 1832. Schiller in his historical dramas had become thoroughly romantic by the time he wrote *William Tell* (1804). Heinrich Heine, a rebellious exile in Paris, was composing sentimental German lyrics in the 1820's. But it was French lyric poetry that under romantic influence reached new heights with Alfred de Musset, Alfred de Vigny, and Victor Hugo. Hugo won even greater fame with his dramas like *Hernani*, which at its production in 1830 started a riotous demonstration among the classicist critics, and with his historical novels such as *Notre Dame de Paris* and *Ninety-Three*.

Nor was romanticism in literature confined to western Europe. In Russia, Pushkin wrote romantic poems in the manner of Byron and historical dramas in imitation of Shakespeare, infusing both with Russian spirit and his own genius. Gogol gained distinction with romantic tales of country life, and with his masterpiece *Dead Souls*, a series of humorous and unflattering sketches of provincial society. In Poland, Mickiewicz glorified the Polish countryside in his historical poems. In Italy, Manzoni turned from classicism to romantic poetry and wrote the greatest Italian novel of the century, *I Promessi Sposi*. Elsewhere—in Spain, Portugal, Austria, Scandinavia—romantic writers broke loose from the classical tradition in poetry, drama, and the novel.

Pictorial art was less rapidly affected by romanticism than literature. Though they showed signs of the new tendencies, artists such as David or Ingres continued to paint in the classical tradition, while sculptors like Canova or Thorwaldsen sought to make their statues even more severely classical than those of the Renaissance. But the English painters Constable and Turner and the Frenchman Delacroix brought romanticism into painting by emphasis on vivid color, nature, history, and, in the case of the last, violent action. When François Rude was set to work on the sculptures for Napoleon's Arch of Triumph at Paris he put into them an intensity of emotion and dramatic action that was typically romantic.

At first in the nineteenth century, architecture tended to adhere to a severe classicism—the so-call "pure Greek." But before long the new vogue of the middle ages, exemplified by the success of Scott's novels, produced a tremendous interest in, and revival of, medieval gothic architecture. All sorts of buildings from churches to private homes were constructed in some approximation to the gothic style. When, after a

Immanuel Kant. After a painting done in 1791.

Courtesy Bettmann Archive

fire, the British houses of parliament were rebuilt in the 1840's, the new edifice was gothic.

Music went romantic earlier than pictorial or monumental art. Though the towering genius of Beethoven defies classification, his later work contains distinctly romantic as well as classical elements. Clearly romantic in their colorful melodies and their escape from restraining rules were such German composers as von Weber, Schubert, and Mendelssohn. Italian opera also became quite romantic, both in manner and subject, with the work of Rossini, Bellini, and Donizetti. The last based one of his most popular operas, *Lucia de Lammermoor*, on an historical novel by Sir Walter Scott.

B. Philosophy and Religion

In some ways Immanuel Kant (1724–1804) represented the culmination of the rationalist philosophy of the seventeenth and eighteenth centuries. Seeking to approach God and religious truth by reason, Kant decided that some features of the universe and of human experience can not be discovered or understood by rational processes. He concluded that God, the freedom of the human will, and the immortality of the soul are known by man, not through reason, but through a sort of inner moral instinct. This doctrine, that certain vital truths transcend human reason, is described, in some forms, as transcendentalism, and in others as "idealism." Kant's emphasis on the moral duties of man and his concepts of "spirit" and "will" paved the way for such a disciple as Fichte, who stood for a kind of transcendental pantheism and applied his philosophical "idealism" to the practical task of arousing German patriotism against Napoleon.

In the chair of philosophy at the university of Berlin, Fichte was succeeded by Hegel, who was at once an "idealist" and a mystic. Hegel's eloquent use of semi-scientific, semi-poetic phrases, his personification of abstract forces, his constant reference to "spirit"—world spirit, time spirit, national spirit, and so on—stirred romantic if somewhat misty thoughts in his hearers and readers. His emphasis on freedom gave hope to many liberals, while his survey of world history with its conclusion that the peak of the progress of the human spirit had been reached in the contemporary Prussian monarchy, where "man as man is free," reassured conservatives. Hegel thought that progress took place by a process which he called dialectic: a situation (thesis) gives rise to its negation (antithesis), and the two fuse to create a new situation (synthesis).

While philosophy was moving toward romantic "idealism," trends in religion were also distinctly away from the rationalism of the eighteenth century. Indeed, the period of romanticism witnessed a remarkable religious revival, a renewed faith in the supernatural and in Christianity, and a special emphasis on mystical religious experience. This was helped undoubtedly by current disillusionment about rationalism and also by romantic interest in the middle ages.

In the era of Napoleon, when Pope Pius VII was a prisoner of the Emperor and revolutionary ideas were in the ascendant, it had seemed to many persons as if Catholic Christianity were decaying and before long might disappear. But the years after 1815 produced a remarkable restoration of Catholic influence and prestige. The quiet dignity with which the Pope resisted Napoleon's persecution won general respect. When he returned to Rome in 1814, he formally reconstituted the Society of Jesus which had been suppressed forty-one years earlier. With France he continued the Napoleonic concordat, and with other Catholic states he concluded similar agreements. With Protestant Prussia, he negotiated a friendly agreement for the regulation of Catholic affairs in that country.

Under Pius VII a number of intellectuals of other faiths or of no faith were converted to Catholicism, and defenders of it wrote books which met with an enthusiastic response. In 1817 appeared *Du Pape* by a French scholar, Count Joseph de Maistre, which upheld the ancient claims of the papacy, insisted that the pope was infallible in matters of faith and morals, and argued that the way to care for the ills of the world was to recognize the pope as the supreme and inspired head of all Christian nations.

Even more influential was Chateaubriand's *Le Génie du Christianisme*, published in 1801, which, with glowing figures of speech, upheld Catholicism as the historic religion that had produced the best in European civilization. Inspired by such works, many Catholics in France and other lands ceased to feel that they were on the defensive against rationalist attacks. In most Catholic countries, moreover, the authorities, in their efforts to suppress liberalism, gave support to the church and strengthened the control of the clergy over education.

England was deeply affected by the religious revival in a number of ways. At the death of John Wesley in 1791 there had been, in Great Britain, about 77,000 Methodist church members. So rapidly did the movement grow in ensuing years that by 1837 they numbered over 300,000. The rise of the Methodists wrought changes in the Anglican Church, which began to show a new interest in popular preaching and evangelical religion. Alongside the Methodists, other evangelical sects, like the Baptists, grew in numbers and activity.

But a counter tendency soon manifested itself in the "Oxford movement." At the University of Oxford a group of young clergymen headed by John Henry Newman and Edward Pusey, who were disturbed by rationalism, liberalism, and the effects of evangelical Protestantism, began to stress the historic, traditional, and Catholic elements in the Anglican Church. In a series of famous tracts during the 1830's they stressed the authority of the Church as against the individual or the Bible and upheld the view that the Anglican Church was a branch of the "undivided Catholic Church." In 1845, Newman's search for religious authority convinced him that ultimately it was to be found only in the voice of the pope, and he joined the Catholic Church. A considerable number followed him, with consequent strengthening of the Catholic Church in English-speaking countries. At the same time, other leaders of the Oxford Movement, including Pusey, remained in the Anglican Church, and strove to make it more Catholic in its beliefs and ceremonies. Thus there arose, within the Anglican Church, an Anglo-Catholic "high church" party which combated both the severely Protestant "low church" and the looser "broad church" groups

In Germany the earlier "pietism" waned, and the Lutheran churches remained closely bound to, and supervised by, the governments of the various states. Doctrinal differences had so far lost their meaning, however, that the civil authorities were able forcibly to unite the Calvinist and Lutheran churches in Prussia and several other German states. On the whole it was in the new "idealist" philosophy, rather than within established Protestant churches, that religious impulses of the romantic period found chief expression in Germany.

C. Contribution of Romanticism to Nationalism and Liberalism

So closely related were nationalism and romanticism in the era of Metternich that it is difficult to separate them. Nationalism was romantic, and most romanticism was nationalist. Everywhere, devotees of romanticism displayed patriotic emotions and sentiments. Usually they extolled the common people of their respective nationalities. Frequently they ransacked historical records to find evidence of their nation's glorious deeds in the past. As heirs to the fervor engendered in the Revolutionary and Napoleonic eras, the patriotic romantics glorified the nation, its language, its culture, its folk songs, its past, with an ardent and often poetic emotionalism. In those countries which were already national states, romantic nationalism strengthened patriotic devotion to the fatherland. Not infrequently, political and religious conservatives were just as patriotic and romantically nationalistic as the liberals or the radicals. In lands still divided into various states, like Italy and Germany, or subject to foreign rule, like Poland and Czechoslovakia, romantic nationalism led to intense and often revolutionary movements for unification and liberation.

Nationalists and romantics could join with enthusiasm in exalting folk culture—the myths, ballads, proverbs, dances, customs, and costumes of the several European peoples. The more scholarly could investigate the peculiarities of local laws and

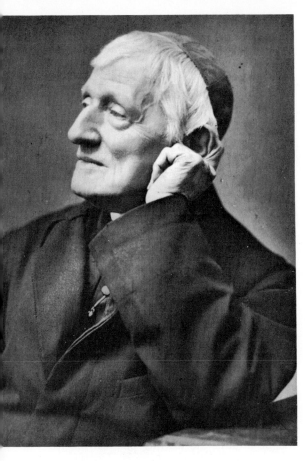

John Henry, Cardinal Newman. From a photograph (1887).

Courtesy Bettmann Archive

institutions or devote themselves to the study of the national language in its varieties and dialects. In this connection the fashion was more or less set by Jacob Grimm, who was the author of an elaborate *German Grammar*, a detailed *History of the German Language*, and an imposing *German Dictionary*. In addition, Grimm collected fairy tales that he found current among the people and wrote a history of the pre-Christian myths and religion of the Germans. The same sort of work was done with great diligence and more or less success for France, England, Hungary, Czechoslovakia, Poland, Russia, Finland, Bulgaria, and almost every other European nation.

Romanticism and nationalism shared an enthusiasm for history. National pride prompted historical research, and romantic interest in the past built up national pride. Stein, the German patriot, sponsored a project for publishing all the source materials for the ancient and medieval history of Germany, and the first volume of the great resulting collection, *Monumenta Germaniae Historica*, appeared in 1826. Soon Great Britain and France had commissions of scholars at work on the publication of their medieval documents. It was indeed an age of history. In Germany, Niebuhr and Ranke; in Britain, Carlyle and Macaulay; in France, Michelet and Guizot: these were busy preparing monumental historical works. If some like Niebuhr turned to ancient history, or, like Carlyle, wrote mainly of foreign countries, still in most histories the patriotic note was seldom absent and it was often dominant. Indeed, histories were frequently the means by which the patriotism of "oppressed," or subject, peoples was aroused. Thus, Francis Palacky stirred the Czechs with his five-volume *History of the Bohemian People*, which began to appear in 1836.

In France or Great Britain, conservatives could join with liberals in nationalist manifestations. But in Italy or Germany or Poland, liberals were the outstanding nationalists, for national unification or liberation could be attained only by upsetting the conservative *status quo* which Metternich was so vigorously maintaining. It seemed clear that national unity in Germany and Italy, or national liberation in Poland or Czechoslovakia, could be gained only by revolution. There were moderate liberals and nationalists who hoped to obtain their goals by the slow process of education and reform. But in the divided and subjected countries most nationalists and liberals were perforce revolutionaries.

Revolutionary activity had to be carried on underground. Frequently its leaders were in exile. There was often a romantic note in their work. There were oaths taken by the dim light of candles and signed in blood. There were secret passwords and handclasps. There were meetings in the woods or in caverns. There were symbols like skulls and naked daggers. But in spite of all such trappings, the work was deadly serious.

As a conspicuous example of the romantic nationalist revolutionary, we may mention Joseph Mazzini (1805–1872). A native of Genoa and the son of a university professor, he early became both a liberal and a nationalist. As a young man he joined the secret revolutionary society of the *Carbonari,* and took part in its activities, and was betrayed to the authorities while initiating a new member. Jailed for six months without trial, he was finally released, but under so many restrictions that he went into exile in France. In 1831 he projected a new non-secret organization, "Young Italy." It was composed of intellectuals under forty years of age, who would conduct an incessant campaign among all Italians for the purpose of instilling in them the desire to liberate their country from foreign and domestic tyrants and to unify it into a democratic "Roman Republic." In 1833 Mazzini was sentenced to death *in absentia,* for his part in an abortive revolutionary movement in the Sardinian army. By word and pen, Mazzini worked for his cause. He was not a good organizer, and the groups of collaborators he gathered shifted and changed. But he did inspire large numbers of Italians and fire them with the flame of his purpose. The flood of pamphlets, newspapers, letters,

and instructions which he poured into Italy from his exile in France and England slowly bore fruit—but fruit that was one day to be bitter in his mouth, for nationalism was to prove stronger than liberalism, while to Mazzini the two were inseparable.

There was an engaging quality in the teachings of Mazzini. The banner he designed for "Young Italy" bore on one side the words "Unity" and "Independence," and on the other, "Liberty, Equality, and Humanity." Even his nationalism had a broadly international aspect. Though, as he once said, he "loved Italy above all earthly things," he dreamed of a Europe that would be a peaceful brotherhood of free nations. In 1834 he organized "Young Europe," an association "of men believing in a future of liberty, equality, and fraternity for all mankind, and desirous of consecrating their thoughts and actions to the realization of that future."

D. Scientific Progress

While romantic, liberal nationalists sought to alter the existing political order,

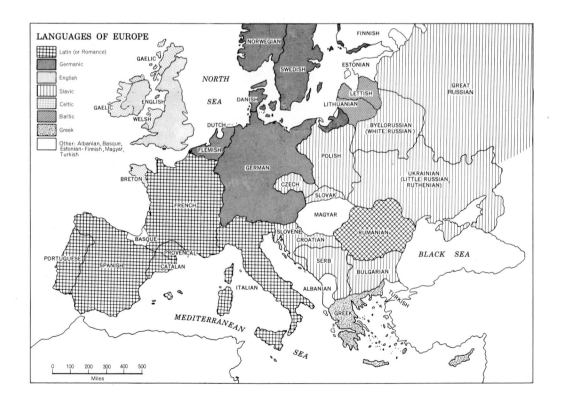

scientists in their laboratories and observatories were extending the boundaries of knowledge. The scientific work of the seventeenth and eighteenth centuries was carried ahead, and a peculiar phenomenon of modern times became evident—that of accelerating tempo. One scientific discovery led to others, and each of these to still others, so that as the nineteenth century progressed science made ever more rapid advance.

When the century opened, two famous French professors, Lagrange and Laplace, were systematizing and developing the work of preceding mathematicians and scientists since the time of Newton. Lagrange, who in 1793 had devised the metric system of weights and measures for the French government, perfected a series of mathematical innovations, some of them very useful for astronomical calculations. His friend Laplace devoted his chief attention to astronomy and published between 1799 and 1825 his five-volume *Celestial Mechanics*. In it he gave convincing mathematical proof of Newton's principle of gravitation and worked out many of the implications of Newton's theories. In another work he put forward his celebrated "nebular hypothesis," an ingenious supposition as to the way in which the whole solar system developed from a vast, whirling, gaseous cloud.

In the footsteps of these French scientists followed Leverrier, director of the observatory at Paris. By mathematical calculations he showed in 1845 that there must be another unseen planet in the solar system out beyond Uranus and he predicted its orbit. The next year occurred one of the great triumphs of modern astronomy when the new planet, which was given the name of Neptune, was actually observed close to the spot which Leverrier had foretold.

In physics, the early nineteenth century witnessed a rapid development of thermodynamics, optics, magnetism, and electricity. Thermodynamics, the study of the mechanical action of heat, became a subject of much interest as the use of the steam engine developed. Earlier physicists had thought of heat as a subtle fluid which they called "caloric." But that it was a form of motion, rather than a substance, was demonstrated by an American, Benjamin Thompson, who in 1798 presented to the Royal Society in

London a paper entitled *Enquiry concerning the source of heat which is excited by friction*. A loyalist at the time of the American Revolution, Thompson had gone to England and later to Bavaria, where he gained the title of Count Rumford. His work was carried on by Sir Humphrey Davy in England, and in France by Carnot, son of the Jacobin statesman. In 1843, James Joule upheld the view that, whenever mechanical force is expended, an exact equivalent of heat always results. He had already been able to show that electrical energy, like mechanical, had its equivalent in heat. His name has been given to a scientific unit of energy—the joule.

From the work of these men, scientists were able to formulate two great principles of physics. The "first law of thermodynamics," that of the "conservation of energy," was largely a discovery of Helmholtz, who read a paper on the subject in 1847. It held that the quantity of energy which can be brought into action in the whole of nature is unchangeable and can neither be increased nor diminished. Four years later William Thomson, better known by his later title of Lord Kelvin, stated the "second law of thermodynamics," that of the "dissipation of energy," that, while the sum total of energy in the universe is unchangeable, the amount of energy available is constantly diminishing by a continual degeneration into non-available energy such as "dissipated" heat.

But what were perhaps the most exciting developments of the time in physics were in the field of electricity. In the eighteenth century Franklin had shown that lightning was an electric phenomenon; Galvani had experimented with the action of electricity on the muscles of frogs; Volta had in 1799 devised the voltaic pile, a sort of dry cell; and there had been much experimenting with the static electricity of "Leyden jars." But in the nineteenth century, electricity rapidly ceased to be a laboratory curiosity and became an important new force. In 1820 Ampère suggested the use of electricity for sending messages, and in the 1830's practical systems of telegraphy were developed by Wheatstone in England, and Morse in America. Already, Sir Humphrey Davy and others had been producing electric cur-

Samuel F. B. Morse (1791–1872). Self portrait.

rents from improved voltaic piles, and it was quickly shown that such currents could decompose chemical compounds and also be used for electroplating one metal with another. In 1808 Davy produced an electric arc light between two carbon poles.

In 1819 a Dane, Oersted by name, showed that, since an electric current affected a compass needle, electricity and magnetism were related. This connection was investigated by Michael Faraday, who in a series of brilliant experiments produced magnetism by electric currents and discovered the principle of the electric motor and the dynamo (1831). With the development of the dynamo, electric current could be generated in larger quantities and more easily than by the voltaic pile. Experiments of all sorts with electricity and even its industrial use became much more practicable.

Through the work of chemists and physicists, an old idea dating back to the ancient Greeks was definitely established in the nineteenth century. Philosophers and scientists had often speculated as to whether the matter of the universe might not be made up of minute particles or "atoms." About 1803, John Dalton, arguing from facts of chemistry, persuasively presented the idea that all matter consists of atoms, that the atoms of various chemicals are distinguished from each other by different relative weights, and that atoms combine in definite relationships to form compounds. At almost the same time, an Italian nobleman, Count Avogadro, at the University of Turin, demonstrated that gases consist of minute particles which he called "molecules" and proposed the hypothesis that "equal volumes of gases, under the same conditions of temperature and pressure, contain the same number of smallest particles or molecules." For a time there was confusion in terminology between Dalton's "atoms" and Avogadro's "molecules." But gradually "atom" came to be accepted as the name of the smallest unit of simple elements, while "molecule" was used for a unit composed of two or more atoms in a gas or in a compound.

Organic chemistry was actually born in 1828, when Friedrich Wöhler showed that urea, a substance hitherto thought of as purely animal, could be artificially synthesized from chemicals in the laboratory. The old distinction between living creatures and inorganic substances was thus broken down. Apparently, everything was made of chemical elements and compounds. Wöhler likewise helped to establish another connection between chemistry and living matter, for he did some work with Justus von Liebig, whose experiments at the universities of Giessen and Munich showed that vegetables require certain chemicals in order to grow well. Liebig's efforts paved the way for the development of chemical fertilizers, which eventually revolutionized modern agriculture.

Meanwhile biologists and botanists were making strides in knowledge of animals and plants. Lamarck, in his *Natural History of Invertebrate Animals*, not only gave a wealth of detailed information about various forms of life, but proposed a general theory, which, though not entirely new, was to undergo significant development in ensuing years. This was the idea of evolution—that one species of animals is derived from another, and that "higher" forms develop out of "lower" forms. The idea was significant, but Lamarck's suggestions as to how evolution took place proved mistaken. He held that need felt in an animal body tends to produce a new organ, which use develops, and that such changes can be passed on to succeeding generations. In short, he erroneously believed that "acquired characteristics" are inherited.

In geology, the outstanding scientist was Sir Charles Lyell. In 1830 he published his classic *Principles of Geology, an attempt to explain the former changes of the Earth's surface by reference to causes now in operation*. His basic idea was not new, for James Hutton in a book published forty-five years earlier had held similar views. But Lyell reenforced Hutton's argument by a wealth of scientific observations and presented it in a lively and entertaining style. It was Lyell's contention that the present surface of the earth was the product, not of past floods and catastrophes or of special acts of the Creator, but rather the result of observable forces that were still in operation—winds, frost, rain, streams, ice, volcanoes, earthquakes. Coal came from buried vegetation, fossils from buried plants and animals, and they had been buried not by a catastrophe but by natural agents. Mountains had been lifted by the slow folding of the earth's crust; valleys had been formed by the erosion of rivers. It had all been a slow, continuous, evolutionary process.

Another scientific landmark, this one in the field of embryology, is attributable to a physician, Dr. von Baer, who worked in East Prussia and Russia. His *Letter on the Egg of Mammals* (1827) pointed out that human beings, in common with all other mammals, and with birds, fishes, and reptiles, are reproduced by the fertilization of eggs. Baer's later work and that of other scientists were improved in accuracy and range by the development in the 1830's of the compound microscope. And it was the improved microscope that enabled Theodor Schwann to discover in 1837 that yeast is made up of living organisms. Two years later he formulated the highly significant "cell theory," that all living things originate and grow tiny structural units, or "cells."

Basically, the newer developments in science militated against the emotional and mystical impulses of the era of romanticism. As some of the mysteries of nature were cleared up and some of its marvels better understood, there was a renewed tendency on the part of many intellectuals to become indifferent, if not actively hostile, to current conceptions of religion and the supernat-

ural. Over against the romantically inspired religious revival of the era, a new generation of skeptics, absorbed in science, turned from those things which they felt man could not know positively to fields like chemistry or physics which, they thought, contained the factual and the certain. In a sense this trend was a continuation of the influence of Newtonian physics on the eighteenth century, which had seen thinkers move from Christian faith to Deism and even to Atheism. But science was now scoring so many triumphs that its prestige was affecting a larger number of persons. When combined with the development of industry, which will be discussed in the next chapter, the influence of science in the nineteenth century was toward materialism—a paramount interest and faith in those things which man can detect with his senses and examine in the laboratory.

Disciples of Nature. Caricature of romantic painters by Honoré Daumier (d. 1879).

CHAPTER 45

Advance of Machine Industry

A. Early Stages

The term "industrial revolution" is so well established in historical usage that it cannot be readily abandoned, although there is some reason for doing so. The process of improving manufacturing techniques, developing the factory system, and increasing industrial output has been long and slow, whether in England or in the world at large. In England it can be traced back at least to the mid-sixteenth century and is still continuing. What is spread over four centuries is hardly a "revolution."

The "industrial revolution" used to be assigned to eighteenth-century England. Sometimes such dates as 1740–1800 or 1760–1820 were specified, with emphasis on certain inventions in the cotton and metal industries, on the building of roads and canals, and on the Watt steam engine. But it was gradually realized that, while cotton and iron manufacture did grow rapidly in the eighteenth century, the period of real mechanization and mass production came after 1800 or even after 1820. In 1800 the power loom was not yet in practical use, the processes of steel manufacture were still costly and slow, and only a few score low-power Watt steam engines were in operation. The building of roads and canals in eighteenth-century England only repeated what had been done in France in the seventeenth century. The real revolution in transportation came after 1830 with the introduction of the railway and the steamship.

If the term "industrial revolution" is to be used, it should be applied to the period in which a country is fairly rapidly changed over from predominantly agricultural and commercial pursuits to those of mechanized industry. In England this change occurred, roughly speaking, between 1830 and 1870. Before 1830 most Englishmen were still engaged in farming or in trade. By 1870, most Englishmen were connected in one way or another with mechanized industries. That the change—the "industrial revolution"—took place originally in England, is attributable to the fact that certain prerequisites for it had been more completely fulfilled there than in any other country. These prerequisites, which must be briefly examined, may be listed under six heads: capital, labor, techniques, resources, transportation, and markets.

1. Capital. For intensive industrialization, capital in large quantities is necessary to build factories and machines, to hire workers, and to buy raw materials. This was available in England as profit from the successful British commerce of the seventeenth and eighteenth centuries and from the capitalist type of agriculture which grew up especially after 1740 in connection with the enclosure movement. In England, moreover, the use of capital was expedited by the Bank of England, by efficient handling of governmental finances, and by the rise of a London money market where bills could be discounted and shares bought and sold. The British coinage and paper money were on a sound basis from the early eighteenth cen-

James Watt. Sir Francis Legatt Chantry (d. 1842).

tury onwards, save for a brief period during and after the Napoleonic wars. Just when the need for financing industry was becoming great, joint stock banks other than the Bank of England were legalized (1826). In the ensuing decades the formation of joint stock corporations for industry, commerce, and finance was made simple and easy. It must be noted, however, that much of England's industrial capital was self-generated. That is, a manufacturer, starting with a small capital, enlarged his plant by plowing back his profits into the business.

2. *Labor.* Workers for the new English industries of the nineteenth century came from a number of sources. The British population was growing rapidly. It almost doubled in the eighteenth century, and doubled again in the first half of the nineteenth, despite considerable emigration. There was some immigration into England of Continental European labor in the eighteenth, and of Irish in the nineteenth, century. Perhaps most important of all, labor was made available for factory-production through the gradual destruction of the old peasant farming as a result of the enclosure movement and capitalist agriculture.

3. *Techniques.* England, in the late eighteenth and early nineteenth centuries developed techniques, processes, and machines necessary for large-scale industry. France was probably ahead of England in technology as late as 1750. Afterwards England rapidly outstripped all rivals. The story of the cotton textile inventions is familiar, though it has probably been unduly conventionalized, and the work of a number of inventors has been attached to a single name. In any case, the flying shuttle (John Kay, 1733), the spinning jenny (James Hargreaves, about 1767), the water frame (Richard Arkwright, 1769), the spinning "mule" (Samuel Crompton, 1779), the power loom (Edmund Cartwright, 1785), the cotton gin (Eli Whitney, 1792, in the United States), the cylindrical calico printing machine (Thomas Bell, 1785), and chemical bleaching and chemical dyes—all these had been developed before the end of the eighteenth century. They had been successfully grouped in factories operated by water or even steam power, and cheap large-scale production in factories had put out of business the small-shop and the home production of cotton thread. In the early nineteenth century, the factory cotton industry grew by leaps and bounds. By 1835 there were nearly 106,000 power looms in the British Isles.

The story of the metal industries is almost as familiar. Shortage of wood to make charcoal for the smelting of iron ore, impelled experimentation with coal, which had been mined in ever-increasing quantities in England since the sixteenth century. The Darbys at Coalbrookdale, in the first half of the eighteenth century, attained success in this endeavor by transforming coal into coke and then using a strong blast of air in the smelting process. English iron production had been declining for lack of charcoal; it was rejuvenated after the mid-eighteenth century by the use of the Darby's coke-blast process and by a series of other inventions and improvements: John Smeaton's air pump (1760), the reverberatory furnace, "puddling," and the rolling mill (all developed by Henry Cort and Peter Onions about 1783), James Watt's steam hammer, Huntsman's steel process (about 1740), the hot blast (Nielson, 1828). By the early nineteenth century, iron was being pro-duced in rapidly increasing quantities. From it were made the new machines. Enthusi-asts were urging the use of iron for bridges, for ships, and even for coffins.

In the eighteenth century the power most generally used was, as in the past, that of man, mules, wind, or water. A steam (or atmospheric) engine—the Newcomen—had been invented in the early 1700's, but its use was restricted to pumping water out of mines. It was vastly improved upon by James Watt's engine, patented in 1769 and first put to industrial use in 1776. By the first decade of the nineteenth century, steam was becoming a major motive force. No longer did a mill have to be located beside a running stream. Steam engines were being put on boats (Robert Fulton's *Clermont*, 1807), and the first moderately successful locomotive was made by George Stephenson in 1814. Watt had encountered difficulty in making his early engines for lack of proper machine tools. But gradually this was surmounted by the development and use of drills, lathes, the slide rest, and stamping presses.

4. *Resources.* England was well endowed with just the resources needed for indus-trialization. Its climate was damp enough to be highly suitable for mechanical spinning and weaving. Its water power was ample. More important, England was abundantly endowed with iron and coal.

5. *Transportation.* With its many ports and extensive shipping, Great Britain was well equipped, by the eighteenth century, for sea-borne transport. Then, during the latter half of the century, Britain modern-ized its medieval inland transportation by the construction of a network of roads and canals. Since no part of England is much more than sixty or seventy miles from salt water, these roads and canals soon put many inland towns in a position to share in the growing British trade.

6. *Markets.* England and Scotland, since the Act of Union of 1707, had constituted a consolidated open market, free of tariffs. To them, Ireland was united in 1800, giving English industry a still more extensive home market. English merchants had opened up channels of trade to all Europe, to North America, to Africa, and to the Far East before the mid-eighteenth century. After-wards, British markets continued to expand. The United States kept on buying British goods, even after the American Revolution. India bought more and more British wares, especially the new, cheap cottons. The Spanish colonies were opened to British commerce in the period of the French Revolution and Napoleon, and Britain in-creased its trade with them when they became independent countries in the 1820's. All over the world, from Canton to Buenos Aires, and from Capetown to North Cape, British commerce, from the begin-ning of the nineteenth century, had no serious competitor.

Thus by 1815 or 1839, England had all the prerequisites for the rapid growth of large-scale factory production. She had them more fully than any rival. She had already undergone a certain degree of indus-trialization in cotton textiles and the metal trades. In the ensuing decades she was to become indeed the workshop of the world. She was to undergo her "industrial revolu-tion" a generation ahead of any other major country. When this revolution was under way in England (and later in other countries) it proved to be self-generating, self-perpetuating, self-reinforcing. Once in-dustry really got going, there was a sort of take-off into more rapid, more extensive in-dustrialization. The point of take-off seems to be that at which the new industry begins to produce at such a rate that it can pro-vide large quantities of capital for further industrial expansion. That point came in England about 1830.

B. Industrial Revolution in England

The industries already developed in Eng-land expanded with amazing rapidity after 1830. For example, English exports of cot-ton goods rose in value from 19 million pounds sterling in 1830 to 56 million in 1870. In 1821, England bought 93,500,000 pounds of raw cotton from America, her principal source of supply. By 1859–1860 such purchases ran well over a billion pounds. In 1871, moreover, 88 per cent of all workers in the cotton industry were employed in factories.

Iron progressed almost as fast. British production of pig iron rose from 750,000 tons in 1830 to six million in 1870. Coal production similarly increased from 26 million tons in 1830 to 110 million forty years later. In the metal industries, the biggest advance was the improvement of methods for large-scale conversion of iron into steel. The Bessemer process, introduced in 1856, was rapid and inexpensive. It made steel available for machinery, rails, and ships, and steel was stronger and more durable than iron. Then to the Bessemer process was added the Siemens-Martin "open hearth" process in the 1860's, while in the 1870's the Thomas-Gilchrist developments made it possible to use iron ores with a high phosphorous content. Between 1856 and 1870, the price of steel was cut in half in England.

In the same period, factory organization and machine production were applied to such old and formerly small-scale industries as shoe-making, brewing, flour-milling, and furniture-making. Production of arms and munitions was likewise revolutionized both by mechanization and by new inventions such as the percussion cap (as against the flintlock), the rifle (as against the musket), and breech-loading (as against muzzle-loading). In 1862 an American, Richard Gatling, invented a machine gun which would fire 350 shots a minute. With the "Gatling gun," the "industrial revolution" was carried into warfare.

New industries came into existence alongside the older ones. In the 1840's growing urban demand, increasing scientific knowledge, and better methods of producing glass jars and tin receptacles permitted the introduction of canned foods. By the 1860's fresh fruits, fish, and vegetables were being canned in considerable quantities, and "extract of beef," just invented by the German scientist Liebig, was enjoying a popularity quite out of line with its nutritional value. Gail Borden in America had just patented "condensed milk," and dried milk was first made in England in 1855.

From the making of coke for iron smelting, there developed a new industry, for, in producing coke, coal gas is released. A gas-lighting company was incorporated in London in 1812. Gas was first used for cooking in 1832. By the mid-century many streets and many homes were being lighted by it, and "gas works" and gas tanks disfigured most of the larger cities.

But scientific progress in the field of electricity was already preparing a rival to gas. The invention of the carbon arc light and improved dynamos made electrical lighting practicable by 1870, and the invention of the incandescent lamp in 1878 put it in widespread use. Meanwhile, electricity was being widely employed for the electroplating of metals as early as the 1850's, and in the previous decade the telegraph had spread a network of wires over the face of Europe. Together with a submarine cable to America, successfully laid in 1866, the telegraph made it possible to get news transmitted with unheard-of rapidity and gave a stimulus to newspapers, which were likewise aided by mechanical steam presses and cheaper paper.

A new industry that arose between 1830 and 1870 was photography. Though the first crude photograph had been made in 1822, it was a Frenchman, Daguerre, who rendered the process practicable. By 1839 he could "take pictures" in thirty minutes; and "daguerreotype" was long a synonym for photograph. In 1841 Fox Talbot, an Englishman, developed a faster process; and a decade later, almost instantaneous photography was realized. Henceforth the new art developed swiftly as a great commercial industry.

The invention, by the American Charles Goodyear in 1839, of a process of vulcanizing rubber in order to make it stronger and more elastic laid the foundation of another new industry. By the 1860's there was a marked growth of factories for the production of rubber articles, but the great days of rubber still lay ahead. Similar was the story of petroleum products. In the 1850's a Scottish industrial chemist, James Young, discovered how to make naphtha, lubricating oils, paraffine, and kerosene by distilling crude oil. Gradually these new products found a market, and kerosene or "coal oil" was especially popular for use in lamps. World production of petroleum, a mere two thousand barrels in 1857, rose to five and a half million in 1870. Only ten years later it would be thirty million.

The mechanization of industries, old and

Locomotives of 1831 and 1893 as displayed at the Chicago World's Fair, 1893.

Courtesy Bettmann Archive

new, produced what amounted to another profession—that of engineer. Originally, engineers had been men who designed and constructed fortifications and engines of war. But as industrial invention proceeded and became more complicated, it gave rise to "civil engineers" trained to plan and build roads, docks, canals, aqueducts, drainage systems, lighthouses, etc. In 1828 the civil engineers of London formed a society. But rather rapidly the engineers became more specialized. Some, dealing with steam engines, machine tools, mill work, and moving machinery in general, became "mechanical engineers." Others, busying themselves with the technical problems of mines, became "mining engineers." By 1870 there were "marine engineers," "sanitary engineers," "chemical engineers," and "electri-

cal engineers." In a way the engineers were a link between industry and science. Many of them were competent scientists and some of them made significant contributions. Gradually science and industry became closely interlocked.

Probably even more "revolutionary" than the rapid progress of industry, between 1830 and 1870, were the startling improvements in transportation. In 1830 men still went afoot, or rode on horseback or in carriages. In 1870 they and their goods could be whisked about at previously unheard-of speeds over shining roads of rails. The first steam railway was that between Stockton and Darlington in England, opened in 1825, with stationary engines to draw the cars over the hills and locomotives to pull them on level stretches. In 1830, the Liverpool-

Manchester line was inaugurated, and on it Robert Stephenson's improved locomotive, the *Rocket,* covered the forty-mile distance in an hour and a half. The success of this venture ushered in a period of extensive railway building. There were forty-nine miles of steam railways in 1830 in England. In 1870 there were 15,300 miles. Small lines were consolidated into larger systems, and London was linked with all the major English and Scottish cities. Locomotives were vastly improved, railway building techniques developed, and speed and safety increased.

The revolution in ocean transportation was slightly slower. In 1838 two ships crossed the Atlantic under steam power, the *Sirius* in eighteen days, and the *Great Western* in fifteen days. Two years later Samuel Cunard inaugurated the first regular trans-Atlantic steamship service. In the 1850's, the screw-propeller was widely adopted in place of the earlier paddle wheels, and iron began to replace wood as the building material for the larger ships. In 1858, when an iron liner, the *Great Eastern,* was constructed with a gross tonnage of 18,337, a horsepower of 11,000, and a speed of thirteen knots, it was regarded as a triumph of marine engineering. The number of British steamships increased from 298 in 1830 to 3,178 in 1870, and their net tonnage rose in the period from 30,339 to 1,112,934. But it was not until the 1880's that the tonnage of Britain's steamships surpassed that of her sailing vessels.

Not only was there a shift from sail to steam. There was a remarkable growth of the merchant marine as a whole. The tonnage of British ships more than doubled between 1830 and 1870, and just at the end of the period the opening of the Suez canal in 1869 gave another impetus to sea-borne transport. The swift decrease of the costs of shipping goods by water made it possible for England to sell its wares, even bulky ones of iron, all over the world, and also made it easier and less expensive to import both raw materials like cotton and wool, and food like wheat.

The impact of industry, science, and cheap transportation on English agriculture worked first in one direction, then in the other. By the enclosure movement and the new techniques of the eighteenth century,

British farming had been changed over into a large-scale, profit-making enterprise. High prices in the Napoleonic era had brought wealth to the landowners, but in the twenty-five years after 1815, prices were relatively low, workers were drawn off into the growing factories, and competition of cheap food from the continent was increasing. For a while, agricultural profits were low.

But from 1840 to 1874, British farming became very profitable once more, despite the repeal of the corn laws in 1846. Machinery, applied to agriculture, drastically cut labor costs. In 1853 the "Crosskill reaper" was perfected in England, and at about the same time the "McCormick reaper" began to be imported from America. Moreover, Liebig's work on fertilizers had practical effect. Manufacture of superphosphate of lime was begun in England (1846), use of nitrate of soda grew, and guano from Peru was imported in swiftly increasing amounts. As the age of chemical and mechanical agriculture advanced, the crops of the English landlords rose while their labor costs dropped. They did very well till about 1874, when a combination of diseases among their animals and the impact of cheap food imported on steamships from Russia, Argentina, United States, Canada, and Australia brought depression.

If the big landlords were seeking and making profits in the period from 1830 to 1870, they were merely reflecting the fact that England had become by this time a thoroughly capitalist country. To older capitalists who had made money by commerce and banking, had been added new industrial capitalists. The factory and the machine gradually supplanted the old craftsman and the artisan, for these could not afford to buy the new machines nor could they compete with them. Work in homes and small shops declined, nor could the putting-out system face the competition of the factory. The changes thus wrought were far-reaching. No longer was ownership of tools and shops spread among thousands of workers. The factories and machines were owned by a relatively small number of industrial capitalists, men who brought together labor, raw materials, and machines in a single spot and organized the production and sale of goods.

The early industrialists had often been poor men, like Arkwright or Watt, who, starting in a small way, by intelligence and persistence and (sometimes) ruthlessness, built up a factory. Rapidly, however, the "self-made" men were joined by those who already had wealth from land or trade or inheritance and who now "invested" in factories and shared the profits. As joint stock companies grew in number and popularity in the mid-nineteenth century, it became easy for the man with money to "invest" in industry and reap the profits, while the technical work of production and management was carried on by hired employees of the corporation. There were, of course, risks. Many enterprises failed. To the capitalists, it seemed that the risks they ran justified the rewards they got. In any event, industrialization greatly increased the amount of capital in England. One estimate is that it rose from 1,500 million pounds sterling in 1750 to 2,500 million in 1833, and 6,000 million in 1865.

C. Spread of Machine Industry to the Continent

England was so closely bound to the Continent by commercial ties that industrialization of the former was certain to affect the latter. Machines, such as water frames of the Arkwright type, were introduced sporadically into France and the Belgian Netherlands in the latter part of the eighteenth century. As early as 1781 an English iron master founded the famous metal and munitions works at Creusot north of Lyons and installed a steam engine there. Coke smelting was employed at Creusot in 1810, and though the enterprise declined when munitions orders fell off at the close of the Napoleonic wars, it was later revivified by the Schneider family and became one of the most famous metal works in Europe.

Another Englishman, William Cockerill, mechanic and inventor, constructed in Belgium (at Verviers) in 1799 the first wool-carding and wool-spinning machines on the continent. In 1807 he established a large machine shop at Liége and made a handsome fortune from it. After the peace settlement of 1815, machine production was quickened and extended.

Though the process of industrialization was begun in Belgium well before 1830, it was the ensuing decades that witnessed its triumph. By 1870, Belgium, aided by British investments and engineers, was a nation of foundries, factories, and mines. It was the most densely populated country in Europe. The majority of its inhabitants lived in cities and got their livelihood from industry or trade. As early as 1834, the Belgian parliament adopted a plan drawn up by George Stephenson for the construction of a national system of railways radiating from Liége and Brussels. Through loans floated in England, the plan was speedily carried into effect.

France was more slowly and less completely industrialized. Her traditions of hand-work and luxury manufacture had become solidly entrenched before the political revolution of 1789. Her system of small-scale agriculture had been reënforced by that Revolution. She had lost both colonies and markets during the long wars. She lacked adequate supplies of coking coal, and much of her iron ore had too much phosphorus in it to be useful before the development of the Thomas-Gilchrist process in 1878. Yet the "industrial revolution" gradually penetrated into France. First it affected mining and metallurgy. The output of coal rose from 800,000 tons in 1815 (about the same as in 1770) to 1,800,000 tons in 1830, and of pig iron from 100,000 to 300,000 tons, while the number of steam engines (still used mainly for pumping water out of mines) increased from 16 to 625.

After 1830, with the aid of the business-minded government of Louis Philippe and later subsidies and assistance from Napoleon III, French industries developed behind a wall of tariffs which were maintained at high levels till 1860. Especially vitalizing for industry was the construction of railways, which was begun in 1842 with a line from Paris to Rouen and thence to Le Havre (built by an English company, with English capital, and English engineers and workmen). By 1870 a network of main lines radiated north, south, east, and west from Paris.

From 1830 to 1870 the output of French coal increased from 1,800,000 to 16,000,000 tons, and of pig iron from 300,000 to 1,400,000 tons, while the horsepower of steam engines, other than locomotives, rose from 20,000 to 336,000. After 1840, power-driven machinery began to compete with hand work in the French textile industries. Most of the new factories were concentrated in the north of the country, in Alsace and Lorraine or near Lille, Rouen, and Paris. By 1870, many an urban Frenchman was a machine-tender in a factory, although small shops and the putting-out system still flourished and the bulk of the population was still definitely agricultural.

Germany, despite vast resources of coal and iron, was originally more backward than France. Although some machinery was brought in from England and a few factories were built prior to 1830, there was scarcely a beginning of industrialization till after that date. The formation of a customs union (*Zollverein*), including by 1833 most German states (except Austria), removed many trade barriers. It had been designed primarily to help landowners by enlarging markets for agricultural goods, but it also served to stimulate commerce and to create a desire for improved means of communication. In 1839, with aid from British capital, the first important German railway was built from Dresden to Leipzig, and by the time of the political revolutions of 1848, there were some 4,000 miles of railway connecting Berlin with Hamburg, the Rhine, Prague, and Vienna. In Germany, in contrast to England, Belgium, and France, railway building preceded real beginnings of industrialization, but just as railways speeded up the foundries and factories of those countries, it served to create them in Germany.

German coal output, less than that of France in 1850, rose to 16 million tons in 1860 and to more than 37 million in 1870. Production of pig iron jumped to half a million tons in 1860 and soared to almost two million tons ten years later. Meanwhile, steam-driven machinery was being applied to cotton spinning, and textile factories were springing up in Saxony, Silesia, Westphalia, and the Rhineland. Cotton weaving and the manufacture of other textiles was, however, as late as 1870, still predominantly a hand industry, and 64 per cent of the population of Germany was still classed as rural and agricultural. Germany was clearly beginning to experience her "industrial revolution." But its sweeping consequences were to become obvious only after 1870.

Elsewhere on the continent, large-scale manufacturing, with the factory system and industrial capitalism, appeared only spottily before 1870. There were a few instances in Holland, Sweden, and Spain. There were considerably more in Russian Poland, particularly near Warsaw. Bohemia (especially Prague) and German Austria (especially Vienna) participated somewhat in the new mechanized industry. In the 1850's a few steam engines were brought into northern Italy (Piedmont), and Count Cavour acquired wealth and his first fame as a promoter of industrialization. But, by and large, Europe, with the exception of England, Belgium, France, and Germany, was before 1870 almost as solidly agricultural as it had been a century or two earlier.

D. Accompaniments of Industrialization, and Temporary Triumph of Economic Liberalism

For centuries up to the eighteenth, the population of Europe had been static or only slowly rising. In 1700, it did not number more than 125 million. By 1800, it totaled about 187 million; by 1850, 226 million; and by 1900, 400 million. In a general way, with exceptions as to eastern Europe, this tremendous growth of population occurred in areas where industrialization was taking place. It was probably caused more by a decline in the death rate than by an increase in the birth rate, and seems to have been connected with improved diet and sanitation.

Most of the population growth was centered in cities, which were heavily augmented by influx from rural areas. In Great Britain, London expanded into an urban colossus far overshadowing all other English cities. Old cities like Bristol or Glasgow grew; while new ones, which had been mere villages in the early eighteenth century, came to be great, busy, densely populated centers, as in the case of Liverpool, or Leeds or Sheffield, or Manchester, or Birmingham. Similar changes occurred on the Continent with sensational growth of such cities as Brussels, Paris, Lille, or Berlin. In addition, hundreds of towns grew into cities, and villages grew into towns.

With the rise of the cities came significant changes in the structure of classes. The familiar division of landowner and peasant, merchant and artisan, persisted. But to it was added another division of industrial capitalists (with dependent managers, foremen, engineers, lawyers, etc.) and wage-earning proletarians. By 1870 in England the most numerous type was the "factory hand," the proletarian who owned no property and made his living by a daily labor at some kind of a machine.

Under the new industrialization, the lot of the wage-laborer was hardly a happy one. While the peasant or rural artisan of the eighteenth century had most likely worked long hours and been ill-housed and ill-clad, he had been, to a considerable degree, his own master. He often owned some land, some tools, and a cottage. He had some security. He was part of a friendly community that felt some responsibility for him. The worker in the factories, forges, and mines of the 1840's had few such advantages. He labored twelve or fourteen hours a day at a machine in dismal, unsanitary, and unsafe factories. If he was a miner he worked underground and scarcely saw the light of day. He went to work at the sound of a whistle. He was fined for absence or lateness. He was clad in rags or shoddy cloth. He ate unwholesome food. He lived in a rented room in some sort of human rabbit-warren with much dirt and little or no sanitation. His work was intensely monotonous and he had few amusements. He was often unemployed because the factory owner found it cheaper to hire his wife and children. Even six-year-olds were found useful because of their nimble fingers. The bad living and working conditions of industrial laborers, with the grimy industrial cities, appeared first in Great Britain, but they were duplicated on the continent wherever industrialization occurred.

In earlier rural life, there had always been work to do. But in newer industrialized life there were usually some jobless men—the unemployed. And every few years, there recurred a business "crisis" or "depression" that produced widespread mass unemployment with intense suffering for the hapless urban proletarians. Such depressions occurred in 1818–1819, 1825–1830, 1837, 1847–1848, 1857–1858, 1866–1867, 1873–1878.

On the other hand, the new industrialism was attended by many advantages. Increased production meant increased wealth. The new inventions brought such comforts and improvements as better food, better clothes, running water, gas and electric light. With the growth of science, medical knowledge was advanced. Man could travel speedily. News could be sent almost instantaneously. Machinery was doing some of the back-breaking toil formerly done by man. But at least in the first or second generation of industrialization, these advantages accrued more to the wealthy than to the wage workers.

The way in which the economic life of Europe was developing was explained and defended by British economists of the time, variously known as "economic liberals," the "classical school," or, after the cotton manufacturers who had fought for the repeal of the English corn laws, "the Manchester school." All were deeply influenced by the laissez-faire doctrines of Adam Smith's *Wealth of Nations*,[1] though they made distinctive additions. Malthus promulgated a "law of population," that the number of persons tends to grow faster than the food supply and that over-population can be prevented only by "positive checks" of famine, war, and disease, or by "preventive checks" of continence and abstention from marriage. The poor, said Malthus, were "the authors of their own poverty"—they had too many children. Ricardo argued that "rent" is determined by population growth, forcing use of ever more sterile land for the production of food. He also enunciated an "iron law of wages," that wages tend to fall toward the level of bare subsistence. Nassau Senior demonstrated to his own satisfaction that daily hours of factory labor should not be reduced from fifteen to fourteen, because it was the fifteenth hour which gave the capitalist his needed profit. McCulloch advanced a "wage fund" theory, that there was just so much money to pay the laborers

[1] See above, p. 491.

of a country; if one group of workers succeeded in raising their wages, they were merely reducing the pay of some of their fellow laborers. Meanwhile Jeremy Bentham, philosopher of "utilitarianism," maintained that the application of *laissez-faire* and the ideas of economic liberalism would result in the greatest good for the greatest number of people.

As developed by such British writers, economic liberalism became by the 1830's a well-organized body of doctrine. Like political liberalism, with which it was closely associated, it stressed the individual. It made individual self-interest the motive force of economic life. Again like political liberalism, it stressed freedom—freedom of trade (no tariffs or subsidies), freedom of contract between individuals (no labor unions), freedom from government interference or regulation (*laissez-faire*), freedom of competition (no monopolies, especially none chartered by governments). The economic liberals were the heirs of eighteenth-century thought in that they believed that economic life was guided by supposedly "natural laws," such as "laws" of rent and wages and population. Man could not prevent, though he might impede, the operation of such "laws." The best thing to do was to remove all man-made restrictions and let the "laws" work automatically.

Despite a growing pessimism of classical economics from the time of Malthus and Ricardo (which earned for it the title of "the dismal science"), its doctrine of economic liberalism won many followers. Industrial capitalists found in it justification for the system under which they were growing wealthy, and many statesmen were quite convinced of its validity. Economic liberalism gained firmest foothold and most victories in Great Britain. Between 1800 and 1860, almost all the longstanding British restrictions on private industry and trade were repealed by parliamentary action. Thus disappeared the statute of apprentices, laws regulating woolens, leather, and linens, the assize of bread, navigation acts, tariffs, usury laws, monopolies of East India Company and Hudson's Bay Company, and the Elizabethan poor law. By the time the last of the English import duties (except a few retained for revenue) were removed by the Cobden treaty with France in 1860, England had adopted free trade and *laissez-faire* as thoroughly as any nation has ever done.

In France and Germany, economic liberalism won some converts. Yet it never triumphed completely and many industrialists pleaded for tariff protection against cheap British imports. France kept her high tariffs till Napoleon III reduced them to a moderate level by agreeing to the Cobden treaty in 1860. The German Zollverein tariff of 1834 was a low one—Germany did not yet have many industries to protect. Writers on the continent who espoused economic liberalism usually did so because it seemed consonant with the political liberalism they favored. On the whole, continental countries never adopted economic liberalism with the wholehearted thoroughness evinced by Britain.

E. Protests Against Economic Liberalism

Meanwhile the "dismal science" of liberal economists and the more dismal conditions created by industrialization did not go unchallenged. Among groups in England who reacted against the shocking conditions to which workers were subjected, the following may be mentioned: (1) Political radicals and extreme democrats, like William Cobbett, contended for the rights and the dignity of the common man. (2) Certain clergymen, like Denison Maurice and the novelist Charles Kingsley, thought the squalor and degradation of the working classes unchristian, and urged a "Christian Socialism" of coöperation and profit-sharing. (3) An humanitarian factory owner, like Robert Owen, first improved conditions in his own mills, then tried and failed to secure effective legislation from parliament, then turned to "Utopian Socialism" and endeavored to establish in Britain and America coöperative, agricultural-industrial colonies. (4) Some Tory aristocrats, like Michael Sadler and Lord Ashley, reacting against the growing dominance of middle-class industrialists, wrote books and pamphlets exposing current social ills, and worked for legislation to remedy them. (5) A Tory politician like Benjamin Disraeli felt that the old landed classes must win the support of the lower classes and together limit the excesses of the middle class and strengthen the country by improving social and economic conditions. (6) Miscellaneous persons opposed existing conditions from some special interest in popular education or in public health (7) Persons from among the laboring classes sought to better their lot by political agitation (as with the Chartists), by formation of mutual benefit or coöperative societies (like the coöperative grocery store founded at Rochdale in 1844), and by labor unions (which were partially legalized in England in 1824–1825).

No one of the British groups just listed would have been strong enough to make headway in Parliament, or in the country at large, against economic liberalism, but through joint action advantage could be taken of political circumstances to win some of the measures sought. Thus Great Britain witnessed, even in the period of the triumph of *laissez-faire*, some legislation that went against doctrines of economic liberalism and sought to protect workers or to improve their condition by means of government action.

As early as 1802 a "factory act" limited the hours of labor and regulated the working conditions of pauper-apprentice children who were rented out by the parish authorities to factory owners. Other factory acts in 1819, 1831, and 1833 limited night work and the hours of labor of all children and the employment of children under nine years of age. The act of 1833 was the first important one, for it provided mechanisms of inspection and enforcement. In 1842 an act forbade the employment of women and girls, and of boys under ten, in mines, while subsequent "mines acts" required certain minimum working conditions and precautions against accidents. A supplementary factory act of 1844 limited still further the hours of employment for women and children, and a maximum work-week of sixty hours was provided for them by an Act of 1847. Despite the outcries of economists, this last act, together with later additions, gradually forced a ten-hour day in British industry. Meanwhile a Public Health Act of 1848 sought to improve sanitation, and in the next five years almost two hundred local boards of health were set up. In the

1860's a series of acts was passed to prevent adulteration of food and drink.

Thus before *laissez-faire* completely triumphed in Great Britain by wiping out all the old restrictions that had come down from mercantilist days, new considerations based on the results of industrialism, and new pressures from those who opposed economic liberalism, were already leading to legislation by which the government was newly regulating business and interfering with its functioning. Very gradually the condition of urban workingmen was improved.

On the continent, criticism of industrialism and its attendant economic liberalism was more radical than in England, but for a considerable time it was less productive of protective legislation for workingmen. Of the distinctive critical movements which originated on the continent, the following may here be mentioned:

1. "Utopian Socialism" was advocated by a number of persons, including the Frenchman Charles Fourier, who pleaded for a new social organization based on coöperative communities raising their own food and making their own goods.

2. A variety of "radical" opponents of economic liberalism offered various criticisms or alternatives. A Swiss, Sismondi, insisted that the equitable distribution of goods was just as needful as their increased production. A German, Friedrich List, questioned the "laws" of the classical economists, especially their doctrine of free trade, and urged that economic regulation, including tariff protection, should be utilized to promote nationalist development. The Frenchman, Louis Blanc, who was particularly shocked by unemployment, preached the "right to work" and proposed coöperative factories to be guaranteed by the state. He was a kind of "state socialist." Another Frenchman, Proudhon, was the father of "anarchism." He wanted to abolish all compulsion by state or church, and, with it, all private ownership (though not private use) of property, and to make credit available to everyone without interest charges.

3. "Social Catholicism," led by such persons as Ozanam in France and Bishop Ketteler in Germany, combated on moral and religious grounds the individualism and

selfishness of industrialists and urged state intervention and a revival of guilds in order to safeguard the working classes. The liberalism which Gregory XVI condemned in the 1830's included economic liberalism.

4. "Marxian Socialism" or "Communism" was derived from the middle-class German writers Karl Marx and Friedrich Engels, who lived and worked in exile, chiefly in England. Their views were first set forth clearly in the *Communist Manifesto* (1848), and later elaborated in *Capital*, the first volume of which appeared in 1867. Marx and Engels believed that history was the story of the struggle between economic classes. The bourgeois capitalists, they claimed, had defeated the old feudal classes in the French Revolution, but immediately had to face a new struggle with the industrial proletariat. The proletarians were exploited by the capitalists, the fruits of their labor were taken from them, and they were ravaged by unemployment. But they were growing in number and discipline and would shortly seize power from the bourgeoisie, probably by violent social revolution.

None of the foregoing movements accomplished very much in the early period of industrialization on the Continent, but the last three laid foundations for influential popular action after 1870.

CHAPTER 46

Liberal and Nationalist Revolutions of 1848-1849

A. The February Revolution at Paris and Creation of the Second French Republic

By 1847 the groups in France which opposed King Louis Philippe were becoming stronger and more vocal. Prevented by press censorship from expressing its views in print, the opposition voiced its demand for electoral reform at a series of political banquets held at Paris and in the provinces. In alarm the government forbade a "monster banquet" at Paris scheduled for February 22, 1848. This prohibition precipitated another Paris revolution—the "February Revolution" of 1848.

On February 22 angry workers, reckless students, and earnest liberals crowded the streets shouting for reform. The next day as the tumult continued, Guizot, the prime minister, ordered the National Guard to restore order. But soon the guardsmen were joining the crowds in the popular cry, "Down with Guizot." Guizot resigned. The rioting might then have subsided, had not some soldiers guarding Guizot's residence fired into a crowd of boisterous demonstrators, killing twenty-three and wounding thirty others. For a moment the crowd was stunned. Then in a rage it bore off the corpses for all Paris to behold.

Dawn of February 24 found the streets of Paris ominously barricaded by workmen and placarded with such signs as, "Louis Philippe massacres us as did Charles X; let him go join Charles X." Prudent as always, Louis Philippe tarried only long enough to abdicate in favor of his ten-year-old grandson, the Count of Paris, and then, as "Mr. Smith," he drove off in a closed carriage to follow Charles X to England.

The Count of Paris was ignored, and a "provisional government" installed itself at the city hall in Paris. It was an odd mixture, for it included the Catholic liberal poet Lamartine, the Jacobin republican Ledru-Rollin, the socialist Louis Blanc, and a workingman, Albert. So unpopular had Louis Philippe become that even extremists, legitimists on the right and anarchists like Proudhon on the left, rallied temporarily to the new government. Since two monarchies had failed in thirty-three years, a republic seemed the only practicable solution. So the provisional government proclaimed France a republic—the second republic in French history. But what kind of a republic would it be?

At the outset the Second French Republic was impelled by the Paris proletariat in a radical and socialist direction. It is to be noted that this revolution was the first in Europe to have a definitely socialist tinge, though, oddly enough, because Louis Philippe had alienated Catholics, it was almost the only European revolution of the period which was not marked by a good deal of anti-clericalism.

The provisional government ordered the election of a National Assembly by universal manhood suffrage. The National Guard, hitherto reserved to the middle classes, was opened to all citizens. "National workshops," in response to demands of Louis

Guizot. By Honoré Daumier
(d. 1879).

Blanc and his followers, were promised to guarantee work for everyone. A commission was set up to develop a program of social reform. From February to May there was the utmost enthusiasm among socialists, radicals, and workmen in Paris and in some of the other towns and cities. Liberty trees were planted. Red flags of revolution were flown. Proudhon and his followers openly attacked the system of private property.

But all was not well with the revolution. Blanc had urged workshops which would be coöperative and productive factories. Instead, the "national workshops" of 1848 were really work projects such as digging trenches, improving parks, and the like. They had little utility, and were only an excuse for paying the unemployed a dole of two francs a day. Moreover, the elections for the National Assembly in May showed that the rest of France was much less revolutionary than Paris. The peasants and property owners of the provinces elected men who were on the whole republican, but conservative as to social and economic matters. They looked with much fear on "red" Paris. They were prepared to defend private property. They had no desire to spend public funds in doles for the workers of Paris. One of the first things that the Assembly

did when it met at Paris in June 1848 was to abolish the so-called "national workshops."

The withdrawal of the wages of two francs a day meant starvation for many of the Parisian workmen, who were well aware of the conservative intentions of the National Assembly. Once again, rebellion flared up and barricades were built in the streets. The Assembly, in alarm, entrusted dictatorial powers to General Cavaignac, who called out regular troops and bourgeois national guardsmen to put down the rioting. In a futile effort to prevent bloodshed, the archbishop of Paris lost his life. For three days, the terrible "June days" (June 24–26, 1848), there was fierce and stubborn fighting in the streets of Paris. In the end, the forces of "order" triumphed. Some of the rebels were shot, and 4,000 were transported to penal colonies overseas. Louis Blanc fled to England. Proudhon was jailed. The socialist side of the February Revolution was liquidated.

With the "red menace" of socialism thus eliminated, the National Assembly proceeded during the summer and autumn of 1848 to lay the foundations of the Second French Republic in line with the ideas of moderate, bourgeois liberals. Much emphasis was put on "the family, rights of property, and public order." At the same time, concessions were made to the workers by establishing a "commission of thirty" to study social reforms; to Catholics, by promising more religious teaching in the schools; to humanitarian liberals, by abolishing slavery in the colonies, freeing the press from censorship, and doing away with capital punishment; to Jacobin democrats, by adopting a democratic republican constitution.

This constitution of 1848 provided for a president with a term of four years, and for a one-house legislature, both to be elected by universal manhood suffrage. The president would choose his own cabinet (as in the United States), but he might not veto an act of the legislature and he would not be eligible for reëlection. The National Assembly arranged for elections to take place in December 1848.

B. Revolutionary Wave Throughout Central Europe

There had been signs in the years just before 1848 that central Europe was restive under the bonds of Metternich's conservative system. When news of the February Revolution in Paris spread quickly over Europe along the railways and telegraph lines that had recently been built, the latent restiveness became widespread revolt.

Revolt occurred throughout the Austrian domains. On March 3, 1848, Louis Kossuth, an Hungarian patriot and advanced liberal, called upon Metternich to grant to Hungary a free parliament and self-government. Eight days later a group of Czech liberals in Prague made like demands in respect of Bohemia. On March 13 a turbulent mob of students and workers clashed with police in the streets of Vienna.

Metternich called out the civic guard. But it refused to disperse the crowds that gathered around the imperial palace; while a deputation urged the Emperor Ferdinand I to dismiss Metternich at once. Assured that his hour had at last arrived, the white-haired old minister presented his resignation. His residence was already sacked and burning. On March 14, 1848, he hurriedly departed from Vienna for London. Metter-nich, the veteran foe of revolution, was fleeing for his life before a revolution.

By the time Metternich reached safety in London a little more than a month later, the revolutionary storm was racking, not only the chief cities of the Habsburg Empire, but all central Europe as well. At Vienna, promptly after the flight of Metternich, Ferdinand I named a liberal ministry, freed the press, authorized a national guard, and promised a constitution. In April he promulgated a constitution. But the Viennese liberals, now in control of the capital city and backed by the new national guard, were unwilling to accept a constitution which was granted by the Emperor and might later be revoked by him. They forced him to convene a Constituent Assembly, so that the new constitutional government would be based on the people's, not the monarch's, will. Ferdinand, practically powerless, retired to Innsbruck, and in July 1848 the Assembly met in Vienna. It had been elected nominally by universal manhood suffrage, but in fact largely by bourgeois voters. It represented all the Habsburg Empire save only Hungary and Lombardy-Venetia, where other plans were afoot.

In Hungary, in March and April of 1848, the liberals organized their own revolution. It was arranged that the Hungarian Diet would meet annually and include representatives of middle-class taxpayers as well as the hitherto dominant landowners. It would make laws for Hungary, and to it an Hungarian ministry, separate from the Austrian, would be responsible. Ferdinand, yielding to pressure and panic, was persuaded to appoint the first such Hungarian ministry, and it included leading Hungarian liberals like Kossuth and Francis Deák. Revolutionary legislation was rapidly enacted. The press was freed; a national guard was organized; serfdom, feudal privileges, and the exemption of nobles from taxation were abolished. Though no step was taken to depose the Emperor Ferdinand as King of Hungary, the liberal government at Budapest adopted a national flag and otherwise acted as a free national state. Backed by the liberals at Vienna, the Hungarians felt it safe to ignore the hostility of the King at Innsbruck.

In Prague, too, liberals—both Czech and German—seized the opportunity offered

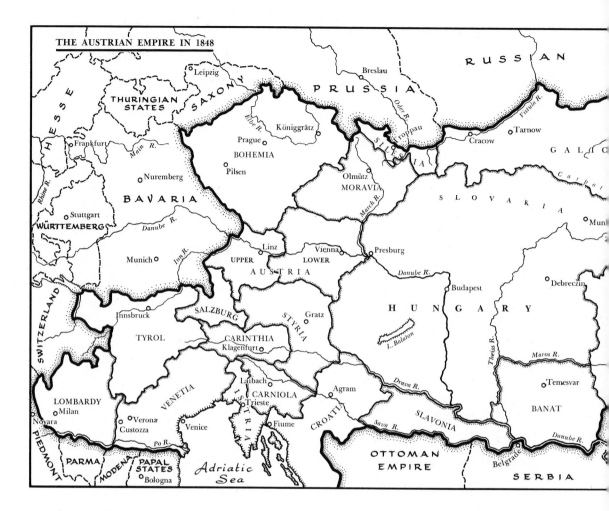

THE AUSTRIAN EMPIRE IN 1848

them to set up a separate ministry for Bohemia, to transform the local Diet into a national parliament, and to create a national guard. In April, the Emperor felt compelled to agree in general terms to this autonomous, liberal regime for Bohemia. But the German liberals at Vienna and the Hungarian liberals at Budapest were not eager to see the Czechs or other Slavs obtain real self-government. The Czech liberals and nationalists accordingly convoked at Prague, in June 1848, a Pan-Slavic Congress consisting of Czech, Slovak, Polish, Yugoslav, and Russian delegates to devise measures which might assure liberty and autonomy to the Slavic peoples, especially those within the Habsburg Empire.

In Italy, a revolt had broken out within the kingdom of the Two Sicilies even before the February Revolution at Paris, and in January 1848 King Ferdinand II was forced to accept a liberal constitution. Influenced by events in France, the King of Sardinia-Piedmont, Charles Albert, promulgated a liberal constitution, called the *Statuto*, on March 4, 1848. Then with the collapse of Metternich's power at Vienna and the ensuing confusion, the tide of liberal and national revolution rolled all over Italy.

At Milan, the populace, after five days of street fighting (March 18–22), expelled General Radetzky and his Austrian garrison, and cheered for the transfer of Lombardy from Austria to Sardinia. At Venice, under the leadership of Daniel Manin, a patriotic liberal, the townspeople drove out the Austrain officials and proclaimed the restoration of the Venetian republic. But if the Austrians had been expelled from some of the larger cities, they still had in Lombardy a large army, which might be used to reestablish Austrian rule. To get rid of this threat and drive the Austrians from Italy, Charles Albert of Sardinia declared war on Austria,

But when crowds flocked to the palace square to applaud him, they were received with musket-shots from his royal guard. Again the barricades went up and street-fighting broke out, in which two hundred citizens lost their lives. On March 19 the King showed a change of heart. He called off his troops, appointed a liberal ministry, and convoked a Constituent Assembly. The Assembly was elected by universal manhood suffrage and met in Berlin in May 1848. It was overwhelmingly liberal.

In the smaller German states, simultaneous revolutionary movements met with similar success. In Bavaria, the liberals compelled King Louis I to abdicate in favor of his son, Maximilian II, who swore to uphold and liberalize the constitution which had been granted thirty years earlier. In Baden, Württemberg, Hesse, Hanover, Saxony, Nassau, Brunswick, and the petty Thuringian States, the rulers were frightened into appointing liberal ministries, promising constitutional government, and granting freedom of the press. In Bremen, Hamburg, and Lübeck riots led to a liberalizing of the governments of these "free cities," which had long been ruled by wealthy oligarchies.

On the borders of Germany, both Denmark and Holland were affected by the liberal upheaval. The Danish King Frederick VII promised liberal rioters (March 21, 1848) to summon a constitutional convention. It met in October, and drafted a constitution which was put into effect in June 1849. The Dutch King William II put himself at the head of the liberal movement and sanctioned in October 1848 a constitution, which transformed the old States-General into a national parliament.

Even England did not wholly escape the effects of the general commotion of 1848. The Chartists, reawakened by liberal successes on the continent, prepared a petition for a democratic reform of parliament and planned to present it with a tremendous demonstration. The ministry and upper classes were alarmed. The aged Duke of Wellington was called upon to defend the government with regular troops and 170,000 special middle-class constables. But rain dampened the ardor of the Chartists and the demonstration fizzled out.

March 23, 1848. To his army of 60,000 men, were soon added detachments from the Two Sicilies, the Papal State, Tuscany, and Lombardy. Charles Albert captured the fortified town of Peschiera from Radetzky at the end of May. It looked as if Italy was well on the way to securing both liberal government and national independence.

Meanwhile, Metternich's fall was the signal for rejoicing and for liberal (and national) revolution throughout Germany. The most sensational upheaval was in Prussia. King Frederick William IV of Prussia was a romantic and somewhat dramatic prince, who, though arbitrary and paternalistic by nature, had indulged in some mildly liberal gestures. He was much surprised when his "beloved" Berliners took to rioting and erecting barricades (March 15–17, 1848). To quiet the excitement he promised to convene a Prussian Parliament and to work for a national union of Germany.

The revolts which swept the continent of Europe were not only liberal, but nationalist. In Italy, many patriots rallied behind Charles Albert to win national freedom and unity under the banner of the house of Savoy. In Germany, popular demands grew urgent that something be done to unify the separate states into a single nation. In response, the new liberal governments of the several states instructed their delegates in the Diet of the loose German Confederation at Frankfurt to authorize the democratic election of a National Assembly to devise a new federal government for the whole of Germany. Elections were duly held in Austria, Prussia, and other German states, and, since many conservatives refrained from voting, the liberals won a large majority. In May 1848, the representatives came together at Frankfurt, and the body is known in history as the Frankfurt Assembly.

The Diet of the German Confederation ceased to function. The new Frankfurt Assembly proceeded to proclaim a German National Empire and to select a temporary administrative head for it in the person of a liberal Habsburg prince, the Archduke John of Austria. It then set to work to draw up a constitution. From the start, most of the members assumed that the new Germany, like the old Confederation and the older Holy Roman Empire, would include Austria—not the whole Austrian Empire, but the German part of Austria centering in Vienna—that it would be a federation something like the United States, and that the central government would be monarchical but parliamentary and liberal. The task of writing such a constitution was both difficult and delicate, and there was much difference of opinion as to whether the emperor of Austria or the king of Prussia should be the new German emperor.

On the new constitution and the negotiations connected with it, the Frankfurt Assembly labored for a year. Meanwhile, in December 1848, it reached agreement on a document called the "Fundamental Rights of the German Nation." This statement was similar, in a general way, to the French "Declaration of the Rights of Man and of the Citizen" of 1789, though it was more detailed, more frankly nationalist, and at the same time less dogmatically democratic. It was in fact the classic expression of the middle-class, liberal nationalism of the mid-nineteenth century. It summed up the hopes and dreams of 1848. With it as a guide, the new nation which the Assembly was striving to create would have been both constitutional and liberal.

C. Nationalist Conflicts and Conservative Reaction

During the first half of 1848, liberalism made startling advances all over Europe. Then it began to suffer setbacks which wiped out most of the liberal gains. The explanation, both of the rapid liberal victories and of the subsequent defeats, lies in the very nature of the revolutions of 1848. They were primarily urban, middle-class affairs. The cities spoke first and loudly in favor of a new liberal regime. Then in due course the countryside of conservative landowners and peasants spoke less noisily but with greater weight.

The rural areas were rooted deep in traditional ways and usages. The great majority of the inhabitants of Germany, the Austrian Empire, and Italy belonged to agricultural classes. They distrusted townsfolks. They respected the clergy. They had a lingering regard for their landlords. Most of the clergy and landowners were hostile to revolutionary change, and in the course of time they rallied to the support of the bureaucrats and army officers, who, though pushed aside in the first stages of the upheaval, were likewise opposed to revolution. Moreover, even the cities were divided by cleavages between bourgeois and workers, and between radicals and moderates. As the revolutions made rapid progress, many middle-class moderates drew back in alarm. Then, too, while the liberals could appeal to national sentiment, so could the conservatives. Before long the masses of people, rural and urban, were being urged to prop up their tottering governments for the sake of national strength and prestige.

The first serious setback to the liberal revolutionary movement in central Europe occurred in Bohemia. Here in June 1848 the Austrian governor and army commander, Prince Windischgrätz, enraged by

ITALIAN STATES IN 1848-1849

a renewal of rioting in Prague in which his wife had been killed, acted decisively to "restore order." His troops, backed by German elements in the province who had become alarmed by the increasing power of the Slavic Czechs, subdued Prague, dispersed the Pan-Slavic Congress, and overthrew the revolutionary liberal government. Liberal reforms were revoked, and Bohemia placed under martial law.

The next important setback was in Italy. Here the army of Charles Albert of Sardinia was weakened by the withdrawal of contingents from central and southern Italy. Both Pope Pius IX and King Ferdinand II of the Two Sicilies were frightened by "excesses" of the revolutionaries and continuance of domestic "disorder," and Ferdinand wanted all his troops to restore absolutism in his kingdom. In July 1848 a reënforced Austrian army under Radetzky decisively defeated the Italian army of Charles Albert at Custozza. Charles Albert agreed to an armistice and Radetzky reoccupied Milan and all Lombardy.

This serious reverse to the cause of Italian liberty and unity aroused Italian extremists to frantic endeavors. At Rome, the liberal papal minister, Rossi, was assassinated in November 1848. Pope Pius IX, disillusioned with liberalism and in fear of his life, fled from the city. In February 1849 a republic was proclaimed at Rome, and Mazzini assumed the leadership. Radical republicans likewise seized control of Florence and Naples and temporarily transformed them into republics. Charles Albert, driven on by the threat of a similar republican outbreak in his kingdom of Sardinia, renewed the war with Austria. But in March 1849, at Novara, he suffered a second and quite overwhelming defeat at the hands of Radetzky. Forced to conclude a humiliating peace with Austria, Charles Albert abdicated in favor of his son, Victor Emmanual II, but did not revoke the Piedmontese constitution (*Statuto*). The victorious Austrian army could now be utilized to suppress the revolutionary republics.

In May 1849 the King of the Two Sicilies and the Grand Duke of Tuscany were restored to their thrones by force of arms. Venice, blockaded by land and sea, surrendered to the Austrians. As for Rome,

French troops, sent under circumstances which we shall presently note, overthrew Mazzini's republic at the end of June and reinstated Pope Pius IX in his temporal domains. By the summer of 1849 all Italy was once again under traditional control. Republicanism was stamped out, and, except under Victor Emmanuel in Sardinia, liberalism was suppressed.

The Austrian restoration in Italy was rendered easier by the triumph of conservative reaction in Austria itself. The successes of Windischgrätz and Radetzky in June and July 1848 had heartened the Emperor Ferdinand at Innsbruck and his conservative supporters, for it was clear that loyal troops could be used successfully to repress revolution. Events in Hungary likewise played into the conservatives' hands. The revolutionary government under Kossuth at Budapest was characterized not only by liberalism, but also by an intense Hungarian nationalism. It outraged Austrians by its separatist tendencies, and it aroused violent opposition of the Croats, Serbs, Slovaks, and Rumanians under Hungarian rule, for it showed no

Joseph Mazzini. From a photograph.

Courtesy Bettmann Archive

Louis Kossuth. From a daguerreotype.

Courtesy Bettmann Archive

"order was restored," was to persuade Emperor Ferdinand to abdicate in favor of his eighteen-year-old nephew, Francis Joseph, and then to have the new Emperor annul the liberal concessions which the old one had made. He allowed the Austrian constitutional convention to continue its debates a while longer. But he ignored the document it prepared, and proclaimed a conservative constitution by his own authority. Eventually he withdrew even this concession to liberalism.

Schwarzenberg likewise began a vigorous offensive against the Hungarians, and sent Windischgrätz and his army to support Jellačić who was already invading Hungary. Kossuth replied by proclaiming Hungary an independent republic (April 1849) and by stirring the people to patriotic armed resistance. For a time the invading armies were held at bay. But Schwarzenberg asked and obtained the assistance of an additional army from the Russian Tsar Nicholas I, who was eager to suppress all revolution in central Europe lest a new revolt should occur in Poland. By August 1849 the three invading armies had overcome resistance in Hungary. Kossuth fled into exile. The liberal constitution was abolished. Once again Hungary was ruled as an Austrian province.

The success of the conservative forces in Italy and throughout the Habsburg Empire had a profound influence in restoring confidence to the conservatives in Germany. By the late summer of 1848, King Frederick William IV of Prussia yielded to two pressures to defy the liberals. One was pressure from Great Britain, France, and Russia to end the war on Denmark which at the request of the Frankfurt Assembly he had been waging to free the "German" duchies of Schleswig and Holstein from Danish rule. The other was pressure from conservative classes at home—landowners, Protestant clergy, army officers, civil servants—to check the liberal Prussian Constituent Assembly, which was voting to abolish the nobility, to make the King a mere figurehead, and to send a Prussian army to help the liberals in Vienna. In the autumn of 1848 Frederick William IV felt strong enough to act. He ousted the liberal ministry and installed a conservative one under the reactionary Count Brandenburg. He withdrew his troops

tendency to make any concessions to their national sentiments and demands. These anti-Hungarian nationalists found an able champion in Joseph Jellačić, a Croatian soldier and patriot, who pointed out to the Emperor that the Croats and other Slavs would make common cause with Austria against the Hungarian pretensions. In September 1848, Jellačić was made governor of Croatia and authorized to attack Hungary with a Slavic Austrian army which would be aided by German Austrian troops from Vienna.

The liberals of Vienna sought to prevent the despatch of troops against the Hungarian liberals. A mob hanged the minister of war to a lamp post and seized the imperial armory. But on Vienna were already converging the army of Windischgrätz from Bohemia and that of Jellačić from Croatia. To assist the Viennese "rebels," marched a Hungarian army. But it was defeated and turned back by Jellačić. On the last day of October 1848, Windischgrätz beat down the resistance at Vienna and occupied the city by force. A score or so of radical leaders were executed and the liberal government was supplanted by a reactionary ministry headed by Prince Felix Schwarzenberg, brother-in-law of Windischgrätz and disciple of Metternich.

Schwarzenberg's first important act, once

from Denmark and used them to overawe the Constituent Assembly and the people of Berlin. When these acts caused no serious tumult, the King dissolved the Constituent Assembly and drafted a constitution which left real power in his hands and those of the ministers he chose. It did provide for a legislature which would be consulted on some matters, but by a peculiar "three-class system" two thirds of that body represented those who paid two thirds of the taxes—the upper class and the wealthiest part of the middle class.

The triumph of reaction in Prussia and Austria left the liberal majority of the Frankfurt Assembly in a most awkward position. In a desperate attempt to save the situation, the Assembly offered the crown of the projected new German Empire to the Prussian King, hoping that his romantic attachment to nationalism and his desire for personal glory would outweigh his growing aversion to liberalism. Frederick William IV hesitated. But he received ominous warnings from the Austrian Prime Minister Schwarzenberg and from the Russian Tsar Nicholas. In April 1849 the Prussian King denounced the constitution that had been drawn up by the Frankfurt Assembly and refused, as he said, "to pick up a crown out of the gutter."

In a despairing protest against the now obvious failure of the Frankfurt Assembly, liberal extremists tried in May 1849 to install republics in the Rhineland, Silesia, Saxony, and Baden, but these were quickly suppressed by Prussian troops. Many of the liberal leaders who escaped jail or execution fled into exile. Not a few found refuge in the United States.

Though now a foe of all liberalism, Frederick William IV was still haunted by the dream of uniting Germany under Prussian leadership. Accordingly, he proposed a plan for a close union of all the German states, except Austria, with himself as president. Some of the states accepted and sent delegates to a meeting of the parliament of the new "German Union" at Erfurt in 1850. But Austria, with conservatism triumphant at home, was in a position to reassert her old leadership in Germany. Schwarzenberg would not permit the union of Germany under Prussia and a Hohenzollern emperor.

For a time in 1850, it looked as if war would break out between Austria and Prussia. Schwarzenberg had the support of the south German states and of others like Saxony, which feared Prussia. It seemed likely, too, that Russia would support Austria. In the face of such powerful opposition, the Prussian King backed down. In November 1850 Frederick William IV signed the treaty of Olmütz with Austria. By its terms, the "German Union" under the presidency of Prussia was dissolved, and the previous "German Confederation" under the presidency of Austria was restored. There was no provision for a popular parliament. Instead, the Diet of delegates of the princes was reconstituted, and, acting under instructions from the now conservative governments of Austria and Prussia, it formally repealed the "Fundamental Rights of the German Nation" and set up a special commission to purge any state constitution of "revolutionary novelties."

D. Transformation of the Second French Republic into Another Napoleonic Empire, and General Restoration of "Law and Order," 1850–1852

The revolutionary upheaval of 1848 was over by 1850, and the regime of Metternich to a large degree reëstablished. Even in France, the revolutionary gains of 1848 did not endure. The elections held in December of 1848 for the presidency of the new Republic produced a curious result. General Cavaignac got one and a half million votes; Ledru-Rollin received 370,000. But five and a half million ballots were cast for Louis Napoleon Bonaparte, nephew of the Emperor Napoleon. Louis Napoleon, after a youth spent in exile and some adventures as a member of the Carbonari in Italy, had set himself seriously to the work of being the heir of the Napoleonic tradition. He had dabbled in military matters. He had written a book on poverty and social reform. He had steadily cultivated the Napoleonic legend, compounded of fact and fiction, of liberalism and dictatorship. Twice—at Strasbourg in 1836, and at Boulogne in 1840—he had tried to organize armed risings against the government of Louis Philippe.

Both attempts had been ludicrous fiascos. After the second, Louis Napoleon had been imprisoned for six years, and had escaped to England in the disguise of a stone-mason.

In 1848 came his opportunity. He had not been in France during the June days, and so had not alienated the workers by siding against them. Yet he was known to be a friend of law and order. If the Emperor Napoleon had stood for anything, it had been firm rule. Perhaps his nephew would bring peace at home and respect abroad. What especially helped Louis Napoleon was fear of the "red menace," the "ugly threat of socialism," on the part of the middle-class, the landowners, and most Catholics. Some of the radical republicans laughed at Louis Napoleon's candidacy for the presidency. His amazing success at the polls turned their amusement to dismay.

Once installed as President, Louis Napoleon set himself to increase his popularity and simultaneously to control police and army. To strengthen Catholic support, he sent to Rome the French military expedition which in June 1849 ousted Mazzini's republic and reinstated Pope Pius IX. Similarly he approved the Falloux Law of 1850, which removed the restrictions imposed by Guizot under Louis Philippe on Catholic schools. At the same time, to ensure support of urban workers, Louis Napoleon sponsored legislation which limited the hours of work (to twelve a day), restricted child labor, and improved the distribution of poor relief. To satisfy the bourgeoisie, he showed himself a friend of property, order, and business interests.

So conservative, on the whole, was Louis Napoleon's attitude that he might have lost the sympathy of workers and of liberals, had he not adroitly utilized a dispute with the national legislature, in which conservatives had a majority. In 1850 the legislature passed a law restricting the suffrage to taxpayers who had lived for three years in the same district, thus disenfranchising a third of the voters—mostly urban workers. The President gave willing ear to protests against this law and promptly declared that he could not permit the legislature to deprive millions of Frenchmen of the right to vote. In November 1851 he demanded that the legislature reëstablish universal suffrage.

Napoleon III. By Jean Baptiste Carpeaux (d. 1875).

When it refused to do so, he executed, on December 2, a *coup d'état*.

This seizure of power was skillfully managed. Police and troops overawed all opposition. A manifesto proclaimed a temporary dictatorship, the dissolution of the Assembly, and the restoration of universal suffrage. Censorship prevented counter agitation. The most notorious critics of the President, such as Adolphe Thiers and Victor Hugo, were hustled out of the country. On December 21 the French people in a plebiscite voted, by 7,500,000 to 640,000, to empower President Louis Napoleon to prepare a new constitution for the Second Republic. He had won conservatives by standing firm for internal order, and liberals and radicals, by sponsoring universal suffrage.

The new constitution, modeled closely on Napoleonic precedent, gave the President a term of ten years and put so much power in his hands and in those of the Council of State appointed by him that he became virtually a dictator. The next year, Louis Napoleon devoted to propaganda. He appealed to national pride. He spoke honeyed words to peasants, to artisans, to capitalists, to rich and poor, to reactionaries and radicals, to believers and agnostics. He organized demonstrations at which he was greeted with cries of "Vive l'empereur." His reward was speedy and complete. On December 2, 1852, he became, through a new national plebiscite, Napoleon III, Emperor of the French.

The Second Republic was thus changed to the Second Empire, a dictatorship only partially concealed by the national plebiscites and the continued existence of a national legislature which had no real power. The February Revolution had, in a little over four years, resulted in a regime even less democratic than that of the monarchy which it had replaced.

Yet the revolutionary upheaval of 1848 left some liberal gains in Europe. In the Austrian Empire, the conservatives did not reëstablish serfdom, which had been abolished by the liberal governments. Henceforth the peasants were free to buy and sell land and to move from place to place. From the revolutions, moreover, there survived some form of constitutional government, if not in the Austrian Empire, at least in Sardinia-Piedmont, Switzerland, Holland, Denmark, and Prussia.

The enduring gains of liberalism were but scanty. By its manifold failures in 1848 and 1849, liberalism was discredited and driven underground again in France as well as in Central Europe. Yet behind the scenes it was by no means dead; if the liberals of the 1860's were less vocal than those of 1848, they became slowly more influential.

One of the factors that thwarted a liberal triumph in 1848 was clearly nationalism. Though liberals and nationalists had joined hands to start and carry on many of the revolutions, occasions had quickly arisen where national interests ran counter to liberal aims. "Liberal" Prussia had in 1848 fought "Liberal" Denmark in the name of German nationalism. "Liberal" Hungary, identified with Magyar nationalism, had aroused the nationalist opposition of liberal Croatians and other Slavs. German liberals in Bohemia, alarmed by the rapid rise of Czech nationalism, had thrown in their lot with the conservatives of German Austria. Worst of all, the struggle of Austria with Prussia for leadership in the unification of Germany had confused all the issues and resulted in thwarting liberalism, as well as nationalism.

Had the Frankfurt Assembly succeeded in its liberal national work, the subsequent history of Germany, and of Europe too, might have been very different. Had Germany been united under liberal auspices, then the whole weight of nationalism and patriotism would have been behind the new liberal state, and Germany might have remained liberal as well as nationalist.

After 1848, liberalism and nationalism displayed some tendency to split apart and take separate roads. Nationalists showed themselves ready to sacrifice liberalism to attain national ends; and during ensuing decades some of them tended to invoke "blood and iron," rather than "liberty, equality, and fraternity."

CHAPTER 47

Liberal Nationalist Regime of Napoleon III

AND CREATION OF NATIONAL STATES OF ITALY
AND RUMANIA

A. Napoleon III's Domestic Policies

We have already seen how the "Napoleonic legend," the fear of the "red menace," the blunders of the republican legislature, and his own crafty maneuvers combined to enable Prince Louis Napoleon Bonaparte to overthrow the Second French Republic and to make himself in 1852 the Emperor Napoleon III. His regime was essentially a dictatorship. He organized an effective secret police; he controlled the press; he manipulated elections by the use of "official candidates"; he dominated the legislature and the whole government down to the provincial prefects and mayors; and he jailed or exiled his most outspoken critics. He made much of the army and of old Napoleonic soldiers.

Napoleon III tried to make his dictatorship acceptable to both radicals and conservatives. On the one hand, he preserved at least the illusion of universal manhood suffrage and called the Second Empire "the final flower of the French Revolution." On the other hand, he resolutely defended "order"; and his marriage in 1853 with the beautiful Eugénie, a Spanish countess, gave him an Empress whose charm helped to make the French court once more the center of European styles and fashions.

The Emperor was favorably impressed by the contemporary vogue of economic liberalism. In politics, he was hardly a liberal, but in economics he was even more liberal than Louis Philippe or Guizot. Legislation designed to aid business was the order of the day. Railway lines were multiplied and consolidated. The formation of stock companies was made easier. The Bourse, or stock exchange, became ever more active as the capital market boomed (and occasionally crashed). Government regulation of business was reduced. A system of savings banks was established. Even the tradition of high tariffs was broken, when Napoleon III cut the French import duties to a maximum of 30 per cent (after five years, to 25 per cent) in the Cobden treaty with Great Britain (1860). Despite plaintive outcries of some manufacturers, the Emperor proceeded in the 1860's to conclude low-tariff treaties with the German Zollverein, and with Belgium, Italy, Switzerland, Austria, Sweden, Spain, and Portugal. His initiative seemed to be ushering in an era of freer trade for all Europe.

Napoleon III also sponsored a remarkable series of public works to stimulate industry and commerce and to provide employment for labor. Harbors were improved, swamps drained, roads repaired, and the network of railways completed. In Paris, vast sums of money were spent on constructing broad boulevards and magnificent public buildings under the supervision of the Emperor's devoted friend, Baron Haussmann. The French capital thus became the most beautiful and attractive city in the world, a mecca for tourists and pleasure seekers. The imposing new opera house,

The Paris Opera House.
Courtesy Bettmann Archive

with its ornate architecture and glaring gas lights, was a symbol of the Second Empire.

Napoleon III, unlike Louis Philippe, did not forget the workers. He chatted familiarly with them and drank toasts to them. He subsidized their organizations. It was for the working class, he affirmed, that his government of cheap bread, public works, and national holidays existed. With all this talk, there was some actual labor legislation, just enough to encourage the proletariat and not enough to alienate the bourgeois liberals. One law permitted workers to form coöperative societies for buying and selling. Another partially legalized trade unions and recognized for the first time (though under severe limitations) the right to strike. A third extended workmen's voluntary insurance, with state guaranties, against death and industrial accidents.

Napoleon III took special care to reassure the peasants who still constituted a majority of the French population. He repeatedly affirmed his devotion to the principle of private property and his interest in the vineyards and wheatfields of the peasants. He encouraged railway construction, he said, the better to get their goods to market. He lowered tariffs, the better to sell their products in England. The Emperor likewise took pains to favor the Catholic Church. He strengthened the hold of the clergy on the universities and public schools in France, maintained French troops at Rome for the protection of the pope, and in general posed as the champion of Catholic Christianity.

For the first time since the advent of Napoleon I, it seemed as though France had a government that could secure internal peace and order, rise superior to factional quarrels, and reconcile divergent political, economic, and social interests. To most Frenchmen and most Europeans, the rule of Napoleon III seemed eminently successful, and France was widely regarded as the strongest country on the continent of Europe. But to some degree these appearances were deceptive. The Second Empire bears a superficial resemblance both to the Empire of the first Napoleon and to regimes of twentieth-century dictators. In techniques and methods, it forms a sort of link between them. It was characterized by a suppression of political liberty through censorship, secret police, and a sham constitution. It paid homage to democracy by plebiscites but thwarted all real democracy in both local and national governments. To make up for the loss of liberty, it emphasized material well-being and sought by propaganda, often inconsistent and in many cases not backed by action, to keep the support of all groups and classes however divergent their interests. Yet there was much more liberalism in the regime of Napoleon III than in the later dictatorships of Communists and Fascists. There was comparatively little dictation in economic matters, and less interference with personal liberties. Moreover, through the whole period of the Second Empire there were strong currents of opposition to it at home as well as abroad.

Doubtless Napoleon III was sincerely pacific at heart, and he aspired to be the champion of nationalities. He lacked the martial zeal of the born soldier, and he had an un-Napoleonic aversion to the sight of battlefields and the smell of gunpowder. Yet circumstances and his own ambition and heritage involved him in a series of wars. And it was war which eventually engulfed him and ended the Second French Empire.

B. The Crimean War, National Emergence of Rumania, and Napoleon III's Colonial Ventures

From the beginning of his rule, Napoleon III made friendship with Great Britain a keystone to his diplomacy. At the same time, his relations with the Tsar Nicholas I of Russia were distinctly unfriendly. The Tsar had been reluctant to recognize the Second Empire; his tariffs irked French business men; his religious intolerance irritated French Catholics; his stern measures with the Poles outraged French liberals. But it was a quarrel between Roman Catholic and Eastern Orthodox monks in Palestine which ignited the latent hostility between Russia and France. The Tsar had long been interested in carving up the Ottoman Empire, whose Sultan he described as the "sick man of the East." When Russia denounced the Sultan's inability to keep peace in the Holy Land and demanded that Russia be allowed to "protect" the Christians in the Ottoman Empire. Napoleon III encouraged the Sultan to resist.

The dispute presented a seemingly golden opportunity to the French Emperor. A war with autocratic, intolerant Russia—the power which had defeated Napoleon I, created the Holy Alliance, and crushed the Poles—would be popular at home and in western Europe with both liberals and Catholics. Moreover, he could count on British support, for if English liberals were pacific, they were also anti-Russian. It was becoming a major point of British policy to bolster up the decaying Ottoman rule so as to prevent aggressive Russia from becoming too strong in the eastern Mediterranean and threatening the British route to India. Consequently, Great Britain backed French insistence on the preservation of the integrity of the Ottoman Empire. For reasons of its own, which we shall note later, Sardinia espoused the Franco-British cause, while Austria, torn between gratitude for Russian help in 1849 and fear of Russian advance in the Balkans, preserved a troubled neutrality. Prussia was friendly to Russia but inactive.

War began between the Ottoman and Russian Empires in 1853. France and Great Britain joined the Turkish side in 1854, and Sardinia in 1855. It was easy to declare war but a little difficult to find a place to fight. At length the French and British sent a joint expedition into the Black Sea and attacked the Crimea. Since military operations were confined mainly to this peninsula, the conflict is known as the Crimean War. It is notable as the first significant struggle between major European powers after 1815. It was marked by gross military inefficiency on both sides. Sickness caused more deaths in the armies than bullets. At length, the Allies captured Sevastopol, and in 1856 Russia sued for peace. The Crimean War cost half a million lives and two billion dollars.

Napoleon III had the satisfaction of holding the peace conference at Paris. In the settlement arrived at, Russia agreed to respect the integrity of the Ottoman Empire, to renounce any claim to protect its Christian inhabitants, to restore to it a small slice of territory in Bessarabia, and not to keep any warships in the Black Sea. An international commission was created to supervise the free navigation of the Danube. Thus the Ottoman Empire was preserved, and Russia was checked. Napoleon III was cheered by returning veterans. In the midst of the popular applause, a son—the Prince Imperial—was born to the Emperor and Empress. Fortune smiled upon the Emperor of the French and lured a pacifist on to further wars.

Emperor Maximilian of Mexico. From a photograph.

One by-product of the Crimean War won Napoleon III considerable prestige with liberals and nationalists, even if it eventually weakened the Ottoman Empire, for which the war had supposedly been fought. This was the formation and unification of Rumania. The Rumanians were a people speaking a Latin language and inhabiting the Ottoman principalities of Moldavia and Wallachia and the Russian province of Bessarabia. Affected by the doctrines of nationalism, the Rumanians were eager to establish a free and united Rumania. At the peace conference, Napoleon III insisted on adding part of Bessarabia to Moldavia and securing for the Rumanian principalities a large measure of autonomy within the Ottoman Empire. In 1858 he secured from the Sultan and the great powers a general recognition of the right of each of the Rumanian principalities to elect its own parliament and choose its own prince, though it was expressly provided that Moldavia and

Wallachia should not be united. The Rumanian leaders neatly got around this provision by having the two principalities choose one and the same prince, Alexander Cuza. In 1861–1862, Napoleon III again showed his benevolent interest in the Rumanians by persuading the powers to recognize not only the one prince, but also the fusion of the two parliaments into a united Rumanian parliament. The Second French Empire thus helped to create the modern national state of Rumania.

Meanwhile, Napoleon III was showing his interest in colonial affairs. He completed the pacification of Algeria in 1857, and the next year established a permanent civil government there under Marshal MacMahon. He dispatched naval expeditions to occupy various islands in the Pacific, notably New Caledonia (1853). He joined with the British in a military demonstration against China, which extorted from the Chinese government the treaties of Tientsin (1860), opening several ports to European trade and promising security to Christian missionaries in the interior. South of China, the Emperor laid the foundations of a large French colonial domain, for in 1858 he sent an expedition into Annam and Cochin-China to avenge the murder of some French missionaries, and five years later he established a French protectorate over Cambodia.

One colonial undertaking, in the long run, failed miserably, though at the start it appeared a brilliant project. It was a plan to take over the republic of Mexico, which was torn by internal strife. The time seemed opportune, for the United States was too involved in its Civil War (1861–1865) to interfere. In 1861, Benito Juarez, an Indian in blood and a radical in policy, had won his way to power in Mexico. He inaugurated a series of anti-clerical "reforms," such as suppression of religious communities, confiscation of church lands, and institution of civil marriage. In addition, Juarez repudiated the foreign loans contracted by the preceding conservative regime.

Napoleon III joined with Great Britain and Spain to seize the Mexican customs houses by force, so as to compel Juarez to recognize the debts Mexico owed abroad. Within four months, a compromise satisfactory to Spain and Great Britain was reached and these powers withdrew their forces. But the French troops stayed on, since Napoleon III had more elaborate plans afoot. He did not intend to make Mexico an outright French colony, for a step so drastic might well have aroused violent opposition from other countries, but rather to install a puppet regime subservient to France. By so doing, he was confident that he would please French Catholics, who felt that their church would thereby be relieved of persecution in Mexico and also French business men, who would find continuing opportunities for lucrative investment in Mexican mines, railways, and agriculture. Accordingly, in the autumn of 1862, the French Emperor sent to Mexico a force of 30,000 French veterans. Though they required constant reënforcements, the French army captured Mexico City in June 1863 and drove Juarez into the mountain fastnesses of the north. Casting around for a ruler for Mexico, Napoleon III hit upon the Archduke Maxmilian, brother of the Austrian Emperor Francis Joseph.

But the "great idea of his reign," as Napoleon III termed it, proved disastrous. From the outset, Maximilian, who became "Emperor of Mexico" in 1864, was in a precarious position. His regime was unpopular even among Mexicans who disliked Juarez. The French troops, hampered by rough country and lack of communications, encountered difficult guerilla warfare. Most important of all, the end of the American Civil War (1865) enabled the United States to reassert the principle of the Monroe Doctrine and to back up its protests with very real threats. Whereupon, Napoleon III faced about and gradually recalled his expeditionary forces. The last of them left Mexico in February 1867. Maximilian, who was gallant or foolhardy enough to remain behind, was soon captured and shot, and Juarez was reinstated as president.

The Mexican venture of the French was not only disastrous in itself. It was a veritable boomerang against Napoleon III. The restoration of Juaraz brought in Mexico a renewal of anti-Catholic legislation and repudiation of the franchises recently acquired by French financiers. In France, there was dismay at the blood and money that had been uselessly expended, while ardent Cath-

olics and bourgeois liberals alike grew increasingly critical of the Emperor.

C. Unification and National Independence of Italy

The failures of Charles Albert of Sardinia and of revolutionary liberals like Mazzini in 1848–1849,[1] did not destroy the movement for the unification of the Italian peninsula into a single nation. In fact, the ensuing period witnessed such an intensification of nationalist agitation that it has been called the *risorgimento* (resurrection).

There had been serious disagreement among Italian patriots about methods of achieving national unity. Mazzini from exile continued to urge the formation of a liberal democratic republic. One of his most vigorous followers was Joseph Garibaldi, a native of Nice, who had fought in South America, against Austria in north Italy in 1848, and against the pope in central Italy in 1849. For a time Garibaldi was a refugee in New York, but in 1854 he returned to Italy to await a new opportunity to strike for national freedom.

Another method had been advocated by a Piedmontese priest named Gioberti, who sought to reconcile nationalism and liberalism with traditional religion, and proposed a federation of existing Italian states under the presidency of the pope. This had appealed to many persons among the clergy and upper classes, but any popular support for it was lost after 1849 by the ultra-conservatism of Pope Pius IX.

A third group of nationalists had urged the creation for all Italy of a liberal, constitutional monarchy under the king of Piedmont-Sardinia, and after 1849 this group gained strength at the expense of the others. Republicanism waned as a natural reaction to its excesses and failures in 1848–1849. Federalism practically collapsed in the face of Pius IX's hostility. On the other hand, despite the failure of King Charles Albert of Sardinia to make headway against Austria and his abdication in 1849, his successor, Victor Emmanuel II, attracted an ever increasing number of supporters by reason of his retention of liberal constitu-

[1] See above, p. 606.

Cavour.

Alinari Photograph

tional government and of his personal reputation for bluff honesty.

In Count Camillo di Cavour, King Victor Emmanuel had a first-rate assistant. From his youth an admirer of French culture and British political and economic liberalism, Cavour was first known as an improving landlord, as a promoter of factories and railway building, and as editor of *Il Risorgimento*, a famous journal which urged liberal and constitutional reform in Piedmont-Sardinia to prepare it for leadership in all Italy. With the establishment of constitutional government in the kingdom, Cavour came rapidly to the fore in politics. He entered the cabinet in 1850, and in 1852 became prime minister and minister of foreign affairs. At these posts, he remained, with one brief interruption, till his death nine years later.

As premier, Cavour strove to promote the material welfare of the country in current British fashion. Tariffs were lowered, industry and transportation improved, and public finances reformed. At the same time, he sought to reduce the influence of the church by restricting its privileges, expelling the Jesuits, and suppressing some of the monas-

tic establishments. His ideal, he said, was "a free church in a free state."

Despite formidable obstacles that stood in his way, but aided greatly by the National Society which had largely superseded Mazzini's Young Italy, Cavour worked steadily for the cause of Italian unity. Since he was convinced that Italy could be united only by the defeat of Austria, for which defeat foreign aid would be necessary, he turned his attention to the diplomatic field. In 1855 he took Sardinia into the Crimean War as an ally of France and Great Britain, hoping that Austria would join the Russian side. Austria disappointed him by remaining neutral, but at least Cavour won a hearing for Italian problems at the peace table, where he explained at length and in angry tones the injustice of Austrian rule in Italy.

Aided by the popularity of Piedmont-Sardinia among liberals in France, Cavour then set to work to gain the help of Napoleon III against Austria. Though the French Emperor had been an Italian Carbonaro in his youth, though he had Italian blood in his veins, though his cousin ("Napoleon II") had as a baby been entitled "King of Rome," he hesitated until a fanatical Italian nationalist, named Orsini, threw a bomb at him in January 1858. Napoleon III quickly made up his mind to risk offending the pope and French Catholics by aiding Italian liberals and nationalists.

A secret meeting between Cavour and the Emperor took place at Plombières in July 1858. Napoleon III agreed to assist Sardinia in driving Austria out of Lombardy and Venetia and to sanction the creation of a single north Italian state. Cavour agreed to arrange it so that Austria would seem the aggressor in the war, and then to cede to France the Alpine duchy of Savoy and the Mediterranean port of Nice. Forthwith, Cavour set about irritating Austria by ostentatious military preparations and a haughty diplomatic tone.

In April 1859 Austria sent Sardinia an ultimatum demanding immediate demobilization. Cavour rejected the ultimatum, and war began with Austria on one side and Sardinia and France on the other. It lasted from April to July and constituted the first major step on the road to Italian liberation and union. Hailed with enthusiasm by the Italians, Napoleon III and Marshal Mac-Mahon led a French army into Piedmont, where they united with a Sardinian army under Victor Emmanuel II and General La Marmora. In June the Austrians, defeated at Magenta and Solferino, abandoned Milan and fell back upon the strong fortresses of Venetia.

Napoleon III had promised to "free Italy from the Alps to the Adriatic." But the defeats of the Austrians had inflamed Italian nationalism, and patriots in central Italy were demanding that Modena, Parma, Tuscany, and the Papal State be incorporated into a union under Victor Emmanuel II, as well as Lombardy and Venetia.

French Catholics were alarmed at this threat to the Pope's temporal power, and one French bishop, from the pulpit, branded Napoleon III as "the modern Judas Iscariot." The French Emperor, himself, was much upset by the carnage he had witnessed in the battles already fought, and by indications that Prussia might join Austria against him. Moreover, he apparently envisaged some sort of federal, rather than a united, Italy. For these reasons, he decided to call a halt to the war, and, in July 1859, he concluded with the Emperor Francis Joseph at Villafranca an armistice, whereby it was agreed that Lombardy should be ceded to Sardinia, Austria should retain Venetia, the rulers of central Italy would be reinstated in their duchies, and the

UNIFICATION OF ITALY, 1859-1870

Pope would become president of an Italian federation.

Thus Napoleon III fulfilled only half his bargain with Cavour. It was the turn of Italian patriots and French liberals to denounce the French Emperor. Cavour in disgust resigned his offices. But Victor Emmanuel had no alternative. He acceded to the terms of the truce, which was ratified in November by the treaty of Zurich.

Napoleon III and Francis Joseph, however, had not reckoned with the resolution of Italian patriots, nor with the skill with which Cavour, who returned to office, conspired with the liberal and radical leaders of central Italy. The inhabitants of the duchies and of part of the Papal State drove out their rulers and governors, established revolutionary governments, held plebiscites, and voted to join the kingdom of Sardinia. Cavour, in the name of his King, sent commissioners to take charge of these regions.

At first, Napoleon III refused emphatically to recognize such an exercise of the "right of national self-determination." But Cavour drove a shrewd bargain. With deep regret, he offered the French Emperor Nice and Savoy (just as if Napoleon III had carried out the original agreement to free Venetia as well as Lombardy), if France would recognize the annexation to Sardinia of Tuscany, Parma, Modena, and the papal province of Romagna. In the treaty of Turin (March 1860), Napoleon III accepted this deal. Still another plebiscite was held in Savoy and Nice, and they were "restored to France," to which they had belonged briefly in the time of the French Revolution and Napoleon I. Thus Napoleon III made a tangible territorial gain for France. But the costs were rather high. French liberals and French Catholics now distrusted him more than ever. Italian patriots, who, like Garibaldi, a native of Nice, thought Napoleon had reaped a shameful reward for a half-completed bargain, denounced him. Even Victor Emmanuel II was deeply pained at parting with Savoy, the ancestral home of his family. And affairs in Italy had gotten almost completely out of French control.

Close on the heels of the unifying movement in northern Italy came a similar development in the south, led this time by Garibaldi rather than Cavour. In the Two Sicilies, Francis II had succeeded Ferdinand II in 1859, but had made no change in the tyrannical system of government. Garibaldi, with the connivance of Cavour, assembled at Genoa a volunteer army of about a thousand "redshirts." In May 1860 they sailed to Sicily where they were welcomed by enthusiastic revolutionaries. In a remarkable campaign, in which his forces grew steadily, while those of Francis II were weakened by desertion, Garibaldi made himself master of the island. Then he crossed over to the mainland and in September took possession of Naples. Francis II retired to the fortress of Gaeta.

Garibaldi's swift victories and romantic personality made him such a popular idol that he could easily have become republican dictator of all south Italy. To avoid such an eventuality, Cavour despatched a Sardinian army southward. When the army crossed into papal territory, all the European powers, except Great Britain and Sweden, withdrew their diplomatic representatives from Turin. But Cavour announced the annexation of the entire Papal State except the city of Rome and its immediately surrounding territory. The Sardinian forces went on into southern Italy and, on November 7, Garibaldi and Victor Emmanuel II rode side by side through the streets of Naples. Despite his radical advisers, nationalism was now stronger with Garibaldi than republicanism. He resigned his authority into the hands of Victor Emmanuel II, and, refusing all titles and honors, retired to his home.

Though Napoleon III made the gesture of sending a fleet to Gaeta, he could not stem the tide. The British persuaded the French Emperor to withdraw his ships, the blockade of the fortress was completed, and it fell at last in February 1861. Already a plebiscite had ratified the annexation of the Two Sicilies to Sardinia; a parliament representing all Italy, save Rome and Venetia, had met in Turin; and Victor Emmanuel II had been proclaimed King of the new Italian nation.

For three months Napoleon III did not

Garibaldi. From an engraving.

Courtesy Bettmann Archive

was himself engaged in a desperate war. Over the protests of Pope Pius IX and a show of armed resistance ordered by him, Italian troops took Rome in September 1870, and in 1871 it became the capital of the united kingdom of Italy.

Thus Napoleon III, the chief instrument in the early stages of the unification of Italy, appeared to be its chief obstacle in its later phases. His venture into Italian politics gained him relatively little. Not only had he helped to create on the borders of France a single centralized state where formerly there had been several weak ones, but he had alienated Catholic opinion by his action in 1859, and liberal opinion by his wavering but conservative policies thereafter. He did have the territorial gains of Nice and Savoy.

D. Decline and Fall of the Second French Empire

Mexico and Italy were not the only explanations of the decline of Napoleon III's popularity at home and his prestige abroad. In the 1860's he was aging rapidly, and disaffection was growing within France. Conservatives were talking about the desirability of bringing back either a "legitimate" Bourbon king (grandson of Charles X) or a "liberal" Orleanist king (grandson of Louis Philippe). Many Liberals, including professional men and journalists, were leaning toward republicanism and lending support to the party which hitherto had comprised only doctrinaire radicals and ill-organized workingmen. In other words, the national combination which had backed the Emperor was falling to pieces, and there were reëmerging the factions of royalists and republicans which had existed before his advent.

recognize the new kingdom of Italy, and he continued to maintain a French garrison at Rome to defend the Pope. The French Emperor, once the hero of liberals and nationalists, had now been forced into a conservative position by preventing the Italians from making Rome their capital.

Cavour did not live to see the final triumph of his policies, for he died in June 1861. The completion of Italian unity fell to other hands. Venetia was won in 1866, when Italy joined Prussia in a war on Austria. Through an agreement with the Italian government, Napoleon III withdrew the French troops from Rome in 1866, but he sent a military force back the next year to defeat an armed incursion led by Garibaldi. This second French garrison was withdrawn only in 1870 when Napoleon III

The rising tide of opposition and its danger to the Second Empire were disclosed by the parliamentary elections of 1869. Despite governmental manipulation, fifty royalists and forty republicans were returned, and the opposition vote rose everywhere (but especially in the cities) to unheard-of proportions. Being an opportunist, Napoleon III responded by deciding to "liberalize" his government, and he at once made a number of concessions. He eased the press censorship. He promised to abandon the practice of paying election expenses of "official" candidates for the legislature. He agreed that his ministers should be responsible to the legislature rather than to himself. And he appointed a prime minister, Émile Ollivier, who formerly, as a liberal royalist, had bitterly criticized the imperial regime, but who now seconded the plan of Napoleon III to establish a "Liberal Empire."

Through the collaboration of Ollivier and the Emperor, a new "liberal" constitution for the Second Empire was drawn up. It embodied the concessions already made and assigned much of the power formerly exercised by Napoleon and his Council of State to the legislature. Such reforms might conciliate the liberal royalists, but they satisfied neither the legitimist royalists nor the republicans. The latter, in fact, redoubled their subversive agitation, openly attacking the Emperor in newspapers, speeches, and demonstrations.

The new constitution was submitted to a plebiscite in May 1870. Though the opposition vote declined from the high point of the previous year, it still reached ominous proportions. Seven million votes were cast in favor of the constitution, one and a half million against it. Nearly two million qualified voters stayed away from the polls.

Whether the "Liberal Empire" would have been a success, no one can tell, for other events intervened. But those very events were affected by internal conditions in France. There was one point on which Frenchmen were approaching agreement— opposition to the political unification of Germany under Prussian auspices. French liberals detested Prussia as a reactionary state. French Catholics disliked Prussia for its intolerant Protestantism. French patriots feared the rise of a powerful nation across the Rhine, for since Richelieu's day a weak Germany had been considered an advantage and safeguard for France. French imperialists (including the Empress) thought a successful patriotic war would ensure the popularity and continuance of the Empire.

Napoleon III had no stomach for war with Prussia. He was broken in health,

and troubled by recollections of his previous wars. He knew, moreover, that France had no friend in Europe on whom she could count for sure support in a crisis. Yet he was aware, too, that if the gamble of a war with Prussia succeeded, it might bring glory to the Empire and assure the succession of his son,. the Prince Imperial.

The Prussian prime minister at the time was the astute Bismarck, who believed that the unification of Germany could be completed only by a successful war with France, and he found a pretext for it in a complication arising in Spain. Spanish liberals had organized a revolution in 1868 and ousted the arbitrary and dissolute Queen Isabella II. They were seeking a new sovereign who would be liberal and constitutional. After receiving refusals from several European princes, the Spanish liberals offered the crown to Prince Leopold of Hohenzollern-Sigmaringen, a Catholic cousin of William I, the King of Prussia. Prince Leopold, not too eager for Spanish adventures, declined the offer. But Bismarck, scenting the possibilities of the situation, procured a renewal of the invitation and its acceptance by the prince (July 2, 1870).

Pressed by his wife, his ministers, and popular sentiment, Napoleon III took a strong stand and professed to see in the acceptance a projected union of Germany and Spain reminiscent of the empire of Charles V and menacing to France. He sent strong protests to the Prussian and Spanish governments, and on July 12 it was announced that Prince Leopold had withdrawn his acceptance. If the French Emperor had let well enough alone, he would have emerged the victor in a minor diplomatic skirmish. But he was urged by his advisers to push the matter further and to administer to Prussia a stinging diplomatic defeat. The French ambassador to Prussia was instructed to obtain from William I an official public promise that he would never permit a Hohenzollern to become a candidate for the Spanish throne.

The ensuing interview between the Prussian King and the French ambassador at the summer resort of Ems was indecisive. When the persistent ambassador requested another interview, the King merely stated that he was leaving Ems and could not receive him. The news of this rebuff was sent to Bismarck in a telegram by one of the King's aides. Bismarck, who was consulting the Prussian military chiefs at the time, was at first in despair, for the matter seemed ended. Then he saw a possible plan to bring on war. He secured the assurances of the military leaders that all was in readiness for the conflict. Then he gave the telegram to the press, not in its original form, but so edited by omissions as to seem very abrupt, an insult to the French ambassador. The amended telegram was nicely calculated to have the effect, in Bismarck's own cynical words, "of a red rag on the Gallic bull."

The report of the Ems despatch, published in Paris on July 14, the French national holiday, threw France into an angry frenzy. That night Napoleon acceded to popular clamor and to the counsel of his ministry, and decided on war. The next day the French legislature, with only a few dissenting votes, authorized a formal declaration of war against Prussia. The third—and last—of the European wars of the Second Empire was beginning.

The Empire entered the Franco-Prussian war (1870–1871) with much enthusiasm, but with little else. Austria and Italy, like Russia and Great Britain, remained aloof. French mobilization went badly. The attempt to use the railways led to traffic jams. Supplies were piled up in one place, while troops were shifted to another. Early in August 1870 Marshal MacMahon suffered such a reverse at the hands of the invading Germans that he was obliged to withdraw his army from the greater part of Alsace and fall back on Châlons. On August 18 another French army under Marshal Bazaine was defeated by the Germans under Moltke in a bloody battle at Gravelotte in Lorraine, and shut up in the fortress of Metz. In this crisis MacMahon advised Napoleon III to pull back the French armies to Paris and reorganize them there for a decisive battle. But when the Emperor wired the plan to the Empress Eugénie, whom he had left as regent at the capital, she replied that a general retreat would mean the overthrow of the Empire and

that he should go forward to relieve Metz.

Napoleon and MacMahon, with heavy hearts, moved their inferior forces down the Meuse river seeking to find a place where they might cross and drive back the Germans. At Sedan, almost down to the Belgian border, they made a despairing attempt, September 1–2, 1870. Outnumbered, outgeneraled, and finally encircled, the Emperor at length stopped the slaughter by surrendering with 81,000 men. The battle of Sedan ended the first phase of the Franco-Prussian war, which had so far lasted barely six weeks.

The battle of Sedan also ended the Second Empire. On September 4, when it became generally known in Paris that the main French army had been captured and that the Emperor himself was a prisoner, a self-appointed group of republicans, among whom Léon Gambetta was conspicuous, proclaimed at the city hall the deposition of the Emperor and the establishment of a republic—the Third French Republic. The Empress Eugénie hastily fled, with the aid of an American dentist, to England. A government of national defense was constituted to rule France until peace could be restored and the nation consulted on the making of a permanent constitution for the country.

The adventure of the Second Empire was over. Its promises of peace and stability had been belied. Whatever it had done for the internal development of France had been compromised by its wars and the disaster of 1870. The experiment of peaceably turning a dictatorship into a constitutional, liberal empire was a failure.

Napoleon III himself was released by the Germans at the close of the war. He went to die in England (1873), and his ill fortune pursued his son, for the Prince Imperial ("Napoleon IV") was killed fighting for the British against the Zulus in South Africa in 1879. The Empress Eugénie lived till 1920, long enough to see republican France revenge her husband by conquering imperial Germany. But for the Bonapartes, there was no renewal of the extraordinary circumstances which had enabled the nephew of Napoleon I to dominate France from 1848 to 1870.

William I, flanked by Moltke and Bismarck. Reinhold Begas (d. 1911).

CHAPTER 48

Creation of the Hohenzollern German Empire

AND THE HABSBURG DUAL MONARCHY OF AUSTRIA-HUNGARY

A. German Nationalism and the Prussian Bismarck

In Germany, as in Italy, the events of 1848–1849 [1] did not mean the end of agitation for national unification. As with Italy, the big obstacle to a unified German state was Austria, though here the Austrian role was somewhat different. In Italy, Austria was a foreign power occupying part of the peninsula and dominating much of the rest. In Germany, Austria proper was German in language and for centuries had been part of the Holy Roman Empire, and latterly of the German Confederation. Now Austria faced a dilemma. She wanted to retain her traditional leadership in Germany. Yet she could not bring into a German nation her millions of non-German subjects (Hungarian, Czech, Slovak, Polish, Croatian). German national sentiment which had been aroused against Napoleon in the triumphant War of Liberation, never died down, and during the ensuing age of romanticism it continued to inspire patriotic songs and societies. Scholars joined poets in glorifying the German nationality, its language and customs, its history and mission.

Important to at least the middle class were developments which indicated that national unity would be profitable as well as romantically desirable. In 1818, Prussia had substituted for her previous multiplicity of provincial tariffs a single one. This was low on manufactured goods and lower still

---

[1] See above, pp. 607–608.

on raw materials, but it taxed goods passing in transit through Prussian territory and hence provided Prussia's neighbors with a special inducement to join her economically. Between 1819 and 1826, a number of minor German states which had territories enclaved (completely surrounded) by Prussia accepted her tariffs and formed a customs union (*Zollverein*) with her. Then between 1829 and 1833, a number of the central states adhered to the union, and in the latter year even the southern states of Bavaria and Württemberg entered it.

Thus was inaugurated an enlarged *Zollverein* in which most of Germany was included, with a single set of customs duties on its exterior frontiers. In the next twenty years all the remaining states were incorporated save only Austria and Hamburg. Though not originally designed as such, the *Zollverein* proved to be a powerful instrument in uniting Germany and in increasing the influence of Prussia. The same end was also served by the construction of railways, which by 1860 bound all the German states closely together.

There were, however, forces other than Austrian influence which worked against German unity. One was fear and dislike of Prussia on the part of many Germans. Another was religious difference and conflict between Catholics and Protestants. A third was "particularism," the loyalty of the citizens of each of the separate states to it and to its ruler, their pride in local history, their preference for their own dialects and customs. Particularism was especially strong

623

in the Catholic states of the south, of which Bavaria was the chief. Such was the general situation in Germany in the 1850's and 1860's. Liberal revolution in 1848 had failed to bring unity. It remained for the strong-arm tactics of a cynical conservative to succeed where liberals had failed. This was Bismarck.

Otto von Bismarck belonged to the class of land-owning north-German squires (or Junkers) who had long served the Prussian monarch in army, Lutheran church, and civil administration. Though deeply attached to Prussia and its king, Bismarck had led an unruly life as a young man and had even been dismissed from the civil service for "deficiency in regularity and discipline." His marriage in 1847 to the pious daughter of another landlord had steadied him and confirmed his devotion to the Lutheran state church and to ultra-conservative principles. During the upheavals of 1848–1849, he vigorously opposed the liberals. He offered to bring his peasants to Berlin to

defend King Frederick William IV and was one of two in the Prussian legislature who refused to vote thanks to the King when he promised to grant a constitution.

Bismarck scoffed at the Frankfort Assembly; and, while reluctantly accepting the Prussian constitution of 1850, he aided in forming a Conservative party to resist liberalism and to defend the royal power, the agricultural interests, the army, and the Lutheran Church. From 1851 to 1862, he was active and eminently successful in the Prussian diplomatic service. As Prussian delegate in the German Diet at Frankfurt, and as Prussian ambassador to St. Petersburg and Paris, he gained a deep knowledge of German and of European affairs.

Bismarck's great opportunity came as the result of a conflict between the Prussian King William I (Prince-Regent 1858–1861, King, 1861–1888) and the Prussian legislature. William I was far from brilliant, but he was hard-working and pertinacious; and above all he was a soldier with an absorbing

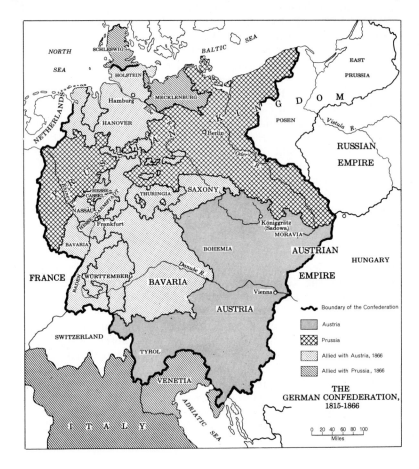

THE GERMAN CONFEDERATION, 1815–1866

Bismarck. Franz von Lenbach (d. 1904).

Courtesy Bettmann Archive

passion for all matters military. As soon as he came to power, William I set about reforming and expanding the Prussian army with the aid of a gifted chief of staff, General Helmuth von Moltke, and a very able minister of war, Albrecht von Roon. To finance the army reforms, the King asked the legislature in 1861 for more money. This the legislature, under the influence of liberals, refused. Whereupon the King dissolved the legislature. The ensuing elections returned 100 conservatives, 25 moderate liberals, and 235 progressives—the last a new political party consciously modeled after the British Liberal party, and resolved to force liberal principles and real parliamentary government on the King. Thus an impasse was reached. William I, Moltke, and Roon were determined to push through the army reforms. The party with an overwhelming majority in the legislature was determined to prevent them from doing so.

To break the deadlock, William I, on Roon's advice, summoned Bismarck to be his chief minister. Bismarck's policy was summed up, a bit ominously, in his famous sentence, "Not by speeches and majority resolutions are the great questions of the time decided—that was the mistake of 1848 and 1849—but by blood and iron." Unable to get favorable action from the Progressive majority, he proceeded, with the King's consent, to govern Prussia without a legal budget and without a parliament. As a virtual dictator and in flat violation of the constitution, he levied and collected taxes and put through the whole program of military reform. The Progressives grumbled, and liberals in other German states heaped abuse on Bismarck. But Bismarck was confident that the liberals at home and abroad were more vocal than dangerous. He worked on the dubious principle that the end justifies the means. He would overcome his opponents by his very success. In the new army he had a powerful instrument for effecting German national unification under conservative Prussian leadership.

B. The Danish War of 1864, and the German Civil War of 1866 Between Prussia and Austria

As a first step in his plan, Bismarck precipitated a war between Denmark on the one hand and Austria and Prussia on the other. The excuse for the war lay in the complicated question of the duchies of Schleswig and Holstein. These duchies, which contained a large German population, had already occasioned a brief war in 1848. That conflict had been settled when the Great Powers forced through a compromise highly favorable to Denmark, for the Danish king remained sovereign of the duchies while promising not to incorporate them into the rest of his kingdom. In 1863, King Frederick VII of Denmark died, and his successor, Christian IX, under the pressure of nationalist demands from his Danish subjects, broke the compromise agreement by accepting a new constitution which unified the political institutions of Denmark and the two duchies.

The response in Germany was a wave of patriotic agitation against Denmark. In it, Prussia and Austria competed for leadership, and in 1864, they both went to war with Denmark. The Danes fought heroically. But this time they got no foreign help, and, overborne by sheer numbers, they had to submit to the terms of the treaty of Vienna, imposed on them in October 1864. The treaty gave Schleswig and Holstein to Austria and Prussia. As Bismarck anticipated, the two victors were soon at odds over the division of the spoils, for while Austria, backed by the German Confederation, wanted to make a separate state out of the duchies, Prussia refused to do so. The dispute was only temporarily patched up by the Convention of Gastein in 1865, according to which Holstein would be administered by Austria, and Schleswig by Prussia.

Bismarck was determined to bring about a war between Prussia and Austria. But before doing so he wanted to make sure that Prussia would get foreign help and Austria would not. He was fairly certain that Great Britain and Russia would remain neutral. France was more doubtful.

In October 1865, at Biarritz, Bismarck made vague hints of "compensations" to Napoleon III, so as to forestall French interference in the early stages of the war. Bismarck counted on such a quick victory by the reformed Prussian army that there would be no later stages and thus no opportunity for France to intervene successfully. From Italy, Bismarck obtained more than mere neutrality. He secured an alliance against Austria. So sure was Bismarck of his ability to start the war when he wished, that the alliance ran for only three months beginning in April 1866. If within that time war broke out between Prussia and Austria, Italy promised to join the former. As a reward she would get Venetia from Austria.

Bismarck proceeded to stir up trouble for the Austrians in Holstein. When Austria responded by appealing to the German Confederation, Bismarck declared that such an appeal violated the Convention of Gastein, and he sent Prussian troops to occupy Holstein and oust the Austrians.

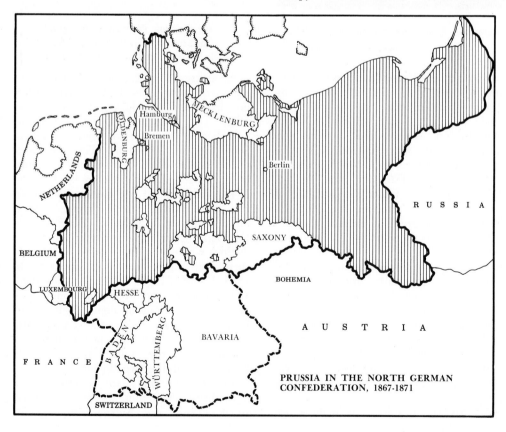

PRUSSIA IN THE NORTH GERMAN CONFEDERATION, 1867-1871

At the same time he proposed a reform of the German Confederation and the exclusion of Austria from it. Austria called on the Confederation to reject the reform and to mobilize against Prussia. Most of the states sided with Austria, because of the particularist fears of Prussian dominance. Liberals opposed conservative Prussia, and Catholics sympathized with Catholic Austria.

Bismarck then announced that Prussia was seceding from the Confederation, and would fight a "defensive" war against Austria and her German allies. Italy, of course, was soon found on the Prussian side. Despite the ruthless cynicism with which Bismarck precipitated the war, he managed so skillfully and concealed his moves so well that public opinion in most foreign countries favored Prussia.

The actual war, between Prussia and Italy on the one hand and Austria, Bavaria, Hanover, Saxony, Baden, Württemberg, and some lesser German states on the other, was of such surprisingly short duration (June 15 to July 26, 1866) that it is usually called the "Seven Weeks' War." Austria, though less well prepared for war than Prussia, defeated the Italians on land and sea. But in the main campaign in Bohemia, the Austrians were overwhelmed in the battle of Sadowa (or Königgrätz) on July 3, 1866. This battle was so decisive that it led to the end of the war, to drastic rearrangements in Italy, Austria, and Germany, and to a tremendous increase in the military reputation of Prussia.

By the final treaty of Prague (August 1866), Austria was obliged to cede Venetia to Italy and Holstein to Prussia, to pay a small indemnity, and to consent to the dissolution of the German Confederation. The German states north of the Main were to enter a "closer union" with Prussia. Those south of the Main were to form a union of their own. From both groups Austria was to be excluded. But Bismarck did not wish to make a mortal enemy out of Austria. He had gained his end by getting her shut out of German affairs despite her thousand years of participation in them. His territorial demands were therefore moderate, and he vetoed the idea of a triumphal Prussian parade through Vienna.

Bismarck made separate treaties with the south German states of Bavaria, Baden, Württemberg, and Hesse-Darmstadt, by which they lost virtually nothing, for he wanted to win their friendship.

The north German states which had sided with Austria came off much worse. Prussia annexed outright, not only Schleswig-Holstein, but also Hesse-Cassel, Nassau, the free city of Frankfurt, and the kingdom of Hanover (since 1837 separated from the crown of England and under its own ruler). These additions of five million subjects and 27,000 square miles of territory made Prussia for the first time a compact and continuous state stretching from Russia and Denmark to France and the Main River. Henceforth, with Austria excluded, two-fifths of the area and two-thirds of the population of Germany belonged to Prussia.

The lesser German states north of the Main which were not annexed by Prussia—twenty in number—were formed by Bismarck, in 1867, into a new and closely knit North German Confederation. Each state retained a measure of local autonomy but all were subordinated to a federal government with the King of Prussia as hereditary "President" and with a two-house legislature. Prussia clearly dominated the new organization.

C. The Franco-Prussian War of 1870–1871, and Creation of the German Empire

Amid the enthusiasm occasioned by victory over Austria, Bismarck made his peace with the Prussian legislature. Dazzled by the success of his policies, the Progressive party abandoned its opposition and voted a bill of indemnity which gave Bismarck legal forgiveness for his unconstitutional behavior in the past. Indeed, many Progressives now discovered that they were more nationalist than liberal. When the federal parliament of the North German Confederation was formed, a new party became very active in it and collaborated closely with Bismarck. It was called the National Liberal Party. Many of its members were former Progressives.

In the states south of the Main, there was still much distrust and dislike of Bis-

Parisians partonizing a butcher shop selling cat and dog flesh during the siege, 1870–1871. From a contemporary drawing.

Courtesy Bettmann Archive

marck and of Prussia among liberals, Catholics, and particularists. A step toward closer cöoperation between the northern confederation and the southern states was taken in 1867, when a joint customs parliament was created to discuss common tariff problems. But it limited itself strictly to such matters, for the southern states were jealously guarding their political independence. To Bismarck, it seemed clear that only a big patriotic enterprise such as a victorious war against a common foreign foe could bring Bavaria, Württemberg, Hesse-Darmstadt, and Baden into union with Prussia. As preparation for just such a war, certain bungling attempts of Napoleon III to obtain "compensation" in 1867 so alarmed the south German states that Bismarck was enabled to conclude secret defensive alliances with them.

We have already mentioned Bismarck's role in precipitating the Franco-Prussian War in 1870 over the question of the Hohenzollern candidacy for the Spanish throne.[1] When France declared war, the south German states honored their treaties of alliance and joined with Prussia against France. Their troops shared with the Prussians in the victories which ensued.

After the surrender of Napoleon III at Sedan, the German armies moved rapidly on to Paris, which was soon encircled and

[1] See above, pp. 620–621.

besieged. Peace might have been quickly negotiated had not Bismarck let it be known that Germany must be "safeguarded" in the future by "recovering" Alsace-Lorraine from France. The French government, unwilling to blight the new republic at the start by such a cession of territory, fought on under the inspiring leadership of Léon Gambetta. Escaping from Paris in a balloon, Gambetta raised fresh troops, who, to the surprise of the Germans, won some successes, although they were unable to relieve Paris. Strasbourg had already surrendered in September, and Metz was yielded up in October through the cowardice (if not treachery) of Marshal Bazaine.

Paris held out until January 27, 1871, and then surrendered only because its people were freezing and starving. Four days afterwards, an armistice was arranged, in order to permit the election of a French National Assembly which would have authority to conclude peace. The preliminary peace terms, agreed to at Versailles by Bismarck and Adolphe Thiers, head of the French provisional government, were reluctantly ratified by the new Assembly in March. The final peace treaty was signed at Frankfurt in May 1871.

By the treaty of Frankfurt, France ceded to Germany all of eastern Lorraine, including the fortress of Metz, and all of Alsace except Belfort, a fortress which had heroically withstood a German siege. To retain Belfort and its environs for France, Thiers had to permit a triumphal parade of the German conquerors through Paris. In addition, France agreed to pay a war indemnity of five billion francs. German troops remained in occupation of northern France till this sum was paid in full (1873). In the course of the war the Germans had lost 28,000 dead and 101,000 other casualties. The French losses were 156,000 dead, 143,000 wounded or disabled, and 720,000 surrendered or interned.

Of the numerous and far reaching results of the Franco-Prussian War, the most striking was the fulfillment of Bismarck's plan for the establishment of a German Empire under Prussian and Hohenzollern leadership. Just as Bismarck had foreseen, the triumphantly successful war in which South Germans fought shoulder to shoulder with Prussians aroused throughout the country a wave of popular patriotic ardor strong enough to overcome particularist sentiments, princely jealousies, liberal suspicions, and Catholic misgivings. By November 1870, while the war was still in progress,

Bismarck negotiated treaties of union between the North German Confederation and the southern states of Bavaria, Württemberg, Baden, and Hesse-Darmstadt. These treaties, duly ratified by the respective sovereigns and parliaments, simply extended the North German Confederation so as to include the southern states, and changed its name to the "German Empire" (*Deutsches Reich*). The King of Prussia, instead of being "President of the Confederation," was henceforth to be "German Emperor."

By a curious coincidence the solemn ceremony of inaugurating the German Empire was held on January 18, 1871, exactly 170 years after the Prussian Hohenzollerns had assumed the title of king.[1] And by the irony of fate, since the Germans were still besieging Paris, it was held in the Hall of Mirrors in the palace of Louis XIV at Versailles, "in the ancient center," the official German report explained, "of a hostile power which for centuries had striven to divide and humiliate Germany." There, surrounded by

---

[1] See above, p. 447.

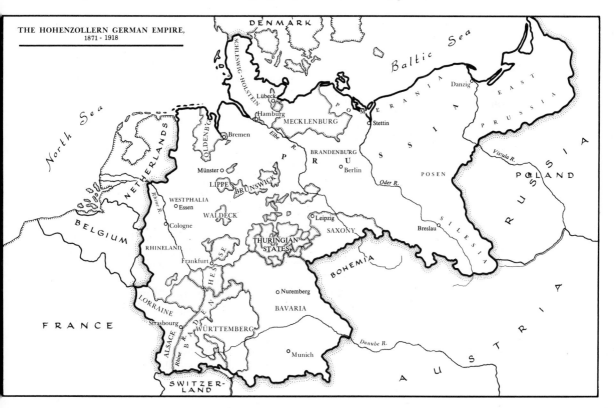

THE HOHENZOLLERN GERMAN EMPIRE,
1871 - 1918

Emperor Francis Joseph of Austria-Hungary.

Courtesy Bettmann Archive

German princes and generals, Bismarck read the imperial decrees which set the seal of success on the first part of his life work.

The Franco-Prussian War had other results than the unification of Germany and the formation of the German Empire. In taking Alsace-Lorraine from France, Bismarck over-reached himself, though he would no doubt have taken western Lorraine as well had he known how valuable the Thomas-Gilchrist process would soon make its abundant iron ore. But moved by the advice of his military counselors, Bismarck was willing to risk permanent French hostility in order to give Germany a more defensible frontier across the Rhine. He got the frontier, and he also got the hostility.

The Franco-Prussian War ushered in a new era. It broke the long peace (1815–1870) among the major powers of western

Europe. It created a new and very potent nation, the German Empire. It emphasized once more the value of large, well-trained, and well-equipped armies. It aroused a fiercer nationalism not only in victorious Germany and defeated France but also in the rest of Europe. In short it sowed many of the seeds which were bitterly reaped in the twentieth century.

D. Creation of the Dual Monarchy of Austria-Hungary

In the Austrian Empire, the Seven Weeks' War resulted in drastic changes. The Hungarians, defeated in their bid for independence under Kossuth in 1849, had been restive under Austrian rule. There had been some fear at Vienna that they would prove rebellious in the crisis of 1866. But under the leadership of Francis Deák, they fought loyally in the disastrous war. It was Deák's belief that Hungary would best serve its interests by a partnership with Austria rather than by revolt against her. Indeed, the Magyars (Hungarians) had at least one major interest in common with the German Austrians, for they were both eager to hold down the subject Slavic peoples.

Deák's gamble in getting Hungary to support Austria in 1866 was successful. The military catastrophe of that year followed so closely the defeat of 1859 in Italy, that a reorganization of the Habsburg Empire was obviously necessary. In accomplishing this, it seemed less drastic to transform the Empire into a dual monarchy by granting autonomy to the Magyars, than to form a five-part federation by recognizing the claims of Poles, Czechs, and Yugoslavs as well. Accordingly, after due negotiations, a new political arrangement for the Austrian Empire was worked out by the *Ausgleich* (Compromise) of 1867. The Habsburg dominions were divided into two parts: (1) the "Empire of Austria," embracing Austria proper, Bohemia, Galicia, Carniola, and the Tyrol; (2) the "Kingdom of Hungary," including Hungary proper with its crown lands of Croatia, the Banat, and Transylvania. Each part would have a constitution and parliament of its own, and each would be independent of the other in

EUROPE IN 1871

most respects. Yet the two would be united by a common ruler—to be known under the dual title of "Emperor of Austria and King of Hungary"—and by a common army, common foreign relations, and certain common ministers.

Thus was the Austrian Habsburg Empire transformed into the Dual Monarchy of Austria-Hungary. The Seven Weeks' War had proved advantageous to Hungarian as well as German nationalism. The Dual Monarchy, though it was to endure for fifty-one years, contained a fatal defect. It did not recognize the national aspirations of the Slavic peoples who were left under what they regarded as the alien (and in the case of Hungary, tyrannical) rule of Germans and Magyars.

The Slavs who came off best in the new scheme of things under the Habsburg Emperor-King were the Poles and the Croats. The Poles of Galicia were given some political and economic liberty in 1868 by the Austrians and, indeed, were so favored that they coöperated with Vienna in holding down the Czechs and Slovenes. The Croats were the most western and advanced of the southern Slavs, and therefore the most likely to agitate politically and make trouble for the Magyar rulers at Budapest. They were predominantly Roman Catholic rather than Orthodox in religion, and, unlike their fellow Serbs, they used the Roman rather than the Greek alphabet. Hungary appeased them to a degree by granting Croatia some local autonomy in 1868. As for the Czechs in Bohemia and their kinsmen the Slovaks in Hungary, they were treated more or less like inferior and subject peoples within the Dual Monarchy. They responded by agitations at home and by intrigues with Slavic Russia abroad.

SELECT SUPPLEMENTARY READINGS FOR PART IX

Chapter 44. On romanticism: H. N. Fairchild, *The Romantic Quest* (1931); Oliver Elton, *Survey of English Literature, 1780–1830*, 2 vols. (1920); and appropriate chapters in Kuno Francke, *History of German Literature* (4th ed., 1901); C. H. C. Wright, *History of French Literature* (new ed., 1925); J. Pijoan, *History of Art*, vol. III (1928); J. Barzun, *Romanticism and the Modern Ego* (1943); A. Einstein, *Music in the Romantic Era* (1941); H. R. Hitchcock, *Architecture: Nineteenth and Twentieth Centuries* (1958). On science: H. S. Williams, *Story of Nineteenth-Century Science* (1900); J. D. Dampier-Whetham, *History of Science and Its Relations with Philosophy* (2nd ed., 1932); R. H. Shryock, *The Development of Modern Medicine* (1936); E. Nordenskiold, *History of Biology* (1928); J. R. Partington, *A History of Chemistry*, vol. IV (the 19th century) (1964); S. P. Thompson, *Faraday* (1898); J. T. Merz, *A History of European Thought in the Nineteenth Century*, 4 vols. (2nd ed., 1912–1928).

Chapter 45. G. N. Clark, *The Idea of the Industrial Revolution* (1953); W. O. Henderson, *Britain and Industrial Europe, 1750–1870* (1954); J. K. Finch, *Engineering and Western Civilization* (1951); C. Singer, E. J. Holmyard, A. R. Hall, T. I. Williams, eds., *A History of Technology*, 5 vols. (1955–1958), vol. IV, *The Industrial Revolution* (c. 1750 to c. 1850); F. C. Dietz, *The Industrial Revolution, 1750–1927* (1927); J. L. and B. Hammond, *Rise of Modern Industry* (1926); C. S. Abbot, *Great Inventions* (1932); W. Bowden, *Industrial Society in England Toward the End of the Eighteenth Century* (1925); L. C. A. Knowles, *Industrial and Commercial Revolutions in Great Britain During the Nineteenth Century* (1921) and *Economic Development in France, Germany, Russia, and the United States* (1932); H. D. Fong, *Triumph of the Factory System in England* (1930); J. H. Clapham, *Economic History of Modern Britain*, vol. II, *Free Trade and Steel* (1932), and *Economic Development of France and Germany, 1815–1914* (3rd ed., 1928); H. J. Habakkuk and M. Postan, eds., *The Cambridge Economic History of Europe*, vol. VI (1965); F. A. Nussbaum, *History of the Economic Institutions of Modern Europe* (1933); Sir Leslie Stephen, *English Utilitarians*, 3 vols. (1902); C. R. Fay, *The Corn Laws and Social England* (1932); C. S. Orwin and E. H. Whetham, *History of British Agriculture, 1846–1914* (1964); William Cunningham, *Rise and Decline of the Free Trade Movement* (1912); B. L. Hutchins and A. Harrison, *History of Factory Legislation* (3rd ed., 1926); John Morley, *Life of Richard Cobden* (1903); J. L. and B. Hammond, *Lord Shaftesbury* (1924); Sidney and Beatrice Webb, *History of Trade Unionism* (rev. ed., 1920); H. A. Clegg *et al.*, *A History of British Trade Unions Since 1889*, vol. I, *1889–1910* (1964); W. S. Sanders, *Trade Unionism in Germany* (1916); A. F. Weber, *The Growth of Cities in the Nineteenth Century* (1899).

Chapter 46. P. S. Robertson, *Revolutions of 1848* (1952); A. Whitridge, *Men in Crisis: the Revolutions of 1848* (1949); J. A. R. Marriott, *The French Revolution of 1848 in Its Economic Aspects*, 2 vols. (1913); D. C. McKay, *The National Workshops, a study in the French Revolution of 1848* (1933); L. A. Loubère, *Louis Blanc* (1961); F. A. Simpson, *Rise of Louis Napoleon* (1925); H. von Treitschke, *History of Germany in the Nineteenth Century, 1815–1848*, 7 vols. (tr. 1915–1919); K. R. Greenfield, *Economics and Liberalism in the Risorgimento, a Study of Nationalism in Italy, 1814–1848* (1934); G. Salvemini, *Mazzini* (1920); H. A. L. Fisher, *The Republican Tradition in Europe* (1911); J. L. and B. Hammond, *The Age of the Chartists, 1832–1854* (1930); A. Briggs, ed., *Chartist Studies* (1959).

Chapter 47. R. C. Binkley, *Realism and Nationalism* (1935); *New Cambridge Modern History*, vol. X (1960); G. P. Gooch, *The Second Empire* (1960); A. L. Guerard, *Napoleon III* (1942); Philip Guedalla, *The Second Empire* (1928); F. A. Simpson, *Louis Napoleon and the Recovery of France, 1848–1856* (1923); J. M. Thompson, *Louis Napoleon and the Second Empire* (1954); T. Zeldin, *Emile Ollivier and the Liberal Empire of Napoleon III* (1963); F. C. Palm, *England and Napoleon III* (1948); H. B. Parkes, *A History of Mexico* (1950); W. R. Thayer, *The Life and Times of Cavour*, 2 vols. (1911); D. Mack Smith, *Cavour and Garibaldi, 1860* (1954) and *Garibaldi* (1956); Bolton King, *History of Italian Unity, Being a Political History of Italy from 1814 to 1871* (1899); H. Acton, *The Last Bourbons of Naples (1825–1861)* (1961); G. M. Trevelyan, *Garibaldi and the Thousand* (1909) and *Garibaldi and the Making of Italy* (1911); T. W. Riker, *The Making of Roumania* (1931); H. C. F. Bell, *Life of Palmerston* (1941).

Chapter 48. H. Friedjung, *The Struggle for Supremacy in Germany* (tr. 1935); W. O. Henderson, *The Zollverein* (1939); W. H. Dawson, *The German Empire, 1867–1914*, 2 vols. (1919); R. H. Lord, *The Origins of the War of 1870* (1924); L. D. Steefel, *Bismarck, the Hohenzollern Candidacy, and the Origins of the Franco-Prussian War of 1870* (1962); O. Pflanze, *Bismarck and the Development of Germany: the Period of Unification, 1815–1871* (1963); M. Howard, *The Franco-Prussian War: the German Invasion of France, 1870–71* (1961); F. Darmstaedter, *Bismarck and the Creation of the Second Reich* (1948); W. O. Henderson, *The Zollverein* (1960).

Suez Canal.
*Courtesy
Bettman Archive*

PART X
PROGRESSIVE AND

From Bismarck
to Lloyd George

IMPERIALIST EUROPE, 1871–1914

THE LAST PART of the nineteenth century was an era of optimism. After 1871, it began to seem as if the age of major wars was over. In one country after another democracy made visible progress. At the same time, the spread of industrialization and the resultant increase in the output of goods seemed to usher in a period when poverty would be reduced and human well-being forwarded. Cheap food from North America and Australia, if it raised some problems for the landowners of England, improved the diet of the workers in the cities.

Meanwhile, science was making such spectacular advances that it seemed to many as if the day was not far off when the whole of the universe could be explained in the materialistic terms of matter and motion. With science, medicine and public health progressed significantly and, as the death rate dropped, population grew even more rapidly than it had in the past. A portion of the increasing numbers emigrated to America; an even larger proportion moved into the expanding cities.

But as the vision of a peaceful, prosperous, expanding world, guided by science and supplied by machine industry, developed in men's minds, there were some dark spots which people strove to forget. Conditions in the city slums were in many countries so sordid that there were attempts to improve the lot of the worker through "social legislation." It seemed, moreover, as if progress were focussed in western Europe, for in the east, particularly in the empires of the Romanovs and the Ottoman sultans, there was no democracy, relatively little industry, and scant attention to the needs or desires of the lower classes.

There was a renewal of the European imperialism of the seventeenth and eighteenth centuries. It had seemed, about 1860, as if the day of building colonial empires might be over, as if there were a general agreement that colonies did not pay and were not worthwhile. But partly because of the rapidly rising nationalism after the unification of Italy and of Germany, and partly because of the tremendous growth of industry and commerce, there was, in the last three decades of the century, a new struggle for colonies in which Africa was partitioned and much of Asia and Oceania brought under European sway.

During the whole period, Great Britain enjoyed a very special preëminence. A leader in democracy and liberalism, she had made her advances since the seventeenth century without revolution. Her industry was the best developed in the world. Her commerce, guarded by the largest of all navies, traversed the seven seas almost without rival. London was the world center for banking, finance, and insurance. People of all lands turned to England as the outstanding example of a modern nation.

CHAPTER 49

Democracy in Western Europe

A. The Shining Example of Britain

Throughout the last half of the nineteenth century, Great Britain was the model which most other countries sought to copy. They looked with envy upon her far-flung empire, her mighty navy, her incomparable industry and commerce, her foreign investments, her growing population. Somehow her success in these many lines seemed to be connected with her parliamentary government, which showed itself able to move toward liberal democracy without revolution, and with her cabinet system, which seemed flexible enough to meet every expanding need.

To be sure, Britain preserved more of the class structure of the eighteenth century than countries like Belgium or Holland or even France. She was very slow in creating a system of free public education. In social legislation she lagged behind Germany. But these were merely illustrations of the gradualness of development which seemed part of the secret of British success.

The Victorian compromise, initiated by the reform of 1832,[1] did not last to the mid-point of Queen Victoria's reign (1837–1901). By 1867 the pressure from the laboring classes for the extension of the suffrage was getting too strong to be resisted. In the previous year, the Liberals and their rising leader Gladstone, who had proposed a slight parliamentary reform, had been driven from office on that issue. But popular demonstra-tions increased to the point of violence, and in 1867 the Conservative prime minister, Lord Derby, authorized his chief lieutenant, Disraeli, to introduce a new and still mod-erate reform bill. To embarrass the Con-servatives, Gladstone, aided by Radical Liberals, proposed a number of amendments to broaden the bill. Rather than allow the Liberals to get credit for a popular reform, Disraeli accepted the amendments and se-cured the passage of the bill, which was by now a good deal more radical than Glad-stone's original proposal. Thus was the reform of 1867 enacted through competi-tion between the two parties. Democratic in trend, it almost doubled the electorate by giving the franchise to most urban work-ingmen.

Five years later, under Gladstone's aus-pices, the secret ballot was introduced. Then in 1884, the Liberals put through the third great parliamentary reform of the nine-teenth century by extending the vote to rural workers and bringing Great Britain fairly close to universal manhood suffrage. In 1885 the Conservatives sponsored a sup-plementary reform, providing that members of the House of Commons would be chosen by approximately equal districts of about 50,000 people each. Thus Britain achieved a very considerable degree of the political democracy for which the Chartists had pleaded forty years earlier.[2]

If the lower classes got the vote, the upper and wealthier classes still retained

---

[1] See above, p. 570.

[2] See above, p. 571.

political predominance. They completely controlled the House of Lords. They occupied most seats in the House of Commons. They held nearly all cabinet offices. Yet in the party competition of upper-class leaders, there was a growing tendency to seek lower-class votes by making campaign promises, and sometimes the promises were kept. Gradually, therefore, Britain achieved a measure of social reform, and, contrary to the principles of economic liberalism, the government increased its intervention in economic matters for the benefit of workers.

The outstanding political leaders in the period after the reform of 1867 were William E. Gladstone and Benjamin Disraeli. Gladstone was prime minister from 1868 to 1874, from 1880 to 1885, in 1886, and from 1892 to 1894, while Disraeli was prime minister in 1868 and from 1874 to 1880. Gladstone professed devotion to the liberal principles of peace, *laissez-faire*, and humanitarianism; he disapproved of imperialism and was most happy when arguing for "retrenchment" (economy) in the home government. Disraeli, on the other hand, believed that the upper and lower classes should coöperate to restrain the triumphant middle class and to preserve the traditional English institutions of monarchy, Anglican Church, and landed aristocracy; and in the 1870's he started Britain off on a new stage of imperialist expansion and stressed the importance of India in the British Empire by adding "Empress of India" to Queen Victoria's other titles.

The issues which separated Gladstone and Disraeli were not really as deep as they appeared to the Liberals and Conservatives of the time. Both parties were committed to maintenance of things as they were. Both parties were willing to accept changes of necessity or for political advantage. The most burning disputes were over Ireland, which was poverty-stricken, depopulated since the potato famine of 1845–1846, and economically exploited by absentee landlords and Anglican churchmen. When the Irish became sufficiently violent, or sufficiently organized, something had to be done for them, though concessions were usually accompanied by "coercion acts." In 1869 Gladstone prevailed on parliament to disestablish the Anglican Church in Ireland,

Queen Victoria.

so that Catholic Irishmen were no longer required to pay for the support of Protestant churches and ministers. A Land Act of 1870 forbade arbitrary evictions of Irish tenants, arbitrary raising of rents, or failure to reimburse the tenant for improvements he had made. Another Land Act of 1881 granted Irish peasants the "three F's" for which they were then agitating—fair rent, fixity of tenure, and free sale.

But it was a political situation which gave weight to Irish demands. In the general election of 1885, an Irish Nationalist party, which had been organized and was led by Charles Stewart Parnell, obtained a balance of power between the evenly matched Liberal and Conservative parties. Whereupon Gladstone, anxious for Irish support of himself and the Liberal party, acceded to Parnell's demand for "home rule" for Ireland, and in 1886 introduced such a bill in Parliament. By doing so, however, Gladstone split the Liberal Party, as Peel had earlier split the Conservative Party.

A group of liberals led by Joseph Chamberlain and calling themselves Liberal Unionists, joined the Conservatives in voting down home rule. For the next twenty years the Conservatives, supported by the Liberal Unionists, were in office continuously, except for 1892–1895, when Gladstone again introduced a home rule bill and got it through the Commons only to have it defeated by the Lords. But while the Conservatives stood firm against home rule, they made some concessions to Ireland. Thus they sponsored a series of land purchase acts which wrought a veritable social revolution in Ireland by advancing government funds (on easy terms) to Irish tenants and thus enabling them to buy out their landlords and become peasant proprietors.

There were other British reforms. An Education Act of 1870 gave increased support to the old religious schools and inaugurated a system of state schools (called "board schools"). Full legal recognition was granted to labor unions by an act of 1871, and before the end of the century unionism had spread from the skilled crafts to semiskilled factory workers, and to unskilled laborers as well. Slowly the pressure of lower class voters, of trade unions, and of social reformers made itself felt. Before he devoted himself to the Irish question and an unsuccessful attempt to reëstablish English tariffs, Joseph Chamberlain made a reputation for "municipal socialism" by reforms he instituted as mayor of Birmingham. In the Conservative party, Lord Randolph Churchill led a group of "Tory Democrats" who worked for social legislation.

Disraeli.

The period from 1873 to 1896, marked by these democratic, social, and educational reforms, was a difficult one in some ways for Great Britain. World prices were low. Profits in trade and commerce dwindled. British agriculture, in the face of overseas competition of cheap wheat and frozen meat, ceased to be profitable. Germany and the United States were becoming serious competitors in manufacturing. But all this was relative, and after 1896, as prices rose again, Britain made handsome profits once more from industry and commerce if not from farming.

B. The Third French Republic

The Third Republic in France was proclaimed amidst the gloom attending the defeat at Sedan in 1870. It was organized by a National Assembly elected to ratify an humiliating peace with Germany, and comprising an anti-republican majority. And in its first days, it was torn by civil as well as foreign war. Yet, though no other French régime since 1789 lasted more than eighteen years, the Third Republic endured for seventy.

When the National Assembly was elected in 1871, the royalists were eager to make peace, while the republicans, unwilling to saddle the new republic with the shame of defeat, wished to continue the war. Since the country was sick of war, it voted heavily for the peace party and, out of 650 deputies elected, some 400 were royalists. This majority naturally refused to sanction the republic. It made the peace and appointed Adolphe Thiers as "head of the executive power" to keep the throne warm for a king, who, it was expected, would soon occupy it. But meanwhile the masses of Paris, distrustful of the royalist Assembly, ravaged by economic distress, and injured by the Assembly's decision not to pay wages to national guardsmen any more and to enforce the payment of debts and rent which had been suspended, rallied to the support of the city Commune (city government) in armed revolt against the National Assembly. In April and May 1871, the city, which had so recently been besieged by Germans, underwent a second siege. The attacking French army sent by Thiers fought fiercely, and the "Communards" resisted furiously. In desperation, Parisian extremists slew the hostages they held, including the archbishop of Paris, and burned a number of public buildings, including the palace of the Tuileries. But at last they were overwhelmed. The Commune was crushed and its surviving leaders were killed or exiled.

Having crushed the Parisian radicals, the National Assembly turned to the business of establishing a permanent government. It soon found itself facing a nearly insoluble problem, for, though its majority was royalist, this was divided into two almost equal camps. "Legitimists" wanted the Count of Chambord (grandson of Charles X) as king, while "Orleanists" wanted the Count of Paris (grandson of Louis Philippe). For months the two factions wrangled, until in 1873 they were temporarily shocked into joint action by Thiers's announced conversion from royalism to republicanism. Outraged, they ousted Thiers and elected in his stead the staunchly royalist Marshal Mac-Mahon. Soon afterward they agreed upon a compromise: the childless Count of Chambord would become King, and the Count of Paris would be his heir. But this was upset by the rock-ribbed conservatism of the prospective king, who declared that the flag of France under his rule would be the white banner of the Bourbons, symbol of the old regime. Such a seemingly insignificant point proved a major stumbling block, for it meant that the Count of Chambord, as "Henry V," would try to take France back to the days before 1789, and the majority of Frenchmen, including French royalists, had moved too far along the road of liberal democracy for any such retreat.

With the failure of the royalist plan, the National Assembly set about organizing a French republic. But the royalist majority still hoped to fashion the republic so that it could easily be transformed into a monarchy after the death of the aging Count of Chambord. In November 1873 the Assembly made MacMahon "President of the Republic." In January 1875, by the narrow margin of one vote, it provided for the election of future presidents. Three more "constitutional laws" in 1875 completed the framework of government. Filled in by precedent, interpretation, and amendment, they were all the constitution which the Third Republic ever had. The laws provided for a two-house legislature (Senate and Chamber of Deputies), a ministry responsible to the legislature, and a president elected for a seven-year term by the two houses meeting jointly. On paper, the president seemed to enjoy considerable powers. In practice, authority rested with the parliament.

In the first elections under the new system, France showed its true sentiments by electing a majority of republican deputies, among whom Gambetta was foremost. But MacMahon was unwilling to accept this verdict, and on May 16, 1877, he appointed a royalist ministry, dissolved the Chamber of Deputies, and ordered new elections. Both MacMahon and Gambetta toured the country in a spectacular campaign. The republicans won a decisive victory, and MacMahon had to appoint a republican ministry. Two years later, after the republicans gained control of the Senate, they were able to force MacMahon out of the presidency and to put in a colorless politician named Grévy. One result of the "sixteenth of May" was that no future president dared to used his power to dissolve the Chamber. Another was a tendency to elect undistinguished and "safe" men as presidents.

Thus by 1879 republicans finally controlled the Third Republic. During the ensuing decade they consolidated the new regime. They made the tricolor the national flag, the Marseillaise the national anthem, July 14 the national holiday, and Paris (instead of Versailles) the national capital. They made the Senate wholly elective instead of partly appointed. They passed laws guarantying freedom of speech, assembly, and the press. At the same time they assailed Catholic "clericalism" as an enemy of republicanism. Under the leadership of Jules Ferry, they passed a series of educational laws designed to restrict church schools and to erect a system of national non-religious lay education. They banned many of the religious orders. They made civil marriage compulsory.

From 1879 the Third French Republic showed two interesting peculiarities. The

General Boulanger.

first was an apparent instability arising from the large number of political parties, or "groups." Few of the ministries lasted more than a year. Many endured only a few weeks or months. But policy was actually stable, because a new ministry usually contained a number of ministers from the preceding one and represented merely a slight reshuffling of cabinet posts. The second peculiarity was a tendency to move toward the left (radicalism). The major republican group of the 1880's, led by men like Gambetta and Ferry, was called "Opportunist," since it had no fixed programs other than republicanism and anti-clericalism. To the left of the Opportunists were the "Radicals," including Georges Clemenceau. By the 1890's these were growing in strength, and to their left, socialist groups were emerging.

In the first twenty years after 1879 the Opportunists guided the destinies of the republic. They led it into new imperialist adventures, which we shall note later. They favored business by raising tariffs on industrial products, subsidizing shipping, and constructing public works. They helped agriculture, first by substituting a host of indirect taxes for the land taxes, then by subsidies and aid to peasant coöperative and credit associations, and finally by protective tariffs. The Méline tariff of 1892 represented a major decision. By placing heavy duties on such products as wheat, meat, and sugar, it indicated that the French (unlike the British) were determined to preserve the peasantry and to keep agriculture prosperous even if it meant expensive food for the rest of the population.

There was a good deal of opposition to the Republic, even after 1879, and within the next twenty years this assumed serious proportions on two occasions. One was the Boulanger Affair, and the other the Dreyfus Affair.

General Boulanger, a radical republican at the start and war minister in 1886–1887, became popular with patriots by championing a "war of revenge" against Germany, and before long he was intriguing with conservative elements to make himself a dictator, presumably in Napoleonic fashion. In 1889 he was elected to the Chamber from Paris by a huge majority, and might then have successfully executed a *coup d'état*. But he lacked courage, and when the government ordered his arrest he fled the country. In 1891 the "brave general" committed suicide in Brussels.

More serious was the Dreyfus Affair. In 1894 a secret court-martial of the French army convicted a certain Captain Alfred Dreyfus (a French Jew) and sentenced him to life imprisonment on Devil's Island (near French Guiana). A little later, when question was raised about evidence used at the trial, the general public divided sharply between "Dreyfusards" and "Anti-Dreyfusards." The former, contending that Dreyfus was innocent, included the majority of republicans; the latter, holding that he was guilty, embraced foes and critics of the republic—a noisy group of anti-Semites, most royalists, many Catholics, and officers intent upon upholding the "honor of the army." As proofs eventually accumulated in favor of Dreyfus's innocence, he was brought back to France and retried in 1899, but so intense was the feeling against him in the army that he was again found guilty, though "with extenuating circumstances." Whereupon he was pardoned by the

President of the Republic, and in 1906 was completely exonerated and restored to military rank.

The Dreyfus Affair had several important consequences. (1) The republic was strengthened. (2) Royalists were discredited, and weeded out of the army. (3) Opportunists who had shilly-shallied in the case were supplanted by Radicals who, with some Socialist support, became the leading political group. (4) Anti-clericalism was greatly intensified, so much so, that in the ensuing years the triumphant Radicals expelled almost all religious orders from France (1901), made provision (1904) to prevent clergymen from teaching even in church schools, and, by abrogating the Concordat of 1801, separated church from state (1905).

C. Other Successes of Liberal Democracy

In the latter part of the nineteenth century, while liberal democracy was the rule in Great Britain and France and partially recognized in Germany, it made notable progress elsewhere in western Europe. In Italy, there were special difficulties. There was cleavage between the progressive industrial north and the backward agricultural south, and there was papal hostility to the new Italian kingdom. Pope Pius IX refused to recognize Italy's forceful seizure of Rome in 1870 and became "the prisoner of the Vatican." The Italian government attempted to meet the impasse by a "law of papal guaranties," which promised sovereign independence to the Pope within the Vatican and granted him an annual subsidy in return for the territory he had lost. Pius IX promptly rejected the law, refused the subsidy, and forbade Catholics to participate in Italy's political life. Though the Pope's attitude strengthened his international position by making it clear that he was not subservient to the Italian government, it created grave difficulties for Italy. It was not until 1929 that an amicable settlement was reached between Italy and the Vatican.

Despite these difficulties, parliamentary government made considerable progress in Italy. There were a number of parties, which in general fell into two groups: the Right, whose strength lay in the industrial north; and the Left, led by middle-class intellectuals and lawyers from the south. The Right was perhaps a shade more aristocratic and less anti-clerical than the Left. But both were very much like the liberal republicans of France. The Right was in power from 1870 to 1876, and the Left for most of the next twenty years. One of the Left prime ministers, Crispi, led Italy into an ill-fated imperialist attempt to seize Ethiopia. The Ethiopians crushed the Italian expeditionary force at Adowa (1896), and the discredited Left was out of power for the next seven years.

Both Right and Left sought to better Italian economic life by constructing railways, subsidizing shipping, and granting tariff protection to industry. Despite Italy's lack of coal and iron, some progress was made, slowly before 1896, and rapidly thereafter. Yet lack of opportunity at home led millions of Italians, especially from the south, to emigrate to Argentina, Brazil, and the United States. In 1900, about 350,000 left the country; and in 1910 the figure rose to 530,000.

In both Spain and Portugal, liberalism made some advance. Spanish liberals ousted Queen Isabella II in 1868. But attempts to establish a constitutional monarchy under another dynasty were succeeded by still more disastrous attempts to found a republic. After much disorder and fighting, the Bourbon monarchy was restored in 1875 in the person of Isabella's son, Alphonso XII. For the next thirty-five years, Spain was nominally a liberal constitutional monarchy. Actually it was ruled by a group of military and political chieftains whose power rested on the indifference of the masses and the support of the army. Some were called Liberal, others Conservative, and they cheerfully shared the spoils of office with each other. Republicans continued their propaganda and helped to force the adoption of universal manhood suffrage in 1890. To counterbalance the votes of city workers, who were becoming more revolutionary (whether they wanted a republic, socialism, or provincial autonomy), the Conservatives made the suffrage compulsory in 1907 so as to oblige the more conservative peasants to vote. An unsuccessful war of 1898 against the United States lost Spain most of her remaining colonies, and proved a blow to her national pride and to the monarchy.

Conditions in Portugal were much like those in Spain after 1875. In general the ministers were less efficient and more corrupt. In addition, King Charles I was personally licentious and extravagant. In 1907 he tried to quell factional strife by giving dictatorial powers to the prime minister, but in the next year both Charles and his eldest son were assassinated in the streets of Lisbon. The monarchy staggered along till 1910, when it was overthrown by a revolt which made Portugal a republic.

By the late nineteenth century, both Belgium and Holland had become liberal, constitutional monarchies much like Britain. In Belgium the Liberal party was in power most of the time from 1847 to 1884, but its anti-clerical tendencies gave rise to a strong Catholic party which controlled the government for the next thirty years. In Holland, though the suffrage was gradually broadened, the sovereign could still initiate and veto legislation. More thoroughly democratic was Switzerland, which adopted the referendum (1874), permitting the people as a whole to vote on laws, and also the initiative (1891), enabling a specified number of citizens to force the submission of a measure to such a vote.

In Denmark, King Christian IX (1863–1906) waged a long contest with the lower house of the national legislature. Till 1901 he succeeded in ruling in a more or less autocratic manner, but in that year he was compelled to appoint a ministry representing the majority of the lower house. It was not until 1914–1915 that the age for voting was cut from thirty to twenty-five and the upper house of the legislature made wholly elective. Norway and Sweden were ruled by the same king, but with separate ministries and legislatures from 1815 to 1905. In this arrangement, the Swedes had the better of the bargain, for they held chief positions in the joint army and diplomatic services. Growing Norwegian nationalism finally led to a separation of the two countries. In 1905, the Norwegians proclaimed their independence and chose the second son of the Danish king as their ruler. Sweden reluctantly consented. Universal manhood suffrage was established in Norway in 1898, and in Sweden in 1907.

By 1914 all the countries of western Europe seemed committed to political democracy. Almost all of them had something approaching universal manhood suffrage. All of them had constitutions, even though Britain's was unwritten. Most of them had governments responsible to the national legislatures, though this was not true of Germany and did not mean much in Spain or Portugal. All of them recognized personal liberties of speech, press, religion, and assembly.

D. Controlled Democracy in Germany under Bismarck

The new German Empire represented a nice compromise between nationalism and federalism, and between divine-right monarchy and popular government. In the Empire were twenty-five states besides the "imperial territory" of Alsace-Lorraine. Each state retained its respective duke, grandduke, or king, and its control over such local matters as direct taxation, education, public health, police, and landholding. Certain special privileges were conceded to some of the states. Thus Bavaria retained control of its own post offices, railways, and army (in peace time), and in Saxony the supreme court of the Empire was located. The federal, imperial government had authority over foreign affairs, military matters, foreign and domestic commerce, and criminal and civil law. For the Empire as a whole, laws were to be made by a two-house legislature: a *Bundesrat* (Federal Council), composed of agents of the various state governments; and a *Reichstag* (Imperial Parliament), elected democratically by all males over twenty-five years of age.

While democracy was recognized in the manner of electing the Reichstag, it was restricted by limiting the power of that body, for the imperial ministry, headed by a chancellor, was responsible not to it but to the Emperor. Moreover, Prussia, still under the undemocratic constitution of 1850, was given a major role in the Empire. Not only was the Prussian king, as emperor, empowered to appoint and dismiss the chancellor of the Empire at will, but usually the imperial chancellor and the prime-minister of Prussia were one and the same person. The agent of the king of Prussia in the Bundesrat was given enough votes to enable him to veto any reduction in the army or in taxes or any amendment to the imperial constitution which the majority in the Reichstag might approve. To conduct the new imperial machinery, from the key position of the chancellorship, the Emperor William I, appropriately enough, selected Bismarck, and the statesman who had created the German Empire guided its destinies for almost twenty years afterwards.

Within a short time the governmental machinery of the new Empire was organized and perfected. The legal systems of the several states were replaced by uniform codes of law for the whole Empire. Imperial coinage supplanted the coins of the various states. An imperial bureau unified the state railroads and coördinated them with the military, postal, and telegraphic services. Control of banks was transferred from the state governments to the Bundesrat, and an Imperial Bank (Reichsbank) was set up.

To safeguard the new Germany, Bismarck turned to both diplomacy and military preparedness. In the field of foreign relations, he strove to keep France isolated so that she would have no allies if she were tempted to start a "war of revenge." At the same time, he extended the Prussian system of compulsory military service to the whole Empire, and the peace strength of the army was fixed at 400,000. Though the Chancellor would have liked to have the army appropriations made permanent, the Reichstag would grant them only for seven (later five) years at a time. But Bismarck soon learned to get the appropriation renewed each time by arranging a "war scare" at the right moment. The German military machine was always growing, never shrinking, after 1871.

In putting through his various policies, Bismarck had the support of the bourgeois National Liberal party, and of the Free Conservative party, which was composed mainly of Prussian landlords. The other major parties were the Old Conservative, made up largely of "old fashioned" Prussian squires, Lutheran clergymen, and army officers, and the Progressive party, drawn chiefly from middle-class liberals. The former was too Prussian to sympathize with Bismarck's all-German mood after 1871, and too reactionary to approve his gestures toward democracy. On the whole, however, it went along with him on most matters and backed him vigorously in his army policy. But the Progressives, who were pacifist and wanted a really democratic and liberal government, were a thorn in Bismarck's flesh. It was a relief to him that their strength was gradually waning. There were minor groups, too, who opposed Bismarck in the Reichstag. In 1875 the radical followers of Karl Marx and the more moderate followers of Ferdinand Lassalle united to form a Social Democratic party. Thereafter there were always some Socialist deputies to criticize the government and plead the cause of the workers. There were, in addition, small groups of deputies from Hanover, Schleswig, Prussian Poland, and Alsace-Lorraine, who represented people more or less unhappy under Prussian rule. Sometimes they were aided in fighting the Chancellor by deputies from the south who were eager to preserve "states' rights" or the Catholic religion from Prussian and Protestant interference.

Bismarck was particularly nettled by the Catholic, states' rights group; and his desire to repress it by striking at the Catholic Church was shared by a majority in both the Reichstag and the Prussian parliament. To many German Protestants, the Catholic Church seemed a foreign organization standing in the way of German nationalism. To many German liberals, Pope Pius IX seemed a reactionary trying to compensate for his loss of temporal power by asserting an ever greater spiritual authority. From 1872 to 1880 Bismarck waged a kind of war in Prussia and throughout Germany against the Catholic Church. On this point, the Progressives heartily approved of the Chancellor's policy, and one of them gave the conflict a high-sounding name by which it has since been known—the *Kulturkampf* (struggle for civilization).

In 1872, Bismarck began the fight by expelling the Jesuits from Germany and breaking off diplomatic relations with the pope. Then in Prussia, he put through (1873–1874) the so-called "May Laws" or "Falk

Laws," which provided that every Catholic clergymen must be a German citizen educated in German public schools and universities, and must be certified or "authorized" by the Prussian government. Ecclesiastical seminaries were put under state control, and Catholic preparatory schools for the clergy were banned. Religious instruction, even in Polish-speaking areas, was to be given in German. Backed by the pope, the German bishops condemned this legislation. Whereupon the Prussian parliament forbade "unauthorized" persons to exercise church functions and made refractory clergymen subject to loss of citizenship, imprisonment, or exile. With such severity were these measures enforced that within a single year six Catholic bishops were jailed and Catholic public worship ceased in more than 1300 parishes. In 1877, every Prussian Catholic bishop and hundreds of priests were in prison or exile, and lay Catholics were being rapidly weeded out of the civil service.

With unexpected unanimity, German Catholics fought back against Bismarck's anti-Catholic legislation. Encouraged by the pope and their "martyred" bishops, they rallied in support of "administrators" who by stealth took the place of the bishops and kept the church organization functioning. In politics they supported Catholic leaders, like Windthorst from Hanover, who were building up a distinctively Catholic party—the so-called Center Party. The new party demanded not only the repeal of the anti-Catholic laws but also a broad program of social reform. In 1874 it polled one and a half million votes and elected ninety deputies. Before long, Windthorst was skillfully lining up support from all the groups hostile to Bismarck and even from some of the Protestant Conservatives who were alarmed by the general anti-religious implications of the anti-Catholic legislation.

Finally, Bismarck decided that opposition on the religious issue was endangering his other policies. He also began to feel that Marxian Socialism was an even greater menace than Catholic Christianity. Accordingly, in 1880, he secured from the Prussian parliament authorization to use his discretion in enforcing the May Laws. Diplomatic relations with the Vatican were presently resumed, and in 1886 the most oppressive anti-Catholic measures were repealed. Bismarck thus confessed that his *Kulturkampf* had been a failure. From his standpoint it was even worse, for it raised up a new and well-organized Catholic party which was soon working with democrats and socialists to secure political and social reforms.

E. Bismarck and Socialism

Bismarck was correct in his belief that the Socialists were gaining in strength, for, as Germany became increasingly industrialized, the urban proletariat grew by leaps and bounds, and within it the Socialists obtained many converts. As we have seen, industrialism had made considerable progress in Germany before 1870. Afterwards its growth was phenomenal. It was stimulated by the French war indemnity, aided by national unity, fostered by government assistance, and forwarded by the discoveries of German scientists. German pig iron production rose from 1,400,000 metric tons in 1870 to almost eleven million in 1905, by which time it surpassed Great Britain's. German steel output by 1895 was greater than British. German coal production multiplied nine times between 1860 and 1900. By 1895 nearly seven million workers were employed in German industry and less than thirty-seven per cent of the population was making its living from agriculture.

Germany, coming late into the field, got off to a very good start in the newer industries, at the same time that she was making such rapid progress in the old. In photographic goods and optical instruments, in electrical products, and in chemicals, Germany held a commanding position by 1900. In many lines, from novelties to cutlery and from toys to textiles, the Germans won markets by making a relatively good product at a very cheap price. The government encouraged the business men to get together in associations or "cartels" to eliminate competition, fix prices, and expand sales abroad. Railway rates were cut on goods for export. Consuls with business experience were stationed in foreign cities, and schools were established to train salesmen for work abroad.

As trade and commerce grew, the German cities increased in size and number.

Between 1870 and 1900 German population rose from forty-one to fifty-six million and most of the growth was concentrated in cities. From the 1840's to the early 1880's many Germans had emigrated to foreign lands. In the peak year the number leaving the country had topped 200,000. But after 1880, economic opportunities increased so rapidly at home that emigration diminished. The German peasant seeking to better himself went no longer to North or South America, but to thriving industrial, mining, or commercial centers in his own country, such as Hamburg, Leipzig, Essen, Stuttgart, Cologne, or Berlin.

With industrialization and urban life, there came for workers new problems of unsanitary housing, long hours, insecurity, and the like. Many laborers embraced the teachings of the Socialists as a promising way out of their troubles. In 1877, the newly united Social Democratic party polled a half million votes and elected twelve deputies to the Reichstag. The doctrines which these Socialists preached—revolution, class conflict, thoroughgoing social and political democracy, abolition of private property, internationalism, and pacifism—were the very opposites of Bismarck's ideas and to him they seemed destructive to the state, the family, and civilization itself. He was outraged by the propagandist speeches of the Socialist deputies and by their opposition to every measure he sponsored. He therefore sought to suppress Socialism in two ways: to crush it by force, and to kill it by kindness.

In 1878 there were two unsuccessful attempts by madmen to assassinate the venerable Emperor William I. Bismarck made use of the resulting public excitement by claiming that the insane men were associated with the Socialists. He dissolved the Reichstag and secured the election of a new one which shared his opinion of the Social Democrats. At once, over the protests of Catholic Centrists and of Progressives, the majority of Conservatives and National Liberals passed a severe law against Socialist propaganda. Though enacted at first for only four years, it was reënacted several times and remained in effect till 1890. It forbade the circulation of Socialist books, pamphlets, and newspapers, empowered the police to break up Socialist meetings and suppress Socialist publications, and put the trial and punishment of Socialist offenders in the hands of the police.

Yet here again Bismarck failed. The more rigorous was the enforcement of the law against the Socialists, the more effective became their propaganda and the example of their "martyrs,"—and the more solid and influential became the Social Democratic party. The party maintained its organization in Germany, waged a war of words against Bismarck from neighboring countries, and even increased its representation in the Reichstag. In 1881 it won twelve seats in that body, and by 1890 it won thirty-five.

But Bismarck did not rely on repression alone. He realized that the workers had many just grounds for complaint. As a "junker" landlord he had no great sympathy for the new industrial capitalists. As a nationalist and militarist he wanted the mass of the German people to be strong, healthy, and contented. In addition, Bismarck thought that by removing the most acute economic grievances of the laboring class, he could make it loyal to the state and immune to Socialist propaganda. Consequently, in the 1880's he sponsored an elaborate and well-considered program of social legislation—a kind of "new deal"—which was eventually imitated in most other industrial countries, in the United States, for example, some fifty years later. For this program, he secured support from the Conservatives who believed in the old Prussian tradition of benevolent paternalism and from the Catholic Center Party which was pledged to work for social reform.

In 1883 a law established insurance for workers against sickness. The next year employers were compelled to insure their employees against accidents. In 1887 the labor of women and children was drastically limited, the hours of work were restricted in various industries, Sunday was set aside as a day of rest, and an elaborate system of government regulation and supervision of factories and mines was set up. In 1889 arrangements were made to insure laborers against old age and inability to work. Thus by 1890 the German workers were better protected against exploitation and were

Dropping the Pilot. Cartoon in *Punch*, March, 1890.

more secure from the misfortunes of industrial life than their fellows in any other country. But instead of killing Socialism, this legislation, put through by the conservative Chancellor, seemed to have the opposite effect. The Socialists called the new laws half-measures and pleaded for more drastic reform.

Even before Bismarck tried to win the support of labor for the imperial government, he took another step designed in some degree to benefit the industrialists. The *Zollverein* had in general pursued a policy of low tariffs, but as German industry grew, it seemed desirable to help it to compete against older British industries by giving it an assured position in the home market. In addition, Bismarck wanted to get revenues for the imperial government without the necessity of levying assessments on the various states, which controlled local taxation. For these reasons, and against opposition of the Progressives, who believed in free trade, Bismarck in 1879 put through a much higher tariff on industrial goods.

This change did give effective protection to many German industries, but it did not help agriculture which was suffering from overseas and Russian competition. Bismarck, as a conservative and landowner, sympathized with the agricultural classes, wished to preserve a balance between agriculture and industry, and hoped, for military reasons, to keep Germany from becoming dependent on food from abroad. Accordingly in 1885 and 1887, he secured the passage of tariffs which greatly raised the import duties on agricultural products, and especially on grain. This policy served to prevent a decay of German agriculture comparable to that which occurred in England.

Austria and Italy had raised their customs duties in 1878, a year before Bismarck's first protective tariff. But it was Bismarck's action which seemed to set off a wave of higher tariffs all over Europe, and reversed the trend toward freer trade so noticeable in the 1860's. Of the major countries, only Great Britain clung to the "liberal" principles of free trade.

Against Danes, Poles, and Hanoverians who persisted in their objections to Prussian rule, Bismarck directed repressive legislation. In the Polish areas, he not only tried to force the use of the German language and to prevent hostile political activity, but also to transfer farms from Polish to German ownership. Alsace and Lorraine received some favors, but the hostility of their deputies in the Reichstag convinced Bismarck that he was right in treating them as conquered provinces and not as equals of the other German states. Toward the Jews, Bismarck was none too kindly disposed, though for political and financial reasons he refrained from public attack on them and even rebuked Adolf Stöcker, a Lutheran chaplain of William I, for his anti-Semitic activities in the 1880's. Nevertheless the bitterly anti-Jewish agitation of Stöcker and the anti-Semitic party (called National Socialist) which he founded were quite in accord with the illiberal attitude of the Chancellor toward most minority groups in Germany.

William I, whom Bismarck had made Emperor and with whom he had worked so long, died in 1888. He was succeeded by his son Frederick, but within a few months he too died, and was succeeded by his son, William II. The new Emperor was a young man with the same ideas on divine-right monarchy and the importance of the army as had characterized William I, but with a vanity, volubility, and impulsiveness which irritated the aging Bismarck. At the start, William II announced that he was going to continue the Chancellor in office and follow his advice. But Bismarck was set in his ways and used to running things, while William II was eager to try new ways and to be the directing force in the government. From the standpoint of the Emperor it soon became a question of "whether the Hohenzollern dynasty or the Bismarck dynasty should rule."

In March 1890 friction between the young Emperor and the old Chancellor reached a climax. They differed on Germany's policy toward Russia. They differed on the anti-Socialist policy. To check Bismarck, William II ordered that cabinet ministers should have access to him directly rather than through the Chancellor. Bismarck declined to accede to the order and William II demanded his resignation. The "Iron Chancellor" retired to his estates, where, until his death at the age of eighty-three (1898), he lived in more or less open criticism of the Emperor.

When Bismarck retired in 1890, his task was done. He had founded the Hohenzollern German Empire and put his stamp upon it. It was indeed fateful that the new Germany was created by a conservative Junker who believed in blood and iron, who distrusted democracy, and who thought that the end justified the means.

CHAPTER 50

Relative Backwardness of Eastern Europe

A. The Russian Tsardom

While western Europe was moving toward political democracy, the Russian Empire remained autocratic. Its core was the "Great Russian" nationality, stretching out in all directions from Moscow; but by the mid-nineteenth century the expansion of the country had brought under Russian rule not only such closely related Slavic peoples as "Little Russians" (Ukrainians) and "White Russians" (Byelorussians), but many other European peoples, including Finns, Estonians, Latvians, Lithuanians, Poles, and Rumanians, besides a bewildering variety of Asiatic peoples living east of the Urals in Siberia or Turkestan. Both the Great Russians and the subject peoples were ruled autocratically by civil and military agents of the Tsar, though the Finns retained some local self-government throughout the century, and the Poles until 1831.

The Tsar Alexander I (1801–1825) had shown some sympathy with liberalism in his early years, but the reign of his sucessor, Nicholas I (1825–1855), was one of stark reaction. He stifled liberal criticism in Russia by use of secret police. He wiped out Polish liberties after the insurrection of 1831. Though he aided the Greeks in gaining their independence in 1829, he helped to prevent the Hungarians from gaining theirs in 1849. In 1850, Russia was an autocracy as despotic as that of Peter the Great.

Nicholas I died in the midst of his unsuccessful Crimean War against the Ottoman Empire, Great Britain, and France.

His successor, Alexander II (1855–1881), was faced with the necessity, not only of signing a humiliating peace treaty, but of allaying criticism and discontent within Russia. Though the Russian middle class of officials, professional men, business men, and intellectuals was relatively small, it was becoming more vocal. One group with whom Nicholas I had sympathized was that of the "Slavophiles," for they believed in resisting western influences and glorifying things Russian, such as the Orthodox Church and the autocratic rule of the Tsar. Another group, the so-called "Westernizers," wished to modernize Russia by importing western science, laws, industry, and education, and to develop within the Empire some such constitutional government as existed in Great Britain or France.

To these Westernizers, Alexander II made certain significant concessions between 1861 and 1864. One of the most notable was his abolition of serfdom. Though there were areas held by free peasants and by Cossacks, nine-tenths of the land of Russia was owned in 1855 by the imperial family and some 100,000 noble families. These estates were tilled by serfs, who formed the great majority of the Russian population. Part of the produce of the fields went to the landlord. Part went to the support of the peasant village communities, or *mirs*. The serfs were bound to the soil. They paid the landlord dues in money, kind, and labor. Some two million household serfs who held no land were virtually slaves, whose services could be rented out like those of horses or oxen. The situation

Tsar Alexander II.
Courtesy Bettmann Archive

in this respect was worse than that of western Europe in the early middle age. Though there were exceptions, most of the Russian serfs lived in squalor, ignorance, and poverty.

First the Tsar freed the serfs on the imperial estates. Then, in the face of dogged opposition from landowners, he promulgated a decree of general emancipation in 1861. The decree abolished all legal rights of the landlords over the persons of his serfs. It gave personal freedom but no land to the household serfs. The serfs who were working on the large estates received not only freedom, but an interest in a portion of the land, which was bought from the nobles with money advanced by the government and then turned over to the village communities (*mirs*) to be parcelled out among the peasants. The whole process was very complicated and there were some in-

justices. Many peasants received too little land to afford them a living. Many landlords did not have adequate labor to work their fields. The peasants were left with a consuming hunger for more land. They were burdened by the annual payments which they had to make to the government to refund to it the purchase price of the lands. While they were freed from the authority and courts of the nobles, they were subjected to the harsh and often corrupt rule of imperial officials, judges, and tax collectors. Nevertheless, the benefits of even such emancipation as this soon showed themselves in gradually enlarged areas under cultivation, greater yield of taxes, growth of grain exports, and slowly improving conditions for the peasantry.

Another "westernizing" reform of Alexander II was the establishment of provincial assemblies. A decree of 1864 provided that each district of the thirty-four provinces, or "governments," of Russia, should have a local assembly, or *zemstvo,* composed of landed nobles and of delegates indirectly elected by townsfolk and peasants. For its district, each *zemstvo* would have authority to levy taxes, and to supervise public works, churches, schools, prisons, poor relief, and public health. Optimistic "Westernizers" thought this reform might lead to constitutional government.

Likewise the Tsar reformed the judicial system. A decree of 1862 transferred the trial of civil and criminal cases from imperial administrative officials to law courts modeled after those of western Europe. At the bottom were justices of the peace. Then came district and circuit courts. A senate acted as final court of appeal. With the decree were issued instructions for codifying the laws, establishing jury trials for criminal cases, and holding trials in public rather than in secret. But exception was made in the case of political offenders. These would still be subjected to secret, arbitrary trials by administrative officials.

Alexander II also did something to encourage elementary and technical schools, construction of railways, and development of mines. But by 1865 his reforming zeal was spent, partially as a result of a Polish revolt in 1863, which, though forcefully suppressed with comparative ease, indicated to him that western ideas were dangerous. From 1865 to 1905, the rule of Russia under Alexander II and his successors, Alexander III (1881–1894) and Nicholas II (1894–1917), was thoroughly reactionary. Critics of the government and zealous reformers were ruthlessly silenced by execution, imprisonment, or exile to Siberia. Discontent was driven underground into revolutionary secret societies, which occasionally committed acts of terrorism against the authorities. One such act occurred in 1881, when the assassination of Alexander II brought Alexander III to the throne.

Under Alexander III the policies of the Russian autocracy were both reactionary and nationalist. Centralization of administration reduced the authority of the *zemstvos* and brought even the *mirs* under government supervision. The educational system was carefully controlled from elementary school through university. The press was subjected to drastic censorship. And everywhere were agents of the secret police ready to pounce on reformers or critics of the government. In behalf of nationalism, a policy called "Russification" was pursued. It was an effort to impose the language and the Eastern Orthodox Christianity of the Great Russian people on other nationalities within the Empire. Russian sectarians who had split off from the Orthodox Church, "Uniates" (Eastern Christians reunited with the papacy), Roman Catholics (in Poland and Lithuania), and Protestant Lutherans (in the Baltic provinces) were all persecuted or harassed, in order to force them into the Orthodox fold. Similar attempts were made to enforce the use of the Great Russian language by Poles, Lithuanians, Ukrainians, and other subject peoples. One phase of Russification was persecution of Jews. They were forbidden to hold land (1882). They were ordered to live in a special district called the Jewish Pale (1890). Officials permitted or even encouraged anti-Jewish riots (*pogroms*) accompanied by the plundering and burning of Jewish property and the massacre of Jews. So intense was the persecution that in the single year 1891 some 300,000 Polish and Russian Jews emigrated from Russian territory, many of them to the United States.

In carrying out his repressive policies, Alexander III used throughout his reign, in important posts, two energetic men who were as enthusiastic as he about the bolstering of autocracy and the suppression of dissent. One was Viatscheslav Plehve (1846–1904). A lawyer of Lithuanian stock, trained at the universities of Warsaw and St. Petersburg, he organized the police throughout the Empire so well and used the ministries of justice and interior so effectively that agitation of all sorts was to a degree driven underground. Ironically enough he was, in the end, killed by the bomb of a revolutionist. The other was Constantine Pobyedonostsev (1827–1907). A teacher of civil law at Moscow, he became the tutor of Alexander III and from 1880 to 1905 was Procurator of the Holy Synod. In this position he made attempts to improve the religious education of the Orthodox clergy. But he also sought to use them and their church as instruments of propaganda for the Tsardom and for Russification. To him, as he makes clear in his *Reflections of a Russian Statesman*, western liberal and democratic innovations like jury trial and freedom of the press were dangerous if not downright immoral.

The advent of Nicholas II to the imperial throne in 1894 brought no change in policy. Centralization, repression, and Russification continued. The new Tsar was mystical and fatalistic, weak and obstinate, and much under the influence of his neurotic wife, who, though a granddaughter of the English Queen Victoria, was passionately devoted to Russian autocracy and the Orthodox Church.

Yet under Alexander III and Nicholas II events were taking place that in the long run would contribute to the downfall of the Tsarist regime in Russia. The country was undergoing industrialization, especially in textiles and metallurgy. Railways were being built. Population was growing, from 57 million in 1850, to 103 million in 1900, and to 130 million in 1914. While it continued to be largely agricultural, by 1914 one seventh of it lived in cities as against only a tenth in 1874, and one seventh of so big a population was no small number. The Empire now had as many town dwellers as France and many more factory towns than Italy.

Closely associated with the industrialization of Russia was Count Sergei Witte (1849–1915). Of Dutch extraction, he was a native of Tiflis, where his father was a government official. He began his career as a conservative journalist, but before long he became interested in railways and finance. Appointed to the imperial service by Alexander III, he continued in it for more than a decade under Nicholas II. Though an apostle of Slavophile political conservatism, Witte was an ardent advocate of western industrial and commercial development. First as head of the railway bureau, later as minister of finance, he worked for the construction of railways, and for policies of economic nationalism favorable to big business. He stabilized the currency, gave bounties to new industries, and provided protection for old ones. He sponsored some regulation

Count Sergei Witte.

of factories and some social insurance. Among his varied achievements were the construction of the Trans-Siberian railway and the introduction of the government monopoly of the sale of vodka. Despite all he did to strengthen Russia economically, he was so clearly identified with the "Westernizing" movement that, in 1906, he was forced out of office by reactionaries who had the ear of the Tsar.

In 1861, Russia had 700 miles of railway; in 1882, 15,000 miles. By 1914 the figure rose to 47,000 miles. Though it could hardly compare with Britain or Germany, Russia was already a significant producer of iron and textiles. In fact, by the early twentieth century Russia had undergone the early stages of an industrial revolution. It had developed a transportation system, a factory system, and a body of more or less skilled workers to a degree that made possible additional and more rapid industrialization. It is worth noting that the government played a larger part in this movement than in many other countries. The first railroads, for example, had been built by private capital, but usually with a guarantee by the state of a return on the money invested. In 1881, the imperial government went further and decided on outright state ownership of the railways.

As the twentieth century opened, Russia was politically an autocracy comparable with that of Louis XIV. Economically, it was a vast land of peasant agriculture, with industrialized islands bound together by a network of railways. Socially, it was primarily a peasant country with a strong land-owning nobility whose main function was still service of the state, especially in the army. But it had a growing bourgeoisie, a considerable number of intellectuals dissatisfied with the political backwardness of the nation, and a rising proletariat already infected with revolutionary teachings.

B. Disruptive Nationalism in Austria-Hungary

The Dual Monarchy of Austria-Hungary showed tendencies both like those of western and like those of eastern Europe, with Austria more typical of the west and Hungary of the east. By 1867 Austria-Hungary was thrust out of both Germany and Italy. Henceforth, its attention was focussed on its own domains and on the hope of repairing its fortunes by expansion in the Balkans. But in the Balkans it encountered mounting native nationalism and growing Russian ambition, while at home it had to cope with a trend toward industrialization, liberalism, and democracy and a most ominous rising tide of nationalism among its own subject peoples.

During the period from the *Ausgleich* in 1867[1] to the World War of 1914, Austria-Hungary was ruled by the Emperor Francis Joseph (1848–1916), who sought to maintain the traditions and ceremonies appropriate to the most renowned of all the ruling houses, the Habsburgs.[2] He had had to grant constitutional government to both Austria and Hungary. But in both countries, the parliaments were long dominated by the landowning nobility and the upper middle class; and the Emperor retained the right to veto legislation and to maintain in office ministries of which the majority of the parliaments did not approve.

The legislatures of the two parts of the Dual Monarchy were supposed to settle their differences and jointly to supervise

[1] See above, pp. 630–631.
[2] See picture of Francis Joseph, above, p. 630.

the imperial ministries of army, finance, and foreign affairs through an odd kind of joint parliament called the "Delegations," consisting of sixty representatives from the Austrian parliament and sixty from the Hungarian. They met alternately in Vienna and in Budapest. The Austrian delegates used German; the Hungarian, Magyar. Each group normally met in a separate chamber and communicated with the other in writing. In cases of failure to agree, they did meet together, but only to vote, not to debate. Such a clumsy mechanism was scarcely sufficient to cope with the increasing problems that kept arising between Austria and Hungary.

Austria, particularly in the neighborhood of the cities of Vienna and Prague, witnessed a considerable development of factory industry and of an urban proletariat, while Hungary remained more thoroughly agricultural and almost feudal in character. This difference helped to make the *Ausgleich* of 1867 an uneasy compromise. Austria wanted a protective tariff on industrial products; Hungary wished to protect farm products. The solution, which was worked out in the 1880's and which satisfied neither country, was to protect both. There were disputes, too, about the army, for the Hungarians wanted their regiments commanded exclusively by Magyars and all military orders given in the Magyar language. There was friction also about the central bank established in Vienna in 1878, about the negotiation of commercial treaties, and even about foreign policy. Yet the existence of the Dual Monarchy brought many advantages, since it maintained a large area of central Europe as an economic unit without barriers to trade. It supported a great capital at Vienna where the arts and sciences flourished amidst a conglomerate population from all parts of the Empire. And the joint strength of Austria and Hungary was sufficient to give the monarchy considerable weight among European great powers.

In the 1870's Austrian politics were much influenced by a Liberal party with anti-clerical tendencies which ran counter to the country's long Catholic tradition. But the next decade saw the rise of a Catholic party, called Christian Socialist, which was headed by a Viennese lawyer named Karl Lueger.

It won a large following among the peasantry and the lower middle class, and allies from among Catholic Poles and Czechs. Under stimulus from the Christian Socialists in the 1880's, trade unions were legalized, factories and mines regulated, working hours limited, and the labor of women and children restricted. As mayor of Vienna, Lueger made that city famous for its municipal ownership and operation of public utilities. But there was an ominous note in his leadership, for he won many followers by his passionate attacks on Jews and "Jewish capitalism." It was in the atmosphere of anti-Semitism abetted by Lueger that Adolf Hitler grew up.

In the 1880's and 1890's, the Austrian government had tried making some concessions to its subject nationalities—Czechs, Italians, Slovenes, Rumanians, Ruthenians, and Poles. It allowed relatively free use of their respective languages. It split the University of Prague into two parts, one German and one Czech. It permitted the local administrations of such cities as Cracow, Prague, and Trieste to be managed respectively by Poles, Czechs, and Italians. But all concessions only led to a demand for more and it seemed clearly impossible to give political power to the subject peoples. The Germans in Bohemia would have resented Czech rule, while the Poles would have opposed any liberties for the Ruthenians in Poland, and the Italians in Istria would have opposed rule by the Yugoslavs.

Pressure from the lower classes produced an important extension of the franchise in 1896. In 1907 universal manhood suffrage was granted and voting was made compulsory. By this time, however, Marxian Socialism was spreading among urban workers. The election of 1907 returned to the Austrian parliament 115 Christian Socialists, 62 Liberals, and 87 Socialists. These parties all found their strength in the German-speaking parts of Austria. But the rise of nationalism was ominously evidenced by an array of deputies who represented not parties, but nationalities, each eager for cultural and in some cases political autonomy. There were 82 Czech deputies, 72 Poles, 37 Slovenes, 30 Ruthenians, 15 Italians, 5 Rumanians, and 5 Jewish Zionists, a total of 246 as against 264 for the "German" parties. Yet neither the Emperor nor his advisers made any serious attempt to solve the national problem confronting Austria.

The Hungarians, too, had difficulties with subject nationalities. But they ruled with a harsher hand. They strove to impose their own Magyar language on Slovaks, Croatians, and Rumanians under their control. They abolished all local self-government in the Rumanian districts, and restricted the local autonomy that had been granted the Croatians. They kept the suffrage so limited that in 1910 there were only one million voters (chiefly Magyar) in a population of twenty million. They retained political power firmly in the hands of the Hungarian landowners and their middle class allies.

Imperial parliament building, Vienna.

Courtesy Bettmann Archive

Sultan Abdul Hamid II.

Courtesy Bettmann Archive

C. *Disruptive Nationalism in the Ottoman Empire and the Balkans*

While Austria-Hungary had its troubles in the late nineteenth century, the Balkan peninsula verged toward chaos as Ottoman rule gradually crumbled away. The Ottoman Sultan Abdul Hamid II began his reign in 1876 by making a pretense of adopting western institutions. He promulgated a constitution of the liberal type. But it was almost at once suspended and for thirty years it remained a dead letter. From the outset, too, the Sultan was faced with insurrections of Bulgarians and Bosnian Serbs and with Russian aggression. An ensuing Russo-Turkish war of 1877–1878 resulted in a crushing defeat for the Ottoman Empire. True, the Sultan gained interested diplomatic support of Great Britain and Austria-Hungary, who insisted, at the international congress of Berlin (1878), on softening the harsh peace conditions which Russia had demanded. But for this aid, the Sultan had to agree to British occupation of Cyprus and to Austrian administration

of the Yugoslav provinces of Bosnia, Herzegovina, and Novibazar. He also had to promise to coöperate with the great powers on a program of internal reforms, and Ottoman finances were so disrupted by the war expenditures that the country was practically mortgaged to foreigners. In 1881 control of the finances was entrusted to a commission of foreign bankers.

In addition, the treaty of Berlin of 1878 gave marked impetus to the most disruptive force at work in the Balkans—nationalism. The Sultan was compelled to recognize the complete independence of Rumania, Serbia, and Montenegro, the full autonomy of a part of Bulgaria, and a measure of autonomy for the remaining part (Eastern Rumelia). Each of the Balkan peoples at once sought, by means of propaganda, secret societies, conspiracies, and armed bands, to realize its national ambition for expansion. In vain the Sultan tried to play off the great powers against each other, especially Russia against Austria-Hungary. In vain he called in German experts to reorganize his army and his treasury. In vain did he employ terrorism, a spy system, and even massacres. The Ottoman Empire continued to crumble.

In 1882, Great Britain effected a military occupation of Egypt and established a virtual protectorate over that dependency of the Ottoman Empire. But the loss was nominal rather than real, for Egypt had been more or less independent since the early part of the century. In the Balkans, however, the decay of Ottoman rule was more meaningful. The semi-autonomous province of Eastern Rumelia revolted in 1885 and secured union with the principality of Bulgaria. Serbia, seeking "compensation" for this addition of territory by its neighbor, attacked Bulgaria and was soundly beaten. Thus Bulgaria was not only enlarged but also strengthened by a successful war, though it did not become completely independent under its own tsar till 1908.

Greece, independent since 1832, made some modest acquisitions of territory. Great Britain turned over to it, in 1864, the Ionian Islands, and, as a result of the Congress of Berlin, Greece obtained Thessaly on its northern boundaries in 1881. In 1896 the Greeks in Crete revolted, and the next

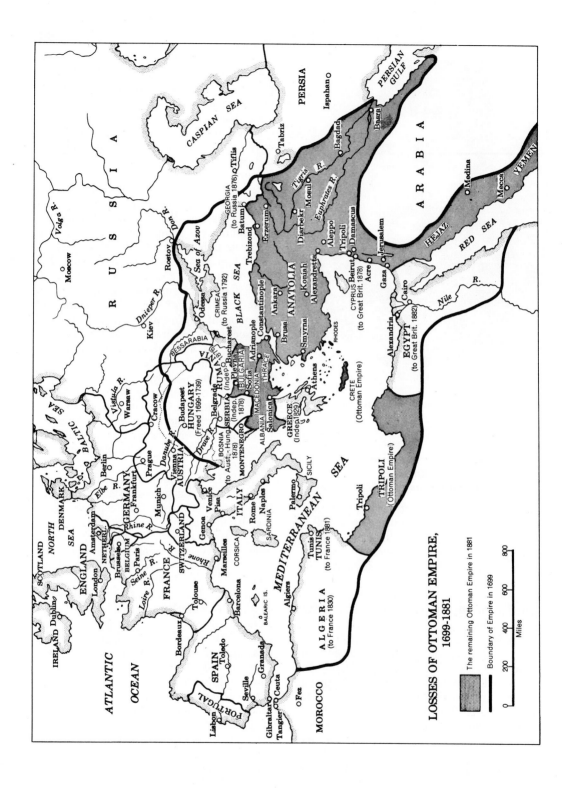

LOSSES OF OTTOMAN EMPIRE,
1699-1881

The remaining Ottoman Empire in 1881

Boundary of Empire in 1699

Miles

0   200   400   600   800

year the kingdom of Greece went to war with the Ottoman Empire on their behalf. This time the Turkish army put up a firm and successful fight. But when the Turkish army advanced on Athens, Russia, Britain, France, and Italy intervened and stopped the Graeco-Turkish War. Greece was compelled to pay an indemnity and to cede a little territory in the north. But Crete was made autonomous, put under the protection of the intervening powers, and given a son of the Greek king as its governor. In 1905 another Cretan insurrection led to an increase in Greek control of the island, for, though the fiction of the Sultan's suzerainty was maintained, Greece was permitted to appoint the Cretan governor and to drill the militia and provide officers for it. One effect of the Cretan developments was to bring to the fore an outstanding Greek patriot and statesman, Eleutherios Venizelos (1864–1936). A leader in the rising of 1896, he became the chief political figure in Crete, and so great was his popularity in Greece itself that he was summoned to Athens to be premier in 1910.

Within the Balkan countries there were many similarities of development. Each brought in a foreign prince to rule it: Greece, the Danish George I (1863–1913); Rumania, the Hohenzollern German Charles I (1866–1914); Bulgaria, the German Alexander I (1879–1886), and then another German, Ferdinand I (1887–1918). Only in Montenegro and Serbia did native dynasties rule. In the former Nicholas I (1860–1918) came from a local family of princes. In the latter the throne was fought over by two rival families whose founders had played leading roles in securing Serbian independence—the Karageorges and the Obrenovićs. The Obrenović dynasty ruled from 1817 to 1842, and from 1859 to 1903; the Karageorge dynasty, from 1842 to 1859 and after 1903. The sway of the Obrenovićs in the second half of the nineteenth century was punctuated by occasional Karageorge insurrections, which kept the country in turmoil, and by brutal assassinations, one in 1868 and another in 1903.

Most of the Balkan countries had constitutions, parliaments, and theoretically responsible ministers. But rule was actually by factions rather than by parties. The leaders generally came from a thin upper crust of urban professional men. The influence of foreign countries played a major role in the factional politics. Despite the building of some railways and a few scattered factories, the rural life of the peasants was little changed by independence. Some schools were opened, but the great masses of the people remained illiterate.

In each Balkan country there was an intense desire to expand frontiers so as to add areas claimed for racial, linguistic, or historic reasons. One warred, openly or secretly, with another; and all cast longing eyes on territory still held by the dwindling Ottoman Empire.

Thus western Europe—industrial, democratic, and liberal—had, on its southeast border, a Balkan region which was backward, chaotic, and tumultuous. The implications of the disintegration of the Ottoman Empire were already making themselves felt. Russia and Austria were competitively seeking to gain strength by expanding their influence over the newly emerging Balkan nations. These now constituted a veritable powder magazine, highly dangerous to international peace. It would presently set all Europe in flames.

President Krueger visits his troops during Boer War.

Courtesy Bettmann Archive

CHAPTER 51

Arms, Alliances, and the New Imperialism

A. Competitive Armaments and International Alliances of the Bismarckian Era, 1866–1893

Prussia demonstrated in 1866 and 1870 what could be accomplished by a well-equipped and well-trained army based on conscription. In the ensuing decades, nearly every European state, save Britain, organized a national army based on compulsory service of all able-bodied males. In some states men had to serve one year in the military forces, in others two or three. More and more, Europe came to resemble a great armed camp with bayonets glinting along the frontiers and artillery roaring in the annual maneuvers and war games. This militarism was definitely competitive. If one country increased the size of its standing army, its neighbors felt compelled to enlarge theirs. If one nation developed an improved rifle or machine gun, all the others strove to acquire a still better one.

Britain alone continued to rely on the old-fashioned, small professional army, because her position as an island made a navy much more important to her than land forces. For many years, the British navy was unchallenged as mistress of the seas. To compete with Britain in this sphere seemed hopeless and unnecessary. But in 1898, the German Emperor William II, influenced by the writings of an American naval officer, Captain Alfred Mahan, who in a series of books was stressing the importance of sea power in warfare, and backed by aggressive German nationalism, decided

to follow the advice of his naval secretary, von Tirpitz, and to build up a great German navy. Beginning with laws enacted in 1898 and 1900, Germany created an imposing fleet of battleships, cruisers, submarines, and destroyers, second only to Britain's. In the fifteen years after 1898, Germany's annual naval expenditures rose from 30 million to 120 million dollars. Britain at once responded by increasing the number and size of her warships, so that in 1913 her naval expenditures were more than double those of Germany. Meanwhile, other nations—France, Italy, Japan, and the United States—were enlarging their navies. Naval force thus became an object of international competition like armies.

From 1871 to 1914, there were numerous war scares in Europe, but no actual wars save in the Balkans. For the first twenty years of the period, it was Bismarck (who previously had precipitated three wars) who did most to maintain peace. He now felt that it would best serve German ends. The keystone of his foreign policy was to keep France diplomatically isolated, so as to prevent her securing allies with whose aid she might wage a war of revenge on Germany. With this end in view, he developed a new kind of alliance. Before 1870, alliances had almost always been temporary affairs entered into during the actual course of a war or when an outbreak of hostilities seemed imminent. Bismarck, after the successful Franco-Prussian war, proceeded to negotiate alliances in peacetime designed to create a permanent line-up of powers which

659

by its very strength could prevent war or, if need be, ensure victory.

In 1872 Bismarck arranged a conference in Berlin of Emperor William I of Germany, Emperor Francis Joseph of Austria, and Tsar Alexander II of Russia, to advertise to the world the cordial relations between the three powers of central and eastern Europe. The next year the members of this so-called Three Emperors' League formally agreed to work together to preserve peace and, if war should threaten, to consult together "to determine a common course of action." Despite strained relations between Russia and Austria at the time of the Russo-Turkish War of 1877–1878, the Three Emperors' League was renewed in 1881 and lasted until 1887 when it was superseded, for another three years, by a special Reinsurance Treaty between Germany and Russia.

Meanwhile in 1879 Bismarck negotiated a close defensive alliance between Germany and Austria-Hungary. This, by the inclusion of Italy in 1882, was expanded into a Triple Alliance which, repeatedly renewed, lasted until 1915. Moreover, so long as Bismarck remained at the helm in Germany, he could count, in any threatened conflict, on the neutrality of Great Britain if not on its active coöperation.

The isolation of France, so carefully secured by Bismarck, did not long survive his fall in 1890. The Tsar Alexander III of Russia was troubled by the refusal of the Emperor William II of Germany to renew the "Reinsurance Treaty." Slavophiles were urging that "Holy Russia" be purged of German cultural influence. Russian economic interests complained about the high German tariffs on wheat and rye established in 1885 and 1887. Moreover, Russia needed foreign capital to enable her to build railways and factories, to equip her armies, and to stabilize her currency. Bismarck had discouraged German loans to Russia. But what the Berlin Bourse withheld, the Paris money market supplied, and by 1890 Russia was already financially dependent on France. It must be remembered, too, that since the eighteenth century the Russian nobility had been brought up to speak French, and many spoke it in preference to Russian, while Paris and the French Riviera were favorite playgrounds for Russian grand dukes and lesser nobles.

The Tsar Alexander III disliked and distrusted the democratic politics of France. But the other forces at work gradually overcame his scruples. An informal diplomatic *entente* (understanding) between France and Russia was inaugurated in 1891. In 1893, by a military convention, Russia promised to aid France in case she were attacked by Germany, while France promised to help Russia in similar circumstances. Thus was inaugurated the Dual Alliance; and henceforth Europe was split between it and the Triple Alliance.

B. Sources of Renewed Imperialism

From 1815 to 1880, there was a slackening in colonial activities of the great powers. France lost all but the remnants of her earlier overseas empire; Spain retained only fragments of hers. Portugal's colonies, after Brazil broke away, consisted only of stagnant trading posts. To be sure, Holland still held a large domain in the East Indies, and Britain's empire encircled the globe. But the theories of *laissez-faire* were opposed to colonialism. Economic liberals pointed out that colonies were useful only for trade and this could be had without the maintenance of expensive political and military control. In addition, the example of the United States, of the Spanish American colonies, and of Brazil seemed to indicate that, once colonies had matured, they would sever their ties with the mother country and "fall away like ripe pears dropping off a tree."

Yet even in the period of waning interest in imperialism, there was some colonial activity. France, as we have seen, got complete control of Algeria in the years following 1830, and under Napoleon III acquired colonies in the Pacific and Indo-China, not to mention the ill-starred attempt to make a protectorate of Mexico.

For Great Britain, the possession of an extensive empire raised numerous problems. In Canada, conflict between royal governors and provincial assemblies led at length to a brief rebellion (1837). As a result, a commission headed by Lord Durham was sent to investigate Canadian grievances. In 1839 Durham published a lengthy report in which he advocated the union of the Canadian colonies and the grant to them of responsible government under a royal governor who should be, like the British king, a mere figurehead. Ten years later, Canadian self-government was formally recognized by the British parliament. And once this principle was sanctioned for Canada, it was soon applied elsewhere. Between 1850 and 1875, responsible self-government was granted to all the major, white-inhabited, British colonies.

But the teeming peninsula of India presented a far more difficult problem. Until past the middle of the nineteenth century the British East India Company, under general supervision of the government in London, had exercised political powers. In 1857 native unrest flamed into a revolt led by native troops (sepoys) and called therefore the Sepoy Mutiny. With some difficulty the rising was put down and the mutineers punished. The next year the British parliament deprived the Company of its political powers and vested control in a cabinet minister in London and a viceroy in India, each assisted by a small council. Though it gave no self-government to India, the Act of 1858 envisioned the possibility that some day such a grant would be made.

Even while popular interest in colonies was lessening, Britain kept acquiring new ones, for her far-flung older possessions made it easy, and sometimes defensively needful, to appropriate additional territories. Thus, for example, Britain added New Zealand (1840), Hong Kong (1842), Natal (1843), the Malay States (1874), and the Fiji Islands (1874). In addition, the older colonies received a heavy immigration from the British Isles, as Irishmen were impelled by famine to leave home, and Englishmen and Scots by bad conditions accompanying industrialization. There was heavy migration to Canada, South Africa, New Zealand, and Australia. The discovery of gold in Australia and in British Columbia, about 1850, led to a rush of gold-seekers to those areas.

During the 1870's there was a shift in the attitude toward colonies, not only in Britain under Disraeli's influence, but in other countries as well. By 1880, the new imperialism was gathering strength, and in the ensuing twenty-five years there was a scramble among the major powers to appropriate "unoccupied" or "backward" regions. In this period practically all Africa was partitioned among the rival imperialist nations, and many areas in Asia and the Pacific were seized. Though the chief competitors were Britain, France, and Germany, other nations were infected by imperialist fever. It is not easy to determine what led to this rather sudden change of attitude, for it was and is still clear that most colonies do not "pay" in the ordinary sense of bringing in more money than they cost. But some of the explanations which have usually been offered are these:

1. Economic. The return to high tariffs in Europe in the late 1870's and in the 1880's tended to close European markets to foreign industrial products at the very time when the growing industrialization of France, Germany, the United States, and Italy was greatly increasing the potential industrial output, and when the rise of industrial rivals was forcing the British to worry about opportunities to sell their goods. In the same period, the decline of world prices was accompanied by a prolonged depression, which, with only a few short breaks, lasted from 1873 to 1896, when the increased output of gold from South Africa tended to raise prices and stimulate business. Industrial countries eagerly turned to a search for new markets. To many, it seemed that colonies, under one's own political control, provided the safest and best kind of markets, since in them no hostile nation could put up prohibitive tariffs.

With the improvement of ocean transportation, even distant overseas colonies took on a new importance as sources of cheap food, tropical goods, and raw materials. There was growing demand not only for cotton, wool, and minerals, but for relatively new products such as palm oil, bananas, rubber, or guano, and for older ones like coffee and tea. From its own colonies, a nation might advantageously secure such goods and also ensure the dominance of its own merchants and ships in the carrying trade. The improvements in transportation (steamships) and communication (cables and telegraphs) made it much easier to acquire and govern distant overseas areas.

The same sort of explanation applies in the matter of investments. As low prices after 1873 cut profits of the new industrialists, these began to look about for new opportunities to invest their capital at more attractive rates of return. Before 1870 much money was loaned at high rates to Spanish American and other undeveloped foreign countries. But the defaults on these debts were so frequent that many capitalists welcomed the chance to invest in colonial enterprises (railways, mines, plantations) where political control seemed to give a greater assurance of safety, while need for capital kept the rate of return high.

2. *Social*. The maturing of industrial economy in Great Britain, and to a lesser degree in Germany, seemed to reduce the opportunities of quick advancement at home for ambitious young men of good education and family. Such men were the ones who traditionally could expect to find successful careers in colonial armies, governments, and business enterprises. At the other end of the scale, colonies held promise of draining off surplus population of depressed or unemployed classes, though actually there was never much emigration to tropical areas, which were the main object of the new imperialism.

3. *Political and military*. Great Britain could always find an excuse for taking a new colony in her need for coaling stations, seaports, and naval bases. Once Germany began to develop her merchant marine, and later her navy, she could advance similar reasons. With France, the fact that the country was being rapidly outstripped in population by Germany made peculiarly attractive the idea of recruiting dusky soldiers overseas. There was widespread feeling that possession of a colonial empire added to a country's influence and prestige.

4. *Nationalist*. For renewed European imperialism after 1870, there is doubtless some validity in all the reasons advanced under the three headings above. Yet there is also much of the fallacious. Colonies did not form as good markets, sources of food and raw materials, or fields for investment as did independent countries like Russia, Brazil, Argentina, or the United States. Emigration to colonial areas was relatively light after 1870. Colonies were as often political and military liabilities as they were assets.

The real driving force behind the new imperialism came from the rise of intense nationalism. The fact that Britain possessed a great empire led other countries to want one. There was a notable fascination in seeing new areas on the map colored pink or green or blue like the mother country. There was a strong feeling that an advanced and cultured nation had an obligation to spread its language and superior culture to "backward" peoples of the earth. This idea of "civilizing mission" was often mixed up with Christian missionary zeal and activity, or with the humanitarian heritage of the eighteenth-century "Enlightenment."

As the nationalism of the European nations grew more vigorous after 1870, it found outlet, not only in political speeches, military competition, and economic rivalry at home, but also in expansion overseas. National pride was swelled by raising the flag over territories whose names had the day before been unknown to the patriotic masses. National honor could be vindicated by avenging a murdered trader or missionary.

The new imperialism was all a little vague, especially as to facts and figures. But it was a rosy and compelling vision to statesmen and to newspaper readers of Europe in 1890. If liberals still raised voices against imperialist ventures, their laments were now usually drowned out by the swelling chorus of popular patriotic approval.

C. Partition of Africa

In the 1870's, except for a few coastal areas, Africa was still a dark and little known continent. Rich in resources and inhabited mainly by Negro tribes whose primitive weapons were no match for modern rifles and machine guns, it formed a most attractive sphere for the new colonial activity. Strangely enough, however, the scramble to seize and divide Africa was

Leopold II of Belgium.
Courtesy
Bettmann Archive

begun not by the great powers but by the ruler of one of the lesser countries. This was Belgium's King Leopold II (1865–1909), who was a shrewd business man as well as a rather dissolute monarch. He became interested in Africa in a curious way.

In 1840 a Scottish physician and missionary named David Livingstone had gone to Africa. In the ensuing three decades he won fame by his exploring expeditions in the south-central part of the continent and by his discovery of Lake Nyasa and of the upper courses of the Zambesi and Congo rivers. Toward the close of his life, Dr. Livingstone was reported lost in the jungle, and a New York newspaper proprietor capitalized the widespread interest in the missionary's fate by despatching an ad-

venturous Anglo-American journalist, Henry Stanley, to find him. Stanley "found" Livingstone in 1871, and then engaged in a series of important explorations of his own, which he described in thrilling fashion in his book *Through the Dark Continent*. Unable to get backing for his plans in either America or Great Britain, Stanley eventually obtained the ear of King Leopold II of Belgium and aroused his interest in the Congo River region.

Leopold, with much talk of scientific purposes, organized a private commercial company, with himself as president and chief stockholder. Through Stanley and other agents, native Congo chieftains were beguiled into turning over their lands to the company, and the work of exploiting the rubber and other products of the region

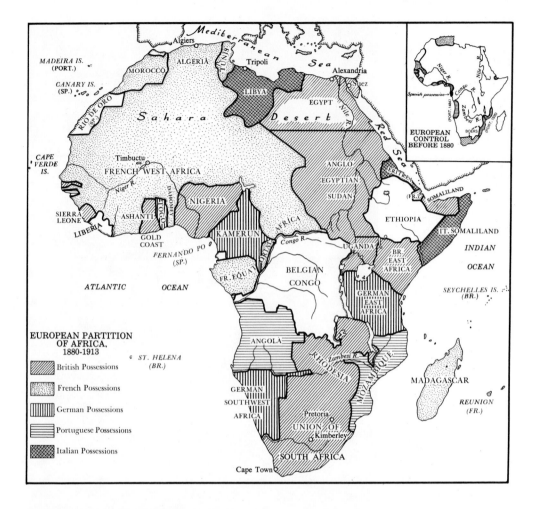

MADEIRA IS. (PORT.)

CANARY IS. (SP.)

CAPE VERDE IS.

SIERRA LEONE

LIBERIA

ATLANTIC OCEAN

EUROPEAN PARTITION OF AFRICA, 1880-1913

○ ST. HELENA (BR.)

British Possessions

French Possessions

German Possessions

Portuguese Possessions

Italian Possessions

Mediterranean Sea

Algiers

MOROCCO   ALGERIA   TUNIS   Tripoli

Sahara   LIBYA   Desert

Alexandria   Suez

RIO DE ORO

Timbuctu

FRENCH WEST AFRICA

Niger R.

ASHANTI

GOLD COAST

FERNANDO PO (SP.)

DAHOMEY

NIGERIA

KAMERUN

FR. EQUA.

EGYPT

ANGLO-EGYPTIAN SUDAN

ERITREA

(FR.) SOMALILAND

ETHIOPIA

IT. SOMALILAND

Congo R.   UGANDA

BR. EAST AFRICA

BELGIAN CONGO

GERMAN EAST AFRICA

PORT. AFRICA

Nile R.

Red Sea

INDIAN OCEAN

SEYCHELLES IS. (BR.)

ANGOLA

RHODESIA

Zambesi R.

MOZAMBIQUE

MADAGASCAR

REUNION (FR.)

GERMAN SOUTHWEST AFRICA

Pretoria

UNION OF Kimberley

SOUTH AFRICA

Cape Town

EUROPEAN CONTROL BEFORE 1880

Niger R.   Nile R.

Spanish possession   Congo R.

(PORT. 1482)   Zambesi R.

BOERS   (PORT. 1505)

by forced labor was begun. Leopold's venture raised some questions among the other powers, and an international congress was convened at Berlin in 1885. It sanctioned the erection of Leopold's African holdings into the "Congo Free State" and laid down a few simple rules to be observed by nations acquiring African territory.

Into the Congo Free State, Leopold poured considerable capital. But he was soon reaping a rich reward. Rubber exports soared in value from $30,000 in 1886 to ten million dollars in 1908. By the latter date, however, there were numerous disclosures of outrages visited upon the natives and of the virtual enslavement of laborers who gathered the rubber. Insistent demands for sweeping reform in the Free State arose both outside and inside Belgium. Leopold yielded to public opinion, and, in return for a handsome financial compensation, transferred the Congo Free State to the Belgian

government. In what was henceforth called the Belgian Congo, Belgium thus acquired a colonial empire with an area almost eighty times her own.

But the Congo was merely a start. In the incredibly brief space of twenty-seven years, beginning in 1885 with the international congress at Berlin and ending in 1912 when Morocco passed finally under Franco-Spanish rule, the whole of Africa (save only Ethiopia and Liberia) was taken over by European countries. By 1914, of the continent's eleven and a half million square miles, the French held almost four million, the British three and three-quarters million, the Germans nine hundred thousand, the Belgians about nine hundred thousand, the Portuguese eight hundred thousand, the Italians six hundred and fifty thousand, and the Spanish a hundred thousand. Liberia remained independent because of the friendly interest in it of the United States;

Ethiopia, because of its defeat of the Italians at Adowa in 1896.

The lion's share in the partition went to Britain and to France, which had already had African holdings before 1880—Britain in the Cape Colony at the extreme south, and France in Algeria at the extreme north and in Senegal on the west coast. But Germany, after Bismarck's reluctant conversion to colonialism, got no mean extent of territory in the competition.

In tropical central Africa, the technique of acquisition was much the same. Selecting a spot, preferably one where his nation had some previous association through missionary or trading activities, the colonizer (soldier, explorer, adventurer, or official government agent) went in among the natives and persuaded their chieftain to affix his mark to a treaty turning over the territory to a European power.

In this manner, Karl Peters, by a dozen treaties secured in ten brief days, acquired for a German company 60,000 square miles in east Africa in 1884. The next year he prevailed upon Bismarck to take the company and its land under the formal protection of the German government, and within five more years, by methods similar to those of Peters, German East Africa was expanded into an imperial domain of 200,000 square miles. In much the same fashion, de Brazza of France snatched the northern part of the Congo basin from Stanley's hands, while German agents north and south of the Congo region were acquiring Kamerun and German Southwest Africa.

When the scramble in equatorial Africa was over by the 1890's, the Germans possessed, on the west side, Togoland in addition to Kamerun and German Southwest Africa; the French owned the French Congo, Dahomey, Senegal, the Ivory Coast, and French Guinea; and the British held Gambia, Sierra Leone, the Gold Coast, and Nigeria. The Portuguese had expanded their coastal trading posts into the extensive territory of Angola south of the Congo Free State, while the Spanish held Rio de Oro opposite the Canary Islands and the tiny Rio Muni in the mid-continent. On the east side of Africa, the Portuguese enlarged their old holdings on the coast to include all of Mozambique. To the north

of this was German East Africa, and still farther north was British East Africa. Thence onward to the Red Sea, Somaliland was divided among the Italians, the British, and the French, while on the Red Sea itself the Italians held the torrid coastland of Eritrea.

The conditions under which northern Africa was partitioned were somewhat different, for along the Mediterranean coast were more or less civilized Moslem countries. One of these, Algeria, had been appropriated by France long before 1870. In 1881 the French statesman Jules Ferry despatched a military expedition from Algeria into the troublesome neighboring state of Tunisia and obliged its Moslem ruler— the bey—to submit to a French protectorate. From Tunisia and Algeria, the French pushed southward, exploring along caravan routes and establishing military posts in the enormous expanse of the Sahara desert and the western Sudan, until at length they linked up their northern African colonies with their equatorial ones like French Congo and the Ivory Coast. Thus most of the great northwest shoulder of Africa came under French control.

Egypt, exploited by foreigners since the time of ancient Greeks and Romans, likewise fell prey to the new imperialism. Under its Turkish ruler, Ismail, who assumed the title of Khedive, Egypt loosened the bonds that previously tied it to the Ottoman Empire and appeared to be progressing toward full independence. But Egypt acquired new significance from the hundred-mile Suez canal which was constructed by a French company, largely financed by the Khedive through loans contracted on exorbitant terms in Europe, and opened by a gala fete in 1869. The British had originally shown slight interest in the canal, imagining it would prove impracticable. Once it was built, however, it provided a short and vital route between England and India. In 1875 Ismail, unable to meet the interest on his loans from Europeans, was desperate for money. He sought relief by selling his large holdings of shares in the Suez Canal Company, and the British government bought them.

Egyptian finances went from bad to worse, and in 1876 Ismail turned them over to a "dual control" of French and British agents. Three years later, when he tried to get rid of the foreigners, he was deposed. His successor had to submit once more to the dual control, but some of his subjects resented it, and in 1882 they revolted.

Though the French, in a momentary reaction against imperialist projects, refused to use force, the British bombarded Alexandria. A British army occupied the country, suppressed the revolt, and restored the Khedive to nominal rule, while imposing on him the duty of doing what the British told him to do. In this manner was established what amounted to a British protectorate over Egypt. The Khedive continued to "reign," but a British army remained and British "advisers" made all important decisions. Some notable reforms were instituted. Finances were put in order, the administration of justice improved, and irrigation works instituted. Moreover, a representative assembly was created in 1883, and in 1913 it was given limited legislative powers.

Up the Nile lay the Egyptian Sudan, which the British practically abandoned in 1885 after a fanatical native leader, "the Mahdi," had annihilated an Egyptian garrison, under a British general, at Khartum. But in 1898, when a French expedition under Captain Marchand proceeded overland all the way from the Congo to the upper Nile valley and at the little village of Fashoda in the Egyptian Sudan hoisted the French flag and claimed the territory for France, Great Britain insisted that the area was in its sphere of influence and sent against Captain Marchand a larger expedition with bigger guns under General Kitchener. The two commanders dealt politely with each other, while they sought instructions from home by telegraph. For a time there was a serious war scare, but eventually the French government withdrew Marchand and his men, and an Anglo-French treaty of 1899 recognized British predominance in the Egyptian Sudan.

D. British-Boer Conflict in South Africa

In South Africa, British expansion involved conflict with white people of European stock—the Boers, descendants of Dutch colonists of the seventeenth and eighteenth centuries. During the Napoleonic wars, Great Britain had taken Cape Colony from Holland. The Dutch farmers resented British rule, and when their Negro slaves were freed by the government in London in 1833, a large number of the Boers quit Cape Colony, "trekking" (emigrating) to Natal, and thence northward to the Orange and Vaal rivers. The British tried to extend their rule wherever the Boers trekked. They annexed Natal in 1843 and five years later claimed the settlements on the Orange and Vaal rivers. But the Boers in the north stubbornly withstood the extension of British rule, and in the early 1850's Britain acknowledged the independence of the Transvaal Republic and the Orange River Free State. Though in 1877 the British tried to reassert their claim to the Transvaal, the Boers defeated a small British force at Majuba Hill (1881). Gladstone, still representing anti-imperialist liberal doctrines, withdrew the British troops and recognized anew the country's virtual independence.

Elated by their success, ignorant of the full power of Britain, fanatical in their devotion to Calvinism, the Boer farmers

Cecil Rhodes. From a bust by Henry Pegram.

became more truculent and even dreamed of expelling the British from all South Africa. But the discovery of diamonds at Kimberley (about 1870) and of gold in the Rand region (1886) brought numerous foreign fortune hunters, most of them British. Among them was Cecil Rhodes, who won enormous wealth in gold and diamond mines and became the outstanding promoter, financier, and statesman of South Africa, and a leading exponent of aggressive British imperialism. In 1889 he organized the British South Africa Company which acquired title to a vast area of unsettled land and began developing this territory, later known as Rhodesia. From 1890 to 1896 Rhodes, as prime minister of Cape Colony, schemed to take over the Dutch republics of Transvaal and the Orange River Free State. He dreamed, too, of extending British sway northward and of building a Cape-to-Cairo railway. He is best remembered in the United States for the endowment he left after his death to bring young American "Rhodes Scholars" to study at Oxford where they might learn to understand Britain and to advance Anglo-American friendship.

By annexing Zululand in 1887, the British shut off the Transvaal from the sea, and in 1895 a certain Dr. Jameson, a friend of Rhodes, responding to complaints of British gold-seekers who were denied citizenship by the Boers, led an armed raid into the Transvaal with the avowed purpose of overthrowing its government. Though the Jameson raid failed of its purpose, it greatly embittered relations between the British and the Transvaal government headed by Paul Krueger, a hardy old Dutch pioneer. At last in 1899 the republics of the Transvaal and the Orange River Free State, in alliance, went to war with Great Britain. At the outset the Boers took the offensive and won some brilliant victories. But though they knew the country as only frontiersmen can and had able generals like Louis Botha and Christian de Wet, they could muster only an ill-equipped and irregularly formed army of 40,000 men or less.

The British, stirred by their defeats, raised volunteers in Britain, Canada, Australia, and New Zealand, and eventually poured an army of 350,000 men into South Africa under the command of Lord Roberts and Lord Kitchener. It was an odd, elusive, bushwacking war, with the Boers retreating into the hinterland only to sweep out on isolated British detachments, and it was long and bitterly fought. Even after Pretoria, the capital of Transvaal, fell, a sort of fierce guerilla warfare ensued for two years. Finally the weight of numbers and equipment told, and in May 1902, by the treaty of Vereeniging, the Boers laid down their arms on condition that the British respect the Dutch language and grant self-government to the former Dutch republics. The British lived up to their pledge.

Despite the lingering hostility of the Boers, a plan for confederation of South Africa won approval and was ratified by the British parliament in 1909. By it, Cape Colony, Natal, Transvaal, and the Orange River Free State were formed into the Union of South Africa, a union modeled after the Dominion of Canada. In a sense the formation of the federation was a triumph for the Boers. They elected a majority of the members of the Union Parliament and one of their number, General Louis Botha, who had fought valiantly against the British, became prime minister and remained in office till his death in 1919. He was succeeded by another Boer, General Smuts, who likewise had fought against Great Britain. Anti-British sentiment did not altogether die among the Boers, and in both the First and Second World War, there was, at the start, serious difficulty in securing South African support for Great Britain.

The Boer War had many repercussions on Britain. The physical examination of volunteers for the army showed the ravages of two generations of slum-living and factory work on the health of the British lower classes and gave a marked impetus to social legislation and town planning designed to remedy conditions. The war provided an opportunity for anti-imperialists to point out the costs, the dangers, and the wastefulness of imperial expansion.

But anti-imperialist criticisms were drowned out by the rising chorus of patriotic enthusiasm. Young newspaper correspondents like Winston Churchill sent back from the battlefields glowing accounts of British bravery, and Rudyard Kipling, who had been telling in prose and verse of the romance and color of British rule in India, turned his attention to South Africa. Newspaper readers were provided a highly flavored and much romanticized version of the glories of imperialist expansion.

E. Imperialism in Asia, the Pacific, and the Caribbean

If the last years of the nineteenth century and the first years of the twentieth witnessed intensive imperialist activity in Africa, other sections of the world were by no means neglected. Germany, Great Britain, and the United States vied with each other in economic penetration of Latin American countries by selling goods and making loans there. The United States in 1898 fought a brief war with Spain over conditions in Cuba. At the end of the conflict, Cuba was given independence qualified by certain American controls, and the United States took possession of Puerto Rico, Guam, and the Philippines. In 1898 Hawaii was likewise annexed, and in 1899–1900 the United States shared with Britain and Germany in the partition of the Samoan Islands.

By 1900 almost all the Pacific Islands had been taken over by European nations or the United States. Britain and France, first in the field, got the majority. But Holland still held the major part of the extensive and very valuable East Indies, and Germany not only secured a portion of New Guinea, and of the islands to the northward, and the two largest islands of the Samoan group, but purchased in 1899 the Caroline Islands from Spain.

On the mainland of Asia, Europeans were also extending their sway. Russia was colonizing Siberia, which had been enlarged by the forced cession from China of all territory north of the Amur river (1858). Britain moved outward from India by taking over Burma and Baluchistan in the 1880's and the Malay States north of Singapore. France added Annam and Tonkin (1884) to Cochin-China and Cambodia, thus creating an extensive Indo-Chinese domain, which was partly a colony and partly a protectorate. But the really

crucial question from the 1890's onwards was whether foreign powers would seize and partition the gigantic and decaying Chinese Empire. Here a new imperialistic competitor entered the scene. It was Japan.

Japan had closed itself off from Europeans (save for a Dutch trading post) from the seventeenth century till 1853–1854, when an American Commodore, Matthew Perry, "opened" Japan and negotiated a treaty permitting American ships to use Japanese harbors. Other nations quickly obtained similar concessions, and Japan experienced an inrush of western influences. In the ensuing decades, Japan underwent a veritable revolution. The emperor (or mikado) was restored to the authority long exercised in his name by "shoguns"; feudalism was ended; western industrialism, education, and militarism were imported and adapted to native traditions. Japanese pride in their race and their history soon found expression in something much akin to western nationalism and imperialism.

Britain had wrested Hong Kong from China in 1842, and other nations had secured special rights in the "treaty ports." But the real despoilment of China was begun by the Japanese. In 1894–1895 Japan waged war on China and by the peace treaty detached Korea from the Chinese Empire (she did not annex it outright till 1910), acquired the large island of Formosa, and obtained Chinese recognition of her rule in Ryukyu islands, including Okinawa. Japan would likewise have taken over the Liaotung peninsula and Port Arthur, had not Russia, backed by France and Germany, intervened. At this point, European countries rushed in to acquire, by lease, control of Chinese port areas. Britain got Weihaiwei; France, Kwangchow; Germany, Kiaochow. Russia, having prevented Japan from taking the Liaotung peninsula and Port Arthur, leased them for herself (1898).

The Chinese Empire, under the weak rule of the Manchu dynasty, was without military power to resist foreign aggression, and pleas of the United States for an "open door" in China for all foreign traders went more or less unheeded. In 1900 a Chinese patriotic anti-foreign society, called the "Boxers," committed outrages on foreigners which led to a joint British-French-German-

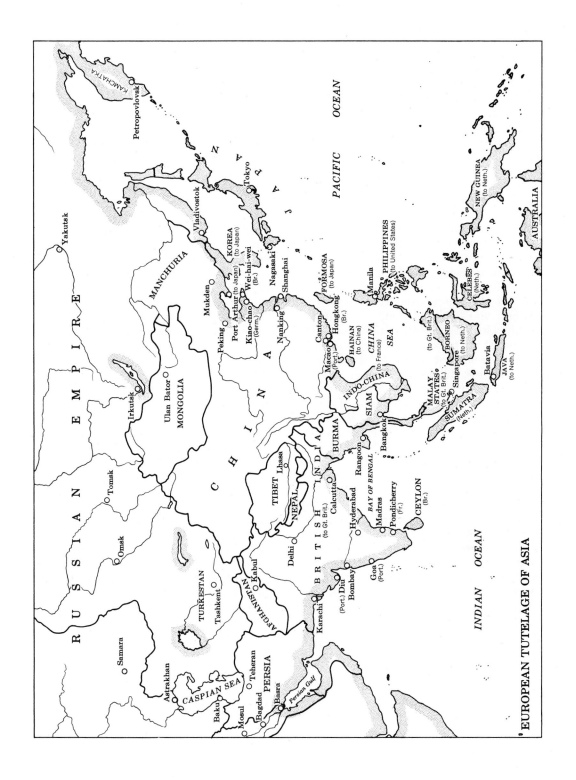

KAMCHATKA

Petropavlovsk

PACIFIC OCEAN

Yakutsk

JAPAN

Tokyo

Vladivostok

KOREA (to Japan)

NEW GUINEA (to Neth.)

AUSTRALIA

R U S S I A N   E M P I R E

MANCHURIA

Mukden

Port Arthur (to Japan)

Wei-hai-wei (Br.)

Kiao-chao (Germ.)

Nagasaki

Shanghai

Nanking

FORMOSA (to Japan)

PHILIPPINES (to United States)

Manila

Irkutsk

Peking

Canton

Hongkong (Br.)

Macao (Port.)

HAINAN (to China)

CHINA SEA

CELEBES (Neth.)

Ulan Bator

MONGOLIA

C H I N A

BORNEO (to Neth.)

Tomsk

INDO-CHINA (to France)

MALAY STATES (to Gt. Brit.)

Singapore (to Gt. Brit.)

Batavia

SUMATRA (Neth.)

JAVA (to Neth.)

TIBET

Lhasa

NEPAL

I N D I A

BURMA

SIAM

Bangkok

Rangoon

Omsk

BAY OF BENGAL

Calcutta

TURKESTAN

Tashkent

AFGHANISTAN

Kabul

Delhi

B R I T I S H   INDIA (to Gt. Brit.)

Hyderabad

Madras

Pondicherry (Fr.)

CEYLON (Br.)

Samara

Astrakhan

CASPIAN SEA

Baku

PERSIA

Teheran

Karachi

Diu (Port.)

Bombay

Goa (Port.)

INDIAN OCEAN

Mosul

Bagdad

Basra

Persian Gulf

EUROPEAN TUTELAGE OF ASIA

American-Russian-Italian-Japanese military expedition that captured Peking and exacted a large indemnity.

After Russia secured Port Arthur, it became clear that she had designs on Manchuria and Korea. This brought her into conflict with Japan. For the ensuing Russo-Japanese War (1904–1905), Japan was well prepared. Her army had been doubled between 1895 and 1904 and its equipment vastly improved. Japan began the war, without any declaration, by a surprise attack on Russian ships at Port Arthur. Russia fought at a serious disadvantage, for her trans-Siberian, single-track railway was not sufficient to handle war traffic and her navy was defeated by the Japanese. The war was marked by Japanese land victories at Port Arthur and Mukden, and by internal troubles in Russia. But Japan was well-nigh exhausted when the conflict was brought to a close through the mediation of the American president, Theodore Roosevelt, in 1905. The treaty of Portsmouth (N. H.) transferred the leased areas of Port Arthur and the Liaotung peninsula from Russia to Japan. Japan likewise re-acquired the southern half of Sakhalin Island, which had been ceded to Russia back in 1875. Russia promised, moreover, not to interfere in Korea or Manchuria.

While such developments were occurring in eastern Asia, the western fringe of the continent also witnessed the clash of imperialist interests. Moving in from the south, Great Britain acquired between 1839 and 1901 a series of protectorates from Aden at the foot of the Red Sea to Kuwait at the head of the Persian Gulf, and sought to extend its influence northward into Persia (Iran). Meanwhile Russia was pressing southward into Persia, intervening in local politics and seeking concessions. Finally in 1907 Russia and Britain agreed to divide up Persia into "spheres of influence." Russia was to have the north, Britain the south, while both could operate in the center.

Everywhere the Europeans went in their imperialistic advances into Africa, Asia, and the Pacific Islands, they carried the blessings and the curses of modern civilization. They brought in new diseases and improved medicines to cure them. They brought the Christian religion and sectarian disputes. They brought in modern industry and the exploitation of workers in factories. They brought improved agriculture and forced labor on plantations. Though the French and the Portuguese treated civilized colored peoples more or less as equals, the British, Americans, and Germans drew a sharp "color line" and were apt to live like exclusive aliens in the midst of native peoples.

But in the balance sheet of imperialism, some things must be entered on the credit side of the ledger. The imperialist powers built roads and canals, ports and railways. They "opened up" many backward and isolated areas. They introduced modern sanitation and medical knowledge. To some degree they succeeded in educating the natives, in implanting some knowledge of Christian ideals, and in instilling such Western ideas as those of democracy and nationalism, which would eventually prove dangerous to the occupying powers.

CHAPTER 52

Revolutionary
Cultural Developments

A. In Science

Science had made dazzling advances in the period between the French Revolution and the middle of the nineteenth century.[1] This progress was accelerated in the years from 1850 to 1914. There were new discoveries of great importance, and every phase of life—health, food, transportation, industry, agriculture, education, philosophy, religion —was increasingly affected by the impact of science. Scientific research became firmly established in universities and as an adjunct of business enterprises. Scientific knowledge (of greater or less accuracy) was spread among the masses by schools, books, lecturers, and newspapers. The physical conditions and the intellectual climate of European life were increasingly shaped by the onward march of science.

For influence on later thought, the most significant scientific development of the period was the idea of evolution and theories as to how it took place as propounded by Alfred Russel Wallace (1823–1913) and Charles Darwin (1809–1882). For Wallace, the theory was to some degree a flash of inspiration. For Darwin, it was the result of careful observation in the South Seas (1831–1836) and suggestions drawn from Lamarck, Lyell, and Malthus's *Essay on Population*. With due credit to Wallace, who had also been reading Malthus, Darwin set forth his new ideas in his chief work, *On the Origin of Species by Means of Natural Selection, or the Preserva-*

[1] See above, pp. 582–586.

tion of Favored Races in the Struggle for Life (1859). Darwin held that the separate species of animals and plants were not the results of special acts of creation, but that they had "evolved" from earlier species by natural processes. Of these processes, "natural selection" was the most important. The argument ran like this. All individuals vary from each other. Certain of these variations will favor the individual's survival in its struggle to live and reproduce. Such favored individuals will survive longer and have more offspring. Thus the advantageous variation will tend to be fixed in the species, and as such variations accumulate a new species will be developed from the old one. The idea of "evolution" was by no means new. But here was a seemingly simple and natural way to explain how it could come about.

On the popular mind, Darwinian biology made a most profound impression. A philosopher like Herbert Spencer tried to shape all history and all thought into a Darwinian pattern. Publicists attempted to apply Darwinism to the evolution of nations and classes and to justify aggressive nations or capitalists as evidencing "survival of the fittest" in a "struggle for existence."

While all this pseudo-Darwinism was being spread about, actual Darwinian biology was undergoing important modifications. The central fact of biological evolution came to be accepted by all reputable scientists, and the discovery of skeletal remains of prehistoric human beings or near-human beings in England, France,

Germany, and far-off Java indicated that man as a physical being was descended from some earlier form of life. But it was demonstrated that "acquired characteristics" could not be inherited, as Lamarck and Darwin had imagined. And an Austrian Augustinian monk, Gregor Mendel, by a series of experiments on sweet-peas in the garden of his monastery, indicated that evolution is more likely to occur by sudden leaps or "mutations" than by gradual change. Clearer understanding was reached of the mechanism of heredity.

If biology made the most impact on the minds of people, it was probably medicine that affected their lives most directly. Before 1870, Lister and Pasteur had laid foundations for antiseptic surgery and the germ theory of disease. In the ensuing decades medical knowledge advanced by leaps and bounds, and medical practice was revolutionized. Pasteur himself developed a method of immunization against rabies. The bacilli of cholera, lockjaw, diphtheria, bubonic plague, and other diseases were isolated. The means of transmission of typhoid fever (polluted water, milk, etc.) and of malaria and yellow fever (mosquitoes) were detected. Innoculations were developed, and preventive measures taken. Along with these advances came others in

Louis Pasteur.

Photograph from Underwood and Underwood, New York

surgery, such as those which made appendectomy a relatively simple and (by the use of anaesthetics) painless operation. Such progress was soon reflected in a falling death rate in all civilized countries. For example, in Germany it dropped from 25.3 per thousand in 1881 to 11.1 in 1930.

In physics and chemistry, progress was no less notable. Hertz discovered the "ether waves" that Marconi presently utilized for wireless telegraphy (1895). Modern radio was made possible through the vacuum tube which grew out of the work of two British scientists, Thomson and Richardson, and was invented by De Forest in the United States (1907). Röntgen discovered X-rays in 1895, while Pierre Curie and his wife Marie isolated radium from pitchblende three years later. Meanwhile other scientists were beginning to open up the field of sub-atomic physics and to show that the atom itself was made up of a nucleus and of electrons. As for chemistry, it was yoked ever more closely to industry. Factories turned out chemical products cheaply and in large quantities. Organic and inorganic compounds were synthesized. One of the most significant achievements was the development, on the eve of World War I, of processes by which nitrogen in the air could be turned on a commercial scale into either munitions or fertilizers.

In the realm of psychology, Wilhelm Wundt, "the father of physiological psychology," indicated in his major book (1872) a physical basis for thought and behavior and a relationship of human minds to those of lower animals. Under his leadership, psychology turned from introspection to observation and from speculation to experiment, and became a laboratory science.

At the end of the nineteenth century, just when it seemed to many persons as if scientific progress might speedily lead to a new synthesis of human thought, which would be strictly materialistic and deterministic, any such outcome was rendered dubious by novel developments in physical science. In the very last year of the century, Max Planck advanced a new notion called the "quantum theory," according to which energy is given off by a vibrating body in little lumps or packets or units (called quanta) and not steadily or with a wavelike

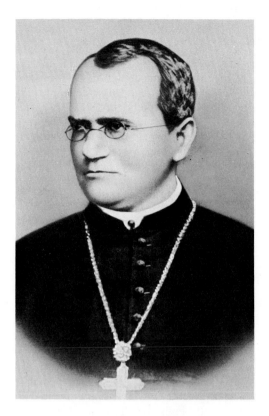

Gregor Mendel (d. 1884).

Courtesy Bettmann Archive

ebb and flow as the older physics had assumed. Planck's work soon received confirmation and extension from a wide variety of sources. Investigations of stellar spectra and of the sun bore out the new ideas and it came to be held that heat and light from the sun and other stars, never satisfactorily explained by the older physics, arose from energy given off by atoms as they changed from one state to another. Work with radium also demonstrated that the old idea of the immutability of elements was not correct. Radium itself is always breaking down into lead, and other elements like uranium undergo similar disintegration. On the eve of the first World War, the "new physics" was already unsettling the minds of scientists and casting doubts on long accepted axioms.

Another shock to nineteenth-century physics came from the Michelson-Morley experiment in 1887. Michelson and Morley, two American scientists, showed that the ether, long assumed to be the medium in which light waves (and later radio waves)

undulated, could not be detected, and therefore could not be held to exist. This conclusion eventually led Albert Einstein to propound his "Special Theory of Relativity" in 1905 and his "General Theory of Relativity" in 1915. According to Einstein, Newtonian physics had been guilty of a kind of scientific provincialism. It had treated motion in space either as relative to our own solar system, or later as relative to a great motionless ocean of ether filling all space. Now that the idea of ether had to be discarded, Einstein worked out ways of stating motion so that the statement would be equally correct for an observer on the Earth, or on Sirius or some other star. These statements involve very elaborate mathematical concepts. They use the velocity of light as an absolute (the same for all observers) and they make time a fourth dimension (in addition to length, breadth, and thickness). Einstein's "Relativity" did not change ordinary measurements on earth, but it did alter astronomical concepts.

While physicists and astronomers were plunging deeper into an un-Newtonian world of electrons, relativity, and space-time, psychology too was undergoing revision. From the time of Hobbes and Locke, man had been regarded as a thoroughly rational animal. The social sciences, like economics, had been built on the notion that man made rational choices and behaved in a logical manner. Now this was changed, partly through the work of Wundt's disciples, who stressed the animal character of man's mental behavior, and partly through the rise of psychiatry and "psychoanalysis." The latter, as practiced by Sigmund Freud, showed that a good deal of human behavior springs from unconscious or subconscious sources—repressed sexual urges, forgotten childhood experiences, suppressed fears and conflicts. Altogether, the newer psychology indicated that man is only a partly rational animal, and that much of his behavior is conditioned not by logical thought but by psychological forces of which he is partly or wholly unaware.

Influenced by these trends, sociologists contended that human groups are just as lacking in rationality as individuals. From such work, together with the development of modern advertising, were derived techniques for influencing mass behavior, which were to be tentatively tried out in World War I and used with appalling effects in the 1930's.

B. In Technology

As science progressed, it produced a continuing and increasing impact on industry. New processes were evolved; new ideas were applied; new products were developed; the total volume of production increased with startling rapidity.

Coal and iron had been the basis of the Industrial Revolution and they remained basic in the swift advance of industrialism. British production of coal grew from 110 million tons in 1870 to 265 million in 1910, and of pig iron from six to nine million tons. But in Germany, output rose in the same period even faster. That of coal increased from 37½ million tons to 222 million, and that of pig iron from two to almost fifteen million tons. By 1910, not only had Britain lost her industrial predominance, but so had Europe, for in that year the United States was producing 415 million tons of coal and more than 27 million tons of pig iron.

The application of the Bessemer and Siemens processes made it easy to produce steel from iron in large quantities and cheaply. Cheap steel made it possible to expand the railroads and to build steamships. By the 1890's, a revolution in ocean transportation had taken place; the sailing ship was being driven from the seas by the faster and more reliable steamship.

Cheap steel also made possible all sorts of machinery, and improved machine tools like the power lathe and the power press made for better and more precise machines. Britain's power looms in the cotton industry increased from 475,000 in 1870 to 700,000 in 1910. But whereas they had constituted far more than half the world total at the former date, they were only thirty per cent of it at the latter. Moreover, a new factor was appearing in the world of textiles. A French nobleman, Count Hilaire de Chardonnet had patented, in 1884, a process for making a fiber resembling silk

from wood pulp. By 1910, some two and a half million pounds of "artificial silk" or "rayon" were being produced, by the Chardonnet process, and a good deal more by the British "viscose" process. And such amounts were merely an augury of the great expansion of the synthetic fiber industry that was to come. Moreover, textiles, old and new, were no longer being dyed by the old natural coloring agents like indigo, but rather by a profusion of new chemical dyes, often derived from coal tar.

Even more revolutionary was a new force which man was beginning to master. Electricity had been known since the eighteenth century, and the principle of the dynamo to generate it had been discovered by Faraday in 1831. But a whole series of developments, inventions, and adaptations were necessary before electricity could be widely used. Electric motors and dynamos were common by the 1890's. Electric lighting, which had begun with the use of the arc light in the 1870's, began rapidly to oust gas jets with the invention of the incandescent bulb by Thomas Edison in 1879. Three years earlier, Alexander Graham Bell had exhibited the first telephone, and before the end of the century telephone lines stretched for thousands of miles through Europe and America. These continents had been linked by a cable in 1866. But communications across oceans were eventually made much easier by the invention of radio or "wireless" in 1895 by Guglielmo Marconi. The uses of electricity seemed endless, for it could be applied to vacuum cleaners, sewing machines, stoves, refrigerators, trolley cars, railways, and industrial machinery. The age of electricity was even symbolized by the substitution in New York in 1888 of electrocution for hanging as the means of executing criminals.

Local transportation was much affected by improvements in the bicycle which gave it a great popularity in the years after 1890. But even more significant was the development of the automobile. After a variety of experiments in the 1880's, practicable automobiles were introduced in the 1890's. At first, France took a lead in producing them, but by 1910, the United States was making 181,000 each year, three fourths of the world output. And already some were Fords, for by that time Henry Ford was introducing the assembly line techniques of mass production that were to make cheap cars possible.

Though some of the early automobiles were powered by steam or electricity, the rapid improvement of the internal combustion gasoline engine soon made it not only the most efficient motive power for cars, but also available for other uses. Motor boats were not uncommon by 1900, and before that date the Count von Zeppelin and the Brazilian Santos-Dumont were experimenting with motor driven dirigible balloons. While "zeppelins" proved practicable, and truly successful flights were being made by 1906, the future lay with heavier-than-air craft. The first airplane flight was in 1903 by a machine constructed by the American brothers Wilbur and Orville Wright. In 1909, the French aviator Blériot flew a monoplane across the English Channel from Calais to Dover. The age of aviation was dawning.

A competitor to the gasoline engine was the internal combustion engine using heavier oil for fuel and fired by compression. It was developed by the German Rudolf Diesel in the 1890's, and was soon applied to ships, locomotives, and the generation of electricity. Another power source for dynamos was the steam turbine. Though the principle of the turbine is as old as the windmill, it remained for Sir Charles Parsons, an English engineer, to adapt it to steam in the 1880's. As turbines were improved they turned out to be much more efficient for many uses than the old Watt-type steam engine.

In other fields, too, innovation proceeded apace and one improvement led to another. For example, from wood pulp or cellulose, "celluloid" was first made in the United States in 1869. From cellulose, artificial silk was produced, as we have seen. From cellulose, too, was made in 1887, by George Eastman, the roll film which dramatically improved and speeded the processes of photography, made the simple camera possible, and permitted the development of the motion picture by Thomas Edison (1891) and others. But even more important, ways of making paper from wood pulp were developed in the 1880's that made it much cheaper than the earlier rag paper. Cheap paper meant cheaper magazines, books, and newspapers. The invention of a machine for setting type, the linotype, by Mergenthaler, a German-born American, in 1885 made it still less expensive to produce printed matter. Similarly the typewriter developed in the 1870's and 1880's made correspondence easier and created not only the new profession of typist, but opened up ever growing possibilities of employment for women.

Not all the new inventions were designed for peaceful purposes. Both the zeppelin and the airplane were capable of military use. Alfred Nobel, a Swedish chemist, intended dynamite for peaceful ends when he introduced it in 1867, but his invention ushered in a new era of high explosives. Sir Hiram Maxim, an American who became a British subject, invented the first truly automatic machine gun in 1884 and later an explosive called cordite. His brother, Hudson Maxim, developed a smokeless powder, and his son, Hiram Percy Maxim, created the Maxim silencer for making firearms noiseless. It was an American, too, John Holland, who in 1875 made the first practical submarine. By 1900, most of the great powers were adding them to their navies.

This incredible series of inventions and technological changes did not consist in a series of isolated events. They tended to be interconnected and one development led to another and the two of them to a third. Automobiles forced the improvement of highways, tremendously stimulated the rubber industry, and greatly expanded oil production and refining. But the improvement of small electric motors made the "self-starter" possible and led to a more rapid increase in automobile production. Or again, steamships made it possible for Great Britain to import much of its food, and, at the same time, shipbuilding became a major industry in Britain.

Taken as a whole, the scientific, industrial, and technological developments in western Europe and the United States from 1870 to 1914 changed the way of living of the peoples concerned much more than they had been changed in the two centuries preceding 1870. They permitted an astounding increase in population. The population of Germany, for example, grew from 40 million to 65 million in the forty years after 1870. They led to rapid enlargement of cities and a relative (and often an absolute) decline in the rural areas. In Germany there were in 1870 eight cities of over 100,000 inhabitants. In 1910 there were forty-one. Moreover, the growing cities were linked together by rapid transportation (trains, ships, automobiles) and by rapid communications (telegraph, cable, telephone, radio). In them dwelt vast masses of people, most of them industrial workers of one sort or another. These new urban masses were better educated than previous generations, for state-supported education was becoming more general and more democratic. But they were also easily influenced by the strident slogans of the new mass media like the cheap newspapers. Europe was rapidly becoming richer and more prosperous. It was also getting to be less stable as the unrooted city-dweller replaced the old-time peasant as the typical European.

C. Materialism in Philosophy and Realism in Literature and Art

Amid the sensational advances of science and industry in the latter half of the nineteenth century, there was a vogue for "materialism" in philosophy and for "realism" in literature and art. Broadly speaking, materialism meant an explanation of everything by reference only to forces detectable by human senses, and a consequent ignoring of spiritual concepts.

Evolutionary thought as applied, not only to the origin of man and animals, but to the geologic features of the earth, the formation of the solar system, and the development of human society and institutions (including law, government, the family, language, and religion), seemed to many persons to provide a satisfactory explanation of how things got to be as they are, without the help of any supernatural Creator. This was apparently reënforced by developments in anthropology, archaeology, and biblical criticism.

Archaeologists uncovered a vast mass of data about primitive and prehistoric man. Anthropologists made elaborate studies of primitive myths and religions and of primitive cultures. Critics subjected the Bible to a searching investigation as a document in the evolution of religion. Some of this "higher criticism" was done in a reverent spirit, but much of it with a feeling of antipathy to revealed religion.

The outstanding philosopher of Darwinian materialism was Herbert Spencer. In 1860 he issued the prospectus of his *Synthetic Philosophy*, an enormous work in ten volumes, upon which he was engaged for the next thirty-six years. In it he applied the principles of evolution to philosophy, psychology, sociology, and ethics. He held that everything, organic and inorganic, had evolved naturally by a progression "from the homogeneous to the heterogeneous," from the undifferentiated to the highly specialized. Behind this evolution Spencer thought there was an unknowable power or cause, but in his work he focussed his attention on knowable combinations of matter and motion. To him society was an evolving organism, religion originated in the worship of ancestral ghosts, and the industrial competition and extreme individualism of the capitalist age was an example of the "struggle for existence."

If trends of the nineteenth century led to materialism in fields of thought, they tended to produce a new "realism" in literature. To be sure, there was much surviving romanticism in all countries. Rudyard Kipling was quite romantic about British imperialism, Robert Louis Stevenson about Scottish history and the South Seas, and Edmond Rostand about French history. But the outstanding movement was toward a realistic treatment of men and society—a realism grimed with factory smoke, sordid with slum-living, and full of toil and sorrow and discouragement. The tendency had been evident in the great English novelists of the mid-century, for, though Dickens, Thackeray, and George Eliot retained romantic elements, they also tried to depict real people, occupied with contemporary problems. If Thackeray often dealt with historical subjects, if George Eliot chose romantic Italy for the setting of some of her books, and if Dickens was frequently sentimental, still Thackeray bitterly satirized the British upper classes, George Eliot put very real country people and poor people in her books, and Dickens exposed the conditions of the working classes with a humor that was sometimes grim.

After the mid-century, realism steadily gained ground. Flaubert in *Madame Bovary* gave an intensely sordid picture of French country life and human passions. Even more consciously realistic was Émile Zola, who in the years after 1871 turned out twenty somber volumes in which he traced the lives of several generations of a French family and sought to portray every phase of French life and society. Anatole France, with a glittering and facile style that won him fame and fortune, mingled witty satires and philosophical and critical works with realistic novels dealing both with contemporary life and historical scenes.

In England, George Meredith employed realism in a psychological analysis of his characters, while Thomas Hardy devoted his talents to studies of the fateful workings of the "struggle for existence" in village and peasant life in the English countryside of "Wessex." Psychological analysis of the upper classes was carried further by Henry James, who was born in America but lived in England, while social criticism reached a high point in the pungent dramas of George Bernard Shaw, published with long expository introductions, and in the fantasies and novels of H. G. Wells.

The Norwegian Ibsen carried realism on the stage to a new peak in his grim dramas. In Germany, Sudermann wrote both dramas and plays about city dwellers, while Hauptmann turned to a realistic presentation of peasant life. In Russia, a whole galaxy of novelists endowed that country with a great literature, much of it terribly realistic in its portrayals of peasants and nobles, officials and intellectuals, and gloomy with an oppressive sense of the social problems that weighed on the country. The greatest of all the Russians was Leo Tolstoy, whose *War and Peace* is an immense and incomparable panorama of Russia at the time of the Napoleonic invasions. In his later life Tolstoy turned to pacifism and a kind of revolutionary, Christian mysticism.

Against the major realistic trend in European letters was a series of reactions or counter trends of some significance. One was toward "symbolism," which sought "not a literal exactness but a suggestive use of words." It was exemplified in France by the poetry of Mallarmé and Verlaine, and in England by the prose of Walter Pater and the verse of Swinburne. Symbolism at length degenerated into "art for art's sake," a conscious decadence, an emphasis on form rather than content, in a school known as that of the *fin de siècle* (end of the century), which reached its zenith in the affectation and the wit of Oscar Wilde.

Painting may have been prevented from going realistic in the same way as literature by the invention of photography. When a camera could reproduce a scene with exactness, pictorial artists, if they were to surpass the machine, had to seek for more than accuracy. The major school of painters of the late nineteenth century was that of the French "impressionists," who sought by a skillful use of light, shade, and color to give a sense of how an object looked at a fleeting instant. Impressionism was akin to symbolism in literature. It sought to suggest the reality more vividly than could classical accuracy of line and brushwork. Among prominent "impressionists" were Édouard Manet, Claude Monet, and Auguste Renoir.

The impressionists were succeeded by "post-impressionists." Among these were Cézanne, who by thick layers of paint, slight distortions, and careful draftsmanship, tried to give greater solidity to his paintings; Gauguin, who fled from Paris to the South Seas and turned out canvases that were a luxuriant riot of tropical colors and dusky-skinned natives; and Vincent Van Gogh, a Dutch pastor's son who, half-insane, painted startling but most effective pictures with great blobs of fierce color often laid on with a palette knife rather than a brush.

The music of the age of realism remained predominantly romantic. Such were the operas of Richard Wagner, with their emphasis on medieval German folk lore; of Verdi, with their patriotic Italian sentiment; and of Saint-Saens and Massenet in France. Romantic, with an emphasis on German and Hungarian nationalism, was the music of Brahms, and likewise the compositions of those who sought inspiration in national

Count Leo Tolstoy. From a portrait painted in 1887 by I. J. Repine.
Courtesy
Bettmann Archive

folk music like the Czech, Dvorak, and the Norwegian, Grieg. Romantic too was the Russian school exemplified by Tschaikovsky. There was, however, some turning away from romantic music. The outstanding innovator was Claude Debussy, who began experimenting impressionistically with unusual scales and the use of dissonances and who paved the way for the "modern" music of the twentieth century.

Of all the arts, architecture was the most confused. Gothic in the best romantic tradition vied with classical temples, Byzantine basilicas, French châteaux, Swiss chalets, and Georgian country homes. Spain, Italy, and even Egypt and Japan supplied architects with more or less unfortunate inspirations. There was a continuing tendency to use classic models (rather freely) for public

buildings—banks, courts, memorials, city halls, post offices, and the like. But private homes were constructed in almost every conceivable style.

Gradually, however, new materials like steel and concrete, and the need of erecting buildings suited to some special purpose—railway stations, grain-elevators, factories—gave rise to the modern tendency toward functionalism, the adaptation of the edifice to its use.

The confusion in architecture reflected the lack of guidance in an age which was losing old faiths and not finding new ones. Science and materialism could change human life, but somehow they could not infuse it with inspiration. Realism sought to depict life as it was, rather than to lead men toward something better.

D. Marxian Socialism to the Fore

In the 1830's and 1840's there had been a series of radical protests against the growing capitalism and advancing industrialism of western Europe. There had been the Utopian socialism of Fourier and Owen, the anarchism of Proudhon, the social workshops of Louis Blanc. To a certain degree opposition to entrenched wealth and power had mingled with the liberal and romantic nationalism of revolutionaries like Mazzini. In the latter half of the nineteenth century, radical protests continued, but on the whole they tended to be swallowed up in Marxian socialism.

Karl Marx (1818–1883) was a native of Trier in Rhenish Prussia and the son of a Jewish lawyer. For revolutionary activities he was forced to leave Germany and spend most of his life in exile in Paris, in Brussels, and after 1849 in London. In 1844 in Paris, Marx met Friedrich Engels, the son of a wealthy German manufacturer. They found their ideas to be much alike and henceforth collaborated closely in writing and other activities. Of the two, Marx was undoubtedly the more intelligent, and his reputation has tended to obscure that of Engels. But it should be remembered that Engels had an incisive mind and shared in the authorship of all Marx's major works.

The first important production of the collaborators was the *Communist Manifesto*, published in the revolutionary year of 1848. It was called "Communist" to distinguish it from the writings of contemporary Utopian socialists. Later, after the Utopians faded out of the picture, Marx and Engels called themselves Socialists. The *Manifesto* was a ringing call to the European laboring class to rise in revolt. It concluded with the summons, "The proletarians have nothing to lose but their chains. They have a world to win. Workingmen of all countries, unite–" Though this document defined the basic position of Marx and Engels, their teachings were later elaborated in other writings, especially in the massive three-volume treatise *Capital*, of which the first volume was published by Marx in 1867, and the others after his death by Engels.

In the socialist movement of the last half of the nineteenth century Marx played a multiple role: 1. He was its scholar. During his long years of exile in London, Marx familiarized himself with the peculiar economic history of England, and concluded from it that as other countries became industrialized they would follow the English pattern. For his philosophic ideas and "dialectic" method, Marx drew heavily on Hegel,[1] but, whereas Hegel had seen spiritual forces as shaping material conditions, Marx believed that material conditions molded spiritual forces. Marx was also indebted for some of his ideas to the British classical economists, especially Ricardo.

2. Marx expounded a new theory of history. It has been variously called "economic determinism," "historical materialism," and the "economic interpretation of history." Marx held that economic factors determined the form and nature of all historical development, whether of law, government, art, literature, religion, or social institutions. Among economic factors, the most important were what Marx called the "relations of production," that is, who owned the means of production (land, factories, and the like), and how they were exploited. Whence resulted a struggle—or series of struggles—between economic classes. For centuries a developing bourgeoisie had struggled against the nobles and the feudal relations of production. At last in the French Revolution, they had pulled down the feudal nobility and created a capitalist society. But no sooner was the bourgeoisie in power than it was confronted with a new struggle against the rising proletariat.

3. Marx was an insistent prophet. From his historical analysis, he argued that, as time went on, big capitalists would absorb smaller ones until at last a stage of monopoly capitalism would be reached in which there would be a very few, but very powerful, bourgeois capitalists. Meanwhile the proletariat of workers would be growing in size, as peasant farmers were forced to become agricultural laborers and as small capitalists lost their shops and became wage workers. At length the proletariat, overwhelming in numbers, disciplined by factory work, and organized by socialist leaders,

---

[1] See above, p. 579.

would rise up in revolution and overthrow the few remaining monopoly capitalists. The struggle would be bitter, for the capitalists would still control government, army, police, courts, churches, schools, and newspapers. But the triumph of the proletariat would be inevitable. In most countries the revolution would be a violent one. In a few democratic nations like Britain, it might possibly be accomplished by ballots, without violence.

Marx thought 1848 might be the year of the great revolution, and, though disappointed in this, he still imagined he would live to see proletarian seizure of power. Once the laborers had overthrown the bourgeoisie, Marx expected that there would be a period of a "dictatorship of the proletariat," during which the victors would forcefully liquidate the institutions of capitalist society and stem any attempts at counter revolution. Then would be ushered in a classless, socialist state, in which all the people would own the means of production and exploit them for the benefit of all. The class struggle would be at an end, for there would be only one class.

4. Marx attempted revolutionary organization. Though he believed that a successful proletarian revolution was inevitable, he felt it could be speeded by an organized party of class-conscious socialists who accepted his interpretation of history and his prophecies. In 1848, Marx had attracted little attention. But as industrialism progressed, he won followers, impressed by his ideas and attracted by their seemingly "scientific" nature. In 1864 Marx helped to found an International Workingmen's Association, usually called the "First International." It was composed of groups from various European nations and the United States, and it held several international congresses. It stressed the international aspect of socialism and denounced religion, militarism, and nationalism as capitalist devices to delude the workers. Though it succeeded in spreading the Marxian teachings, the First International remained small and poor. It was rent by internal dissension, and weakened by national passions aroused in the Franco-Prussian War and by disillusionment with the ensuing failure of the Paris Commune. It was formally dissolved at a meeting of a few faithful assembled at Philadelphia in 1876.

Failure of the "First International" did not mean failure of Marxian socialism. In most European countries, socialist parties were formed and gradually grew. By the end of the 1880's these commanded the loyalty of many workingmen and some bourgeois intellectuals. They were supported (especially in Germany) by affiliated trade unions. They could boast parliamentary representatives, newspapers, and paid propagandists.

In 1889 delegates of socialist parties from different countries met in Paris and formed a new federation, usually termed the "Second International," which maintained a central office and held a series of congresses until the World War of 1914. But the real strength of socialism lay in the growing parties within each country. In Germany, by 1914, the Social Democrats were the largest party, with 110 members in the Reichstag representing four and a quarter million voters. To attain such popularity the Socialists sometimes compromised their principles. Many of them tended to work for reform and social legislation rather than for revolution. Some thought that socialism could best be achieved by democratic processes. Disputes over compromises and tactics led to repeated splits and controversies among the Marxians. In Germany, though the party held together, its right wing tended to follow "revisionist" or "reformist" ideas of Eduard Bernstein, who urged collaboration with bourgeois parties to put through social reforms, advocated the achievement of socialism by ballots, not violence, and even challenged such basic Marxian tenets as the tendency of capital to concentrate in fewer hands.

Though Marxian socialism after 1870 tended to swallow up all other movements of radical protest against industrial capitalism, there were some extreme left-wing trends that broke away from and even opposed Marxism. Prince Peter Kropotkin won some followers to his doctrine of anarchism. More important was the "syndicalist" or "direct-action" movement which emerged in the late 1890's in France, Italy, and Spain and was represented somewhat later by the I.W.W. (International Workers of the World) in the United States. It kept out of politics and devoted itself to the economic and "moral" preparation of the proletariat for a "general strike" which would usher in a social revolution. In Spain syndicalism fused with anarchism to form curious radical offshoots of the main Socialist movement.

Both in its regular and its irregular forms, the Socialism of the late nineteenth century was as thoroughly materialistic as any capitalist counting his profits or any philosopher seeking to explain the universe in terms of matter and motion. It insisted that the effective forces in the world were material. It denounced religion as an opiate with which the bourgeois tried to dope the proletarians. It advocated the use of material means to gain material ends. The classless state of the socialist dreams was a thoroughly materialistic paradise where the ownership of capital by all would give material goods to all.

E. Impact on Christianity

Since the seventeenth century, there had been rising religious skepticism and indifference in western Europe. They were accelerated by the "enlightened" philosophers of the eighteenth century and by the French Revolution. They were temporarily retarded by the evangelical movements (like pietism and Methodism), and by the romantically inspired religious revival after 1815. Then in the late nineteenth century they received powerful new stimuli from the material progress that came with industrialism, and from the materialist philosophy that was associated with the advance of the natural sciences.

By the 1890's large numbers of the middle classes and of intellectuals were quite indifferent in matters of religion. Some of them might still go to church out of habit, or they might stay at home and let their wives and daughters go for them. There was also a growing group distinctly hostile to religion. Some were anti-clericals, who assailed the "reactionary" influence of the clergy, or saw possible political advantage in attacking organized religion. Others, like the Marxian socialists, thought of churches as tools of the capitalists used by them to

keep the workers quiet and orderly. Still others felt that religion consisted of outworn superstitions at variance with, and opposed to, the findings of modern science.

Intellectually, the churches probably lost most ground by opposition of some of their leaders to certain developments of science. The doctrine of evolution, with its insistence on the animal origin of human beings and its denial of the literal accuracy of the story of creation as told in *Genesis*, was opposed by some Catholics and even more strenuously by many Protestants. Similarly, the findings of geologists as to the age and development of the earth were denounced by many churchmen. It was frequently said that "science" and "theology" were at war with each other.

The Catholic Church was confronted in the nineteenth century by political as well as intellectual difficulties. Pope Pius IX (1846–1878), despite his early liberalism, was driven into a conservative position by his experiences with the revolutions of 1848–1849. While he strengthened the church by concordats with Catholic countries and by reëstablishing Catholic hierarchies in England and Holland, he issued a series of documents against liberalism which culminated in a famous encyclical, *Quanta Cura*, and an accompanying *Syllabus of Errors* (1864).

In the encyclical, Pius IX condemned modern liberal ideas of extreme individualism and the supremacy of the secular state over the church, and lauded the earlier ideal of the "Christian state." The *Syllabus* listed in abbreviated form "the principal errors of our time" which had latterly received papal condemnation. The "errors" included those of freethinkers and agnostics who denied or doubted the divine origin and mission of the church; those of materialists who repudiated the spiritual or subordinated it to the physical or temporal; those of anti-clericals and nationalists who sought to restrict the church and exalt the lay state; those of the liberals and the indifferent who thought one religion as good as another, held that the church should be a private, voluntary association, and imagined that the pope should reconcile himself to "modern civilization."

In 1869, while discussion of the *Syllabus* was still heated, Piux IX convened a general council of the Catholic Church, the first such council since that of Trent three centuries before. The Vatican Council, attended by nearly eight hundred prelates from all over the world, reaffirmed and deepened the traditional teaching of the church on the relationship between faith and reason. But its most striking achievement was the definition in July 1870, despite earnest preliminary opposition from a minority of its members, of the dogma of papal infallibility. It was solemnly proclaimed, as a "dogma divinely revealed," that the pope is infallible when he speaks *ex cathedra,* that is officially as the "pastor and doctor of all Christians," regarding faith or morals. The dogma was denounced by Protestants, liberals, agnostics, and nationalists, and was utilized for anti-clerical campaigns in France, Italy, and Spain, and in the *Kulturkampf* in Germany. And simultaneously the Italian government forcefully seized Rome from the Pope.

The successor of Pius IX was Leo XIII (1878–1903), who was a first-rate scholar and a sympathizer with democracy and social reform. In the intellectual sphere, while he stood firm for the historic dogmas of Catholic Christianity, he promoted the renewed study of the writings of St. Thomas Aquinas, who had taught that science and religion could not be in basic conflict since truth is one. In political matters, Leo XIII continued to condemn the "errors" denounced by Pius IX and to insist on the "right" of the church to a privileged position in the state and in education. At the same time he encouraged the formation of popular and democratic Catholic parties in Belgium, Austria, and Germany, advised French Catholics to support the Third Republic, and expressed admiration for the constitution of the United States.

In social and economic problems, Leo XIII showed keen interest. He encouraged the development of a Catholic "social" movement which sought to combat both economic liberalism and Marxian socialism and to christianize industrial society. To this movement which had been gathering headway, especially in France and Germany since the 1870's, Leo XIII in 1891 gave a guiding charter in a famous encyclical, *Rerum Novarum.* Against the Marxians, this document defended private property as a natural right and the family as the cornerstone of society. It condemned the exaltation of the state, economic determinism, and the doctrine of the class struggle. Against the economic liberals, it held that labor is not a commodity and that the state should prevent exploitation of workers, encourage collective bargaining, and enact social legislation. Specifically the encyclical urged the wider distribution of private property, the fostering of trade unions and cooperatives, the restriction of labor by women and children, and the assurance of a "living family wage."

If the Catholic Church was weakened under Leo XIII and his successor, Pius X (1903–1914), by anti-clerical legislation in traditionally Catholic lands like France, Spain, Portugal, and Latin America, and by continued strife with the Italian state, it was strengthened by the growth of Catholicism in traditionally Protestant countries like England, Holland, Canada, Australia, and the United States. Pius X was faced with a special problem in the rise of "modernism" within the church. Its advocates sought to modify Catholic teaching so as to bring it into line with what they regarded as the findings of science and of the "higher criticism" of the Bible. Though "modernism" proved troublesome, Pius X stood firm against it, excommunicated some of its outstanding leaders, and reaffirmed the traditional position of the church. It thus ceased to be a significant movement in Catholic Christianity at the very time when it was becoming influential in Protestant churches.

The first reaction of most Protestants to "Darwinism" and the "higher criticism" was, generally speaking, one of hostility. But shortly, as materialism progressed and the new science was popularized, they produced more complex reactions, so that by about 1900 three distinct movements were obvious in nearly all Protestant churches.

First, a minority of Protestants, including a relatively large proportion of intellectuals, moved toward an agnostic position. Unable to square the Bible with science, they threw over the former. Some of them sought refuge in "ethical culture," "unitarianism," or in a vague pantheism.

Second, at the opposite extreme, large

numbers of devout Protestants, relatively more numerous among the masses and in agricultural areas, were impelled to take a *fundamentalist* position. Holding the Bible to be literally inspired, they denounced any scientific explanation which contradicted or questioned their own traditional interpretation of that sacred book.

Third, a gradually growing number of Protestants became *modernist,* that is, they remained Protestant Christians in name and in actual church membership, but they tended to neglect church creeds and dogmas and the Bible itself, and to emphasize the beauty of Christianity and its ethical teachings as a guide to moral conduct. Innumerable as were the shades of modernism within the Protestant churches, they were almost all marked by an evolutionary attitude toward religion in general and Christianity in particular. Such an attitude marked a sharp reversal in the traditional Protestant habit of seeking pure religion by a return to primitive Christianity and a dependence on the authority of the Bible. It also involved a sharp reversal in the original Protestant emphasis on faith as against "good works." As the faith of Protestants in creeds and dogmas declined, they threw themselves with increasing vigor into good works of all sorts. They worked for social reform, foreign missions, popular education, public health, organized recreation, and against alcoholism, political corruption, and juvenile delinquency. Many churches became social centers of recreation and organized charity. Special Protestant organizations were developed such as Young Men's Christian Association, Salvation Army, etc.

Neither among the Protestants nor among the Catholics was there any unified reaction to the age of materialism. Religion appeared to be on the defensive, in a world that was responding more and more to nonreligious stimuli. For the first time in more than fifteen hundred years, Western European civilization seemed to be ignoring the Christian heritage to which it had been born and in which it had been nurtured.

Yet in one respect historic Christianity was not on the defensive in the decades that followed 1870. Both Catholics and Protestants engaged in a greatly expanded missionary effort that affected almost every part of the world. Using both institutions founded in earlier periods, the Congregation of the Propaganda (1622), the Society for the Propagation of the Faith (1822), the Society of Foreign Missions at Paris (1658), together with the old orders (Jesuits, Franciscans, Dominicans) and new societies like the White Fathers established in France (1868) for work in Africa, the Catholic Church developed a missionary enterprise of very considerable proportions. By 1910, some 41,000 persons were working in Catholic missions in Africa, Asia, and Oceania. Nor was this mission work without significant effects. Though except in the Philippines there had been relatively few Catholics outside of America and Europe in the middle of the century, it was estimated that in 1900 there were two and a quarter million in India, more than a million in China, two and a half million in Africa, sixty thousand in Korea, and a like number in Japan.

Before 1790 there had been relatively little Protestant missionary activity among non-European peoples. But in the next decade missionary societies were formed in England by the Baptists, by the Presbyterians and Congregationalists, and by the Anglicans. The movement spread to the United States, and before the middle of the nineteenth century there were numerous Protestant missionary groups competing with each other and with the Catholics in an effort to evangelize the people of the non-European world. The scope of this effort expanded greatly in the last decades of the century as new lands were explored and opened up. In 1910, there were some 18,000 active Protestant missionaries, and by this time some form of Protestantism was the religion of a million and a half people in India, two and a half million in Africa, a quarter of a million in China, and eighty thousand in Japan.

Both Catholics and Protestants also paid some attention to "home missions." Devoted priests and ministers tried to bring religion into the lives of the industrial workers in the city slums. They set up chapels and settlement houses and sought to give guidance and comfort to those who were crushed and oppressed by the changing society of the western world.

Lloyd George.

Photograph from Underwood & Underwood, New York

CHAPTER 53

Peace Movement and Spasmodic Violence

AT THE TURN OF THE CENTURY

A. Progress of Democratic Social Reform, Particularly in Britain

The twentieth century opened with general optimism. Peace reigned among major European countries. The progress of industry and agriculture seemed to be ushering in a new period of abundance. Science was conquering disease. Democracy was advancing. Social reforms were being accomplished by legislation. Prophets of war and revolution seemed like pessimists left over from another and less enlightened era. Was not the eighteenth-century dream of peaceful and rapid progress at last being realized?

Great Britain still led the way in economic and political life. London was the economic heart of the world from which radiated the arteries of commerce and finance. In British politics, significant changes were taking place. Marxian socialism had never won much of a place in British life, though it had inspired the formation of a small "Social Democratic Federation" in 1881. More important were the "Fabian" Socialists, a group of intellectuals, including Shaw and Wells, who preached socialization by gradual reform. Still more important was the steady growth of the trade union movement, which before 1890 had been confined mainly to the skilled trades, but afterwards came to include a large proportion of unskilled labor as well. In 1892 there had been 1,500,000 trade-union members in Great Britain. Twenty-one years later there were over 4,000,000.

In 1893 Keir Hardie, a Scottish miner, had tried to take the trade unionists into politics by forming an "Independent Labor Party." But it made little progress before 1901, when the House of Lords, acting as the supreme court of law, decided (in the so-called Taff Vale decision) that a trade union was legally liable for damages arising from any strike conducted by its members. Almost at once, the trade unions, Independent Labor Party, the Social Democratic Federation, and the Fabian Society formed a coalition known as the Labor Party, which in 1906 elected twenty-nine members of parliament and in 1910 forty-two members. A new force thus arose in British politics, a force which pushed the older parties, especially the Liberals, into sponsoring vigorous measures for social reform.

The Conservative Party, long in power, found itself by 1906 seriously divided over imperialism and tariff protection, and compromised by the Taff Vale decision. In the elections of that year, it campaigned for the imposition of tariffs so that preferential treatment could be granted the colonies, while the Liberals fought back with their old slogan of a "free breakfast table" (no tariffs on food) and a promise to repeal the Taff Vale decision by legislation. The Liberals won a resounding victory, which brought them to power and kept them there for a decade. Between 1906 and 1914 they put through a series of significant acts.

In aid of trade unions, the Liberals reversed the Taff Vale decision by the Trade

Disputes Act of 1906, authorized payment of salaries to members of the House of Commons in 1911 so that poor unionists could afford to sit there, and in 1913 strengthened the Labor Party by allowing the use of union funds in elections. A Workmen's Compensation Act extended the principle of the employer's liability for injuries to his laborers. A Labor Exchange Act set up free, public employment bureaus. A Trade Boards Act arranged for the fixing of minimum wages in "sweated industries." In 1912 minimum wage legislation was enacted for the benefit of coal miners. Meanwhile, a series of laws was passed for the benefit of children, old people, and the health of the public. One act enabled local school boards to give free lunches to under-nourished school children. Another sought to improve many phases of the life of children by providing free medical attention, better recreational facilities, and special treatment for juvenile delinquents. An Old Age Pensions Act set up a system of relief for aged persons. A Housing and Town Planning Act aimed at eliminating slums. Capping the whole series of social enactments, a National Insurance Act (1912) provided health insurance for most workers and unemployment insurance for many.

Taken as a whole, this legislation marked an important step towards the socializing of Britain. Opposition to it grew into a fierce controversy over the "Lloyd George Budget" of 1909. Lloyd George, a gifted Welshman, had long been interested in land reform and social legislation. As Chancellor of the Exchequer in the Liberal cabinet, he decided to kill a number of birds with one stone by submitting to Parliament a frankly radical budget, proposing a steeply graduated income tax, a heavy inheritance tax, a tax on unused land designed to break up great estates, and special taxes on motor cars and other luxuries. With the revenues thus to be secured chiefly from the wealthy, Lloyd George planned to finance the Liberal program of social legislation.

By a party vote, the House of Commons passed the 1909 budget. But the Conservative majority in the House of Lords rejected it, despite the long tradition against interference by the upper house with finance bills. Each side said that the other was trying to overthrow the British constitution, and the ensuing elections in 1910 were hotly fought. The Liberals lost ground, but with the aid of Labor allies and the Irish (to whom they promised "home rule") they retained control of the Commons. With minor modifications, the Lloyd George budget was passed again, and this time the Lords did not venture to reject it.

But the fight over the budget led to another fight of a constitutional nature over the House of Lords. The Liberals put through the House of Commons a bill drastically limiting the powers of the upper house. It was rejected by the Lords, and new elections were held in December 1910. The results were about the same as before, with the consequence that the Lords finally gave way and consented to the enactment of the "Parliament Act." This provided: (1) that finance bills passed by the Commons would become law without the approval of the Lords; (2) that other public bills would become law even though rejected by the Lords, if they were passed by the Commons in three successive sessions with at least two years elapsing between the first and the third passage; (3) that general elections for the Commons would be held at least every five (instead of every seven) years. Thus the House of Lords was left with only a suspensive veto over most bills and no veto at all on financial measures. The democratic House of Commons was supreme.

The British reforms were more or less duplicated in other major European countries. Between 1900 and 1914 the movement toward democracy registered important victories. Universal manhood suffrage was established in Austria, Sweden, and Italy. Portugal became a republic in 1910, and even Russia, after 1905, was toying with liberal constitutional reforms.

There was also widespread pressure for social legislation on the part of both Socialist and Catholic parties and of the growing trade union movement. The growth of unionism was indeed an outstanding feature of the period. In Germany the number of union members rose from about 350,000 in 1891 to over 3,000,000 in 1913, and in France it increased from 150,000 in 1904 to 400,000 in 1912. The social legislation

Industry. By Preston Dickinson.

Courtesy Whitney Museum of Fine Arts, New York

of the period followed the pattern set in the 1880's in Germany and after 1905 in Great Britain. Almost every industrial country enacted some scheme for insuring workers against sickness, accidents, death, old age, and unemployment. Trade unions were completely legalized, their funds protected, the right to strike recognized, and collective bargaining encouraged. Education for children was made free and compulsory in most countries, and many enactments were designed to protect women and children. Public health was the aim of measures on housing, sanitation, water supply, medical service, and the purity of food and drugs.

The optimists in 1913 could point with

enthusiasm to the progress made in recent years. It seemed as if Europe was adjusting itself to the new industrialism. It was eliminating the ills of urban life and many of the hardships and uncertainties that had faced factory workers. It was spreading ever more widely the benefits derived from increased production and from modern science. It was doing all these things, moreover, through democratic means, through legislation passed by parliaments ever more responsive to the popular will.

B. General Material Progress

Between 1890 and 1910 world production of pig iron increased from 27,500,000 metric tons to 66,250,000. Of this latter figure Britain produced a little less than a sixth, Germany a good deal more than a fifth, France about a sixteenth, and the United States considerably more than a third. In coal production in 1913, though Britain still led Europe with almost 300,000,000 metric tons, its total output was less than half of that of the United States. But in merchant shipping and commerce, Britain still triumphantly led all the world. In 1914 over 44 per cent of the steamships of the world were British. Germany came second with 11 per cent. No other country had more than 4.6 per cent. World trade (in contemporary dollars) had risen from 14.8 billion in 1880 and 20.1 billion in 1900 to 40.4 billion in 1913. Of this, 17 per cent was British, 15 per cent American, 12 per cent German, and 7 per cent French.

In Britain the number of cotton spindles increased from 36,700,000 in 1870 to 53,500,000 in 1910, and the number of power looms from 475,000 to 700,000 in the same period. But whereas in 1870 Britain had dominated cotton textile production, by 1910 only about 40 per cent of the spindles and 30 per cent of the looms were hers. Most of the rest were distributed among the United States, Germany, France, Italy, Russia, Austria, Spain, India, and Japan. In 1885 British foreign investments had totaled £1,302,000,000. In 1913 they amounted to £3,763,000,000 and represented, it was estimated, a quarter of Brit-

ain's national wealth. But France had become a major lender, too, and her investments abroad in 1913 amounted to almost half as much as those of Great Britain. Germany, Switzerland, and Holland were now lenders also, although their foreign investments together were not as large as those of France.

Such figures as the foregoing indicate a number of things. (1) World production and trade were growing very rapidly. (2) Britain's share, while still most impressive, was becoming proportionately less, as Germany, France, and the United States increased their portions. (3) World industry and commerce had so developed that the whole earth was bound together by the buying, selling, and transportation of goods. National self-sufficiency was gone. Each country depended more or less on its neighbors and on distant lands, not only for food or raw materials or manufactured goods, but also for markets in which to sell its own products.

This dependence was less marked in the case of great continental powers like Russia or the United States. It was more marked in the case of Germany, and most in the case of Great Britain. Britain paid for her imports of food and raw materials by exports of manufactures, by sale of shipping, banking, and insurance services, and by income from investments abroad.

The progress of science, industry and the arts was periodically put on show in great World Fairs, or International Exhibitions. The first notable exhibition of the sort had been that in London in 1851, when crowds came to admire a "Crystal Palace" of glass and iron. But it had been surpassed by the Paris fairs of 1878 (for which the Trocadero Palace had been built) and of 1889 (at which the great spidery Eiffel Tower had been the object of much attention). Dozens of other exhibitions, including those at Philadelphia (1876), Sydney (1881), Amsterdam (1883), Chicago (1893), Bucharest (1894), and Berlin (1896), gave the various nations a chance to vie with each other in displays of manufactured goods, agricultural products, artistic handicrafts, and exotic wares from overseas, while African villages, Japanese pagodas, artificial lagoons, wild animals, and scores of other attractions were designed to lure visitors in hordes. The fairs continued into the twentieth century (Buffalo 1901, St. Louis 1904, Liége 1905, Milan 1906, Dublin 1907, London 1908, Seattle 1909, etc.), though it seemed that the Paris Exhibition of 1900 was almost unsurpassable. It occupied 549 acres, had 211 pavilions, attracted almost forty million paying visitors, and cost more than 200 million francs. At it almost every civilized nation and a great many of the colonies put on exhibits designed to sell goods or to indicate the development of the arts and sciences.

The world fairs somehow symbolized the interdependence of the nations of the earth, their willingness to coöperate, and their general spirit of optimism. There seemed indeed ample reason to look forward to the future with hope and confidence. Science was opening up new vistas; medicine was prolonging human life; industry was providing ever-increasing wealth and giving the lie to the Marxists who insisted that the lot of the workingman would ever grow worse. Education was more general; democracy and parliamentary government were coming to seem the norm; order, law, and justice were more and more characteristic of the European and Western world. It seemed reasonable for men, in 1910, to believe that those trends which had been evident since 1815 and increasingly clear since 1870 would continue indefinitely into the future. It was not only possible, but easy, to envision a world where poverty and disease had been conquered, where educated voters elected wise and just men

The Eiffel Tower. Maurice Utrillo (d. 1955).

to rule them, and where the various nations worked together peacefully for the benefit of all mankind.

C. The Peace Movement

The very interdependence of the nations of the world in industry, trade, and finance convinced many persons that there would never be another major war. This was re-enforced by movements deliberately designed to maintain world peace and increase world coöperation. The idea of a Concert of Europe in which the Great Powers would act together, did not die with Metternich. All the major nations were represented at the Congress of Paris (1856) which ended the Crimean War, at the Congress of Berlin (1878) which readjusted the Balkan situation, and at another Congress of Berlin (1884–1885) which laid down rules for the opening up of Africa. The great powers of Europe at a Congress in Brussels agreed in 1890 to end the traffic in arms and liquor with African natives. They acted together with Japan and the United States to end the Boxer disturbances in China in 1900. Paralleling this European coöperation were periodic Pan-American conferences at which all American nations amicably discussed matters of common interest.

Peaceful international coöperation was becoming the rule in many matters. In 1864, for humanitarian purposes, a congress at Geneva set up an international Red Cross society, which soon had branches in almost every country. Most nations joined a Telegraph Union (1875) and a Postal Union (1878), and many agreed to standardized patent laws (1883) and uniform copyright laws (1887).

As early as 1816 a peace society had been founded in England, another was instituted at Geneva in 1828, and a third at Paris in 1841. Thenceforth, and especially after 1878, associations of professed pacifists multiplied throughout the Western world, until in 1914 there were some 160 of them with numerous branches and many members. International congresses of pacifists were held, and a permanent peace headquarters maintained at Berne. To the peace movement, several great industrialists made notable contributions. For example, the Swedish Alfred Nobel willed the major part of the princely fortune he amassed from the manufacture of dynamite and other high explosives, to establish prizes for those who forwarded the cause of international peace as well as for those who promoted science and literature. Likewise, Andrew Carnegie, a Scottish-American steel magnate, established and heavily endowed a special peace "foundation" and built a "temple of peace" at the Hague.

In 1899 the Tsar Nicholas II, eager to cut down the military burden on his budget and to increase Russia's international prestige, convoked an international peace conference at the Hague to try to reach some agreement for a reduction of armaments. Twenty-six sovereign nations of Europe, Asia, and the Americas were represented. It proved impossible, because of mutual suspicion and jealousies, to agree on any general limitation of arms. But steps were taken to restrict the use of certain weapons in war, to codify international law with regard to war, and to establish at the Hague an international court of arbitration to which the nations might submit their quarrels.

In 1907, prompted by the American President, Theodore Roosevelt, Nicholas II summoned a second peace conference at the Hague. This time, forty-four governments were represented. Again it proved impossible to establish a general limitation of armaments, but humane amendments were added to the "laws" of land and sea warfare, an international prize court was provided for, and conventions were adopted requiring that wars be begun by formal declarations and restricting the use of force in the collection of foreign debts. It was recommended that similar conferences be held at regular intervals in the future.

D. Unsettling Domestic Violence

If, in the decade before World War I, peace and democracy seemed to be in the ascendant, there were signs of impending difficulties. Liberal democrats had held that education and democracy would raise the tone and dignity of politics, that calm de-

King Cophetua and the Beggar-Maid. A 1908 cartoon from *Punch* on Prime-Minister Asquith's lukewarm attitude toward woman suffrage.

bate would be the method of solving disputes, and that the masses, once they were literate, would respond soberly to reasonable arguments. But even in liberal Britain there were signs of stress and strain and ominous notes of violence.

There was serious trouble, for example, in Ireland. Irish nationalists had been much disappointed at Gladstone's failures to put through a home rule act. One of them, who was convinced by these failures that new tactics were necessary, was Arthur Griffith, who, in his newspaper, the *United Irishman*, established in 1899, advocated cultural, economic, and political independence for Ireland. In 1906 a new party was formed under Griffith's leadership. It took the Gaelic name of *Sinn Fein* ("we ourselves").

Meanwhile the bulk of the Irish nationalists continued to work for home rule by parliamentary means under the leadership of John Redmond. They were able to secure some local self-government for Ireland (1898) and two important land purchase acts (1896, 1903) designed to provide the Irish peasantry with farms. But more they could not get, until the Liberals, after the 1910 elections, found themselves in need of Irish votes. The Irish supported the Lloyd George budget and the Parliament Act. In return, Asquith, the Liberal prime minister, put through the House of Commons an Irish Home Rule bill in 1912. It was rejected by the House of Lords, passed again by the Commons (1913), and again turned down by the Lords. One more passage by the Commons in 1914 and it would become law, despite the upper house.

In Ireland itself, while the Sinn Fein group denounced the Home Rule Bill of 1912 as a weak compromise, Ulster Protestants, under the militant leadership of Edward Carson, swore by a "solemn covenant" to resist the Catholic majority and never to submit to an Irish parliament; and they raised a volunteer army of 100,000 men. In response, Sinn Feiners joined with other Irish nationalists to form a force of "Irish Volunteers." By 1914, violent clashes were occurring and civil war seemed near at hand—so near that Germans thought Britain was immobilized by the threat. But when foreign war actually came, Redmond and his Irish followers rallied to the British cause. The Home Rule bill was passed again and made law, but its execution was suspended for the duration of the war.

On the continent, most of the violence came from extreme radicals, from the left wing of the labor movement, and from Balkan nationalists. Between 1890 and 1914, anarchists assassinated several prominent political figures, including King Humbert of Italy (1900), the Empress Elizabeth of Austria (1898), President Carnot of France (1894), President McKinley of the United States (1901), King Charles I of Portugal (1908), and a number of Russian officials and grand-dukes. The support of anarchism waned somewhat after 1900, but syndicalists with doctrines which glorified violence, or "direct action," took their place. Under syndicalist influence, a great railway strike was organized in France (1909). It was stopped only when the premier, the former socialist Aristide Briand, mobilized part of the army and thus put many of the strikers in uniform and under military discipline.

In the name of nationalism, much violence was done. Nationalistic Russians murdered Jews and oppressed subject peoples like the Poles or the Finns. Pan-German Prussians tried to suppress Polish political activities by force. Turks massacred Armenians and other Christians. Serbs, Bulgarians, Greeks, and Rumanians resorted to strong-arm methods in Macedonia and elsewhere to further their nationalistic aims. Others who did not so often employ violence urged war or revolution. There were Frenchmen who dreamed of a "revenge" war to recover Alsace-Lorraine, Italians who hoped to fight Austria to win *Italia irredenta* ("unredeemed Italy," areas inhabited by Italians but still under Austrian rule), Serbs who cast covetous eyes on Bosnia and Herzegovina, Czechs and Poles who longed to oust their foreign rulers. Left-wing Socialists all over Europe worked for a revolution that would redden the streets with bourgeois blood.

Outwardly Europe appeared calm, peaceful, progressive. But within, to those aware of forces at work, it seemed a seething mass of class and nationalist discontent, ready to boil over into turmoil and chaos.

Émile Zola. Aubrey Beardsley (d. 1898).

SELECT SUPPLEMENTARY READINGS FOR PART X

General. C. J. H. Hayes, *Political and Cultural History of Modern Europe*, vol. II (1939); S. B. Clough and C. W. Cole, *Economic History of Europe* (1952); R. C. Binkley, *Realism and Nationalism, 1852–1871* (1935); C. J. H. Hayes, *A Generation of Materialism, 1871–1900* (1941); *New Cambridge Modern History*, vol. XII (1960).

Chapter 49. James Bryce, *Modern Democracies*, 2 vols. (1921); J. W. Derry, *A Short History of Nineteenth-Century England* (1963); B. Tuchman, *The Proud Tower* (1966); R. C. K. Ensor, *England, 1870–1914* (1936); Esme Wingfield-Stratford, *The Victorian Sunset* (1932); Anthony Wood, *Nineteenth Century Britain, 1815–1914* (1960); G. M. Young, *Victorian England* (1936); S. Nowell-Smith, ed., *Edwardian England, 1901–1914* (1964); C. Petrie, *The Victorians* (1961); E. R. Norman, *The Catholic Church and Ireland in the Age of Rebellion (1859–1873)* (1965); G. Slater, *The Growth of Modern England* (1939); J. P. Mackintosh, *The British Cabinet* (1962); J. C. Carr and W. Taplin, *History of the British Steel Industry* (1962); A. M. McBriar, *Fabian Socialism and English Politics, 1884–1918* (1962); M. Cole, *The Story of Fabian Socialism* (1961); J. H. Clapham, *The Economic Development of France and Germany* (1936); G. Wright, *France in Modern Times: 1760 to the Present* (1960); D. W. Brogan, *France Under the Republic, 1870–1939* (1940); S. B. Clough, *France, a History of National Economics, 1789–1939* (1939); R. E. Cameron, *France and the Economic Development of Europe, 1800–1914* (1961); R. H. Soltau, *French Parties and Politics, 1871–1921* (1922); Benedetto Croce, *A History of Italy, 1871–1914* (1929); R. Albrecht-Carrié, *Italy from Napoleon to Mussolini* (1950); W. H. Dawson, *The German Empire, 1867–1914*, 2 vols. (1919); E. Eyck, *Bismarck and the German Empire* (1950).

Chapter 50. M. Karpovich, *Imperial Russia, 1801–1907* (1932); S. Pushkarev, *The Emergence of Modern Russia, 1801–1917* (1963); J. D. Clarkson, *A History of Russia* (1961); G. T. Robinson, *Rural Russia Under the Old Regime* (1932); G. Fischer, *Russian Liberalism* (1958); H. Seton-Watson, *The Decline of Imperial Russia, 1855–1914* (1952); T. H. von Laue, *Sergei Witte and the Industrialization of Russia* (1963); S. Harcave, *First Blood: the Russian Revolution of 1905* (1964); R. A. Pierce, *Russian Central Asia, 1867–1917: a Study in Colonial Rule* (1960); H. W. Steed, *Hapsburg Monarchy* (1919); J. Redlich, *Emperor Francis Joseph of Austria* (1929); Oscar Jaszi, *Dissolution of the Hapsburg Monarchy* (1929); R. Kann, *The Multinational Empire: Nationalism and National Reform in the Hapsburg Monarchy, 1848–1918*, 2 vols. (1950); P. G. J. Pulzer, *The Rise of Political Anti-Semitism in Germany and Austria* (1964); A. J. May, *The Hapsburg Monarchy, 1867–1914* (1951); C. A. Macartney, *Hungary: a Short History* (1962); Ferdinand Schevill, *History of the Balkan Peninsula* (rev. ed., 1933); C. and B. Jelavich, eds., *The Balkans in Transition* (1963); D. C. Blaisdell, *European Financial Control in the Ottoman Empire* (1929); E. E. Ramsaur, Jr., *The Young Turks* (1947).

Chapter 51. W. L. Langer, *European Alliances and Alignments, 1871–1890* (1931); R. J. Sontag, *European Diplomatic History, 1871–1932* (1933); P. T. Moon, *Imperialism and World Politics* (1926); R. G. Trotter, *The British Empire-Commonwealth* (1932); Mary E. Townsend, *Rise and Fall of Germany's Colonial Empire, 1884–1918* (1930); H. I. Priestley, *France Overseas, a Study of Modern Imperialism* (1938); T. F. Power, *Jules Ferry and the Renaissance of French Imperialism* (1945); F. H. Skrine, *The Expansion of Russia, 1815–1900* (3rd ed., 1915); R. J. S. Hoffman, *Great Britain and the German Trade Rivalry, 1875–1914* (1933); Herbert Feis, *Europe, the World's Banker, 1870–1914* (1930); E. M. Winslow, *The Pattern of Imperialism* (1948); J. Schumpeter, *Imperialism and Social Classes* (1955); R. Robinson *et al., Africa and the Victorians: the Climax of Imperialism in the Dark Continent* (1961); W. L. Langer, *The Diplomacy of Imperialism* (1951); G. Sansom, *A History of Japan, 1615–1867* (1963); J. T. Pratt, *The Expansion of Europe in the Far East* (1947); R. P. Masani, *Britain in*

India (1960); T. R. Metcalf, *The Aftermath of Revolt, India, 1857–1870* (1964); J. Marlowe, *World Ditch: the Making of the Suez Canal* (1964); R. A. Oliver, *Sir Harry Johnston and the Scramble for Africa* (1957); S. G. Millin, *Rhodes* (1952); L. M. Thompson, *The Unification of South Africa, 1902–1910* (1960); Eric Walker, *A History of Southern Africa* (1957); L. H. Palmer, *Indonesia and the Dutch* (1962).

Chapter 52. On Science, in addition to works cited for chapter 44, see F. A. Lange, *History of Materialism and Criticism of Its Present Importance* (3rd ed., 1925); E. Boring, *History of Experimental Psychology* (1929); A. N. Whitehead, *Science and the Modern World* (1926); Jacques Barzun, *Darwin, Marx, Wagner, the Fatal Legacy of "Progress"* (1941) and *Race, a Study in Modern Superstition* (1937); W. M. Simon, *European Positivism in the Nineteenth Century* (1963); C. Singer, E. J. Holmyard, A. R. Hull, T. I. Williams, eds., *A History of Technology*, 5 vols. (1955–1958), vol. V, *The Late Nineteenth Century* (c. 1850 to c. 1900); E. Diesel, G. Goldbeck, and F. Schildberger, *From Engines to Autos* (1960). On Marxism, see Isaiah Berlin, *Life of Marx* (1939); G. D. H. Cole, *What Marx Really Meant* (1934); G. Lichtheim, *Marxism: an Historical and Critical Study* (1961); H. Collins and C. Abramsky, *Karl Marx and the British Labour Movement: Years of the First International* (1965); Karl Federn, *The Materialistic Conception of History* (1939); G. M. Stekloff, *History of the First International* (1928); W. H. Dawson, *German Socialism and Ferdinand Lassalle* (1888). On Anarchism: E. H. Carr, *Michael Bakunin* (1937); G. Woodcock, *Anarchism, a History of Libertarian Ideas and Movements* (1962). On the churches and religion: K. S. Latourette, *History of the Expansion of Christianity*, vol. IV (1941); E. T. Gargen, *Leo XIII and the Modern World* (1961); Adrian Fortescue, *The Orthodox Eastern Church* (2nd ed., 1908); S. W. Baron, *Social and Religious History of the Jews*, vol. II (1937); and articles in the *Catholic Encyclopedia*; J. Hennessy, S. J., *The First Council of the Vatican: the American Experience* (1963).

Chapter 53. J. Swain, *Beginning the Twentieth Century, a History of the Generation That Made the War* (1933); E. P. Cheyney, *Modern English Reform, from Individualism to Socialism* (1931); C. R. Fay, *Coöperation at Home and Abroad* (4th ed., 1939); A. P. Higgins, *The Hague Peace Conferences* (1909); F. S. L. Lyons, *Internationalism in Europe, 1815–1914* (1963); D. C. Somervell, *Modern Britain, 1870–1939* (1941); E. C. Wingfield-Stratford, *The Victorian Aftermath, 1901–1914* (1933); Francis Hackett, *Ireland, a Study in Nationalism* (1918); G. Dangerfield, *The Strange Death of Liberal England* (1935); R. Jenkins, *Asquith* (1965).

From William II
to Hitler

The German "War Lords."

Photo by Underwood & Underwood, New York

v. Mackensen   v. Moltke   Kronprinz Wilhelm   v. François   v. Falkenhayn   v. Beseler   v. Bethmann-Hollweg
              v. Preussen   Ludendorff   v. Einem
v. Bülow   Kronprinz Rupprecht Herzog Albrecht   v. Kluck   v. Emmich   v. Haeseler   v. Hindenburg   v. Heeringen
          v. Bayern   v. Württemberg Kaiser Wilhelm II.   v. Tirpitz

PART XI

WORLD WAR I

Hitler addressing a youth parade at Nuremberg, 1936.
Courtesy Wide World Photos

AND ITS AFTERMATH

THE LATEST AGE—the twentieth century—marks, in some respects, the greatest advance and the highest achievement of European, or Western, civilization. This is doubtless so in science and technology, and likewise in popular aspiration for fuller, freer, and richer life. In other respects, however, the age suggests comparison with the early middle age (the "Dark Age") or with the ancient age of Eastern Mediterranean empires. Its violences are even more deadly and destructive, its instability as manifest, and its dictatorships as despotic.

The age opens with optimism inherited from the previous century concerning material progress and democratic politics. It also opens with portents, similarly inherited and now multiplying, of international conflict. While seeming progress is made in extending liberalism and nationalism into eastern Europe, the fate of the old border-empire of Austria becomes a very real issue between Germany and Russia, and hence between their respective allies in the game of power politics.

For over four years, from 1914 to 1918, is waged a war involving every great power of Europe, together with Japan and the United States, and most lesser nations of the world. It is called the First World War. Strictly speaking, it was not the first war fought globally, but it was quite unprecedented in its magnitude and destructiveness.

There follows a decade of renewed hope and optimism. Old empires are broken up, their subject nationalities liberated, and the European state-system put squarely on a national basis. Within the new nations, as within older ones, democracy is well-nigh universally professed and individual liberty pledged. And to preserve peace and prevent recurrence of war, a league of nations is fashioned. Democracy and peace, it is imagined, will stimulate the art as well as the technology of a dawning new era.

Already, however, Western democracy has failed to take root in Russia, and, instead, a novel type of dictatorship is forcefully fastened upon it—Marxian, "popular," and "totalitarian." Presently, amid deteriorating economic conditions in central Europe, dictatorships, ostensibly anti-Marxian but equally totalitarian and fiercely nationalist, are installed in Italy and Germany and are imitated, in greater or lesser degree, in many smaller countries. All such dictatorships represent a repudiation of traditional Western liberty, and the major ones are antagonistic to the Judaeo-Christian spiritual heritage. Without scruples, they exalt militarism, make propaganda a fine art, and readily employ force and violence alike in domestic and in international affairs.

The example of the dictatorships of eastern and central Europe tends to widen the gulf in western Europe between "Left" and "Right," to impair the operation of remaining democratic government, and to break down the League of Nations. Only when the democratic Western powers are exasperated beyond endurance by aggression of the totalitarian dictatorships, particularly by Nazi Germany, do they abandon compromise and go to war.

CHAPTER 54

Toward World War I

A. Russo-Japanese War and Revolt in the Russian Empire

As we have seen, Russian expansion in Asia had, in 1904, brought the empire of the Tsars into armed conflict with the rising power of the vigorous and intensely nationalistic Japanese; and this led to an internal upheaval in European Russia. We have already noticed that the Russian peasants were left unsatisfied by the land settlement which accompanied their emancipation in 1861.[1] Then, too, by the end of the nineteenth century a Social Democratic party was winning urban workers to Marxian Socialism. Peasant dissatisfaction was exploited by a Social Revolutionary party, which, adapting Marxian teachings to the traditions of Russian agricultural life, proposed that the land be given to those who actually worked it. Simultaneously, a Constitutional Democratic ("Cadet") party had appeared among middle-class "Westernizers," and the policy of "Russification" pursued by Alexander III and Nicholas II had aroused bitter resentment among "subject peoples" in the Empire—Poles, Finns, Letts, Lithuanians, Jews, Georgians, Armenians, etc.

All the latent opposition to the autocratic Tsardom became active as soon as it was borne in upon the Russian people that they were suffering one reverse after another in the war with Japan. Naturally enough the Tsar's government was blamed. Middle-class liberals held political banquets and

[1] See above, p. 650.

made provocative speeches. Workers staged political strikes at Moscow, Vilna, and other industrial centers. At St. Petersburg a procession of strikers, led by an Orthodox priest named Gapon, was fired on by troops while on its way to present a petition to the Tsar. The resulting bloodshed earned for that day (January 22, 1905) the title of "Red Sunday." The Tsar's uncle, the Grand Duke Sergei, was assassinated in Moscow in February 1905, and other political murders ensued. Armed outbreaks occurred in Poland and the Caucasus. The state railways could be operated only under martial law. The universities were closed. Most significant of all, in rural districts bands of peasants, under Social Revolutionary leaders, wandered about pillaging and burning the mansions of noble landlords and country gentlemen.

Faced with growing disorder, the Tsar made concessions. Hoping to appease the subject peoples, he promised religious toleration, permitted the use of Polish in private schools, and relaxed the enforcement of anti-Jewish legislation. Hoping to quiet the peasants, he cancelled the arrears they owed on the payments to the state for the land they had received. Hoping to win over the liberals, he consented to respect legal formalities in the trial of political offenders and promised to work out a plan for constitutional government. After further hesitation and delay and further rioting and disorder, the Tsar announced in August 1905 that he would establish a parliament, or Imperial Duma.

In October 1905, Nicholas II issued a kind of constitution in the form of a "manifesto," guaranteeing personal liberties of conscience, speech, and association, establishing moderately popular franchise for the election of the Duma, and clearly stating that henceforth no law would be valid without the Duma's consent. In December the Tsar was prevailed upon to grant practically universal manhood suffrage for Duma elections, and (in March 1906) he provided a two-house parliament by designating the Duma as the lower chamber and the old Council of State as the upper chamber. Of the latter, now to be called the Council of the Empire, half the members would be appointed, and half elected indirectly by certain privileged classes. Meanwhile a general strike in Finland led the Tsar to reëstablish the Finnish Estates General suppressed in 1899; and, when it proceeded to draft a modern, liberal constitution, the Tsar ratified it.

In Russia, however, the revolutionary upheaval soon spent its force. The conclusion of peace with Japan in the autumn of 1905 ended the series of defeats, reduced the pressure on the government, and released troops for the "restoration of order" at home. Many Russians were tired of foreign war and domestic rioting. The revolutionary elements fell to quarreling among themselves. Extreme (Bolshevik) Social Democrats clashed with moderate (Menshevik) Social Democrats, and both were in conflict with the Social Revolutionaries, while all the radicals were distrusted by the liberals. The liberals themselves disputed about the Duma and the policies it should pursue. The Constitutional Democrats thought the Tsar's decrees were merely a first step in the right direction, and hoped that the Duma would draw up a constitution that would make the Russian government like the British. A rival group, called "Octobrists," were content to accept the Tsar's "October Manifesto" as definitive, even though it made the Duma only a mild check on the autocracy.

As the revolutionary elements fell to quarreling, reactionary elements in Russia plucked up courage, closed their ranks, and prepared to fight for the preservation of the autocracy, the great landed estates, and the

traditional regime as a whole. Landlords, officials, courtiers, army officers, Slavophile patriots, and numerous Orthodox clergymen organized a "Union of the Russian People," which early in 1906 began a counter-revolutionary movement. "Black bands" or "black hundreds," as certain agents of the Union were popularly called, terrorized radicals and incited mob violence against Jews. Leaders of the Union put pressure on the Tsar to withdraw the concessions he had made, and Nicholas II showed himself more amenable to conservative than he had

Peasant Bargemen of the Volga. I. J. Repine (d. 1930).

been to liberal influence. In the decree of March 1906 establishing the Council of the Empire, he forbade the new parliament to discuss constitutional laws, asserted his own autocratic control of military and foreign affairs, and authorized imperial ministers to promulgate laws when the Duma was not in session, and to proceed on the basis of the old budget if in any year a new budget was not approved. Then Nicholas II installed as premier an energetic conservative, Peter Stolypin.

Stolypin repressed revolutionary agitation

and treated quite cavalierly the Duma which had been elected and had assembled at St. Petersburg in May 1906. When the Cadet and Social Revolutionary majority in the Duma proposed parliamentary control of the imperial ministers and a program of land reform to break up large estates, Stolypin rejected their proposals, dissolved the Duma, and ordered new elections. Thereupon, two hundred Cadet members of the Duma, in imitation of the Tennis Court meeting of the French deputies in 1789, assembled at Viborg in Finland and drew

Nicholas II. Valentine Syerov (d. 1911).

up a manifesto calling on the Russian people to refuse taxes and military service till the Tsar's government should respect the Duma. The Viborg manifesto produced only a feeble response. Its authors were disfranchised; the Cadet clubs were suppressed; the few attempts at insurrection were put down; some revolutionaries were executed and many others banished.

Despite governmental interference, the opponents of autocracy obtained a majority in the second Duma, which met in March 1907. Again there was a collision between the ministers and the legislature. Again the government dissolved the Duma. This time, however, Nicholas II issued a new "constitutional law" obviously intended to assure the election of future Dumas which would not oppose the government. The suffrage was elaborately restricted. Electoral districts were redrawn so that conservative rural voters could swamp the radically inclined cities.

The new system worked as Nicholas II and Stolypin intended. The third Duma, chosen in October 1907, contained an overwhelming majority of Conservatives and Octobrists, who were quite willing to have the Duma restricted to a consultative role. Outside the Duma, revolutionary opposition continued from radicals and members of the subject nationalities, but it no longer terrified the government. The revolutionary upheaval of 1905 had subsided and left behind only the democratic reforms in Finland and a slightly altered form of imperial government which the official almanac of 1907 appropriately described as "a constitutional monarchy under an autocratic Tsar."

B. Diplomatic Crises Over Morocco and the Balkans

We have seen in an earlier chapter how the Triple Alliance of Germany, Austria, and Italy was balanced in the 1890's by the Dual Alliance of France and Russia.[1] For a time, Great Britain tended to coöperate with the former, but as naval rivalry developed with Germany, it veered toward the Dual Alliance. In 1904, negotiations between Britain and France, by settling colonial disputes between them, linked them in

[1] See above, p. 660.

an *Entente Cordiale* (friendly understanding). It was not an alliance, but it rapidly developed into something closely approaching one, for the two countries supported each other in one diplomatic crisis after another, and, under Sir Edward Grey, the British Foreign Minister, military and naval "conversations" were initiated which by 1912 resulted in "understandings" as to how the two countries would support each other in case of war. Britain agreed to protect the French Channel and North Sea coast by her navy in the event of war between France and Germany, so as to enable the French to concentrate their fleet in the Mediterranean.

The *Entente* was soon extended by the inclusion of France's ally, Russia. The defeat of Russia by Japan in 1905 eased British fear of Russian advances in Asia. With French encouragement, Britain and Russia settled in 1907 their pending conflicts in Asia. Henceforth, the Triple Alliance of Germany, Austria, and Italy was confronted by the Triple Entente of France, Russia and Great Britain, with Japan as a close associate of the latter. Moreover, Italy was not wholly loyal to the Triple Alliance, for in 1902 she secretly joined France in a mutual pledge of neutrality if either should be attacked. Though the line-up of the European great powers was reasonably clear by 1908, it must be remembered that the exact terms of most of the treaties and understandings were secret. This secrecy tended to increase mutual suspicion and fear, and in ensuing crises no nation was quite sure where its enemies or even its supposed friends stood.

Between 1905 and 1913 there were recurrent diplomatic crises. Some had to do with Morocco, and others with the Balkans. All were settled by diplomatic means without bringing about a war among the major nations. But each might have caused a war; each shook the foundations of European peace; each alarmed statesmen and lent weight to the arguments of those who pleaded for bigger armies and navies.

The French had long been increasing their influence in Morocco, and by 1905 the French foreign minister, Delcassé, had plans well advanced for the establishment of a French protectorate over the greater part of that country. He secured the assent of Italy (1900), and of Britain (1904), and he reached an agreement with Spain, whereby the Spanish would be given a protectorate over the part of Morocco not appropriated by France. Morocco was a backward and brigand-ridden country, and, though its independence had been affirmed by an international congress at Madrid in 1880, its fate seemed to Delcassé to concern only France and Spain.

The German chancellor, Bülow, thought otherwise. He was eager to check France by asserting Germany's interest in Morocco and to weaken the entente between France and Great Britain. Picking a favorable moment, just three weeks after the defeat of France's ally, Russia, by the Japanese at Mukden, he arranged to have the German Emperor William II land at Tangier and ostentatiously salute the Sultan of Morocco as an "independent" ruler in whose lands "*all* foreign nations" would enjoy equal rights.

There followed a brief moment of awful suspense. Then Delcassé resigned and France agreed to submit the whole Moroccan question to an international congress. The congress met at Algeciras in Spain in 1906 and proved a disappointment to Bülow. Britain consistently backed France, and so did Italy. The final agreement, while paying lip service to the independence of the Sultan and the "open door" for the commerce of all nations in Morocco, authorized the French and Spanish to instruct and officer a native police force and to oversee the execution of "reforms." Thus, to all

Luncheon of the Boating Party. Pierre Auguste Renoir (d. 1919).

Photo by Lewis P. Woltz; courtesy Phillips Memorial Gallery, Washington, D.C.

intents and purposes, despite Bülow's efforts, the Algeciras conference resulted in a French victory.

Another and acute Moroccan crisis was precipitated in 1911 when the French sent an army to Fez "to restore order," and Germany despatched a warship, the *Panther,* to the port of Agadir, ostensibly to safeguard German mining interests, but with a significant hint that the warship would be withdrawn only when the French left Fez. So grave was the situation that military preparations were hurried forward in France and Germany. Russia was not sufficiently recovered from the Japanese war to promise much assistance, but the British proclaimed their full support of France.

After some bickering and much tension, a Franco-German convention was concluded, whereby Germany promised not to oppose the establishment of a French protectorate in Morocco, and France agreed to maintain the "open door" there. In addition, as a sort of bribe, which represented a real reward to the Germans for their obstructive tactics, France ceded to Germany two strips of French Equatorial Africa. Though both Moroccan crises were thus resolved without war, they served to quicken hostility between Germany and France and to consolidate the friendship of France and Great Britain. Germany by her strong-arm methods assumed, in the eyes of the outside world, something of the role of a bully.

Even more disquieting than the Moroccan crises were those in the Balkans, where Austria-Hungary and Russia were the major opponents rather than France and Germany, though the two latter nations were involved through their efforts to support their respective allies. Germany had special motives for backing up Austria, since she was eager to spread her own influence in the Ottoman Empire. In 1899 the Emperor William II paid a ceremonious visit to the Sultan. From 1903 Germans were involved in plans for building a "Berlin-to-Bagdad" railway. German officers were training the Turkish army.

A major crisis in the Balkans occurred in 1908, when Austria-Hungary took advantage of a Turkish revolution to annex outright the Serb-speaking provinces of Bosnia and Herzegovina, which she had been "administering" under the provisions of the treaty of Berlin,[1] and which Serbia coveted. A storm of indignation arose in Serbia, which aroused sympathetic response in Russia. But Germany announced her firm intention of giving full military support to Austria-Hungary. Russia, still not fully recovered from the Japanese war, had to give way and Serbia was compelled to promise that she would not countenance anti-Austrian propaganda and would live on "good neighborly terms" with the Dual Monarchy. Peace was preserved. But Russia and Serbia, humiliated by the incident, drew closer together; and Serbia was swept by a fierce wave of expansionist nationalism.

By 1911, the international situation was extraordinarily perilous. Recurrent crises in Morocco and the Balkans had cost every great power some measure of prestige. Germany had been outplayed in Morocco by France and Britain. But France had been forced to cede African territory to Germany, and Britain had lost influence in the Ottoman Empire. Russia had been outplayed in the Balkans by Austria-Hungary and Germany, but was now backing Serbia and was resolved not to be outplayed again. Germany was coming to believe that, instead of exercising predominance in Europe as she had done in the days of Bismarck, she was now "encircled" by a ring of potentially hostile powers. But the more a great power was threatened with the loss of prestige, the less yielding and conciliatory it was likely to be.

C. Revolution in the Ottoman Empire, and the Italian and Balkan Wars of 1911–1913

Three years after the Russian revolutionary upheaval of 1905, the Ottoman Empire underwent a revolution. Since the 1890's there had been movements aimed at reforming and modernizing the Empire. The most vigorous in its radicalism and nationalism was that of the "Young Turks," led by Enver Bey, who formed a revolutionary "Committee of Union and Progress." In July 1908, this committee, with the

[1] See above, p. 655.

support of the army, executed a *coup* at Salonica, proclaimed in force the long-suspended constitution of 1876, and threatened the Sultan Abdul Hamid II with deposition if he should offer resistance. Thoroughly frightened, the Sultan endorsed the restoration of the constitution, abolished the censorship, and put a Liberal, Kiamil Pasha, at the head of the ministry.

The new regime failed to maintain internal order or to prevent foreign aggression; and in 1909 Enver and the committee executed a second *coup*, deposed the Sultan, and put in his place his mild-mannered brother, Mohammed V. The liberal cabinet of Kiamil Pasha was replaced by a Young Turk ministry, and the parliament was transformed into a National Assembly. From 1909 to 1918 the government of the Ottoman Empire was practically a military dictatorship headed by Enver Bey (who soon was promoted to be Enver Pasha). The aim of the Young Turks was a vigorous nationalism. They planned to "Turkify" the Empire by forcing all its peoples to use the Turkish language, to accept a system of national education, and to serve in a common national army. Though they had the existing army back of them, the program of the Young Turks was impracticable, for there were too many Christians and non-Turkish Moslems in the Empire who were opposed to it; and such opposition was encouraged from abroad.

In September 1911 Italy suddenly announced her intention of annexing the Ottoman north African provinces of Tripoli and Cyrenaica. The Young Turk government replied by a resolute declaration of war and sent Enver Pasha to undertake the defense of the provinces. But the war resulted in a double loss for the Turks. Enough Turkish troops could not be sent to Africa to prevent Italy from making good her conquest there. But enough were sent to encourage the Balkan nations to attempt to seize lands of the Ottoman Empire in Europe. Before the Turco-Italian war was ended in October 1912 by the treaty of Lausanne, which gave Italy Cyrenaica and Tripoli and permitted her to administer the Dodecanese Islands in the Aegean, the Balkan War of 1912–1913 had begun. The Ottoman Empire was in its death throes.

Shrewdly sizing up the growing weakness of the Empire, King Ferdinand of Bulgaria organized a Balkan League of Bulgaria, Serbia, Greece, and Montenegro. After feverish military preparations, it attacked the Ottoman Empire in October 1912. The Turks brought back Kiamil Pasha as prime minister, won some diplomatic support from the Great Powers, terminated the war with Italy, and threw all their military strength into the defense of their European territories. But in spite of these efforts, the Balkan allies, to everyone's surprise, overwhelmed the Turkish resistance, captured Salonica and Monastir, overran Macedonia, and by March 1913 the Bulgarians were in possession of Adrianople, while the Serbs took Scutari in April. Finally in May 1913 Enver Pasha had to accept the peace terms of the Balkan League as amended by the great powers, even though the Ottoman Empire thus lost all its European territory save Constantinople and a narrow strip along the Bosporus and Dardanelles.

It was one thing to despoil the Turks and quite another to divide the booty, for not only were Balkan allies very jealous of each other, but Austria-Hungary was determined to prevent the enlargement of a pro-Russian Serbia. In this determination, Austria was backed by Germany and Italy and opposed by Russia and France. For a time it seemed as if the major powers would go to war over the Balkan problem. But at last a compromise was reached. Serbia was allowed to expand southward but was barred from the Adriatic by the erection of an independent state of Albania under a German prince.

If a world war was thus staved off, another Balkan war was let loose. Serbia, deprived of the portion of Albania she had expected, demanded a part of Macedonia which had been tentatively assigned to Bulgaria, and Greece was at odds with Bulgaria over the division of Thrace. By June 1913 Serbia and Greece were fighting Bulgaria and they were soon joined by Rumania, which, though hitherto passive, was fearful of an enlarged Bulgaria. The Turks, hopeful of regaining some of their losses, likewise threw their troops against Bulgaria. In July 1913 the Turks recaptured Adrianople,

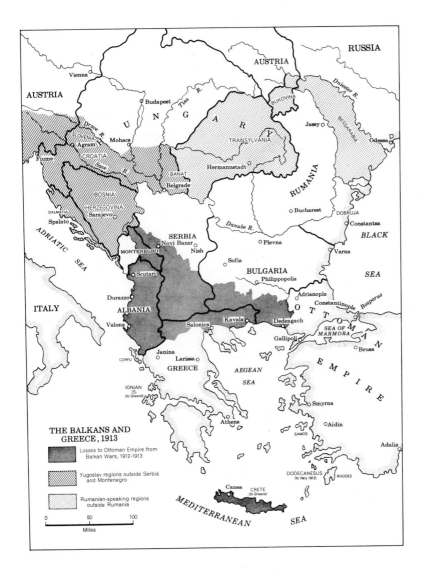

THE BALKANS AND
GREECE, 1913

- Losses to Ottoman Empire from Balkan Wars, 1912-1913
- Yugoslav regions outside Serbia and Montenegro
- Rumanian-speaking regions outside Rumania

0   50   100
Miles

while the Greeks, Serbs, and Rumanians were closing in on the Bulgarian capital of Sofia. Unable to secure aid from the great powers, King Ferdinand of Bulgaria had to make peace. The treaty of Bucharest in August 1913 reassigned the spoils of the previous war. Serbia got a large chunk of Macedonia. Greece secured Crete, southern Epirus, southern Macedonia (including Salonica), and part of western Thrace. Bulgaria retained a bit of Macedonia and the region of central Thrace. But to Rumania, Bulgaria had to cede her northeastern territory of Dobruja and subsequently she had to give back Adrianople to the Turks.

By the two wars of 1912–1913, all the Balkan states were enlarged at the expense of the Ottoman Empire, and a new nation, Albania, was created. But Bulgaria was left feeling cheated and revengeful. The nationalism, the jealousies, and the rivalries of the Balkan countries were greatly intensified. And the great powers eyed each other with ever greater suspicion and hostility. The Balkan Wars proved a prelude to much vaster conflict.

D. Multiple Origins of World War I

The First World War scarcely deserves the title, for the War of the Spanish Succession, the Seven Years' War, and the

Memorial to Peter I, King of Serbia 1903–1918 and of Yugoslavia 1918–1921. Ivan Mestrovic (d. 1962).

Napoleonic conflicts had all been struggles waged on the high seas and on several continents. But because of its magnitude, the number of participants, the costs in men and money, and the ending of a long period of comparative peace, this war seemed to contemporaries to be of a completely new order. Its origins were multiple, and their general nature may be indicated as follows:

1. Diplomatic. We have seen how, between 1891 and 1914, the great powers of Europe had become aligned in two camps, each bound by secret engagements, and each jealous and suspicious of the other. We have seen likewise how a series of crises, especially those connected with Morocco and the Balkans, heightened the tension between Triple Entente and Triple Alliance. By 1914, each group of powers felt cheated or thwarted, and unwilling to make the kind of concessions necessary to surmount the next crisis by compromise. Diplomacy certainly did not cause the World War, but it helped to create a situation in which it could take place.

2. Political and Nationalist. Behind most of the occurrences which led toward the war lay political rivalries and nationalistic aspirations. It was the excesses of modern nationalism which induced democratic and not-so-democratic statesmen to squabble over their nations' interests in Africa, Asia, and the Balkans. It was nationalism which made the French long to recover Alsace-Lorraine, and the Russians to extend their control southward. It was nationalism which embittered the rivalries of states like Great

Britain and Germany and encouraged them to military and naval competition. Most important of all, nationalism was an explosive force which had already disrupted the Ottoman Empire and now seriously threatened the integrity of other conglomerate Empires—most notably the Austrian, but even, perhaps, the Russian. Nationalistic Serbia, fresh from helping to break up the Ottoman Empire, was aflame with zeal to expand at the expense of the Austrian Empire; and the statesmen of the latter made frantic efforts to safeguard it against any nationalist dissolution.

3. *Economic.* Deeply ensnarled with other factors were those of an economic nature. Germany and Great Britain were engaged in industrial and commercial competition. Germany by great efforts was gaining ground. Britain was in danger of losing her preëminent position. Such economic contention led to friction and suspicion between the two nations and prepared the people of one to look upon people of the other as rivals. In lesser degree there were similar economic rivalries between Russia and Germany, between France and Germany, and so on. Excited by nationalistic propaganda, economic rivalry became just as real as the bonds of economic solidarity that held nations together.

4. *Military.* From the rising nationalist sentiments and the anarchical state of international relations arose military and naval rivalries that themselves led toward war by making Europe an armed camp and putting in the hands of each country a military machine ready for use. More than anything else perhaps, naval rivalry embittered Anglo-German relations, while the competitive race in land armies and armaments increased fear and hostility among all the continental countries. Advice of general staffs was usually asked in each diplomatic crisis, and sometimes, as in the case of Austria or Russia, the military experts found reasons for urging steps more warlike than those advocated by diplomats or politicians. Indeed, the balance of military power on the continent was close enough to make each nation fearful lest another obtain the advantage by a headstart in mobilization.

5. *Social.* There was a wide variety of social factors. They ranged from a belief in "social Darwinism"—that the fittest nation (in a military sense) would survive and grow, or that war was a healthy part of the "struggle for existence"—to a belief in the superiority of the French or German or Russian or some other "culture." They included unfortunate effects of mass journalism in an age of literacy, and of patriotic oratory in a period of democracy. Basically, the decline of Christian faith among many people helped to create a mood in which war was less shocking to the ethical sense of mankind. In a materialist world, what was wrong with the use of material force to gain material ends?

Unsuspected by masses of Europeans still basking in the declining sun of "peace and prosperity," war clouds were gathering in 1914 on every horizon.

Archduke Francis Ferdinand of Austria and his wife.

Photo by Underwood & Underwood, New York

CHAPTER 55

World War I, 1914–1918

A. Outbreak of the War: Central Powers versus Allied and Associated Powers

On June 28, 1914, the Archduke Francis Ferdinand, nephew of the Emperor Francis Joseph and heir to the thrones of Austria and Hungary, was assassinated, together with his wife, in the Bosnian town of Sarajevo, by a band of nationalist Serbs. The assassination evoked a storm of indignation in Austria-Hungary and invited the Austrian foreign minister, Count Berchtold, to have a reckoning with Serbia. It is now known that the assassins, though natives of Bosnia and thus subjects of the Habsburg Empire, were members of a Serbian secret society, the "Black Hand," that they had been armed and trained in Serbia, and that they had been assisted by high officers in the Serbian army. It is also fairly certain that important Serbian officials, including the prime minister, had foreknowledge of the conspiracy and yet gave the Austrian government no adequate warning.

At the time, despite his suspicions, Count Berchtold could get no proof of the complicity of the Serb government. But determined to crush Serbia, he proceeded as if he had the necessary evidence. With some difficulty, he won over the Hungarian premier and the Emperor Francis Joseph to his plans. On July 5–6, an emissary of his secured from the German Emperor William II a pledge of un-

qualified support for Austria in any action she might take against Serbia. This "blank check" with which Germany underwrote Berchtold's schemes was a serious mistake, since William II, though eager to back up his Austrian ally and to avenge the Archduke, does not appear to have wanted a major war at this juncture.

Having gained the support of Germany, Berchtold presented Serbia, on July 23, with an ultimatum, acceptance of which he demanded in forty-eight hours. In it he called upon Serbia to suppress anti-Austrian propaganda, to dismiss anti-Austrian officials, and to accept the aid of agents of the Austro-Hungarian government in repressing the revolutionary movement which sought to gain for Serbia lands of the Dual Monarchy. On July 25 the Serbian government replied, accepting all demands that would not impair its "independence and sovereignty" and offering to refer disputed points to the Hague Court or to an international conference. At the same time, the Serbs ordered the mobilization of their army. Whereupon the Austro-Hungarian government pronounced the Serbian reply evasive, broke off diplomatic relations with Serbia, and likewise ordered mobilization. War was clearly impending between Austria and Serbia.

But a vaster war was also impending. The Russian government felt that if it stood aside and let Austria crush Serbia, Russian prestige in the Balkans would be shattered. From the French President

Raymond Poincaré, who was paying a state visit to St. Petersburg, Russia received assurance of French support. France had no eagerness for war, but feared lest she lose her ally or the alliance lose prestige. On July 26 the British Foreign Minister, Sir Edward Grey, urged that a conference of diplomats try to find a peaceful solution to the crisis. France and Italy responded in a favorable manner. But Germany, afraid that at such a conference she would be outplayed as at Algeciras in 1906,[1] replied that the dispute concerned only Austria and Serbia and hence that the other powers should strive merely to "localize" the dispute, that is, to keep the war a small one. With this evidence of Germany's support, Austria declared war on Serbia on July 28.

Events then marched fast. Amidst frantic diplomatic efforts to preserve peace, military preparations were pushed ahead with feverish haste. On July 29, when news of the Austrian declaration of war reached St. Petersburg, the Tsar Nicholas II was prevailed upon to order a general mobilization of the Russian army. That evening, von Moltke, German chief of staff and nephew of the Prussian commander in 1870, argued in a council at Potsdam that war was inevitable and that Germany should mobilize at once.

That night, William II, alarmed at the prospect of war, tried to persuade Austria to negotiate with Russia and begged the Tsar to take no military measures which "would precipitate a calamity we both wish to avoid." But it was too late to swerve Berchtold from his course, and, when the Tsar tried to change the general mobilization to a partial one, the Russian foreign minister, urged on by the Russian military men who had no plans for a partial mobilization, soon persuaded him (July 30) to renew the orders for general mobilization. Russian mobilization transformed the Austro-Serbian war into a general conflict. Von Moltke now had no difficulty in convincing William II that Germany could not delay her own mobilization without risking disaster. On July 31 Germany

presented Russia with a twelve-hour ultimatum demanding immediate demobilization. Russia did not reply. Germany declared war.

Germany knew that war with Russia was almost certain to involve France. Accordingly on July 31, Germany presented an eighteen-hour ultimatum to France, demanding that she should declare her neutrality. Had France agreed, Germany would then have demanded the right to occupy the French fortresses of Toul and Verdun till peace was restored. But France did not agree. Instead, she merely stated on August 1 that she "would consult her interests" and at once began mobilization. On August 3, 1914, Germany declared war on France.

The British on the whole were sympathetic to France, and Sir Edward Grey on August 2 told the Germans that Britain would not tolerate naval attacks on the French coasts or shipping. But there was strong pacifist sentiment both among the people and in the cabinet. Germany, however, soon solidified British opinion against her, for on August 2 she occupied the neutral Grand Duchy of Luxembourg, and presented a twelve-hour ultimatum to Belgium requiring free passage of German troops across Belgian territory. The Belgian government refused and appealed to Britain, which, with Prussia and the other great powers, had guaranteed Belgian neutrality in 1839. Aroused by this violation of international law, and by the threat to the Low Countries whose independence Great Britain had always sought to maintain, the British government declared war on Germany at midnight on August 4. In his disappointment, the German Chancellor, Bethmann-Hollweg, berated the British ambassador for Britain's going to war "just for a scrap of paper."

The major contestants were now at war with each other. But gradually other nations were drawn into the conflict. On August 7, tiny Montenegro joined her fellow Yugoslav state of Serbia against Austria-Hungary. Japan, perceiving a chance to advance her interests, declared war on Germany on August 23. The Ottoman Empire, hoping to regain its recently lost territories, signed

---

[1] See above, p. 704.

A Dawn in 1914. After an etching by the British artist C. R. W. Nevinson.

on August 1 a secret treaty of alliance with Germany, and on October 29 bombarded Russian Black Sea ports, thus forcing the Entente powers to declare war. At the outbreak of the conflict, Italy and Rumania, though nominal allies of the Central Powers, remained neutral on the ground that the war was not defensive on the part of Germany and Austria-Hungary. Thus Italy lived up to a secret agreement of 1902 with France. Soon, both sides were bidding for the support of these neutrals and in the game of promising bribes the Entente Allies had the advantage, for they

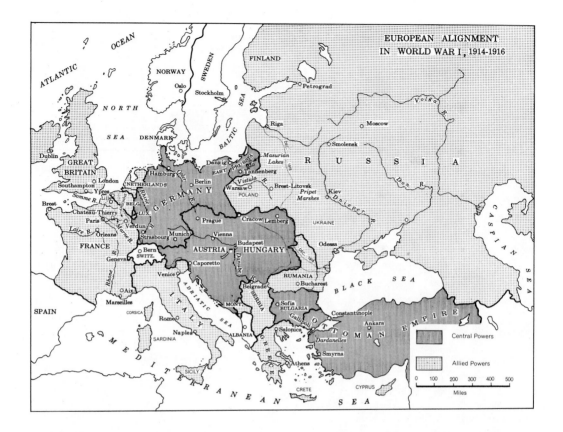

could agree to give to Italy long-coveted blocks of Austrian territory, and to Rumania large slices of Hungarian lands.

In April 1915, Italy signed a secret treaty with the Allies at London, whereby she was promised financial aid and territory in Africa as well as in Austria and the Ottoman Empire, if she would come into the war. On May 23, despite the fact that the armies of the Allies were suffering reverses, Italy declared war on Austria. Italy's entrance was balanced to some degree by the fact that Bulgaria, still smarting from her losses in 1913 and encouraged by German victories, allied herself with the Central Powers in September 1915, in return for promises of territorial gains, and on October 14 declared war on Serbia. Rumania held off until 1916, by which time the pro-German King Ferdinand had been succeeded by his pro-Ally nephew Carol and the Allies had won some encouraging victories. In return for promises of territorial extensions, Rumania declared war on Austria on August 27, 1916. By this time Portugal, long an ally of Britain,

had declared war on Germany (March 9, 1916). Thus all Europe, save Scandinavia, Holland, Switzerland, and Spain, was engaged in the struggle, for the Allies were using Greek territory for operations as early as 1915, though they did not force that country formally into the war till July 1917.

At the outbreak of the war the American President, Woodrow Wilson, had proclaimed the neutrality of the United States and had urged its people to be "neutral in fact as well as in name." As the war progressed, however, such neutrality proved difficult to maintain. Britain halted and searched American ships and seized contraband cargoes. But such violations of American rights could be paid for, later, in cash. More serious were the sinkings of American ships by the submarines with which Germany fought the British blockade. Against such sinkings, Wilson protested sternly, and likewise against the sinking of British vessels with American cargoes and passengers aboard. On May 7, 1915, the British liner "Lusitania" was sunk with the loss of about a hundred

American lives. Backed by the growing pro-Allied sympathy at home, Wilson took a strong stand and forced Germany to promise to refrain from sinking merchant vessels without providing for the safety of the passengers.

Thus the action of the United States put a stop to the one effective German weapon against the British blockade. But early in 1917 Germany announced her intention of resuming unrestricted submarine warfare. The German leaders felt sure that Britain could be starved into submission before American aid could be effective. The United States at once broke off diplomatic relations with Germany, and, when the Germans carried out their threat of sinking merchantmen regardless of the flag they flew or the passengers they carried, the United States declared war on Germany, on April 6, 1917. In the following months a number of Latin American countries, together with Siam, Liberia, and China, followed the lead of the United States. The whole world seemed to be arraying itself on the side of the Allies.

B. First Stage (1914–1916), from German Success to Deadlock

The war came as a terrific shock to Europe. In an instant, dreams of peaceful progress evaporated. Yet everywhere, stirred by patriotic sentiments, people rallied to the support of their respective governments. Pacifism evaporated, and neither the Christian churches nor the Socialist parties were able to maintain any international solidarity. It was quickly apparent that nationalism was the strongest sentiment in Europe.

At the start, it was generally expected that the war would be a brief one, and for a time German successes were such that it seemed as if the conflict might be ended in a few months. The German military plan was to strike first and with superior strength in the west against France, and then when France was crushed, to turn eastward and overwhelm Russia. In pursuit of this plan, huge German armies advanced rapidly through Belgium, overcoming all resistance there, and driving French armies and a

British "expeditionary force" backward toward Paris. Only a few days after the outbreak of hostilities, the German commander-in-chief, von Moltke, wired the Emperor William II, "In six weeks the whole story will be concluded."

But the Germans were overconfident. They made tactical blunders. They allowed a gap to open up between two of their advancing armies. On September 6, almost in sight of Paris, they were halted by the French and the British and in the next three days, in a series of actions known as the Battle of the Marne, they were forced to retreat. By September 14 the Germans were on the defensive.

The "miracle of the Marne," as the French called it, prevented a speedy German victory and produced a stalemate. Both sides rapidly extended their lines and dug themselves in, until a series of entrenched armies opposed each other from the North Sea coast of Belgium to the Swiss border. A war of movement and maneuver had been expected. Instead, it was now trench warfare, in which the machine gun was king, and advance obtainable only by appalling casualties. As the war progressed, attempts were made to break up the trench warfare by heavy artillery barrages, by the use of poison gases (Germans), and by tanks (British). But until 1918 none of these attempts achieved more than partial and momentary success. The western front was deadlocked.

It was otherwise in the east. At the start of the war, the Russians, with surprising speed, invaded Austrian Galicia and German East Prussia. In Galicia, they met with success, but in East Prussia their early advance was turned into a crushing disaster involving the loss of 300,000 men and vast amounts of material, when the Germans under Generals Hindenburg and Ludendorff routed one Russian army and broke up another in the battles of Tannenberg (August 26–31, 1914) and the Masurian Lakes (September 5–15, 1914).

The Austrians not only were defeated in Galicia, but their invasion of Serbia was checked and then pushed back. The Germans, even though it meant weakening the west front, had to come to their aid. In a great offensive at Gorlice (May 1915)

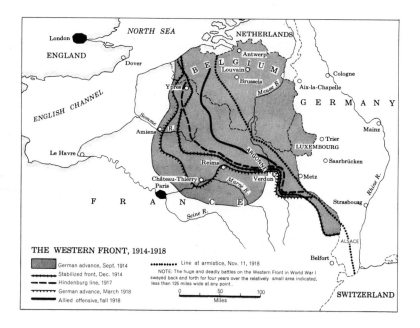

THE WESTERN FRONT, 1914-1918

Line at armistice, Nov. 11, 1918

German advance, Sept. 1914

Stabilized front, Dec. 1914

Hindenburg line, 1917

German advance, March 1918

Allied offensive, fall 1918

NOTE: The huge and deadly battles on the Western Front in World War I swayed back and forth for four years over the relatively small area indicated, less than 125 miles wide at any point.

0   50   100

Miles

the Germans and Austrians under General Falkenhayn pushed back the Russians and exploited this success so well that by September 1915 all Poland and most of Lithuania were in the hands of the Central Powers. Though Italy declared war on Austria, the Austrians for almost a year easily held their mountainous frontier against the Italians.

Fresh from his eastern victories, Falkenhayn hurried west in September 1915 with reserve troops and checked a French offensive in Champagne. Then joined by Bulgaria, Germany and Austria turned on the stubborn Serbs. By the end of the year they had overrun all Serbia and Montenegro and occupied Albania as well. Linked up by land with the Ottoman Empire, the Central Powers now were dominant from the Persian Gulf to the North Sea, and their improved position was emphasized by a British failure. Early in 1915, in a plan inspired by Winston Churchill, a Franco-British fleet attempted to force the Dardanelles in order to open a short supply route to Russia, which was already desperately short of munitions. The attempt failed, and a costly landing on the Gallipoli peninsula was held in check by the Turks under German leadership. In December 1915 the whole venture was abandoned.

In February 1916, the Germans opened up a tremendous offensive on the western front, designed to take the French fortress of Verdun and to "bleed France white" in the process. A gigantic battle dragged on from February to July, but in face of heroic French defense, the Germans failed to take Verdun. On both sides, the losses in men were staggering. In May the Austrians weakened their Russian front for a drive on Italy. But though the Italians retreated at first, they soon held, and the Austrians had to shift troops back to the Russian front to try to stem a Russian offensive under General Brusilov that won back most of Galicia. The victories of Brusilov, and of an Italian counter-offensive that gained the key city of Gorizia, helped to persuade Rumania to come into the war (August 1916). But the Rumanians had waited too long. An Austro-German army under Falkenhayn quickly overran Rumania, so that, by the end of 1916, its resources of oil and wheat were at the disposal of the Central Powers.

By this time, such resources were becoming of crucial importance. At the beginning, all the participants, even Germany, were ill-prepared for a long war. But once it was realized that the struggle would be long and very costly, every belligerent undertook an economic mobilization. Never before had governments been so active nor their influence so pervasive. If at first they hesitated and fumbled, gradually their efforts became more effective. Germany was first, and most perfectly, organized. In Austria-Hungary more than 80 "centrals" were set up to handle various phases of production and distribution. France established a whole series of committees, commissions, and "offices." Britain had "control boards" and committees composed of representatives of capital, labor, and the state. Even corrupt and backward Russia tried to organize its economic effort through a "central war industries committee" instituted in May 1915.

Among the Central Powers, Germany was clearly the leading partner, though she sometimes had difficulty in keeping Austria in line. Among the Allies there was a difficult task of coördination which was handled with only partial success. The Allied military command was not unified till the last months of the war. In the economic field there was earlier and better coöperation. Britain and France established commissions to make common purchases, and a joint agency for control of ships and shipping which served not only to speed supplies to France or Britain, but also to discipline neutral powers by cutting off their imports and exports.

In the economic warfare between the Allies and the Central Powers, the most effective weapons were, respectively, the British blockade and the German submarines. By its control of the sea, Britain captured or sank or drove into hiding practically all German ships. Gradually, by a system of control and inspection, she throttled even the imports Germany could get via neutral countries like Holland or Sweden. Within the bonds of the British blockade, Germany writhed to no avail. She was short of food (desperately so by 1918), short of copper, oil, and rubber; and *ersatz* (substitute) products by no means filled the gap. On only one occasion did Germany challenge the British fleet, the basis of the blockade. That was off Jutland at the end of May 1916. In a great naval battle, a German fleet which had ventured out into the North Sea encountered a British armada. The British lost more ships and lives. But the German warships retreated to their home harbors and did not again emerge.

If Germany was strangled by the blockade, Britain was vulnerable as an island. By commerce raiders, floating mines, and especially by submarines, the Germans sought to destroy the shipping by which England drew on the outer world for food and supplies. In April 1917 submarine warfare reached a peak, and one ship out of four that left the British Isles was torpedoed. If the Germans could have redoubled their efforts, Britain might have been put out of the war. But the British (and now the Americans as well) met the threat by a gigantic shipbuilding campaign, by anti-submarine weapons (depth bombs, wire nets, listening devices), and by sending vessels in convoys guarded by warships. The crisis was past and before the war was over 200 German submarines were destroyed. But the shipping losses of the Allies (especially of Britain) were staggering. Before the end of the war they amounted to about 6,000 vessels totaling almost fifteen million tons, or some three-fifths of the shipping with which the Allies had begun the war.

C. The Russian Revolutions of 1917

By 1917 the Allies were generally victorious outside the European Continent. The Japanese had seized the German treaty ports in China and the German islands in the Pacific. British, French, and Belgians had captured all the German colonies in Africa, except German East Africa, and this could not hold out much longer. In the Near East, the British, after a series of failures in 1915, had captured Bagdad and most of Mesopotamia (Iraq); and in 1917, under General Allenby, and with Arab support, they conquered Palestine.

Within Europe the Allies were less successful. True, the Central Powers had experienced discouragement in 1916 by the failure of the Verdun campaign, by heavy losses from a British offensive on the Somme, and by the entrance of Rumania into the war. Falkenhayn had been dismissed from chief command (August 1916), and Hindenburg (with Ludendorff) had been made virtually a military dictator. Under Hindenburg's guidance, the Germans on the western front early in 1917 retreated to the heavily fortified "Hindenburg Line." Thereby they gave up about a thousand square miles of territory, but straightened their lines and conserved their waning man-power. Some of the German Socialists and Centrists commenced to clamor for peace, while the new Emperor of Austria, Charles I (1916–1918), began secret but fruitless peace negotiations with the Allies.

Nevertheless the Central Powers were clearly dominant throughout the Balkans. They had pressed the Russians far back and were easily holding the Italians in check. Germany was in a strong defensive position in the west, and its leaders hoped that unrestricted submarine warfare would bring success in 1917. Such was the general situation when a series of events in Russia proved as encouraging to the Central Powers as it was discouraging to the Allies.

Since 1915 things had been going from bad to worse in Russia. Brusilov's victories in 1916 had been more than offset by the incompetence and corruption of the Tsarist regime. The Russian armies were desperately short of munitions and supplies. In vain, the Cadets and Octobrists in the Duma urged the establishment of constitutional government and a responsible ministry. The Duma was dissolved and its members sent home or jailed. In vain, a convention of *zemstvos* endorsed the Duma's recommendations. It too was dissolved. In vain, Russian patriots of all classes pleaded for reforms. The Tsar and his government went on with their incompetent blundering.

During the winter of 1916–1917 popular disaffection overspread Russia. The subject nationalities grew restless. The middle classes grumbled. There were riots of peasants and strikes of workers. Revolution was precipitated by the decrees of the autocratic government on March 11, 1917, that the Petrograd strikers should go to work and that the recently reassembled Duma should again go home. The strikers refused to obey and won over to their side the soldiers

upon whom the government relied to suppress them. They formed a revolutionary "soviet" (or council) of soldiers and workingmen. The Duma likewise refused to obey, and, by agreement between it and the Petrograd Soviet, a provisional government was set up on March 14 under the chairmanship of Prince George Lvov, a liberal landlord. The next day a deputation waited on the Tsar at Pskov and obtained his abdication.

The provisional government at once proclaimed freedom of speech, press, association, and religion. It released political prisoners, permitted the return of political exiles, restored full autonomy to Finland, and promised it to Poland. It announced that a National Constituent Assembly would shortly be elected by universal manhood suffrage to draw up a constitution for Russia. At the same time, it strove to infuse new energy into Russia's prosecution of the war.

There was momentary rejoicing among the Allies, for they imagined that a democratic Russia would fight more vigorously than an autocratic one. In this, they were grievously disappointed. For three years Russia had suffered heavier losses than any other country. The masses were sick of war and soldiers wanted to get home. The provisional government could not agree on a program of reform or resist the pressures of the "soviets of soldiers, workers, and peasants" that were everywhere being formed. In May the discouraged Prince Lvov resigned and was succeeded by Kerensky, a member of the Social Revolutionary party.

Kerensky brought several moderate (Menshevik) Socialists into the ministry, but he failed to halt the subversive activities of the most radical group of Socialists, the "Bolsheviks" or "Communists." These were skillfully led by Nikolai Lenin (revolutionary name of Vladimir Ulyanov), who had returned from exile in Switzerland under a safe conduct from the Germans who were eager to foment further troubles in Russia, and by Leon Trotsky (revolutionary name of Lev Bronstein), who came back from exile in America. The Bolsheviks were a tiny minority of the population, and even of the proletarian and middle-class

Nikolai Lenin.
Courtesy
Bettmann Archive

radicals. But they had a philosophy, a program, and a technique of revolutionary organization. They got their members into key positions within the soviets at Petrograd, Moscow, and elsewhere. They urged a dictatorship of the workers and no compromise with capitalism. They proposed the nationalization of all factories and landed estates. For the war-weary population they promised a cessation of hostilities. For the hungry workers they promised food. Lenin's slogan, "Peace! Land! Bread!" struck deep chords among the Russian people and evoked favorable response from multitudes who were quite hazy about the principles of Marxian Socialism.

Kerensky vainly begged the Allies to consent to a general peace "without annexations or indemnities." He vainly tried to combat both Bolshevik and German propaganda and to restore discipline in the faltering Russian armies. He vainly launched a desperate offensive in July 1917. The Russian troops mutinied. The Austrians recovered all of Galicia. The Germans captured Riga and penetrated into Estonia.

In November 1917 a second revolution occurred in Russia. Kerensky's provisional government was overthrown, and Lenin, at the head of the Bolsheviks and working through the local soviets, took charge of affairs. One of the first acts of the new Communist regime was to agree to a truce with Germany and Austria-Hungary; and in March 1918, after protracted wrangling, a peace treaty was signed at Brest-Litovsk by Russia on one side and Germany and her allies on the other.

The peace thus dictated by Hindenburg and Ludendorff was harsh in the extreme and showed what the Allies might expect if they were defeated. It involved what amounted to a partition of the Russian Empire. Poland, Lithuania, and the Latvian province of Courland were ceded outright to Germany and Austria. Bessarabia was turned over to the Central Powers for transfer to Rumania. Armenian districts south of the Caucasus were surrendered to Turkey. Finland, Estonia, the Latvian province Livonia, and the huge area of the Ukraine were detached from Russia and recognized as independent states under German protection.

Rumania, completely isolated by the defection of Russia and largely in the hands of the Central Powers, felt obliged to sue for peace and to agree to a treaty which was imposed upon her at Bucharest in March 1918. Thereby Rumania yielded Dobruja to Bulgaria and certain mountain passes to Austria-Hungary. But in return for pledges of close coöperation with Germany and Austria, Rumania was promised Bessarabia.

Thus in 1917–1918 the Allied eastern front completely collapsed. Germany was free to devote her attention to the western front, and Austria-Hungary, though torn by a rising tide of nationalism among her subject peoples, had only to stand firm against Italy.

D. Last Stage (1917–1918): Defeat and Collapse of the Central Powers

The withdrawal of Russia from the war was a blow to the Allies. Yet before the treaty of Brest-Litvosk was signed, other events were turning the balance against the Central Powers. The Allies were receiving increasingly effective aid from the United States, first in ships, food, and munitions, but by 1918 in men as well. Disaffection was spreading rapidly among Poles, Czechs, and other subject peoples of Austria-Hungary. The German submarine campaign was not achieving its object,[1] but the British blockade was depriving Germany of direfully needed food and materials. The Allied war-aims set forth by

---

[1] The toll of Allied shipping taken by German submarines declined from four million tons in the first half of 1917 to two and a quarter million in the second half of 1917, and to a scant two million in the first half of 1918.

President Woodrow Wilson of the United States in his "fourteen points" of January 1918, strengthened morale of Allied peoples and correspondingly weakened that of peoples within the Central Powers. These points may be summarized thus:

1. "Open covenants of peace, openly arrived at," and no secret diplomacy in the future;
2. Freedom of the seas in peace and war;
3. Removal of economic barriers to the interests of subject peoples;
4. Reduction of armaments;
5. Impartial adjustments of colonial claims with due regard to the interests of subjected peoples;
6. Evacuation of Russian territory with full opportunity for Russia to determine her own future development;
7. Evacuation and restoration of Belgium;
8. Evacuation and restoration of French territory, and the return of Alsace-Lorraine to France;
9. Readjustment of Italian frontiers along clearly recognizable lines of nationality;
10. Autonomous development for the peoples of Austria-Hungary;
11. Evacuation and restoration of Serbia, Montenegro, and Rumania, an outlet to the sea for Serbia, interrelations of the Balkan states according to historical lines of allegiance and nationality;
12. Secure sovereignty for the Turkish parts of the Ottoman Empire, autonomy for the other portions, freedom of shipping through the Straits;
13. Establishment of an independent Poland with all territories inhabited by indisputably Polish population and with access to the sea;
14. Formation of a general association of nations to guarantee "political independence and territorial integrity to great and small states alike."

As their submarine campaign weakened and their man-power lessened, the Germans

under Hindenburg and Ludendorff made a supreme effort to smash the Allied armies in France before the full weight of American man-power became effective. In March 1918 they smote the British trenches in the valley of the Somme with a terrific assault and plowed through to Amiens. In April, they hit the British west of Lille and gained some fifteen miles. In May, with the last of their reserve troops and with boys called to military service ahead of time, they struck the French along the Aisne and fought their way forward to Château-Thierry on the Marne only forty-odd miles from Paris. Here, Marshal Ferdinand Foch who had been named commander-in-chief of all the Allied armies, checked the Germans with the help of fresh American troops.

The furious drives and sledge-hammer blows of the Germans in the spring of 1918 netted them considerable territory, as well as prisoners and guns, and served to restore the western front almost to what it had been in 1914 on the eve of the first battle of the Marne. But they were supremely expensive, for they were accompanied by a frightful loss of life not only of French and British but of Germans as well, and German man-power was running low. In June the Germans could still push forward near Noyon another six miles. But a similar effort in July, aimed at Reims, encountered unyielding resistance and was quickly succeeded by a great Allied counter-offensive. Meanwhile, in June, an Austrian offensive against the Italians along the Piave River had been stopped and turned back. The day of military successes for the Central Powers was over, and the final triumph of the Allies began.

In 1918 the war governments of the Allies were in strong hands. Wilson directed the American effort. Lloyd George headed the ministry in Great Britain. Italy had a vigorous prime minister in Orlando. In France, the aged Clemenceau was virtual war dictator, with a fierce will to victory. The Allies now had satisfactory coördination in both military and economic matters, and their troops were at last well supplied with munitions of all sorts. Thanks to conscription in the United States, there were

a million American soldiers in France by July 1918, and in the next four months that number was doubled.

Having checked the Germans in the second battle of the Marne (July 1918), the Allies, flushed with victory and guided by the master hand of Foch, hammered at the German lines everywhere in France. While Franco-British armies recaptured Cambrai and Lille, Franco-American armies forced the Germans from St. Mihiel and cleared them out of the Argonne. By the end of October, the Germans had been driven almost completely out of France, and compelled to evacuate most of Belgium. Along the whole western front they were retreating so rapidly as to resemble a rout.

Meanwhile in the Near East, the British were pressing Turkey hard. With Arab aid they overran all Palestine and advanced into Syria. In October 1918, they captured both Damascus and Aleppo. From Salonica an Allied army, under a French general, Franchet d'Espérey, struck north, in September 1918, against the Bulgarians. Within two weeks Macedonia was cleared and Bulgaria itself was tottering.

Almost simultaneously, Austria-Hungary collapsed. Encouraged by Allied victories in the west and in the Balkans, the Czech and Yugoslav deputies in the Austrian parliament on October 1, 1918, proclaimed the right of their peoples to self-determination. On October 18, a declaration of independence was issued by the provisional government of the "Czechoslovak Republic" headed by Thomas Masaryk, an outstanding Czech scholar and patriot. Eleven days later the Croatian Diet voted to break its ties with Hungary and to join Serbia in creating a union of all Yugoslavs. The Rumanians reëntered the war and invaded Hungary. The Italians advanced into the Austrian provinces of Istria and the Tyrol.

The confederacy of the Central Powers, which had stood like a granite fortress for four years, was finally crumbling. Its armies were defeated and demoralized. Its generals were discredited. Its monarchs and statesmen were panic-stricken. Its peoples were clamoring for peace. Bulgaria, the last to join the confederacy, was the first to quit it. She surrendered unconditionally to the Allies on September 30, 1918. A month later, the Ottoman Empire and Austria-Hungary followed suit. Germany was left to end the First World War as best she could.

Already, in August 1918, General Ludendorff had told William II that the war was lost, and at the end of September, prostrated by the news of Bulgaria's surrender, he had besought the Emperor to make peace at once. William II responded by appointing a liberal chancellor, Prince Maximillian of Baden, and instructing him to negotiate with the Allies. After a month's interchange of notes between Prince Maximillian and President Wilson, the Allies agreed to make peace on the basis of the "fourteen points," subject to reservations on the fate of Austria-Hungary and on an explicit pledge of German reparation "for all damage done to the civilian population of the Allies." On this basis an armistice between Germany and the Allies was signed on November 11, 1918, in a railway car on a siding in the forest of Compiègne in northern France. But by this time revolutionary movements and naval and military mutinies in Germany had brought about the downfall of the imperial German government and the succession of a republican and socialist government. It was consequently the latter which signed the armistice. William II had already taken refuge in Holland.

In accordance with the armistice, the Allies occupied the left bank of the Rhine. To the Allies, moreover, Germany surrendered all her war material, though most of the German naval ships were sunk by their officers at Scapa Flow (June 1919). The confederacy of the Central Powers, broken and disarmed, lay prostrate at the feet of the triumphant Allies.

The First World War lasted four years and fifteen weeks. It was waged by thirty nations, including all the great powers. Sixty-five million men bore arms in it. Eight and a half million were killed, twenty-nine million were wounded, captured, or missing. The direct costs of the war have been estimated at something like 200 billion dollars. Its indirect costs in property and lives are incalculable.

With the First World War, an era ended, an era of optimism and "progress." The new age that was dawning began with high hopes at the peace conference, but those hopes soon gave way to disillusionment. For the next two decades Europe was in an unstable equilibrium, which, when it finally broke down, plunged the world into a second and even greater disaster.

CHAPTER 56

Peace Settlement of 1919–1920

A. Paris Peace Conference and Treaties

Paris and its environs were naturally chosen as the setting for the peace conference following the First World War. It was decided in advance by the victorious Allies that they would first reach agreement among themselves on peace terms and afterwards summon the vanquished Central Powers, beginning with Germany, to accept the terms. Accordingly, the conference was formally inaugurated by an assemblage of eminent Allied representatives on January 18, 1919, in the Hall of Mirrors at Versailles, where, forty-eight years earlier to the day, Bismarck had proclaimed the German Empire. Altogether, the participating "allied and associated nations" numbered thirty-two. But in all ensuing negotiations, the crucial decisions were made by the "Big Three"—Wilson for the United States, Clemenceau for France, and Lloyd George for Great Britain.

After four months of incessant labor and spasmodic disputing, the draft of a peace treaty with Germany, 80,000 words in length, was submitted to, and endorsed by, the conference in a formal plenary session on May 6, 1919. The next day German delegates were admitted and presented with the draft. They protested that it was intolerably severe and that it violated the "fourteen points." The Allies made only minor concessions, and at length on June 23 a German Constituent Assembly at Weimar voted to accept it unconditionally. Five days later the treaty was signed in a solemn ceremony in the Hall of Mirrors at Versailles.

With the completion of this "treaty of Versailles" with Germany, the major work of the conference was done and its leading figures went home. But others stayed on and labored over the settlements with the remaining defeated states. Peace was formally concluded with Austria in September 1919 (treaty of St. Germain); with Bulgaria in November 1919 (treaty of Neuilly); with Hungary in June 1920 (treaty of the Trianon); and with Turkey in August 1920 (treaty of Sèvres). The last never really went into effect. The others, including that with Germany, endured for two decades. Since they were all signed in the vicinity of Paris, they may be called collectively the Peace of Paris. Into each was written a "covenant" providing for the establishment of a League of Nations and a Permanent Court of International Justice, which we shall discuss later.

By the treaty of Versailles, Germany ceded Alsace-Lorraine to France, the towns of Eupen and Malmédy to Belgium, the province of Posen and a strip running to the sea through West Prussia (the Polish corridor) to Poland. The town of Memel was ceded to the Allies, and was appropriated by Lithuania in 1923, as partial compensation for Polish seizure of Vilna. Further, Germany agreed to the holding of plebiscites to determine the fate of East

Prussia, Upper Silesia, and Schleswig. East Prussia voted to remain German; the northern third of Schleswig joined Denmark; Upper Silesia, after much disorder, was arbitrarily divided between Germany and Poland. Danzig became an international "free city," and the coal region of the Saar was placed for fifteen years under the administration of the League of Nations and the economic control of France.

In addition, Germany yielded all her overseas empire. Her lease of Kiaochow and privileges in Shantung were transferred to Japan, and also her Pacific islands north of the equator. The German portion of Samoa went to New Zealand, and the other German possessions south of the equator in the Pacific were transferred to Australia. German Southwest Africa was assigned to the Union of South Africa; German East Africa to Great Britain (save for the northwest corner which went to Belgium); Kamerun and Togoland were divided between Britain and France. In most cases the powers receiving German colonies did so, not as absolute sovereigns, but as "mandatories"

of the League of Nations, to which they promised to give periodic accounts of their stewardship.

Germany recognized, moreover, the independence of Poland, Czechoslovakia, and German Austria, denounced the treaties of Brest-Litovsk· and Bucharest, and gave the Allies a free hand to settle affairs in eastern Europe. Militarily Germany promised to abolish conscription, reduce her army 'to 100,000 men, raze all fortifications for thirty miles east of the Rhine, reduce her navy to six battleships, six light cruisers, and twelve torpedo boats with no submarines, to abandon military and naval aviation, demolish the fortifications of Heligoland, open the Kiel canal to all nations, build no forts on the Baltic, and surrender her transoceanic cables. Though Germany expressly consented to the trial of the former Kaiser and other "war criminals," Holland refused to surrender William II, and attempts by the Allies to prosecute other offenders were soon abandoned.

By a special section (the "war guilt clause"), Germany was compelled to

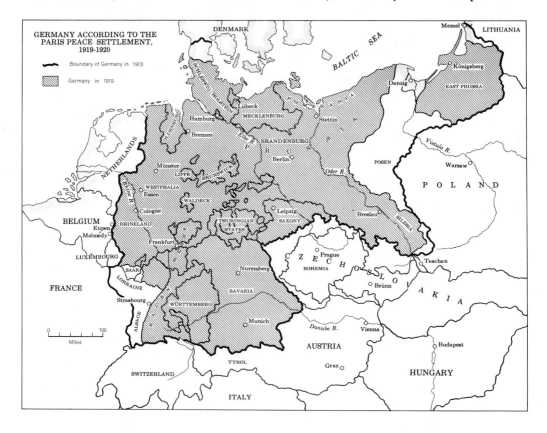

The "Big Four" at the Peace Conference 1919. Left to right, Premiers Lloyd George, Orlando, and Clemenceau, and President Wilson.

Photo by Underwood & Underwood, New York

acknowledge responsibility for bringing on the First World War and to promise "reparations" for the damage done to Allied civilians and their property. On this account she was to make an immediate payment of five billion dollars and such further payments as the Allied Reparations Commission should direct. In the meantime she was to make payments in goods of all sorts —ships, railway equipment, cattle, coal, books, etc.—as compensation for the destruction she had wrought. The total amount of reparations was left unsettled. It was to be the most that Germany could pay. Until the treaty was executed in full and the reparations paid, the Allies might occupy the left bank of the Rhine and bridgeheads on the right bank, although, if Germany were fulfilling her obligations, partial evacuation would take place within fifteen years.

The treaties with other defeated powers followed in a general way the pattern of the treaty of Versailles with Germany, and involved a drastic rearrangement of the map of Europe. By the treaty of St. Germain, Austria recognized the independence of Hungary, Czechoslovakia, Poland, and Yugoslavia, and ceded to them and to Rumania and Italy the bulk of the old territories of the Dual Monarchy. Austria was left as a small, independent, German-

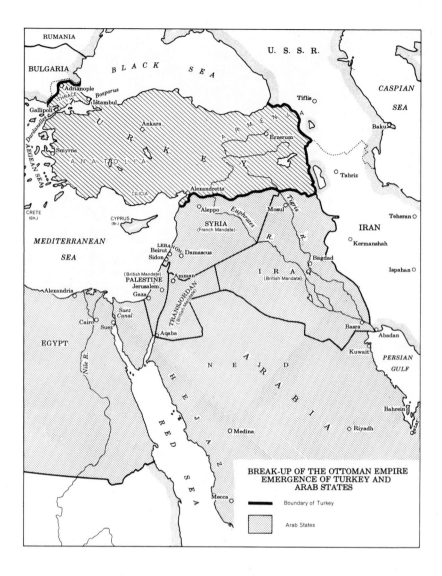

RUMANIA

BULGARIA

BLACK SEA

U. S. S. R.

CASPIAN SEA

Adrianople
Bosporus
THRACE
Gallipoli
Istambul
Dardanelles
AEGEAN SEA
Smyrna
ANATOLIA
CILICIA
Ankara
TURKEY
Erzerum
ARMENIA
Tiflis
Baku
Tabriz
Alexandretta

CRETE
(GK.)
CYPRUS
(Br.)
Aleppo
Euphrates
Mosul
Tigris
SYRIA
(French Mandate)

MEDITERRANEAN SEA
LEBANON
Beirut
Sidon
Damascus
R.
IRAN
Kermanshah
Teheran
Ispahan
IRAQ
(British Mandate)
Bagdad

Alexandria
(British Mandate)
PALESTINE
Jerusalem
Gaza
Amman
TRANSJORDAN
(British Mandate)

EGYPT
Cairo
Suez
Suez
Canal
Aqaba
Basra
Abadan
Kuwait
PERSIAN GULF

Nile R.
HEJAZ
NEJD
ARABIA
Bahrein
Qatar

RED SEA
Medina
Riyadh

Mecca

BREAK-UP OF THE OTTOMAN EMPIRE
EMERGENCE OF TURKEY AND
ARAB STATES

━━━ Boundary of Turkey

▨ Arab States

speaking state with an area and a population about the same as Portugal's. She was deprived of seaports, and her army was restricted to 30,000 men. Her formerly great capital city of Vienna now resembled a head without a body.

From Bulgaria were taken, by the treaty of Neuilly, most of the lands she had won in the Balkan War of 1912–1913 and all her World War conquests. Dobruja went to Rumania, most of Macedonia to Yugoslavia, the Thracian coast to Greece.

By the treaty of the Trianon, Hungary was stripped of almost all her non-Magyar subjects and many who were Magyars. The Slovak provinces went to Czechoslovakia. Transylvania was ceded to Rumania.

Croatia was yielded to Yugoslavia. Hungary shrank from an imperial domain of 125,000 square miles to a little land-locked state of 36,000 square miles, and from a population of twenty-two million to one of eight million.

Determination of the fate of the Ottoman Empire was delayed by acute quarrels between France and Britain and between Italy and Greece, as well as by the existence of two rival Turkish governments, the Sultan's at Constantinople and that of Mustafa Kemal, an army officer and ardent nationalist who established a revolutionary republican regime at Ankara in Asia Minor. At length in August 1920 the Allies signed a treaty at Sèvres with the Sultan, by which the Arab state of Hejaz, east of the Red Sea, and Armenia, in Asia Minor, would be independent. Palestine, Mesopotamia, Trans-Jordania, and Syria would become mandates, the first three of Britain, the last of France. Cilicia would be a sphere of influence for France, and southern Anatolia for Italy. Smyrna, Thrace, Adrianople, Gallipoli and the Aegean islands would be ceded to Greece. The Straits would be demilitarized and internationalized. Of all the conquered countries, Turkey alone, under the vigorous Mustafa Kemal, was able to resist the execution of the peace terms imposed on it. Armenia did not become independent. Adrianople and Smyrna remained Turkish. The spheres of influence did not materialize. The Straits were not demilitarized or internationalized.

The reason why Mustafa Kemal was able to oppose the peace settlement lay in the fact that the Allies had demobilized their forces, while he had an army still in being. He wiped out the Armenian Republic, compelled the Italian troops to leave southern Anatolia, and obliged the French to end their occupation of Cilicia. The French, Italians, and Russians all began to treat directly with Mustafa Kemal, but the British encouraged the Greeks to attempt, in 1921, to enforce the terms of the treaty of Sèvres by armed might. The Turks in a vigorous campaign drove the Greeks out of Asia Minor, and in November 1922 occupied Constantinople and deposed the Sultan Mohammed VI. The success of Mustafa Kemal and his Turkish Nationalists led to new and difficult negotiations. Eventually in July 1923 at Lausanne in Switzerland another treaty was signed. It ended the Turkish Empire, and made Turkey a more or less consolidated national state. Turkey resigned all claims to Hejaz, Palestine, Trans-Jordan, Mesopotamia, and Syria, but kept the whole of Anatolia and also Cilicia, Adalia, Smyrna, Constantinople, Gallipoli, Adrianople, and eastern Thrace— a total area of about 300,000 square miles with a population of some thirteen million.

The peace settlement of Paris and the later treaty of Lausanne did not resolve all questions, but they did establish a political framework and a territorial settlement for Europe. Unlike the settlement at Vienna,

a hundred years earlier, they made some attempt to redraw the map of Europe along lines of nationality. This proved very difficult; and the new nations that sprang from the Peace of Paris were required to sign "minority treaties" guaranteeing civil equality and cultural opportunities to national minorities within their borders.

B. The New Nations

Several nations gained independence in 1919–1920 as a result of the partial breakup of the Russian Empire. Finland, long used to some degree of autonomy under the tsars, established a successfully functioning political democracy, and, like the neighboring Scandinavian states, achieved a quiet prosperity based in part on co-operative enterprises. Latvia and Estonia became democratic republics, and so did Lithuania. In the last named country there was much political turbulence, aggravated by the Polish seizure (1920) of Vilna, the city claimed by the Lithuanians as their capital.

To reconstitute an independent Poland had seemed impossible in 1913, for it required the dissolution of the three Empires of Russia, Germany, and Austria. Yet this actually occurred in the course of the First World War. For some time afterwards there was fighting between the Poles and the Russians, but at length, by a treaty signed at Riga in March 1921, Communist Russia recognized the independence of Poland and accepted a compromise frontier well to the east of that (the Curzon line) tentatively suggested earlier by the Allies.

With an area of about 150,000 square miles and a population of about thirty million, Poland was the largest of the new states of central Europe. But it had been grievously devastated by war, and its electorate and parliament were split into an extraordinary number of political factions whose chronic rivalries made successful constitutional government difficult. From 1926 until his death in 1935, Marshal Josef Pilsudski, Polish hero of the First World War, exercised a kind of veiled military dictatorship, and during these years considerable progress was made in breaking up large landed estates and in promoting popular education.

In the new nation of Czechoslovakia, which emerged from the disruption of Austria-Hungary, democratic practices were steadily adhered to, despite difficulties with neighboring countries and with a large minority of "Sudeten" Germans in Bohemia, and despite differences between Catholics and Socialists and between Czechs and Slovaks. The personal prestige of Thomas Masaryk, who was in a very real sense the "father of his country" and its president until 1935, combined with the parliamentary skill of other leading statesmen to preserve democratic government. Political stability was enhanced by a modest but solid prosperity based in part on reforms which gave land to the peasants and on industrial development, especially the large-scale production of munitions and shoes.

Both post-war Austria and post-war Hungary, now stripped of their subject peoples, were essentially new states. Austria was harried by adverse economic conditions, centering in depressed Vienna, whose fac-

tories were cut off from their former markets and sources of supply and whose people for the most part joined the Social Democratic party. Rural and provincial Austria remained Catholic and tended to vote for the Christian Socialist party. Immediately after the war the Social Democrats were the largest party and governed the country in a coalition with the Catholics. But from 1922 to 1930, the Christian Socialists in coalition with the smaller Nationalist Party were in charge of affairs. Aided by loans from abroad, Austria struggled along until 1931, when, caught in the backwash of the world depression, her economic difficulties led her into political troubles which were soon gravely complicated by pressures from abroad.

Hungary after a brief experience of Communist dictatorship fell into the hands of reactionary aristocrats led by Admiral Horthy and Count Stephen Bethlen. From 1920, Hungary was technically a "constitutional monarchy," without a king and with Horthy as "regent." There was little real democracy, for power rested with the great landowners and wealthy bourgeois. There

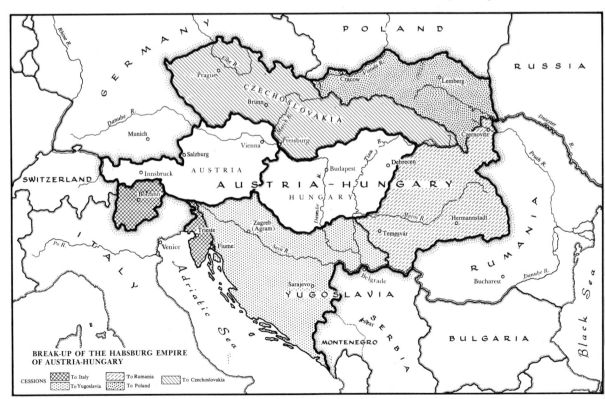

BREAK-UP OF THE HABSBURG EMPIRE
OF AUSTRIA-HUNGARY

CESSIONS   To Italy   To Rumania   To Czechoslovakia
           To Yugoslavia   To Poland

was much bitter nationalism summed up in the slogan "No! No! Never!," which referred to the loss of territory imposed on Hungary at the end of the war.

Yugoslavia, which was Serbia enlarged by territories transferred from Austria-Hungary, was deeply troubled by differences in religion, culture, and politics among its constituent peoples—Serbs, Croats, and Slovenes. The Serbs were Orthodox in religion and "backward" in economics and culture. The Croats and Slovenes were Catholic in religion and more progressive. In addition, there were more than a million Moslems, mainly in the province of Bosnia. The Croatians urged a federal state and home rule for Croatia. The more numerous Serbs insisted on a centralized administration. This difference, intensified by religious, educational, and economic disputes, led to bitter quarrels and even fights among the deputies in the Chamber at Belgrade. Violence reached a peak in 1928, when Stefan Radić, the Croatian leader, and several of his lieutenants were killed. Whereupon, early in 1929, King Alexander, supported by the army, dissolved the parliament, suppressed the constitution, proclaimed himself dictator, and repressed all criticism and dissent.

Rumania, with her area and population doubled as a result of the First World War, was almost a new state. Vexed by minorities which constituted two-ninths of her population, the government sought to win the support of the peasantry by a drastic policy of breaking up large estates. But in so doing it roused the ire of former landlords. Though nominally democratic, Rumania was actually ruled by cliques of professional politicians, some of them notoriously corrupt. Moreover, there was trouble with the crown, for after the death of Ferdinand I (1927), he was succeeded, not by his son Carol who had been legally debarred from the succession because of his infatuation with a woman of doubtful reputation, but by Carol's son, Michael. In 1930, however, Carol, with the support of army officers, seized the throne, and the government became more arbitrary and irresponsible.

One of the most vigorous of the smaller countries in the post war period was Turkey.

Cut down to a population overwhelmingly Turkish, intensely nationalist, infused with patriotic pride by the victory over the Greeks in 1921–1922, and possessed of a beloved leader in Mustafa Kemal, Turkey made rapid progress. Nominally Turkey was a constitutional, democratic republic, but actually it was a nationalistic dictatorship under Mustafa Kemal, who proceeded rather rapidly to westernize the country. The sultans had been religious leaders (caliphs) as well as political rulers. Mustafa Kemal abolished the caliphate (1924), reduced the role of the Moslem religion, substituted western law for that based on the Koran, abolished the wearing of the fez and the veil, changed from the Arabic to the Roman alphabet, prohibited polygamy, emancipated women, adopted the western calendar, developed public education, introduced the metric system of weights and measures, and in 1932 brought Turkey into the League of Nations. Few countries have been transformed so fast or so successfully. Turkey began to look toward the future not the past. It built railways, dams, electric plants, and irrigation projects. It organized a compulsory exchange of minority populations with Greece, by which a million Greeks, resident in Turkey, were sent to a homeland they had never known, and 400,000 Turks, resident in Greece, were brought to Turkey. It put down by force revolts of the stubbornly Moslem Kurds. It developed a lively and relatively free press. When Kemal died in 1938, he left a strong country and one that moved, though fitfully, toward a more democratic government.

Of the national states which were newly constituted or newly enlarged in 1919–1920, only Czechoslovakia and Finland made a real success of democratic republican government. In the rest, for a variety of reasons, including internal conflict and fear of foreign nations, the trend was toward some sort of arbitrary or dictatorial rule. It seemed as if democracy was something that could not be attained suddenly, but rather must grow by a slow evolution nurtured by experience. It is possible that greater prosperity in the new nations might have led to a longer maintenance of popular government. But despite moments of economic well-being in the 1920's, a serious depression harrassed Europe most of the time in the two decades after 1919. Even the older democracies had their troubles in the post-war world.

C. France and Great Britain

Though victorious in the war and re-possessed of Alsace-Lorraine, France faced a multitude of grave problems after 1919. At the start, the most pressing seemed to be the rehabilitation of her devastated areas in the north, the cost of which she expected Germany to bear. In 1920, after much haggling, the Allies agreed that France should get 52 per cent of German reparations, and the next year the total of these was fixed at thirty-two billion gold dollars. But it was one thing to determine the debt and another to collect it. There were serious obstacles to accepting payments in kind, for free importation of such commodities as coal, steel, or machines from Germany threatened to ruin corresponding English and French industries. Money payments proved no less difficult, for Germany could not make them unless she had a large favorable balance of trade, and this could be secured only by letting her win back all her pre-war markets and many new ones. Against any such outcome, France, as well as the United States and many other countries, quickly erected high tariff walls. In 1922 Germany declared her inability to make further payments. Whereupon French troops occupied the German industrial district of the Ruhr. But the Germans met this step with well-organized "passive resistance," and the French found it as difficult to secure payments by force as by negotiation.

In 1924, an international commission of experts headed by an American banker, Charles Dawes, devised a plan whereby German payments would be spread over a long period of years. France withdrew her troops from the Ruhr, and for a while the "Dawes Plan" seemed to work fairly well. But the Germans were irked by the economic controls it imposed, and the transfer of payments was still difficult. In 1929, a second commission of experts headed by

another American, Owen Young, recommended that the reparation payments be reduced to eight billion dollars spread over the next fifty-eight years. This proposal, together with provision for the Allied evacuation of the occupied areas of the Rhineland, was embodied in an international agreement signed at the Hague in 1930.

But in the very next year, in the face of world-wide depression, Germany declared herself unable to meet even the Young Plan payments. At the suggestion of the American President Herbert Hoover, Germany's creditors granted her a temporary moratorium, and in 1932 they agreed to scale the remaining reparations payments down to 700 million dollars, if at the same time the United States would forgive the war debts (totalling over ten billion dollars) owed by the various Allied nations to it. This the United States refused to do. Whereupon the Allied countries (except Finland) stopped payments to the United States as Germany had stopped payments to them. Practically, though not legally, both reparations and interallied war debts, which had so long weighed down the economy of the world, were thus wiped off the slate.

The total of reparation payments actually made by Germany was about six and a half billion gold dollars, of which over a third represented American loans to Germany that were not repaid. Meanwhile, French reconstruction was financed less by receipts from Germany than by domestic taxes, loans, and issuance of paper money, which brought on an inflation that reduced the value of the franc by four-fifths and bore hard on the salaried classes and on all those who lived on savings or fixed incomes.

Meanwhile, in the international sphere, France sought to bolster her position and ward off any German "war of revenge" by a system of alliances. She contracted a formal military alliance with Belgium in 1920, with Poland in 1921, and with Czechoslovakia in 1924. The last-named country had already formed, in 1920–1921, a "Little Entente" with Rumania and Yugoslavia for the purpose of safeguarding the territories they had each acquired from Hungary. This arrangement helped France

A Figure. Henri Matisse
(d. 1954).

to enlarge her circle of alliances by drawing into it Rumania in 1926 and Yugoslavia in 1927. But in the event, the alliances proved slender reeds to lean on, for not only did France have to continue to strengthen her allies by costly loans, but the countries of eastern Europe (except Czechoslovakia) were drawn in the 1930's by economic motives towards Germany, which promised them a better market for their goods than France.

In internal politics, France oscillated between the Right and the Left, with the Left tending to gain strength. The Right parties, or "National Bloc," controlled the government from 1919 to 1924. But the failure of Poincaré's strong policy toward Germany brought in the "Cartel of the Left" in the elections of 1924. It proceeded to adopt a conciliatory attitude toward Germany, and in 1925 it agreed to the "Locarno Pact," whereby Germany entered the League of Nations, while Germany, France, and Belgium promised to respect their mutual frontiers, and Italy and Britain guaranteed the arrangement. In the crisis of financial inflation, however, the Left failed to command popular support, Poincaré was recalled to the premiership, and parties of the Right won the elections of 1928. The Left again triumphed in 1932, and once more in 1936.

In Great Britain, the political scene was marked by the almost complete disintegration of the Liberal party. Its old faith in free trade seemed no longer tenable, for in the post-war world Great Britain was in a precarious economic position. Her veins of iron and coal were running thin. She had lost markets to the United States and Japan. The new countries were trying to build up their own industries behind protective tariffs. Unemployment hung like an ominous cloud over the British Isles. In 1921, two million workers were idle in a country of only forty-two million people. Even in 1928, a boom year in most lands, the number of British unemployed hovered close to the million mark.

The Lloyd George coalition government, which had triumphed in the "khaki election" of 1918, made the peace. It reluctantly recognized the Irish Free State as a separate dominion (1921). It extended social insurance for labor and greatly increased the government subsidies ("doles") for unemployment payments to workers. But in 1922, the coalition broke up and in the ensuing election the Liberals won only

118 seats in the Commons against 347 for the Conservatives and 142 for the Labor party.

Britain had already adopted some emergency tariffs. Now the Conservatives under Stanley Baldwin came out for thoroughgoing protection as a cure for Britain's ills, and an election was fought on the issue in 1923. The Conservatives lost some 90 seats, while the Laborites gained fifty, with the result that early in 1924 Britain's first Labor cabinet was formed under Ramsay MacDonald. But this was short-lived, for it was dependent on Liberal support, and when MacDonald decided to recognize the Bolshevik government of Russia the Liberals deserted him.

New elections in 1924 gave a thumping majority to the Conservatives, and a second Baldwin government lasted until 1929. It fought and beat a "general strike" of the workers arising from unemployment in the coal mines. It extended the suffrage (1928)

League of Nations Buildings at Geneva.

Courtesy Wide World Photos

to all women on the same basis as men. In foreign affairs, it pursued a cautious policy, hostile to Russia, friendly to Germany, and not too coöperative with France. In domestic matters it tried to improve economic conditions by gingerly experimenting with housing and the "rationalization" of industry and by "sound" financial policies.

In the regular general election of 1929, Labor won a plurality and Ramsay MacDonald formed a second ministry. But his government almost at once ran into an acute economic crisis resulting from the worldwide depression which began in 1929. MacDonald tried no radical reforms and his careful policies met with little success. When, in 1931, he proposed drastic economies in governmental expeditures including the "dole" to the unemployed, he split the Labor party. Only a minority under the name of National Laborites stuck with the prime minister. But instead of resigning, MacDonald invited Conservatives and Liberals to join with him in forming a "national government" to meet the economic crisis, and in the ensuing election his coalition won a sweeping victory. But the chief beneficiaries were the Conservatives, who almost doubled their representation.

A protective tariff was now enacted, and in 1931 the so-called Statute of Westminster recognized the self-governing dominions of the British Empire (Canada, Australia, New Zealand, South Africa, and Ireland) as "nations" grouped in a "Commonwealth," and bound together only by ties of sentiment, by allegiance to a common king, and by occasional conferences. In 1935, Stanley Baldwin replaced MacDonald as prime minister, and the Conservatives won the election of that year.

D. The League of Nations

The First World War created a widespread demand for some sort of association of nations to preserve world peace. Various plans were proposed by statesmen and publicists. But it was Woodrow Wilson who was most insistent on providing for a definite League of Nations by a solemn international "Covenant" incorporated in the Paris peace settlement of 1919–1920.

The Covenant provided for an international body of two houses—an Assembly in which every nation had one vote, and a Council in which the great powers had permanent seats and a few lesser powers held temporary elective seats. In addition, there were a Secretariat staffed by officials with headquarters at Geneva; a Court of International Justice at the Hague for the settlement of disputes; and an International Labor Office designed to further interests of labor all over the world. Though in some ways the League resembled an international government, it was in reality much more like a continuous conference of diplomatic agents of the various states. Its main purpose was to prevent war, but it also had special duties imposed on it by the treaties of 1919–1920, and was expected to promote general international coöperation.

The Covenant obligated the member nations "to respect and preserve as against external aggression" each other's "territorial integrity and political independence." It required the submission of disputes to arbitration, and, if arbitration failed, to the Council. Members were forbidden to wage war in contravention of a unanimous decision by the Council, and provision was made for economic and military measures ("sanctions") against recalcitrant states, whether members or non-members. All treaties contrary to the League were to be abrogated and all treaties old and new were to be registered with the League Secretariat. The League was to push forward the reduction of armaments, to administer Danzig and the Saar, and to supervise mandated colonies.

In January 1920, at the call of President Wilson, the League of Nations was formally inaugurated at Paris with an initial meeting of the Council, and the first Assembly convened at Geneva in the following November. By this time all the Allies in the First World War, except the United States and Russia, had joined the League; and the invited neutrals brought the number of members to forty-two. It was ironical that the United States, whose President had taken the leading part in launching the League, should have held aloof from it.

The reason for this was that unfortunately the League became an issue of American partisan politics, and in the presidential election of 1920 "isolationist" foes of the League triumphed.

Other states were admitted to the League from time to time, for example, Germany in 1926 and Russia in 1934. By 1935, there were sixty-two members: twenty-eight in Europe, twenty-one in America, eight in Asia, three in Africa, and two in Australasia. But there were also significant secessions. Above all, the continuous abstention of the United States was calamitous for the League.

Despite its weaknesses, the League accomplished a great deal. The Secretariat gathered and published much useful data about world conditions. The League supervised the repatriation of 400,000 prisoners of war belonging to twenty-six nationalities. It aided in caring for refugees. It helped in the financial rebuilding of Austria and Hungary. It conducted plebiscites with impartiality and successfully administered Danzig and the Saar. Through its agencies, it did much to check the spread of typhus and the international traffic in opium. Through its commission on intellectual coöperation, it brought together scientists and scholars from all parts of the world and facilitated the exchange of scientific, artistic, and literary information and the movement of students and teachers from one country to another. Through its associated Labor Office, it promoted international collaboration in collecting facts and in dealing with problems of industrial labor. Through the Court of International Justice, a considerable number of controversial matters were successfully arbitrated, and through special committees a start was made toward a codification of international law.

Thus the League proved a valuable and indeed indispensable instrument of international coöperation. But its record in its primary function of settling disputes which might lead to war was not so shining and by the mid-1930's was beclouded. A few minor disputes it settled: between Finland and Sweden over the Aland Islands (1920); between Poland and Germany over their boundary in Upper Silesia (1921); between Greece and Bulgaria over border incidents (1925); between Peru and Colombia over a border province (1933). In dealing with disputes affecting major powers, the League was far less effective. It ended a dispute between Great Britain and Iraq over the Mosul oil fields, but it did so only by a pro-British decision. In 1923, when Poland, backed by France, was in conflict with Lithuania over Vilna, League mediation was pushed aside and Poland's seizure of the city was upheld by an independent agreement among France, Britain, and Italy. In the same year, in a violent quarrel between Greece and Italy, the Italians seized the Greek island of Corfu, and ignored the League. Only through the mediation of France and Britain was Italy persuaded to evacuate Corfu, and then on terms necessitating Greek acceptance of Italy's major demands. In the 1930's the League was flouted with impunity by Japan, Germany, and Italy.

In respect of disarmament, the failure of the League was well-nigh complete. Outside its framework, a conference of naval powers at Washington in 1921–1922 agreed to a limitation of battleship tonnages to a ratio of 5 for Great Britain, 5 for the United States, 3 for Japan, 1.67 for France, and 1.67 for Italy, but no agreement was reached about limitation of light cruisers (advocated by the United States) or prohibition of submarines (urged by Britain). At a second naval conference at Geneva in 1927, the United States and Britain still could not agree about cruisers. They finally reached an agreement at a third conference at London in 1930, but Japan now acquiesced most reluctantly, while France and Italy refused altogether. Consequently the London commitments bound only three of the five naval powers and were further weakened by an "escalator clause" which permitted a nation to exceed the specified tonnage totals if it thought its "national security" was "materially affected" by the naval building of another country.

In the matter of land armies, even less progress had been made. In 1925 the League created a special commission to study the problem, which proved to be

Self Portrait. Vincent Van Gogh (*d.* 1890).

extraordinarily complicated and difficult, especially in view of the fears of some nations like France and the ambitions of others like Germany and Italy. After five years of labor, the Commission brought forth a draft treaty providing for limitations "in principle" of number of men under arms and of expenditures for armaments. But it included also an "escape clause" pro-posed by the United States and permitting any country to "suspend temporarily" any restriction imposed on it by the treaty. The long awaited Conference on Disarmament met in Geneva in February 1932 to discuss and improve the draft treaty. All League members were represented, and also the United States and Russia.

The Conference was protracted. In vain

the American President Hoover proposed a cut of one third in the armies of all countries. In vain the British prime minister, MacDonald, urged a standard army of 200,000 men for each of the major powers. Each proposal aroused fears or suspicions. In October 1933, Germany, now dominated by Adolf Hitler, impatiently quit the Conference and announced her purpose of rearming without regard to restrictions of the Versailles treaty. In the summer of 1934, Britain acknowledged the failure of the Conference. It then faded away, and in 1935 Germany independently reëstablished the kind of army which she had in 1914.

E. Economics and Culture After World War I

Despite its devastation, World War I increased the productive capacity of major nations and in some lines stimulated scientific advance. Internal difficulties removed Russia from world trade, and most of the countries of Europe were upset by currency inflation, violent in defeated lands like Germany and Austria, partial among victors like France and Italy. Inflation enabled Germany to slough off its internal debt, but most other countries, especially Britain, staggered along under a tremendous burden of indebtedness. Reparations and war debts complicated international finance. Agricultural reforms in central and eastern Europe produced a more equitable distribution of land, but often decreased productiveness since the new peasant proprietors lacked capital.

By 1926, despite difficulties, general European production, including even Russia's, approximated pre-war levels, and for the next three years comparative prosperity reigned; political tensions eased somewhat; international relations improved; people became optimistic. Then in the autumn of 1929, the American stock market crashed; business slackened, unemployment rose, and the United States experienced a prolonged depression. As American loans to Europe ceased, as American purchases of European goods fell off, and as American tourists to Europe thinned out, the depression rapidly overspread Europe. Internal and international friction increased, and in gloom and mutual suspicion Europe moved down the slope toward catastrophe.

Unsettled economic and political conditions after the First World War were reflected by a notable unsettling in art and literature. In painting there were numerous conflicting tendencies. "Cubism," inaugurated by a Spaniard in Paris, Pablo Picasso, utilized planes, straight lines, and geometrical forms. "Futurism," developed mainly in Italy, criticized the "static" quality of past painting and tried to show objects in motion, frequently by duplicating them in slightly altered positions. "Surrealism" attempted to depict a Freudian character of the human mind by showing incongruous objects associated in a wildly dreamlike manner. Less extreme artists, Henri Matisse for example, followed lines laid down before the war by post-impressionists like Cézanne and Van Gogh.

Architecture, though much of it was still traditional, developed a "modernist" school which achieved some striking results. "Modernism" in architecture was born of attempts to realize the potentialities of new materials like steel and concrete. It was fathered by designers of skyscrapers, office buildings, garages, and factories, with an eye upon the uses to which such edifices were put. It was consolidated into a "school" and achieved its greatest popularity in Germany. By 1930, many of the new buildings all over Europe were "modern" and "functional," with great sweeping planes, geometrical forms, and many windows.

In popular music, American jazz swept Europe, and syncopated rhythms were common not only along the Mississippi but on the Danube, the Seine, and the Thames. Serious composers like the Austrian Arnold Schönberg moved toward "modernism" in music, using dissonance, abandoning old harmonic relationships, employing novel sound effects, and trusting often to "natural inspiration."

The literature of the era was chaotic. Spread of literacy had greatly increased the size of the reading public, and if many were satisfied with daily newspapers and trashy magazines or novels, others created a demand for almost every conceivable type of book. There was a vogue for non-fiction works on travel, history, economics, politics, and especially biography. One trend, represented by Lytton Strachey's *Eminent Victorians*, was toward "debunking" great figures of the past by stressing their oddities and shortcomings. There were also many realistic but nostalgic works, such as those of the French Marcel Proust or the German Thomas Mann.

Most striking of all, though not very popular, were a number of authors who experimented with words, figures of speech, punctuation, capitalization, and all the old rules of writing. Some of them like Gertrude Stein and James Joyce carried their experiments so far that many of their works became partly or wholly incomprehensible to the average reader. Likewise, there was a notable vogue of the introspective novel, exploring and emphasizing the vagaries, rational and non-rational, of the human mind.

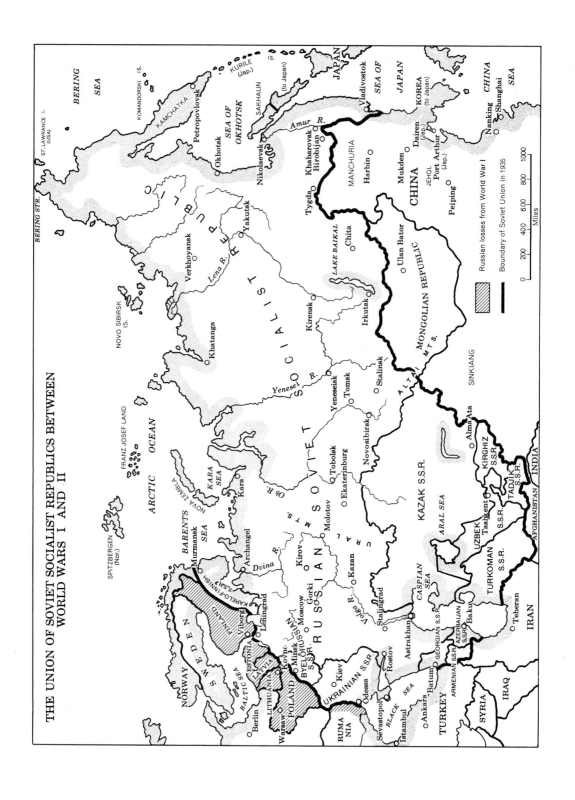

THE UNION OF SOVIET SOCIALIST REPUBLICS BETWEEN
WORLD WARS I AND II

Russian losses from World War I

Boundary of Soviet Union in 1935

0   200   400   600   800   1000
Miles

CHAPTER 57

Rise of Communist, Fascist, and Nazi Dictatorships

A. Communist Russia and the Soviet Union

At the close of the First World War, liberal democracy was the rule in every country of Europe except Russia. Here, it had been promised by the popular revolution of March 1917 which overthrew the autocratic tsardom, but the promise was nullified by the *coup d'état* and revolution of November 1917 which inaugurated a forceful dictatorship. This was called a "dictatorship of the proletariat." It was really a dictatorship of the Bolshevik Communist leader, Lenin, actively supported by a small but fanatical following, and employing methods of the utmost ruthlessness. It was more despotic than any recent European regime. It proved to be the forerunner of other dictatorships, which, whatever their professed principles might be, would copy its practices, and not only repudiate liberal democracy at home but oppose it abroad.

Just prior to Lenin's seizure of power, a Constituent Assembly had been freely and democratically elected. As it contained relatively few Bolsheviks, it was dissolved when it tried to meet in January 1918. Meanwhile the country at large was being terrorized. Nobles, landowners, army officers, and priests who would not accept the new regime were driven into exile or put to death. The ex-Tsar, his wife, and children were slaughtered. All dissident groups, including Cadets, Social Revolutionaries, or Menshevik Socialists, were mercilessly crushed.

Lenin's withdrawal of Russia from the First World War and his making peace with the Germans in March 1918, coupled with his repudiation of debts and his strident preaching of world revolution, angered the Allies and prompted them to give financial and military aid to "white" opponents of the "red" dictatorship. For the next two or three years Russia was prey to spasmodic civil war and foreign intervention, and also to a famine which in 1921–1922 carried off some five million people.

Yet the dictatorship triumphed. The Allies were too sick of war and too divergent in purpose to sustain any effective intervention in Russia. On the other hand, Lenin had in Leon Trotsky an exceptionally able war minister who successfully organized, equipped, and inspirited a remarkable "red army." And masses of Russian peasants and workers rallied to the support of the dictatorship lest its overthrow involve a reversal of its decrees for the break-up of large landed estates and the confiscation of privately owned factories. By 1921 domestic opposition was overcome and foreign interference ceased. In 1924 the Russian Communist regime was formally recognized by Great Britain, France, and Italy, and ten years later by the United States.

A kind of constitution for the Communist regime was promulgated in 1923. It provided for several "Soviet Socialist Republics," joined together in a "Union," and each guaranteed some measure of cultural nationalism. At first there were

739

Stalin at the 16th Congress of the Russian Communist Party. Painting by A. Gerasimov.

Courtesy Bettmann Archive

four of these, but by 1936 they numbered eleven.[1] Nominally the form of government for both the Union and the several constituent states was democratic. Persons over eighteen years of age who were engaged in "productive work" or enlisted in the army could vote for members of local "soviets." Local soviets chose delegates to regional soviets, and these elected deputies to a congress of soviets in each state and to an All-Union Congress of Soviets for the whole federation.

In practice, however, there was little more of democracy than of personal liberty under the Communist dictatorship. Many classes of persons were definitely debarred from voting: former tsarist officials, clergymen, employers of labor, private traders, well-to-

do peasants (*kulaks*). And all who could vote found themselves obliged to vote for nominees of the small minority belonging to the Communist party.

No other party was allowed to exist, and no person might belong to the Communist Party unless he avowed unquestioning faith in the principles of Marx and Lenin, promised the strictest obedience to party discipline, and proved his zeal during a probationary period. All members had to be continuously "active" and "above reproach." Their organization paralleled the governmental structure of the Union. Local party "cells" in factories, offices, or villages sent delegates to regional committees, which in turn were represented in an All-Union Party Congress. This Congress elected a Central Committee with a supreme "political bureau" of nine members. Here rested the center of authority for the entire Soviet Union, for the "political bureau" proposed major policies for the country and utilized the party machinery, along with elaborate espionage and censorship, with secret police

---

[1] (1) Russia, with its capital at Moscow, and embracing ninety per cent of the area and nearly seventy per cent of the population of the entire Union; (2) Ukraine, with capital at Kiev; (3) White Russia, with capital at Minsk; (4) Georgia; (5) Azerbaijan; (6) Armenia; (7) Turkoman; (8) Uzbek; (9) Tajikistan; (10) Kirghiz; (11) Kazakstan.

and arbitrary arrests and executions, to secure unquestioning adoption of such policies at any point from the local soviets up to the All-Union Congress. Though in theory they were separate, the party and the government were so intertwined as to be practically indistinguishable. He who controlled the party, controlled the country as a supreme dictator.

First the dictator was Lenin, who was both prime minister of the government and president of the party's political bureau, but by 1922 he was suffering from overwork and was partially paralyzed. There ensued a bitter rivalry for the succession between Trotsky, the war minister, and Stalin (Joseph Dzugashvili), scion of a Georgian peasant family and secretary of the Central Committee of the party. When Lenin died in 1924, Stalin's control of the party machinery and his popularity with the party members enabled him to become the acknowledged dictator. Trotsky was expelled from the government in 1924 and from the party in 1927. In 1929 he fled into exile and was murdered in Mexico eleven years later. By a series of "purges," his followers and other dissidents were rooted out of the government and the party.

During the first years of Soviet rule in Russia an attempt was made to apply the principles of Marxian socialism in thoroughgoing fashion. Private property was confiscated; debts repudiated; land, mines, and factories nationalized. But peasants disregarded the nationalization of the land, and took it for themselves. Workers' committees who strove to run the factories often lacked technical competence. The country as a whole was racked by civil war, foreign intervention, disease, and famine. The grain harvest of 1921 was only two-fifths that of 1913, and the transportation system was in a state of almost complete breakdown.

In the circumstances, Lenin proclaimed in 1921 a "new economic policy" (NEP). This, while preserving a communistic basis in public ownership of the major means of production, promised liberal rewards for Russian and foreign technicians, permitted small scale private production and trade, and allowed the peasants to rent land, hire labor, and sell their crops to private traders. The NEP stimulated production, both agricultural and industrial, and helped Russia to recover from the worst effects of war.

But to Stalin and other leaders, the NEP was only a temporary makeshift. To realize their ambition of making Russia a great industrial country and of socializing agriculture as well as industry, they worked out a series of "Five Year Plans." Under these, Russia did become a great industrial nation. Between 1928 and 1938 its production multiplied almost five times. By the latter date Russia was the fourth nation in the world in industrial output, being surpassed only by the United States, Germany, and Great Britain. In iron, steel, and certain other commodities, Russia was ahead of Britain.

Socialization of agriculture encountered special difficulties. Before the end of the first "Five Year Plan," it was decided to liquidate the kulaks (well-to-do peasants who had prospered under the NEP) and ruthlessly to push forward the creation of collective farms. Hundreds of thousands of kulaks were dispossessed and sent into exile or to concentration camps. Many peasants slaughtered and ate the livestock that was about to be confiscated and collectivized. As a result, there was more famine, especially during 1932–1933 in the Ukraine, where large numbers starved to death. But socialization was achieved, whatever the costs. By 1936, over 98 per cent of all tilled land was in state or collective farms, and agricultural production was again increasing.

The Communist dictatorship of the Soviet Union persistently endeavored to suppress all varieties of historic Christianity. It closed most of the churches, persecuted priests, forbade missionary enterprise, and denied advancement to practicing Christians. At the same time, it sponsored a "Society of the Godless" and the stream of propaganda by which this organization helped to de-Christianize the youth of the Soviet Union.

The dictatorship zealously promoted popular literacy. Thousands of schools—primary, secondary, and technical—were established. Scientific institutes were organized, and research conducted, especially along practical lines. Radio stations, newspapers, and books multiplied. Schooling was free at all levels, but, like all publicity and intellectual activity in the Soviet Union, it was subject to official censorship and propaganda and dominated by the Marxian ideas and approved policies of the Communist party.

In 1936 the Soviet Union adopted a new constitution, broadening the franchise and containing a declaration of individual liberties. It was largely "window dressing," however. Actually the dictatorship of Stalin and his Communist party continued as before.

There was some alteration of internal policy at about this time. National patriotism, which previously had been scorned, was now inculcated. Differentials in compensation for various sorts of labor were widened, until the bureaucracy of officials and managers was so well-paid that "socialist millionaires" became possible. Piecework wages, and what would be called in capitalist lands the "speed up," were introduced. Russia under Stalin was moving away from Lenin's principles of 1917, and the trend was now toward some form of state capitalism and an intensification of nationalism.

The Communist dictatorship in Russia had significant influence outside. Its example and propaganda served to split off from foreign Socialist parties, which were normally democratic, new Communist parties that were pro-Russian and anti-democratic. These were federated in 1919 in a "Third International" (Komintern), with headquarters at Moscow, in competition with the "Second International" of the more moderate Socialists. Through the Komintern, the Russian dictatorship directed the policies and activities of sizeable Communist parties in Germany, France, Italy, and most other countries on the European continent. Thereby it rendered the operation of liberal democracy more difficult in those countries, not only directly, but also indirectly by stimulating counter activity on the part of anti-democratic conservatives and reactionaries.

B. Fascist Italy

Among countries fatefully affected by the rise of totalitarian dictatorship, Italy was one of the most conspicuous. The Italian government which waged the First World War was liberal and democratic, and the first general election after the close of that struggle seemed to indicate that Italy, like Britain and France, would continue to adhere to liberal democracy. In addition to a slender majority of old-line Liberals in the newly elected Chamber of Deputies, there were increased numbers of Social Democrats and also a large representation of a new Catholic Popular party, led by Don Sturzo and committed to democracy.

Conditions in Italy were not conducive to orderly progress. Many patriots blamed the existing regime for Italy's relative military weakness in the war and for her failure in the ensuing peace negotiations to get as much territorial extension in Africa and the Near East as they thought she should have. The majority of Italian Socialists, influenced by example and propaganda of Lenin's Bolshevik dictatorship in Russia, turned Communist and abandoned democratic methods in favor of "direct action." They instigated a series of strikes, accompanied by much violence, and in many instances they dispossessed owners of factories and assumed control.

Against such extremes of "Right" and "Left," the Liberal ministers from 1919 to 1922 were unable or unwilling to take any effective action. They disputed among themselves, while the domestic situation grew rapidly worse. The budget was unbalanced, the public debt large, the currency inflated. The balance of trade was highly unfavorable; and rising tariff walls abroad, together with America's refusal to receive any more immigrants (who might have sent remittances home) and Italy's need for foreign raw materials, rendered improvement well-nigh impossible.

The circumstances provided opportunity for an ambitious man, Benito Mussolini. Son of a blacksmith and himself an elementary school-teacher in his early years, he was, before the war, a left-wing Socialist, vehemently anti-Catholic and anti-imperialist. He served a jail-sentence for pacifism, lived for a time in exile, and at length became editor of the official publication of the Italian Socialists. During the war he became an ultra-patriot, broke with the pacifist majority of his party, served in the trenches as an ordinary soldier, and founded a newspaper through which he exerted ever widening influence. He now urged the employment, in behalf of an intensive nationalism, of essentially the same tactics as the Communists used; and for such a program he gained support of restless demobilized soldiers, dissatisfied white-collar workers, youthful intellectuals, and groups of frightened business men. His movement was called "Fascism."

Mussolini greeting crowds at the 15th anniversary of the founding of the Fascist party.

Courtesy Bettmann Archive

The word Fascism was derived from the *Fascio* (or "club") which Mussolini organized at Milan in 1919 and which gave rise, during the next two years, to a network of similar *fasci* all over Italy. In November 1921 these were consolidated into a political party, with Mussolini at its head and with a wealth of symbolism and ceremonial. Fascists wore black shirts in imitation of Garibaldi's red shirts, and revived the ancient Roman usages of saluting with outstretched arm and carrying as their emblem the *fasces* of the Roman lictors.

With mounting enthusiasm and violence and with perfected organization, Fascism gathered momentum during 1921–1922, while its opponents—Liberal, Socialist, and Catholic—remained divided and irresolute. In October 1922 the Fascists held a great congress at Naples, paraded the streets, and listened to a grandiloquent speech by Mussolini, who declared, "Either the goverment will be given to us or we shall march on Rome." Then as the Liberal prime minister resigned, Fascist crowds moved on Rome by train and auto. The regular army stood aside, and King Victor Emmanuel III asked Mussolini to form a ministry. Whereupon the Fascist leader extorted from the terrified parliament a grant of dictatorial powers.

Fascists were speedily put into key positions throughout the country, and given a monopoly on propaganda. Socialists were suppressed and their strikes stopped. For a brief time, following the murder of the Socialist leader Matteoti, the opponents of Fascism threatened to coalesce in dangerous unity. But by strict censorship and forceful police measures, Mussolini weathered the storm and followed it up with a veritable reign of terror. Opponents were imprisoned or exiled. Critics were silenced.

By a series of enactments from 1925 to 1928 Mussolini consolidated his dictatorship. Political parties other than the Fascist were banned. Censorship was tightened. "Seditious" persons were subjected to summary "justice." Mussolini as prime minister of the state and "leader" (*Duce*) of the Fascist party was authorized to initiate legislation and appoint local officials. Elections for parliament were transformed to a

744

mere "yes" and "no" vote on a list of Fascist candidates.

Formally, Italy continued to be a "constitutional" monarchy. The king was still nominal sovereign. A parliament still existed. But actually the whole government was dominated by the Fascist party, which, like the Communist party in Russia, consisted of a small minority, and which was similarly organized, with local groups, provincial federations, and Grand Council. As chairman of the Grand Council and prime minister of the country, Mussolini centered all power in his hands. To enforce his will he had not only the governmental agencies but a special Fascist militia. To win the loyalty of the youth and to train future members of the party, quasi-military organizations were set up for boys and young men.

Mussolini and his Fascist dictatorship sought to gain the support of workingmen by undertaking social changes and substituting a "corporate" state for the previous liberal state. Non-Fascist trade unions and all strikes were banned in 1926, but at the same time were organized thirteen "syndicates" (six of employers, six of employees, and one of professional men), under whose auspices tribunals were established to settle labor disputes.

Mussolini sought also to win the approval of Italian Catholics by negotiating with Pope Pius XI the Lateran treaty of 1929, which recognized the sovereign independence of the papal state of "Vatican City," and likewise a concordat, which regulated relations between state and church within Italy and promised the latter important functions in education. It was not long, however, until the church and the Fascist party were at odds over the schools and the youth organizations. Catholicism and totalitarian dictatorship were fundamentally incompatible.

Nationalism was continually emphasized by Mussolini and the Fascists. Italians were ceaselessly reminded of their past greatness and future destiny as a nation. For patriotic reasons as well as to give work to the unemployed, the government fostered a great variety of public works. Pride in the past was stimulated by repairing and unearthing ancient Roman monuments and erecting grandiose memorials. Faith in the future

Pope Pius XI.
Courtesy Bettmann Archive

was aroused by a host of "modern improvements." Railways were refurbished, palatial steamships built, marshes drained, electric power plants constructed. As far as might be, Mussolini aimed at economic self-sufficiency for Italy.

Closely associated with nationalism, was an ostentatious militarism. The army was increased and its equipment improved. Military reviews were staged. Special youth organizations trained small boys in the manual of arms. In speeches, Mussolini ranted about war and the warlike virtues and tried to fill Italians with an unaccustomed martial ardor. And related to this militarism was an aggressive imperialism.

C. Republican Germany and Its Difficulties

German defeat in the First World War brought about, in November 1918, the overthrow of the Hohenzollern Empire which Bismarck had created in 1871, and the substitution of a provisional republican government headed by Friedrich Ebert, a prominent Socialist. Not all Germans took kindly to the change. There was opposition from a monarchist "Right," which comprised former Conservatives (now renamed "Nationalists") and former National Liberals (reorganized by a wealthy industrialist, Gustav Stresemann, as a "People's" party).

There was also opposition from an extreme "Left," composed of Socialists who sympathized with Bolshevik Russia and wanted to effect a thoroughgoing social revolution in Germany by means of a similar dictatorship. At first, it was this Communistic opposition which made chief trouble for the provisional government by inciting workers to riot and revolt. It was promptly and sternly suppressed, however, by Ebert with the support of a majority of Socialists, who were resolved to maintain the tradition of their party as Social Democratic.

Meanwhile the provisional government sponsored the election, by universal suffrage, of a National Constituent Assembly. Coöperating with Ebert and the Social Democrats in support of democracy and republicanism were the Catholic Centrists and the Progressives (now known simply as "Democrats"); and this coalition obtained an overwhelming majority of the popular electorate and hence dominated the Assembly, which met at Weimar in February 1919, ratified the treaty of Versailles in June, and completed a constitution in July.

The Weimar constitution of the new German Republic was thoroughly democratic. While it retained the federal organization of the previous Empire it lessened the powers of the several states and broadened those of the central government. In the latter, it entrusted legislative power to a two-house legislature composed of a Reichstag, representing the people, and a Reichsrat, representing the states. The executive authority was vested in a president, elected by the people for seven years, and in a chancellor and ministry responsible to the Reichstag. The suffrage was granted to all adult citizens of both sexes. The constitution included a detailed and liberal bill of rights, and provisions for the initiative, referendum, and recall, for proportional representation of all parties, and for a National Economic Council, representative of labor and capital, to advise on social and economic legislation. Similar changes at the same time in the state constitutions of Prussia, Bavaria, Saxony, and all others, seemed to guarantee the democratic character of the whole German Republic.

Grave difficulties confronted the German Republic. Internally, there was continuing embittered opposition of a monarchist and nationalist "Right" and of a communist, pro-Russian "Left." In foreign affairs, Germany was penalized and fettered by the terms of what seemed to most of its people a harsh and unjust peace treaty. To make matters worse, the country's economic position was extremely precarious.

There was currency inflation, which reached a climax in 1923, when a basketful of notes would not buy a dozen eggs, and a cow or a chair could be procured only for billions or even trillions of marks. While public indebtedness (war bonds, etc.) was wiped out, so too were savings accounts, life insurance, and investments of the middle class. Though the currency was stabilized on a new basis by 1924, Germany never recovered from the effects of the inflation. The German bourgeoisie had lost so much of its money and property that it remained a middle class only in its psychology. It was restive and eager to regain its lost status.

For a time the Republic appeared to gather strength. As "Leftist" insurrection had been suppressed in 1919, so a "Rightist" attempt at a *coup d'état* (the "Kapp Putsch") was thwarted in 1920 by a general strike of Socialist workers. Then, from 1924 to 1929, when the inflation and the Ruhr occupation were over and the Dawes Plan and Locarno agreements in effect, matters perceptibly improved. Despite frequent changes of ministry, the governing coalition of Centrists, Democrats, and Socialists retained a comfortable majority. At the general elections of 1924 the coalition polled 18 million votes out of 29 million cast. Four years later it polled almost 23 million out of 31 million. Besides, the People's party was now coöperating, and its leader, Stresemann, was chancellor in 1923 and then foreign minister until his death in 1929. At the same time, economic conditions improved somewhat. Germany gradually regained a considerable part of her foreign markets despite high tariffs in many countries. American loans enabled her to meet her reparations payments. And the towns, states, and national government were able to borrow heavily for public works.

Then came the financial crash of 1929, ending American loans and creating a most fateful economic depression in Germany. Unemployment, which even in 1928 had amounted to 1,350,000, rose to 3,150,000 in 1930, and to 5,600,000 in 1932. Such depression served to bring out inherent weaknesses of the Weimar Republic. The coalition which so far had triumphantly maintained it, now weakened and tended to disintegrate. Some of the Democrats, as well as most of the People's party, turned toward the "Right" and helped to swell the opposition from that quarter, while a growing number of Social Democrats heeded propaganda from Moscow and, under the leadership of Ernst Thälmann, a Hamburg mechanic, definitely joined the Communist opposition on the "Left." These organized local "cells" and regional "soviets." In 1930 they polled 4½ million votes, and in 1932 nearly 6 million. They took orders from Moscow, preached internal revolution and external coöperation with Russia, and stubbornly refused to work with the democratic Socialists or support the republic.

While the subversive activities and propaganda of the Communists were dangerous, so too, increasingly, was the opposition of the Nationalist Right. Here the original core of hostility to the republic consisted of Junkers (landed Prussian aristocrats), long identified with the monarchy, the army, and the civil service. They were scandalized by the defeat of German arms, and the overthrow of the Hohenzollern Empire. They chafed at the military and other restrictions of the Versailles treaty, and they eagerly put forward the myth that the German armies had never been defeated but had been "stabbed in the back" on the home front by traitorous Socialists and internationally minded Jews and Catholics.

It was the Junkers who provided the leadership of the Nationalist Party. At first, the following of this party was not impressive. In 1920, though it polled some 4 million votes in the general election, it was discredited by the failure of the Kapp Putsch. Another *coup* was attempted at Munich in 1923 by an odd team of nationalist fanatics, the renowned and elderly General Ludendorff and the youthful and hitherto unknown Adolf Hitler. Both were arrested, and Hitler was imprisoned.

Early in 1925, by clever maneuvering, the Nationalists obtained an ominous success. They put forward as their candidate for President of the Republic, to succeed the Socialist Ebert, who had just died, the aged war-hero, Field-Marshal Hindenburg, who; thanks to his personal popularity, won the election. Hindenburg's basic loyalties were those of a Junker—to empire, army, landed aristocracy, and Lutheran Church. Yet during the seven years of his first presidential term he observed his oath to uphold the republic and loyally coöperated with the republican majority in the Reichstag.

In 1932 Hindenburg was reëlected as the candidate of the republican coalition against candidates that stood for dictatorship rather than for democracy. One of these was the Communist Thälmann and the other the "Nationalist Socialist" (or Nazi) Hitler. A year later the democratic German Republic was practically ended by Hindenburg's delivering it to Hitler.

D. Nazi Germany

Adolf Hitler was born in Austria in 1889 of a lower middle-class family. He grew up with only ordinary schooling, and as a young man eked out a meager livelihood in an architect's office in Vienna and as a free-lance illustrator in Munich, solacing himself with devotion to Wagner's operas and Nietzsche's philosophy of the super-man. He became an ardent German nation-alist, adoring "Aryan" Germany, despising the polyglot Austrian Empire, and detest-ing Jews, Socialists, liberals, and pacifists. He served in the German army throughout the First World War. He was wounded and gassed, and for his valor he was awarded the Iron Cross. But he was not promoted beyond the rank of corporal.

At the close of the war, Hitler joined with a handful of youthful army acquaint-ances to form the "National Socialist" (or "Nazi") party, whose "unalterable pro-gram," adopted in 1920, was a mixture of radicalism and nationalism. It denounced the Versailles treaty, demanded the union of all who spoke German in a Greater Ger-many, and insisted on the return of Ger-many's lost colonies and the full rearma-ment of Germany. It assailed German Jews as aliens who should be denied citi-zenship. It condemned liberalism and par-liamentary democracy. It proposed eco-nomic reforms designed to appeal to both the workers and the lower middle classes: abolition of unearned income, of depart-ment stores, and of land speculation.

Hitler speedily assumed leadership of the group and discovered that he had ora-torical ability. By "letting himself go" in frenzied recital of the woes of Germany and in fierce denunciation of Jews and foreigners, he could attract and stir large audiences and exercise over them an almost hypnotic influence. The attempted Nazi *coup*, with General Ludendorff, at Munich in 1923 (the "Beer Hall Putsch") fizzled miserably, but it gained notoriety for Hitler and his ideas. A kind of bible for Nazism, under the title of *Mein Kampf* (My Battle), was written by Hitler while in jail.

Hitler and his lieutenants built the Nazi party along lines already adopted and tested by the Communists in Russia and the Fascists in Italy, with local cells, youth organizations, party guards (the *Schutz-staffeln*, or S. S.), and "storm troops" (the *Sturmabteilung*, or S. A.). They adopted a brown-shirt uniform and the emblem of a black swastika on a red field. They indulged in most strident propaganda and violent tactics, terrorizing their opponents and dis-regarding law and personal rights. The party attracted many jobless youths, discontented war veterans, and impoverished bourgeois, but prior to 1929 it had relatively slight electoral success and was deemed less dan-gerous to German democracy than its Com-munist rival.

Nazi opportunity came with the eco-nomic depression of 1929. Hitler won most of the lower middle class, and new allies among aristocrats of the conservative Na-tionalist party, who thought they could use him for their own ends. Even industrial and commercial magnates began to support him as a barrier against the rising tide of Communism.

In the elections of 1930, while the Cen-ter Party more than held its own, the vote of the People's and Democratic parties fell off by 1¼ million, that of the Socialists by a half million, and that of the conservative Nationalists by two million. But the Com-munists gained a million votes, and the Nazis almost six million. The radical "left" and the radical "right" were winning mass support at the expense of the democratic coalition. From 1930 to 1932 the republi-can government, under Chancellor Hein-rich Brüning, was dependent on wavering coöperation of the Social Democrats and support of the ultra-conservative President Hindenburg.

Brüning and other republicans worked manfully for Hindenburg's reëlection to the presidency in 1932. Thälmann, the Com-munist candidate, polled 3,700,000 votes, and Hitler, 13,400,000. But Hindenburg won with 20,000,000 votes. Once reëlected, Hindenburg, out of growing senility or deep-seated prejudices, began to give heed to Junker aristocrats who surrounded him. He dismissed Brüning and appointed as Chancellor Franz von Papen, who had allied himself with the conservative Nationalists and who now, with the aid of General Kurt von Schleicher, executed a military *coup* against the Socialist premier and police officials of Prussia. The Socialists, receiving no aid from the Communists, meekly sur-rendered their posts. But from ensuing gen-eral elections, neither Papen nor Schleicher (who succeeded him in the chancellorship) could obtain anything like a majority of Conservative supporters in the Reichstag.

Eventually, conservative Nationalists convinced Hindenburg that their cause could best be served, and any Communist dictatorship most surely prevented, through collaboration with Hitler's Nazi party, which, with the conservative Nationalists, now commanded a parliamentary majority. Accordingly, on January 30, 1933, the senile President dismissed Schleicher and appointed Hitler chancellor.

It had taken Lenin and Mussolini several years to crush opposition and establish their respective dictatorships. Hitler did likewise within a few months. From the start, he regarded his Nationalist allies in the ministry and the Reichstag as merely a convenient link with Hindenburg and legality. The important thing was that he now commanded the public police as well as his own storm troops; and these were ruthlessly employed to terrorize opponents and assure to the Nazis a majority in elections scheduled for March 1933. Just prior to this election the Reichstag building was burned, undoubtedly by Nazis, although at the time Hitler made political capital out of it by blaming it on the Communists. Out of 39 million votes, the Nazis polled 17 million, and their Nationalist allies some 3 million. It was by no means an overwhelming electoral victory for Hitler, but it sufficed.

A week later, Hindenburg decreed that the Republican flag (black, red, gold) be hauled down and replaced by two flags, that of the old German Empire (black, white, red), and the swastika of the Nazis. On April 1, 1933, the Reichstag voted to delegate its powers for four years to the Hitler government. Thus began what the Nazis called the Third Empire, counting as its predecessors only the old Holy Roman Empire and that of Bismarck and William I.

The revolution which inaugurated the "Third Empire" was attended by intense popular excitement skillfully worked up and exploited by the new regime. Press, radio, cinema, and public meetings were all used for intensive propaganda. One of Hitler's chief lieutenants, Joseph Goebbels, exhibited a veritable genius for showmanship, and under his guidance a whirlwind of hysteria swept the country. Deprived by censorship of all impartial news and critical

opinion, many Germans, even normally sober and sensible ones, began to believe implicitly in Nazi propaganda and especially in the genius of "The Leader" (*Der Führer*), Adolf Hitler.

The hysteria of the Nazi revolution was heightened by spectacular anti-Semitism. Jews (and Christians with Jewish blood) were dismissed from all public posts. Jewish shops were looted. With sporadic intensifications, the persecution continued until thousands of Jews fled abroad, while others were immured in concentration camps and brutally tortured. This ruthless anti-Semitism was embodied at length in a code of public laws, while youths were encouraged to despise and even to destroy Jewish books, art, and music.

Meanwhile, Hitler consolidated his hold on the governmental machinery. His associate, Hermann Göring, was made premier of Prussia, and the rest of the states were subjected to other leading Nazis. The Nationalist party and the People's party were absorbed by the Nazis, while all other parties were abolished. Labor unions were dissolved and "replaced" by a "German Labor Front" completely dominated by Nazi officials. Marxian books were burned. Strikes were forbidden.

By November 1933 Hitler was ready to seek national endorsement of what he had done. He held simultaneously the election of a new Reichstag and a plebiscite on Germany's withdrawal from the League of Nations. The results as given out by the Nazis, who superintended the polls, were 40½ million "yes" and 2 million "no" on withdrawal from the League, and 39½ million ballots for the Nazi list of Reichstag candidates as against 3½ million "blank" or "spoiled."

When Hindenburg died in 1934, Hitler became president as well as chancellor of Germany, and this step was endorsed by another plebiscite. In the same year he crushed opposition within the Nazi party and conspirators outside it by a "blood purge" in which a number of leading Nazis and non-Nazis like Schleicher were murdered.

From 1934 to 1939, the story of the Nazi dictatorship was one of strengthening hold on Germany. The government was com-

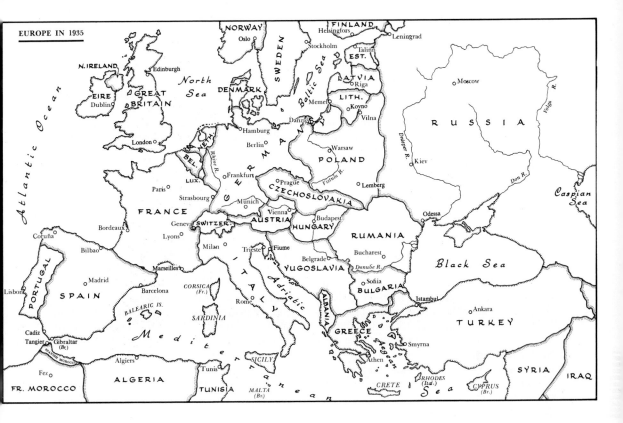

pletely centralized; the old rights of the states were eliminated; new districts were set up and put under Nazi *gauleiters* who firmly carried out Hitler's will. The new regime, like the Russian or Italian, was thoroughly totalitarian in that it denied individual rights and regulated all domestic activities, social, political, economic, cultural. Those who ventured to oppose or criticize it, including a considerable number of Catholic and Protestant clergy, were imprisoned or executed. Some fled the country and found refuge abroad.

The dictatorship ended unemployment by a program of public works, and especially of rearmament, which it began secretly in 1933 and openly not long afterwards. Fortifications were constructed, munitions factories built, a whole military aircraft industry established. Compulsory military service was reinstituted and gradually Germany moved onto a war footing. The whole economy of the country was brought under state control. Exports were pushed, especially to the Balkans, while imports were regulated so as to stockpile war material. Eventually it was foreign war, not domestic revolt, which brought Nazi Germany to an inglorious end.

E. Wide Trend Toward Dictatorship

The trend toward dictatorship and the abandonment of democratic and constitutional forms of government was by no means confined to Russia, Italy, and Germany. It had seemed in 1920 as if the whole world were moving toward liberal democracy. But the next two decades saw a major reversal as country after country developed some type of authoritarian or dictatorial rule, usually with a definite admixture of control by the military. So strong, however, was the popular belief in democracy that the dictators almost without exception cloaked the new methods of governing in the trappings of the liberal institutions that had been evolved since 1789—constitutions, plebiscites, elections, bills of rights, legislatures chosen by a broad electorate, and the like.

In Hungary a liberal government under Count Michael Károlyi (1918) and a

Communist dictatorship under Béla Kun (1919) were quickly succeeded by monarchy without a king organized by a group of aristocrats, and approved by an election (1920). Admiral Horthy became "Regent," and in 1921 Count Stephen Bethlen was made premier. In fact, for ten years, Bethlen, supported by the well organized National Unity party, ruled in a thoroughly arbitrary fashion, as did his successor (1932), Julius Gomboes. Similarly in Poland, the large number of parties and factions made government ineffective under the very democratic constitution of 1921, and Marshal Pilsudski, a general as well as a former Socialist and revolutionary, assumed control in 1926. Sometimes as war minister, sometimes as premier, Pilsudski was in fact the dominating figure in Poland until his death in 1935. Just before he died, he secured the adoption of a new constitution which provided for the continuation of a qualified dictatorship.

In the Balkan countries, likewise, democratic procedures tended to give way to authoritarian techniques. The Rumanian constitution of 1923 had democratic features, including universal suffrage, but it gave the king the power to appoint and oust ministers without reference to the legislature. Indeed King Carol II did succeed for periods (1931–1932, 1938–1940) in ruling quite arbitrarily. There was, moreover, a strong reactionary party, the Iron Guards, which wanted to establish a thoroughly Fascist kind of government. Bulgaria in the post-war period moved from a nominally democratic government, that was often in the control of reactionaries, to authoritarian rule, whether by army officers (1934–1935) or by the King, Boris III (after 1935). It was the monarch, too, who in Yugoslavia became in effect the dictator, for in 1929, Alexander I with the support of the army dissolved the parliament, suspended the constitution, and suppressed all dissent. A new constitution two years later, though it had liberal features, in reality confirmed royal control. Albania likewise became a kind of royal dictatorship when a young Moslem and army officer, Ahmed Zogu, who had been elected president in 1925, proclaimed himself King Zog I in 1928. In Greece, on the other hand, it was a premier,

General John Metaxas, who eventually installed a dictatorship in 1936 and had himself made premier for life in 1938. Greece came to this solution only after a stormy period of confused political strife both as a monarchy (till 1924 and again after 1935) and as a republic (1924–1935). We have already noted that the Turkish post-war leader, Mustafa Kemal, was in fact a dictator, though toward the end of his life he was developing some of the elements that might make democratic government possible.

It was not only in the troubled areas of central Europe and the Balkans that democracy seemed to be weakening in the years after 1920. In the new Baltic countries, which had adopted radically democratic constitutions, the paralyzing agitation of Communists, Fascists, and dissident democrats led to the establishment of dictatorial rule in Lithuania (1926), Latvia (1934), and Estonia (1934). Even Finland, which was sturdily republican, had to adopt rather arbitrary techniques to repress dissident extremists of the right and of the left. At the other corner of Europe, in Portugal, General Antonio Carmona seized the presidency (1926), revised the constitution in a Fascist direction, and got himself continued as president with nearly complete dictatorial powers. In 1928, he brought into the government a professor of economics from the University of Coimbra, Dr. Antonio de Oliveira Salazar, who as premier was soon managing the dictatorship and continued to do so after Carmona's death in 1951. In Spain, the course of events was both more troubled and more violent. The constitutional monarchy there under King Alphonso XIII was weakened by increasingly unsuccessful military operations in Morocco, and in 1923 the King connived at the establishment of a military dictatorship under a nobleman and army officer, Primo de Rivera. But Primo's attempts to make a Fascist corporate state of Spain won little popular support, and when he resigned in 1930, the democratic constitution was restored. The next year the monarchy was abolished, the King driven out, and a republic established. It, in turn, was to endure for only eight years, and, after a bloody civil war, to give way to another dictatorship under General Francisco Franco.

The trend away from democracy was by no means confined to Europe. Iran was a more or less constitutional monarchy under its Shah Ahmed in 1921. But in that year an able general, Reza Pahlavi, took over the government. First as war minister, then as premier (1923), he organized a strong, nationalist rule, and in 1925 he arranged the deposition of Ahmed and had himself made Shah. He was in fact a military dictator. In China, a republic had been established by the democratic leader Sun Yat-sen in 1911. But for years China was in a state of near chaos with rival governments, independent "war lords," and the infiltration of Russian and Japanese agents. Finally, with the backing of Sun Yat-sen's Kuomintang party, an able general, Chiang Kai-shek, came to the fore and installed a Nationalist government at Nanking in 1927 and at Peking the next year. Peking was renamed Peiping. Nanking was made the capital, and Chiang was made President of the Republic. Conditions were, however, so unsettled, and pressure from the Russians and Japanese so continuous, that Chiang ruled as a military, nationalist dictator rather than as a democratic, constitutional leader.

Developments in Japan seemed superficially different. After World War I, the Japanese constitutional empire appeared to be stable enough and increasingly democratic. Universal manhood suffrage was, for example, granted in 1925, and for some years the government was controlled in turn by the Seiyukai (conservative) and the Menseito (liberal) party. But there was much corruption, and nationalist and militarist groups and individuals were increasingly dissatisfied with the government and its policies. In 1931, the Japanese army, without approval from the appropriate ministries, began hostilities against the Chinese in Manchuria—an undeclared war that was eventually to merge into World War II. The next year the Menseito party leader and the Seiyukai premier were both assassinated. Thereafter, the government was in the hands of violently nationalist army and navy officers who believed in, and increasingly used, thoroughly dictatorial procedures.

Thus the trend toward authoritarian rule, in one form or another, was world-wide in the two decades after 1920. Only the old and stable countries of western Europe, Scandinavia, and North America, plus one new nation, Czechoslovakia, remained democratic during that period. Far from "making the world safe for democracy," World War I led to an era in which democracy weakened or disappeared in a number of countries where it had been at least partially established in 1914—Japan, Italy, Spain, Portugal, Greece. It seemed as if the confused conditions of the world were an invitation for strong men, army officers, and nationalist parties to seize power and to exercise it in an authoritarian fashion. Once in command, they were often able to retain control and to repress dissent by means of the improved weapons and more effective methods of communication, propaganda, and organization which modern technology had put at their disposal. Or, to state it another way, the rapid changes in society all over the world induced by war, economic development, spreading education, and technological innovation had dissolved the cement that held society together in many countries and had produced a condition of instability which opened the road to ruthless men with motives which varied from the most self-seeking to the most patriotic.

Neville Chamberlain leaving Munich, September, 1938.

CHAPTER 58

Undoing the Paris Peace Settlement

A. Intensifying Economic and Ideological Conflicts

Hopes of the early 1920's that humanity was entering upon an age of assured peace and democratic progress were pretty well dispelled by the mid-1930's. The League of Nations was obviously weakening. Promised limitation of armaments was proving vain, and in the case of the newer totalitarian dictatorships (Russia, Italy, and Germany) military establishments were being strengthened in an increasingly alarming manner.

Everywhere economic nationalism was being competitively practiced. As early as 1922 the United States, despite its being a creditor nation which could be paid only by importation of goods, adopted an intensely protective tariff, and most European countries, in imitation or retaliation, raised their tariffs. Such tariff conflict became acute and bitter following the depression of 1929. Again the United States led the way, and, against the advice of prominent economists, raised its import duties sharply in the Hawley-Smoot tariff of 1930. France inaugurated a policy of admitting only specified quotas of certain foreign goods. Great Britain adopted a protective tariff in 1932. The Netherlands and most other countries on the Continent were soon copying France, while Britain by the Ottawa agreements (1932) sought to raise a tariff barrier around the whole British Empire.

Quotas and tariffs were supplemented by currency restrictions. In the 1920's almost all European countries worked their way back to an international gold standard, but after 1929 every nation began to tinker with its money in the hope that, by cheapening it, prices could be raised at home and unemployment relieved by expanding sales abroad. Britain went off gold in 1931, the United States in 1933. With these pivots of world economy loosened, all other countries went the same way, and further competitive reductions in the value of national currencies were made. International exchange was disrupted, and most countries restricted the export of money. World economy was breaking up into national units and associated "blocs."

In coping with depression and unemployment at home, countries were driven not only to restrictions on trade and finance, but also to the assumption of increasing control over all phases of economic life. Agricultural subsidies, labor legislation, and governmental direction of industry grew rapidly in importance and scope.

Complicating the economic depression and conflict of the 1930's was an intensifying ideological conflict. Instead of the liberal and democratic Europe which had been expected at the close of the First World War, there was now a Europe in which liberal democracy was retreating before a rapid advance of dictatorship. The newer dictatorship was of two main types: (1) Marxian or Communist, as in Russia; and (2) Fascist or Nazi, as in Italy and

Germany. Each of these was to its followers a veritable religion, inspiring them with fanatical devotion, and each claimed to be absolutely opposed to the other. Yet, while one represented an extreme "left" and the other an extreme "right," they both employed essentially the same organization and methods and both were thoroughly hostile to liberal democracy.

Though neither type of dictatorship permitted any domestic dissent or criticism, both fostered the spread of their respective ideologies abroad, and this the democracies could not prevent without violating their distinctive liberalism. Thus, while no democratic parties existed in Russia, Italy, or Germany, nearly all democratic countries had Communist and Fascist parties, denouncing each other but both working to subvert the democratic regimes that harbored them. In the United States and most democratic countries of western Europe along the Atlantic seaboard, the subversive parties were vocal but not immediately menacing. Elsewhere, however, they tended to paralyze the orderly operation of democratic government and to provoke forceful action against them leading to at least partial dictatorship. This actually occurred in Poland, Lithuania, Latvia, Estonia, Rumania, Yugoslavia, Austria, Hungary, Bulgaria, Greece, Turkey, and Portugal.

In Spain, King Alphonso XIII had connived at the establishment of a dictatorship by General Primo de Rivera which lasted from 1923 to 1930. In 1931 a revolution ousted the King and established a republic. Though this endured for eight years, it was torn by bitter conflict between "left" and "right." A "leftist" revolt was suppressed with bloodshed in 1934. A "rightist" revolt in 1936 led to three years of civil war.

B. Weakness of the League of Nations, and Japanese Seizure of Manchuria

The Paris peace-settlement of 1919–1920, with the Covenant of the League of Nations, was supplemented in the 1920's by the so-called "Nine-Power" treaties (1922) designed to maintain the integrity of China and the *status quo* in eastern Asia, and also by the "Kellogg-Briand" pact (1928) by which all countries pledged themselves to "renounce the use of war as an instrument of national policy." By 1935, however, Germany was repudiating the peace settlement which she had promised to observe, while Japan and Italy were waging wars against fellow members of the League of Nations. Thenceforth, matters went from bad to worse, and violence or the threat of violence increasingly dominated world affairs.

The sequence of these sorry events was initiated by Japan in 1931. Though she had signed the Nine-Power treaties, joined the League, and adhered to the Kellogg-Briand pact, she was ambitious to control China. She already had important investments in Manchuria and a hold on its strategic railways, but it appeared difficult for her to gain more, because of her international commitments, and because the Chinese Nationalist government of Chiang Kai-shek was consolidating its hold on China and insisting on the maintenance of Chinese sovereignty over Manchuria. In Japan the more or less liberal leaders who had signed the peace pacts were being harassed by extreme nationalists, who resorted to assassination and terrorism, and who succeeded in establishing in the spring of 1932 what amounted to a military dictatorship.

Already hostilities had been opened in Manchuria. In September 1931, to "protect" Japanese property, to "repress banditry," and to "restore order," Japanese troops attacked Chinese forces, and, expanding their hold rapidly from the railway zones, soon overran the entire territory and drove out the Chinese governor and his forces. China appealed to the League of Nations, and a League commission, after six months' investigation, recommended that Japan be censured and Manchuria be given an autonomous government under Chinese sovereignty. Japan ignored the recommendations, resigned from the League, and proceeded with the plans of her militarists in Manchuria.

The League, unable to agree on any joint action or "sanctions" against Japan, contented itself with expressing regret. Unavailing, too, were China's pleas to the United States under the Nine-Power

Generalissimo Chiang Kai-shek reviewing his staff officers, 1940.

Courtesy Wide World Photos

treaties and the Kellogg-Briand pact, though the American government did announce the "Stimson doctrine," to the effect that it would not recognize any territorial changes resulting from aggression in violation of treaties. The simple fact of the matter was that only force applied by a great power could have checked Japan. The United States, Great Britain, and France were too busy with the problems of depression and those created by the rise of dictatorships in Europe to be willing to use force in defense of China. Thus the basic principles of the League and of international peace were sacrificed, and Japan pursued her aggressive way unhindered.

In 1932 Japan set up a puppet government in Manchuria under the ex-Emperor of China, Henry Pu-yi, renamed the country Manchukuo, and recognized it as "independent." In response, the Chinese organized a patriotic boycott of all Japanese goods. But this action only inspired Japan's military clique, now firmly in the saddle at Tokyo, to further aggression. A Japanese expeditionary force landed at Shanghai, and Japanese armies occupied the Chinese province of Jehol south of Manchuria. At length in 1933 the Chinese government of Chiang Kai-shek, powerless to resist and without aid from abroad, consented to a truce which left Jehol and Manchuria in Japanese hands. The United States and the League of Nations merely withheld recognition of the new Japanese-dominated state of Manchukuo.

Sure now that she could proceed without interference from the great powers, Japan in 1934 denounced the Washington and London naval agreements and started strengthening her navy. The next year, Japanese troops pushed across the Great Wall into the Chinese provinces of Chakar and Hopei and compelled the Chinese government to replace its officials in these provinces and in Peiping and Tientsin with persons acceptable to Japan. Under this pressure from Japan, Chinese patriotic feeling was aroused, and there were signs that the Chinese might achieve political unity and be able to resist further Japanese advances. In 1936 Chiang Kai-shek ended the civil war in Kwantung and the next year reached an agreement with the Communist forces in northwest China for a "united front" against Japan. Whereupon, fighting between Chinese and Japanese troops near Peiping in July 1937 was the signal for the delivery of a Japanese ultimatum to China. When China rejected it, Japan launched an actual, if undeclared, war against China, which continued until it was merged (in 1941) with the greater struggle of the Second World War.

C. Italian Conquest of Ethiopia, and Civil War in Spain

While Japan waged a war of aggression in eastern Asia, Mussolini and Hitler were directing aggressive policies for Italy and Germany in Africa and Europe. Mussolini cherished dreams of expanding Italy's colonial empire. In particular, he cast envious eyes on the independent African kingdom of Ethiopia (Abyssinia), and longed to avenge the defeat it had inflicted on Italy at Adowa in 1896.[1]

In pursuit of his policy, Mussolini negotiated an agreement with Great Britain in 1925, whereby Italy might seek "concessions" in Ethiopia. But Ethiopia, a member

[1] See above, p. 665.

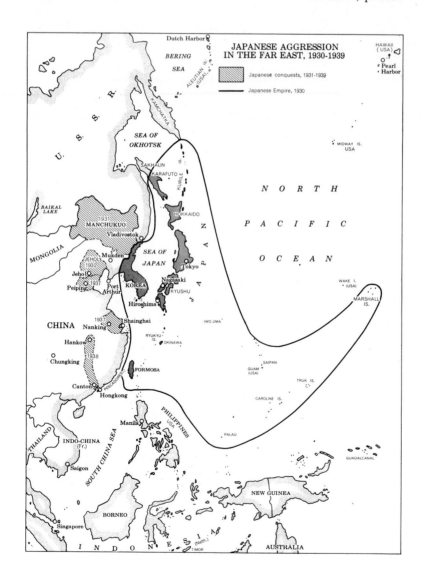

JAPANESE AGGRESSION
IN THE FAR EAST, 1930-1939

Japanese conquests, 1931-1939

Japanese Empire, 1930

Generalissimo Francisco Franco being greeted by Dr. Antonio de Oliveira Salazar.

Courtesy Wide World Photos

of the League of Nations since 1923, promptly protested to that organization, and Italy, posing as a special friend of Ethiopia, signed with it in 1928 a treaty of "perpetual friendship" and arbitration. But still the Ethiopian King, Haile Selassie, doggedly refused all Italian requests for special favors or concessions, and Mussolini gradually reached the conclusion that Italy could gain her ends in Ethiopia only by the use of force.

Such use of force would violate existing treaties and the principles of the League of Nations. But Japan had shown that this could be done with impunity. In January 1935 Mussolini secured from France, which was eager to keep Italian friendship as a check against Hitler's ambitions, an agreement that Italy should have a free hand in Ethiopia. Then alleging the necessity of repressing disorder along the ill-defined border between Ethiopia and the Italian colonies of Eritrea and Somaliland, he despatched an Italian army to east Africa.

Ethiopia appealed to the League and won popular and presently governmental support in Great Britain, which now perceived in Italy's aggressive attitude a threat to its own imperial interests in Egypt, as well as to the cause of collective security. Britain sent a fleet to the Mediterranean and besought the League to take a strong stand. In vain France tried to effect a compromise which would give Italy part of Ethiopia. Mussolini went ahead with his preparations and in October 1935, in flagrant violation of the League Covenant, the Kellogg Pact, and the Italian-Ethiopian treaty, Italian troops invaded Ethiopia, captured Adowa, and pushed on into the interior. Though the natives fought bravely, they had no arms to match the tanks, planes, and artillery of the Italians. By May 1936 Haile Selassie had fled abroad, his capital of Addis Ababa was occupied, and the whole country was formally annexed to Italy. King Victor Emmanuel III assumed the title of Emperor of Ethiopia.

Meanwhile, in October 1935, the League of Nations had pronounced Italy an aggressor. Britain backed the action of the League, and France reluctantly supported Britain. In November, the League voted to apply economic sanctions against Italy, including a ban on the shipment of oil to her. The sanctions caused some distress in Italy, but they failed of their purpose, for they solidified the Italian people in support of Mussolini, while Italy obtained needful war materials from Germany. With scrupulous regard for treaties and international law, Britain made no attempt to shut off the flow of Italian troops and supplies through the Suez Canal.

In Italy's conquest of Ethiopia, as in Japan's war against China, there was ruthless use of force, violation of treaties, and disregard of the League of Nations. Italy responded to her condemnation by the League by merely withdrawing from it in May 1936, and in July the League acknowledged its impotence by rescinding the sanctions against Italy. Aggression scored a notable victory.

No sooner was the Italian conquest of Ethiopia completed than the outbreak of civil war in Spain afforded opportunity for forceful interference on the part of all three of the major European dictatorships—Italy, Germany, and Russia. Ever since the establishment of the Spanish republic in 1931, it had been sorely troubled by conflict between "Right" and "Left," and in 1934 a revolt of the Left had been suppressed with no little bloodshed. Elections early in 1936 gave a majority of seats in parliament (though not quite a popular majority) to a "popular-front" coalition of Leftist groups—Radical Republicans, Socialists, Syndicalists, and Communists—which promised to break up large landed estates, to enforce measures against the church, and to make drastic reductions in the army. Considerable mob violence ensued, and in July 1936 a group of high army officers (who later chose General Francisco Franco as their chief, or *caudillo*) attempted a *coup d'état* against the popular-front government. The *coup* failed of its immediate purpose, but it precipitated an extraordinarily destructive civil war lasting for almost three years (1936–1939).

The Spanish Civil War was primarily a Spanish affair. It was a struggle between the Leftist groups which comprised the "popular front" and were known as "Loyalists," and Rightist groups of Monarchists, Carlists, and Conservative Republicans, which, with a newly created fascist group called the Falange, were known as "Nationalists." Loyalists were stronger in northern and eastern Spain; Nationalists, in western and southern Spain. The former had allies in nationalistic Basques and Catalans; the latter, in the majority of clergy and army officers.

But the Spanish Civil War also had ominous international aspects. Almost from the start, General Franco received aid in men, money, planes, and material from Fascist Italy and Nazi Germany, and gradually his Nationalist movement became popularly identified with the cause of fascist dictatorship. On the other hand, the popular-front government received similar aid from Communist Russia and fell increasingly under its influence, with the result that the Loyalist cause was represented by its adversaries and critics as essentially the cause of Marxian dictatorship. Under Communist auspices, "international brigades" were recruited and sent into Spain to battle anti-Communist "volunteers" and expeditionary Italian and German forces. There was constant danger that the Spanish Civil War might develop into a huge international war involving not only the two contrasting types of dictatorship but also the remaining democratic great powers.

Anxious to avoid entanglement in any such war, and, if possible, to stave it off altogether, the United States strengthened its neutrality legislation, while Great Britain adhered to a similar policy of nonintervention in Spain and sought to persuade other European powers to do likewise. With perfect cynicism the several dictatorships assured Britain they were not intervening or would at once cease to intervene, and then kept on giving aid to one side or the other in Spain. France was less cynical, but its "popular-front" ministry of the time, under Léon Blum, was sympathetic with the Spanish Loyalists and inclined to wink at private violations of public neutrality.

Meanwhile the civil war dragged on in Spain, with fortune slowly favoring the Nationalists. In 1937 Franco accomplished the piecemeal conquest of the Basque provinces in the north, and in March 1938 his armies drove eastward to the Mediterranean and cut off the Loyalist forces in Catalonia from those in the Madrid-Valencia zone. This marked the beginning of the end. During the next year Franco conquered all of Catalonia; and finally, after a twenty-nine-months' siege, Madrid capitulated to him in March 1939. Thousands of Loyalists fled abroad, principally to France, Mexico, and South America. Spain itself was subjected to a military dictatorship of a fascist type.

The outcome of the protracted violence in Spain was as heartening to Mussolini and Hitler as it was uncomfortable for Stalin and ominous for the democracies. Even in Western Europe, on the Atlantic seaboard, dictatorship was now triumphant over liberal democracy; and for any final reckoning with France and Britain (or with Russia), Italy and Germany had gained prestige and valuable military experience.

D. Hitler's Repudiation of the Versailles Treaty

Before he came to power Hitler had won popularity in Germany by denouncing the victors of the First World War and preaching the most intense kind of German nationalism. Once his dictatorship was established, he used the field of foreign relations for a double purpose—to increase his personal prestige with the Germans, and to gain territory and prestige for Germany. His objective was piecemeal destruction of the Paris peace-settlement, and his tactics were unusually simple. He focussed attention on some particular German demand and insisted that when this was granted Germany would live like a good neighbor with the rest of Europe. When it was granted, he proceeded to make a new demand. He was satisfied to obtain his ends by threats and bluster. But he rapidly pushed forward German military preparations in case war should result from his tactics.

Early in his dictatorship, Hitler turned his attention to Austria, his native land, which he was resolved to bring into an *Anschluss* (union) with Germany, contrary to express provision in the treaty of Versailles. He actively encouraged Nazi propaganda within Austria, and connived at an attempted *coup d'état* there in July, 1934, attended by the murder of the Austrian chancellor, Dollfuss. The *coup* failed, partly because the Nazis had insufficient popular support within Austria, and partly because Italy, seconded by Czechoslovakia and France, took a strong stand and threatened war if Germany should take over Austria. Consequently, on this occasion, Hitler backed down; he denied that he had had anything to do with the trouble in Austria or had any intention of annexing that country.

Common opposition to Hitler drew France and Italy temporarily together, and in January 1935 they signed a pact at Rome designed to maintain Austrian independence, give Italy a free hand in Ethopia, and uphold the treaty of Versailles. At the same period, Hitler scored a victory. In the plebiscite held according to the Versailles treaty to determine the fate of the Saar, ninety per cent of the votes were for reunion with Germany, and accordingly, on March 1, 1935, amid much Nazi rejoicing, the Saar was formally turned over to Hitler's Third Empire. Elated by this success (legitimate for once), Hitler intensified Nazi propaganda among German-speaking people outside Germany—in Austria, Danzig, Memel, and the Sudentenland (western fringe) of Czechoslovakia. He made no secret of his hope of absorbing such areas, and even the Russian Ukraine, into his greater Germany.

As if to give speedy effect to this ambitious program, Hitler dramatically announced, on March 16, 1935, Germany's repudiation of all treaty limitations on her armaments, the reëstablishment of universal military service, and the creation of an air force equal to the British or the French. Applauded with patriotic enthusiasm in Germany, Hitler's violation of the Versailles treaty naturally aroused alarm elsewhere. In a conference at Stresa, in April 1935, Mussolini joined the premiers of France and Britain in proclaiming that the three countries would work together to support the League of Nations and the Versailles treaty. In May, France concluded a defensive military alliance with Russia, and Russia made a similar alliance with Czechoslovakia. It seemed as if Nazi Germany might be restrained by joint action of the other dictatorships with the democracies.

In the autumn of 1935, however, Fascist Italy, as we have seen, began her Ethiopian adventure. Mussolini had reason to believe that the French government and possibly the British would regard it with benevolent eyes. But popular feeling in Britain and France opposed the compromises suggested, and regard for the League of Nations and the principle of "collective security" led both countries to participate in the sanctions against Italy. Germany, on the other hand, openly sympathized with the Italians and supplied them with war material. Moreover, Hitler seized the moment when cleavage was widening between Italy on one hand and France and Britain on the other to deliver a major blow at the European treaty structure. In March 1936, German troops marched into the demilitarized zones of the Rhineland in flat violation of both the Versailles treaty and the Locarno pact.

The German general staff had been very reluctant to take this step, fearing that France would fight and defeat the new German armies, which were not yet ready for a major war. Hitler had insisted on the gamble, and fortune favored him. Though the Council of the League of Nations adopted a resolution condemning Germany for violation of treaties, France and Belgium were the only nations at all minded to take any real action, and they were deterred by pacifism at home and indifference abroad. Russia refused to collaborate with France. Italy was now hostile to France. Great Britain was more concerned with Italian aggression than with German. In the circumstances, Germany remilitarized her western frontiers with impunity, while Belgium broke off her military alliance (of 1920) with France and resumed her neutrality. French prestige and the cause of peace suffered a most serious setback.

By October 1936 the course of events brought Germany and Italy into an open accord, the so-called "Rome-Berlin axis." It was the logical result of their close relations during the Ethiopian War, their common disdain for the League of Nations, their opposition to France and Great Britain, their similarity in government and ideology, and their ambitions for expansion.

In November 1936, Germany concluded with Japan an "Anti-Comintern" pact, ostensibly directed against the spread of Russian Communism, but clearly intended to serve Japanese purposes in eastern Asia and German ambitions in Europe; and a year later, Italy adhered to this pact. Thus emerged a new balance of power, with Germany, Italy, and Japan on one hand, and France, Great Britain, and Russia on the other. It was a most precarious balance, however, for continued and effective collaboration of Communist Russia with the western democracies proved well-nigh impossible.

Meanwhile Nazi Germany continued her violations of the treaty of Versailles. In November 1936 she repudiated its provisions for international control of her water-

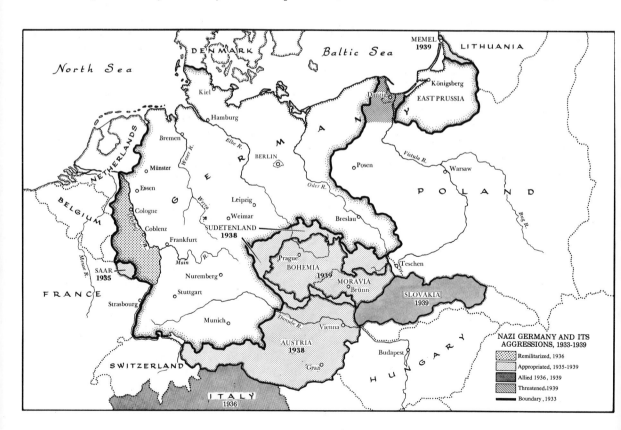

NAZI GERMANY AND ITS AGGRESSIONS, 1933-1939

Remilitarized, 1936
Appropriated, 1935-1939
Allied 1936, 1939
Threatened, 1939
Boundary, 1933

ways. In January 1937 she denounced its clauses charging her with war-guilt. Then early in 1938 she violated its guarantee of Austrian independence. The Austrian Chancellor Schuschnigg had been contending desperately against a rising tide of Nazi infiltration and propaganda in his country. At length in March 1938, when direct overtures to Hitler proved vain, Schuschnigg suddenly called for a plebiscite, in which he hoped to show that most Austrians were opposed to union with Germany, despite the noisy claims of the Austrian and German Nazis. To prevent the holding of the plebiscite, Hitler swiftly occupied helpless Austria with German troops and proclaimed its incorporation in the Nazi German Empire.

Other powers might protest, but Italy, which in 1934 had threatened war to prevent Germany's seizure of Austria, was now so absorbed in Ethopian and Spanish adventures and so closely allied with Germany that Mussolini pretended to approve the extension of the German Empire to the borders of his own country. With Italy acquiescent, the protests of other nations were merely verbal.

Thus Germany by the spring of 1938 had destroyed the restrictive clauses of the treaty of Versailles, helped to discredit the League of Nations, and made considerable territorial gains. Hitler's bloodless successes convinced the German people of his genius, and many of those who did not like his policies of dictatorship and terrorism at home were dazzled and won over by his successes abroad.

E. "Appeasement," Partition of Czechoslovakia, Russo-German Pact, and Outbreak of World War II

From 1935 to 1938, Anthony Eden as British foreign secretary had tended, though somewhat hesitantly, to work with France, the League of Nations, and even Russia in an attempt to check Italy and Germany. But his efforts seemed fruitless, for Italy and Germany drew closer together and won a series of successes in Ethopia, Spain, and Austria. Neville Chamberlain, who succeeded Stanley Baldwin as British prime minister in 1937, dismissed Eden in the spring of 1938 and tried a new tack. While retaining ties with France, he would strive to reach an understanding with Germany and Italy. With Italy he at once negotiated a set of treaties (signed April 1938), by which Italy promised to get out of Spain as soon as possible and to stop anti-British propaganda in Palestine and Egypt. In return, Britain promised to work for general recognition of Italy's conquest of Ethiopia. Amidst recriminations and the despairing protests of the native ex-ruler, Haile Selassie, Great Britain obtained from the League of Nations authorization for individual members to recognize the King of Italy as Emperor of Ethiopia, and herself granted such recognition.

But no sooner was Italy "appeased" than Germany demanded "appeasement." Hitler was following up his success in Austria with virulent propaganda against Czechoslovakia and ostentatious preparation for giving forceful aid to its "oppressed" German-speaking minority—the Sudetens. These were being stimulated by Nazi agents to demand not mere autonomy but outright annexation to Germany. The Czechs mobilized in defense and called on France, Russia, and the Little Entente for their promised assistance. On the other side, Italy and Hungary backed Germany's truculent attitude. For a few days the crisis was acute, war seemed at hand, and popular emotion was intense. Dramatically Chamberlain flew back and forth between England and Germany begging Hitler not to precipitate war, while Daladier, the French premier, flew back and forth between Paris and London. No united stand could be made against Hitler. The position of Russia was uncertain. The Little Entente dared not break with Germany unless France did. France felt horror at the prospect of war, and was determined to stick to Great Britain. Britain imagined that by permitting Germany to annex German-speaking districts of Czechoslovakia, Hitler would be "appeased" and there would be no war.

So the crisis was suddenly ended by an accord signed at Munich in September 1938 by Chamberlain, Daladier, Mussolini, and Hitler, by which peace was maintained but democratic Czechoslovakia was sacrificed. Hitler got a free hand to annex the Sudetenland, which he promptly did. Simultaneously, Poland seized the Teschen district of Czechoslovakia, and Hungary occupied a strip of Slovakia. Altogether, Czechoslovakia lost a third of her territory and no longer had a strategically defensible western frontier. All she received in return was a joint guarantee attached by the four great powers to the Munich pact. Hitler, triumphant, announced he had no further territorial ambitions. Chamberlain, flying back from Munich, declared he had given Europe "peace in our time." Almost everywhere (outside of Czechoslovakia) people hailed the Munich pact with relief. It seemed to remove the threat of war and to indicate that there could be pacific collaboration among the major European powers whether dictatorial or democratic.

How far Hitler could be trusted to observe his pledges was soon apparent. In March 1939, only six months after the Munich pact and without even consulting its other signatories, he completed the partition of Czechoslovakia. With German encouragement, a separatist Slovak cabinet had been set up, and when the Czech prime minister tried to depose its head, Hitler not only forced the Czech government to accede to the Slovak demands but to place itself under his direction. German troops poured into Prague. Bohemia and Moravia were made dependencies of the Third Reich. Slovakia was transformed into a German protectorate. Simultaneously, Hungary seized the Ruthenian province of Carpatho-Ukraine.

These events of March 1939 convinced Neville Chamberlain that Nazi Germany could neither be trusted nor "appeased" by concessions. With dismay he saw Hitler bully Lithuania into surrendering Memel to the Third Reich, while Mussolini, eager to share in spoils of forceful expansion, occupied Albania and added it to Italy. Almost immediately Hitler launched a vituperative campaign against Poland, charging that it was committing "atrocities" against its German minority, and demanding that it agree to German annexation of Danzig and a "rectification" of the Polish Corridor.

This was too much for Chamberlain. In April 1939 he suddenly and radically recast British foreign policy. Great Britain entered into a formal alliance with France and Poland to guarantee one another's independence and territorial integrity, by war if necessary, against any aggression. At the same time Britain announced its readiness to give like guarantees to Rumania, Greece, and Turkey. At long last, a serious attempt would be made to compel Nazi Germany to desist from further treaty violations and aggressions against its neighbors.

It was a belated attempt. The totalitarian dictatorships would hardly have ventured upon their aggressions, if, at the first threat of such aggressions, the democratic great powers had acted in concert and with the superior forces which they then commanded. Combined and resolute action by Great Britain, France, and the United States would almost certainly have prevented the Japanese seizure of Manchuria in 1931, the Italian conquest of Ethopia in 1935, and German rearmament in 1936. As late as the Munich crisis in the autumn of 1938, there was still a good chance that a strong united stand by the democratic powers might have enlisted Russian coöperation and resulted, without war, in halting Hitler and sparing Czechoslovakia.

Why the democratic powers neglected their earlier and more favorable opportunities to stop totalitarian aggression, and why, instead, they followed so long a policy of "appeasement," is explicable primarily by the deep-seated pacifism of their peoples. Democratic peoples were as reluctant to face the threat of war as the dictators were eager to commit aggression. While the latter concentrated upon preparedness for war, the former pressed their governments to cut expenditures for army and navy and to avoid any step which might lead to war. The United States, throughout the 1920's and 1930's, was popularly pacifist and isolationist to an extreme degree. Its criticism of the totalitarian dictatorships and their aggressions was purely verbal; it held aloof from the League of Nations, even from the World Court; it would not consider any joint action with France or Great Britain; it adopted legislation aimed at maintaining a strict neutrality in the event of any foreign war. And the pacifism and practical isolationism of Britain and France were scarcely less pronounced.

Only an accumulation of German aggressions finally brought the British and French governments to the alliance of April 1939 with Poland. The alliance was none too strong. Neither the French nor the British people displayed any enthusiasm about it, and the United States clung to neutrality. On the other hand, Germany had at least potential allies in her Axis associates— Italy and Japan—and perhaps in Spain. She was now once again better armed and equipped for war than the opposing alliance. Under Hitler she had a unity of purpose, command, and enforced public opinion, which the Allies lacked; and her recent annexations had given her a manpower superior to theirs. Moreover, she had a will to war which in Britain and France was still gravely qualified by continuing pacifism and, in France, by bitter partisan strife.

Hitler might yet have hesitated to attack Poland and thus defy France and Great Britain, had it not been for the decisive stand of Communist Russia. During the critical summer of 1939, Stalin and his Foreign Minister Molotov spurned the overtures made to them for Russian coöperation with Britain and France. Already, in the spring of 1939, they had secretly indicated to the Nazi Foreign Office a willingness to arrange, for a price, an entente with Germany. Stalin doubtless believed that, by favoring Germany, he could share in a partition of Poland and have a free hand to recover what the Russian Empire had lost in the First World War along the Baltic and Black Seas. And by maintaining a nominal neutrality while the Nazi dictatorship was locked in what he imagined might be a gigantic and exhausting struggle with the western democracies, he would be able at the close of the struggle to dominate all Europe in the interest of the Soviet Union, communism, and his own dictatorship.

At first, Hitler hesitated to negotiate with a Russian regime which he heartily disliked and which in the past he had stridently denounced. But as the crisis developed, he perceived advantages in a deal with Russia and pushed the negotiations for it. Consequently, late in August, a "non-aggression pact" was concluded at Moscow between Russia and Germany, and proclaimed to the world. Accompanying it were secret articles which provided for a partition of Poland, allowed Russia a free hand in the Baltic states, and promised Germany a copious supply of foodstuffs, petroleum, and other needful war supplies from Russia.

This Russo-German pact was a signal to Stalin that he might proceed with forceful aggressions of his own. It was also the final signal for Germany's attack on Poland and the outbreak of war. Hitler was now assured that he would have collaboration, not opposition, in the east, and that in the west, especially in France, military effort against him woud be impeded by an extreme Fascist "Right" sympathetic with Nazi Germany and still more by an extreme "Left" of pro-Russian Communists who would follow directions from Moscow and obediently acclaim the new German-Russian pact.

On September 1, 1939, scarcely more than a week after the German-Russian pact, and without any formal declaration of war, German armies invaded Poland. Two days later, Great Britain and France, honoring their treaty obligations, declared war on Germany. It was the beginning of what is termed the Second World War.

SELECT SUPPLEMENTARY READINGS FOR PART XI

General. C. J. H. Hayes, *Contemporary Europe since 1870* (1958); S. B. Clough and C. W. Cole, *Economic History of Europe* (1952); *The Columbia Encyclopedia; New Cambridge. Modern History*, vol. XII (1960).

Chapter 54. B. Romanov, *Russia in Manchuria, 1892–1906* (1952); J. A. White, *The Diplomacy of the Russo-Japanese War* (1964); M. T. Florinsky, *Russia, a History and an Interpretation*, vol. II (1953); Hugh Seton-Watson, *Decline of Imperial Russia, 1865–1914* (1953); W. L. Langer, *The Diplomacy of Imperialism, 1890–1902*, 2 vols. (1935); B. E. Schmitt, *Triple Alliance and Triple Entente* (1934) and *The Annexation of Bosnia* (1937); E. C. Helmreich, *The Diplomacy of the Balkan Wars, 1912–1913* (1938); George Young, *Nationalism and War in the Near East* (1915); R. J. Sontag, *European Diplomatic History, 1871–1932* (1933); W. C. Buthman, *Rise of Integral Nationalism in France* (1939); R. Albrecht-Carrié, *Italy from Napoleon to Mussolini* (1950); R. A. Kann, *The Multinational Empire, Nationalism and National Reform in the Habsburg Monarchy*, 2 vols. (1950); K. S. Pinson, *Modern Germany* (1954); M. Dill, Jr., *Germany, a Modern History* (1961); L. L. Snyder, *From Bismarck to Hitler, the Background of Modern German Nationalism* (1935); R. W. Tims, *Germanizing Prussian Poland, 1894–1919* (1941); B. Lewis, *The Emergence of Modern Turkey* (1961).

Chapter 55. C. R. M. F. Crutwell, *A History of the Great War* (1936); B. H. Liddell Hart, *History of the World War* (1935); C. J. H. Hayes, *Brief History of the Great War* (1920); S. B. Fay, *Origins of the World War*, 2 vols. (1930); B. E. Schmitt, *The Coming of the War, 1914*, 2 vols. (1930); T. G. Frothingham, *Naval History of the World War*, 3 vols. (1924–1926), and *The American Reinforcements in the World War* (1927); B. W. Tuchman, *The Guns of August* (1962); R. Gibson and M. Prendergast, *German Submarine War, 1914–1918* (1931); N. N. Golovine, *The Russian Army in the World War* (1931); F. P. Chambers, *The War Behind the War, a History of the Political and Civilian Fronts* (1939); Charles Seymour, *American Diplomacy During the World War* (1934); D. Howarth, *The Desert King: Ibn Saud and His Arabia* (1964); W. H. Chamberlin, *The Russian Revolution, 1917–1921*, 2 vols. (1935); E. H. Carr, *A History of Soviet Russia*, 3 vols. (1950–1964) in 7 parts, vol. I, *The Bolshevik Revolution, 1917–1923*; R. H. Lutz, *Fall of the German Empire* (1932); Z. A. B. Zeman, *The Break-up of the Habsburg Empire, 1914–1918* (1961); W. S. Churchill, *The World Crisis, the Eastern Front* (1931); B. Pares, *The Fall of the Russian Monarchy* (1939); G. F. Kennan, *Soviet-American Relations, 1917–1920* (1956–1958).

Chapter 56. H. W. V. Temperley, *A History of the Peace Conference of Paris*, 6 vols. (1920–1924); E. M. House and Charles Seymour, *What Really Happened at Paris, the Story of the Peace Conference, 1918–1919* (1921); Harold Nicolson, *Peacemaking, 1919* (1939); F. P. Walters, *A History of the League of Nations*, 2 vols. (1952); H. C. F. Bell, *Woodrow Wilson* (1945); R. S. Baker, *Woodrow Wilson, Life and Letters*, 8 vols. (1935–1939); C. K. Webster and S. Herbert, *League of Nations in Theory and Practice* (1933); M. O. Hudson, *Permanent Court of International Justice* (1934); F. G. Wilson, *Labor in the League System* (1934); H. L. McBain and L. Rogers, *New Constitutions of Europe* (1922); B. C. Shafer, *Nationalism, Myth and Reality* (1953); C. J. H. Hayes, *Historical Evolution of Modern Nationalism* (1929); C. A. Macartney, *National States and National Minorities* (1934); A. Rosenberg, *Birth of the German Republic* (1931);

Semi-abstract "modern" sculpture by Amadeo Modigliani (d. 1920).

R. J. Kerner, ed., *Yugoslavia* (1949) and *Czechoslovakia* (1940); G. L. Lewis, *Turkey* (1955); William Miller, *The Ottoman Empire and Its Successors* (3rd ed., 1934); C. L. Mowat, *Britain Between the Wars, 1918–1940* (1955); Arnold Wolfers, *Britain and France Between Two Wars* (1940); J. M. Keynes, *Economic Consequences of the Peace* (1920); J. C. Stamp, *Financial Aftermath of the War* (1932); D. Wecter, *The Age of the Great Depression, 1929–1941* (1948); P. Birdsall, *Versailles Twenty Years After* (1941); C. A. Macartney and A. W. Palmer, *Independent Eastern Europe: a History* (1962).

Chapter 57. On Communist Russia, in addition to works by Chamberlin and Carr cited for chapter 55: M. T. Florinsky, *World Revolution and the U.S.S.R.* (1933) and *Toward an Understanding of the U.S.S.R.* (2nd ed., 1951); Waldemar Gurian, *Bolshevism* (1952) and *The Soviet Union* (1951); Hans Kohn, *Nationalism in the Soviet Union* (1933); M. Fainsod, *How Russia Is Ruled* (1953); A. Balabanoff, *Impressions of Lenin* (1964). On Fascist Italy and Nazi Germany: M. T. Florinsky, *Fascism and National Socialism* (1936); R. Albrecht-Carrié, *Italy from Napoleon to Mussolini* (1950); H. W. Schneider, *Making the Fascist State* (1928); D. A. Binchy, *Church and State in Fascist Italy* (1942); H. Finer, *Mussolini's Italy* (1935); K. S. Pinson, *Modern Germany* (1954); A. Rosenberg, *History of the German Republic* (1936); R. N. Hunt, *German Social Democracy, 1918–1933* (1964); R. T. Clark, *Fall of the German Republic* (1935); Alan Bullock, *Hitler, a Study in Tyranny* (1952); Karl Heiden, *Hitler* (1936); J. W. Wheeler-Bennett, *Wooden Titan, Hindenburg in Twenty Years of German History, 1914–1934* (1936); F. L. Neumann, *Behemoth, the Structure and Practice of National Socialism* (1942); W. L. Shirer, *The Rise and Fall of the Third Reich* (1960); F. Zweig, *Poland Between Two Wars* (1944); E. A. Peers, *The Spanish Tragedy, 1930–1936* (1936); D. A. Puzzo, *Spain and the Great Powers, 1936–1941* (1962); H. Thomas, *The Spanish Civil War* (1961); G. Jackson, *The Spanish Republic and the Civil War* (1965).

Chapter 58. C. J. Haines and R. J. S. Hoffman, *Origins and Background of the Second World War* (1947); Joseph Grew, *Ten Years in Japan* (1943); D. Borg, *The United States and the Far Eastern Crisis of 1933–1938* (1964); Francis C. Jones, *Japan's New Order in East Asia: Its Rise and Fall, 1937–1945* (1954); R. J. C. Butow, *Tojo and the Coming of the War* (1961); H. Feis, *The Road to Pearl Harbor* (1950); D. J. Lu, *From the Marco Polo Bridge to Pearl Harbor: Japan's Entry into World War II* (1961); Arnold Wolfers, *Britain and France Between Two Wars* (1940); M. H. H. Macartney and P. Cremona, *Italy's Foreign and Colonial Policy, 1914–1937* (1938); L. Mosley, *Haile Selassie: the Conquering Lion* (1965); Elizabeth Wiskemann, *The Rome-Berlin Axis* (1949); R. Luža, *The Transfer of the Sudeten Germans* (1964); Keith Feiling, *Life of Neville Chamberlain* (1947); K. Eubank, *Munich* (1963); Kurt von Schuschnigg, *Austrian Requiem* (1946); J. Gehl, *Austria, Germany, and Anschluss, 1931–1938* (1963); R. Machray, *The Poland of Pilsudski, 1914–1936* (1937); R. L. Buell, *Poland, Key to Europe* (1939); R. J. Sontag and J. S. Beddie, eds., *Nazi-Soviet Relations, 1939–1941* (1948); R. A. Divine, *The Illusion of Neutrality* (1962).

The meeting at Yalta. Stalin, Roosevelt, and Churchill.
Courtesy Bettmann Archive

PART XII

WORLD WAR II, 1939–1945

President Kennedy greets Chancellor Konrad Adenauer of West Germany, April 1961.

Courtesy Wide World Photos

From Stalin

to Kennedy

AND SINCE

THE SECOND World War lasts six years from 1939 to 1945 and even surpasses the First in terrifying destruction. At the outset, it is clearly a struggle between democracies and totalitarian dictatorships, with Communist Russia giving support to Nazi Germany and Fascist Italy. Later a rupture between Germany and Russia throws the latter dictatorship into an ill-assorted but eventually victorious alliance with the democracies.

The outcome of World War II raises more questions than it settles. Only two powers are the real victors—totalitarian Russia and democratic America. A new world situation thus arises with two super-powers and a series of countries, new and old, of secondary economic and military potential. The various nations tend to align themselves with one or the other super-power. All western and central Europe—the traditional seat of European and Western civilization—is sorely weakened. Part of it is held to the Russian system by force or fear of force, and other parts are not wholly unreceptive to Russian influence. And between a Communist world and a free world a "cold" war ensues.

Colonial empires overseas break up. Dozens of new nations more or less unready for self-government are created. A brave effort is made to resuscitate an international organization under the name of United Nations. It proves increasingly effective in some spheres and makes progress despite the fact that the world is divided into two alignments. But there remains the question as to whether through it or outside it the nations of the earth can find ways of living together in peace, security, and stability.

Meanwhile, there is rapid progress in science and technology bringing changes more significant and of greater effect on the lives of men than in any previous period of similar duration. Improved communications spread knowledge of the productivity of modern industry and of the standard of living in the advanced countries. The less developed countries undergo a "revolution of expectations" and strive to win for themselves the fruits of the new kinds of production and national independence.

The period is one of change, of hope, of fear. No one can predict the ultimate outcome. Nor is it clear that the highest spiritual values of historic Western civilization can be preserved as its outward forms, its nationalism, its science are spread throughout the world.

CHAPTER 59

World War II, 1939-1945

A. Initial German Successes and Russian Coöperation (1939-1940)

The Second World War began on September 1, 1939, with a slashing German attack on Poland. It proved a very one-sided affair. The invading German armies outnumbered the defending Polish armies almost three to one, and gave brilliant and terrifying demonstration of the new military technique of *Blitzkrieg* ("lightning war"). This involved heavy bombing, by superior air force, of fortifications, roads, railways, industrial plants, power stations, etc., and, amid resulting confusion and destruction, a quick infantry advance spearheaded by a superior and mobile force of armored tanks. Even the weather favored the Germans, for the clear bright days of that September were ideal for air operations, and kept the Polish plains dry and firm for tank maneuvers.

The Poles fought bravely and furiously, and at Warsaw they held out until their capital city was a shambles. It was all in vain. Within a very few days after the initial German attack, the outcome was a foregone conclusion. And in little more than two weeks, Soviet Russian armies were collaborating with the Germans and occupying the eastern part of Poland. Within five weeks all Polish resistance was crushed, the government was in exile, the country partitioned between the dictatorships of Nazi Germany and Communist Russia, and the surviving population subjected to merciless exploitation.

Meanwhile, Poland's allies, France and Great Britain, were powerless to help. Both were astounded by the swiftness and terror of the Blitzkrieg in the East, and quite unprepared to cope with it. They possessed no such numbers of planes and tanks as Germany. Britain, while enjoying naval superiority, had a relatively small and ill-equipped army, the transport of which to the Continent took time. France had a larger army, but it was subordinated to a great system of fortifications (the "Maginot Line") which had been constructed for defensive purposes along the Franco-German frontier after the First World War, and which was paralleled, since the remilitarization of the Rhineland in 1936, by an even stronger German system of fortifications (the "Siegfried Line"). Thus the forces of the Western Allies, if seemingly sheltered from German attack, were practically prevented from invading Germany, and hence from affording any relief to Poland.

This curious situation in the west continued throughout the winter of 1939-1940, with some patrol activity and with occasional dropping of propaganda pamphlets, but without serious fighting. The Allies optimistically hoped that while their armies sat safe behind the fortified frontier, their superior economic and commercial resources would gradually weigh against Germany and bring it to terms. Consequently they tended to overlook the lessons of the German Blitzkrieg in Poland and to neglect taking special precautions against its repetition in the West. They were not sufficiently heedful of their loss of prestige from Poland's subjugation and partition, or of the defeatism spreading within France, or of the ominous activities of the three chief European dictatorships during that winter of 1939–1940.

Nazi Germany was free to transfer its major forces from the east to the west and to increase its already superior number of planes and tanks, preparatory to a supreme effort to overwhelm France. Simultaneously, Mussolini busied himself with denouncing France and laying claims for Fascist Italy to Corsica and Tunis and Savoy and Nice. And the Communist Russian dictatorship of Stalin, in continuing collaboration with Nazi Germany, and with no effective opposition from the Allies, proceeded to tear up treaties and to commit a series of aggressions against all its European neighbors.

Following its seizure and incorporation of eastern Poland, Russia made demands on the three Baltic republics of Lithuania, Latvia, and Estonia which they were in no position to resist and which led to their transformation into Russian "protectorates" with Russian garrisons at strategic points. By agreement with Hitler, the German-speaking minorities in these lands were sent "home" to Germany, and finally, in July 1940, all three countries were incorporated in the Soviet Union.

But this was not all. Russian troops invaded and occupied the Rumanian provinces of Bessarabia and Bukovina; and Rumania, mindful of the fate of Poland, surrendered them to the Soviet Union. Russia likewise made demands on Finland for military and naval bases and for certain outright cessions of territory. Here, however, resistance was encountered, and at the end of November 1939 Russia began a war with Finland by bombing its capital city of Helsinki. In an amazing display of courage and military skill, and with surreptitious aid from the Scandinavian countries, especially Sweden, the Finns withstood for several months Russian invasions from the south, north, and east. But by March 1940, sheer weight of numbers and material bore down the Finns and broke their "Mannerheim Line." Finland surrendered, and on March 12 signed peace terms which yielded to

Winston Churchill.

Courtesy Bettmann Archive

Russia the Karelian peninsula in the south, the Petsamo region in the north, and a naval base close to Helsinki. Communist Russia was now dominant in nearly all the territories it had lost at the close of the First World War; and wherever it newly established itself, it drove existing governments into exile and terrorized the populations.

Shortly after the conclusion of the Russian conquests in eastern and northern Europe, the Germans were ready to strike with overwhelming force in the west. On April 9, 1940, they seized Denmark and launched an air and naval invasion of Norway. At some points, they encountered resistance, but it was confused, and was interfered with by traitors within the country. One of these, a certain Major Vidkun Quisling, was later to enrich modern languages with a new word, for "quisling" came to stand for the "fifth-column" traitor who betrayed his homeland to a foreign country.

For a brief space, it seemed that Great Britain might be able to come to the rescue of Norway. But German air power drove British ships out of the straits between Denmark and Norway, and soon compelled them to quit Norwegian ports. King Haakon VII of Norway fled, and set up a "government in exile" in England, and the greater part of the Norwegian merchant marine continued to carry goods for the Allies.

On May 10, 1940, as a result of the British fiasco in Norway, Winston Churchill succeeded Neville Chamberlain as prime minister of Great Britain. In Churchill the British found a great war leader, capable of uniting the country in the face of disaster and eventually of leading it to victory. Son of an American mother and a father who was descended from the Duke of Marlborough, Churchill had had a long experience in public affairs. He had consistently warned his country of the rising menace of Nazi Germany and had severely criticized Chamberlain's pre-war policy of "appeasement." He now took the helm in Britain's gravest crisis.

B. Fall of France and Isolation of Britain (1940–1941)

On May 10, 1940, the very day on which Winston Churchill became prime minister of Great Britain, the Germans launched an offensive against France. It was not a frontal attack on the heavily fortified "Maginot Line," which would have been much too costly, but rather an outflanking of the Line by a surprise attack through the neutral countries of Holland and Belgium. War was declared by both, but their armed resistance was not great, and it was quickly mowed down by the same sort of Blitzkrieg which the Germans had employed against Poland—a skillful use of air power, lightning movements of armored columns, spearheaded by tanks, some "fifth column" work, the employment of parachute troops, and relentless. pressure against a disorganized foe.

In Holland, German parachutists, wearing Dutch uniforms, hurtled down from the air, while German ground forces, in rubber boots, swarmed across canals and flooded fields. The Rotterdam airfield was captured on the first day, and the city itself was turned to rubble by a murderous and unopposed bombing. Armored columns raced across the country, cutting the Dutch army into bits. Within a week all resistance was. crushed, and Queen Wilhelmina and her government took refuge in England.

Belgian resistance lasted not much longer. At the very start, the Germans captured bridges over the Meuse River and the Albert Canal. British and French troops were pushed forward to help the Belgians hold a second line from Antwerp to Louvain and Namur. But the German armored columns swept through the Ardennes, which the French had thought almost impassable for them, and crossed the Meuse near Sedan. This was a crucial breakthrough. It obliged the armies in Belgium to fall back and it brought the Germans into France beyond the west end of the Maginot Line.

The Germans exploited their breakthrough, not by swinging to the left, toward Paris, as in 1914, but to the right, toward the sea. German spearheads reached Abbeville on May 20 and turned north to Boulogne on the coast. Quickly the million Allied soldiers in Belgium (including the entire British army on the Continent) were cut off from the main French armies, and against them the Germans drove fast and furiously from all directions. On May 27 King Leopold III of Belgium surrendered and became a prisoner of war; and during the next week the British worked manfully with all sorts of water craft to evacuate their army from the port of Dunkirk. The latter had to abandon guns, munitions, and supplies, but, despite almost continuous air attack and shell fire from land, the boats managed to get to England some 225,000 British troops and about 110,000 others (mostly French).

Meanwhile, the same tactics which the Germans used to cut off Belgium and the British were being employed to demoralize, cut through, isolate, and overwhelm the several French armies within France itself.

In vain the French high command was transferred from General Gamelin to General Weygand. The French armies were without adequate planes and tanks, and they employed those they did have ineffectively; they were confused and blocked not only by the Germans, but by enormous numbers of civilian refugees and, in some instances, by internal Communist and "fifth column" activity. And, to cap the climax, Fascist Italy seized the opportunity to join Germany in the attack on France, just as Russia had seized a like opportunity to assist in the destruction of Poland. Italy declared war on France and Great Britain on June 11. Three days later the Germans occupied Paris. French armed resistance was already nearing an end, and the French government moved to Tours and thence to Bordeaux.

France had promised Britain not to make a separate peace, and Churchill flew to Tours with a proposal that France and Great Britain be merged into one country, with one government, and fight on together. There was some discussion of the possibility of removing remnants of French troops and equipment to French North Africa, or of concentrating forces for a final stand in the peninsula of Brittany. To a majority of the French cabinet, such possibilities appeared impractical, and by a vote of 13 to 11 it decided to quit the struggle. Reynaud, the premier who had succeeded Daladier, resigned and was replaced by the aged Marshal Pétain, who had won fame as the defender of Verdun in the First World War. On June 17 the new cabinet asked Hitler for an armistice, and for its conclusion the Germans brought out of a museum the railway car used for signing the armistice of November 11, 1918, which had registered Germany's defeat in the First World War. At the same spot, in the forest of Compiègne, on June 21, 1940, the French delegates signed an armistice that registered the disastrous defeat of their country. A camera at the scene caught Hitler dancing a little jig.

By the terms of the armistice, France north of the Loire River and the entire Alantic coast would be occupied and administered by the Germans; the remainder would have a measure of autonomy; the country would have to pay heavy "costs of occupation." To the Germans the price of this sensational victory was comparatively small. They had lost about 25,000 killed and 70,000 wounded. They had captured, killed, or wounded more than two million French soldiers.

The fall of France had several immediate effects. (1) It practically ended the Third French Republic. Marshal Pétain obtained from the Parliament a grant of dictatorial power, which he used to set up at Vichy an essentially fascist regime for the part of France left him by the armistice. For a time, most Frenchmen regarded Pétain as a patriot who only awaited a favorable chance to strike back at the Germans. Gradually, however, as certain high officials of his regime, especially Pierre Laval, urged "collaboration" with the Germans, there developed in France an "underground" resistance, some of which was brought into clandestine contact with a "Free France" group that the British government collected and sponsored in London under the leadership of General DeGaulle.

(2) Italy formally entered the war on the side of her Axis partner, and undertook to dominate the Mediterranean. Expeditionary forces were despatched to Italian North Africa to oppose the British in Egypt and, if possible, to deprive them of the Suez Canal, while diplomatic pressure was exerted on Spain to get it to enter the war, seize Gibraltar, and thus close the western end of the Mediterranean to the British.

(3) Throughout the European continent Germany and collaborating Russia were now all-powerful, less than a year after the outbreak of war. They had partitioned Poland between them; and while Russia had appropriated Lithuania, Latvia, and Estonia, and despoiled Finland and Rumania, Germany had conquered Norway and Denmark, Holland and Belgium, and now France; and Italy was her active ally. And for self-preservation, other and lesser powers now felt constrained to hold aloof from Great Britain and to be friendly with the Axis. Hitler acted as a kind of arbiter among the nations of central and east-central Europe. For example, he directed a veritable partition of Rumania, agreeing to Russian seizure of Bessarabia and to

Bomb destruction in London. St. Paul's Cathedral is in the background.

Courtesy Wide World Photos

Hungary's annexation of part of Transylvania. In vain the Rumanian government expressed dissatisfaction. German "tourists" filtered into the country and in September 1940 abetted a *coup d'état* which sent King Carol into exile and eventually established a pro-Nazi dictatorship.

(4) Great Britain was left without allies and was separated from Germany's triumphant forces only by the narrow waters of the British Channel. The whole Atlantic coastline of Europe from Norway to southernmost France was in German hands, and all the resources, factories, and labor of western and central Europe were at Germany's disposal. Britain had suffered the loss of the best part of its war-equipment (except planes) during the rout in Belgium and the evacuation from Dunkirk, and considerable time would be required to replace it.

There is little doubt that Germany might have overwhelmed its one remaining foe if it had concentrated its attention, for a year after June 1940, on preparations for an actual large-scale invasion of England—building and marshalling transports along the Continental coast and providing them with adequate airplane coverage and submarine protection for the crossing. That Germany did not do this, is mainly attributable to a naive belief of Hitler and some of his chief advisers that a devastating air attack on Britain would suffice to bring it to terms.

The Germans opened their air attack on British coastal towns on August 8, 1940, and early in September extended it, with some 1,500 planes, to London. Then until the late spring of 1941 British cities were under more or less continuous air attack. Some 50,000 high explosive bombs (not counting incendiaries) fell on London.

Coventry was almost obliterated. Ports and manufacturing cities, such as Cardiff, Portsmouth, Swansea, Glasgow, Liverpool, Manchester, and Sheffield were badly battered. Some 40,000 persons were killed and twice as many wounded.

Yet the air attack of Germany on Britain failed. First, it failed because the British still had a sizeable defensive air force, which, during 1940–1941, knocked down three thousand German planes at a loss of less than a thousand to themselves. As Winston Churchill said, in tribute to British flyers, "Never in the field of human conflict was so much owed by so many to so few."

Second, British civilian, as well as air-force, morale proved tough and firmly resistant. When Britain stood alone against a victorious enemy, its people showed their finest qualities.

Third, the British had important resources and manufacturing skill, which enabled them to replace their losses and to add to their airforce and other defenses. Moreover, they still were dominant on the seas and, despite heavy losses inflicted on their shipping by German submarines and planes, they continued to receive invaluable assistance in men and supplies from overseas, especially from the British Dominions of Canada, Australia, and New Zealand.

Fourth, and most significant of all, the British had an increasingly important source of supply in the United States. At the outbreak of the war, most of the American people were isolationist and anxious to keep out of it. But as the Germans scored one triumph after another, alarm grew in the United States, and its sentiment became increasingly pro-British. Under the leadership of President Franklin Roosevelt, it began to give the British "all aid short of war." In September 1940 it turned over to Britain fifty naval destroyers in return for leases on naval bases in Newfoundland and the West Indies. In November it shared its own rapidly rising production of war material on a fifty-fifty basis with Great Britain, on condition that the latter pay for and transport its share on a "cash and carry" basis. This arrangement was later eased for Britain by a "Lend-Lease Act" passed by the American Congress in March 1941.

Fifth, and last, Germany was diverted in 1940–1941 from concentrating against Great Britain by a number of extraneous developments. Hitler, imagining that he could get full French coöperation from Marshal Pétain which would enable him to shut the British out of the Mediterranean, neglected to force Spain into the war and to secure Gibraltar. Then, too, he found that his Italian ally was so weak and dispirited as to require constant bolstering.

In September 1940, an Italian army under Marshal Graziani, advancing from the North African province of Libya, crossed the Egyptian border and reached Sidi Barrani, while other Italian forces from Ethiopia edged their way into Kenya and the Sudan. Then in October, another Italian army, based on Albania, launched an attack on Greece, partially for conquest and partially as additional aid against the British in the eastern Mediterranean. Both Italian efforts failed dismally. In December 1940 the British in Egypt, under General Wavell, counter-attacked, rolled Graziani's army far back into Libya, and took 130,000 prisoners and much material. Then, between January and May 1941, South African and other British Dominion troops overwhelmed the Italian garrisons in Somaliland, Eritrea, and Ethiopia, and restored Haile Selassie to the throne from which he had been driven five years previously.[1] Meanwhile, by January 1941 the Greeks had decisively beaten the Italians and driven them back into Albania.

In these circumstances, Germany had to pull Italy's chestnuts out of the fire. In February 1941 Hitler sent into North Africa several highly trained and armored German divisions under General Rommel, who replaced the Italian commander and pushed the British back through Libya and far inside the Egyptian frontier. In March 1941 Hitler moved to end the Graeco-Italian conflict by establishing German control in southeastern Europe. He demanded of Bulgaria and Yugoslavia that they grant passage of German troops. King Boris III of Bulgaria readily acceded, and the Regent Paul of Yugoslavia more reluctantly on March 25. In the latter country, however, a popular and army revolt deposed Paul

[1] See above, p. 757.

and led to a brief German-Yugoslav war. Within two weeks the Germans, with their Blitzkrieg, overran Yugoslavia and ended its formal resistance. But in the mountainous wilds of the country, a prolonged guerrilla war continued.

Then into Greece the German war machine proceeded. In vain the British sent an expeditionary force from Egypt to help the Greeks. By the end of April, Greece was overrun and the British saved 44,000 of their force only by another Dunkirk-like evacuation. For a little longer the Greeks, with British aid, clung to Crete, but this too they had to abandon in the face of overwhelming attacks of German airplanes and parachutists.

Yet the very reverses which Great Britain suffered in the spring of 1941 in Greece and Crete were evidence that Germany was far afield from a knock-out blow against England itself. And any such blow was now indefinitely postponed by a break between Germany and Russia.

C. Break between Germany and Russia, and Participation of the United States (1941)

From the summer of 1939 to the spring of 1941 there had been apparently friendly coöperation between Nazi Germany and Communist Russia, with consequences advantageous to themselves and disastrous to the rest of Europe. Then suddenly, on June 22, 1941, the anniversary of Napoleon's break with Russia in 1812, Hitler broke with Stalin and launched a gigantic German invasion of Russia. This marked a radical change in the setting and course of the Second World War.

Stalin and his Communist associates had undoubtedly feigned greater friendship with Hitler and Nazi Germany than they felt, and they were certainly piqued in the spring of 1941 by German military intervention in Bulgaria and Yugoslavia which they thought of as being within Russia's sphere of influence. Fundamentally, of course, they sought to serve Russian and Communist ends, not

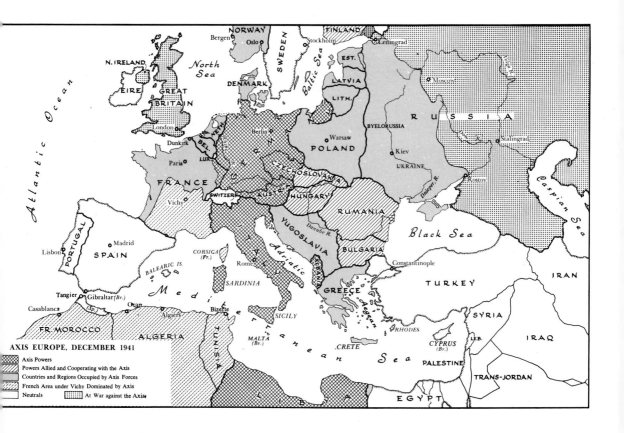

AXIS EUROPE, DECEMBER 1941

Axis Powers
Powers Allied and Cooperating with the Axis
Countries and Regions Occupied by Axis Forces
French Area under Vichy Dominated by Axis
Neutrals   At War against the Axis

Hitler's; and if at any time fortune should cease to smile on Hitler, they would be pretty sure to be his enemies instead of his friends. Yet, whatever may have been their ultimate intentions, they were hardly minded to break with Hitler in June 1941. The break was on the other side.

Hitler had long been obsessed with anti-Slavic, as well as anti-Communist, feeling, and his pact of 1939 with Communist Russia was only a needful temporary expedient. He was convinced that sooner or later Germany must fight Russia for the hegemony of Eastern Europe, and particularly for the rich agricultural region of the Ukraine; and the moment now seemed propitious. Germany had quickly overwhelmed every nation with which her army grappled, including the reputedly great military nation of France, while Russia had experienced much difficulty in subduing petty Finland. Hence, a German war against Russia should be brief and highly successful. It could be represented as a "crusade against the red menace," and as such would enlist sympathy throughout western Europe. Hitler felt sure that once he had crushed Russia he could make some sort of reasonable peace with Great Britain. If the British proved unduly stubborn he would have the resources and the security to bring about Britain's defeat at his own leisure.

The sudden break of Hitler with Stalin in June 1941 had numerous repercussions. Churchill, speaking for Great Britain, declared: "Any man or state who fights against Nazidom will have our aid. Any man or state who marches with Hitler is our foe. . . . We shall give whatever help we can to Russia and to the Russian people." In France, the Communists quickly changed their earlier pacifist and pro-German stand into an active resistance to the Germans. American Communists, who until June 1941 had been denouncing the war as an imperialist conflict from which America should remain isolated, now called loudly for all-out aid to Russia and Britain. On the other hand, countries which had been despoiled by Russia between 1939 and 1941, such as Finland and Rumania, actively supported Germany in warring on Russia, as also did Hungary and Bulgaria.

Germany gave promise in 1941 of repeating in Russia what had been done in Poland in 1939 and in France in 1940. Its armies, using the tactics of the Blitzkrieg, with planes and tanks, rapidly pierced the protective belt of East Poland and the former Baltic republics and pushed deep into Russian territory. In less than four weeks, German armies hammered into Smolensk. Then, as their central thrust slowed down a hundred miles from Moscow, they launched a drive to the south which engulfed Kharkov and reached Rostov at the mouth of the Don. They occupied all of the rich agricultural and industrial Ukraine. Simultaneously, other German armies in the north swept forward to the very gates of Leningrad.

In early October the Germans resumed their direct drive on Moscow, and by the end of the month they had it partially encircled. By late November it seemed as though they must shortly capture it and oblige Stalin to sue for peace. The moment was opportune for an associate of the Axis—faraway Japan—to merge its protracted war with China into a general drive for supremacy in Asia and the Pacific.

Already in July 1941, Japan had taken advantage of the fall of France to obtain military and naval bases in French Indo-China; and shortly afterwards, in pursuit of what it euphemistically termed the establishment of a "co-prosperity sphere" throughout eastern Asia, it adopted an aggressive attitude toward the Dutch East Indies. The United States and Great Britain were alarmed, and both countries imposed a partial embargo on shipments to Japan. The Japanese response was the installing, in October, of a new and bellicose premier in the person of General Tojo and his despatching, in November, of a pretended "peace mission" to the United States. This was merely a cover. The Japanese government decided to strike while Russia was being overborne by Germany, while Britain was isolated and seemingly powerless, and while the United States was unprepared. On December 7, without any declaration of war, Japanese planes made a surprise attack on the American fleet at Pearl Harbor in Hawaii, destroyed a considerable part of it, and won temporary naval supremacy in the Pacific.

On December 8 the United States and Great Britain declared war on Japan. Three days later Germany and Italy declared war on the United States. The Second World War was now indeed global. Every major power was engaged in it.

As Germany won notable initial successes in Russia, so Japan won similar successes in the Pacific. By the end of December 1941 the Japanese were in Siam and were threatening Burma. They captured Guam and Wake Island from the Americans and Hong Kong from the British. In another month they had overrun most of the Philippine Islands, and by the middle of February 1942 they had reduced the great British fortress and naval base of Singapore.

D. Passing of Axis Powers from Offensive to Defensive (1942–1944)

The Axis powers of Germany, Italy, and Japan maintained offensives throughout the greater part of 1942. Though they were now opposed by an alliance of Great Britain, Russia, and the United States, the latter continued to suffer reverses.

The Japanese, between January and March, conquered Burma, thereby cutting the main supply-route over the Burma Road to China, and at the same time threatening India. They defeated a combined Dutch, American, British, and Australian naval force in the strait of Macassar, in the Dutch East Indies, and on March 1 effected a landing on Java. Within the next few weeks they overwhelmed the Dutch, took possession of nearly all the extensive Malay archipelago, and menaced Australia. In May they forced the surrender of Bataan and Corregidor, the last American footholds in the Philippines.

In Europe, the Germans had met with more stubborn resistance in Russia than they anticipated, and although their armies in 1941 had conquered the Ukraine and gotten to the gates of Leningrad and Moscow, they not only received no peace plea from Stalin, but were actually pushed back a bit during the ensuing winter by a Rus-

President Franklin D. Roosevelt signing the declaration of war against Japan.

Courtesy Bettmann Archive

sian counter-offensive. By the spring of 1942, however, they had recovered and were making new advances. They still failed to take either Leningrad or Moscow, but they overran the Crimea and captured Sevastopol. Then, in the summer, they made two extensive drives. One was southward, netting them Rostov and carrying them hundreds of miles into the Caucasus with its rich oil fields. The other was eastward between the Donetz and the upper Don, and on to Stalingrad on the Volga.

In North Africa, there had been fluctuations in the desert fighting between the British, based on Egypt, and the Italians and Germans, based on Tripoli. In January 1942 the latter were driven back from the Egyptian frontier, but in the summer, under command of the German General Rommel, they returned, recrossed the frontier, and advanced to El Alamein, only sixty miles from Alexandria. Axis conquest of Egypt and the Suez Canal seemed imminent.

In the latter part of 1942 each of several offensives of the Axis powers was halted and changed into a defensive operation; and the Allies began important offensives of their own. The main reason for this change was that, whereas the Axis at the start had been better prepared for war, possessing superiority in planes, tanks, guns, and munitions, and having more technically trained men, it was now being equalled and surpassed in all these respects by its foes. Russia not only had an extraordinarily large pool of man-power, but it removed many of its vital industrial plants out of reach of the invader and mightily expanded them. It also received enormous quantities of war material from Great Britain and especially from the United States.

The United States performed industrial prodigies. Once it was tooled up for war production on a mass basis, it turned out, from 1942 to 1945, a gradually overwhelming avalanche of weapons—over 400,000 planes, 70,000 naval craft of all types, 80,000 landing craft, 8,000 cargo ships, nearly 2 million heavy machine guns, over 2 million sub-machine guns, 12 million rifles and carbines, nearly 6 million bombs to be dropped by aircraft, half a million depth charges for use against submarines, 110 million grenades, 86,000 tanks, nearly 2½ million trucks. By 1945, much more than half the war-production of the world was in America.

Nor was it merely a matter of quantity. Coming into the war late, the United States was able to focus its production on the latest models. The Germans improved their tanks more rapidly than the Americans. But in planes, the bombers and fighters of the United States surpassed those of their opponents. On both sides scientists were mobilized and developed new weapons of offense and new mechanisms of defense. But in the long run the achievements of the British and Americans overshadowed even the most spectacular German inventions, such as the jet-propelled flying bomb and the rocket bomb.

The farthest extension of Japanese conquests was reached in June 1942. In that month American fleet-based planes, in the crucial naval battle of Midway, stopped a major Japanese thrust at Hawaii. In August, American marines landed at Guadalcanal in the Solomon Islands, and held it against repeated counter-attacks in the autumn.

Germany's second-year offensive against Russia was halted by fierce, protracted, and eventually successful. Russian resistance at Stalingrad. In November the Russians struck back against the Germans with a well-prepared counter-offensive, which encircled a German army of some 300,000 men and compelled its surrender at the end of January 1943. The defense of Stalingrad, and the succeeding Russian counter-attack, marked the turning point of the war on the eastern front, if not of the whole war.

In Egypt, the invading Germans and Italians were finally driven back by the British from El Alamein in a spectacular battle of tanks. It began in October 1942 and resulted in heavy losses for General Rommel and his retirement to fortified positions four hundred miles west of Egypt. Stalin, to relieve his hard-pressed Russians, had been urging Britain and America to assume an offensive in Europe and to open a "second front" in France. In 1942, however, Roosevelt and Churchill were agreed that sufficient men, ships, planes, and materiel for such a difficult operation were not yet available. Instead, they decided to seize French North Africa, preparatory to an attack on what Churchill called the "soft under-belly" of the Axis through Sicily and Italy. The British drive westward from Egypt was deemed a part of this plan.

On November 8, 1942, an Anglo-American expedition, carried by hundreds of craft and protected by heavy naval escort, effected landings near Casablanca on the Atlantic coast and at Oran and Algiers on the Mediterranean. It had been feared that Spain, under General Franco, might seriously interfere with the operation. This did not occur, however, and what difficulty the landing forces had was not with Spaniards but with French units loyal to Marshal Pétain. Even this difficulty was soon surmounted through special agreement between Admiral Darlan, representing at the moment the Vichy regime in North Africa, and General Dwight Eisenhower, who was commander-in-chief of the Anglo-American forces. Subsequently, Darlan was assassinated, and in time a "Free French" government was established at Algiers under General de Gaulle.

Meanwhile, the Allied seizure of French North Africa had repercussions within France. The Germans swiftly reacted by seizing the part of France which, in accordance with the armistice, had remained under French (Vichy) administration. They completely discredited the Vichy regime, rendered Marshal Pétain virtually a prisoner, and gave a big impetus to the French resistance movement and its eager coöperation with the Allies.

For a time, Rommel's army of Germans and Italians put up a stubborn fight in Tunisia against the British advancing westward from Egypt and Libya, and the Americans pressing eastward from Algeria. At length the Allies effected a juncture, and on May 6, 1943, they won a decisive victory. The city of Tunis and the naval base of Bizerte fell to them, and within a week German resistance in Africa ceased.

With North Africa entirely in their hands, the Anglo-American forces prepared for the next operation. On July 9, 1943, after prolonged air bombing, they landed in Sicily and quickly overcame the Italian defense. But German forces, which had been evacuated from North Africa, fought fierce rearguard actions across Sicily and safely reached the mainland. Sicily itself, within forty days, was an Allied conquest.

The defeats in Africa and Sicily produced important results among the Italians, who, as a people, had not been enthusiastic about Mussolini's getting them into the war. There were mutterings even inside the Fascist party. On July 24, 1943, at a meeting of the Fascist Grand Council, a motion was passed asking King Victor Emmanuel to assume real leadership. Mussolini was arrested; the King placed the government in the hands of Marshal Badoglio; and Fascism was outlawed.

Badoglio then opened secret negotiations with the Allies. The Germans still had large forces in Italy, and the Allies demanded "unconditional surrender," as Roosevelt and Churchill had agreed to do in a meeting the previous winter at Casablanca. The ne-

gotiations were kept secret until the Allies actually landed in Italy on September 9, 1943, when it was announced that Badoglio and the King had agreed to an armistice, amounting to unconditional surrender. The Germans, however, were not caught napping. They had already taken over the defense of southern Italy and they moved quickly to seize control of the entire peninsula. Thus Italy was in an odd position. It had signed an armistice, but it was largely in German hands. Mussolini escaped to the north to conduct a sort of phantom puppet government for the Germans.

The Anglo-American army put ashore on the beaches of Salerno on September 9, met fierce German opposition. It was supported by planes from Sicily and by heavy fire from naval vessels, but its position was difficult until it was joined by a British army which had taken the southern ports of Taranto, Brindisi, and Bari, and moved rapidly northward. By October 1 the Allied forces captured Naples, but not before the Germans had destroyed the port facilities and wrecked much of the city.

The mountainous nature of the Italian peninsula and the skillful defense of the Germans made Allied advance northward extremely difficult. In January 1944 the Allies tried to hasten matters by a landing behind the German lines at Anzio. But the Germans reacted so quickly as to imperil the landed troops, and the Anzio expedition was not safe until May when it was joined by the main Allied army which had been painfully pushing forward. This had been delayed by a heavily fortified German "Gustav Line" which ran through Cassino. It was not until May 11 that the Gustav Line was breached. Then Cassino was finally taken and the Anzio beachhead relieved; and on June 4, 1944, the Allied forces entered Rome. But the German General von Kesselring dexterously extricated his troops and prepared new defense lines still farther north.

One of the factors which made von Kesselring's retreat inevitable, despite his military skill and the advantages of the terrain he defended, was an increasing difficulty in securing supplies from Germany. This difficulty in turn arose from the rising tempo with which Allied bombers were striking at production centers and transportation lines in Italy and more especially in Germany. As early as May and June of 1942 the British staged three raids of a thousand bombers each on Cologne, Essen, and Bremen. Afterwards, improved airplane design and increased production, plus the participation of the American air force, rendered such heavy bombing more frequent and more destructive. British bombers specialized in night raids; American, in daytime operations. By early 1943 Germany was subjected on successive days to "round the clock" bombing, and the bomb-carrying capacity of the planes was gradually increased.

The main targets of the Allied air forces were submarine pens and other German installations on the Channel Coast, German industries with special emphasis on refineries and synthetic fuel plants, and railways and other means of communication. Germany was not "knocked out" from the air, but the bombing did produce shortages and a creeping paralysis of communications which seriously hampered the German armies.

Growing Allied air power paid another dividend. Air patrols from Newfoundland, Iceland, North Ireland, and later from the Azores (with Portugal's permission), together with the use of "baby flattop" carriers, checked the submarine menace. In May 1943 the Germans for the first time lost more submarines than they put into operation. Thenceforth the threat to Allied shipping decreased, though it was held in check only by constant vigilance.

While the western Allies were clearing the Mediterranean, concluding an armistice with Italy, and bombing Germany, Russia was likewise scoring notable successes. At the beginning of 1943, while one German army was being crushed at Stalingrad, another was being driven out of the Caucasus. The siege of Leningrad was broken on January 18, and in early March the threat to Moscow was practically ended.

Throughout the spring and summer of 1943 there was heavy fighting in southern Russia, with certain towns and areas changing hands several times. Finally, in the autumn, energetic Russian offensives captured Kharkov, the strategic railway junc-

tion of Bryansk, and the city of Smolensk, which had been the German eastern headquarters in 1941-1942, and pushed the Germans out of the Donetz basin. In November 1943 they won the Ukranian capital of Kiev.

By June 1944 the Russians had cleared the Nazis out of most of the territory held by the Soviet Union in 1938. In the south they had advanced into pre-war Rumanian and Polish territory. In the center they had liberated much of White Russia. In the north they had come nearly to the old Estonian border. They had inflicted tremendous losses on the Germans which the Nazis could in no wise repair. These successes they had achieved by remarkable strategy, by hard fighting, and by an ability to maintain supply lines with few railways. This last ability was greatly enhanced by American motor trucks shipped to them by the tens of thousands under the Lend-Lease arrangement and brought in from Arctic Ocean ports and by an overland route which had been opened up through Persia.

Though President Roosevelt had made the crucial decision of devoting the bulk of American resources to the prosecution of the war in Europe and to such enterprises as the landings in North Africa and the invasion of Italy, the year 1943 and the first half of 1944 were not without gains in the Pacific against the Japanese, made possible by a growing control of the air and of the sea. During the summer and fall of 1943, American forces extended their hold in the Solomons by taking New Georgia and the air base at Munda, together with adjacent islands. In November, American marines captured airfields on Bougainville. Already a most effective naval and military strategy was being worked out. Instead of painfully digging out the Japanese garrisons on every island, General MacArthur, the American commander in the Pacific, was content to seize key airfields and ports, isolating other Japanese contingents, cutting their supply lines, and leaving them to wither away. Thus Rabaul, the principal Japanese base on New Britain, was rendered ineffective in December.

Early in 1944 the Americans struck into territory that had been Japanese before Pearl Harbor by capturing the atoll of

General Dwight D. Eisenhower.

Courtesy Bettmann Archive

Kwajalein in the Marshall Islands. Thereby they secured a base for bombing the Japanese at Truk in the Carolines and for a further push which took them to Saipan in the Marianas by the summer of 1944. Despite isolated Japanese garrisons in the southwest Pacific, the war there was now essentially over. The American forces were in a position to strike for the recovery of the Philippines, and they had covered the longest and hardest part of the sea-and-air road leading to Tokyo.

E. Allied Victory (1944–1945)

On June 6, 1944, the very day on which the Germans evacuated Rome, American and British (including Canadian) forces landed in France. This was the greatest water-borne invasion of history. It began with air and naval bombardment of fifty miles of Normandy beaches and the dropping of paratroopers behind the coast line; and presently, despite stout German resistance, it secured a strong Allied foothold in the Cherbourg peninsula. Thence was launched an offensive with planes and tanks which beat the Germans at their own Blitzkrieg, threw them into disorder, and obliged them during the next two months to quit Paris and the greater part of France.

By mid-September it was obvious that the Allies were closing in upon Germany and that its defeat was only a matter of months. In France, the Anglo-American invasion from the west was linked up with another which came from a recent landing in the south on the Mediterranean coast near Toulon. Together the invaders numbered over two million, and already they had practically liberated France, pushed into Belgium and Luxembourg, freed Brussels and Antwerp, and entered Holland and even Germany itself.

At the same time, the Allied forces in Italy had pressed the Germans northward from Rome through very difficult mountainous terrain and had come in sight of the Po valley. The Russians, too, were driving successfully, and in overwhelming force, from eastern Europe. In August 1944, Russian armies broke through to the Baltic west of Riga, pushed into East Prussia, overran eastern Poland, and reached the Vistula River both above and below Warsaw. Simultaneously another Russian army entered Rumania and occupied Bucharest. In September, Finland surrendered anew on Russia's terms, while Russian troops penetrated into Bulgaria, Yugoslavia, Hungary, and Czechoslovakia.

In the autumn and early winter of 1944, Nazi Germany made a supreme effort to hold off the victoriously advancing Allies. Russian advance in the east was almost everywhere slackened and halted. Allied advance from the south was stopped by the German "Gothic" line in north Italy. Allied advance from the west was arrested and actually turned back in the so-called "Battle of the Bulge," which was fought in December and which temporarily brought the Germans back into Belgium. Germany, however, could not maintain for long a counter-offensive or even a defense on so many fronts. Its war material, its manpower, and its morale were now vastly inferior to the Allies'.

Early in 1945 Allied offensives were resumed and went on unrelentingly to the end. The Russians captured Warsaw in January, Budapest in February, Danzig in March, Vienna in April. In April the Allies in Italy took Bologna, crossed the Po, and reached Milan. Meanwhile, Allied forces in the west, now including substantial French contingents, wiped out the "Bulge," reached Cologne in March, gained control of the Rhineland and the Ruhr in April, and on April 25 made first contact with the Russians near Leipzig.

On May 2, the German army in Italy surrendered. Already a group of Italian Communists had seized Mussolini fleeing toward the Swiss border, and had slain him and hung up his body for public execration in Milan.

On May 2, Berlin fell. The western Allies might have taken it, but by previous agreement they left it to the Russians, who mowed down the final furious resistance of frenzied Nazis. Hitler perished miserably amid the ruins. On May 7, German military and naval commanders met Allied commanders at Reims and agreed formally to unconditional surrender. Allied victory was complete in Europe.

Victory in the Pacific over Japan was yet to be achieved, but by May 1945 it was in clear prospect. The United States now possessed super-abundant naval and air strength. It had reconquered almost all of the Philippines since October 1944. It had obtained bases for effective bombing and eventual invasion of Japan by conquering Iwo Jima in February 1945 and Okinawa in April. In May the British recovered most of Burma; and the Chinese, aided by American supplies, were cutting the Japanese off from Indo-China and regaining some of their own coastal territory.

A large-scale invasion of Japan was planned for the autumn of 1945, but it proved unnecessary. By midsummer, the incessant bombing of the country convinced many responsible Japanese, including the Emperor Hirohito, that further fighting was futile and that they should sue for peace. On August 8 the hopelessness of the odds against them was emphasized by Russia's formally declaring war against Japan and ordering an advance into Manchuria and Korea. The final determinant was the atomic bomb, the outcome of several years' secret labor by American, British, and Canadian scientists and engineers. Two such bombs were dropped on Japan, with the most terrifying results: one on August 6, destroying the city of Hiroshima and killing some 66,000 civilians; the other on August 9, laying Nagasaki in ruins and killing 40,000.

An underwater atomic blast in Bikini Lagoon, July 25, 1946.

Courtesy Wide World Photos

The next day, Japan offered to surrender, on the one condition that its Emperor was not molested. The surrender was agreed to by the Allies on August 14, 1945, and shortly afterwards American troops, under General MacArthur, occupied Japan. This marked the end of World War II.

The costs of the war can never be accurately determined. To the American people alone, the immediate and direct cost of the war was over a million casualties, including nearly 400,000 deaths, and a financial expenditure of something like 350 billion dollars. The direct expenditure of other countries has been estimated at a trillion (1,000 billion) dollars, while loss of property must run to another trillion, and of human lives into the millions.

Three major contributions to final Allied victory may be discerned: first, the stubborn courage of the British during the year in which they stood alone against the triumphant Axis; second, the vast man-power, relentless defense, and strategically skillful attacks of the Soviet Union which wore down the Germans; third, the vast productive capacity of the United States which provided the materials for victory.

President Harry Truman addressing first session of the United Nations at San Francisco, 1945.

Courtesy Wide World Photos

CHAPTER 60

Immediate Outcome of World War II

A. Peace Plans and the United Nations

During the course of the war, shortly after Germany's attack on Russia, but while the situation of England still seemed dark indeed, President Franklin Roosevelt and Prime Minister Winston Churchill had met at sea in August 1941. One of their purposes was to formulate a statement of the objectives of the anti-Nazi powers, which would, at the same time, influence neutral opinion and form a general basis for the post-war settlement. It was to some extent modeled after Wilson's famous and influential "Fourteen Points," but it was much less specific.

The "Atlantic Charter," as it was called, declared that the United States and Great Britain sought no additional territory, and that if any territorial changes were made at the end of the war they should be in accord with the freely expressed wishes of the peoples concerned. It went on to reaffirm the right of all peoples to choose their own form of government, to promise the restoration of freedom to countries that had been conquered, and to assert that all nations, victors or vanquished, should have access to raw materials. It proclaimed that all nations must be secure within their own boundaries, and must be afforded the means of freeing their citizens from fear and want; that the seas must be free; and that ultimately the use of force must be abandoned among nations, though, pending the establishment of general security, na-

tions threatening aggression must be disarmed.

The hopes for democracy, security, and peace, thus enshrined in the Charter, fitted well the mood of the Allied governments in exile. At a conference in London, in September 1941, Belgium, Poland, Czechoslovakia, Yugoslavia, Greece, and others accepted the principles of the Charter as a basis for the post-war settlement. After the entrance of the United States into the war, there was a gradual drawing together of the powers arrayed against Germany, Italy, and Japan. Poland and Russia had already signed a declaration of friendship. In May 1942, Great Britain and Russia signed a twenty-year treaty of alliance. At the same time, "full understanding" was reached between the United States and Russia. Important conferences were held by Roosevelt and Churchill in 1943 at Casablanca, at Washington, and at Cairo; and Stalin joined them at Teheran in late November 1943 and at Yalta early in 1945. Though for the most part these consultations had to do with immediate war needs and strategy, some agreements were made looking to eventual arrangements for peace.

In November 1943, the foreign secretaries of Great Britain, the United States, Russia, and China met at Moscow and asserted the need of establishing as soon as practicable a permanent "international organization" of "all peace loving states." At the Teheran Conference, the next month, Roosevelt, Churchill, and Stalin called for "a world family of democratic nations." The implementation of these ideas was pushed forward at the Dumbarton Oaks Conference in Washington (August–November 1944), where representatives of the Big Three and China drafted a Charter for the United Nations—a name supplied by President Roosevelt. The draft, with only minor amendments, was adopted by a conference at San Francisco (April–June 1945) of fifty-one nations arrayed against Germany, Italy, or Japan, and it went into effect on October 24, 1945.

The initial members were the fifty-one represented at San Francisco.[1] But it was provided that others, including enemy states, might subsequently become eligible for membership. One of the anomalies in the original membership was the inclusion, at Stalin's insistence, of the Ukraine and Byelorussia, though these were integral parts of the Soviet Union. For a full decade afterwards, as a result of friction between the Soviet Union and the Western powers, only nine additional nations were admitted: Afghanistan, Iceland, Sweden, Thailand, Pakistan, Yemen, Burma, Israel, and Indonesia.

Not until the end of 1955 was a compromise reached whereby sixteen other nations were admitted: Albania, Austria, Bulgaria, Cambodia, Ceylon, Eire, Finland, Hungary, Italy, Jordan, Laos, Libya, Nepal, Portugal, Rumania, and Spain. Other admissions gradually followed, chiefly of newly independent states in Asia and Africa, until by 1962 the United Nations had a total and truly worldwide membership of 104. Still excluded were Communist China and the divided countries of Germany, Korea, and Vietnam.[2]

[1] Argentina, Australia, Belgium, Bolivia, Brazil, Byelorussia, Canada, Chile, China (Nationalist), Colombia, Costa Rica, Cuba, Czechoslovakia, Denmark, Dominican Republic, Ecuador, Egypt, El Salvador, Ethiopia, France, Great Britain, Greece, Guatemala, Haiti, Honduras, India, Iran, Iraq, Lebanon, Liberia, Luxembourg, Mexico, Netherlands, New Zealand, Nicaragua, Norway, Panama, Paraguay, Peru, Philippines, Poland, Saudi Arabia, South Africa, Syria, Turkey, Ukraine, Uruguay, U.S.A., U.S.S.R., Venezuela, Yugoslavia.

[2] The members, as of mid-1966, are listed in the rear end papers of this volume.

In a general way, the United Nations bore a close resemblance to the League of Nations. It had a General Assembly in which each nation had one vote, and a Security Council of eleven, including five permanent members (Great Britain, China, France, Russia, and the United States) and six members (ten after 1966) elected for two-year terms by the Assembly. By a most important provision, any permanent member may veto any action by the Security Council save only in the case of a merely "procedural" matter. A Secretariat under a Secretary General performs administrative and technical tasks.

In practice, the successive Secretaries General, Trygve Lie of Norway, Dag Hammarskjöld of Sweden, and U Thant of Burma, have been important not only as administrators but also as representatives and spokesmen of the whole organization. An Economic and Social Council of eighteen members elected by the Assembly seeks to improve world health, economic, social, and educational conditions. Related to the U.N. are a dozen special agencies, among them: a United Nations Educational, Scientific and Cultural Organization (UNESCO); a Food and Agricultural Organization; an International Labor Organization; an International Civil Aviation Organization; an International Monetary Fund; and a World Health Organization.

Directly responsible to the Assembly, is a Trusteeship Council designed to safeguard the interests of colonial peoples, previously supervised by the League of Nations, or taken from former holders as a result of the Second World War. The Assembly likewise chooses an International Court of Justice of fifteen members who are empowered to decide international disputes of a justiciable nature and to render advisory opinions. Under the Security Council are an Atomic Energy Commission to deal with the development and use of atomic power, and a Military Staff Committee composed of representatives of the major powers and charged with planning and directing military action against aggressor nations. Provision is also made for international armed forces to be used at the discretion of the Security Council; and these have been drafted and employed in Korea and the Congo. The United Nations also intervened more or less effectively to limit strife or aggression in Iran, Greece, Palestine, Indonesia, and India-Pakistan (twice: 1947–1949, 1965). It successfully administered Libya and transformed it in January 1952 into an independent nation. But its major importance has not been in settling disputes or preventing conflicts. Rather, it has been significant as a world forum and through the work of its agencies. As a meeting place for the nations in times of tension, it has permitted small countries to be heard. It has focussed on some problems what amounts to a world opinion, whose weight even the great powers feel. It has compelled the powers great and small to make known their position—to stand up and be counted—on a host of issues.

Even more important has been the quietly effective work of many of the United Nations' agencies. The Relief and Rehabilitation Administration (UNRRA) distributed in 1945–1946 one and a quarter billion dollars' worth of aid to war-ravaged countries. The International Monetary Fund has slowly furthered the cause of monetary stability. The International Bank had by 1966 provided loans for rehabilitation and development to some seventy countries for a total of more than nine billion dollars; and the International Children's Emergency Fund (UNICEF) had assisted child health, welfare, and nutrition programs aiding more than a hundred million children in 116 countries and territories.

The World Health Organization (WHO) has provided information, supplies, and technical skills to fight a dozen endemic diseases such as malaria and yaws. UNESCO has assisted libraries, reduced illiteracy, provided for the translation of important works, and greatly accelerated the interchange of scholarly knowledge. All the while, other organs like the International Civil Aviation Organization, the International Atomic Energy Agency, the Universal Postal Union, the World Meteorological Organization, the Commission on Narcotic Drugs, and the International Telecommunication Union have been carrying forward in unspectacular but vital areas the whole idea of international coöperation.

With its headquarters in New York in an impressive glass-walled building, with its pale blue flag emblazoned with a polar map of the world between two olive branches, with its postage stamps designed to symbolize international coöperation, the United Nations had taken on by 1955 many of the attributes of an enduring institution.

In June of that year its tenth anniversary was marked by a special meeting in the city of San Francisco, its birthplace.

The speeches, which were numerous and eloquent, could almost be summarized as follows: the United Nations had not fulfilled all of the hopes of the year 1945; the world situation had thwarted it in its major role as a peace-maker; but it had accomplished much; there was new hope for the future of man; and in any case this organization was a continuing symbol of man's aspirations for a world at peace.

B. Weakened Europe and Shift in the Balance of Power

It was a war-ravaged and weakened Europe that played a part in the founding of the United Nations. Destruction wrought by war, especially by air bombardment, was tremendous. Nor was the devastation confined, as in the First World War, to limited areas; rather, it was widespread over most of Europe—in Britain, the Low Countries, Norway, France, Italy, all Central Europe, Greece, the Balkans, and the greater part of European Russia. Many major cities were totally or in large part destroyed.

And, since the Second World War was more truly global than the First, much destruction had also taken place on a large scale in Japan, China, and the Philippines. Economic and social conditions were terrifying. Food, fuel, and fibers were wanting or in short supply in all the war-torn countries. Devastated nations, faced by a gigantic task of rehabilitation, were without many of the requisites for it. Farmers lacked tools, machinery, livestock, fertilizer, and seed. Undamaged factories lacked raw materials and coal. Many people, undernourished, ill-housed and ill-clad, lacked vitality. The transportation systems were in chaos. Inflation in greater or lesser degree was universal, and the prices of available goods soared in black markets, despite rationing and price controls.

Aggravating the chaotic conditions was the problem not only of returning millions of demobilized soldiers and prisoners of war to peaceful pursuits, but also of caring for many millions of "displaced persons"— Jews and others ejected by the Nazis; Poles expelled from the part of their country appropriated by Russia; Germans ousted from East Prussia, Silesia, and the Sudetenland; Arabs ejected from Palestine; and many a political refugee. A decade after the end of the war it was estimated that there were still two million homeless persons.

The defeated powers were not merely weakened and ravaged; they were prostrate. Germany, Austria, Italy, and Japan were occupied by military forces of the victor nations—Austria and Germany by France, Britain, Russia, and the United States; Italy by Britain and the United States; Japan by the United States; and Poland, Rumania, Bulgaria, and Hungary by Russia. There were some attempts to punish the defeated. Russia in particular removed a good deal of machinery and other capital goods from Germany. In the vanquished countries, all weapons of war were removed or destroyed, armed forces were disbanded, and war-factories were dismantled. At Nuremberg, beginning in November 1945, leading German Nazis were tried by the victors as "war criminals." Eleven were sentenced to death. Similar trials were conducted by the United States in Japan and by local or national courts in several countries. Continuing attempts were made to de-Nazify Germany by removing all Hitler's devoted followers from positions of importance. But vengeance was quickly overshadowed by the practical problems of reorganizing governments, local and national, reëstablishing transportation, providing some sort of housing, and feeding the people.

If the defeated nations were prostrate, some of the victors were in little better state. The end of the war saw neither Great Britain nor France in a position to play effectively the role of a great power. Britain had political stability, but was unable to feed itself or to produce enough exports to secure the needed food. Loans from the United States and Canada in 1945–1947, totaling some five billion dollars, were all that enabled the British to purchase needed food, raw materials, and other goods. The task of rebuilding its cities and rehabilitating its industries strained every resource of the country and it had little to spare for military or diplomatic purposes. At the same time, as we shall see, a large part of the British Empire was cutting itself loose from the homeland. France was an even worse case, for it had most of the problems faced by the British and, in addition, it could not achieve a strong, stable, and effective government.

In terms of sheer strength, either military or economic, Great Britain and France were no longer great powers. Japan, Italy, and Germany were even weaker and were in the control of their conquerors. China was lapsing into civil strife more debilitating than foreign war. Whereas in 1939 it had been possible to count seven great powers (or eight if China were included), by 1946 there were only two left—Russia and the United States. Russia had suffered much in the war. It had had untold millions of military and civilian casualties. Many of its great cities had been devastated and its factories destroyed. But it had built up new industrial potential behind the Urals. It had created and maintained a massive army and a mighty air force. It had untold resources within its expanding boundaries. It had a young and growing population. And it espoused the ideology of Marxist Communism, which if it was more or less identical in practice with Russian nationalism and imperialism and if it meant ruthless and bloody dictatorship at home, could still be exported to the discouraged and downtrodden in other lands as a gospel of economic and social democracy and justice. The Russian Soviet State had been born (as Lenin had predicted it might be) from the chaos produced by World War I. Stalin and his followers had no doubt that, in like fashion, opportunities would be offered by the aftermath of World War

II. Russia kept her armed forces and her war industry substantially intact in the years following 1945.

The United States emerged from the war more powerful even than Russia. It had suffered no war damage and relatively small loss of human life. It had dramatically and massively increased its industrial output. It had by far the most potent navy and air force in the world and it had by far the best equipped army. But the American people were eager for peace. They were optimistic about their ability to cooperate with the Russians in making a secure and stable world, just as they had worked with them to defeat Hitler. They wanted the soldiers, sailors, and airmen returned to civilian life as rapidly as possible. Thus it was that in 1946 and 1947 the great American military machine was taken to pieces. Tanks and planes and ships and artillery were junked. The armed forces were cut back to a small size. The nation strove to return to a peace basis as quickly as possible. By 1948, there was only one great military power—Russia. Its armed might, nevertheless, was to a considerable degree counterbalanced by the fact that the Americans still had a monopoly (and a stockpile) of the fantastic new weapon, the atom bomb. Until Russia matched the United States in atomic strength it could not venture too freely to use its military might.

In the United States itself, leadership fell to President Harry Truman, who had succeeded to the office on the death of President Franklin D. Roosevelt on April 12, 1945. Under Truman the demobilization took place with less dislocation than had been expected. Soon the factories of the country were pouring out a spate of goods—automobiles, refrigerators, textiles, tractors, radios, washing machines—to make up for the wartime deficit. Soon new types of goods like plastics and television sets were added to the flow. As the gross national product and per-capita income rose to unprecedented heights, the world, including many Americans, waited uneasily to see if the United States would not slump from fabulous prosperity into another and worse depression than that of 1929–1933. The

Russians were confident that this would happen, for Marxist theory insisted that the "contradictions of capitalism" were bound to produce ever more frequent and ever more severe economic crises. But the reforms of the prewar and war period in economic matters and the extremely varied nature of the economy had by now created a stability that stood the country in good stead. Though there were minor recessions, they were short-lived. The sheer weight of post-war production made the United States as important in the economic sphere as its atom bombs made it in the military.

C. Failure to Effect a General Peace Settlement

The Atlantic Charter of 1941 had set forth some of the general principles which, it was hoped, might be embodied in a peace settlement. Other and more specific points were agreed on at some of the wartime conferences. At Cairo in November 1943, Roosevelt and Churchill agreed for their respective countries to seek no territorial gains, and promised Chiang Kai-shek that Japan would lose all areas acquired since 1895, with Formosa going to China, and Korea becoming independent. At Teheran (1943) the same leaders, with Stalin, promised to maintain after the war "the independence, sovereignty, and territorial integrity of Iran." More important were the decisions reached by the Big Three at Yalta in February 1945.

Though the atomic bomb was then in the making, its success was by no means assured, and Roosevelt and Churchill were told by their military advisers that Russian help would shorten the war against Japan and save innumerable casualties. During the Yalta meeting, therefore, in return for a promise of Russian aid against Japan once the European war was over, the American President and the British Prime Minister promised Stalin that Russia would receive the Kurile Islands and the southern half of Sakhalin from Japan, and control, at China's expense, of Outer Mongolia, Port Arthur, Dairen, and the Manchurian railways, and that they would persuade China to accept this settlement. Stalin agreed that in the liberated countries of Europe self-government should be restored and free elections held. As to Poland, it was arranged that Russia might continue to hold eastern Polish territory up to the old "Curzon line," that Poland would be compensated by being given German areas to the west and north, and that the Poles should be allowed to choose their own government at free elections with universal suffrage and a secret ballot. Germany, it was agreed, should be divided into zones and occupied by Russia, Great Britain, the United States, and possibly France; its war factories should be dismantled, and it should be made to pay heavy reparations with half of them going to Russia.

When Germany had been defeated and another conference was necessary in August 1945, to implement the Yalta agreements, Roosevelt had died and Churchill had lost the general elections in England. At the Potsdam Conference, therefore, it was President Harry Truman and Prime Minister Clement Attlee who met with Stalin. At this meeting the zones of military occupation were delimited, with Russia holding the eastern part, Britain, France, and the United States holding the west, and Berlin (embedded in the Russian eastern zone) under joint control. Pending a final peace treaty, German frontiers were tentatively set along the Oder and Neisse rivers. Russia got the northern half of East Prussia. Poland, in compensation for its territorial losses in the east to Russia, received Danzig, Upper and Lower Silesia, eastern Brandenburg, most of Pomerania, and the southern part of East Prussia. France recovered Alsace-Lorraine; Belgium, Eupen and Malmédy; and Czechoslovakia, the Sudetenland. The much disputed Saar was put in the French zone and two years later it was detached from the rest of Germany and united economically with France, while remaining politically autonomous.

The losses to Germany in territory were much more severe than after World War I. In 1937 Germany had comprised some 182,000 square miles. What was left of it in 1945 amounted to about 137,000 square miles, with 42,000 (population about 17,-500,000) in Russian hands and 95,000

square miles (population 49,000,000) under control of the Western Allies. It is to be noted that most of German industry lay in the Allied zones in the west, but it was agreed that the remaining war plants and war potential should be dismantled and destroyed.

At the Potsdam Conference it was also arranged that Austria should be detached from Germany, but that it should be divided into four zones for occupation by the victors. The Russian zone in the east included the oil fields and some of the most important industrial and agricultural areas.

In eastern Europe and the Balkans, the matter of military occupation was settled not so much by agreement as by the situation itself. Russian armies were in effective control of Hungary, Bulgaria, and Rumania. Here they were to stay, and, as we shall see, to secure the creation of satellite governments managed from Moscow. The situation in Poland and Czechoslovakia was more complicated, but in the end came to the same result. Thus Russia from 1945 on was overwhelmingly dominant in all of eastern and much of central Europe.

At Potsdam it had been agreed to proceed at once with the drafting of peace treaties with Italy, Rumania, Bulgaria, Hungary, and Finland. The actual drafting of the treaties proved difficult and led to much dispute among the Allies. But eventually definitive treaties were agreed on and were signed at Paris in February 1947. All of them provided for reparations, most of which were to go to Russia. Italy was to pay 360 million dollars, Bulgaria 70 million, Hungary, Rumania, and Finland 300 million each. In each country, the size of any future armed forces and the amount of military material were drastically limited. A number of territorial changes were imposed. Italy lost all its colonies. Part of Venetia Giulia and some Adriatic islands went to Yugoslavia and some small frontier areas to France. Long-disputed Trieste was placed under international control. The Dodecanese Islands and Rhodes were turned over to Greece. Hungary was forced to return Transylvania to Rumania and a small region to Czechoslovakia. Rumania in turn lost Bessarabia and Bukovina to

Russia, and the southern part of Dobruja to Bulgaria. Finland had to cede to Russia the Petsamo province and a large part of Karelia and also to grant to Russia a naval base dominating the Gulf of Finland.[1] Bulgaria lost no territory and made the gain indicated above. The United States had no part in the treaty with Finland since it had never declared war on that country.

In the negotiation of these treaties there were some traces of principle, for regard was occasionally paid to history and nationality. But for the most part they recognized the actual post-war situation and took account of Russia's military predominance in eastern Europe and the military and strategic needs of the great powers. They legally established peace over much of Europe. But the terms of the treaties were in many ways less important than the developing realities of international power politics.

[1] Russia, seeking Finnish favor, agreed in 1955 to return the naval base.

D. Communist Conquest of Eastern Europe

It is a curious fact that Communism, which claims to be social and economic democracy, has always been imposed by armed force. In the post-war period, Russia, instead of liquidating its army, used it ruthlessly to create Communist regimes in countries adjoining its territories. During the war, Russia had crushed and annexed the republics of Latvia, Lithuania, and Estonia. In the years after 1945, it created dependent, "satellite," Communist regimes in Poland, Czechoslovakia, Hungary, Rumania, Bulgaria, Albania, and East Germany. There was no pretense of free and democratic elections with a secret ballot even when these had been promised (as at Yalta in the case of Poland).

The technique of establishing a Communist puppet regime in an area occupied or influenced by Russian armed forces varied somewhat from country to country, but the general pattern soon became familiar. The existing or provisional government

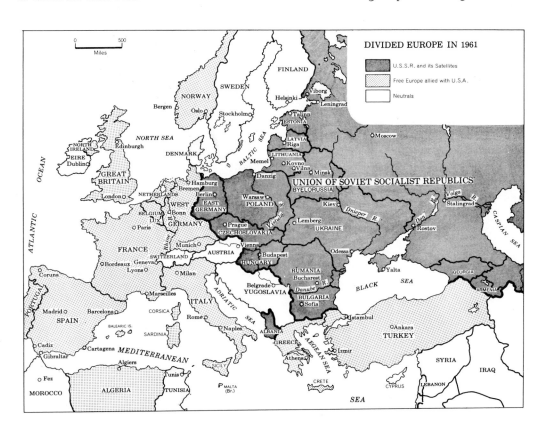

would first be denounced as fascist and reactionary and would be superseded by a coalition "popular front" cabinet in which Communists held key positions, such as minister of interior (in charge of the police) and minister of information (in charge of propaganda). Then the Communist ministers, backed by military aid, pressure, or threats from Russia, and led by a native who had been trained in Leninist tactics in Moscow, would get rid of their non-Communist fellow ministers and establish an authoritarian government. Next a constitution like that of the Soviet Union would be drawn up and ratified by an election theoretically democratic but actually controlled. Finally the disciplined Communist party, even though a small minority, would take complete control and more or less rapidly liquidate all opposition parties and leaders. Thereafter, it was easy to control the schools, universities, newspapers, courts, and communications, to terrorize the churches, to suppress civil liberties, and to establish a thoroughgoing dictatorship, which would take orders from Moscow in both internal and external matters.

It is not hard to understand why the Western democracies did not at first oppose this new type of imperialism by which Russia extended its sway over neighboring peoples—not remote and backward tribes, but civilized folk with proud traditions of culture and independence. They trusted that the wartime coöperation with Russia could be maintained in the post-war years and that Russia would live up to the commitments it had made at Yalta and Potsdam and in endorsing the United Nations Charter. They demonstrated this trust by a speedy disarmament which left them incapable of intervening forcibly, especially in areas near to Russia. They had raised no serious objections to the outright annexation by Russia of eastern Poland, northern East Prussia, Carpatho-Ruthenia (from Czechoslovakia), and Bukovina and Bessarabia (from Rumania). They had entrusted the sole military occupation of east-central Europe to Russia and were in no position to prevent what ensued, save by the use of military force which they were no longer willing or able to apply.

Thus it was that much of what they had fought for (such as an independent Poland) was lost in the peace. The case of Poland was particularly poignant.

During the war when the Polish government-in-exile at London had objected to the idea of permanent Soviet annexation of eastern Poland, Russia had recognized a pro-Soviet "provisional government" at Lublin headed by a Polish Communist, trained in Moscow, Boleslav Beirut. At Yalta, Stalin had persuaded Roosevelt and Churchill to recognize Beirut's government, provided non-Communist members were added to it and free elections were held. In August 1945, the Beirut government ceded to Russia 70,000 square miles of Polish territory in the east.

The next year "the capitalist system" was abolished. Non-Communists were added to the government but were hemmed in and kept quite without power. Elections were held in 1947 under the dominance of police, troops, and disciplined Communist party members. The National Assembly, thus elected, adopted a constitution like that of Russia, with Beirut as president. The Communist and Socialist parties were merged (1948). Non-Communist parties were destroyed and their leaders driven into exile or put to death. Pressure was applied to the Catholic Church to prevent its interference with developments, and the Catholic primate, Cardinal Wyszynski, with several other bishops, was imprisoned. A marshal of the Russian army, Konstentin Rokossovsky was made Polish Minister of National Defense. The Poles might regret their independence and chafe under the new bonds they bore, but the Russian grip on the Polish satellite was firm.

Despite the presence of Russian troops and organized pressure from a Communist minority, Hungary strove to maintain a democratic and independent government in 1945. Elections in November of that year gave the democratic elements a large majority in the National Assembly. A liberal republican constitution was adopted, and Ferenc Nagy, a leading democrat, became premier. But a *coup d'état* in May 1947 ousted the Nagy cabinet. By the middle of 1949 Hungary had a Communist constitution, a single Communist party,

Three Musicians. Pablo Picasso, painted in 1921.

Courtesy Museum of Living Art

and close ties with Russia. All domestic dissent had been crushed. Cardinal Mindszenty, who had been a stalwart opponent of the Nazis, was condemned in February 1949 to life imprisonment and many another Hungarian patriot suffered a like or worse fate.

In Bulgaria, George Dimitrov, a Communist returning from Russia, forced his way, with the help of Soviet troops, into the government, and dominated a referendum which in September 1946 dethroned the youthful King Simeon II (who, in 1943, had succeeded his father Boris III). Controlled elections, the next month, enabled the Communists to take over the government, to found another "people's republic," and to reduce the opposition to impotence. The next year, the leader of the democratic Agrarian party was executed and a constitution of the Soviet type was adopted.

In Rumania, elections held in November 1946 put Communists in the government. Led by Peter Groza, the premier, and Ana Pauker, a fanatical disciple of Stalin, and supported by Russian troops, they forced the abdication of King Michael at the end of 1947. By 1952 all parties other than the Communist "People's Democratic Front"

had been completely eliminated and in that year a Russian-type constitution was put into effect.

The story in Albania was much the same. After the Germans had been driven out (by the end of 1944), a provisional government was established by a Russian protégé, Enver Hoxha. It was recognized by Russia, and also by the United States and Great Britain with the added proviso that free elections must be held. But the elections were not free, and American and British recognition was withdrawn. Nonetheless, with Russian support, King Zog was formally deposed (December 1945), and a "people's republic" under the dictatorship of Hoxha was set up. The 1945 constitution was modeled after that of the Soviet Union and the army was closely tied to that of Russia.

The case of Czechoslovakia is parallel. In 1945, its government-in-exile under President Beneš returned home. Under compulsion it ceded the province of Ruthenia to Russia, and established (in 1946) a six-party coalition cabinet in which the leading figure was a Russian-trained Communist, Klement Gottwald. Backed by pressure from Moscow, the Communists slowly gained control over the government and over the entire country. In February 1948, by a *coup d'état* which met with little opposition and secured the reluctant consent of Beneš, this control was made complete. In March, Jan Masaryk, liberal foreign minister, and son of the heroic founder of the Czechoslovak republic, ended his life under mysterious circumstances. He had hoped to make his country a political and cultural link between the east and the west, but the Russians wanted puppet states not links. In June Beneš felt compelled to turn the presidency over to Gottwald, who promptly promulgated a Soviet-style constitution and proceeded to eliminate all opposition.

The events in Yugoslavia form a significant variation on the theme, for in that country there were in existence, at the end of the war, native armed forces with a good deal of equipment and a strong spirit of patriotism. There had been, in Yugoslavia, during the war, rival resistance movements. One was headed by General Draja Mikhailovich, loyal to King Peter II and the government-in-exile in London; the other led by Joseph Broz, a Russian-trained Communist popularly known as Marshal Tito. In 1944, Russia persuaded Great Britain and the United States to insist on a merger of the two movements, with the result that, after the withdrawal of the German troops, King Peter was obliged to appoint Tito prime minister. Using his governmental powers and armed forces, Tito saw to it that the Communists won the elections of November 1945. The monarchy was abolished and the Federal People's Republic of Yugoslavia established. During the ensuing year, opposing factions were destroyed, General Mikhailovich was executed, and the Catholic primate, Archbishop Stepinac, was sentenced to sixteen years in prison.

So far the story is like that of the other satellites. But during 1947 and 1948 as the Russians sought to confirm their control over yet another puppet, things did not work out as expected. Tito and the Yugoslavs were at first much favored by the Russians: for example, Belgrade was made the headquarters of the Communist international organ—the Cominform. But as Russian "advisers" and secret police moved

President Eduard Beneš of Czechoslovakia, 1945.

Courtesy Wide World Photos

into the country, Tito reacted against the Russians. In June 1948, he and his government were denounced in vitriolic terms by the Cominform and many expected that he would soon be replaced by another leader more amenable to Soviet control. Instead, he was able to maintain his position and to retain the loyalty of the Yugoslav Communists and the army. The break between Russia and Yugoslavia soon appeared complete, and Tito was wooed and supported with economic aid and military supplies by the Western democracies even though his regime was a dictatorship and its principles and techniques were Communist. Not until 1955 did the Russians seek to heal the breach with Tito and it was then clear that they were willing to accept Yugoslavia as a smaller partner rather than a satellite. Tito seemed eager to continue in an independent position in which he could obtain advantages from both the Soviet Union and the Western powers. Though Tito and his ministers were convinced Communists and though they often talked as if they were the most rigid and extreme Marxists, still as time passed they allowed economic experiments that were quite unlike the Russian system. There was, indeed, some private ownership and a good deal of decentralization in industry and commerce, and peasant proprietorship of the land was widespread.

Altogether, between 1939 and 1948, Russia, in an imperialist expansion movement almost unparalleled in history, had been able to ring itself about on the west, first with a band of territory seized and absorbed (Lithuania, Latvia, Estonia, Petsamo province, part of Karelia, eastern Poland, part of East Prussia, Ruthenia, Bukovina, Bessarabia) and then to add to that ring another outer one of firmly controlled satellite puppet states (Poland, Czechoslovakia, Hungary, Rumania, Bulgaria). Albania was an exception in not being contiguous to Russian controlled territory, but this situation arose only from the fact that Yugoslavia had been able to assert its independence from Russia. In terms of Russian propaganda, this expansion was the "liberation of peoples from capitalist domination," the "establishment of peoples' democracies," the spreading of the "socialist revolution," and the safeguarding of the "Communist homeland" by interposing territorial barriers between it and the "aggressive" and "warmongering" capitalist West. To a more impartial view it seemed like the ruthless exploitation of cynical diplomacy and armed force to further the cause of Russian nationalistic imperialism. The Soviets had expanded Russian territory and control far beyond the farthest limits ever dreamed of by the most fanatical of the Russian nationalists of the days before 1914.

E. Communist Triumphs in East Asia

As things turned out, the greatest Communist successes in the post-war period were scored not so much in Europe as in Asia. It was in Asia, too, that the most acute crises arose and that the "cold war" was attended by a series of hot "shooting" wars.

At Yalta, in 1945, Stalin may have thought that the government of Chiang Kai-shek and his nationalist Kuomintang party would dominate China after the war. At any rate, Stalin pledged Russian support to Chiang Kai-shek, and Russia and the Nationalist government of China negotiated a treaty in 1945. What actually happened, therefore, may have been a surprise to the Russians, but they were certainly quick to take advantage of it.

During the war, Chiang's government had been opposed not only by the Japanese but also by Communist forces, under the Moscow-trained Mao Tse-tung, who dominated areas in the northwest of China, whither they had been driven in previous years. Weakened by the long war, by inflation and corruption, and by the dissatisfaction of some elements of the population, Chiang Kai-shek's Nationalists encountered grave difficulties in coping with the Communist army which had been extending its sway in the last years of the war, and which, in the immediate post-war period, was making still more advances.

When the Chinese Communists showed themselves stronger than had been expected, the Russians at once began to support them with arms taken from the Japanese, and with technical assistance, though at the same time Russia continued to loot Manchuria of all the machinery that could be carried away. By 1949, Mao and his Communist armies were winning victory after victory. They captured Tientsin and Peiping in January, Nanking in April, and by December were substantially in control of the whole of continental China. Chiang Kai-shek, his government, and the remnants of his armies were forced to take refuge in Formosa (Taiwan), so recently reacquired by China from Japan.

Thus China, with its extensive territories, its rich resources, and its population numbering over half a billion, came under Communist sway. In September 1949 a government of the Soviet type was organized, and the next February a treaty of mutual aid and friendship was signed by Russia and Communist China. In the ensuing years, Russia supported the Chinese with military equipment, goods, technical assistance, and advisers. In 1951, the Chinese felt strong enough to expand into Tibet and to set up

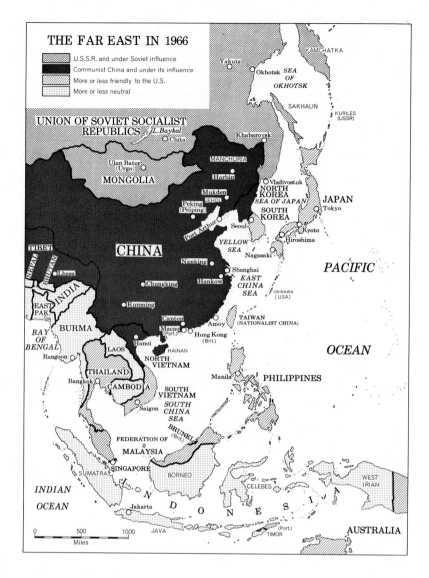

THE FAR EAST IN 1966

U.S.S.R. and under Soviet influence
Communist China and under its influence
More or less friendly to the U.S.
More or less neutral

a puppet government there. Before many years were out the Chinese were deporting Tibetans, bringing in Chinese, liquidating the "wealthy" peasants and destroying the Buddhist monasteries and other religious centers. The Tibetans rose in hopeless revolt, but without success. In 1959 the Dalai Lama, who had been both the political and religious leader of the country, fled to India, whither he was followed by thousands of refugees unwilling to submit to Communist rule.

Meanwhile in China the new regime was consolidating itself rapidly and successfully. Foreigners were driven out. Christian missionary enterprise was stopped. The merchant class and landowners were destroyed or "re-educated" in work camps. The peasants were forced into communal life on collective farms and employed on giant projects of flood control and irrigation. Industry, both of the household and factory type, was stimulated. Vast campaigns of Communist education and propaganda were undertaken. The developments were similar to those in Communist Russia, but Mao and his followers claimed to be even purer and more rigorous in their Marxism than their Russian comrades. In any case, China was already overshadowing all other Communist regimes in the world, save only the Russian.

Nor were the expansionist tendencies of Communism in Asia confined to the seizure of Tibet. Even before that move had been made, Korea had become the object of a major Communist drive. It had been arranged at the Cairo Conference in 1943 that Korea should be independent, and at the close of the war the victors proceeded on this basis. But like Germany, Korea was divided into zones of military occupation. That part of the country north of the thirty-eighth parallel (containing most of the mineral and industrial resources of the country) was entrusted to Russia, while the area south of that parallel (containing the best agricultural land) was to be held by the United States. The Russians at once set about transforming their half of the country into a puppet Communist state despite the fact that the native population, the United States, and the United Nations all wanted Korea to be a unified nation. In the South, the Republic of Korea was set up in 1948 after an elected national assembly had drawn up and adopted a democratic constitution and chosen Syngman Rhee, a veteran patriot, as its first president.

In December 1948 the Soviet Union withdrew its army of occupation from North Korea. It could afford to do so, for it had organized there not only a dependent Communist regime, but also a large native army indoctrinated in Communist ideology and well armed. The withdrawal was, moreover, useful for Russian propaganda purposes, since it could be hailed as proof of the Soviet Union's respect for the "freedom" of Asian peoples, in contrast with the "imperialism" of the Western powers and especially of the United States. Not to be outdone in championship of freedom for Asiatics, the United States followed the Russian example, and in June of 1949 with-drew its occupation forces from South Korea. It left there, however, to defend the Republic, only a relatively small and very scantily supplied native army. It was in this same year that Mao and his Communists triumphed in China and were soon recognized not only by Russia and its satellites, but also by Great Britain (anxious over the fate of Hong Kong) and·by other countries including India.

Alarmed by the Communist success in China, President Truman and his Secretary of State, Dean Acheson, adopted a policy designed to arrest Communist expansion in Asia no less than in Europe. In May 1950, the American government promised active aid to French Indo-China (Vietnam) in suppressing native rebellion and warding off aggression by Communist China. But Indo-China proved not to be the immediate object of Communist conquest.

In the early morning of June 25, 1950, without previous warning North Korean Communist armies, many thousand strong, crossed the thirty-eighth parallel and swept into South Korea. Taken by surprise and desperately short of arms and munitions, the forces of the republican government of South Korea could not withstand the attack. In four days, they lost the capital city of Seoul and were in full retreat. Communist conquest of all Korea appeared imminent and it seemed likely that Russia and Communist North Korea would be able to present the world with an accomplished fact which no one would feel called upon to alter by armed force. This would doubtless have been the result if the United States had not intervened, with results which will be discussed later.[1]

---

[1] See below, pp. 814–817.

General Charles de Gaulle.

Courtesy French Embassy Press and Information Division. Copyright Paris-Match

CHAPTER 61

Post-War Free Europe

A. Democratic Britain

The democracies of western Europe emerged from the war in a sorry state. Democracy itself had been weakened, for if it had fought off the Nazi-Fascist attack from the Right in a prolonged and bloody struggle, it now had to confront an invigorated Communist menace from the Left. Communism usually feeds and grows on human misery and there was misery aplenty in post-war Europe. Moreover, the military victory of Russia added to the prestige of Communism. In many countries, too, the Communists, after the German attack on Russia, had won popularity by their vigor and courage in the underground resistance movements.

Thus in most of the Western countries, while the right-wing reactionaries of the fascist type were non-existent or discredited, the Communists were, save in Britain, an important political factor. In France and Italy the Communists were especially numerous and well organized. In several countries democratic strength came from Catholic parties which had become more radical in their demands for social reform, but were firm in their defence of political democracy, religion, the family, private property, and the dignity and integrity of the individual. Another element of democratic strength was the Socialist parties, including the British Labor Party, for if some leftist elements in them flirted continuously with the Communists, the majority believed steadfastly in democratic political methods and procedures. Parties such as the Conservatives in Britain and the Radical Socialists in France seemed weaker immediately after the war, but tended to gain in strength as time passed.

In July 1945, while the war in the Pacific was still going on, British elections gave the Labor Party some 390 out of 640 seats in the House of Commons. Thus Winston Churchill, despite his contributions to victory, was pushed from power and replaced as prime minister by the Labor leader, Clement Attlee. Labor used its parliamentary success to advance its program of socializing the basic industries. One by one it nationalized the Bank of England, the coal mines, communications, the railways and long-distance trucking, the iron and steel industry, civil aviation, electricity and gas. Medicine was also nationalized or socialized, and the extension of social legislation promised the British a security "from the cradle to the grave."

But the problems of post-war Britain were not the same as those of the nineteenth century in which socialization had seemed a hopeful remedy. Britain had lost much of its overseas investment and its shipping; New York, not London, was the financial center of the world; the Empire was falling to pieces; iron-ore reserves were running out and coal had to be secured from thinner and deeper veins. In such circumstances the British problem was to create enough goods and services to sell abroad so that sufficient food and raw materials could be purchased. The socialized industries, coal for example, seemed no more productive than under private ownership. Rationing, import restrictions, and high taxes had to be used to keep consumption down, so that for some years after the war, the British continued under wartime austerity. Repeatedly, Britain had to be helped by loans and subsidies from the United States.

Amid these difficulties the British maintained their courage and their solidarity. Indeed, they accomplished much that seemed to them to be constructive. The National Insurance Act and the National Health Service Act (both of 1946), with the Family Allowance Act of 1945, raised the standard of living of the lower classes. Drastic income and inheritance taxes reduced the importance of established wealth. Subsidies kept the price of food relatively low. The Town and Country Planning Acts (1947) provided for rational procedures in rebuilding the cities and in the use of land. Agriculture was regulated and subsidized to increase productivity. Education at all levels was extended and higher education was made available to a much larger proportion of the youth. The pound was devalued to aid exports.

Slowly British productivity increased until by 1953 it was well above pre-war levels. Despite recurring crises, the balance of trade improved and less dependence on American aid was necessary. But progress was too slow and the results of the nationalization of industry were discouraging. In the elections of 1950, the Labor Party was able to retain only a minute majority in the House of Commons. The Labor Party, moreover, was divided into factions. That led by Prime Minister Attlee decided to slow the progress of socialism and to continue coöperation with the United States, while the left-wing under Aneurin Bevan espoused opposing policies. Hoping to improve his majority, Attlee called for special elections in the fall of 1951. But the results were a victory for the Conservatives who gained a slender majority of 19 in the House. Winston Churchill returned to the post of Prime Minister. Thus the famous war leader was in office when King George VI died in February 1952 and was succeeded by his twenty-five-year-old daughter, who was crowned as Elizabeth II with traditional panoply and pomp.

The Conservatives retained all the social legislation passed by the Laborites. But they returned the iron and steel and trucking industries to private ownership, reduced food subsidies, slowly eliminated rationing, and sought to stimulate private enterprise. Prosperity increased in Britain and there was full employment, rising industrial production, and an improvement in the housing situation. It was difficult to say how much of the betterment arose from the Conservative policies and how much from world conditions. But in any case when Churchill (now a Knight of the Garter and thus Sir Winston) resigned in the spring of 1955, Sir Anthony Eden, his successor as the Conservative Prime Minister, called special elections at the end of May. Aided by the continued split in the ranks of Labor, the Conservatives tripled their majority in the House of Commons.

Despite this initial success and despite the favorable reaction of the British people to increasing prosperity and a retreat from socialism, Sir Anthony Eden was soon in trouble. In July of 1956, President Abdul Nasser of Egypt nationalized the Suez Canal and seized the assets of the Canal Company. Nasser was planning to construct a gigantic high dam on the Nile at Aswan. He had had indications of support by loans from Great Britain, the United States, and the International Bank. When those offers were withdrawn, he responded by taking over the Canal. At the same time, the continuing border troubles between Egypt and Israel grew in intensity. At the end of October, Israel invaded Egypt and was soon supported by the air and land forces of Britain and France. Both the United Nations and the United States objected so strongly that the invaders had to accept a cease-fire agreement and to withdraw their forces. A United Nations emergency force superintended the withdrawal and policed the frontier, while the Canal which had been blocked by the Egyptians was cleared under United Nations supervision.

Eden's participation in this venture had

Queen Elizabeth II.

Courtesy
British Information Services

been motivated by a sense of the importance of the Suez Canal to Britain and by the difficulties of dealing with Nasser. The adventure came to nought because the aggressive use of force to settle a dispute shocked world and American opinion and seemed too perilous in an age of atomic weapons. Though he had the approval of some elements of the Conservative Party, Eden's prestige declined so fast and so far that he was compelled to resign in January of 1957. He was succeeded by Harold Macmillan.

Under Macmillan's quiet but firm guidance, the Conservatives rather rapidly regained the support that the Suez fiasco had temporarily lost them. They were strengthened by divisions in the Labor Party on the foreign policy issues and on the question of retreating from socialism at home. They were strengthened further by the steadily increasing income of the average Briton who found himself able to buy television sets, refrigerators, and even automobiles. New elections were held in October 1959. The Conservatives won again, with a majority of some hundred members in the House of Commons. This third successive victory for one party was almost without precedent in modern times and led to renewed quarreling and questioning in the ranks of defeated Labor.

In the ensuing years the Conservative Party was gradually weakened by De Gaulle's veto (1963) of Macmillan's proposal that Britain join the Common Market, by unsavory scandals that touched even a cabinet member, and by continuing economic difficulties which centered in an unfavorable balance of payments tending to drain off the British gold reserve. In October of 1963, Macmillan resigned for reasons of health and was succeeded by Sir Alec Douglas-Home, who gave up his peerage (he had been Earl of Home) so that he might sit in the House of Commons. Twelve months later, an election ended the thirteen years of Conservative rule and brought in a Labor government under Harold Wilson. Though Labor's majority of four in the Commons was minute, Wilson proceeded to govern vigorously and to take stern measures on the economic front. Nationalization of industry was rather soft-pedaled, but social legislation was somewhat strengthened and labor unions were favored. New elections, in 1966, gave Labor a majority in the Commons of nearly a hundred, and discoveries of great gas deposits in the North Sea and Yorkshire brightened the long-run economic prospects.

B. The Fourth and Fifth French Republics

The economic problems in post-war France were not dissimilar from those in Great Britain. But the political developments were quite different. The French elected a National Assembly in October 1945. It chose General De Gaulle as head of a provisional government and, amid growing strife among the political parties, it drafted a new constitution providing for a weak executive and an all-powerful legislature. De Gaulle protested and resigned, and a popular plebiscite, in May 1946, rejected the new constitution. A new Assembly drafted another constitution creating only a slightly stronger executive. This document, establishing the Fourth French Republic, was adopted by plebiscite in October 1946, but with little popular enthusiasm. The vote was nine and a quarter million for it, eight million against it, with eight and a half million abstaining. The new constitution replaced the former

Chamber of Deputies by a National Assembly elected by universal suffrage including women, and the former Senate by a Council of the Republic, chosen by indirect election and having only advisory powers. The president was still elected as previously, for seven years, by the two houses. As in the past he could act only with the consent of the ministry, and thus the National Assembly was supreme.

In the first two assemblies and in the first legislature elected under the constitution, the three major parties were the Communist, the Socialist, and the Popular Republican Movement (M.R.P.), a liberal democratic Catholic party which included many of the former leaders of the resistance against the Germans. The Socialists, the M.R.P., and the Radical Socialists (mildly conservative democrats) united to elect a Socialist, Vincent Auriol, as the first President; he was succeeded in 1953 by René Coty. Meanwhile, in 1946, a fourth major party of conservative followers of De Gaulle emerged. It was called the *Rassemblement du Peuple Français* (R.P.F.). But it refused to participate in ministries, gradually split into factions, and lost influence.

Racked by inflation, pinched by a continuing shortage of food and raw materials, torn by dissensions left over from the war period, threatened by Communists on the left and the R.P.F. on the right, French governments had a difficult time in the post-war years. France was governed for the most part by a coalition of the Socialists, the M.R.P., and the Radical Socialists (who were slowly gaining strength). But there were differences within the coalition. The Radical Socialists disliked the social legislation and the high taxes favored by the Socialists and the M.R.P. The Socialists and Radicals opposed the M.R.P. on state aid for Catholic schools. All three feared to support deflationary legislation lest they lend strength to the Communists.

The tendency to temporize and the disputes among the ruling parties led to an instability of ministries no less notable than under the Third Republic. There were, for example, eight premiers between 1948 and 1953. Even Mendès-France, a Radical, who became premier in June 1954, and, with much popular backing, espoused a policy of liquidating French commitments in Indo-China and inaugurating needed economic reforms at home, could not retain office for even a year. Elections held in January 1956 resulted in gains for the Communists and for a new right-wing party headed by a youthful tax critic named Poujade. The National Assembly appeared much too divided to provide a stable government.

Underneath the political instability, however, improvements were taking place. The currency inflation was at length checked, though the franc was stabilized at about one-fourteenth of its pre-war value. Hydro-electric plants were built. Agricultural machinery was widely introduced. Industrial production was increased. Public health was bettered. The birthrate rose. By 1955, France was more prosperous than it had been at any time since the First World War. By 1965, the French were enjoying a standard of living unprecedented in that country. Housing projects rose in the suburbs. New broad highways were swarming with automobiles. The consumption of meat and milk was rising rapidly. Workers even had to be imported from other lands to till the fields and man the busy factories.

But despite the economic development, there was one problem so difficult, so divisive, and so acute that it led to one political crisis after another and finally to the liquidation of the Fourth Republic. This was the problem of North Africa and in particular of Algeria. In 1955 France ruled North Africa from the boundaries of Libya to the Atlantic Ocean. Tunisia and Morocco were technically protectorates, the former under a bey, the latter under a sultan. But in fact, both were dominated by France. Against the French there was growing Arab and Moslem nationalist agitation of such violence that at length the French government was compelled to yield. By a treaty of March 1956 the protectorate established in 1911 was ended and the independence of Morocco was recognized. The Sultan, Mohammed V, who had played an important role in resistance to the French, changed his title to King. At his death in 1961 he was succeeded by his son. Similarly, Tunisia became independent in 1956. But here the bey was deposed and a republic was proclaimed with Habib Bourguiba, who had been the leader of the Neo-

Destour or nationalist party, as President.

Such a solution was not as practicable for Algeria. It had been invaded, "occupied," "annexed," "subdued," and "pacified" between 1830 and 1871, and its northern region had in 1947 been divided into *départements* and declared to be a part of metropolitan France, though it had also a certain degree of autonomy. Beginning in 1954, nationalist agitation in Algeria passed into a violent stage, and for the next seven years the French army was engaged in a fierce and large-scale guerrilla war against the Algerian "rebels"—a war that cost billions of dollars and thousands of lives. What complicated the problem was that more than a million of the ten million inhabitants of Algeria were European. Some French families had lived there for generations and regarded themselves as Algerian, just as did their Moslem neighbors.

The Algerian issue, moreover, divided France, with all the more conservative or reactionary elements insisting on a solution that would leave Algeria French. The army, too, at some points, seemed unwilling to support any move that might lead toward a French withdrawal from Algeria. A special crisis came in 1958, when it seemed that France was about to lapse into civil war. It was solved by the reëmergence of General De Gaulle. In May, pro-Gaullist army and civilian groups seized power in Algeria. In June De Gaulle became premier of France with the approval of the National Assembly. In September a new constitution prepared by De Gaulle was approved by an overwhelming majority of the voters, and the General himself was elected President of the Fifth Republic in December. The new constitution gave greatly increased powers to the executive branch of the government and in particular to the President. De Gaulle used them to quiet the political turmoil, to repress dissent, to order the finances, and to attempt to bring the Algerian strife to an end. In early 1961, by another overwhelming vote, the French people supported the President's Algerian policies. With this mandate, De Gaulle proceeded to negotiate with the Algerian nationalists (the F.L.N. party, or National Liberation Front) and with its "government in exile" under "premier" Ferhat

Abbas. In April another threatening revolt in Algeria, led by four French generals and backed by some professional elements of the army, collapsed in a few days, and by its failure further strengthened De Gaulle. After a national referendum in July of 1962, which gave him well-nigh total support, De Gaulle proclaimed Algeria independent.

The new constitution of 1958, which had, in effect, liquidated the Fourth Republic and inaugurated the Fifth, provided also for new arrangements for the French Community—the former overseas colonies. It had been voted on in these territories as well as in France and had won approval, save in French Guinea, which chose to sever all ties with France immediately. The new provisions applied mainly to Africa, since French Indo-China had already been transformed into independent nations and since Martinique, Guadeloupe, Réunion, and French Guiana had, in 1947, been given the status of overseas departments of France. By 1966, fifteen former French African colonies had become independent states. In 1962, De Gaulle put through a constitutional amendment which provided for the direct election of the president of France by popular suffrage. The first such election was held in December of 1965, with De Gaulle himself as the leading candidate. He was the victor, but only after he had failed to secure a majority in the first election and had, therefore, to participate in a two-candidate run-off in which he secured fifty-five per cent of the ballots cast. Thus De Gaulle became the first French president to be elected by a vote of the people since Louis Napoleon in 1848. The election showed, however, that De Gaulle's opposition to European unity, the Common Market, and the United States was less popular than he had thought. It also marked the end of a period of political apathy in France in which party strife had been quiescent and in which the government, backed by a docile National Assembly, had sought to foster the growing internal prosperity of France and to check the inflation which accompanied that prosperity. It seemed likely that new and active political groupings of the left, right and center were beginning to emerge.

In the foreign field, the policies De Gaulle had been pursuing led some of his opponents to insist that he was suffering from delusions of grandeur both as to himself and as to France. His aim was clearly to make France a strong and independent nation with leadership of sorts in world affairs and preëminence in western Europe. He insisted on making and exploding atom bombs (the first in 1960) so that France might have a "striking force" and be a nuclear power along with Britain and the United States. He sometimes wooed West Germany, sometimes rebuffed it. He made friendly gestures to Russia (1965–66). He blocked the entrance of Great Britain into the Common Market. He sought to reduce the influence, economic and political, of the United States in Europe and opposed its policies as to Vietnam. He recognized Communist China (1964). He tried to prevent any erosion of French national sovereignty by international organizations—the United Nations, NATO, the Common Market— thereby weakening them and checking the trend toward unity in the world, the Atlantic nations, and Europe. Thus it seemed to many that the last of the great leaders of World War II, in striving to win for France the kind of strength, glory and prestige that a Louis XIV might have sought, had forgotten the lessons of two great wars as well as the debt that the French owed the British and the Americans for aid in those conflicts.

C. Italy and Other Free Countries of Western Europe

Defeated Italy had many problems in common with France. Like France, for example, it had a large and disciplined Communist party eager to foment disorder and revolution and always ready to follow the dictates of Russia. In 1946 King Victor Emmanuel III, in an effort to preserve the Italian monarchy, had abdicated in favor of his son, who became King Humbert II. But a popular vote went in favor of a republic and Humbert abdicated in his turn. It seemed possible at the start that the Republic would be a Communist one, for many Italians turned to Communism, in reaction against discredited fascism, as a quick road to economic improvement, and as a method of winning the support and

Foreign ministers Alcide de Gasperi of Italy and Robert Schuman of France, 1951.

friendship of victorious Russia. In the elections for the Constituent Assembly in June 1946, out of a total of 556 members the Communists under Palmiro Togliatti got 104 seats and the Socialists under Pietro Nenni, who was prepared to work with the Communists, got 115 seats. The largest party opposing them was the Christian (Catholic) Democratic Party led by Alcide de Gasperi, who succeeded in winning the support of the smaller liberal parties and some right-wing Socialists who broke with Nenni. In 1947, De Gasperi was able to form an anti-Communist coalition with a slender majority.

De Gasperi secured the reluctant ratification of the peace treaty with the Allies, the withdrawal of the Anglo-American forces of occupation, and the adoption of a new constitution (December 1947). The new government consisted of a Chamber of Deputies elected by universal suffrage, a Senate chosen partly by the people and partly by regional councils, a president elected for seven years by the parliament plus some regional representatives, and a cabinet responsible to the legislature. The ensuing elections in 1948 were critical. The

United States played a role by providing for economic aid to Italy and proposing with Britain and France that the peace treaty be revised to give Trieste to Italy. In the event, De Gasperi's Christian Democrats won 306 of the 574 seats, and the Communists and Nenni Socialists only 182. As President was chosen Luigi Einaudi, a political liberal who was definitely anti-Communist. De Gasperi remained as premier till August 1953, not quite long enough to see a settlement negotiated in October 1954 by which the city of Trieste was turned over to Italy, though most of the surrounding territory went to Yugoslavia. He was succeeded by other Christian Democrats, the first of whom was Giuseppe Pella at the head of an all-Christian-Democratic cabinet, and the second, Mario Scelba with a coalition cabinet. The elections of 1953 had given the Christian Democrats 261 members out of 590, while the Communists got 143 and the Nenni Socialists secured 75. In the elections of 1958, the democratic parties of the center increased their margin in the Chamber, and the Christian Democrats continued to provide the premiers. The president elected in 1955, Giovanni Gronchi, belonged to the same party, as did his successor, Antonio Segni, elected in 1962.

That same year saw a marked shift, called "the opening to the left," in the political scene. After much soul searching on both sides, the Christian Democrats and the Nenni Socialists agreed to collaborate on a program calling for more planning, more nationalization of industry and more independent regional administration. When the Communists gained a million votes in the general elections of 1963 and the collaborating parties lost some ground, they drew even closer together. Nenni entered the government of the Christian Democrat premier, Aldo Moro and his fellow Socialist, Giuseppe Saragat, became foreign minister. The next year, Segni had to resign for reasons of health, and after twenty ballots, with many Christian Democrats abstaining, Saragat was elected president by the Chamber of Deputies and the Senate meeting in joint session.

Italy in the post-war period faced not only problems produced by the war—rebuilding factories and housing, paying reparations, fighting off the threat of internal Communism—but also others of longer standing—overpopulation, scanty resources, large estates inefficiently farmed. Every cabinet promised land reform, but progress was slow. Industrial development, sparked by aid in goods, money, and technical skills from the United States, did slowly cut down unemployment. Italian manufactured goods —textiles, shoes, typewriters, motor scooters, small automobiles—began to compete in the world markets. In 1963, for example, Italy exported almost three hundred thousand automobiles. Indeed, so rapid was the expansion of production that Italy began to suffer from inflation and the accompanying economic dislocations. But most of the growing industrial activity was in the north. Thus the contrast between that prosperous region and the area south of Rome, where unemployment continued at a high level, became more and more painful. As a result, scores of thousands of Italian workers moved from the south to the north, and others emigrated, on a more or less temporary basis, to Switzerland and the Common Market countries. So great was the prosperity of the Western world and so many the historic attractions of Italy that more

than twenty million tourists went thither each year. In the cultural field, Italy scored many post-war triumphs. Italian movies were exported in large numbers, Italian novels were translated into many languages, Italian clothing styles for women began to compete with those of Paris.

The smaller democratic countries of western Europe confronted many of the same problems as the larger ones, and like them responded in a variety of ways. The Low Countries had been overrun by the Germans and fought over in the later stages of the war. Belgium rapidly stabilized its currency, checked inflation, and, supported by the prosperity of the Belgian Congo, rich in uranium and copper, made a rapid recovery. It was governed after the war by the Christian Social (Catholic) and Socialist parties. But these fell into a dispute over King Leopold III, who had surrendered, perhaps precipitately, to the Germans in 1940. A crisis was averted when the King, in July 1951, abdicated in favor of his son Baudouin. But a new one threatened at the end of 1960, when, shaken by the loss of the Congo and by internal disputes between the Christian Social party and the Socialists and between the French-speaking and the Flemish-speaking citizens, the country was paralyzed by a series of prolonged strikes. But the next year, after general elections, the coalition of the Christian Social and Socialist parties was patched up and continued to govern, though disputes and violence went on over the language issue, even after a law of 1961 made Flemish the sole official language in the north, and French in the south, with Brussels as a bilingual area. The French-speaking (Walloon) minority kept pressing for a federal state, split along language lines. Gradually relations with the now independent Congo improved and many Belgian technicians, civilian administrators and teachers returned there to help the new country. In 1964, Belgian paratroopers were dropped at Stanleyville in a partially successful attempt to rescue European hostages held by Congolese rebels. This venture was backed by the United States and strongly opposed by most of the independent African states.

In the Netherlands, recovery after the war was at first slow, for the loss of the Dutch empire in Indonesia required painful

Football. A modernist painting by André Lhote.

adjustments. Friction with Indonesia continued until the Netherlands, under pressure from the United States and others, ceded West New Guinea (West Irian) in 1962 to the United Nations to be turned over the next year to the Indonesian government. Diplomatic relations between the two countries were resumed in 1963. In 1948, the revered Dutch queen, Wilhelmina, abdicated for reasons of age and health and was replaced by her daughter, Juliana. The government of the Netherlands was conducted by a coalition of parties headed by the Catholic People's Party, which secured the most members in the Second Chamber of the States-General in the general elections of 1959 and again in those of 1963. Economic conditions were improved somewhat after 1948 by the creation of the Benelux Customs Union (with Belgium and Luxembourg) and after 1958 by the success of the Common Market. Prosperity was likewise greatly enhanced for the Netherlands by the discovery (1963) and development of vast natural gas deposits.

Other small countries that had been involved in the war included Finland, Denmark, and Norway. Despite its defeat by Russia, its proximity to that country, and the territorial concessions that had been wrung from it, Finland steadfastly clung to its independence and to a democratic form of government. Ruled by a coalition of Socialists, Agrarians, and Liberals under a Socialist president, Juho Paasikivi (elected 1945 and again in 1950), the Finnish people by heroic efforts paid their reparations to Russia and strove to keep the peace with their mighty neighbor. This they did with such success that in 1956 the ten-year treaty of assistance and friendship signed in 1948 was extended to 1975. At the same time, the Soviet Union returned to Finland the Porkkala area which it had obtained in 1944. Under President Kekkoren (elected in 1956 and again in 1962), Finland's policy of coöperation with both the Soviet Union and the West was continued. The elections of 1962 somewhat weakened the left parties in the two-hundred-member, one-house Parliament, and in 1964 a new government based on a rightist coalition was formed, only to be succeeded in 1966 after new elections by a left coalition in which the socialists predominated.

In agricultural Denmark, post-war recovery was fairly rapid, but the country emerged from occupation by the Germans shorn of its most important overseas dominion, for Iceland in 1944 had voted to become an independent republic. Denmark was governed after the war by a succession of coalition cabinets under Social Democrat, Liberal, and Liberal-Conservative leaders. A modernized constitution adopted in 1953 changed the national legislature to a one-chamber instead of a two-chamber body and made Greenland, which had been a colony, into a full-fledged member of the Danish Commonwealth with elected representatives in the parliament. The elections of 1964 left the Social Democrats as the largest party and they formed a new government, though they had only seventy-six of the 179 members in the Folketing (parliament). In Norway, the Labor Party secured a majority in the first post-war election and conducted the government (save for a brief interlude in 1963) until its defeat in the elections of 1965. When the king, Haakon VII, died in 1957 at the age of eighty-five, he was succeeded by his son, Olav V. In both Denmark and Norway, Communists were unable to muster more than a small fraction of the voters. But in Finland they elected a substantial minority of the deputies in the Diet. The elections of 1962, for example, returned forty-seven Communists out of a total of two hundred.

The five countries of Western Europe which had remained neutral during the war —Sweden, Switzerland, Eire (Ireland), Portugal, and Spain—were confronted after 1945 by problems rather different from those faced by the nations which had been involved in the conflict. They had no devastation to make good. But they did have to adjust to a situation in which they could no longer make high profits by exports to the warring countries. Sweden, troubled as to how to conduct its diplomacy as between Russia and the Western democracies, was governed by Social Democratic cabinets and continued to develop its democratically planned economy and welfare state. The elections of 1964 showed the Social Democrats again to be stronger than the next three parties (Liberals, Centrists, Conservatives) combined. Like the other Scandinavian countries, Sweden strongly supported the United Nations and supplied observers (Cuba, 1962) and even troops (Congo, 1960) for its peace-keeping operations. Switzerland maintained its traditional federal democracy and rapidly built up its exports of clocks, watches, machinery, textiles, chemicals, drugs, electrical goods and scientific instruments. So prosperous, indeed, did Swiss industry become that large num-

bers of Italian and other workers were imported. By 1966, the presence of so many aliens had become a social and a political problem. Eire secured its complete and final independence from Britain in 1948. De Valera, leader of the nationalistic Fianna Fail Party, alternated with John A. Costello of the more moderate Fine Gael Party as premier in the post-war years. In 1959, De Valera became president after a hard-fought election.

The Iberian neutrals, Spain and Portugal, can hardly be counted among the democratic countries, for they both retained their pre-war dictatorial regimes. The Spanish government of General Franco was long treated by the Western democracies as an outcast both because of its alleged fascist nature and wartime sympathy with Hitler. But the Spanish people, eager to prevent a renewal of civil war, acquiesced in the Franco regime. In 1947 a "succession law" was endorsed by popular vote. It provided that in case of the death or incapacity of the Chief of State, a regency council would propose a king or regent who must be accepted by two thirds of the Cortes (or parliament, established in 1942). By 1956, negotiations between Franco and the royalist pretender to the throne had progressed far enough to make it seem likely that the Spanish monarchy would eventually be restored. By then, moreover, Spain was being wooed and supported by the United States in its efforts to build an anti-Russian coalition. And though Spain had been specifically and ostentatiously barred from membership in the United Nations in 1945 by the Western democracies as well as by the Communist Soviet Union, it was admitted without serious opposition ten years later. Funds from the United States for air bases and other military installations were, by 1961, having a signficant effect on the Spanish economy. In industry, agriculture, transportation and the general standard of living, a significant improvement was apparent. Further, the relatively low cost of travel in Spain brought thither swarms of tourists (some ten million a year) from Western Europe and the United States, and the money they spent was of considerable economic importance. In 1964 a four-year development plan got off to a good start with a rapid increase of industrial production and of foreign investment in Spain. Growing prosperity brought back some of the hundreds of thousands of Spanish laborers who had gone to work in the Common Market countries. Though the Franco government relaxed somewhat its stern controls, it moved quickly to suppress the recurrent strikes and student demonstrations.

In Portugal, Marshal Carmona, who had seized power in 1926, was able, through his control of elections, to retain the presidency for a quarter of a century. But power was actually in the hands of his prime minister, Dr. Antonio de Oliveira Salazar, and no change in this situation was effected by the election of General Francisco Lopes as president in 1951, or that of Admiral Americo Rodrigues Tomas in 1958. Internally, Dr. Salazar maintained his authority by his watchful police and his control of the army, though by 1965, several incidents (including an anti-government manifesto during the carefully controlled elections of that year) had made it clear that there was still a liberal opposition dissatisfied with Portugal's regime. Externally, Salazar coöperated with the Western democracies, but he and his people resented Western sympathy with native unrest in the African colony of Angola and the United Nations' failure to prevent, or to condemn India's forceful seizure of Goa and other coastal enclaves which Portugal had held since the fifteenth century.

Fidel Castro explaining his plans for redistribution of the land to a group of farmers, 1959.

CHAPTER 62

Defense of the Free World

A. American Leadership and the Cold War

In 1945–1946, the United States and the other Western democracies were, on the whole, trustful of Russian intentions and promises, and hopeful that the great powers could work together in coöperation to make "one world" free from aggression and fear. Stalin and his foreign minister, Molotov, said that Russia was "democratic" and "peace-loving." They endorsed the Atlantic Charter and the United Nations. They pledged the Soviet Union to respect the right of liberated peoples to have free elections and to set up and maintain governments of their own choosing. It seemed reasonable to expect that the Western powers could work with Russia on friendly terms. Of course occasional concessions might have to be made on both sides. But not to make concesssions might lead to friction, hostility, and even armed conflict. The prospect of a Third World War, with atomic weapons, was too terrifying to contemplate.

For a brief time such optimism seemed justified. It was a bit shaken as early as the autumn of 1945 by a Russian attempt to take over the important oil-producing province of Azerbaijan in northern Iran. But in this instance, the Soviet Union yielded to pressure from the United Nations. The troops were withdrawn and optimism reigned again.

Not for long, however. By the end of 1946, it was becoming quite obvious that the Soviet dictatorship attached quite different meanings to "democracy," "free elections," and "self-determination" from those usual in the United States or Western Europe. It became clear, too, that, instead of adhering to its earlier promises and honestly coöperating with the Western democracies for the realization of a free world, Russia was aggressively seeking to transform as much of the world as possible into a Communist empire dependent on Moscow. It was retaining its war-time armies. It was paralyzing the United Nations by the frequent use of its veto in the Security Council. It was fostering subversive Communist movements in other lands, especially France and Italy. It was, as we have seen, imposing puppet Communist governments on one country after another in Eastern Europe. It was directing a continuous and abusive propaganda campaign against the Western nations, and particularly against the United States. These were denounced as war-mongering, capitalistic countries, seeking to obtain more markets so as to bolster up a decaying economic system and hence bent on encircling and throttling the "homeland of socialism," the Soviet Union. If Russia did join, after much haggling and delay, in making peace treaties in 1947 with Italy, Hungary, Bulgaria, Rumania, and Finland, it became evident that it would agree to no reasonable settlement of peace terms with Germany.

With Austria the situation was somewhat different. For ten long years Austria had been subjected to a four-power (British, French, American, and Russian) occupation, with joint control of Vienna by the four. The Austrians had nonetheless been able to organize a democratic republic governing the whole country and to arrange for fairly free trade and travel among the several zones. The new Austrian government had been organized by a respected socialist statesman, Dr. Karl Renner, who became its first President. It had been governed in the succeeding years by a cabinet representing a coalition of the Popular (Catholic) and the Socialist parties. In three elections (1945, 1949, 1953) the Communist party had not been able to elect more than four or five deputies out of a total of 165. Starting with United Nations' help in 1946, Austria had received much foreign aid in food and goods, and by 1955 had achieved a modest level of prosperity. The Western powers were eager to end the occupation, but in scores of meetings, held off and on through the post-war years, the Soviet representatives always interposed some frustrating obstacle that made the negotiations abortive and fruitless. Russia seemed to resent the failure of Communism to attract support from the Austrian people. It appeared anxious to maintain troops in Austria so as to have a good excuse for keeping other military detachments in Hungary and Rumania as lines of communication from Russia to Austria. It insisted on retaining control of Austrian industries and oil wells which it had seized in 1945 as belonging to Nazi Germany. Great, therefore, was the surprise in the West when, at further meetings in the spring of 1955, the Russians showed themselves conciliatory on the points they had so long, so stubbornly, and so unreasonably upheld. Greater even was the astonishment, when in May a treaty was actually signed between the four powers and Austria with provision for ending the occupation and neutralizing the country.

But if, at long last, the Soviet Union showed itself willing to reach an agreement on Austria, still in other directions it continued to evince unyielding hostility to the Western powers. Opinion in the Western countries was most affected by the manner in which Czechoslovakia was taken over by the Communists. By then (1948) it was clear that the Soviet Union was implacably hostile to the democracies and was in fact engaged in what came to be termed a "cold war" (as opposed to a "hot" or shooting war) against them. Eastern Communist Europe was cut off from the West by what Winston Churchill called an "iron curtain," for the Russians, with the utmost severity, restricted travel, trade, and communication in the lands they controlled. Historic ties were broken. The continent of Europe stood divided into two parts, the one free, the other subject to the dictates of Communist Moscow.

The first significant American countermove came in 1947. Russia had recently denounced its non-aggression treaty with Turkey and was demanding from that country territorial concessions and a share in the control of the straits leading from the Black Sea into the Mediterranean. At the same time it was inciting Yugoslavia (still under Moscow's influence), Albania, and Bulgaria to give military assistance to a Communist insurrection in Greece. Great Britain had helped to free Greece from the Germans in 1944 and to reëstablish order there, but it now lacked the resources to protect Greece or Turkey from Communist aggression by Russia and its Balkan satellites. Into the breach, with British approval, stepped the United States. In March 1947, President Truman asked the American Congress for funds for troops and supplies to oppose Communism in Greece and Turkey. In May, the so-called "Truman Doctrine" (that the United States would use its economic strength to arrest the advance of Communism) was endorsed and an initial appropriation of 400 million dollars was made.

In the event, American aid was sufficient to turn the tide in both cases. It enabled Greece to suppress the internal Communist menace and the guerrillas operating in the border areas, to improve economic conditions, and to maintain an orderly democratic government. In the ensuing years, Greece gradually grew in economic strength and stability assisted by continuing American aid and a tremendous increase in the tourist business. When King Paul died in 1964, he was succeeded by his twenty-three-year-old son, Constantine, who in the next

General George C. Marshall, Chief of Staff of the U.S. Army during World War II, and after it both Secretary of State and Secretary of Defense.

Courtesy Wide World Photos

military aid and ECA was replaced by the Mutual Security Agency (MSA) at the end of 1951, it spent twelve and a half billion dollars, and the money and goods which it provided were of incalculable value in rebuilding a prosperous West Europe and greatly lessening the want and misery on which Communism thrives. Nor was American aid confined to Europe. Over the years much went to Asiatic countries such as Pakistan and Nationalist China, and under President Truman's "Point Four Program" (announced in 1949) technical assistance and financial help were extended to underdeveloped areas. In 1953, MSA and the Point Four Program were consolidated into the Foreign Operations Administration (FOA), which in turn became the International Coöperation Administration (ICA) and then the Agency for International Development (AID). Gradually, as Europe recovered, more and more of the assistance was channeled to the underdeveloped countries of Asia, South America and Africa. By 1966, foreign aid of all types from the United States had totaled more than one hundred billion dollars and was continuing at the rate of more than three billion dollars a year.

Foreign aid to strengthen the nations not in the Communist camp was a supplement to political and military alignments. In April 1949, moreover, the United States entered into a twenty-year defensive alliance with a number of Western nations—Canada, Great Britain, France, Italy, Norway, Iceland, Denmark, Netherlands, Belgium, Luxembourg, and Portugal. The pact established a "North Atlantic Treaty Organization" (NATO), with an executive committee of foreign ministers, a defense council of war ministers, and a military committee of chiefs of staff. To the European members of NATO, the United States, in October 1949, granted an initial subsidy of a billion dollars to help them rearm. Supervision of the planning and coördination of the defense efforts was entrusted to the American General Dwight Eisenhower.

Greece and Turkey were later admitted to NATO, and the United States by special agreement with Spain secured air and naval bases in that country to supplement the defense of Western Europe and the Mediterranean. When General Eisenhower re-

year won a long parliamentary battle against the ambitious prime minister Papandreou for control of the army. Turkey, too, was enabled to withstand the Soviet pressures and focus its efforts on internal political and economic problems.

A second step was taken by the United States in June 1948, when Truman's Secretary of State, General George C. Marshall, proposed a plan for giving American aid to other European countries. Russia was invited to participate, but it denounced and rejected the "Marshall Plan" and prevented all satellites (plus Finland) from accepting American help. The plan was accepted by France, Great Britain, and fourteen other European nations. And it was implemented in the United States by the Foreign Assistance Act of 1948 under which was set up an Economic Coöperation Administration (ECA), headed by Paul Hoffman, to administer the European Recovery Program (ERP). Before the emphasis turned to

turned home in 1952 to be elected President in succession to Harry Truman, supreme command of the NATO military forces was turned over to another American, General Matthew Ridgway.

As a supplement to NATO a Council of Europe was also organized in 1949. It represented an expansion of the alliance which had been created at Brussels the previous year by France, Great Britain, and the Benelux countries. It did not include Canada, the United States, or Portugal, but it did eventually include, in addition to the other NATO countries, Eire, Sweden, and West Germany.

Thus free Europe drew together to defend itself against Soviet pressure and the threat of Russian expansion. But the military situation was changed dramatically in September 1949, when President Truman announced that an atomic explosion, presumably that of an atom bomb, had taken place in Russia. Up to this point it had been possible to believe that Russia would be restrained in its use of force by fear of the atomic bomb stockpile in the hands of the United States. Now it became easy to envision a day when Russia, equipped with a number of the new bombs, might use them suddenly in a surprise attack, or a situation in which neither side would use such weapons for fear of retaliation. Moreover, it soon became clear that the atom bomb, producing its effects by atomic fission, had been much surpassed in power by a hydrogen fusion bomb, and there were rumors of even more deadly missiles—a cobalt bomb and an uranium fission-fusion bomb. In addition, it was no longer necessary to deliver bombs by means of airplanes, for both Russia and the United States were developing rockets capable of journeys into space with bombs as warheads. That the Russians were technically very competent in this field was demonstrated dramatically, on October 4, 1957, when they launched an artificial satellite called "Sputnik I" which circled the earth every ninety minutes for three months. The United States sent its first satellite (Explorer I) into orbit in January 1958, and in the ensuing years, the two powers launched into space scores of vehicles for scientific, military and propaganda purposes. By 1966, some five hundred man-made objects were orbiting the earth.

The French added a satellite to this circling hardware late in 1965.

The change in the military picture led the United States to propose as early as 1950 that West Germany be rearmed, and that a German army be included in the plans for defense of the West. France, always fearful of a militarized Germany, countered by suggesting that a European army be established with only small German units scattered through it. Thereby the creation of powerful military forces under German command could be avoided. In 1952 this proposal was made part of a treaty setting up a European Defense Community (EDC), but ratification of the treaty proved difficult and France eventually rejected its own plan. Then Sir Anthony Eden, British Foreign Minister, in a suprising reversal of traditional policy, offered to keep British troops on the continent indefinitely if Western Europe could reach an understanding on an appropriate defense system which would include Germany. Finally, agreements were signed at Paris in 1954, by which West Germany was recognized as a sovereign state, given the right to have armed forces, and admitted to NATO. The Brussels treaties of 1948 were to be expanded into a defensive alliance to be called the Western European Union with Italy as well as West Germany included. Agreement to these proposals was secured from the countries concerned during 1955. Arrangements were made to end the occupation (save in divided Berlin) by France, Britain, and the United States, though it was understood that their troops would remain there as part of the European defense system. In 1955, West Germany set about recreating an army. Conscription was introduced in 1957, and the number of soldiers was raised so that, by 1966, the German Federal Defense Force numbered more than four hundred thousand men.

All was not completely harmonious within NATO, however. After De Gaulle came to power, he pressed for a larger role for France and for less complete integration of the NATO forces in Europe. He reënforced his position by pushing forward French development of atomic devices to such a point that France was able to detonate an atomic bomb in the Sahara desert

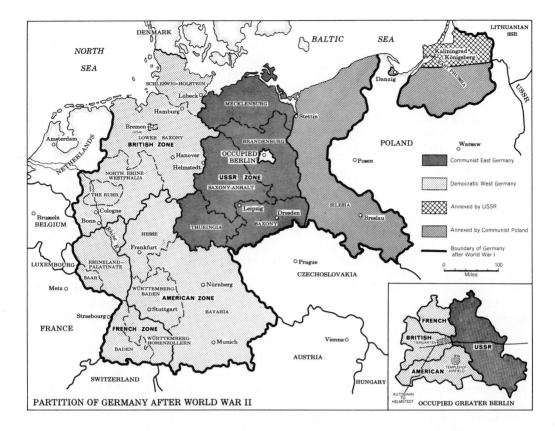

early in 1960. Britain had already set off several atomic bombs and a hydrogen bomb as well (in 1957).

B. Divided Germany

From the very close of the war the problem of Germany intensified the tension between the Soviet Union and the Western powers. At first, the problem concerned matters of military occupation. The division into zones was awkward enough with the British occupying the northwest, the French the west and southwest, the Americans the center and south, and the Russians the northeast. But even more awkward was the fact that Berlin, under the joint control of the occupying nations, lay deep in the Russian zone, though access to it for the other powers was pledged by Russia. The city of Berlin was divided into two zones, the western under French-British-American control, the eastern under Russian.

At the start, the four powers coöperated in trying "war criminals" and "de-Nazify-ing" Germany. The Russians took all the machinery they could lay their hands on as reparations, but the Western Allies seemed not unwilling to have Germany kept weak. They agreed in 1946 on the abolition of the historic state of Prussia and the division of Germany into seventeen states—five in the eastern Russian zone, the others in the west. The Russians in their zone set about creating a Communist regime subservient to Moscow, and the Americans busied themselves trying to democratize theirs and to break up the great industrial cartels into competing units.

But as the tone changed from one of hesitant coöperation to one of "cold war," policy toward Germany changed also. The Western powers began to see in Germany a possible counterweight to Soviet influence in central Europe. Gradually it became their policy to work for a strong and stable Germany. Inflation was checked and the currency stabilized. Relief materials and "Marshall Plan" credits were poured into the country. And the Germans responded. A decade after the close of the war West Germany was the most prosperous and productive country in western Europe. With factories rebuilt, its industrial output was far above that of pre-war years, and its exports were rising. It had even been able to absorb into useful employment a large number of the millions of German refugees who had fled from East Germany, the Baltic countries, the Sudetenland, and the German areas seized by Communist Russia and Poland.

Meanwhile, West Germany was achieving a very considerable degree of political stability. The occupying powers sponsored democratic constitutions and elections in the several states and in 1948 a democratic election for an Assembly that met at Bonn and drew up a federal republican constitution. Under this constitution, a Federal Diet was elected in 1949, consisting of 139 Christian Democrats, 131 Social Democrats, 52 Liberals, and 80 others including 14 Communists. A coalition cabinet was formed with the sturdy, seventy-three-year-old Christian Democratic leader, Dr. Konrad Adenauer, as Chancellor. In East Germany, on the other hand, the Russians allowed no free elections. They sponsored, rather, the creation of a Social Unity Party led by a Communist, Otto Grotewohl. A People's Council was appointed in 1948. The next year it was converted into a People's Chamber which promulgated a constitution of the Soviet type for the "German Democratic Republic" in the Russian zone. East Germany, which had always been largely agricultural, experienced no such economic recovery as did West Germany.

As West Germany grew stronger and more prosperous, the Russians cut it off more and more strictly from East Germany by commercial barriers and frontier restrictions. In March 1948 they virtually ended the period of coöperative occupation by walking out of the Allied Control Council. In June, they tried to drive the Western officials from Berlin and to end the joint control by shutting off all access to it from the west by highway, railroad, or water. The Western Allies, unwilling to use force, found an answer in the "airlift." For a year, American and British planes flew in all the food, fuel, and raw materials needed by West Berlin. Checkmated and realizing the propaganda value of the airlift for the

Western democracies, since it was a peaceful yet dazzling display of logistical skill and of air power, the Russians eventually gave in and in 1949 again opened the roads to Berlin.

The policy of the West German government at Bonn was coöperation with the Western powers. These, more and more eager for a strong West German ally and convinced that Russia would not agree to a peace treaty, proclaimed in 1951 an end to the state of war with Germany. The growing coöperation between the Federal Republic of Germany and the Western nations was marked by a rapprochement even with France. One of the difficult problems was that of the Saar which after the war had been made semi-autonomous but united economically with France. But by an agreement reached in 1956 between France and West Germany the Saar was joined to the latter, politically in 1957 and economically in 1960.

Adenauer, the leader of the Christian Democrats, remained as Chancellor until the latter part of 1963, when, at the age of eighty-seven, he reluctantly turned over his office to Dr. Ludwig Erhard, who had been his minister of Economic Affairs. Adenauer could look back on his achievements with justified satisfaction, for under him the "miracle of Germany" had taken place. In the fourteen years of his chancellorship, wartorn, defeated, divided and devastated West Germany had achieved not only a booming prosperity but also a respected place in the councils of Europe. Hard-fought elections in 1965 endorsed the rule of the Christian Democrats and left Erhard still in power.

In the post-war years there were signs that all was not well in East Germany. As the country was subjected to the standard apparatus of a Communist police state, with control in the hands of a single party (the Socialist Unity Party) and "order" maintained by a ministry of state security, a militarized "People's Police," and a large army provided with Soviet equipment, the contrast with the freedom and prosperity of West Germany became more and more glaring. There was a steady stream of refugees, numbering sometimes more than a thousand a day, who left the Russian zone to find haven in West Germany. Finally in June of 1953, when the East German gov-

President Kennedy near the Wall in Berlin, June 1963.

ernment sought to increase production by decree, without increasing wages, violent riots broke out in East Berlin and other East German cities. They were suppressed, but only by the use of force and in a bloody fashion. The constant flight of East Germans to the West weakened the economy and advertised the unpleasantness of life under Communist rule. Then in August of 1961, the East Germans closed the border to the West and overnight built a wall dividing their sector of Berlin from the Western section. Despite all precautions, enforced with bullets, refugees continued to trickle through the barrier. "The Wall," indeed, became a symbol, for the whole world, of Communist oppression. On one dramatic occasion, this symbolism was clear for all to see, when President John F. Kennedy (June, 1963) visited West Berlin and in sight of the Wall talked of freedom to a cheering multitude.

C. The Korean War

The most acute episode of the post-war struggle in Asia between the Communist bloc and the free world arose from the conflict over Korea which for more than three years turned the cold war into a hot one. As we have seen above,[1] on June 25, 1950, armies of Communist North Korea swept over the thirty-eighth parallel in a massive thrust into South Korea. On the morrow of the invasion, President Truman took the courageous decision of ordering armed American resistance to the aggression. Troops, planes, munitions were hurried to Korea from General MacArthur's command in Japan and were gradually added to directly from the United States. The Con-

---

[1] See p. 797.

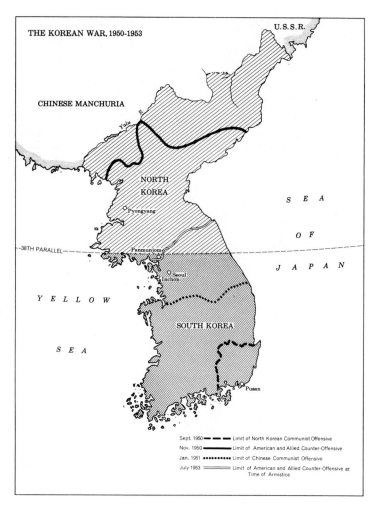

THE KOREAN WAR, 1950-1953

U.S.S.R.

CHINESE MANCHURIA

Yalu R.

NORTH KOREA

Pyongyang

S E A

O F

-38TH PARALLEL-

Panmunjom

J A P A N

Seoul
Inchon

Y E L L O W

SOUTH KOREA

S E A

Pusan

Sept. 1950 ▬ ▬ ▬ Limit of North Korean Communist Offensive
Nov. 1950 ▬▬▬ Limit of American and Allied Counter-Offensive
Jan. 1951 ●●●●●●●● Limit of Chinese Communist Offensive
July 1953 ═══════ Limit of American and Allied Counter-Offensive at Time of Armistice

gress later approved the President's decision, and in July voted large increases in the armed forces of the United States.

Truman also immediately laid the problem of the Korean invasion before the Security Council of the United Nations. Through the fortuitous circumstance that the Russian delegate had walked out (in protest against the refusal to admit Communist China), there was no Soviet representative to exercise the veto. On June 27, therefore, the Security Council, with Russia absent and Yugoslavia abstaining, declared that North Korea had broken the peace, directed it to withdraw its troops from South Korea, and urged all United Nations members to help South Korea to repel the invasion. Collective action by United Nations' forces was authorized, with General MacArthur in command. In the event, sixteen members sent military forces (though most of them were merely of token size), and thirty-seven others contributed supplies, medical equipment, or the like. The brunt of the war was borne by the United States and South Korea.

During the summer of 1950, the North Korean invaders made steady progress southward. By early September they had pushed the South Korean and American forces into the southeastern corner of the country. But by this time, American reinforcements were arriving in sufficient number to turn the tide. General MacArthur launched a counter-offensive with surprise landings at Inchon, a hundred miles behind the fighting front. It recaptured Seoul, and at the end of September, in conjunction with the South Koreans, it drove the invaders back of the thirty-eighth parallel. The allies continued to advance through North Korea, and on November 21 they reached the Manchurian frontier. It seemed as if the Korean War was about to end with the complete and decisive defeat of Communist aggression.

The Communists of North Korea were indeed routed. But already Chinese Communist armies, with Russian equipment, had been massing behind the Manchurian border for a new and fiercer offensive. On November 26, a quarter of a million men, plentifully supplied with planes and tanks, crossed the frontier and threw back the American, South Korean, and United Nations forces with heavy losses. On they pressed, conquering all North Korea, capturing Seoul again and carrying the war even further southward.

The Korean War, and especially this second phase of it, had peculiar international aspects. There was no doubt that the Soviet Union inspired the aggression and supplied the weapons for it. Nor was there any doubt that the Chinese government of Mao Tse-tung was fighting the United Nations in Korea. Yet there was no declaration of war on either side and little disposition to call Russia to account. There was widespread fear that otherwise the conflict could not be "localized" in Korea and would bring on another world war. The British and other governments of Western Europe were especially fearful lest American aid and interest be diverted from them to the Far East; and, besides, the Indian and other Asian governments showed an embarrassing tenderness toward both Communist China and Communist Russia. No government which had previously recognized Mao's regime in China broke off diplomatic relations with it even when its armies were fighting the United Nations forces in Korea. Some even supported the Russian contention that Communist China should supplant the Nationalist Chinese government as a member of the United Nations and of the Security Council.

All this influenced and handicapped the United States government in its conduct of the Korean War. General MacArthur was kept on the defensive and was strictly debarred from bombing Chinese bases and supply lines in Manchuria and from using the Chinese Nationalist army on Formosa. When he complained publicly about these and other restrictions, President Truman replaced him by General Matthew Ridgway.

Meanwhile, American reinforcements continued to pour in, and eventually the Chinese invasion into South Korea was halted and turned back. Once more Seoul was recaptured by the United Nations forces. By autumn of 1951 the contending armies were facing each other along a battle-scarred and bloodily contested line across Korea close to the thirty-eighth parallel, but north of it in the east and south of it in the west. In September, in an effort to halt the carnage and with the sanction of the United Nations, the United States opened truce negotiations with the army commanders of Communist China and North Korea. These, intent upon gaining time, strengthening their forces, and improving the positions they held, greatly prolonged the negotiations. As the discussions dragged on, sporadic fighting continued, and it was not until July 27, 1953, that an armistice was signed at Panmunjom.

One of the difficult questions in negotiating the armistice had been the problem of the repatriation of prisoners of war. The Communists wanted the Chinese and North Korean prisoners turned over to them, but it was clear that many of them did not want to return to their Communist-ruled countries. The United States, therefore, insisted that each prisoner be allowed to choose whether to go home or not. In the end, a United Nations repatriation commission supervised the whole matter. The Communists were shocked and the world surprised to learn that more than 21,000 Chinese and North Koreans refused to be repatriated. The armistice left the line between North and South Korea in approximately the position attained by military force.

Once hostilities were ended the United States set to work immediately to assist in the economic rehabilitation of South Korea. But the task in that war-torn country was a formidable one. An attempt to turn the armistice into a more permanent peace at a nineteen-nation conference (which included Communist China), in Geneva in 1954, broke down when the Communists refused to accept the idea of genuinely free elections throughout Korea and argued that the United Nations as an "aggressor" should be debarred from further activity

there. There was much left to be settled
in regard to Korea, despite the war which
had lasted more than three years and cost
the United States a third as many casualties
as World War II.

Bolstered by American economic and
military aid, South Korea made some progress under its aging President, Dr. Syngman
Rhee, who had been elected in 1948 and
re-elected in 1952, 1956, and 1960. But
since corruption was rampant and inefficiency widespread, much of the American
assistance was frittered away. The government more and more employed police
methods to suppress opposition and rigged
elections to stay in power. Finally in April
1960, student demonstrations and growing
protest drove the President from power in
a relatively peaceful revolution. The constitution was amended to place power in
the hands of the cabinet rather than the
president, and Dr. John M. Chang became
premier. The new government attempted
to rule in a more democratic fashion, but
it was faced with the continuing and difficult problems of poverty and lack of education. In 1961, the government was overthrown and rule came into the hands of a
military junta—headed by General Pak
Chung Hi—which avowed as its objectives
economic improvement, opposition to Communism and the suppression of corruption.
It forcefully eliminated from the political
scene all who might oppose it. Efforts were
made to restore democratic rule and political
parties. But it was General Pak (now retired
from the army) who was elected president,
under a new constitution, in October of
1963. Under the new civilian government,
real progress began in education, in administration, and on the economic front. Japan
and Korea, in the face of opposition in both
countries, settled a long list of disputes by
signing a treaty of friendship and coöperation in 1965.

D. Democratic
Japan

The Korean War, and the loss of China
to Communism which had preceded it,
worked a dramatic change in the American
attitude and policy toward Japan. After
the close of World War II, the United
States had been chiefly concerned with

eliminating Japan as a threat to the peace
of Asia and of the Pacific. The American
occupation under General Douglas MacArthur had tried "war criminals," purged the
government, education, and business of
right-wing nationalists and militarists, reformed the land system to encourage small
peasant landholdings, broken up the big
business combines, outlawed the nationalist Shinto religion and the emperor-
worship connected with it, and arranged
for the writing, acceptance, and promulgation of a new democratic constitution. So
thorough was the purge of rightist elements in schools, universities, labor unions,
and agricultural coöperatives, that many of
these were left in the hands of Socialists.
The constitution (effective in 1947) retained the emperor, but with no more
power than the British sovereign. By the
constitution, Japan renounced war and the
use of force in international affairs, and the
maintenance of armed forces was prohibited. Meanwhile, the United States supported the Japanese people by importation
of food and raw materials, and sought to
improve public health and economic conditions.

After 1949 American policy toward
Japan underwent a drastic change. Japan
began to seem like a bulwark against the
advance of Communism in Asia. In 1950,
the United States approved the creation of a
national "police" force that much resembled an army, and pressed for the creation
of armed forces (despite the constitutional prohibition) until in 1954 legislation
was enacted providing for military, naval,
and air "defensive" forces.

Though the occupation of Japan was
under American auspices, it was supervised
by an Allied Council for Japan in Toyko
and a Far Eastern Commission (composed
of representatives of the United States, Australia, Canada, Nationalist China, France,
Great Britain, India, the Netherlands,
New Zealand, the Philippines, and Russia)
meeting in Washington. Lack of agreement
within the Commission long prevented the
preparation of a peace treaty. But in 1950,
despite Russian objections, President Truman decided to go forward with this task
and appointed a mission under John Foster
Dulles (later Secretary of State under President Dwight Eisenhower) to negotiate a

treaty with Japan and the other interested powers.

The treaty was eventually signed in September 1951 at a conference in San Francisco by Japan and almost fifty other countries. Russia refused to sign and India to attend. China was not party to the proceedings because there was disagreement among the Allies as to which of its governments—Nationalist on Taiwan or Communist on the mainland—was the legal and therefore recognizable government. By the treaty, the state of war with Japan was ended and its full sovereignty reëstablished. Its losses of territory were confirmed: the Kurile Islands and the southern half of Sakhalin went to Russia; the Pacific islands, "mandated" to Japan after World War I, were entrusted to the United States; Taiwan was assigned to Nationalist China; and Korea was to be independent. Reparations in goods and services were to be arranged for by Japan with its former enemies. At the same time the United States concluded a mutual assistance pact with Japan, by which the latter's independence and territorial integrity were guaranteed, but the United States was allowed to retain military and naval bases in Japan and to continue its occupation of Okinawa and the other Ryukyu Islands. A similar pact was made by the United States with the Philippines, and the United States resumed its support of Chiang Kai-shek and his nationalists on Taiwan. At the end of 1956, Japan was admitted to the United Nations.

In the years after the end of the American occupation, Japan entered upon a period of tremendous economic growth and prosperity. In part, this development arose from the continuing flow of American funds for the bases on Japanese territory. In part, it came from the fact that Japanese debts had been liquidated by inflation and that the cost of maintaining military forces had been greatly reduced. But it was also due to the energy and skill of the Japanese people, to the fact that machinery and other equipment destroyed in the war were replaced by the most modern facilities for production, and to improvements in the quality of Japanese goods (textiles, toys, electronic devices, automobiles, optical instruments, cameras, etc.) which found them an increasing market in the United States, Europe, and Asia. There was, indeed, almost a vogue for things Japanese in America. The occupation troops had come to like the Japanese, whose stylized good manners and way of life in their homeland made a most favorable contrast to their ruthlessness in war abroad. In any case, many Americans became enthusiastic about Japanese architectuure, prints, gardens, and flower arrangement.

The enthusiasm was not wholly reciprocated in Japan. If the Japanese became more and more westernized and welcomed such American innovations as television and electrical kitchen equipment, still, on the other hand, there was a considerable growth of anti-American sentiment, not unnatural after military defeat and occupation by the victors. Most of the students were, moreover, so imbued with Marxist ideology that in the teeth of the contrary facts they thought of the United States as "imperialist" because it was "capitalist" and Russia as not "imperialist" because it called itself "socialist." There was even some feeling that Japan should draw closer economically to Communist China.

The post-war cabinets in Japan were in the hands of the conservative party (Liberal-Democrats) supported by the business elements in the cities and the peasant-farmers of the countryside. The opposition was largely composed of Socialists of varying hues, though there was some Communist leadership among students, teachers, and labor unions. Under such premiers as Yoshida, the government was cautiously coöperative with the United States. Anti-American feeling became a major political factor, when in the face of rising and vocal opposition the premier, Nobusuke Kishi, forced through, in early 1960, the ratification of a new mutual security treaty with the United States. It reduced the role and influence of America in Japan, but not enough to satisfy its critics. Matters came to a head when riots by students and others forced the cancellation of a proposed goodwill visit of President Eisenhower to Japan in 1960. As a result, Kishi was compelled to resign. But the ensuing elections in November confirmed the continuing control of the conservative Liberal-Democrats under a new premier, Hayato Ikeda, as did further elections in July 1962 and November 1963.

Soviet Premier Nikita Khrushchev speaking in Leipzig, 1959.

Courtesy Wide World Photos

Ikeda's government negotiated favorable trade agreements with Britain, Australia, the Soviet Union and even Communist China. Prosperity, with some ups and downs, continued to grow dramatically, so that when Ikeda resigned at the end of 1964, for reasons of health, industrial production as against 1955 had more than tripled and per capita income had more than doubled. Ikeda was succeeded by Eisaku Sato of the same party (Liberal-Democrat). Japan's recovery and progress were on display for all the world to see when the Olympic games were held in Tokyo in October 1964.

E. From Stalin to Khrushchev

An event in 1953 seemed briefly to give promise of altering the character of the cold war and of changing conditions in the Soviet Union and in the neighboring countries that it dominated. That event was the death of Stalin from a brain hemorrhage on March 5. Stalin had been all-powerful in the Soviet Union before World War II, but after it he had the added prestige of military victory and of imperial success— the annexation of some 260,000 square miles of territory with more than twenty million inhabitants, the creation of a ring of satellite states in the west, and the triumph of Communism in China and North

Korea. Russian propaganda and folklore made Stalin into such a superman that sometimes it seemed as if he were being confused with God.

During eight years following World War II, there is little doubt that Stalin dictated the policy of Russia both internal and external. He was responsible for both its successes (the creation of the satellites) and its mistakes (miscalculations in respect to Yugoslavia and to the American reaction to the invasion of South Korea). He was responsible for the cold war and for Russia's strategy in it. It was Stalin, too, who decided to keep up Russia's military strength, maintaining a big army, enlarging the navy (especially as to submarines) and the air force, pushing forward atomic weapon research, and emphasizing heavy industry (for war material) as against light industry (for consumer goods). As always in a dictatorship, where censorship reigns, there were inexplicable events. Writers, composers, and scientists gained favor, or lost it, at the whim of the Dictator, for failing to understand or to follow the party line as he drew it. There was a definite trend toward anti-semitism in government circles, despite the Soviet preachments about racial equality. There seemed to be at least a temporary relaxation of government drive against religion; some Orthodox churches, monasteries, and seminaries were reopened and a few shrines were restored. Most curious of all was the arrest in January 1953 of nine physicians high in official circles who were charged with plotting the death of important officials. (The doctors were released in April 1953, shortly after Stalin's death, with the explanation that the charges were mistaken.)

There was clearly some confusion in the Kremlin when Stalin died. But it was shortly announced that he would be succeeded by a five-man group, consisting of Georgi M. Malenkov as premier, and four deputy premiers—Vyacheslav Molotov as foreign minister, Marshal Nikolai Bulganin as defense minister, Laurenti Beria as minister of internal affairs and head of the secret police, and Lazar Kaganovich in charge of economic affairs. That there was a continuing, if hidden, struggle for power became evident in July when Beria was arrested, and he and his followers "purged." His fall was accompanied by the rise of Nikita Khrushchev, secretary of the Communist Party (the position through which Stalin had attained power). There was, at the same time, a significant increase in the importance of military men, indicating perhaps that the new government felt the need of special support from the army. In any case, Marshal Voroshilov was soon made president of the Presidium of the Supreme Soviet, a post much like that of president in other European republics. Malenkov was demoted from the premiership in February 1955 and replaced by Marshal Bulganin, and Marshal Georgi Zhukov took charge of the military.

At the Soviet Party Congress in Moscow in 1956, in a long, detailed, and surprising speech, Khrushchev denounced Stalin and his regime. Stalin, he said, had used cruel and ruthless procedures that were inappropriate to Communism. He had created a one-man rule based on a "cult of personality." He had by police methods interfered improperly with the lives of the people and with orderly government. This bitter attack on "Stalinism" led to hopes and stirrings both in Russia and in the satellite nations. In Poland, where the majority of the people were still devoutly Roman Catholic and intensely patriotic, there had long been restiveness under the domination of Communist leaders chosen by and subservient to Russia. In June 1956, massive riots of workmen broke out in Poznan and there were troubles in other cities. The risings were suppressed by force, but only after numbers of people had been killed, wounded, or imprisoned.

The Polish situation was sufficiently ominous to force a change in Soviet policy. Wladyslaw Gomulka, a Polish Communist leader who had been jailed because of his anti-Russian, or at least anti-Stalinist, tendencies, was allowed to become party leader in October and to take over control of the government. In the ensuing months a compromise was developed by which the Polish government under Gomulka was allowed a good deal of leeway on matters of internal policy, in return for relatively strict adherence to the Russian position on external matters. Under Gomulka the government was throughly Communist, but it allowed more personal freedom, including some freedom of speech and of religious worship. The attempt to collectivize the farms was more or less abandoned. Cultural relations with the Western nations were to some degree renewed. The Poles, under the shadow of Soviet armed might, remained deeply nationalistic, and thought of themselves as better off than in the days of Stalin.

A major factor in leading the Soviet government to accept the modified situation in Poland was the even more serious challenge that it had to face at the same time in Hungary. The rule of Russia's puppets in Hungary had been even tougher than in Poland. When the premier, Imre Nagy, showed some signs of relaxing economic pressures and controls in 1955, he was ousted. But during the next year there was growing unrest and opposition to the secret police and to the Communist Party. Imre Nagy was allowed to resume the premiership in October 1956. But the unrest spread, workers' councils were formed, and when the police fired on a crowd there was open and armed rebellion. Everywhere the revolution seemed to be making progress and there were even reports that the Russian troops in Hungary were hesitant about firing on the people. But the revolt was quieted on October 28, when Nagy announced that Russia had promised to remove all Soviet troops from the country. By a monstrous act of treachery, however, the Soviet Union sent in new and reliable forces with tanks and artillery, surrounded Budapest, and on November 4 attacked.[1] There was heroic resistance and thousands of Hungarian patriots died in a vain effort to maintain their briefly enjoyed independence. Budapest and the other cities were subdued. Nagy was imprisoned and eventually executed (1958). Tens of thousands of Hungarians fled the country. The Russians put into power a premier they could rely on, Janos Kadar, who proceeded slowly but surely to liquidate the opposition to Communist rule.

One factor in the Hungarian crisis was that those who rose in revolt and, with inadequate weapons and organization, fought heroically for freedom fully expected some sort of aid, at least in arms, from the Western powers. But the United States and the other NATO countries apparently feared that any move would precipitate a general and atomic war. They were, moreover, inhibited by another crisis, that of Suez, which occurred at exactly the same time.[2] The Suez conflict not only separated the United States from France and Great Britain and occupied the attention of the United Nations, but to a degree it prevented the world from becoming fully aware of the ruthless way in which Russia put down the Hungarian revolt.

Those who expected that the Polish and Hungarian difficulties would discredit the new leadership in Russia that had seemed to pave the way for them by a relaxation of pressures were surprised to find that Khrushchev was able gradually to consolidate his position. In March 1958, the Supreme Soviet elected Khrushchev premier and it was soon apparent that he was in firm control of the Russian governmental machinery and of the Communist Party in the Soviet Union. One after another possible rival to Khrushchev, such as Zhukov, Bulganin, Malenkov, and Molotov, was either liquidated or demoted. And the body of the once god-like Stalin was removed from its shrine beside Lenin's in Moscow's Red Square.

Yet the Russian people seemed quite resigned and generally loyal to the regime. They were now used to it, and thoroughly indoctrinated by it. Moreover, they benefitted from rising Russian industrial production and consequent improvement in the standard of living, and they felt patriotic satisfaction in Russian achievements in the fields of science and engineering in general and in astronaut accomplishments in particular.

The decade under Khrushchev demonstrated, however, that there were three major weaknesses in the generally strong position of the Soviet Union. The first was in the area of agriculture. From Lenin on, policy had tended to favor heavy industry as against the production of consumer goods and all industry as against agriculture. Agricultural output, therefore, lagged behind in a most serious fashion. From the start of his period of power, Khrushchev sought to remedy the situation by pushing the "virgin lands" program, under which hitherto unplowed land was utilized for the production of wheat and other food crops. But the program failed because of insufficient fertilizer, inadequate incentives to the farmers, unscientific seed selection and unfavorable climatic conditions. In 1963, grain production fell more than twenty per cent below the previous year, and, to feed its people, the Soviet Union had to import more than eight million tons of grain in 1963–1964 from Australia, Canada, and the United States. Such imports were, moreover, continued in the following years.

The second weakness lay in the primitive and uncertain methods by which power was passed from one leader to the next. By 1964, dissatisfaction with Khrushchev was growing in the top levels of the Soviet government and the Communist Party. It was felt that he had made mistakes in foreign affairs with Cuba, China, and the satellite countries (especially Rumania), that he had committed errors in economic planning and organization (especially in agriculture) and that he had even permitted the rise of a "personality cult" not unlike what he had deplored in the case of Stalin. On October 13, 1964, Khrushchev was summoned back to Moscow from a vacation and, under circumstances that are still mysterious, was forced to resign and go into secluded retirement. Khrushchev was replaced in his crucial

---

[1] See picture of Russian tanks in Budapest, below, p. 864.

[2] See below, p. 845.

position as secretary of the Communist Party by a former associate, an engineer named Leonid Brezhnev, while an economic planner, Alexei Kosygin, became chairman of the Council of Ministers. There were further changes among the top-level officials, though Anastas I. Mikoyan was not replaced as president until December 1965. But it gradually became evident that the Soviet Union now was under the two-man leadership of Brezhnev-Kosygin. The way in which Khrushchev so suddenly disappeared from the Russian scene gave rise to questions and dissatisfaction in many Communist parties all over the world, some of which had had difficulty in transferring their loyal allegiance from Stalin to Khrushchev.

The third weakness lay in the growing inability of the Russian Soviet regime to dominate other Communist governments as it had under Stalin. Beginning in 1949, when it had become clear that the Chinese Communists were going to triumph, the Soviet Union had aided and supported their new government with loans, military equipment, technicians and trade. But ever conscious of the relatively sparse population of Siberia, the teeming hordes of Chinese, and Siberia's long frontier with China, the Russians had refused to provide China with the most sophisticated weapons or to help them to make an atom bomb. Gradually a coolness developed between the two countries. By 1961, they were displaying sharp differences in ideology, with the Chinese claiming to be purer Marxists and urging violent revolution in all non-Communist areas, even at the risk of large-scale war, and the Russians seeing merits in "peaceful coexistence" and emphasizing economic development. At first, the Russians denounced and then broke off relations with tiny Albania, which, oddly enough, sided with China, while the Chinese attacked Yugoslavia for its "revisionism," or lukewarm Marxism. One result was that Yugoslavia and the Soviet Union patched up their quarrels (1962). But it soon became clear that what Mao and Khrushchev were really disputing about was the leadership of the Communist world. The only national Communist parties that definitely lined up with the Chinese were those of North Vietnam, North Korea, and Albania. But in other countries the Chinese had much influence, and many Communist parties soon were divided into pro-Peking and pro-Moscow wings. Though they showed hostility to India (as a threat to their leadership in Asia), the Chinese Communists sought diligently to create strong ties with the colored peoples of the world. Just two days after Khrushchev's resignation Chinese prestige and self-confidence were greatly enhanced by the fact (expected for some weeks) that they were able to detonate an atom bomb. Indeed, the two events were perhaps not unrelated, for Khrushchev may have underestimated the ability of the Chinese to create atomic devices, and this bad guess may have been one of the charges against him.

Meanwhile, Russia's ability to dictate to its own satellites slowly diminished and some of them began to pursue national rather than Soviet aims. Rumania, for example, began in 1963 to show itself restive as to the policies of the Moscow-dominated economic association (COMECON). It opposed the Russian efforts toward greater centralization and insisted on building up its own industrial strength, making some friendly gestures toward Peking, welcoming tourists from Western Europe, and seeking to increase its trade with non-Communist countries. In short, the Soviet Union was becoming the leader, not the master, of the Communist nations and this leadership was being challenged by China.

F. Latin America in Evolution

During World War II, Latin America had been relatively quiet, relatively prosperous, and coöperative with the United States and its allies. But the post-war period was one of rapid change. Airplanes opened up quick access to many parts that had been remote. Industry began to develop significantly in countries like Brazil and Mexico. Better communication in the form of motion pictures, radio, and eventually television made many people dissatisfied with the rather low standard of living prevalent outside the wealthy sections of the large cities. There was also a general feeling that the "good neighbor" policy developed by President Franklin D. Roosevelt had been replaced by one of neglect on the part of the United States.

And it was a fact that American attention was so highly focussed on Europe and later on Asia that not much economic aid flowed into Central or South America.

The problems of Latin America were manifold and varied. In Mexico, for example, there was a shortage of good land, though improved techniques were rapidly increasing agricultural output. In Colombia and Brazil, on the other hand, the question was how to proceed with the development of much unexploited territory. But, in general, there were many difficulties shared by most of the Latin American countries. One was inadequate education. Literacy was generally low, and even where it was not, secondary school, university, and technical (medical, engineering) education was deficient, and there were insufficient numbers of trained people. Another difficulty was the rapidly growing population. Introduction of improved public health techniques and the elimination of major diseases, such as yellow fever, smallpox, and malaria, had resulted in a drastic reduction of the death rate without a corresponding decrease in the birth rate. Yet industry and agriculture were not growing fast enough to take care of the increased numbers and at the same time to produce a rapid improvement in the standard of living. Mexico with a population in 1965 of some 40 million was, for example, growing at the rate of a million a year. And it was estimated that forty per cent of the Latin American population was under fifteen years of age.

There were also continuing problems of political stability. In the immediate postwar period a number of the Latin American countries were under regimes that somewhat resembled European dictatorships, though they were often based on older local traditions and customs. In 1953, for example, Argentina was ruled by Juan D. Peron, Paraguay by Fredrico Chaves, Venezuela by Marcos Perez Jimenez, Colombia by Rojas Pinilla, Cuba by Fulgencio Batista, the Dominican Republic by Rafael Trujillo, and a number of other Latin American countries had quasi-dictatorial regimes, as in Brazil where Getulio Vargas had been in control with only a five-year interruption since 1933.

During the ensuing years there was a trend away from dictatorship, and in most instances it was replaced by a more liberal regime, as in Venezuela, Colombia, Brazil, and Argentina. In Paraguay, however, one dictator was merely replaced by another (Alfredo Stroessner) after a revolt in 1954, and in the Dominican Republic Trujillo remained in power until his assassination in 1961. Often, as in Venezuela, the Catholic Church aided and supported the change to a democratic regime.

There was a continuing tendency, however, for democratic regimes to be ousted, from time to time, by the military, who then formed juntas which governed for longer or shorter periods. Thus the military ruled Argentina in 1962–1963, and again after a coup in mid-1966; Peru likewise in 1962–1963, preceding the election of President Belaunde; Ecuador after 1963; and Boliva after 1964. Brazil was an important example. There a bloodless revolution in 1964 under Marshal Humberto Castelo Branco overthrew the left-leaning regime of João Goulart (which had been leading the country into economic disaster). Applying stern economic measures against inflation, the new regime ruled the nation in a firm but increasingly undemocratic manner. In 1965, after unsatisfactory state elections, political parties were suppressed and the government became more dictatorial. Mexico, continuing under successful one-party rule in which the military played only a minor role and democratic forms were maintained, displayed vigorous economic progress. After the ousting of Rojas Pinilla (1957), Colombia worked out a compromise by which the two major parties took turns at holding the presidency. In Venezuela, for the first time in its history, a legally elected president (the reform-minded Romulo Betancourt) served out his term, and, despite persistent violence and disorders inspired by Communists, he duly transferred power to his legally elected successor (Raul Leoni) in 1964. Uruguay, though gradually encountering more and more economic difficulties, continued along the democratic road under its peculiar nine-man executive. A shining example was Chile, with its long tradition of law, order and democracy. There, the distinguished president Jorge Alessandri was succeeded in 1964 after a very hard-fought election by a Christian Democrat, Eduardo Frei, who de-

President Kennedy greets President Alessandri of Chile on the White House lawn, December 1962.

cisively defeated a Communist-Socialist candidate. Frei's victory constituted the first triumph of a Christian Democrat party in Latin America. He promised thorough-going economic and social reform, but insisted that he would carry it through in a democratic fashion.

A special instance of the ousting of a dictator, and his supplanting by another, was that of Cuba. Here people grew more and more dissatisfied with the harsh and corrupt rule of General Batista. The opposition gradually drew together under the leadership of Fidel Castro who, with small forces, waged a long guerrilla warefare against the government from the mountains of the Oriente Province. At first the United States preserved relatively strict neutrality, but by 1958 it was clear that the forces of young (thirty-one years old) Castro were securing aid from sympathizers and others on the American main-

land. Finally, on the first day of 1959, Batista fled the country and the revolutionary forces took over. Castro himself became premier and practical dictator. It was soon apparent that his regime was under Communist influence. Opponents were executed in large numbers. A drastic land reform law was decreed (May 1959). And before long Castro was pursuing a definitely anti-United States policy. The property of American individuals and business firms was confiscated or nationalized, and the Dictator made long and bitter speeches in which he blamed the United States for all of Cuba's ills. President Eisenhower cut drastically the amount of sugar which Cuba, under a quota, had been permitted to export to the United States on favorable terms and finally, late in 1960, broke off diplomatic relations with Castro's government.

Meanwhile, the Soviet Union, Communist China, and Czechoslovakia had been making friendly gestures toward Cuba, selling it needed oil and machinery, buying its sugar, and providing it with arms and technicians. Khrushchev took repeated opportunities to display his support of Cuba and in July 1960 declared that Russia would retaliate if the United States intervened in Cuba. Castro, in turn, publicly acknowledged in 1961 that from the outset he had been a convinced Communist, and he redoubled his Communist propaganda, strengthened his revolutionary militia, pushed his educational reforms, and instituted severe rationing and other social and economic controls.

The existence of the Castro regime in Cuba led to two crises. The first occurred in 1961, when anti-Castro refugees, with the help of the United States, organized a small-scale armed invasion of Cuba at the "Bay of Pigs." The expected assistance from the people of Cuba did not materialize. The whole venture was a fiasco, and one that enhanced Castro's prestige, united the Cuban people and stimulated anti-United States feeling throughout Latin America. The second crisis with Cuba came in October 1962, when it seemed for a week that the world was sliding over the brink into an all-out nuclear war. On October 22, President Kennedy announced that flights over Cuba had proved the Russians to be installing missiles and bases there capable of launching an atomic attack on the United States. He then instituted a naval blockade of the island designed to prevent the arrival of further weapons from Russia, and from the Organization of American States secured a unanimous vote supporting him. The world seemed to hold its breath waiting to see if there would be violent contact between Russian and American ships. But the Soviet vessels drew back. There were complicated negotiations involving exchanges of letters between Khrushchev and Kennedy and interchanges between the Secretary-General of the United Nations, U Thant, and Castro. At length, it became clear that without consulting Castro, Khrushchev was going to withdraw the missiles. On November 2, President Kennedy announced that the Cuban bases were being dismantled. Six days later he reported that Soviet ships were actually taking away the missiles. Thus by

restrained firmness on the part of the United States, disaster had been avoided. But it was clear that if Khrushchev had not yielded, President Kennedy would have felt compelled to use armed force to liquidate the threat from Cuba. During the crisis, the United States had offered to guarantee the territorial integrity of Cuba if adequate inspection and controls were set up by the United Nations or otherwise. Since Castro would not agree to such inspection, the United States continued aerial surveillance of the island.

If there were divisions and troubles in the Western Hemisphere, there was also some effort, outside Cuba, to improve communication and increase coöperation. There was a definite tendency for most of the Latin American nations most of the time to follow the lead of the United States in crucial votes in the United Nations, but if these states were eager for American loans and economic support they were also alert to resist any symptoms of "Yankee imperialism" or "dollar diplomacy." And there was in some of the countries an increasing, even threatening, amount of Communist infiltration and propaganda.

There were certian formal developments of note. As far back as 1890, the Pan-American Union had been created and occasional Inter-American Conferences had been held. The ninth such conference was opened at Bogotá, Colombia, in March 1948. Though it was interrupted by a local political outbreak, fostered by Communists and involving bloody riots, it transformed the Pan-American Union into the "Organization of American States" dedicated to the peaceful settlement of controversies among members, mutual support against aggression, non-intervention in each other's domestic affairs, and opposition to totalitarianism. These principles, especially non-intervention, had already been enshrined in the Treaty of Rio de Janeiro in 1947. The tenth conference took place six years later (1954) at Caracas in Venezuela, with all members represented except Costa Rica. The American Secretary of State Dulles spent most of his effort securing the passage of an anti-Communist resolution, which was eventually adopted by a vote of seventeen to one (Guatemala opposing, Mexico and Argentina abstaining).

Guatemala's vote on the Dulles resolution of 1954 reflected the growing influence of Communism on the government of that country's president, Jacobo Arbenz Guzman. In June of the same year Guatemala was "invaded" from Honduras by anti-Communist military forces, armed largely from the United States. In the event, the anti-Communist forces were triumphant within ten days. Arbenz fled and was eventually replaced in the presidency by Carlos Castillo Armas, an army officer, who outlawed Communism and promised democratic government.

In 1956, at a meeting in Panama, the heads of nineteen American states drew up and signed a declaration of principles for the Organization of American States, including mutual help and non-intervention. In 1960, the Organization of American States condemned the Dominican Republic for supporting a plot to assassinate the president of Venezuela and also took a stand against the attempt of China and Russia to inject themselves into the affairs of the Americas. Various efforts by member nations of the Organization of American States to mediate between the United States and Cuba were unsuccessful. But the whole Castro situation so focussed the attention of the United States on the Latin American nations that President Eisenhower approved a plan involving a half a billion dollar program of economic and other aid to them. In his inaugural address and early press conferences President Kennedy in 1961 indicated that he would go forward vigorously with that program, and this he did, for in August of 1961 at a conference in Punta del Este (Uruguay), the United States launched the Alliance for Progress. This was a plan for coöperation in the economic development and social betterment of Latin America. Under it the United States, for the next decade, pledged ten billion dollars in aid, to be partially matched by the Latin American nations, themselves, which also promised to push internal reforms in spheres such as landownership, taxation and education. In the three fiscal years 1963–1965, the United States actually committed almost four billion dollars in aid under the Alliance for Progress. By 1965, when, at another meeting in Rio de Janeiro, the American Secretary of State, Dean Rusk,

pledged the continuance of the Alliance beyond 1971, considerable progress in many Latin American lands was visible in the fields of housing, education and economic development. But the full effect of American help was often hampered by persistent trade deficits in the recipient countries and by political instability, inflation and the slow pace of reform in matters like taxation. American aid actually reached the figure of a billion dollars a year or more. It came in many guises, such as loans, grants and technical assistance from AID; loans from the Inter-American Bank and its Social Progress Trust Fund; the World Bank (International Bank for Reconstruction and Development) and its International Finance Corporation, and the International Monetary Fund. Some of these sources were international; but the United States provided a major part of the money in most cases. The United States also gave or loaned vast quantities of excess agricultural products under Public Law 480, which at the same time reduced surpluses at home, and abroad provided school lunches and fed millions of hungry people. When President Kennedy visited Venezuela, Colombia (1961) and Mexico (1962), he was hailed with spontaneous and overwhelming enthusiasm in vivid contrast to the rough treatment accorded Vice-President Nixon in Peru and Venezuela in 1958. To the Latin-Americans, Kennedy seemed a symbol of youth, hope and peace.

There were other crises that shook the O.A.S. One came in January 1964 in Panama, where there had long been agitation for the revision of the Canal Treaty with the United States, so as to secure more clearly defined sovereignty and greater income. The trouble started when some American students defied regulations and hoisted the stars and stripes at their high school in the Canal Zone. But it quickly assumed alarming and bloody proportions as Panamanian mobs attacked the zone. Twenty-five people (including four U.S. soldiers) were killed before order was restored, and it was some weeks before negotiations among Panama, the United States and the O.A.S. resulted in agreements which led to discussions on the revision of the treaty. Though impartial investigations later exonerated the United States of the charge of using undue military force against the crowds, the whole episode left unpleasant memories in Latin America.

More serious and more prolonged was the crisis in the Dominican Republic. That country had been in an unstable condition after the death of the dictator Trujillo in 1961. Elections in 1963 had brought to the presidency a liberal intellectual, Juan Bosch. But he was ousted in the same year by the military, who replaced him by a civilian junta. Troubles within the junta and opposition within the nation led, in April 1965, to a revolution in which the military were opposed by leftish elements and by supporters of Bosch. The military controlled most of the country. Their opponents held a section of Santo Domingo, the capital city. When the fighting became serious and bloody, and when it seemed to President Johnson that Castro-type Communists might gain power, he sent in American troops to restore order. Though he later secured O.A.S. support and Brazil supplied soldiers for the occupation, President Johnson was widely accused in Latin America of having resorted to old-style, unilateral intervention. Nonetheless, internal peace was gradually restored, a compromise government was installed, and elections were held in 1966.

In face of all the problems it confronted, the O.A.S. continued to function with some effect in settling disputes and encouraging coöperation. At a meeting of the O.A.S. foreign ministers in Rio de Janeiro in November 1965, the suggestion of an Inter-American Peace Force to intervene in situations like that of the Dominican Republic did not receive enough support to be carried forward. It looked too much like intervention. But steps were taken to strengthen the O.A.S. organizationally and to provide for more frequent high-level meetings. Meanwhile the Economic Commission for Latin America (ECLA), an organ of the United Nations, was facilitating coöperation in the economic sphere. The Central American Common Market (El Salvador, Guatemala, Nicaragua, Honduras, Costa Rica) made considerable progress in production, economic integration, and also in education. The Latin American Free Trade Association (LAFTA), which included the South American countries (plus Mexico and minus Venezuela) and which likewise aimed at integration, moved forward more slowly. Despite all the plans, all the effort, all the organizations, and all the outside help, it was clear that the goal of prosperity and stability for Latin America would be attained only through a long and arduous struggle.

Though not even a member of the O.A.S., Canada was a factor of increasing importance in the Western Hemisphere and in the world. During the years after World War II, it entered upon a period of remarkable growth and prosperity. Its population rose from fourteen million in 1951 to almost twenty million in 1966, it had one of the highest standards of living in the world, and it made a sustained and successful effort to enlarge and improve its secondary and higher education. Canada's proximity to the United States brought to it much American capital which speeded the development of its rich resources in minerals, oil, gas, water power and timber. It was the best customer of the United States, and the United States was its best customer. Many Canadians were, indeed, irked by their country's economic (and some thought cultural) dependence on its neighbor to the south; but coöperation between the two nations, in defense and other matters, was close and usually friendly. In 1957 Canada had been ruled for twenty-two years by its Liberal Party, though the veteran prime minister, Mackenzie King, had been replaced in 1948 by L. S. St. Laurent. The long reign was ended by a victory of the Progressive Conservatives under J. G. Diefenbaker, which was resoundingly confirmed by new elections in 1958. Diefenbaker, however, in the long run was unable to consolidate his support and the Liberals returned to power in 1963, though with only a plurality of seats in the House of Commons. The new prime minister, Lester B. Pearson, strove to turn the plurality into a majority by elections in 1965, but failed to do so. A persistent problem remained the agitation for more cultural, linguistic, and even economic autonomy by the French-speaking population of Quebec.

G. West European Coöperation

If there were signs of growing coöperation as well as troubles in the Americas, there was an even more marked drawing together of the nations of Western Europe for peaceful purposes as well as to resist the Russian threat. In addition to the various efforts, discussed above, to coördinate the military strength of the democracies—NATO, and the Western European Union [1]—several organizations were set up to exploit American aid under the Marshall Plan coöperatively and to improve economic conditions in the countries involved. The Organization for European Economic Coöperation, with headquarters in Paris, worked closely with corresponding American agencies. Its success was evident in the rapid rise of industrial, mineral, and power output, the increased agricultural production, and declining unemployment in Western Europe after 1948. Similar coöperation through the European Payments Union eased the problems of international payment for goods and stimulated the flow of trade.

More significant, perhaps, was the "Schuman Plan," put forward by a French foreign minister, Robert Schuman, in 1951 and effective in 1953.[2] Under this plan, embodied in a fifty-year treaty among Belgium, France, Italy, Luxembourg, Netherlands, and West Germany, there was created a "European Coal and Steel Community." Its object was to stimulate and regulate the production of coal and steel and to set up a unified market for these products in the countries involved, by eliminating tariffs, quotas, subsidies, and other restrictive practices. The Community is administered by a High Authority of nine members, chosen by the respective countries but with not more than two coming from any one country. The Authority makes decisions by a majority vote and can enforce them by fines. It is empowered to take almost any action in its sphere of influence—the production and distribution of coal and steel. Thus the nations involved gave up a considerable degree of sovereignty over a vital industrial area for the sake of integrating production, so long hampered by the national boundaries which cut across the veins of coal and iron ore.

The Council of Europe, established in 1949, had more sweeping objectives, but was able to accomplish less than the Schuman Plan. Because its membership overlapped so much with NATO, it excluded defense from its spheres of interest and left military coördination to SHAPE (Supreme Headquarters Allied Powers Europe) near Paris. It was supposed to seek greater political unity and economic and social progress. It operated through a Council of Ministers and a Consultative Assembly. From its first meeting at Strasbourg (August 1949) the Assembly seemed to many to foreshadow a parliament of the "United States of Europe" which might some day come into being, for it included representatives from almost all the countries of western Europe.

For its seventeen members (Austria, Belgium, Cyprus, Denmark, France, West Germany, Great Britain, Greece, Iceland, Ireland, Italy, Luxembourg, Netherlands, Norway, Sweden, Switzerland, Turkey) the the Council of Europe serves much the same purpose as does the Organization of American States for the American republics. It maintains contacts with UNESCO and other international organizations. It established a Court of Human Rights in 1959 to uphold the Human Rights Convention to which all its members save France had adhered. Since individual citizens of some of the countries can appeal directly to the Court, it is, like the Council, a supra-national entity. In addition to this convention, the Council has adopted more than thirty others dealing with matters of international concern from automobiles to university students. Though the Council has elaborated a constitution for eventual union and has promoted discussion of topics having to do with European coöperation, it has remained important chiefly as a sketchy embodiment of the dream of unity.

Much more significant has been the thrust toward greater economic coöperation. Out of the Marshall Plan and the developments it engendered grew the Organization for European Economic Coöperation (OEEC) which included all the European countries outside the Communist sphere save Finland, and with which the United States, Canada, and Yugoslavia are associated. The OEEC worked in various matters through offshoot organizations such as the European Nuclear Energy Agency, the European Productivity Agency, the

---

[1] See above, p. 814.

[2] See his picture, above, p. 805.

From an Office Window. By C. R. W. Nevinson.

European Monetary Agreement (which in 1958 superseded the European Payments Union), and the European Conference of Ministers of Transport. The OEEC was governed by a Council with a representative from each member nation. Its decisions were binding but had to be unanimous. During 1960 a treaty was negotiated which had the effect of replacing the OEEC with a new body, the Organization for Economic Coöperation and Development. But OECD differs from OEEC chiefly because the United States and Canada are included as full members rather than as associates. The treaty was ratified by the United States early in 1961.

The formation of the European Coal and Steel Community led to increases in production. Steel output rose from 42 million metric tons in 1952 to about 81 million in 1964. Investment and research increased, unprofitable coal mines in Belgium were closed down, and arrangements were made so that displaced laborers could cross international boundaries. It was the success of the European Coal and Steel Community that led to a further and even more important step toward the economic unity of western Europe. Under the leadership of Paul Henri Spaak of Belgium and after several conferences, the Treaty of Rome creating the Common Market was drawn up and signed in 1957 and went into effect at the start of the next year.

The Common Market (or European Economic Community) consists of six nations—France, West Germany, Italy, Belgium, the Netherlands, and Luxembourg. By the treaty they agreed to a progressive reduction of tariffs among themselves and a gradual movement toward conformity in their external tariffs and internal social and economic legislation. By 1966, successive cuts in import duties had lowered tariffs within the Common Market to twenty per cent of the 1957 level, and trade among the members had increased by more than one hundred and sixty per cent in the same period. When the process is complete in 1970, the six countries will form a free trade

General Carlos Romulo of the Philippines addressing the United Nations General Assembly after his election as its president, Sept. 20, 1949. At his left is Trygve Lie, U.N. Secretary-General.

Courtesy Wide World Photos

area and an economic unit. Greece became an associate member in 1962, as did Turkey two years later. The Common Market also entered into trade agreements with Israel (1962) and Lebanon (1965). The Common Market Commission administers the treaty, reports to the Council of Ministers of the EEC, and works with the Coal-Steel High Authority. Arrangements were made to associate eighteen African countries with the Common Market and to provide funds for their economic growth (through a Development Fund) as well as for investment in the home countries (through a European Investment Bank). A Court of Justice was created to handle disputes and enforce decisions. Thus in the economic sphere the EEC represents a truly supra-national body and a real step toward unity in western Europe. The Treaty of Rome created, moreover, for its six signatories the European Atomic Energy Community (Euratom). This organization conducts research, maintains a common market for nuclear materials, and seeks to develop atomic power.

From the start, Great Britain was torn by a desire to belong to the Common Market and a fear lest membership in it would impair its economic relationships with the overseas nations of the British Commonwealth. After much hesitation and negotiation, the British decided at first to stay out and, as a counterweight to the Common Market, they formed in 1960 the European Free Trade Area, often referred to as the "Outer Seven" in contrast to the "Inner Six." EFTA was composed of Great Britain, Denmark, Norway, Sweden, Switzerland, Austria, and Portugal. It has a looser organization than the EEC and fewer supra-national features. But it, too, aims at a gradual reduction in tariffs and the creation of a free trade area. By the end of 1964, intra-EFTA tariffs had been reduced by seventy per cent and trade within the group had increased eighty-five per cent since 1958. The Seven emerged from World War II in somewhat better economic condition than the Six. The Six, however, have been developing faster since the mid-1950's than the Seven. Indeed, the spectacular increase in prosperity, production and per capita income within the EEC has offered a shining example of the fruits of economic coöperation and has illustrated the advantages of large markets as against small ones in the modern world of mass production. But both the progress of the Common Market and the trend toward European unity were checked by the nationalistic attitude of General De Gaulle. When, in 1962–1963, Prime Minister Macmillan reversed his country's former policy and sought for it admission to the EEC (despite protests from the Commonwealth), De Gaulle vetoed this proposal and kept Great Britain out. That many of the French favored a strengthening of the Common Market and disapproved of their president's opposition to greater European political and economic unity was indicated by the surprising num-ber of votes against De Gaulle in the preliminary and run-off elections of December 1965.

De Gaulle's policies were not the only evidence of persistent nationalism in the economic sphere. As far back as 1947, there had been established the General Agreement on Tariffs and Trade (GATT) designed to reduce import duties and remove barriers to commerce. The original twenty-three nations had grown to sixty-four by 1965, with thirteen others participating in one way or another. President Kennedy had sought through GATT to bring about drastic reductions in tariffs and other trade barriers. But when, after his death, the "Kennedy Round" of negotiations actually got under way in 1964, selfish national interests slowed progress to a snail's pace and limited the extent and nature of the tariff reductions.

CHAPTER 63

REACTION AGAINST WESTERN IMPERIALISM AND

Emergence of Free Nations throughout the World

A. General Factors

The war from 1939 to 1945 was more truly a *world* war than its predecessor from 1914 to 1918 and its effects were deeper and more widespread. World War I had been primarily a European struggle with only incidental campaigning in Asia and Africa; and the chief change it had wrought outside of Europe was merely the transfer of German colonies and Turkish dependencies to the victorious powers. The break-up of the Austrian, Russian, and Ottoman empires and the recognition, in the European peace-settlement of 1919–1920, of the principle of national self-determination had indeed stimulated nationalistic movements in the Near East and the Far East, especially among Turks, Arabs, Persians, Indians, and Chinese. But until World War II, the Western powers had retained enough strength and prestige to maintain their overseas imperial sway with only minor concessions to native nationalism.

World War II was quite another story. The nationalism of peoples previously subject to Western imperial rule was immensely stimulated by the ease with which

Asiatic Japan ousted the French from Indo-China, the British from Malaya and Burma, the Dutch from Indonesia, and the Americans from the Philippines, all accompanied by the slogan "Asia for the Asians" and by the establishment of native, though puppet, governments. Nor did the eventual defeat of Japan profit the former imperial powers, since the United States, which was clearly the major factor in the victory, was reacting strongly against imperialism, and since France, Britain, and the Netherlands were too weak and distracted to make a major effort to repress the persistent and militant demands of their colonial subjects for national independence.

These demands were encouraged, moreover, when the United States fulfilled its earlier promise and recognized the Philippines as an independent republic on July 4, 1946. Assisted by economic, financial, and military aid from the United States, the Philippine government, under successive presidents—Manuel Roxas, Elpidio Quirino, Ramón Magsaysay, Carlos Garcia, and Ferdinand Marcos—made progress in the rehabilitation of the country and the suppression of the Communist-inspired guerrilla bands, the so-called "Huks." In for-

835

eign affairs, the Philippines, being culturally the most "Wsetern" of Asiatic countries, coöperated with the Western democracies.

Other factors, too, were at work to alter the non-European world and to liquidate the overseas empires of the Western nations. One was the matter of race or color. It happened that the European imperial nations were all composed of white people, whereas their colonies and dominions in Asia and Africa were the home of colored races, black, brown, and yellow. Many countries in Latin America, too, had populations largely or partly of American Indian or Negro blood. "Color bars," by which natives were excluded from white clubs, shops, and hotels, had been common particularly in the British colonies, and the conscious superiority with which the "sahib" treated the people he ruled had galled the pride of the indigenous populations. The Japanese, moreover, had, during World War II, made much of the fact that they were ousting the whites from the areas they had long been exploiting. The French, it is true, had no "color bar" and tended to treat colonials as equals if they had learned to speak and read French and had absorbed French "civilization." It was similar with the Portuguese. But opportunities to be "assimilated" were very limited for Asians and Africans.

Working in the same direction was what has been called the "revolution of expectations." During World War II, the native populations of Africa, Asia, and Oceania were introduced to modern technology as well as modern weapons. Melanesians learned to drive jeeps and Tunisian Arabs to service airplanes. The improvements in communications and the development of mass media (picture magazines, radio, comic books, television) made Asians and Africans vividly aware of the standard of living of the peoples of the industrialized countries. And the way the European and American soldiers lived, ate, dressed, and used machines on bases throughout the world was a telling reiteration of what the mass media taught. Sensing that other ways of life were possible and that disease, hunger, and poverty were not a necessary constant accompaniment of human existence, the peoples of the underdeveloped

countries became eager for rapid improvement of their lot. To almost all of them it seemed that the first step toward such improvement was national independence.

The "cold war" added difficulties to the post-war situation outside of Europe and often lent them a special urgency. Part of the Marxist doctrines of the Communists dealt with imperialism and held that it was the last stage of "monopoly capitalism" when capitalist countries, having exhausted their home markets, turned to exploit peoples overseas and to fight over the loot. The theory was demonstrably untrue, for it could be shown that the home markets of the industrialized countries continued to grow in importance and that the colonies almost invariably cost more than they yielded. It was clear, moreover, that the new imperialists were the Communists themselves, for Russia was ringing itself with satellite states and keeping them under iron control, while China was expanding into North Korea, Tibet, and North Vietnam.

Nonetheless, the Marxist ideas constituted an easy explanation for past ills and put the blame for the backwardness of the underdeveloped countries on the Western colonial powers. The Communist propaganda spoke in appealing terms of "social justice," "economic democracy," the "overthrow of capitalism," and the "establishment of socialism." And Moscow-trained Communists were available to provide leadership to subversive movements in every new nation. In addition, the Russians had an appealing story to tell. They had been a backward and exploited people until 1917. They had made themselves into a great industrial and military power by adopting Communism. They stood ready, in the name of the brotherhood of all workers, to help the emerging countries travel the same road. Russia was, in fact, almost always seeking to strengthen itself by any available means. Russian policy was intensely nationalistic and imperialist. But the siren song of its propaganda sounded sweet to peoples emerging from colonialism. Despite the efforts of the Western nations, the economic aid they gave, and their counter-propaganda for real democracy and freedom, the Communists scored successes from Indonesia to Cuba.

Thus the world picture as it took shape

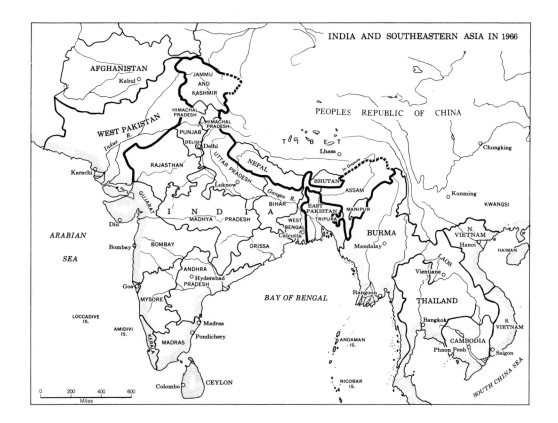

in the post-war years from the East to the West Indies was in some respects clear. Western imperialism, which had begun in the sixteenth century and waned in the early nineteenth century, but which had revived with renewed vigor from 1875 to 1914, was disappearing. Subject peoples were gaining nationhood. The former imperial powers were increasingly reluctant to use force to quell native agitation or uprisings. Nationalism was triumphant in Asia and Africa. The remnants of the old colonial empires seemed definitely outdated. The "colonial revolution," one of the great, epoch-making movements of modern times, was substantially complete by 1966, when even tiny colonies like Gambia (with a population of less than 325,000), the Maldive Islands (about 100,000 people), and Mauritania (about 770,000) had become independent nations. As one new country after another joined the United Nations the problems before it became increasingly those of encouraging the economic and social development of the peoples who were securing independence and nationhood.

B. India and Southeastern Asia

Winston Churchill had said, during the war, that he did not purpose to preside over the dissolution of the British Empire. But during the immediate post-war years almost all of Britain's huge Asiatic possessions obtained independence. The Labor government then in office was neither minded nor able to repress by force the native people bent on securing national freedom. For example, nationalist movements throughout India now reached such intensity as to induce the British Parliament to enact an Indian Independence Act, which became effective in August 1947. This did not provide for a united India, but, recognizing the profound religious differences and prejudices between Hindus and Moslems, it set up two states: (1) Pakistan, chiefly Moslem, consisting of two separate parts in the northeast and northwest of the peninsula, comprising together 365,000 square miles and a population of about 100 million by 1966; and (2)

Federal India, mainly Hindu, covering the much larger remainder, with 1,250,000 square miles and about 450 million inhabitants in 1966. Both states accepted a merely nominal membership in the British Commonwealth, and Federal India loosened even this tie by adopting, in 1950, a constitution which rejected the Crown and proclaimed a Republic.

Both States had very serious domestic problems. India under the leader of its dominant Congress Party, Jawaharlal Nehru, strove to operate politically as a democracy, and to cope with grave economic and social conditions and with an extremely low standard of living and a very high degree of popular illiteracy. Pakistan, under Mohammed Ali Jinnah and his successors in leadership of the Moslem League and of the country, had to face similar difficulties and, in addition, that of administering two widely separated regions.

To add to their troubles, Pakistan and India engaged in disputes (sometimes accompanied by bloodshed on both sides) over boundaries between them, over which should gain posession of the mountainous territory of Kashmir, and over tariffs and other economic matters. While in foreign policy Pakistan leaned toward the West, India under Nehru attempted to maintain a "neutralist" position between the Communist and the democratic powers. Nehru succeeded in getting France to surrender the few coastal trading posts it had retained since the destruction of its Indian empire in the eighteenth century.[1] Portugal, however, was less compliant, and only at the end of 1961, and then only after armed Indian attacks, did it surrender its small sixteenth-century enclaves (including Goa).

In making India into a strong and united nation, Nehru and the Congress Party faced a most difficult problem because of the historic local divisions of the country. To a degree a solution was found by adopting a federal system, with many spheres of activity (such as agriculture, public order, education, and health) reserved to the fifteen states and six union territories. More difficult was the language situation. In Europe, over the centuries,

language boundaries had come to coincide more or less with national boundaries and language had become an important element in national patriotism. But within India itself, the 1951 census listed 845 languages or dialects. Moreover, these languages belong to three quite different linguistic families—Indo-European (including Hindi, Bengali, Bihari, Marathi, Gujerati, and Urdu), Dravidian (including Tamil and Telegu), and Munda (with ten different dialects). Of these, Hindi, with Urdu, is spoken by about forty-five per cent of the population, and Hindi has been proclaimed the "official" language of India, though English continues to be used for all official purposes, including speeches in Parliament, and is in fact the only medium through which many Indians can communicate with each other. It was hoped that through mass schooling Hindi might become the national language and English be relegated to a secondary role. But attempts to enforce the official use of Hindi after 1964 led to strikes and riots, and the use of English was continued.

In 1958, following much disputing and rioting among the linguistic groups, India's political map was redrawn so that the majority of the population in each of the states would speak, if not a single language, at least closely related dialects. Exceptions were made for Bombay and Punjab. Rioting continued in the former between the nineteen million people speaking Gujerati and the thirty million speaking Marathi, until finally in 1960 Bombay had to be split into the two states of Maharashtra and Gujerat. In Punjab demands for separate statehood grew louder from the religiously separate Sikhs. Thus in some senses India is not a national state on the European model but a federated empire of national states, held together by ties of history, religion, a common colonial past, and a common means of communication for the educated—the English language.

The basic domestic problems confronting Nehru as the Prime Minister of the second most populous nation on earth had to do with administration, industry, agriculture, education, and health. In all these fields, though the difficulties were immense, impressive progress was made. India had inherited from the British a well-organized

---

[1] See above, p. 474.

Prime Ministers Harold Macmillan of Britain and Jawaharlal Nehru of India, 1961.

Courtesy Wide World Photos

administration and trained Indians to man it. But use was also made of British and other foreign experts hired to perform special functions. Much of the industry of the country was nationalized, though a considerable private sector existed. Under successive five-year plans (the fourth began in 1966) the government sought to develop the country's productivity by controlling foreign exchange, by regulating imports and exports, and by investing heavily in new factories and mines. In this task it was aided by loans and grants from the United States, Britain, and Russia. In agriculture, too, there was considerable advance. Old crops were improved, new ones were introduced, better techniques of cultivation were employed, and large-scale irrigation projects were inaugurated. But after twenty years of independence, the per capita annual income of the Indian citizen was far less than the monthly income of an inhabitant of the British Isles. The population increase each year, moreover, tended to eat up the added foodstuffs produced and to hold down the rise of per capita income. Indeed, even in good years India had to import quantities of food, and in bad years the imports became massive. Much of the needed wheat and rice was secured from the United States under the foreign aid and Food for Peace programs. Up to 1966, India had thus received more than two and a half billion dollars'

worth of foodstuffs. In 1964, for example, India got some fifteen per cent of the United States wheat crop.

Though Nehru always claimed to support non-violence in the tradition of Gandhi, he was not above using force for nationalist ends. In the face of pressure from the United States, Great Britain, and other countries, he sent in troops in 1961 to take over the tiny Portuguese colonies (left over from the sixteenth century) of Goa, Daman, and Diu. Internally the Congress party remained in firm control, though there was a vociferous minority of Communists on the left and some small-scale opposition from the right as well. In foreign affairs Nehru sought to maintain a "neutralist" position and to align himself with neither side in the "cold war." But, perhaps because he had been much influenced by Marxism, he in general seemed more critical of the Western powers than of the Communists down to 1956. The evidence of the ruthlessness of Russian imperialism in that year in the case of Hungary had considerable influence on the Indian leaders, and their doubts about Communism were reënforced by China's complete control of Tibet after 1959. In 1962, the threat on the northern mountain frontier became much more serious when Chinese troops invaded India at various points and defeated the Indian defending forces. Nehru rallied his people and secured arms from both Great Britain and the United States. Suddenly, after ten weeks of sporadic fighting, Peking announced a withdrawal and a cease-fire. But the border situation remained ominous and unstable.

In May of 1964, Nehru died at the age of 74, and all India was plunged into mourning. As a great, popular, national hero, Nehru could not be replaced, but he was succeeded as prime minister by one of his quietly able supporters, Lal Bahadur Shastri. The very next year Shastri was confronted by a mounting crisis that quickly turned into a war. It arose over Kashmir (technically Jammu and Kashmir), a mountain state in the north, between India and Pakistan, with a population predominantly Moslem, but with an hereditary ruler who was Hindu. Immediately after they secured their independence in 1947, India and Pakistan began to dispute the possession of Kashmir. Fighting occurred and was stopped only by the intervention of the United Nations. A cease-fire line was established which gave most of the territory to India. Both sides agreed to a plebiscite when conditions should permit. Thereafter, Pakistan appealed repeatedly to the United Nations to arrange such a plebiscite, while India gradually came to take the position that Kashmir was permanently and definitively part of India. In 1965, Pakistan began to support various subversive movements in Indian-held Kashmir and sent in "infiltrators." Full-scale fighting broke out in August, not only in Kashmir but at other points on the India-Pakistan frontier. Both governments roused their people to patriotic frenzy and both launched major attacks with tanks and planes. Great Britain and the United States withheld aid from both sides and with Russian support sought to stop the conflict. China, siding definitely with Pakistan (with which it had been maintaining increasingly cordial relations since 1962), threatened India from the north. After some weeks of inconclusive struggle—in which both sides claimed victories—and after the intervention of the Secretary-General of the United Nations, U Thant, a cease-fire was agreed to. But skirmishes and forays continued in Kashmir and along the border. Finally, early in 1966, President Ayub of Pakistan and Premier Shastri of India met in Tashkent in the Soviet Union with the Russian premier,

Kosygin, acting as mediator. After days of negotiation an agreement was reached by which both countries undertook to withdraw their troops to the positions held before the fighting started and to recognize their obligation under the United Nations charter to settle all disputes peacefully. Dramatically, Shastri died of a heart attack the night after the end of the meeting. He left the Kashmir question with no definitive solution yet in sight. His successor was Mrs. Indira Gandhi, Nehru's daughter, who despite economic difficulties and threatened famine quickly showed herself to be a capable political leader.

In addition to the awkwardness created for Pakistan by the fact that it consisted of two distinct territorial units separated by nearly a thousand miles and united mainly by a common devotion to the Moslem religion, there were other difficulties that arose from the scanty resources of West Pakistan and the fact that the Moslem inhabitants had been little given to commerce and industry. The death of Mohammed Ali Jinnah in 1948 left Pakistan without a leader of the stature and popularity of Nehru. Not until 1956 was it possible to adopt a constitution, and its effectiveness was short-lived. Growing economic problems, corruption in government at all levels, the failure of outside aid from the United States to raise the standard of living very much, and increasing popular unrest all led to a situation in October 1958 in which the president, Iskander Mirza, felt compelled to suspend the constitution and oust the cabinet. Within a few weeks the government was turned over to General Mohammed Ayub Khan, who ruled firmly but with the avowed intention of educating the country toward democratic, constitutional government. In 1959 a new "four-level" political system was announced with a good deal of democracy in the villages and more indirect rule above. In 1960 Ayub Khan was elected president. Under him a drastic land reform was promulgated, other reforms in finance, law, education, and economic matters were inaugurated, and a moderately democratic constitution was established (1962). Under two successive five-year plans (ending in 1965) and with much financial and technical assistance from the United States, agricultural production, industrial output and national income increased notably. But economic progress was compromised by developments in foreign affairs. Fear of conflict with India led to excessive military expenditures and to a rapprochement with Communist China, which in turn led to a decrease in financial and military aid from the United States. The actual war with India in 1965 diverted attention and resources from the crying economic and social needs of the country.

Like India and Pakistan, the other former British colonies of Southeast Asia gained independence after World War II. Burma and Ceylon were freed in 1947 and organized new governments along democratic lines the next year. Burma became an independent republic, while Ceylon chose to remain within the British Commonwealth, though it gradually restricted British influence and even forced the British to give up their naval base at Trincomalee. In 1960, a woman, Mrs. Sirimavo Bandaranaike, the widow of the former premier who had been assassinated, became prime minister. Burma was harassed by internal conflicts and fell under military rule from 1958 to 1960 and again after 1962. Both countries externally developed friendly relations with the Communist nations and internally displayed a trend toward socialism, a trend that seemed checked, temporarily at least, in Ceylon by the defeat of Mrs. Bandaranaike's government in the elections of March 1965.

For the Federation of Malaya, independence was somewhat more delayed, partly because of the racial divisions within its territories, and partly because of a long drawn out struggle against Communist guerrillas. But in 1957 it became a limited constitutional monarchy under its own Paramount Ruler. Singapore, with a population of more than a million and a half, at first was a state within the Federation. It became self-governing in 1959 and an independent nation in 1965, because the predominance of Chinese within its population made coöperation with the other, more Malayan states increasingly difficult. In 1963 the Federation was joined by the former British colonies of Sabah (previously North Borneo) and Sarawak and changed its name to Malaysia. The tiny oil-rich colony of Brumei, enclaved in Sarawak, remained out-side the enlarged Federation. From the start, President Sukarno of Indonesia opposed the formation of Malaysia and harassed Sabah and Sarawak by armed border raids. Malaysia has a population of some nine million people, a third of them Chinese.

In the Pacific Ocean the major British countries, Australia and New Zealand, retained their position in the Commonwealth with no thought of any other course since they had long since won complete self-government and were bound to Britain by economic ties as well as by sentiment. New Zealand, for example, continued to send more than half its exports to, and to get more than half its imports from, the mother country, which was also the leading customer and supplier of Australia. Both countries associated themselves with the United States through a defense pact called ANZUS (Australia, New Zealand, United States) and through SEATO. Australia was ruled after 1949 by a Liberal-Country party coalition under Robert Gordon Menzies as prime minister until he was replaced in 1966 by his treasurer, Harold Holt. In the elections of 1958 and 1963, it again won a substantial majority in the federal House of Representatives. During the years after the war, Australia made rapid progress in industrial production, in part perhaps because it modified its immigration policy and welcomed immigrants, especially from the British empire. Between 1945 and 1966 some two million new settlers arrived and the total population of Australia rose to over eleven million. The standard of living in Australia compared very favorably with that of the most advanced countries.

New Zealand was likewise prosperous, though it remained predominantly agricultural. Dairy production has become more important in recent years, but the major export items, meat and wool, are still derived from sheep-raising. The original Polynesian inhabitants (the Maoris) of the islands, who constitute seven per cent of the population of about two and a half million, have full citizenship. Some of them have served in Parliament and have held important official positions. Even more than Australia, New Zealand is notable for an elaborate system of social security protecting the people from problems of illness, unemployment, accident, and old age. The

Labor party which had been responsible for much of the social legislation won a slender majority in the one-house legislature in the elections of 1957, but lost to the more conservative Nationalists in 1961 and again in 1963.

Thailand (formerly Siam) shook off Japanese rule in 1945, signed a treaty of friendship with Britain and India the next year, and set about coping with internal difficulties. The troubles were serious and were punctuated by assassinations and *coups*. Though technically a limited monarchy operating under an interim constitution (of 1959), Thailand is actually under control of the military and is periodically disturbed by their intrigues and by scandals affecting them.

The Far Eastern empires of the Dutch and of the French were liquidated more definitively and less smoothly than that of the British. In Indonesia, native nationalism, stimulated by the Japanese occupation, became militant in Java. In August, 1945, nationalists led by Achmed Sukarno seized power from the Japanese and proclaimed the "Republic of Indonesia" with its center in Jakarta (the former Batavia) and with a claim of sovereignty over Sumatra and Madura as well as Java. The next year another nationalist government, with its capital at Macassar, was set up for East Indonesia—Celebes, the Moluccas, and the Lesser Surdas. The Dutch sought to oppose these developments with armed force, and at one point (1948) captured the Republican leaders including Sukarno. Meanwhile the United Nations had intervened, and in 1949 the Security Council induced the government of the Netherlands to recognize the independence of a new Indonesian state including all the former Dutch territories except Dutch New Guinea. In 1950, the Republic of Indonesia became the sixtieth member of the United Nations.

Lack of trained leadership made the establishment of a stable government difficult; there was continued friction with the Netherlands over New Guinea; and the Indonesians in reacting against the old style colonial imperialism were gullible about accepting Communist ideas and leadership. Under Sukarno, who was elected president at the end of 1949, there were continuing economic and political diffi-

culties for the Indonesians who numbered nearly ninety million. There was even a serious revolt in 1952 with resistance continuing on Celebes until 1961. As president, Sukarno was, at various periods, sometimes more and sometimes less radical and sometimes more and sometimes less democratic. But he continued to work with the Communists and, after 1959, moved toward "guided democracy," which was his name for a quasi-dictatorship. He continued to stir up Indonesian nationalism by incessant demands that the Netherlands cede the western part of New Guinea which he called West Irian. This the Dutch refused to do until 1962, when, under pressure from the United Nations, they yielded the territory. It was administered for a few months by the United Nations, then turned over to Indonesia. Despite this victory, Sukarno's policy grew more and more pro-Communist and anti-Western. The British embassy was attacked by a mob (1963) and United States cultural centers were similarly wrecked (1964). Amidst deteriorating economic conditions, Sukarno adopted and pursued against the new nation Malaysia a policy of "confrontation" which included guerrilla-type raids on the Malayan mainland. In October 1965 the Indonesian army crushed a Communist Party attempt to take over the government by force. Under General Nasution (Minister of Defense), whom the Communists had tried to assassinate, military officers took control of the government, killed or imprisoned Communist leaders, and strove to liquidate the Party. But Sukarno remained in office because of his widespread popularity, though the new government reversed many of his policies. In mid-1966, it ended the difficulties with Malaysia and it showed itself more friendly to the United States and western European countries.

The French in Asia faced much the same problems as the Dutch in Indonesia. In 1946 they had reassumed control of their principal Asiatic colony, Indo-China, including the three states of Vietnam (formerly Annam), Laos, and Cambodia. But they at once confronted strong opposition in the north led by Ho Chi Minh, a Communist. Soon they were in open conflict with the Communist-led forces, called Vietminh. The French tried to cater to native nationalism by supporting the Vietnamese titular Emperor (Bao Dai) and according various degrees of autonomy to the three states. But they could not end the struggle with Ho Chi Minh, who created the "Democratic Republic of Vietminh"; and the war went on with the French making little progress and Vietminh, supported by China and Russia, gaining in strength. By 1954, defeats for the French, despite some aid from the United States, had cumulated to a point where they were willing to abandon Indo-China. This step was consummated under the leadership of the French premier Pierre Mendès-France. An accord was reached at Geneva by which Vietnam was divided into a northern part under Ho Chi Minh and Communist rule, and a southern part, which ousted Bao Dai, became a republic and was to some degree dependent on economic and military help from the United States. Under Ngo Dinh Diem as president, South Vietnam continued to be harried by Communist guerrillas (called Vietcong), as did the small neighboring kingdom of Laos. There, despite military support from the United States, the government of Laos was so ineffectual that Communist rebels, supported by North Vietnam and by Red China, made considerable progress during 1960 and became a subject of international negotiation in 1961. Cambodia declared itself an independent kingdom in 1953 and was admitted to the United Nations two years later.

Thus the story of the post-war years in Southeast Asia was one of the liquidation of the Western colonial empires, the emergence of new nations imbued with an intense nationalism not always grounded in history or cultural unity, and the intrusion of the cold war as the Communist powers sought for points where expansion of their dominance was possible and as the democratic countries attempted to check and contain this new imperialist advance.

Gradually this cold war turned hot. Cambodia remained "neutral" but coöperated more and more with North Vietnam, with Communist China, and with the Vietcong guerrillas in South Vietnam. Laos was torn by internal strife, and part of the country fell under control of Communists supported by North Vietnam. But it was in South Vietnam that a real war slowly developed. From 1955 on, President Eisenhower sent military advisers in considerable numbers to help train the South Vietnamese army and to assist it in suppressing the Vietcong. Under President Kennedy, aid in men and weapons was increased as the Vietcong gained control over more and more rural areas. In 1963, Ngo Dinh Diem was assassinated and was succeeded by a series of governments usually under military officers. Meanwhile the Vietcong, aided by a steady flow of men and supplies from North Vietnam, continued to make headway. Finally, in 1965, President Johnson committed United States troops to combat. By the end of that year, there were some two hundred thousand American soldiers, marines, and airmen in South Vietnam. American planes were bombing military targets in North Vietnam, American navy vessels were shelling shore points, hard fighting was going on in various parts of South Vietnam, and casualties were mounting rapidly. The United States repeatedly declared its willingness to negotiate. But North Vietnam, under Ho Chi Minh, would settle for nothing less than a withdrawal of United States forces and a triumph of the Vietcong and Communism in South Vietnam, while the United States was striving for an independent South Vietnam which would check the spread of Communism in southeast Asia. Attempt after attempt at mediation by various countries and by the United Nations failed before this impasse of conflicting aims. In many non-Communist nations, and even among some sections of opinion in the United States, there was criticism of American policy.

C. The Near and Middle East

In the post-war period, Egypt was the most important of the Arab nations. Its intense nationalism took an anti-British form, and from 1946 onward there were riots against the British and attempts to secure their withdrawal from the Suez Canal Zone.[1] In 1951, the government of King Farouk denounced the Anglo-Egyptian treaty of 1936, and the troubles grew more intense until much foreign property was destroyed in Cairo in January 1952. The

---

[1] See above, pp. 800–801.

U.S. infantrymen debark from helicopters in battle area of South Vietnam, December 1965.

Courtesy Wide World Photos

King attempted to ease the situation, but he was ousted in July by a group of nationalist army officers under General Naguib, who seized control of the government and in 1953 made Egypt a republic. The next year Naguib was replaced as premier by another officer, Gamal Abdel Nasser, under whom an agreement was reached with Britain for the evacuation of the Suez Canal Zone. Meanwhile Britain and Egypt were disputing also over the status of the jointly ruled Sudan. In 1953 agreement was reached to establish self-government in the Sudan and after three years to let the Sudanese decide their political future. In 1956, after a plebiscite, the Sudan was proclaimed independent. It fell under the military rule of General Abboud for a while (1958–1964), and it was troubled by risings of its southern Negro tribes who objected to the dominance of the northern Arabs.

Meanwhile, Nasser had become more or less a dictator as well as a vehement nationalist. Not only was he the leader of the sole political party, that of National Union, but also he was elected President of Egypt in 1956. Nasser preached pan-Arab nationalism and sent his emissaries throughout the Arab lands, with such effect that in 1958 Syria, through geographically separated from Egypt by Israel and Jordan, joined it to form the United Arab Republic. Both the Southern Region (Egypt) and the Northern Region (Syria) retained some separate features. There was, for example, a flag for each as well as one for the united republic. But both were ruled by Nasser, and in 1960 a joint parliament, two thirds Egyptian, one third Syrian, was elected to exercise certain restricted powers. The Union was short-lived, however. In 1961 Syria seceded and restored an independent government.

Emperor Haile Selassie of Ethiopia welcomed by President Nasser of Egypt at the Cairo airport, 1959.

Courtesy Wide World Photos

In foreign affairs Nasser, with some success, sought in Egypt to play off the Communist bloc against the Western powers. He did, indeed, receive economic aid from both, without committing himself to either. Distrustful of what he was getting from the Communist powers, the United States at length withheld a large loan it had promised him toward the construction of a huge dam on the Nile at Aswan. Whereupon, in 1956, Nasser sought compensation by seizing the Suez Canal and appropriating its revenues. A brief but stormy international crisis ensued. While Israeli troops invaded the Sinai peninsula, a Franco-British naval force took possession of the Canal. Against such use of force, with attendant bloodshed, the United States protested; and so too, curiously enough, did Communist Russia, then engaged in bloody suppression of revolt in Hungary.[1] The upshot was fairly prompt withdrawal, under United Nations' auspices, of the invaders, and acquiescence in control of the Suez

[1] See above p. 824.

Canal by Egypt, which continued to deny the Canal's use to Israel. After much negotiation, Nasser paid the stockholders of the Canal company twenty-eight million British pounds as compensation for its seizure. With Soviet help he went ahead with the construction of the Aswan high dam and the irrigation works it would make posisble. The relations of the U.A.R. (Egypt) with the Soviet Union varied from friendly to hostile in the ensuing years, but with aid from both sides and despite nationalization of most business (1961–1963), considerable economic progress was visible.

One of the major concerns of all the Arab countries was the development of the Jewish state of Israel in Palestine. Great Britain, confronted by the rival nationalisms of Jews and Arabs and unable to reconcile them, surrendered its mandate over Palestine in May 1948. At once the independent Jewish republic of Israel was proclaimed at Tel Aviv. Arab natives of Palestine, supported by the bordering Arab states, strove to destroy Israel by armed force. But the Israelis fought back with

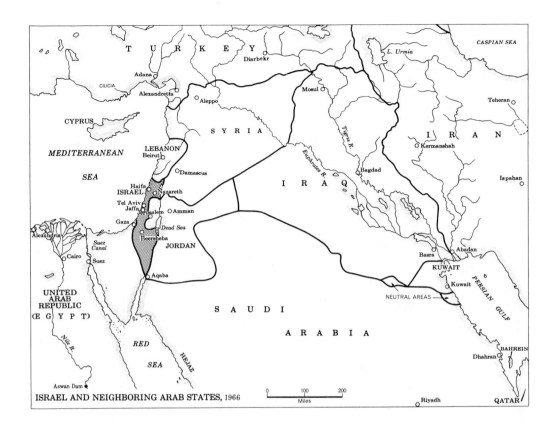

ISRAEL AND NEIGHBORING ARAB STATES, 1966

much success, and finally in January 1949 a truce was arranged through the United Nations. Jordan was left in possession of an eastern strip of Palestine, including the "old city" of Jerusalem; Egypt retained a southeast coastal strip; but some 8,000 square miles went to the new state. In 1949, Israel adopted a democratic constitution and elected the veteran Zionist leader, Chaim Weizmann, as President. Peace did not reign, however, for the ensuing years were punctuated by bloody border incidents, for which responsibility seemed to lie with both Israelis and Arabs. Nor was any solution found for the problem of the thousands of Arab refugees from Palestine.

Though the Arab states were so hostile that they pretended that Israel did not exist and Egypt prevented the use of the Suez Canal by Israeli shipping, yet Israel made rapid economic progress under the long premiership of David Ben-Gurion, who first took office in 1948 and resigned in 1963. Irrigation, improved techniques, and pioneering communities greatly increased agri-

cultural production. Infusions of dollars from the United States expanded such industries as textiles and building materials. The army was maintained on an efficient level because of the almost continual strife, including border incidents, with the neighboring Arab states.

One of Israel's neighbors, oil-rich Iraq, underwent a violent revolution in 1958. King Faisal II was assassinated; a republic was proclaimed; and General Abdul Karim Kassim took power. Though Iraq flirted with the Soviet Union, it retained some of its connections with the West, and though there was some internal pressure for union with Egypt and Syria, it maintained its independence. Kassim himself was overthrown and executed in a *coup d'état* in 1963. There was another *coup* later in the year, and the the ensuing governments were dominated by the military. Similarly, Jordan, though harried both by Communists and by a pro-Nasser party, was able to stay independent under King Hussein I, who had succeeded to the throne in 1952. Jordan did, however, end its close military ties with Britain.

Lebanon, where the government represented a precarious balance between the evenly divided Christian and Moslem influences, faced a revolt against its pro-Western regime in May 1958. President Chamoun appealed to the United States for help and President Eisenhower responded by sending in a detachment of marines. Order was gradually restored; there was little bloodshed; and a new president was chosen who was reasonably satisfactory to the various factions. His successor was elected peaceably in 1964.

The non-Arab nations of the Near and Middle East also underwent difficulties and encountered crises. Iran in 1946 was threatened from the north when Russia failed to withdraw troops stationed there during the war. Pressure from the Security Council of the United Nations resulted in the recall of these forces. But urged on by nationalism, Iran in 1951, under a premier named Mossadegh, seized the great British-owned oil industry. Production ceased for lack of technicians. But eventually the Shah, Mohammed Riza Pahlevi, ousted Mossadegh; and an agreement was worked out with the British so that production was resumed in 1955. With some attempts at land reform by the Shah, and considerable help from the United Nations and the United States, gradual economic progress was apparent in the ensuing years. Under three successive development plans (the last for 1962–1968) supported in part by the government's oil revenues, dams and roads were built and irrigation greatly extended.

Turkey grew in strength in the post-war years. It stood off Russian demands for territorial and other concessions in 1945–1950, supported in the latter years by military and economic aid from the United States. It developed its industry, improved its agriculture, and in 1946 permitted the appearance of a Democratic Party opposed to the dominant People's Party. In the free elections of 1950, the Democratic Party won a resounding victory and took over the reins of government, with Celâl Bayar succeeding Ismet Inönü as president and Adnan Menderes becoming premier. Under Bayar, Turkey coöperated willingly with Britain and the United States while maintaining its own intense nationalism. The Democratic Party again swept the polls

in 1954 and in 1957. But its rule became gradually more restrictive and repressive and some of its grandiose economic plans fizzled out despite American aid. In May 1960, there were riots and student protests, until a group of army officers under General Cemal Gursel staged a rapid coup and took over the government. After a long trial, a number of members of the previous government were condemned to prison and three, including Menderes, were executed. A new and democratic constitution was adopted in 1961 and under it the followers of Menderes, now organized in the Justice Party, won a resounding victory in the elections of 1965.

The eastern Mediterranean island of Cyprus, which had been governed by Great Britain since 1878, became independent in 1960. In the preceding post-war years it had been racked by violence on the part of those who wanted union with Greece and by disputes between the four fifths of the population who were Greek Christians and the one fifth who were Turkish Moslems. According to the compromise eventually reached, Cyprus was to be a republic with a constitution guaranteeing certain rights to the Turkish minority, and the British would retain a naval base. The Greek Orthodox Archbishop Makarios was elected president of the new nation. But bloody violence between the Greek and Turkish inhabitants recurred. Though Makarios, in 1963, accepted Greek, Turkish and British troops under British command to restore order, fighting continued and it seemed likely that Turkey and Greece might interfere. Even after the United Nations sent in a peace-keeping force of Canadian, Finnish and Irish soldiers, there was more bloodshed. Repeated efforts at mediation produced no solution, but a truce arranged late in 1964 brought an uneasy peace to the island.

Egypt's nearest neighbor in North Africa, Libya, was not returned to Italy after the war, but rather emerged as an independent kingdom under the leader of the Senussi tribes. After a brief period under the guidance of the United Nations, Libya became fully sovereign in 1952. The country's apparent lack of resources was dramatically remedied in 1958–1959 by the discovery of vast oil deposits and their rapid development by international oil companies.

At the end of 1964, production had risen to a million barrels a day.

Matters did not go forward so smoothly in the rest of North Africa. As we have seen, first Tunisia, then Morocco, won independence, while a struggle for it raged in Algeria. The struggle here was a long, bloody, and complicated one. The complexity and difficulty were results of a whole series of conflicting interests—French *vs.* Arab, town-dwellers *vs.* country folk, Moslem *vs.* Christian.

With dogged pertinacity, General De Gaulle strove to settle affairs by establishing an independent Algeria, but one that would coöperate with France and accord equal rights to its large minority of French settlers. Eventually, in March 1962, a "cease-fire" was agreed to and arrangements were made for the holding of plebiscites in both France and Algeria to determine the future relationship between the two countries. In France, last-ditch reactionaries sought to change the trend of events by bombings and terrorism, but the vote in both countries was overwhelming. On July 3, De Gaulle declared Algeria independent. After a prolonged political struggle and some violence and fighting, Algeria came under the control of Ahmed Ben Bella, who was able to put down opposition and organize a one-party government with strong socialist tendencies. Though Ben Bella visited Castro in Cuba (1963) and showed friendship to Communist countries, he began to work out coöperative arrangements with France, which were made somewhat easier by the fact that most Europeans had fled from Algeria before or after independence. In June 1965, Ben Bella was overthrown in a bloodless *coup* by his own Defense Minister, Colonel Houari Boumédienne, a man of somewhat more conservative stamp. In October 1965, a pact was ratified between France and Algeria. It provided that France should develop the vast oil resources of Algeria and receive much of the production, while in turn, France agreed to give Algeria substantial economic and financial aid.

D. New African States

Africa, south as well as north of the Sahara, presented in the post-war period a confusing picture of turmoil and change, of which the most striking feature was the emergence of a whole series of new countries from colonialism to independence. The fate of the former Italian colonies had been referred to the United Nations. Libya became independent in 1952. Italian Somaliland was joined to the British Somaliland Protectorate and became independent as the Republic of Somalia in 1960. Eritrea was federated with Ethiopia in 1952 but retained a degree of autonomy until 1962.

The vast empire of France in Africa had been a concern to the French at the close of World War II. They then attempted to solve all their colonial problems by providing in the constitution of the Fourth Republic for a "French Union" composed of the mother country, overseas "départements" (Algeria, Martinique, Guadeloupe, Réunion, Guiana), "associated territories" (French West Africa, French Equatorial Africa, Madagascar, Comoro Islands, French Somaliland, New Caledonia, French Oceania), and "associated states" (Morocco, Tunisia, Vietnam, Cambodia, Laos). But the winds of nationalism were blowing strong and, as we have seen, the Indo-Chinese states, Morocco, and Tunisia had soon to be recognized as independent. It was, moreover, the bloody struggle in Algeria that brought down the Fourth Republic in France and led to the creation of the Fifth.

De Gaulle's 1958 constitution replaced the "French Union" with the "French Community," which bore a certain resemblance to the British Commonwealth of Nations. It retained the "overseas départements" of the Union and the non-African overseas territories, but the African territories were given the opportunity to choose independence and all of them did so. By 1966, these fifteen new nations were grouped in three different categories. The Central African and Malagasy (Madagascar) Republics and the Republics of Congo (Brazzaville) Gabon, Senegal and Chad remained as members of the French Community, under constitutional provisions adopted in 1960, with a status something like that of dominions in the British Commonwealth. Outside the Community, but maintaining "special relationships" and defi-

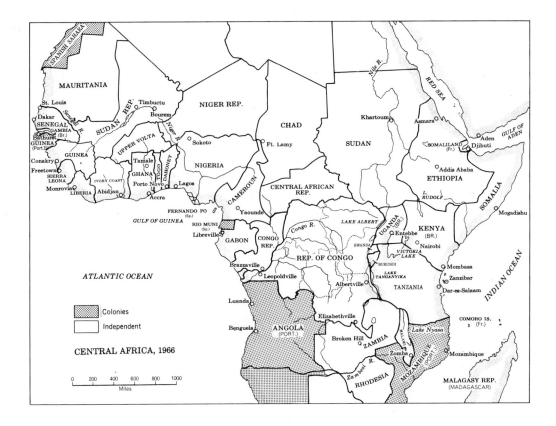

MAURITANIA
St. Louis
Dakar
SENEGAL
GAMBIA (Br.)
Bathurst
GUINEA (Port.)
Conakry
Freetown
SIERRA LEONE
Monrovia
LIBERIA
GUINEA
Senegal R.
SUDAN REP.
UPPER VOLTA
IVORY COAST
Abidjan
Accra
GHANA
Tamale
Porto Novo
Lagos
TOGO
DAHOMEY
Niger R.
Timbuctu
Bourem
Sokoto
NIGER REP.
NIGERIA
CAMEROUN
FERNANDO PO (Sp.)
RIO MUNI (Sp.)
Libreville
GABON
GULF OF GUINEA
Yaounde
CENTRAL AFRICAN REP.
CHAD
Ft. Lamy
SUDAN
Khartoum
Asmara
SOMALILAND (Fr.)
Aden
Djibuti
GULF OF ADEN
RED SEA
Addis Ababa
ETHIOPIA
L. RUDOLF
UGANDA (Br.)
Entebbe
KENYA (BR.)
Nairobi
SOMALIA
Mogadishu
Nile R.
Congo R.
LAKE ALBERT
RWANDA
BURUNDI
VICTORIA LAKE
Mombasa
Zanzibar
Dar-es-Salaam
INDIAN OCEAN
ATLANTIC OCEAN
CONGO REP.
REP. OF CONGO
Brazzaville
Leopoldville
Albertville
LAKE TANGANYIKA
TANZANIA
Luanda
Benguela
ANGOLA (PORT.)
Elizabethville
Broken Hill
ZAMBIA
Zambezi R.
RHODESIA
Lake Nyasa
Zomba
MALAWI
MOZAMBIQUE (PORT.)
Mozambique
COMORO IS. (Fr.)
MALAGASY REP. (MADAGASCAR)
SPANISH SAHARA

Colonies
Independent

CENTRAL AFRICA, 1966

0   200   400   600   800   1000
Miles

nite links with France, were the Republics of Ivory Coast, Dahomey, Upper Volta, Mauritania, Niger, and Cameroun (a federation of the former British and French trust territories). These twelve (plus Togo) were all members of an association for coöperative purposes—the African and Malagasy Union for Economic Coöperation. In a third group were the Republics of Guinea, Mali and Togo, which have with France merely agreements to coöperate in certain fields. From 1958 to 1963 Guinea had maintained an attitude of hostility to France. Mali and Senegal had joined briefly (1959–1960) in the Federation of Mali. These new countries ranged in population from Gabon with less than half a million people to the Malagasy Republic with some six million, and in area from Togo with about twenty thousand square miles to the Republic of the Niger with almost half a million. All of them adopted distinctive flags, national anthems, constitutions, and a republican form of government modeled more or less on that of France. But many of them tended to move toward a one-party system,

and in some (Togo, Central African Republic, Upper Volta and Dahomey, for example) governments were overthrown by more or less violent military coups.

In most of these republics there was an élite group, educated in France. From it and from French-trained army officers and sub-officers, the new governments were staffed. Government business and foreign affairs were usually carried on in French and there was considerable assistance from French experts and technicians. Senegal, with its great sea and air port of Dakar, had the largest group of educated and competent people since it had been in touch with European civilization for more than four centuries and had enjoyed a degree of self-government for many years. There was a tendency in most of these countries to stress their African nature—their *negritude*—and to search the scanty records of the past so as to create a historical background. All of them tended to work with the other new African nations, especially in the United Nations where they joined in denouncing the segregationist policies of South Africa and Southern Rhodesia. This coöperation was formalized in 1963 at a conference in Addis Ababa by the foundation of the Organization of African Unity with thirty member nations. It was modeled on the Organization of American States. Some of the former French colonies (Guinea, Mali, and Congo, for example) flirted off and on with the Communist countries and sought aid from both Russia and China. A number of them received technical assistance from Israel.

Since the boundaries of the new countries were often not meaningful on a geographic, tribal or linguistic basis, since some of them, now separate areas, had been administered together by the French, and since all of them were relatively small and had limited resources, there was a tendency for them to draw together in groupings of various sorts. All of them, save Mali and Guinea, were given the status of associates with the European Economic Community (Common Market). All of them, again minus Mali and Guinea (but plus Rwanda, which had formerly been Belgian), became members of the African and Malagasy Union for Economic Coöperation which runs the multinational airline *Air Afrique* and whose heads of state meet in semiannual conferences. In addition, there are the Customs and Economic Union òf Central Africa (Central African Republic, Congo, Gabon, Chad, Cameroun) with a common external tariff since 1966; the *entente* (agreement to work together) of Ivory Coast, Dahomey, Upper Volta and Niger; the customs union of Senegal, Mali, Ivory Coast, Dahomey, Upper Volta, Niger and Mauritania; and the West African monetary union of Senegal, Mauritania, Ivory Coast, Upper Volta, Niger, Dahomey and Togo. Despite the skillful leadership of a few statesmen (such as Felix Houphouet-Boigny of Ivory Coast) despite all efforts at coöperation, and despite external aid from many sources, it gradually became clear that the road to stability, prosperity, and progress was, for small, new, underdeveloped nations, long, slow and difficult.

The formation of new African states out of former British colonies took place more gradually than in the case of the nations derived from French holdings. Ghana, the former Gold Coast, became an independent country within the British Commonwealth in 1957, and its first president, Kwame Nkrumah, strove not only to develop his own country along Communist lines but also to play a leading role in African affairs and in any pan-African movements that might arise, until he was ousted by a military coup in 1966. His successors turned Ghana away from coöperation with the Communist countries.

Federal Nigeria, composed of Northern, Western, and Eastern Regions and with an area of nearly 400,000 square miles and a population of some fifty-six million, secured independence in 1960 but retained membership in the British Commonwealth. The Northern Region is the largest in area and population and predominantly Moslem, but it is also the most backward. Sierra Leone, tucked in between Guinea and Liberia, became independent in 1961. The British trust territory of Cameroon voted in its northern section to join Nigeria and in its southern part to unite with Cameroun. Despite regional and tribal rivalries, Nigeria, the largest of the new countries, with a sizeable group of educated leaders, made progress, politically, economically, and in the establishment of schools and universities, a progress that was marred by violence in the hard-fought elections of 1965 in which the government used strong-arm tactics against the opposition party. The disorder culminated in a military coup early the next year. The overthrow of the existing government reflected the tribal tensions among the various geographic areas. During the early stages of the coup, a number of leaders were assassinated, including the prime minister, Sir Abukar Tafawa Balewa and the premier of Northern Nigeria. The new government ruled with a firm hand and sought to end corruption, but in its turn was overthrown by another military group.

In British eastern Africa, Tanganyika (the former German East Africa) became independent at the end of 1961 under the able guidance of its leading statesman, Julius Nyerere. In December 1963, Zanzibar likewise became independent. A month later, its sultanate was overthrown and a "People's Republic" was formed which called in advisers from Communist China, Cuba, and East Germany. After some weeks of disorder,

President Kwame Nkrumah of Ghana with Dag Hammarskjöld, Secretary-General of the United Nations.

Zanzibar united with Tanganyika to form Tanzania but continued to pursue a policy of friendship with the Communist countries. Uganda secured its independence in 1962 as, in the following year, did Kenya, where the first president of the new republic was Jomo Kenyatta. Though he had been the leader of the Mau Mau terrorists who had fought against the British, he soon showed himself to be a leader of considerable skill and wisdom. The new East African states (Tanzania, Uganda, Kenya) transformed the old East Africa High Commission into the East African Common Services Organization, which handles railways, harbors, posts, airlines, telephones, telegraphs, weather-forecasting, and some aspects of finance for all three countries, which also form a single trade unit. The prime-minister of Uganda, in 1966, ousted the king and installed military rule.

The developments in the British territories south of Tanzania were more complicated. In 1953, Southern Rhodesia, Northern Rhodesia and Nyasaland were put together in a self-governing federation with the hope that a solution could be worked out for the relationship between Negroes and whites. The stumbling block proved to be Southern Rhodesia, where a white minority of less than a quarter million controlled the Negro majority of almost four million and was unwilling to give up its dominance. As a result the federation broke up and, in 1964, copper-rich Northern Rhodesia became the independent nation of Zambia under a Negro government headed by President Kenneth Kaunda, a situation accepted by the white minority (about seventy-five thousand in a population of more than three and a half million). Similarly, Nyasa, where there were less than ten thousand whites in a population of nearly three million, became independent in 1964 under the name of Malawi, with Dr. Hastings Banda, a Negro physician, who had been trained in the United States, as its first prime minister. But in Southern Rhodesia no parallel solution could be found. The British government refused to grant independence without assurances that provisions would be made for eventual government by the Negro majority. These the ruling whites would not give. Finally, in November 1965, the Prime Minister of Southern Rhodesia (now called just Rhodesia), Ian Smith, issued a unilateral declaration of independence, which Great Britain refused to recognize. Pressured by the United Nations and backed by the United States, Britain then began to apply economic sanctions against Rhodesia. Some of the African nations (including Tanzania) broke off relations with Britain on the grounds that its government was not acting with sufficient force and firmness.

So sweeping was the trend toward independence that even the tiny British colony of Gambia (in West Africa) and the still smaller colony of Malta (in the Mediterranean) became separate nations in 1964. Somewhat earlier (1962), far across the Atlantic, both Jamaica and Trinidad secured their independence. An attempt to form a West Indies Federation based on the two latter was short-lived. British Guiana (now Guyana) became independent in 1966. All the former British colonies that became separate countries were admitted to the United Nations. All of them (save Rhodesia) remained within the British Commonwealth, though some—like Jamaica, Trinidad, Malawi, Malta, and Gambia— became self-governing dominions, but still received a governor general from Britain; while others—like Uganda, Nigeria, Ghana, Kenya, Tanzania and Zambia—became republics with their own presidents.

The race question, so difficult in Rhodesia, also caused a member nation to leave the British Commonwealth. In the Union of South Africa the general elections of 1948 drove from the premiership the moderate General Smuts, and replaced him by a rabid Boer nationalist, Dr. Daniel Malan. The latter, with his Afrikaaner Nationalist party, proceeded to implement anti-British, anti-Negro, and anti-United Nations policies. Against the protests of the United Nations, the mandated territory of Southwest Africa was annexed. Drastic legislation to insure racial segregation (*apartheid*) and white supremacy was passed. Native protests were ruthlessly repressed. The economy fared better than might have been expected because of the extensive uranium deposits which gave South Africa another commodity much in demand. Finally, in 1955, the Boer nationalists succeeded in packing the Senate so that they could proceed with their unconstitutional plan of taking the right to vote away from the only segment of the colored population to which the suffrage had previously been extended. Thereafter the *apartheid* policy became more and more oppressive and led to riots and demonstrations which were so ruthlessly suppressed, with much bloodshed by troops and police, that questions were asked and motions introduced in the United Nations, and the public opinion of the world was outraged. Matters came to a head in March 1961 at a meeting of the prime ministers of the British Commonwealth nations including those form Ghana and Nigeria. The Prime Minister of the Union of South Africa, Dr. Hendrik Verwoerd, a stern advocate of *apartheid*, found himself alone when he sought to defend his country's racial policies. He, therefore, announced South Africa's withdrawal from the Commonwealth. And a subsequent plebiscite ratified its adoption of the status of a totally independent republic. Yet this step was merely the culmination of a long trend, for the British flag, the British national anthem, and allegiance to the Queen had already been eliminated, and decimal currency had replaced pounds, shillings, and pence.

Compared to the former British and French colonies, the transition to independence of the Belgian Congo in Africa was both confused and painful. The Belgians rather hastily yielded to the vociferous clamor and granted independence in 1960. Elections were held; but almost at once the country, with very few trained native leaders, and with bitter memories of the oppressive rule of Leopold II of Belgium, lapsed into chaos. Soon the Congo became a sort of pawn in the cold war, for in the autumn of 1960, the Soviet Union seemed on the point of taking control by flying in "technicians," while the United States sought to prevent such a development. Meanwhile, European missionaries, teachers and settlers were being attacked and murdered in various parts of the country. Into this confusion and disorder, with American support but Russian opposition, the United Nations moved. It dispatched a multi-national armed force

Demonstration in Leopoldville in the Congo, 1960.

Courtesy Wide World Photos

composed largely of Asians and Africans; it sent in experts to operate the public services; and it provided food, supplies, and funds. But the local troubles were unabated. The president, Joseph Kasavubu, was jealous of the prime minister, Patrice Lumumba, who favored the Communists; and both were opposed by Moise Tshombe, who headed Katanga, the wealthiest and best developed of the six large provinces of the country. Tshombe was determined that Katanga should secede from the Congo and constitute an independent state, and with the aid of Belgian and other interested persons he raised troops and defied the central government. In efforts to negotiate a settlement Lumumba was murdered on a trip to Katanga and Hammarskjöld, the U. N. Secretary-General, perished in a plane crash. Eventually (1963) the U. N. troops completed the occupation of Katanga. Tshombe fled to Europe, while Lumumba's successor as prime minister, Cyrille Adoula, ousted the Soviet Embassy and with much help

from the United Nations strove to restore order and improve economic conditions. In 1964, the U. N. military forces left, a new constitution was adopted, and Tshombe returned to succeed Adoula as the head of an interim government. Using white mercenary troops, he sought to put down rebel forces in Katanga. When it seemed likely that these rebels would murder a number of European hostages whom they held, Belgium, with help from United States planes, flew in paratroopers who held Stanleyville long enough to evacuate some two thousand Europeans. They were too late to save one hundred and eighty of the hostages. During 1965, Tshombe gradually ended the rebel threat and brought a semblance of peace to the troubled country. But after indecisive parliamentary elections he was ousted by President Kasavubu, who in turn was deposed (November 1965) by General Joseph D. Mobuto, commander in chief of the army. Mobuto seized power, canceled the scheduled presidential elections, and announced that he himself would hold the presidency for the next five years. It seemed likely that it would take longer than that to bring stability and order to the Congo.

The countries of Rwanda and Burundi, which had formed part of the German East Africa, and then had been held by Belgium first as a League of Nations mandate and later as a United Nations trust territory, were also not without their share of troubles after they were given independence in 1962. The chief difficulty arose from the ancient animosity between the Watutsi (a Nilotic tribe), who had been the rulers for centuries, and the much larger Bantu tribe of the Wahutu, who had been the exploited subjects. An uprising of the Wahutu in 1959 had overthrown the Watutsi feudal hierarchy in Rwanda. After independence, Rwanda became a republic with the Wahutu in control, while Burundi remained in the hands of the Watutsi as a constitutional monarchy with an hereditary king (called the Mwami). In the ensuing years, some hundred and fifty thousand Watutsi fled from Rwanda to Burundi and other nearby areas. After an unsuccessful invasion of Rwanda by Watutsi refugees, the Wahutu massacred many of the Watutsi who had remained there, and twelve thousand more fled (1964). This tribal strife caused the failure of a customs and monetary union (1962–1964) of Rwanda and Burundi and was, perhaps, responsible for the assassination of the prime minister of Burundi in 1965. Later in the same year, after an unsuccessful uprising, the Watutsi in Burundi executed scores of Wahutu leaders.

By 1966, the great African empires of Britain, France, and Belgium had been liquidated, though of the British holdings there were remnants left—the territories of Basutoland, Bechuanaland, and Swaziland, in or adjoining South Africa, still administered by British commissioners but scheduled for independence. Surviving also were the relatively unimportant Spanish holdings of Ifni and Spanish Sahara on the westward bulge of the continent and further south Spanish Equatorial Africa (consisting of Rio Muni, on the mainland, and Fernando Po, an island in the Gulf of Guinea). Portugal likewise retained Portuguese Guinea, the Cape Verde Islands and the islands of San Tome and Principe. Much more important

as exceptions to the end of colonialism were the great Portuguese holdings of Angola on the west coast and Mozambique on the east coast, plus Southwest Africa, the former German colony now held by the Union of South Africa, to which it had been given under a mandate by the League of Nations. In most of these were signs of unrest as the ardor for freedom, independence, nationhood, and the ending of colonialism was communicated even across guarded borders and to natives who had been held down by repressive rule.

In the case of the Portuguese territories, the issues were complicated by the fact that they were not technically colonies but overseas provinces of the mother country. They had been founded over four centuries ago and consequently had been held longer than the African possessions of any other Western nation. Portugal was very proud of them and very reluctant to part with any of them. They meant prestige and some profit to the mother country. Political and other rights had been granted in them to all natives who had been assimilated to Portuguese culture in language and by education, although the number of such persons was small, since educational opportunities for the native population were limited. Actual native unrest and revolt did develop, especially in northern Angola, where they echoed the situation in neighboring Congo. These risings (1961–1963) were put down by military force with much bloodshed despite aid from other African countries. The policy of suppression by Dr. Salazar's dictatorial Portuguese government, the general reaction against colonialism, and the sympathy of the new African nations led the repeated anti-Portuguese resolutions in the Assembly of the United Nations. Agreement seemed general that Portuguese rule should be ended. But just how this was to be accomplished was much less clear.

E. Special Problems Confronting the New Nations

In all the new nations in Africa, in the colonies approaching nationhood, and in those where a national future is not yet certain, there are problems of tribalism, language differences, and in some instances religious problems. Some units are wholly or partly Moslem; others were partly Christian and partly pagan. Some are split into cohesive tribal groups that may vary in size from a few score families to millions of people; and among these tribes there are ancient rivalries and hatreds. Most difficult of all, perhaps, is the language problem. In Ghana, with less than five million inhabitants, more than twenty vernaculars are spoken and the government radio broadcasts in six African languages. In certain parts of Nigeria it is possible to find, within a comparatively small area, half a dozen villages speaking not different dialects but quite different languages. Similar situations exist almost everywhere in Africa south of the Sahara.

On the educational and practical side, it is probable that most of the former colonies will use for some time to come a European language for education beyond the primary schools, for governmental purposes, and for communication across the linguistic barriers. The former British colonies will use English and the former French colonies French. The situation on a smaller scale resembles that in India described above.

On the political side, the tribal and language situation gives rise to three different kinds of nationalism. One is represented by such contemporary African leaders as Kwame Nkrumah in Ghana, Sékou Touré in Guinea, Tom Mboya in Kenya, Julius Nyerere in Tanganyika, and Mamadou Dea in Senegal. They and their colleagues have been educated in English or French schools. They not only aspire to liberate the former colonies and transform them into free and independent national states modeled more or less after those in Europe, but also to repress native tribalism, which they regard as an outwarn survival from more primitive and barbaric times.

A second kind of nationalism is tribalism itself. Some of the tribes are large enough to have a real sense of unity and sometimes close affiliations with other tribes. Thus the Mau Maus who terrorized Kenya in the 1950's were an oath-bound unit of Kikuyu, Meru, and Embu tribes. Their nationalist movement was crushed only after much bloodshed and the jailing of 60,000 tribesmen. Again, Negro tribesmen vigorously and persistently opposed the incorporation of Nyasaland into a federation with the white-ruled Rhodesias. In Rwanda the conflict is between two tribal groups—the tall and lordly Watutsi and the shorter and less warlike Wahutu whom they had enslaved. Some of the troubles in the former Belgium Congo have arisen from the fierce hostility to each other of tribes like the Lulua and the Baluba.

The third type of nationalism is pan-African. There is a dream, which some African statesmen pursue with fervor and to which almost all give at least lip service, of a united Africa from the Mediterranean to the Cape of Good Hope, or perhaps, at the minimum, from the southern limits of the Sahara to the northern boundaries of the Union of South Africa. It is a natural hope, when the pride of the Negro has been awakened and his dignity recognized, when there is talk of an African spirit and an African "soul," when it is clear that the new African nations are for the most part too small to be truly viable economic units, and when it is to be feared that the emotions and traditions of tribalism could split Africa into hundreds of tiny and warring units. There are African leaders who believe that once colonial rule has been completely ended, the new states will more or less naturally group themselves into federations and the federations into a continental confederation. But it is likewise held by others that the political, economic, linguistic, tribal, and religious tendencies toward separatism must long prevail and entail sorry strife.

In the whole picture of disintegrating colonial empires and the disappearance of European rule, there are several interesting aspects. Colonialism had served to export to Asia and Africa a number of thoroughly West European ideas and institutions. Some of these, like liberty, equality, nationalism, have turned out to be the very notions that have brought an end to colonial rule. Others, like democracy, constitutionalism, patriotism, justice and the rule of law, even where grafted into a thoroughly alien civilization, have turned out to be integrating forces and ideals toward which some of the emerging peoples could strive. Liberal democracy has seemed to be one of the hardest to achieve; and in most of the new nations, from South Vietnam to Ghana, from Indonesia to Guinea, from Pakistan to

DEVELOPED AND
UNDERDEVELOPED NATIONS

Developed

Partially developed

Underdeveloped

The categories of development are approximate and are based on
education and national product per capita.

the Sudan, there has been some version of rule by the strong leader (often a military man) in a more or less authoritarian fashion.

Another development that appeared as the colonial empires were liquidated has been the importance of education. What the new nations wanted most was to share in modern material civilization with its many benefits—health, ample food, material goods, rapid transportation, easy communication, leisure, amusements. But modern civilization clearly requires skilled administrators, professional men, and technicians. Such people are the product of a long and complicated educational process. And the new nations have had the most variant degrees of popular education. The success of the emerging countries would seem to depend, partly on whether they can retain the services of trained Europeans, but even more on how many of their own people are properly trained and educated.

Thus the difficulties in the Belgian Congo have been clearly related to the fact that there were, at independence, fewer than twenty native university graduates in the whole country, while the temporary stability of Nigeria could be accounted for by the fact that it had some thousands. India or Ceylon were well provided with educated personnel compared to Indonesia or Cambodia. One of the major problems for East Africa (Kenya, Tanganyika, Uganda) was how to remedy rapidly a deficiency of adequately trained persons. In fact, for almost all the emerging nations the crucial question is whether or not an appropriate educational system can be created rapidly enough to cope with the problems of the years that lie ahead.

A related question is that of economic development. A requisite for the creation of a modern industrial country is the investment of large amounts of capital in dams, factories, mines, roads, and power plants. Such capital can be derived from saving by the people, but only if they can be persuaded or compelled to hold down their current consumption; and this is most difficult when the standard of living is low and the eagerness for more goods great. In the Communist countries consumption has been regulated by planning, discipline, and force. In non-Communist lands, while there has

been a good deal of planning, efforts have been made to secure saving by persuasion. The two models have been the relative freedom of the United States and the policed state of the Soviet Union. Most of the new countries prefer freedom, but they are impressed by the success of Russia which, in less than half a century, has turned itself from a backward and poor country to a relatively modern and prosperous one, through the discipline imposed by the Communist Party.

Another source of capital for investment is a favorable balance of payments in international trade and transactions. A few countries with a highly salable export crop or product could sometimes achieve such a balance, as with Ghana when cocoa prices were high. But for most nations to secure a favorable trade balance, it would be necessary to hold down imports and thus again to restrict consumption. A third source of capital is loans or gifts from nations and investments by private firms or persons. Private investment is both difficult and risky in new countries, but on the governmental side the United States has poured large quantities of capital into the emerging nations as outright gifts, as "hard" loans to be repaid in dollars, and as "soft" loans to be repaid in the local currency and often over long periods. The motives of the United States have been partly humanitarian, partly military, partly political. Russia, in this phase of the cold war, has given economic aid on a smaller scale but with considerable propaganda effect. Great Britain invested large amounts in the former British colonies, as did France in the former French colonies.

Other sources of investment have been international. They include the International Bank for Reconstruction and Development (and its affiliate, the International Finance Corporation), the International Development Association (related to the U. N.), the Special Fund of the United Nations, and the Inter-American Bank (with its Social Progress Trust Fund). The sums involved in economic aid have been large. By 1966 the International Bank had made loans totaling more than nine billion dollars. In that year alone the various forms of assistance to other lands from the United States amounted to some four billion dollars. But the question remained as to whether even such massive infusions of capital could speed the development of the new lands rapidly enough to meet the rising expectations of their peoples.

Whatever their educational or economic status, the emerging nations have set much store by membership in the United Nations, and by 1966 the number of members had reached one hundred and seventeen. In the Assembly, Guinea's vote counted as much as Great Britain's, and Ceylon's as much as Russia's. The United Nations meetings, moreover, constituted a forum where small countries could state their views and make their complaints. On cold war issues their votes were often wooed in a pleasant fashion by the great powers. Some of the agencies of the United Nations were also in a position to be most helpful to underdeveloped countries. In this category were particularly notable FAO (Food and Agriculture Organization), UNESCO (United Nations Educational, Scientific and Cultural Organization), and WHO (World Health Organization).

When it is remembered that the charter of the United Nations was signed originally in June of 1945 by fifty-one nations, the doubling of its membership can be thought of as a symbol of much that happened in the post-war world—the breakup of the colonial empires, the emergence of new and independent countries, the needs of the underdeveloped areas. In fact, all the problems posed by the two decades after the close of World War II were clearly not going to be solved by the end of the century.

CHAPTER 64

Aspects of Contemporary Civilization

A. Continuing Cold War

Two decades after the close of World War II it was clear that the Western civilization that had developed in Europe during the previous twenty-five centuries had, in one respect or another, spread into the most remote and isolated areas of the world. In New Guinea and Papua, the Australians were trying to introduce western-style democracy; Christian missionaries were to be found almost everywhere; jet airplanes roared into new airfields high in the Andes or the Himalayas; Congolese killed each other with Russian or American weapons; Indian parliamentary leaders debated issues in English; Chinese peasants strove to understand the writings of Karl Marx. Not only had Western ways penetrated into every clime, but also most of the backward or underdeveloped countries were striving, or at least wishing, for the benefits of modern industrialization. Former head-hunters wanted to ride in jeeps; naked tribesmen hoped that their radios could be replaced by television sets.

But the world, instead of being united by common ways of doing things and common desires, was divided politically and ideologically into three camps—the Commu-nist, the Democratic, and the Neutral. Of the neutral countries, India was the largest and most important. Its neutralism was a matter of philosophy as well as of political strategy. But many other countries, like Ghana, Egypt, or Afghanistan, were willing and indeed eager to accept economic help from both camps. Yugoslavia talked a vigorous brand of Communism, but maintained friendly relations with, and received help from, the Western powers. Finland was tied intellectually to the West but geographically to Russia. Switzerland was strictly neutral by tradition and Austria by recent treaty settlement. Other nations, while more or less neutral, leaned to one of the two sides. Thus Iran, Japan, and Pakistan worked closely with the democratic countries, while Cuba identified itself with the Soviet Union. Most of the new African countries tried to stand aside from the struggle and to focus on their own development, while most of the Latin American countries worked with the United States, though in many of them there were parties or elements that were sympathetic to Russia or China or Cuba.

The blocs were not, however, as clearly defined as they had been in 1950 or 1960. Among the democratic countries of Europe, fear of a Soviet invasion had declined and economic strength had grown tremendously. France was pursuing an independent policy, and NATO seemed shaky and less important. The Communist bloc was even more clearly divided, since China, claiming to stand for a sterner, starker, Stalinist-type Marxist line, was engaged in bitter ideological dispute with the Soviet Union. Little Albania sought to follow China's lead, and China was active in Communist propaganda in Cuba and other Latin American countries. Nonetheless, as the original Communist nation—"the homeland of socialism"— as the largest geographically, the most developed industrially, and the most powerful militarily of all the Communist states, the Soviet Union was by far the most important element in determining their doctrine and deciding their policies. Most of the Communist parties, all around the world, still gave their allegiance to, and took their orders from Moscow.

Part of Russia's prestige arose from its success in World War II, its absorption of Lithuania, Latvia, and Estonia, its domination of the surrounding satellite countries from Poland to Bulgaria, its ruthless suppression of dissent in Hungary. Part came from its remarkable advances in science symbolized by its space vehicles. Part could be attributed to its obvious military strength and the effectiveness of its machinery for espionage and propaganda. But there were two other major factors in Russia's influence throughout the world. One was the Marxist-Leninist philosophy which, though it dated from the mid-nineteenth century, seemed modern in backward countries. By ignoring the unfulfilled prophecies of Marx and his outworn economics and by stressing his attacks on the exploitation of the workers and Lenin's hostility to colonialism and imperialism, the Russians were able to tell an appealing story to the underdeveloped lands. The story was, moreover, a very simple one that anyone could grasp. It "explained" the political, economic, cultural, and social situation. It attributed poverty and backwardness to exploitation by the former colonial powers, the capitalists, and the big landowners. It scoffed at religion and all non-material factors or forces. It presented itself as "scientific" and it insisted that the trend of history was inexorably with and toward Communism.

The second factor was Russia's economic progress. Starting out in 1917 not much better off than some of the underdeveloped nations, the Soviet Union had transformed itself into a great industrial power. It had done so by planning and by holding down consumption so as to increase investment in factories, dams, and mines. That it had also done so by eliminating individual freedom, sternly mobilizing the workers, and "liquidating" all who objected or dissented (kulaks, Ukrainians, Kazakhs, Cossacks, etc.) was less stressed by the Russians. Yet the results were clear. The Soviet Union could produce satisfactory tanks and trucks, airplanes and submarines, cameras and television sets. For a while it led the world in missile engineering and space vehicles. Khrushchev had probably not exaggerated very much when in 1960 he claimed that the national income of the Soviet Union was increasing at the rate of eight per cent a year. And it was estimated that the rate of investment (for future production) was higher than in any other land.

The center and keystone of the democratic nations, on the other hand, was the United States. Territorially it was much less extensive than Russia. In population it was smaller than the Soviet Union and, by a wide margin, than China or India. But industrially it towered above all other countries—so much so that in some lines (e.g., automobiles) it could equal all the rest of the world combined. Its standard of living was far higher than even advanced nations like Great Britain or France. It could afford to spend some fifty billion dollars a year on defense. Its intervention had been decisive in World War II both in the east and in the west. It had, moreover, welded together a slightly uneasy military alliance (NATO) in Europe and a rather ineffectual one (SEATO) in Asia. It maintained military and air bases round the world from Spain and Libya to Okinawa and the Philippines. It had poured military and economic assistance into dozens of countries in the amount of scores of billions of dollars.

But if its industrial might lent it prestige, the wealth of the United States made it an object of envy and criticism. The standard of living of its foreign-based soldiers contrasted unpleasantly with that of the local inhabitants. The careless spending of its

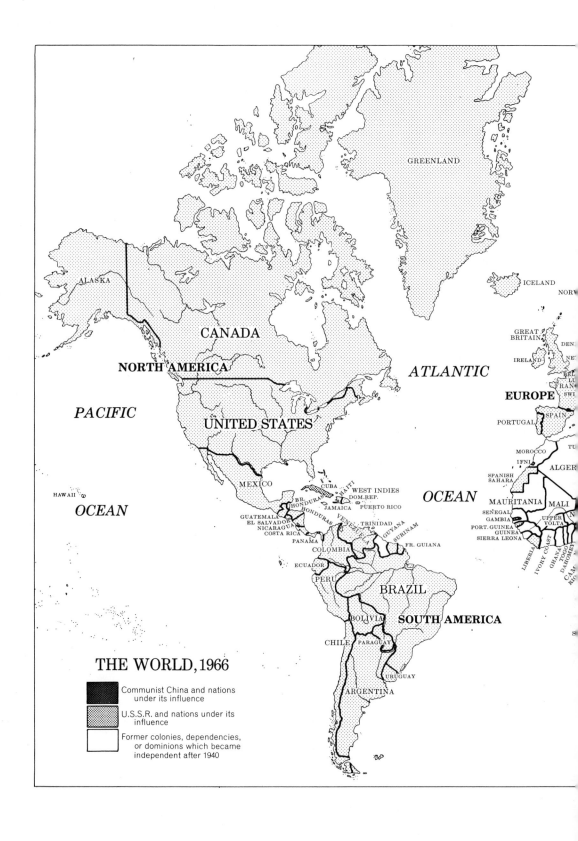

GREENLAND

ICELAND

NOR

ALASKA

CANADA

GREAT
BRITAIN
IRELAND

DEN

NE
BEL
LU
FRAN
SWI

NORTH AMERICA

ATLANTIC

EUROPE

PACIFIC

UNITED STATES

PORTUGAL

SPAIN

MOROCCO

IFNI

ALGER

TU

HAWAII

OCEAN

MEXICO

OCEAN

SPANISH
SAHARA

MAURITANIA

MALI

CUBA
HAITI
WEST INDIES
DOM.REP.
JAMAICA PUERTO RICO

GUATEMALA
EL SALVADOR
NICARAGUA
COSTA RICA
PANAMA

BR.
HONDURAS
HONDURAS

VENEZUELA

TRINIDAD

GUYANA

SURINAM

FR. GUIANA

COLOMBIA

SENEGAL
GAMBIA
PORT. GUINEA
GUINEA
SIERRA LEONE

UPPER
VOLTA

N

LIBERIA

IVORY COAST

GHANA

TOGO

DAHOMEY

CAM
RO

ECUADOR

PERU

BRAZIL

BOLIVIA

SOUTH AMERICA

CHILE

PARAGUAY

URUGUAY

ARGENTINA

THE WORLD, 1966

Communist China and nations
under its influence

U.S.S.R. and nations under its
influence

Former colonies, dependencies,
or dominions which became
independent after 1940

Russian tanks guard the Budapest Station during the Hungarian rising, 1956.

Courtesy Wide World Photos

millions of tourists aroused mixed feelings in many lands. Moreover, some great powers of the pre-1914 period (Great Britain, France, Germany, Japan) found it a little hard to adjust to a situation in which war and circumstance had reduced them to second- or third-rate status. Its very pre-eminence, moreover, made the United States the prime target for the propaganda, the criticism, and the diplomacy of the whole Communist bloc. Red China, for example, despite the long history of friendship between the American and Chinese people, chose as the enemy against whom its citizens must be aroused, not the waning British Empire, which still held Hong Kong, but rather the United States.

The United States had certain advantages in the ideological struggle. It had been the first nation to throw off colonial rule, to establish modern republican government, to develop a workable democracy, to live under a constitution, to respect a bill of rights, and to fuse peoples of the most variant races, religions, and origins into a viable whole. It had been, furthermore, for almost two centuries a symbol of freedom and of opportunity for the oppressed peoples of every land. Its example had much to offer to other countries.

But it had certain disadvantages. The American people were so used to democracy that they had become a little unready to expound its virtues. Though they were making progress, they had been unable wholly to solve the problem of race relations. Despite their instinctive anti-colonialism, they often found themselves in a position where it seemed important to defend an allied or friendly nation against the attacks of aspiring colonial peoples. And although they believed deeply in democracy, the exigencies of international politics, military diplomacy, and the cold war often led them to accept or even support the dictatorial rule of a strong man if he seemed likely to keep his country aligned with American interests.

Perhaps most difficult of all, the United States appeared to the rest of the world as the prime example and the chief defender of "capitalism," and most Americans were prepared to proclaim themselves supporters of "capitalism" and "free enterprise." Here a real misunderstanding of words was involved. For the African, the Asian, and for many Europeans, "capitalism" meant the kind of system that Karl Marx had seen and described in Great Britain in the mid-nineteenth century. It implied a greedy and exploiting class of capitalists who, in their search for profits, disregarded human welfare, the workers' rights, and the national interest. It implied, moreover, that labor was unorganized and helpless, that the independent farmer was so impoverished that he was being driven from the land, that urban living conditions were dismal and unhealthy, and that the government operating under the philosophy of *laissez-faire* was both unwilling and unable to do anything about the situation. To many, in addition, "capitalism," in line with the theories of the Russian Lenin, was seeking by every possible means to exploit overseas workers through political or economic imperialism because home markets, composed of underpaid workers, were exhausted. The very phrase "free enterprise" recalled to some minds Marx's comment about labor which was "free" to sell itself for low wages and to starve in slums.

To the American, on the other hand, "free enterprise" meant an economy, still competitive, in which the individual still had opportunity to organize and develop a business. To him, "capitalism" meant the system under which the United States was operating in the mid-twentieth century and which was in some respects further removed from the England of 1850 than was Soviet "Communism." In the United States of the 1960's the workers were organized in powerful labor unions which were sometimes dominant and occasionally domineering. The high wages of labor had produced an enormous and continually expanding home market not only for food, clothing, and housing but also for automobiles, television sets, and outboard motor boats. The government was active in every phase of economic life. It organized some businesses and participated in others (mixed corporations). It took half of the profits of business through a corporation tax. It subjected the

rich to income taxes that rose in a steep graduation to 70% on the very affluent, and it broke up the estates of the wealthy through heavy inheritance taxes. Nor was its action predominantly negative, for an elaborate system of social security had been established which protected most people from the worst misfortunes of industrial life. And in 1965, President Johnson put through a program designed to aid disadvantaged youth, improve economic conditions in backward areas, enforce the civil rights of Negroes, and provide medical care for the elderly. The farmer, moreover, was the object of such extensive subsidies that a good many uneconomic units were kept in existence. And banking, public utilities, stock markets, food and drug businesses, and many others were under strict regulation to protect the citizenry.

Thus when an Indonesian or an African from Ghana or a Japanese labor leader talked about American capitalism and imperialism he had one kind of a picture—largely incorrect and outdated—in mind, whereas the American, whether a member of the United States Information Service or a private individual, had quite another. If in the cold war the average Russian thought of himself as standing against capitalism, imperialism, and war and for socialism and the world-wide liberation of the laboring masses, the average American believed that his country was opposing Communism, irreligion, and war and was supporting freedom, law, justice, democracy, and respect for the individual human being. The Russian was convinced of the "aggressive" purpose of the democratic powers because of their military alliances and the American bases that ringed the Soviet homeland. The American was equally convinced that his country would never start a war and was seeking merely to check the ruthless advance of the Soviet Union which had in two decades absorbed or subjected Latvia, Lithuania, Estonia, Poland, Czechoslovakia, Rumania, Bulgaria, and Hungary, and the expansion by force of arms of world Communism which had in the same period taken over China, North Korea, Albania, North Vietnam, Tibet, and Cuba and had made threatening progress in Guinea, Mali, Nepal, Laos, Afghanistan, Indonesia, Ghana, and other lands. It seemed clear to the American, for example, that Russia had been prepared to exploit the disorder in the Congo in 1960–1961 by sending in "technical advisers," military and para-military contingents with a view to gaining control there, and had been checked only by the action of the United Nations.

From 1961 to 1963, the image of the United States in the rest of the world was dramatically improved by the personality and actions of President John F. Kennedy. The fact that he was the first Roman Catholic president in a predominantly Protestant country seemed in itself to indicate that the United States had reached a new level of religious understanding and accord. He was the first world leader who had fought at the front in World War II and thus knew at first hand the terrors of modern warfare. He was young, vigorous, attractive, incisive and realistic with a kind of tough idealism and a profound faith in freedom and democracy. While eager to stimulate the social, cultural and economic progress of the United States, he made clear his intent to assist the less developed nations, as, for example, in the Alliance for Progress and in the Peace Corps (which by 1966 had more than ten thousand volunteers contributing significantly to the improvement of conditions in forty-six countries). Despite the fiasco of the Bay of Pigs, President Kennedy was able to convince the world that his country wanted peace. He was particularly effective in personal contacts with the many statesmen who came to Washington from Europe, Latin America, Africa and Asia, though when he met with Khrushchev in June of 1961 in Vienna, the only agreement they could reach was to move toward a neutral status for Laos. The good impression that Kennedy made initially was reënforced by his restraint in handling the crisis of the Berlin Wall (August 1961), his firmness in the matter of the Congo (1961), and his firmness and restraint in the missile confrontation in Cuba (October 1962). The President's assassination in Dallas, Texas, in November 1963, was received with sorrow and shock around the world, even in Communist countries. President Lyndon Johnson continued Kennedy's policies at home and abroad, and, after his overwhelming victory in the elections of 1964, was able to put

through a broad program of domestic legislation. Under his leadership great progress was made in bettering the status and defending the rights of Negroes.

B. Competition in Armaments and Production

During the decade of the 1950's the armament race between the opponents in the cold war underwent a series of changes. Intensified by the Korean War, it had seemed to slacken after the death of Stalin and the peace in Korea (1953). Then gradually it intensified once more, as it became apparent that the Soviet Union and the Western powers were not going to be able to reach agreement or even an understanding on the status of Berlin and Germany, on disarmament, or on the cessation of atomic tests. The hopes that Khrushchev would be more conciliatory than Stalin were gradually belied as the line he followed became tougher and harder, perhaps under pressure from some elements in the Soviet government, perhaps lest the Chinese Reds, by being more aggressive, should seize the ideological leadership of the Communist world.

As the armament competition became more intense after 1955, it also changed in character. During the preceding years the Russians had focussed on land armies, tanks, artillery, and submarines as well as airplanes. The United States, while maintaining strength in other branches and putting some trust in the forces of its NATO allies, had placed its main reliance on long-range planes capable of delivering atomic bombs. But it slowly became clear that the weapon of the future was the missile, whether with an atomic or a conventional warhead. All sorts of missiles were developed by both sides—ground to air, air to air, air to ground, ground to ground—for different purposes. The whole picture changed dramatically in October 1957 when the Soviet Union put into orbit around the Earth an artificial satellite (Sputnik I). Such a feat demonstrated clearly that there was no place in the world that could not be reached by a missile from any other spot on Earth. There were, to be sure, engineering problems to be solved and ever greater accuracy to be sought, but it was evident that the day would come when the long-range bomber as an offensive weapon would be supplemented and then replaced by the missile. The United States immediately stepped up its program and hastened the development of missiles of various sorts, including those to be launched from deep underground pits and from submarines.

Indeed, the whole armament picture was in a state of flux. On the one hand, after the United States exploded the first thermonuclear bomb at Eniwetok in the Pacific in 1952 and the Russians developed similar devices, it became clear that the opponents in the cold war could destroy each other and perhaps through radioactive "fallout" eliminate most, or even all, life on earth. On the other hand, all attempts to reach disarmament agreements failed of success, in part at least because the United States insisted on close inspection to make sure that enforcement was adequate, while Russia would not accept more than token inspection. Even in the matter of atomic bomb tests, though Russia, Britain, and the United States temporarily stopped making them, agreement proved impossible because of differences on the question of detection and enforcement, particularly in respect to underground explosions. But the negotiations begun at Geneva in 1958 among the three nations went on and on. Meanwhile, in February 1960, France set off, in the Sahara, its first atomic bomb and thus became the fourth nation with "atomic capability." The fifth was Communist China, which exploded its first atomic device in 1964 and its second in 1965.

In 1960 Prime Minister Khrushchev announced that as a result of the changeover to rockets, missiles, and nuclear weapons the armed forces of the Soviet Union would be reduced from the 1959 level of 3,623,000 to 2,423,000 for the 1960–1962 period. The estimate of Russian defense expenditures for 1960 was seventeen per cent of the national governmental revenue. In the United States in the same year more than half of the Federal budget was for defense. France, fighting a continuing war in Algeria, put about one third of its governmental expenditures into its armed forces, while Great Britain allocated about one fourth of its revenue to military purposes. Thus even with the changing nature of armament competition, it remained a very heavy burden on the major countries, save some of those that had been defeated in World War II, notably Japan, Italy, and West Germany. A number of the new nations, too, sought to create armies and air forces larger than necessary and too expensive for an underdeveloped economy.

In 1961, tension grew again, since the Soviet Union was threatening to sign a peace treaty with East Germany and thus to revise the status of West Berlin. Khrushchev announced an increase of almost thirty per cent in military expenditures and resumed nuclear tests with about fifty explosions, some of them larger than any earlier blasts. President Kennedy reluctantly ordered increased defense spending and the resumption of atomic-bomb testing. But after the Cuban crisis of 1962, United States-Soviet relations improved somewhat and long negotiations led to a treaty prohibiting all nuclear test explosions save those underground (which produce no fallout). It was signed in Moscow in August 1963 by Great Britain, the United States, and the Soviet Union. Other nations were invited to adhere and almost all did so except France and Communist China. The test ban treaty was one of President Kennedy's outstanding achievements and one of his last, for it went into effect just forty-three days before his death. After 1963, little progress was made on disarmament. Indeed, the undeclared war in Vietnam led to a major increase in military spending by the United States.

International competition also existed in more peaceful fields. Improvement in statistics and in economic analysis made it easier to get figures not only for industrial production but also for G.N.P. (gross national product—all goods and services) and for other global figures. Because the free world and the Communist world were both seeking to impress the new nations, there were frequently battles of figures on increased production, total production, G.N.P., total investment, and the like. In essence, western Europe and the United States still led by wide margins in most areas of production. But Russia had become the second most important industrial nation and was growing faster than the older industrial countries particularly in terms of percentages, since the base from which they were calculated was smaller. Indeed, in the campaign for the presidency of the United States in 1960, Senator John F. Kennedy, as candidate, had made a major issue of the point that the recent rate of growth of the American G.N.P. (between two and three per cent) had not been large enough. The rate soon began to improve. It grew to 7.7. per cent in 1962, 6.7 per cent in 1964, and with an increase of 7.4 per cent in 1965, the G.N.P. of the United States rose to the astounding figure of $676 billion. Since prices were also edging up, the growth in real terms was slightly less—5.6 per cent in 1965, for example. One persistent problem created difficulties in the 1950's and 1960's. Though the United States was exporting more goods than it was importing, the expenditures of its millions of tourists and its extensive military and aid programs abroad produced large deficits in its total balance of foreign payments. As a result there was a continuing drain of gold out of the country. By pressure both through taxes and voluntary restrictions the payment deficit for 1965 was reduced to a billion and a quarter dollars. But the problem remained at least partially unsolved.

Some comparative figures given in the table at the bottom of the page portray the production situation in the 1960's. The figures gathered by the Statistical Office of the United Nations are for 1963 and in millions of metric tons (of 2,205 lbs.) unless otherwise indicated.

Such figures do not tell the whole story. Production, especially industrial production, was expanding more rapidly in the countries that had more recently been developing large-scale manufacturing (U.S.S.R., Japan, Mexico) than in the older industrial nations. But Italy, West Germany, and France were showing very considerable gains in industrial output as they built new, modern, and large-scale plants. In all industrial countries there was a pronounced shift to new types of production such as electronics (television sets), plastics, and synthetics (rubber, nylon). Production of electricity seemed a fairly good index of the degree of industrialization. A little of it was being produced by atomic energy plants, but most was still thermal (coal) or hydroelectric (water power). Russia was determined to overtake the United States in production both to provide goods for its own people and to influence the new nations. But despite its larger resources in land and people, it seemed unlikely that the Soviet Union could catch up with the United States in most lines before the 1970's or even later.

In another area there was some difference of opinion as to the advantages of growth.

	U.S.[7]	U.S.S.R.	U.K.	W.Ger.	France	Italy	Japan	World
Wheat	31.0	70.1 [1]	3.0	4.9	10.2	8.1	.7	250.3
Meat	13.9	9.1	2.0	3.0	3.0	1.0	.5	67.7
Electricity [2]	1011.2	412.4	173.6	147.3	88.2	71.3	160.2	2849.2
Crude Petroleum	372.0	206.0	.1	7.3	2.5	1.8	.8	1303.5
Coal	430.5	395.1	198.9	142.8	47.8	.6	52.0	1929.0
Cement	61.6	61.0	14.1	29.2	18.1	22.1	29.9	368.0
Steel	99.1	80.2	22.9	31.6	17.6	10.2	31.5	386.6
Aluminum	2.1	1.0	.03	.2	.3	.09	.2	4.4
Motor Vehicles [3]	9.1	.6	2.0	2.7	1.7	1.2	1.4	20.5
Air Transport [4]	81.0	[5]	9.6	2.6	6.0	3.1	3.1	147.0
Radio and Television [6]	27.3	7.3	4.4	5.5	5.0	2.3	22.9	[5]

[1] Figures are for 1962.
[2] Billions of kilowatt hours.
[3] Millions of motor vehicles.
[4] Billions of passenger-kilometers.
[5] Not reported.
[6] Millions of receivers produced.
[7] In 1965 the United States produced some 119 million metric tons of steel, 2.5 million metric tons of aluminum, and 9.3 million motor vehicles.

The twentieth century witnessed a veritable explosion in population as the death rate (especially for infants) was reduced by improved medical techniques, better public health measures, and a higher standard of living. At the same time, the birth rate continued at high levels in underdeveloped countries (Latin America, India, China, Indonesia) and, surprisingly enough, rose markedly after World War II in countries like the United States and France. The estimated population of the world was about three and a third billion by 1966. If the growth rate of the 1960's (about 1.9 per cent) is maintained, the number of people on earth will greatly exceed six billion in the year 2000. Ceylon can be taken as an illustration of the problem. Life expectancy there was 32 years in 1921. By 1954 it was 60 years. The Ceylonese death rate dropped from 19.8 per thousand in 1946 to about ten by 1960 as a result of the elimination of malaria and the establishment of better public health procedures. But the birth rate remained at the high level of 35 per thousand. From 1958 to 1963, the population of Ceylon grew at the rate of 2.5 per cent a year, from 9,388,000 to 10,625,000.

In Japan, though there was a sharp drop in the death rate in the years after 1946, the birth rate also decreased sharply and thus the rate of increase in the population was moderate. India grew by 50 million people between 1958 and 1963, reaching a total of 460 million and a density of 151 per square kilometer (as compared with 20 in the United States and 87 in France), and could have almost 700 million inhabitants by the year 2000 if such growth continues. It is estimated similarly that mainland China may grow from something like 650 million in 1960 to more than 1.6 billion at the end of the century.

In Western countries like France or the United States, many people welcomed the increasing population as a sign of national health and a source of national strength. In lands like Russia and China, which adhered to the Marxist philosophy, any fears about population growth were denounced as neo-Malthusian and the view was upheld that under socialism added population is an asset, though Communist China by 1966 had changed its official view and was trying to check population growth. But in India,

Pakistan, and other countries with an already dense population and an eagerness to raise the general standard of living, there were widespread fears that the additional population would consume most of any increases of production—that is, that the necessity of feeding, housing, and clothing the added millions of people would reduce the chances of raising the per capita income. In Mexico, where the rate of population increase of 3.2 per cent a year could raise the population from 38 million in 1963 to more than 123 million by the year 2000, similar fears were expressed, as they were in South America where the population could grow from 140 million in 1960 to 394 million four decades later. On the other hand, many people held that improvements in agriculture, science, and industry would make it possible both to feed ever increasing numbers and to raise the general standard of living at the same time.

C. New Marvels of Science and Technology

Ever since the eighteenth century, science (and with it technology) had been advancing at an ever increasing rate. In the twentieth century, and especially after World War II, this acceleration of progress was evident in the most varied fields. Science became a factor in the cold war. The United States studied its science and engineering education to make sure it was not falling behind Russia's. So many men and women were engaged in scientific pursuits that it was estimated that ninety per cent of all the scientists who had ever lived were alive in 1960.

The understanding of the atom that had made possible the atomic and the thermonuclear bomb progressed rapidly both on the theoretical and the experimental fronts. The results were a little confusing. The work of Sir Ernest Rutherford, Niels Bohr, and others had led, by the 1920's, to a fairly simple concept of the atom as being composed of a positively charged proton as a nucleus with negatively charged electrons revolving around it, something like a miniature solar system. Further developments made it clear that the atom, and particularly its nucleus, was much more complex. In 1927 the German physicist Heisenberg

Albert Einstein. Emil Orlik (d. 1932).

announced his "principle of indeterminacy" which indicated that it was impossible to know at the same time where an electron was in its orbit and how fast it was going. Before long it became clear that electrons had to be treated as if they were both particles of matter and also of radiation. New atomic particles—neutrons, neutrinos, positrons, mesons, etc.—were discovered, until by 1966 there were more than thirty of them with which physicists had to deal by means of newly created mathematical techniques such as quantum mechanics and new instruments like cloud chambers, betatrons, cyclotrons, and mass spectrometers. In the light of the new discoveries matter became something quite different from the hard particles governed by the laws of Newtonian physics which the nineteenth-century scientists had discussed. Rather it partook more of the nature of radiation, fields of force, and the like, and it could be shown that even the hardest substance, like steel, was almost entirely empty space. Indeed it was discovered that there is anti-matter. It was shown that there exist protons with a negative charge instead of a positive, and electrons with a positive instead of a negative. If a normal proton encounters a negative one,

both are annihilated in a flash of energy. Rapid progress was also made in solid state physics, and the transistor based on this development revolutionized the electronics industry. Another startling discovery was that of lasers—beams of one color, coherent light that could carry messages and even drill holes.

The tremendous advances in the understanding of the nature of matter[1] made possible rapid progress in other fields. It became evident that the light and heat of the sun and other stars were the result of atomic processes, and it was possible to determine with some certainty what those processes were and how they could account for astronomical phenomena such as *novae* and the variation in star types from white dwarfs to red giants. The new field of radio astronomy grew in importance, since it was discovered that many bodies in space emit radio waves as well as light. In 1963, a new astronomical phenomenon was observed, the "quasar" or quasi-stellar object. These are very bright entities out at the edge of observable space that for their size emit fantastic amounts of energy. The new discoveries led to new theories as to the origin of the universe. One, the "big bang" hypothesis, held that the universe had begun in a gigantic explosion billions of years ago. In chemistry the work on the atom not only gave an understanding of chemical reactions, the nature of chemical bonds, and the relationship of one element to another, but also made it possible by techniques such as the bombardment with atomic particles to change one element to another, to create radioactive isotopes, and also to produce new radioactive elements.[2]

An isotope is one of two or more forms of a chemical having the same number of protons in the nucleus and thus the same atomic number, but differing in the make-up of the nucleus and thus in atomic weight. It was found that there were almost

---

[1] Basic contributions to the "new physics" had been made earlier in the twentieth century by Einstein. See above, p. 673.

[2] Neptunium, 1940; Plutonium, 1940; Americum, 1944; Curium, 1944; Berkelium, 1950; Californium, 1950; Einsteinium, 1954; Fermium, 1954; Mendelevium, 1955; Nobelium, 1957; Lawrencium, 1961 with atomic numbers higher than that of uranium.

Radio telescope
at Stanford University
in California.

*Courtesy
Wide World Photos*

three hundred stable isotopes of the various elements and some eight hundred radioactive isotopes which decayed into other forms in periods ranging from a fraction of a second to hundreds of years. The use of radioactive isotopes opened up new fields in biology, physiology, botany, and even archaeology. It became possible, for example, to introduce radioactive isotopes into a fertilizer and then trace the part of the plant in which they appeared. Or again, by studying the content of carbon 14 in a piece of wood or textile it was shown that its date could be determined with some accuracy back for several thousand years. By a similar technique the temperature of the sea water in which tiny shells were formed millions of years ago could be accurately ascertained.

The new knowledge and the new methods led to the creation of a number of previously undeveloped sciences or combinations of sciences ranging from biochemistry to astrophysics and from biophysics to paleobotany. Revolutionary advances were made in biology through the study of hor-

mones, enzymes, and nucleic acids by biochemical and biophysical techniques. One field, genetics, profited especially from the new developments and techniques. Before World War II, T. H. Morgan and others experimenting with fruit flies had greatly advanced the understanding of heredity and the role of genes and chromosomes in determining the traits of an individual. Now, with the aid of short wave radiation, electron microscopes, radioactive isotopes, and the like, it became possible to determine much more accurately how genetic differences were actually transmitted and imprinted in the cells. One of the startling advances in the new field of molecular biology was the discovery that two nucleic acids, D.N.A. (deoxyribonucleic acid) and R.N.A. (ribonucleic acid), played a crucial part in setting the genetic characteristics of living things, from microbes to men. Similarly, the role of viruses and how they affected healthy cells and caused diseases became clearer. The rapid increase of understanding of genetics made possible the development of disease resistant plants (blight-proof potatoes, rust-proof wheat) and more productive strains (hybrid corn), which, taken together with improvements in cultivation, irrigation, and fertilization, greatly raised agricultural output.

Hand in hand with the new knowledge in biology and chemistry went startling advances in medicine. Physicians in the twentieth century were able to understand many diseases and pathological conditions in a thoroughly scientific manner. Part of the improvement arose from better diagnosis made possible by equipment such as the cardiograph or the X-ray camera. Part of it depended on the isolation, identification, and often the synthesis of substances which control physiological processes. Thus vitamin C was shown to prevent scurvy, and more than a dozen other vitamins were discovered and their importance determined. Adrenalin was found to affect allergic conditions, insulin (1922) to control diabetes, cortisone (1936) to alleviate rheumatic pains.

Perhaps even more significant was the development of new drugs and of antibiotics. The "sulfa drugs" were discovered and some of them were proved to be most efficacious against the bacteria that cause pneumonia, diphtheria, and other diseases. Even more marvelous were the antibiotics, of which the first was penicillin, discovered in 1929 and put to medical use during World War II. It was followed by many others such as streptomycin, aureomycin, terramycin, etc. Taken together they formed a more effective weapon against infection and disease than any that had ever before been available to physicians. Still other drugs, many of them "tranquilizers," were found to be useful in the treatment of mental disease, and drugs began to be employed with much success even against tuberculosis.

Vaccination against smallpox had been in use since the early part of the nineteenth century and the Pasteur treatment against hydrophobia since the latter part. But the twentieth century saw the development of preventive treatments based on vaccines or other immunizing injections against a wide variety of ailments ranging from diphtheria and scarlet fever to allergies, yellow fever, and eventually (1953) infantile paralysis. New chemicals were of aid in combating insect-borne diseases. DDT had been discovered in 1874 but had not been used as an insecticide until 1939. By employing it, louse-borne diseases like typhus could be controlled and mosquito-borne malaria could be substantially eliminated. Surgery kept pace with general progress in medicine, and by the mid-twentieth century, brain, heart, and other operations of incredible delicacy were being performed in an almost routine manner. And it was found that plastic parts could sometimes be used to repair living tissue, such as the heart and the arteries. The medical advances were of great effect also in the fields of public health and sanitation. The provision of pure water, the adequate disposal of wastes, and the protection of foods all helped to save millions of lives.

As in medicine, so in technology, progress in the sciences led in the twentieth century, rather rapidly, to momentous changes. Many of them had to do with the development, improvement, and diffusion of nineteenth-century inventions. Thus the telephone (1876) became so common that it was estimated that there were about 175 million (half of them in the United States) in 1965. Radio (1895) led to the development of world-wide broadcasting systems, radar (1925), television (1926), and systems for the automatic guidance of airplanes and missiles. The first clumsy airplane flown by the Wright brothers at Kitty Hawk in 1903 had, less than sixty years later, given way to jet planes capable of carrying more than a hundred passengers at six hundred miles an hour or with a single pilot at more than five times that speed. The jet plane, in effect, shrunk the world to a tiny fraction of its former size. Modern man could get from New York to Capetown or Karachi faster than his father could have gone from New York to Chicago, or than George Washington could have traveled from New York to Baltimore. The first automobile had been produced in the 1880's. In 1965, the United States alone had some ninety million motor vehicles, and had for the transportation of people and goods a highway system of roads, turnpikes, parkways, and throughways totaling more than three million miles, constructed with the aid of giant earth-moving machines which did the work of hundreds of men. The first crude phono-

Electronically controlled line of machine tools checked by a single engineer.

graph of 1877 had, seventy-five years later, developed into the high-fidelity set capable of reproducing music with uncanny accuracy. Celluloid (1870) had been superseded by scores of plastics for a wide variety of purposes. Synthetic fibers such as "nylon," "dacron," and "orlon" had almost replaced natural silk by 1960 and were competing with the older fibers like wool and cotton. In 1963, in the United States alone, almost 1.8 million tons of synthetic rubber were produced.

Though much of the technological advance in the twentieth century was based on earlier developments, there were whole industries that were substantially new, including plastics, synthetics, biological chemicals, frozen foods, and electronics. The electronic industry, made possible in good part by the invention of the three-element vacuum tube (1906), was revolutionized after 1948 by the development of the simpler and smaller transistor. The use

of transistors made possible the creation of relatively compact computers or "electronic brains" which could store and report information, perform routine operations, and rapidly make mathematical computations which would take a man many years to complete. In the 1960's, such computers not only speeded scientific progress but also took over a great area of governmental and business activities, such as accounting and inventory control. The whole development of atomic ventures, ranging from engines to drive submarines and surface ships, to atomic power plants, and to the production of radioactive isotopes, arose after the explosion of the first atom bomb (1945), which had been soon superseded (1952) by the thermo-nuclear or hydrogen bomb thousands of times more destructive.

Equally dramatic was the rapid evolution of rockets and missiles. While rockets had been known and used for military and other purposes for hundreds of years, it was the

Gemini 7 in space, photographed from Gemini 6, December 17, 1965.

Courtesy
Wide World Photos

work of Robert H. Goddard (1882–1945) in Massachusetts that led to a renewed interest in them. He was, for example, the first to launch a liquid fuel rocket. Developments in World War II rapidly indicated that rockets could be used not only for long-range intercontinental missiles but also for space exploration. In this field the Russians leaped into the lead by launching on October 4, 1957, an artificial satellite, Sputnik I, which continued in orbit around the earth for three months. Before the end of 1960 the Russians had put six satellites in orbit, while the United States had sent up more than two dozen, much smaller than those of the Russians but usually heavily instrumented to send back information about radiation and other conditions in space. During the same period the Russians sent out three space probes, one of which, Lunik II, encircled the moon on September 13, 1959, while the United States launched two, again smaller in size. In April 1961, the Soviet Union put a space vehicle into orbit with a man (Yuri A. Gagarin) aboard, who successfully returned to earth after one revolution around the world. In February 1962 the United States safely put a marine officer (John Glenn) in space three times around the earth.

The competition in space exploration led thereafter to even more rapid and more startling advances. The Russians sent up Vostoks III and IV, which orbited within a few miles of each other (1962). The first female astronaut, Valentina Tereshkova did a three-day flight (1963). The Voskhod flew sixteen orbits with three men aboard (1964). And Alexei Leonov, in a space suit, spent ten minutes outside his space craft (1965). The United States launched manned flights of six orbits (1962) and of twenty-two orbits (1963). Edward White took a "space walk" of twenty minutes (1965). And most spectacular of all, two manned space craft, Gemini 7 and Gemini 6, navigated to a rendezvous within a few feet of each other (1965). Meanwhile, scores of other launchings were made for scientific and experimental purposes. A Tiros series was sent aloft by the United States for weather observation and prediction. Other vehicles—Echo, Relay, Telstar, Syncom, and finally Early Bird (1965)—were sent up for communication purposes and made possible direct television between Europe and America. Russian craft, Lunik III and Zond III, photographed the invisible side of the moon, while an American series (Rangers 7, 8, and 9) took thousands of close-up pictures of the front side. Both countries launched Mars probes (1964). The American craft was more successful and sent back twenty-one photographs of that planet, some at a distance of less than six thousand miles. An earlier American Venus shot (1962) sent back much information. The indications were that neither planet was capable of supporting life. President Kennedy had suggested that the Soviet Union and the United States coöperate in putting a man on the moon. But since the Russians preferred competition, each country went on with the race and hoped for success before 1970. The Russians scored an important "first" in this contest when, in February 1966, one of their space craft made a "soft landing" on the moon and sent back pictures of its surface, a feat soon duplicated in an improved fashion by the United States.

All the technological and scientific advances gave rise to one momentous fact. Both agricultural and industrial output could be greatly increased without any corresponding increase in, and in fact often a decrease in, the amount of human labor required. Agricultural production per man-hour was raised rapidly not only by the use of machines for plowing, sowing, cultivating, reaping, and preliminary processing, but also by the use of better crop varieties and improved cultivation techniques. The results were startling where the new methods were applied. In the United States the number of persons employed in agriculture dropped from 12.5 million in 1930 to less than five million in 1966, but in the same period agricultural production increased dramatically. That of corn more than doubled. Wheat increased more than twenty-five per cent, and the number of cattle grew by about sixty per cent.

The growth of industrial output was even more startling. It arose not only from the application of new scientific knowledge, devices, and techniques, and from the use of machinery, but also from the introduction of new managerial methods. From the beginning of the twentieth century up to World War II, some of the major increases in production were achieved through new techniques of "mass production." Some of them, such as interchangeable parts, had been used in the nineteenth century. But their importance grew rapidly after 1900. The development of the "assembly line" for the manufacture of automobiles by Henry Ford in Detroit just before World War I was a striking example. After 1945 a new kind of innovation in production became significant. This was "automation," a system whereby, for the most varied processes of manufacture, control, and inspection, machines and electronic devices replaced human beings. Through "feedback" techniques the machines could keep track of their own operation and alter it as might be necessary. In all sorts of industries —textiles, chemicals, petroleum refining, plastics—automated factories with only a few supervisory workers could steadily turn out vast quantities of goods. While automation progressed most rapidly in the United States because of the high cost of labor, it also developed to a very considerable degree by 1966 in Germany, Great Britain, France, and other countries. Automation was not so evident in Russia but mass-production methods were widely employed there.

Taken together, the new methods and techniques, the new power sources like oil, electricity, and atomic energy, the application of scientific knowledge, the development of new kinds of production (automobiles, airplanes, synthetics, plastics, electronics, etc.) constituted an industrial revolution in the twentieth century which made the changes in the nineteenth century seem puny by comparison. A few simple statistics will illustrate the magnitude of the movement. Between 1920 and 1959 in the United States the production of electricity increased eighteenfold, of aluminum more than two hundred and eighty fold, of paper more than fivefold, of electric refrigerators more than seven-hundredfold, and in the twelve years from 1947 to 1959

American Airlines Terminal, J. F. Kennedy Airport, New York. Architects, Kahn and Jacobs.
Note abstract design in glass that dominates facade.

	Great Britain	France	Germany [1]	U.S.S.R.
Steel in millions of metric tons				
1937	13.1	7.9	20.0	17.8
1963	22.9	17.6	31.6	80.2
Automobiles and trucks in thousands				
1937	445	200	332	199
1963	2,012	1,707	2,662	587
Electricity in billions of kilowatt hours				
1927	10.9 (1928)	11.4	12.4	1.7
1938	30.7	19.3	55.2	36.4
1963	173.6	88.2	147.3	412.4

[1] West Germany after 1945.

D. Social Sciences and Philosophic Speculation

The rapid advances in science and technology in the twentieth century, taken together with the wars, the vast political changes, and the general instability, had profound effects on the non-scientific areas of human endeavor. The "social scientists" tried to become more scientific, and the phrase "behavioral sciences" came into use to express the hope that sociology, anthropology, and psychology could be more like physics or biology in their ability to control and formulate their data and to make generalizations and predictions.

Economics did in fact become more scientific. Aided by significant improvement in the gathering of statistics and by very rapid development of refined statistical techniques, economists were able to work effectively with concepts such as the "level of prices," the "index of production," "gross national product," "national income." Economic theory likewise advanced as its practitioners, such as J. M. Keynes in Britain and J. M. Clark in the United States, improved the methods of analysis. Governments and business turned more to economists for an understanding of what was happening and what might occur as a result of changes in policy. Down to World War II, and especially in the 1930's, economists had been particularly interested in business cycles and depressions, their causes and their nature. But after 1945 the general upsurge of production and prosperity and the mildness of the economic recessions that occurred reduced the urgency of those problems, while the war-time and post-war inflations and exchange difficulties increased the attention paid to monetary and fiscal policy. It came to be widely believed, moreover, that governments, by their monetary and tax policies, by deficit spending, by subsidies and social expenditures, by public works and other devices, could stimulate growth, maintain prosperity, and bring about a considerable degree of stability. Such indeed, seemed to be the case in France, West Germany and the United States, for example.

Political science and sociology made less progress in the direction of becoming scientific or developing tenable theories. But

the index of industrial production rose by more than sixty per cent. In 1951 it took 568,000 American workers to produce 105 million tons of steel. In 1961 it required only 450,000 to produce the same amount.

What was happening in the United States was more or less duplicated in the other industrial countries. In Russia the percentage rise in output was even steeper, partly because the base was smaller. But the absolute amounts also became massive after World War II. The figures on the opposite page indicate the changes in an old industry like steel and new ones like automobile production and electricity.

both came to use, with some effect, statistics derived from polls or otherwise to describe and analyze human behavior. Both remained predominantly descriptive and both were hard put to it to keep up with the rapid tempo of political and social change in the twentieth century. Political scientists, influenced perhaps by the rise of dictatorships after World War I, became more interested in political realities as against forms. They strove to understand the actualities of political power, where it lay, and how it was exercised.

There was great activity in the field of history, which expanded to include a vast deal of writing about the Americas, Africa, and Asia, whereas before 1900 strictly European history had seemed of overwhelming importance. Several attempts were made, with indifferent results, to describe the movement of all human history. These included Oswald Spengler's pessimistic *The Decline of the West*, written after World War I, and Arnold Toynbee's elaborate *Study of History* (1934–1954).

Archaeology, using new scientific techniques like carbon 14 dating, greatly expanded knowledge of ancient peoples, not only of the Mediterranean world but also of India and the Americas. Anthropology progressed in two directions. It made much clearer the evolution of early man, and it studied intensively and sympathetically surviving primitive peoples who had now been brought into contact with modern civilization. Some of the concepts derived from this latter field proved to be equally applicable to advanced nations, and the field of cultural anthropology became a most active one.

Psychology seemed to move in two directions in the twentieth century. On the one hand it developed as a science based on laboratory experiments and careful observation. The Russian Ivan Pavlov had begun, before 1900, to describe human behavior in terms of observable phenomena rather than consciousness, and he originated the concept of the "conditioned reflex." This approach was carried further by a host of other workers such as the American John B. Watson whose school of psychology was called "behaviorism." Rather different were the Germans, Kurt Kaffke, Max Wertheimer, and Wolfgang Köhler, who gained insights into human actions by studying great apes and other animals and who developed "gestalt psychology" emphasizing patterns as against simple reflexes. Psychological tests were worked out and much used, especially in the United States.

On the other hand, one side of psychology developed into psychiatry which built up effective techniques for curing mental illness but was subjective and indeed almost poetic rather than scientific. The father of psychiatry was Sigmund Freud, an Austrian physician, who before 1900 was stressing the unconscious and subconscious factors (especially sexual urges) in human behavior and curing patients by "psychoanalysis."[1] His followers split into several schools, two of them led by former associates of Freud, C. G. Jung and Alfred Adler who stressed other factors more than sex. Adler, for example, invented the notions of the "inferiority complex" and the "defense mechanism" to explain the ways in which people acted. Jung recognized the importance of the human soul and of spiritual factors. Psychoanalysis, whether Freudian or post-Freudian, became very influential in many fields because of its stress on the non-rational origins of human action.

Indeed it was becoming evident, even before World War I, that there was a trend away from the rationalism and determinism of the eighteenth and nineteenth centuries. The Italian sociologist Vilfredo Pareto was stressing the non-rational bases of group behavior. Georges Sorel, a French engineer, was emphasizing the importance of myth in motivating masses of people. Modern advertising was already learning that an appeal to the emotions was more effective than a reasoned argument. The rise of nationalism, so important in leading to the two world wars of the era, and so accentuated by both of them, was clearly a non-rational phenomenon, though politicians were able to take advantage of it and to use it in a thoroughly rational and calculating fashion.

In philosophy there were some attempts to push forward down the road of rationalism. The British Bertrand Russell, for example, who made distinguished contributions to mathematics, tried to bring the precision of that field into his philosophy

---

[1] See above, p. 673.

of "logical atomism" and into his development of a "symbolic logic" which would not depend on words, colored as they are by emotion, by their cultural connotations, and by their history. His work was carried further by the Austrian Ludwig Wittgenstein whose "logical positivism" was so rational that it became almost anti-rational in its insistence that most communication in words is meaningless. In his later years, after World War II, Wittgenstein withdrew from some of the extreme positions he had taken, but not before he had given added impetus to the growing attempt to reach understanding of various subjects by linguistic analysis. In addition, some Christian philosophers like Jacques Maritain, who harked back to the tradition of Thomas Aquinas, appeared as the chief defenders of human reason against critics of the most varied sort. The Marxist philosophers, who were of course the only kind allowed in Communist countries, thought of themselves as materialistic and deterministic in their point of view and scientific and rational in their procedures. But as a matter of fact, Marxism was so dated by the mid-twentieth century that its methodology was antiquated, its assumptions contrary to fact, and its support based on political rather than intellectual grounds.

An important and typical twentieth-century school of philosophy was pragmatism. Though similar to the fictionalism of the German scholar, Hans Vaihinger, it was principally American in origin and was developed by such thinkers as C. S. Peirce, William James, and John Dewey. The pragmatists saw truth more as a process than an end, as changing rather than as absolute. What "worked," what advanced understanding and knowledge was for them "true" until something that worked better was developed. Pragmatism was thus related to the experimental laboratory procedures of science.

But even more typical of the twentieth century were thinkers whose approach was non-rational, anti-rational, or meta-rational (beyond reason). Two philosophers, both French, may serve as illustrations, the one active before World War I, the other active after World War II. Henri Bergson (1850–1941) seized on biology as a way to escape from the rigid and rational determinism imposed by nineteenth-century physics. In his *Creative Evolution* (1907) he sought to sweep away both physics and logic. To him, the "vital urge" (*élan vital*) of the biological organism was all important. Instinct and intuition were far more significant than reason. There might be final causes and ultimate goals but they mattered little, for immediate causes and goals were ever molded anew by creative evolution as it proceeded. Jean Paul Sartre (*b.* 1905), whose school of thought came to be known as "existentialism" and won many followers in the 1950's, especially among writers, harked back to a Danish Protestant theologian of the nineteenth century, Sören Kierkegaard, who had sharply distinguished between knowledge and faith and between thought and life. With this as a starting point, Sartre maintained that the only certainty was human existence and experience. One could be properly skeptical about knowledge, reason, ideals, and almost everything else. Indeed the only real argument against suicide was that there is inherent in human existence a kind of stoic courage and a dumb ability to endure.

Church of Notre-Dame de Royan (1958). Guillaume Gillet, architect.

CHAPTER 65

Religion and Art in an Age of Confusion and Change

A. Religion

The rationalistic and atheistic attacks on religion which had characterized the closing decades of the nineteenth century, and the first of the twentieth,[1] lost some of their cogency with the waning, after World War I, of faith in human reason and in the ability of natural or social science to provide ultimate answers or goals. But traditional Christianity (and Judaism also) had new foes and faced new difficulties. One was indifference. A large number of people in the Western world simply ceased to think much about religious matters and devoted themselves to other concerns, or they held that material and secular matters were so important that religion could be relegated to a minor role. Couldn't the national state do whatever worthwhile educational and charitable work the churches had been doing, and do it better?

Another and peculiarly devastating development was the repudiation of Christianity, whether Catholic, Orthodox, or Protestant, by large sections of the industrial working class. This occurred chiefly in the large cities and overgrown suburbs on the European continent, though to some extent in Great Britain and in Latin America; probably the United States was least affected. It was the result in part of past neglect on the part of the churches themselves, and in part of effective propaganda of Marxian Socialism, with its emphasis on materialism, class-warfare, and eventual glorious triumph of the proletariat, and with its denunciation of supernatural religion as an "opiate," a "tool of capitalism."

The pseudo-religious nationalism which appeared after World War I in Fascist Italy and Nazi Germany was essentially anti-Christian. To be sure, Mussolini tried to conciliate the church and win its support by negotiating the Lateran treaty with the Vatican,[2] but the papacy reacted vigorously against his attempts to lessen its influence. In the case of Germany under Hitler, there was forceful suppression of Christian dissent or criticism. Here, too, in pursuit of a most un-Christian and inhuman "racialism," there was, during Hitler's dictatorship, a terrible many-sided persecution of Jews (including Christians with any Jewish ancestry), climaxed during World War II by mass extermination of an estimated five or six million in the most dreadful secret torture chambers and roasting ovens.

---

[1] See above, pp. 681–683.

[2] See above, p. 744.

Communist Russia, though less affected by such "racialism," had been, from the start in 1917, the determined and persistent foe of Christianity and has worked steadily to supplant it, among the masses, with atheism. The Russian Communists have barely tolerated the Orthodox Church, reducing it to the status of a private society, preventing any propaganda or public teaching by it, and turning many of its cathedrals and other places of worship into museums, atheistic centers, or government buildings. Within the Soviet Union, Protestantism, which used to be freely practiced in the Baltic provinces, has been even more seriously handicapped than Orthodoxy. Catholic bishops and priests have been killed or exiled and Catholic worship, once widely observed by the so-called "Uniates" in the Ukraine and Byelorussia, has been stopped altogether except in one or two small churches in Moscow that are attached to foreign embassies and are served by closely watched foreign priests.[1]

Similar policies have been followed since World War II by Communist regimes wherever they have been intruded: in the satellite states of eastern Europe, and also in China, North Korea, and North Vietnam. So far, results have varied, depending on the strength of religious loyalty in the several nations. Communist China and its satellites have rigorously persecuted all kinds of Christianity and killed, imprisoned, or expelled all foreign missionaries. In Poland, on the other hand, the Catholic Church under the leadership of Cardinal Wyszynski of Warsaw was strong enough to obtain some concessions and a degree of freedom from Communist domination. In Czechoslovakia, there is bare toleration of Catholic and Protestant churches, and likewise of Orthodox churches in Yugoslavia, Rumania, and Bulgaria. In an attempt to smite the Catholic Church in Yugoslavia, its Primate, Archbishop Stepinac, was arrested by Tito's regime in 1946, tried on false charges of being pro-Nazi, and condemned to prison at hard labor for sixteen years; he was transferred to "house arrest" five years later, and died in 1960, a Cardinal of the Roman Church and a Christian

martyr. In Hungary both Protestants and Catholics held gallantly to their faith, and for it both suffered grievously. For example, the strong-willed Catholic leader, Cardinal Mindszenty, who had been imprisoned during World War II for opposing the Nazis and Fascists was imprisoned for life in 1948 for opposing the Communists; freed amid popular acclaim by the brief revolt at Budapest in October 1956, he escaped certain death on its suppression by taking asylum in the United States legation.

Despite the best efforts of Christian leaders, and the valiant stand of Christian followers, the Communist campaign against supernatural religion and in behalf of atheism cost Christianity the loss of large numbers of former adherents. In the Soviet Union the remaining Orthodox faithful consisted mostly of elderly people; and in the Communist satellites many of the younger generation were being weaned away from Christian practice. Nor was this all. De-Christianization was an obvious fact among the fairly large numbers of Communists in the West, especially in Italy, France, and Latin America.

Yet Christian losses were counterbalanced—and probably more than counterbalanced—by renewed Christian vitality and certain positive gains. The major Churches met the problems and crises of the age under notably able and devoted leadership. There were especially gifted and heroic clergymen among both Protestant and Orthodox Christians. And the Roman Catholic Popes, since Leo XIII, have been men of great intelligence and spirituality, foresighted and devout: the saintly Pius X (1903–1914), the conciliatory Benedict XV (1914–1922), the scholarly Pius XI (1922–1939), the wise Pius XII (1939–1958), the beloved John XXIII (1958–1963), and the scholarly and thoughtful Paul VI (1963–   ).

In certain respects the intellectual climate of the period after World War II has been more favorable to Christianity than that of the era before World War I. The newer physics has undermined, among thoughtful persons, the earlier belief in the stability of matter: the older materialism now seems rather simple and naive. Natural scientists are less certain of themselves. Many phenomena, formerly regarded as

---

[1] For further details about the anti-religious campaign in Russia, see above, p. 741.

Karl Barth, Swiss theologian on his 70th birthday, May 10, 1956.

Courtesy Wide World Photos

doubts concerning some of the optimistic teachings of earlier social scientists. Many persons, too, who had been uninterested in religion have been led by the human depravity evidenced in Hitler's concentration camps, by the ethical questions raised by the atomic bombing of the civilians of Hiroshima, or by the studied deceit and ruthlessness of the Communists, to think about ultimate human values and the traditional spiritual bases of civilization. Some came to believe that only in the tenets and ethics of Christianity could be found a cure for the destructiveness and chaos of the twentieth century.

There was corresponding intellectual vitality among religious thinkers, and renewed emphasis on theology not only in the Catholic Church but in Protestantism which had tended before the World Wars to neglect theology in promoting liberalism and social service.[1] A leading apostle of the newer tendency was Karl Barth (*b.* 1886), a German-Swiss neo-Calvinist and determined foe of Hitler. Barth insists that the time has come for the churches to return to an enlightened fundamentalism, to firm belief in divine Providence and in the Scriptures as God's word to man. But Barth's fundamentalism differs from the earlier sort in that it is set forth in the full light of recent science and philosophy. Probably his most famous follower in the United States is Reinhold Niebuhr (*b.* 1892). Among Catholics, perhaps Jacques Maritain (*b.* 1882) is the best known of a group of intellectuals seeking to adapt traditional theology to contemporary thought and needs.

Both Catholics and Protestants now strove, actively though belatedly, to evangelize the urban working classes. Pope Leo XIII's encyclical on labor, which had had slight effect when first issued (1891), was reënforced and rendered more influential by encyclicals of Pius XI (1931) and John XXIII (1961). There was a similar drive on the part of Protestant groups. And there were noteworthy results. The thriving labor movement in the United States remained respectful of religion, and so also did a considerable part of the British trade unions, while throughout western Europe a Chris-

fully explained, are becoming less explicable. Nor is evolution a troublesome scientific idea now to thoughtful Christians, whether Catholic or Protestant. For example, the eminent French scientist Lecomte du Noüy (1883–1947) held in his *Human Destiny* that evolution could not have occurred by blind chance, but only through divine guidance, and the millions of years it had taken to create man would be as a day—or nothing—to a timeless being like God. Lecomte du Noüy further believed that, with the appearance of *homo sapiens,* evolution ceased being physical so far as man was concerned and became spiritual, with Christ the perfect summation. Similarly, the distinguished paleontologist Pierre Teilhard de Chardin (1881–1955), in his somewhat unorthodox thinking, considered evolution as a divine process. All of which is a far cry from the "warfare of science and religion" of seventy years earlier.

Besides, the intervening two World Wars, with their attendant political, economic, and social changes, have raised grave

---

[1] See above, pp. 682–683.

Albert Schweitzer (d. 1965). Alsatian Protestant missionary, physician, scholar; in Equatorial Africa since 1913.

tian trade-union movement emerged which, though having fewer members than the Socialist and Communist unions, was growing and could vie with them, and even exert some influence on them. In the United States during the 1960's, Catholics and Protestants, both clergymen and laymen, played a most active role in the movement to protect the civil liberties and defend the human rights of the American Negroes.

Missionary enterprise was pressed as never before by both Catholic and Protestant and, as far as possible, by Eastern Orthodox Christians. There was a serious setback to it—a practical stoppage—in Communist China, but missionaries who were prevented from serving there only swelled the numbers working elsewhere—in Japan, South Korea, Taiwan, Indo-China, or India, for instance. Of course, Christian missions now have to cope throughout Asia and Africa not only with Communist propaganda and threats against them, but also with native nationalist suspicion that they are allies and agents of Western imperialism. In Africa, too, they are in competition with an advancing tide of Moslem missionary effort. Yet Christian gains have been notable. According to the 1964 Yearbook of the *Encyclopaedia Britannica*, there are, outside of Europe and America, some 68 million Catholics, 26 million Protestants, and eight million Eastern Orthodox—an

estimated total of more than a hundred million professed Christians.

It is an interesting and important fact that, despite losses, Christianity's stronghold has remained in the Western world of Europe and America, and that the Christian Churches—Catholic and Protestant alike—have come to accept and lend support to the cause of human liberty. As atheism is the hallmark of the Communist world, so, it may be said, Christianity is unmistakably part and parcel of the free world. Nowadays, democratic Christian political parties flourish throughout Western Europe, and the free world's foremost statesmen are practicing Christians. Notable in the years after World War II were, for example, such Catholic leaders as De Gasperi, Adenauer, De Gaulle, and Kennedy.

The United States has become not only the leading defender of the free world but the country with the largest number of professed Christians. In 1965 this number was estimated to include more than 68 million Protestants, almost 47 million Catholics, and over 3 million Eastern Orthodox. There were also more than 5½ million Jews. In the world as a whole, there were nearly a billion professing Christians, including some 572 million Roman Catholics, 220 million Protestants, and 141 million members of Eastern Orthodox Churches. There were thought to be about 446 million Moslems, 387 million Hindus, 159 million Buddhists, and 13 million Jews. In addition, there were, especially in Communist lands, large but uncertain numbers of atheists.

Two notable movements have characterized the Christian churches in recent times; the one, liturgical; the other ecumenical. Catholic and Orthodox have been used, from time immemorial, to "liturgies," that is, to set forms of public worship, especially in the celebration of Mass or the Eucharist. In the present century, the Catholic Church has moved steadily, particularly under Popes Pius X, Pius XII, John XXIII, and Paul VI toward restoring its liturgy to earlier and simpler usage and securing greater lay participation in it. Quite as noteworthy has been the trend, under "high church" influence, to vivify and extend liturgical observance in Anglican and Lutheran Churches and to a remarkable extent in other Protestant churches. Apparently it has popular appeal. And in this connection, we should add that nowadays new church buildings, whether Catholic or Protestant, are often constructed in ultra-modernist styles and adorned with examples of the latest art.

The ecumenical movement looks toward mutual understanding and coöperation, and perhaps eventual union, among the Christian churches. It is a response to the obvious need for common defense against aggressive Communist materialism and atheism and for common action in the missionary field. It has come conspicuously to the fore among Protestants. In 1908 some twenty-five denominations formed a "Federal Council of the Churches of Christ in North America," and in 1922 an "Ecumenical Christian Conference on Life and Work," held at Stockholm, was attended by delegates of thirty-one non-Catholic bodies. Then in 1948, after World War II, a "World Council of Churches" was created by a meeting at Amsterdam of representatives of 150 Protestant and Eastern Orthodox churches from some forty-four countries. At its Second Assembly (Evanston, Illinois, 1954), there were delegates from 163 member churches and at the Third Assembly (New Delhi, 1961), twenty-three more churches were added, including the Orthodox Church of Russia. The World Council maintains headquarters at Geneva, and, though it has no legislative power over its member churches, it promotes coöperation in the "spread of evangelism, interchurch aid and reconstruction, study of religious and social issues, and growth of ecumenical consciousness among church members."

Protestants are still much divided among themselves on matters of doctrine and organization. But the rancor that once marked their interrelations is now a matter of history, and a few actual unions have latterly been effected. Thus Anglicans have joined with Presbyterians and other Protestants to form a "United Church" in India; and in the United States the Reformed and Congregational Churches have merged into a "United Church of Christ."

As for the Catholic Church, it has an ecumenical movement of its own. It increasingly emphasizes its world-wide and

Laurian Cardinal Rugambwa, Bishop of Rutabo, Tanganyika, and Archbishop Mark Mihayo (at left) of Tabora, Tanganyika, at the first inter-territorial Episcopal Conference of the East African Catholic hierarchy.

Courtesy Religious News Service Photo

supra-national nature. With its general administration now concentrated, under the papacy, in the diminutive but independent Vatican City, it yet is in close touch with the world outside through its diplomatic corps, through regular visits to Rome of its thousands of bishops and of mass pilgrimages, through the dozens of national colleges it maintains at Rome for the advanced training of priests, and through representatives on its highest counselling body—the College of Cardinals—of a widening diversity of nations. Under Pope John XXIII and again under Paul VI the number of Cardinals was increased. After the Consistory of February 22, 1965, the College of Cardinals had 103 members. They included 32 Italians, 34 other Europeans, 6 Americans, 3 Canadians, 13 from Latin America, 9 from Asia and the Middle East, 5 from Africa (of whom 2 were Negroes), and one Australian. Six of the Cardinals came from Communist countries (China, Czechoslovakia, Hungary, Poland, Ukraine, Yugoslavia).

The most important religious development of the twentieth century ("the event" Karl Barth called it) was the Second Vatican Council (1962–1965). It was the first such gathering since the Vatican Council of 1869–1870, and the second since the Council of Trent (1545–1563). It was notable for its size and for the broad range of topics discussed. Some 2,500 patriarchs, cardinals, archbishops, bishops, religious superiors, experts (or *periti*), and observers (including Protestants and representatives of the Eastern Orthodox Churches) attended it. Six thousand speeches were written and 1,400 were delivered. The Council Fathers cast 1,200,000 individual ballots on the matters laid before them. Vatican II was even more notable for the great work it accomplished, summed up by the Italian word *aggiornamento*, the bringing up to date of the Roman Catholic Church.

The idea of summoning the Council occurred in January 1959 to Pope John XXIII, who had won the affection and respect of all people by his warm personality and his embodiment of Christian charity and love. It met on October 11, 1962, and after Pope John's death (June 3, 1963), it was reconvened in three more annual sessions by his successor, Pope Paul VI. It closed on December 8, 1965, after adopting sixteen important documents (four constitutions, nine decrees, three declarations) which covered a tremendous variety of subjects—liturgy, divine revelation, the Church in the modern world, religious education, the role of the laity, ecumenism, missionary activity, Church organization, religious liberty and others. Unlike some earlier councils which had issued anathemas against dissidence, Vatican II was infused with a spirit of tolerance and understanding. In fact, during its course Pope Paul and Patriarch Athenagoras of Constantinople voided the mutual excommunications that had marked the separation of the Eastern and the Western Churches in the year 1054. And in the last days of the Council, Paul VI joined with Orthodox and Protestant churchmen in an interfaith prayer service at the basilica of St. Paul's Outside the Walls. During the Council, moreover, Pope Paul indicated that there would be a reform of the Curia (the central government of the Church) and, as a first step, modernized the Holy Office, changing its name to the Congregation for the Doctrine of the Faith and stressing its positive role as against its traditional function of the repression of error. He likewise announced the establishment of a synod of bishops to assist him in ruling the Church.

The notable accomplishments of the Council were legion. It strengthened the tradition of the "collegiality" of the bishops —that is the idea that they should share in the governance of the Church. It authorized the use of the vernacular languages in the Mass. It stressed and enhanced the role of the laity. It denounced anti-Semitism. It greatly advanced the cause of ecumenism, emphasizing how much all Christians hold in common, encouraging dialogue and joint action with non-Catholics, and expressing respect for the reverent religious spirit embodied in some non-Christian religions. It upheld religious liberty and opposed coercion of the individual conscience and the infringement of human dignity.

The trend toward ecumenism and a greater role for the Church as a supranational world organization was dramatized by Paul VI through his visits to the Holy Land (January 1964), to India (December 1964), and to the United Nations Assembly in New York (October 1965) where

Pope Paul VI addresses the General Assembly of the United Nations, October 4, 1965.

he addressed a moving plea to the representatives of more than a hundred countries. "No more war," he said. "War never again. Peace, it is peace that must guide the destinies of people and of all mankind."

The ecumenism, so forwarded by Vatican II, had been visible even before it convened. The noteworthy lessening in tension between Catholics and Protestants had, for example, been symbolized by the election, for the first time in history, of a Catholic, John F. Kennedy, to the presidency of the predominantly Protestant United States, and by the friendly call in 1960 on Pope John by the Archbishop of Canterbury, spiritual head of the Anglican communion. To be sure, it was a courtesy call, without doctrinal discussion, but there had been no such courtesy shown on either side since the sixteenth century.

As to the followers of the other major supernatural religions, it must be borne in mind that they, like the Christians, faced problems and dangers in a troubled world. The number of Jews in Europe has notably declined as a result of the Hitlerian massacres, of Soviet discrimination, and of emigration to the United States and to Israel. In Israel and elsewhere there is division, moreover, between religious Jews (Orthodox or Reformed) and nationalistic Zionist Jews more or less indifferent to religion. Contemporary Moslems are similarly divided by national lines, sectarian differences, and greater or lesser devotion, but, generally speaking, their common belief in God and the Prophet Mohammed renders them naturally averse to atheistic communism and hence potential allies of the Christian free world.

As the twentieth century has progressed, the basic religious issue has ceased to be opposition between science and theology. Rather the conflict is between atheism and supernaturalism. It is whether in the long run an exclusively "this-worldly" faith like

Geoffrey Francis Fisher, Archbishop of Canterbury, 1945–1961.

Courtesy Wide World Photos

Marxian Communism can and will provide the masses of mankind with a satisfying substitute for "other-worldly" faith which from earliest times to now humanity has cherished.

B. Literature

Literature has responded to the violence and the rapid change of the latest age, though in a very real sense the nineteenth century continued up till 1914. English novelists like Joseph Conrad (Polish by birth), H. G. Wells, John Galsworthy, and Thomas Hardy, playwrights like George Bernard Shaw, short story writers like Rudyard Kipling, and poets like John Masefield continued in the literary veins and traditions established before 1900, as did authors like Anatole France and Romain Roland in France and Thomas Mann in Germany. But by the time of World War I new winds were beginning to blow.

In 1913 Marcel Proust published in France the first volume of his great novel *A la Recherche du Temps Perdu*, of which the seventh and last did not appear until after his death in 1922. The work is a metic-

ulous chronicle of the doings of people in high society, but it is notable for its delicate, searching psychological analysis of character, subtle use of symbols and metaphors, and emphasis on sex. While Proust's volumes were appearing, the Irishman William Butler Yeats was publishing books of poetry more obscure than his earlier work but fascinating and powerful in their involved use of myth and symbol. Even more significant, perhaps, was James Joyce, whose *Portrait of the Artist as a Young Man* (1916) and, more especially, *Ulysses* (1922) had a profound influence on later novel writers. The latter book is related in structure to Homer's epic, but it tells the events of a single day in Dublin and does so by attempting to reproduce the "stream of consciousness" of the individual mind with all the leaps, quirks, subconscious associations, sex preoccupations, and obscurities that occur in thought. Even earlier and with more emphasis on sex, D. H. Lawrence in his novels like *Sons and Lovers* (1913) or *Women in Love* (1921) had shown some of the same tendencies. Still more microscopic in their psychological analysis were the novels of Virginia Woolf, such as *Mrs. Dalloway* (1925) and *To the Lighthouse* (1927). Joyce in his later works experimented in such daring fashion with words and language that they are too difficult for the ordinary reader unless he has the help of an elaborate commentary.

From the 1920's onward, novels, except those written frankly for entertainment, became more and more psychological. Many authors used Freudian or other psychoanalytical ideas to probe or display human motives, and symbols rather than expositions to give insights. Some seemed more interested in turning their own psyches inside out than in communicating with the reader. But each showed his own individual variation. Roger Martin du Gard in France and Sinclair Lewis in the United States were more realistic; André Gide (France) more perverse and more interested in style; Franz Kafka (Germany) more enigmatic in his nightmarish depictions of the tragic and incomprehensible predicament of modern man; Ernest Hemingway (United States) more preoccupied with war and violence; William Faulkner (United States) more fascinated by symbols; Graham Greene (Britain) more concerned with sin and salvation; Boris Pasternak (Russia) more perturbed by the fate of the individual in an age of mass social movements; Albert Camus, Jean Paul Sartre, and André Malraux (all French) were more existentialist. In England, after World War II, "angry young men" wrote novels of vivid protest against the drabness of lower-class and middle-class life. There was, too, a persistent stream of books about the war itself, stressing more often the grim realities than the drama or the heroism.

What was true of twentieth century novels was also true of dramas. Eugene O'Neill's plays, produced in the United States from 1916 on into the 1930's, were gripping but often grim portrayals of psychological conflicts, as were those of Tennessee Williams a generation later. The Italian Luigi Pirandello wrote dramas like *Right You Are if You Think You Are* (1922) which left the audience to choose one of a good many possible interpretations of the piece. Sartre and Camus wrote plays as existentialist as their novels. Jean Giraudoux modernized old myths with French wit and satire, and in both Europe and America there arose a "theater of the absurd"—plays related to existentialism but confusing in their use of symbols and their exploration of psychotic and neurotic minds. Many of the plays, like many of the novels, were transformed into motion pictures with more or less success. Though spectacles and action dramas were most popular with the audiences, the fuller and deeper possibilities of the screen were sometimes exploited by the Germans before Hitler, the Russians before Stalin, the Italians in the early 1950's, and the "new wave" of French producers at the end of that decade.

Poets became more and more interested in myth, ambiguity, and symbol. Many of them looked back with admiration to the French Baudelaire (1821–1867) or Rimbaud (1854–1891) or were influenced by the German R. M. Rilke (1875–1926), all of whose poems had used a wealth of symbolism. Many followed Joyce in experimenting with words and language or used poems as a means of self-expression rather than communication. A seeming exception

was the American Robert Frost, but his artistic simplicity was deceptive, for there were depths of metaphoric and symbolic meaning in his poems. Though Thomas Stearns Eliot, American-born Briton, was in the forefront in the new trends and in his analysis of the modern age, he differed from many in that his poems were usually infused with religious feeling, as were his poetic dramas like *Murder in the Cathedral* (1935) or *Cocktail Party* (1949). So extreme was the experimentation with words of Gertrude Stein, an American who lived most of her adult life in Paris and whose poems appeared in the 1920's and 1930's, that conservatives refused to recognize her work as poetry.

C. Painting and Sculpture

If experimentation was common in literature, it was even more evident in the field of painting. In the years preceding World War I the impressionist and post-impressionist painters mentioned previously [1] were still active, and Paris was still the center of art activity as it had been since the mid-nineteenth century. But there soon appeared new and more advanced schools of painting which moved further and further away from any attempt at realistic representation of scenes and objects. Inspired by Cézanne's view that everything in nature is "modeled on the lines of the sphere, the cone, and the cylinder," Pablo Picasso, a young Spanish artist working in Paris, began about 1910 trying to reduce everything he depicted to geometrical form. Other artists—Georges Braque, Juan Gris, Fernand Leger, Francis Picabia—were moving in the same direction. Their approach quickly came to be known as "cubism." Their paintings tended to minimize color and to emphasize shapes, planes, and angles to a point so abstract that the subject was no longer recognizable. A painting by Marcel Duchamp called *Nude Descending a Staircase*, which caused a great stir when exhibited in the United States in 1913, had in it no recognizable human figure nor any staircase. Though the cubists, and especially Picasso, were moving in other directions

---

[1] See above, p. 677.

The Black Circle (1924).
Watercolor by Wassily
Kandinsky.

*Courtesy Museum of
Modern Art, New York*

by the early 1920's their work had great influence on later developments in painting and in modern design.

A contemporary and not wholly dissimilar school was "futurism." In 1909, the Italian poet Filippo Tommaso Marinetti issued a manifesto calling for a new philosophy of art consonant with the machine age and insisting on the beauty of such things as "a racing car rattling along like a machine gun." Stimulated by his ideas, five Italian painters issued the next year their own proclamation calling for a revolt against tradition ("Burn the Museums") and urging the portrayal of machines and motions. These five—Umberto Boccioni, Carlo Carrà, Luigi Russolo, Gino Severini, Giacomo Balla—soon attracted followers who like them attempted to paint the dynamism of the machine age. As with the cubists, their subjects are often presented as abstractions, but they put so much emphasis on color, rhythm, and movement that some of their paintings convey a sense of excitement that is almost frenzied. Though the group was broken up by World War I, its influence on later artists was important.

The same period of feverish experiment

spawned a half dozen other "schools" of painting, including orphism (1912), synchronism (1913), vorticism (1914), dadaism (1916), and in Russia rayonism, suprematism, and constructivism. Of all these the two most important were fauvism and expressionism. Fauvism began as a revolt against impressionism about 1906 and won its name because some critics derisively called its adherents *fauves* (wild beasts) after seeing the paintings of their first major exhibit in Paris. But a number of the *fauves*—Raoul Dufy, André Derain, Georges Rouault, Maurice de Vlaminck—went on to achieve distinctive styles and eventual fame, and Henri Matisse had great influence because of his ability to use strong and vivid color with striking effect. While most of the others tended more or less toward abstractions, Matisse,[2] though he used distortion of line, form, and perspective, usually portrayed a recognizable subject.

Expressionism was a German school which grew up after 1908 under the leadership of Oscar Kokoscha and Max Pechstein. By heightened color, distorted figures, and

---

[2] See above, p. 731.

the abandonment of perspective, it sought to express the personal emotions of the artist, emotions which might range all the way from mystic tenderness to fierce violence. From it developed several subgroups, of which the most significant was the "Blue Riders"—Franz Marc, Wassily Kandinsky, Paul Klee, Aleksei von Jawlensky. Many of their paintings moved toward abstract exercises in color and form as with Kandinsky, though Klee and others remained somewhat more representational.

A slightly later movement was surrealism which arose after 1922. Often using a technique of almost photographic realism, the surrealists tried in their work to plumb the depths of the subconscious mind. Their paintings bring together incongruous objects meticulously painted so that the effect is often that of a dream or a nightmare. Among the most noted of these artists were Salvador Dali, Joan Miro, and Jean Arp. Dali's *The Persistence of Memory*, also popularly called *Wet Watches*, attracted wide public attention. Though not strictly of the school, the Russian Marc Chagall and the Italian Giorgio de Chirico were influenced by it.

After the period of ferment, artists in the ensuing decades went off in various directions, mostly those that had been indicated by experiments undertaken in the years 1908 to 1925. Picasso, for example, painted in a dozen different veins, almost always with a touch of genius. In Mexico there developed after 1920 a distinguished school of artists who painted vivid pictures (including murals and mosaics) much influenced by the pre-Columbian art of the American Indians. Diego Rivera, Jose Clemente Orozco, David Alfaro Sigueiros, and Rufino Tamayo often sought to expose the evils of capitalism and to celebrate the triumphs of the Mexican Revolution.

In the United States there had developed before World War I a group of notable artists, including Arthur B. Davies, George Bellows, Maurice Prendergast, and William Glackens, who were influenced by the newer tendencies and who, because they sometimes chose unromantic subjects, were called by critics "the Ashcan School." Art was much stimulated in America by the public subsidies of the depression period, but it was hard to put it into categories or schools until the abstract expressionists arose in the years between the wars. They used all the color and emotion and violence of the German expressionists but were strictly nonrepresentational. Sometimes, as with one of their leaders, Jackson Pollock, they did not use brushes but squeezed the paint directly from tubes or swished it from cans to get sweeping and dramatic effects. The vogue of abstract expressionism, which influenced Europe as well as America, was followed in the 1960's by various movements. Among them were "pop art," in which the most everyday objects, such as tin cans or advertisements, were portrayed with careful realism, and "op art" in which lines and geometrical figures were meticulously arranged to produce optical effects or illusions.

Sculpture in the twentieth century evidenced most of the same tendencies as painting. It moved away from realistic representations and toward abstractions. It frequently used distortions of various sorts and it was much influenced by an increasing acquaintance with primitive work such as the wood carvings of Africa or Polynesia. Before World War I the most influential sculptor was probably the French Auguste Rodin (1840–1917) who was both a realist and a romantic. The blurred outlines of his figures emerging from the rough stone are sometimes reminiscent of the impressionist painters. His *Man with a Broken Nose* is thoroughly realistic, while his famous *Thinker* suggests the evolution of man from the lower animals. The Croatian Ivan Meštrović, who won Rodin's praise, is notable for the powerful emotions portrayed in his work and for the strong effects he achieved by distortion. With remarkable originality his sculptures are at the same time "primitive," "archaic," and "abstract." More clearly "primitive" was Aristide Maillol whose massive women seem like the fabled earth mothers of ancient times. But the dominant trend was toward abstraction, as is shown in the work of the Italian Amadeo Modigliani who began his career as a post-impressionist painter but soon passed from cubist painting to a kind of cubist sculpture using simple geometrical forms. Even more abstract were the works of Jacob Epstein, born in New York but

An abstract expressionist painting by Jackson Pollock, entitled Number 1. 1948.

working mainly in London. His sculptures were at first greeted with derision but won increasing appreciation, and he himself after World War I did bronze portraits in a more traditional manner.

By the mid-century many "sculptors" were producing works in varied materials from cement to scrap iron which portrayed form or flight or the semblance of motion but which no longer bore any relationship to natural objects. Some of them moved (mobiles), others got their effect by lighting, and still others were elaborate mathematical constructs of wire and metal.

Taken as a whole, modern art has expressed the chaos, the confusion, the questing, the uncertainty, the dynamism, the change of the twentieth century. It has revolutionized design. It has proved itself capable of creating exciting decorative effects. It has served to express the artist's reaction to the world he lives in whether it be denial, frustration, antipathy, or even acceptance. Sometimes, as with the Mexican school, it can be used as a medium of propaganda.

It can communicate, at least in some instances, a mood or an emotion. But it is less clear that it can set up true communication, particularly in the realm of ideas, between the painter and his audience, for in most instances the viewer is free to react or interpret in his own way with no assurance that he has fathomed the artist's intent.

D. Architecture and Music

Architecture has changed more slowly than painting, for many twentieth-century buildings have been erected in one or another of the Western traditions—classical, neo-classical, gothic, Georgian, etc. But there is also a definite "modern architecture," variant in expression but tending to exploit the new materials that have become available to the architect, such as steel, aluminum, plastics, cinder blocks, plywood, glass, reënforced or pre-stressed concrete, and so on. There has also been a strong tendency toward simplicity, an emphasis on geometric form (perhaps related to cubism), and functionalism. In fact, one of the most important new ideas has been the famous dictum "Form follows function." Many of the newer buildings have emphatic vertical lines, wide spans, the slim supports made possible by the use of steel and apparently unsupported elements cantilevered out into space. The new materials also have made possible a variety of constructions other than buildings, such as dams, highways, and bridges.

As early as 1890, the American architect Louis Henry Sullivan (1856–1924) had designed the steel-frame Wainwright Building in St. Louis in such a fashion that its functional structure was evident. His American successors like Frank Lloyd Wright carried modernism much further. Wright's buildings, from the Imperial Hotel in Tokyo (1922) to the spiraled Guggenheim Museum in New York (1959), almost invariably show imagination as well as the modern tendencies. Similarly, the Swiss architect Charles Edouard Jeanneret, who called himself LeCorbusier, always showed, from his pavilion at the Paris Exhibition of 1925 to his housing project at Marseille and the city of Chandigar he designed in India, a resourceful inventiveness in the new vein, often standing his buildings on stilts to create ground level space and vistas. Very influential also was Walter Gropius. Winning a reputation with his Fagus factory buildings in Germany (1912), he created the Bauhaus Institute of architecture first at Weimar and then (1925) at Dessau. Leaving Hitler's Germany, he came to the United States where his teachings, his opposition to all non-functional ornamentation, and his insistence on simplicity had a strong impact on the younger generation of architects—though there were those who thought his edifices too stark. By 1966, Brasilia, the half-finished new capital of Brazil, was a monument to the new architecture, while in New York the boxlike glass and steel skyscraper had become almost a cliché. There developed, indeed, as a reaction a tendency to relieve the modern starkness by the most various decorative elements—texture, color, shadows, grilles, murals, reflecting pools, mosaics, sculpture, and even ornamentation.

Music in the twentieth century showed conflicting tendencies. For most concerts and operatic performances the predominant fare continued to be the "classical music" of the eighteenth and nineteenth centuries. There was an increasing vogue for the works of Bach and a growing interest in the music of the centuries before 1700. On the other hand, the world was swept, beginning shortly before 1920, by a remarkable enthusiasm for American jazz—popular music with a syncopated rhythm sometimes varied by extemporization. It developed from "ragtime" and owed much to Negro musicians and thus perhaps ultimately to Africa. Some jazz, such as *St. Louis Blues* by W. C. Handy or the more elaborate *Rhapsody in Blue* by George Gershwin, won the status of "classics" of this genre. Various subvarieties of jazz, "hot," "swing," "sweet," "boogie-woogie," "rock and roll," in their turn enjoyed popularity throughout the whole world. Jazz, indeed, poured out of phonographs, radios, and dance halls from Singapore to Helsinki and from Capetown to Tokyo. Even in Russia, where there was a tendency to regard jazz as American, capitalist, and degenerate, it had its devotees among young people. After four decades jazz seemed still so much in favor

Le Corbusier examining the model of an all glass apartment house designed by him, 1935.

Courtesy Wide World Photos

that it could be denominated *the* popular music of the century.

But there was also another kind of "modern music" which won growing acceptance as the twentieth century progressed, and was more and more presented as part of serious concerts. Moving on from the tendencies evident in earlier composers such as Claude Debussy (1862–1918), who had experimented with dissonances and unusual scales, younger men became more daring. Thus the Russian Igor Stravinsky created a sensation with his *Firebird* (1910) and his *Rite of Spring* (1913), musical ballets which startled contemporaries by their freedom in rhythm and harmony, by their impetuous violence, and by their brilliant coloring. A series of composers in the ensuing years experimented in a daring fashion with the traditional musical forms and techniques, and some even sought to introduce city noises or factory sounds or new electronic effects into their works.

Some composers, like the Russians Dimitri Shostakovich and Sergei Prokofiev, the German Paul Hindemith, or the American Walter Piston, created works that were recognizably connected with the older musical traditions though often inventive and experimental in new veins. Others, like the Hungarian Béla Bartók, were highly individualistic in their innovations. Still others, led by Arnold Schönberg, sought to find greater freedom for creativity by escaping entirely from the classical tonality in works that were subjective, emotionally violent, and even neurotic, and that were perhaps related to German expressionism in painting. In the 1920's Schönberg began employing a twelve-tone technique in which he was no longer bound by the old octave arrangement of notes. He had followers like Anton Webern and Alban Berg (who wrote a full length opera, *Lulu*, in the twelve-tone scale); and his atonalism influenced still others such as Bartók and the American Roger Sessions.

Thus as the second third of the twentieth century drew toward a close, it was clear that all the arts had changed dramatically. A critic from the 1890's would scarcely have recognized as art, much less have understood, a large portion of the painting, sculpture, poetry, or music of the

1950's and 1960's. All the arts were reflecting the confusion, the uncertainty, and the tension of their times. They were reflecting, moreover, the industrial civilization of which they were part, with its enormous cities, its mechanized transport, its mass communication media, its great factories. They were profiting greatly, too, from some of the changes that had taken place. The steady shortening of the work week in the advanced countries gave many people the time to enjoy or even practice the arts, while the new inventions brought within the reach of almost the whole population what had previously been available only to an elite. Thus, if most motion pictures and television performances were superficial and tawdry, still the best made good drama available to millions. Similarly, color reproductions of paintings by improved processes increased the accessibility of the art of all the past ages, while the phonograph, the radio, and television could bring the best as well as the most popular in music to a very wide audience. Down to the twentieth century the arts had been mainly for the delectation or amusement of the upper classes, which constituted only a small fraction of the whole population. By the 1960's they were at least available to the masses.

E. "Summits" and Interaction of Historic Civilizations

After 1948 when the Communist seizure of control in Czechoslovakia convinced the Western powers that their hopes for peaceful coöperation with the Soviet Union were unlikely to be realized, international politics and indeed the whole world picture were dominated by the conflict between the East (Russia and her satellites and later China) and the West (United States and associated nations). Sometimes the struggle was muted and, as after Stalin's death, there were expectations of a change in Russian policy. Sometimes the contention was open and violent as in the Korean War. But in either case it went on and on with no end in sight.

Though the conflict was, from the Russian point of view, between capitalism and Communism, such was hardly the case, for differences in the internal economic systems are no bar to external coöperation and even friendship. Actually the East and the West were at odds because they had radically different ideologies and moralities, and because the Communists firmly believed that they must spread their system to all countries by any means from the support of internal subversion and disorder to straightforward military conquest. The Communist outward thrust was indeed the most grandiose imperialist effort in the history of mankind, for it aimed at the conquest of the whole world. And despite Communist slogans and preachments, the effort was in some senses old-fashioned, since it was shaped and colored by Russian nationalism save where it was dominated by Chinese nationalism.

Several times the world struggle came to a sharp focus in what have come to be called "summit conferences," since these have brought together the topmost authorities of the major nations. The pattern of such meetings was probably influenced by precedents from World War II when the major allied leaders had gathered to shape policies and reach agreements—Cairo 1943, Teheran 1943, Yalta 1945, Potsdam 1945. In August 1959, President Eisenhower flew to Europe for conferences with Adenauer, Macmillan, and DeGaulle. The next month Khrushchev came to America and conferred with the American President at Camp David in Maryland. The discussions led to no important understandings but seemed to generate a feeling of greater friendliness, and they paved the way for arranging, at Khrushchev's urging a further meeting to be held at Paris in May 1960.

But when the four leaders (Eisenhower, De Gaulle, Macmillan, and Khrushchev) had actually come to Paris, the Russian premier deliberately broke up the meeting. His excuse was that the United States had been flying observation planes over Russian territory in violation of international law and that one of them had been shot down some two weeks before. He demanded that Eisenhower halt the flights and apologize. The American President did agree to the former demand but not to the latter, and the meeting ended in bitter words. Tensions were increased when in July the Russians shot down another American plane,

this time over international waters, and when Khrushchev came to a United Nations meeting in New York in September. At this gathering the Russian premier heckled his opponents, displayed violent ill temper, demonstrated his support for Castro, and denounced the attempts of the United Nations to bring order to the Congo. In particular, Khrushchev attacked Dag Hammarskjöld, the Secretary-General of the United Nations, and urged that he be replaced by a three-man committee composed of a representative of the East, one of the West, and one of the neutral powers. Since the suggestion was that such a committee could make decisions only unanimously, the arrangement would have given the Soviet Union a veto over all actions. Soon Russia was proposing similar committees for other international purposes, such as the policing of a ban on nuclear bomb testing—a subject which had been long and fruitlessly discussed in meetings at Geneva.

Despite the tense and unpromising atmosphere generated, another summit meeting was arranged. John F. Kennedy, the new American President elected in November 1960, wished to take stock of the Russian leader. And Khrushchev had given some indications that he thought he might be able to reach agreement more easily with Kennedy than with Eisenhower. President Kennedy, therefore, flew to Europe in May 1961 and conferred with De Gaulle in Paris, Macmillan in London, and Khrushchev in Vienna. Both Khrushchev and Kennedy proved adamant on major issues and the only understanding reached was that Laos should be "neutralized." East-West tension, increased by the Berlin Wall (August 1961) and by the Soviet renewal of nuclear testing (October 1961), reached a terrifying climax in the Cuban missile crisis (October 1962). Thereafter, there seemed to be a gradual relaxation of which the test-ban treaty (1963) was perhaps the first fruit.

Whether tense or relaxed, the power struggle was now being enacted on a world stage. Up to 1914 or even 1945, there had existed a sort of international system based on Europe, though ever since 1500 progressively affecting other continents. On the eve of World War II five of the seven nations which were accounted "great powers" were European: Great Britain, France, Germany, Italy, and Russia. At its end, four of these, and also Japan, had fallen from their high position and had become secondary to two "super powers," the American United States and the Eurasian Union of Soviet Socialist Republics. But in the 1960's this situation, too, seemed to be undergoing a change as conditions in the world at large slowly gave a new and more confused aspect to the cold war and blurred its outlines. Four developments were especially significant. First, the conflict between Russia and China had split the solidity of the Communist bloc. Each country was denouncing the other and seeking support from Communist parties everywhere and from the smaller nations. Russia was obviously concerned that, in the future, China, growing in power, might press against the long Soviet frontier in Asia. Second, Western Europe had recovered so far and grown so strong that it no longer felt completely dependent on the United States and was less willing (especially in the case of France) to accept American leadership. Its fears of a Russian invasion had declined. Only the division of Germany and the problem of Berlin kept it from settling down in the glow of prosperity engendered by the success of the Common Market. Third, the world was slowly adjusting to the situation in which a major (and therefore atomic) war seemed unlikely, if not unthinkable. At the same time it had become clear that minor wars with conventional weapons were going to go on and on as in the case of Korea, the Congo, Vietnam and Kashmir. Armies were still important in internal coups and nationalistic border clashes. Fourth, the developing countries of Asia, Africa and Latin America, courted so eagerly by both the Communists and the Free World, were making it more and more evident that they were concerned with, and occupied by, their own problems. They saw little advantage in lining up with one side or the other in the cold war, and even the attempt to form a solid neutralist bloc did not meet with much success. All these factors were slowly making the world struggle more four-sided than two-sided. While the Soviet Union and the United States were still clearly the superpowers, Western Europe (with Britain) seemed to be emerging as a third, and China (no longer accepting Russian leadership) counted almost as a fourth by its sheer weight of population and its long-run potential. In this confusing world picture it seemed likely that most of the hundred smaller nations would be content to stand aside and to accept help from any source.

The emergence of the new nations was in itself a factor of change as was their admission to the United Nations. Thereby this organization has been altered from a predominantly European-American and racially "white" affair to a truly world-wide one, including Afro-Asian peoples of color. The newly independent nations, generally speaking, are devoted to the organization and rely upon it to safeguard them and give them help and prestige. At the same time some, in pursuit of nationalist ends, have showed themselves willing to violate United Nations' charter injunctions against using force. India, for example, has resorted to force in Goa against Portugal; Indonesia has used it against Malaysia; India and Pakistan have fought each other. It may turn out that the U. N. has been weakened by its increase in numbers and by the fact that tiny new states like Malta or Cyprus have one vote in the Assembly just like Italy or India. But the U. N. has weathered many vicissitudes and seems slowly to be strengthening its peace-keeping and peace-making abilities.

The world of the last third of the twentieth century is bound together not only by membership in the U. N. and by the modern technology of jet planes and communication satellites but also by participation in Western civilization, for this civilization is not a thing of the past. Its material features are now common property, or at least they represent common goals, of all peoples. Nor should its abiding spiritual aspects be overlooked. Nations in Asia and Africa of quite different background and civilization have derived from several generations, if not centuries of European tutelage and colonialism, a knowledge of European ideas and a habit of copying European manners and customs. Christianity, native of the West, has exerted greater influence on the historic religions of the East than these have exercised on Christianity. It does seem likely that the coming decades and even centuries will witness not the supersession of Western civilization, with its long past and high values, but rather the continuation and expansion of its influence in every continent as a major element in an evolving world civilization.

SELECT SUPPLEMENTARY READINGS FOR PART XII

Chapter 59. H. C. O'Neil, *A Short History of the Second World War* (1950); Winston Churchill, *Memoirs of the Second World War*, 6 vols. (1948–1953); Floyd Cave *et al.*, *Origins and Consequences of World War II* (1948); A. R. Buchanan, *The United States and World War II*, 2 vols. (1964); W. Ansel, *Hitler Confronts England* (1960); A. S. Milward, *The German Economy at War* (1965); V. Rowe, *The Great Wall of France* (1961); P. Carell, *The Foxes of the Desert* (1961); G. A. Harrison, *Cross-Channel Attack* (1951); W. H. McNeill, *America, Britain and Russia, Their Cooperation and Conflict, 1941–1946* (1953); H. Feis, *Japan Subdued: the Atomic Bomb and the End of the War in the Pacific* (1961); M. Jakobson, *The Diplomacy of the Winter War: an Account of the Russo-Finnish War, 1939–1940* (1961); B. H. Liddell Hart, *The Revolution in Warfare* (1947); S. E. Morison, *The Two-Ocean War: a Short History of the United States Navy in the Second World War* (1963); Alexander Werth, *Twilight of France* (1942); Paul Farmer, *Vichy, Political Dilemma* (1955); W. L. Langer, *Our Vichy Gamble* (1947); R. Wohlstetter, *Pearl Harbor, Warning and Decision* (1962); J. R. Deane, *The Strange Alliance* (1947); J. H. Wuorinen, *Finland and World War II* (1948); R. E. Sherwood, *Roosevelt and Hopkins* (1948); D. D. Eisenhower, *Crusade in Europe* (1948); S. E. Morison, *History of United States Naval Operations in World War II*, several vols. (1947 ff.); J. P. Baxter, 3rd, *Scientists Against Time* (1946); H. R. Trevor-Roper, *The Last Days of Hitler* (1947); R. Hilberg, *The Destruction of the European Jews* (1961); H. Feis, *Japan Subdued* (1961); J. B. Collier, *The Defense of the United Kingdom* (1957); S. E. Morison, *American Contributions to the Strategy of World War II* (1958); R. A. Watson-Watt, *Three Steps to Victory* (1958); B. H. Liddell Hart, *The Soviet Army* (1956); A. Clark, *Barbarossa, the Russian-German Conflict, 1941–45* (1965); L. Collins and D. Lapierre, *Is Paris Burning?* (1965).

Chapter 60. J. B. Harrison, *This Age of Global Strife* (1952); W. C. Langsam, *The World Since 1919* (1954); Avery Vandenbosch and Willard Hogan, *The United Nations* (1952); Eugene Chase, *The United Nations in Action* (1951); Carnegie Endowment for International Peace, *United Nations Studies*, 8 vols. (1947–1956); F. H. Hinsley, *Power and the Pursuit of Peace* (1963); R. B. Russell, *A History of the United Nations Charter: the Role of the United States, 1940–1945* (1958); H. Feis, *Between Peace and War: the Potsdam Conference* (1960); B. Moore, *Soviet Politics, the Dilemma of Power* (1950); D. J. Dallin, *The New Soviet Empire* (1951); Z. K. Brzezinski, *The Soviet Bloc: Unity and Conflict* (1960); C. A. Manning, *The Forgotten Republics* (1952) (Baltic states annexed by Russia); V. S. Vardys, ed., *Lithuania Under the Soviets* (1965); H. L. Roberts, *Rumania* (1951); F. A. Váli, *Rift and Revolt in Hungary* (1961); D. A. Schmidt, *Anatomy of a Satellite* (1963); R. L. Wolff, *The Balkans in Our Times* (1956); J. Korbel, *The Communist Subversion of Czechoslovakia, 1938–1948* (1959); G. Ionescu, *Communism in Rumania, 1944–1962* (1964); C. G. Haines, ed., *The Threat of Soviet Imperialism* (1954); M. Beloff, *Soviet Policy in the Far East, 1944–1951* (1953); R. L. Walker, *China Under Communism* (1955); J. Ch'ên, *Mao and the Chinese Revolution* (1965); A. D. Barnett, *Communist China and Asia* (1960); H. E. Richardson, *A Short History of Tibet* (1962); G. F. Kennan, *American Diplomacy, 1900–1950, and the Challenge of Soviet Power* (1951); J. F. Byrnes, *Speaking Frankly* (1947); W. B. Smith, *My Three Years in Moscow* (1950); A. B. Lane, *I Saw Poland Betrayed* (1948); Waldemar Gurian, ed., *Soviet Imperialism* (1953); Hugh Seton-Watson, *The East European Revolution* (1950); J. P. Nettle, *The Eastern Zone and Soviet Policy in Germany, 1945–1950* (1951).

Chapter 61. M. A. Fitzsimons, *The Foreign Policy of the British Labor Government, 1945-1951* (1953); Hajo Holborn, *Political Collapse of Europe* (1951); T. L. Jarman, *A Short History of Twentieth-Century England* (1963); D. C. Somervell, *British Politics Since 1900* (1950); M. Bruce, *The Coming of the Welfare State* (1961); S. D. Bailey, *Parliamentary Government in the Commonwealth* (1952); C. P. Kindleberger, *Economic Growth in France and Britain, 1851-1950* (1964); E. M. Earle, ed., *Modern France, Problems of the Third and Fourth Republics* (1951); F. R. Willis, *France, Germany and the New Europe, 1945-1963* (1965); F. Goguel, *France Under the Fourth Republic* (1952); E. J. Furniss Jr., *De Gaulle and the French Army* (1964); M. Einaudi and F. Goguel, *Christian Democracy in Italy and France* (1952); M. Einaudi *et al.*, *Communism in Western Europe* (1951); A. Werth, *France 1940-1955* (1956); R. Aron, *France Steadfast and Changing: the Fourth to the Fifth Republic* (1960); P. M. Williams and M. Harrison, *De Gaulle's Republic* (1960); S. B. Clough, *The Economic History of Modern Italy* (1964); M. Grindrod, *The Rebuilding of Italy: Politics and Economics, 1945-1955* (1955); G. Mammarella, *Italy After Fascism: a Political History, 1943-1963* (1964); D. L. Horowitz, *The Italian Labor Movement* (1963); A. C. Jemolo, *Church and State in Italy, 1850-1950* (1960); N. Andren, *Government and Politics in the Nordic Countries: Denmark, Finland, Iceland, Norway, Sweden* (1964); I. Andersson, *A History of Sweden* (1956); J. H. Wuorinen, *A History of Finland* (1965).

Chapter 62. Dexter Perkins, *American Approach to Foreign Policy* (1952); H. S. Truman, *Memoirs*, 2 vols. (1955-1956); T. C. Sorenson, *Kennedy* (1965); H. A. Kissinger, *Nuclear Weapons and Foreign Policy* (1957); P. M. S. Blackett, *Atomic Weapons and East West Relations* (1956); H. L. Ismay, *NATO, the First Five Years, 1949-1954* (1954); R. Ritchie, *NATO: the Economics of an Alliance* (1956); H. A. Kissinger, *The Troubled Partnership, a Re-Appraisal of the Atlantic Alliance* (1965); D. Middleton, *The Atlantic Community* (1965); S. E. Harris, *The European Recovery Program* (1948); G. Freund, *Germany Between Two Worlds* (1961); O. E. Clobb, *20th Century China* (1964); B. L. Schwartz, *Chinese Communism and the Rise of Mao* (1950); K. S. Latourette, *The American Record in the Far East, 1945-1951* (1952); T. Tsou, *America's Failure in China, 1941-1950* (1963); D. Rees, *Korea: the Limited War* (1964); L. M. Goodrich, *Korea, Collective Measures Against Aggression* (1953); W. G. Beasley, *The Modern History of Japan* (1963); R. Leckie, *Conflict: the History of the Korean War, 1950-53* (1962); E. O. Reischauer, *The United States and Japan* (1950); Sir George Sansom, *The Western World and Japan* (1950); F. S. Dunn, *Peace-Making and the Settlement with Japan* (1963); H. M. Vinacke, *The United States and the Far East, 1945-1951* (1952); K. Kawai, *Japan's American Interlude* (1960); L. M. Goodrich, *Korea: a Study of U.S. Policy in the United Nations* (1956); F. Tannenbaum, *Ten Keys to Latin America* (1962); D. E. Worcester and W. G. Schaeffer, *The Growth and Culture of Latin America* (1956); J. J. Johnson, *The Military and Society in Latin America* (1964); R. E. Poppino, *International Communism in Latin America, 1917-1963* (1964); D. Lewis, *Five Families, Mexican Case Studies in the Culture of Poverty* (1959); H. F. Cline, *Mexico: Revolution to Evolution, 1940-1960* (1962); T. L. Smith, *Brazil: People and Institutions* (1954); A. P. Whitaker, *Argentina* (1964); J. R. Scobie, *Argentina: a City and a Nation* (1964); A. H. Robertson, *The Council of Europe* (1956); H. L. Mason, *The European Coal and Steel Community* (1955); W. Diebold, Jr., *The Schuman Plan: a Study in Economic Coöperation, 1950-1959* (1959); Isaiah Frank, *The European Common Market* (1961); S. N. Fisher, ed., *France and the European Community* (1964); G. L. Weil, ed., *A Handbook on the European Economic Community* (1965); A. Zurcher, *The*

Struggle to United Europe, 1946–1958 (1958); H. A. Schmitt, *The Path to European Union: from the Marshall Plan to the Common Market* (1962).

Chapter 63. C. J. H. Hayes, *The Historical Evolution of Modern Nationalism* (1955) and *Nationalism, a Religion* (1960); H. Kohn, *The Age of Nationalism, the First Era of Global History* (1962); S. C. Easton, *The Twilight of European Colonialism: a Political Analysis* (1960); G. E. Taylor, *The Philippines and the United States* (1964); R. Heussler, *Yesterday's Rulers: the Making of the British Colonial Service* (1963); G. Wheeler, *The Modern History of Soviet Central Asia* (1964); V. A. Smith, *The Oxford History of India* (1957); P. F. Griffiths, *Modern India* (1957); Khalid Bin Sayeed, *Pakistan: the Formative Phase* (1961); S. Arasaratnam, *Ceylon* (1964); W. L. Holland, ed., *Asian Nationalism and the West* (1953); B. Harrison, *South-East Asia: a Short History* (1954); D. G. E. Hall, *A History of South-East Asia* (1955); J. F. Cady, *Southeast Asia: Its Historical Development* (1964); D. Lancaster, *The Emancipation of French Indochina* (1961); B. B. Fall, *The Two Viet-Nams* (1963); J. M. Gullick, *Malaya* (1963); N. J. Ryan, *The Making of Modern Malaya: a History from Earliest Times to the Present* (1963); G. M. Kahim, *Nationalism and Revolution in Indonesia* (1952); Alastair M. Taylor, *Indonesian Independence and the United Nations* (1960); J. D. Legge, *Indonesia* (1964); G. E. Kirk, *A Short History of the Middle East* (1957); George Lenczowski, *The Middle East in World Affairs* (1952) and *Russia and the West in Iran* (1949); P. Avery, *Modern Iran* (1965); Majid Khadduri, *Independent Iraq, 1932–1958: a Study in Iraqi Politics* (1960); G. H. Torrey, *Syrian Politics and the Military, 1945–1958* (1964); P. Seale, *The Struggle for Syria: a Study of Post-War Arab Politics, 1945–58* (1965); Norman Bentwich, *Israel* (1953); C. Sykes, *Crossroads to Israel* (1965); M. H. Bernstein, *The Politics of Israel: the First Decade of Statehood* (1957); C. Issawi, *Egypt in Revolution: an Economic Analysis* (1964); K. Wheelock, *Nasser's New Egypt* (1960); L. D. Epstein, *British Politics in the Suez Crisis* (1964); J. Eayrs, ed., *The Commonwealth and Suez: A Documentary Survey* (1964); K. H. Karpat, *Turkey's Politics* (1959); M. Halpern, *The Politics of Change in the Middle East and North Africa* (1963); W. A. Hance, *The Geography of Modern Africa* (1964); Jane S. Nickerson, *A Short History of North Africa* (1961); R. Oliver and J. D. Fage, *A Short History of Africa* (1962); M. Khadduri, *Modern Libya: a Study in Political Development* (1963); G. K. N. Trevaskis, *Eritrea, a Colony in Transition, 1941–52* (1960); C. H. Moore, *Tunisia Since Independence* (1965); D. E. Ashford, *Political Change in Morocco* (1961); T. L. Hodgkin, *Nationalism in Colonial Africa* (1956); J. Hatch, *A History of Postwar Africa* (1965); W. M. Macmillan, *The Road to Self-Rule: a Study in Colonial Evolution* (1959); Z. K. Brzezinski, *Africa and the Communist World* (1963); G. H. T. Kimble, *Tropical Africa*, 2 vols. (1960); D. L. Wiedner, *A History of Africa South of the Sahara* (1962); Rupert Emerson, *From Empire to Nation* (1960); J. Duffy and R. A. Manners, *Africa Speaks* (1961); P. Neres, *French Speaking West Africa: from Colonial Status to Independence* (1962); *The African Nations and World Solidarity* (1961); L. H. Gann, *A History of Northern Rhodesia: Early Days to 1953* (1963); T. M. Franck, *Race and Nationalism: the Struggle for Power in Rhodesia-Nyasaland* (1960); K. Ingham, *A History of East Africa* (1963); E. J. Huxley, *Race and Politics in Kenya* (1956); G. Bennett, *Kenya: a Political History, the Colonial Period* (1963); A. J. Wills, *An Introduction to the History of Central Africa* (1964); D. E. Apter, *The Gold Coast in Transition* (1955); M. Crowder, *A Short History of Nigeria* (1962); V. T. LeVine, *The Cameroons from Mandate to Independence* (1964); C. Young, *Politics in the Congo: Decolonization and Independence* (1965); A. P. Merriam, *Congo: Background of Conflict* (1961); R. Lemarchand, *Political Awakening in the Belgian Congo* (1964);

E. W. Lefever, *Crisis in the Congo: a United Nations Force in Action* (1965); C. Carter, *The Politics of Inequality: South Africa Since 1948* (1958); R. First, *Southwest Africa* (1963); T. Okuma, *Angola in Ferment: the Background and Prospects of Angolan Nationalism* (1962); J. Duffy, *Portugal in Africa* (1962); K. M. Pannikar, *Afro-Asian States and Their Problems* (1960); D. Lowenthal, ed., *The West Indies Federation: Perspectives on a New Nation* (1961); E. S. Mason, *Foreign Aid and Foreign Policy* (1964); *Statesman's Yearbook; World Almanac; Annual Register of World Events.*

Chapter 64. See works cited for Chapters 60–63. In addition: H. W. Forbes, *The Strategy of Disarmament* (1962); H. A. Kissinger, *Nuclear Weapons and Foreign Policy* (1957); G. W. Elbers and P. Duncan, *Scientific Revolution: Challenge and Promise* (1959); P. Frank, *Modern Science and Its Philosophy* (1962); C. T. Chase, *The Evolution of Modern Physics* (1947); F. S. Taylor, *History of Industrial Chemistry* (1957); C. J. Singer, *A History of Biology* (1950); R. H. Shryock, *A History of Modern Medicine* (1947); B. and J. Lovell, *Discovering the Universe* (1964); P. Joubert, *Rocket* (1957); Eugene M. Emme, ed., *The History of Rocket Technology* (1964); M. Alperin *et al.*, eds., *Vistas in Astronautics* (1958, ff.); A. E. Jones, *The Life and Work of Sigmund Freud*, 3 vols. (1953–1957); B. Berelson and G. A. Steiner, *Human Behavior: an Inventory of Scientific Findings* (1964). See also *Statesman's Year Book*, United Nations' reports and documents, and current periodicals, such as the *Scientific American.*

Chapter 65. Christopher Dawson, *The Dynamics of World History*, ed. by J. J. Mulloy (1956), and *Understanding Europe* (1960); M. D. Shulman, *Beyond the Cold War* (1966); J. Macquarrie, *Twentieth Century Religious Thought* (1963); Reinhold Niebuhr, *Faith and History* (1949); A. S. Nash, ed., *Protestant Thought in the Twentieth Century* (1951); J. N. Moody and J. G. Lawler, *The Challenge of Mater et Magistra* (1963); R. B. Kaiser, *Pope, Council and World* (1963); Waldemar Gurian and M. A. Fitzsimons, eds., *The Catholic Church in World Affairs* (1954); K. S. Latourette, *Christianity in a Revolutionary Age*, vols. IV–V, *Since 1914* (1962); R. Tobias, *Communist-Christian Encounter in East Europe* (1956); A. H. Barr, *Masters of Modern Art* (new ed., 1958); B. S. Myers, *Modern Art in the Making* (1959); M. Raynal, *History of Modern Painting*, 3 vols. (1949–1950); W. Haftmann, *Painting in the Twentieth Century* (1960); O. W. Larkin, *Art and Life in America* (1949); A. C. Ritchie, *Sculpture of the Twentieth Century* (1952); C. Seymour, Jr., *Tradition and Experiment in Modern Sculpture* (1949); H. E. Reed, *A Concise History of Modern Painting* (1959); P. S. Hansen, *An Introduction to Twentieth Century Music* (1961); N. Slonimsky, *Music Since 1900* (1949); A. Copland, *Our New Music* (1941); H. R. Hitchcock, *Architecture: Nineteenth and Twentieth Centuries* (1958); J. M. Richards, *An Introduction Modern Architecture* (1956); C. Jones, *Architecture Today and Tomorrow* (1961).

The Coronation of Elizabeth II in Westminster Abbey, June 2, 1953.

Courtesy Wide World Photos

APPENDIX

APPENDIX

Select List of European Sovereigns

I. EMPERORS

Roman

Augustus, 27 B.C.–14 A.D.	Hadrian, 117–138	Philip, 244–248
Tiberius, 14–37 A.D.	Antoninus Pius, 138–161	Decius, 249–251
Gaius, 37–41	Marcus Aurelius, 161–180	Aurelian, 270–275
Claudius, 41–54	Commodus, 180–193	Diocletian, 284–305
Nero, 54–68	Septimius Severus, 193–211	Constantius, 305–311
Vespasian, 69–79	Caracalla, 211–217	Constantine, 311–337
Titus, 79–81	Macrinus, 217–218	Constantius II, 337–361
Domitian, 81–96	Elagabalus, 218–222	Julian, 361–363
Nerva, 96–98	Alexander Severus, 222–235	Valens, 364–378
Trajan, 98–117	Maximinus, 235–238	Theodosius, 379–395

East Roman (Byzantine)

Arcadius, 395–408
Theodosius II, 408–450
Marcian, 450–457
Leo I, 457–474
Zeno, 474–491
Anastasius I, 491–518
Justin I, 518–527
Justinian, 527–565
Justin II, 565–578
Maurice, 582–602
Heraclius, 610–641
Justinian II, 685–711
Leo III, 717–741
Constantine VI, 780–797
Irene, 797–802
Nicephoras I, 802–811
Leo V, 813–820
Michael III, 842
Basil I, 867–886

West Roman

Honorius, 395–423
Valentinian III, 423–455
Julius Nepos, 474–475
Romulus "Augustulus,"
  475–476

Frankish Roman

Charlemagne, 800–814
Louis, the Pious, 814–840
Lothair, 840–855
Louis II, 855–875
Charles II, the Bald, 877–881
Charles III, the Fat, 881–887

East Roman (Byzantine)—Cont.

Constantine VII, 912–959
Nicephoras II, Phocas,
  963–969
Basil II, 976–1025

Constantine IX, 1042–1054
Isaac I, 1057–1059
Romanus IV, 1067–1071
Alexius I, Comnenus, 1081–
  1118
John II, 1118–1143
Manuel I, 1143–1180
Andronicus I, 1183–1185
Isaac II, 1185–1195
Alexius III, 1195–1203

Michael VIII, Palaeologus,
  1259–1282
Andronicus II, 1282–1328
Andronicus III, 1328–1341

John V, 1341–1391
Manuel II, 1391–1425
John VI, 1425–1448
Constantine XI, 1448–1453

Holy Roman (German)

Henry I, the Fowler, 919–936	SAXON
Otto I, the Great, 936–973	"
Otto II, 973–983	"
Otto III, 983–1002	"
Henry II, 1002–1024	"
Conrad II, 1024–1039	FRANCONIAN
Henry III, 1039–1056	"
Henry IV, 1056–1106	"
Henry V, 1106–1125	"
Lothair II, 1125–1137	"
Conrad III, 1138–1152	HOHENSTAUFEN
Frederick I, Barbarossa, 1152–1190	"
Henry VI, 1190–1197	"
Philip of Swabia, 1198–1208	
Otto IV, 1208–1215	GUELF
Frederick II, 1220–1250	HOHENSTAUFEN
Conrad IV, 1250–1254	"
Rudolf I, 1273–1291	HABSBURG
Adolf, 1292–1298	NASSAU
Albert I, 1298–1308	HABSBURG
Henry VII, 1308–1313	LUXEMBOURG
Louis IV, 1314–1347	BAVARIAN
Charles IV, 1347–1378	LUX-BOHEMIAN
Wenceslas, 1378–1400	"
Sigismund, 1410–1437	"
Albert II, 1438–1439	HABSBURG
Frederick III, 1440–1493	"

Holy Roman (German)

Maximilian I, 1493–1519
Charles V, 1519–1556
Ferdinand I, 1556–1564
Maximilian II, 1564–1576
Rudolf II, 1576–1612
Matthias, 1612–1619
Ferdinand II, 1619–1637
Ferdinand III, 1637–1657
Leopold I, 1658–1705
Joseph I, 1705–1711
Charles VI, 1711–1740
Charles VII, 1742–1745
Francis I, 1745–1765
Joseph II, 1765–1790
Leopold II, 1790–1792
Francis II, 1792–1806

Austrian

Francis I, 1804–1835
Ferdinand I, 1835–1848
Francis Joseph, 1848–1916
Charles I, 1916–1918

Ottoman (Turkish Sultans)

Mohammed II, 1451–1481
Bayezid I, 1481–1512
Selim I, 1512–1520
Suleiman II, the Magnificent, 1520–1566
Selim II, 1566–1574
Murad III, 1574–1595
Mohammed III, 1595–1603
Murad V, 1623–1640
Ibrahim, 1640–1648
Mohammed IV, 1648–1687
Mustapha II, 1695–1703
Ahmed III, 1703–1730
Mahmud I, 1730–1754
Othman II, 1754–1757
Mustapha III, 1757–1773
Abdul Hamid I, 1773–1789
Selim III, 1789–1807
Mahmud II, 1808–1839
Abdul Medjid, 1839–1861
Abdul Aziz, 1861–1876
Abdul Hamid II, 1876–1909
Mohammed V, 1909–1918
Mohammed VI, 1918–1922

Russian (Tsars)

Ivan III, the Great, 1462–1505
Basil IV, 1505–1533
Ivan IV, the Terrible, 1533–1584
Theodore I, 1584–1598
Boris Godunov, 1598–1605
Michael Romanov, 1613–1645
Alexius, 1645–1676
Theodore II, 1676–1682
Ivan V, 1682–1689
Peter I, the Great, 1682–1725
Catherine I, 1725–1727
Peter II, 1727–1730
Anna, 1730–1740
Ivan VI, 1740–1741
Elizabeth, 1741–1762
Peter III, 1762
Catherine II, the Great, 1762–1796
Paul, 1796–1801
Alexander I, 1801–1825
Nicholas I, 1825–1855
Alexander II, 1855–1881
Alexander III, 1881–1894
Nicholas II, 1894–1917

French (Napoleonic)

Napoleon I, 1804–1814
Napoleon III, 1852–1870

German (Hohenzollern)

William I, 1871–1888
Frederick III, 1888
William II, 1888–1918

II. POPES (Partial List)

Peter, d. about 67 A.D.
Clement I, 88–97
Alexander I, 105–115
Sixtus I, 115–125
Pius I, 140–154
Soter, 166–175
Victor I, 189–199
Calixtus I, 217–222
Urban I, 222–230
Stephen I, 254–257
Felix I, 269–275
Marcellus I, 308–309
Sylvester I, 314–336
Julius I, 337–352
Liberius, 352–366
Damasus I, 366–384
Innocent I, 401–417
Leo I, 440–461
Symmachus, 498–514
Vigilius, 537–556
Gregory I, 590–604
Boniface IV, 608–615
Honorius I, 625–640
Martin I, 649–654
Eugene I, 654–657
Agatho, 678–682
Leo II, 682–683
Sergius I, 687–701
Gregory II, 715–731
Gregory III, 731–741
Zacharius, 741–752
Stephen III, 752–757
Paul I, 757–768
Hadrian I, 772–795
Leo III, 795–816
Gregory IV, 827–844
Leo IV, 847–855
Nicholas I, 858–867
John VIII, 872–882
Formosus, 891–896
John X, 914–928
John XII, 955–963
Sylvester II, 999–1003
John XIX, 1024–1032
Benedict IX, 1032–1045
Leo IX, 1049–1054
Gregory VII, 1073–1085

Urban II, 1088–1099
Paschal II, 1099–1118
Honorius II, 1124–1130
Innocent II, 1130–1143
Eugene III, 1145–1153
Hadrian IV, 1154–1159
Alexander III, 1159–1181
Lucius III, 1181–1185
Celestine III, 1191–1198
Innocent III, 1198–1216
Honorius III, 1216–1227
Gregory IX, 1227–1241
Celestine IV, 1241
Innocent IV, 1243–1254
Alexander IV, 1254–1261
Urban IV, 1261–1265
Clement IV, 1265–1271
Gregory X, 1271–1276
John XXI, 1276–1277
Nicholas III, 1277–1281
Martin IV, 1281–1285
Honorius IV, 1285–1288
Nicholas IV, 1288–1292
Celestine V, 1294
Boniface VIII, 1294–1303
Benedict XI, 1303–1304
Clement V, 1305–1314
John XXII, 1316–1334
Benedict XII, 1334–1342
Clement VI, 1342–1352
Innocent VI, 1352–1362
Urban V, 1362–1370
Gregory XI, 1370–1378
Urban VI, 1378–1389
Boniface IX, 1389–1404
Innocent VII, 1404–1406
Gregory XII, 1406–1417
Martin V, 1417–1431
Eugene IV, 1431–1447
Nicholas V, 1447–1455
Calixtus III, 1455–1458
Pius II, 1458–1464
Paul II, 1464–1471
Sixtus IV, 1471–1484
Innocent VIII, 1484–1492
Alexander VI, 1492–1503
Pius III, 1503

Julius II, 1503–1513
Leo X, 1513–1521
Hadrian VI, 1522–1523
Clement VII, 1523–1534
Julius III, 1550–1555
Marcellus II, 1555
Paul IV, 1555–1559
Pius IV, 1559–1565
Pius V, 1566–1572
Gregory XIII, 1572–1585
Sixtus V, 1585–1590
Urban VII, 1590
Gregory XIV, 1590–1591
Innocent IX, 1591–1592
Clement VIII, 1592–1605
Paul V, 1605–1621
Gregory XV, 1621–1623
Urban VIII, 1623–1644
Innocent X, 1644–1655
Alexander VII, 1655–1667
Clement IX, 1667–1670
Clement X, 1670–1676
Innocent XI, 1676–1689
Alexander VIII, 1689–1691
Innocent XII, 1691–1700
Clement XI, 1700–1721
Innocent XIII, 1721–1724
Benedict XIII, 1724–1730
Clement XII, 1730–1740
Benedict XIV, 1740–1758
Clement XIII, 1758–1769
Clement XIV, 1769–1774
Pius VI, 1775–1799
Pius VII, 1800–1823
Leo XII, 1823–1829
Pius VIII, 1829–1830
Gregory XVI, 1831–1846
Pius IX, 1846–1878
Leo XIII, 1878–1903
Pius X, 1903–1914
Benedict XV, 1914–1922
Pius XI, 1922–1939
Pius XII, 1939–1958
John XXIII, 1958–1963
Paul VI, 1963–

III. OTHER SOVEREIGNS

Kings of England

William I, 1066–1087,	NORMAN
William II, 1087–1100,	"
Henry I, 1100–1135,	"
Stephen, 1135–1154,	"
Henry II, 1154–1189,	ANGEVIN
Richard I, 1189–1199,	(PLANTAGENET)
John, 1199–1216,	"
Henry III, 1216–1272,	"
Edward I, 1272–1307,	"
Edward II, 1307–1327,	"
Edward III, 1327–1377,	"
Richard II, 1377–1399,	"
Henry IV, 1399–1413	LANCASTER
Henry V, 1413–1422,	"
Henry VI, 1422–1461,	"
Edward IV, 1461–1483,	YORK
Edward V, 1483,	"
Richard III, 1483–1485,	"
Henry VII, 1485–1509,	TUDOR
Henry VIII, 1509–1547,	"
Edward VI, 1547–1553,	"
Mary I, 1553–1558,	"
Elizabeth I, 1558–1603,	"
James I, 1603–1625,	STUART
Charles I, 1625–1649,	"
(Cromwell)	"
Charles II, 1660–1685,	"
James II, 1685–1688,	"
Mary II, 1689–1694,	"
William III, 1689–1701,	ORANGE
Anne, 1701–1714,	STUART
George I, 1714–1727,	HANOVER
George II, 1727–1760,	"
George III, 1760–1820,	"
George IV, 1820–1830,	"
William IV, 1830–1837,	"
Victoria, 1837–1901,	"
Edward VII, 1901–1910,	SAXE-COBURG
George V, 1910–1936,	WINDSOR
Edward VIII, 1936,	"
George VI, 1936–1952,	"
Elizabeth II, 1952–	"

Kings of France

Hugh Capet, 987–996,	CAPETIAN
Robert, 996–1031,	"
Henry I, 1031–1060,	"
Philip I, 1060–1108,	"
Louis VI, 1108–1137	"
Louis VII, 1137–1180	"
Philip II, Augustus, 1180–1223,	"
Louis VIII, 1223–1226,	"
Louis IX, 1226–1270,	"
Philip III, 1270–1285,	"
Philip IV, the Fair, 1285–1314,	"
Louis X, 1314–1316,	"
Philip V, 1316–1322,	"
Charles IV, 1322–1328,	"
Philip VI, 1328–1350,	VALOIS
John, 1350–1364,	"
Charles V, 1364–1380,	"
Charles VI, 1380–1422,	"
Charles VII, 1422–1461,	"
Louis XI, 1461–1483,	"
Charles VIII, 1483–1498,	"
Louis XII, 1498–1515,	"
Francis I, 1515–1547,	"
Henry II, 1547–1559,	"
Francis II, 1559–1560,	"
Charles IX, 1560–1574,	"
Henry III, 1574–1589,	"
Henry IV, 1589–1610,	BOURBON
Louis XIII, 1610–1643,	"
Louis XIV, 1643–1715,	"
Louis XV, 1715–1774,	"
Louis XVI, 1774–1792,	"
(Revolution and Napoleon)	"
Louis XVIII, 1814–1824,	"
Charles X, 1824–1830,	"
Louis Philippe, 1830–1848,	ORLEANS

Kings in the Iberian Peninsula

Castile

Alphonso V, 999–1027
Ferdinand I, 1028–1065
Alphonso VI, 1065–1109
Alphonso VII, 1137–1157
Alphonso VIII, 1158–1214
Henry I, 1214–1217
Ferdinand III, 1217–1252
Alphonso X, 1252–1284
Sancho IV, 1284–1296
Ferdinand IV, 1296–1312
Alphonso XI, 1312–1350
Peter I, 1350–1368
Henry II, 1368–1379
John I, 1379–1390
Henry III, 1390–1406
John II, 1406–1454
Henry IV, 1454–1474
Isabella I, 1474–1504
Philip I, 1504–1506

Aragon

Alphonso I, 1104–1134
Alphonso II, 1162–1196
Peter II, 1196–1213
James I, 1213–1276
Peter III, 1276–1285
Alphonso III, 1285–1291
James II, 1291–1327
Alphonso IV, 1327–1336
Peter IV, 1336–1387
John I, 1387–1395
Martin I, 1395–1410
Ferdinand I, 1414–1416
Alphonso V, 1416–1458
John II, 1458–1479
Ferdinand II, 1479–1516

Portugal

Alphonso I, 1112–1185
Sancho I, 1185–1211
Alphonso II, 1211–1223
Sancho II, 1223–1248
Alphonso III, 1248–1279
Diniz, 1279–1325
Alphonso IV, 1325–1357
Peter I, 1357–1367
Ferdinand I, 1367–1383
John I, 1385–1443
Alphonso V, 1443–1481
John II, 1481–1495
Manuel I, 1495–1521
John III, 1521–1557
Sebastian, 1557–1578
Henry, 1578–1580
(*To Spain, 1580–1640*)
John IV, 1640–1656
Alphonso VI, 1656–1667
Peter II, 1667–1706
John V, 1706–1750
Joseph, 1750–1777
Peter III, 1777–1786
Maria I, 1786–1816
John VI, 1816–1826
Peter IV, 1826
Maria II, 1826–1853
Peter V, 1853–1861
Louis I, 1861–1889
Charles I, 1889–1908
Manuel II, 1908–1910

Spain

Ferdinand V, 1506–1516	
Charles I, 1516–1556	
Philip II, 1556–1598,	HABSBURG
Philip III, 1598–1621,	"
Philip IV, 1621–1665,	"
Charles II, 1665–1700,	"
Philip V, 1700–1746,	BOURBON
Ferdinand VI, 1746–1759,	"
Charles III, 1759–1788,	"
Charles IV, 1788–1808,	"
Joseph, 1808–1813,	BONAPARTE
Ferdinand VII, 1813–1833,	BOURBON
Isabella II, 1833–1868	
Amadeo, 1870–1873,	SAVOY
(*Republic, 1873–1874*)	
Alphonso XII, 1875–1885,	BOURBON
Alphonso XIII, 1886–1931,	"

Kings in Scandinavia

Denmark	Norway	Sweden
Harold, 935–985		
Svend, 985–1014	Olaf I, 996–1000	Olaf, 993–1024
Knut, 1014–1035	Olaf II, 1016–1029	
Hardiknut, 1035–1042	Magnus, 1035–1047	
Svend II, 1047–1076	Harold III, 1047–1066	
	Magnus III, 1095–1103	
Waldemar I, 1157–1182	Magnus V, 1161–1184	Eric IX, 1150–1162
Knut VI, 1182–1202		
Waldemar II, 1202–1241	Haakon IV, 1217–1262	Earl Birger, 1248–1266
	Haakon V, 1299–1319	Magnus, 1279–1290
Waldemar IV, 1340–1375	Haakon VI, 1350–1380	
	Olaf III, 1380–1387	Albert, 1365–1388
	Margaret, 1387–1412	Gustavus I, Vasa, 1523–1560
	Christian I, 1448–1483	Eric XIV, 1560–1568
	Hans, 1483–1513	John III, 1568–1592
	Christian II, 1513–1523	Gustavus II, Adolphus, 1611–1632
	Frederick I, 1523–1533	
	Christian III, 1533–1559	Christina, 1632–1654
	Frederick II, 1559–1588	Charles X, 1654–1660
	Christian IV, 1588–1648	Charles XI, 1660–1697
	Frederick III, 1648–1670	Charles XII, 1697–1718
	Christian V, 1670–1699	Frederick I, 1720–1751
	Frederick IV, 1699–1730	Adolphus, 1751–1771
	Christian VI, 1730–1746	Gustavus III, 1771–1792
	Frederick V, 1746–1766	Gustavus IV, 1792–1809
	Christian VII, 1766–1808	Charles XIII, 1809–1818
	Frederick VI, 1808–1839	
Christian VIII, 1839–1848	Charles XIV, 1818–1844	
Frederick VII, 1848–1863	Oscar I, 1844–1859	
Christian IX, 1863–1906	Charles XV, 1859–1872	
Frederick VIII, 1906–1912	Oscar II, 1872–1907	
Christian X, 1912–1947		
Frederick IX, 1947–	Haakon VII, 1905–1957	Gustavus V, 1907–1950
	Olaf V, 1957–	Gustavus VI, 1950–

Kings of Poland, Bohemia, and Hungary

Poland

Boleslav I, 992–1025
Casimir I, 1025–1058
Boleslav II, 1058–1091
Boleslav III, 1102–1139
Ladislas I, 1306–1333
Casimir III, 1333–1370
Louis of Hungary, 1370–1382
Ladislas II, 1386–1434
Ladislas III, 1434–1444
Casimir IV, 1447–1492
John Albert, 1492–1501
Sigismund I, 1506–1548
Sigismund II, 1548–1572
Henry of Valois, 1573–1574
Stephen Bathory, 1575–1586
Sigismund III, 1587–1632
Ladislas IV, 1632–1648
John II Casimir, 1648–1668
John III Sobieski, 1674–1696
Augustus II of Saxony, 1697–1733
Augustus III, 1733–1763
Stanislaus II, Poniatowski, 1763–1795

Bohemia

Bretislav I, 1037–1055
Vratislav II, 1061–1092
Bretislav II, 1092–1110
Vladislav I, 1111–1125
Sobeslav, 1125–1140
Vladislav II, 1140–1173
Ottakar I, 1197–1230
Wenceslas I, 1230–1253
Ottakar II, 1253–1278
Wenceslas II, 1278–1305
Wenceslas III, 1305–1306
John of Luxembourg, 1310–1346
Charles, 1346–1378
Wenceslas IV, 1378–1419
Sigismund, 1419–1437
Albert, 1437–1439
Ladislas, 1440–1457
George Podiebrad, 1458–1471
Vladislav III, 1471–1516
Louis, 1516–1526
Ferdinand of Austria, 1526–1564
(*Same Rulers as Austria, 1526–1918*)

Hungary

Stephen I, 997–1038
Andrew I, 1046–1066
Ladislas I, 1077–1095
Koloman, 1095–1116
Bela III, 1173–1196
Andrew II, 1205–1235
Bela IV, 1235–1270
Ladislas IV, 1272–1290
Andrew III, 1290–1301
Charles I, 1308–1342
Louis I, 1342–1382
Sigismund, 1387–1437
John Hunyadi, 1446–1456
Matthias I, 1458–1490
Vladislav of Bohemia, 1490–1516
Louis of Bohemia, 1516–1526
Ferdinand of Austria, 1527–1564
(*Same Rulers as Austria, 1527–1918*)

Kings of Prussia after 1701

Frederick I, 1701–1713
Frederick William I, 1713–1740
Frederick II, the Great, 1740–1786
Frederick William II, 1786–1797
Frederick William III, 1797–1840
Frederick William IV, 1840–1861
William I, 1861–1888
Frederick III, 1888
William II, 1888–1918

Kings of Savoy and Italy after 1701

Victor Amadeus II, 1675–1730
Charles Emmanuel III, 1730–1773
Victor Amadeus III, 1773–1796
Charles Emmanuel IV, 1796–1802
Victor Emmanuel I, 1802–1821
Charles Felix, 1821–1831
Charles Albert, 1831–1849
Victor Emmanuel II, 1849–1878
Humbert I, 1878–1900
Victor Emmanuel III, 1900–1945
Humbert II, 1945–1946

Modern Sovereigns of Other European States

Dutch Netherlands

Same as Spain, 1504–1581
William of Orange, the Silent, *Stadholder,* 1581–1584
Maurice, 1584–1625
Frederick Henry, 1625–1647
William II, 1647–1650
John DeWitt, Grand Pensionary, 1650–1672
William III, *Stadholder,* 1672–1702 (K. of England, 1689–1702)
John William, 1702–1711
William IV, 1711–1751
William V, 1751–1795
Republic, 1795–1806
Louis Bonaparte, *King,* 1806–1810
To France, 1810–1813
William I, *King,* 1813–1840
William II, 1840–1849
William III, 1849–1890
Wilhelmina, 1890–1948
Juliana, 1948–

Belgium

Same as Spain, 1504–1713
Same as Austria (Holy Roman Empire), 1713–1797
To France, 1797–1815
To Dutch Netherlands, 1815–1830
Leopold I, 1831–1865
Leopold II, 1865–1909
Albert I, 1909–1934
Leopold III, 1934–1951
Baudouin I, 1951–

Serbia (Yugoslavia)

Karageorge, *Prince,* 1812–1813
Miloš Obrenovic, 1817–1839
Milan, 1839
Michael, 1839–1842
Alexander Karageorgevic, 1842–1859
Michael Obrenovic, 1860–1868
Milan I, 1869–1889; *King,* 1882–1889
Alexander, 1889–1903
Peter Karageorgevic, 1903–1921
Alexander I, 1921–1934
Peter II, 1934–1945

Greece

To Ottoman Empire, 1400–1821
Otto I, 1832–1862
George I, 1863–1913
Constantine I, 1913–1917
Alexander I, 1917–1920
Constantine I, 1920–1922
George II, 1922–1924
(*Republic,* 1924–1935)
George II, 1935–1947
Paul I, 1947–1964
Constantine XIII, 1964–

Rumania

Alexander John Cuza, *Prince,* 1859–1866
Carol I, *Prince,* 1866–1881, *King,* 1881–1914
Ferdinand, 1914–1927
Michael, 1927–1930
Carol II, 1930–1940
Michael, 1940–1947

Bulgaria

Alexander of Battenberg, *Prince,* 1879–1886
Ferdinand, *Prince,* 1887–1908; *Tsar,* 1908–1918
Boris III, 1918–1943
Simeon II, 1943–1946

Samson and the lion (c. 1300) depicted in a
Medieval German bronze aquamanile.

Museum of Fine Arts, Boston

INDEX

A

*A*achen, 123, 124. *See* Aix-la-Chapelle
Abbasid dynasty, 104, 107
Abboud, General Ibrahim, 844
Abdul Hamid II, Sultan, 655, 706
Abelard, Peter, 233, 241–242
Abu Bakr, Caliph, 104
Abu'l-Abbas, Caliph, 104
Abyssinia. *See* Ethiopia
Academy, French, 418, 423–424
Acadia, 459, 460. *See* Nova Scotia
Acheson, Dean, 797
Acre, 177
Act of Abjuration, 388; of Settlement, 513; of Succession, 362; of Supremacy, 362, 365; of Uniformity, 365, 509; of Union, 513
Actium, battle of, 35
Adalbert of Prague, 147
Adams, John, 521
Adams, Samuel, 516
Addison, Joseph, 478
Adelaide, Empress, 143
Aden, 670
Adenauer, Konrad, 767, 816, 884, 895
Adhemar of Puy, Bishop, 169
Adler, Alfred, 878
Adolf of Holstein, 176
Adoula, Cyrille, 853
Adowa, 642, 665, 756
Adrianople, battle of (378), 66; treaty of, 566
Aeschylus, 22
Aetius, 68
Africa, 71, 662–668, 848–857
Agadir, 705
Agathias, 95
Agincourt, battle of, 281
Agricola, Rudolph, 316
Agriculture, medieval, 154–159, 198–199, 266–268; modern, 367, 475–477, 592, 875
Ahmed, of Persia, 751
AID, 813, 829
Aids, feudal, 133–134
Air warfare, 773. *See* Atomic bomb
Aistulf, King, 118

Aix-la-Chapelle, treaty of (1668), 426; (1748), 468; conference of (1818), 562. *See* Aachen
Akkad, 7–8
Alais, peace of, 418
Alamans, 63–64, 68
Aland Islands, 734
Alans, 66, 67
Alaric, 66, 67
Alaska, 461
Alba, Duke of, 386–387
Albania, 750, 762, 774, 791, 793, 825
Albany Congress, 471
Albert II, Emperor, 292
Albert "the Bear," of Brandenburg, 176
Albert, Bishop, 176
Albert of Hohenzollern, 352
Albert, workingman, 599
Alberti, Leon Battista, 315, 319, 322–323
Albertus Magnus, 242
Albigensians, 206, 234, 235–236
Al-Biruni, 108
Albornoz, Cardinal, 309, 327
Albuquerque, 348
Alchemy, 108
Alcuin, 123–124, 125
Aldhelm, 97
Aldine Press, 316
Aleppo, 180
Alessandri, Jorge, 826
Alexander, "the Great," 24–25, 33
Alexander III, Pope, 176, 216–217, 227, 237
Alexander VI, Pope, 303, 310, 346
Alexander I, of Bulgaria, 656
Alexander I, of Russia, 550, 553, 554, 557, 559, 564, 649
Alexander II, of Russia, 649–651, 660
Alexander III, of Russia, 651, 652, 699
Alexander I, of Yugoslavia, 729, 750
Alexander Cuza, of Rumania, 614
Alexander Nevski, 223

Alexandria, 25, 26, 90, 103
Alexius Commenus I, Emperor, 154, 168, 169, 224
Alexius I, of Russia, 43
Al-Farabi, 108
Alfred "the Great," of England, 126, 127, 146
Algebra, 107
Algeciras, conference of (1906), 704–705, 712
Algeria (Algiers), 571, 614, 660, 665, 778, 804
Alhambra, 108, 109
Ali, Caliph, 104
Al-Khwarizmi, 107
Allenby, General, 717
Alliance for Progress, 829, 866
Alliances, international (1871–1914), 659, 703–705, 708
Almeida, 348
Alphabet, Cyrillic, 88, 151
Alphonso V, of Aragon, 302
Alphonso X, of Castile, 211
Alphonso, "the Magnanimous," 309, 315
Alphonso XII, of Spain, 642
Alphonso XIII, of Spain, 750–754
Al-Razi, 108
Alsace, 342, 402, 468, 628–629
Alsace-Lorraine, 643, 648, 723, 730, 790
Altenberg, 217
Alvarez de Piñeda, 346
Amalfi, 189
Ambrose, Saint, 44, 59, 60
Amenophis IV, Pharaoh, 10
America, 303, 346, 377, 389–390, 453–461
Amherst, Jeffrey, 518
Amiens, 226; treaty of, 547
Ammianus Marcellinus, 58
Amorites, 7
Ampère, 583
Amsterdam, 273, 408, 454, 455, 456
Amur, 461
Anabaptists, 355, 366
Anarchism, 597, 680–681, 692
Andrew II, of Hungary, 222
Angelico, Fra, 320, 324
Angevins, 201–202

UNITED NATIONS

NATIONS UNIES 聯

NACIONES UNIDAS 合

ОБЪЕДИНЕННЫЕ НАЦИИ 國